P9-DNS-775

FIFTH EDITION

Adapted Physical Education and Sport

Joseph P. Winnick, EdD

The College at Brockport,
State University of New York

EDITOR

Human Kinetics

Library of Congress Cataloging-in-Publication Data

Adapted physical education and sport / Joseph P. Winnick, EdD., editor. -- 5th ed.
  p. cm.
 Includes bibliographical references and index.
 ISBN-13: 978-0-7360-8918-0 (hard cover)
 ISBN-10: 0-7360-8918-7 (hard cover)
 1. Physical education for people with disabilities. 2. Sports for people with disabilities. I. Winnick, Joseph P.
 GV445.A3 2010
 371.9'04486--dc22

2010016597

ISBN-10: 0-7360-8918-7
ISBN-13: 978-0-7360-8918-0

Copyright © 2011, 2005, 2000, 1995, 1990 by Joseph P. Winnick

All rights reserved. Except for use in a review, the reproduction or utilization of this work in any form or by any electronic, mechanical, or other means, now known or hereafter invented, including xerography, photocopying, and recording, and in any information storage and retrieval system, is forbidden without the written permission of the publisher.

Notice: Permission to reproduce the following material is granted to instructors and agencies who have purchased *Adapted Physical Education and Sport, Fifth Edition:* pp. 485-486 and 607-613. The reproduction of other parts of this book is expressly forbidden by the above copyright notice. Persons or agencies who have not purchased *Adapted Physical Education and Sport, Fifth Edition* may not reproduce any material.

The Web addresses cited in this text were current as of April 2010, unless otherwise noted.

Acquisitions Editor: Kathy Read; **Developmental Editor:** Melissa Feld; **Assistant Editor:** Rachel Brito; **Copyeditor:** Alisha Jeddeloh; **Indexer:** Betty Frizzéll; **Permission Manager:** Dalene Reeder; **Graphic Designer:** Fred Starbird; **Graphic Artist:** Dawn Sills; **Cover Designer:** Keith Blomberg; **DVD Face Designer:** Susan Rothermel Allen; **Photographer (cover):** Phil Cole/ Getty Images; **Photographer (interior):** © Human Kinetics, unless otherwise noted; **Photo Asset Manager:** Laura Fitch; **Visual Production Assistant:** Joyce Brumfield; **Photo Production Manager:** Jason Allen; **Art Manager:** Kelly Hendren; **Associate Art Manager:** Alan L. Wilborn; **Printer:** Courier Printing

Printed in the United States of America   10 9 8 7 6 5 4 3 2

The paper in this book is certified under a sustainable forestry program.

Human Kinetics
Web site: www.HumanKinetics.com

United States: Human Kinetics
P.O. Box 5076
Champaign, IL 61825-5076
800-747-4457
e-mail: humank@hkusa.com

New Zealand: Human Kinetics
P.O. Box 80
Torrens Park, South Australia 5062
0800 222 062
e-mail: info@hknewzealand.com

Canada: Human Kinetics
475 Devonshire Road Unit 100
Windsor, ON N8Y 2L5
800-465-7301 (in Canada only)
e-mail: info@hkcanada.com

Europe: Human Kinetics
107 Bradford Road
Stanningley
Leeds LS28 6AT, United Kingdom
+44 (0) 113 255 5665
e-mail: hk@hkeurope.com

Australia: Human Kinetics
57A Price Avenue
Lower Mitcham, South Australia 5062
08 8372 0999
e-mail: info@hkaustralia.com

E5008

Special Olympics

Through a vision born in her own backyard in Rockville, Maryland, Eunice Kennedy Shriver (1921-2009) changed the lives of millions of people with intellectual disabilities worldwide as well as the lives of all who volunteer or work on behalf of those with disabilities. From the time of her brother John F. Kennedy's presidency, she worked diligently to ensure the passage of every major piece of legislation on behalf of people with disabilities and develop grassroots programs to show the world that people with disabilities can learn, perform, contribute, and change our lives for the better. We dedicate this book to the memory of Eunice Kennedy Shriver, whose amazing life and accomplishments as the founder of Special Olympics changed the world for the better as few others in history have.

Contents

Chapter 4

Measurement, Assessment, and Program Evaluation 59
Manny Felix and Garth Tymeson

Chapter 5

Individualized Education Programs 79
Manny Felix and Garth Tymeson

Chapter 6

Behavior Management 101
E. Michael Loovis

Chapter 7

Instructional Strategies for Adapted Physical Education . . 119
Douglas H. Collier

part two
Individuals With Unique Needs
149

Chapter 8
Intellectual Disabilities 151
Patricia L. Fegan

Chapter 9
Behavioral Disabilities 173
E. Michael Loovis

Chapter 10
Autism Spectrum Disorders . . . 195
Cathy Houston-Wilson

part three
Developmental Considerations
377

part four

Activities for Individuals With Unique Needs
441

Preface

It is with a great deal of satisfaction and motivation that I write this preface for the fifth edition of *Adapted Physical Education and Sport*. When I wrote the preface for previous editions, I was confident that these books would benefit children with unique physical education needs by providing clear and concise information for teachers and others who provide quality services. In this fifth edition, the book is further developed and, at times, reorganized to meet today's trends in adapted physical education and sport. This preface identifies and explains major influences on the content and organization, briefly summarizes new and continuing features, provides an overview of the parts of the book, and closes with some comments about the value of adapted physical education and sport in the lives of young people today. As the editor, I strongly welcome comments on the book's strengths and suggestions for improvement.

LEGISLATION: A MAJOR INFLUENCE ON THIS BOOK

There are many factors that shape the emphasis, approach, content, and organization of any book. This book is influenced by original and current versions of landmark laws: the Individuals with Disabilities Education Act (IDEA) and the Individuals with Disabilities Education Improvement Act (IDEIA). These laws were originally signed in 1975 as PL 94-142, the Education for All Handicapped Children Act. The second important legislation is section 504 of the Rehabilitation Act (originally passed in 1973 as PL 93-112).

One of major purposes of IDEA is to ensure that all children with disabilities have available to them a free public education that emphasizes special education and related services to meet their unique needs. IDEA makes it clear that the special education to be made available includes physical education, which in turn may be specified as adapted physical education. As is communicated in this book, regulations associated with IDEA define physical education as the development of physi-

cal and motor fitness, fundamental motor skills and patterns, and skills in aquatics, dance, and individual and group games and sports (including intramural and lifetime sports). In this book, adapted physical education is defined in a manner consistent with key provisions of the IDEA definition, including the scope of physical education presented in the definition. This book helps schools and agencies in each state to develop and implement physical education programs for students with disabilities consistent with federal legislation and students with other unique needs.

The emphasis on the identification of unique needs, which is part of the IDEA definition of special education, is emphasized in this book. This book includes numerous ways of adapting physical education to meet individual needs. One of the most important concepts associated with federal legislation is the requirement of individualized education programs (IEPs) designed to meet the unique needs of children. In chapters 5 and 21, detailed information is presented about components and strategies for developing IEPs, 504 plans, and individualized family service plans (IFSPs).

In IDEA, the disabilities of children aged 3 to 21 are identified and defined. Information related to physical education is presented in this book in regard to each of the specific disabilities identified in the law. IDEA also defines infants and toddlers (birth to age 2) with disabilities. One entire chapter on physical education services related to infants and toddlers is presented.

Both IDEA and section 504 require that education be provided in the most normal, integrated setting appropriate. In regard to physical education, this book encourages education in regular environment to the extent appropriate. The book prepares readers for working in inclusive environments, with extensive discussions about inclusion in several chapters. However, it recognizes that education in the least restrictive environment is the law of the land and also prepares readers to provide services in other settings. In regard to sport, this book recommends an orientation to sport that enables and encourages participation in a variety of settings and responds to the requirement of equal opportunity for participation in extracurricular experiences.

Therefore, this book responds to legislative requirements in many ways. These include compatibility with the definition of special education, the requirement of identifying unique educational needs of the student within the context of a broad program of physical education, the requirement for IEPs, education in the most integrated setting possible, and equal opportunity for extracurricular experience. Because of the orientation of this book, educators can be most confident that they are implementing programs that respond to the societal needs that are expressed through legislation.

NEW FEATURES IN THIS EDITION

Many changes affecting adapted physical education and sport have occurred subsequent to previous editions of this book. Chapters have been updated or revised to incorporate these changes. The inclusion movement continues to expand and thrive, and more and more involvement of students with disabilities is occurring in regular physical education and sport settings. Following an introduction to inclusion with emphasis on the functions of teachers for successful inclusion, several chapters in the book focus on practices and applications relevant to inclusion.

Because individuals with disabilities are increasingly involved in sport, this book includes a separate chapter on adapted sport (chapter 3). Advances regarding classification, sport organizations, national governing bodies, and the Paralympic Games are dramatic, and this chapter has been revised to communicate the changes. The chapter continues to be guided by unique and contemporary orientations to sport adapted for people with unique needs. The chapter increases attention to adapted sport as a part of in-school programs, including interscholastic programs.

Although all chapters have been updated, major revisions are provided in several chapters. The chapter on measurement and assessment (chapter 4) and the chapter on IEPs (chapter 5) have been written by two authors new to the text: Dr. Manny Felix and Dr. Garth Tymeson. They have significantly updated chapter 4 to reflect recent advances in measurement and assessment. The Brockport Physical Fitness Test (BPFT), a criterion-referenced, health-related physical fitness test appropriate for young people with disabilities, is introduced in the

chapter, and a DVD of the test is included in the back of the book. Chapter 5 has also been updated with particular attention to the development of IEPs. The chapter continues to prepare teachers for IEP development, including technological advances. A particularly noteworthy element that has been added is the increased attention given to the strengths or positive abilities and interests of the student in setting goals and objectives. This is particularly important in developing transitional programs and involvement in athletic pursuits.

In the last few years, more and more attention has been given to autism. In response, Dr. Cathy Houston-Wilson has continued her development of a practical, user-friendly chapter focusing on the implications of this condition for the teaching of physical education. Also in this fifth edition, separate chapters have been written on visual disabilities, deafness, and deafblindness by one of the foremost authorities in the United States, Dr. Lauren J. Lieberman.

The increased attention on positive behavior support (PBS) and ways to provide for students with behavioral disabilities consistent with IDEA has resulted in more attention on this topic in both chapters 6 and 9.

CONTINUING FEATURES

In this and previous editions of this book, many of the chapters have focused on physical education and sport rather than merely structuring the book by the names of disabilities. The latter approach traditionally has been associated with a medical model for the structuring of knowledge rather than a more educationally oriented model. On the other hand, relevant information regarding disabilities including characteristics is presented in the text so that relationships between disabilities and implications for physical education and sport may be drawn and understood.

This edition retains focus on physical education for people from birth to age 21. No attempt is made to address the entire age span of people with disabilities, although much information in the book is relevant to the entire age span. Although this book focuses on the areas of physical education and sport, it also includes information relevant to allied areas such as recreation and therapeutic recreation.

A feature that has been continued in this edition is the presentation of resources with each chapter. The presentation of written, audiovisual, and electronic resources in the text and instructor guide will be of much interest and helpful to both students and instructors.

This fifth edition continues two elements designed to enhance reader understanding: opening chapter vignettes and application examples within chapters. The opening vignettes present real-life scenarios that introduce one or more chapter concepts to be discussed. Application examples provide readers with the opportunity to explore real-life situations and see how the concepts in the text can be applied to situations to solve the issues at hand.

An online instructor guide has again been developed to accompany this book. For each chapter, the instructor guide provides objectives, suggestions for learning and enrichment activities, resources, and PowerPoint presentations. Because it is so important for college students to be aware of people with disabilities and to teach and interact with them in a positive manner, the instructor guide includes additional ideas to provide these opportunities. The guide also includes some ideas for an introductory course related to adapted physical education and sport as well as a sample course syllabus. Finally, an electronic bank of test questions has been included that may be used to develop quizzes, exams, or study questions.

PARTS OF THE BOOK

The book is presented in three parts. Part I, Foundational Topics in Adapted Physical Education and Sport, encompasses chapters 1 though 7, which introduce the reader to adapted physical education and sport. This part includes chapters on adapted sport, IEPs, measurement and assessment, and behavior management. Part I ends with chapter 7, which identifies strategies for instruction in adapted physical education.

Part II, Individuals With Unique Needs, includes 11 chapters. This section covers all the disabilities specifically defined in IDEA, and one chapter relates to students with temporary disabilities and special conditions. These chapters provide an understanding of disabilities, how they relate to physical education and sport, and educational implications associated with each disability covered. As appropriate, particular attention is given in each chapter to inclusion and sport programs.

The third part of the book, Developmental Considerations, includes four chapters. Chapters 19 through 22 in this part cover motor development, perceptual–motor development, adapted physical education for infants and toddlers, and children in early childhood programs.

Part IV, Activities for Individuals With Unique Needs, includes chapter 23 through 29. These chapters present physical education and sport activities for both school and out-of-school settings. A key aspect of this part is the presentation of specific activity modifications and variations for the populations involved in adapted physical education and sport. This part concludes with a chapter on wheelchair sport performance. Part IV in particular serves as an excellent resource for teachers, coaches, and other service providers long after they have left colleges and universities and are involved in providing quality programs for young people.

The appendixes consist of the latest definitions regarding infants, toddlers, and children with disabilities in IDEA; a list of addresses for organizations associated with adapted physical education and sport; information related to the BPFT; and a scale to rate or evaluate adapted physical education programs. Each of these complements information presented in the main body of the book. Also, as mentioned earlier, a DVD is included with the text that offers an audiovisual presentation of the BPFT.

CLOSING

As opportunities in adapted physical education and sport have increased, there has been a realization that people with disabilities are really people with abilities and individual differences who are capable of much more than society has ever believed. With greater participation, the value of physical activity has been more clearly recognized and accepted. More than ever before, young people with disabilities, parents, medical professionals, educators, and others are recognizing the tremendous value of physical education and sport today. This recognition and acceptance extend throughout the world, as clearly demonstrated at international symposia related to adapted physical activity and international competition in sport.

As the field of adapted physical education and sport has advanced, many recognizable subspecialties have emerged. Thus, I continue to assemble top people in their areas of expertise to serve as a team of authorities who draw on many years of experience in adapted physical education and sport to contribute to the book.

This book has been designed to be comprehensive, relevant, and user friendly. It has been designed as both a resource and text for adapted physical education and sport. As a resource, this book aids teachers, administrators, and other professionals as they plan and provide services. As a text, it can be used to prepare students majoring in physical education, recreational sport management, special education, and related disciplines. Although the book can serve many purposes, its primary thrust is its emphasis on providing quality services to people with unique physical education needs, differences, and abilities.

Joseph P. Winnick

Acknowledgments

Boni B. Boswell—I wish to extend a warm thanks to Joe Winnick for the opportunity to contribute to this book and for his ongoing support of dance in the schools. Also, I am grateful to the many students at East Carolina University who have reviewed this work and shared their creativity and humor.

Douglas H. Collier—I would like to thank Joe Winnick for bringing me on board and for his thoughtful and positive contributions to the chapter I wrote and to our profession. Thanks also to my wonderful wife Chris for her constant support and friendship.

Patricia L. Fegan—Appreciation is extended to Joe Winnick for allowing me to continue as part of this incredible writing team and for writing the section on cognitive development in chapter 8. Very special appreciation is extended to the 11,000 athletes of Special Olympics Maryland who make me smile every day and inspire me by their greatness.

Manny Felix—I genuinely thank Dr. Joe Winnick not only for allowing me the professional opportunity to be part of an excellent adapted physical education textbook but also for his personal mentorship in the development of the assessment chapter. I extend my gratitude to Dr. Frank Short, who provided an excellent template of the assessment chapter through his earlier versions from previous editions. I thank my wife, Cindy, and our children, Lexie, Becky, and Michael, who have always supported me in my professional career.

Cathy Houston-Wilson—I would like to thank Joe Winnick for giving me the opportunity to contribute to this text. I would also like to thank my family, Kevin, Meagan, Shannon, and Kiera, for their love and support, with a special thanks to my mom, Marie Maxwell, who lives in our hearts forever.

Luke E. Kelly—I would like to thank the graduate students at the University of Virginia who serve as a sounding board for my ideas and as reviewers of my drafts. I would also like to thank Andrew, Zachary, and Melissa for their continuing support and for being the source of inspiration for my work.

Francis M. Kozub—I would like to thank Mary, Patrick, and Jesse for their patience throughout my career. Specifically, I would like to acknowledge Mary's editorial contributions to this book and many other publications over the years.

Barry W. Lavay—I would like to thank Joseph Winnick for providing me with the opportunity to contribute to this book and for his major contributions, over the years, to the adapted physical activity profession. I would like to acknowledge my students and colleagues, who continue to challenge me to learn and grow as a professional. A special thanks to my mother and father, who at a young age instilled in me the importance of receiving an education. I want to thank my family, my wife, Penny, and children, Nicole and Danielle, who have always been supportive of my work and who, most importantly, make life special.

Monica Lepore—I wish to thank the children and families in the WCU Wednesday night adapted physical education program for their dedication to the professional preparation of my teacher certification students, and a thank-you goes out to my WCU adapted physical education minors for teaching in the program. In addition, I would like to thank my family, Maria, Anne, Pat, Frank, Donna, and Dylan, for their unwavering support and love.

Lauren Lieberman—I would like to acknowledge the students from the Perkins School for the Blind for their assistance in teaching me much of what I know about sensory impairments. I would also like to thank all of the administrators, specialists, counselors, and campers from Camp Abilities for continuing to show the world what children who are visually impaired, blind, or deafblind can do in the area of sport and recreation. Special thanks to Dr. Carol Greer, an educational audiologist from the Board of Cooperative Educational Services in Rochester, New York; Lori Reich, a teacher who is hard of hearing from San Diego; Dr. Barry Lavay, a professor of adapted physical education from California State University; and Dr. Katrina Arndt from St. John Fisher College in Rochester, New York, a specialist on transition and higher education for students who are deafblind, for their feedback on chapter 13. Special thanks to Dr. Jim Mastro, professor of adapted physical education and a Paralympic athlete from Bemidji State University, and to Dr. Francis Kozub at SUNY Brockport for chapter 12. I would also like to thank Dr. Kathleen Ellis from West Chester University for her generous assistance in writing my chapters.

E. Michael Loovis—I would like to thank Don Krebs, president of Access to Recreation, Inc., and Mary Goff Hipp formerly from Fieldstone Farm Therapeutic Riding Center for their assistance in acquiring the photographs used in chapter 27. Also my thanks to Joe Winnick for his assistance with reconceptualization of chapter 9.

John C. Ozmun and David L. Gallahue—Our chapter is dedicated to Dr. Harold "Hal" Morris, a dear friend and respected colleague, whose commitment and devotion to the roles of scholar, leader, mentor, and friend were unsurpassed. In addition, we would like to thank our families for their unwavering love and support.

Michael J. Paciorek—I would like to express my sincerest thanks to one of my best friends and colleagues in helping me with this chapter, Jeff Jones, director of BlazeSports Institute for Applied Science. I appreciate your efforts and friendship. I would also like to acknowledge the efforts of Susan Katz at the United States Olympic Committee and Diane Doyle of *Sports 'N Spokes*. Most of all I would like to acknowledge the great contribution by my wife Karen. Her comments, suggestions, and encouragement helped me greatly. Thanks to Joe Winnick for his leadership and contribution to adapted physical activity.

David L. Porretta—Recognition and appreciation go to USA Volleyball, Össur Americas, and Challenge Publications, Ltd./Palaestra for providing selected chapter photos. Also, a special thanks goes to Joseph Winnick for inviting me to participate in this and previous editions of the book.

Francis X. Short—Appreciation is extended to Joe Winnick for all the constructive criticism on my chapter, to Lauren Lieberman and the campers

and staff of Camp Abilities, and to all the folks at Human Kinetics for their hard work on the text.

Christine B. Stopka—This chapter was made possible by the outstanding work by Dr. Paul Surburg (original chapter author) and Dr. Luke Kelly (pediatric orthopedic content from former chapter 22); the current author is very appreciative of their generous and invaluable contributions to this chapter and this textbook.

Garth Tymeson—I sincerely thank Joe Winnick for inviting me to contribute to this text and for his influence on my professional development. In addition, I need to acknowledge Frank Short for his excellent contributions to the individualized education program chapter in this and previous editions. Finally, deepest appreciation is extended to my wife, Martha, who keeps me in adapted physical education reality with her creativity and teaching excellence with PK-12 students.

Joseph P. Winnick—I wish to acknowledge the wonderful support and cooperation I have received from the outstanding authors involved in this edition. I very much appreciate the help and support I have received from many persons at SUNY Brockport.

Abu B. Yilla—This work extends the work of Dr. Colin Higgs from the second edition of this book. Dr. Higgs' permission, contributions to this chapter, and personal support of my professional activities are greatly appreciated. Also, the contribution of William Hernandez of Per4Max Medical, who provided valuable information and images for this chapter, needs to be recognized. The support of the Dallas Wheelchair Mavericks basketball team and the department of kinesiology at University of Texas at Arlington are also appreciated, as is the assistance of Dr. Winnick and his graduate students at SUNY Brockport.

Lauriece Zittel—I would like to thank Joe Winnick for the opportunity to contribute to this edition of the text. A special thanks to my precious Claire Anne—you have shared your life, love, and development. I am learning so much as I watch you move through your early childhood years.

part one

Foundational Topics in Adapted Physical Education and Sport

Part I of this book, consisting of seven chapters, introduces adapted physical education and sport and presents topics that serve as a foundation for the book. Chapter 1 defines adapted physical education and sport and offers a brief orientation concerning its history, legal basis, and professional resources. Programmatic planning, inclusion, and qualities of service providers are also introduced. In chapter 2, the focus shifts to the organization and management of programs. Topics include programmatic and curricular planning and guidelines for the organization and implementation of adapted physical education programs. Chapter 3 emphasizes information pertaining to adapted sport. Following a brief introduction, the chapter covers the status of and issues associated with adapted sport, from local school and community programs to Paralympic Games. Preparing physical educators to enhance the involvement of people with disabilities in sport is stressed in the chapter. Vital to the development of adapted physical education programs are several concepts related to measurement and evaluation, and chapter 4 discusses measurement, assessment, and evaluation and recommends specific strategies in regard to adapted physical education. Chapter 5 contains a detailed discussion of individualized education programs developed for students with unique needs, including section 504 accommodation plans. Chapter 6 emphasizes basic concepts and approaches related to methods of managing behavior. Chapter 7 discusses instructional strategies related to adapted physical education.

The information in part I relates to planning, assessing, prescribing, teaching, and evaluating adapted physical education. It includes information related to overall program planning (chapters 1 and 2), student assessment and program evaluation (chapter 4), individualized education programs (chapter 5), instructional strategies (chapter 7), and program organization and management (chapter 2). A chapter on behavior management is included in the foundational area before chapter 7 because of its importance in both shaping appropriate social behavior and its influence in facilitating skill acquisition.

chapter 1

Introduction to Adapted Physical Education and Sport

Joseph P. Winnick

Adapted physical education and sport programs relate to the unique needs and abilities of individuals, which vary widely. What is not often known is that people with disabilities who are involved in physical activity and sport achieve goals that many would think are impossible. For example, Ernst Van Dyk (South Africa) and Jean Driscoll (USA) attained record times in the Boston Marathon of 1 hour, 18 minutes, and 27 seconds and 1 hour, 34 minutes, and 22 seconds, respectively, using wheelchairs. Jim Abbott, a pitcher for the New York Yankees who was born without a right hand, pitched a no-hitter against the Cleveland Indians in 1993. Wilma Rudolph—despite birth defects and polio—was a triple gold medalist in the 100-meter, 200-meter, and 400-meter relays in the 1960 Olympics in Rome. Tom Dempsey, born with only half a right foot, set a National Football League record in 1970 for the longest field goal kicked (63 yd, or 58 m). Casey Martin, who has a serious impairment of his leg associated with Klippel-Trenaunay-Weber syndrome, gained fame as a gifted golfer. These examples demonstrate what individuals with disabilities can achieve when opportunities are provided.

People who pursue a career of teaching physical education and coaching sports typically enjoy physical activity and are active participants in physical education and athletics. Often, however, they do not become knowledgeable about adapted physical education and sport until they prepare for their careers. With increased awareness, they realize that people with unique needs might exhibit abilities ranging from very low to extremely high. As they gain experience, students begin to appreciate that people with a variety of unique needs are involved in adapted physical education and sport. They learn that those with unique needs include people with and without disabilities.

If physical education and sport opportunities are offered in educational institutions and other societal entities, they must be made available to all students, including those with disabilities. It is neither desirable nor permissible to discriminate on the basis of disability in regard to these opportunities. Provisions should be made to offer equivalent as well as identical services so that equal opportunity for equal benefits may be pursued. Adapted physical education and sport has evolved as a field to meet the unique physical education and sport needs of participants. This chapter introduces the reader to adapted physical education and sport.

MEANING OF ADAPTED PHYSICAL EDUCATION

Because people use different terms to mean the same thing (and different definitions to mean the same term), it is important to clarify the definition of adapted physical education. **Adapted physical education** is an individualized program including physical and motor fitness, fundamental motor skills and patterns, skills in aquatics and dance, and individual and group games and sports designed to meet the unique needs of individuals. Typically, the word *adapt* means "to adjust" or "to fit." In this book, the meaning of *adapt* is consistent with these definitions and includes modifications to meet the needs of students. It encompasses traditional components associated with adapted physical education, including those designed to correct, habilitate, or remediate. Adapted physical education is viewed as a subdiscipline of physical education that provides safe, personally satisfying, and successful experiences for students of varying abilities.

Adapted physical education is generally designed to meet **long-term unique needs** (more than 30 days). Those with long-term unique needs include people with disabilities as specified in the Individuals with Disabilities Education Act (IDEA). (The Individuals with Disabilities Education Act [IDEA] may also be cited as the Individuals with Disabilities Education Improvement Act [IDEIA]. In this text, it will be referred to as IDEA.) According to IDEA, a **child with a disability** means a child with mental retardation, hearing impairment including deafness, speech or language impairment, visual impairment including blindness, serious emotional disturbance, orthopedic impairment, autism, traumatic brain injury, learning disability, deafblindness, or multiple disabilities or other health impairments that require special education and related services (OSE/RS, 2006). The term *child with a disability* for a child aged three to nine years may, at the discretion of the state and the local educational agency, include a child experiencing developmental delays as defined by the state and as measured by appropriate diagnostic instruments and procedures in one or more of the following areas: physical development, cognitive development, communication development, social or emotional development, or adaptive development. This child, by reason thereof, needs special education and related services (OSE/RS, 2006).

Adapted physical education might also include **infants and toddlers** (children under three years of age) who need early intervention services because (1) they are experiencing developmental delays in cognitive development, physical development, communication development, social or emotional development, or adaptive development or (2) they have a diagnosed physical or mental condition that has a high probability of resulting in developmental delay. At the discretion of the state, adapted physical education might also include at-risk infants and toddlers (IDEA, 2004). The term **at-risk infant or toddler** means a child under three years of age who would be at risk of experiencing a substantial developmental delay if early intervention services were not provided (IDEA, 2004).

Adapted physical education may include individuals with disabilities as encompassed within section 504 of the Rehabilitation Act of 1973 and its amendments. Section 504 defines a person with a disability as anyone who has a physical or mental impairment that substantially limits one or more major life activities, has a record of such an impairment, or is regarded as having such an impairment. Although every child who is a student with a disability under IDEA is also protected under section 504, all children covered under 504 are not necessarily students with a disability under IDEA. Students with disabilities who do not need or require services under IDEA are, nonetheless, entitled to accommodations and services that are necessary to enable them to benefit from all programs and activities available to students without disabilities.

Adapted physical education may include students who are not identified by a school district as having a disability under federal legislation but who have unique needs that call for a specially designed program. This group might include students restricted because of injuries or other medical conditions; those with low fitness (including exceptional leanness or obesity), inadequate motor development, or low skill; or those with poor functional posture. These students might require individually designed programming to meet unique goals and objectives.

According to IDEA, students aged 3 to 21 with disabilities must have an **individualized education program** (IEP) developed by a planning committee. In developing an IEP, physical education must be considered, and the IEP might include specially designed instruction in physical education. IEPs should also consider needs in extracurricular activities, including participation in sport. Athletes with disabilities are encouraged to include goals related to sport in an IEP. IDEA also requires the development of an **individualized family service plan** (IFSP) for infants and toddlers with disabilities (OSE/RS, 2006). Although physical education services are not mandated for this age group, they may be offered as part of an IFSP. In accordance with section 504 of the Rehabilitation Act of 1973 and its amendments, it is recommended that an accommodation plan be developed by a school-based assessment team to provide services and needed accommodations for students with disabilities. Although not covered by federal law, an **individualized physical education program** (IPEP) should also be developed by a planning committee for those who have a unique need but who have not been identified by the school as having a disability. Each school should have policies and procedures to guide the development of all individualized programs. More specific information on the development of programs and plans is presented in chapters 4 and 5 (ages 3-21) and chapter 21 (ages 0-2).

Consistent with the least restrictive environment (LRE) concept associated with IDEA, adapted physical education may take place in classes that range from **integrated** (i.e., regular education environments) to **segregated** (i.e., including only students receiving adapted physical education). Although adapted physical education is a *program* rather than a *placement*, it should be understood that a program is directly influenced by placement (the setting in which it is implemented). Whenever appropriate, students receiving an adapted physical education program should be included in regular physical education environments with appropriate support service if needed. Although an adapted physical education program is individualized, it can be implemented in a group setting and should be geared to each student's needs, limitations, and abilities.

Adapted physical education should emphasize an **active** program of physical activity (figure 1.1) rather than a **sedentary** alternative program. The program should be planned to attain the benefits of physical activity through meeting the needs of students who might otherwise be relegated to passive experiences associated with physical education. In establishing adapted physical education programs, educators work with parents, students, teachers, administrators, and professionals in various disciplines. Adapted physical education may employ developmental (bottom-up), community-based, functional (top-down), or other orientations and might employ a variety of teaching styles. Adapted physical education takes place in schools and other agencies responsible for education. Although adapted physical education is educational, it draws on related services (more on related services in chapter 2 and later in this chapter), especially medical services, to help meet instructional objectives and goals.

In this text, adapted physical education and sport are viewed as part of the emerging area of study known as **adapted physical activity**, a term that encompasses the comprehensive and interdisciplinary study of physical activity for the education, wellness, sport participation, and leisure of individuals with unique needs. Adapted physical activity encompasses the total life span, whereas **adapted physical education** focuses only on the ages of 0 to 21. Although adapted physical education may exceed the minimal time required by policies or law, it should not be supplanted by related services, intramurals, sport days, athletics, or other experiences that are not primarily instructional.

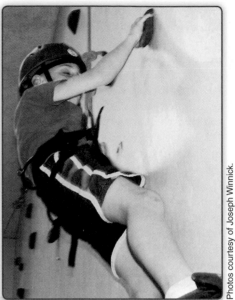

Photos courtesy of Joseph Winnick.

FIGURE 1.1 Examples of active adapted physical education: *(a)* Athlete with a unique extracurricular need participates in an IEP; *(b)* student with a visual impairment confidently scales a wall.

ADAPTED SPORT

Adapted sport refers to sport modified or created to meet the needs of individuals with disabilities. Based on this definition, for example, basketball is a regular sport and wheelchair basketball is an adapted sport. Goalball (a game created for people with visual impairments in which players attempt to roll a ball that emits a sound across their opponents' goal) is an adapted sport because it was created to meet unique needs of participants with disabilities. Individuals with disabilities may participate in regular sport or adapted sport conducted in unified, segregated, individualized, and parallel settings. Winnick (2007) has offered an adapted interscholastic model for sport, which is discussed in chapter 3. Also present in chapter 3 is a sport integration continuum.

Adapted sport encompasses disability sport (e.g., Deaf sport), which typically focuses on segregated participation in regular or adapted sport. Although **disability sport** terminology has been used as a term encompassing sport related to individuals with a disability, **adapted sport** terminology is preferred for the following reasons: It is consistent with the terms *adapted physical education* and *adapted physical activity*, it focuses on the modification of sport rather than on disability, it encourages participation in the most normal and integrated environment, it is consistent with normalization theory, it promotes the creation of

sport opportunities, and it provides an opportunity for the pursuit of excellence in sport throughout a full spectrum of settings for participation. This orientation to adapted sport is consistent with the sport integration continuum and the adapted interscholastic model for sports presented in chapter 3. It is believed that these models will lead to more participation in sport by individuals with disabilities as well as to more creative offerings and grouping patterns related to sport at every level of participation. Adapted sport terminology supports the development of excellence in sport while promoting growth in sport participation within many settings.

Adapted sport programs are conducted in diverse environments and organizational patterns for a variety of purposes. Educational programs are generally conducted in schools and may include intramural, extramural, and interscholastic activities. Intramural activities are conducted within schools, involve only pupils enrolled in that school, and are organized to serve the entire school population. Extramural sport activities involve participation of students from two or more schools, and they are sometimes conducted as play days or sport days at the end of instructional or intramural sessions. Interscholastic sports involve competition between representatives from two or more schools and offer enriched opportunities for more highly skilled students. Adapted sport activity might also be conducted for leisure or recreational purposes within formal, open, or unstructured programs; as a part of the lifestyle of individuals or groups; or for wellness, medical, or therapeutic reasons. For example, sport or adapted sport might be used as part of recreational therapy, corrective therapy, sport therapy, or wellness programs. In general, involvement in sport or adapted sport has several purposes. In this book, the focus is on adapted sport in educational settings and in regional, national, and international competition under the governance of formalized organizations promoting sport for individuals with disabilities. Winnick (2007) uses the term **electronic sport** to encompass individual and team performance and results that are communicated electronically to a coordinating center. For example, the time of a 17-year-old female performing in an 800-meter wheelchair competition is transmitted to regional, state, and national centers.

PLANNING: PURPOSES, AIMS, GOALS, AND OBJECTIVES

An important step in providing a good adapted physical education program is planning. A plan provides the direction of the program and includes identifying its purpose, aims, goals, and objectives. The purpose of a program should be consistent with the mission of its organization and with the general physical education or sport program avail-able for students without disabilities. In this book, it is assumed that the purpose of adapted physical education is to promote **self-actualization**, which in turn promotes optimal personal development and contributes to the whole of society. This purpose is consistent with the humanistic philosophy interpreted by Sherrill (2004), who says that humanism is a philosophy that pertains to helping people become fully human, thereby actualizing their potential for making the world the best possible place for all forms of life.

There is no universal model or paradigm related to purposes, aims, goals, or objectives in adapted physical education. The framework presented in figure 1.2 is offered as a skeletal reference for physical education programs and is consistent with federal legislation and the orientation used in this book. Figure 1.2 encompasses the statement of purpose as well as the aims, goals, and content areas of a program. This framework assumes that the adapted physical education program is part of the total school physical education program. In essence, the program strives to develop participants to their maximum.

In this orientation, the physical education and sport program aims to produce physically educated people who live active and healthy lifestyles that enhance their progress toward self-actualization. The National Association for Sport and Physical Education (NASPE) has developed six content standards to reflect what the physically educated person should be able to know and do (see sidebar).

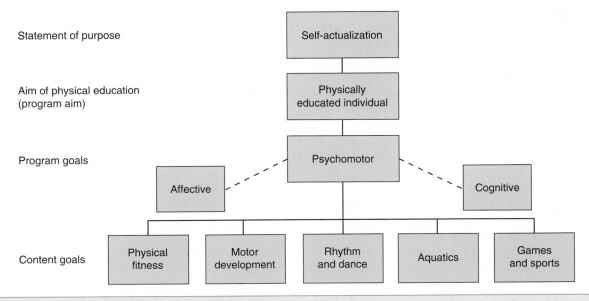

FIGURE 1.2 Aims and goals for an adapted physical education program.

NASPE Content Standards

The physically educated person does the following:

Standard 1—demonstrates competency in motor skills and movement patterns needed to perform a variety of physical activities.

Standard 2—demonstrates an understanding of movement concepts, principles, strategies, and tactics as they apply to the learning and performance of physical activities.

Standard 3—participates regularly in physical activity.

Standard 4—achieves and maintains a health-enhancing level of physical fitness.

Standard 5—exhibits responsible personal and social behavior that respects self and others in physical activity settings.

Standard 6—values physical activity for health, enjoyment, challenge, self-expression, and social interaction.

Reprinted from NASPE, 2004.

The development of a physically educated person is accomplished through experiences associated with goals and objectives related to psychomotor, cognitive, and affective domains of learning. In this paradigm, program goals are accomplished by education of and development through the psychomotor domain. In figure 1.2, education *of* the psychomotor domain is represented by solid lines connecting content and program goals. Development *through* the psychomotor domain is represented by dotted lines among cognitive, affective, and psychomotor development areas.

Program goals are developed through content areas in the physical education program. Content areas related to psychomotor development may be grouped in many ways. Figure 1.2 shows five content goals areas: physical fitness, motor development, rhythm and dance, aquatics, and games and sports. These content areas are consistent with the definition of physical education associated

with IDEA. Each of these content areas includes developmental areas of sport skills. For example, aerobic capacity might be a developmental area under physical fitness, and basketball is a sport within the content area of group games and sports.

The content goals shown in figure 1.2, as well as goals in affective and cognitive domains, may serve as annual goals for individualized programs. Specific skills and developmental areas associated with these goals may be used to represent short-term objectives. For example, an annual goal for a student might be to improve physical fitness. A corresponding short-term objective might be to improve health-related flexibility by obtaining a score of 20 centimeters on a sit-and-reach test. Objectives can be expressed on several levels to reflect the specificity desired. The emphasis given to the three developmental areas in a program should be on the student's needs. An adapted physical education program is established to meet objectives unique for each student.

In general, the purpose, aims, and program goals are the same for regular and adapted physical education. Differences between these programs exist mainly in the content goals, specific objectives, and performance standards and benchmarks. For example, goalball may be a content goal for individuals who are blind, and an objective might relate to throwing and blocking. Teachers may select test items and standards that assess functional as well as physiological health, which relate to health-related physical fitness. Other differences might include the time spent on instructional units or objectives and the scope of the curriculum mastered.

SERVICE PROVIDERS

People who provide direct services are the key to ensuring quality experiences related to adapted physical education and sport. These providers include teachers, coaches, therapists, paraeducators, and volunteers. In regard to teachers, it must be emphasized that adapted physical education and sport is provided not only by educators who specialize in this field but by regular physical educators as well. If services were provided only by specialists in adapted physical education, relatively few students would be getting services because there are too few specialists in adapted physical education.

To meet the needs of children in adapted physical education and sport, teachers of physical education must assume responsibility for all children they teach. Each teacher must be willing to contribute to the development of each student. This requires a philosophy that looks toward human service and beyond win–loss records as the ultimate contribution in one's professional life. Success for *all* students in physical education requires an instructor who has appropriate professional knowledge, skills, and values as well as a caring and helping attitude. A good teacher or coach of children recognizes the development of positive self-esteem as important and displays an attitude of acceptance, empathy, friendship, and warmth while ensuring a secure and controlled learning environment. The good teacher or coach of adapted physical education and sport selects and uses teaching approaches and styles beneficial to students, provides individualized and personalized instructions and opportunities, and creates a positive environment in which students can succeed. The good teacher or coach uses a praising and encouraging approach and creates a positive educational environment in which all students are accepted and supported.

People studying to become teachers often have little or no experience working with students with unique physical education needs. It is important to take advantage of every opportunity to interact with individuals with disabilities, to describe the value of physical activity to them, and to listen to their stories about their experiences in adapted physical education and sport. Being involved in disability awareness activities and having an opportunity to function as if one has a disability provides important insights and values to prospective teachers.

BRIEF HISTORY OF ADAPTED PHYSICAL EDUCATION

Although significant progress concerning educational services for individuals with disabilities has been relatively recent, the use of physical activity or exercise for medical treatment and therapy is not new. Therapeutic exercise can be traced to 3000 BC in China. It is known that the ancient Greeks and Romans also recognized the medical and therapeutic value of exercise. However, the idea of physical education or physical activity to meet the unique educational needs of individuals with disabilities is a recent phenomenon. Efforts to serve these populations through physical education and sport have been given significant attention only during the 20th century, although efforts began in the United States in the 19th century.

Beginning of Adapted Physical Activity

In 1838, physical activity began receiving special attention at the Perkins School for students with visual disabilities in Boston. According to Charles E. Buell (1983), a noted physical educator with a visual impairment, this special attention resulted from the fact that Samuel Gridley Howe, the school director, advocated the health benefits of physical activity. For the first eight years, physical education consisted of compulsory recreation in the open air. In 1840, when the school was moved to South Boston, boys participated in gymnastic exercises and swimming. This was the first physical education program in the United States for students who were blind, and, by Buell's account, it was far ahead of the physical education in public schools.

Medical Orientation

Although physical education was provided in the early 1800s to people with visual impairments, as well as people with other disabilities, medically oriented gymnastics and drills began in the latter part of the century as the forerunner of modern adapted physical education in the United States. Sherrill (2004) states that physical education prior to 1900 was medically oriented and preventive, developmental, or corrective in nature. Its purpose was to prevent illness and promote the health and vigor of the mind and body. Strongly influencing this orientation was a system of medical gymnastics developed in Sweden by Pehr Henrik Ling and introduced to the United States in 1884.

Shift to Sport and the Whole Person

From the end of the 19th century into the 1930s, programs began to shift from medically oriented physical training to sport-centered physical education, and concern for the whole child emerged. Compulsory physical education in public schools increased dramatically, and training of physical education teachers (rather than medical training) developed for the promotion of physical education (Sherrill, 2004). This transition resulted in broad mandatory programs consisting of games, sports, rhythmic activities, and calisthenics designed to meet the needs of the whole person. Students unable to participate in regular activities were provided corrective or remedial physical education. According to Sherrill, physical education programs between the 1930s and the 1950s consisted of regular or corrective classes for students who today would be described as normal. Sherrill (2004) has succinctly described adapted physical education during this time in the United States:

> Assignment to physical education was based upon a thorough medical examination by a physician who determined whether a student should participate in the regular or corrective program. Corrective classes were composed of limited, restricted, or modified activities related to health, posture, or fitness problems. In many schools, students were excused from physical education. In others, the physical educator typically taught several sections of regular physical education and one section of corrective physical education each day. Leaders in corrective physical education continued to have strong backgrounds in medicine and physical therapy. People preparing to be physical education teachers generally completed one university course in corrective physical education. (p. 18)

Emerging Comprehensive Subdiscipline

During the 1950s, more and more students described as handicapped were being served in public schools, and the outlook toward them was becoming increasingly humanistic. With a greater diversity in pupils came a greater diversity in programs to meet their needs. In 1952, the organization American Association for Health, Physical Education and Recreation (AAHPER), now known as the American Alliance for Health, Physical Education, Recreation and Dance (AAHPERD), formed a committee to define the subdiscipline and give direction and guidance to professionals. This committee defined adapted physical education as "a diversified program of developmental activities, games, sports, and rhythms suited to the interests, capacities, and limitations of students with disabilities who may not safely or successfully engage in unrestricted participation in the rigorous activities of the regular physical education program" (Com-

mittee on Adapted Physical Education, 1952). The definition retained the evolving diversity of physical education and specifically included students with disabilities. *Adapted physical education* still serves today as the comprehensive term for this subdiscipline, although it is not limited to people with classified disabilities.

Recent and Current Status

With the impetus provided by a more humanistic, more informed, and less discriminatory society, major advances continued in the 1960s. Many of these advances were associated with the Joseph P. Kennedy family. In 1965, the Joseph P. Kennedy, Jr. Foundation awarded a grant to AAHPERD to launch the Project on Recreation and Fitness for the Mentally Retarded. The project grew to encompass all special populations, and its name was changed in 1968 to the Unit on Programs for the Handicapped. As director of the unit, Dr. Julian U. Stein dramatically influenced adapted physical education at every level throughout the United States.

In 1968, the Kennedy Foundation exhibited further concern for individuals with mental retardation by establishing the Special Olympics. This program grew rapidly, with competition held at local, state, national, and international levels in an ever-increasing range of sports. During the mid-1960s, concern for people with emotional or learning disabilities had a significant effect on adapted physical education in the United States. The importance of physical activity for the well-being of those with emotional problems was explicitly recognized by the National Institute of Mental Health (NIMH) of the U.S. Department of Health and Human Services (DHHS) when it funded the Buttonwood Farms Project. The project, conducted at Buttonwood Farms, Pennsylvania, included a physical recreation component. This project was valuable for recognizing the importance of physical activity in the lives of individuals with disabilities, bringing the problems of seriously disturbed youths to the attention of educators, and developing curricular materials to prepare professionals in physical education and recreation for work with this population.

During the same era, adapted physical education gained much attention with the use of perceptual–motor activities as a modality for academic and intellectual development, particularly for students with learning disabilities. The contention that movement experiences serve as a basis for intellectual abilities has lost support in recent years. However, the use of movement experiences, including active games, for the development and reinforcement of academic abilities appears to be regaining popularity and research-based support.

Current direction and emphasis in adapted physical education are heavily associated with the right to a free and appropriate education. Because of litigation and the passage of various federal laws and regulations in the United States, progress has occurred in both adapted physical education and sport. This legal impetus has improved programs in many schools and agencies, extended mandated physical education for individuals aged 3 to 21, stimulated activity programs for infants and toddlers, and resulted in dramatic increases in participation in sport programs for individuals with disabilities. Legislation has also resulted in funds for professional preparation, research, and other special projects relevant to the provision of full educational opportunity for individuals with unique needs. Finally, the impact of federal legislation and a strong belief in the right to and value of an education in the regular educational environment have resulted in a significant movement toward inclusion regarding the education of children with disabilities in the United States. Dramatic advocacy and progress have increased relative to the offering of adapted sport opportunities in secondary schools (Frogley and Beaver, 2002; Winnick, 2007; Vaughn, 2007). The elements of modern direction and emphasis mentioned here are covered in detail in several parts of this book.

Recent and Current Leaders

As fields of study emerge, evolve, and mature, people always appear who have provided leadership and achieved excellence in the field. These individuals serve as role models for contributions to philosophy, theoretical foundations, research, programs, teaching, and other services to the field. In regard to adapted physical education, the periodical *Palaestra* has identified 10 people who made significant contributions to adapted physical education in the late 20th century throughout distinguished careers. Their class of 1991 leaders included David M. Auxter, Slippery Rock University in Pennsylvania; Lawrence Rarick, University of California at Berkeley; Julian U. Stein, AAHPERD and George Mason University; Thomas M. Vodola, Township of Ocean School District in New Jersey; and Janet Wessel, Michigan State University. In the next decade, *Palaestra* selected the following nationally and internationally recognized people as leaders in the field of adapted physical education: David Beaver, Western Illinois University; Gudrun Doll-Tepper, Free University of Berlin; John Dunn, Oregon State University; Claudine Sherrill, Texas Women's University; and Joseph P. Winnick, State University of New York, College at Brockport. Detailed accomplishments of the 2000 group are presented in the summer 2000 issue of *Palaestra* ("Leadership in disability sport," 2000).

The American Association for Physical Activity and Recreation (AAPAR) has created the Julian U. Stein Lifetime Achievement Award to give recognition to sustained lifetime leadership to the field. The holders of this award (Stein, Sherrill, Winnick, Auxter, and Seaman) are presented in figure 1.3. Although these leaders have been recognized, it is important to realize that they constitute a tiny percentage of the people making significant contributions at many levels every day in the field of adapted physical education.

a   b   c   d   e

Photos courtesy of Julian Stein, Claudine Sherrill, Joseph Winnick, David Auxter, and Janet Seaman.

FIGURE 1.3 Recent and current leaders of adapted physical education: *(a)* Julian U. Stein, *(b)* Claudine Sherrill, *(c)* Joseph Winnick, *(d)* David Auxter, *(e)* Janet Seaman.

INCLUSION MOVEMENT

Inclusion means educating students with disabilities in a regular educational setting. The movement toward inclusion was encouraged by and is compatible with the LRE provisions associated with IDEA. Education in the LRE requires, to the maximum extent appropriate, that children with disabilities be educated with children without disabilities. However, according to LRE provisions in IDEA, a continuum of alternative environments (including segregated environments) may be used for the education of a student if those are the most appropriate environments. A recommended continuum is presented in figure 2.1 (p. 24). The inclusion movement has also been given impetus by many who believe that separate education is not an equal education and that the setting of a program provided for a child significantly influences that program. In the United States today, all but a small percentage of students with disabilities attend schools with peers without disabilities. This is the reality of inclusion and is why appropriately prepared educators are required. Although this book prepares teachers to serve children in all settings, it gives special emphasis to the skills and knowledge needed to optimally educate children with disabilities in regular educational environments.

LITIGATION

Much has been written about the impact of litigation on the guarantee of full educational opportunity in the United States. The most prominent of cases, which has served as an important precedent for civil litigation, was *Brown v. Board of Education of Topeka* (1954). This case established that the doctrine of separate but equal in public education resulted in segregation that violated the constitutional rights of black students. Two landmark cases also had a heavy impact on the provision of free, appropriate public education for all children with disabilities. The first was the class action suit of *Pennsylvania Association for Retarded Children v. Commonwealth of Pennsylvania* (1972). Equal protection and due process clauses associated with the Fifth and Fourteenth Amendments served as the constitutional basis for the court's rulings and agreements. The following were among the rulings or agreements in the case:

- Labeling a child as mentally retarded or denying public education or placement in a regular setting without due process or hearing violates the rights of the individual.

- All mentally retarded children are capable of benefiting from a program of education and training.

- Mental age may not be used to postpone or in any way deny access to a free public program of education and training.

- Having undertaken to provide a free, appropriate education to all its children, a state may not deny mentally retarded children the same.

A second important case was *Mills v. Board of Education of the District of Columbia* (1972). This action, brought on behalf of seven children, sought to restrain the District of Columbia from excluding children from public schools or denying them publicly supported education. The district court held that, by failing to provide the seven children with handicapping conditions and the class they represented with publicly supported specialized education, the district violated controlling statutes, its own regulations, and due process. The District of Columbia was required to provide a publicly supported education, appropriate equitable funding, and procedural due process rights to the seven children.

From 1972 to 1975, 46 right-to-education cases related to people with disabilities were tried in 28 states. They provided the foundation for much of the legislation to be discussed in the next section.

LAWS IMPORTANT TO ADAPTED PHYSICAL EDUCATION AND SPORT

Laws have had a tremendous influence on education programs for students with disabilities. Since 1969, colleges and universities in many states have received federal funds for professional preparation, research, and other projects to promote programs for individuals with disabilities. Although the amount of money has been relatively small, physical educators have gained a great deal from that support. The government agency most responsible for administering federally funded programs related to adapted physical education is the Office of Special Education and Rehabilitative Services (OSE/RS) within the U.S. Department of Education.

Four laws or parts of laws and their amendments have had significant impact on adapted physical education and adapted sport: IDEA, section 504 of the Rehabilitation Act of 1973, the Olympic and Amateur Sports Act, and the Americans with Disabilities Act (ADA). In January of 2002, PL 107-110, the No Child Left Behind Act of 2001 (NCLB), was signed into law to ensure that all children have a fair, equal, and significant opportunity to obtain a high-quality education. The provisions of NCLB emphasize the attainment of academic achievement standards and academic assessment that affect students in special education. Although the central thrust of NCLB has less impact on adapted physical education and sport than the other four laws have, it is clear that NCLB must be coordinated with the other laws. Table 1.1 shows a time line marking important milestones along with brief statements describing the importance of these laws.

Individuals With Disabilities Education Act

A continuing major impetus related to the provision of educational services for students with disabilities is PL 108-446, the Individuals with Disabilities Education Improvement Act of 2004. Definitions associated with this law, which is cited herein as IDEA, can be found in appendix A. This act expanded on the previous Education for All Handicapped Children Act and amendments. However, IDEA reflects the composite and the most recent version and amendments of these laws (table 1.1). This act was designed to ensure that all children with disabilities have access to a free appropriate public education that emphasizes **special education** and **related services** designed to meet their unique needs and prepare them for employment and independent living (see sidebar).

In this legislation, the term *special education* is defined to mean specially designed instruction at no cost to parents or guardians to meet the unique needs of a child with disability, including instruction conducted in the classroom, in the home, in hospitals and institutions, in other settings, and in physical education (OSE/RS, 2006). IDEA specifies that the term *related services* means transportation and such developmental, corrective, and other supportive services as are required to assist a child with a disability to benefit from special education, including speech-language pathology and audiology services, psychological services, physical and occupational therapy, recreation (including therapeutic recreation), early identification and assessment of disabilities in children, counseling services (including rehabilitation counseling), orientation and mobility services, and medical services for diagnostic and evaluation purposes. Related services also include school health services, social work services in school, and parent counseling and training (OSE/RS, 2006). The act also ensures that the rights of children with disabilities and their parents or guardians are protected and helps states

Table 1.1 Legislative Time Line: 1973-2008

Law	Date	Importance
PL 93-112, Rehabilitation Act of 1973	1973	Section 504 of this act was designed to prevent discrimination against and provide equal opportunity for individuals with disabilities in programs or activities receiving federal financial assistance.
PL 94-142, Education for All Handicapped Children Act of 1975 PL 101-476, Individuals with Disabilities Education Act of 1990 (IDEA) PL 108-446, Individuals with Disabilities Education Improvement Act of 2004 (IDEIA)	1975	These acts and their amendments are designed to ensure that all children with disabilities have available a free appropriate public education that emphasizes special education (including physical education) and related services designed to meet their unique needs.
PL 95-606, Amateur Sports Act of 1978 PL 105-277, Ted Stevens Olympic and Amateur Sports Act of 1998	1978	These acts coordinate national efforts concerning amateur activity, including activity associated with the Olympic Games. As a result of this legislation, USOC took over the role and responsibilities of the United States Paralympic Committee.
PL 101-336, Americans with Disabilities Act (ADA)	1990	This act extended civil rights protection for individuals with disabilities to all areas of American life.

Highlights of the Individuals With Disabilities Education Act

IDEA and its rules and regulations require the following:

- A right to a free and appropriate education
- That physical education be made available to children with disabilities
- Equal opportunity for nonacademic and extracurricular activities
- An individualized program designed to meet the needs of children with disabilities
- Programs conducted within the LRE
- Nondiscriminatory testing and objective criteria for placement
- Due process
- Related services to assist in special education

and localities provide education for all individuals with disabilities. In addition, IDEA has established a policy to develop and implement a program of early intervention services for infants and toddlers and their families.

Definition and Requirements of Physical Education in IDEA

Regulations associated with IDEA (OSE/RS, 2006, p.18) define physical education as the "development of (a) physical and motor fitness, (b) fundamental motor skills and patterns, and (c) skills in aquatics, dance, and individual and group games and sports (including intramural and lifetime sports)." This term includes special physical education, adapted physical education, movement education, and motor development. IDEA requires that special education, including physical education, be made available to children with disabilities and that it include physical education specially designed, if necessary, to meet their unique needs. This federal legislation, together with state requirements for physical education, significantly affects physical education in schools. Readers should notice that

the definition of adapted physical education used in this book closely parallels the definition of physical education in IDEA.

Free Appropriate Public Education Under IDEA

The term *free appropriate public education* means special education and related services (1) are provided at public expense, under public supervision and direction, and without charge; (2) meet the standards of the state's educational agency; (3) include preschool, elementary, or secondary school education in the state involved; and (4) are provided in conformity with an IEP (OSE/RS, 2006).

Least Restrictive Environment

IDEA requires that education be conducted in the LRE. Education in the LRE means that students with disabilities are educated with students without disabilities and that special classes, separate schooling, or other removal of children with disabilities from the regular physical education environment occurs only when the nature or severity of disability of a child is such that education in regular classes with the use of supplementary aids and services cannot be achieved in a satisfactory way (OSE/RS, 2006).

Relevant to education in the most appropriate setting is a continuum of instructional placements (see figure 2.1), which range from a situation in which children with disabilities are integrated into a regular class to a very restrictive setting (out-of-school segregated placement).

Focus on Student Needs and Opportunities

IDEA implicitly, if not explicitly, encourages educators to focus on the educational needs of the student instead of on clinical or diagnostic labels. For example, as the IEP is developed, concern focuses on present functioning level, objectives, annual goals, and so on. The associated rules and regulations also indicate that children with disabilities must be provided with an equal opportunity for participation in nonacademic and extracurricular services and activities, including athletics and recreational activities.

Section 504 of the Rehabilitation Act

The right of equal opportunity also emerges from another legislative milestone that has affected adapted physical education and sport. Section 504

APPLICATION EXAMPLE

Student Placement

Setting: Individualized program planning committee meeting

Student: A 10-year-old with behavior problems, inadequate physical fitness (as evidenced by failing to meet specific or general standards on the Brockport Physical Fitness Test), and below-average motor development (at or below one standard deviation below the mean on a standardized motor development test)

Issue: What is the appropriate setting for instruction?

Application: On the basis of the information available and after meeting with the parents and other members of the program planning committee, the following plan was determined:

▶ The student will receive an adapted physical education program.

▶ The program will be conducted in an integrated setting with support services whenever the student's peer group receives physical education.

▶ The student will receive an additional class of physical education each week with two other students who also require adapted physical education.

of the Rehabilitation Act provides that no otherwise qualified person with a disability, solely by reason of that disability, be excluded from participation in, be denied the benefits of, or be subjected to discrimination under any program or activity receiving federal financial assistance (Workforce Investment Act of 1998).

An important intent of section 504 is to ensure that individuals with a disability receive intended benefits of all educational programs and extracurricular activities. Two conditions are prerequisite to the delivery of services that guarantee benefits to those individuals: Programs must be *equally effective* as those provided to students without disabilities, and they must be conducted in the *most normal and integrated settings* possible. To be equally effective, a program must offer students with disabilities **equal opportunity** to attain the same results, gain the same benefits, or reach the same levels of achievement as peers without disabilities.

To illustrate the intent of section 504, consider a student who is totally blind and enrolled in a course in which all other students in the class are sighted. A written test given at the end of the semester would not provide the student who is blind with an equal opportunity to demonstrate knowledge of the material; thus, this approach would not be equally effective. By contrast, on a test administered orally or in Braille, the student who is blind would have an equal opportunity to attain the same results or benefits as the other students. In giving an oral exam, the instructor would be giving equivalent, as opposed to identical, services. (Merely identical services, in fact, would be considered discriminatory and not in accord with section 504.) It is neither necessary nor possible to guarantee equal results; what is important is the equal opportunity to attain those results. For example, a recipient of federal funds offering basketball to the general student population must provide wheelchair basketball for students confined to wheelchairs, if a need exists.

A program is not equally effective if it results in indiscriminate isolation or separation of individuals with disabilities. To the maximum degree possible, individuals with disabilities should participate in the LRE, as represented by a continuum of alternative instructional placements (see chapter 2).

Compliance with section 504 requires program accessibility. Its rules and regulations prohibit exclusion of individuals with disabilities from federally assisted programs because of architectural or other environmental barriers. Common barriers to accessibility include facilities, finances, and transportation. Money available for athletics within a school district cannot be spent in a way that discriminates on the basis of disability. If a school district lacks sufficient funds, then it need not offer programs; however, it cannot fund programs in a discriminatory manner.

In accordance with section 504, children with disabilities who do not require special education or related services (not classified under IDEA) are still entitled to accommodations and services in the regular school setting that are necessary to enable them to benefit from all programs and activities available to students without disabilities. Every student with a disability under IDEA is also protected under section 504, but all students covered under section 504 are not necessarily students with a disability under IDEA.

Section 504 obligates school districts to identify, evaluate, and extend to every qualified student with a disability (as defined by this act) residing in the district a free and appropriate public education, including modifications, accommodations, and specialized instructions or related aids as deemed necessary to meet their educational needs as adequately as the needs of students without disabilities are being met. School districts across the United States are now developing section 504 accommodation plans to provide programmatic assistance to students so that they have full access to all activities. For example, a 504 plan related to physical education might seek specialized instruction or equipment, auxiliary aids or services, or program modifications. A sample 504 plan is presented in chapter 5.

The Rehabilitation Act is complaint-oriented legislation. Violations of section 504 may be filed with the United States Office for Civil Rights (OCR), and parents may request under section 504 an impartial hearing to challenge a school district's decision regarding their children.

Olympic and Amateur Sports Act

The Amateur Sports Act (ASA) of 1978 (PL 95-606), amended by PL 105-277, the Ted Stevens Olympic and Amateur Sports Act of 1998, has contributed significantly to the provision of amateur athletic activity in the United States, including competition for athletes with disabilities. This legislation has led to the establishment of the United States Olympic Committee (USOC) and gives it exclusive jurisdiction over matters pertaining to U.S. participation and organization of the Olympic Games, the Paralympic Games, and the Pan American Games, including representation of the United States in the Games. USOC encourages and provides assistance to amateur athletic programs and competition for amateur athletes with disabilities, including,

where feasible, the expansion of opportunities for meaningful participation in programs of athletic competition for athletes without disabilities. Additional information about the Paralympics is presented in chapter 3.

Americans with Disabilities Act

In 1990, PL 101-336, the Americans with Disabilities Act (ADA), was passed. Whereas section 504 focused on educational rights, this legislation extended civil rights protection for individuals with disabilities to all areas of life. Provisions include employment, public accommodation and services, public transportation, and telecommunications. Related to adapted physical education and sport, this legislation requires that community recreational facilities, including health and fitness facilities, be accessible and, where appropriate, that reasonable accommodations be made for individuals with disabilities. Physical educators must develop and offer programs for individuals with disabilities that give them the ability to participate in physical activity and sport experiences within the community.

HISTORY OF ADAPTED SPORT

Deaf athletes were among the first Americans with disabilities to become involved in organized sport at special schools. As reported by Gannon (1981), in the 1870s the Ohio School for the Deaf became the first school for the Deaf to offer baseball, and the state school in Illinois introduced American football in 1885. Football became a major sport in many schools for the Deaf around the turn of the century, and basketball was introduced at the Wisconsin School for the Deaf in 1906. Teams from schools for the Deaf have continued to compete against each other and against athletes in regular schools.

Beyond interschool programs, formal international competition was established in 1924, when competitors from nine nations gathered in Paris for the first International Silent Games (now known as the Deaflympics). In 1945, the American Athletic Association of the Deaf (AAAD) was established to provide, sanction, and promote competitive sport opportunities for Americans with hearing impairments.

The earliest formal, recorded athletic competition in the United States for people with visual disabilities was a telegraphic track meet between the Overbrook and Baltimore schools for the blind in 1907. In a telegraphic meet, local results are mailed to a central committee, which makes comparisons to determine winners. From this beginning, athletes with visual disabilities continue to compete against each other and against their sighted peers.

Since the 1900s, wars have provided impetus for competitive sport opportunities. Sir Ludwig Guttmann of Stoke Mandeville, England, is credited with introducing competitive sport as an integral part of the rehabilitation of veterans with disabilities. In the late 1940s, Stoke Mandeville Hospital sponsored the first recognized games for wheelchair athletes. In 1949, the University of Illinois organized the first national wheelchair basketball tournament, which resulted in the formation of the National Wheelchair Basketball Association (NWBA). To expand sport opportunities, Ben Lipton founded the National Wheelchair Athletic Association (NWAA) in the mid-1950s. This organization has sponsored competitive sport at state, regional, and national levels for participants with spinal cord conditions and other conditions requiring wheelchair use. Another advancement was the creation of the National Handicapped Sports and Recreation Association (NHSRA). This organization—known today as Disabled Sports USA (DS/USA)—was formed by a small group of Vietnam veterans in the late 1960s. It has been dedicated to providing year-round sport and recreational opportunities for people with orthopedic, spinal cord, neuromuscular, and visual disabilities.

Special Olympics—created by the Joseph P. Kennedy, Jr. Foundation to provide and promote athletic competition for individuals with mental retardation—held its first international games at Soldier Field in Chicago in 1968. (A symbol for Special Olympics is shown in figure 1.4.) Special Olympics has served as the model sport organization for individuals with disabilities through its leadership in direct service, research, training, advocacy, education, and organizational leadership.

During the last quarter of the 20th century, other national multisport and unisport programs have been formed. These have expanded available sport offerings to an increasing number of individuals with disabilities. The latest opportunities have been organized for athletes with visual impairments, cerebral palsy, closed head injury, stroke, dwarfism, and other conditions.

The evolution of sport organizations within the United States has led to greater involvement in international competition. In fact, many American sport organizations have international counterparts (see chapter 3). Especially notable in this regard is the International Paralympic Committee (IPC), discussed in chapter 3. American organizations that participate in international games are also listed in chapter 3. These organizations are multisport programs—that is, several sports are included as a part of these programs. In addition to multisport organizations, several organizations are centered on single sports, such as the NWBA. An important movement is underway today in which sport programs traditionally offering programs for athletes without disabilities are organizing opportunities and competition for athletes with disabilities. This approach reduces the need for sport organizations organized primarily for types of disability. Some of these programs are associated with international competition. Unisport organizations provide excellent opportunities for athletes with disabilities, and several of these organizations are identified in other chapters and appendix B of this book.

In the past few years, much of the impetus for sport for athletes with disabilities has been provided by out-of-school sport organizations. Although developing at a slower rate, other opportunities have begun to surface throughout the United States in connection with public school programs. An important milestone came in 1992 when Minnesota became the first state to welcome athletes with disabilities into its state school association. This made Minnesota the first state in the nation to sanction interschool sport for junior and senior high school students with disabilities. More recently, a Georgia-based nonprofit organization titled the American Association of Adapted Sports Programs (AAASP) has been developed to build interscholastic sport leagues for students with physical disabilities or visual impairments. This group has developed a model for other programs throughout the country to imitate. This organization has joined forces with Project ASPIRE (Adapted Sports Programs In Recreation and Education) to promote programs. AAASP has been endorsed by AAPAR.

A few states now organize statewide competition for athletes with disabilities. Some of these are combined with community-based sport programs, and others are provided independently of other organized sport programs. Finally, sport programs in rehabilitation settings for members of

Photo courtesy of Zurab Tsereteli.

FIGURE 1.4 This symbol of the Special Olympics was a gift of the former Union of Soviet Socialist Republics on the occasion of the 1979 International Special Olympic Games, hosted by the State University of New York, College at Brockport. The artist is Zurab Tsereteli.

communities are emerging in major cities in the United States. More detailed information on these programs is presented in chapter 3.

PERIODICALS

The increased knowledge base and greater attention to adapted physical education and sport in recent years has been accompanied by the founding and development of several periodicals devoted to the subject. Among the most relevant of these are the *Adapted Physical Activity Quarterly*, *Palaestra*, and *Sports 'N Spokes*. Other periodicals that publish directly relevant information from time to time include the *Journal of Physical Education, Recreation and Dance*; *Strategies*; *Research Quarterly for Exercise and Sport*; *Journal of Visual Impairment and Blindness*; *Journal of Learning Disabilities*; *American Annals of the Deaf*; *Teaching Exceptional Children*; *American Journal of Mental Deficiency*; *Journal of Special Education*; *Therapeutic Recreation Journal*; *Journal of the Association for Persons with Severe Handicaps*; *Clinical Kinesiology*; and *Physical Educator*.

ORGANIZATIONS

The American Alliance for Health, Physical Education, Recreation and Dance (AAHPERD) is an important national organization that makes significant contributions to programs for special populations. AAHPERD has many members whose primary professional concern lies in adapted physical education and sport. They are primarily associated with AAHPERD as part of AAPAR. Over the years, its many publications, conferences, and conventions have given much attention to adapted physical education and sport—not only on the national level but also within the state, district, and local affiliates of the organization. Its professional conferences and conventions are among the best sources of information on adapted physical education and sport, and it is expected that it will continue to provide key professional services and leadership in the future.

The National Consortium for Physical Education and Recreation for Individuals with Disabilities (NCPERID, or the Consortium) was established to promote, stimulate, and encourage professional preparation and research. The organization was started informally in the late 1960s by a small group of college and university directors of federally funded professional preparation or research projects seeking to share information. Its members have extensive backgrounds and interests in adapted physical education and therapeutic recreation. They have provided leadership and input on national issues and concerns, including the development of IDEA and its rules and regulations; federal funding for professional preparation, research, demonstration projects, and other special projects; and monitoring of legislation. The Consortium holds an annual meeting and publishes a newsletter.

The International Federation for Adapted Physical Activity (IFAPA), which originated in Quebec, has expanded to a worldwide organization with an international charter. Its primary service has been to sponsor a biennial international adapted physical activity symposium. In alternating years, symposia organized by IFAPA are also held in other regions throughout the world. The North American Federation of Adapted Physical Activity (NAFAPA) is the North American affiliate of IFAPA. The organization primarily solicits memberships from allied health therapists, therapeutic recreators, and adapted physical educators. With its international dimensions, IFAPA can disseminate valuable knowledge throughout the world.

As mentioned earlier, the OSE/RS, part of the U.S. Department of Education, is responsible for monitoring educational services for individuals with disabilities and for providing grants to colleges and universities to fund professional preparation, research, and other special projects.

As mentioned earlier, a private organization that has made a monumental contribution to both adapted physical education and sport is Special Olympics, Inc., founded by Eunice Kennedy Shriver. Although its leadership in providing sport opportunities for individuals with intellectual disabilities is well known, this organization has provided much more to adapted physical education and sport. Specifically, Special Olympics has played a key role in the attention to physical education in federal legislation and the provision of federal funding for professional preparation, research, and other projects in federal legislation through its advocacy activities. The organization has provided a worldwide model for the provision of sport opportunities, and its work is acknowledged in several sections of this book. In appendix B, many other organizations that promote, advocate, and organize physical education and sport opportunity are listed.

SUMMARY

Over the past few years, increased attention has been given to adapted physical education and sport. This chapter presented a brief history of this field. Information regarding program direction was presented, and the importance and characteristics of those providing services in this field were recognized. The chapter stressed the importance of litigation, legislation, and the inclusion movement on programs affecting individuals with disabilities. Finally, periodicals and organizations significant to adapted physical education were identified and described.

REFERENCES

Brown v. Board of Education of Topeka, 347 U.S. 483 (1954).

Buell, C.E. (1983). *Physical education for blind children.* Springfield, IL: Charles C. Thomas.

Committee on Adapted Physical Education. (1952). Guiding principles for adapted physical education. *Journal of Health, Education and Recreation, 23* (15), 15-28.

Frogley, M., & Beaver, D. (2002). Is the time right for interscholastic athletics for student-athletes with disabilities? *Palaestra, 18,* 4-6.

Gannon, J.R. (1981*). Deaf heritage: A narrative history of deaf America.* Silver Spring, MD: National Association for the Deaf.

Individuals with Disabilities Education Act Amendments of 2004 (IDEA) (PL 108-446), 20 U.S.C. 1400 (2004).

Leadership in disability sport, adapted physical education, and therapeutic recreation. (2000). *Palaestra, 16* (3), 48-52.

Mills v. Board of Education of the District of Columbia, 348 F. Supp. 966 (1972).

National Association for Sport and Physical Education. (2004). *Moving into the future: National standards for physical education: A guide to content and assessment.* Reston, VA: National Association for Sport and Physical Education.

No Child Left Behind Act of 2001 (NCLB Act). Pub. L. 107-110, 115 Stat 1425 (2001).

Office of Special Education and Rehabilitative Services (OSE/RS), 34 CFR 300 (2006).

Pennsylvania Association for Retarded Children v. Commonwealth of Pennsylvania, U.S. District Court, 343 F. Supp. 279 (1972).

Sherrill, C. (2004). *Adapted physical activity, recreation and sport: Crossdisciplinary and lifespan* (6th ed.). Boston: McGraw Higher Education.

Ted Stevens Olympic and Amateur Sports Act of 1998, U.S.C.A. 220501 et seq.

Vaughn, B. (2007). A response to Joseph P. Winnick (Letters to the Editor). *Palaestra, 23* (3), 16.

Winnick, J.P. (2007). A framework in interscholastic sports for youngsters with disabilities (guest editorial). *Palaestra, 23* (2), 4, 9.

Workforce Investment Act of 1998 (PL 105-220), Sec 401 et seq. (1998).

Winnick, J.P., Auxter, D., Jansma, P., Sculli, J., Stein, J., & Weiss, R.A. (1980). Implications of section 504 of the Rehabilitation Act as related to physical education instructional, personnel preparation, intramural, and interscholastic/intercollegiate sport programs. In J.P. Winnick & F.X. Short (Eds.), *Special athletic opportunities for individuals with handicapping conditions.* Brockport, NY: SUNY College at Brockport (ERIC Ed210897) or *Practical Pointers, 3* (11), 1-20.

This chapter provides a full position paper related to section 504 of the Rehabilitation Act of 1973.

WRITTEN RESOURCES

American Association of Adapted Sports Programs (AAASP), P.O. Box 538, Pine Lake, GA 30072; phone: 404-294-0070; e-mail: AAASP@bellsouth.net; Web site: www.AAASP.org.

This is a nonprofit organization that builds interscholastic sport leagues for students with physical disabilities or visual disabilities. Sports include beep baseball, indoor wheelchair soccer, wheelchair basketball, power wheelchair hockey, and track and field.

Block, M.E. (1995). American with Disabilities Act: Its impact on youth sports. *Journal of Education, Recreation and Game, 66* (1), 28-32.

This article summarizes major parts of the act and answers questions on how the act affects youth sports.

Metro Association for Adapted Athletics. Rich Matter, Minnesota State High School League, phone: 763-560-2262, ext. 497; e-mail: rmatter@mshsl.org.

This organization provides leadership and organizes interscholastic athletic opportunities for students with disabilities in the state of Minnesota.

ELECTRONIC RESOURCES

Challenge Publications: www.palaestra.com.

This is the home of *Palaestra*, published by Challenge Publications, P.O. Box 508, Macomb, IL 61455.

Human Kinetics: www.humankinetics.com.

This is the home of the *Adapted Physical Activity Quarterly*, published by Human Kinetics, P.O. Box 5076, Champaign, IL 61825-5076.

National Center on Physical Activity and Disability (NCPAD): www.ncpad.org.

NCPAD provides information and resources to enable people with disabilities to become as physically active as possible.

Paralyzed Veterans of America: www.pva.org.

This is the Web site of *Sports 'N Spokes*, published by the Paralyzed Veterans of America, 2111 East Highland Ave., Ste. 180, Phoenix, AZ 85016-4702.

PE Central: www.pecentral.org.

This site provides up-to-date information on developmentally appropriate programs for school-aged children. It offers resources and lesson ideas for regular and adapted physical education classes.

PE Links 4 U: www.pelinks4u.org.

Provides seven sections related to physical education that offer links, resources, and suggestions for programs.

Project ASPIRE: www.aaasp.org.

Through Project ASPIRE, the AAASP joins forces with leading authorities in sport and physical fitness to lay the foundation for a network of school-based adapted athletic programs across the United States.

Program Organization and Management

Joseph P. Winnick

J immy, an elementary student with cerebral palsy, could definitely benefit from an individualized program to meet his physical education needs. Unfortunately for Jimmy, there is a great deal of confusion at his school. Is he eligible for adapted physical education? In what setting should his program be implemented? What should he be taught? How much time should he receive in physical education? Should he receive physical therapy? In Jimmy's school, these issues are not unusual—the same questions arise every time a student with a unique need enrolls. Should Jimmy's school have written guidelines to improve the educational process for Jimmy and other students? The answer is yes, and this chapter provides information to help develop these guidelines.

The information in this chapter will help schools organize and manage programs and write guidelines reflecting policies and procedures for implementing adapted physical education programs. The guidelines can be a part of the overall plan for physical education or part of a separate document. In either case, guidelines should reflect current laws, rules and regulations, policies, procedures, and best practices.

PROGRAM AND CURRICULUM PLANNING

An important early step for organizing and managing programs and developing guidelines is to identify the purpose, aims, goals, standards, and objectives for physical education. As part of this step, the similarities and differences between regular and adapted physical education should be addressed. This provides a good beginning framework for a program. There is no universal model for this framework, so educational entities must establish or adopt their own. A sample framework for adapted physical education is presented in the first chapter of this book and is outlined in figure 1.2. This framework can be adapted for use for a school plan. It also serves as the structure for this book.

ADMINISTRATIVE AREAS RELATED TO PROGRAM ORGANIZATION AND MANAGEMENT

Personnel who administer school programs must develop procedures for organizing and implementing an adapted physical education program. These administrators must ensure that the resources at their disposal adequately meet the needs of the students they serve. They should have procedures in place to identify students who should receive adapted physical education programs, and they should have a plan for selecting settings most appropriate for instruction. Because of the current emphasis on inclusion, understanding and promoting inclusion is an important consideration in implementing programs. Administrators must

ensure that appropriate class sizes and groupings are provided, schedules are developed to meet student needs, mandated time requirements are met, sport opportunities are provided, and programs are appropriately funded and conducted in accessible facilities. In the next few pages these areas are addressed in more detail.

Identifying Students for Adapted Physical Education

In identifying students for an adapted physical education program, it is important at the outset to determine who is eligible. In some instances, the decision is obvious, and an elaborate system of identification is not necessary. In other instances, determination of a unique need can be made only after assessment data are analyzed and compared with the criteria established to determine a unique need.

An adapted physical education program is for students with unique needs who require a specially designed program exceeding 30 consecutive calendar days. In selecting candidates for such a program, procedures, criteria, and standards for determining unique needs are important (see chapters 4 and 5). The inability to attain health-related, criterion-referenced physical fitness standards appropriate for the individual is an example of a criterion for establishing a unique need. A unique need is exhibited because individual students are expected to meet standards appropriate for them.

Many procedures are used to identify students who require adapted physical education in a school. These procedures are associated with **Child Find**, a program that tries to determine which children in a school have unique needs, as referred to in the Individuals with Disabilities Education Act (IDEA). The procedures might include screening

- all new school entrants,
- students with disabilities,
- all students annually,
- referrals, or
- students requesting exemption from physical education.

An important Child Find activity is the screening of all new entrants to the school. For transfer students, records should be checked to determine if unique needs in physical education have been previously identified. In the absence of such information, the school, as part of its procedures, might decide to administer a screening test, particularly if a unique physical education need is suspected.

A second Child Find source is a list of enrolled students identified as having a disability in accordance with IDEA. Every student who has been so identified and whose disability is frequently associated with unique physical education needs should be routinely screened. Many children with disabilities have participated in preschool programs, and records from these programs might indicate children with unique physical education needs.

A third activity is the annual screening of all students enrolled in school. Such a screening might involve informal observation as well as formal testing. Conditions that might be detected through informal screening and possibly warrant in-depth evaluation include disabling conditions, obesity, clumsiness, aversion to physical activity, and postural deviations.

Many students are referred to adapted physical education. School guidelines should permit referrals from

- parents or guardians;
- professional staff members in the school district;
- physicians;
- judicial officers;
- representatives of agencies with responsibility for student welfare, health, or education; and
- students themselves (if they are at least 18 years of age or are emancipated minors).

Referrals for adapted physical education should be received by a specifically designated person in each school.

Medical excuses or requests for exemption from physical education should lead to referrals for adapted physical education. When an excuse or request is made, immediate discussion with the family physician might be necessary to determine how long adaptation might be required. For a period shorter than 30 consecutive days, required adjustments can be determined by the regular physical education teacher by following established local policies and procedures. If the period is longer than 30 consecutive days, the procedure for identifying students for adapted physical education for a school district should be

followed. Typically, these procedures may involve a planning committee.

Instructional Placements for Physical Education

Students who are referred or are otherwise identified as possibly requiring a specially designed program should undergo a thorough assessment to determine if a unique need exists. Suggested procedures for assessment appear in chapters 4 and 5. Once it is established that students have unique physical education needs and require an adapted physical education program, they must be placed in appropriate instructional settings. It must be emphasized that adapted physical education may be implemented in a variety of settings. In accordance with IDEA, children with disabilities must be educated with students who are not disabled and in the least restrictive environment (LRE) to the maximum extent appropriate. To comply with the LRE requirement, various authors have proposed options on a continuum of instructional arrangements. Typical options on a continuum of instructional arrangements appear in figure 2.1. The number of options available is less important than the idea that students will be educated in the regular setting (to the extent appropriate and possible) and in the environment most conducive to their advancement. The continuum presented in figure 2.1 clearly depicts more possibilities than integrated or segregated placement alone and thus is consistent with IDEA.

The three levels at the base of the continuum provide placement in a regular educational environment, and it is within these levels that the continuum is consistent with education in inclusive environments. Level 1 placement is for students without unique needs or those whose short-term needs are met in the regular physical education program. This placement is also appropriate for students with unique needs requiring an adapted education program that can be appropriately implemented in the regular physical education setting.

Level 2 is for students whose adapted physical education programs can be met in a regular class environment with support services. For example, some students might function well in a regular class if consultation is available to teachers and parents. In another instance, regular class placement might be warranted if a paraprofessional or an adapted physical education teacher can work with the student with unique needs.

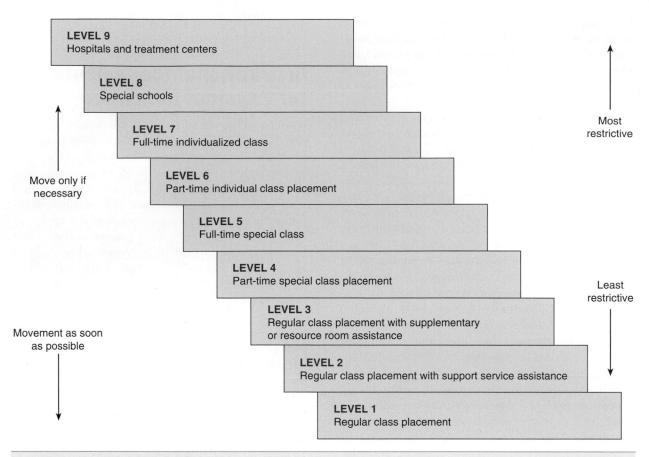

LEVEL 9
Hospitals and treatment centers

LEVEL 8
Special schools

LEVEL 7
Full-time individualized class

LEVEL 6
Part-time individual class placement

LEVEL 5
Full-time special class

LEVEL 4
Part-time special class placement

LEVEL 3
Regular class placement with supplementary
or resource room assistance

LEVEL 2
Regular class placement with support service assistance

LEVEL 1
Regular class placement

Most
restrictive

Least
restrictive

Move only if
necessary

Movement as soon
as possible

FIGURE 2.1   A continuum of alternative instructional placements in physical education.

Level 3 is a regular class placement with supplementary or resource room assistance. Supplementary services can be provided each day or several times a week as a part of or in addition to the time scheduled for physical education. Where indicated, the student might spend a portion of physical education time supervised in a resource room.

Students who require part-time special class placement represent level 4. Their needs might be met at times in an integrated class and at other times in a segregated physical education class. The choice of setting is determined by the nature of the student needs.

Level 5, full-time placement in a special class, is appropriate for those whose unique needs cannot be appropriately met in the regular physical education setting. Levels 6 and 7 are appropriate when part-time or full-time individual class placement is necessary.

Levels 8 and 9 reflect instructional placement in which needs must be met outside the regular school. In level 8, instruction might take place in special schools; in level 9, instruction might occur in hospitals, in treatment centers, or even at a student's home. Students in levels 8 and 9 might be placed outside the school district. In such cases, the local school system is still responsible for ensuring that appropriate education is provided.

Inclusion

Within the past decade, more and more students with disabilities have been educated in regular educational environments. **Inclusion** has been one of the most powerful educational movements over the last 25 years. The movement is not specifically advocated as a part of IDEA, but it is consistent with the requirement in the act that students with disabilities be educated alongside students without disabilities to the maximum extent appropriate. A key foundation of inclusion is the belief that a separate education may not be equal.

Although inclusion has been and continues to be a powerful force, its definitions and interpretations are varied. As defined in chapter 1, inclusion means educating students with disabilities in regular educational settings alongside students without disabilities. However, proponents of inclusion believe that more than integration comes into play. Craft (1996, p. 57) states that "inclusion is a set of attitudes that together provide a welcoming and supportive educational environment, one that is respectful and appreciative of individual differences, and one in which all students participate regardless of gender, race, motor ability, or challenging condition (disability)."

Total inclusion differs from the LRE approach in that the LRE approach advocates education in the most integrated and appropriate environment. Thus, some acceptable placements are not in a regular education environment. Inclusion is consistent with LRE in that both approaches recognize the importance of support services for successful implementation in regular education settings. Placing students in integrated settings without needed support services is sometimes referred to as *dumping* (i.e., combining students with and without unique educational needs but not providing appropriate support services for the students who need them).

Advocates of the inclusion movement point to many benefits for students. They believe that inclusion is advantageous for several reasons:

- It provides students with a more stimulating and motivating environment.

- It provides increased opportunities for students with disabilities to develop social skills and age-appropriate play skills.

- It promotes the development of friendships among students with and without disabilities.

- It provides skilled role models, which fosters the development of skills in all developmental domains.

Those less supportive of the inclusion movement name the following possible problems in inclusive education:

- Students with disabilities might receive less attention and time on task than their classmates do.

- Some teachers are not adequately prepared for successful inclusion and do not possess the interest and motivation to teach in inclusive settings.

- Students without disabilities will be held back in their educational development.

- Inclusion is too expensive if it means providing support services and decreasing class sizes.

- School districts use the inclusion movement as a way of saving money by combining students with and without disabilities but not providing support services for successful educational experiences for all students.

Although these views are held by some, education in the most normal integrated setting possible is a legal right in the United States and must be supported.

This section of the chapter focuses on inclusion for physical education instruction, but integration and inclusion have relevance for sport also. Schools have a responsibility to provide both curricular and extracurricular experiences in the most integrated settings possible. This is reflected in this book by the use of the term *adapted sport* rather than *disability sport* when referring to sport opportunities for individuals with disabilities. A need exists to examine and provide opportunities in sport that include both individuals with and without disabilities in regular or inclusionary settings. The term *disability sport* implies a single sport setting. Use of this term to refer to all sport related to individuals with disabilities impedes creativity and participation in unified sport and in unified sport settings. Chapter 3 presents a sport integration continuum that reflects an inclusionary view that is less confining than an orientation that emphasizes disability. Of course, this movement toward a more inclusionary sport must not necessarily impede the aim for excellence that is characteristic of many segregated sport opportunities. Athletes with disabilities should be encouraged to develop themselves optimally to participate at the highest level of athletic excellence, even though the setting might be segregated.

Functions of Teachers of Adapted Physical Education

This section discusses key functions performed by teachers and others that contribute to successful teaching of adapted physical education. These functions include identifying unique needs, determining appropriate instructional settings and supplementary or support services, selecting strategies for individualizing instruction, adapting activities, preparing students without disabilities for inclusion, and preparing support personnel.

Identify Unique Needs

The first step is to identify the unique needs of the student. Once this is accomplished, the program content and objectives can be most appropriately selected. The identification of unique needs is basic to adapted physical education. In the absence of unique needs, the physical education that is appropriate is regular physical education. Sample guidelines for the determination of a unique physical education need are presented in chapter 4. Several chapters in this book include information to help identify, clarify, and meet unique needs.

Determine Appropriate Instructional Settings and Support Services

Once unique needs are recognized, settings for instruction and supplementary or support services are identified. Possible settings are presented in figure 2.1 on page 24. Settings for instruction depend on the support or supplementary services required. Support services might include ways to promote individualized attention through team teaching, peer tutoring, teaching assistants, paraprofessionals, or volunteers. In addition to support services, there might be a need to identify and provide section 504 accommodations for students with disabilities to promote interaction. Examples include interpreters; facilities, equipment, or supply modifications; and even rule modifications. Examples of supplementary services include physical, occupational, or recreation therapy; orientation and mobility training; and extended services in physical education.

Individualize Instruction

The ability to individualize instruction is an important skill for teachers implementing programs. Individualization occurs when teachers make modifications in their objectives, methods of assessment, content, instructional materials, teaching styles, and instructional strategies and methods. Chapter 7 includes a detailed discussion of instructional strategies to meet individual differences. Strategies for individualization will vary and build on the curricular content and objectives appropriate for each student. Inclusionary curricular options modified from the suggestions of Craft (1996) include the following: the *same curriculum content* with objectives the same or different from other students in the class, a *multilevel curriculum* in which specific skills or activity levels are varied to meet specific objectives but in which the content areas are the same for all students, a *modified curriculum* in which activities are adapted to meet the same or different goals or objectives, and a *different curriculum* in which the activities pursued are different in order to meet the same or

FIGURE 2.2 Mixed cycling.

Photo courtesy of Joseph Winnick.

different goals or objectives. Figure 2.2 presents an example of mixed or parallel inclusive cycling to pursue aerobic objectives. Figure 2.3 shows tandem and cooperative cycling conducted in an inclusive manner to reach aerobic objectives.

Adapt Activities

Another critical function is to adapt activities. Adapting activities increases the likelihood that students with varying abilities will have the same

a

b

FIGURE 2.3   (a) Tandem and (b) cooperative cycling.

Photos courtesy of Joseph Winnick.

opportunity to participate and gain equal benefits from participation (see the application example). Of course, not all adaptations are equal, lead to the same results, or are good. For example, allowing a student using a wheelchair to play in a traditional basketball game involving nine students without disabilities might jeopardize the education and safety of the players and is probably not a good modification strategy. Permitting a double dribble in a basketball game by a student with low cognitive functioning might be considered a good strategy by some teachers and students but be viewed as unfair by others. With this in mind, it is useful to evaluate adaptations using established criteria. For the purpose of this book, the following criteria are suggested for determining good adaptations in settings including students receiving adapted physical education. A good adaptation does the following:

- Promotes interaction and interplay—good adaptations enhance coaction, cooperation, competition, and reciprocity to the extent appropriate.
- Meets the needs of all students in the class—good adaptations meet the needs of all students and do not jeopardize the education of any student in class.
- Improves or maintains self-esteem—good adaptations improve or maintain the self-esteem of all students. Adaptations should not embarrass or inappropriately draw attention to students.

- Provides physical activity—good adaptations promote physical activity for all classmates as much as possible (e.g., elimination-type activities would be contraindicated).
- Provides a safe experience for all—good adaptations sustain a safe environment for all participants.

Modifications to guide the adaptation of physical activities have been directly or indirectly categorized in many ways. Lieberman and Houston-Wilson (2009) suggest four modification areas for adapting activities: equipment, rules, environment, and instruction. Each modification area involves a change or variation so that students with unique needs might be better able to participate in skills or games. As an example, table 2.1 provides some ways that the activities associated with softball can be modified using the four categories. The modifications may be applied to most or all physical activities and to one or more individuals participating in the activity. This book provides adaptations for physical education and sport based on these modification areas and others.

Although adapting physical activities via the four modification areas is a useful approach, adaptations can be enhanced in other ways as well. The sidebar presents seven helpful techniques to promote the integration of students with and without disabilities into physical education activities. These techniques may also be evaluated using the criteria for good adaptations presented earlier. The first suggested technique is to permit the sharing, substitution, or

APPLICATION EXAMPLE

Inclusion

Setting: Seventh-grade physical education class

Student: 13-year-old student with intellectual disabilities and limitations in motor coordination

Unit: Basketball

Task: Dribble the ball around five cones in a weaving manner, return, give the ball to the next person in line, and then sit at the end of the line.

Application: The physical educator might include the following task modifications:

▶ Permit the use of either the same or alternating hands.
▶ Permit the skipping of alternating cones or increase the distance between cones.
▶ Use a different ball size.
▶ Dribble for a shorter distance around fewer cones.
▶ Dribble at varying speeds.

Table 2.1 Modifications of Softball Activities

Category	Modifications
Equipment	Beep balls, auditory balls, bright balls, Nerf balls, Wiffle balls, large balls, buzzers on bases, large bases, tee, large plastic bats, light bats
Rules	Hit off a tee, five-strike rule, no strikeout, three swings and no strikes, running with a partner
Environment	Shorter distance between bases, increased number of players in a game, reduced number of bases, batting cages, smaller field, partner activities
Instruction	Physical assistance, peer tutors, teaching in Braille, task analysis, sign language, hand signals, verbal cues, demonstration, auditory cues, one-on-one instruction

Data from Lieberman, 2009.

interchange of duties in an activity. This technique is patterned after the idea of a pinch hitter or a courtesy runner in softball. In an inclusive setting, for example, a runner without disabilities might run to first base after a nonambulatory student strikes a softball from a tee, or a runner who is blind might run bases with a sighted partner.

A second helpful technique is to select activities in which contact can be made and maintained with an opponent, partner, small group, or object. Children with auditory or visual impairments might engage successfully in such activities as tug of war, chain tag, square dancing, and wrestling because continual contact is made with partners, team members, or opponents. Children with visual impairments might use a rail to guide their approach while bowling.

A third helpful technique is to modify activities in such a way that all participants assume an impairment or disability. If not overused, this strategy can be useful in educating all children. Students without disabilities might simulate lower-limb impairments during an activity by hopping on one foot; they could also close their eyes or be blindfolded while playing Marco Polo in a pool.

The next technique is a procedure generally recommended in regular physical education—that is, to modify or avoid elimination-type games or activities. In dodge ball, for example, rather than being eliminated from play when hit by a thrown ball, children might become throwers standing behind their opponents' end line or simply have a point charged against them. In a game of Jump the Shot, the winner could be the one who makes contact with the shot the least number of times rather than the last person remaining in the activity.

Inclusion is sometimes promoted when play areas are reduced for students with limited movement capabilities. For example, a student with a below-the-knee amputation and a prosthesis might successfully play tennis, badminton, or volleyball in a court that is narrower than normal. Years ago, American football players with vision impairments played on fields 10 yards (9 m) wide. Reducing the size of play areas might be advisable to decrease activity intensity for children exhibiting cardiopathic disorders, severe forms of diabetes, or other conditions affected by exercise intensity.

The next technique is to emphasize abilities rather than disabilities. For example, Deaf children or those who have vision impairments might be more successfully included in activities if auditory or visual cues or goals are used. Instead of running to a line, students with impaired vision might be asked to run toward a bell, horn, whistle, drum, or clapping sound. Students with impaired vision might also shoot baskets, perform archery, or play shuffleboard if an auditory goal locator is placed near the target. Students with severe movement restrictions using wheelchairs might play a game in which the winner is the one who most closely predicts her time in negotiating 100 yards (91 m), thus practicing cognitive abilities.

A final recommended technique, and perhaps the most helpful, involves modifying activities by giving handicaps. This strategy is based on competition in games such as bowling or golf where handicaps are given to even the playing field. In a running relay, for example, a child with a lower-limb impairment is given a distance handicap and runs a shorter distance or is given a head start. In a basketball shooting contest, a student with less ability might participate by standing closer to the basket using a smaller ball or shooting at a larger rim. When playing Wiffle ball, students with eye–hand coordination deficits might be permitted to use a much larger plastic bat. In tennis, a player using a wheelchair might be permitted to strike the ball after it has bounced twice. In these instances, the idea is to see who can participate or win under the conditions determined at the outset.

Techniques for Integrating Students With and Without Disabilities Into Physical Education Activities

- Permit the sharing, substitution, or interchange of duties in activities.
- Select activities in which contact is made and maintained with an opponent, partner, small group, or object.
- Modify some activities in a way that allows students without disabilities to assume disability.

- Modify or avoid elimination-type games and activities.
- Reduce play areas if movement capabilities are limited.
- Modify activities to use abilities rather than disabilities.
- Modify activities by giving handicaps.

Prepare Regular Physical Education Students for Inclusion

A fifth key function for successful inclusion is preparing regular physical education students for an inclusionary physical education experience. It is commonly accepted that positive experiences and disability awareness contribute to overall peer acceptance and healthy attitudes toward people with disabilities and their involvement in physical education and sport activities. Block (2007), who uses the term *general education*, has suggested several disability awareness activities for students without disabilities:

- Invite guest speakers with disabilities who have had successful experiences in physical education and sport.
- Role-play activities.
- Discuss current attitudes held by students regarding people with disabilities.
- Discuss role models who are successful in physical education and sport.
- Teach general information about specific disabilities and how they are acquired.
- Provide general education on how students can help people with unique physical education needs learn and participate successfully in activities.
- Encourage students to provide support and help students with disabilities feel accepted in an inclusive environment.

A positive example set by the teacher is certainly a key factor for successful inclusion and acceptance by regular physical education students. The teacher should clearly convey that students with disabilities are individuals who belong in an inclusive society unless their unique educational needs cannot be met in that setting and that they should not be regarded as intruders dumped into a regular classroom.

Prepare Support Personnel

A sixth function of teachers implementing adapted physical education is to prepare support personnel. Successful teaching frequently depends on the provision of appropriate support services. Support services might be quite varied and might involve teaching assistants, paraprofessionals, related service professionals, adapted physical educators, volunteers, students, and others. To optimize the use of support personnel, the teacher needs to be confident that the personnel are prepared to provide their unique contributions. The nature of the preparation will vary according to the role that support personnel provide and the background of each contributor. Readers are referred to the writings of Block (2007) and Lieberman (2007) for detailed information regarding the preparation of support personnel.

Class Size and Type

Class size is an important variable to consider when placing students in instructional settings. Unfortunately, class sizes for physical education are often excessive. If quality instruction is expected, class sizes should not exceed 30 students in regular settings. When students with unique needs in physical education are included in the general education environment, the number of students in the class must be adjusted according to the nature of the disability and supplementary aides and services should be available. Special or separated classes should not exceed 12 students, and this number should be reduced to 6 or fewer students when extraordinary needs are exhibited. In some rare instances, individualized instruction is warranted. The number of students in classes should be adjusted based on the number of professionals, paraprofessionals, and aides available to provide assistance. Chronological age affects placement as well. Age differences within a class should never exceed three years unless students are 16 or older. School officials should know and comply with their state laws and regulations governing class size and composition. Each school district should specify policies regarding class sizes and support services and apply them equitably to physical education classes and other areas of the school curriculum.

Scheduling

Scheduling must be considered when making decisions regarding the setting for instruction. There are many approaches to scheduling that can accommodate various instructional arrangements. One effective method is to schedule supplementary and resource services for adapted physical education at the same time as regular physical education. A large school might have four physical education teachers assigned to four regular settings during a single period along with a fifth teacher assigned to provide adapted physical education services. Other instructional arrangements might provide extra class time or alternative class periods to supplement participation in regular physical education classes. In one scheduling technique used in elementary schools, a child placed in a special academic class joins an appropriate regular physical education class. This arrangement meets the student's need to be integrated in physical education while receiving special support in academic areas. Schools in which students are permitted to elect courses or units often have fewer scheduling problems because students may choose activities that fit their schedule and that they can participate in with little or no adjustment needed.

Time Requirements

Time requirements for adapted physical education must be clearly specified in school plans. The frequency and duration of the required instructional program should at least equal that of students receiving regular physical education. If state time requirements for regular physical education instruction are specified for various grade levels, and if adapted physical education students are placed in ungraded programs, the school's guidelines should express equivalent time requirements, using chronological age as the common reference point. A district plan should communicate the federal requirements for physical education.

Physical education should be required of all students and should be adapted to meet unique needs. In cases of temporary disability, it is important to ascertain how long the student will require an adapted physical education program, and a standard should be set to distinguish temporary and long-term conditions. For this book, a short-term condition (e.g., a sprained ankle) ends within 30 consecutive calendar days and can be accommodated by the regular physical education teacher. To the extent possible and reasonable, participation in physical activity rather than alternative sedentary experiences should be required.

School districts also need to deal with the issue of permitting participation in athletic activities, such as a soccer game or practice, as a substitute for active time in physical education class. Although coordination of instruction and sport participation (regular or adapted) is necessary, substitution should not be made unless it is approved in the student's individualized education program (IEP) and the practice fits in with the overall physical education plan of the school district. In most cases, the substitution of athletics for physical education is not recommended and should not be permitted.

School districts must also clarify and coordinate instructional time requirements with related services. For instance, time spent in physical therapy must not supplant time in the physical education program. If appropriate guidelines are developed, few, if any, students should be exempt from physical education.

Sport Programs

An adapted physical education plan should include general guidelines on sport participation and its relation to the physical education program. In view of the details involved in implementing a comprehensive extracurricular sport program, a specific operating code should also be developed. It is recommended that the extracurricular sport program be established on the assumption that the sport program and the adapted physical education program are interrelated and interdependent. Extracurricular programs, including interscholastic programs, should build on the basic instructional program in adapted physical education and should be educational. Students with disabilities should have equal opportunity to attain the same benefits from extracurricular activities as their peers without disabilities.

A sport program should emphasize the well-being of the participants in the context of games and sports. It is also important to ensure participation to the extent possible and reasonable. Health examinations before participation and periodically throughout the season, if necessary, promote safe participation. Athletes with disabilities should receive, at minimum, the same medical safeguards as other athletes.

For an interscholastic program with several schools participating, it is important to have a written statement of the principle educational goals as agreed to by the board of education, the administration, and other relevant individuals or groups. The statement should reflect a concern for student welfare, an interest in the educational aspects of athletic competition, and a commitment to the development of skills that yield health and leisure benefits both during and after the school years.

Over the past few years, increased attention has been given to providing sport opportunities for individuals with disabilities. In response to the intent of section 504 of the Rehabilitation Act of 1973 and IDEA, educational and extracurricular opportunities must be provided in the least restrictive (most normal and integrated) setting possible. Chapter 3 presents a framework for a sport continuum to promote integration to the maximum extent possible, guide decisions on sport participation, and stimulate the provision of innovative opportunities. Also in chapter 3 is a model for interscholastic adapted sport offerings. By their very nature interscholastic activities involve experiences of individuals and teams in different schools. Thus, there is a need for planning, coordination, and implementation at local, regional, county, and state levels. Additional information is presented in chapters 1 and 3 in this book.

Facilities

The facilities available for conducting programs in adapted physical education and sport might significantly affect program quality. The school athletic facilities should be operated in a way that makes them readily accessible to students with disabilities;

in fact, section 504 rules and regulations prohibit exclusion of individuals with disabilities from federally assisted programs because of architectural, program, or other environmental barriers. Provision of access may dictate structural changes in existing facilities. All new facilities should be constructed to ensure accessibility and usability.

In planning facilities in which to conduct adapted physical education and sport programs, attention must be given to indoor and outdoor areas, including teaching stations, lockers, and restrooms. Indoor facilities should have adequate activity space clear of hazards or impediments. The environment must have proper lighting, acoustics, and ventilation. Ceiling clearance should permit appropriate play. Floors should have a finish that enables all kinds of ambulation. When necessary, protective padding should be placed on walls. There should be plenty of space for wheelchairs to pass and turn.

As is true of indoor areas, outdoor areas should be accessible and properly surfaced. Facilities should be available and marked for activities, including special sports. Walkways leading to and from outdoor facilities should be smooth, firm, free of cracks, and at least 48 inches (122 cm) wide. Doorways leading to the facilities should have at least a 36-inch (91 cm) clearance and be lightweight enough to be opened without undue effort; when possible, doorways should be automatically activated. Water fountains with both hand and foot controls should be located conveniently for use by individuals with disabilities. Colorful signs and tactual orientation maps of facilities should be posted to assist individuals with visual disabilities.

Both participants in adapted physical education and athletes need adequate space for dressing, showering, and drying. Space must be sufficient for peak-use periods. The design of locker rooms should facilitate ambulation and the maintenance of safe and clean conditions. Adequate ventilation, lighting, and heating are necessary. The shower room should be readily accessible and provide enough showerheads to accommodate everyone. The facilities should be equipped with grab rails. Locker rooms should include adequate benches, mirrors, and toilets. People with disabilities frequently prefer horizontal lockers and locks that are easy to manipulate. Planning must ensure that lockers are not obstructed by benches and other obstacles. All facilities must be in operable condition. Well-designed restrooms should have adequate space for manipulation of wheelchairs, easily activated foot or hand flush mechanisms, grab rails, and toilets and urinals at heights that meet the needs of the entire school population.

Swimming pools are among the most important facilities. Pool design must provide for safe and quick entry and exit (refer to chapter 25 for additional information). Water depth and temperature should be adjustable to meet learning, recreational, therapeutic, and competitive needs. Careful coordination of pool use is usually necessary to accommodate varying needs. Dressing, showering, and toilet facilities must be close by, with easy access to the pool.

Students in adapted physical education and sport programs must have equal opportunity to use integrated facilities. Too often, segregated classes in physical education for students with disabilities are conducted in boiler rooms or hallways. Administrators need to offer classes so that students with disabilities have the opportunity to attain the same benefits from school facilities as students without disabilities. Failure to do so is discriminating and demeaning to both students and school personnel.

Budget

An equitable education for a student with unique needs is more costly than that of a student without unique needs. To supplement local and state funds, the federal government has several programs that provide money for the education of people with unique needs. Funds associated with IDEA are specifically earmarked. To facilitate the receipt of federal funds for physical education, physical educators must be sure that they are involved in IEP development.

Funds associated with IDEA are available to help provide for the excess costs of special education (i.e., costs that exceed student expenditure in regular education). These funds flow through state education departments (which are permitted to keep a certain percentage) and on to local education agencies. This flow-through money can be used to help cover excess costs already assumed by states. Because adapted physical education involves students both with and without disabilities, it is less discriminatory for schools to fund teachers in physical education, whether regular or adapted, from the same local funding source than to rely on federal money. This is justifiable because states are responsible for the education of all their students.

In addition to meeting needs identified in IEPs, funding must support the preparation of teachers to provide quality services in adapted physical education and sport. For example, funds are needed for in-service education, workshops, clinics, local meetings, professional conferences and conventions, program visitations, and so on. Schools also need funds to maintain up-to-date libraries and reference materials.

Interscholastic teams made up of students with disabilities must receive equitable equipment, supplies, travel expenses, officials, and so on. Although the funding level for curricular and extracurricular activities in a local community is not externally dictated, available funds cannot be used in a discriminatory fashion (e.g., available to males but not females, or available to students without disabilities but not to students with disabilities).

HUMAN RESOURCES

A quality program in adapted physical education and sport depends to a great extent on the availability of quality human resources and the ability of involved personnel to perform effectively within a group. People are needed to coordinate and administer services, fulfill technical and advocacy functions, and provide instruction. Many of these functions are carried out in important committees. To provide high-quality services for adapted physical education and sport, the teacher must work with various school and IEP committees. In doing so, it is helpful to understand roles and responsibilities and to realize that the concern for students with unique needs is shared by many. This section identifies key personnel and discusses their primary roles and responsibilities. Many perform their responsibilities by serving on committees identified in chapter 5.

Director of Physical Education and Athletics

Although not a universal practice, it is desirable for all aspects of physical education and sport programs to be under the direction of an administrator certified in physical education. Such centralization enhances coordination and efficiency in regard to personnel, facilities, equipment, budgeting, professional development, and curriculum. The director of physical education and athletics should oversee all aspects of the program, including the work of the coordinator of adapted physical education, if that position exists.

Because adapted physical education and sport is often in the developmental stage and not a well-advocated part of the total program, the physical education director needs to demonstrate genuine concern and commitment to this part of the program. A positive attitude serves as a model for others. With the assistance of other administrative personnel, the director can help the program in adapted physical education and sport by ensuring adequate funding, employing qualified teachers, and providing support services. The director must also be knowledgeable about adapted physical education and sport to work effectively with individuals and groups outside the department. The director must work with other directors, coordinators, school principals, superintendents, and school boards and must have positive professional relationships with medical personnel. Other important relationships are those with parents, teachers, students with disabilities, and advocacy groups. For this reason, the director of physical education and sport must stay informed about all students who are identified as having unique needs.

Adapted Physical Educator or Coordinator

To provide a quality comprehensive school program in adapted physical education and sport, schools are advised to employ a qualified teacher of adapted physical education to provide direct teaching responsibilities and program coordination and leadership. In a small school, this might be a part-time position; in larger schools, a full-time adapted physical education teacher or coordinator might be needed. Although most states do not require a special endorsement, credential, or certification to teach adapted physical education, it is best to select someone who has considerable professional experience. If possible, the teacher or coordinator should have completed a recognized specialization or concentration in adapted physical education and, where applicable, should meet the state competency requirements for certification. If a school cannot employ a person who has preparation in adapted physical education, the teacher's or coordinator's duties should be entrusted to someone who demonstrates genuine interest in the field.

The role and functions of the teacher or coordinator depend on the size of the school, the number and types of students with disabilities within the school population, and the number and types of students involved in adapted physical education and sport. Generally, however, the teacher or coordinator needs to assume a leadership role in various functions associated with adapted physical education and sport. The specific functions often differ

Characteristics of a Good Consultant

- Establishes a positive rapport in the consulting environment.
- Is prepared in the field of consultation.
- Has a passion for the consulting role.
- Encourages others to provide information and share ownership of results.
- Works as an equal rather than as an authority.
- Asks for feedback during the consultancy (helping) process.
- Establishes trust.
- Employs empathetic listening.
- Plans programs jointly.
- Accepts constructive criticism.

more in degree than in kind from those performed by regular physical educators. Table 2.2 identifies typical functions associated with adapted education and sport and indicates who is responsible for those functions. Functions may overlap or be shared; specific lines of demarcation should be drawn to suit local conditions.

A function that adapted physical educators are increasingly called on to do is to serve as a consultant or resource person for a school or school district. It would be ideal if every school district employed one or more people with a background and interest to serve not only as a teacher but also as a resource person. Colleges and universities preparing adapted physical education specialists are increasingly putting more attention on preparing students for the consulting role. Consultants are expected to serve as resource people or helpers to regular physical educators and anyone else who affects the quality of services in physical education and sport. They should be able to assess needs, plan and implement programs, and evaluate educational experiences. Consultants might provide information on many topics, including information on disabilities and implications for teaching physical education; ways of adapting methods, activities, and assessment practices and procedures for students with unique needs; strategies for controlling student behavior; information regarding recent legislation affecting students receiving special education; and information on developing individualized education and 504 plans for students with disabilities. Some characteristics of a good consultant are presented in the sidebar.

Regular Physical Educator

Although adapted physical educators are sometimes employed by a school, the regular physical educator plays a vital role in implementing quality programs in adapted physical education and sport. Table 2.2 presents several functions that are shared by or are the primary responsibility of regular physical educators. For example, they play an important role in screening. They might also implement instructional programs in integrated environments and help implement sport programs. One of the most important tasks is referral of students to appropriate committees. In the area of management or leadership, regular physical educators generally play a secondary role. With the present-day trend of including more and more students with disabilities in regular classes, it is often the responsibility of regular physical educators to implement and oversee such programs.

Table 2.2 Primary Responsibility for Functions Relevant to Adapted Physical Education and Sport

Function	Responsibility	
	Regular physical educator	Adapted physical educator or coordinator
MEASUREMENT, ASSESSMENT, EVALUATION		
Student screening	X	X
In-depth testing		X
Student assessment and evaluation		X
Adapted physical education or sport program evaluation		X
TEACHING OR COACHING		
Implementation of instructional programs for students with short-term unique needs	X	
Implementation of instructional programs to meet long-term unique needs in integrated environments	X	X
Implementation of instructional and sport programs with guidance of adapted physical educator	X	
Implementation of adapted sport programs		X
MANAGEMENT AND LEADERSHIP		
Consultation		X
In-service education		X
Advocacy and interpretation		X
Recruitment of aides and volunteers		X
Chairperson of adapted physical education committee		X
Liaison with health professionals	X	X
Referral and placement	X	X
Organization of adapted sport program		X

Nurse

The school nurse is an allied health professional with an important part in the successful development and implementation of adapted physical education and sport programs. The nurse must be knowledgeable about the adapted physical education and sport program and, ideally, should serve on the committee on adapted physical education. By helping to convey information required for individual education planning, the nurse can be a valuable resource. If time permits, the school nurse can assist the physical education staff in testing students, particularly in the case of postural screening. The nurse can also keep medical records, communicate with physicians, and help parents and students understand the importance of exercise and physical activity.

Physicians

Physicians have an important relationship with the adapted physical education and sport program. The physician's role is so important that it is often addressed in federal, state, or local laws, rules, and regulations. In some instances, states look to a designated school physician for the final decision on participation in athletic opportunities. School physicians also provide and interpret medical information on which school programs are based. Using this information, the IEP planning groups plan appropriate programs. The responsibility for interpreting the adapted physical education and sport program for family physicians and other medical personnel also lies with the school physician.

In states where physical education is required of all students, physicians must know and support laws and regulations. They must be confident that if a student is unable to participate without restriction in a regular class, adaptations will be made. Physicians should be aware of how physical education and adapted physical education have changed over recent years and should understand their role and responsibilities within the existing programs.

One of a physician's important functions is to administer physical examinations. Examination results are used as a basis for individualized student evaluation, program planning, placement, and determination of eligibility and qualification for athletic participation. It is desirable for students with unique physical education needs to receive an exam every three years, beginning in the first grade. Exams should be annual for those assigned to adapted physical education because of medical referrals. School districts that do not provide physical exams should require adequate examination by the family physician. For students covered by IDEA, medical examinations must be given in accordance with state and local policies and procedures. For athletic participation, exams should be administered at least annually.

Coaches

Adapted sport programs should be operated under the direction of qualified school personnel. When an adapted program includes interscholastic athletic teams, standards for coaches must be consistent with those for the regular interscholastic athletic program. Teachers certified in physical education may be permitted to coach any sport, including those whose participants have disabilities. Ideally, coaches of teams composed primarily of players with unique needs should have expertise in adapted physical education.

Coaches must follow acceptable professional practices. These include maintaining a positive attitude; insisting on good sportsmanship, respect, and personal control; and continuing to improve professionally through in-service programs, workshops, and clinics.

Related Services Personnel

Under IDEA (Office of Special Education and Rehabilitative Services [OSE/RS], 2006), related services include transportation and other developmental, corrective, and supportive services required to help children with disabilities benefit from special education. Related services include speech-language pathology and audiology services; psychological services; physical and occupational therapy; recreation, including therapeutic recreation; early identification and assessment of disability in children; counseling services, including rehabilitation counseling; orientation and mobility services; and medical services for diagnostic and evaluation purposes. Related services also include school health services, social work services in schools, and parent counseling and training.

Related service providers who significantly influence physical education include occupational and physical therapists. According to the rules and regulations for the implementation of IDEA, occupational therapy includes improving, developing, or restoring functions impaired or lost through illness, injury, or deprivation; improving ability to perform tasks for independent functioning when functions are impaired or lost; and using early intervention to prevent initial or further impairment or loss of functioning. The same rules and regulations define physical therapy as services provided by a qualified physical therapist. These services have traditionally included physical activities and other physical means for rehabilitation prescribed by a physician. The rules and regulations specify that recreation includes assessment of leisure function, therapeutic recreation services, recreation programs in schools and community agencies, and leisure education.

Much has been written about the relation of adapted physical education to physical and occupational therapy. The lines of responsibility among these areas are often blurred. One thing that is clear is that related services must be provided if a student requires them to benefit from direct services. For example, both physical and occupational therapy must be provided to the extent that a student needs them to benefit from physical education or other direct services in the school program. IDEA specifies that physical education must be made available to children with disabilities. Also, states have their own requirements concerning the provision of physical education. Clearly, physical therapy and adapted physical education are not identical, and related services should not supplant physical education or adapted physical education, which are direct services under IDEA.

Several assumptions about the role of physical education might underlie the decision of who will design programs to improve the physical fitness of students with disabilities. First, it is the physical educator's responsibility to design these programs. Thus, the physical educator is involved with the development of strength, endurance, cardiorespiratory endurance, and flexibility (range of motion). Her responsibility concerns both affected and unaffected parts of the body. For example, students with cerebral palsy should be helped to maintain and develop their physical fitness. When dealing with the affected parts of the body, the physical educator should consult and coordinate with medical or related service personnel in program planning and implementation.

Sometimes improvements in physical development cannot be attained by a physical educator using the usual time allotments, methods, or activities associated with physical education. In such cases, physical or occupational therapy can enhance physical fitness development. Activities

included in the physical education programs of students with disabilities should be those that are typically within the scope of physical education. These are the kinds of activities subsumed under the definition of physical education in the rules and regulations of IDEA and included in the scope of physical education, as described in chapter 1.

Although the physical educator involves children in exercise, it is important not to limit physical education to an exercise prescription program. Instead, the physical educator must offer a broad spectrum of fun and well-liked physical education activities. Children who require exercise lasting an entire physical education period should meet this need in class time added to the regularly scheduled physical education period, or it should be a provided service. This approach would permit involvement in a broad spectrum of activities within the regularly scheduled physical education class. Physical educators should help students appropriately use wheelchairs and supportive devices in physical education activities. Thus, they must be knowledgeable about wheelchairs and other assistive devices. However, it is not their responsibility to provide functional training in the use of those aids for basic movement or ambulation.

Physical educators must consult physicians and other medical personnel as they plan and implement programs. Such consultations should be consistent with the adapted physical education program of the school.

Although much can be written concerning roles and responsibilities, often the quality of services provided depends on the interpersonal relationships of service providers. Successful situations are those in which professionals have discussed their roles and responsibilities and work hard to deliver supportive services to benefit students with unique needs.

Paraeducators

Paraeducators and many other support personnel play a vital role in adapted physical education and sport. Paraeducators should provide assistance in instructional and extracurricular experiences for the classroom. They should be provided at a ratio that is consistent with the other subject areas in state laws, rules, regulations, and guidelines. Qualifications should be in accord with appropriate state and local regulations. Ideally, paraeducators will enhance and support other support personnel, including instructional volunteers, tutors, coaches, or officials who serve to enhance the learning environment. Paraeducators should be prepared for their roles and responsibilities (Lieberman, 2007), and their efforts should be valued and recognized.

GENERAL PROGRAM EVALUATION

At the beginning of this chapter, the importance of guidelines for program organization and management were stressed. This chapter has presented background information that can be used to develop such guidelines. Once in place, the guidelines can serve as a basis for program direction, implementation, and general program evaluation. Program evaluation might encompass the total physical education program or just the adapted physical education portion. Ideally, the guidelines should be evaluated at five-year intervals and draw on data collected from a variety of relevant sources.

Appendix D presents a sample rating scale to assess six essential areas related to program organization and management: curriculum, required instruction, attendance, personnel, facilities, and administrative procedures. This appendix contains a series of criteria statements that reflect guidelines suggested in this chapter relative to these areas. The entire scale or parts may be used to collect data for program evaluation. An instrument for evaluation is least threatening if used for self-appraisal and as a point of departure for identifying and discussing strengths and weaknesses and developing a schedule to remedy weaknesses and reinforce strengths. The areas of evaluation in appendix D related to program organization and management supplement the instructional and standards-based assessment and evaluation discussed in the program evaluation section in chapter 4.

SUMMARY

Well-organized and well-managed programs for adapted physical education are built on solid policies and procedures, which are enhanced and characterized by written guidelines on how to implement programs. This chapter has provided information that may be used for the development of programs and program guidelines. Information has been presented in four categories: program and curriculum planning, administrative procedures and program implementation, human resources, and general program evaluation.

REFERENCES

Block, M.E. (2007). *A teacher's guide to including students with disabilities in general physical education.* Baltimore: Paul H. Brookes.

Craft, D.H. (1996). A focus on inclusion in physical education. In B. Hennessy (Ed.), *Physical education source book.* Champaign, IL: Human Kinetics.

Lieberman, L.J. (Ed.). (2007). *Paraeducators in physical education.* Champaign, IL: Human Kinetics.

Lieberman, L., & Houston-Wilson, C. (2009). *Strategies for inclusion: A handbook for physical educators* (2nd ed.). Champaign, IL: Human Kinetics.

Office of Special Education and Rehabilitative Services (OSE/RS), 54 CFR (2006).

WRITTEN RESOURCES

Block, M.E. (2007). *Including students with disabilities in general physical education* (3rd ed.). Baltimore: Brooks.

This source helps teachers include students with disabilities in regular physical education settings. Included are topics on planning, assessment, instruction, adaptation, and safety.

Craft, D.H. (Ed.). (1994). Inclusion: Physical education for all. *Journal of Physical Education, Recreation and Dance, 65* (1), 22-56.

This periodical provides a special issue on inclusion, including information on making curricular modifications, promoting equal-status relationships among peers, and teaching collaboratively with others as well as research on inclusion, ideas on infusion, and experiences implementing inclusion in two schools.

Lieberman, L.J. (Ed.). (2007). *Paraeducators in physical education.* Champaign, IL: Human Kinetics.

This manual is a training guide on the roles and responsibilities of paraeducators in physical education.

Lieberman, L., & Houston-Wilson, C. (2009). *Strategies for inclusion: A handbook for physical educators* (2nd ed.). Champaign, IL: Human Kinetics.

This source provides background information and strategies for successful integration of a child with disabilities into a traditional physical education setting and contains teachable units that include assessment tools for curriculum planning.

Sherrill, C., & Megginson, N. (1984). A needs assessment instrument for local school district use in adapted physical education. *Adapted Physical Activity Quantity, 1,* 147-157.

This includes a checklist for evaluating school district needs related to adapted physical education.

Winnick, J.P. (2008). Rating scale for adapted physical education. Unpublished manuscript. Brockport, NY:

The College at Brockport, State University of New York.

This rating scale can be used as a self-assessment instrument on which to base evaluation of an adapted physical education program. The scale presents criteria statements reflecting guidelines implicitly suggested in this chapter. The rating scale can be found in appendix D.

3

Adapted Sport

Jeffrey Kling is of average intelligence, but he has a hearing impairment, cerebral palsy, and poor motor skills, for which he receives physical therapy. He is a student with a disability and is eligible for services as outlined in IDEA. During the ninth grade, Jeffrey was required to complete a 1-mile run for his physical education class. It took him the entire class to accomplish this requirement. Jeffrey's physical education teacher encouraged him to try out for the cross country team the next year. He and his father trained hard during the summer, and as a 10th-grader, Jeffrey earned a letter as a member of his high school cross country and track teams, coming in last in every race.

Before the start of the 11th grade, Jeffrey's parents met with Mentor, Ohio, school officials and submitted proposed goals and objectives for Jeffrey's individualized education program (IEP) that addressed his need to run cross country. The school district officials refused to discuss the appropriateness of these goals and objectives as a part of the IEP. Additionally, the request to run cross country was denied because the Ohio High School Athletic Association (OHSAA) has an age limit for participation in athletic events (similar to most states): If a student enrolled in high school attained the age of 19 before August 1, that student would be ineligible to participate in high school interscholastic athletics in the calendar year. Jeffrey missed the date by 16 days. His parents requested a due process hearing to decide whether the school district, by failing to consider the parents' request to make an individual determination about the need for interscholastic cross country and track, denied Jeffrey free and appropriate public education, and whether a school district, subject to federal law (Individuals with Disabilities Education Act [IDEA]), can summarily reject a special education program that contains an interscholastic athletic component in reliance on the rules of a private voluntary athletic association (OHSAA) (Siegel, 2000; Stewart, 2001). After reading the chapter, refer to the results of due process and court decisions relevant to the Jeffrey Kling case toward the end of the chapter.

This chapter discusses the implications of Jeffrey's case and provides information on the responsibility of physical educators in providing meaningful sport participation and training opportunities for students with disabilities. It presents a continuum of sport participation and identifies many multi- and unisport organizations available for individuals with disabilities. Athletic participation for students with disabilities is a logical extension of any good physical education program. Although participation in sport programs should not be used as a substitute for adapted physical education, after reading this chapter teachers should be able to provide parents and students with information on the many sport resources available. Throughout this chapter, keep in mind that the concepts of least restrictive environment and free and appropriate public education also apply to athletic opportunities.

Although medical personnel and educators have seen for many years the potential that sport participation has for students with disabilities, opportunities for such participation have been slow to develop (Murphy & Carbone, 2008). Limited sport opportunities have been available for older participants for some time, but interscholastic sport opportunities for children with disabilities are only now beginning to emerge. High school students with disabilities have a strong desire to participate in serious athletics similar to those available for students without disabilities. As noted in chapter 1, U.S. legislation affirms the rights of students with disabilities to have equal access and opportunities to physical education, intramural, and interscholastic sport programs.

As defined in chapter 1, adapted sport refers to sport modified or created to meet the unique needs of individuals. For many people, the definition of adapted sport refers only to competitive athletic opportunities. Although this chapter focuses on those opportunities to a great degree, the physical educator should refer to adapted sport in the broadest sense possible and use it to encompass not only competitive athletic experiences but also leisure-time recreational pursuits that enable a student with a disability to practice healthy living outside the school setting. Adapted athletics should be viewed as legitimate, serious sport and competition of high quality; it should not be seen as only a social experience.

INTEGRATION CONTINUUM

Over the past few years, increased attention has been given to providing sport opportunities for people with disabilities. In response to section 504 of the Rehabilitation Act of 1973, educational and extracurricular opportunities must be provided in the least restrictive (most normal and integrated) setting possible, on the basis of a continuum of settings ranging from the most restrictive (segregated) to the least restrictive (integrated). Winnick (1987) offers a five-level integration continuum for sport participation that includes regular sport with accommodation, regular and adapted sport, integrated adapted sport, and segregated adapted sport (see figure 3.1).

The integration continuum, which relates to the provision of programs in the least restrictive environment, encompasses opportunities in intramural and interscholastic programs and out-of-school sport and leisure programs. (For purposes of this book, all are included under the designation of sport.) The athlete has many options available to participate in regular sport or adapted sport through a five-level continuum. Regular sport implies that the athlete with a disability can participate in a sport without modifications. Adapted sport implies that the athlete with a disability competes in a regular sport with the aid of an assistive device (e.g., sled hockey) or rule modification (e.g., smaller field, smaller goal, and fewer players for soccer players with cerebral palsy) or that the athlete participates in a sport designed for a particular disability, such as wheelchair rugby (a sport for quadriplegics who use wheelchairs) or goalball (a game for people with visual impairments). Information on specific activities may be found in chapters 24 through 29.

Levels 1 and 2 of the continuum are regular sport settings distinguished only by a need for accommodation. The most appealing option is regular sport. In regular sport, the setting is integrated. People with disabilities are provided equal opportunities to qualify for participation at these levels. An example of level 1 participation would be an athlete with intellectual disabilities running the 800-meter dash for her high school track team or an athlete with an amputation playing on the local youth baseball team. Although it is rare for an athlete with a disability to participate at the Olympic level, amputee

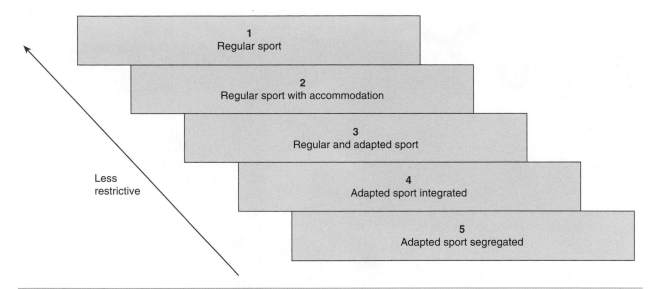

FIGURE 3.1 An integration continuum for sport participation.

Reprinted, by permission, from J.P. Winnick, 1987, "An integration continuum for sport participation," *Adapted Physical Activity Quarterly,* 4: 158.

athlete Natalie Du Toit of South Africa qualified and participated in the 2008 Beijing Olympic Games in marathon swimming. Du Toit was provided with no accommodation during competition.

In accordance with section 504, schools and agencies should provide modified or special activities only if the following four criteria are met (Department of Health, Education, and Welfare, 1977; Winnick et al., 1980):

- Programs and activities operate within the most normal and appropriate setting.
- Qualified students with disabilities are not denied opportunity to participate in programs and activities that are not separate and different.
- Qualified students with disabilities are able to participate in one or more regular programs and activities.
- Students with disabilities are appropriately placed in full-time special facilities.

A bowler who is blind competing against sighted athletes with only the accommodation of a guide rail falls under level 2. Other examples might include an athlete with a physical disability participating on a high school track team while using a field or throwing chair (figure 3.2), or a blind swimmer competing with sighted swimmers while using tap sticks to know when to begin flip turns. In making accommodations at level 2,

section 504 rules and regulations require that any accommodation provided be reasonable and allow individuals with disabilities an equal opportunity to gain the same results as other participants in an activity. At the same time, accommodations should not give an unfair advantage to an individual with a disability. In the case of the bowler who is blind, the guide rail substitutes for vision for the purpose of orientation to the target; for the field athlete, the throwing chair provides the stability needed during competition. Because the activity remains essentially unchanged for all participants and no undue advantage is given, this accommodation constitutes regular sport participation.

Perhaps the most well-publicized and controversial level 2 situation occurred when professional golfer Casey Martin was denied participation on the Professional Golfers' Association (PGA) tour in the spring of 1998. Martin, who has a rare circulatory disorder in his leg that makes it painful to walk moderate distances without severe pain, uses a cart when golfing. The PGA alleged that the use of a cart constituted an unfair advantage and fundamentally altered the nature of the game. The U.S. Supreme Court ruled 7–2 that the Americans with Disabilities Act (ADA) required the PGA to allow Martin to ride in a golf cart between shots at PGA tour events. In delivering the majority opinion, Justice John Paul Stevens said that allowing Martin to use a golf cart is not a modification that fundamentally alters the nature of the sport. Title III of the ADA, modeled

Courtesy of Paraplegia News; PVA Publications.

FIGURE 3.2 A sitting javelin competition can be conducted concurrently with high school track and field meets for students without disabilities.

on Title II of the Civil Rights Act, prohibits discrimination based on disability in places of public accommodation. By its "plain terms, it prohibits the PGA Tour from denying Martin equal access to its tours on the basis of his disability" (*PGA Tour v. Martin*, 2001).

Level 3 includes both regular and adapted sport conducted in settings that are partly or fully integrated. Those with a disability compete against or coact with all participants in a contest, including competitors with and without disabilities. For instance, an athlete participating in a wheelchair (adapted sport) might compete against all runners in a marathon, including athletes with and without disabilities; athletes without disabilities run on foot (regular sport). Additionally, an athlete without a disability and an athlete with a disability might play together as doubles partners in tennis. The ambulatory partner is permitted one bounce before returning the volley (regular sport); the wheelchair tennis player is permitted two bounces (adapted sport). This option involves both people with and without disabilities as part of the same team or

group. In today's school environments, this clearly can and should be encouraged. When a school district or a combination of schools (intermediate school districts) is unable to or elects not to field an entire team of students with disabilities, the unified option can be employed.

The Special Olympics Unified Sports program is another example of athletes with and without disabilities participating together. Unified Sports, begun in 1989, is a program that places athletes with intellectual disabilities and their peers without intellectual disabilities on the same team for training and competition. Athletes benefit from physical and mental challenges by participating in competitions organized by Special Olympics or by community sport organizations. The use of Unified Sports rules and guidelines on age and ability grouping help ensure that all athletes play a meaningful role on the team. Special Olympics now offers Unified Sports for all its summer and winter sports.

Level 3 also includes situations in which an athlete participates part time in regular sport and part time in adapted sport. For example, a person who is blind might participate in regular competition for powerlifting but in adapted sport competition for goalball. Level 3 activities show either athletes with and without disabilities integrated and participating in regular sport and adapted sport, respectively, *or* athletes with disabilities participating part time in adapted sport and part time in regular sport.

At level 4, athletes with and without disabilities participate in a modified version of the sport. Competition or coaction must include both a participant with a disability and a participant without a disability. One example is a game of tennis in which athletes with and without disabilities use wheelchairs in their competition against opponents who are likewise in wheelchairs.

At level 5, athletes with disabilities participate in adapted or regular sport in a totally segregated setting. The Challenger division created by Little League Baseball for athletes with physical disabilities is a level 5 example outside of scholastic sport. The Challenger division provides boys and girls with disabilities the opportunity to experience the emotional development and the fun of playing Little League Baseball. This program provides every child with the opportunity to participate in a structured athletic program. The Illinois wheelchair basketball program, the sports included in the Minnesota State High School League, and the sports associated with the Georgia High School Association model provide examples of level 5 segregated sport in interscholastic settings.

The conceptual framework for the sport continuum is based on degree of integration (with coactor or competitor) and sport type (traditional or adapted). The continuum stresses association or interaction among athletes with and without disabilities—the key ingredient in integration. To some extent, the continuum reflects severity of disability and ability to compete, but at times it may be less responsive to this concern. This is because the nature of the disability and the ability to perform are greater factors than severity of condition.

ADAPTED INTERSCHOLASTIC MODEL FOR SPORTS

The integration continuum just described provides an opportunity for more creative solutions in providing serious interscholastic high school sport

opportunities for athletes with disabilities. In 2007, Winnick provided such a creative framework, the Adapted Interscholastic Model for Sports (AIMS), to help guide the development and implementation of interscholastic sport based on his original work with the integration continuum. This framework provides a variety of options geared to the needs and abilities of participants; encourages movement toward participation in the least restrictive, most normal setting; emphasizes sport rather than disability; and encourages the use of modern technology for implementation (Winnick, 2007). The framework modifies the integration continuum to deal with serious elite athletes who wish to participate in interscholastic sport. It builds on the integration continuum but focuses on providing serious interscholastic sport opportunities using options of electronic, parallel, segregated, unified, and regular sport, many of which can be administered as a part of the program of the state high school athletic association. Regular sport corresponds to levels 1 and 2 in the integration continuum, unified and parallel sport correspond to levels 3 and 4, and segregated sport is identical to level 5.

A creative option suggested by Winnick (2007) in this framework that addresses the issue of individual sport is the use of electronic sport. This option is patterned after the telegraphic sport conducted in the United States 100 years ago. The earliest formal recorded athletic competition in the United States for people with visual disabilities was a telegraphic track meet between the Overbrook and Baltimore schools in 1907. In this meet, local results were mailed to a central committee, which made comparisons to determine winners. This option is particularly important for people with disabilities participating individually or on teams participating independently from opponents and electronically communicating their results to a central coordinating organization. Team and sport events that lend themselves nicely to this option include bowling; field activities such as the shot put, high jump, and long jump; track activities such as the 100-meter, 200-meter, 400-meter, and 800-meter events or even the 26-mile marathon; and powerlifting events such as the squat, bench press, deadlift, and so on. Once performance scores are determined, they are matched with individual and team classifications and further associated with age, gender, and so on. With present technology, winners in categories are determined and results are available at the school district, county, state, or even national level.

SPORT ORGANIZATIONS

As legislation has led to more inclusion in all aspects of daily living, an explosion has occurred in the number of organizations that provide sport programming for individuals with disabilities. These can be categorized into multisport and unisport organizations.

Community-Based Multisport Organizations

Multisport organizations provide training and athletic competition in sports for individuals with a particular disability. For instance, the BlazeSports National Disability Sports Alliance (BNDSA), formerly the United States Cerebral Palsy Athletic Association (USCPAA) and now a division of BlazeSports America, provides competition in 10 sports for people who have cerebral palsy, stroke, or traumatic brain injury. These organizations serve in much the same capacity as sport national governing bodies for athletes without disabilities: They oversee the development and conduct of their sports and promote athletic involvement for their members. In addition to the athletic competition involved, athletes have used these organizations as support groups and discussion forums. There are seven multisport disabled sport organizations affiliated with the United States Olympic Committee (USOC), including the BlazeSports National Disability Sports Alliance (BNDSA); Dwarf Athletic Association of America (DAAA); Disabled Sports USA (DS/USA); Special Olympics, Inc. (SOI); United States Association of Blind Athletes (USABA); USA Deaf Sports Federation (USADSF); and Wheelchair and Ambulatory Sports, USA (WASUSA).

Each organization provides sport opportunities in different ways. Some organizations, such as BNDSA, rely on sport technical officers to oversee programs; others, such as WASUSA and USADSF, are divided into sport federations. The USADSF operates outside the International Paralympic Committee (IPC). Their athletes compete internationally in the Deaflympics (formerly the Deaf World Games) and do not compete in the Paralympic Games. Each of these sport organizations is affiliated with an international counterpart for world competition (see table 3.1). More information on multisport organizations can be found in the later chapters on specific disabilities.

Table 3.1 Relationship Among USOC Disabled Sport Organizations and IOSDs

American sport organization	IOSD	Disability areas
BlazeSports National Disability Sports Alliance (BNDSA)*	Cerebral Palsy-International Sports and Recreation Association (CP-ISRA)	Cerebral palsy, traumatic brain injury, stroke survivors
Disabled Sports USA (DS/USA)*	International Wheelchair and Amputee Sports Federation (IWAS)	Spinal cord injured, amputee, dwarfism, other wheelchair users
Dwarf Athletic Association of America (DAAA)*	IWAS	Spinal cord injured, amputee, dwarfism, other wheelchair users
Special Olympics, Inc. (SOI)***	International Sports Federation for Persons with Intellectual Disability (INAS-FID)	Intellectual disabilities
United States Association of Blind Athletes (USABA)*	International Blind Sports Federation (IBSA)	Visual disabilities
USA Deaf Sports Federation (USADSF)**	International Committee of Sports for the Deaf (CISS)	Deafness
Wheelchair and Ambulatory Sports, USA (WASUSA)*	IWAS	Spinal cord injured, amputee, dwarfism, other wheelchair users

*Paralympic-affiliated organization.

**Non-Paralympic organization (participates in the Deaflympics).

***Special Olympics, in conjunction with the USOC, has assumed the responsibility for athletes with intellectual disabilities participating in the United States.

Unisport Organizations

Unisport organizations promote sport participation in a single sport, either for a single disability or for multiple disabilities. For instance, North American Riding for the Handicapped Association (NARHA) offers therapeutic and competitive horseback riding for people regardless of disability. The Handicapped Scuba Association International (HSA) offers individual and instructor training programs in a similar manner, whereas Achilles Track Club affiliates offer road-racing opportunities for athletes with disabilities. Examples of unisport organizations that promote one sport for people with disabilities include the United States Quad Rugby Association (USQRA), the United States Sled Hockey Association (USSHA) (see figure 3.3), and the National Beep Baseball Association (NBBA), to name a few.

OLYMPIC AND AMATEUR SPORTS ACT AND USOC

A brief history of the adapted sport movement was presented in chapter 1, but the Amateur Sports Act of 1978, amended in 1998 as the Olympic and Amateur Sports Act (within the Omnibus Appropriations Bill), is perhaps the one piece of legislation that provided the catalyst for the explosion in adapted sport. Sponsored by former senator Ted Stevens of Alaska, this legislation reorganized the USOC and administration of amateur sport in the United States. The amended act strengthened the linkage between the USOC and athletes with disabilities by including the Paralympic Games and amateur athletes with disabilities within the scope of the act and within the USOC. With the available resources and prestige attached to the USOC, sport organizations for people with disabilities have more opportunities in building their programs. The USOC constitution was rewritten to reflect the new commitment to adapted sport and intent of the law (USOC, 1998):

> To encourage and provide assistance to amateur athletic programs and competition for amateur athletes with disabilities, including, where feasible, the expansion of opportunities for meaningful participation by such amateur athletes in programs of athletic competition for able-bodied amateur athletes.

U.S. PARALYMPICS

Thanks to the enactment of the Amateur Sports Act, the USOC mission includes responsibilities for development and training of athletes with disabilities. U.S. Paralympics, established in 2001 as

Jim West/age fotostock

FIGURE 3.3　The United States Sled Hockey Association is an example of a unisport organization.

a division of the USOC, provides sport opportunities to the 21 million Americans with disabilities by operating programs in four areas (http://usparalympics.org).

Community Programs

A key goal of the USOC is to increase the availability of Paralympic sport programming for Americans with physical disabilities through grassroots programming and outreach initiatives. Through partnerships with existing organizations, as well as the development of new programs, the USOC Paralympic division is targeting program expansion into 250 American cities by 2012.

Paralympic Academy

The Paralympic Academy is a three-tier program with state, national, and international events. Students with physical disabilities (aged 12-18), as well as the teachers and coaches who instruct them, are selected for participation. Local academies are hosted by community organizations that specialize in Paralympic sport programs. These are typically one-day clinics that serve as an introduction to Paralympic sport.

USOC Paralympic Military Program

The Paralympic movement was founded through a rehabilitation program developed for wounded World War II veterans. Returning to its roots, the Paralympic Military Program provides postrehabilitation support and mentoring to American service members who have sustained physical injuries (see figure 3.4). Veterans are introduced to Paralympic sport techniques and opportunities through clinics and camps. They are connected with ongoing Paralympic sport programs in their hometowns. The program is not just about sport; it is also about attitude, camaraderie, and healthy, active lifestyles.

Elite Athlete and Team Support

The USOC and U.S. Paralympics work with both sport national governing bodies and disabled sport organizations to provide support services to elite athletes with disabilities in training and competing in the Paralympics and other quadrennial games for athletes with disabilities. The USOC Disabled Sports

FIGURE 3.4 The USOC Paralympic Military Program offers sport opportunities for injured war veterans.

Photo courtesy of Tom Kimmell Photography.

Services department manages the internal activities necessary to promote this process and addresses all issues related to national Paralympic concerns.

The USOC works with both the sport national governing bodies and the disabled sport organizations to support services for elite athletes with disabilities in training and competing in the Paralympics and other quadrennial games.

ROLE OF NATIONAL AND INTERNATIONAL GOVERNING BODIES

National governing bodies and international federations are organizations dedicated to the development and promotion of specific sports. These organizations generally sanction competitions and certify officials. By law, each of the national governing bodies affiliated with the USOC must allow participation by people with disabilities and assume a greater responsibility for elite athletes with disabilities. National governing bodies and international federations now routinely include information on adapted sport participation through the use of subcommittees, information on specific programming options, or the inclusion of adapted sport rules. For example, the United States Racquetball Association (USRA) includes wheelchair racquetball rules in their official rulebook. Some sport organizations have merged with other organizations, such as the National Foundation of Wheelchair Tennis (NFWT) merging with the United States Tennis Association (USTA) in 1998, to offer expanded programming for athletes with disabilities. Similar mergers have occurred at international levels as well.

INTERNATIONAL ORGANIZATIONS OF SPORT FOR THE DISABLED

An International Organization of Sport for the Disabled (IOSD) is an independent organization recognized by the International Paralympic Committee (IPC) as the sole representative of a specific disability group to the IPC. The IPC currently recognizes four IOSDs: the Cerebral Palsy International Sports and Recreation Association (CPISRA), the International Blind Sports Federation (IBSA), the International Sports Federation for Persons with Intellectual Disability (INAS-FID), and the International Wheelchair and Amputee Sports Federation (IWAS).

PARALYMPIC GAMES

The Paralympic Games (*para* meaning "equal to") are the equivalent of the Olympic Games for athletes with physical disabilities or visual impairments. Individuals with hearing impairments compete in the Deaflympics. The Paralympics began in 1948, when the Stoke Mandeville Games were held in Aylesbury, England. This was the same year the 14th Olympic Games were held in London. The idea of holding these events is attributed to a physician, Sir Ludwig Guttman, who included sport in his rehabilitation for injured World War II veterans.

The first Paralympic Summer Games were held in Rome in 1960, the same year that the Italians hosted the 17th Olympic Games (the first winter Paralympic Games were held in Sweden in 1976). These first summer Paralympic Games drew 400 athletes representing 23 countries. Since then, the Olympic and Paralympic Games have led a paral-

lel existence, being held in the same city or same country whenever possible. The 1988 Seoul Games marked the beginning of the modern Paralympic Games, the first time the term *Paralympics* was used.

The 1992 Barcelona Paralympics marked the first time that a joint Olympic and Paralympic Committee was used. International Olympic Committee (IOC) president Juan Antonio Samaranch was so deeply moved and impressed by the caliber of the Barcelona Paralympic Games, he decreed that after 1996 all bids for the Olympic Games must be submitted by joint Olympic and Paralympic Committees. "The Paralympic Games have been as successful as the Olympic Games," said Samaranch, "that it is an indication that we must take another look at, and think seriously about the subject of disabled people. It was the same organizing committee and the same volunteers that worked out very well" (Samaranch, 1992). Most Olympic Games since have included two demonstration events for athletes with physical disabilities: the 1,500-meter wheelchair race for men and the 800-meter wheelchair race for women. Although full inclusion and merger with the Paralympic Games might not be possible, the recognition of events for athletes with disabilities in the Olympic Games demonstrates the strides made toward the recognition of athletes with disabilities as elite athletes. The 2008 Paralympic Games in Beijing included over 4,000 athletes from 150 countries.

The Paralympic Games, which began as an event with strong social implications and therapeutic ends, has become the most important sporting event for people with disabilities. Every four years the participation of elite athletes at the Paralympic Games provides proof of the progress being made in terms of competitiveness and athleticism. The countless records broken and the marks achieved, as well as the increase in international attention, further demonstrates the great success of the Games and the overall development of disability sport.

The IPC is the global governing body of the Paralympic Movement. The IPC organizes the Summer and Winter Paralympic Games every four years, and it serves as the international federation for 12 sports, for which it supervises and coordinates the world championships and other competitions. The governance of 26 sports (20 Paralympic Summer sports, 5 Paralympic Winter Sports, 1 non-Paralympic sport) falls under the responsibility of various bodies (table 3.2). Every country that participates in the Paralympic Games has a national counterpart to these federations.

Table 3.2 **Paralympic Sport and Sport Governance**

Sport	Sport governance	Season
Alpine skiing	International Paralympic Committee (IPC)	Winter
Archery	International Archery Federation (FITA)	Summer
Athletics	IPC	Summer
Biathlon	IPC	Winter
Boccia	Cerebral Palsy International Sports and Recreation Association (CPISRA)	Summer
Cycling	International Cycling Federation (UCI)	Summer
Equestrian	International Equestrian Federation (FEI)	Summer
Five-a-side football (soccer)	International Blind Sports Federation (IBSA)	Summer
Seven-a-side football (soccer)	CPISRA	Summer
Goalball	IBSA	Summer
Ice sledge hockey	IPC	Winter
Judo	IBSA	Summer
Powerlifting	IPC	Summer
Shooting	IPC	Summer
Swimming	IPC	Summer
Nordic skiing	IPC	Winter
Rowing	International Rowing Federation (FISA)	Summer
Sailing	International Foundation for Disabled Sailing (IFDS)	Summer
Table tennis	International Table Tennis Federation (ITTF)	Summer
Volleyball (sitting)	World Organization Volleyball for Disabled (WOVD)	Summer
Wheelchair basketball	International Wheelchair Basketball Federation (IWBF)	Summer
Wheelchair curling	World Curling Federation (WCF)	Winter
Wheelchair dance sport (non-Paralympic sport)	IPC	Summer
Wheelchair fencing	International Wheelchair and Amputee Sports Federation (IWAS)	Summer
Wheelchair rugby	IWAS	Summer
Wheelchair tennis	International Tennis Federation (ITF)	Summer

CLASSIFICATION

Classification systems are used widely in sport to allow for a fair and equitable starting point for competition (Richter et al., 1992). Youth football requires a minimum and maximum weight of players, whereas youth soccer and baseball might have age and gender restrictions, all with the purpose of providing maximum enjoyment and fairness and preventing injuries. Classification is an ongoing process that may be reviewed throughout the athlete's career.

Within a specific type of disability is a wide continuum of ability or physical characteristics. For instance, the levels of acuity among people with visual impairments vary significantly, as do the levels of functional ability among people with cerebral palsy. This kind of continuum of functional ability is common to athletes with and without disabilities.

It is accepted that some form of classification or groupings must be used for athletes with disabilities, but which is the most equitable classification to use remains a topic of debate and complexity. Classification systems that were begun years ago continue to evolve. Classification systems are generally of two types: medical and functional.

Medical classification verifies minimum disability and is not concerned with the functional ability of the athlete (Davis & Ferrara, 1996). Examples include the level of visual acuity for a blind athlete, the level of a spinal cord injury, or the location of an amputation (see figure 3.4). These kinds of evaluation provide a medically related equal starting point for competition. Success or failure in competition then depends on the physical skill and the level of training of athletes.

Functional classification systems identify how an athlete performs specific sport skills (Davis & Ferrara, 1996). Functional systems combine medical information with performance information to evaluate an athlete's sport-specific skills and medical condition required in an event. For instance, classifiers might observer athletes with cerebral palsy performing their sport to determine range of motion and physical capabilities prior to classification. This classification system can be used for both single disability and cross-disability competitions. In other words, function is primary and medical condition is secondary.

Special Olympics uses a classification system based on age, gender, and past performances. Other classification systems for athletes with disabilities are presented in several chapters in this book.

Whichever classification system is used, the system should ensure that the training and skill level of the athlete become the deciding factor in success, not the type or level of disability (Paciorek & Jones, 2001). Sport or health care professionals who have completed a certification course perform classification for national and international competition. Classifiers usually consist of physicians, physical therapists, occupational therapists, and others knowledgeable in kinesiology and disability, and they can receive local, national, or international levels of certification. Classifications related to specific disabilities can be found in other chapters of this book.

SCHOOL AND COMMUNITY-BASED ADAPTED SPORT PROGRAMMING

Although international competitions such as the Paralympic Games, Special Olympics World Games, and Deaflympics tend to receive much media attention, few athletes with disabilities have the necessary skills or opportunity to participate in these elite events. The majority of athletes with disabilities participate in grassroots and youth sport programming in their communities. These typically include recreation and park district programs, parent-sponsored sport programs, cross-disability sport programs affiliated with rehabilitation centers, and sports available through public school athletic programs (see figure 3.5). Community-based programs continue to evolve, such as BlazeSports America, a nonprofit organization that improves the lives of youths and adults with physical disability through sport and healthy living. BlazeSports provides sport training, competitions, summer camps,

St. Petersburg Times/Zuma Press/Icon SMI

FIGURE 3.5 Adapted sport programming is most often offered in communities. Here a park district teamed up with Paralympic Sport Tampa Bay to offer a summer basketball clinic.

and other sport and recreational opportunities for youths and adults with spinal cord injury, spina bifida, cerebral palsy, traumatic brain injury, muscular dystrophy, amputation, visual impairment or blindness, and other physical disabilities.

Section 504 of the Rehabilitation Act of 1973 and the ADA have had great implications for the sport participation of young people with disabilities (Storms, 2007). These complementary antidiscrimination pieces of legislation require agencies that provide sport programs, whether they receive federal funds or not, to provide equivalent opportunities to people with disabilities. No sport program may discriminate against players or coaches with disabilities, including school-based programs. All players have the right to play on recreational sport teams and must be afforded the opportunity to try out for select or premier teams, even if segregated programs such as Little League Challenger baseball leagues are available (Block, 1995). Schools, recreation programs, and communities must make reasonable accommodations to ensure that people with disabilities have equal access to programs. Reasonable accommodations might require purchasing an adapted piece of equipment, such as a wider bench for a powerlifter with a spinal cord injury, or providing facilities that are readily accessible to people with disabilities, such as the community fitness center.

REGULAR SPORT PARTICIPATION

Jeffrey Kling (who was featured at the beginning of the chapter) and other athletes with disabilities will continue to experience barriers in their attempts to participate in regular sport opportunities. No numerical data are available on participation of young people with disabilities in regular sport, though anecdotal records suggest that participation continues to increase despite these barriers. Reports of high school athletes with disabilities participating in cross country, swimming, track and field, and even football are highlighted in newspapers across the United States. Many sport organizers are making reasonable accommodations for athletes with disabilities. Runners who are blind are being allowed to run track and cross country with sighted guides in mixed competition. Wrestlers who are blind are allowed to use a touch start. Athletes with amputations and those with intellectual disabilities participate on track and field and football teams. Various accommodations are being

made in recreation programs without fundamentally altering competition. League officials must continue to consider and implement commonsense changes that enable a student with a disability to meet the same eligibility requirements that other team members must meet.

Although not specifically addressed in the ADA, the implications of this law prevent discrimination against coaches and athletes in youth sport programs (Block, 1995). Various court cases have upheld the right of baseball coaches who use wheelchairs to coach on the field (*Anderson v. Little League*, 1992; *Barrios v. California Interscholastic Association*, 2002), the right of wheelchair athletes to compete alongside runners without disabilities (Norman, 2007), and the case of *Kling v. Mentor School District* that challenged arbitrary age restrictions for athletes with disabilities in high school sports (Siegel, 2000). These cases illustrate the confusion that exists regarding people with disabilities participating in regular sport. According to the National Federation of High Schools (NFHS), high school athletes with disabilities must meet the same eligibility standards for participation as required of all athletes, including grade point average and submission of a medical clearance form from a physician. The NFHS advocates development of adapted sports programs while recognizing the budgetary and logistical challenges (NFHS position paper, 2007). According to the NFHS, federal statutes (ADA, IDEA, and section 504) guarantee that local public school systems will be required to develop and implement interscholastic athletic programs for students with disabilities. Increased numbers of athletes with disabilities participating in regular sport will continue at a slow pace as more students are included in regular education environments, sport organizers become educated about disability rights, and court decisions clarify the existing confusion.

Over the past few years, much of the impetus for sport for athletes with disabilities has been provided by out-of-school sport organizations. Although developing at a slower rate, other opportunities have begun to surface throughout the United States in connection with public school programs (Matter, Nash, & Frogley, 2002). An important milestone was reached on November 11, 1992, when Minnesota became the first state to welcome athletes with disabilities into its state high school association. The Metro Association for Adapted Athletics (MAAA) is a member of the Minnesota State High School League, which operates the adapted athletics program statewide for high school students with disabilities. This move made Minnesota the first in the nation to sanction interscholastic sport for middle and high school students with disabilities.

In the spring of 2008, Maryland passed the Fitness and Athletics Equity for Students with Disabilities Act, which requires schools to allow athletes with disabilities to play wheelchair basketball or tennis, to swim, or to otherwise play sports, either among themselves or side by side with students without disabilities (Williams, 2008). The act allows students with disabilities to try out for teams and to use modifications, accommodations, or aids they usually use to play the sport. Modifications or aids might include wheelchairs, artificial limbs, interpreters for Deaf students, and sound-emitting equipment for students with visual impairments. This makes Maryland the first to require schools to create equal athletic and physical education opportunities for students with disabilities. With the passage of this law, Maryland could soon become the leader in providing scholastic adapted sport opportunities.

In another example of legislation advocating for interscholastic adapted sport programs, the New Jersey State Legislature has passed initial legislation requiring the New Jersey State Interscholastic Athletic Association (NJSIAA) to establish adapted athletic programs. Sponsored by Assemblyman Fred Scalera, the legislation would direct the NJSIAA to work with the American Association of Adapted Sports Programs (AAASP) to establish interscholastic athletic programs adapted for participation by student athletes with physical disabilities or visual impairments and to support the efforts of participating school districts that implement adapted athletics programs. The bill also would require coaches in an adapted athletic program to receive specialized training for the program.

The AAASP was formed in 1980 in DeKalb County, Georgia, as an after-school program for students with physical disabilities in grades 1 through 12. In 2001, the AAASP and the Georgia High School Association (GHSA) formed an alliance to promote the AAASP adapted sport model (along with its sister program, Project Aspire) as a viable component of the overall athletic structure of the state. In this parallel relationship, the GHSA looks to the AAASP for guidance in adapting sports for students with physical disabilities or visual impairments within high schools. The GHSA has designated the AAASP as the official sanctioning and governing body for Georgia's interscholastic adapted athletics (AAASP, 2008).

In 2006, the AAASP partnered with the Alabama High School Athletic Association in developing an interscholastic sport program for students with disabilities (Hennie, 2006). Winnick's framework (2007) enhances creativity and attention to these emerging programs and initiatives.

Since 1992, the Connecticut Interscholastic Athletic Conference (CIAC) has had a partnership with Special Olympics to offer Unified Sports programming. Participation is open to all public and parochial schools in Connecticut. At the elementary level, students engage in noncompetitive athletic activities designed to develop skills in a variety of sports; middle and high school students compete in statewide Unified Sports tournaments. The CIAC currently holds tournaments in basketball, soccer, softball, and volleyball. The program boasts the participation of 1,300 athletes and 120 schools throughout the state.

A few other states now provide statewide competition for athletes with disabilities. According to Frogley and Beaver (2002, p. 4-5), "these attempts have centered more on accepting certain events within already staged state championships, rather than the adoption of a state-wide program of interscholastic competition for student-athletes with disabilities, and have thus failed to provide comprehensive state-wide opportunities for competition." For example, Iowa offers limited track and field competition at state high school championships, and New York offers regional and statewide competition for young people with physical and sensory disabilities in connection with its Empire State Games for the Physically Challenged. These Games, conducted with government financing, serve as an alternative to the Empire State Games for athletes without disabilities. The Illinois High School Association has become the first state to add wheelchair basketball as part of their programming (Matter, Nash, & Frogley, 2002). Currently 150 student-athletes are registered, with full-season play beginning in 2005; the sport is sponsored and administered by the IHSA (M. Frogley, pers. comm.).

Since 2001, WASUSA and the Glenn D. Loucks Games have run an integrated elite high school track meet in White Plains, New York. For 41 years, the Loucks Games have attracted the top high school athletes from the northeastern United States. With the inclusion of a wheelchair division, this meet is the country's only integrated nonstate high school track meet (Scorecard, 2002).

Because of the tremendous health benefits, sport programs in rehabilitation settings are also increasing (Paciorek & Jones, 2001). Most of the larger programs are centered in major cities. Examples include the Wirtz Sports Program at the Rehabilitation Institute of Chicago's Center for Health and Fitness; the Roosevelt Warm Springs Institute for Rehabilitation in Warm Springs, Georgia; the Shepherd Center in Atlanta, Georgia; and the Craig Rehabilitation Hospital in Denver, Colorado. These centers generally offer multisport cross-disability programming for members of the community.

TRANSITION SERVICES

Important goals of physical education and adapted physical education programs are to provide students with the functional motor skills, knowledge, and opportunities necessary for lifelong, healthy, independent living. Adapted sport programs can play a vital role in assisting with independent living and should be seen as a logical extension of the school-based program. These programs should provide for a clear transition between the school and community living. IDEA is very clear on the transition issue and mandates that a statement be provided of the transition service needs for students beginning no later than age 16 and beginning at age 14, and when determined appropriate, a statement of needed transition services for the child including interagency responsibilities or any needed linkages between the school and community living. Please see the application example for more details.

Although IDEA specifies that a transition plan must be provided at least by age 16, transition services in physical education and sport should begin at a much earlier age to foster independence and inclusion in community living. Taking into account the needs and desires of each student, the physical educator should use the IEP to identify and recommend extracurricular programs, including intramurals and sport. These activities promote the goals of adapted physical education as well as those of occupational and physical therapy. Physical therapists can play a large role by assisting with the athletes' exercise and conditioning program.

APPLICATION EXAMPLE

Transition Services

Setting: Individualized education planning committee meeting

Child: 17-year-old student with spina bifida who is a wheelchair user

Issue: At the beginning of the meeting, the student's parents ask about an educational program to teach their child about community recreation opportunities.

Application: Because federal law requires that transition services be included in a student's IEP at age 16, the physical educator has already considered the available options. The IEP contains goals and objectives relating to the following information:

▶ Each week the student will be exposed to various community recreation opportunities. The student and other classmates will leave the school for community recreation programs. The students will attend swimming and fitness classes at the local fitness facility, where they will receive instruction on the use of the equipment.

▶ The IEP includes goals and objectives related to participation in a recreational activity such as bowling.

▶ The physical educator has also planned trips to the adapted sport program at the local rehabilitation hospital, where the student will participate in the competitive sport programs of sitting volleyball and sailing.

▶ The physical educator has also collaborated with the special education resource teacher to include instruction on using public transportation to get to recreational programs.

Linking these interdisciplinary services makes for a greater chance that the recommendations will be implemented. Once parents are aware of programs available for their child, they often have more influence than teachers in encouraging school officials to develop such opportunities. Adapted physical education and adapted sport can provide a vital link in the transition plan to assist the person with a disability in becoming fully integrated into community life (Megginson & Lavay, 2001).

ROLE OF THE PHYSICAL EDUCATOR IN ADAPTED SPORT

Opportunities for students without disabilities to participate in sport and leisure programs within and outside of school are well documented. Most middle and high schools provide a full range of sports for the interested student. Opportunities for students with disabilities, however, are not always apparent or available. Although federal legislation supporting these programs has been available since 1973, many schools have been slow to respond to the needs and desires of their students with disabilities. Many court cases have documented the rights of students with disabilities to have access to the same quality of programs available to students without disabilities.

As long as physical educators do not understand the important role they play in promoting sport participation for students with disabilities, students such as Jeffrey Kling will sit idly by the sidelines, watching others and wondering what it feels like to experience the thrill of participation and competition. Physical educators have the responsibility to provide specific goals and objectives related to sport participation in the IEP. Physicians and parents of children with disabilities can also be enlisted to advocate for sport opportunities (Murphy & Carbone, 2008).

The unqualified success of national and international sport events for people with disabilities, such as the Paralympics, Deaflympics, and Special Olympics, has documented the ability of people with disabilities to become elite athletes who train and compete just as hard as their counterparts without disabilities. Television and media exposure of adapted sport continues to improve. The highly publicized 2001 Supreme Court case involving golfer Casey Martin's successful attempt to compete in the PGA while using a golf cart, as well as other lower court cases, emphasize that people with disabilities can compete in regular competitions if reasonable accommodations are provided that do not change the nature of the sport or alter the skill required.

No longer should one equate disability with lack of ability. Elite athletes with disabilities complete the wheelchair marathon in less than 90 minutes, athletes who are blind complete bicycle races of 80 miles (130 km) or more, athletes with cerebral palsy play soccer at a high level, and athletes with amputations run the 100-meter dash in times less than 2 seconds off the Olympic record. Competitions such as goalball, wheelchair rugby, and Special Olympic gymnastics now draw large numbers of spectators. People with disabilities are more visible in communities, such as wheelchair users playing tennis, children with cerebral palsy playing soccer or baseball, and people who are blind riding tandem bikes. It is clear that people with disabilities have the same desires and needs to participate in adapted sport as people without disabilities. The physical educator plays a vital role in helping to make this happen (see figure 3.6).

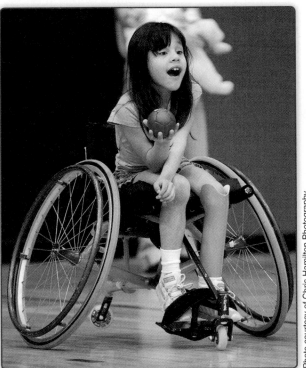

FIGURE 3.6 Physical educators play a large role in developing lifelong sport skills for students.

Photo courtesy of Chris Hamilton Photography.

WHAT ABOUT JEFFREY KLING'S CASE?

Legislation supporting athletic participation of people with disabilities has had a dramatic impact on participation levels over the past 35 years. The ruling in the *Kling v. Mentor School District* case might have far-reaching implications and precedence. According to the ruling, under applicable federal statutes and regulations, the IEP team—and *not* the OHSAA—are charged with the responsibility to determine the need for a student with a disability to participate in interscholastic athletics. Where OHSAA rules conflict with or are more restrictive than IDEA and thereby operate to prevent compliance with IDEA, such conflicts shall be resolved in favor of IDEA (Siegel, 2000; Stewart, 2001).

With regard to the age limitation, the OHSAA's position was that the age-19 rule establishes a threshold standard through which to achieve desired goals of safety and fairness and is cast in concrete, without exception. Petitioners define this as administratively convenient. The court's position was that the athletic association inappropriately used the ease of administration to justify the lack of a waiver provision. In other words, the association and its members did not wish to be burdened by a case-by-case analysis of an individual student-athlete's particular situation. "The court wonders what either institution's (i.e., the school district or the OHSAA) mission may be if it is not the welfare and education of individual students" (Siegel, 2000).

Insofar as the OHSAA rules are more restrictive than IDEA and thereby operate to prevent compliance with IDEA, Jeffrey is not obligated to follow them. Notwithstanding the fact that the Mentor and Mayfield school districts are members of the OHSAA, the age-19 rule cannot be blindly accepted and obeyed. Private agreements containing items inconsistent with federal law do not take precedence, and to the extent the terms of the agreement cause an actor to violate the law, they are not enforceable (*Shelley v. Kramer*, 68 S Ct. 836, 1948).

School administrators, physical educators, and athletic directors should review policies for athlete participation and ensure that the rules are reasonable and sensible. School personnel should review individual cases to meet the needs of all students and not be blinded by past practice and inflexible rules. Administrators should be guided by best practice, not past practice. As the number of students with disabilities who are included in neighborhood schools increases, so does the likelihood that these students will want opportunities to participate in interscholastic activities.

SUMMARY

In the past 35 years, many advances have occurred in adapted sport. Federal legislation, work of advocates and professional sport organizations, increased awareness of health benefits by physical educators and medical personnel, and involvement with the USOC are some reasons for the growth of adapted sport. Global conflicts have led to the development of specific adapted sport programs and advanced prosthetics for injured war veterans. Many opportunities exist today for people with disabilities to participate in sport and leisure activities throughout communities. Opportunities exist at regional, national, and international levels for people interested in elite levels of competition through multi- and unisport organizations. Interscholastic models exist that may enhance the development of interscholastic programs for people with disabilities. Based in part on the *Kling v. Mentor* decision, state legislatures are recognizing the rights of students with disabilities to participate in interscholastic sport programs.

Physical educators must be resource people. They need to be aware of the programs in their communities for their students with disabilities to take the skills and knowledge they have acquired in adapted physical education and use them. Goals and objectives related to sport should be an important part of the IEP for students who have disabilities.

REFERENCES

American Association of Adapted Sports Programs (AAASP). (2008). Retrieved from www.aaasp.org.

Anderson v. Little League Baseball, Inc., 794 F.Supp. 342 (Dist. Ariz. 1992).

Barrios v. California Interscholastic Association, 277 F.3d 1128 (9th Cir. 2002).

Block, M.E. (1995). Impact of the Americans with Disabilities Act (ADA) on youth sports. *Journal of Physical Education, Recreation and Dance, 66* (1), 28-32.

Davis, R., & Ferrara, M. (1996). Athlete classification: An exploration of the process. *Palaestra, 12* (2), 38-44.

Department of Health, Education, and Welfare. (1977). Education of handicapped children. *Federal Register*, *42* (163), 42434-42516.

Downs, C. (2007). The Little League Challenger division ensures children with disabilities opportunities to play ball. *Palaestra*, *23* (4), 20-24.

Frogley, M., & Beaver, D.P. (2002). Editor's corner: Is the time right—interscholastic athletics for student-athletes with disabilities? *Palaestra*, *18* (2), 4-5.

Hennie, M. (2006). Improving athletic opportunities for students with disabilities. *Palaestra*, *23* (3), 20-25.

Huebner, C. (2003). U.S. Paralympics Forum. *Palaestra*, *19* (2), 9.

Matter, R., Nash, S., & Frogley, M. (2002). Interscholastic athletics for student-athletes with disabilities. *Palaestra*, *18* (3), 32-38.

Megginson, N.L., & Lavay, B.W. (2001). Providing disability sport opportunities in adapted physical education. *Palaestra*, *17* (2), 20-26.

Murphy, N.A., & Carbone, P.S. (2008). Promoting the participation of children with disabilities in sports, recreation, and physical activities. *Pediatrics*, *121* (5), 1057-1061.

National Federation of High Schools (NFHS). (2007). Position paper. Retrieved from www.nfhs.org.

Norman, G.C. (September 2007). Adapting sports for the mobility-impaired. *Maryland Bar Bulletin*.

Paciorek, M.J., & Jones, J.A. (2001). *Disability sports and recreation resources* (3rd ed.). Traverse City, MI: Cooper.

PGA Tour v. Martin, 532 U.S. 661, (2001). United States Supreme Court Decision. Rehabilitation Act of 1973. Revisions of 1998, 29 U.S.C. Chapter 16.

Richter, K.J., Adams-Mushett, C., Ferrara, M.S., & McCann, B.C. (1992). Integrated swimming classification: A faulted system. *Adapted Physical Activity Quarterly*, *9*, 5-13.

Samaranch, J.A. "Closing Ceremonies, Paralympic Games." Barcelona, Spain, September 14, 1992.

Scorecard. (2002). Elite wheelchair track meet. *Sports 'N Spokes*, *28* (5).

Shelley v. Kramer, 334 U.S. 1, 68 S.Ct. 836, 92 L. Ed. 1161 (1948).

Siegel, N.G. (2000). Kling vs. Mentor School Board. Retrieved from www.nessasiegel.com/kling_vs_mentor.htm.

Stewart, D.A. (2001). The Power of IDEA: Kling vs. Mentor School District. *Palaestra*, *17* (4), 28-30, 32.

Storms, T. (2007). The wheels of justice turn in adapted interscholastic sport-making progress. *Palaestra*, *23* (3), 4-5.

United States Olympic Committee (USOC). (1998). USOC Constitution. Colorado Springs: Author.

Williams, J. (2008, August 31). School programs for disabled taking shape. *Baltimore Sun*, A11.

Winnick, J.P. (1987). An integration continuum for sport participation. *Adapted Physical Activity Quarterly*, *4*, 157-161.

Winnick, J.P. (2007). A framework for interscholastic sports for youngsters with disabilities. *Palaestra*, *23* (2), 4, 9.

Winnick, J.P., Auxter, D., Jansma, P., Sculli, J., Stein, J., & Weiss, R.A. (1980). Implications of section 504 of the Rehabilitation Act as related to physical education instructional, personnel preparation, intramural and interscholastic/intercollegiate sport programs. *Practical Pointers*, *3* (11), 1-20.

WRITTEN RESOURCES

Davis, R. (2011). *Teaching disability sport: A guide for physical educators* (2nd ed.). Champaign, IL: Human Kinetics.

This is an excellent resource for physical education teachers or recreation specialists to help establish a comprehensive physical education program for students with and without disabilities using the medium of sport. The book describes many disability sports and how activities can be modified and taught in physical education settings.

DePauw, K.P., & Gavron, S.J. (2005). *Disability and sport* (2nd ed.). Champaign, IL: Human Kinetics.

This source gives readers an understanding of the historical context for sport today and trends for the future, an awareness of sport modifications, and a multitude of sport opportunities available for people with disabilities.

Paciorek, M.J., & Jones, J.A. (2001). *Disability sports and recreation resources*. Traverse City, MI: Cooper.

This is a complete resource guide that provides information on 47 sport and recreation activities for people with disabilities. Information is provided on adapted equipment and manufacturers, disabled sport organizations, and national governing bodies.

chapter 4

Measurement, Assessment, and Program Evaluation

Manny Felix and Garth Tymeson

In a recent district physical education staff meeting, you were given the task of developing testing policies and procedures to identify children who may be eligible for adapted physical education services. You were given this lead role because you had just graduated with a teaching emphasis in adapted physical education and held state certification in it. In the past, the special education director of the district or the principal of the school would simply tell the physical education teachers which students would be in adapted physical education for the year. School district personnel and many parents knew that this was not the legal process in determining who needs adapted physical education, but physical education teachers had neither the knowledge about the role of tests in the special education process nor the access to appropriate test instruments.

Until now, that is—now that you have been hired to teach in and direct the adapted physical education program. The school district, including the administrators, special education teachers, physical education teachers, related service personnel, and parents, are relying on your leadership to improve the program. What testing policies and procedures would you recommend for determining eligibility for adapted physical education, identifying physical education needs, and monitoring physical education progress? How would these policies and procedures comply with current legislation and best practices? This chapter will help you answer these questions.

Measurement and assessment serve significant purposes in physical education. One critical purpose in adapted physical education, to assist in determining eligibility for adapted physical education, is alluded to in the previous scenario. The Individuals with Disabilities Education Act (IDEA) requires periodic measurement and assessment throughout the special education process in order to ensure that an appropriate education, including physical education, is provided. This chapter identifies concepts of measurement and assessment as they relate to adapted physical education. Major topics include terminology, test standards and approaches, testing and assessment used in adapted physical education, test instruments, and program evaluation.

TERMINOLOGY

Many terms are inappropriately used synonymously in the physical education profession. It is important to distinguish among tests, measurement, evaluation, and assessment. **Test** refers to instruments, protocols, or techniques used to measure a quantity or quality of properties or attributes of interest (Lacy & Hastad, 2007). For example, a flexibility test may require the use of a sit-and-reach box and a specific protocol (e.g., one leg at a time, hold on fourth stretch) in order to gather measurement data. Of course, there are several ways to test for and measure a desired characteristic. For instance, in addition to skinfold measurements, body fat can be measured by other clinical methods such as hydrostatic underwater weighing or bone densitometry, but these methods are not feasible for the physical educator. **Measurement** simply refers to the process of collecting data on the property or attribute of interest (Lacy & Hastad, 2007). For instance, when a skinfold test is used, the measurement is expressed in millimeters, giving an indication of the attribute of body fat.

Evaluation and **assessment** are synonymous terms that include the process of interpreting the measurement data and making a judgment by comparing results with predetermined criteria or objectives (Lacy & Hastad, 2007). For example, a 15-year-old student with intellectual disability runs the 20-meter PACER test and receives a score of 30 laps. This measurement score can then be compared to a predetermined standard (such as 33 laps when using the Brockport Physical Fitness Test

[BPFT]). Because this student's score does not meet the predetermined standard, it indicates that the student does not have a level of aerobic functioning necessary for good health. Had the student's score been higher than the predetermined standard (>33 laps), then the interpretation would have been different (i.e., the performance score indicates adequate levels of aerobic functioning consistent with good health). Evaluation and assessment of scores thus facilitate objective decisions such as educational decisions regarding eligibility, program planning, placement, and performance goals. In the previous example, since the student lacks adequate aerobic functioning, it may be decided that her measurable individualized education program (IEP) goals and objectives should address the need to improve cardiorespiratory fitness.

STANDARDS FOR ASSESSMENT

In order to evaluate performance scores and subsequently make appropriate assessment decisions, it is necessary to understand standards of performance. Standards most commonly used to evaluate test scores in physical education may be norm referenced or criterion referenced. Most test instruments use either norm or criterion referencing or both for evaluation of student scores.

Norm-Referenced Standards

Norm-referenced standards allow comparison of one student's performance against the performance of others from a particular peer group with similar characteristics (e.g., a 10-year-old girl's score will be compared with other 10-year-old girls' scores). Norm-referenced standards allow for evaluation statements such as, "Tucker's object-control motor area of functioning is above average for boys his age," "Tamiko is two years behind her age group in locomotor skill functioning," and "Tim's abdominal curl-up performance score places him at the 21st percentile compared to other boys his age." Examples of norm-referenced standards include percentiles, chronological age norms, T-scores, z-scores, and other test-specific standard scores (Wood & Zhu, 2006).

Norm-referenced standards are generally established by testing large numbers of subjects from specifically defined population groups. The distribution of these test scores should be consistent with normal curve theory. Through statistical analyses, scores are summarized and percentiles and standard scores are then derived by age and gender. Norm-referenced standards are usually associated with standardized testing approaches discussed later in this chapter.

Criterion-Referenced Standards

Whereas norm-referenced standards allow comparison of individual performance scores with other scores of a comparable group, **criterion-referenced standards** allow comparison of individual scores to some absolute level of mastery or predetermined criterion. This mastery score represents a minimally acceptable level of performance for the test instrument or item. Mastery scores can be determined by expert judgment, research data, logic, experience, or other means (Wood & Zhu, 2006).

An example of criterion-referenced standards is the running test item (table 4.1) from the Test of Gross Motor Development (TGMD-2). The TGMD-2 is a test instrument commonly used in adapted physical education to measure locomotor and object-control functioning in children 3 to 10 years of age (Ulrich, 2000). When the test item is implemented, the child's performance is compared to the performance criteria listed. Thus, TGMD-2 individual test-item scores are criterion referenced. (However, summative scores on the TGMD are norm referenced.)

In the past, many tests used norm-referenced standards that generated percentile scores. For instance, on a fictitious health-related physical fitness test a student received a 30 percent body-fat measurement, which placed this person at the 50th percentile based on age and gender. Although the 50th percentile is statistically average (most people will score near the average), the score does not necessarily mean that it is healthy. In this case, some people might misinterpret that 30 percent body fat is at an adequate level of health since the percentile score is average. One advantage of using criterion-referenced standards is that a performance score is not compared with others but instead with a mastery level that has been deemed acceptable.

Recently, greater attention has been placed on the use of tests with criterion-referenced standards for determination of unique needs and instruction in physical education. The Fitnessgram 8.4 (Cooper Institute for Aerobics Research, 2007) is a good example. Standards associated with the Fitnessgram test represent a level of performance that is indicative of good health and improved physical function. For each test item (table 4.2), standards for a healthy fitness zone are provided by gender and age (5 to 17+ years). The healthy fitness zone is defined by a lower-end score and an upper-end score. All students are encouraged to achieve at least the lower-end criterion, which would mean their score is at least at a level associated with good health for that area of fitness. Little or no emphasis may be placed on going beyond the upper-end criterion, however, because most health-related objectives can be attained simply by staying within the healthy fitness zone. (At times, it may be inappropriate to exceed performance outside health fitness zones, such as exceeding a recommended score on the trunk lift or having extremely low levels of body fat, particularly in females). Similar to the Fitnessgram, the BPFT is criterion referenced with established healthy fitness zones, but the standards are uniquely organized not only by age and gender but also by disability. As exemplified by these two tests, criterion-referenced standards can be associated with standardized tests, but they can also be found with some of the alternative testing approaches discussed later in this chapter.

Table 4.1 Criterion-Referenced Measurement of the Run on the TGMD-2

Performance criteria	Trial 1	Trial 2	Score
1. Arms move in opposition to legs, elbows bent	0	0	0
2. Brief period where both feet are off the ground	1	1	2
3. Narrow foot placement landing on heel or toe (i.e., not flat-footed)	1	1	2
4. Nonsupport leg bent approximately 90 degrees (i.e., close to buttocks)	1	1	2
Skill score			6

Scoring: 0 = criterion not exhibited; 1 = criteria exhibited.

Table 4.2 Fitnessgram and BPFT Test Items Arranged by Fitness Components

Fitnessgram	BPFT
Aerobic capacity • PACER • Mile run • Walk test	Aerobic functioning • PACER (20 m and 16 m) • Mile run • Target aerobic movement test
Muscular strength, endurance, and flexibility • Curl-up • Trunk lift • Push-up • Modified push-up • Pull-up • Flexed arm hang • Back-saver sit-and-reach • Shoulder stretch	Musculoskeletal functioning • Reverse curl • Seated push-up • 40 m push or walk • Wheelchair ramp test • Push-up • Modified pull-up • Dumbbell press • Bench press • Dominant grip strength • Flexed arm hang • Extended arm hang • Trunk lift • Curl-up • Modified curl-up • Target stretch test • Shoulder stretch • Modified Apley test • Modified Thomas test • Back-saver sit-and-reach
Body composition • Percent fat (triceps and calf skinfolds) • Body mass index	Body composition • Skinfolds (triceps and calf, triceps and subscapular, or triceps only) • Body mass index

Standardized Testing Approaches

Standardized testing involves implementation of previously established test procedures and protocols (found in test administration manuals) in controlled environments in order to objectively collect data. In this manner, students are tested in exactly the same way under exactly the same conditions. By controlling, or standardizing, the environment, validity and reliability (including objectivity) of the test results are maximized. Standardized testing frequently is used to determine if a student is making reasonable progress on skill and fitness development compared with similarly defined students (e.g., by age and gender) or with levels of achievement thought to be appropriate for students with certain characteristics. In doing so, standardized testing is often used for eligibility and placement decisions when school districts use specific objective criteria (e.g., two standard deviations below the mean, below the 20th percentile) to determine eligibility for adapted physical education.

Although standardized testing approaches may be appropriate for the general student population, a physical educator must be careful not to indiscriminately use this approach with some students with disabilities since unique physical, cognitive, and behavioral characteristics may reduce the validity of the test result. Some test instruments that have been standardized with the general population in mind are now suggesting test modifications for use with students with disabilities. Also, some tests (and consequently their test procedures) have been specifically developed for students with and without disabilities. The BPFT is a good example of this. A few of the many tests of physical fitness, motor development, and sport skills that use standardized testing are described later in the chapter.

Alternative Approaches

Alternative testing refers to the gathering of data through a variety of testing means and environmental conditions. For example, a checklist that identifies presence or absence of key throwing components (e.g., opposition, weight transfer, follow-through) may be used when the student is engaging in throwing practice trials during a lesson activity, during a tee-ball modified activity, or even during a more formal one-on-one testing situation. In any of these situations, data can be collected. Alternative testing methods often include the use of observations, checklists, rubrics, task analyses, and portfolios. Some of these techniques are alternative strategies to tests that use standardized approaches.

Because some standardized test items are not natural or authentic and thus are less helpful in identifying appropriate instructional needs, proponents for alternative strategies suggest that testing physical education content in real-world settings is a more effective way to align testing with instruction. This may be even more appropriate for students with disabilities due to varying abilities and instructional needs. **Authentic testing** refers to testing in real-world environments or activities. Authentic testing can be more efficiently aligned to directly measure the skills that students need for successful participation in physical education. Techniques associated with authentic assessment are briefly discussed next.

Checklists

Checklists indicate the presence or absence of essential behaviors or characteristics in a list format. No attempt is made to determine the extent or quality of the characteristic. They are simply checked to indicate whether or not the characteristic is exhibited (Lund, 2000). Checklists are particularly helpful when using task analysis. An example of a simple checklist is provided in figure 4.1. A point-system checklist is a variation where points are assigned to behaviors or characteristics. This may be useful for teachers if numerical grades are given. Checklists are appropriate if the intent is to simply tell what students can do; however, if the intent is to determine the quality of performance, then analytic rating scales would be more appropriate. When used in authentic teaching situations, checklists can be a valuable and practical tool to identify instructional needs.

Rubrics

Rubrics are rating scales that distinguish among varying levels of performance or skill through clear performance criteria. When using rubrics, the scorer can make accurate, consistent, and objective judgments about the quality of performance. By using rubrics, teachers can identify what skills a child is able to perform on functionally relevant physical education content and present the quality performance level of that skill. A major advantage of using rubrics (and checklists) is the ease with which curricular-embedded, measurable IEP goals and objectives can be assessed.

An analytic rating scale is one type of rubric that uses ratings such as excellent, good, fair, and poor to distinguish degrees of performance. Rubrics can either be quantitative (numerical) or qualitative. Quantitative rubrics (refer to figure 4.2) use numbers to distinguish levels of performance, whereas qualitative rubrics (refer to figure 4.3) use words or adjectives to differentiate performance. One of the distinct advantages of testing and evaluating through rubrics is that students and teachers know what performance needs to be exhibited in order to get the best possible score. For instance,

---

Wheelchair Basketball Checklist: Recovering the Ball From the Floor With the Wheel

Yes	No	
_____	_____	Approaches ball with adequate speed.
_____	_____	Upper body leans toward ball side of wheelchair.
_____	_____	Reaches for ball with extended arm and palm of hand facing the wheel.
_____	_____	Forces ball with hand against push rim or spokes while wheelchair is moving.
_____	_____	Allows ball to reach top of wheel using wheel momentum and steady placement of hand against push rim or spokes.
_____	_____	Rotates hand under the ball to place ball on lap.

FIGURE 4.1 A simple checklist where the user simply checks whether or not the characteristic is present.

Behavioral Rating in Physical Education

Scale: 1 = very poor; 2 = poor; 3 = adequate; 4 = good; 5 = very good; NA = not applicable

Desired behaviors	1	2	3	4	5	NA
RESPONDING TO THE TEACHER						
Quietly listens to instruction.						
Follows directions in a timely manner for introductory activities.						
Follows directions in a timely manner for skill development.						
Follows directions in a timely manner for games and sports.						
Stops and listens during activity transitions.						
Uses positive or neutral language with teacher.						
Willing to accept help when needed.						
Other (specify):						
RELATING TO PEERS AND EQUIPMENT						
Works cooperatively with a partner when asked.						
Works cooperatively with a group (>2) when asked.						
Uses positive or neutral comments to peers.						
Displays sportsmanship by avoiding conflict with others.						
Does not become frustrated with group performance outcomes.						
Helps others when appropriate.						
Uses equipment appropriately.						
Other (specify):						
EFFORT AND SELF-ACCEPTANCE						
Quickly begins activity once instructed to do so.						
Stays on task during motor-engaged activities.						
Stays on task during non-motor-engaged activities.						
Willing to improve own performance; strives to be successful.						
Does not become frustrated with own performance outcomes.						
Other (specify):						

FIGURE 4.2 Sample quantitative rating scale rubric.

Game-Play Rating Scale

Component	Peewee	Rising star	Collegiate	Olympic
Positioning	Frequently flat-footed; waits for play or is not aware of upcoming plays.	Occasionally uses correct position; often waits for play.	Demonstrates correct positioning on offense and defense; anticipates play.	Demonstrates use of strategies during game play while maintaining a high level of intensity.
Skill mechanics	Avoids using skills.	Occasionally exhibits proper skill mechanics.	Frequently uses proper skill mechanics.	Demonstrates proper skill mechanics consistently.
Rules	Does not adhere to rules.	Occasionally adheres to rules.	Usually adheres to rules.	Adheres to rules on a regular basis.
Team play	Demonstrates poor sportsmanship or teamwork skills.	Shows little tendency toward sportsmanship or teamwork skills.	Cooperates with teammates and demonstrates good sportsmanship.	Organizes teammates toward a positive common goal.

FIGURE 4.3 Sample qualitative rating scale rubric.

in the basic game-play rubric (figure 4.3), performance is judged to be in one of the four levels of performance for each content area of game play (e.g., positioning, skill mechanics). With this particular rubric, content areas can be evaluated as students play an actual game; thus, evaluating can be unobtrusive and take place in a more natural environment.

Often, rubrics can be easily modifiable for students with disabilities. For example, a rubric where a level of performance characteristic is stated as "moves into position quickly" could be modified to read "wheels into position" or "attempts to move into position." Another example of a modification might be the substitution of a beach ball for a regulation volleyball when using a volleyball rubric. Similar to these examples, physical educators may need to make modifications to existing rubrics in order to test students with disabilities on functionally relevant skills and content. This may be necessary especially when using ecological task analysis (ETA) in teaching.

For physical education content that is unique and personalized to the student (e.g., effective wheelchair propulsion and agility, behavior in physical activity settings), a rubric may need to be created to address the specific area of need. Creating well-written rubrics is worthwhile if the rubric allows for more effective educational decision making and enhanced instruction. Steps and hints for developing rubrics can be found in a recommended resource by Lacy and Hastad (2007).

Task Analysis

Task analysis can be used as an alternative assessment strategy to identify movement capabilities and limitations as well as consequent instructional needs. The process of task analysis involves breaking down a movement skill into its component parts. Assessment of tasks involves determining which tasks are attained. The value in determining specific parts of a task that a student can and cannot perform lies in the determination of appropriate instructional content. For more information on the development and use of task analysis, refer to chapter 7.

Portfolios

Portfolios consist of a purposeful, integrated collection of exhibits and work samples showing effort, progress, and achievement (Melograno, 2006). An authentic picture of student achievement is presented through pieces of evidence rather than simply through some kind of grade. In adapted physical education, teachers can identify any number of items that students can choose to include in their physical education portfolio. Examples include digital media, test results (including standardized tests), teacher observations, peer evaluations, rating scales, checklists, journals, self-reflections, self-assessments, student projects, and activity logs.

Materials, however, are not just dumped into a portfolio. Teachers must establish criteria for what goes in the portfolio and how it will be evaluated. One common way to organize the portfolio is by standard and sample benchmarks (Melograno, 2006). The contents of a portfolio will vary depending on the student's age and cognitive ability as well as the purpose of the portfolio. Portfolios should reflect assessments and performances related to all three domains of behavior (cognitive, affective, psychomotor), adapted as necessary for students with disabilities. For instance, a rubric addressing behavioral characteristics might be appropriate to demonstrate affective functioning in physical education and subsequently may be added to a student's portfolio.

Synthesis

The push for alternative or authentic types of assessment has gained momentum in adapted physical education. Authentic approaches hold promise for directly linking testing and learning. When conducted properly, authentic approaches inform students of their progress (which, to a large extent, they monitor themselves) and what they need to work on next. Testing and learning become seamless because students learn, in part, from the testing program.

Alternative approaches, however, are not without limitations. Many alternative approaches rely heavily on subjective observation. As Hensley (1997) has noted, such assessment practices "have frequently been criticized on the basis of questionable validity and reliability, being susceptible to personal bias, generosity error (the tendency to overrate), lack of objective scoring, as well as the belief that they are conducted in a haphazard manner with little rigor" (p. 21). Furthermore, both IDEA and the No Child Left Behind Act require that the unique needs of young people be determined using valid, reliable, objective, and nondiscriminatory instruments, and authentic assessment strategies often do not meet these criteria.

Consequently, it is recommended that measurement and assessment strategies include both standardized and alternative approaches. Two continua influence the selection of tests in adapted physical education. One relates to the extent of its psychometric properties (including validity and reliability) and the other relates to the extent of its authentic properties. There tends to be a relation between these variables. Because the establishment of appropriate levels of validity and reliability requires controlled circumstances, tests with stronger psychometric qualities tend to have lower authentic qualities. Conversely, those with stronger authentic qualities tend to have weaker psychometric properties.

Of course, teachers should attempt to select tests that have at least acceptable levels of both types of properties. Test selection, however, will also be influenced by the purpose of the testing. When important educational decisions pertaining to a student (e.g., eligibility for adapted physical education) are based on testing, the teacher should give preference to tests with stronger psychometric properties. When a student is learning a skill to be used in a particular context (e.g., dribbling a basketball for eventual use in a game situation), the teacher should give preference to tests with stronger authentic properties to monitor student progress. The application of both standardized and alternative assessment strategies in adapted physical education is explored further in the next section.

TESTING AND ASSESSMENT IN ADAPTED PHYSICAL EDUCATION

There are many reasons for testing and assessing in physical education, including increasing motivation, determining strengths and weaknesses, classifying students, determining degree of achievement, evaluating instruction and programs, predicting future success, and conducting research designed to answer questions and solve problems (Miller, 2002). In adapted physical education, testing and assessment strategies are often employed to assist in the determination of unique need (eligibility for services and, subsequently, placement) and in providing a basis for instruction. The relation of testing and assessment to these functions is discussed in the following sections.

Determination of Unique Need

Students suspected of having unique physical and motor needs should be referred to appropriate personnel within the school for further testing. Increasingly, more school districts are using response to intervention (RTI) strategies before referrals are processed. RTI consists of tiers of intervention strategies that can be employed in the regular education classroom with the intent to determine if struggling learners require specialized services (Council for Exceptional Children

[CEC], 2007). Thus, the referral process does not mean automatic entry into special education. Referrals must document the reasons why the student should be considered for further testing. Testing and assessment at the referral level, usually called **screening** or **informal assessment**, document the need for an in-depth evaluation to determine if the student has a unique need in physical education.

Determining unique need is critical for two reasons. First, a student must have a unique need to be eligible for adapted physical education. This is true both for students considered to have disabilities under IDEA and for those without disabilities who have unique physical education needs. Second, once a unique need is determined, the need serves as the basis for developing measurable IEP goals.

In dealing with the question of eligibility, a distinction must be made between an adapted physical education *program* and the instructional *placement* to which a student is assigned. A student might qualify for an adapted program but may receive the program services in a regular class placement. Thus, placement is established after the IEP goals have been determined. When a student is referred for possible adapted physical education services, the school district must first formally determine whether or not the student is eligible for the adapted physical education program. It will be necessary for the adapted physical educator to conduct more thorough, formalized assessments to determine if the student has a unique need. In the absence of a medical referral, the criteria for entry into the adapted program (in most cases) should be based primarily on psychomotor performance. Usually, measurement and assessment for the purpose of determining program eligibility should focus on standardized testing (i.e., tests with strong psychometric properties and standards for evaluation). Most districts have established eligibility criteria, and teachers are expected to follow those district policies.

Some states and many school districts have developed criteria for admission into adapted physical education. For instance, in order for a student with a documented disability to be eligible for adapted physical education in the state of Minnesota, the student must either fall one and a half standard deviations below the mean on a standardized psychomotor evaluation or fitness test that is administered individually by an appropriately licensed teacher, have documentation of inadequate development, or exhibit limited achievement and independence in regular physical education based on at least two of the following: motor and skill checklists; criterion-referenced measures; parent and staff interviews; informal tests; medical history or reports; systematic observations; social, emotional, and behavioral evaluations; and deficits in achievement related to the defined curriculum (Minnesota Department of Education, 2007).

In states without such criteria, it is recommended that school districts adopt specific criteria for eligibility in adapted physical education. It is also recommended that districts consider one or more of the following criteria for eligibility based on test results that measure aspects of physical education:

1. Low motor development. The student exhibits a motor delay of at least two years or performance is one standard deviation below the mean in motor development.

2. Low motor skill performance. The student fails to meet age- or grade-level competencies or criterion-referenced standards in one or more physical education content areas.

3. Low health-related physical fitness. The student does not meet specific or general standards of health-related physical fitness.

Because formal testing often takes place under artificial conditions, districts might consider additional salient criteria. For example, corroboration of standardized test results through observational techniques, authentic test results, or a temporary trial placement might also be required. Also, behavioral and communication needs may be considered when making professional judgments regarding eligibility. These factors are reflected in criteria used in determining eligibility for adapted physical education in Minnesota. Thus, a variety of relevant professional judgments can supplement eligibility criteria and decision making. Other examples of these considerations include the following:

1. Need for a specially designed physical education program recommended by an individual education planning team

2. Need for safe participation

3. Medical condition or disability that affects participation in physical activity

4. Need for a specially designed program to meet unique needs (strengths) for intramural and interscholastic sport experiences

Once eligibility has been established based on a documented unique need, appropriate goals and objectives are written. Chapter 5 reviews aspects of writing measurable and observable annual goals and short-term objectives. Once goals and objectives are written to address the student's unique needs, the most appropriate educational placement in the least restrictive environment is selected. The first placement consideration should be the regular class environment. Teachers should attempt to modify activities and instructional methodologies so that the student's goals can be met in the regular class.

Although there is one primary criterion for admission into the program (i.e., performance), there are several considerations in the selection of the appropriate placement. Placement, for instance, might depend in part on what is being taught in the regular class. A student who uses a wheelchair, for instance, could probably meet appropriate goals for individual sports (e.g., swimming, weightlifting, track and field) in a regular placement. But the same student might be assigned to a more restrictive setting when team sports (e.g., volleyball, soccer, football) are played in the regular class (although alternative activities also could be offered within the same placement). Another important consideration during placement is the input of the student and his parents. Whatever placement is selected, the student should be comfortable with it. In some cases, when students are unable to understand concepts or safety considerations being taught in the regular class or if there are behavioral or other affective concerns, students might need to be assigned to a more restrictive placement (see the continuum of alternative instructional placements in chapter 2).

Measurement in the Affective Domain

Students with disabilities, with or without unique needs in the psychomotor domain, might be placed in more restrictive physical education settings if they have unique needs in the affective domain. The affective (or social–emotional) domain is broad and encompasses elements such as attitudes, interests, values, beliefs, and personality, among others, but social behavior is the element of the affective domain that often gets the greatest attention in schools. The ability (and willingness) to follow directions, take turns, respect others, play fair, and demonstrate sportsmanship, for instance, is important in physical education and community-based physical activity settings.

Although physical educators can certainly make observations relative to a student's behavior in physical activity settings, it is unlikely they will administer any standardized tests to help determine a unique need in the affective domain. Such an assessment is most likely conducted by a school psychologist and might include the administration of tests such as the Vineland Social Maturity Scale or the Behavior Assessment System for Children. Physical educators would more likely assess behavior in an authentic context and, as such, would develop their own rubrics, checklists, task analyses, or rating scales to measure behavior. Refer to figure 4.4 for a behavioral rating scale that can be used in physical education.

Physical educators might also be involved with functional behavioral assessment (FBA), which is designed to gradually reduce unwanted behaviors while also increasing more desirable behaviors (U.S. Department of Education, 2005). In FBA, data such as frequency of behaviors, response rates, intervals, time sampling, durations, and latency periods are commonly gathered. The collection of behavioral data through the use of rubrics and FBA processes can lead to individualized behavioral intervention plans deemed necessary for the child to achieve educational success. Behavioral intervention plans based on FBA are covered in greater depth in chapters 6 and 9.

Providing a Basis for Instruction

The role of measurement and assessment does not stop after the student has been assigned an adapted physical education program. Progress on annual goals established for the student should be monitored throughout the year. As suggested earlier, alternative tests can be used for this purpose. For instance, students can work (individually, in pairs, or with the teacher) from task sheets or cards that include rubrics or task analyses for a particular activity. Teachers help students devise practice regimens that promote learning, as evidenced by scoring at a higher level on the rubric or by demonstrating previously missing techniques on the task analysis. Skills learned in practice situations also need to be transferred to natural environments, such as daily activities, games, and sports.

At the conclusion of the instructional program or unit, the teacher should conduct final testing to determine the student's exit abilities. In some cases, grades are awarded based on this final assessment. Whether the program is graded or not, progress

Affective Domain Criteria

Etiquette

▶ Respects others' personal space and boundaries.

▶ Honors activity dynamics.

▶ Conforms to standards of conduct of the sport.

Fairness

▶ Plays fair.

▶ Accepts defeat and does not complain.

▶ Accepts victory and does not gloat.

Communication With Peers

▶ Encourages others.

▶ Accepts skill levels of others.

▶ Assists others in reaching personal success.

▶ Uses active listening, positive words, and body language respectfully.

Communication With Instructor

▶ Uses active listening, positive words, and body language respectfully.

▶ Accepts coaching cues in a positive manner.

▶ Responds to instruction and seeks clarification.

▶ Remains on task.

Scoring

Each of the four categories is rated on multiple occasions as follows:

A = appropriate = always meets behavioral criteria.

NI = needs improvement = sometimes meets behavioral criteria.

I = inappropriate = never meets behavioral criteria.

FIGURE 4.4 Sample rating scale for the affective domain.

Reprinted with permission from *Journal of Physical Education, Recreation & Dance*, a publication of the American Alliance for Health, Physical Education, Recreation and Dance, 1900 Association Dr., Reston, VA 20191 (www.aahperd.org).

should be evaluated in terms of the written goals and objectives. For nongraded situations, Melograno (2006) suggests a progress report form that lists the student's goals as a checklist on which teachers can check "achieved," "needs improvement," or "working to achieve" for each goal listed. Summary sheets from portfolios can also be used for evaluating exit abilities. Some teachers might choose to give awards to students on the basis of their final test performances.

Meeting District and State Testing Requirements

IDEA requires that students with disabilities be included in state- or district-wide assessment programs (National Dissemination Center for Children with Disabilities, 2010). These assessment programs include tests that are periodically given to all students in order to measure achievement in academic areas, including physical education. Because IDEA states that students with disabilities should have as much involvement in the general curriculum as possible, a child who is receiving instruction in the general curriculum could take the same standardized test that the school district or state gives

to children without disabilities. Accordingly, the IEP must indicate how the child is participating in state- or district-wide assessments. Participation in a state- or district-wide test can fall under one of following three options (National Dissemination Center for Children with Disabilities, 2010):

1. Participation in the same standardized test— The same test and testing methods that are given to peers without disabilities are given to the student with a disability who receives special education services. An example might be that a school district physical education program requires fitness testing at various grade levels. Beginning at the ninth grade, all students, including those who receive special education services, perform the 20-meter PACER test to measure aerobic capacity.

2. Appropriate accommodations are provided— In order to enable children with disabilities to participate in such general assessments, appropriate accommodations may be necessary. The IEP team specifies what accommodations that child will need in order to participate. For instance, instead of the 20-meter PACER test, a student with a disability might be accommodated by allowing him to perform the 16-meter version with the assistance of a peer tutor. This particular test would allow

for appropriate evaluation according to disability-specific standards.

3. An alternative test is given—The IEP team may determine that the student cannot participate in a particular state- or district-wide test, even with modifications. If this is the case, the team must include a statement in the IEP explaining why the test is not appropriate for the student and how she will be assessed instead. The child is then tested using an alternative method that measures the same content area. In the case of measuring aerobic capacity by using the PACER test, aerobic capacity may possibly be measured by bike or arm ergometry, swim tests, or the target aerobic movement test (as described in the BPFT).

TEST INSTRUMENTS USED IN ADAPTED PHYSICAL EDUCATION

Many published tests are available to physical educators. Most of these tests are considered more standardized than alternative; that is, most published tests tend to have established levels of validity and reliability, provide norm-referenced or criterion-referenced standards, and require controlled testing environments. Some of these tests, however, do contain alternative elements such as rubric scoring systems (e.g., TGMD-2) or task-analysis sequences and checklists (e.g., Special Olympics coaching guides).

Available tests in physical education measure a range of traits and abilities. Most, however, fall within five traditional areas of physical and motor development and ability: reflexes and reactions, rudimentary movements, fundamental movements, specialized movements (including sport skills, aquatics, dance, and activities of daily living), and health-related physical fitness. (Note that these categories are somewhat arbitrary and do not encompass all possibilities. In some situations, for instance, teachers might routinely test and assess the posture or the perceptual–motor abilities of their students.) More recently, a sixth area, physical activity, has gained attention. The rest of this section is devoted to a discussion of tests or measures from these six areas. One instrument from each area is highlighted. The highlighted instruments are meant to be representative of a particular content area and are recommended or used by many adapted physical educators. Other tests are available within each area, and teachers always have the option of designing alternative measures to augment or replace published instruments. In adapted physical education, there are always circumstances when published instruments prove to be inappropriate for a particular student, and teachers must modify or design instruments in accordance with the student's abilities. (Additional tests are listed in the resources section of this chapter.) The application example illustrates how tests can be used.

Measuring Reflexes and Reactions

The measurement and assessment of primitive reflexes and postural reactions is becoming increasingly common in adapted physical education, particularly in early intervention and childhood programs. (See chapter 19 for information on reflexes and reactions.) As educational services are extended to infants and toddlers, as well as to those with more severe disabilities (especially those that are neurologically based, such as cerebral palsy), physical educators need to understand the influence of reflexes and reactions on motor development milestones and motor skill learning.

Because primitive reflexes normally follow a regular sequence for appearing, maturing, and eventually disappearing, they are particularly helpful in providing information on the maturation of the central nervous system. If a primitive reflex persists beyond schedule, presents an unequal bilateral response (e.g., present on one side but absent or not as strong on the other), is too strong or too weak, or is completely absent, then neurological problems might be suspected. When primitive reflexes are not inhibited, they will undoubtedly interfere with voluntary movement because muscle tone involuntarily changes when reflexes are elicited. The Milani-Comparetti Motor Development Screening Test is a good example of an instrument that identifies reflexes and reactions.

Milani-Comparetti Motor Development Screening Test for Infants and Young Children

■ **Purpose:** The Milani-Comparetti test (Stuberg et al., 1992) is designed to assess motor development in young children from birth to 24 months. Although the instrument has obvious use for infant and toddler programs, the inclusion of several

APPLICATION EXAMPLE

Measurement and Assessment

Setting: A new 10-year-old student with mild intellectual disabilities received special education services, including adapted physical education, at his previous school. As a matter of policy, the district will reevaluate the student before deciding on proper programs and placements. A physical education teacher is invited to be a member of the IEP team.

Issue: How should the physical educator determine if the student should be assigned to the adapted program?

Application: The physical educator might do the following:

▶ Administer the BPFT to determine if the student's fitness is sufficiently developed. (The expectation would be that the student would achieve at least specific standards for children with intellectual disabilities.)

▶ Administer the TGMD-2 to determine if fundamental movements are completely developed. (Maximum or near-maximum scores would be expected for a 10-year-old.)

▶ Compare standardized test results (i.e., BPFT and TGMD) with the district guidelines or criteria for adapted physical education.

▶ Place the student in a trial placement (or placements) and collect authentic assessment data. (Determine, for instance, if the rubrics being used by other members of the class are reasonably appropriate, with or without modification, for the new student.)

▶ Consider all assessment data when formulating a recommendation for the IEP team.

---

reflexes and reactions in the battery makes it appropriate for older developmentally delayed children as well, especially those with cerebral palsy.

■ **Description:** There are 27 items associated with this test. Nine of the items are classified as spontaneous behaviors, which test for head control in four postures (vertical, prone, supine, and pulled from supine), body control in three postures (sitting, all fours, and standing), and two active movements (standing from supine and locomotion). The remaining 18 items are evoked responses and test 5 primitive reflexes (hand grasp, asymmetrical tonic neck, moro, symmetrical tonic neck, and foot grasp) and 13 righting, parachute, or tilting reactions. In evaluating most of the spontaneous behaviors, testers are required to evaluate the progression of development. For instance, for all-fours, the child progresses from a prone position propped up by forearms and hands, to hands and knees, and finally to hands and feet (i.e., plantigrade). For evoked responses, the tester need only note whether the reflex or reaction is absent or present. Age norms are associated with each of the test items.

■ **Reliability and validity:** Interobserver and test–retest data provide evidence of acceptable levels of reliability. Age norms were established based on the performance of 312 subjects. Content validity is claimed based on general acceptance of test items by physicians and therapists.

■ **Comment:** The primary advantage of the Milani-Comparetti is its relative ease of administration, which is due, in part, to the limited number of test items. Physical and occupational therapists are likely to have experience with this test and might be resources for the adapted physical educator.

■ **Availability:** Munroe-Meyer Institute, University of Nebraska Medical Center, 985450 Nebraska Medical Center, Omaha, Nebraska 68198-5450. Web site: www.unmc.edu/media/mmi/pdf/mediacatalog2008.pdf.

Measuring Rudimentary Movements

Rudimentary movements are the first voluntary movements (see chapter 19). Reaching, grasping, sitting, crawling, and creeping are examples of rudimentary movements. Most instruments that assess rudimentary movements do so in some kind of developmental milestone format—that is, a series of motor behaviors associated with specific ages are arranged chronologically and tested individually. By determining which behaviors the child can perform, the teacher can estimate the child's developmental age (because each milestone has its own age norm) and can provide future learning activities (i.e., the behaviors in the sequence that the child cannot currently do). The Peabody Developmental Motor Scales (PDMS-2) is an example of this approach, with some additional enhancements (other instruments are discussed in chapters 21 and 22).

Peabody Developmental Motor Scales

■ **Purpose:** The PDMS-2 (Folio & Fewell, 2000) assesses the motor development of children from birth to 83 months in both fine and gross motor areas. Items are subcategorized into the following six areas: reflexes, stationary (balance), locomotion, object manipulation, grasping, and visual–motor integration.

■ **Description:** The PDMS-2 encompasses 249 test items (mostly developmental milestones) across the six motor areas. The items are arranged chronologically within age levels (e.g., 0-1 month, 6-7 months, 18-23 months), and each is identified as belonging to one of the six categories being assessed (e.g., reflexes, locomotion). It is recommended that testers begin administering items one level below the child's expected motor age. Items are scored from 0 to 2 according to specified criteria. Testing continues until the ceiling-age level is reached (a level for which a score of 2 is obtained for no more than 1 of the 10 items in that level). Composite scores for gross motor quotient (reflexes, balance, locomotion, and object manipulation), fine motor quotient (grasping and visual–motor integration), and total motor quotient (combination of gross and fine motor subtests) are possible.

■ **Reliability and validity:** Empirical research has established adequate levels of reliability and validity. Information is provided for subgroups as well as for the general population.

■ **Comment:** The PDMS-2 appears to have certain advantages over other rudimentary movement tests. First, the large number of test items represents a larger sample of behaviors than exist in many other tests. Second, the six categories help teachers pinpoint exactly which areas of gross motor development are problematic. Finally, the scoring system and availability of normative data provide the teacher with more information on student performance than many other tests do. Supplementary materials, including a software scoring and reporting system and a motor activity program, also are available in conjunction with PDMS-2.

■ **Availability:** Pro-Ed, 8700 Shoal Creek Boulevard, Austin, TX 78757-6897. Web site: www.proedinc.com/customer/productView.aspx?ID=1783.

Measuring Fundamental Movements

The critical window of opportunity, the time during which experience has the most influence on developing fundamental motor skills, seems to be the early childhood and early elementary years. Fundamental movements skills can be classified as locomotor (traveling, e.g., jumping), nonlocomotor (stationary, e.g., one-foot balance) or manipulative (object control, e.g., throwing). Some fundamental movement test instruments measure how far the performance has progressed along a motor continuum, but most use a point system to evaluate either the process of the fundamental movement or its product. Process-oriented approaches generally attempt to break down (or task analyze) a movement into its component parts and then evaluate each component individually. This approach assesses the quality of the movement, not its result. Product-oriented approaches are concerned primarily with outcome. Product-oriented assessment is more concerned with the quantity of the movement (e.g., how far, how fast, how many) than with its execution. The TGMD-2 emphasizes a process-oriented approach to the assessment of fundamental movements.

Test of Gross Motor Development-2

■ **Purpose:** The TGMD-2 (Ulrich, 2000) was designed to measure gross motor content frequently taught in preschool and early elementary grades, including special education; to be used by various professionals with a minimum amount of training; to use both norm-referenced and criterion-referenced standards; and to place a priority on the gross motor skill sequence rather than the product of performance.

■ **Description:** The test measures locomotor (six test items) and object-control skill functioning (six test items) and provides an overall indication of gross motor functioning. Locomotor subtest items include the run, gallop, hop, leap, horizontal jump, and slide. Object-control subtest items consist of the two-hand strike, stationary dribble, catch, kick, underhand roll, and overhand throw. For each skill, the tester is provided with performance criteria used to assess the child's performance. Children receive 1 point for meeting each performance criteria given for each of two trials allowed. These criterion-based scores can be added and compared to norm-referenced standards in order to make summative evaluations regarding locomotor, object-control, and overall gross motor performance. Percentiles, standard scores, and chronological age equivalents can be determined for assessment purposes.

■ **Reliability and validity:** Reliability coefficients are quite high (generally .84 to .96). Acceptable levels of content-related, criterion-related, and construct-related validity are provided.

■ **Comment:** The sound process of test construction should provide the user with a good deal of confidence that scores obtained by children accurately reflect their fundamental movement abilities. Availability of both criterion-referenced and norm-referenced standards enhance the capability of the test to support eligibility, placement, IEP planning, and instructional decisions. Test scores allow for easy monitoring of student progress and reporting to parents.

■ **Availability:** Pro-Ed, 8700 Shoal Creek Boulevard, Austin, Texas 78757. Web site: www.proedinc.com/customer/productView.aspx?ID=1776.

Measuring Specialized Activity Movements

Of the six content areas described in this section, specialized movements present the greatest challenge for making summary statements relative to assessment and for choosing one test instrument as an example. This is because of the wide variety of possible physical education and sport activities that could be tested under this heading. Sport skills tests can take many forms, but often they are criterion referenced and teacher constructed (in fact, many teachers prefer to use authentic techniques to assess game and sport skills). Teachers who work with students with disabilities who compete in special sport programs, including those offered by multisport organizations (e.g., BlazeSports National Disability Sports Alliance [BNDSA]), are encouraged to develop their own tests specific to the event in which the athlete competes. One example of a sport skills test that can be used with athletes with disabilities comes from the Special Olympics coaching guides.

Sport Skills Program Guides

■ **Purpose:** Special Olympics, Inc., provides coaching guides that can complement or supplement existing physical education and recreation programs for people with disabilities (aged eight and older) in sport skills instruction.

■ **Description:** Guides are provided for 29 sports and recreation activities. Although the guides are not test instruments per se, authentic assessment is a critical aspect of the instructional programs recommended in the guides. Assessments consist of both task analyses and checklists. Testers check off task focal points that the student is able to perform. For instance, in athletics there are 14 test items corresponding to track and field events. Within each checklist, testers check the focal points an athlete can demonstrate (e.g., "Performs a single-leg takeoff for a running long jump.").

■ **Reliability and validity:** No information has been reported, but content validity probably could be claimed because the checklists reflect sport skills task analyses developed by content (specific sport activity) experts in the field.

■ **Comment:** A primary advantage of the coaching guides is convenience—a teacher or coach can adopt the existing task-analysis curricula for many sport activities and further modify accordingly for specific students and situations if needed. The program has been used with participants with intellectual disabilities for some time and has been shown to have good utility for that group. A disadvantage is that neither reliability nor validity of the various test instruments has been formally established.

■ **Availability:** Special Olympics, Inc., 1325 G Street, Suite 500, Washington, DC 20005. Web site: http://info.specialolympics.org/Special+Olympics+Public+Website/English/Coach/Coaching_Guides/default.htm.

Measuring Health-Related Physical Fitness

Because health-related physical fitness is an increasing concern in the health and well-being of young people, it is crucial to use fitness tests that provide meaningful data and allow sound instructional decision making. Over the years many standardized tests of physical fitness have become available to teachers. The BPFT is one test that is recommended to measure and assess the health-related physical fitness of young people with disabilities. The BPFT (Winnick & Short, 1999a) extends the health-related, criterion-referenced approach to young people with disabilities. A DVD on the BPFT has been included with this text.

Brockport Physical Fitness Test

■ **Purpose:** The BPFT (Winnick & Short, 1999a) provides a health-related, criterion-referenced physical fitness test appropriate for young people (aged 10-17) with and without disabilities.

■ **Description:** The test battery includes 27 test items (refer to table 4.2) from which teachers can choose. (A brief description of all test items can be found in appendix C, and many are demonstrated in the video clips presented on the DVD.) Typically, students are tested on four to six test items from three components of fitness: body composition, aerobic functioning, and musculoskeletal functioning (muscular strength, endurance, and flexibility). Although specific test items are recommended for children with intellectual disabilities, cerebral palsy, visual impairments, spinal cord injuries, and congenital anomalies and amputations, teachers are encouraged to personalize testing. Personalization involves identifying health-related concerns pertaining to the student, establishing a desired fitness profile for the student, selecting components and subcomponents of fitness to be assessed, selecting test items to measure those components, and selecting health-related, criterion-referenced standards to evaluate fitness. Thus, teachers have the option to modify any of the elements of the testing program as outlined in the test manual. Both general-population and disability-specific standards are available for assessment and evaluation. A general standard is one appropriate for the general population and has not been adjusted in any way for the effects of a disability. A specific standard is one that has been adjusted for the effects of a disability. Specific standards are available only for selected test items for particular groups of people.

■ **Reliability and validity.** The test items in the BPFT have been shown to be valid and reliable through various studies. Evidence for validity and reliability is provided in a lengthy technical report published in a special issue of the October 2005 *Adapted Physical Activity Quarterly* (Winnick, 2005).

■ **Comment:** The BPFT was patterned after the Fitnessgram, and many of the standards, especially for the general population, were adopted from that test. Thus, teachers in inclusive settings should find it relatively easy to use both tests as necessary. In addition to the test manual, a training guide is also available (Winnick & Short, 1999b).

■ **Availability:** Human Kinetics, P.O. Box 5076, Champaign, Illinois 61820. Phone: 800-747-4457. Web site: www.humankinetics.com/products/showproduct.cfm?isbn=0736078983.

Measuring Physical Activity

Much research has established the positive relation between regular physical activity and health, and many physical education programs are promoting physically active lifestyles as a primary goal of the program. Consequently, it is becoming increasingly important for physical educators to find ways of measuring physical activity that describe the status of a student's activity level and ways of documenting changes in that level. At present, four types of activity measures are available to teachers: heart rate monitors, activity monitors (e.g., pedometers, accelerometers, motion sensors), direct observation, and self-report instruments (Welk & Wood, 2000). Despite their accuracy, heart rate monitors have limited applicability in school situations because of the cost and limitations (only a few children can be measured at one time). Pedometers are relatively inexpensive, are accurate, and have good utility for measuring walking activity, but they do not have broad applicability in measuring general physical activity. Coding student activity through direct observation is not expensive, but it can be time consuming because only a few children can be monitored at one time by a trained observer. (These three approaches—heart rate monitors, activity monitors, and direct observation—might be more effective in settings with fewer students.)

Self-report instruments are the most appropriate means of measuring physical activity in most school settings. Self-report instruments require students to recall and record their participation in physical activity over a set amount of time (usually from one to seven days). Although many self-report instruments are available (see Welk & Wood, 2000, for examples), all seek to quantify the frequency, intensity, and duration of students' physical activity. If students with disabilities have difficulty with self-reports, teachers or parents might need to provide an estimate of the information instead. A computer software program, Activitygram, provides teachers with an easy method for measuring student physical activity.

Activitygram

■ **Purpose:** Activitygram (Cooper Institute for Aerobics Research, 2007), a program associated with Fitnessgram, records, analyzes, and saves student physical activity data and produces reports based on that data.

■ **Description:** Activitygram is part of the Fitnessgram 8.4 test program. The program prompts participants to recall their physical activities over the previous two or three days in 30-minute time blocks. Students select activities from within six categories: lifestyle activity, active aerobics, active sports, muscle fitness activities, flexibility exercises, and rest and inactivity. Students are also asked to rate the intensity of the activity (light, moderate, vigorous). Activitylog, a related component of Activitygram, allows students to track their physical activity (in step counts or minutes of activity) and to set personal goals and challenges. Activitygram and Activitylog printed reports provide an analysis of activity habits and personalized messages that give suggestions to increase or maintain physical activity. Recommendations are based on national guidelines developed by the Council on Physical Education for Children (COPEC), a division of the National Association for Sport and Physical Education (NASPE).

■ **Reliability and validity:** Because of the subjective nature of self-report measures, measurement error may reduce validity. Nevertheless, the Previous Day Physical Activity Recall instrument, on which the Activitygram program is based, has been shown to provide valid and reliable estimates of physical activity and also accurately identifies periods of moderate to vigorous activity (Weston, Petosa, & Pate, 1997). Measurement error can be minimized when parents, teachers, and others can verify activity measures.

■ **Comment:** Although designed primarily with students without disabilities in mind, the Activitygram can be useful for students receiving adapted physical education. Specific activities will vary (e.g.,

running versus pushing a wheelchair), but the six categories of physical activity are appropriate for most students with or without disabilities. Younger children and those with intellectual disabilities, however, might have trouble recalling and entering activity data. Peer tutors, teacher aides, or parents could be prepared to make direct observations and could enter the data on behalf of a student who has difficulty using the system.

■ **Availability:** Human Kinetics, P.O. Box 5076, Champaign, Illinois 61820. Web site: www.humankinetics.com/products/showproduct.cfm?isbn=9780736068567.

PROGRAM EVALUATION

One of the time-honored purposes of measurement in physical education is program evaluation. As used in this section of the book, the term *program evaluation* relates to the evaluation of instructional programming. Other aspects of a program, including management and organization, can be evaluated in other ways; see chapter 2 and appendix D. Program evaluation seeks to answer the question, "Is the physical education program doing what it purports to be doing?" This kind of information, of course, is important to teachers because if the answer to this question is, "No," then changes need to be made in order to improve the program.

Program evaluation, however, can also have a powerful public relations function in schools. Physical education teachers are all too familiar with attacks on their programs by administrators or school boards when fiscal or instructional resources are limited. Unfortunately, physical education has not always been able to successfully defend against these attacks. For instance, in 2007, high school student participation in daily school physical education was only 30 percent (U.S. Department of Health and Human Services [DHHS], 2008a). To improve this statistic and others like it, physical educators must overcome perceptions that their programs are merely playtime, glorified recess, or open recreation. Physical educators, certainly, must build good programs, but it is insufficient for them to simply claim the program is effective—they must objectively demonstrate that it is effective.

To conduct program evaluation, program goals must be in place. These goals might be determined locally (in a specific school or school district), statewide, or even nationally. A school district, for instance, might choose to adopt the NASPE content standards (NASPE, 2004) for its program goals or aims. These six standards are as follows:

1. Demonstrates competency in motor skills and movement patterns needed to perform a variety of physical activities.
2. Demonstrates understanding of movement concepts, principles, strategies, and tactics as they apply to the learning and performance of physical activities.
3. Participates regularly in physical activity.
4. Achieves and maintains a health-enhancing level of physical fitness.
5. Exhibits responsible personal and social behavior that respects self and others in physical activity settings.
6. Values physical activity for health, enjoyment, challenge, self-expression, or social interaction.

Although helpful in articulating a direction for a program, these standards in their current form may be too broad to be used for program evaluation. It is up to the local physical education staff to operationalize the standards in ways that can be measured and evaluated. Examples of how staff might establish operational definitions for a few of the NASPE standards are provided in the following list.

Standard 1

To evaluate standard 1, the terms *competency* and *variety* must be defined. For instance, a district might choose to define beginning, intermediate, and advanced competencies for the motor skills and movement patterns taught in its curriculum and might simply define variety by the number of activities for which some level of competency is claimed. So, physical education staff might rework standard 1 as follows:

By the end of the year, at least 80 percent of all eighth-graders will master all beginning-level competencies in at least three sports and all intermediate-level competencies in at least one sport.

If staff members can specify beginning, intermediate, and advanced competencies for a variety of sports taught in the curriculum, they can adopt specific program levels of accomplishment for specific grades so that perhaps by graduation the program goal might be for 80 percent of the students to have met beginning-level competencies

in at least 10 activities, intermediate in at least 5, and advanced in at least 3. This, then, would be the district's operational definition for reaching NASPE standard 1. Students and teachers could develop portfolios that follow students through their school years, with teachers helping students to acquire additional competencies in various sports as they move toward graduation.

Standard 3

Physical education staff might decide to adopt the Centers for Disease Control and Prevention (CDC) and American College of Sports Medicine (ACSM) joint physical activity guidelines for its secondary students as follows (USDHHS, 2008b):

For grades 7 to 12, 90 percent of all students will perform at least 60 minutes of daily moderate-intensity physical activity during the school year.

The Activitygram computer program could be used to monitor progress on this program goal, although teachers might want to interact with students to encourage accurate self-reporting. Pedometers are relatively inexpensive and are becoming increasingly popular in schools. Some models record exercise time, which would be useful in evaluating this standard.

Standard 4

Computer software associated with Fitnessgram (Activitygram) and the BPFT (Fitness Challenge) could be used to evaluate a program goal based on standard 4. Fitness Challenge, for instance, provides a report that summarizes the performance of all class members for all items in the test battery. Physical education staff might operationalize standard 4 as such:

At least 80 percent of all students aged 10 to 17 will meet either minimal general or specific health-related physical fitness standards for their age, gender, and, as appropriate, disability on at least one measure of aerobic functioning.

Other program goals could be written for other components of fitness and monitored with help from Activitygram or Fitness Challenge. Because Fitness Challenge includes both general and specific standards, it is useful in inclusive settings.

As a final note on program evaluation, program goals that have been operationally defined for a general physical education program might not always be useful in evaluating an adapted physical education program. In the absence of general program goals that might apply to a diverse student body in adapted physical education, teachers could choose to report program evaluation data as a function of success in meeting students' short-term objectives on their IEPs (see chapter 5). Such a program goal might read as follows:

> At least 80 percent of all short-term physical education objectives appearing on a student's IEP will be achieved for at least 90 percent of students enrolled in adapted physical education.

These short-term objectives would be based on the alternative or standardized measurement strategies discussed in this chapter.

SUMMARY

Measurement and assessment serve several important functions in adapted physical education. Most significantly, they are a means for determining whether a student has a unique need in physical education, and they provide a foundation for structuring learning experiences and monitoring progress. Measurement and assessment strategies range from techniques with stronger psychometric properties conducted in less natural environments (standardized assessment) to those with weaker psychometric properties conducted in more natural environments (authentic assessment). Each of these approaches has strengths and weaknesses and should be selected in accordance with the purposes of the assessment. These approaches are best combined to yield a more accurate picture of the student's level of performance.

Ordinarily, assessment in adapted physical education should focus on physical fitness and motor development and ability (including reflexes, rudimentary movements, fundamental movements, activities of daily living, sport skills, aquatics, and dance, as appropriate). Standardized tests are commercially available for each of these areas and are especially useful for summative purposes, such as determining unique need. Standardized tests, however, might be inappropriately used with students with disabilities and not provide a basis for instruction and learning. Authentic techniques may be used when standardized tests are inappropriate, and they are especially useful for formative or instructional purposes, such as monitoring student progress on a daily basis. Test data generated from the assessment of individual students can be aggregated to yield information on the effectiveness of the physical education instructional program.

REFERENCES

Cooper Institute for Aerobics Research. (2007). *Fitnessgram/Activitygram test administration manual* (4th ed.). Champaign, IL: Human Kinetics.

Council for Exceptional Children (CEC). (2007). CEC's position on response to intervention (RTI): The unique role of special education and special educators. Retrieved July 2, 2008, from www.cec.sped.org/AM/Template.cfm?Section=Search&section=Issue_4&template=/CM/ContentDisplay.cfm&ContentFileID=2666.

Folio, M., & Fewell, R. (2000). *Peabody developmental motor scales* (2nd ed.). Austin, TX: Pro-Ed.

Hensley, L. (1997). Alternative assessment for physical education. *Journal of Physical Education, Recreation and Dance, 68* (7), 19-24.

Lacy, A., & Hastad, D. (2007). *Measurement and evaluation in physical education and exercise science* (5th ed.). San Francisco: Benjamin Cummings.

Lund, J. (2000). *Creating rubrics for physical education.* Reston, VA: NASPE.

Melograno, V. (2006). *Professional and student portfolios for physical education* (2nd ed.). Reston, VA: NASPE.

Miller, D. (2002). *Measurement by the physical educator.* New York: McGraw-Hill.

Minnesota Department of Education. (2007). *Developmental adapted physical education.* Retrieved July 2, 2008, from www.education.state.mn.us/mdeprod/groups/Compliance/documents/Form/000831.pdf.

National Association for Sport and Physical Education (NASPE). (2004). *Moving to the future: National standards for physical education* (2nd ed.). Reston, VA: Author.

National Dissemination Center for Children with Disabilities. (2010). Accommodations in Assessment. Retrieved April 16, 2010 from www.nichcy.org/educatechildren/iep/pages/accommodationsinassessment.aspx.

Stuberg, W., Dehne, P., Miedaner, J., & Romero, P. (1992). *Milani-Comparetti Motor Development Screening Test for infants and young children* (3rd ed.). Omaha: Munroe-Meyer Institute for Genetics and Rehabilitation.

Ulrich, D. (2000). *Test of gross motor development* (2nd ed.). Austin, TX: Pro-Ed.

U.S. Department of Education. (2005). *Individuals with Disabilities Education Act amendments of 2004.* Volume 70, Number 118. 34 CFR Part 300. Washington, DC: Author.

U.S. Department of Health and Human Services (USDHHS). (2008a). *Healthy People 2010 progress review: Physical activity and fitness.* Atlanta: DHHS, CDC, National Center for Chronic Disease Prevention and Health Promotion (NCCDPHP).

U.S. Department of Health and Human Services (USDHHS). (2008b). *Physical activity guidelines for Americans.* Atlanta: DHHS, CDC, NCCDPHP.

Welk, G., & Wood, K. (2000). Physical activity assessment: A practical review of instruments and their use in the curriculum. *Journal of Physical Education, Recreation and Dance, 71* (1), 30-40.

Weston, A., Petosa, R., & Pate, R. (1997). Validation of an instrument for measurement of physical activity in youth. *Medicine and Science in Sports and Exercise, 29* (1), 138-143.

Winnick, J. (Ed.). (2005). Introduction to the Brockport Physical Fitness technical manual [Special issue]. *Adapted Physical Activity Quarterly, 22* (4).

Winnick, J., & Short, F. (1999a). *The Brockport physical fitness test manual.* Champaign, IL: Human Kinetics.

Winnick, J., & Short, F. (1999b). *The Brockport physical fitness training guide.* Champaign, IL: Human Kinetics.

Wood, T., & Zhu, W. (2006). *Measurement theory and practice in kinesiology.* Champaign, IL: Human Kinetics.

WRITTEN RESOURCES

Brigance Inventory of Early Development—Revised. (1999). Curriculum Associates, Inc., P.O. Box 2001, North Bellerica, MA 01862. Web site: www.curriculumassociates.com/products/detail.asp?title=BrigIED2.

This is a criterion-referenced assessment of more than 200 skills in 11 major areas, including preambulatory motor, gross motor, and fine motor skills. Designed for ages birth to 7 years.

Denver Developmental Screening Test (Denver II). (1989). Denver Developmental Materials, Inc., P.O. Box 371075, Denver, CO 80237. Web site: www.denverii.com/DenverII.html.

Developmental milestones for normal gross motor development; age norms up to 6 years.

Lacy, A., & Hastad, D. (2007). *Measurement and evaluation in physical education and exercise science* (5th ed.). San Francisco: Benjamin Cummings.

This book focuses on measurement and evaluation in many activity and physical education settings.

President's Challenge. (2008). President's Council on Physical Fitness and Sports, 200 Independence Avenue SW, Room 738H, Washington, DC 20201. Web site: www.presidentschallenge.org/index.aspx.

This is a physical activity and physical fitness awards program. Five awards are available—three related to physical fitness (including the Presidential Physical Fitness Award), one to health-related physical fitness, and one to maintaining a physically active lifestyle.

ELECTRONIC RESOURCES

American Association for Physical Activity and Recreation (AAPAR). (2007). Adapted physical education assessment scale II. Web site: www.aapar-apeas.org/index.html.

This is a standardized motor performance test for students aged 4.6 to 17 years. The test measures four areas of motor performance (perceptual motor function, object control, locomotor, and physical fitness) as well as adaptive behaviors. This norm-referenced test is based on scores of students in the general school population and has been used to identify students who need adapted physical education services.

Fitness Challenge software. (1999). American Fitness Alliance, Youth Fitness Resource Center, P.O. Box 5076, Champaign, IL, 61825-5076.

This computer software program supports the BPFT. It prints goals, results, and fitness plans for individual students, and separate reports can be generated for instructors or parents. Also includes the technical manual for the BPFT, which provides validity and reliability information.

Fitnessgram 8.4 software. (2009). American Fitness Alliance, Youth Fitness Resource Center, P.O. Box 5076, Champaign, IL, 61825-5076.

Provides a sophisticated computerized system for administering the Fitnessgram. Includes both teacher and student components. The student component allows students to enter their own test scores and track their progress. It also provides a system for monitoring their levels of physical activity through Activitygram, a subcomponent of the software.

Note: The authors sincerely thank Francis X. Short, professor, State University of New York, College at Brockport, for his contributions in this chapter in earlier editions.

5

Individualized Education Programs

Manny Felix and Garth Tymeson

Martha Shockley, a general physical education teacher at a local elementary school, was doing some work on the computer at home when her husband looked over her shoulder.

"What's all this?" he asked.

"I'm revising annual IEP goals for Kyle, one of my students," she said. "I have a special education IEP team meeting after school tomorrow."

"All that stuff is for one student?"

"Yeah, but it's not that much—mostly test results, a copy of his current IEP goals, and some notes I've made on the progress he's making on his annual physical fitness, sport skills, and swimming goals. All the information is on the computer so it can be quickly and easily revised. I'm part of a team of teachers and other professionals who develop, implement, monitor, and revise his IEP."

"Is an IEP like a lesson plan that I write for my students in history classes?"

"No. I still write lesson plans to teach skills needed to achieve content area goals on the IEP. Mostly the IEP lists the student's measurable annual goals and the resources that the school district provides the student to work toward achieving the goals. Parents also have input, and sometimes the student participates in the IEP meeting. We use the IEP to monitor progress during the school year and to plan for the future of the students as they transition to new education levels and programs. It's also used as a basis for quarterly report cards like those of all other students."

"Sounds like a lot of work for one student."

"Well, it does take a little time, but it's really important to develop an individualized program for a student with a unique need in physical education. The special and general education classroom teachers, parents, principal, physical therapist, and other staff work with me as a team. Besides, an IEP is required by law for eligible children with disabilities. I wish all kids, including our own, could have this type of individualized program so their personal instructional needs were addressed."

"Required by law? So, what happens if Kyle doesn't achieve the measurable annual goals as your IEP team planned? Can teachers get in trouble?"

"You can relax," Martha laughed. "They won't send me to detention or the Big House if Kyle does only one curl-up or doesn't run a four-minute mile! I review the goals on a regular basis and make teaching adjustments in order to best provide movement experiences in physical education to meet Kyle's unique needs."

U.S. education laws require that eligible students with disabilities receive individualized programs to meet their unique needs. Depending on age and other factors, a student's individualized program might be developed in the form of an individualized education program (IEP), an individualized family service plan (IFSP), or a section 504 accommodation plan. Further, students who are not disabled but who have unique needs in physical education might also have individualized programs developed for them. Such programs, though not required by federal law, are recommended in this text and are called *individualized physical education programs* (IPEPs). This chapter provides an overview of these programs and discusses in detail the requirements and procedures for developing IEPs, section 504 plans, and IPEPs.

OVERVIEW OF INDIVIDUALIZED PROGRAMS

The foundation of special education services required by the Individuals with Disabilities Education Act (IDEA) is the provision of an IEP. Often called the heart of IDEA, an IEP is a comprehensive written document used to describe the process of providing services and the detail of what those services will include (Norlin, 2007). The most recent amendments to IDEA in 2004 reaffirmed the importance of IEPs for providing free appropriate public educational services for students with disabilities in their least restrictive environment (U.S. Department of Education, 2006). An IEP describes the student's present levels of academic achievement and functional performance, identifies measurable annual goals, and lists the types, frequencies, and durations of educational services to be provided to meet personalized goals. IDEA requires that educational teams develop IEPs for all eligible students with disabilities between the ages of 3 and 21.

IDEA also has provisions for addressing the developmental needs of infants and toddlers with disabilities. Local agencies may provide early intervention services for infants and toddlers in accord with state discretion. These services are detailed in an IFSP, a document written for all eligible participants. (The IFSP is described in chapter 21.) Thus, IDEA addresses the needs of students from birth to 21 years of age who meet the criteria of infants, toddlers, and children with disabilities as defined by the act (see chapter 1 for an overview of disabilities defined in IDEA).

Some students with disabilities, however, might not meet the eligibility criteria to qualify for federally mandated special education services provided by IDEA. Students with conditions such as HIV or AIDS, asthma, seizure disorder, diabetes, attention deficient/hyperactivity disorder (ADHD), or mild physical or learning disabilities may not require intensive special education services. These children may not be eligible for special education IEPs, but they might be entitled to appropriate accommodations and services tailored to meet their needs as provided in a section 504 disability accommodation plan (see chapter 1 for a description of section 504 of the Rehabilitation Act). These 504 plans often include accommodations for the physical education and extracurricular participation needs of students.

In physical education there might be a third group of students (in addition to those covered by IDEA and section 504) who require individualized programs. These students do not qualify as having a disability that affects their education as defined under federal law, but they do have unique needs in physical education. Students who are recuperating from injuries, are recovering from noncommunicable diseases, are overweight, have low skill levels, or have deficient levels of physical fitness might fall into this category based on district criteria. Although this group of students is not covered by federal law, it is recommended that school districts develop IPEPs to document programs modified to meet students' unique physical education needs.

Whether or not a student is deemed to have a disability under the provisions of IDEA or section 504, physical education teachers should provide an individualized program if the student has a unique need. A unique need is apparent when a student cannot safely or successfully participate in the regular physical education program. Figure 5.1 summarizes the individualized programs that are either required or recommended for students with disabilities and other unique needs in physical education.

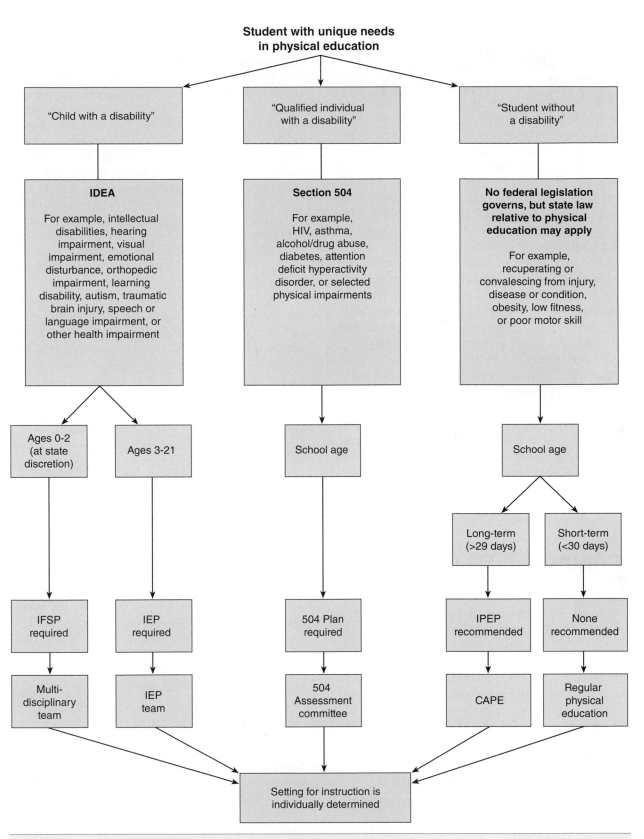

FIGURE 5.1 Individualized programs for students with unique needs in physical education.

STUDENTS WITH DISABILITIES: THE IEP DOCUMENT

The IEP is a specially designed educational program for any child identified as having a disability by the school district in accordance with IDEA. An IEP is a comprehensive written document for each child with a disability that is developed, implemented, reviewed, and revised in a meeting (U.S. Department of Education, 2006), and it describes the free appropriate public education for an eligible child with a disability as defined by IDEA. School districts may develop their own IEP document format; thus it is not unusual for neighboring districts to use different IEP forms. Although formats vary, each IEP must include certain components. Refer to the U.S. Department of Education Web site (http://idea.ed.gov/static/modelForms) for a model IEP form.

The IEP contains information about the entire instructional program for a student. Physical education, if determined to be part of the IEP, is only one of many content areas of this comprehensive document. To efficiently manage these documents, an increasingly common practice by school districts is to have IEPs on secure Internet-based programs that allow teachers and other school personnel to develop, monitor, revise, and complete IEPs from a computer.

COMPONENTS OF THE IEP

Although school district IEP forms might include additional information and vary in format, IDEA requires an IEP to contain several specific components. Each of these required components is discussed here, and, if appropriate, sample physical education information that might be included in an IEP is discussed and shown in figure 5.2.

Statement of Child's Present Levels of Academic Achievement and Functional Performance

Every IEP must include a statement of the child's present levels of academic achievement and functional performance, including how the child's disability affects her involvement and progress in the general education curriculum or, for preschool children, how the disability affects participation in appropriate activities (U.S. Department of Education, 2006). The present level of performance (PLP) component is used to establish the student's baseline educational abilities and is where all relevant evaluation and background information is presented. This evaluation information has two purposes: (1) to determine if a child has a disability (this is especially critical during the student's initial evaluation and formal reevaluations, which must take place at least once every three years) and (2) to determine the educational needs of the child. The PLP should also note how the disability affects the child's participation and success in the general education curriculum (curriculum for children without disabilities).

The PLP is the cornerstone of the IEP. Information presented in all subsequent IEP components is related to the PLP content. If the PLP is not properly determined, chances are the student's specially designed instructional program will not be the most appropriate. PLP statements should be data based, objective, observable, and measurable (Capizzi, 2008). Ordinarily, the PLP component consists primarily of test results, which can come from standardized tests with performance norms or criteria or from less formal teacher-constructed tests (including authentic assessments).

Both standardized and authentic assessment results have roles to play in the IEP. When the purpose of the evaluation is to determine if the student qualifies as a child with a disability with a unique educational need (especially during the initial evaluation and any triennial reevaluations), the assessment instruments must be technically sound and validated for the purposes for which they are used. Standardized tests are more likely to address these considerations than less formal, teacher-constructed tests. These tests must be given as described by the specific directions of the authors and by qualified personnel knowledgeable in the content area. On the other hand, teacher-constructed tests (i.e., authentic assessments) can be helpful in clarifying the educational needs of the child. In fact, IDEA requires current classroom-based assessments and observations as part of the evaluation of any student under consideration for special educational services. Authentic assessment techniques that are curriculum embedded are more likely to address this concern than commercially produced, standardized tests that are most often used for initial decisions on special education eligibility.

Individualized Education Program (Physical Education Content)

Student's name: Kyle Hernandez

Age: 16 (student with Down syndrome; moderate cognitive disability)

Present Levels of Performance

1. Completes 28 laps in the 20 m PACER test (Brockport Physical Fitness Test [BPFT] specific standard is 38 laps). Kyle demonstrates a well-coordinated, mature running pattern but needs a peer-buddy to run with him during the test to motivate him and keep him from stopping and sitting when reaching end lines.

2. Performs 20 modified curl-ups (exceeds the BPFT specific standard but does not meet the minimal general standard of 24). Demonstrates very good form for curl-ups.

3. Successfully performs the trunk lift at 12 in. (30 cm; BPFT general standard is 9-12 in., or 23-30 cm).

4. Back-saver sit-and-reach score for both right and left sides is 8 in. (20 cm; BPFT general standard is 8 in.).

5. Averages 4,700 steps per day on a pedometer. General recommendation is about 10,000 per day.

6. Scores 1 (out of a possible 3) on the overhand throwing rubric. (Characteristics: Ball is brought behind the head in preparation and release is high over the shoulder, steps forward with the leg on the same side as the throwing arm, trunk rotation is limited in preparation and during throw, trunk flexes slightly in follow-through.)

7. Throws a baseball a distance of 30 ft (9 m) (average of five trials) using an overhand pattern.

8. Scores 3 (out of a possible 10) on the overhand throwing accuracy test (target is 4 ft by 4 ft [1.2 m by 1.2 m] with the bottom line 2 ft [0.6 m] from the floor; student stands 30 ft [9 m] away and attempts to throw an indoor baseball to the wall target 10 times, earning 1 point for each successful throw).

9. Averages three inappropriate social behaviors or physical provocations (hitting, pushing others) per physical education class.

10. Swims 25 m in 45 seconds using the front-crawl stroke with inconsistent rhythmic breathing (typically holds breath and lifts head to breathe; when prompted to breathe to the side, he can do so but usually reverts to holding breath and lifting the head after the first stroke); arm strokes barely break surface of water, with irregular flutter kick often characterized by bicycle kicking; body position is less than horizontal due to lifting the head out of the water and inadequate flutter kicking; overall stroke technique appears to be inefficient and counterproductive to forward propulsion; endurance is good; does not fatigue or stop while swimming 25 m. He is very motivated and cooperative in the aquatic setting, and he has excellent water adjustment skills.

Effect of disability on involvement and progress in the general education curriculum: Kyle has Down syndrome with moderate cognitive disability. His disability generally contributes to lower performance in physical fitness and sport activities since he has difficulty understanding rules, concepts, and strategies of many curricular units, which at times makes it difficult to interact with his peers without disabilities. His muscle tone is poor (very hypotonic), he is overweight, and he tires easily. Kyle sometimes requires physical assistance or prompting when participating in physical education and is occasionally physically aggressive toward other students. With assistance, he can participate in several regular physical education units (mostly those focused on individual sports; he demonstrates little positive participation or interactions in team-oriented units).

Measurable Annual Goals and Short-Term Objectives

Note: Goals 1 and 2 are written in the traditional format that includes related short-term instructional objectives; goals 3 through 6 are written in the multi-element format discussed in this chapter and do not have accompanying objectives or benchmarks.

Goal 1. Kyle will improve his aerobic functioning.

(continued)

FIGURE 5.2 Sample physical education information for an IEP.

Short-Term Objectives

1.1 With a peer buddy running side by side, during three consecutive class days Kyle will run 30 laps of the 20 m PACER without sitting between laps.

1.2 Kyle will run 35 laps of the 20 m PACER with a peer buddy during three consecutive class days.

1.3 Kyle will independently run 40 laps of the 20 m PACER during three consecutive class days.

Goal 2. Kyle will improve his overhand throwing ability as demonstrated by scoring a 3 on the throwing technique rubric during three consecutive class days.

Short-Term Objectives

2.1 Kyle will score a 3 on the overhand throwing rubric. (Characteristics: Arm is swung backward rather than upward, ball is above the throwing elbow, throwing elbow moves horizontally during throw, thumb points down in follow-through, trunk rotates in preparation, throwing shoulder drops slightly in preparation, foot opposite the throwing arm steps forward with weight transfer from back foot to front.)

2.2 Kyle will throw a baseball overhand 50 ft (15 m) 8 out of 10 trials during three consecutive class days.

2.3 Kyle will score 7 out of 10 on the throwing accuracy test from 30 ft (9 m) during three consecutive classes.

Goal 3. By June 2010, following verbal instructions, Kyle will demonstrate improved abdominal muscular strength and endurance by achieving minimal general standards on the BPFT (will perform at least 24 modified curl-ups) when assessed by his adapted physical education teacher.

Goal 4. By December 2010, when provided with daily verbal reminders based on his behavior intervention plan at the start of class, Kyle will decrease his inappropriate behaviors in physical education as demonstrated by having two or fewer physical provocations with peers per 45-minute class for three consecutive class periods.

Goal 5. By June 2010, when assisted by a family member or friend, Kyle will increase his daily out-of-school physical activity by achieving an average of 7,000 steps for five consecutive days as measured by a pedometer (measurements taken at home by parents at night and reported to adapted physical education teacher via e-mail).

Goal 6. By May 2010, following verbal instructions, Kyle will swim 25 m in less than 40 seconds using the front crawl, demonstrating at least 10 consecutive correct rhythmic breathing sequences to the same side, with both arms emerging fully out of the water with each stroke while continuously performing proper straight-legged flutter kick during three consecutive classes, as assessed by the adapted physical education teacher.

Procedures for Measuring and Reporting Child's Progress to Parents

Criteria for evaluation of progress are contained in the measurable goals and short-term objectives. Progress on the goals and objectives will be monitored monthly or during the appropriate curriculum unit. A written report describing Kyle's progress on his goals and objectives will be sent to the parents at least quarterly (or at the same time as report cards for students without disabilities). A final assessment will be conducted during the week of June 1. The BPFT, pedometer readings, swimming skills rubric, and three throwing tests will be used for this evaluation. The teacher will maintain a daily record of Kyle's physical provocations to determine a three-day analysis of inappropriate behaviors.

Statement of Services and Supplementary Aids

Kyle will receive adapted physical education services with his intact special education class three times during the six-day high school class cycle, 35 minutes each class (except when participating in general physical education units). In addition, Kyle will participate in the regular physical education class (45 minutes per class period) during personal fitness, softball, swimming, and adventure education units. No special equipment or aids are required, but a trained peer tutor will be assigned to Kyle during

FIGURE 5.2   *(continued)*

the units in the general physical education class. It is important for Kyle to be in regular physical education class during appropriate units so he can observe socially appropriate behaviors.

Statement of Participation in Regular Education Settings

To best meet Kyle's needs, he will be placed in a combination of adapted physical education and regular physical education for participation with other students without disabilities. During the personal fitness, softball, swimming, and adventure education curriculum units, Kyle will receive 100 percent of his physical education program in a placement with peers without disabilities (the regular education setting).

Assessment Accommodations

The BPFT includes appropriate accommodations for health-related fitness assessment in accord with the Fitnessgram test that is administered at the high schools in the district (e.g., the curl-up to measure abdominal strength is modified so that the hands slide along the thighs to the knee rather than sliding across a strip placed on the floor). The swimming skills rubric is used by all students in high school. The three overhand throwing tests (technique, distance, accuracy) are modified from those ordinarily administered at the elementary level but were deemed appropriate for Kyle given his interest in baseball. Kyle currently cannot score on the baseball skills test routinely given at the secondary level.

Schedule of Services

Kyle will have adapted physical education from 9:30 to 10:05 a.m. every other day during the six-day cycle. During the personal fitness, softball, swimming, and adventure education units, he will attend the regular physical education class from 1:15 to 2:00 p.m. on three days during the six-day class cycle.

Transition Services

Kyle loves baseball, frequently attends games with his family, plays baseball video games, and watches games on television. In the spring and summer, Kyle will participate in the community-based Challengers baseball program for the first time. Development of baseball skills, with an emphasis on throwing, will take place in his adapted physical education class. Rules of the game will be reinforced both in physical education and at home. Mr. Hernandez (Kyle's father) will spend additional time each weekend working on batting skills (off a tee and underhand pitch). During the winter Kyle will accompany his older brother to the Snap Fitness Center at least two days a week after school (for strength and aerobic activities). This will provide formal exposure to community physical activity facilities for Kyle's future use. Mrs. Hernandez will take Kyle for walks around the community after dinner at least three times per week. It is also recommended that Kyle's parents consider enrolling him in Special Olympics swimming and other activities where he could compete and continue to increase his physical activity in community-based settings.

FIGURE 5.2 *(continued)*

PLP information should be presented in a way that places the student on a continuum of achievement—that is, the test results shown should discriminate among levels of ability. For this reason, tests on which students can only attain either minimum (0 out of 10) or maximum (10 out of 10) scores are not very helpful in determining PLP (although some criterion-referenced tests might simply have pass–fail standards). Also, in situating a student on this performance continuum, the PLP component should note what the student *can* do, not just what he cannot do. It is important to provide positive performance information, including behavioral aspects of participation, to parents and other IEP team members. Finally, PLP information should be presented in a way that is immediately interpretable; it should not require additional detailed explanation from the teacher.

When standardized test results are included, it is helpful when percentiles, criterion-referenced standards, or other references are presented as well as the raw scores; teacher-constructed tests should be adequately described so the conditions can be replicated at a later date. (See chapter 4 for information on measurement and assessment in adapted physical education.)

Statement of Measurable Academic and Functional Annual Goals

Every IEP requires a statement of measurable annual goals that describe what a student is expected to achieve in a specific content area in a given year. These goals are designed to meet the child's needs that result from disability in order to enable the child to be involved in and make progress in the general curriculum and to meet the child's other educational needs that result from disability (U.S. Department of Education, 2006).

Some professionals write IEP goals as general statements that give direction to instructional programs, followed by several more specific and measurable short-term objectives or benchmarks related to the goal. Examples of these general goal statements are "To improve physical fitness," "To develop a front-crawl stroke," or "To increase gross motor skill performance." This traditional practice of writing general goals is changing as a result of reauthorized federal legislation (IDEA, 2004) that does not mandate short-term objectives for IEP goals, outcomes of court cases, and more stringent accountability practices in special education (Norlin, 2007). Annual IEP goals are now often written in a much more measurable and specific format, sometimes without objectives or benchmarks. However, states still have the choice of requiring school districts to include short-term objectives or benchmarks for IEP goals. In addition, school districts may opt to include short-term objectives or parents may request that they be included to more easily monitor progress toward a goal. This chapter provides examples of both formats: multielement annual IEP goals that are specific and do not include short-term objectives and IEP goals that are traditional (general or broad statements) and accompanied by short-term objectives or benchmarks as progress markers. Figure 5.2 provides examples of traditional and multielement annual IEP goals.

Writing Traditional Annual IEP Goals

When IEP goals are accompanied by related short-term objectives or benchmarks, the goals are written in a more general format compared with the specific, measurable goals presented in the six-element format (see page 87). For example, IEP goals written in a more traditional or general format might look like this:

- Marissa will improve her fundamental movement patterns.
- Ryan will increase his level of physical activity in out-of-school settings.
- Kyle will improve his striking skills for application during individual sports.

These broad goals must be following by measurable and specific benchmarks used to assess progress toward the annual goal. As with all IEP goals, they should give guidance to the instructional program, be based on the child's unique need as identified in the PLP data, and relate to a goal content area that is agreed upon by the IEP team, including parents.

Although IDEA no longer requires short-term objectives or benchmarks for annual goals unless the child takes alternative assessments aligned with alternate achievement standards, many professionals and school districts encourage their use to assist with measuring student progress (Bateman & Herr, 2006; Jung, 2007). In addition, parents may request short-term objectives or benchmarks on an IEP. Teachers should follow school district policies and format when writing goals, short-term objectives, and benchmarks for their students' IEPs.

Though similar in concept for measuring progress, there is a difference between short-term objectives and benchmarks in IEPs. Both must be measurable and are used to determine how well the student is progressing toward an annual goal. Short-term objectives break down skills described in the annual goal into discrete parts, and they are progressively more challenging steps toward the goal. Benchmarks indicate the amount of progress the child is expected to make within a specified part of the year (National Dissemination Center for Children with Disabilities, 1999). Benchmarks and short-term objectives focus on the same skills, but the criterion, or level of proficiency, will change to measure progress toward goal attainment (Downing, 2008). For example, a short-term objective related to improving the overhand throw may be written as: "When given a verbal prompt and handed a 12-inch (30 cm) softball, Marissa will throw overhand with arm–leg opposition using her dominant hand, and she will demonstrate across-the-body follow-through 8 out of 10 times." All short-term objectives must clearly describe the action, conditions, and criterion in order to be measurable. These three aspects relate to information presented in the six-element format discussed in the following section (will do what, under what conditions, and at what level of proficiency).

Benchmarks related to the same goal for overhand throwing may include statements regarding how far and how accurate student throws will be at the end of each month (time period):

- By October 1, Marissa will throw a tennis ball overhand 10 feet (3 m) and hit the target 5 out of 10 trials.

- By December 1, Marissa will throw a tennis ball overhand 20 feet (6 m) and hit the target 7 out of 10 trials.
- By March 1, Marissa will throw a tennis ball overhand 30 feet (9 m) and hit the target 9 out of 10 trials.

Just as an annual goal must relate to PLP information, short-term objectives and benchmarks must relate to the IEP goal. If an annual goal stresses the content area of eye–hand coordination, the short-term objectives or benchmarks must include eye–hand coordination skills such as dribbling, catching, and striking. The student's baseline (pretest) ability must also appear in the IEP as part of the PLP component. For example, a short-term objective might specify that a student will be expected to do 15 curl-ups in 60 seconds at some future date, but this statement has little meaning unless it is known how many curl-ups the student can do now (baseline or pretest). An easy way to write a short-term objective is to take a well-written multielement IEP goal statement (see next section), copy the information from elements 3 and 4 (what action or skill and under what conditions), and make a reasonable change in the criterion or proficiency. The teacher must use professional judgment based on experience to determine what constitutes a reasonable expectation for improvement. It should be noted that although goals, short-term objectives, and benchmarks are helpful in identifying activities to be conducted in class, they are primarily used to prioritize content and measure student progress, not to replace carefully designed daily lesson plans.

Writing Multielement Annual IEP Goals

Well-written, measurable goals are one of the most critical aspects of an IEP and should contain specific, meaningful information. When writing annual IEP goals that will not have related short-term objectives, the following six elements are recommended by Kosnitsky (2008):

1. By when
2. Who
3. Will do what
4. Under what conditions
5. At what level of proficiency
6. As measured by whom or what

The following information describes each of these elements as used when writing measurable annual IEP goals.

By when: This can be written as a date or length of time for intervention. For example, a goal may state "By May 2010" or "In 24 weeks." Since goals must be written annually, school districts will often use a time period aligned with yearly IEP reviews or meetings. The time period could also coincide with when the school district needs to report academic progress to parents, or it could align with the length of the instructional intervention within a curriculum unit. School districts usually have a recommended format that teachers follow for this time factor and other IEP annual goal elements.

Who: An IEP goal is written for a specific student to describe what that person will be expected to accomplish in one school year. The IEP document will likely contain information about others who provide supports and services for the student, but goals must be written for individual students.

Will do what: This element states the areas of need inferred from the PLP in the form of skills or behaviors that can be changed, observed, and measured. A guide for teachers writing this element of measurable goals is to ask themselves, "What will I see if the student meets the goal?" (Kosnitsky, 2008). Areas of need in physical education include health-related fitness components, aquatic skills, fundamental motor patterns, team and individual sport skills, and community-based physical activity participation, among others.

Under what conditions: This element of the goal specifies what must be present for the student to perform the targeted skill or behavior at the desired level. The condition often describes the environmental arrangements or degree of assistance needed by the student (e.g., "given a verbal prompt and visual demonstration," "when given a tennis racket and verbal instructions"). Conditions could also include the assessment circumstances (e.g., "while participating in a game of five-on-five soccer with peers," "given a plastic baseball bat," "while in a prone position with a flotation device around the waist in water that is 5 ft [1.5 m] deep"). Changes in the conditions can have a major impact on the difficulty of the desired task. If the conditions are not precisely specified, it is difficult to determine how the student is to perform the task and what the student's real ability is for that task. Many times learning conditions are taken for granted. However, these specifics need to be part of a measureable IEP goal in order to objectively document student progress.

At what level of proficiency: Often called the *performance criteria*, this element determines the change the IEP team expects the student will attain based on the instruction during the IEP cycle. There are no strict guidelines or right or wrong standards for establishing criteria. Critical factors used to set the level of proficiency or criteria include the student's baseline or PLP; frequency, duration, and intensity of instruction; criterion or norm-referenced standards appropriate and attainable; type of task or behavior being taught; support services and assistance available; and meaningful and realistic circumstances regarding the area of need.

As measured by: Measurability requires information such as how progress is assessed, who will collect data, where and when data are attained, and what assessment will be used to gather data. Some school districts use IEP forms that allow for this information to be placed in other sections and not directly in the goal statement. The following sample goals contain this information, but it can be removed if a district uses another format or if it is included in another section of the IEP document.

These sample measurable annual IEP goals are written in the multielement format:

- By June 2009, given a plastic baseball bat and verbal prompts, Ryan will properly hold the bat, position himself next to home plate, and strike a 12-inch (30 cm) stationary plastic ball off a tee 8 of 10 times for a distance of at least 25 feet (7.5 m), demonstrating weight shift and shoulder and hip rotation, when assessed by his physical education teacher with a rubric during a team sport unit.

- By October 2009, while wearing goggles and participating in an aquatics unit in regular physical education, Marissa will swim underwater in water that is 5 feet (1.5 m) deep, secure with her hand five diving sticks (one at a time) from an area 10 feet by 10 feet (3 m by 3 m) in less than 1 minute, and swim to the surface and side of the pool when assessed by a paraprofessional using an aquatic skills rubric.

- By November of 2010, Michael will improve his abdominal strength as demonstrated by independently completing 15 standard curl-ups in less than 60 seconds with legs bent at knees, starting with back flat on the floor and reaching with hands so fingertips slide on the floor and touch a pad 5 inches (13 cm) away under the legs as measured by the adapted physical education teacher using the Brockport Physical Fitness Test (BPFT).

In contrast to these measurable IEP goals, the following goal statements are not measurable or appropriate because they are vague and arbitrary.

- Lexi will practice cardiorespiratory endurance this year.
- Kyle will participate in a team sport to enhance his self-esteem.
- Cindy will continue a fitness program to improve abdominal strength.
- Jose will work on his striking skills for community-based sport participation.

Measuring and Reporting Progress to Parents

An advantage to writing measurable, observable, and specific IEP goals (and if necessary, short-term objectives or benchmarks) is the resulting information they can provide when reporting student progress toward annual goals at planned intervals. This progress documentation must be shown to parents and should be reported in objective terms and measures (as opposed to subjective and vague statements). In most cases, progress is determined by testing the written goals or short-term objectives or benchmarks. The evaluation should indicate the extent to which the progress is sufficient to enable the student to achieve the goals by the end of the year. Evaluation can be scheduled to occur at any time within 12 months from the time the IEP takes effect (the entire IEP must be reviewed at least annually and student disability status at least every three years).

School district IEP forms contain a section where teachers record how and when progress toward a goal will be measured. In addition, the IEP will state how often and when progress is to be reported to parents. This will generally take place at the same time as other quarterly or periodic school reports, such as school report cards. Time periods for reporting this information are determined by state or school requirements. This ensures that IEPs are used, goals and objectives or benchmarks are monitored by teachers, and parents are provided with required progress reports toward meeting annual goals. Although IDEA does not require report cards or quarterly reports, this practice aligns well with progress reporting for all students, with or without special education needs (Norlin, 2007). Parental notification of the progress of a student with a disability should occur at least as often as parents are routinely informed of the progress of a student without disabilities (e.g., the frequency of regular report cards).

Statement of Special Education and Related Services and Supplementary Aids and Services

Another required component of the IEP is a statement of the specific special education and related services and supplementary aids and services to be provided to the student (or on behalf of the student) as well as a statement of the program modifications or supports for school personnel that will be provided for the student. These services, aids, and supports should be based on peer-reviewed research to the extent practicable and are provided to enable the student to make progress toward the annual goals, to be involved and make progress in the general education curriculum as well to participate in extracurricular and nonacademic activities, and to be educated and to participate with other students with and without disabilities (U.S. Department of Education, 2006).

Once the PLP is determined and measurable annual goals are written, decisions must be made regarding the student's educational placement, any additional services to be provided, and the use of special instructional media and materials. The placement agreed upon should be the least restrictive environment for the student.

In addition to appropriate placement, other direct special education and related services might be prescribed. A **special education service** refers to instruction designed to meet the unique needs of a student with a disability that directly affects educational goals, such as physical education. Provisions for this service must be specified in this component of the IEP. Most school district IEP forms will have a section or boxes to check that indicate the type of physical education program in which the student will participate. For some students, both regular and adapted or specially designed physical education may be provided based on skill level, units of instruction, age, and other factors. A **related service** is designed to help the student with a disability to benefit from special education. Examples include physical therapy, therapeutic recreation, occupational therapy, psychological services, and speech therapy. Not all special education students need or qualify for related services. However, physical education is a direct special education service (part of a required

free appropriate public education), not a related service, and should be addressed on the IEP when appropriate (see sidebar).

In some cases, modified physical education equipment (e.g., beep baseball, audible goal locator, snap-handle bowling ball, bowling ramp) and special support personnel (e.g., teacher assistants, paraprofessionals, peer tutors, volunteers) are required for the education of students with disabilities. These should also be listed in this IEP component.

Statement of Participation in Regular Settings and Activities

It is preferred that the student participate in the regular program with peers without disabilities to the maximum extent possible. The IEP must contain an explanation of the extent, if any, to which the child will not participate with children without disabilities in the regular class and in other extracurricular and nonacademic activities (U.S. Department of Education, 2006). If a child is removed from the regular physical education setting to participate in an adapted or specially designed physical education program, for instance, it must be noted in this component of the IEP. Usually this explanation includes a percentage of time the student is excluded from (or included in) the regular educational setting and for what kinds of activities or curricular units. It must be remembered that an adapted physical education program may be provided in a variety of settings, including an inclusive setting.

Statement of Alternate Assessment Accommodations

Another required IEP component is a statement of any individual appropriate accommodations that are necessary to measure the academic achievement and functional performance of the child on state- and district-wide assessments of student achievement. Further, if it is determined that the child will not participate in a particular assessment, the IEP must state why the child cannot participate in the regular assessment and why the selected alternative assessment is appropriate for the child (U.S. Department of Education, 2006). Thus, if a school district routinely administers

An Important Question: When Is Physical Education Included in the IEP?

When must physical education be described or referred to in the IEP? The answer depends on the type of program the student is in (U.S. Department of Education, 1998).

■ **Regular physical education with students without disabilities.** If a student with a disability can participate fully in the regular physical education program without any special modifications to compensate for the student's disability, it is not necessary to describe or refer to physical education in the IEP. On the other hand, if some modifications to the regular physical education program are necessary for the student to be able to participate in that program, those modifications must be described in the IEP.

■ **Specially designed physical education.** If a student with a disability needs a specially designed physical education program, that program must be addressed in all applicable areas of the IEP (e.g., present levels of educational performance, goals, objectives; services to be provided).

■ **Physical education in separate facilities.** If a student with a disability is educated in a separate facility, the physical education program for that student must be described or referred to in the IEP. However, the kind and amount of information to be included in the IEP depends on the physical motor needs of the student and the type of physical education program to be provided. Thus, if a child at a residential school for Deaf students is able to participate in that school's regular physical education program (as determined by the most recent evaluation), then the IEP need only note such participation. On the other hand, if special modifications are required for the student to participate, those modifications must be described in the IEP. Moreover, if the student needs an individually designed physical education program, that program must be addressed under all applicable parts of the IEP.

physical education tests (physical fitness, fundamental motor skills, sport skills, aquatics, and so on) to its students, the appropriateness of those tests for a student with a disability must be considered. In this case, test item accommodations or substitutions must be explained as necessary and noted on the IEP (refer to chapter 4 for more details about alternative assessments and test accommodations).

Schedule of Services and Modifications

The IEP must include the projected date for the beginning of the special education and related services and modifications listed earlier in the IEP and the anticipated frequency, location, and duration of those services and modifications (U.S. Department of Education, 2006). This component would include details of the specially designed physical education schedule for the student. The number of minutes per week of physical education instruction should be listed in this IEP component.

Transition Services

The IEP also requires the following, beginning not later than the first IEP to be in effect when the child turns 16 (or younger, if determined appropriate by the IEP team) and updated annually thereafter: (1) measurable postsecondary goals based on age-appropriate transition assessments related to training, education, employment, and, where appropriate, independent living skills and (2) a statement of needed transition services, including courses of study, needed to assist the student in reaching those transition goals (U.S. Department of Education, 2006). This component includes goals, services, and actions to help the student transition successfully from the school-based educational program to a community-based option that will occur no later than age 22. Many students, for instance, might eventually be enrolled in vocational training programs, some might go on to college, and others might enter alternative adult service programs (e.g., group homes, sheltered workshops). School personnel attempt to prepare students for the most appropriate option once they age out of school.

For physical education teachers, transition programs include extending opportunities for physical activity into community settings. Examples of IEP goals during this important transition phase could include participation in community-based adapted sport, extracurricular and other nonacademic activities, recreation, or leisure programs designed to enhance physical fitness, motor ability, sport skills, social skills, or community adjustment. Adapted physical educators planning for community transition should conduct student interviews or administer surveys to determine the sport, recreation, or leisure interests of their students (and their families); take field trips to expose students to community-based, physical activity–related facilities and programs; compile an inventory of community-based, physical activity–related facilities and programs that can be matched with student interests, abilities, and resources; and work with community-based, physical activity–related service providers to expand the possibilities for people with disabilities (Modell & Megginson, 2001).

Although IDEA requires only that transition services be included in the IEP (either as a separate component, as described here, or embedded in other components of the IEP), some authorities (e.g., Krebs & Block, 1992; Piletic, 1998) have suggested the development of an individualized transition plan (ITP) to address this important element of a student's physical education. An ITP might list community transition goals, the necessary steps for achieving the goals, and, because IDEA defines transition services as a coordinated set of activities, identify the people responsible for each of the activities (see the application example). Planning for lifetime physical activity as part of transition services is important for students with disabilities, and it should be part of the required IEP document.

Transfer of Rights at Age of Majority

The final required component of an IEP states that beginning not later than one year before the child reaches the age of majority under state law, the IEP must include a statement that the child has been informed of his rights under IDEA, if any, that will transfer to him on reaching the age of majority (age 18 in most states). This aspect of the IEP deals with legal rights of students, and school districts will have a process in place to monitor this requirement.

DEVELOPMENT OF THE IEP

Procedures for developing an IEP vary slightly from state to state and even among school districts within a state, but essentially the process involves two steps: determining if the student is eligible for special education services and developing the most appropriate program, including establishing measurable annual goals and determining appropriate placement. The IEP development process usually begins with a referral. Any professional staff member at a school who suspects that a child might possess a unique educational need can refer the child for an evaluation to determine eligibility for special education. A physical education referral should outline the reasons a disability is suspected, including test results, records, or reports; attempts to remedy the student's performance; and the extent of parental contact before the referral. A sample referral form is shown in figure 5.3. Parents might refer their own children for evaluation when they suspect a problem, and when parents enroll a child in a new school, the district will frequently ask them if they feel their child might have a disability. Physicians and judicial officers sometimes make referrals as well.

IDEA requires an IEP team, consisting of one or both of the student's parents, at least one regular education teacher, at least one special education teacher, a representative of the school district qualified to provide or supervise the provision of special education, someone who can interpret the instructional implications of evaluation results (this may be one of the other school team members), the child with a disability (whenever appropriate), and other appropriate individuals at the discretion of either the parents or the school who have knowledge or special expertise regarding the child, including related service personnel (U.S. Department of Education, 2006). The title of the IEP team or committee varies from state to state. For instance, the team may be called the *committee on special education, multidisciplinary team,* or *admission, review, and dismissal committee.*

In many cases the IEP team will determine unique needs by assessing the results of standardized tests. But before reaching a final decision, the team also considers other information, such as samples of current academic work and functional performance; the role of behavior, language, and communication skills on academic performance; the amount of previous instruction; and anecdotal accounts, including parental input. Based on the information gathered and the ensuing discussion,

APPLICATION EXAMPLE

Physical Education Transition Services

Issue: The physical education teacher of a 16-year-old female student with a disability must consider strategies for transitioning to community-based physical activity programs as part of her IDEA-required IEP.

Application: The teacher might consider the following steps:

▶ Interview the student to determine her physical activity preferences, experiences, and abilities (including those related to sport, physical recreation, and physical activity-related leisure).

▶ Contact her family, siblings, friends, and teachers to determine their physical activity interests and current and future expectations for the student relative to community-based physical activity, sport, recreation, and leisure.

▶ Contact representatives from relevant community-based, physical activity–related agencies to determine the feasibility of having the student participate in their programs, including the identification of necessary support (e.g., equipment or procedural modifications, human assistance such as a peer mentor). Are there physical activity programs in place for students with disabilities?

▶ Write a physical activity–based ITP that includes measurable goals (e.g., participate appropriately in the open swim program or in the fitness center at the local recreation center), activities to meet the goals (e.g., transportation; checking in; locker-room use, including using the locker, changing clothes, and using the showers; swimming skills; pool rules and etiquette), and identification of the people responsible for supporting each activity, including evaluating the student's progress in the activity (e.g., physical education teacher, special education teacher and paraprofessionals, community service provider, family members, peer mentors, volunteers).

▶ Design a school-based physical education curriculum unit that teaches the necessary skills to support transition goals (e.g., swimming skills, pool rules, fitness center behaviors, etiquette).

▶ Teach those skills in the community-based setting whenever possible (e.g., at the pool of the local recreation center rather than at the school pool).

▶ Evaluate progress on the transition goals regularly, as stated in the student's IEP.

the IEP team decides if the student has a disability and thus is qualified for special education; if so, the team recommends a program and a placement setting based on the IEP that is developed.

The IEP is a negotiated document—both the school and the parents have input into its development and must agree on its contents before it is signed and implemented. In the event that the two parties cannot agree on the IEP content, IDEA provides procedures for resolving the disagreement. These **due process** procedures are designed to protect the rights of the child, the parents, and the school district as well as to ensure fairness to all parties involved (figure 5.4). The IEP requires the school to provide a free appropriate public education, including special education, related services, and supplementary aids and services listed in the IEP, but it does not guarantee the child will achieve the goals in the document. The responsibility of the district is limited to ensuring that all involved personnel make good-faith efforts to assist the student in achieving IEP goals (Norlin, 2007).

Department of Physical Education Referral Form

This form should be used by teachers or administrators of physical education and others to refer students with unique needs to chairpersons of CSE, CPSE, CAPE, or the school building administrator. Referrals should be processed through the office of the adapted physical education coordinator to the director of physical education, who shall forward the referral to the appropriate people. Referrals may be made to change the program or placement of the student or for any other action within the jurisdiction of the CSE, CPSE, or CAPE.

Faculty member making referral: Date:

Student referred: Age: Gender:

Present physical education class (if any):

Student's primary or homeroom teacher:

A unique physical education need has been identified for the student:

By the CSE?   Yes   No

By the CPSE?   Yes   No

By the CAPE?   Yes   No

If no, give reasons for believing a unique physical education need exists.

Give test results, records, or reports upon which a referral is based.

Describe previous attempts to remediate student's performance.

Has parental contact been made?   Yes   No
If yes, describe:

If a recommendation for placement or other action is included as a part of this referral, indicate the recommendation:

Referral processed by: Referral initiated by:
(Director of physical education):   (Staff member):

Legend: CSE—Committee on Special Education
CPSE—Committee on Preschool Education
CAPE–Committee on Adapted Physical Education

FIGURE 5.3   A sample referral form for adapted physical education.

IEP sequence

Due process procedures

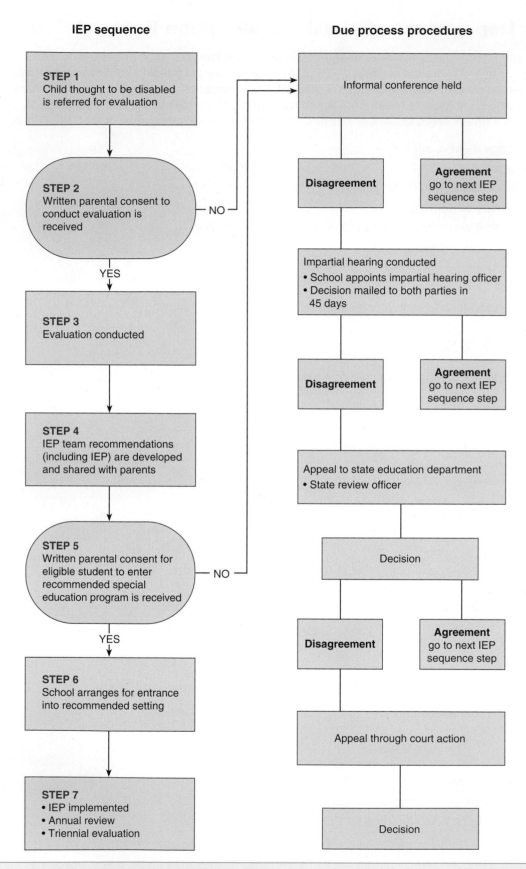

FIGURE 5.4 Sample IEP sequence and due process procedures.

SECTION 504 AND THE ACCOMMODATION PLAN

Although section 504 of the Rehabilitation Act of 1973 is more than 30 years old, its implications and requirements are still important in physical education (French et al., 1998). Because the definition of a qualified individual with a disability in section 504 is broader than the definition of a child with disability in IDEA, some students with disabilities will not have IEPs (under IDEA) but nevertheless might require appropriate accommodations and services (U.S. Department of Education, 2005). These accommodations and services must be documented in a section 504 accommodation plan.

Unlike the IEP, 504 plans do not have mandated components and, consequently, school districts usually develop their own. A sample 504 plan is presented in figure 5.5. A 504 plan template for a student with diabetes can be found at www.diabetes.org/assets/pdfs/schools/504-adanasndredf-2007.pdf.

Section 504 Accommodation Plan

Name: Date of birth: Grade:

School: Date of meeting:

1. Describe the nature of the problem.

2. List evaluations completed, including dates of each evaluation.

3. List the basis for determining that the child has a disability (if any).

4. Describe the nature of the child's disability.

5. Does the disability affect a major life activity? If so, explain how.

6. List the accommodations (e.g., specialized instruction or equipment, auxiliary aids or services, program modifications, and so on) the team recommends as necessary to ensure the child's access to all district programs.

Review and reassessment date: (must be completed)

Participants (name and title):

cc: Student's cumulative file

Attachment: Information regarding section 504 of the Rehabilitation Act of 1973 due process notice

Date:

FIGURE 5.5   Sample 504 accommodation plan.

The plan is developed by a committee consisting of at least two school professionals (e.g., teachers, nurses, counselors, administrators) familiar with the student and the school district's 504 officer (French et al., 1998). (School districts with more than 15 employees are required to have a 504 officer to monitor the implementation of section 504.) Technically, section 504 does not require a full evaluation by a multidisciplinary diagnostic team, but clearly the assessment should focus on areas of student need that might necessitate assessment by more than one professional.

The elements of the 504 plan found in figure 5.5 are self-explanatory, but note that item 5 ("Does the disability affect a major life activity?") is particularly important. To meet the definition of a qualified person with a disability under section 504, the student must have a physical or mental impairment that substantially limits one or more major life activities (Norlin, 2008). Usually the accommodations listed in the plan (see item 6 in figure 5.5) are selected to help the student benefit from instruction in the regular education classroom. More restrictive educational placements (those apart from peers without disabilities), although possible, would have to be justified.

STUDENTS WITHOUT DISABILITIES WHO HAVE UNIQUE NEEDS

As mentioned at the beginning of this chapter, students without disabilities who have unique needs in physical education are not covered by IDEA or section 504. School districts, however, still must provide an appropriate education for these students.

It is recommended that school districts establish a **Committee on Adapted Physical Education (CAPE)** to address unique needs of students without disabilities in physical education. This committee should consist of at least three members: the director of physical education or designee, the school nurse, and the teacher of adapted physical education. When possible, the student's regular physical education teacher should also be a member of the committee, and a school administrator should be available for consultation. The function of this committee is to determine the student's eligibility for an adapted program; define the nature of that program, including placement; and monitor the student's progress. A recommended procedure is outlined in figure 5.6 and discussed in the following seven steps. These may be modified as necessary to meet the needs of the school district.

■ **Step 1.** Referrals to the CAPE ordinarily are made to the chairperson of the committee by a physical educator, family physician, parent, or even the student when it is felt that the student has a unique need in physical education. The committee should consider only those referrals in which the needs are believed to be long term (more than 30 days).

■ **Step 2.** When the CAPE receives a referral form from a source other than the parents, the committee should notify the parents of the referral and indicate that an adapted program will be considered. The notification should point out that physical education is a required subject area under state law (where applicable) and that blanket excuses, waivers, or substitutions are not appropriate options; that development of an adapted program would not mean that the district considers the student to have a disability under IDEA or section 504; and that any change in program will be reviewed regularly (at least annually). Parents should also be invited to submit their own concerns or aspirations for their child's physical education program.

■ **Step 3.** In the case of a medical excuse or referral, the CAPE should contact the family physician to determine the nature of the condition or disease and the impact on physical education. The CAPE should also consult the student's regular physical education teacher to determine the student's performance level and any difficulties the student experiences in the current program. It might also be necessary to conduct additional testing to better understand the student's strengths and weaknesses.

■ **Step 4.** After considering all the information collected in step 3, the CAPE must decide if a specially designed (adapted) program is appropriate. If the student does not have a unique need, the parents are informed, and the process is over. If, however, the student is eligible for an adapted program, the committee must develop an IPEP for the student. The IPEP is similar to the IEP and should include program goals, PLP (including any medical limitations), short-term objectives, placement and schedule of services, and a schedule for review. Again, parents should be consulted for input on goals and activities for the IPEP.

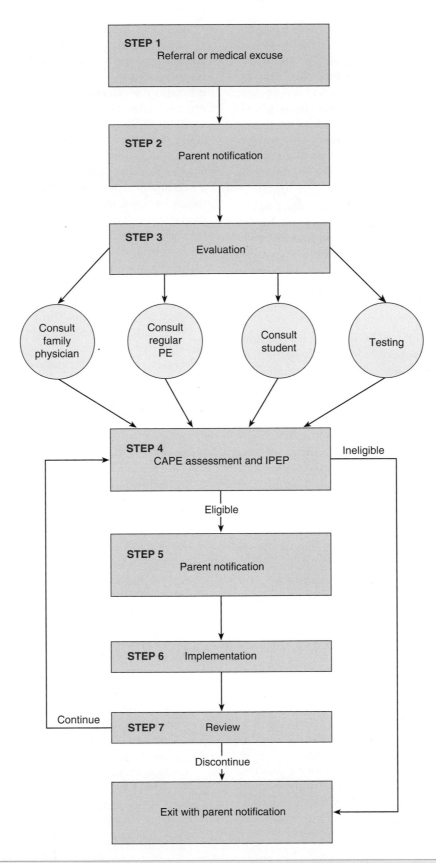

STEP 1
Referral or medical excuse

STEP 2
Parent notification

STEP 3
Evaluation

Consult family physician

Consult regular PE

Consult student

Testing

STEP 4
CAPE assessment and IPEP

Ineligible

Eligible

STEP 5
Parent notification

STEP 6   Implementation

Continue

STEP 7   Review

Discontinue

Exit with parent notification

FIGURE 5.6   A recommended procedure for evaluating the need for adapted physical education services for students without disabilities.

■ **Step 5.** Parents are notified of the CAPE's decision. If the student is eligible, parents should receive an explanation of the adapted program and a copy of the IPEP. It is also recommended that the regular physical education teacher and, in the case of a medically initiated referral, the family physician receive copies of the IPEP as well. (The district should have due process procedures comparable to those depicted in figure 5.4 in case the parents do not agree with the committee's decision or with the program outlined in the IPEP.)

■ **Step 6.** The adapted program described in the IPEP is implemented. Most IPEPs can probably be implemented in an integrated placement. In cases in which a one-to-one or segregated placement is recommended, however, school districts must obtain parental permission before changing the placement, unless the board of education has other procedures in place that are appropriate.

■ **Step 7.** The IPEP will be in effect for the time specified under the schedule for review section. At the conclusion of this time, the CAPE evaluates the student's progress and decides whether to continue or discontinue the program.

Formation of a CAPE is solely at the discretion of the school district and is not required by law. Districts must recognize, however, that a student need not be classified as having a disability to possess a unique need in physical education. Once that notion is acknowledged, it is incumbent on districts to develop procedures to ensure that such students receive an appropriate education. Given the mounting prevalence of obesity and secondary conditions in the United States, for instance, the IPEP provides an option for schools looking to help all students address serious health and physical activity–related problems.

SUMMARY

Students might be eligible for adapted physical education if they exhibit a unique physical education need. IDEA and section 504 of the Rehabilitation Act of 1973 provide procedures for modifying educational programs for students with disabilities. These individualized programs are implemented as written documents required by the legislation. Infants and toddlers (birth to age two) who meet the criteria established by IDEA may receive early intervention services under the act. These services must be documented in an IFSP. (The development of an IFSP is covered in chapter 21.)

Similarly, individualized programs for qualified children (aged 3-21) also are governed by IDEA. In this case, however, the individualized program is documented in an IEP. The details of physical education services for eligible students with disabilities must be described in these IEPs. Not all students with disabilities qualify for services under IDEA, but they might still be entitled to special accommodations or services under section 504. These modified programs must be described in a section 504 accommodation plan. Finally, there might be students without disabilities in a school district who have unique needs in physical education. These students would not qualify for services under either IDEA or section 504 but might still require a modified physical education program. Although not required by law, it is suggested that districts develop written IPEPs to document the adapted physical education program.

Note: The authors sincerely thank Francis X. Short, State University of New York, College at Brockport, for his contributions in this chapter and earlier editions.

REFERENCES

Bateman, B., & Herr, C. (2006). *Writing measurable IEP goals and objectives* (2nd ed.). Verona, WI: Attainment Company.

Capizzi, A. (2008). From assessment to annual goal: Engaging in a decision-making process in writing measurable IEPs. *Teaching Exceptional Children, 41* (1), 18-25.

Downing, J. (2008). *Including students with severe and multiple disabilities in typical classrooms* (3rd ed.). Baltimore: Brooks.

French, R., Henderson, H., Kinnison, L., & Sherrill, C. (1998). Revisiting section 504, physical education and sport. *Journal of Physical Education, Recreation and Dance, 69* (7), 57-63.

Individuals with Disabilities Education Act Amendments of 2004 (IDEA) (PL 108-446), 20 U.S.C. 1400 (2004).

Jung, A. (2007). Writing S.M.A.R.T. objectives and strategies that fit the R.O.U.T.I.N.E. *Teaching Exceptional Children, 39* (4), 54-58.

Kosnitsky, C. (2008). *IEP goals that make a difference: An administrator's guide to improving the process.* Horsham, PA: LRP.

Krebs, P., & Block, M. (1992). Transition of students with disabilities into community recreation: The role of the adapted physical educator. *Adapted Physical Activity Quarterly, 9* (4), 305-315.

Modell, S., & Megginson, N. (2001). Life after school: A transition model for adapted physical educators.

Journal of Physical Education, Recreation and Dance, 72 (2), 45-48, 53.

National Dissemination Center for Children with Disabilities (NICHCY). (1999). *Individualized education programs: Briefing paper.* Retrieved from www.nichcy.org. Washington, DC: Author.

Norlin, J. (2007). *What do I do when: The answer book on individualized education programs* (3rd ed.). Horsham, PA: LRP.

Norlin, J. (2008). *Extended school year services under the IDEA and Section 504: Legal standards and case law.* Horsham, PA: LRP.

Piletic, C. (1998). Transition: Are we doing it? *Journal of Physical Education, Recreation and Dance,* 69 (9), 46-50.

U.S. Department of Education. (1998). *Federal Register,* 34 CFR Ch. III, July 1, 1998.

U.S. Department of Education. (2005). Protecting students with disabilities: Frequently asked questions about Section 504 and the education of children with disabilities. Retrieved from www.ed.gov/about/offices/list/ocr/504faq.html.

U.S. Department of Education. (2006). *Federal Register,* Part II, 34 CFR Parts 300 and 301. Final regulations for IDEA 2004—Individuals with Disabilities Education Improvement Act of 2004—PL 108-446. Retrieved from www.ed.gov/legislation/FedRegister/finrule/2006-3/081406a.pdf.

WRITTEN RESOURCES

Kowalski, E., Lieberman, L., & Daggett, S. (2006). Getting involved in the IEP process. *Journal of Physical Education, Recreation and Dance,* 77 (7), 35-39.

This article discusses numerous strategies for the regular physical educator to become more knowledgeable and active in IEP development, implementation, and revision.

National Association of State Directors of Special Education. (2006). *The Individuals with Disabilities Education Act: Comparison of IDEA regulations (August 3, 2006) to IDEA regulations (March 12, 1999).* Retrieved from www.nasdse.org. Alexandria, VA: Author.

This document provides a detailed side-by-side comparison of the implementation of federal regulations for the two most recent reauthorizations of IDEA. The comparison allows for easy identification of changes.

Norlin, J. (2008). *What to do when: The answer book on section 504* (3rd ed.). Horsham, PA: LRP.

This resource addresses issues related to section 504 and the education of students with disabilities in an easy-to-use question-and-answer format. A separate chapter on extracurricular activities includes guidance on interscholastic sport, field trips, and other noneducational services.

ELECTRONIC RESOURCES

Building the Legacy: IDEA 2004. Office of Special Education Programs, U.S. Department of Education. Web site: http://idea.ed.gov/explore/home.

This site contains numerous resources on the IEP process, including sample forms, questions and answers, learning modules, instructional videos, PowerPoint presentations, most recent IDEA changes, and final regulations.

Council for Exceptional Children (CEC). Web site: www.cec.sped.org.

This site provides a catalog of books and resources related to the special education process and IEP development.

IDEA Partnership. Web site: www.ideapartnership.org.

This site contains extensive materials on all aspects of educating students with disabilities, including development of individualized education programs, model IEP forms by the U.S. Department of Education, IEP requirements and practices, and instructional resources.

Individualized Education Programs. http://idea.ed.gov/explore/view/p/%2Croot%2Cdynamic%2CTopicalArea%2C1%2C.

This site contains questions and answers, presentations, teacher training manuals, video clips, and other IEP resources from the U.S. Department of Education.

IRIS Center (IDEA 2004 and Research for Inclusive Settings. Web site: http://iris.peabody.vanderbilt.edu.

This site presents materials for faculty and professional development providers for the preparation of current and future school personnel who work with students with disabilities in inclusive settings.

National Center for Learning Disabilities. Understanding the Standards-based Individualized Education Program (IEP): www.ncld.org/images/stories/Publications/AdvocacyBriefs/UnderstandingStandardbasedIEP/UnderstandingStandards-BasedIEPS.pdf.

This site provides guidance for the development of IEPs for student with learning disabilities.

U.S. Department of Education. (2005). Protecting students with disabilities: Frequently asked questions about section 504 and the education of children with disabilities. www.ed.gov/about/offices/list/ocr/504faq.html.

This site expands on section 504 and provides guidance for eligibility and section 504 plan development.

Behavior Management

E. Michael Loovis

Mr. Smith is the physical education teacher at Middlefield Junior High School. He has been assigned an eighth-grade class into which several students with behavioral disorders have been integrated. Although the class is reasonably well behaved, one student, Robert, has a difficult time staying on task, and he is constantly uncooperative, often getting into arguments with other students. Mr. Smith has instituted a token economy system such that time on task and reduced frequency of uncooperative behavior earn points. The system is displayed on a clipboard that Mr. Smith carries and is available for Robert to assess his performance during class. During the first day that the token economy was in effect, Mr. Smith noticed that Robert was paying attention to his instructions and participating effectively in drills. Mr. Smith walked up to Robert and said, "Good work, Robert, you've earned a point." Then Mr. Smith placed 1 point on the chart. A little later Robert told a teammate that he had done a good job. Mr. Smith approached Robert and said, "That was a very nice thing to say to Sam; you've just earned another point."

At this rate Robert has a good chance to earn 3 points, which is the number required to exchange points earned for backup reinforcers. Robert had previously determined what those reinforcers would be with help from Mr. Smith. If Robert earns the prescribed number of points, he can redeem them for the opportunity to choose from a menu of reinforcers that include his choice for culminating activity of the day, free time in the gym on Friday, and serving as captain for his group during the next class session. Successful implementation of this behavior modification strategy will result in Robert's staying on task and eliminating or significantly reducing the number of times he gets into arguments with classmates.

For years, educators confronting inappropriate behavior have used a host of behavior management practices, in worst cases including corporal punishment, suspension, and expulsion. In most cases, these practices are **reactive**—that is, a particular method is applied after a particular misbehavior has occurred. However, many of the problems that educators face on a daily basis could be prevented if the educators took a more **proactive** approach toward managing student behavior. Implicit in this statement is the discontinuation of ineffective practices. For example, it is difficult for a physical educator to establish an appropriate instructional climate in a self-contained class for students with behavior disabilities when several students persist in being verbally and physically abusive toward the teacher and other class members.

From another perspective, behavior management interventions include "all those actions (and conscious inactions) teachers . . . engage in to enhance the probability that children, individually and in groups, will develop effective behaviors that are personally fulfilling, productive, and socially acceptable" (Walker, Shea, & Bauer, 2007, p. 7). For example, a behavior management approach can help a physical educator determine the appropriate level at which to begin instruction in golf for students with intellectual disabilities and to maintain the students' enthusiasm for learning the activity over time. Behavior management has also been used to teach those social behaviors considered essential to performance in school, at home, and in other significant environments. This chapter offers several proactive approaches to help teachers and coaches achieve the goals and objectives of their programs in a positive learning environment. Physical educators probably use an eclectic or pragmatic approach to behavior management, depending on what they perceive works best in a given situation. In this chapter, the following approaches are highlighted: applied behavior analysis, psychoeducational, psychodynamic, ecological, biogenic, and humanistic.

APPLIED BEHAVIOR ANALYSIS

According to Cooper, Heron, and Heward (2007), applied behavior analysis (ABA) is a "scientific approach for discovering environmental variables that reliably influence socially significant behavior and for developing a technology of behavior change that takes practical advantage of those discoveries" (p. 3). More specifically, ABA is the application of reinforcement learning theory derived from operant psychology. ABA includes such procedures as **respondent conditioning** (the automatic control of behavior by antecedent stimuli), **operant conditioning** (the control of behavior by regulating the consequences that follow a behavior), **contingency management** (the relation between a behavior and the events that follow it), and **behavioral modeling**, also called **observational learning** (learning through observing another person engaged in a behavior).

All of these procedures have one thing in common: the planned systematic arrangement of consequences to alter a person's response (or at least the frequency of that response). As it relates to an IEP designed to improve physical fitness, this arrangement could involve the use of rewards to encourage students with intellectual disabilities to engage in sustained exercise behavior when riding stationary bicycles. It could also mean establishing a contract with a student who has cerebral palsy to define a number of tasks to be completed in a unit on throwing and catching skills.

To understand ABA, one must understand some basic terminology. On the assumption that behavior is controlled by its effect on the environment, the first step toward understanding the management of human behavior is to define the stimuli that influence people's behavior. A measurable event that might have an influence on behavior is referred to as a **stimulus**.

Reinforcement is a stimulus event that increases or maintains the frequency of a response. In physical education, reinforcement may be thought of as feedback provided directly or indirectly by the teacher or coach. Reinforcers can be physical, verbal, visual, edible, or active. Examples of reinforcers include a pat on the back (physical), an approving comment such as "Good job!" (verbal), a smile (visual), a piece of candy (edible), or a chance to bounce on a trampoline (active). All of these examples are usually considered positive reinforcers. Positive reinforcers, or rewards, are stimuli that students perceive as good—that is, as something they want. If a response occurs and it is positively reinforced, the likelihood of the response recurring under similar circumstances is maintained or increased. For example, a teacher might praise a student who demonstrates appropriate behavior during instruction in the gym. If praise is positively reinforcing to that student, the chances of the student's attending to instruction in the future are strengthened. **Positive reinforcement** is one of the principles of operant conditioning described in this section. Certainly positive reinforcement is the preferred strategy in adapted physical education; to the extent possible, the entire instructional experience should be positive. Figure 6.1 illustrates this principle as well as the others examined in this chapter. The presence of aversive stimuli—something students want to avoid—is commonly called **negative reinforcement**. If a response occurs and it successfully averts a negative stimulus, the likelihood of the desired response recurring under similar circumstances is maintained or increased.

Because positive and negative reinforcement might produce similar results, the distinction between them is not always readily apparent. An example might clarify the difference. Suppose that a student has been talking to a friend and distracting the teacher and the rest of the class while the teacher is explaining a lesson. If the teacher warns that continued talking will result in after-school detention or a low grade for the day (possible aversive stimuli), and if the student perceives the stimuli as something to avoid, then the likelihood that the student will attend to instructions will increase. By listening in class, the student will avoid staying after school or having her grade reduced. This is an example of negative reinforcement because the stimulus increases the likelihood of a desired behavior through the avoidance of an aversive consequence rather than the presentation of a positive one.

Just as teachers and coaches seek to maintain or increase the frequency of some behaviors, they might want to decrease the occurrence of others. When the consequence of a certain behavior has the effect of decreasing its frequency, the consequence is called **punishment**. Punishment can be either the presentation of an aversive stimulus (type I punishment) or the removal of a positive stimulus (type II punishment). The intention of punishment is to weaken or eliminate a behavior. The following scenario illustrates the effect of punishment on the student from the previous example. The student has been talking during instructional time. The teacher has warned the student that continued talking will result in detention or a grade reduction. The student ignores the warning and continues to talk. The consequence for talking when she is supposed to be listening will be the presentation of one of the two aversive stimuli.

A slightly different scenario illustrates the notion of punishment as the removal of a positive stimulus. Our student, still talking after the teacher's warning,

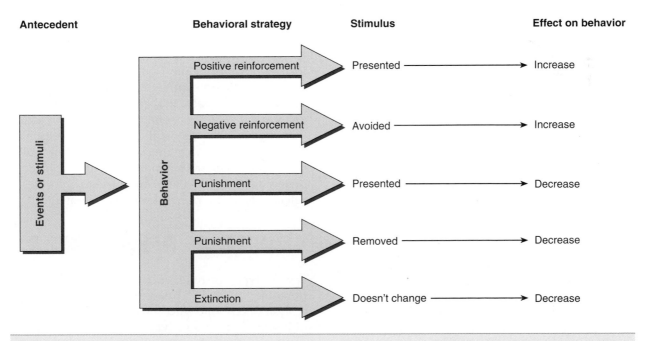

FIGURE 6.1 Principles of operant conditioning.

is punished by being barred from a five-minute free-time activity at the end of class—an activity perceived as a positive stimulus. The removal of this highly desirable activity fits the definition of punishment and weakens or eliminates the disruptive behavior in future instructional episodes.

In contrast to punishment, withholding of reinforcement after a response that has previously been reinforced results in **extinction** or cessation of a behavior. Extinction differs from punishment in that no consequence follows the response; a stimulus (aversive or positive event) is neither presented nor taken away. For example, teachers or coaches who pay attention to students when they clown around might be reinforcing the very behavior they would like to see eliminated. If they ignore (i.e., stop reinforcing) the undesired behavior, the behavior will probably decrease in frequency.

Applied behavior analysts have begun to emphasize the importance of **antecedent events** or **stimuli** in controlling human behavior. These events or stimuli that occur before the behavior of interest signal an opportunity for a consequence (see figure 6.1). This recognition of the importance of antecedent events has led applied behavior analysts to think in terms of a behavioral paradigm or sequence that recognizes the three-term contingency of antecedent-behavior-consequence (ABC).

Antecedent events that stimulate the occurrence of certain behavior consist of actions such as questioning, prompting or cueing techniques employed by the teacher (opportunities to respond to academic requests, or OTRs), demonstrations of appropriate behavioral responses prior to students engaging in practice, or announcements from the teacher about the appropriate manner for transitioning from one activity to another. For example, a teacher asks a student to identify one of the two types of serves in badminton (antecedent), the student responds with the correct answer (behavior), and the teacher tells the student that the answer is correct and says, "Nice job!" (consequence). (Note that antecedents in the ABA context are not to be confused with intrapsychic causes for aberrant behavior that are prevalent in psychoanalytic theories.)

In addition, behavioral outcomes that are functionally related to antecedent events can involve changing the environment in ways that stimulate behavior to occur. For example, before the initiation of a lesson, a teacher could partner a student who is known to be disruptive with a peer who in the past has had a calming influence on the student while engaged in physical activity (antecedent). The student with the disruptive behavior participates in relative calm and finishes the lesson without being disruptive (behavior), and the teacher rewards the student with five minutes of free time at the end of class (consequence).

With the reauthorizations of the Individuals with Disabilities Education Act (IDEA) in 1997 and again in 2004, emphasis has been placed on one of the most powerful tools of ABA, namely, functional behavioral assessment (FBA). IDEA 2004 mandates "a functional behavioral assessment, behavior intervention services and modifications, that are designed to address the behavior violation so that it does not recur" (Section 615 (k) (1) (F) (i)).

Antecedent events have gained greater clarity in light of the positive behavioral interventions and supports (PBIS) movement. PBIS and ABA parallel each other in the sense that they start with an examination of the three-term contingency (ABC) and conclude with a behavioral intervention plan designed to either promote more positive behaviors or eliminate problematic behaviors. Chapter 9, Behavioral Disabilities, provides an in-depth discussion of PBIS and its emphasis on FBA and behavior intervention plans, both of which rely heavily on identification of antecedent events that control a student's behavior.

Table 6.1 summarizes the basic strategies of ABA. Each principle has a specific purpose, and application of the principles requires that teachers or coaches analyze behaviors carefully before attempting to change them.

The examples provided in table 6.1 illustrate the range of learning principles available to teachers and coaches who want to change student behaviors. No one principle is the best choice all the time; which one to apply depends on the specifics of the situation. Later in this chapter (and again in chapter 9, p. 185), recommendations are provided that originate from the work of Dunn and Leitschuh (2006). After reading the section on their rules of thumb (chapter 9), readers are encouraged to review table 6.1 to better understand the role of selected learning principles in ABA strategies.

TYPES OF REINFORCERS

Several types of reinforcers can be used in ABA, including primary (unconditioned), secondary (conditioned), and vicarious reinforcers. The use of highly preferred activities to control the occurrence of less preferred responses, known as the **Premack principle**, is another reinforcer.

Table 6.1 Behavior: Consequences, Classification, and Probable Effect

Behavior	Consequences	Classification	Effect
Susan engages effectively in drills.	Teacher praises Susan.	Positive reinforcement	Susan will continue to do well in drills.
Juan forgets to wear his gym uniform.	Teacher suggests that next time he will lose 5 points.	Negative reinforcement	Juan will wear his gym uniform.
Tenora forgets her tennis shoes for the second day in a row.	Teacher deducts 5 points from her grade.	Punishment (type I)	Tenora will not forget her shoes next class.
Bill makes aggravating noises during class.	Teacher ignores Bill's noises.	Extinction	Bill will stop making noises during class.
Chris is overly aggressive during game play in class.	Teacher withdraws opportunity to participate in free time at end of class.	Punishment (type II)	Chris will tone down his aggressiveness during game play.

■ *Primary reinforcers.* **Primary (or unconditioned) reinforcers** are stimuli necessary for survival. Examples include food, water, and other phenomena that satisfy biological requirements such as the needs for sleep, warmth, and sexual stimulation.

■ *Secondary reinforcers.* **Secondary (or conditioned) reinforcers** acquire their reinforcing properties through learning. A few examples are praise, grades, money, and completion of a task. Because secondary reinforcers must be learned, stimuli or events must often be paired repeatedly with other primary or secondary events before they will become reinforcers in their own right.

■ *Vicarious reinforcers.* The essence of **vicarious reinforcement** is in observing the reinforcing or punishing consequences of another person's behavior. As a result of vicarious reinforcement, the observer will either engage in the behavior to receive the same positive reinforcement or avoid the behavior to avert punishment.

■ *Premack principle.* According to the Premack principle (Premack, 1965), activities that have a high probability of occurrence can be used to elicit low-probability behaviors. To state it another way, activities that an individual or group prefers can be used as positive consequences or reinforcers for activities that are not especially favored.

SCHEDULES OF REINFORCEMENT

When using the ABA approach, the teacher or coach must understand when to deliver a reinforcer to attain an optimal response. During the early stages of skill acquisition or behavior change, it is best to provide reinforcement after every occurrence of an appropriate response. This is called **continuous reinforcement**. After a behavior has been acquired, continuous reinforcement is no longer desirable or necessary. Behavior is best maintained not through a process of continuous reinforcement but through a schedule of intermittent or partial reinforcement. Several types of intermittent schedules exist, but the two most common are ratio and interval schedules.

In **ratio schedules**, reinforcement is applied after a specified number of defined responses have occurred. **Interval schedules**, on the other hand, provide reinforcement when a specified time has elapsed since the previous reinforcement. Thus, a ratio schedule is based on a preestablished number of responses, whereas an interval schedule is based on time between reinforcements. Associated with each of these major schedule types are two subtypes: **fixed** and **variable**. When these types and subtypes are combined, four alternatives for dispensing reinforcement are available. Both fixed and variable ratio schedules of reinforcement produce high response rates (e.g., providing praise an average of every second successful throw or every third successful throw). In the case of interval reinforcement, a fixed schedule produces a high response rate just before the time for the next reinforcement. Conversely, there is a cessation of responding after reinforcement (e.g., praising the first successful throw at the end of each one-minute interval). Variable intervals of reinforcement, on the other hand, produce consistent response rates because the person cannot predict when the reinforcer will be dispensed (e.g., praising the first successful throw at the end of an average three-minute interval).

PROCEDURES FOR INCREASING BEHAVIOR

Once it is determined that a behavior not currently in a student's repertoire is desired or that the frequency of a behavior needs to be altered, the targeted response must be defined in measurable and observable terms. This response will be an observable instance of performance having an effect on the environment. After clear identification has been made, behavioral intervention can begin. The following discussion highlights several popular strategies for increasing desirable behavior, including shaping, prompting, chaining, modeling, token economy, fading, and contingency management.

■ *Shaping.* The strategy of **shaping** involves administering reinforcement contingent on the learning and performance of sequential steps leading to development of the desired behavior. Shaping is most often employed in the teaching of a new skill. Once the terminal or desired behavior has been learned, it is no longer necessary to perform all steps in the progression. For example, the use of shaping to teach a dive from a 1-meter board might include the following progression: kneeling dive from a 30-centimeter elevation, squat dive from a 30-centimeter elevation, standing modified dive from a 30-centimeter elevation, squat dive from the 1-meter diving board, and standing modified forward dive from the diving board. Once the dive from the 1-meter board has been learned, there is no longer any reason to perform the steps in the progression.

■ *Chaining.* Unlike shaping, which consists of reinforcing approximations of a new terminal behavior, **chaining** develops a series of discrete portions or links that, when tied together, lead to enhanced performance of a behavior. Chaining is distinct from shaping in that the steps necessary to achieve the desired or terminal behavior are performed each time the response is emitted. In shaping, the steps in the progression are not considered essential once the terminal behavior has been mastered.

There are two types of chaining: forward and backward. In forward chaining, the initial step in the behavioral sequence occurs first, followed by the next step, and so forth until the entire sequence has been mastered (see the application example). A student learning to execute a layup from three steps away from the basket would take a step with the left foot, take a step with the left foot while dribbling once with the right hand, repeat the previous step and add a step with the right foot, and repeat the previous step with an additional step and jump off the left foot up to the basket for the layup attempt. In some cases a student's repertoire is limited, or the last step in the sequence is associated with a potent reinforcer. Under these circumstances, it might be necessary to teach the last step in a behavioral sequence first, followed by the next-to-last step, and so on until the entire sequence is learned. This is called *backward chaining*.

■ *Prompting.* Events that help initiate a response are called **prompts**. These are cues, instructions, gestures, directions, examples, and models that act as antecedent events and trigger a desired response. In this way the frequency of responses and thus the chances of receiving reinforcement are increased. Prompting is crucial in shaping and chaining procedures. Prompts can be thought of as a system of more or less intrusive or direct cues. They are arranged in descending order of intrusiveness, from verbal to visual to physical assistance. The object of the system of least prompts is to encourage a response by using the least intrusive or direct cue; for example, a student who requires a visual prompt from a teacher is receiving a less intrusive prompt than one who requires physical assistance to perform the same behavior. Another form of prompting commonly used during instruction with individuals with mental retardation and autism is redirection. The purpose of a redirect is to communicate an alternative means to engage the learner's attention on the task at hand. The redirect can be in the form of a physical or gestural cue, including pointing, touching materials, or touching the person's hand (if touching can be tolerated) (Jones, 1998).

■ *Fading.* The ultimate goal of any procedure to increase the frequency of a response is for the response to occur without the need for a prompt or reinforcer. The best way to reach this goal is with a procedure that removes or fades the prompts and reinforcers gradually over time. **Fading** reinforcers means stretching the schedule of reinforcement so that the student must perform more trials or demonstrate significantly better response quality in order to receive reinforcement. For example, someone who has been receiving positive reinforcement for each successful basket must now make two baskets, then three baskets, and so on before reinforcement is provided.

APPLICATION EXAMPLE

Behavior Management

Setting: An elementary physical education class

Student: A 9-year-old student with high functioning autism with delays in throwing and catching

Unit: Fundamental motor skills and patterns

Task: Throwing with a mature, functional throw—at the very least stepping with the leg opposite the throwing arm

Application: The physical educator might do any of the following:

▸ Use forward chaining of the throwing mechanics.

▸ Use a visual prompt, such as a footprint, to aid in the stepping action.

▸ Use continuous reinforcement until correct throwing is well established.

▸ Fade the visual prompt (e.g., footprints) as the student becomes more consistent in performance.

■ *Modeling.* The strategy of **modeling** is a visual demonstration of a behavior that students are expected to perform. From a behavioral perspective, modeling (similar to vicarious reinforcement) is the process in which a person watches someone else respond to a situation in a way that produces reinforcement or punishment. The observer thus learns vicariously.

■ *Token economy.* Tokens are secondary reinforcers that are earned, collected, and subsequently redeemed for a backup reinforcer. Tokens, which might be poker chips or checkmarks on a response tally sheet, are earned and exchanged for consumables, privileges, or activities, which are the backup reinforcers. A reinforcement system based on tokens is called a **token economy**. Establishment of a token economy includes a concise description of the targeted behavior or behaviors along with a detailed accounting of the tokens administered for performance of targeted behaviors.

■ *Contingency management.* When teachers change a behavior by providing a stimulus contingent on the occurrence of a desired response, they are practicing **contingency management** (Walker, Shea, & Bauer, 2007). The most sophisticated form of contingency management is the behavior contract. The contract (which is an extension of the token economy) specifies the relation between behaviors and their consequences. The well-developed contract contains five elements: a detailed statement of what each party (i.e., student and teacher) expects to happen; a targeted behavior

that is readily observable; a statement of sanctions for failure to meet the terms of the contract; a bonus clause, if desirable, to reinforce consistent compliance with the contract; and a monitoring system to keep track of the rate of positive reinforcement given (Kazdin, 2001). An example of a behavior contract appears in chapter 9, page 181.

PROCEDURES FOR DECREASING BEHAVIOR

On occasion, the behavior of an individual or a group needs to be decreased. Traditionally, decreasing the frequency of behavior has been accomplished using extinction, punishment, reinforcement of alternative responses, and time-out from reinforcement. In this section, positive management techniques are stressed since they have been successful in reducing or eliminating a wide range of undesirable behaviors. Moreover, these techniques model socially appropriate ways of dealing with troublesome behaviors and are free of the undesirable side effects of punishment. Reinforcement is ordinarily viewed as a process to increase, rather than decrease, behavior. Consequently, extinction and punishment are most often mentioned as methods for decreasing behaviors. In this section, the use of reinforcement techniques to decrease behavior (Cooper et al., 2007) will be emphasized. These techniques either deliver or withhold reinforcement based on whether or not a predetermined frequency or quality of behavior has been achieved.

■ *Reinforcement of other behavior.* Reinforcing a student for engaging in any behavior other than the targeted behavior is known as **differential reinforcement of other behavior**. The reinforcer is delivered as long as the targeted behavior (e.g., inappropriate running during the gym class) is not performed. Thus, the student receives reinforcement for sitting on the floor and listening to instructions, standing quietly and listening to instructions, sitting on the bleachers and listening to instructions—anything other than inappropriate running during class. This reinforcement has the effect of decreasing the targeted response.

■ *Reinforcement of incompatible behavior.* This technique reinforces behaviors that are directly incompatible with the targeted response. For example, a student has a difficult time engaging cooperatively in games during physical education class; the opposite behavior is playing cooperatively. The effect of reinforcing cooperation during game playing is the elimination of the uncooperative response. Unlike reinforcement of other behavior, this strategy defines diametrically opposed behaviors—playing uncooperatively versus playing cooperatively—and reinforces instances of positive behavior only.

■ *Reinforcement of low response rates.* With a technique known as **differential reinforcement of low rates of responding**, a student is reinforced for gradually reducing the frequency of an undesirable behavior or for increasing the amount of time during which the behavior does not occur. For instance, a student who swears an average of five times per day would be reinforced for swearing one less time (i.e., four times). This schedule would be followed until swearing is eliminated completely.

The three techniques just discussed use positive reinforcement to decrease the frequency of undesirable behavior. Research does suggest, however, that acceptable levels of behavior might not be achieved without a punishment component (Lerman & Vorndran, 2002). For example, in cases in which the factors that maintain behavior cannot be identified or controlled or in which rapid behavior suppression is necessary to prevent physical harm, punishment might be part of the behavior management strategy. In recognition of the breadth and diversity of ABA techniques, more traditional methods of decreasing inappropriate behaviors will now be described.

■ *Punishment.* Normally, punishment is thought of as the presentation of an aversive consequence contingent on the occurrence of an undesirable behavior (type I). In the Skinnerian (or operant psychology) tradition, punishment also includes the removal of a positively reinforcing stimulus or event (type II), which is referred to as **response cost**. In either case, the person is presented with a consequence that is not pleasing or is deprived of something that is pleasing. For instance, a student who is kept after school for being disobedient is most likely experiencing punishment. Likewise, the student who has failed to fulfill a part of the contingency contract in the class and thus has lost some hard-earned tokens that buy free time in the gym is experiencing punishment. Response cost is most effective when used in combination with systematic reinforcement of appropriate behavior (Thibadeau, 1998). In each case the effect is to reduce the frequency of the undesirable behavior.

Walker and colleagues (2007) detail the advantages and disadvantages of using punishment. One advantage is the immediacy of its effect; usually, an immediate reduction occurs in the response rate. Punishment can also be effective when a disruptive behavior occurs with such frequency that reinforcement of an incompatible behavior is not possible and when a behavior must be temporarily suppressed while another behavior is reinforced. The disadvantages of punishment are numerous, including undesirable emotional reactions, avoidance of the environment or person producing the punishment, aggression toward the punishing person, modeling of punishing techniques by the person who is punished, and reinforcement for the person who is delivering the punishment. Additionally, physical punishment might result in physical abuse, although that may not have been the intent. For these reasons positive reinforcement is strongly encouraged in physical education for students with disabilities. Emphasis should always be on creating positive instructional environments that promote successful experiences.

■ *Time-out.* Time-out is an extension of the punishment concept, which often involves the removal of a positive event. The **time-out** procedure is based on the assumption that some positive reinforcer in the immediate environment is maintaining the undesirable behavior. In an effort to control the situation, the student is physically removed from the environment and consequently deprived of all positive reinforcement for a specified time. The three types of time-out are observational, exclusion, and seclusion (Lavay, French, & Henderson, 2006). In observational time-out, the student is removed from an activity but is permitted to watch as classmates engage in the lesson. Exclusion time-out, on the other hand, isolates the student within the physical education setting without opportunity to observe what is going on in the lesson. Finally, seclusion time-out completely isolates the student, removing him from the physical education setting.

USES OF APPLIED BEHAVIOR ANALYSIS IN PHYSICAL EDUCATION AND SPORT

Most people, including parents, teachers, coworkers, and students, use some form of ABA daily. In ordinary situations, however, the use of ABA might not be thorough and regular. On the other hand, the deliberate application of reinforcement learning principles in an attempt to change behavior is a systematic, step-by-step procedure. According to Block (2007), evidence supports the use of ABA in both segregated and inclusive programs for students with special needs. A classic example of ABA in adapted physical education is the work of Dunn and Leitschuh (2006), who developed a data-based gymnasium (DBG) for teaching students with severe disabilities in physical education. Successful implementation of the DGB depends on systematic use of the behavioral principles discussed in this section. Additionally, Dunn and colleagues have provided rules of thumb that guide the use of behavioral techniques in teaching skills and changing social behaviors. These include the use of naturally occurring reinforcers such as social praise or an extinction (i.e., ignoring a behavior). Tangible reinforcers such as food, toys, or desirable activities, which are earned as part of a token economy, are not instituted until it has been demonstrated that the consistent use of social reinforcement or extinction is ineffective.

In skill-acquisition programs, task-analytic phases and steps are individually determined, and students move through the sequence at a rate commensurate with their ability. For example, a **phase** for kicking with the toe of the preferred foot consists of having students swinging the preferred kicking leg backward and then forward, contacting the ball with the toes of the foot and causing the ball to roll toward the target. **Steps** represent distances, times, or numbers of repetitions that might further subdivide a particular phase (e.g., kicking the ball with the toe of the preferred foot a distance of 10, 15, or 20 ft [3, 4.6, or 6 m]). Decisions about program modifications or changes in the use of behavioral strategies (rules of thumb) are made on an individual basis after each student's progress is reviewed. Further discussion of the DBG and the rules of thumb for managing inappropriate behavior in physical education with students with severe disabilities can be found in chapter 9.

Advantages of ABA include the following:

■ It considers only behaviors that are precisely defined and capable of being seen.

■ It assumes that knowing the intrapsychic cause of a particular behavior is not a prerequisite for changing it; however, this is no way diminishes the importance of understanding the antecedents that may cause the behavior.

■ It encourages a thorough analysis of the environmental conditions and factors that might influence the behavior in question—that is, the antecedents.

■ It facilitates functional independence by employing a system of least prompts—that is, a prompt hierarchy is used that is ordered from least to most intrusive.

■ It requires precise measurement to demonstrate a cause-and-effect relation between the behavioral intervention and the behavior being changed.

Disadvantages of ABA that should be considered before implementing such a program include the following:

■ The actual use of behavioral principles in a consistent and systematic manner is not as simple as it might seem.

■ Behavioral techniques might fail when what is thought to be the controlling stimulus is not so in reality (e.g., a Premack reinforcer falsely constructed on the assumption that a student prefers a particular activity is destined to be unsuccessful).

■ Behavioral techniques might not work initially, requiring more thorough analysis by the teacher to determine if additional techniques would be useful; this can entail implementing a new approach immediately, if necessary.

Example of Applied Behavior Analysis

The process for implementing a behavioral system, ABA, requires reasonably strict adherence to several well-defined steps. The following example illustrates the teaching of a skill using the three-term contingency (ABC) and a limited number of behavioral principles. A similar process is outlined in chapter 9 using FBA and a behavior intervention plan to remediate an aberrant social behavior.

Identifying the behavior: Standing long jump

Establishing the baseline: In a pretest condition, the student is observed on three occasions performing the long jump with faulty mechanics, most notably in the takeoff and landing portions of the jump.

Objective: When requested to perform a standing long jump, the student jumps a minimum of 3 feet (1 m), demonstrating appropriate form on takeoff, in the air, and on landing.

Choosing the reinforcer: The teacher determines that social reinforcement (verbal praise) is effective.

Scheduling the reinforcer: The teacher decides to use continuous reinforcement

initially and then switch to a variable ratio as learning and performance increase.

Prompt: Using the system of least prompts, the instructor employs prompts in order from least to most intrusive: (1) "Please stand behind this line and do a standing long jump" (verbal prompt); (2) "Please stand behind this line, bend your knees, swing your arms backward and forward like this, and jump as far as possible" (verbal plus visual prompt); and (3) "Please stand behind this line, bend your knees, feel how I'm moving your arms so they swing back and forth like this, and jump as far as possible" (physical guidance prompt). In this example, prompts serve as antecedent events that cause the behavior to occur.

Behavior: The student acknowledges the prompts, assumes the correct position, and executes the long jump as intended.

Reinforcement: The teacher says, "Good job!" (verbal reinforcement).

Subsequent behavior: The student likely maintains or improves the performance.

OTHER APPROACHES

The management of behavior has been the concern of individuals and groups with various theoretical and philosophical views. No fewer than five major approaches have been postulated to remediate problems associated with maladaptive behavior. Two models (either singly or in combination) guide most educational programs today (Hallahan & Kauffman, 2003): the behavioral and psychoeducational approaches. The behavioral approach, ABA, has already been discussed. The psychoeducational approach will be discussed in the next sections along with the psychodynamic, ecological, biogenic, and humanistic approaches. These interventions are discussed only briefly. Resources are suggested at the end of the chapter for those who wish to further explore a particular intervention and its primary proponents.

Psychoeducational Approach

The psychoeducational approach views inappropriate behavior as students' maladaptive attempts to cope with their environment; it assumes that academic failure and misbehavior can be remediated directly if students are taught how to achieve and behave effectively. This approach emphasizes the education of the student's whole self, balancing the educational and psychological perspectives. It focuses on the affective and cognitive factors associated with the development of appropriate social and academic readiness skills useful in home, school, and community. Its proponents recognize that some students do not understand why they behave as they do when their basic instincts, drives, and needs are not satisfied. Psychoeducation is concerned with the here and now. Although it acknowledges the influence of past events on a student's behavior and psyche, it is less concerned with explanations for this behavior; identifying the student's potential for education and emphasizing learning abilities are more important functions of this approach. Diagnostic procedures include observational data, measures of achievement, performance in situations requiring particular skills, case histories, and measures of general abilities.

The psychoeducational approach focuses on strengthening the student's self-esteem and her relationships with teachers. This is accomplished through compensatory educational programs that encourage students to acknowledge that what they are doing is a problem, to understand their motivations for behaving in a certain way, to observe the consequences of their behavior, and to plan alternative ways of behaving in similar circumstances.

When a behavioral crisis occurs, a teacher trained in the psychoeducational approach conducts a **life-space interview**, a term first used by Redl (1952). More recently it was renamed *life-space crisis intervention*. The purpose of the life-space crisis intervention is to help the student either overcome momentary difficulties or work through long-range goals.

The psychoeducational approach assumes that making students aware of their feelings and having them talk about the nature of their responses will give them insight into their behavior and help them develop control. This approach emphasizes the realistic demands of everyday functioning in school and at home as they relate to improving inappropriate behaviors. Among several strategies teachers can use to implement the psychoeducational approach are self-instruction, modeling and rehearsal, self-determination of goals and reinforcement standards, and self-reward.

Teachers are in an advantageous position to encourage students to use self-instructional strategies. This means helping students reflect on the steps of good decision making when it is time to learn something new, solve a problem, or retain a concept. The process involves teaching students to listen to their private speech, or those times when they talk either aloud or subvocally to themselves. An example of private speech would be when a person makes a faulty ceiling shot in racquetball and says, "Come on, reach out and hit the ball ahead of the body!" Self-instruction can be as simple as a checklist of questions for students to ask themselves when a decision is required: What is my problem? How can I do it? Am I using my plan? How did I do? These are the types of questions asked within the self-instructional process.

In the modeling and rehearsal strategy, students who have a difficult time controlling their behavior watch others who have learned to deal with problems similar to their own. Beyond merely observing the behavior, the students can see how the models respond in a constructive manner to a problematic situation. Modeling could include the use of relaxation techniques and self-instruction. Students can also learn appropriate ways of responding when time is provided to mentally rehearse or practice successful management techniques. Much of the modeling and rehearsal strategy is steeped in Bandura's (1977) work on social learning theory and Goldstein and his colleagues' (1980) cognitive-behavioral procedures known as *skillstreaming*.

Another strategy that has proven effective in helping students control their behavior works by including them in the establishment of goals, reinforcement contingencies, or standards. An example of this process occurs when a group of adolescents with behavior disabilities determines which prosocial behaviors each member needs to concentrate on during an overnight camping trip. Likewise, the group establishes the limits of inappropriate behavior and decides what the consequences will be if anyone exceeds these limits.

A final strategy used in the psychoeducational approach is self-reward, which involves preparing students to reward themselves with some preestablished reinforcer. For example, a student who completes the prescribed tasks at a practice station might immediately place a check on a recording sheet posted at that station. When the checkmarks total a specified number, the student is thus instrumental not only in seeing that the goal of the lesson is achieved but also in efficiently implementing the reinforcement process.

Psychodynamic Approach

Most closely associated with the work of Freud, the psychodynamic approach has evolved as a collection of many subtheories, each with its own discrete intervention. For example, Adlers' social discipline approach, Roger's person-centered theory, and Glasser's reality therapy were all spawned from psychodynamic theory (Cullinan, 2007). The focus of this approach is the cause of psychological dysfunction. Specifically, the psychodynamic approach strives to improve emotional functioning by helping students understand *why* they are functioning inappropriately. This approach encourages teachers to accept students but not their undesirable behavior. It emphasizes helping students develop self-knowledge through close and positive relationships with teachers. From the psychodynamic perspective, the development of a healthy self-concept, including the ability to trust others and have confidence in one's feelings, abilities, and emotions, is integral to normal development. If the environment and significant others are not supportive, anxiety and depression might result. Self-perceptions and perceptions of others can become distorted, and the result might be impaired personal relationships, conflicting social values, inadequate self-image, ability deficits, and maladaptive habits and attitudes.

In an attempt to identify the probable intrapsychic causes of inappropriate behavior, the psychodynamic approach uses diagnostic procedures such as projective techniques, case histories, interviews, observational measures of achievement, and measures of general and specific abilities. Ideally, the cause of the psychic conflict is identified through interpretation of diagnostic results and an analysis of prevailing symptoms. Once the primary locus of the emotional disturbance is known, an appropriate treatment can be determined.

Conventional pyschodynamic treatment modalities include psychoanalysis, counseling interviews, and psychotherapeutic techniques (such as play therapy and group therapy). Treatment sessions involve the student alone, although some therapists see only the parents. Recently, family therapy has become popular, with students and parents attending sessions together. Regardless of how the session is configured, it is designed to help students develop self-knowledge.

The psychodynamic approach, including psychoanalysis and psychotherapy, is not regarded as an exemplary approach to intervention. Teachers might be employed at settings in which this approach is advocated, but such settings are usually directed by psychiatrists. Overall, it is not a common approach in traditional educational settings (Cullinan, 2007). The psychodynamic approach has several inadequacies that include the following: diagnostic study is time consuming and expensive, the results of diagnostic study yield only possible causes for emotional conflict, and therapeutic outcomes are similar regardless of the nature of the intervention—whether students are seen alone or with parents, in play therapy or in group counseling.

There are several misconceptions about the psychodynamic approach. Teachers should be aware that implementation of psychodynamic theory does not preclude working with groups. Its primary goal

need not be increasing students' personal awareness. And teachers do not need to be permissively accepting, deal with the subconscious, or focus on problems other than those that are real concerns in the present situation.

Ecological Approach

The ecological approach assumes that behavioral problems are caused by a disturbance in the student's environment or ecosystem. In effect, the student and the environment influence each other in a reciprocal and negative manner (i.e., some characteristic of the student disturbs the ecosystem, and the ecosystem responds in a way that causes the student to further agitate it). "The problem arises because the social interactions and transactions between the child and the social environment are inappropriate" (Hallahan & Kauffman, 2003, p. 222). Said another way, a student's problems are affected by the environment; the student is not the only one causing the problems. For example, a student who cannot get to class on time and thus is in conflict with teachers might be reflecting the disdain in his culture for punctuality rather than disrespect for the teacher or the school schedule.

Evaluative procedures for assessing the causes of disturbed behavior are difficult at best. Educators have purported to use a five-phase process for collecting ecological data: describing the environment, identifying expectations, organizing behavioral data, summarizing the data, and establishing goals.

Additionally, the Behavior Rating Profile (BRP-2) examines behaviors in several settings from several points of view. The profile consists of three student rating subscales, one teacher rating scale, one parent rating scale, and a sociogram (a diagram that uses connecting lines to indicate choices made in groups). The purpose of the profile is to define deviant behavior specific to one setting or to one person's expectations (Brown & Hammill, 1990).

The goal of the ecological approach is not simply to stop a disturbed or unwanted behavior but to change an environment, such as the home, in substantive ways. This is important if the environment is to continue supporting desirable behavior once the intervention is withdrawn. Generally speaking, the focus of intervention within the ecological approach is on one or more environments. Interventions that focus on only one environment, however, are frequently unsuccessful, given that the behavior in question is prominent in more than just one location (Cullinan, Epstein, & Lloyd, 1991). For example, if a student is experiencing the same problems at home and in school, intervention must address how the behavior will be handled in both places. This is a particularly difficult issue since students are permitted to behave in one way at home only to find that the behavior is inappropriate and not tolerated in school. This could create a conflict between the school and the family that could necessitate working not only with the student but also family members.

Educational applications of the ecological approach are designed to make environments accommodate students rather than helping students fit in environments. In a classroom, this might require physical and psychological adaptations, such as individual or small-group work areas, time-out areas, or reinforcement centers. This approach entails having teachers create environments in which students succeed rather than anticipate failure. Changes in the home ecosystem might require parental involvement (e.g., talking with parents), respite care, or family therapy. At times, changes in several ecosystems are required (e.g., home, school, and community).

Of interest are present-day attempts to establish ecologically based programs, including the establishment of PBIS. To develop an effective behavioral intervention, educators must engage in a three-step process: Perform a functional assessment of the student's behavior, determine and implement intervention strategies, and evaluate the results. Assessing the student's behavior includes observation and recording of behavior patterns in several settings (e.g., classroom, playground, cafeteria, gym) with the intention of profiling the student's conduct. Establishing a baseline helps teachers understand either why a student is behaving in a certain way or who is controlling or reinforcing a student's behavior.

After completing the functional assessment, the teacher develops and implements an intervention. The intervention should set realistic goals, including the acceptance of behaviors that would ordinarily not be appropriate. For example, a student who fights with a certain teammate each time she misses a shot during a basketball drill might realistically be permitted to shout or curse at that teammate as long as she does not physically assault her. After a while, shouting and cursing would be similarly faded. As many people as possible who work with the student should develop the intervention plan. Behavioral interventions must be team based so that the student experiences consistency. The student should also participate in developing the behavioral intervention.

Evaluation of the intervention plan is the final step. Teachers assess how effective the plan is and if modifications are necessary. Most experts agree that evaluation should occur monthly, if not weekly. It is obvious that the process involved in PBIS mirrors the steps used in implementing an ABA program. It is equally obvious that PBIS is influenced by a confluence of approaches, in this case ABA and the ecological approach. An in-depth explanation and illustration of PBIS, including the articulation with ABA, can be found in chapter 9, Behavioral Disabilities.

Biogenic Approach

The central focus of the biogenic approach is neurophysiological dysfunction. Closely associated with the medical model, this approach relies on diagnostic techniques that explore signs and symptoms. Physicians attempt to localize problems using neurological soft signs (e.g., the results of gait and postural assessments); timed, repetitive movements; and visual motor sequencing tasks. Lack of definitive results might prompt the use of electroencephalography (EEG), computed tomography (CT), or magnetic resonance imaging (MRI) if lesser diagnostics prove uneventful. Identification of students with disabilities in this realm is made on the basis of general behavioral characteristics (e.g., hyperactivity, distractibility, impulsiveness, emotional lability) and specific functional deficits (e.g., disorders in perception, language, motor ability, and concept formation and reasoning). The manifestation of these characteristics and deficits is attributable to injury or damage to the central nervous system.

The biogenic approach places considerable importance on etiological factors. The integrity of the central nervous system is assessed on the basis of performance in selected activities or tests, such as walking a line with eyes closed, touching a finger to the nose, or reacting to stimuli such as pain, cold, and light. Additionally, a neurological examination including an EEG is often part of the diagnosis. Following diagnosis, treatment might include drug therapy, surgical procedures (e.g., removal of a tumor), physical therapy, sensory integrative therapy, or developmental training.

A major strategy associated with the biogenic approach is drug therapy (though the use of drugs to control or modify behavior cuts across several behavioral approaches). Students are medicated for the management of such challenges as short attention span, distractibility, impulsiveness, hyperactivity, visual motor impairments, and large motor coordination problems. "Data . . . point to the increasingly widespread use of psychopharmacologic medications, with as many as 2-4% of children in general education, 15-20% of children in special education, and 40-60% of children in residential facilities receiving medication treatment" (Konopasek & Forness, 2004, p. 353). Psychotropic drugs represent the major category of substances used to control emotional, behavioral, and cognitive changes of people with disabilities. These drugs include medications typically classified as antipsychotic, antianxiety, antidepressant, antimania, stimulant, or sedative–hypnotic. The most common categories of psychotropic drugs for the purpose of this discussion are stimulants, neuroleptics, and antidepressants.

■ *Stimulants.* Stimulants are administered primarily for the management of attention deficit/hyperactivity disorder (ADHD). ADHD is the only condition other than obesity and narcolepsy for which there is FDA approval for the use of stimulants. The most frequently prescribed family of stimulants is the methylphenidate hydrochlorides. These include Ritalin (the most commonly prescribed), Concerta (a long-acting form prescribed for children under six years of age), Metadate CD, Metadate ER, Focalin, and Methylin ER (Schatzberg, Cole, & DeBattista, 2003). All of these drugs are adjunctive therapy and are used with students who experience moderate to severe hyperactivity, short attention span, distractibility, emotional lability, and impulsiveness. Although it seems contraindicated to treat an overactive child with stimulants, these drugs increase concentrations of dopamine, norepinephrine, and serotonin. Increasing these neurotransmitters improves cognition, memory, and attention (Konopasek & Forness, 2004). Possible side effects include loss of appetite, weight loss, stomachache, headache, irritability, anxiety, and insomnia. These effects are more profound in individuals with intellectual disabilities (Arnold et al., 1998).

■ *Neuroleptics.* These drugs, also called tranquilizers, remain the most widely prescribed class of psychotropic medications for individuals with intellectual disabilities. They are also used to control bizarre behavior in psychotic adults. In children they are used to control hyperactivity, aggression, self-injury, and stereotypic behavior. Tranquilizers are classified as either major or minor. Major *tranquilizers*, also called *antipsychotics*, include such drugs as Mellaril (thioridazine hydrochloride), Thorazine (chlorpromazine hydrochloride), and

Haldol (haloperidol), all of which are prescribed for the management of psychotic disorders, including severe behavior disorders marked by aggressiveness and combativeness (Baumeister, Sevin, & King, 1998). Possible side effects of the major and minor tranquilizers include dizziness, drowsiness, vertigo, fatigue, diminished mental alertness (which could impair performance in physical activities), tardive dyskinesia (involuntary movements of the tongue and facial muscles), and movement disorders, referred to as the *extrapyramidal effect*.

■ *Antidepressants.* Antidepressants are prescribed to adults to alleviate depression. In children they have a more diverse function, including not only the management of obsessive–compulsive disorder (OCD), affective disorders, and ADHD but also the treatment of nocturnal enuresis and, to a lesser extent, ritualistic behavior, self-injurious behavior, and aggression. Perhaps because of the documented side effects of antidepressants—ataxia, muscle weakness, drowsiness, anxiety, sleep disruption, decreased appetite, increased blood pressure, and mental dullness (Sovner et al., 1998)—physical educators and coaches should know when students are receiving such medication. Commonly prescribed antidepressants include Anafranil (clomipramine) and Tofranil (imipramine), which is used for ADHD where patients show excessive side effects or fail to respond favorably to stimulants.

Humanistic Approach

Based on the work of Maslow (1970), the humanistic approach has as its basis the self-actualization theory. Five primary human needs are identified in ascending order, including physiological needs, safety, belongingness and love, esteem, and self-actualization. According to this theory of motivation, humans seek to meet unsatisfied needs at progressively higher levels as lower needs are met. For example, someone lacking food, safety, love, and esteem would probably hunger for food more strongly than for anything else. But when the need for food is satisfied, the other needs become stronger. In the need hierarchy, self-actualization is the fulfillment of one's highest potential. Maslow considered the following to be attributes of self-actualized people: accepting, spontaneous, realistic, autonomous, appreciating, ethical, sympathetic, affectionate, helpful, intimate, democratic, sure about right and wrong, and creative.

Self-actualization is the process of becoming all that one is fully capable of becoming. In large measure self-actualization is developed naturally by people without disabilities. People with disabilities, on the other hand, might not achieve the same relative status of self-actualization as their peers without disabilities because they sometimes lack the intrinsic motivation and external assistance to become all they are capable of becoming. The desire to move people with disabilities toward self-actualization is supplied, at least initially, by those who care about them as individuals first and foremost and as individuals with disabilities to a secondary degree.

In the sixth revision of her text on adapted physical education, Sherrill (2004) and colleagues have continued to draw extensively and build on self-actualization theory of Abraham Maslow, as well as the noted psychotherapist Carl Rogers' concept of the fully functioning self and newer sources in attitude theory and disability studies, to guide a humanistic orientation to adapted physical education in general and to affective development in particular. Sherrill is not only the spokesperson for the humanistic philosophy but also its instrumentalist in that she applies its concepts in the gym and on the field. In an effort to demonstrate how the humanistic philosophy can be translated into action, Sherrill and her colleagues suggest that teachers and coaches of students with disabilities do the following:

■ To the degree possible, use a teaching style that encourages learners to make some of the major decisions during the learning process. This implies that students should be taught with the least restrictive teaching style or one that most closely matches their learning styles.

■ Use assessment and instruction that are success oriented. If tasks are sufficiently broken down (i.e., task analyzed), positive reinforcement and success will characterize the learning environment. No matter where students score in terms of the normal curve, they have worth as human beings and must be accepted as such.

■ Listen to and communicate with students in an effort to encourage them to take control of their lives and make personal decisions affecting their physical well-being. Counseling students to become healthy, fit, and self-actualized requires the skills of active listening, acceptance, empathy, and cooperative goal setting. Such interaction helps people with disabilities reinforce their internal locus of control.

■ Use teaching practices that enhance self-concept. The following practices are recommended: Show students that someone genuinely cares for them as human beings; teach students to care about each other by modeling caring behavior in daily student and teacher interactions; emphasize social interaction by using cooperative rather than competitive activities; and build success into the instructional plan through the careful use of task and activity analysis.

Hellison (2003) is another physical educator who has been instrumental in disseminating the humanistic viewpoint. He has developed a set of alternative goals or levels for physical education that focus on human needs and values rather than on fitness and sport skill development per se. Hellison has applied the model in a basketball unit that is described in chapter 9. The levels are developmental in nature and reflect a loosely constructed level-by-level progression of attitudes and behaviors. Specifically, they include self-control and respect for the rights and feelings of others, participation and effort, self-direction, and caring and helping.

SUMMARY

Behavior management approaches have been used successfully to facilitate skill acquisition and enhance social behavior, either directly through systematic manipulation of content or indirectly through arrangement of antecedents and consequences of performance to produce more motivation. Additionally, lack of discipline has been identified as one of the most significant problems confronting public school teachers. An equally significant problem is how to replace old, worn-out thinking about how discipline should be delivered in favor of effective, proactive practices.

A number of behavior management systems are available that can significantly affect skill acquisition or reduce the need to discipline students. As students with behavior disabilities are integrated into a regular class and demonstrate persistent disruptive behavior, a behavior management program designed to alleviate the problem might include any of the following: ABA using FBA and behavior intervention plans; a psychoeducational approach using the life-space interview; a psychodynamic approach incorporating play therapy; a biogenic approach using medication; a humanistic approach using self-actualization, self-concept, and attitude theory; an ecological approach using a behavior intervention plan that includes the school as well as the student's home and community environment; or an eclectic use of these approaches, which is the more common scenario in adapted physical education. Physical educators use mainly ABA, humanistic, and psychoeducational approaches, depending on the setting.

REFERENCES

Arnold, L.E., Gadow, K., Pearson, D.A., & Varley, C.K. (1998). Stimulants. In S. Reiss & M.G. Aman (Eds.), *Psychotropic medication and developmental disabilities: The international consensus handbook* (pp. 229-257). Washington, DC: American Association on Mental Retardation (AAMR).

Bandura, A. (1977). *Social learning theory.* New York: General Learning Press.

Baumeister, A.A., Sevin, J.A., & King, B.H. (1998). Neuroleptics. In S. Reiss & M.G. Aman (Eds.), *Psychotropic medication and developmental disabilities: The international consensus handbook* (pp. 133-150). Washington, DC: AAMR.

Block, M.E. (2007). *A teacher's guide to including students with disabilities in general physical education.* Baltimore: Paul H. Brookes.

Brown, L.L., & Hammill, D.D. (1990). *Behavior rating profile: An ecological approach to behavioral assessment* (2nd ed.). Austin, TX: Pro-Ed.

Cooper, J.O., Heron, T.E., & Heward, W.L. (2007). *Applied behavior analysis* (2nd ed.). Upper Saddle River, NJ: Pearson Education.

Cullinan, D. (2007). *Students with emotional and behavioral disorders* (2nd ed.). Upper Saddle River, NJ: Pearson Education.

Cullinan, D., Epstein, M.H., & Lloyd, J.W. (1991). Evaluation of conceptual models of behavior disorders. *Behavioral Disorders, 16,* 148-157.

Dunn, J.M., & Leitschuh, C. (2006). *Special physical education* (8th ed.). Dubuque, IA: Kendall/Hunt.

Goldstein, A.P., Sprafkin, R.P., Gershaw, N.J., & Klein, P. (1980). *Skillstreaming the adolescent: A structured learning approach to teaching prosocial skills.* Champaign, IL: Research Press.

Hallahan, D.P., & Kauffman, J.M. (2003). *Exceptional learners: Introduction to special education* (9th ed.). Needham Heights, MA: Allyn & Bacon.

Hellison, D.R. (2003). *Teaching responsibility through physical activity* (2nd ed.). Champaign, IL: Human Kinetics.

Individuals with Disabilities Education Act Amendments of 2004 (IDEA) (PL 108-446), 20 U.S.C. 1400 (2004).

Jones, M.M. (1998). *Within our reach: Behavior prevention and intervention strategies for learners with mental retardation and autism.* Reston, VA: Division of Mental Retardation and Developmental Disabilities of the Council for Exceptional Children.

Kazdin, A.E. (2001). *Behavior modification in applied settings* (6th ed.). Belmont, CA: Wadsworth/Thomson Learning.

Konopasek, D.E., & Forness, S.R. (2004). Psychopharmacology in the treatment of emotional and behavioral disorders. In R.B. Rutherford, M.M. Quinn, & S.R. Mathur (Eds.), *Handbook of research in emotional and behavioral disorders* (pp. 352-368). New York: Guilford Press.

Lavay, B.W., French, R., & Henderson, H.L. (2006). *Positive behavior management in physical activity settings* (2nd ed.). Champaign, IL: Human Kinetics.

Lerman, D.C., & Vorndran, C.M. (2002). On the status of knowledge for using punishment: Implications for treating behavior disorders. *Journal of Applied Behavior Analysis, 35,* 431-464.

Maslow, A.H. (1970). *Motivation and personality* (2nd ed.). New York: Harper & Row.

Premack, D. (1965). Reinforcement theory. In D. Levine (Ed.), *Nebraska symposium on motivation.* Lincoln, NE: University of Nebraska Press.

Redl, F. (1952). *Controls from within.* New York: Free Press.

Schatzberg, A.F., Cole, J.O., & DeBattista, C. (2003). *Manual of clinical psychopharmacology* (4th ed.). Washington, DC: American Psychiatric Publishing.

Sherrill, C. (2004). *Adapted physical education, recreation, and sport: Crossdisciplinary and lifespan* (6th ed.). St. Louis: McGraw-Hill.

Sovner, R., Pary, R.J., Dosen, A., Geyde, A., Barrera, F.J., Cantwell, D.P., & Huessy, H.R. (1998). Antidepressants. In S. Reiss & M.G. Aman (Eds.), *Psychotropic medication and developmental disabilities: The international consensus handbook* (pp. 179-200). Washington, DC: American Association on Mental Retardation.

Thibadeau, S.F. (1998). *How to use response cost.* Austin, TX: Pro-Ed.

Walker, J.E., Shea, T.M., & Bauer, A.M. (2007). *Behavior management: A practical approach for educators* (9th ed.). Upper Saddle River, NJ: Prentice-Hall.

WRITTEN RESOURCES

Hall, R.V., & Hall, M.L. (Eds.). (1999). *How to manage behavior series* (2nd ed.). Austin, TX: Pro-Ed.

This series consists of 15 self-instructional manuals that cover a broad range of behavioral topics, including selecting reinforcers; planning generalization;

using group contingencies; using planned ignoring; using positive practice, self-correction, and overcorrection; and using prompts to initiate behavior. Each manual provides a clear definition of the procedure, examples of how the procedure is used, and opportunities for the reader to respond in a programmed text format.

Lavay, B.W., French, R., & Henderson, H.L. (2006). *Positive behavior management in physical activity settings* (2nd ed.). Champaign, IL: Human Kinetics.

This manual describes in greater detail many of the approaches suggested in this chapter. It likewise provides many practical examples of how to manage behavior in the physical education settings.

AUDIOVISUAL RESOURCES

Almost everything you ever wanted to know about motivating people: Maslow's hierarchy of needs. (Videotape, 1987). Salenger Educational Media, 1635 12th Street, Santa Monica, CA 90404.

Basic needs such as food, shelter, security, recognition, and achievement are reviewed in light of Maslow's hierarchy of needs; their meaning for motivation in organizational settings is analyzed and illustrated using dramatized incidents. Running time is approximately 16 minutes.

Applied behavior analysis in natural settings. (Videotapes, 2006-2008). Behavior Analysis Association of Michigan, Department of Psychology, Eastern Michigan University, Ypsilanti, MI 48197.

This series of 32 video vignettes describes such topics as discrete trial training, manding, prompting, reinforcement, teaching play skills, and managing problem behavior.

Differential reinforcement. (Videotape, n.d.). Utah Personnel Development Center, 2290 East 4500 South, Suite 220, Salt Lake City, UT 84117.

This video explains and demonstrates the variety of differential reinforcement strategies that are discussed in this chapter.

Teaching people with developmental disabilities. (Videotape, 1988). Research Press, Box 31775, Champaign, IL 60820.

This film is a hands-on training program illustrating how to use task analysis, prompting, reinforcement, and error correction to teach functional skills to people with mild to moderate developmental disabilities. Running time is approximately 88 minutes.

ELECTRONIC RESOURCES

The Life Space Interview and Life Space Crisis Intervention, http://maxweber.hunter.cuny.edu/pub/eres/EDSPC715_MCINTYRE/LSI.html.

This site provides extensive information about the life-space interview and how it's conducted.

Medline Plus Drugs, Supplements, and Herbal Information, www.nlm.nih.gov/medlineplus/druginformation.html.

This site allows practitioners to search for information on psychotropic drugs, including brand names, descriptions, proper use, precautions, and side effects.

PsychoEd.Net, www.psychoed.net.

This site provides information about psychoeducation. It is oriented toward educators of moderately and severely emotionally disturbed students. Child care workers and mental health professionals might also find this information helpful. Psychoeducational approaches helpful for troubled children and youth are presented.

chapter 7

Instructional Strategies for Adapted Physical Education

Douglas H. Collier

Mr. Ellis, the newly hired physical education teacher, was discouraged. "Whenever Peter and Jasmine come to physical education, I just get this tight feeling across my chest. Yes, I know I should be able to accommodate them, and I'd like to be able to, but I just don't feel qualified, so I get nervous. Peter has been diagnosed with Asperger syndrome and Jasmine has Down syndrome. That's as much as I know. Oh, yes—I get an aide when they come to the gym with their 30 classmates. So, the students have Asperger syndrome and Down syndrome. What am I supposed to do with that information? On the one hand, I'm glad they're in the physical education class with their buddies. On the other hand, I wish I had better ideas of how to work with them. Do I change my approach? My curriculum? What if the other students get angry or bored? What if I don't have time for all of the others? Boy, with all the different skill levels and learning styles, I wish that I'd been a little better prepared."

Teaching physical education effectively and efficiently so that students learn and retain meaningful content is a challenging undertaking made even more so by the increasing diversity of the student body (Siedentop & Tannehill, 2000). Although, as outlined in chapter 2, multiple physical education environments exist for students with identifiable disabilities, these students are frequently being integrated into their neighborhood schools and are being taught in the same classes as their peers without disabilities (Block, 2007; Dunn & Leitschuh, 2006). Thus, planning and presenting appropriate physical education content require more attention to individual differences than ever.

This type of planning does *not* mean coming up with a laundry list of instructional modifications based on perceived characteristics of a particular disability type. For example, it would be inappropriate to say, "If she's been diagnosed with autism, I'd better avoid physical prompts. Given he has Down syndrome, I'll expect oppositional behavior." Instructional decisions are not based only on a student's medical or behavioral diagnosis; rather, they are also predicated on the learning style, strengths, and shortcomings of the student as well as the objectives of the class. For example, some students with autism learn more effectively through a command style of teaching, whereas other students with the same diagnosis learn more effectively when given options on how to perform a given skill. Langendorfer (1985) has eloquently noted that physical educators have long known that all students come to physical education with different strengths, learning styles, and rates of learning and that the effective teacher takes these differences into account when planning, delivering, and assessing content.

Teaching quality physical education classes to typically developing students is a demanding undertaking that requires motivation, an extensive knowledge base, lots of practice, and appropriate feedback from skilled observers. When the classes include students with unique needs—whether the setting is integrated or segregated—the heterogeneity of classes clearly is increased, as is the challenge for effective teaching. Siedentop and Tannehill (2000) have noted that a committed and competent physical education teacher has extensive skills in the areas of conceiving and planning the curricula, managing behavior and teaching the content, optimizing the program through appropriate administration, and creatively linking the school program to community opportunities. These skills are required to an even greater degree when teaching students with unique needs. As well, the physical education teacher who works with students with unique needs faces additional challenges that have not been traditionally emphasized in teacher preparation programs. These challenges include writing goals and objectives for individualized education programs (IEPs) or individualized family service plans (IFSPs), adapting activities, task analyzing activities (breaking skills into smaller parts), providing appropriate prompting, training and managing volunteers, working with parents and allied professionals as part of an interdisciplinary team, and effectively managing idiosyncratic or challenging behavior.

This chapter provides information that directly relates to effectively instructing learners with unique needs. This information will assist teachers in structuring a physical education environment that optimizes learning.

PHILOSOPHICAL APPROACHES TO ADAPTED PHYSICAL EDUCATION AND SPORT

Teachers of adapted physical education who implement effective individualized physical education programs believe in each participant's inherent worth and are dedicated to the development of their students' full potential. These general characteristics are present in two primary orientations that have influenced adapted physical education over the past few decades—**humanism** and **applied behavior analysis** (ABA). Although humanism and ABA (also called *behavior therapy, behaviorism,* and *behavior modification*) have different traditions and emphases and often use different empirical tools, they share a commitment to providing the most advanced and highest quality instruction for people with and without disabilities. Both traditions emphasize nonaversive, affirming teaching strategies in terms of both skill acquisition and the management of challenging behaviors.

Teachers who embrace the humanistic approach as well as those who view themselves as applied behavior analysts recognize the inherent challenges of teaching learners with unique needs and believe that, despite these challenges, all learners are entitled to respect. Instructional methodologies that best allow people to be self-reliant and productive while maintaining individual dignity are hallmarks of first-rate programs that embrace these philosophical perspectives. Although often cast as an either–or proposition, the thoughtful practitioner is able to embrace the best of each tradition without hypocrisy. Indeed, from an ethical and at times strategic perspective, proponents of each tradition have much in common. Both orientations, as noted, stress the importance of human dignity. There have been social policies and movements as well as economic priorities that have marginalized people with disabilities. Practitioners from both the humanistic and ABA perspectives stand together in creating appropriate environments where people with unique needs can live full, positive, and valued lives.

Humanistic Philosophy

Humanism emphasizes the pursuit and teaching of such qualities as creativity, choice, awareness, and personal and social responsibility. It is a hopeful and extremely positive view of human beings, holding that everyone—including people with unique needs—has the capacity to develop a positive self-image, be self-determining, and be intrinsically motivated. Practitioners and researchers adhering to a humanistic philosophy view development in a holistic fashion; that is, mind, body, and spirit cannot be divided. Thus, educational experiences are designed to benefit the whole person. For instance, a catching activity would be constructed so that the student would be appropriately challenged physically, intellectually, and affectively. The activity by nature would promote and preserve self-esteem (Sherrill, 2004). According to Rogers and Stevens (1967, p. 2), "An assumption unusual in psychology today is that the subjective human being has an important value which is basic; that no matter how he may be labeled and evaluated he is a human person first of all, and most deeply."

Humanistic philosophy began in the late 1950s with the work of Abraham Maslow (1908-1970) and Carl Rogers (1902-1987), two of the intellectual leaders of the movement. Their work in the area of human motivation, Maslow's self-actualization theory (Maslow, 1987), and Rogers' (1980) fully functioning self theory gave humanistic psychology its initial momentum. These researchers viewed human nature as essentially good, positing that all people have a substantial capacity to be self-determining.

Maslow's self-actualization theory guides practitioners who embrace a humanistic approach to physical education. Evolving from his writings on the hierarchy of human needs, self-actualization theory hypothesizes that basic physiological needs such as thirst and hunger must be taken care of before the more creative or aesthetic needs can be satisfied (see figure 7.1). What Maslow referred to as *deficit needs* (physiological, safety, belonging, and esteem) must be taken care of hierarchically and generally require help from significant others in a student's environment (e.g., parents, teachers, peers). Once these deficit needs have been taken care of, self-actualization (fulfillment of one's potential) can take place. Self-actualization, referred to as *being needs*, is intrinsically motivated and is possible to attain once self-esteem has been achieved.

This hierarchy has implications for adapted physical educators. As students with unique needs take part in physical education, it must be established that physiological needs (e.g., food, water, appropriate medication, temperature) have been met. The teacher of adapted physical education meets these needs at times. With regard to safety, adapted physical educators must go beyond physical considerations and address the psychological climate of the gymnasium. Are the students with unique needs learning in an environment free from

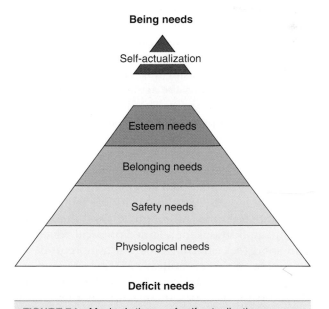

Being needs

Self-actualization

Esteem needs

Belonging needs

Safety needs

Physiological needs

Deficit needs

FIGURE 7.1 Maslow's theory of self-actualization.

Based on Maslow, 1987.

anxiety and confusion? Have learning and assessment activities been selected that build trust and confidence and set the student up to succeed? In terms of Maslow's third tier, belonging, are students with unique needs accepted and appreciated by their peer group and teachers for who they are and not for what they can do? Students must feel safe and accepted before they can benefit from instruction that will improve competence and lead to enhanced self-esteem.

People with unique educational needs often demonstrate low fitness and movement skill levels and, at times, little motivation to improve. They might have done poorly in the past, possibly in a public forum, and see no reason for this state of affairs to change. It is up to the skilled teacher to construct meaningful learning experiences designed for learner success. Once basic self-esteem needs are met, the student might be led to "feelings of self-confidence, worth, strength, capability, and adequacy, of being useful and necessary in the world" (Maslow, 1987, p. 21). This arrival at the self-actualization level (further subdivided into the self-actualization, enlightenment, and aesthetic–creative levels) can be attained only to the degree that a student feels at home in the world.

Carl Rogers, Maslow's contemporary, also made significant contributions in the areas of education, special education, and rehabilitation. Although known primarily for his client-centered approach to counseling, Rogers' (1980) **fully functioning self** theory presents a perspective that influences the education of people with disabilities. Rogers stressed the need for teachers to be warm, empathetic, and genuine as well as accepting of the learner—unconditionally. The theory of the fully functioning self suggests that people have both an **ideal self** and an **actual self**. The closer the match between the ideal and the actual self, the more fully functioning a person is. This ideal human condition results in a person who is open to experience, expresses feelings freely, acts independently, is creative, and lives a rich life. Movement toward this point of development requires **self-acceptance** as well as the unconditional acceptance of significant people in the student's life, including family members and teachers. Although Rogers' theory has strong implications for adapted physical education and sport (see Sherrill, 2004, for a more in-depth treatment of these implications), as a humanistic psychologist, his greatest contribution might be the strong emphasis he placed on the ethical treatment of all people and a recognition of their inherent worth.

Applied Behavior Analysis

There is a rich tradition of employing the principles of ABA to the teaching of physical education to students with unique needs (Alberto & Troutman, 2008; Dunn & Leitschuh, 2006). Succinctly stated, ABA involves changing behavior through the careful application of learning principles.

B.F. Skinner's work (1980) has been applied widely in the teaching of students with disabilities. Skinner stressed the importance of the consequences of a person's actions—that is, what takes place after the behavior—on learning. His work demonstrated that **carefully selected consequences** could change the likelihood of the behavior that preceded it. Although consequences can be negative (punishing), thus resulting in a decrease of the behavior, educators working with students who have unique needs should concentrate on positively reinforcing (rewarding) behaviors that are helpful to the student, thus increasing the likelihood they will occur again.

The educational approach for students with unique needs that uses strategies derived from ABA principles is commonly known as *behavior modification*. Unfortunately, this term might conjure up images of punitive, controlling interventions. Although in the past, these powerful procedures have at times been used inappropriately (too much reliance on punitive consequences), teachers educated in the use of behavioral interventions apply them ethically and positively with an eye on improving a learner's skills. By using this effective and ethical approach to teaching, many teachers have helped students significantly increase their repertoire of socially valued and individually meaningful abilities; as a result, the students live their lives with dignity and as self-reliant members of society.

Although teachers routinely employ behavioral principles, they often do not know that they are doing so. Without being aware of it, a teacher might reward (reinforce) a behavior, leading to an unexpected increase. For example, every time Peter called out, Mrs. Allen stopped the lesson and said, "Peter, we're all tired of you calling out. Please stop." Although Mrs. Allen felt she was firmly and effectively dealing with his behavior, Peter thought all the individual public attention was great. As a result of Mrs. Allen's attention, Peter called out even more.

As noted, the ABA approach to teaching physical education and sport to students with unique needs shares with the humanistic approach a positive and ethical approach to developing meaningful skills. In the area of behavior management, increased attention has been given to positively and proactively dealing with problematic behavior through an approach referred to as *positive behavior support* (PBS) (Carr et. al., 1999; Safran & Oswald, 2003; Stormont et al., 2008). Coming from an ABA perspective, PBS focuses on teaching prosocial skills as opposed to employing aversive and exclusionary practices. To begin with, the antecedents and consequences thought to affect a precisely described behavior are carefully examined (i.e., functional behavioral assessment). Subsequently, data-based interventions are put into place. These positive, skill-building interventions may include teaching the student new skills and changing certain facets of the environment (e.g., task demands, curriculum, instructional pace). An important aspect of PBS is ongoing monitoring of the intervention with respect to its effectiveness. To summarize, PBS focuses on setting up environments that prevent the likelihood of problematic behavior and teaching meaningful academic, affective, and communicative skills that are effective alternatives to the problematic behavior being demonstrated.

Clearly, the humanistic and ABA traditions, along with other approaches in this text (discussed in chapter 6), are relevant to skill acquisition and behavior management. When teaching adapted physical education and sport, the practitioner must remain open-minded and, when appropriate, take the best elements of each tradition. The underlying goals of humanism and ABA are not mutually exclusive. Within an individualized approach to teaching, the needs of students must guide teachers' choices. This text focuses on both approaches and subscribes to an eclectic perspective in implementing instruction. Chapters 6 and 9 include more information about the humanistic and ABA perspectives.

SYSTEMATIC TEACHING: HOW TO FACILITATE MOTOR LEARNING

Experts in the teaching of movement skills have stressed the importance of examining variables that relate to the learner, the task, and the environment when designing learning opportunities for students with unique needs (Newell, 1986; Reid, pers. comm., October 7, 2003). These three variables are not independent of one another; rather, they interact in sometimes complex ways, as shown in figure 7.2. Variables that relate to the learner include age, body build, gender, socioeconomic class, culture, attitudes, actual and perceived competence, creativity, motivations, disability, and ability. Some of these variables might change over the course of a unit or lesson, depending on the situation. For example, students with Down syndrome might be excited about taking part in a jump rope activity, but after 10 minutes of doing the same thing with little success, their motivation level, as well as their perceived competence in jumping rope, might dwindle considerably. Conversely, students with cerebral palsy might come into the gym dreading the thought of taking part in line dancing, but given an excellent breakdown of the skill, some thoughtful peer tutoring, and great tunes, their motivation to participate might increase dramatically.

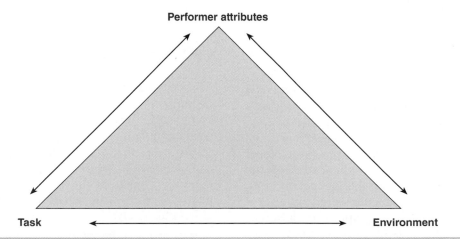

FIGURE 7.2 Interaction of performer, environment, and task.

Based on Newell, 1986.

When examining environmental variables, educators must think beyond the physical. Although the indoor or outdoor setting, facilities, equipment, space, floor surfaces, lighting, and temperature must be considered, it is also imperative that teachers of adapted physical education carefully consider the emotional environment. Do activities take place in a positive, affirming environment in which individual differences are embraced? Is there mutual respect? Are all students treated with dignity? Along with making sure the physical environment is safe and appropriate, effective teachers must also monitor the environment for emotional safety (Sherrill, 2004).

The third variable—the task—gets at the curriculum. Are the movement skills of interest and use to the students? Do instructors teach skills because they enjoy them or because it's always been done that way? Or do they teach a skill because it is valued by the student, the family, or the community and will be useful now or in the next likely educational placement?

Research in the disciplines of motor learning, motor development, motor control, biomechanics, physiology, special education, and pedagogy has uncovered certain principles that can help significantly in the teaching and learning of movement skills. Keeping in mind the interaction of variables related to the learner, the environment, and the task to be accomplished, Dunn (1997) has compiled a list of motor skill tenets.

■ *Growth and maturation influence the ability to learn a movement skill.* It is detrimental to the physical and emotional well-being of students to pressure them to take part in tasks that they are not ready to accomplish motorically, cognitively, or socially. Although teachers should organize learning environments in which students can explore their movement potential, they must carefully consider cognitive, affective, and physical limitations.

■ *Mechanical and physiological principles of movement dictate the best way to perform a given skill.* The laws of stability and motion, along with clearly established physiological principles of exercise, apply to all people regardless of functional level or disability. For example, the principle of stability posits that balance is enhanced when the center of gravity falls within the base of support. This principle should be considered when, for example, students with amputations are asked to perform movement skills in a gym or pool.

■ *Reinforcement and repetition are needed when learning a new skill.* As discussed earlier in this chapter and in other chapters in this book, it is imperative to identify consequences that will increase the likelihood that a response will take place. Although being intrinsically motivated by taking part in an activity is preferred, this is often not the case, especially with students with intellectual disabilities. Thus, it is necessary to find extrinsic reinforcers that are effective and apply them appropriately. In terms of repetition, students with unique needs must have multiple opportunities to perform a given movement skill. Too often, a student will not get enough opportunities to practice, making it unlikely the skill will be established. The teaching situation must allow for plenty of perfect practice (practicing a skill accurately). Practice sessions must be structured so that students have the opportunity not only to repeat a given skill several times but to repeat it in a stimulating, exciting activity in which their attention is focused on the relevant cues.

■ *Emotion affects the process of learning motor skills.* During the learning of a given movement skill, extreme emotion (particularly anxiety, fear, embarrassment, or humiliation) negatively affects the learning process. As mentioned, the teacher of adapted physical education must be aware of the emotional atmosphere of the class and work hard to establish a positive tone conducive to learning. Students might respond differently to the same situation, so the teacher must be aware of each student's individual response. For example, although Miriam doesn't mind one bit when Alex and Stan good-naturedly joke with her about missing the target during a throwing activity, the same comments made to Nick result in a decreased desire to participate and occasionally in physical aggression toward Alex and Stan.

■ *Success at a given task leads to improved learning.* As the adage goes, "Success breeds success." Activities should be chosen and taught such that students will perform them with a high degree of success. To increase the likelihood of success, prompts should be used effectively, and more complicated tasks should be broken down into smaller, more manageable parts. Teachers can also set up tasks that are self-adjusting. For example, students would choose a larger or smaller target depending on their previous success. Remember that reinforcers must be chosen carefully and provided effectively.

■ *Learning takes place more quickly when practice sessions are separated by adequate rest.* Students learn more quickly when their interest is high and fatigue is not an issue. Even a well-designed activity loses its appeal if it goes on too long. Students with intellectual or physical disabilities are often in poor physical condition (Seidl, Reid, & Montgomery, 1987). Thus, keeping instructional sessions short with brief rest breaks and changing activities (even slightly) leads to increased learning. An associated benefit is a reduction in behavior problems because frustration, boredom, and fatigue are minimized.

▪ *Motor skills that are overlearned are retained longer.* Overlearning is the process of repeating a task until its performance is automatic, with no need for conscious effort. Although the point at which a skill becomes automatic varies from student to student, those with intellectual disabilities generally require more repetitions than their peers without disabilities need. An example of an over-learned skill is cycling. Children who ride bikes frequently during their later elementary and middle school years can easily pick up the skill after many years of not riding.

When considering these tenets, note that much of the research presented has been conducted with people who are developing typically, as opposed to those with identifiable disabilities. Although students with unique needs are more similar to their typically developing peers than not and thus it makes sense that these findings apply, additional research with a wider range of subjects with identifiable disabilities will significantly increase the knowledge base.

MEETING INDIVIDUAL DIFFERENCES

A major focus of this text is help the reader address individual differences in a way that leads to significant educational gains for students with unique needs. In the context of this chapter, the word *unique* applies not only to a student's needs but to *all* of the student's attributes. As previously mentioned, teachers must focus on a learner's distinct learning style, strengths, and limitations. Although a thorough understanding of the etiology and characteristics of a given disability (e.g., autism or cerebral palsy) is important—and extensively covered in this text—an excellent understanding of the person standing in the gym is more important still. To borrow a phrase from research, as teachers, our unit of analysis is one—we look at students as individuals first and foremost.

A number of philosophical and practical initiatives in the area of special education inform what and how educators teach students. These approaches are as critical to learning in the gymnasium as they are to learning in the classroom.

Accountable and Accessible Instruction

For all students to reach their academic potential, it is clear that what educators teach and how they teach it must be of the highest quality. To ensure that this is the case, physical educators must not only use state-of-the-art approaches as identified by best practices in the field and empirical research but also carefully assess the progress of their students. As wonderful as the gymnasium might look and as exciting as the activities might be, the proof of an excellent program is whether or not the students are learning meaningful content. To this end, carefully designed assessments must be administered regularly (Friend, 2008). If adequate progress is not being made, the assessments will demonstrate this, and modifications to curricula and the educational approach can be made. Given the range of learners with unique needs taking part in physical education, it is imperative that practitioners develop the skills to identify the appropriate assessments and make the necessary modifications to obtain meaningful information regarding their students' progress (Smith et al., 2008).

Universal Design for Learning

For much of the 20th century, many physical educators have come from the perspective that learners with unique needs require a specialized curricula designed for their unique needs. Educators now posit that most students with unique needs take part in the same curriculum as their typically developing peers, with accommodations and modifications made as necessary (Friend, 2008; Smith et al., 2008). This approach is in accord with the principle of inclusion. As Friend (2008) has noted, if students with unique needs are to be meaningfully integrated into the larger society and not marginalized, it only makes sense that they are exposed to the same core curriculum as their typically developing peers.

Universal design for learning (also referred to as *universal design for instruction*) suggests that instruction should be designed from the start with *all* learners in mind. As opposed to coming up with a tag game that works for most typically developing students and then wondering how the game could be modified for learners with unique needs, universal design would involve designing a game from the beginning that accounts for the unique needs and attributes of all learners. The principles of universal design apply to all facets of education, including architectural considerations, materials and implements, instructional approaches, and assessment. As well as being of practical benefit, the principles of universal design are of ethical and philosophical importance. All learners are equally valued and are considered from the beginning.

Differentiated Instruction

A consistent theme throughout this book is that learners often have a unique set of attributes that must be taken into account when teaching. More specifically, for optimal learning to take place, teachers must differentiate their approach based on the skills and deficits a student presents. Many aspects of the learning process can be modified to enhance instruction (Tomlinson & McTighe, 2006). The skilled educator keeps in mind the learner's abilities and makes changes in the instruction on an individual (that is, differentiated) basis. For example, when Juan comes up to bat in a softball game, his inability to clearly see the pitched ball while standing at the plate makes it tough for him to drive the ball, even though his timing and eye–hand coordination is excellent. It makes sense at this time to use a slightly larger ball with red seams so that Juan can pick it up a little earlier. That's all he needs to be successful in the game. As the year progresses, his ability to see the ball improves to the point where the assistive device isn't required and, therefore, it disappears. As noted earlier, modifications are used only as needed.

Evidence-Based Practices

As discussed earlier in this chapter, it is essential that physical educators teach in a fashion that allows the learner to achieve their potential. To do so, the Individuals with Disabilities Education Act (IDEA) and No Child Left Behind Act encourage the use of evidence-based practice, which means carefully gathering data to help decide what to teach and how that teaching should take place as well as using programs and strategies that have demonstrated effectiveness. Over the past three or four decades, many educational interventions have been proposed that do not have strong support

with regard to their effectiveness. By definition, students with unique needs are at greater risk than the general population, and thus teachers must be thoughtful and rigorous when deciding which approaches they adopt.

Response to Intervention

Because of a need to identify students who may be at educational risk, a framework referred to as *response to intervention* (RTI) has been advocated. Consistent with an emphasis on individualized, evidenced-based instruction, RTI carefully integrates assessment and intervention in such a way that student learning is maximized and behavior problems are minimized from an early age. When appropriately implemented, RTI has the potential to improve the educational experiences and learning of *all* students and to identify at a much earlier point those learners who are at risk for failure. This relatively recent option is in accordance with No Child Left Behind and the 2004 reauthorization of IDEA.

Although much about RTI is appealing for the general physical educator as well as the adapted physical education specialist, a major selling point is the early use of valid and reliable curriculum-based assessments that inform specific interventions. Equally important, the RTI approach requires ongoing monitoring to ensure that teaching is resulting in improvements in the targeted movement skills and that needed interventions are implemented appropriately. This has been referred to by RTI adherents as *continuous progress monitoring*. If adequate progress is not being demonstrated (and the interventions have been carried out appropriately), modifications to either the instructional approach or the goals must be made. These points are, of course, in accord with evidence-based practice, as previously discussed in this chapter.

An ancillary benefit of the RTI model is that, along with a much earlier identification of students at risk, learning deficits will be effectively addressed within a regular education placement—that is, in an integrated classroom setting along with typically developing peers. If there is a need for a more intensive educational approach, often involving a lower student-to-teacher ratio, it is provided within the RTI framework. Generally, needs are addressed within a three-tiered intervention approach (Mellard & Johnson, 2007; Friend, 2008) wherein more intensive and structured interventions are provided based on well-thought-out assessment data. This important component of RTI is outlined in figure 7.3. With respect to physical education, the three-tiered intervention approach would work in the following way:

1. All students in the school would be given valid and reliable movement evaluations. Based on this initial screening, a subset of at-risk students would be identified. These students would receive personalized movement instruction within the regular physical education setting (tier 1), with their progress on deficient areas being monitored weekly for five to eight weeks. If progress is low after this period of research-based instruction, the student will enter tier 2. Between 75 and 85 percent of students are in tier 1.

2. Within tier 2, students receive extensive small-group instruction, along with the instruction previously given within tier 1. This small-group instruction will take place for 10 to 20 weeks with progress being assessed weekly. If progress is strong, the student will once again be provided with tier 1 services, receiving high quality, personalized instruction within the regular physical education setting without the need for small-group intervention. If they are not maintaining an appropriate rate of improvement in tier 1, they will be provided with tier 2 services again.

3. If a student's response to tier 2 intervention is not adequate as demonstrated by a lack of improvement on valid and reliable assessments performed weekly, the student then receives a comprehensive evaluation involving a multidisciplinary team. The result of this evaluation may point to instruction at tier 3. Within tier 3, a more intensive instructional program is put into place, often involving one-to-one interventions outside of the regular education setting in accord with an IEP. In many cases, tier 3 interventions are done in addition to the instruction given within the regular education setting (tier 1).

As pointed out by Winnick (pers. comm., August 20, 2009), these principles may sound familiar to physical educators who have for many years thoughtfully applied a systematic, problem-solving approach to teaching adapted physical education. This approach involves screening to determine if there is a problem, defining and analyzing the problem, developing an intervention plan, and regularly evaluating whether the plan has been effective. What the RTI approach offers is a clear framework to work within.

It is evident from the literature associated with special education that RTI has predominantly addressed academic performance and social

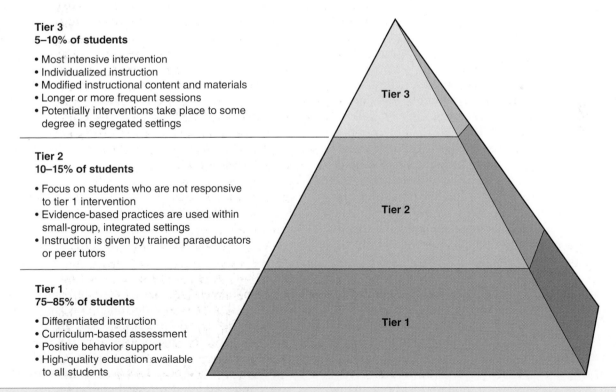

Tier 3
5–10% of students

- Most intensive intervention
- Individualized instruction
- Modified instructional content and materials
- Longer or more frequent sessions
- Potentially interventions take place to some degree in segregated settings

Tier 2
10–15% of students

- Focus on students who are not responsive to tier 1 intervention
- Evidence-based practices are used within small-group, integrated settings
- Instruction is given by trained paraeducators or peer tutors

Tier 1
75–85% of students

- Differentiated instruction
- Curriculum-based assessment
- Positive behavior support
- High-quality education available to all students

FIGURE 7.3 The three-tiered approach of the RTI model.

behavior. However, the principles apply equally to the physical education setting, and physical educators must be familiar with RTI because behavioral intervention plans are involved in physical education. Although to this point RTI has not been emphasized in physical education, the principles and the framework associated with it may be advanced and employed in the development of movement skills as taught within the physical education setting.

Physical educators historically have been involved in universal assessment and screening within the regular physical education setting. The evolving practices associated with RTI, developed to more appropriately meet the needs of students, deserve serious consideration and study on the part of physical educators.

CURRICULAR OPTIONS: WHAT TO TEACH?

Along with a thorough understanding of *how* to effectively teach students with disabilities come the equally important decisions regarding *what* should be taught—that is, decisions on the curriculum. One way to address individual differences, as touched on in chapter 2, is to individualize and formalize objectives and activities.

Given that a significant number of students with disabilities are taught with their typically developing peers in inclusive physical education settings, curricular modifications are often appropriate. Four categories have been suggested that allow for the meaningful integration of students with unique needs. These curricular categories include the same curriculum, multilevel curriculum, modified curriculum, and different curriculum. The *same curriculum* suggests that students with disabilities follow an identical curriculum to that of their typically developing peers, although their objectives might be different from those of the other students. Within the *multilevel curriculum* option, the student with a disability follows the regular physical education curriculum with activity modifications made as necessary (e.g., if a student with Down syndrome is playing a small-sided game of volleyball, she might serve from a distance closer to the net than regulation). Master teachers generally have activity modifications or options available for all students, thus appropriately challenging them at their own developmental level. In this way, everyone in the class is accommodated without anyone being singled out.

A *modified curriculum,* appropriate for some students with more severe disabilities, is used when the regular physical education curriculum is at least partly inappropriate for a student given his unique IEP objectives. However, these IEP objectives can be related to the curricular goals being followed by the rest of the class. For example, Peter, a sixth-grade student with cerebral palsy, is working on the grasp and release of a tennis ball to knock down 3 bowling pins, whereas the other students are rolling plastic bowling balls down a 15-foot (4.6 m) alley to knock down 10 bowling pins. In this example, Peter's unique IEP objective (working on grasp and release) overlaps with bowling, part of the general sixth-grade physical education curriculum. The activity Peter is doing is different but related to what the other students are doing—that is, all students are working on modified bowling tasks.

When the unique physical education needs of a student with an identifiable disability cannot safely and meaningfully be overlapped with the regular physical education curriculum, work on unique IEP objectives might have to take place away from the main physical education activity. In other words, the student might take part in an entirely *different curriculum.* In this case, the student with a disability works on skills unrelated to the curriculum pursued by other students in the class. For example, while classmates are playing small-sided games of ultimate Frisbee, the student with a disability is working on upper-body strength through an individualized weight training program. This is not necessarily an all-or-nothing proposition; alternative activities might be necessary for part of the curriculum but not for others. Block (2007) has suggested that peers without disabilities rotate away from their activities and take part in the alternative activity (e.g., weight training) for a set amount of time. In this way, all students receive the benefit of interacting with all class members while working on meaningful activities. As always, teachers must carefully examine task, environmental, and performer variables when deciding which curricular approach is the most appropriate for a given student at a given time.

A fundamental question related to curriculum concerns whether specific functional, age-appropriate movement skills should be the focus of instruction (a **top-down approach** to teaching) or whether it is more appropriate to follow a developmentally focused curriculum (a **bottom-up approach**). Adapted physical education researchers and practitioners advocating the top-down approach target the movement and recreational skills a person needs to learn in order to independently recreate in the community. The curricular emphasis is on teaching age-appropriate leisure skills valued by the person, her family, and the community at large. The learner's abilities and shortcomings with regard to the skill being taught are carefully examined, and educational experiences are designed to achieve the end result. If a valued leisure skill in Shannon's family is playing two-on-two basketball on the driveway with her dad, mom, and sister, all the subskills needed to play (e.g., dribble, pass, shoot, rebound within a two-on-two game) will be carefully examined in relation to Shannon's demonstrated abilities. If Shannon needs to work on passing the ball accurately with pace at the right time, this skill will be directly taught. Teaching age-appropriate and valued leisure skills in real-world contexts is a hallmark of the top-down approach.

Those who advocate a bottom-up perspective (also called a **developmental approach**) also believe that the ultimate goal of adapted physical education is to prepare students to engage in recreational and sport skills independently. Kelly (1989a) and Graham, Holt-Hale, and Parker (2006) view the bottom-up approach as providing students with a broad foundation of fundamental movement skills during the elementary years. These foundational skills are then combined into games, dance, and athletics during the middle and high school years. Although the focus is on providing instruction in many developmentally appropriate movement skills, if a student is considered at risk, a physical education teacher using the bottom-up approach will intervene earlier rather than later in order to identify the building blocks (neurological, reflexive, or motor) that are lacking and to select activities to remedy the observed shortcomings, thus enabling participation in chronologically and developmentally appropriate movement activities. Moving back to the driveway basketball game, the teacher using a bottom-up approach must be sure that Shannon has mastered the locomotion and object-control abilities important for success in basketball before she plays a two-on-two game.

As is often the case in teaching adapted physical education, an open-minded and eclectic approach is recommended. If the student is very young and the disability (or delay) is minimal, the bottom-up approach might be best. Conversely, if a student has significant physical or intellectual deficits, spending extensive time on the fundamental building blocks likely means the student will not be taking part in meaningful, socially valued activities with typically developing peers. When making decisions about what to teach, always keep in mind individual characteristics and values as well as the unique ecology surrounding the learner.

ACTIVITY MODIFICATIONS

When deciding on the most appropriate curricular approach and activities to meet the student's learning goals, it might become apparent that modifications of activities are necessary if the student is going to participate successfully. There are many strategies on which to base modifications. Lieberman and Houston-Wilson (2009) have suggested that **activity modifications** can be broken down into four categories: equipment, rules, environment, and instruction. The game of softball provides examples of activity modifications for students with various disabilities. If a student has below-average intellectual abilities, the rules might be simplified, whereas for those with visual impairments, the base paths could have a different texture than the field, and the ball and bases might include sound devices. If a student struggles with muscular strength, the bat or ball could be lighter; for students who have decreased coordination or cardiorespiratory fitness, reducing the distance between bases could help; and modified rules for making outs might help players with limited mobility compete at their highest level of ability.

Modifications do not have to affect every component of an activity; they should be limited to those necessary to meet individual needs. Modifications to equipment, rules, or activity parameters must be done cautiously and carefully, keeping in mind the educational experiences of both the students for whom the modifications are being made and their classmates. When modifying an activity, the educator should try to stay as close to the traditional activity as possible. An example of an activity modification for a student with a visual impairment in an archery class is described in the activity modification application.

TEACHING STYLE

"Teaching functions are usually performed within an instructional framework—a delivery system for getting content to the learner. . . . Many factors influence the choice of a teaching strategy, including the content itself, the characteristics of the learner, and the objectives and preferences of the teacher"

APPLICATION EXAMPLE

Activity Modification

Setting: High school physical education class

Student: A 17-year-old who is legally blind with a visual acuity of 2/200

Issue: Modifications for safe and successful inclusion of a student with visual impairment into indoor archery unit

Application: After discussion among the physical education teacher, the student with the visual impairment, and class members, the following policies are instituted:

- ▶ Arrows of the student with visual impairment will be identified with Braille tape by the arrow notch.
- ▶ A special target face will be used on which each scoring area will have a different texture.
- ▶ A raised rope will be used by all students as the shooting line.
- ▶ The archer with visual impairment will use an *L*-shaped wood template to align his feet and the target.
- ▶ A tape recorder will be attached to the back of the target to give auditory direction for the archer.
- ▶ A rope will be attached to the target, and foot templates will be placed on the ground to allow independent movement between the target and the shooting line.
- ▶ No one will go past the shooting line until an audible signal to retrieve arrows is given.
- ▶ Classmates will volunteer to assist with scoring, finding stray arrows, and so on when asked by the student with visual impairment.

(Rink, 2002, p. 177). Regardless of the teaching style and the format of the class, it is imperative that teachers consider the instructional and managerial tone of the physical education class. The tone is independent of both style and format and can range from punitive to positive. Some teachers of adapted physical education would be considered upbeat and excited, whereas others would be best described as relaxed. Some teachers interact frequently with students, and others do so much less. Teachers might be extremely demanding or laidback. Their tone might even vary within and between classes, depending on the context.

Students are exposed to this tone in large- and small-group settings as well as during individual interactions. When describing the tone of the class, terms such as *businesslike, demanding, aloof, warm,* and *caring* are often used. It is, of course, possible to be effective using a businesslike demeanor. It is also possible to be perceived as caring and nurturing and be equally effective. Physical educators working with students with unique needs must ensure that the tone in the classroom is accurately recognized. Furthermore,

they should be aware of the effect—both positive and negative—that tone has on the students. If a particular tone is ineffective for a given student, the teacher should be prepared to modify it. For example, a teacher might accurately perceive himself as nurturing and caring. However, this laidback approach might result in some students being off task because they perceive (mistakenly) that it's okay to goof around because Mr. C doesn't mind. Simply stated, the tone affects student achievement and their desire to spend time in physical education.

As used in this chapter, teaching style refers to how the teacher organizes and delivers instruction to learners. Table 7.1 presents an overview of teaching styles.

There is no one best style; rather, effective instructors adapt their instruction to variables that include personal skills and preferences, the nature of the content, the characteristics of the learners, and the teaching context. In regard to personal skills and preferences, Siedentop and Tannehill (2000) have pointed out that teachers perform better when they are comfortable with and believe

Table 7.1 Teaching Styles

Reproductive styles (teacher-mediated instructional formats)	Productive styles (student-mediated instructional formats)
Command	Guided discovery
Practice or task	Convergent discovery
Reciprocal	Divergent discovery
Self-check	
Inclusion or invitation	

Mosston and Ashworth, 2002.

in the style being used. For example, if they feel pressured to use a more student-directed approach but are not convinced of its efficacy, teaching results will likely suffer. This is not to suggest that teachers should not attempt teaching styles they are less comfortable with, but experimentation in this area should be the result of professional development and reflection, not an administrative directive.

Certain content and objectives are more effectively taught via one teaching style than another. If, for example, a goal is to teach students how to throw a disk using a backhand motion and a forehand motion (the flick), a command style would probably be the most appropriate approach. If, later in the unit, the objective is to decide which motion is most appropriate given the defense being played, a convergent discovery style might be most effective. Clearly, teaching basic movement skills for a given activity is a different proposition than teaching higher-level strategies (Siedentop & Tannehill, 2000). Often, there is not one correct way to solve a movement task. Rather, one movement might be more appropriate than another, depending on the situation. Although a teacher could point out which method would work the best in a given situation, students who learn through active experimentation are potentially more invested in their learning and retain the learning longer. Further, the domain (cognitive, affective, or psychomotor) that emphasizes the goals of the class should be considered. If, for example, students are working together to solve a movement task, a student-directed style, such as cooperative learning, might be more appropriate.

The learner's characteristics are a third consideration, particularly when learners have identifiable disabilities. But teachers should take care not to jump to conclusions. An intellectual disability, for example, is not a sufficient reason to rule out a more student-centered teaching style. However, if behaving appropriately is an issue, where a student struggles with attending to the task at hand,

a teacher-mediated instructional format might be the best approach. Conversely, students who have a physical disability resulting in unique movement patterns might benefit more from a student-mediated instructional format that allows them to discover effective solutions themselves (with support).

Ultimately, when it comes to choosing a teaching style, teacher attributes, comfort level, lesson goals, and learner attributes must be considered. Although it can be challenging to do so, using multiple styles within a given class is frequently the most effective approach. For example, while the majority of the class might be exploring (convergent discovery) how angling a disk alters how it flies through the air, a student with an intellectual disability might be receiving direct instruction (command style) on a backhand throw. As a second example, while most of the class is learning how to serve a tennis ball (command style), one student in a wheelchair, a second with cerebral palsy, and a third whose injured back does not allow a turn of the shoulders might be encouraged to discover unique patterns that allow for fast and accurate serves (divergent discovery). In general, the more severe the intellectual disability, the more direct the teaching style.

The effectiveness of a teaching style ultimately depends on the learner and learning outcomes. Is there a considerable amount of academic learning time? Do students demonstrate a willingness to take part in the activities? Are goals of the unit being met? Ongoing program assessment regarding these questions aids in choosing the best styles of teaching.

CLASS FORMAT

Class format is an important instructional consideration related to teaching style (Block, 2007; Graham et al., 2006). This section presents nine formats that have been effectively used in teaching adapted physical education.

One-to-One Instruction

To promote acquisition, maintenance, and generalization of skills, students receiving adapted physical education sometimes require a 1:1 student-to-teacher ratio. This format allows for a highly individualized teaching session as well as multiple opportunities for the learner to respond. An approach to one-to-one instruction that is extremely successful in teaching students with more severe disabilities is discrete trial teaching (DTT) (Koegel et al., 1982). Later in this chapter, this approach will be presented in considerable depth. In physical education settings, one-to-one instruction can be implemented by the physical education teacher, a trained teaching assistant, a parent, or a trained peer tutor.

Small-Group Instruction

Within a small-group instruction format, 2 to 10 students generally work with one teacher or teaching assistant. This format allows for more independent work and the opportunity to teach students how to interact appropriately with their peers.

Large-Group Instruction

In this format, the entire class participates at the same time under the direction of one or more teachers or teaching assistants. Clearly, it is of great importance to monitor a given student's progress while in a large-group format in order to offer the appropriate amount and type of individualized support.

Mixed-Group Instruction

Within a mixed-group approach, a variety of formats are used during the same class session. This format is particularly effective when students demonstrate different learning characteristics or are working toward different instructional objectives.

Peer Teaching or Tutoring

When peer teaching or tutoring takes place, lower-skilled students are taught by their more highly skilled classmates or by highly skilled students from other classes. A second approach—classwide peer tutoring or reciprocal teaching—uses all students in the class as both tutors and tutees.

Self-Paced Independent Work

As the name of this format suggests, self-paced independent work involves students working on their personal goals mostly by themselves. Often, task cards or input from the teacher or teaching assistant help keep the students focused and on task. In conjunction with task cards, communication boards and visual schedules are particularly effec-

tive for students with autism. These approaches are discussed in more depth in chapter 10.

Cooperative Learning

When students use cooperative learning, subsets of students within a given class work together to accomplish shared goals. This format can be particularly effective when the instructional objectives are affective in nature or target the development of social skills.

Reverse Mainstreaming

In this format, students without disabilities join their peers with unique needs in the self-contained class, taking part in movement activities along with them. Although not a substitute for meaningfully integrating students with unique needs into the regular education setting, reverse mainstreaming does provide opportunities for students with and without unique needs to work together. It is important that students with unique needs interact with their typically developing peers because these interactions provide benefits for everyone.

Teaching Stations (Task Teaching)

Teaching stations allow students to work on more than one task at the same time. Teaching stations are particularly effective when teaching a class of diverse learners at different stages of skill development, because stations can be designed to challenge students at their developmental level. Generally, three or more stations are set up throughout the gym, each focusing on a somewhat different skill or skill set. Students are placed into small groups and assigned to a given station. On the teacher's command, or when students have completed specified activities, students rotate to the next station. Siedentop and Tannehill (2000) have noted that under certain conditions, task teaching might occur without using multiple stations. For example, a single station, such as a climbing wall, could accommodate the class at one time. In this case, small groups might work on a set of related tasks, all occurring on the wall. Climbing stations might include a cargo net, climbing wall, and horizontal bouldering wall.

Stations might involve skills related to each other, such as the tasks involved in playing hockey (e.g., shooting, passing, stick handling, and goaltending). Or, they may involve skills that are unrelated, such as having one station devoted to throwing and catching activities and another to jumping rope.

Stations can be organized in a hierarchical, progressive fashion; as students progress in skill level, they move to a station requiring more ability for the given task. Conversely, the next station might not require any prerequisite skill. Regardless of the progressive or nonprogressive nature of the task setup or whether the tasks are related to each other, each station should accommodate students of varying skill levels by including multiple challenges—that is, opportunities for learning are individualized within stations. If juggling is the task at a station, then there should be an opportunity to juggle one ball, two balls, or scarves. If serving a tennis ball is the task, students should have the opportunity to serve from 8 feet (2.4 m) from the net, the service line, and the baseline. With multiple levels of performance, students have the opportunity to select their own entry level. Well-designed stations provide options for students that relate to skill progressions and physical performance criteria. There are also choices regarding types of implements (e.g., tennis racket versus badminton racket), sizes of targets (both service boxes or just one), and numbers of required repetitions. The students are given choices regarding how and where in the progression they will begin the task. Opportunities to custom design individual stations—that is, offer multiple ways to accomplish a given task—make

this approach particularly useful for learners with disabilities.

To let students know what is expected at a given station, effective teachers often supplement verbal descriptions with simple task cards or posters. These cards or posters might use words, pictures, or a combination of the two. (Of course, the developmental level of students in the class must be considered when designing these cards or posters.) As noted, stations can be designed to challenge students with unique needs at their developmental level, offering progressively more difficult challenges within and between stations. Social skills can also be developed as students help each other at the stations. Figure 7.4 provides an example of a task poster.

DISCRETE TRIAL TEACHING

As noted, when working with students with unique needs, teaching must be structured carefully. Of particular importance are individual interactions with students. This instruction has been called

FIGURE 7.4 Task poster for jumping.

formal individual instruction (Dunn, Morehouse, & Fredericks, 1986), an *instructional episode* (Reid & O'Neill, 1989), and *discrete trial training* (Koegel et al., 1982). This chapter uses the term *discrete trial teaching* (DTT).

The discrete trial is based on principles of learning derived from ABA and, although used most extensively with children who have autism, it is effectively used with a range of students. This approach has been used to teach skills including language skills, social skills, and fundamental movement skills. A discrete trial is a structured method that usually involves teaching in a one-on-one situation. Movement tasks are presented to the student in a series of separate, brief sessions. A particular trial can be repeated several times in a row, several times a day, or for several days until the skill at hand is mastered. An important benefit of a discrete trial is the precision and care with which each trial is conducted without sacrificing the important affective component. Specifically, the components of a discrete trial are, in this order: (1) an instruction or environmental cue, (2) an optional prompt, (3) the student's response, (4) consequences, and (5) an intertrial interval (see table 7.2 for an outline).

Instruction or Environmental Cue

The **instruction** or **environmental cue** is an event a learner responds to. Generally, these events are instructions or requests given by teachers, peers, or parents. However, the event could be an environmental cue, such as the blowing of a whistle or the ringing of a bell. For example, when the physical education teacher blows the whistle twice, what should the student do? Sit down on the carpet square? Return to home base? Teaching responses to both instructions and environmental cues is important.

When giving instructions or setting up environmental cues, the teacher must ensure that the student is paying attention. If the student is not paying attention, the odds of a correct response are extremely low. A simple and effective approach is to precede a request by using the learner's name: "Jim, please roll the ball down the alley."

Especially in the beginning of the teaching–learning sequence, instructions should be simple and clearly stated. If the teacher does not present information in a manner that the learner can understand, confusion results. Thus, care must be taken to use language appropriate to the functional level of the learner, emphasizing clarity. Of course, as a student's skill level increases, the teacher should use more complex instructions. The key is to increase the complexity of the instruction systematically, always keeping in mind the skills of the student. Environmental cues may also be made more complex. Although distractions should be minimized initially, they might be systematically added to the learning environment as a student's abilities increase.

Optional Prompt

After the instruction (or environmental cue) is presented, the teacher might provide a prompt to the learner before the response is made. Although the terms *cue* and *prompt* have been used interchangeably in the literature on special education

Table 7.2 Components of a Discrete Trial

Elements	Characteristics to keep in mind
1. Instructional or environmental cue	Salient, easy to discriminate Appropriate to the task Presented when the student is attending
2. Optional prompt	Presented subsequent to or concurrent with instruction Subsequent to or concurrent with the teacher's consequences Presented with an eye to fading
3. Learner's response	Either correct, incorrect, or no response Must be in response to the instruction or environmental cue
4. Consequences	Applied consistently Applied unambiguously Easy to discriminate
5. Intertrial interval	3-5 seconds

and adapted physical education, for the purposes of this chapter, cues refer to environmental information letting learners know what is expected of them. Prompts, on the other hand, refer to extra information—often verbal, visual, or physical—added to the student's environment to ensure a proper response. Frequently used in special education and adapted physical education to teach a range of skills, prompts are a crucial tool in physical education. Prompts are presented at the same time as or immediately following either instruction or the teacher's consequences. If, for example, during a badminton lesson the instructor said to Robin, "Serve the shuttlecock," this would be a cue. If the instructor followed this cue with further verbal information ("Keep your arm and wrist very loose when you serve"), this would be a verbal prompt. After Robin served, the teacher might show her the proper technique, thus providing a visual prompt.

A prompting system proven effective with many learners is the **system of least prompts** (Lieberman & Houston-Wilson, 2009). In this system, only as much verbal, visual, or physical assistance is given as is necessary for a task to be completed successfully. The objective is skilled **independent performance**. A system of least prompts is particularly effective in systematically reducing assistance when each of the major prompting levels (physical, visual, verbal, and no prompts) is further subdivided. For example, at the level of the physical prompt there are three degrees of physical assistance. This precision allows for the careful withdrawal (i.e., **fading**) of assistance, leading to more autonomous performance on the part of the learner. Following is an example of an effective system of least prompts (after Watkinson & Wall, 1982) in which prompts are broken down into four categories: physical, visual, verbal, and no prompts. At any prompt level, the competent teacher will give more or less assistance to a learner depending on the learner's skill level. Examples of the four levels of prompting are provided here.

■ *Physical prompts.* When using physical prompts, the teacher touches the student. This gives a high degree of physical assistance in which, for example, the teacher holds the student at the wrist as a pendulum swing is used to roll a bowling ball and moves the student's arm through the full range of motion. A reduced level of physical prompting might involve moving the student's arm only during the backswing. A further reduction might involve merely touching the student's wrist and applying slight backward pressure to indicate the direction of the backswing.

■ *Visual prompts.* Visual prompts might involve a complete, sometimes exaggerated, demonstration of the skill in question. In the bowling example, if the skill were rolling the bowling ball from a stationary position, the teacher would demonstrate the complete skill, including the initial body position, backswing, follow-through, and release of the ball. As the learner's skill increased, less visual information would be given; for example, the teacher might demonstrate only the follow-through. Still less visual information might involve just pointing to the student's knees as a reminder to get into a deeper crouch.

■ *Verbal prompts.* Verbal prompts include a sound, word, or instruction to focus the student's attention on the key features of the movements required to complete a skill. As with physical and visual prompts, the physical education teacher might give more or less verbal information, depending on the skill level of the learner. In the bowling example, a high degree of verbal prompting would involve a complete description of how to bowl: "Peter, I want you to bend your knees and then smoothly swing your arm backward and then forward." A reduced level of verbal prompt might involve merely a description of the skill to be performed: "Peter, it's your turn to bowl." A further reduction of verbal prompts would be a more general indication that it's Peter's turn to bowl or a motivating phrase: "Peter, what do you do now?" or "Peter, one, two, three, go!"

■ *No prompts.* At this level, the teacher doesn't use a physical, visual, or verbal prompt to help the student perform the skill; rather, the environment is set up to elicit the skill being worked on. One way of eliciting the skill is to place an object in the environment that indirectly encourages performance of the skill. For instance, the student enters the bowling alley from a direction that brings him alongside the bowling ball rack. This is enough of a prompt to pick up the ball and move to the correct lane. Another example would include the student performing the skill (bowling) after watching a peer perform the same skill.

These prompting categories are not mutually exclusive. Often, verbal prompts are paired with demonstrations or with physical prompts. Similarly, physical and visual prompts can be paired. In any case, the teacher must remember that skilled independent performance is the goal and that assistance should be systematically reduced.

To prompt a student effectively, the following guidelines should be kept in mind.

1. Use prompts that are meaningful to the student. Consider the learner's characteristics (skill level, preferred modality, specific disability). For example, if a student is more receptive to visual prompts than to physical prompts, focus on effectively using visual prompts during the instructional episodes. If a student is deaf or hard of hearing, the emphasis might be on visual or physical prompts.

2. Be careful not to underprompt, because this might lead to frequent errors on the part of the learner.

3. Do not overprompt, because students might become reliant on prompts, thus hindering the development of an independently skilled performance. If assistance is not needed, do not give it.

4. Focus the learner's attention on the task. Some learners attend to the prompt being given instead of the task.

5. Make sure the prompt is effective. Adding an ineffective prompt might delay or block learning.

6. Pretest and assess a student carefully before deciding on prompts—some students might need less assistance than first assumed.

7. Fade physical proximity. The distance between the student and teacher is an important variable involving the effectiveness of a prompt and the independence of the learner. As the student becomes more independent, move progressively farther away.

8. Couple appropriate verbal prompting with other prompts. This way, when the physical or visual prompt is reduced or eliminated, the student still responds to the verbal command.

9. Fade verbal prompts. Although learners should eventually be able to respond only to verbal instructions, true independence means performing activities without even verbal help.

Although an optional component of a discrete trial, the ability to effectively prompt and fade prompts is essential for effective teaching.

Learner's Response

Following the instruction (or environmental cue) is the **learner's response**. The learner must be responding to the instructions or environmental cue. If the learner is responding to something other than the intended instruction or environmental cue, the instruction might have to be reconsidered. Were the instructions too complicated? Was the learner attending to something other than the instructions? Was the environment too distracting? Frequently, more than one person is working with a given student. For this reason, criteria for correct responding should be described in detail and made known to all parties before the trials begin.

Consequences (Positive or Corrective Feedback)

The learner can respond in one of three ways during an instructional episode: correctly, incorrectly, or not at all (that is, no response). In any case, after the student's response, the teacher delivers **consequences**, the type depending on the learner's characteristics and response. Consequences should be based on the learner's behavior and be applied consistently and unambiguously. The learner should be able to easily pick out the consequence (i.e., it should be easily discriminable). When a response was correct (e.g., the ball was thrown accurately), this should be clear to the learner by the consequence that is elicited. Conversely, the learner should also clearly understand when a response is incorrect. Correct responses are reinforced when the learner receives positive reinforcement that she values; that is, the reinforcer should be something the student appreciates, not something the teacher appreciates or feels that the student *should* appreciate. For the reinforcement to be consistent and effective, the criteria for correct response have to be well thought through, understood, and consistently used by everyone working with the student. Lack of consistency severely undermines the teaching. If the learner responds incorrectly, either the response is ignored or corrective feedback is given. Any feedback should give the learner specific information about the performance. In general, punishing consequences should not be employed. Information on effectively applying consequences is presented in chapter 6.

Intertrial Interval

Following the consequences is an **intertrial interval**, a brief (three to five seconds) pause between consecutive instructional episodes. This pause lets the student know that a discrete trial has been completed. It also allows time for the reinforcement (e.g., a hug, a high five, a sticker placed in a book) to take place and for the teacher to write down data, if needed, about the instructional episode.

TASK ANALYSIS

Although people perform many activities of daily living without thinking about them much (they occur almost automatically), in reality they are often quite complex, comprising many subtasks. Whereas students with good cognitive, affective, and movement skills are able to learn incidentally from their daily interactions with the environment, especially when the environment is varied and thoughtfully arranged, students with unique needs often require more systematic and planned learning experiences. When combined with effective prompting and reinforcement, task analysis is a powerful strategy to improve the learning of students with unique needs.

Although task analysis involves the careful examination of the factors or skills involved in the performance of a task, the term *task analysis* can be confusing because authors, researchers, and theorists have used it to describe somewhat different processes. Whereas a traditional task analysis (Dunn & Leitschuh, 2006; Reid & O'Neill, 1989) involves identifying components of an activity and then ordering the components according to their level of difficulty (from easiest to most difficult), Herkowitz (1978) has used the term *developmental task analysis* to examine the variety of task and environmental factors that influence motor performance. Short (2004) used the term *biomechanical task analysis* to refer to the focal points of a continuous task, such as a long jump or overhand throw, and Davis and Burton (1991) coined the term *ecological task analysis* (ETA) to describe a system that, along with recognizing the importance of the task to be completed and the environment, gives equal weighting to the attributes of the learner. The following sections will discuss traditional task analysis, biomechanical task analysis, developmental task analysis, and ETA.

Traditional Task Analysis

A **traditional task analysis** breaks a skill down into its tasks or related subtasks. These tasks are arranged into a sequence from easy to difficult, with short-term outcomes determined for each task

and subtask. An effective approach to traditional task analysis involves separating the main task into several related subtasks (figure 7.5). As mentioned, each subtask has components arranged hierarchically from the easiest to the most difficult. Once all the components of a subtask have been mastered, the learner then moves to the first component of the next subtask. Figure 7.5 provides a task–subtask traditional task analysis for jumping rope.

In writing a traditional task analysis, the teacher must clearly identify the main skill and terminal objective as well as any prerequisite skills. All potential steps (tasks and their associated subtasks) should be described in observable behavioral terms, thus aiding in the development of appropriate IEPs and in the assessment of learning. With regard to IEPs, the specificity provided by the task analysis allows for clarity and thus improved communication between team members (i.e., adapted physical education consultant, general physical education teacher, and paraeducators).

There are many benefits to the traditional task analysis, particularly for students who struggle cognitively. First, there is clear recognition of progress by both student and teacher. With progress on meaningful tasks come avoidance of frustration, reduction in off-task behavior, and maintenance of interest in the task on the part of the teacher and the student. As discussed earlier in this chapter, the maintenance of self-esteem is of considerable importance. The mastery of the components of a given task could help empower students. From a teaching perspective, traditional task analysis allows teachers to see that they have more options than they originally believed, leading to a can-do perspective. Traditional task analysis allows the fading of prompts more quickly, thus increasing independence. Progress can be visually charted, thereby aiding communication with parents and other team members. The charting of progress allows clear observation of educational gains, allowing for sound educational decisions. For example, have inappropriate objectives (e.g., given the amount of time available) been pursued? Is the order of components appropriate? Are more steps needed? Fewer steps? Increased level of prompting?

Although an extremely effective educational tool, especially for students with more severe disabilities, the traditional approach to task analysis has been criticized (Davis & Burton, 1991; Dunn & Leitschuh, 2006; Rich, 2000) because it might overemphasize the task while deemphasizing characteristics of the performer and the environment. The teacher must attend carefully to both

Main task: For Mary to jump rope for a full (overhead) turn four times without verbal cues
Prerequisite skills: Ability to jump, ability to stand erect

    I. Jump over painted line (over and back) once without verbal cue.

        a. Walk line down and back heel to toe with verbal cue.

        b. Face line with toes and jump over once with verbal cue.

        c. Stand parallel with line and jump over and back without verbal cue.

    II. Jump over still rope (over and back) twice without verbal cue.

        a. Face rope with toes, jump over once with verbal cue.

        b. Stand parallel with rope and jump over and back with verbal cue.

        c. Stand parallel with rope and jump over and back twice without verbal cue.

    III. Jump over wiggly (snake) rope (over and back) 2 in. (5 cm) off ground without verbal cue.

        a. Jump over wiggly rope on ground once with verbal cue.

        b. Jump over wiggly rope 1 in. (2.5 cm) off ground over and back with verbal cue.

        c. Jump over wiggly rope 2 in. (5 cm) off ground over and back without verbal cue.

    IV. Jump over half-turned rope without verbal cue four times.

        a. Stand and jump on the back swing twice with verbal cue.

        b. Stand and jump on the forward and back swing twice with verbal cue.

        c. Stand and jump on the forward and back swing four times without verbal cue.

    V. Jump rope a full turn overhead four times without verbal cue.

        a. Stand and jump once as the rope makes a full turn with verbal cue.

        b. Stand and jump twice as the rope makes a full turn with verbal cue.

        c. Stand and jump four times as the rope makes a full turn without verbal cue.

FIGURE 7.5 Traditional task analysis for rope jumping.

the environment and the learners. Although it helps to look at already available task analysis, it is important to come back to the idea of **individualized** teaching. Students will likely differ from one another in terms of the type of breakdown needed, the number of components (and their order) that works best for them, and the most effective manner in which the material is presented. Teachers must look at student strengths, shortcomings, and learning styles, and then be thoughtful and imaginative. The traditional approach to task analysis allows for the aforementioned individualization.

Biomechanical Task Analysis

Biomechanical task analysis has been described by Short (2004) as involving "the biomechanical components or 'focal points' of the task (usually in chronological sequence) so that an 'idealized performance' is described" (p. 59). A biomechanical task analysis for the one-handed backhand stroke in tennis might include the following focal points:

Watches ball throughout the skill.

Moves quickly to ball using proper footwork.

Racket is brought back early in the sequence (early racket preparation).

Body is positioned with hips and shoulders perpendicular to the net.

Weight transfers to front foot at ball contact with rotation of hips and shoulders.

Ball is ahead of hips at contact.

Wrist is firm at contact.

Opposite arm is away from body for balance.

Follow-through is high with hand finishing at or above the shoulder.

Using this analysis, the student would become aware of which aspects of the backhand he has to work on. Assessment and instruction can take place in either a naturalistic environment (while playing or rallying) or in a more controlled, closed environment (the ball being carefully fed to the student).

Although frequently used (and found in many books on adapted physical education and special education), both traditional task analysis and biomechanical task analysis have been criticized for two reasons. According to Davis and colleagues (Balan & Davis, 1993; Davis & Burton, 1991), although traditional task analysis and biomechanical task analysis generally describe the components of the task accurately, they often do not take into account the capabilities (or limitations) of the learner. Second, the traditional approach to task analysis is primarily teacher directed, whereby the teacher specifies how a given skill is to be performed. Taylor, Goodwin, and Groeneveld (2007), Balan and Davis (1993), and others have championed an approach to task analysis (ETA) in which the characteristics of individuals (as well as their choice of movement pattern) has much say with regard to how a given task is accomplished.

Developmental Task Analysis

Herkowitz (1978) has pointed out that a number of task and environmental factors can influence motor performance, and by being aware of these factors, the teacher of adapted physical education may modify them to make the activity easier or more challenging for a student. **Developmental task analysis** has two components: **general task analysis** (GTA) and **specific task analysis** (STA). GTA (table 7.3) outlines all of the task and environmental factors that influence the performance of students in the general movement categories (e.g., throw, strike, jump). Under each of these factors, modifications are given from the most simple to the most difficult.

Once teachers of adapted physical education have a good understanding of how task and environmental factors can influence movement proficiency through GTA, they can develop an STA to look at how specific factors influence movement skill. For example, in regard to throwing, if an instructor decides that it would be beneficial to examine the effect of object size on the learner's performance, the information presented with the STA will be much more precise than information provided by a GTA. Instead of referring generally to ball size (small, medium, large), the instructor precisely manipulates the size (6 in. [15 cm], 8 in. [20 cm], or 12 in. [30 cm]). Clearly, other variables (e.g., weight) may also be manipulated. Through the careful identification and manipulation of important variables, it is possible to break down and sequence tasks that are appropriate for given students regardless of their functional level.

Ecological Task Analysis

Whereas Herkowitz's developmental task analysis attends to important task and environmental factors, **ecological task analysis** (ETA) takes the consideration of interacting factors one step further by carefully examining the learner. An underlying practical and theoretical underpinning of ETA is the belief that "that motor skills, the movement form, and performance outcomes are results of the dynamic interaction (constraints) between the task goal and conditions, the environmental situation, and the capabilities and intent of the performer" (Balan & Davis, 1993, p. 26).

First introduced by Davis and Burton (1991), ETA comes from the tradition of dynamic systems

Table 7.3 Factors for General Task Analysis (Throwing)

	Size of object being thrown	Distance object must be thrown	Weight of object being thrown	Accuracy required	Speed of target	Acceleration or deceleration of target	Direction in which target is moving
Factors simple to complex	Small	Short	Moderately light	None	Stationary	No movement	No movement
							Left to right
	Medium	Medium	Moderately heavy	Little	Slow	Steady speed	Right to left
				Moderate	Moderate	Decelerating	Toward thrower
	Large	Long	Light or heavy	Much	Fast	Accelerating	Away from thrower

Adapted from Herkowitz, 1978.

(Newell, 1986; Thelen & Smith, 1994) and ecological psychology (Gibson, 1977) in which the characteristics of the performer, task, and environment are believed to interact in important ways and must be taken into account when designing movement tasks. As noted, Herkowitz (1978) presented a model where modifications of the environment were paramount. Davis and Burton extended this work by paying particular attention to the learner's characteristics (also referred to as *intrinsic dynamics*) and how these characteristics affect the strategies and skills used to solve a particular movement task. A significant departure from more traditional approaches to adapted physical education, practitioners and researchers who embrace ETA posit that learners benefit significantly by initially manipulating variables and choosing the manner in which they will solve a given task goal. This element of choice and the process of discovery involved is thought to have multiple benefits in terms of learning movement skills, behaving appropriately (Taylor et al., 2007), maintaining on-task behavior, and increasing self-determination. Instead of being given an optimal solution to a given movement problem, the learner is presented with an array of choices within a well-designed, stimulating environment and is given considerable choice as to how she will proceed. For example, for a striking task, balls of various colors, sizes, and textures; bats of various lengths, widths, and weights; and tees or suspended balls are carefully presented to all students. How Pilar knocks down the pins located on the floor is up to her both in terms of the implements used and the movement form chosen.

Davis and Burton (1991) have characterized ETA as a "process of changing relevant dimensions of a functional movement task to gain insight into the dynamics of the movement behavior of the students and to provide teachers with clues for developing strategies" (p. 160). ETA is a less directive, more student-centered approach to teaching movement skills, one that gives over some control to the student in terms of increased choice. As a result, ETA requires considerable ingenuity and creativity on the part of the teacher with regard to organizing an enticing and rewarding environment.

As both a method of assessment and a method of instruction, ETA has four steps (Balan & Davis, 1993):

1. *Identification of the functional movement task goals that are to be accomplished.* These must be meaningful to the students and their families and may be written as behavioral objectives or

goals. Student input regarding the goals can have a tremendous effect on student interest, thereby positively influencing activity levels and behavior. Although more traditional teaching approaches such as the use of verbal instructions and demonstrations may be used, the emphasis of the ETA approach is on providing rich, responsive, and inviting physical and social environments. Within this environment, students are encouraged to practice clearly enunciated movement tasks in a manner of their choosing given their unique abilities. This includes the movement pattern, implement used, and environment (e.g., small group, individual). When structuring the environment, Balan and Davis (1993) have outlined a number of critical considerations. To begin with, the task goal must be clearly enunciated and student participation invited. There must be enough equipment for all students in the class, and it must allow for student choice (e.g., a variety of dimensions and colors). At this time, students practice the goal task, determining which patterns and implements work the best for them. As an illustration, let us assume that the task goal is for an athlete in a wheelchair to put a shot for distance.

2. *Choice.* Choice includes the skill to be accomplished, movement pattern, environment, and implement. During this step, the student practices the skill to be learned and determines which methods work best for the environmental conditions. To continue the shot-put illustration, the athlete is putting the shot while training for a regional high school track and field competition. She is experimenting with seating arrangements (a standard wheelchair, a racing wheelchair, and an individually designed throwing chair), positions from where she will put the shot (putting the shot while facing the target area versus putting the shot with her back to the throwing area), and throwing motions (her arm straight or bent at the elbow upon release). Because the high school meet in which she'll be competing requires all athletes to use an 8.8-pound (4 kg) shot, she is practicing with this specific weight.

3. *Manipulation.* During manipulation, the teacher modifies relevant task variables in order to provide success and challenge (Balan & Davis, 1993). At this point, the teacher alters dimensions of the environment, task, and even on occasion student characteristics. During this stage, as the teacher manipulates task-relevant variables, movement performance is being observed and compared (qualitatively and quantitatively) in order to determine a student's optimal movement pattern. For example,

having observed the athlete's various attempts, the teacher decides that when the athlete uses the standard wheelchair and puts the shot backward using a straight arm, she is most successful.

4. *Instruction.* Direct instruction should be provided after students have had opportunities to understand the task goal, experiment with movement solutions, and choose the movement or skill by which to accomplish the goals. The athlete's coach now gives her direct instruction (based on best teaching and coaching practices) to prepare her for competition.

In the ETA approach, it is important that the environment allows for maximum participation by providing sufficient space, equipment, and movement options. Student choices must be encouraged and affirmed. As noted, before the teacher provides direct instruction, students should be given ample time to explore choices and achieve a certain level of success.

When compared with traditional task analysis and biomechanical task analysis, ETA places greater emphasis on the specific needs and abilities of the student when selecting task goals, movement choices, and ways by which success is determined. ETA encourages teachers to modify and manipulate variables by establishing direct links among the task, the constraints of the performer, and the environment (Burton & Miller, 1998). Finally, ETA provides students with opportunities to explore and discover their abilities.

A schematic for an ETA model for the assessment and instruction of movement tasks is given in figure 7.6, and an example of ETA is provided in table 7.4. Short (2004) has put forward a biomechanical task-analytic model where significant attention is paid to both environmental and individual (student) factors. This hybrid model combines important elements of both the biomechanical and ecological approaches to task analysis. An example of this model is provided in figure 7.7.

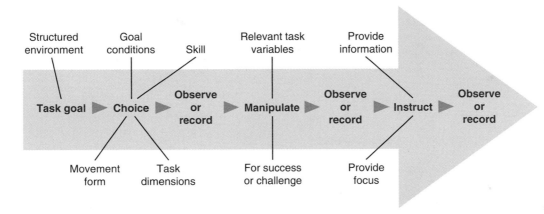

FIGURE 7.6 Schematic for an ETA model for the assessment and instruction of movement tasks.

Reprinted, by permission, from W.E. Davis and A.W. Burton, 1991, "Ecological task analysis: Translating movement theory into practice," *Adapted Physical Activity Quarterly,* 8(2): 154-177.

Table 7.4 **Example of ETA Process: Swimming**

Steps	Application
Selection and presentation of task	Student with a right-arm amputation at the shoulder will independently swim the width of the pool (20 ft [6 m]). Locomotion in water by front float and whip kick, sidestroke, or dolphin kick
Choice	Qualitative criteria for successful completion of the task: efficiency and accuracy of the stroke chosen Quantitative criteria for successful completion of the task: velocity, distance covered, spatial accuracy, and temporal accuracy
Manipulation of relevant variables	Task variables: use of floatation devices, distance to be covered, time constraints in covering the distance, consistency with regard to staying in a given pathway (lane) Environmental variables: water depth, lane width, number of peers present
Instruction	Direct instruction with individualized prompts, reinforcement, and corrective feedback as required

Student's name: _John_   Date of observation: _October 5, 2010_

Observed: ☐ During game ☐ During skills test ☑ During practice

Skill: Forehand stroke in tennis

Performer adjustments necessary? ☐ No ☑ Yes (as indicated next)

☑ Eyes are on the ball throughout the skill.

☑ Moves quickly to the ball using proper footwork.

Self-propels wheelchair; thumb of racket hand is on top of rim or wheel.

☑ Positions body with hips and shoulders perpendicular to the net; knees are bent.

Positions wheelchair at 45-degree angle relative to the net.

☐ Racket is brought back to waist level and parallel with the ground.

Backswing is low to the ground and straight back from rear axle.

☐ Leg drives off rear foot; weight transfers at contact; rotation of hips and shoulders occurs.

Body leans into the shot (toward the net).

☑ Ball is ahead of hips at contact.

Ball is at or slightly ahead of front foot at contact .

☐ Wrist is firm at contact.

☑ Opposite arm is away from body for balance.

Opposite hand is placed on ipsilateral knee or rim for support or balance.

☐ Follow-through is high (hand finishes at or above opposite shoulder).

Environmental factors and modifications:

Court size:	☐ Full court	☑ Half-court	☐ _____
Racket type:	☐ Standard	☑ Junior	☐ Racquetball
	☐ Badminton		
Ball type:	☑ Tennis	☐ Foam	☐ _____
Ball mode:	☐ Hit by opponent	☐ Hit by facilitator	
	☐ Tossed by facilitator	☑ Hit from tee	
_____:	☐ _____	☐ _____	

(Others)

FIGURE 7.7 A biomechanical task analysis that considers the task, the individual, and the environment.

Activity Analysis

Activity analysis is a technique for determining the basic requirements for optimal student success in performing an activity. By breaking an activity into its components, the teacher can better understand the value of a certain activity and modify it to fit a student's needs. Once the needs have been determined, the teacher can use activity analysis to assess whether a given activity can meet these needs.

Activity analysis facilitates the selection of program content based on the teacher's stated objectives. In making the analysis, the teacher must determine the physical, cognitive, social, and administrative requirements for performing the activity. When analyzing an activity from a physi-ological or biomechanical perspective, the teacher should examine such factors as body positions required, body parts used, body actions performed, fundamental movement patterns incorporated, required levels of coordination and fitness, and sensory systems used. Cognitive factors that should be examined include the number and complexity of rules and the need for memorization, concentration, strategies, and perceptual and academic skills. Social factors to consider in activity analysis include the amount and type of interaction and communication required and whether the activity is cooperative or competitive. Such administrative demands as time, equipment, facility needs, and safety factors must also be determined. Table 7.5 shows an activity analysis for table tennis.

Table 7.5 Activity Analysis for Table Tennis

Activity demands	Activity	Table tennis

Physical demands	1. Primary body position required
	2. Movement skills required
	3. Amount of fitness required
	    a. Strength
	    b. Endurance
	    c. Speed
	    d. Flexibility
	    e. Agility
	4. Amount of coordination required
	5. Amount of energy required
		1. Standing
		2. Bending
		3. Minimal fitness level
		    a. Low ability to hold paddle
		    b. Low cardiorespiratory requirements
		    c. Quickness desirable
		    d. Moderate
		    e. High level desirable
		4. Important, especially eye–hand coordination
		5. Little

Social demands	1. Number of participants required 2. Types of interaction 3. Type of communication 4. Type of leadership 5. Competitive or cooperative activity 6. Amount of physical contact required 7. Noise level	1. Two for singles, four for doubles 2. Little; one to one 3. Little verbal; opportunity for nonverbal 4. None 5. Competitive mainly; cooperative if doubles 6. None in singles; much in doubles 7. Minimal
Cognitive demands	1. Complexity of rules 2. Level of strategy 3. Concentration level 4. Academic skills needed 5. Verbal skills needed 6. Directional concepts needed 7. Complexity of scoring system 8. Memory required	1. Moderate 2. Moderate 3. Moderate 4. Ability to count to 21 and to add 5. None 6. All concepts 7. Simple 8. Little
Administrative demands	1. Time required 2. Equipment needed 3. Special facilities required 4. Type of leadership required 5. Safety factors to be considered	1. Can be controlled by score or time 2. Paddles, balls, tables with nets 3. Area large enough to accommodate tables 4. Ability to instruct small group 5. Space between tables

USING SUPPORT SERVICES

To teach physical education skills to students with identifiable disabilities, coteachers, support personnel, aides, volunteers, and peers are needed. The following section outlines their effective use.

Team Teaching

If students with unique needs are in an inclusive physical education class, it is often best for two or more teachers to instruct the class together so that learner differences can be accommodated. This approach, called **team teaching**, is especially important in settings in which educators are not well prepared to work with students who have unique needs. Team teaching is often used in inclusive settings in which teachers of physical education, and perhaps aides, work with children with unique needs to allow them to participate with their peers.

Supportive Teaching

When students with disabilities are included in regular physical education classes, it is often necessary for an aide or a volunteer assistant to help the student. The assistant supports the physical education teacher's efforts to include the child fully in the activity of the regular class and promotes successful participation. The supportive teaching approach is particularly valuable for students just beginning the integration process.

Peer and Cross-Age Tutoring

Peer tutoring involves same-age students helping with instruction. Peer tutors can be used to reduce the student–teacher ratio. Cross-age tutoring programs enlist older students (such as high school juniors or seniors) to work with young children receiving adapted physical education. Cross-age tutoring can provide satisfaction to tutors while increasing the level of learning for students with disabilities. The use of peer-age tutors has become common in inclusive physical education classes. Houston-Wilson, Dunn, van der Mars, & McCubbin (1997) reported that using trained peer tutors to assist students with developmental disabilities resulted in improved motor performance when this technique was used in an integrated setting over 36 days.

PRESCRIPTIVE PLANNING AND INSTRUCTIONAL MODELS

Several curricular models developed since the 1970s have proven successful in providing a quality physical education experience for students with disabilities and have promoted the development of skills needed for inclusion. When used as guidelines, these models can enhance the teaching process and ensure that students with unique needs are taught efficiently and effectively.

■ **Data-Based Gymnasium.** The data-based gymnasium (DBG) is a prescriptive instructional model that provides information on effectively managing the learning environment for students with severe disabilities. The DBG precisely delineates ABA techniques that are effective in accomplishing meaningful learning objectives (see Dunn et al., 1986). The DBG is discussed in other chapters in this book, including chapters 6, 8, and 9.

■ **MOVE.** The Mobility Opportunities Via Education/Experience (MOVE) model is a top-down activity-based curriculum developed to help students with profound disabilities learn the basic motor skills needed for everyday activities in the home and community (e.g., sitting, standing, walking, transferring). MOVE provides a sequence of age-appropriate motor activities valuable to the quest for independence. (For additional information and training locations, contact MOVE International, 1300 17th Street, City Center, Bakersfield, California 93301; phone: 800-397-MOVE; e-mail: move-international@kern.org; Web site: www.move-international.org.)

■ **Moving to Inclusion.** The Active Living Alliance for Canadians with a Disability developed the Moving to Inclusion curriculum, which consists of nine books available in English and French that address a variety of disability groups. These resources are particularly valuable when planning to include students with disabilities in regular physical education classes. (The set is available from the Active Living Alliance for Canadians with a Disability, 720 Belfast Road Suite 104, Ottawa, Ontario K1G 0Z5; phone: 800-771-0663; e-mail: info@ala.ca; Web site: www.ala.ca.)

■ **Special Olympics.** The Special Olympics organization provides a series of sport-specific instructional manuals, each including long-term goals, short-term objectives, skill assessment, task analysis, teaching suggestions, progression charts, and related information. Information is provided about principles of effective coaching, preparing an athlete for competition, nutritional considerations, safety, and risk management. As well, the Motor Activities Training Program (MATP) has been developed for athletes who, because of severe or profound intellectual disability, are unable to take part in official Special Olympics sport competition. The manual for this program provides extensive information regarding the design of individualized training programs that will improve sport skill to the point where the athlete will be able to take participate in the official competitions offered by the Special Olympics. All of the aforementioned information is available at the Special Olympics Web site, www.specialolympics.org.

■ **I CAN.** I CAN (Individualized instruction, Create social leisure competence, Associate all learnings, Narrow the gap between theory and practice) is a comprehensive physical education and leisure skills program for children with unique needs. The program is developmental and provides a continuum of skills from preprimary motor and play skills to sport, leisure, and recreation skills. The achievement-based curriculum (ABC) model (Wessel & Kelly, 1986) is an enhancement of the I CAN curriculum and includes a systematic sequential process that enables teachers to plan, implement, and evaluate instructional programs for students based on selected goals and objectives (Kelly, 1989b; Wessel, 1979).

■ **I CAN Primary Skills K-3.** I CAN Primary Skills K-3 is a physical education curriculum that uses a performance-based instructional model with feedback methods to improve and modify instruction based on student performance from kindergarten through third grade (see Wessel & Zittel, 1998). It includes skill checklists that can be used to collect information for individualizing movement programs.

■ **Smart Start Preschool Movement Curriculum.** This curriculum provides teachers and caregivers with a developmentally appropriate movement curriculum for preschool children of all abilities (see Wessel & Zittel, 1995). Similar to I CAN Primary Skills K-3, Smart Start includes skill checklists that can be used to collect information for individualizing movement programs.

SUMMARY

Many factors affect teaching for physical education and sport. Educators who can thoughtfully and imaginatively use many approaches and match them to the needs of learners are likely to have success. Master educators are always accountable and differentiate their instruction in order to effectively reach all of their students. Keeping in mind principles of universal design, they teach meaningful content in ways that make sense for their students, thus allowing them to more fully adapt their teaching to meet individual needs.

In this chapter, the two major approaches to instruction in adapted physical education and sport—humanism and ABA—were presented. Both approaches inform teaching in a valuable, and often compatible, fashion. Important principles of motor learning that apply to students with unique needs were also discussed. The majority of the chapter examined how to meet the challenge of individual differences in learners. Curricular options, activity modifications, teaching styles, and class formats were discussed, along with several powerful educational tools, such as discrete trial teaching, task analysis, and activity analysis. Also discussed was the importance of using support services, especially with increased teacher–student ratios and a diverse student body. Finally, selected prescriptive planning and instructional models were suggested. Familiarity with these excellent resources helps optimize the learning of students with unique needs.

REFERENCES

Active Living Alliance for Canadians with a Disability. (1994). *Moving to inclusion.* Gloucester, ON: Author.

Alberto, P. & Troutman, A. (2008). *Applied behavior analysis for teachers* (8th ed.). New Jersey: Prentice Hall.

Balan, C.M., & Davis, W.E. (1993). Ecological task analysis approach to instruction in physical education. *Journal of Physical Education, Recreation and Dance, 64* (9), 54-61.

Block, M. (2007). *A teacher's guide to including students with disabilities in general physical education* (3rd ed.). Baltimore: Paul H. Brookes.

Burton, A., & Miller, D.E. (1998). *Movement skill assessment.* Champaign, IL: Human Kinetics.

Carr, E.G., Horner, R.H., Turnbull, A.P., Marquis, J.G., McLaughlin, D.M., McAtee, M.L., Smith, C.E., Ryan,

K.A., Ruef, M.B., Doolabh, A., & Braddock, D. (1999). *Positive behavior support for people with developmental disabilities: A research synthesis.* Washington, DC: American Association on Mental Retardation.

Davis, W. & Burton, A.W. (1991). Ecological task analysis: Translating movement behavior theory into practice. *Adapted Physical Activity, 8,* 154-177.

Dunn, J.M. (1997). *Special physical education: Adapted, individualized, developmental.* Madison, WI: Brown & Benchmark.

Dunn, J.M., & Leitschuh, C.A. (2006). *Special physical education* (8th ed.). Dubuque, IA: Kendall/Hunt.

Dunn, J.M., Morehouse, J.W., & Fredericks, H.D. (1986). *Physical education for the severely handicapped: A systematic approach to a data based gymnasium.* Austin, TX: Pro-ed.

Friend, M. (2008). *Special education: Contemporary perspectives for school professionals* (2nd ed.). Boston: Allyn & Bacon.

Gibson, J.J. (1977). The theory of affordances. In R. Shaw & J. Bransford (Eds.), *Perceiving, Acting, and Knowing: Toward an Ecological Psychology* (pp. 67-82). Hillsdale, NJ: Lawrence Erlbaum.

Graham, G., Holt-Hale, S., & Parker, M. (2006). *Children moving: A reflective approach to teaching physical education* (7th ed.). Boston: McGraw-Hill.

Herkowitz, J. (1978). Developmental task analysis: The design of movement experiences and evaluation of motor development status. In M. Ridenour (Ed.), *Motor development: Issues and applications* (pp. 139-164). Princeton, NJ: Princeton Book Co.

Houston-Wilson, C., Dunn, J.M., van der Mars, H., & McCubbin, J.A. (1997). The effect of peer tutors on motor performance in integrated physical education classes. *Adapted Physical Education Quarterly, 14* (4), 298-313.

Kelly, L.E. (1989a). Instructional time: The overlooked factor in PE curriculum development. *Journal of Physical Education, Recreation & Dance, 60* (6), 29-32.

Kelly, L.E. (1989b). *Project I CAN-ABC.* Charlottesville, VA: University of Virginia.

Koegel, R.L., Russo, D.C., Rincover, A., & Schreibman, L. (1982). *Assessing and training teachers.* In R.L. Koegel, A. Rincover, & A.L. Egel (Eds.), *Educating and understanding autistic children* (pp. 178-202). San Diego: College-Hill Press.

Langendorfer, S. (1985). Label motor patterns, not kids: The developmental perspective for adapted physical education. *Physical Educator, 42* (4), 175-179.

Lieberman, L.J., & Houston-Wilson, C. (2009). *Strategies for inclusion: A handbook for physical educators* (2nd ed.). Champaign, IL: Human Kinetics.

Maslow, A. (1987). *Motivation and personality.* New York: Harper Collins.

Mellard, D. & Johnson, E. (2007). RTI: *A practitioners guide to implementing response to intervention.* Thousand Oaks, Ca: Corwin Press.

Mosston, M., & Ashworth, S. (2002). *Teaching physical education* (5th ed.). San Francisco, CA: Benjamin-Cummings.

Newell, K.M. (1986). Constraints on the development of coordination. In M.G. Wade & H.T. Whiting (Eds.), *Motor development in children: Aspects of coordination and control* (pp. 341-360). Dordrecht, Netherlands: Nijhoff.

Reid, G., & O'Neill, K. (1989). *Adapted aquatics: Promoting aquatic opportunities for all.* Ottawa, Ontario: Canadian Red Cross Society.

Rich, S.M. (2000). *Instructional strategies for adapted physical education.* In J.P. Winnick (Ed.), Adapted physical education and sport (pp. 75-91). Champaign, IL: Human Kinetics.

Rink, J. (2002). *Teaching physical education for learning* (4th ed.). New York: McGraw-Hill.

Rogers, C.R. (1980). *A way of being.* Boston: Houghton Mifflin.

Rogers, C. R. & Stevens, B. (1967). *Person to person: The problem of being human: A new trend in psychology.* Walnut Creek, CA: Real People Press.

Safran, S.P., & Oswald, K. (2003). Positive behavior supports: Can schools reshape disciplinary practices? *Exceptional Children, 69,* 361-373.

Seidl, C., Reid, G., & Montgomery, D.L. (1987). A critique of cardiovascular fitness testing with mentally retarded persons. *Adapted Physical Activity, 4* (2), 106-116.

Sherrill, C. (2004). *Adapted physical activity, recreation and sport: Crossdisciplinary and lifespan* (5th ed.). Boston: WCB/McGraw-Hill.

Short, F. (2004). *Measurement, assessment and program evaluation.* In J.P. Winnick (Ed.), Adapted physical education and sport (pp. 55-76). Champaign, IL: Human Kinetics.

Siedentop, D., & Tannehill, D. (2000). *Developing teaching skills in physical education* (4th ed.). Mountain View, CA: Mayfield.

Skinner, B.F (1980). *About behaviorism.* New York: Alfred A. Knopf.

Smith, T., Polloway, E., Patton, J., & Dowdy, C. (2008). *Teaching students with special needs in inclusive settings* (5th ed.). Toronto: Pearson Education Canada.

Stormont, M., Lewis, T., Beckner, R., & Johnson, N. (2008). *Implementing positive behavior support systems in early childhood and elementary settings.* Thousand Oaks, CA: Corwin Press.

Taylor, J., Goodwin, D.L., & Groeneveld H. (2007). *Providing decision-making opportunities for learners with disabilities*. In W.E. Davis & G.D. Broadhead (Eds.), *Ecological task analysis and movement* (pp. 197-218). Champaign, IL: Human Kinetics.

Thelen, E., & Smith, L. (1994). *A dynamic systems approach to the development of cognition and action*. Cambridge, MA: MIT Press.

Tomlinson, C.A., & McTighe, J. (2006). *Integrating differentiated instruction and instruction by design: Connecting content and kids*. Alexandria, VA: Association for Supervision and Curriculum Development.

Watkinson, E.J., & Wall, A.E. (1982). *PREP: Play skill manual*. Ottawa: CAHPER.

Wessel, J.A. (1979). *I CAN—Sport, leisure and recreation skills*. Northbrook, IL: Hubbard.

Wessel, J.A., & Kelly, L.E. (1986). *Achievement-based curriculum development in physical education*. Philadelphia: Lea & Febiger.

Wessel, J.A., & Zittel, L.L. (1995). *Smart Start: Preschool movement curriculum designed for children of all abilities*. Austin, TX: Pro-Ed.

Wessel, J.A., & Zittel, L.L. (1998). *I CAN primary skills K-3*. Austin, TX: Pro-Ed.

WRITTEN RESOURCES

Please refer to the last section of this chapter (on page 144) for prescriptive planning and instructional models for developing curricula.

Gallahue, D.L., & Donnelly, F.C. (2005). *Developmental physical education for today's children* (4th ed.). Champaign, IL: Human Kinetics.

This source examines the developmental process from the prenatal period through age 12, including a discussion of psychomotor, cognitive, and affective factors influencing the motor development of children. Also described are teaching behaviors and styles that promote effective teaching of students with special needs. A helpful resource in working with children who have developmental delays.

Graham, G., Holt/Hale, S., & Parker, M. (2006). *Children moving: A reflective approach to teaching physical education* (6th ed.). Mountain View, CA: Mayfield.

This comprehensive text on teaching elementary physical education outlines a reflective approach to teaching children. The developmental perspective presented applies to both typically developing children and those with unique needs.

ELECTRONIC RESOURCES

Adapt-talk, a subdivision of PE-Talk and sponsored by Sport-Time International.

Provides an opportunity to discuss adapted physical education challenges with peers and professionals worldwide via e-mail. To subscribe to this service, send an e-mail (type "subscribe" in message) to adapt-talk-digestrequest@lists2.sportime.com.

PE Central: http://pecentral.org.

PE Central is a frequently used online resource for regular physical educators and for teachers who work with students with unique needs. It includes curricular and lesson planning ideas and teaching suggestions.

part two

Individuals With Unique Needs

The first section of this part includes 10 chapters that relate to individuals with disabilities who are specially categorized in accordance with the Individuals with Disabilities Education Act (IDEA). These chapters are followed by a chapter discussing children with unique physical education needs who have not been classified as disabled by IDEA.

The disabilities discussed in the first 10 chapters include intellectual disabilities (chapter 8); behavioral disabilities (chapter 9); autism spectrum disorders (chapter 10); specific learning disabilities (chapter 11); visual impairments (chapter 12); hard of hearing, deafness, or deafblindness (chapter 13); cerebral palsy, traumatic brain injury, and stroke (chapter 14); amputations, dwarfism, and les autres (chapter 15); spinal cord disabilities (chapter 16); and other health-impaired conditions (chapter 17). These chapters examine the etiology of these conditions and the characteristics of affected groups. Particular attention is given in each chapter to implications for physical education, and sport programs associated with disabilities are presented. These chapters are critical for giving service providers the background and understanding they need about the individuals with unique needs they are preparing to serve.

chapter 8

Intellectual Disabilities

Patricia L. Fegan

Loretta Claiborne was born with visual impairments, clubbed feet, and intellectual disabilities in the projects of York, Pennsylvania. After several surgeries to enable vision and correct her clubbed feet, she finally walked at the age of four and talked at the age of seven. Forbidden to participate in school sports because she was in special education, Loretta ran to get away from the bullies. At the age of 18, she became a Special Olympics athlete. Twenty-five years later, in 1996, Loretta received the prestigious Arthur Ashe Courage Award at the ESPN Espy Awards. In 1999, Disney aired a made-for-TV movie about her life, and she appeared on the *Oprah Winfrey Show.*

Along the way, Loretta completed three Boston Marathons, placing among the top 100 of all women each time. In 1988 she finished in the top 25 women in the Pittsburgh Marathon and was named Special Olympics Female Athlete of the Year. In 1991, Loretta was named to the Special Olympics board of directors and was selected by *Runner's World* magazine as the Special Olympics Athlete of the Quarter Century. The following year she was inducted into the York, Pennsylvania, Sports Hall of Fame and the William Penn High School Alumni Hall of Fame—the same high school that barred her from the track team because she had intellectual disabilities.

Loretta introduced then–U.S. president Bill Clinton at the 1995 Special Olympics World Summer Games opening ceremonies in New Haven, Connecticut, and received an honorary doctorate of humane letters from Quinnipiac College in Hamden, Connecticut, becoming the first person with intellectual disabilities to receive an honorary doctorate. The Loretta Claiborne building in York, Pennsylvania, was dedicated in 2001. In 2003, she was awarded a second doctorate of human letters by Villanova University in Pennsylvania. Currently, her uplifting life story is chronicled in the text, *In Her Stride*, a feature title in the WorldScapes literacy series for grades 3 through 6.

One of Loretta's most memorable races was a marathon in Harrisburg, Pennsylvania. Running strong, Loretta noticed another runner beginning to falter. Loretta slowed her pace and stayed with the man throughout the race, encouraging him on; they crossed the finish line together. The other runner? Former world heavyweight boxing champion Larry Holmes! Now a black belt in karate, Loretta still runs and also competes in Special Olympics bowling, figure skating, basketball, golf, soccer, skiing, softball, and swimming.

Intellectual disability is currently in transition regarding terminology, definition, and treatment methods. This chapter presents current trends in definition, classification, and teaching techniques. As appropriate, the term *intellectual disabilities* is used. However, the term *mental retardation* is also used, sometimes interchangeably with *intellectual disability*, because much of the previous literature and best practices have used this term. Additionally, the term *mental retardation* is used by the Individuals with Disabilities Education Act (IDEA) and other groups.

DEFINITION, CLASSIFICATION, AND INCIDENCE

Although there are several definitions and classification systems based on various criteria (e.g., medical condition, IQ score, needed supports), this chapter uses the 2010 definition and classification system developed by the American Association of Intellectual and Developmental Disabilities (AAIDD), which changed its name from the American Association on Mental Retardation (AAMR) in 2007.

Definition

People with intellectual disabilities have diverse abilities and potential, and educators must be prepared to accept this diversity. Intellectual disabilities present a substantial disadvantage to people attempting to function in society. They are characterized by cognitive limitations as well as functional limitations in such areas as daily living skills, social skills, and communication. Over the years, the AAIDD definition of and criteria for classification of intellectual disabilities have changed dramatically, affecting the incidence of intellectual disabilities.

To define the disability of mental retardation, IDEA uses the American Association on Mental Deficiency definition of mental retardation (Grossman, 1973) and adds a phrase on how it affects educational performance: "Mental retardation means significantly subaverage general intellectual functioning, existing concurrently with deficits in adaptive behavior and manifested during the developmental period, that adversely affects a child's educational performance" (IDEA, 2004). This definition doesn't differ much from the 2010 AAIDD definition of intellectual disability, which states, "Intellectual disability is characterized by significant limitations both in intellectual functioning and in adaptive behavior as expressed in conceptual, social, and practical adaptive skills. The disability originates before age 18" (Schalock et al., 2010, p. 13).

Thus, three criteria must be met in order for someone to have mental retardation. The first, significant limitations in intellectual functioning, refers to a person scoring two or more standard deviations below the mean on a standardized intelligence test that is normed on the general population, including people with and without disabilities. Two intelligence tests used extensively throughout the world are the Stanford-Binet V and the Wechsler Intelligence Scale for Children (WISC-III).

The second criterion, significant limitations in adaptive behavior as expressed in conceptual, social, and practical adaptive skills, refers to a person scoring two or more standard deviations below the mean on a standardized assessment measuring the collection of skills a person learns in order to function in everyday life:

Conceptual skills include language, reading and writing, money concepts, and self-direction.

Social skills include interpersonal skills, responsibility, self-esteem, naïveté, obeying of rules and laws, and avoidance of victimization.

Practical skills include activities of daily living, occupational skills, and maintenance of safe environments.

Limitations in adaptive behavior affect performance in daily life and the ability to respond to changes in daily life and the environment.

The third criterion is that the disability originates before the age of 18. Conception through age 18 is considered the developmental stage and is the phase of the life cycle prior to adulthood. It is during this time that various developmental processes are being achieved. Adverse influences occurring during this time of brain growth and development may negatively affect these developmental processes. However, as long as the potential for continued growth exists (until about age 18), compensatory actions may occur to counteract these adverse influences and improve the ultimate structure and function of the brain. Thus, a person with normal intellectual functioning who sustains a brain injury or trauma after age 18 (adulthood), rendering deficiencies in both intellectual and adaptive behavior, is not considered to have an intellectual disability.

Classification and Description

Many systems exist for classifying intellectual disabilities: intelligence quotient (IQ), intensity of needed supports, behavioral systems, and etiological systems. The International Classification of Diseases (ICD) of the World Health Organization (WHO, 2001) and the American Psychiatric Association's *Diagnostic and Statistical Manual of Mental Disorders, Fourth Edition* (*DSM IV*) (APA, 2000) use intelligence test scores to determine the severity of intellectual disabilities (table 8.1).

Although classification systems are necessary for service reimbursement, research parameters, service provision, and communication about selected characteristics, they also stigmatize people by assigning labels that tend to trigger behavioral expectations and negative emotional reactions by others. Labels are also erroneously used as a global summary about people with intellectual disabilities when in reality they reflect little information about the individual and thus have little application when developing support needs based on individual strengths and limitations.

The 2010 AAIDD classification system is multidimensional. It is based on five dimensions of human functioning and the patterns and intensity of supports that enable individuals to participate in home and community life along with medical and behavioral support needs (Schalock et al.,

2010). **Supports** are the resources and strategies that promote the development, education, interests, and well-being of a person and enhance individual functioning. Thus, once the diagnosis of intellectual disability has been made, an assessment in each of the five dimensions influencing human functioning is made. These five dimensions include

1. intellectual ability;
2. adaptive behavior;
3. health (includes physical, mental, and positive health and etiology practices);
4. participation (refers to roles and interactions in the areas of home living, work, education, leisure, and spiritual and cultural activities); and
5. context (the interrelated conditions within which people live their everyday lives).

Lastly, AAIDD's Supports Intensity Scale (Thompson et al., 2004) provides normative data on support needs in 49 life activities grouped into six components as well as a supplemental Protection and Advocacy Scale. These six subscales include

1. home living,
2. community living,
3. lifelong learning,
4. employment,
5. healthy and safety, and
6. social.

The percentile measures and standard scores derived from the Supports Intensity Scale are also used for AAIDD's multidimensional classification system. This shift from a one-dimensional IQ-based classification system to a multidimensional one incorporating patterns and intensity of support needs reflects the shift in focus from students with deficits to students with extraordinary support needs to successful functioning in physical education and the general curriculum.

This chapter uses AAMR's 1992 intensity of support needs when describing students with intellectual disabilities. There are four support intensities:

- **Intermittent supports** are episodic and short term; most are provided on an as-needed basis. These are usually supports required during a job loss, medical emergency, or other life crisis.
- **Limited supports** are more consistent over time but are still time limited. They require few staff members and minimal cost, such as

Table 8.1 Classification of Mental Retardation Based on IQ Scores

Mental retardation level	Intelligence test score
Mild mental retardation	IQ 50-55 to 70-75
Moderate mental retardation	IQ 35-40 to 50-55
Severe mental retardation	IQ 20-25 to 35-40
Profound mental retardation	IQ below 20-25

time-limited employment training or transition support from school to adulthood.

- **Extensive supports** are not time limited and are characterized by regular (daily) involvement in some (though usually not all) environments. Examples are long-term home-living support, ongoing special education classes, and employment in special centers.

- **Pervasive supports** are constant, highly intense, and potentially life sustaining; they are provided across all environments. Pervasive supports involve several people, significant costs, and significant intrusiveness in the person's life.

There are instances in this chapter, however, when classification by IQ level is used because it was the classification system used in the reported research.

Incidence

According to normal probability theory, it is estimated that 2.28 percent of the total population (with no known organic dysfunction) of any society has intellectual disabilities (2.15 percent plus .13 percent equals 2.28 percent). It is also estimated that .76 percent of the total population has known organic dysfunction that causes intellectual disabilities. These figures (2.28 percent plus .76 percent rounded to 3.0 percent) are used to estimate the incidence of people with intellectual disabilities in a particular geographic area (figure 8.1). The actual

number of children and adults with intellectual disabilities receiving services through the educational system or governmental services systems is often much less than 3 percent of the population. This is because most people with intellectual disabilities do not need special services and thus are not on any lists identifying them. For example, during the 2005-2006 school year, states reported serving 556,000 students with intellectual disabilities, or 1.1 percent of the total student enrollment (National Center for Education Statistics [NCES], 2007).

CAUSES OF INTELLECTUAL DISABILITIES

Disorders causing intellectual disabilities are generally categorized according to when in the gestation they occur—prenatally, perinatally, or postnatally. Prenatally, there are more than 750 genetic disorders associated with intellectual disabilities that fall into three types of genetic disorders: single-gene disorders, chromosomal disorders, and multifactorial inheritance (inheritance of genetic and nongenetic factors), each of which is thought to contribute a small amount toward intellectual disability (Harris, 2006). Prenatal environmental factors such as malnutrition, drugs, toxins, and maternal diseases also may cause intellectual disabilities. Perinatal causes of intellectual disabilities include placental insufficiency, abnormal labor and delivery, obstetrical trauma, neonatal seizures, infections, head trauma at birth, metabolic disor-

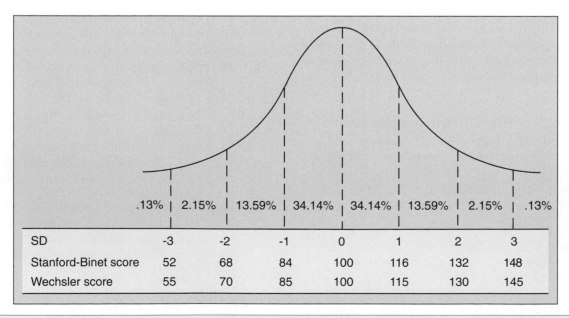

SD	-3	-2	-1	0	1	2	3
Stanford-Binet score	52	68	84	100	116	132	148
Wechsler score	55	70	85	100	115	130	145

.13% | 2.15% | 13.59% | 34.14% | 34.14% | 13.59% | 2.15% | .13%

FIGURE 8.1 The normal curve and IQ scores.

ders, and nutritional disorders. Traumatic head injuries, infections, degenerative disorders, seizure disorders, toxic metabolic disorders, malnutrition, and environment deprivation are postnatal cases of intellectual disabilities (Luckasson et al., 1992).

The most prevalent known cause of intellectual disabilities is **fetal alcohol spectrum disorders** (as much as 1 in 250 births), in some studies accounting for up to half of all people with intellectual disabilities (Centers for Disease Control and Prevention [CDC], 2005). Sophisticated genetic mapping research has determined that **X-linked disorders** are the most prevalent inherited disorders leading to intellectual disabilities. Fragile X syndrome (FXS) is caused by excessive repetitions of three DNA nucleotides on the long arm of the X chromosome, one of the pair of chromosomes that determines gender. About 1 in 129 women and 1 in 800 men are carriers. Carriers often develop fragile X–associated tremor ataxia syndrome (FXTAS) later in life. Full blown FXS affects 1 in 3,600 boys, causing autism spectrum disorders in about one-third of them (Hagerman, 2007). This means that FXS is the most common known cause of autism as well as the most common inherited cause of intellectual disabilities. Seizures, anxiety disorders, and ADHD are also prevalent. Although FXS occurs just as frequently in girls, they tend to be less severely affected by it (Beckett, Yu, & Long, 2005). Other well-known X-linked disorders are Duchenne muscular dystrophy and hemophilia.

COGNITIVE DEVELOPMENT

The 2010 AAIDD definition of intellectual disabilities is functionally and contextually oriented. Although this orientation is useful in determining individual strengths and limitations in present functioning, it is limited for understanding the dynamic nature of intellectual functioning and how it changes from age to age in the developmental process. Such a developmental orientation toward intelligence promotes effective instruction and programming.

To establish developmental orientation, it is necessary to draw on the extensive work of Piaget (1952), who proposed that children move through four stages of cognitive development: the **sensorimotor stage**, the **preoperational stage**, the stage of **concrete operations**, and the stage of **formal operations**. These stages are depicted in table 8.2.

Sensorimotor Stage: Ages 0 to 2

During the sensorimotor stage, children develop, use, and modify their first schemata. For Piaget, schemata are forms of knowing that develop, change, expand, and adapt. A schema might be a simple response to a stimulus, an overt action, a means to an end, an end in itself, an internalized thought process, or a combination of overt actions and internalized thought processes. Examples of schemata include tossing a ball, grasping, and sucking. During the sensorimotor stage, for example, a child develops the schema of grasping, which is internally controlled and can be used in grasping the mother's finger, picking up various objects, or picking up an object from various angles. A schema often functions in combination or in sequence with other schemata, such as when a child throws a ball, an action that combines the schemata of grasping and releasing.

To a great extent, the sensorimotor stage is when a child learns about the self and the environment through the sense modalities. A great deal of attention is given to physically manipulating and acting on objects and observing the effects of such actions. The child is stimulated by objects in the environment and observes how objects react

Table 8.2 Stages of Cognitive and Play Development

Age range (years)	Cognitive developmental stage	Type of play	Play group
0-2	Sensorimotor	Practice play and ritualization	Individual
2-7	Preoperational	Symbolic	Egocentrism and parallel play
3			Reciprocal play (progressive reciprocity in dyads, triads, and the like)
7-11	Concrete operations	Games with rules	Larger group play
11-adulthood	Formal operations		

to actions applied to them. Through exploration, manipulation, and problem solving, children gain information about the properties of objects, such as texture, size, weight, and resiliency, as they drop, thrust, pull, push, bend, twist, punch, squeeze, or lift objects that have various properties. At this stage, children's functioning is largely sensorimotor, with only rudimentary ability to manipulate reality through symbolic thinking. Children functioning at the sensorimotor stage prefer solitary play and benefit from activities that allow them to explore ways to move their body and manipulate objects.

Preoperational Stage: Ages 2 to 7

The preoperational stage includes the preconceptual substage, which lasts to about the age of 4, and the substage of intuitive thought, which spans the ages of 4 to 7. Toward the end of the sensorimotor stage, the child begins to develop the ability to symbolically represent actions before acting them out. However, the symbolic representation is primitive and limited to schemata associated with one's own actions. During the preoperational stage, progress occurs as the child becomes able to represent objects through language and use language in thinking. The child can now think about objects and activities and manipulate them verbally and symbolically. Children are egocentric and unable to view situations from others' perspectives. Children functioning at the early preoperational stage prefer parallel and associative play and enjoy activities that employ rhythms, dance, and make-believe experiences. Language games can help stimulate language development at this stage. Rhythmic dance and low-organization games facilitate cooperative play at the later preoperational stage.

Concrete Operations Stage: Ages 7 to 11

During the stage of concrete operations, children achieve operational thought, which enables them to develop mental representations of the physical world and manipulate these representations in their minds (operations). The fact that operations are limited to those of action, to the concrete, or to those that depend on perception distinguishes this stage from the stage of formal operations. The fact that the child is able to develop and manipulate mental representations of the physical world distinguishes this stage from earlier stages. In the stage of concrete operations, the child is able to

mentally carry through a logical idea. The physical actions that predominated in earlier stages can now be internalized and manipulated as mental actions.

During the concrete operations stage, increased sophistication is present in the use of language and other signs. In the preoperational phase, the child developed word definitions without full understanding of what the words meant. In the stage of concrete operations, language becomes a vehicle for the thinking process as well as a tool for verbal exchange. In this stage, children can analyze situations from perspectives other than their own. This decentering permits thinking to become more logical and the conception of the environment to be more coherently organized. During this stage, children's thinking becomes more consistent, stabilized, and organized. Although children are able to perform the more complex operations just described, they are generally incapable of sustaining them when they cease to manipulate objects or when the operations are not tied to physical actions. Children functioning at this stage of development enjoy lead-up sports and individual and dual activities such as dodgeball, kickball, tag, Simon Says, hide and seek, and so on.

Formal Operations Stage: Age 11 to Adulthood

Children functioning at the stage of formal operations are not confined to concrete objects and events in their operations. They are able to think in terms of the hypothetical and use abstractions to solve problems. They enter the world of ideas and can rely on pure symbolism instead of operating solely from physical reality. They are able to consider all of the possible ways a problem can be solved and to understand the effects of a variable on a problem. Children at this stage can isolate the elements of a problem and systematically explore possible solutions. Whereas children at the stage of concrete operations tend to deal largely with the present, those functioning at the formal operations stage are concerned with the future, the remote, and the hypothetical. They can establish assumptions and hypotheses, test hypotheses, and formulate principles, theories, and laws. They can not only think but also think about what they are thinking and why they are thinking it. During this stage, children are able to use systems of formal logic in their thinking. At this, the last stage of development, they are able to understand and execute complex game strategies of team sport and create movement sequences that interpret a theme, feeling, or event.

Piaget and Play

Piaget called behaviors related to play **ludic behaviors**, which are engaged in to amuse or excite oneself. He held that behaviors become play when they are repeated for functional pleasure. Activities pursued for functional pleasure appear early in the sensorimotor stage. According to Piaget, the most primitive type of play is practice play or exercise play. The child repeats clearly acquired skills (schemata) for the pleasure and joy of it. The infant repeats a movement, such as shaking a rattle over and over, and exhibits pleasure in doing so. This type of play does not include symbolism or make-believe.

Later in the sensorimotor stage, the play in which the child engages is called **ritualization**. More and more schemata are developed and used in new situations. Play becomes a happy display of mastered activities; gestures are repeated and combined as a ritual, and the child makes a motor game of them. As progress is made, the child forms still newer combinations from modified schemata. For example, a child might follow the ritual of sleeping after being exposed to the stimuli associated with sleeping (e.g., pillow, blanket, thumb sucking). Toward the end of the sensorimotor stage, children develop symbolic schemata and mental associations. These symbolic schemata enable them to begin to pretend in play. Some authors refer to symbolic play as *make-believe play*. Throughout the sensorimotor stage, play is individual or egocentric, and there are no rules involved.

The preconceptual stage within the preoperational stage marks the transition from practice play to symbolic play. At the preconceptual stage, play extends beyond the child's own actions. Also, new ludic behaviors appear that enable children to pretend. At ages 4 through 7 (the intuitive thought stage), an advance in symbolic play occurs. The child relates a story in the correct order, is capable of a more exact and accurate imitation of reality, and uses collective symbolism (i.e., other people are considered during play). The child not only begins to play with one or more companions but also continues to display parallel play. In play, the child can think in terms of others, and social rules begin to replace individual ludic symbols. For example, games of tag and games related to the hiding of a moving object are now played. Although play is egocentric, opportunities for free, unstructured, and spontaneous play are important. Children at this level are not positively responsive to intuitive thought. Advancement occurs from egocentricity to reciprocity in play. Thus, opportunities

for cooperative play become appropriate. The collective symbolism associated with cooperative play is at its beginning in this stage. Guessing games, games based on looking for missing objects, games of make-believe, and spontaneous games are stimulating for children during this stage. Responding to tag games, for example, indicates that children are beginning to play with others and to consider others during play.

At the stage of concrete operations, there is an increase in games with rules. Rules might be handed down, as in cultural games, or developed spontaneously. An expansion of socialization and a consolidation of social rules occur. Thus, the playing and construction of group games with rules becomes attractive to children. As the child enters and moves through this stage, play becomes less concerned with make-believe and more concerned with so-called real games. At this stage, play might be structured, social, and bound by rules. Although some children might be ready for such games by age 7, children with intellectual disabilities might not be ready for them until after adolescence, if then.

Application of Cognitive Development to Teaching

Many teaching implications are associated with cognitive theory. Because of space considerations, only a few examples are presented here. First, because language is more abstract than concrete, teachers need to reduce verbalization of instructions and emphasize tactile, kinesthetic, visual, and other more concrete forms of instruction. Children who cannot readily transfer learning or apply past experiences to new situations need more gradual task progressions in smaller sequential steps and need to learn and practice skills in the environments in which they are used. It is also important to consider level of cognitive development in teaching rules and game strategies. As cognition develops, more complex rules and strategies can be introduced.

Knowing the type of play and play groups associated with developmental stages can influence successful participation in games (table 8.2). Individuals at developmental age of 6 or earlier respond with greater enthusiasm for make-believe games played in small groups. Also, language development should be considered in verbalization. For example, it is often helpful to emphasize action words and simple sentences rather than multiple complex sentences when communicating instructions. Demonstrations and physical assistance will facilitate the instructional process. Feedback on the quality of performance should be short and specific. Cognitive theory also serves as a basis for some of the organizational and instructional methods suggested later in the chapter.

CHARACTERISTICS OF PEOPLE WITH INTELLECTUAL DISABILITIES

Intellectual disabilities are multidimensional in that they affect all aspects of a person's life. Following are characteristics typically manifested in people with intellectual disabilities.

Capacity and Rate of Learning

The area in which people with intellectual disabilities differ most from others is in cognitive behavior. The greater the degree of intellectual disability, the lower the cognitive level at which the person functions. Other characteristics affecting learning are a limited ability to generalize information, short attention span, and inability to understand abstract concepts.

Although the learning process and stages of learning are the same for both, children with intellectual disabilities learn at a slower rate than children without intellectual disabilities and thus achieve less academically. The learning rate of children with intellectual disabilities needing intermittent or limited support is usually 40 to 70 percent of the learning rate of children without intellectual disabilities. They may be limited to simpler forms of formal operations, may not be able to progress beyond the level of concrete operations, or may be incapable of surpassing the preoperational substage. Children needing extensive or pervasive support often function at the sensorimotor cognitive stage and may not benefit from traditional schooling. Although self-contained classes and separate schools for children needing extensive or pervasive support exist in most school systems, the primary educational objectives for these children involve mastery of basic life skills and communication skills needed for their care. Adults needing extensive supports might learn to dress, feed, and care for their own hygiene and might even benefit from work activities, but they will most likely need close supervision and care throughout their lives.

Social and Emotional Responses

Although children with intellectual disabilities exhibit the same ranges of social behavior and emotion as other children, they more frequently demonstrate inappropriate responses to social and emotional situations. Because they have difficulty generalizing information or learning from past experiences at the same rate or capacity as children without intellectual disabilities, they are likely to be unprepared to handle all the situations they encounter. Children with intellectual disabilities often do not fully understand what is expected of them, and they might respond inappropriately because they have misinterpreted the situation rather than because they lack appropriate responses.

Educational programs for children with intellectual disabilities should always include experiences to help them determine social behaviors and emotional responses for everyday situations. Personal acceptance and development of healthy social relationships are critical to independence. The reason most people who need intermittent or limited support lose jobs is inadequacy of social skills, such as poor work habits, and an inability to get along with coworkers. On the other hand, when they develop basic social and emotional skills, they are happier and more accepting—and they are a joy to teach in physical activity settings.

Physical and Motor Development

Children with intellectual disabilities differ least from children without intellectual disabilities in their physical and motor characteristics. Although most children with intellectual disabilities display developmental motor delays, they are often related more to limited attention and comprehension than to physiological or motor-control deficits.

Generally, the greater the intellectual disability, the greater the delay in attaining major developmental milestones. As a group, children with intellectual disabilities walk and talk later, are slightly shorter, and usually are more susceptible to physical problems and illnesses compared with other children. In comparative studies, children with intellectual disabilities consistently score lower than children without intellectual disabilities on measures of strength, endurance, agility, balance, running speed, flexibility, and reaction time.

Although many students with intellectual disabilities can successfully compete with their peers without intellectual disabilities, those students needing extensive or pervasive support have a discrepancy equivalent to four or more years behind their peers without intellectual disabilities on tests of physical fitness and motor performance.

The fitness and motor performance of children without intellectual disabilities usually exceeds that of children with intellectual disabilities needing intermittent or limited support, who in turn perform better than children needing extensive or pervasive supports (Gillespie, 2003; MacDonncha et al., 1999; Pitetti, Millar, & Fernhall, 2000). The performance of boys generally exceeds that of girls, with the differences between the genders increasing as the intensity of needed supports increases (Eichstaedt et al., 1991; Londeree & Johnson, 1974). Flexibility and balance seem to be the exceptions. Whereas girls without intellectual disabilities show greater flexibility and balance than boys without intellectual disabilities, boys with intellectual disabilities show greater flexibility and balance than girls with intellectual disabilities. Also, children with Down syndrome exhibit more flexibility than other children with intellectual disabilities (Eichstaedt et al., 1991; Rarick, Dobbins, & Broadhead, 1976; Rarick & McQuillan, 1977). Children with Down syndrome tend to have hypotonic musculature and hypermobility of the joints, which permits them greater than normal flexibility, and, because of weak ligaments and muscles, places them at greater risk of injury.

Winnick and Short (1999a) recommend that children aged 10 to 17 with intellectual disabilities needing intermittent or limited support should achieve levels of aerobic capacity, body composition, flexibility, abdominal strength, upper-body strength, and endurance (necessary for positive health, independent living, and participation in physical activities) approaching the performance levels of their peers without disabilities. Winnick and Short (1999b) also offer activity guidelines for developing these functional and physiological fitness levels in children with intellectual and other disabilities.

Many children with intellectual disabilities are hypotonic and overweight. Nutritional guidance and fitness activities might be necessary to enable a student to perform at a higher level of skill. Disproportionate bodies pose many problems with body mechanics and balance. Activities done on uneven surfaces or requiring rapid change of direction can cause anxiety and pose greater risk of injury and failure. Body alignment may be in a total body slump. Club hands and clubfeet, postural deviations, and cerebral palsy are all prevalent among children with intellectual disabilities, and physical educators must consider these factors when planning each child's program (figure 8.2). Intellectual disabilities often coexist with other disabilities, and the number of coexisting conditions increases with increased severity of intellectual disabilities (Harris, 2006; Murphy et al., 1998), as shown in table 8.3.

Photo courtesy of Special Olympics Maryland.

FIGURE 8.2 Many children with intellectual disabilities have other disabilities as well.

Table 8.3 Coexistence of Intellectual Disabilities With Other Disabilities

Coexisting disability	With mild intellectual disabilities	With severe intellectual disabilities
Autism	9%	20%
Epilepsy	3%-18%	30%-50%
Cerebral palsy	6%-8%	30%-60%
Sensory deficits	10%	17%

DOWN SYNDROME

Down syndrome is the most recognizable genetic condition associated with intellectual disabilities. Because of its prevalence and unique sport and physical education implications, it will be discussed at length here. One in 733 children is born with Down syndrome (National Down Syndrome Society, 2010a). In the United States, about 5,000 such children are born each year. Although fathers are genetically responsible for the abnormality in about 25 percent of all cases, women over the age of 35 present the highest risk (1 in 300) of having a child with Down syndrome. At age 40 the risk increases to 1 in 110 births, and at age 45 the risk is 1 in 35 births (National Down Syndrome Society, 2010b).

Causes

Down syndrome results from one of three chromosomal abnormalities. The most common cause is trisomy 21, so named because of the presence of an extra number 21 chromosome. This results in a total of 47 chromosomes instead of the normal 46 (23 chromosomes received from each parent). A second cause of Down syndrome is nondisjunction, which occurs when one pair of chromosomes fails to divide during meiotic cell division, resulting in 24 chromosomes in one haploid cell and 22 in the other. A third and rare cause of Down syndrome is translocation, which occurs when two chromosomes grow together; they appear to be one chromosome but contain the genetic material of two chromosomes.

Characteristics

Although over 80 clinical characteristics are associated with Down syndrome, the most common physical characteristics are the following:

- Short stature with short legs and arms in relation to torso
- Poor muscle tone
- Flattened facial features
- Eyes slanted upward and outward
- Unusually shaped ears
- Mild to moderate obesity
- Underdeveloped respiratory and cardiovascular systems
- Broad hands and feet with short fingers and toes and a single crease in the palm of the hand

- Poor balance
- Perceptual difficulties
- Poor vision and hearing loss

Many of these characteristics can be seen in figure 8.3.

Many people with Down syndrome also have medical problems. Almost half develop congenital heart disease (Harris, 2006). They are 10 to 15 times more likely to develop leukemia and 62 times more likely to develop pneumonia. Bowel defects requiring surgery and respiratory infections are common (Eunice Kennedy Shriver National Institute of Child Health and Human Development, 2006). People with Down syndrome age more rapidly, and, although estimates vary, 25 percent of people with Down syndrome over age 40 have Alzheimer's disease (Alverez, 2008). This incidence increases with age.

In the United States, a shocking racial disparity exists in the median life spans of people with Down syndrome (Yang, Rasmussen, & Friedman, 2002). A 15-year study of 34,000 people with Down syndrome revealed that the median age at death

FIGURE 8.3 Special Olympics athlete with Down syndrome.

Photo courtesy of Special Olympics Maryland.

for Caucasians with Down syndrome is 50 years, whereas it is 25 years for African Americans and 11 years for people of other races. People with Down syndrome are becoming increasingly integrated into society and its institutions, including schools, health care systems, community living, and the workforce. Although some degree of slow development and learning difficulties is always associated with Down syndrome, attainment and functional ability is much higher than previously thought possible (when people with Down syndrome attended only institutions and segregated schools).

Physical Education Programming

The many medical problems of children with Down syndrome require medical clearance for activity participation and careful planning of the physical education program. Aerobic activities and activities requiring maximal muscular contraction must be adapted and carefully monitored. Muscle hypotonia (low muscle tone) and hypermobility (above-normal mobility) of the joints often cause postural and orthopedic impairments, such as lordosis, ptosis, dislocated hips, kyphosis, atlantoaxial instability, flat pronated feet, and forward head. Exercises and activities that cause hyperflexion are contraindicated because they put undue stress on the body that could result in hernias, dislocations, strains, or sprains. Rather, exercises and activities that strengthen muscles around the joints, thereby stabilizing them, should be encouraged. Poor eyesight and hearing in children with Down syndrome require teachers to employ adapted equipment and teaching strategies typical for those with sensory impairments.

ASSESSMENT

Assessment is necessary to determine the status and needs of students with intellectual disabilities. Children with intellectual disabilities who need only intermittent or limited support can often take the same tests as children without intellectual disabilities. In some instances standardized tests might require modification, or standardized tests designed specifically for students with intellectual disabilities might need to be used. Children with intellectual disabilities needing intermittent or limited support should also be able to complete methods of assessment used with the general student population. However, children needing extensive or pervasive support often lack the physical fitness, motor ability, motivation, and understanding required to perform standardized test items. Winnick and Short (1999a) recommend using task analysis or other measures of physical activity as an alternative to standardized tests to measure the physical fitness of those with such support needs. Pedometers are being used more often to measure involvement in physical activity. Alternative assessments incorporating teacher-developed rubrics, analytic rating scales, and checklists are also appropriate to measure the physical abilities of this population.

Three tests developed specifically for use with students with intellectual disabilities are recommended: the Brockport Physical Fitness Test (BPFT) (Winnick & Short, 1999a), designed to measure health-related physical fitness in students with mild limitations; the Ohio State University Scale of Intra-Gross Motor Assessment (OSU-SIGMA) (Loovis & Ersing, 1979), designed to measure motor development; and the Special Olympics coaching guides (2008a), designed to measure gross motor development and motor and sport skills. Additional information on testing appears in chapter 4.

ORGANIZATIONAL METHODS

Certain organizational methods have proven particularly successful in aiding the learning of students with intellectual disabilities and enabling them to be included in activities. These methods ensure successful positive experiences for students with intellectual disabilities in a physical education class where maximum participation takes place in a controlled environment.

Learning Stations

Learning stations divide the gymnasium or play area into smaller units, each of which is designed for students to learn or practice a specific skill or sport. Students may be assigned to a single learning station for the entire activity period or might rotate from station to station after a set amount of time or after a learning goal has been achieved. In an obstacle course, students usually perform one repetition at each station with a goal of completing all the stations in the shortest amount of time. Learning stations permit flexibility, allow students to progress at their own pace, and provide safe and successful learning experiences for all students, with and without intellectual disabilities. Stations might focus on a theme (e.g., walk in the woods, physical fitness, dance, tennis, motor skills) and promote full integration while accommodating large numbers of students.

Differentiated Instruction

Teaching one lesson to the entire class while meeting the individual needs of each student is an exciting teaching approach called **differentiated instruction**, or multilevel instruction. This approach encourages inclusion of all students because it allows for diverse learning styles and ability among students. The goals and content are the same for all students, but the teacher employs a variety of teaching and presentation techniques such that all students in the class are able to gain varying degrees of knowledge and skill based on their individual abilities. Student practice is also differentiated, allowing for variations in student learning styles, cognitive ability, and motor limitations. Individualized adaptations to the environment, materials, equipment, and rules according to each student's skill level are encouraged. Evaluation of student mastery of skill or knowledge is also differentiated according to individual needs and abilities.

Peer Instruction and Cross-Age Tutoring

One of the most exciting developments in teaching is the use of peers (other students with or without disabilities) to help children with unique needs. It is common for young children to rely on slightly older peers as role models. Cross-age tutoring is an excellent way of providing children with intellectual disabilities role models whom they can imitate. Peer instruction and cross-age tutoring increase personalized instruction time for students with intellectual disabilities.

Community-Based Instruction

Teaching skills in the environment where the skills will ultimately be used is preferable to artificial environments such as the classroom or gym. Students with intellectual disabilities who need extensive or pervasive support do not generalize well from one environment to another, and teaching skills in school environments often entails reteaching the same skills in community

environments. Thus, it is much more efficient to teach skills in environments where they will be used. One of the critical steps in teaching skills in natural environments is identifying and prioritizing environments in which the skills will actually be used. For example, teaching students to access and use community health club facilities, bowling facilities, or pools is preferred to teaching these activities in school gyms or pools. This top-down approach to teaching starts with the end result (bowling at the local bowling center) and works backward to identify all the cognitive, social, physical, and environmental components that need to be taught. This would include, for example, getting to the bowling center, paying for and obtaining the required shoes and bowling ball, bowling 10 frames according to the rules and keeping score, following bowling etiquette, returning the shoes and bowling ball at the conclusion of the game, and getting home. Each of these components may be task analyzed and used for initial assessment, the basis of instruction, and final assessment. The top-down approach to teaching can and should be applied to all sports (Block, 2007).

Partial Participation

If a student with intellectual disabilities can acquire some of the skills needed to participate in an activity, the parts of the skills that cannot be performed can be compensated for through physical assistance, adaptations of equipment, or rule changes. Often, peer tutors can provide physical assistance, and modified equipment and rule changes can allow students to participate in an inclusive setting. For example, a student with cerebral palsy who uses a motorized wheelchair can be assigned a specially lined area of the soccer field. If the soccer ball enters this lined area, the peer tutor stops the ball. The student then has five seconds to maneuver his wheelchair to touch the ball. If the student is successful, the peer tutor then kicks the ball to a member of the student's team. If the student is unsuccessful, the peer tutor then kicks the ball to a member of the opposing team.

INSTRUCTIONAL METHODS

How information is presented to students with intellectual disabilities often makes the difference between success and failure. In general, learning is enhanced if it is fun, ensures success, and keeps the student active. Because students with intellectual disabilities need more time and opportunities to learn new skills, good teachers plan an active class and provide many opportunities for students to practice targeted skills. They will also carefully select teaching methods to match the student's level of cognitive development. The following instructional strategies have proven successful for students with intellectual disabilities.

Concrete and Multisensory Experiences

Because children with intellectual disabilities are slower in cognitive development, their mental operations might be confined to concrete objects and events. Thus, concrete tasks and information are more easily learned and used than their abstract counterparts. Instruction should be concrete, emphasizing only the most important task cues. Because verbalization is more abstract, demonstration or modeling, physical prompting, or manipulation of body parts should accompany verbal instruction. It is vital that demonstrations and modeling are correct so that students do not copy incorrect ways of performing. Verbal instructions and cues should be short (no longer than 30 seconds) and focus on action words; for instance, instead of saying, "Go," say "Run," "Walk," or "Hop."

Data-Based Teaching

Data-based instruction involves monitoring a student's progress and how such factors as environmental arrangement, equipment, task analysis, time of day, levels of reinforcement, and cueing techniques affect progress. By charting student progress, the teacher and student can often determine when an objective will be accomplished (e.g., complete two laps around the track). Cooperative charting by teacher and student can provide the motivation and direction to help a student estimate how long it will take to accomplish any new task, set personal objectives to accomplish a task within a reasonable margin of error, and identify practice techniques for reaching the objectives.

Ecological Task Analysis

Because children with intellectual disabilities are generally unable to attend to as many task cues or pieces of information as children without intellectual disabilities, instructors should break skills down into sequential tasks—either chronologically or from simple to complex components—when

working with children with intellectual disabilities. This ecological task analysis (ETA) must also account for the child's limitations (e.g., intellectual disability, limited range of motion) as well as any environmental factors (e.g., size of ball, speed of ball, length of bat, distance to target) that may influence performance of the task or skill. Planned programs discussed later in the chapter employ task analysis. The tasks selected, the number and variety of choices the learner has, the opportunity to explore and manipulate environmental variables, and the teaching methods selected are all important components of ETA.

Behavior Management

Applying behavior management principles such as cueing, reinforcing, and correcting are critical to the success of task analyzing skills and teaching all the smaller behaviors that enable a student to learn and perform the skill. Behavioral principles must be systematically employed and coordinated. Behaviors to be influenced must be pinpointed and systems designed to promote change in the identified behaviors. Substantial evidence indicates that the shorter the time lapse between student performance and feedback, the more learning is facilitated, especially for people with intellectual disabilities who need extensive or pervasive supports.

Move From Familiar to Unfamiliar

Because students with intellectual disabilities have difficulty applying past experience and previously learned information to new though similar tasks, they are more likely to view each new task as a novel one. Thus, the progression from familiar to unfamiliar must occur gradually and be strongly reinforced. Teachers should begin to teach well within the range of student skill and comprehension. Tasks should be divided into small, meaningful steps; presented and learned sequentially; and rehearsed in total with as little change in order as possible. A word of caution, though: Children with intellectual disabilities often have short attention spans, and although progression to new tasks should be gradual, teachers should plan many activities to keep the student's attention. For example, if the lesson is practicing the fundamental motor skill of hopping, the teacher might need to plan several separate hopping activities in a 20-minute lesson. The use of music and make-believe often improve attention span and involvement. Also, music may be used as a reward when a student achieves an objective or goal.

Consistency and Predictability

Consistency of teacher behavior helps establish and maintain a sound working relationship between teacher and students. When students know what to expect, they can plan their behaviors knowing what the consequences will be. Children with intellectual disabilities are often less flexible in accepting or adapting to new routines. Thus, day-to-day consistency in class structure, teacher behavior, and expectations help promote learning. Teacher behavior should be kind but firm, patient, and always positive when reinforcing desired behaviors and providing feedback on the execution of a skill.

Choice Making

Activities for children with intellectual disabilities are often provided without considering individual preferences. Choice making allows students with little control of their body and environment to have some control of their activity program. It can consist of allowing students to choose which activity they want to play, which ball they prefer, how they would like to be positioned, who they would like to assist them, when they need to stop and rest, and so on. Giving students choices sometimes makes the difference in whether they truly engage in an activity or just go through the motions, and it stimulates language development in students with minimal verbal skills. It is also a key feature of ETA.

Activity Modifications

When challenging skills are modified as necessary, students with intellectual disabilities can often participate successfully in physical education and sport alongside peers without disabilities. This is particularly true for children with intellectual disabilities who have associated health or physical impairments or who need extensive or pervasive supports. Among other ways, activities are often modified by

- substituting fundamental motor skills and patterns for more highly developed sport skills;
- allowing students to sit, hold on to a bar, or hold a peer's hand for support;

- substituting softer, lighter, or slower balls for striking and catching;
- substituting larger balls for kicking and striking;
- substituting shorter, lighter, or broader striking implements;
- substituting stationary or suspended balls for moving balls;
- enlarging the target or goal area;
- reducing the number of players;
- narrowing and shortening the field of play;
- creating safety zones or special zones within the field of play;
- reducing the speed of skill execution or the force required to execute a skill; and
- reducing the distance required for skill execution or lengthening the distance for other students (Block, 2007).

ACTIVITIES

When selecting activities for students with intellectual disabilities, physical educators should be aware of the games, activities, and sports enjoyed by children in the community. These activities are good choices for the physical education class and are consistent with the current emphasis on universal design for learning. Cooperative programming with local recreation agencies can promote successful inclusion of students with intellectual disabilities into structured community-based play groups. Activities should be fun yet challenging to the student with intellectual disabilities. Activities are not fun when they are beyond the understanding and skill of the participants. Music and make-believe help stimulate interest and involvement in games when working with young children.

Activities According to Chronological Age

Instructors should base the activities and skills they teach on a student's chronological age and on activities that the student's peers enjoy. However, students' functional abilities and cognitive development must be considered when determining what teaching methods to employ and how to present skills and activities. Teaching chronologically age-appropriate skills and functional skills frequently used by all students in natural, domestic, vocational, community, and recreational environments minimizes the stigmatizing discrepancies between students with and without disabilities. Conversely, selecting activities based on mental age often involves keeping students needing extensive or pervasive supports at the lower end of the developmental continuum, working on prerequisite skills that are often nonfunctional and unlikely to be used in daily living or in community recreation and sport programs. For example, Duck, Duck, Goose is not an activity for high school students. Rhythm and dance, lifelong sport skills, and fitness activities are age appropriate and can be used in community programs. A particular need of people with intellectual disabilities is to develop the motor skills and physical fitness levels required for optimal vocational training and use of leisure time.

Activities for Students Needing Intermittent or Limited Supports

Teachers should select activities that stimulate language development and problem-solving skills for young students with intellectual disabilities needing intermittent or limited supports. Fun activities that involve make-believe, singing, dancing, and verbalization (e.g., Simon Says or Busy Bee) can help keep their attention and stimulate and reinforce cognitive development. Verbal rehearsal of cues and prompts also stimulates language development. Older students with intellectual disabilities needing intermittent or limited supports often excel in sport; in fact, sport might be their primary avenue for success and self-esteem. They are more likely to be included in physical education classes than in any other subject. Their physical and motor needs are generally similar to those of students without intellectual disabilities, so their physical education activities can often be the same or similar.

Although students needing intermittent or limited supports often excel in physical education and sport, most of them generally do not achieve high skill levels. Still, basketball, soccer, hockey, baseball, and dancing are often popular among adolescents needing intermittent or limited supports, even though concepts of team play, strategy, and rules can be difficult for them to learn. Highly skilled students with intellectual disabilities can learn strategy and rules through concrete teaching strategies. Skill and sport activities such as those fostered by Special Olympics are enjoyable

for students with intellectual disabilities needing intermittent or limited supports.

Activities for Students Needing Extensive or Pervasive Supports

Students needing extensive or pervasive supports have not traditionally been placed into inclusive public school classes but rather into special classes, schools, or institutions. However, more and more of these students are functioning successfully in inclusive classroom settings, particularly when appropriate support systems are in place. Their level of intellectual and motor functioning is basic. Their activity is generally characterized by little student interaction (i.e., parallel play), with most interactions occurring between teacher and student. Children needing extensive or pervasive supports generally need an educational program that includes sensorimotor skills, fundamental skills, movement patterns, and physical and motor fitness development (see the application example).

Sensorimotor programs involve stimulation of the senses so that sensory channels are developed enough to receive information from the environment. Functional senses then permit the child to respond to the environment through movement and manipulation. In these programs, children are taught the normal infant motor progression of head control, crawling, grasping, releasing, sitting, creeping, and standing. Many students with these needs do not walk before age 9, and many never become ambulatory. Children needing pervasive supports might not readily respond to their environment and might exhibit little or none of the curiosity that would motivate them to explore the environment and learn. Even the most rudimentary skills must be taught. Through partial participation and activity modification, many students needing extensive supports can participate in physical education classes alongside peers without disabilities. Many of them enjoy and can benefit from participating in Special Olympics lower-ability sporting events or the Special Olympics Motor Activities Training Program (MATP).

A program with particular relevance for students needing extensive or pervasive supports is the data-based gymnasium (DBG) (Dunn, Morehouse, and Fredericks, 1986), which offers a behaviorally oriented instructional model for teaching students with extensive and pervasive support needs as well as a system for analyzing behavioral principles for

APPLICATION EXAMPLE

Inclusion of Student With Intellectual Disabilities Needing Extensive Supports

Setting: Secondary physical education class

Student: A 14-year-old student with intellectual disabilities who uses a motorized wheelchair and needs pervasive supports

Unit: Basketball

Issue: How to include the student in the basketball game in a meaningful way for both the student and the other basketball players

Application: After consultation with the adapted physical education specialist, the physical educator uses partial participation with peer assistance as follows:

▶ A special area of the basketball court is marked off for use by the student and peer tutor.

▶ If the basketball enters this area, the peer tutor stops the ball. The student has five seconds to maneuver his wheelchair to touch the ball (any challenging task can be used).

▶ If the student is successful, the peer tutor then throws the ball to a member of the student's team. If the student is unsuccessful, the peer tutor throws the ball to a member of the opposing team.

The following suggestions would also work:

▶ Within the special area, set up a target (smaller basket, box, trash can, or the like) and a throwing line that is a challenging distance from the target.

▶ If the basketball enters the special area, the peer tutor stops the ball. The student has 10 seconds to move his wheelchair to the spot where the ball entered the area and then to the throwing line, where he propels either the basketball or a smaller, lighter ball at the target.

▶ If the student hits the target, his team scores a basket. If the student misses the target, the peer tutor throws the ball to a member of the opposing team who is standing underneath the basket.

the socialization of behaviors. Finally, the DBG includes a game, exercise, and leisure sport curriculum. Skills within the curriculum are broken down into tasks and steps sequenced as phases representing shaping behaviors. Students are reinforced for successfully completing tasks that approximate the targeted behavior. The DBG includes a clipboard instructional and management system that helps to identify present status, objectives, and progress on skill development. Although the original text on the DBG is no longer in print, many of the materials and ideas are incorporated in a text by Dunn and Leitschuh (2006).

Mobility Opportunities Via Education/Experience, or MOVE (Move International, 2008), is a top-down, activity-based curriculum for students with extensive and pervasive support needs that combines natural body mechanics with an instructional process that helps students acquire increased amounts of independence necessary to sit, stand, and walk. MOVE uses education as a means to acquire motor skills by having participants practice their motor skills while engaging in other educational or leisure activities. The motor skills sequence is age appropriate and based on a top-down model of needs rather than a developmental sequence of skill acquisition. The motor skills are usable into adulthood and range from levels of zero self-management to independent self-management.

Most students needing pervasive supports are unable to independently perform age-appropriate functional skills. However, the addition of physical assistance and technologies in the form of adapted equipment (e.g., bowling ramp, lowered basketball net), switches, and computers enable many such students to participate in chronologically age-appropriate functional activities in natural environments.

STRATEGIES FOR INCLUSION

About 43 percent of all students with intellectual disabilities receive support services within an inclusive class most of the day, and 50 percent receive specially designed instruction in separate classes within a school most of the day (NCES, 2007). Physical education teachers face the task of providing successful, enjoyable, and challenging learning experiences for all students in inclusive classes. Their teaching strategies must ensure that students with intellectual disabilities will comprehend instructions and achieve success in the inclusive gymnasium. They must also ensure that students without intellectual disabilities accept and respect their peers with intellectual disabilities and understand how they can best support and communicate with them. Teachers can promote integration by using the teaching methods presented earlier.

Many students and adults with intellectual disabilities participate in general school and recreational sport programs. Another inclusive sport opportunity for people with intellectual disabilities is Special Olympics Unified Sports, in which teams are composed of equal numbers of athletes with intellectual disabilities and their peers without intellectual disabilities. Whether participating in general sport programs or in Special Olympics sport programs, all athletes with intellectual disabilities should be able to earn sport athletic letters and certificates, wear team uniforms, ride team buses to competitions, participate and be recognized in school and recreation award ceremonies, and represent their schools or agencies in Special Olympics local, regional, county, and state competitions.

SPECIAL OLYMPICS

Special Olympics, an international sport training and competition program for people with intellectual disabilities aged eight and up, was created in 1968 by Eunice Kennedy Shriver and the Joseph P. Kennedy, Jr. Foundation. The mission of Special Olympics is to provide year-round sport training and athletic competition in Olympic-type sports for children and adults with intellectual disabilities.

Children with intellectual disabilities aged two through seven may participate in the Special Olympics Young Athletes Program (YAP) (Special Olympics, 2008c). YAP is designed for families to play with their young athletes at home and is also appropriate for preschools, schools, and playgroups to use with small groups of young children with and without intellectual disabilities. Children engage in developmentally appropriate play activities designed to foster physical, cognitive, and social development. MATP (Special Olympics, 2004) is a comprehensive motor activity and recreation training curriculum designed for people with pervasive and extensive support needs who do not possess the physical or behavioral skills necessary to participate in Special Olympics official sports. MATP Challenge Days showcase students' achievements and award medals for personal best performance.

Summer and Winter Special Olympics Games are held annually as national, program (state or province), sectional, area (or county), and local competitions. World Summer Special Olympics Games, which take place every four years, began in 1975. World Winter Special Olympics Games, also held every four years, began in 1977. Additional Special Olympics competitions that include two or more sports are defined as tournaments. To advance to higher levels of competition in a particular year (i.e., from local through area and sectional to program competition), an athlete must have trained in an organized training program in the sports in which the athlete is entered for higher-level competition. To advance, athletes are randomly drawn from among all the division winners at the lower level of competition in the sport. Instruction for eight-week training programs is provided in the Special Olympics coaching guides (Special Olympics, 2008b). The Special Olympics coaching guides are helpful in the development of sport skills. Designed for children and adults with intellectual disabilities, the guides are presented in a series of online manuals and videos that present long-term goals, short-term objectives, task-analyzed activities, sport-specific assessments, and teaching suggestions for many sports. Coaching guides are available in all official summer and winter sports.

The showcase for acquired sport skills of Special Olympics athletes in training is the many Special Olympics competitions held throughout the year. These competitions have the excitement and pageantry associated with the Olympic Games, including parading by the athletes, lighting the torch, declaring the Games open, and reciting the Special Olympics oath. In addition to showcasing their skills, Special Olympics athletes often get to meet entertainment and sport celebrities and community leaders, experience new sport and recreational activities through a variety of clinics, enjoy an overnight experience away from home with teammates, and develop the physical and social skills necessary to enter school and community sport programs.

Official (conducted in at least 24 accredited programs from three or more world regions) Special Olympics summer sports are aquatics, athletics, badminton, basketball, bocce, bowling, cycling, equestrian, football (soccer), golf, gymnastics, judo, powerlifting, roller skating, sailing, softball, table tennis, team handball, tennis, and volleyball. Official winter sports include alpine and cross-country skiing, figure skating, speed skating, floor hockey, snowboarding, and snowshoeing. Special Olympics recognized (conducted in at least 12 accredited programs from two or more world regions) sports are cricket, kayaking, and netball.

To provide consistency in training, Special Olympics uses the sport rules of the international sports federation (given the responsibility by the International Olympic Committee [IOC] for handling the technical aspects of Olympic Games) to regulate a sport, except when those rules conflict with the official Special Olympics sport rules (Special Olympics, 2008a).

Special Olympics has developed three programs to help integrate Special Olympics athletes into existing community and after-school sport programs. In the first program, **Sports Partnerships**, students with intellectual disabilities train and compete alongside interscholastic or club athletes. Varsity and junior varsity athletes serve as peer coaches, scrimmage teammates, and boosters during competition. Athletes with intellectual disabilities compete in existing interscholastic or club league competitions. For example, in a track and field meet, the varsity 100-meter race is followed by a Special Olympics 100-meter race. In distance races, all athletes start together. At the end of the meet, individual and school scores are tabulated for varsity and partnership teams. In team sports (soccer, softball, basketball, floor hockey, volleyball), partnership teams compete just before and at the same site as the varsity or junior varsity games.

The second program, **Unified Sports**, creates teams with approximately equal numbers of athletes with and without intellectual disabilities of similar age and ability. Unified Sports leagues can be part of a school's interscholastic, intramural, or community recreation sport program. Currently, these leagues are established in bowling, basketball, golf, softball, volleyball, and soccer (figure 8.4).

The third program, **Partners Club**, brings together high school and college students with

FIGURE 8.4   Special Olympics Unified Sports basketball team.

Photo courtesy of Special Olympics Indiana, Inc.

Special Olympics athletes to perform regular sport skills training and competition and to spend time enjoying other social and recreational activities in the school and community. The Partners Club should be a sanctioned school club with all the accompanying benefits.

Athlete Leadership Programs (ALPs) encourage athlete self-determination, include athletes in policy and program discussions, help athletes discover new roles in Special Olympics, create opportunities for athletes to maximize their potential, and encourage an attitude of service *with* as well as *for* athletes. ALPs include the Global Messenger program (public speaking), Global Athlete Congress, and athletes as Special Olympics board members, coaches, officials, volunteers, employees, and media reporters.

Healthy Athletes screenings take place at Special Olympics competitions and are designed to help Special Olympics athletes improve their health and fitness, leading to an enhanced sport experience and improved well-being. These screening include Fit Feet (podiatry), FUNfitness (physical therapy), Health Promotion (disease prevention), Healthy Hearing (audio), Opening Eyes (vision), Special Smiles (dental), and MedFest (sport physical exams).

PARALYMPIC GAMES FOR PEOPLE WITH INTELLECTUAL DISABILITIES

The Paralympic Games are equivalent to the Olympic Games for the world's top athletes with disabilities. They include athletes with spinal cord injuries, amputations, blindness, deafness, cerebral palsy, intellectual disabilities, and les autres (athletes with a physical disability that does not fall under one of the other categories). Unlike Special Olympics, the Paralympic Games provide international competition only for elite athletes with intellectual disabilities, 15 years and older, who meet minimum qualifying sport standards. They are conducted every four years, just after the Olympic Games and at the same venues.

The Association Nacional Prestura de Servicio (ANDE) and the International Sports Federation for Persons with Intellectual Disability (INAS-FID) held the first Paralympic Games for the Mentally Handicapped in September 1992 in Madrid. At the 1996 Paralympic Games in Atlanta, 56 elite athletes with intellectual disabilities competed in swimming and athletics, and 244 elite athletes with intellectual disabilities competed in athletics, basketball, swimming, and table tennis at the 2000 Paralympic Games in Sydney. Following these Games, the International Paralympic Committee (IPC) suspended INAS-FID from membership because some athletes did not meet the criteria for intellectual disability. INAS-FID and the IPC will reintroduce athletes with intellectual disabilities to competition at the 2012 Paralympic Games (INAS-FID, 2009). INAS-FID continues to conduct world and regional championships in athletics, basketball, cycling, football (soccer), judo, Nordic skiing, swimming, table tennis, and tennis.

SAFE PARTICIPATION

If the physical educator plans activities appropriate to the academic, physical, motor, social, and emotional levels of children with intellectual disabilities, there are few restrictions or contraindications for activity. Special Olympics has prohibited training and competition in certain sports that hold unnecessarily high risk of injury, especially injury that could have lifelong deleterious effects. Prohibited sports are pole vaulting, boxing, platform diving, most martial arts, fencing, shooting, contact football, rugby, wrestling, karate, Nordic jumping, trampolining, and the javelin, discus, and hammer throw. Students with intellectual disabilities may participate in these activities as part of their regular school program.

Most people with Down syndrome have some increased flexibility of joints, called *ligamentous laxity*, which can affect any of their joints. **Atlanto-axial instability** describes an increased flexibility between the first and second cervical vertebrae of the neck. The instability of this joint could place the spinal cord at risk for injury if an affected person were to participate in activities that hyperextend or radically flex the neck or upper spine. About 13 to 14 percent of people with Down syndrome show evidence of instability that is asymptomatic and discovered through X-ray only. The condition can be detected through a physician's examination that includes X-ray views of full flexion and extension of the neck. Only 1 to 2 percent of people with Down syndrome have symptoms that require treatment. Symptoms might include neck pain or persistent head tilt, intermittent or progressive weakness, changes in gait pattern or loss of motor skill, loss of bowel or bladder control, increased muscle tone in the legs, and changes in sensation in the hands and feet. Physical education teachers are encouraged to follow the lead of Special Olympics in restricting students who have atlantoaxial instability from participating in activities that result in hyperextension, radical flexion, or direct pressure on the neck and upper spine. Such activities include certain gymnastics activities, the butterfly stroke, diving, the high jump, heading a soccer ball, alpine skiing, and any warm-up exercises that place stress on the head and neck.

Because many children with intellectual disabilities, particularly those with Down syndrome, are cardiopathic, students should receive activity clearance from a physician. Appropriate activities within the limitations specified by the physician should then be planned.

Another common condition of people with intellectual disabilities is muscular hypotonia (flabbiness). Infants with this condition are often called *floppy babies*. Although hypotonia decreases with age, it never disappears, and hernias, postural deviations, and poor body mechanics are prevalent because of insufficient musculature. Again, physical educators must take care not to plan exercises and activities that are beyond the capabilities of students with muscular hypotonia, because they can lead to severe injury. Abdominal and lower back exercises must be selected with care, and daily foot-strengthening exercises are recommended.

SUMMARY

Intellectual disability is among the most prevalent of disabilities. It is a condition that can be viewed from both functional and developmental perspectives. Intellectual disabilities have many causes, resulting in varied characteristics and affecting success and participation in physical education and sport. This chapter suggested teaching methods, tests, and activities appropriate for this population and briefly reviewed selected sport programs relevant to students with intellectual disabilities. Most people with intellectual disabilities have experienced and continue to experience success in physical education and sport experiences.

REFERENCES

Alverez, N. (2008). Alzheimer disease in individuals with Down syndrome. Retrieved January 13, 2008, from www.emedicine.com/neuro/TOPIC552.HTM.

American Psychiatric Association (APA). (2000). *Diagnostic and statistical manual of mental disorders (DSM IV)* (4th ed.). Washington, DC: Author.

Beckett, L., Yu, Q., & Long, A.N. (2005). The numbers behind Fragile X: Prevalence and economic impact. *National Fragile X Foundation Quarterly, 21*, 18-21. Retrieved from www.fragilex.org/FX_Quarterly_Issue211.pdf.

Block, M.E. (2007). *A teacher's guide to including students with disabilities in regular physical education* (3rd ed.). Baltimore: Paul H. Brooks.

Centers for Disease Control and Prevention (CDC). (2005). Fetal alcohol spectrum disorders. www.cdc.gov/ncbddd/fas/fasask.htm [July 13, 2008].

Dunn, J.M., & Leitschuh, C., (2006). *Special physical education*. Dubuque, IA: Kendall Hunt.

Dunn, J. M., Morehouse, J.W., & Fredericks, H.D. (1986). *Physical education for the severely handicapped*. Austin, TX: Pro-Ed.

Eichstaedt, C.B., Wang, P.Y., Polacek, J.J., & Dohrmann, P.F. (1991). *Physical fitness and motor skill levels of individuals with mental retardation: Mild, moderate, and individuals with Down syndrome: Ages 6 to 21*. Normal, IL: Illinois State University Printing Services.

Eunice Kennedy Shriver National Institute of Child Health and Human Development. (2006). Down syndrome and associated medical disorders. Retrieved June 30, 2008, from www.nichd.nih.gov/publications/pubs/downsyndrome.cfm#DownSyndromeAssociated.

Gillespie, M. (2003). Cardiovascular fitness of young Canadian children with and without mental retardation. *Education and Training in Developmental Disabilities, 38*, 296-301.

Grossman, H.J. (Ed.). (1973). *A manual on terminology and classification in mental retardation* (rev. ed.). Washington, DC: American Association on Mental Deficiency.

Hagerman, R.J. (2007). How do the behaviors seen in persons with Fragile X relate to those seen in autism? Retrieved December 5, 2008, from www.fragilex.org/html/autism.htm.

Harris, J.C. (2006). *Intellectual disability: Understanding its development, causes, classification, evaluation, and treatment*. New York: Oxford University Press.

Individuals with Disabilities Education Improvement Act of 2004, *Public Law No. 108-446,* 118 Stat. 2647 (2004).

International Sports Federation for Persons with Intellectual Disability (INAS-FID). (2009). Joint statement on the re-inclusion of athletes with intellectual disabilities in future Paralympic Games. Retrieved December 5, 2008, from www.paralympic.org/release/Main_Sections_Menu/News/Current_Affairs/2008_09_13_a.html.

Londeree, B.R., & Johnson, L.E. (1974). Motor fitness of TMR vs. EMR and normal children. *Medicine Science and Sport, 6,* 247-252.

Loovis, E.M., & Ersing, W.F. (1979). *Assessing and programming gross motor development for children.* Cleveland Heights, OH: Ohio Motor Assessment Associates.

Luckasson, R., Coulter, D.L., Polloway, E.A., Reiss, S., Schalock, R.L., Snell, M.E., Spitalnik, D.M., & Stark, J.A. (1992). *Mental retardation: Definition, classification, and systems of supports* (9th ed.). Washington, DC: American Association on Mental Retardation.

MacDonncha, C., Watson, A.W.S., McSweeney, T., & O'Donovan, D.J. (1999). Reliability of Eurofit physical fitness items for adolescent males with and without mental retardation. *Adapted Physical Activity Quarterly, 16,* 86-95.

MOVE International. (2008). MOVE overview/information. Retrieved August 4, 2008, from www.move-international.org/about.

Murphy, C.C., Boyle, C., Schendel, D., Decoufle, P., et al. (1998). Epidemiology of mental retardation in children. *Mental Retardation and Developmental Disabilities Research Reviews, 4* (1).

National Center for Education Statistics (NCES). (2007). Digest of education statistics, 2007. Retrieved August 4, 2008, from http://nces.ed.gov/programs/digest/d07/tables/dt07_047.asp?referrer=list.

National Down Syndrome Society. (2010a). About Down syndrome: Down syndrome fact sheet. Retrieved March 14, 2010, from www.ndss.org/index.php?option=com_content&view=article&id=54&Itemid=74.

National Down Syndrome Society. (2010b). About Down syndrome: Incidents and maternal age. Retrieved March 14, 2010, from www.ndss.org/index.php?option=com_content&view=article&id=61&Itemid=78.

Piaget, J. (1952). *The origins of intelligence in children.* New York: International Universities Press.

Pitetti, K.H., Millar, A.L., & Fernhall, B. (2000). Reliability of a peak performance treadmill test for children and adolescents with and without mental retardation. *Adapted Physical Activity Quarterly, 17,* 322-332.

Rarick, G.L., Dobbins, D.A., & Broadhead, G.D. (1976). *The motor domain and its correlates in educationally handicapped children.* Englewood Cliffs, NJ: Prentice-Hall.

Rarick, G.L., & McQuillan, J.P. (1977). *The factor structure of motor abilities of trainable mentally retarded children: Implications for curriculum development.* (DHEW Project No H23-2544). Berkley, CA: Department of Physical Education, University of California.

Schalock, R.L., Borthwick-Duffy, S.A., Bradley, V.J., Buntinx, W.H.E., Coulter, D.L., Craig, E.M., Gomez, S.C., Lachapelle, Y., Luckasson, R., Reeve, A., Shogren, K.A., Snell, M.E., Spreat, S., Tassé, M.J., Thompson, J.R., Verdugo-Alonso, M.A., Wehmeyer, M.L., & Yeager, M.H. (2010). *Intellectual disability: Definition, classification, and systems of supports* (11th ed.). Washington, DC: American Association on Intellectual and Developmental Disabilities.

Special Olympics. (2004). Motor Activities Training Program. Retrieved December 5, 2008, from www.specialolympics.org/Special+Olympics+Public+Website/English/Compete/Sports_Offered/MATP.htm.

Special Olympics. (2008a). Official sports rules, article 1. Retrieved May 23, 2008, from www.specialolympics.org/Special+Olympics+Public+Website/English/Coach/Sports_Rules/Article+I.htm.

Special Olympics. (2008b). Special Olympics coaching guides. Retrieved June 30, 2008, from www.specialolympics.org/Special+Olympics+Public+Website/English/Coach/Coaching_Guides/default.htm.

Special Olympics. (2008c). Young Athletes Program. Retrieved December 5, 2008, from www.specialolympics.org/Special+Olympics+Public+Website/English/Initiatives/Young%20Athletes/default.htm.

Thompson, J.R., Bryant, B.R., Campbell, E.M., Craig, E.M., Hughes, C.M., Rotholz, D.A., Schalock, R.L., Silverman, W.P., Tassé, M.J., & Wehmeyer, M.L. (2004). *Supports intensity scale: Users manual.* Washington, DC: American Association on Mental Retardation.

Winnick, J.P., & Short, F.X. (1999a). *The Brockport Physical Fitness Test manual.* Champaign, IL: Human Kinetics.

Winnick, J.P., & Short, F.X. (1999b). *The Brockport physical fitness training guide.* Champaign, IL: Human Kinetics.

World Health Organization. (2001). *International classification of functioning, disability and health (ICF).* Geneva: Author.

Yang, Q., Rasmussen, S.A., & Friedman, J.M. (2002). Mortality associated with Down syndrome in the USA from 1983 to 1997: A population-based study. *Lancet, 359,* 1019-1025.

WRITTEN RESOURCES

Special Olympics coaching guides. (2010). www.specialolympics.org/sports.aspx.

This is a series of sport-specific instructional manuals. Each manual includes long-term goals, short-term objectives, skill assessments, task analyses, teaching suggestions, progression charts, and related information.

Spirit: The Magazine of Special Olympics. Special Olympics, Inc., 1133 19th Street, NW Washington, DC 20036-3604; phone: 202-628-3630.

A published quarterly by Special Olympics to promote its aims and programs and provide information to participants, volunteers, and others interested in Special Olympics.

AUDIOVISUAL RESOURCES

Building a successful Special Olympics Unified Sports program [DVD]. (2008). Special Olympics, Inc., 1133 19th Street, NW Washington, DC 20036-3604; phone: 202-628-3630.

This is an orientation to Special Olympics Unified Sports programs in schools and in the community. Running time is 22 minutes. Free.

Let's get strong [VHS]. (2001). Commack, NY: Healthy All Over, Ltd., P.O. Box 953, Commack, NY.

This exercise video is designed for people with developmental disabilities. All major muscle groups are targeted for a well-balanced body workout. Running time is 23 minutes.

Let's have fun [VHS]. (2001). Commack, NY: Healthy All Over, Ltd., P.O. Box 953, Commack, NY.

This exercise video is designed for people with developmental disabilities. The low-impact aerobics segment has visual aids to help stimulate imagination. The easy-to-follow routine helps develop a healthier and stronger body, increasing endurance for everyday activities. Running time is 23 minutes.

ELECTRONIC RESOURCES

International Sports Federation for Persons with Intellectual Disability (INAS-FID): www.inas-fid.org.

This is the Web site of the international sports federation for elite athletes with intellectual disabilities. The site provides information on eligibility for competition, member organizations, records and rankings of top competitors, upcoming competitions, and athlete registration.

Special Olympics, Inc.: www.specialolympics.org.

This Web site provides information on Special Olympics worldwide programs, upcoming games and competitions, individual profiles of Special Olympics athletes, links to national and U.S. Special Olympics programs, and how to get involved. It also includes coaching guides and instructional videos in each sport and the official sport rules, which can be downloaded free of charge.

Behavioral Disabilities

E. Michael Loovis

Several students from the seventh-period self-contained class for students with behavioral disorders are standing around before the start of physical education class. Mrs. Thomas, the physical educator, enters the gymnasium, blows her whistle, and says, "Line up and keep your mouths shut!" The students continue talking as they proceed to their predetermined spots on the gym floor where class attendance is taken. Mrs. Thomas yells that she wants the class to "keep their mouths shut and pay attention." Conversation among several students continues and Mrs. Thomas shouts at the group, "Hey, you three, shut your mouths or you're going to the principal's office." None of the students pays any attention to Mrs. Thomas; they continue talking and mimicking her tone of voice. At this point, Mrs. Thomas sends them to the principal's office for the fifth time in two months. As they leave the gym, all three turn toward Mrs. Thomas and say, "Forget you; we'll be back!" They then slam the gymnasium door so hard that the window shatters.

Mrs. Thomas has just had one of what could turn out to be many experiences with students with behavioral disabilities. The keys to teaching these students effectively involve understanding the types of behavioral conditions that exist, how to implement certain instructional strategies to teach students with behavioral disabilities, and how to manage the students' behavior.

The fourth-largest group of young people receiving special education pursuant to the Individuals with Disabilities Education Act (IDEA) are those with emotional disturbances (U.S. Department of Education, 2007). Although the number of students with emotional disturbances increased from 445,000 in 1996 to 489,326 in 2004, the relative percentage when compared with the number of all students aged 3 through 21 served under IDEA remained constant at 8 percent. In the past, these students have been referred to as emotionally disturbed, socially maladjusted, behavior disordered, conduct disordered, and emotionally handicapped. Certain characteristics invariably associated with these students make them stand out. Not all of them exhibit the same characteristics, however; quite the opposite is true. Generally speaking, they tend to demonstrate behavior that is labeled hyperactive, distractive, or impulsive. Some students might exhibit aggression beyond what is considered normal or socially acceptable. Some lie, set fires, steal, and abuse alcohol or drugs. Some might behave in a manner that is considered withdrawn; they might act immature or behave in ways that tend to highlight feelings of inadequacy. The terms **emotional disturbance** and **behavioral disorder** are used synonymously in this chapter.

Another segment of this population might demonstrate behavior directed in a negative way against society; these students are known as juvenile delinquents. Increasingly, others fit the category called *at risk*. These young people are mired in an incompatibility between themselves and school, resulting in low academic achievement and high dropout rates (Sagor & Cox, 2004).

According to IDEA, emotional disturbance is defined as follows (U.S. Department of Education, Office of Special Education and Rehabilitative Services, 2006, p. 15):

> The term means a condition exhibiting one or more of the following characteristics over a long period of time and to a marked degree that adversely affects a child's educational performance:

- An inability to learn that cannot be explained by intellectual, sensory, or health factors
- An inability to build or maintain satisfactory interpersonal relationships with peers and teachers
- Inappropriate types of behavior or feelings under normal circumstances
- A general pervasive mood of unhappiness or depression
- A tendency to develop physical symptoms or fears associated with personal or school problems

Identification of students with emotional disturbance is perhaps the most perplexing problem facing school and mental health professionals. In addition, consideration is given to the ever-expanding number of young people who are at risk. Thus, it is beneficial to understand the three qualifiers that appear in the first paragraph of the federal definition—namely, duration, degree, and adverse effects on educational performance.

- **Long period of time.** This qualifier includes behavioral patterns that are chronic, such as a persistent pattern of physical or verbal attacks on a classmate. It excludes behaviors that could be construed as emotional disturbance but that are situational in nature and thus are understandable or expected. For example, a death in the family, a divorce, or another crisis situation could alter a student's behavior in a way that makes it appear aberrant.

- **Marked degree.** Under consideration here are the magnitude and duration of a behavior. Intensity of behavioral displays, such as intensity of an altercation with a classmate, is considered. For example, a violent physical and verbal attack on a fellow student that requires extensive crisis intervention from teachers and counselors, in contrast to some pushing and shoving, would qualify under this criterion. Also noted is the amount of time a student engages in a particular behavior— for example, if the attacks occur frequently.

- **Adversely affects educational performance.** There must be a demonstrable cause-and-effect relation between a student's behavior and decreased academic performance. This requires, at the very least, determining if students are performing at or near the level they would be expected to attain without a behavioral disorder.

NATURE OF EMOTIONAL AND BEHAVIORAL DISORDERS

When endeavoring to understand students with a mild or moderate behavioral disorder, which is the group most likely to be found in an integrated classroom setting, a behavioral classification appears most serviceable. Quay (1986) conducted the seminal work in dimensional classification. Studies have shown that several dimensions (i.e., conduct disorder, anxiety–withdrawal, immaturity, and socialized aggression) are consistently found in special education classes for students who are emotionally disturbed. In 1987, Quay and Peterson used the revised behavior problem checklist to expand the dimensions identified previously. The six new dimensions (some of which are essentially the same as those listed previously) include the following (pp. 20-22):

- **Conduct disorder** involves attention-seeking behavior, temper tantrums, fighting, disruptiveness, and a tendency to annoy others.
- **Socialized aggression** typically involves cooperative stealing, truancy, loyalty to delinquent friends, associating with bad companions, and freely admitting disrespect for moral values and laws.
- **Attention problems–immaturity** characteristically involves short attention span, sluggishness, poor concentration, distractibility, lethargy, and a tendency to answer without thinking.
- **Anxiety–withdrawal** stands in considerable contrast to conduct disorders, involving self-consciousness, hypersensitivity, general fearfulness, anxiety, depression, and perpetual sadness.
- **Psychotic behavior** involves saying things over and over and expressing strange, far-fetched ideas.
- **Motor excess** suggests restlessness and an inability to relax.

An extension of Quay's work included the identification of two primary dimensions of disordered behavior, namely, externalizing and internalizing (Achenbach et al., 1991). Externalizing behavior involves attacks against others, which parallels Quay and Peterson's original conduct disorder and socialized aggression. Internalizing behavior, on the other hand, involves internal, mental, or emotional conflict, such as depression and anxiety, which approximates Quay and Peterson's anxiety–withdrawal and immaturity dimensions.

Conduct disorders may be classified as either overt or covert (Kauffman & Landrum, 2009) or undersocialized or socialized (Quay, 1986). Undersocialized (overt) behavior—especially behavior that is aggressive—is associated with violence. According to the American Academy of Experts in Traumatic Stress (2003), students who are at risk for violent behavior typically demonstrate behaviors such as the following:

- Expressing self-destructive ideas
- Talking about specific plans to harm oneself or others
- Having difficulty controlling impulses
- Blaming other people and events for their problems
- Engaging in substance abuse

The *Diagnostic and Statistical Manual of Mental Disorders, Fourth Edition* (*DSM IV*) (American Psychiatric Association [APA], 1994) categorizes conduct disorders under four broad headings representing 15 characteristics. A person has a mild conduct disorder if at least 3 symptoms from the list of 15 are present (table 9.1). Four or more symptoms indicate a moderate to severe conduct disorder. Of interest is the relation between oppositional defiant disorder (ODD) and conduct disorder. A significant percentage of children and adolescents who develop conduct disorders also show signs of ODD in early and middle childhood. According to the *DSM IV* (p. 91), ODD is "a recurrent pattern of negativistic, defiant, disobedient, and hostile behavior toward authority figures that persists for at least 6 months and is characterized by the frequent occurrence of at least four of the . . . behaviors" listed in table 9.1.

Psychiatric disorders are another area of concern for teachers in public schools. These disorders are likely to be more disabling and might require special therapeutic and medical treatments. Included in this category of disorders are anxiety disorders (e.g., obsessive–compulsive disorder [OCD] and post-traumatic stress disorder [PTSD]), depression, and other mood disorders (e.g., bipolar or manic depressive disorder) as well as schizophrenic and other psychotic disorders (Forness, Walker, & Kavale, 2003). Combinations of psychopharmacology and behavioral intervention (see chapter 6) are usually employed in the treatment of these disorders.

Table 9.1 *DSM IV* **Diagnostic Criteria for Oppositional Defiant Disorder (ODD) and Conduct Disorder**

ODD	Conduct disorder
Often loses temper.	Often bullies, threatens, or intimidates others.
Often argues with adults.	Often initiates physical fights.
Often actively defies or refuses to comply with adults' requests or rules.	Has used a weapon.
Often deliberately annoys people.	Has been physically cruel to people.
Often blames others for personal mistakes or misbehavior.	Has been physically cruel to animals.
Often touchy or easily annoyed by others.	Has stolen while confronting a victim.
Often angry and resentful.	Has forced someone into sexual activity.
Often spiteful and vindictive.	Has deliberately engaged in fire setting.
	Has deliberately destroyed others' property.
	Has broken into someone else's house, building, or car.
	Often lies to con others.
	Has stolen items of nontrivial value without confronting the victim.
	Often out late without permission, starting before age 13.
	Has run away from home overnight at least twice.
	Often truant, starting before age 13.

CAUSES OF BEHAVIORAL DISORDERS

Several factors conceivably having a causal relationship to behavioral disorders have been identified, including biological, family, school, and cultural factors. In addition, society is slowly becoming aware of children who are at risk. Although space here does not permit a detailed discussion of the factors that place students at risk, broad societal factors have been shown to correlate with poor educational performance. These factors include poverty, minority racial or ethnic group identity, non-English or limited English language background, and specific family configuration (e.g., living in a single-parent household, limited education) (Sagor & Cox, 2004).

Biological Factors

According to Kauffman and Landrum (2009), several biological aberrations might contribute to the etiology of behavioral disorders. These include genetic anomalies, difficult temperament, brain injury or dysfunction, nutritional deficiencies and allergies, physical illness or disability, and psychophysiological disorders. With these factors identified, it is important to reiterate Kauffman and Landrum's (2009) contention, "Although biological processes have a pervasive influence on behavior, they affect behavior only in interaction with environmental factors" (p. 159). On the other hand,

Cullinan (2007) suggests that research supports the proposition that brain disorders can contribute to emotional and behavioral disorders through hereditary and physical influences.

Family Factors

Pathological family relationships are major contributory factors in the etiology of behavioral disorders. Family factors alone do not cause children's disordered behavior, except in complex interactions with other variables. Broken homes, divorce, chaotic or hostile family relationships, absence of mother or father, child abuse, and parental separation might produce situations in which children are at risk to develop behavioral disorders. It is also clear that there is not a one-to-one relation between disruptive family relations and behavioral disorders. Many children find parental discord more injurious than separation from one or both parents. Poverty is another factor statistically correlated with risk of disability (Fujiura & Yamati, 2000). Research also points to a multiplier effect: When two or more factors are present simultaneously, an increased probability exists that a behavioral disorder will develop.

School Factors

It has become increasingly clear that, besides the family, school is the most significant socializing factor for a child. For this reason, the school must shoulder some of the responsibility for causing behavioral disorders. According to Kauffman and Landrum (2009), schools contribute to the development of behavior disorders in several ways:

- Insensitivity to students' individuality
- Inappropriate expectations for students
- Inconsistent management of behavior
- Instruction in nonfunctional and irrelevant skills
- Ineffective instruction in skills necessary for school success
- Destructive contingencies of reinforcement
- Undesirable models of school conduct

Cultural Factors

Frequently, there exists a discrepancy between the values and expectations that are embraced by the child, the family, and the school. Consequently, there is an increased probability that the student will violate dominant cultural norms and be labeled as deviant (Kauffman and Landrum, 2009). Thus, educators should intervene only with behaviors inconsistent with achievement of core educational goals. Behaviors that have a cultural foundation should be evaluated carefully in terms of whether the behaviors are inconsistent with educational goals or whether the behaviors do not conform to educators' cultural mores. In the latter case, disciplining a student would be considered inappropriate.

Part of the problem centers on conflicted cultural values and standards that society has engendered. For example, popular culture has elevated many high-status models whose behavior is every bit as violent as the villains they are apprehending; however, students who engage in similar behaviors are told that their choices are incompatible with society's expectations.

Another problem involves the multicultural perspective, or rather a lack of it. Teachers find it difficult to eliminate bias and discrimination when evaluating a student's behavior. Consequently, students are labeled as deviant when in actuality it is only at school that their behavior is considered inappropriate.

Other cultural factors influencing behavior include the student's peer group, neighborhood, urbanization, ethnicity, and social class. These factors are not significant predictors of disordered behavior by themselves; however, within the context of economic deprivation and family conflict,

they can have an adverse effect on behavior (Kauffman & Landrum, 2009).

A significant sociocultural factor that portrays the relation between aberrant adult behavior and a spiraling incidence of behavioral disabilities is substance abuse. Prenatal exposure to drugs and alcohol affects children in two ways. First, there is an increased incidence of neurological impairment because both drugs and alcohol can cross the placenta and reach the fetus, causing chemical dependency, congenital aberrations, neurobehavioral abnormalities, and intrauterine growth retardation. Second, these children are exposed to family situations that are, at best, chaotic. Typically, they find themselves in the social service system bouncing from one substitute care situation to another. Sinclair (1998) reported that prenatally drug-exposed children in Head Start programs were more likely to be classified as emotionally or behavioral disordered and placed in special education upon entrance into kindergarten.

GENERAL IMPLICATIONS FOR PHYSICAL EDUCATION AND SPORT

Conceptual models that serve as the basis for understanding, treating, or educating students with behavioral disabilities are discussed comprehensively in chapters 6 and 7. These include the psychodynamic, psychoeducational, ecological, biogenic, humanistic, and behavioral approaches to teaching students with behavioral disorders. What follows is a discussion of instructional and managerial strategies that are broadly applied in special education. These strategies can also be used effectively in adapted physical education with students who present mild and severe behavior disorders. See also the application example.

Instructional and Management Considerations

Research confirms that students with emotional disturbance and behavioral difficulties learn best in well-managed environments characterized by effective instruction. In this section, emphasis is placed on instructional and managerial strategies that work for physical educators in both inclusive and segregated settings when teaching students with mild to severe behavior problems.

APPLICATION EXAMPLE

Behavioral Disabilities

Setting: High school physical education class

Student: A 10th-grader with ODD who is frequently verbally and physically abusive to his peers and constantly challenges the authority of the physical educator

Issue: What are some strategies for handling this situation?

Application: The physical educator could try

▶ employing the conflict-resolution process,

▶ examining events or conditions that spark the episodes of abusive behavior,

▶ praising instances of appropriate behavior, and

▶ implementing Hellison's responsibility model.

Differentiated Instruction

Differentiated instruction has been the hallmark of special education in the earliest years of the 21st century. Defined as the "planning of curriculum and instruction using strategies that address student strengths, interests, skills, and readiness in flexible learning environments" (Gartin et al., 2002, p. 8), differentiated instruction acknowledges that there is no one correct way of instructing children, including those with behavioral disabilities. Effective teachers tailor their instructional techniques according to a student's type of behavioral disorder.

In physical education, differentiated instruction should include consideration of the learning environment. Specifically, physical educators should attend to the organization of the gym (e.g., well-established routines, clearly posted rules, and the establishment of a positive instructional climate, including confirmed behavioral expectations). Additionally, arrangement of the environment includes flexible grouping. Students might benefit from large-group instruction, or they might be served better by employing small-group instruction, peer teaching, independent study, one-on-one instruction, or cooperative learning groups. Another way to differentiate is to use multilevel instruction that consists of engaging students in the same curriculum but with different goals and levels of difficulty. For example, in a basketball unit related to learning and performing the jump shot, the physical educator might employ peer teaching, alter the distance from the basket, and reduce the criteria for achievement. Curricular overlapping (Block, 2007) is another modification wherein a student who is unable to participate in the general physical education curriculum works on unique individualized education program (IEP) goals but is accommodated in the regular physical education class (e.g., learning to use a walker while the class participates in a lesson on fleeing and chasing).

Praise

Praise has been documented to have a positive effect on both academic and behavioral outcomes with students with behavioral disorders. However, Sutherland (2000) found that although students complied with teacher requests 80 percent of the time, teachers provided praise only 2 percent of the times that students complied. There is also a potential relation between how much praise is given and whether the praise is given effectively (i.e., conveyed in a tone that is earnest and reinforcing). Kamps, Kravits, Stolze, and Swaggart (1999) demonstrated that multicomponent prevention programs were successful in reducing inappropriate behavior in elementary school children with behavior difficulties. Multicomponent programs employ a combination of social skills training, peer tutoring, and behavior management.

Precision Requests

Special educators have devised programs such as **precision requests**, which have proven effective with students who have serious emotional disturbance and which could easily be used in physical education. Musser, Bray, Kehle, and Jenson (2001) described precision requests as having the following steps:

Step 1: An initial request for compliance is made by saying, "Please." If the student complies, reinforcement is provided. If there is no compliance, step 2 is implemented.

Step 2: A second request is made with the phrase, "You need to ____." If the student complies, reinforcement is provided. If there is no compliance, the final step of the program is implemented.

Step 3: Noncompliance causes the use of reductive techniques such as a time-out.

At the core of effective instruction with students with behavioral disorders is an examination of the ways people communicate. To communicate effectively, people must be able to give and receive information clearly and use the information to achieve a desired result. Giving and receiving information clearly is a goal of effective interpersonal communication that results from active listening.

Active Listening

Three skills are essential to the technique of **active listening**. The first is **attending**, a physical act that requires the listener to face the person speaking, maintain eye contact, and lean forward (if seated). These actions communicate to the speaker that the listener is interested in what is being said. **Listening**, the second skill, means more than just hearing what is being said. It involves the process of decoding, an attempt to interpret what has been said. Consider the following example:

Sender code: "Why do we have to do these exercises?"

Possible receiver decoding:

a. "She doesn't know how to perform them and is embarrassed to admit it."

b. "She's bored with the lesson and is anxious to get to the next class."

c. "She's unclear about why the exercises are necessary and is seeking some clarification."

Suppose that the most accurate decoding was *a* or *c*, but the listener decoded the message as *b*. A misunderstanding would result, and the communication process would start to break down. Such scenarios occur frequently, with neither the speaker nor the listener aware that a misunderstanding exists. The question then becomes, "What can be done to ensure that the correct message is being communicated?" The answer is contained in the third and final step of the active listening process. The third component of active listening is **responding**. The listener sends back the results of the decoding in an attempt to ascertain if there are any misunderstandings. In effect, the listener simply restates the interpretation of the sender's message. For example, in the previous illustration, the listener might say, "You're bored with the lesson and anxious to get to the next class?" If the sender responds, "No," then the receiver can reasonably rule out boredom as a cause for the original statement.

Active listening helps prevent misunderstandings, promotes problem solving, and demonstrates warmth and understanding. As with any new skill, it requires practice for maximum effectiveness.

Verbal Mediation

A second communication technique is **verbal mediation**, which involves students verbalizing the association between their behavior and the consequences of that behavior. Of particular importance is having students take an active role in the verbal mediation process rather than passively hearing teachers make the association for them. The following exchange illustrates verbal mediation. A student has just earned 10 minutes of free time by successfully completing the assigned drill at a circuit training station.

Teacher: "What did you do to earn free time?"

Student: "I followed directions and finished my work."

Teacher: "Do you like free time?"

Student: "Yes, it's fun."

Teacher: "So when you do your work, then you can have fun?"

Student: "Right."

Teacher: "Good for you! Keep up the good work."

In this example, the teacher has promoted the student's verbal mediation of the positive association between the appropriate behavior and the positive consequence.

Conflict Resolution

When teaching students with behavioral disorders, there is a greater-than-average risk of using confrontation to resolve conflict. This does not imply that interpersonal confrontation need be punitive or destructive. On the contrary, a healthy use of confrontation provides the opportunity to examine a set of behaviors in relation to expectations and perceptions of others as well as to establish rules.

The goal of confrontation is resolution of conflicts through constructive behavior change. Several steps are necessary in reaching this desired goal through confrontation: making an assertive, confrontational statement (one that expresses honestly and directly how the speaker feels about another's behavior); being aware of common reactions to confrontation; and knowing how to deal effectively with these reactions.

Although assertive confrontation can be an effective means of resolving conflicts, it requires skillful use of each step in the process. Without question, the most crucial component of the conflict-resolution process is the formulation of an effective confrontational statement. There are three main components, namely, a nonjudgmental description of the behavior causing the problem, a concrete effect that the behavior is having on the person sending the message, and an expression of the feelings produced from the concrete effect of the behavior. Together these components form an **I-message**. When combined with active listening, which further reduces defensiveness, the conflict-resolution process can be an excellent means to avoid major conflicts, as exemplified in the following conversation:

> *Teacher:* "Robert, your disruptive behavior during class is causing me a problem. When you argue and fight with the other students in class, I have to stop teaching. It's distracting to me, and I'm frustrated." (I-message)
>
> *Student:* "I get that stuff at home. I don't need it here."
>
> *Teacher:* "I see. Lately, you're having some problems at home with your parents." (active listening)
>
> *Student:* "My dad and I have been fighting all week."
>
> *Teacher:* "You're really upset about the problem you're having with your father." (active listening)
>
> *Student:* "Yeah! I don't know how much longer I can put up with his bulls—t."
>
> *Teacher:* "So you're angry because of the situation at home, and it's carrying over into school." (active listening)
>
> *Student:* "Yeah! I know you're upset about me fighting and not getting along in class. You know I've tried to get along."

> *Teacher:* "You're a little surprised that it's such a problem for me even though the incidents are not always all that extreme." (active listening)
>
> *Student:* "Well, not really. I see what you're saying. You have to stop teaching and stuff. Mostly I'm taking my anger out on the guys in class. I'll just have to remember that it's not their fault that my dad and me aren't getting along. I'll try harder not to get angry and fight with the guys, okay?"
>
> *Teacher:* "That would sure help me. Thanks, Robert."

In this example, the teacher has used an I-message and the skill of active listening to diffuse a situation that could have erupted into a major confrontation between teacher and student.

Frank, Paget, Bowman, and Wilde (1998) suggest Houdini techniques to avoid destructive confrontational episodes with ODD students. These techniques involve curtailing teacher behaviors that can promote power struggles. For example, teachers should not threaten students, respond emotionally, confront students near their peers, respond quickly, remain in the interaction too long, use bribes, try convincing strategies, or use put-downs. According to the authors, teachers should defuse power struggles by doing the following:

- Use simple directions and choices.
- Make public the consequences for behavior.
- Employ active listening and verbal mediation.
- Give brief and direct instructions in a calm tone.
- Discuss problems with the student in private.
- Walk away from the situation before it gets out of hand.

Behavioral Contracting

Contingency management is especially helpful with students who experience behavioral difficulties. As briefly discussed in chapter 6, a **behavior contract** is a written document that specifies the relation between behaviors and their consequences. An example of a behavior contract is illustrated in figure 9.1.

Physical Restraint and Seclusion

Passage of the Children's Health Act of 2000 (PL 106-310) helped make education and health care more aware of the legal ramifications of using physical restraint and seclusion as a tool for managing the behavior of students with behavioral or mental health difficulties. According to Van Haren and Fiedler (2004), "Physical restraint is defined as restriction imposed by a person that immobilizes or reduces the ability of a pupil to move his or her arms, legs, or head freely" (p. 18). Table 9.2 lists the types of restraint along with their prevailing definition. Van Haren and Fiedler also noted that seclusion should be used as a form of restraint only if it is outlined in the student's IEP.

State education agencies such as the Massachusetts Department of Education have codified the regulatory requirements of PL 106-310 for use by school districts. School personnel receive training annually, including the development of knowledge and skills as they relate to the school restraint policy, methods of preventing the need to physically restrain, types of restraint employed and concomitant safety considerations, administration of restraint based on individual needs and limitations, and documentation and reporting of incidents.

Assessment and Activities

According to Steinberg and Knitzer (1992), effective physical education programs for students with emotional and behavioral disturbances are the exception rather than the rule. They suggest that this is especially perplexing in light of increased academic performance and decreased student absenteeism when students are involved in vigorous and systematic exercise programs. Poor motor performance in students with behavioral disorders is often attributed to indirect factors—attention deficits, poor work habits, impulsivity, hyperactivity, feelings of inadequacy, and demonstration of aggressive behavior—rather than to an innate inability to move well.

Behavior Contract in Physical Education

The terms of this contract are as follows:

The student will earn 1 point for every positive statement or action made to or about an opponent during participation in the class basketball unit. The student must earn 10 points to qualify for free time in the gym on Friday afternoons.

The teacher will record every demonstration of the student's positive interactions as evidenced by the chart publicly displayed in the gym. The teacher will award points during class and supervise free time in the gym on Friday afternoons if the student earns the prescribed number of points.

This agreement is between [student's name] and [teacher's name]. The contract begins on [specify date] and ends on [specify date]. It will be reviewed on [specify date].

Student's signature _____ Date_____

Teacher's signature _____ Date_____

FIGURE 9.1 Behavior contract in physical education.

Table 9.2 Physical Restraint: Types and Definitions

Restraint types	Definition
Mechanical restraint	The use of devices as a means of restricting a student's freedom of movement
Physical escort	The temporary touching or holding of the hand, arm, shoulder, or back for the purpose of inducing a student who is acting out to walk to a safe location
Physical restraint	A personal restriction that immobilizes or reduces the ability of an individual to move the arms, legs, or head freely (does not include physical escorts)
Seclusion	A behavior-control technique involving locked isolation (not including time-outs)
Time-out	A behavior management technique that is part of an approved treatment program and might involve the separation of the student from the group in a nonlocked setting for the purpose of calming (not the same as seclusion)

The approved policies and procedures of a local educational agency should be followed when assessing students with behavioral disorders for the purpose of establishing IEP goals and objectives in physical education. Valid and reliable tests should be used to assess physical fitness and gross motor skills. Instruments such as the Test of Gross Motor Development (TGMD-2) and the Brockport Physical Fitness Test (BPFT) should be used when appropriate. Additionally, ecological or functional assessment techniques might be used when standardized testing protocols are inappropriate. Ecological and functional approaches are discussed in chapter 4.

Exercise programs have been shown to exert a positive influence on disruptive behavior. As little as 10 or 15 minutes of jogging daily has produced a significant reduction in the disruptive behavior of children (Yell, 1988). Elliot, Dobbin, Rose, and Soper (1994) reported a reduction in maladaptive and stereotypic behaviors in adults with autism and intellectual disabilities following vigorous aerobic exercise. Using functional analysis, Roane and Kelley (2008) developed an intervention for decreasing problem behavior during a walking program with a 16-year-old female with developmental and physical disabilities, including self-injurious behaviors.

Depending on students' developmental abilities and behavioral characteristics, they should be placed in a class that can meet their needs. Regardless of placement, the type of programming chosen and the degree of peer interaction are two variables of considerable import. The first area of concern is the program itself. Because some students with behavioral disabilities might demonstrate a lag in physical and motor abilities, the physical educator must provide them with appropriate developmental activities. The emphasis should be on physical conditioning, balance, and basic movement. In this regard, Bar-Eli, Hartman, and Levy-Kolker (1994) determined that goal setting, more specifically the establishment of both short- and long-term goals, produced the greatest increase in performance of a fitness task with a group of adolescent male and female subjects with behavioral disorders. The development of fundamental locomotor and nonlocomotor movements also requires attention. In addition, it might be necessary to emphasize perceptual–motor activities because students with behavioral disabilities often demonstrate inadequacies in this area.

Relaxation is another program component that deserves a special place in the normal movement routine of many students with behavioral disorders. Making the transition from gym to classroom can be difficult for students with hyperactive behavior. This difficulty is not a reason to eliminate vigorous activity from these students' programs; rather, it is a reason to provide additional time, a buffer, during which the students can use relaxation techniques they have been taught. The ability to play effectively is crucial to success in physical education. Because games are a part of the physical education program for most students with behavioral disorders, it is essential for teachers to be aware of the relation between the type of activity chosen and the degree to which inappropriate behavior is likely to occur. The type of programming chosen directly relates to the amount of aggression demonstrated by students during activity. Reduced body contact, simplified rules, and fewer skill requirements are some of the variables that seem to control aggression. Not to be overlooked is the New Games approach (Fluegelman, 1976), which has a cooperative rather than competitive orientation. In light of the problems surrounding self-concept and the antisocial behavior exhibited by some students with behavioral disorders, the least desirable situation is one that prescribes winners and losers or that rewards overly aggressive behavior.

Nontraditional activities such as initiatives and low-ropes challenges also have a place in physical education curricula for students with behavioral disorders. Initiatives are games or other problem-solving activities that foster trust and respect between group members; they provide opportunities to create leadership and team building skills. Cluphf (2003) describes the use of these activities as a useful tool in developing physical skills as well as the value of teamwork and personal persistence in the face of failure.

SPECIFIC APPROACHES FOR PHYSICAL EDUCATION AND SPORT

This section provides two examples of specific approaches used in physical education and sport for students with behavioral disorders. The humanistic orientation can be used with all students, including those who have milder forms of behavioral disorders, and the behavioral approach is employed by educators working with students with both mild and severe behavioral difficulties.

Humanistic Approach

In physical education, students with behavior disabilities ranging from mild to severe can be taught through the humanistic approach. In this context, humanism is applied to skill acquisition and the management of social behaviors. Generally speaking, some techniques suggested by Sherrill (2004) for improving self-concept are singularly applicable with this population; for example, teachers should strive to do the following (p. 234):

■ Conceptualize individual and small-group counseling as an integral part of physical education.

■ Teach students to care about each other and show that they care.

■ Emphasize cooperation and social interaction rather than individual performance.

■ Stress the importance of genuineness and honesty in praise.

■ Increase perceived competence in relation to motor skill and fitness.

■ Convey that they like and respect students as human beings, not just for their motor skills and fitness.

More specifically, the approach outlined by Hellison (2003) has immediate relevance for practitioners confronted with students who are usually high functioning but who lack self-control and consequently present management problems. Hellison has developed a set of alternative goals or levels for physical education that focus on human needs and values rather than on fitness and sport skill development exclusively. The main purpose of Hellison's approach is to develop positive social responsibility. The goals are developmental and reflect a loosely constructed level-by-level progression of attitudes and behaviors. They include self-control and respect for the rights and feelings of others, participation and effort, self-direction, and caring and helping.

Level 0: Irresponsibility. This level defines students who fail to take responsibility either for their actions or inactions; they blame others for their behavior and typically make excuses.

Level I: Respecting the rights and feelings of others. This level deals with the need for control of one's own behavior. Self-control should be the first goal, according to Helli-son, because learning cannot take place effectively if one cannot control impulses to harm others physically and verbally.

Level II: Participation and effort. Level II focuses on the need for physical activity and offers students one medium for personal stability through experiences in which they can engage on a daily basis. Participation involves getting uninterested students to at least go through the motions, experiencing various degrees of effort expenditure to determine if effort leads to improvement and redefining success as a personal accomplishment.

Level III: Self-direction. Level III emphasizes the need for students to take more responsibility for their choices and to link these choices with their own identities. Students at this level can work independently in class and can take responsibility for their intentions and actions. At this level, students begin to assume responsibility for the direction of their lives and to explore options in developing a strong and integrated personal identity. This level includes developing a knowledge base that will enhance achievement of their goals, developing a plan to accomplish their goals, and evaluating their plan to determine their success.

Level IV: Caring and helping. Level IV is the most difficult for students; it is also not a requirement for successful participation in the responsibility model. At this level, students reach out beyond themselves to others, committing themselves to genuinely caring about other people. Students are motivated to give support, cooperate, show concern, and help. Generally speaking, the goal of level IV is the improvement of the entire group's welfare.

Level V: Outside the gym. Level V promotes the opportunity to transfer many of the lessons learned in the gym to other areas of life. It also implies being a role model.

Hellison recognized that these five goals provide only a framework and that strategies must be employed to help students interact with self-control and respect for the rights and feelings of others, participate and show effort, be self-directed, and demonstrate caring and helping behavior on a regular basis. He suggests five interaction strategies to help reach the goals. These include awareness talks (e.g., post levels on gym wall and refer to them frequently), the physical education lesson (e.g., students can be taught to solve conflict during a game), group meetings (e.g., students discuss issues of low motivation or difficulty in being self-directed), reflection time (e.g., students record in a journal or discuss how they did during class in relation to the goals they had established), and counseling time (e.g., students discuss their patterns of abusive behavior and possibly their underlying motives for such behavior). This last strategy gives students the opportunity to talk with the teacher about problems preventing them from achieving their goals within specified levels of the responsibility model. These strategies are "processes for helping students to become aware of, experience, make decisions about, and reflect on the model's goals" (Hellison & Templin, 1991, p. 108). See table 9.3 for a brief examination of the relationship between the levels and strategies in Hellison's model.

Many physical education programs use games to accomplish goals and objectives established for individuals and classes. Because students with behavioral disorders often lack fundamental skills, they frequently are incapable of demonstrating even minimal levels of competence in these games. As a result, they have an increased tendency to act out—perhaps with verbal or physical aggression—or to withdraw, which further excludes them from an opportunity to develop skills.

In an effort to promote the most positive learning environment, Hellison (2003) developed a nontraditional approach to working with at-risk students, using basketball as the primary vehicle for empowering students to learn personal and social values. Employing Hellison's responsibility model (discussed previously) as the philosophical underpinning, the coaching club is a before-school program in Chicago's inner city. It offers students the opportunity to explore movement through a progression of five levels: (I) self-con-

Table 9.3　Hellison's Take Personal and Social Responsibility Model

Strategies	Levels	Examples in physical education and activity settings
Awareness talks	I-V	Verbally remind students during an activity about the levels of responsibility. Model attitudes and behaviors associated with levels during an activity. Conduct student sharing sessions before, during, or after the activity.
Physical activity lesson	I-IV	Students are encouraged to play in a cooperative game. Students are taught how to solve conflict during a game. Students who have been successful in an activity help those who have not been successful.
Individual decision making	I-V	Students who are abusive can choose to sit out of an activity or modify their behavior. A student who chooses to participate in a game of table tennis with friends needs to decide if table tennis is the best way to achieve the goal of increased aerobic capacity.
Group meetings	I and IV primarily II and III potentially	Students discuss what constitutes self-control and the consequences for violating the rules established for participating in the activity. Students verbally evaluate what they thought of the activity that was just completed and the role of the instructor during class.
Reflection time	I-V	Students journal about what occurred during class. Students use a checklist to evaluate the degree to which they were successful in achieving personal goals.
Counseling time	I-V	Teacher and student discuss the student's pattern of aggressive behavior during that day's activity. Teacher and student discuss the amount of effort expended by the student during that day's activity and how it related to the student's personal program goals.

trol, meaning control of one's body and temper; (II) teamwork, meaning full participation by all team members; (III) self-coaching; (IV) coaching another team member; and (V) applying skills learned in the program outside the gym to school, home, and neighborhood. Playing ability is not a prerequisite. This program promotes social responsibility. Likewise, extrinsic rewards are unnecessary because students are motivated to reach level IV (coach) on the evaluation system (Hellison & Georgiadis, 1992, p. 7). Level IV consists of the following:

- Has good attendance.
- Is coachable and on task at practice.
- Does not abuse others or interrupt practice.
- Is able to set personal goals and work independently on these goals.
- Possesses good helping skills (such as giving cues, observing, and giving positive feedback as well as general praise).
- Encourages teamwork and passing the ball.
- Listens to players; is sensitive to their feelings and needs.
- Puts the welfare of players above own needs (such as the need to win or look good).
- Understands that exhibiting these characteristics is the key to being a good coach, regardless of personal basketball ability.

Behavioral Approach

Students with severe behavior disorders require intense programming efforts. This group includes students who are self-indulgent, aggressive, noncompliant, and self-stimulatory or self-destructive (Dunn & Leitschuh, 2006). Using the basic steps of behavioral programming discussed in chapter 6, Dunn and associates developed the data-based gymnasium (DBG). This program incorporates behavioral principles in a systematic effort to produce procedural consistency for teachers who work with students with behavioral disorders and to bring student behavior under the control of naturally occurring reinforcers. To the latter end, instructors use natural reinforcers available in the environment, such as praising a desirable behavior to strengthen it or ignoring an undesirable behavior to bring about its extinction. Tangible reinforcers such as token economies are introduced only after it has been demonstrated that the consistent use of social reinforcement or

extinction will not achieve the desired behavioral outcome.

In an effort to equip teachers with consistent behavioral procedures, Dunn and Leitschuh (2006) use a variety of strategies, including rules of thumb, to apply to inappropriate behavior. For each area of inappropriate behavior (e.g., self-indulgent behavior), there exists a rule of thumb or generally accepted way of responding when certain undesirable behaviors occur. The intent of these rules is to make the development and implementation of a formal behavioral program unnecessary.

- *Self-indulgent behavior.* Behaviors in this category include crying, screaming, throwing tantrums, and performing repetitive, irritating activities or noises. The rule of thumb for handling students who engage in self-indulgent behaviors is to ignore them until the behavior is discontinued and then socially reinforce the first occurrence of an appropriate behavior. For example, one would ignore children's tantrums when they cannot control a play situation with classmates but reinforce with social praise their initial attempts to play cooperatively.

- *Noncompliant behavior.* Noncompliant behaviors include instances when students decline to comply when instructed to do something as well as forgetting or failing to do something because they choose not to do what is asked. Noncompliance also includes doing what is requested but in a less than acceptable way. The rule of thumb is that teachers should ignore noncompliant verbalizations, lead students physically through the task, or prevent students from participating in an activity until they follow through on the initial request. Compliance with any request is immediately reinforced socially. For example, one would physically restrict aggressive play and socially praise a child's positive engagement with a classmate or group.

- *Aggressive behavior.* Verbal or physical abuse directed toward an object or a person is considered aggressive behavior. Examples of aggressive acts include hitting, fighting, pinching, biting, pushing, or deliberately destroying someone's property. The rule of thumb for aggressive behavior is that it is punished immediately with a verbal reprimand and the offending student is removed from the activity. Social reinforcement is given when students demonstrate appropriate interaction with other people or objects. For example, a student who strikes another student is immediately reprimanded verbally (conflict resolution) and is eliminated from the activity (given a time-out; see chapter 6).

■ *Self-stimulatory behavior.* This category includes behaviors that interfere with learning because students become engrossed in the preservative nature of the activities. Examples include head banging, hand flapping, body rocking, and eye gouging. As a rule of thumb, Dunn and associates recommend a formal behavioral program to deal with this type of behavior. An in-depth discussion of formal principles and programs for behavior modification is presented in chapter 6.

POSITIVE BEHAVIORAL INTERVENTIONS AND SUPPORT SYSTEMS

When engaging the topic of positive behavioral interventions and support (PBIS) for the first time, it is important to define its parameters. Positive behavior support (PBS) is "a comprehensive set of strategies meant to redesign environments in such a way that problem behaviors are prevented or inconsequential, and to teach students new skills, make problem behavior unnecessary" (Association of Positive Behavior Support, n.d.). PBS appears to be synonymous with applied behavior analysis (ABA), but in reality, ABA is the root discipline for PBS. PBS uses ABA with particular emphasis on the three-part contingency (i.e., antecedent-behavior-consequence, or ABC).

PBS is required when students' behaviors impede their ability to learn or interfere with others' learning and are caused or related to their disability. In consideration of these needs, school personnel should address individual needs by altering environments and explicitly teaching new skills to students with challenging behaviors so that they genuinely appreciate positive behavior.

Nature of Positive Behavior Support

PBS has its roots in three major sources: ABA, normalization and inclusion, and person-centered values (Carr et al., 2002). The essence of PBS resides in its emphasis on improving the quality of life not only for the students with disabilities but also for those who engage with and support them. PBS recognizes that challenging behaviors do occur; however, an overarching principle of PBS is to intervene when those behaviors are not occurring. It emphasizes positive support tech-niques rather than the traditional use of aversive or negative procedures to control challenging behaviors. The way to accomplish this goal is to teach desirable behaviors. This involves altering or redesigning environments to support appropriate behavior; it encourages and facilitates informed choice making with opportunities to exercise real choices. It means providing appropriate role models, including peers, teachers, and coaches.

Lastly, PBS recognizes the need to respond to and manage crisis situations. For example, when challenging behaviors become extreme, teachers and coaches need to know their options for helping students while being sensitive to protecting students' rights. According to Johnston, Foxx, Jacobson, Green, and Mulick (2006), "It is clear that PBS emphasizes certain values in its approach to services. These values include commitments to respect for the individual, meaningful outcomes, social validation, dignity, normalization, inclusion, person-centered planning, self-determination, and stakeholder participation, among others" (p. 52).

Discipline

After the reauthorization of IDEA in 2004, the rules and regulations for disciplining students with disabilities changed considerably. Several new standards, provisions, and definitions were added. The more notable changes (IDEA, 2004) are detailed here:

■ School personnel now are given new (consistent) authority to determine on a case-by-case basis the necessity for ordering a change in placement for a student with a disability who violates the student code of conduct.

■ School personnel can now remove a student with a disability who violates a student conduct code from an existing placement to an interim alternative education placement, another setting, or suspension for not more than 10 consecutive school days to the extent that such alternatives are applied to students without disabilities.

■ A substantial change in the standard for manifestation determination was established: Within 10 school days of any decision to change the placement of a student with a disability, the IEP team must determine if the misconduct was a manifestation of (i.e., caused by or related to) the student's disability. Table 9.4 illustrates the new standard for manifestation determination when compared with PL 105-17.

■ If the IEP team determines that misconduct was a manifestation of the student's disability, then the team will conduct a functional behavioral assessment and develop a **behavioral intervention plan** (BIP). If a BIP has already been developed, then the IEP team will review the plan and make modifications where necessary. If the student has been removed from the original placement, the student will then be returned to that placement unless the parent and local education agency agree otherwise.

■ A student with a disability can be removed to an interim alternative educational setting (IAES) for not more than 45 days without regard to whether the behavior is determined to be a manifestation of the student's disability for the following: carrying or possessing a weapon; possessing, using, selling, or soliciting illegal drugs; or inflicting serious bodily injury on another person while at school, on school premises, or at a school function.

If students with disabilities violate the school conduct code, they can be suspended for up to 10 days in a school year. Likewise, if students with disabilities are involved with drugs, bring weapons to school, or place themselves or other students in danger, they can be assigned to an alternative placement for up to 45 days. In these cases the IEP team must determine the appropriate IAES, which means the team must determine if the student's misbehavior was a function of a disability (i.e., was the student's ability to understand the consequences of the behavior or to control the behavior subject to disciplinary action impaired?). This process is called *manifestation determination*. If the student's behavior is determined to be related to the disability, the student is subject to IDEA disciplinary procedures. Implementing a two-stage process—namely, conducting a **functional behavioral assessment** (FBA) and designing a BIP—accomplishes this task.

Functional Behavioral Assessment

Students with disabilities (particularly behavioral disorders) who exhibit dangerous or unruly behavior are not exonerated from responsibility for behavior that is considered extreme. The 1997 and 2004 reauthorizations of IDEA created and extended due process policies to ensure that students with disabilities who violate school conduct codes will continue to receive an appropriate education as specified in their IEP. Additionally, the IEP must also specify an appropriate intervention plan to ameliorate the student's challenging behavior.

IDEA requires that prior to expulsion, alternative school placement, or suspension for more than 10 days, a student with a disability must have an FBA, "a systematic method of gathering information about behavior and its relationship with the environment in which it occurs; its goal is to identify the function or purpose that behavior serves for the student under specific environmental conditions" (Payne, Scott, & Conroy, 2007). FBAs can be as simple as the teacher completing a questionnaire or as involved as direct observation for 20 or more hours and experimental manipulation of variables to promote behavioral control.

Cunningham and O'Neill (2007) demonstrated that rating scales, questionnaires, and teacher and student interviews are significantly less effective in functionally analyzing behavior than are direct observation and informal ABC evaluation. For example, a member of the IEP team could observe a student during physical education class and record the frequency of an undesirable behavior, such as physical or verbal abuse during competitive team activities. Additionally, the observer would attempt to identify antecedent events such as occasions when the student is in a one-on-one situation with a particular classmate that might cause an increase in the physical or verbal abuse. See figure 9.2 for an example of an FBA form.

Table 9.4 Changes in the Standard for Manifestation Determination From PL 105-17 to PL 108-446

PL 105-17 (1997)	PL 108-446 (2004)
Was the student's ability to understand the consequences of behavior impaired?	Was the conduct caused by or did it have a direct and substantial relationship to the student's disability?
Was the student's ability to control the behavior subject to disciplinary action impaired?	Was the conduct a direct result of failure by the local education agency to implement the IEP?

Student name: *Seth Zion*   ID: _____   DOB: *3/9/96*   Case manager: *Mrs. Loovis*

Data sources: ☑ Observation I ☑ Student interview I ☑ Teacher interview I ☐ Parent interview I ☐ Rating scales I ☐ Normative testing

Description of behavior:

Student physically and verbally abuses classmates during physical education class.

Settings in which behavior occurs:

Abusive behavior typically occurs during competitive situations (e.g., during a basketball game).

Frequency:

Behaviors occur, on average, at least three times per class period.

Intensity (consequences of problem behavior on student, peers, and instructional environment):

Behavior has resulted in physical injury to several students and a general reluctance on the part of most students to want to compete against Seth.

Duration:

Episodes can be as brief as 10 or 15 seconds in the case of verbal abuse to lengthier confrontations lasting 1 or 2 minutes during physical confrontations.

Previous interventions:

Parent conferences, in-school suspension, and student conference

Educational impact:

Disrupting other peers and failure to make adequate educational progress in physical education

FIGURE 9.2 Sample functional behavioral assessment.

Courtesy of Jeffrey A. Miller at Duquesne University; http://mfba.net/forms.html).

Function of behavior: Specify hypothesized function for each area checked in this section.

☐ *Affective regulation/emotional reactivity (Identify emotional factors, such as anxiety, depression, anger, and poor self-concept, that play a role in organizing or directing problem behavior):*

Student is embarrassed when making mistakes that classmates think are silly.

☐ **Cognitive distortion (Identify distorted thoughts, such as inaccurate attributions, negative self-statements, and erroneous interpretations of events, that play a role in organizing or directing problem behavior):**

☐ **Reinforcement (Identify environmental triggers and payoffs that play a role in organizing and directing problem behavior):**

Antecedents: Engaging in team sports such as basketball.

Consequences: Student uses physical and verbal attacks against classmates to deflect attention away from his fundamentally inadequate motor skills.

☐ **Modeling (Identify the degree to which the behavior is copied, who the student copying the behavior from, and why the student is copying the behavior):**

Not an issue.

☐ **Family issues (Identify family issues that play a part in organizing and directing problem behavior):**

☐ **Physiological/constitutional issues (Identify physiological and personality characteristics, such as developmental disabilities and temperament, that play a part in organizing and directing problem behavior):**

☐ **Communicate need (Identify what the student is trying to say through the problem behavior):**

Student is communicating his embarrassment about his inability to perform basic motor skills.

☐ **Curriculum/instruction (Identify how instruction, curriculum, or educational environment play a part in organizing and directing problem behavior):**

Abusive behavior occurs when instructional expectations exceed his physical and motor abilities.

FIGURE 9.2 *(continued)*

Courtesy of Jeffrey A. Miller at Duquesne University; http://mfba.net/forms.html).

After identifying the student's behavioral difficulty, the IEP team is legally responsible for developing the BIP. Note that IDEA does not specify what components should be detailed in the plan, merely that the plan must be developed (Maag & Katsiyannis, 2006).

Behavioral Intervention Plan

Once the behaviors in question are understood, intervention is designed and implemented. BIPs address students' motives for misbehaving, their likes and dislikes, and the effectiveness of various positive (and negative) reinforcers. BIPs are intended to emphasize positive interactions and behaviors. They should not be designed to punish the student or to catch the student misbehaving. BIPs should also be developed by as many people as necessary who have interactions with the student. It is for this reason that physical educators must understand the purposes and design of the BIP and participate in its implementation.

Scott and Nelson (1999) proposed a process that links FBAs and BIPs. This process involves 10 steps:

1. Determining the function of the undesirable behavior
2. Determining an appropriate alternative behavior
3. Determining how frequently the alternative behavior should occur
4. Developing a teaching sequence
5. Manipulating the environmental context to increase the probability of success
6. Altering the environment to decrease the probability of failure
7. Determining how positive responses will be reinforced
8. Determining consequences for instances of problem behavior
9. Developing a data-collection system
10. Developing goals and objectives in behavioral and measurable terms

In many respects, development and implementation of the 10-step FBA and BIP process parallel the ABA approach outlined in chapter 6. Figure 9.3 is an example of a BIP that has been constructed with consideration of this 10-step process.

INCLUSION

Based on data collected through 2003 (U.S. Department of Education, 2007), students with behavioral disorders are receiving their education in greater and greater numbers in the regular education classroom: 30.2 percent of students with behavioral disorders spend more than 60 percent of the school day in regular classrooms, and another 23 percent spend between 21 and 60 percent of the school day in the regular classroom. Students with behavioral disorders who spend less than 21 percent of the day in regular classrooms equal 33.3 percent. The remaining 16.89 percent receive their education in separate facilities, in residential facilities, and at home or in hospitals (11.96, 3.79, and 1.24 percent, respectively). These data indicate that physical educators are likely to have students with behavioral disorders in their regular physical education classes.

The inclusion of students with behavioral disorders into the regular class should be based primarily on the frequency, intensity, and duration of behavioral episodes. These students will demonstrate behavioral characteristics ranging from mild to severe. For those with mild behavioral profiles, the regular class is easily the placement of choice. The decision becomes more difficult if the student's behaviors are significantly more severe, even with a management plan in effect.

In terms of students with behavioral disorders, inclusion is facilitated much of the time through development and implementation of a BIP. As discussed, these plans detail student expectations and consequences if behavioral expectations are not achieved. Students who have severe behavior disorders such that they are either disruptive and interfere with the operation of the regular class or are harmful to themselves or others might require a segregated approach.

SUMMARY

Behavioral conditions correspond to the categories of behavior disorders and emotional disturbance as defined in IDEA. This chapter provided ideas for teaching and managing students with identified behavioral disorders in physical education classes. Effective interpersonal communication was discussed, specifically, active listening, verbal mediation, and conflict resolution. The work of Hellison and the contributions of Dunn and colleagues were cited as effective approaches in physical education and sport for students with behavioral disorders and students considered at risk.

Physical educators are called on to promote PBS (Safran & Oswald, 2003). They are asked to contribute as members of schoolwide behavior

Behavioral Intervention Plan

Name: Seth Zion

Grade: 6

Age: 12

School: ABC Middle School

Date written: 1/15/2009

Strength of Student

- Wants to be in the general physical education class and generally wants to do the same work as his peers.
- Usually responds well to teachers.
- Enjoys praise and positive, social reinforcement.
- Participates in physical education most days.

Individualized Information About the Student

- Some behaviors associated with conduct disorder are apparent. These include bullying and intimidation, initiating fights, and being physically cruel to classmates.
- Often works and moves slower than peers.
- Has difficulty with tasks necessitating age-appropriate motor skills.

Previously Implemented Interventions

Negative reinforcement, response cost, and positive reinforcement with tangibles. These interventions were not effective.

Problematic Behaviors: Physical and Verbal Abuse Toward Classmates

Baseline: Average of at least three episodes per day for the last three weeks

Function of Behavior

Student uses physical and verbal attacks against classmates to deflect attention away from his fundamentally inadequate motor skills.

Replacement Behavior

Student will use compliments and positive physical gestures that show respect for classmates.

Interventions

A. Student will learn personal responsibility by participating in and progressing through Hellison's model using appropriate levels and strategies.

B. Student will be teamed with peers who understand his challenging behavior and who have volunteered to prompt appropriate behavior.

C. Student is placed in instructional situations that require fewer skills, thus reducing the likelihood of embarrassing mistakes that typically precipitate abusive episodes.

D. Student will receive social praise from the teacher and classmates for each occurrence of desirable behavior.

E. Student's verbal abuse will be ignored; physical attacks will result in a time-out.

Documentation

- Teacher will record the frequency of physical and verbal abuse during scheduled class time.
- Results will be shared with student in an effort to communicate the frequency and perhaps the severity of instances of abuse.
- Teacher will document particular situations or combinations of students that act as antecedents to episodes of abusive behavior.

Amount of Improvement Expected

- No more than one episode of verbal abuse per class session
- Zero instances of physical abuse

FIGURE 9.3 Sample behavior intervention plan.

management systems that not only provide sound and consistent discipline policies but also address the need for positive behavioral instruction. These models (ERIC/OSEP Special Project, 1997) share several features:

- Total staff commitment to managing behavior, whatever approach is taken
- Clearly defined and communicated expectations and rules
- Consequences and clearly stated procedures for correcting rule-breaking behaviors
- An instructional component for teaching self-control and social skill strategies
- A support plan to address the needs of students with chronic, challenging behaviors

REFERENCES

Achenbach, T.M., Howell, C.T., Quay, H.C., & Conners, C.K. (1991). National survey of problems and competencies among 4- to 16-year-olds: Parents' reports for normative and clinical samples. *Monographs of the Society for Research in Child Development, 56* (3), serial no. 225.

American Academy of Experts in Traumatic Stress. (2003). *A practical guide for crisis response in our schools.* Commack, NY: Author.

American Psychiatric Association (APA). (1994). *Diagnostic and statistical manual of mental disorders (DSM IV)* (4th ed.). Washington, DC: Author.

Association of Positive Behavior Support. (n.d.) Retrieved December, 15, 2008, from www.apbs.org/new_apbs/files/Overall%20Glossary.pdf.

Bar-Eli, M., Hartman, I., & Levy-Kolker, N. (1994). Using goal setting to improve physical performance of adolescents with behavior disorders: The effect of goal proximity. *Adapted Physical Activity Quarterly, 11,* 86-97.

Block, M.E. (2007). *A teacher's guide to including students with disabilities in general physical education* (3rd ed.). Baltimore: Brookes.

Carr, E.G., Dunlap, G., Horner, R.H., Koegel, R.L., Turnbull, A.P., Sailor, W., et al. (2002). Positive behavior support: Evolution of an applied science. *Journal of Positive Behavior Interventions, 4,* 4-16, 20.

Cluphf, D. (2003). A low-ropes initiative unit for at-risk students. *Strategies, 17,* 13-16.

Cullinan, D. (2007). *Students with emotional and behavioral disorders* (2nd ed.). Upper Saddle River, NJ: Pearson.

Cunningham, E.M., & O'Neill, R.E. (2007). Agreement of functional behavioral assessment and analysis methods with students with EBD. *Behavioral Disorders, 32,* 211-221.

Dunn, J.M., & Leitschuh, C. (2006). *Special physical education* (8th ed.). Dubuque, IA: Kendall/Hunt.

Elliot, R.O., Dobbin, A.R., Rose, G.D., & Soper, H.V. (1994). Vigorous, aerobic exercise versus general motor training activities: Effects on maladaptive and stereotypic behaviors of adults with both autism and mental retardation. *Journal of Autism and Developmental Disorders, 24,* 565-576.

ERIC/OSEP Special Project. (1997). *Research connections in special education.* Reston, VA: ERIC Clearinghouse on Disabilities and Gifted Education/Council for Exceptional Children.

Fluegelman, A. (Ed.). (1976). *The new games book.* Garden City, NJ: Dolphin Books.

Forness, S.R., Walker, H.M., & Kavale, K.A. (2003). Psychiatric disorders and treatments: A primer for teachers. *Teaching Exceptional Children, 36,* 42-49.

Frank, K., Paget, M., Bowman, B., & Wilde, J. (1998). *Creative strategies for working with ODD children and adolescents.* Chapin, SC: Youthlight.

Fujiura, G.T., & Yamati, K. (2000). Trends in demography of childhood poverty and disability. *Exceptional Child, 66,* 187-199.

Gartin, B.C., Murdick, N.L., Imbeau, M., & Perner, D.E. (2002). *How to use differentiated instruction with students with developmental disabilities in the general education classroom.* Arlington, VA: Council for Exceptional Children.

Hellison, D.R. (2003). *Teaching responsibility through physical activity* (2nd ed.). Champaign, IL: Human Kinetics.

Hellison, D.R., & Georgiadis, N. (1992). Teaching values through basketball. *Strategies, 5,* 5-8.

Hellison, D.R., & Templin, T.J. (1991). *A reflective approach to teaching physical education.* Champaign, IL: Human Kinetics.

Individuals with Disabilities Education Act Amendments of 2004 (IDEA) (PL 108-446), 20 U.S.C. 1400 (2004).

Johnston, J.M., Foxx, R.M., Jacobson, J.W., Green, G., & Mulick, J.A. (2006). Positive behavior support and applied behavior analysis. *Behavior Analyst, 29,* 51-74.

Kamps, D., Kravits, T., Stolze, J., & Swaggart, B. (1999). Prevention strategies for students at risk and identified as serious emotionally disturbed in urban, elementary school settings. *Journal of Emotional and Behavioral Disorders, 7,* 178-188.

Kauffman, J.M., & Landrum, T.J. (2009). *Characteristics of emotional and behavioral disorders of children and youth* (9th ed.). Upper Saddle, NJ: Merrill.

Maag, J.W., & Katsiyannis, A. (2006). Behavior intervention plans: Legal and practical considerations for students with emotional and behavioral disorders. *Behavioral Disorders, 31,* 348-362.

Musser, E.H., Bray, M.A., Kehle, T.J., & Jenson, W.R. (2001). Reducing disruptive behaviors in students with serious emotional disturbance. *School Psychology Review, 30,* 294-304.

Payne, L.D., Scott, T.M., & Conroy, M. (2007). A school-based examination of the efficacy of function-based intervention. *Behavioral Disorders, 32,* 158-174.

Quay, H.C. (1986). Classification. In H.C. Quay & J.S. Werry (Eds.), *Psychopathological disorders of childhood* (3rd ed., pp. 1-34). New York: Wiley.

Quay, H.C., & Peterson, D.R. (1987). *Manual for the revised behavior problem checklist.* Coral Gables, FL: Authors.

Roane, H.S., & Kelley, M.E. (2008). Decreasing problem behavior associated with a walking program for an individual with developmental and physical disabilities. *Journal of Applied Behavior Analysis, 41,* 423-428.

Safran, S.P., & Oswald, K. (2003). Positive behavior supports: Can schools reshape disciplinary practices? *Exceptional Child, 69,* 361-373.

Sagor, R., & Cox, J. (2004). *At-risk students: Reaching and teaching them* (2nd ed.). Larchmont, NY: Eye on Education.

Scott, T.M., & Nelson, C.M. (1999). Using functional behavioral assessment to develop effective behavioral intervention plans: A practical classroom application. *Journal of Positive Behavioral Support, 1,* 242-251.

Sherrill, C. (2004). *Adapted physical activity, recreation and sport: Crossdisciplinary and lifespan* (6th ed.). Madison, WI: Brown & Benchmark.

Sinclair, E. (1998). Head Start children at risk: Relationship of prenatal drug exposure to identification of special needs and subsequent special education kindergarten placement. *Behavioral Disorders, 23,* 125-133.

Steinberg, Z., & Knitzer, J. (1992). Classrooms for emotionally and behaviorally disturbed students: Facing the challenge. *Behavioral Disorders, 17,* 145-156.

Sutherland, K.S. (2000). Promoting positive interactions between teachers and students with emotional/behavioral disorders. *Preventing School Failure, 44,* 110-115.

U.S. Department of Education. (2007). 27th annual report to Congress on the implementation of the Individuals with Disabilities Education Act, 2005 (Vol. 2). Washington, DC: Author.

U.S. Department of Education, Office of Special Education and Rehabilitative Services. (August 14, 2006). Code of Federal Regulations, Title 34, Section 300.530, Assistance to States for the Education of Children with Disabilities. Washington, DC: Author.

Van Haren, B.A., & Fiedler, C. (2004). Physical restraint and seclusion of students with disabilities. *Beyond Behavior, 13 1* (3), 17-19.

Yell, M.L. (1988). The effects of jogging on the rates of selected target behaviors of behaviorally disordered students. *Behavioral Disorders, 13,* 273-279.

WRITTEN RESOURCES

Goldstein, A.P., Sprafkin, R.P., Gershaw, N.J., & Klein, P. (1980). *Skillstreaming the adolescent: A structured learning approach to teaching prosocial skills.* Champaign, IL: Research Press.

This innovative program is designed to help adolescents develop competence in dealing with interpersonal conflicts, increase self-esteem, and contribute to a positive classroom atmosphere.

Kauffman, J.M. (2005). *Cases in emotional and behavioral disorders of children and youth.* Upper Saddle River, NJ: Pearson Education.

This is an adjunct resource that accompanies Kauffman's popular textbook on the same subject matter. Real-life case studies are presented along with questions that can be discussed in class.

Wood, M.M., & Long, N.J. (1991). *Life-space intervention: Talking with children and youth in crisis.* Austin, TX: Pro-Ed.

This is an updated version of the pioneering work of Fritz Redl with emphasis on the intervention, because *crisis* implies verbal intervention. Talking strategies are presented and applied to particular types of problems.

AUDIOVISUAL RESOURCES

Conflict resolution [interactive videodisc]. (1993). University of South Florida, I'm Special Production Network, Tampa, FL 33620-8600.

This level III interactive application (external computer that uses a videodisc player as a peripheral device) teaches students how to send appropriate I-messages, use active listening, and conduct the conflict-resolution process. It is aimed at undergraduate students and career teachers who will teach students with behavioral disabilities.

Understanding the defiant child [VHS]. (1997). Guilford Publications, 72 Spring St., New York, NY 10012.

Dr. Russell Barkley presents a clear and easily understood resource for clinicians, teachers, and parents who must deal with children who have ODD. Using real-life scenes of family interaction and parental commentary, Dr. Barkley helps viewers distinguish ODD from milder forms of misbehavior. The video likewise addresses long-term outcomes for defiant children and the correlation between ODD and ADHD.

ELECTRONIC RESOURCES

Center on Positive Behavioral Interventions and Support: http://pbis.org.

This site is the home of the Center on Positive Behavioral Interventions and Support. It is housed at the University of Oregon but has four partners: the University of Kansas, University of Kentucky, University of South Florida, and University of Missouri. The center disseminates information to schools and families and communicates information regarding the technology of schoolwide positive supports, demonstrating that PBIS is feasible and effective.

chapter 10

Autism Spectrum Disorders

Cathy Houston-Wilson

Dylan is an 11-year-old boy. He enjoys hiking and climbing rocks, the higher the better. His motor skills are average, but he expresses little interest in team sports. His verbal outbursts are mild, and he usually complies with structured tasks. Everything about Dylan is typical for any average 11-year-old boy; however, Dylan does not use language in the conventional manner. He can utter sounds that reflect his feelings (happy, sad, angry) but mostly uses pictures to communicate his wants and needs. He likes things to stay the same and only eats certain foods. His room and his toys are ordered in a certain manner and after he plays with them, they are placed back in the same order as before. These behaviors are indicative of a child with autism.

Marcia, on the other hand, is talkative. Although she is only 12, her vocabulary resembles that of a sophisticated adult. She began talking at an early age, and by age 3 she had taught herself to read. Instead of playing with typical childhood toys, Marcia was more interested in art and artists. She can look at any art history book and tell you the artist of any picture and the history of the artist. Although she is an attractive girl, she has no real friends, but she does not seem to be bothered by that. How can such a bright, beautiful girl have no friends? Marcia has Asperger syndrome.

ylan and Marcia both have behaviors that deviate from typical childhood development. According to the *DSM IV* (American Psychiatric Association [APA], 2000), these two disorders fall under the category of pervasive development disorders (PDD) and include not only autism and Asperger syndrome but also Rett's disorder, childhood disintegrative disorder (CDD), and pervasive developmental disorder, not otherwise specified (PDD-NOS). The term *pervasive* means the condition affects total development. Table 10.1 provides an overview of these conditions.

HISTORY OF AUTISM AND ASPERGER SYNDROME

Although autism was evident for quite some time, it was not until 1943 when Dr. Leo Kanner, a child psychiatrist at John Hopkins University School of Medicine, described the common characteristics of 11 children he had studied between 1938 and 1943. These children were withdrawn and engaged in isolated activities. They did not relate well to people, including their own parents, and they

Table 10.1 Summary of the DSM IV Diagnostic Criteria for Pervasive Developmental Disorders (2000)

Condition	Criteria
Autism	Impairment in social interaction with at least two of the following: • Impairment in the use of nonverbal behaviors such as facial expressions, eye gaze, and body postures • Failure to develop appropriate peer relationships • Lack of spontaneous seeking to share enjoyment, interests, or achievement with other people • Lack of social or emotional reciprocity Impairment in communication with at least one of the following: • Delay in or total lack of the development of spoken language • Marked impairments in the ability to initiate or sustain a conversation with others • Stereotyped and repetitive use of language or idiosyncratic language • Lack of spontaneous make-believe play Repetitive and stereotyped patterns of behavior with at least one of the following: • Preoccupation with one or more stereotyped and restricted patterns of interest that is abnormal in either intensity or focus • Inflexible adherence to specific, nonfunctional routines or rituals • Stereotyped and repetitive motor mannerisms Delays or abnormal functioning in at least one of the following: • Social interaction • Language as used in social communication • Symbolic or imaginative play The disturbance is not better accounted for by Rett's disorder or CDD.
Asperger syndrome	Impairment in social interaction with at least two of the following: • Impairment in the use of nonverbal behaviors such as facial expressions, eye gaze, and body postures • Failure to develop appropriate peer relationships • Lack of spontaneous seeking to share enjoyment, interests, or achievement with other people • Lack of social or emotional reciprocity Repetitive and stereotyped patterns of behavior with at least one of the following: • Preoccupation with one or more stereotyped and restricted patterns of interest that is abnormal in either intensity or focus • Inflexible adherence to specific, nonfunctional routines or rituals • Stereotyped and repetitive motor mannerisms Condition causes clinically significant impairment in social, occupational, or other important areas of function. There is no clinically significant delay in language development. There is no clinically significant delay in cognitive development or self-help skills. Criteria are not met for other specific PDD or schizophrenia.

Condition	Criteria
Rett's disorder	All of the following are used to diagnose the child with Rett's disorder: • Apparently normal prenatal and perinatal development • Apparently normal psychomotor development through the first 5 mo. after birth • Normal head circumference at birth Onset of all of the following after the period of normal development • Deceleration of head growth between ages 5 and 48 mo. • Loss of previously acquired purposeful hand skills between ages 5 and 30 mo. with the subsequent development of stereotyped hand movements • Loss of social engagement • Poor coordination and trunk movements • Severely impaired expressive and receptive language development with severe psychomotor delays
CDD	Apparently normal development for at least the first 2 yr. after birth Clinically significant loss of previously acquired skills (before the age of 10) in at least two of the following areas: • Expressive or receptive language • Social skills or adaptive behaviors • Bowel or bladder control • Play • Motor skills Abnormal functioning in at least two of the following areas: • Impairment in social interaction • Impairment in communication • Stereotyped and repetitive motor mannerisms The condition is not better accounted for by another specific PDD or schizophrenia.
PDD-NOS	This category is used when there is a severe and pervasive impairment in the development of reciprocal social interaction, verbal or nonverbal communication skills, or stereotyped behaviors, but the criteria are not met for a specific PDD, schizophrenia, or other personality disorders.

insisted on routines and displayed unusual body movements, such as flapping their hands. Many of the children could talk, saying the alphabet, for example, or reciting whole books, but they rarely used speech to communicate with others (Ozonoff, Dawson, & McPartland, 2002). In addition, these behaviors were typically exhibited before age 3. Dr. Kanner borrowed the term *autism* from a Swiss psychiatrist who coined the term to describe adults with a certain form of schizophrenia. Dr. Kanner identified these children as having *early infantile autism*. Choosing this terminology proved to be a grave mistake because it led parents to believe that their children were making a conscious effort to withdraw from a hostile and unnurturing environment. Researchers now know conclusively that this is not the case: Autism is not caused by an unloving or unnurturing environment. Thus, the term *autism* has remained, but the descriptor *early infantile* is no longer used (NIMH, 2008a).

For many years, only those children who exhibited the same behavior patterns that Dr. Kanner noted were diagnosed with autism. However, today it is clear that autism ranges in severity, and people with autism can fall anywhere within a spectrum of behaviors, from high functioning ability to low functioning ability. At around the same time that Dr. Kanner first described autism, Dr. Hans Asperger, an Austrian pediatrician, wrote a paper published in 1944 that described a condition that came to be known as Asperger syndrome. The children described by Dr. Asperger were between the ages of 6 and 11 years; these children, despite typical communication and cognitive skills, had significant problems with social interactions. The paper was virtually unknown in the United States and other non-German-speaking countries because the paper was written in German. It was not until 1981 when Dr. Lorna Wing, a prominent British researcher, discovered the paper, summarized it, and noted the similarities between Asperger syndrome and autism. Even today, some people question whether autism and Asperger syndrome are really one condition. Because Asperger syndrome is relatively new to North America, research continues in this area. The greatest similarities between autism and Asperger syndrome can be found in people diagnosed with high-functioning autism (Ozonoff et al., 2002).

AUTISM SPECTRUM DISORDERS

The following section describes each of the five conditions encompassed in the autism spectrum disorders (ASD). It is evident that the characteristics associated with each condition are similar. Although the *DSM IV* clearly distinguishes each condition, there are overlaps. All children with ASD demonstrate deficits in social interaction, verbal and nonverbal communication, repetitive behaviors or interests, and responses to sensory experiences (NIMH, 2008a).

Autism

Of the five PDD conditions, only autism is identified in federal legislation as a specific disability category. The Individuals with Disabilities Education Act (IDEA) (2004) has defined autism as "a developmental disability significantly affecting verbal and nonverbal communication and social interaction, generally evident before age 3, that adversely affects a student's educational performance. Other characteristics often associated with autism are engagement in repetitive activities and stereotyped movements, resistance to environmental change or change in daily routines, and unusual responses to sensory experiences. The term does not apply if a student's educational performance is adversely affected primarily because the student has an emotional disturbance." A student may also be diagnosed with autism after age 3 if she meets the criteria just identified. The following sections briefly describe each of these characteristics.

Communication

According to Friend (2007), about 50 percent of children with autism do not speak at all, and others have echolalic speech (*echolalic* meaning "echo"). For example, if a physical education teacher says, "Ryan, throw the ball," Ryan might repeat word for word the phrase "Ryan, throw the ball" without comprehending what is being asked of him. In other cases, the echolalia might not occur immediately but might come at odd times. A child might recall a TV commercial she saw that morning and begin singing a jingle in the middle of class. In other people with autism who have language skills, the sound of their speech might be flat or monotonous, with no apparent control over pitch or volume. In addition to having speech pattern

problems, some people with autism might not comprehend the social norms of communication and might continue to talk about a preferred topic long after the conversation should have ended. Similarly, a person might stand too close to another person when speaking or might say inappropriate things without realizing the statement will offend others (Friend, 2007).

Social Interaction

As noted in the definition of autism, one of the most noticeable characteristics of people with autism is their inability to develop normal social relationships. Often they prefer to be alone and engaged in isolated activities. They may fail to respond to their name and may avoid eye contact. They show few signs of attachment, and when attachment is observed, it is typically one-sided and unusual. For example, a child might sit on your lap and peck at your cheek. Eye contact is limited, and it often appears as if the child is looking through you rather than at you. Children with autism may also have difficulty developing peer relationships and understanding social cues (Bruey, 2004).

Repetitive Activities and Stereotyped Movements

Repetitive activities such as rocking back and forth in place or twirling and stereotyped movements such as hand flapping may be seen in children with autism. It is unclear why these movements occur, but it is believed that difficulty in processing sensory information may cause some of these reactions (Janzen, 2003). For example, fast flailing movements of the hands could signal agitation or an inability to comprehend what is being asked. Rocking back and forth can be viewed as a calming behavior used to filter out the surrounding environment. Some children may also engage in self-abusive behavior such as biting or head banging. They also tend to have a high tolerance for pain and may derive some form of physical pleasure or self-stimulation from the behavior. Professionals believe that by stimulating pain reactors, a rush of endorphins is released, perpetuating the behavior. Others speculate that self-injurious behavior is a mechanism used to escape an undesirable activity (Bruey, 2004).

Resistance to Change

Resistance to change is often evident in children with autism. They may become agitated if the bus takes a different route to school or if the daily schedule is changed to accommodate a school assembly. Similarly, they may want play objects to be placed in a pattern that only they understand. If the placement of an object is disrupted, they might become agitated. Objects might also be played with in a peculiar manner. For example, children might spin their toys over and over again or look at the toys for hours from various directions. This need for sameness (Bruey, 2004) results from the child's inability to interpret and predict daily occurrences, leading to undue anxiety. In addition, the insistence on sameness often disrupts daily activities and interferes with everyday living.

Sensory Responses

People with autism have difficulty screening out irrelevant information within the environment. Their senses allow them to overattend to some stimuli and underattend to others, thus making it difficult for them to determine the most important part of a task (Ozonoff et al., 2002). In addition, physical pressure may be craved. Some people with autism have been known to lie under couch cushions so that someone can sit on them and squeeze them. It is thought that this tight sensation provides relief from stress. Dr. Temple Grandin, a scholar with autism, created a squeeze box that provides pressure on the body. The person crawls inside the box and is able to self-regulate the amount of pressure given. Research indicates that the squeeze box creates a calming reaction in the people who use it (Bruey, 2004). Other people with autism do not want to be touched at all. Again, this demonstrates the variety among people with autism. Though all have some form of difficulty with sensory stimuli, the degree varies from person to person.

Children with autism have a reduced sensitivity to pain but are abnormally sensitive to sound, touch, or other sensory stimulation (Bruey, 2004). For example, a child with autism may become agitated at the sound of a fire drill or school announcements. Planning for these activities by providing the child with earmuffs or a warning that it will soon be announcement time may help to alleviate the stress. Some children may also find tactile stimulation disturbing and may resist being cuddled or hugged.

These characteristics describe the defining characteristics of autism. In addition, some children with autism may experience swift changes in mood, limited food preferences, sleep distur-

bances, lack of danger awareness, depression, and in some cases seizures and mental retardation (Bruey, 2004).

Asperger Syndrome

Though some people with autism may have attachment difficulties, people with Asperger syndrome can form loving bonds with their family members and other caring adults; however, they tend to have difficulty relating to their peers. The two most common characteristics of people with Asperger syndrome are impaired communication and unusual interests and behaviors.

Communication

People with Asperger syndrome are characterized by their fluent speech and vast vocabulary, but the way they use language typically differs from the norm (Ozonoff et al., 2002). They might talk on and on about a preferred topic, not noticing the disinterest of the other party. They might define terms that do not need defining. Their speech might be extremely loud or so soft that it is difficult to hear what they are saying. People with Asperger syndrome are also quite literal and have difficulty understanding jargon or sarcasm.

Social Interaction

People with Asperger syndrome typically do not follow the conventions of social interaction. They may wish to have friends and be part of a group but because of their inability to adhere to social protocol, such as making eye contact or nodding during a conversation, their success is often limited. In addition, they may be blatantly honest and say things that are inappropriate without realizing the comment was hurtful. They do not seem to understand other people's feelings or point of view; it is difficult for them to put themselves in the other person's shoes. They lack empathy and often do not understand why everyone is upset over something they did or said (Ozonoff et al., 2002).

Interests and Behaviors

Nearly all children enjoy playing computer or video games, but children with Asperger syndrome might engage in this form of activity exclusively, limiting their interactions with peers. They tend to develop strong interests in topics that seem peculiar to others, such as steel mills, botanical classifications, or vacuum cleaners. They can amass a great deal of knowledge about a topic and readily share it with others, but they often cannot see the big picture or interpret the information (Ozonoff et al., 2002). Although a child might recite obscure facts (such as the square footage of every steel mill in the United States), if you ask her which is the largest steel mill, she might become baffled and agitated by the question.

Rett's Disorder

Similar to autism and Asperger syndrome, Rett's disorder, or Rett syndrome, manifests itself during early development and results in atypical behavior. Rett's disorder is rare and affects only girls. The child begins to develop normally for at least the first 6 months of life, but typically between 6 and 18 months the child begins to display autism-like symptoms and begins to regress. Hypotonia (loss of muscle tone) is usually the first symptom noted, along with unusual use of the hands and the ability to speak. Other early symptoms may include problems crawling or walking and diminished eye contact (National Institute of Neurological Disorders and Stroke [NINDS], 2008).

The loss of functional use of the hands is followed by compulsive hand movements that resemble hand wringing and washing. Instead of using their hands for interacting with the environment, children with Rett's disorder repetitively wring, twist, clap, or rub their hands, which obviously interferes with their ability to do most tasks. Additionally, children with Rett's disorder experience slowed brain and head growth, gait abnormalities, seizures, and mental retardation. The child no longer responds to her parents and pulls away from social contact. Previously acquired motor skills are lost as a result of severe apraxia. Eventually, the child will need a wheelchair to ambulate (NINDS, 2008).

Childhood Disintegrative Disorder

Similar to children with the other PDDs that have been discussed, a child diagnosed with CDD begins to develop normally, but this development is followed by a period of regression. Language and cognitive skills are impaired. The typical age of onset is between three and four years, and it affects boys more than girls. At onset, the child begins to withdraw, no longer talks, and loses thinking skills, bowel control, and other abilities. This condition

is rare and results in severe intellectual disabilities (NIMH, 2008a).

Pervasive Developmental Disorder, Not Otherwise Specified

Some people have clear difficulty relating to others, as well as communication problems or repetitive behaviors, but they do not meet the criteria for any other PDD. They fall into the PDD-NOS classification.

ETIOLOGY

No definitive answer has been reached regarding why some children develop ASD and others do not. Some evidence suggests that autism has a genetic link or neurological link, whereas others continue to speculate about vaccinations as a possible cause.

Genetic Link

The majority of ASD cases have genetic causes. The most common genetic link is fragile X syndrome (FXS), a condition that affects both boys and girls but most severely affects boys and causes mental retardation. The National Institute of Mental Health (NIMH) (2008b) estimates that 2.5 to 6 percent of people with autism have FXS, and approximately 25 percent of children with FXS have autism. There is also evidence suggesting that autism might be inherited. A parent who has a child with an ASD has a 2 to 3 percent chance of having another child with an ASD (Bruey, 2004). This number may seem small, but it is 50 percent higher than the chances of parents of a child without an ASD.

Neurological Link

Researchers have also hypothesized that children with ASD have problems with neurotransmitters in the brain whereby messages from the brain are not transmitted properly and have difficulty reaching their destination (Bruey, 2004). In addition, children with ASD have structural differences in their brain compared with those without ASD. Scientists have discovered that children with ASD tend to have smaller heads at birth but then experience rapid growth within the first year. This rapid growth makes learning difficult because the fast pace creates abnormal neural connections, making it difficult to take in information and use it effectively (Courchesne, Carper, & Akshoomoff, 2003).

Vaccination Link

Although a great deal of information is circulating about vaccinations and their link to ASD, the medical community remains steadfast in its assertion that there is no link between vaccinations and ASD (American Medical Association, 2004). The Institute of Medicine reported no relationship between thimerosal, a mercury-based vaccine preservative, and autism, and it also rejected a causal association between the measles-mumps-rubella (MMR) vaccine and autism. By 2000, thimerosal was removed from all childhood vaccines, yet the number of children diagnosed with autism since then has not changed.

INCIDENCE

The Centers for Disease Control and Prevention (CDC) (2008) has estimated that 3 to 6 children out of 1,000 have an ASD (from 1 in 500 to 1 in 150), and males are four times more likely to have autism than females. ASD is now the second most common childhood condition behind intellectual disabilities. Researchers attribute the rise in ASD to changes in the criteria used to diagnose autism along with early detection and identification.

PHYSICAL AND MOTOR CHARACTERISTICS

Although it is clear that people affected by Rett's disorder and CDD have deficits in physical and motor abilities and that those with Asperger syndrome are known to be clumsy, research on people with autism and their physical and motor abilities is inconclusive (Reid & Collier, 2002). Early research by Rimland (1964) concluded that the motor development and movement skills of children with autism followed a typical pattern of development. More recently, Sigman and Capps (1997) stated that children with autism "display well-developed physical and motor coordination and may maintain advanced physical skills through adolescence, a characteristic that differentiates children with autism from those with Asperger Syndrome" (p. 25).

However, after reviewing several studies, Reid and Collier (2002) conclude that "autism is usually associated with movement skill delays and clumsiness" (p. 26), and although there are examples of people with autism who are quite agile and fit, research must continue in this area to determine conclusive results. Additionally, people with autism simply might not be motivated to complete various motor tests or might not understand the purpose in doing so. Finally, little research exists to draw conclusive results in the area of physical fitness. Research does support the use of physical activity to reduce stress and self-stimulatory and destructive behaviors (Levinson & Reid, 1993).

GENERAL EDUCATIONAL APPROACHES

Over the years, many educational approaches have been implemented to aid in the development of people with ASD. Some have been around for some time, whereas others have only been recently introduced. Both parents and professionals continue to search for the best possible approach to help people with ASD live their lives to the fullest and with a degree of normalcy. By far the most popular approaches have been applied behavior analysis (ABA) and the TEACCH (Treatment and Education of Autistic and related Communication-handicapped CHildren) program. More recently, the Developmental Individual-Difference, Relationship-Based Model (DIR), also known as the Floortime approach, and the subsequent affect-based language curriculum have shown promising results as an early intervention strategy. In addition, Carol Gray's social stories and comic strip conversations are being used to effectively communicate with children with ASD. These programs will be reviewed in the following sections.

Applied Behavior Analysis

The ABA approach consists of systematically applying interventions to improve behaviors to a meaningful degree and to demonstrate that the interventions are responsible for improvement (Sulzer-Azaroff & Mayer, 1991). In taking an ABA approach, one must first determine the goal of the intervention. Goals can relate to both behaviors and skills and might include reducing inappropriate behaviors, increasing appropriate behaviors, maintaining appropriate behaviors, generalizing behaviors, teaching new skills, or maintaining learned skills. Once the targeted behavior or skill has been identified, a baseline is determined to note any changes that may result from the intervention. The intervention is then applied and results are documented. Through ongoing assessment, modifications to the intervention can be made.

An important aspect of ABA is noting the antecedent that precedes a behavior or skill performance and the subsequent consequence. Manipulating either of these two variables can also bring about desired changes. Various interventions can be used to shape skills and behaviors, but one intervention strategy that has been used primarily with students with ASD is discrete trial training (DTT) (Lovaas, 1987). In DTT, the instructor gives a prompt to the child to perform a task, such as "Look at me." The instructor then waits for a response. The instructor may repeat the prompt or guide the child to perform the task. The child is then rewarded for either completing the task as requested or completing an approximation of the task. Over repeated trails of various tasks, the child is able to more fully engage in the environment. Forms of this intervention continue to be used today and are more fully discussed in chapter 7.

TEACCH Program

Another popular program used to assist students with ASD is the North Carolina statewide program known as TEACCH, developed by Eric Schopler in the early 1970s. The TEACCH program is based on the concept of teaching based on the culture of autism—that is, teaching based on the needs, interests, and learning style of individuals with ASD. Information is presented visually and in a highly structured and organized manner. *Structured teaching* is a term synonymous with the TEACCH program. The principles of structured teaching include understanding the culture of autism, developing an individualized and family plan for each client, organizing and structuring the physical environment, using visual supports such as daily work schedules to make the sequence of daily activities predictable and understandable, and using visual supports to make individual tasks understandable (Mesibov, Shea, & Schopler, 2005).

The TEACCH program also uses sensory integration therapy to determine the cause of inappropriate behaviors or lack of skill acquisition. It is theorized that sensory overload is often the cause of inappropriate behaviors of people with ASD. For example, if a child is overstimulated in an environment, he might be caused undue stress. Rather than making the child tolerate the environment, he is removed from the environment or the environment is modified. Thus, a hallmark of TEACCH is the emphasis on modifying the environment to enhance learning rather than expecting the child to conform to the traditional way of doing things (Bruey, 2004). The TEACCH program builds on the learning strengths of the learner rather than forcing the learner to conform to socially accepted norms of behavior.

Floortime and Affect-Based Language Curriculum

An exciting early intervention approach for children with autism and other ASD is the DIR or Floortime approach developed by Stanley Greenspan (1998). Floortime is based on Greenspan's theory of six functional milestones necessary for a child to succeed in further learning and development. According to Greenspan (1998, p. 3), these milestones are as follows:

1. The dual ability to take an interest in the sights, sounds, and sensations of the world and to calm oneself down
2. The ability to engage in relationships with other people
3. The ability to engage in two-way communication with gestures
4. The ability to create complex gestures, to string together a series of actions into an elaborate and deliberate problem-solving experience
5. The ability to create ideas
6. The ability to build bridges between ideas to make them reality based and logical

The program requires interactive experiences that are child directed in a low-stimulus environment. Using a child-directed versus adult-directed approach encourages the child to want to relate to the outside world. Time required varies from two to five hours a day. Greenspan advocates that the program begin as soon as possible. He contends that the longer the child is allowed to remain uncommunicative and the more parents lose their sense of their child's attachment, the more deeply the child will withdraw and become perseverative and self-stimulatory. The goal of the program is to transform perserveration into interaction. Once this occurs, the children become more purposeful in their interactions and can imitate gestures, sounds, and play (Greenspan, 1998).

Greenspan and Lewis (2002) have expanded upon Floortime with the Affect-Based Language Curriculum (ABLC). They contend that "affect is more critical for many elements of language acquisition and use than has been traditionally realized" (p. 3). The more the interaction includes affective gesturing, such as pointing, and complex gestures, such as placing a napkin on a plate after finishing eating, the better it will be when words and sentences appear. Greenspan and Lewis recommend using affect and engagement in pleasurable back-and-forth interactions as the foundation for the development of imitation, pragmatics (use of language), and receptive and expressive language.

Gray's Social Stories and Comic Strip Conversations

Carol Gray is credited with introducing the concept of social stories and comic strip conversation, and she has written several books on these topics. A social story is a story written according to specific guidelines to describe a situation in terms of the event or activity (Gray, 2000). The story is created using the student's perspective to make sure the student has all the social information she needs and to present it in an accessible manner. The stories are written in a positive manner and include information on what may happen and why. Social stories are intended for children with ASD who function in the middle to high range of abilities. Comic strips can accompany a social story. Comic strips are visual representations such as drawings, symbols, stick figures, and color that are used to illustrate ongoing communication between parties (Gray, 1994). Social stories can be created for a variety of situations, including developing peer social relationships, developing self-help skills, coping with change, providing feedback, and managing behavior. Social stories and comic strips can also be created for physical education to introduce a new skill or activity. Figure 10.1 depicts a social story and comic strip for encouraging a child with ASD to go swimming.

IMPLICATIONS FOR PHYSICAL EDUCATION

The following section provides an overview of implications for teaching physical education to children with ASD. Specifically, assessment, activity selection, instructional and management techniques, and behavior management techniques are discussed.

Assessment

Reid and O'Connor (2003) provide a model that is potentially useful for assessing the motor skills of children with ASD. Within the model, the instructor examines the interaction of three factors: the student, the environment, and the task. To derive a good understanding of the student, the assessor should seek information from several sources, including parents, teachers, therapists, and aides. Reinforcers and modes of communication should be fully understood before attempting to assess the child. The assessor should also spend time developing a rapport with the child prior to assessment. When beginning the assessment, it is important to start with activities the child understands and is able to perform and then move on to more difficult tasks. It is important to also understand qualities that inhibit or enhance performance. This approach allows for early success and better compliance throughout the assessment.

The second factor that needs to be examined is the environment. Keeping in mind that children with ASD might be hypersensitive to environmental stimuli, the assessor should provide an environment with limited distractions and focus on one task at a time. Environmental cues should be naturally occurring, not forced. For example, if the objective is to assess a child on stair climbing, a slide is preferred rather than an artificial stair device. Using a slide allows the child to climb the stairs to the top of the slide and then slide down; thus, the activity is naturally occurring in the environment and is not contrived.

The final factor to consider in the model is the task. To determine if the task is appropriate, consider the following questions: Is the task age appropriate? Is it functional? Will the information gained assist in the development of individualized education program (IEP) goals and objectives? Will the information be used for program development and instruction? If the answer to any of these questions is yes, then the task being assessed is appropriate. To assess the task, the assessor might use a task-analysis approach in which requisite skills are identified and either further broken down or assessed as a whole. For example, in assessing soccer skills, the assessor would determine the requisite skills for soccer (e.g., dribbling, passing,

It's time for PE.

In PE we are going to go swimming in the pool. First, we have to go to the locker room and change into our swimsuits.

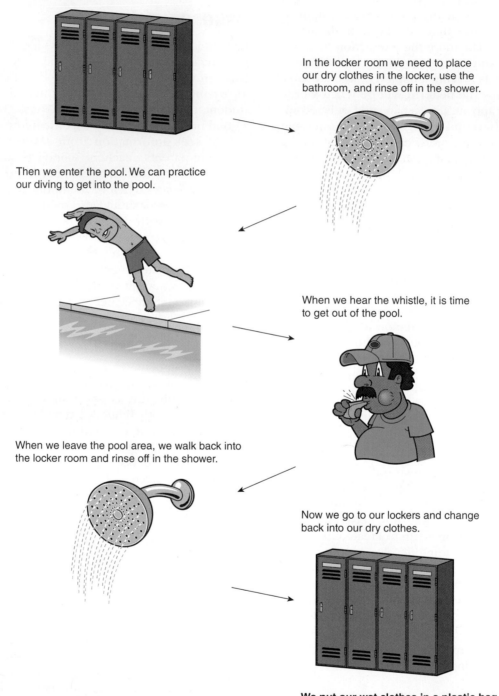

In the locker room we need to place our dry clothes in the locker, use the bathroom, and rinse off in the shower.

Then we enter the pool. We can practice our diving to get into the pool.

When we hear the whistle, it is time to get out of the pool.

When we leave the pool area, we walk back into the locker room and rinse off in the shower.

Now we go to our lockers and change back into our dry clothes.

We put our wet clothes in a plastic bag and leave the locker room with our class.

FIGURE 10.1   This social story and comic strip provide specific guidelines to encourage children with ASD to go swimming.

trapping, shooting). Each of these skills could be broken down into components assessed separately, or the skill could be assessed as a whole. Once the assessment is complete, the information gleaned can be used to develop goals and objectives based on unique needs, serve as a basis for instruction, and aid in activity selection.

Activity Selection

When selecting activities for children with ASD, the most important consideration is the needs and interests of the learners and their families. In addition, the functional value of the activity should be considered. Activities that have a high probability of success for children with ASD are generally more individual, such as swimming, running, and bowling. However, no one should assume that children with ASD cannot participate in and enjoy team sports. Team sports might need modifications to enhance success, but all children should have the opportunity to explore a range of physical education activities.

The learner's age must also be taken into account. Both developmental appropriateness and age appropriateness should always be considered when selecting activities. Although elementary-aged children spend a great deal of time learning and improving their fundamental motor skills, it would be inappropriate to focus on such skills at the middle school or high school level. When selecting activities, instructors should also consider family and community interests. Does the child come from a family that enjoys hiking or skiing? Or is the family more involved in soccer or softball? Considering these factors helps shape the activity selection so that the child with ASD can more fully integrate within the family and community.

One form of movement, known as *sensorimotor activities*, can be especially beneficial to students with ASD. These activities are designed to stimulate the senses with a focus on kinesthetic awareness, tactile stimulation, auditory processing, and visual–motor coordination. Kinesthetic awareness deals with the relationship of the body to space. Examples of kinesthetic activities include jumping on a trampoline, crawling through tunnels, jumping over a rope, and rolling down an incline mat. Tactile stimulation can be enhanced by having the child interact with objects, such as balls with various sizes, shapes, and textures. Auditory processing can be attained by using music and songs that instruct the child in a sequence of movements. Finally, visual–motor coordination can be strengthened by playing an array of games that require tracking, such as kickball, softball, soccer, or lacrosse.

Instructional and Management Techniques

Reid and colleagues have identified several factors to consider when teaching children with ASD (Reid, O'Connor, & Lloyd, 2003). These include allowing time for familiarity with the instructor and the activity, promoting eye contact as much as possible, using clear and consistent cues and prompts, and providing effective reinforcement and feedback. In addition, Houston-Wilson and Lieberman (2003) have identified strategies that can be helpful in teaching children with ASD. They focus on developing an effective communication system through the use of picture and communication boards and organizing the environment through routines and structure. Other variables that contribute to the success of instructing and managing students with ASD include the use of natural environmental cues and task analysis, the correction procedure rule, parallel talk, learning modalities, and support personnel.

Picture and Communication Boards

One of the most common and most successful methods used to teach children with ASD is the use of picture and communication boards (Cohen & Sloan, 2007). Types of pictures include photographs, lifelike drawings, and symbolic drawings. Some children may not yet understand pictures and may need objects to represent them, such as dollhouse furniture or small figures of the object. When pictures are used, it is best to have only one item in the picture because children with ASD have a tendency toward overselectivity, meaning they are not able to screen out irrelevant information. Teachers should help students focus on the most relevant information. For example, if a child is working on basketball skills, it may be preferable not to use a picture of a basketball court with students playing on it because there is too much information on the picture, making it difficult for the child to screen out irrelevant information. Pictures can also be arranged to create a daily, weekly, or monthly schedule. Boardmaker is one of many commercial software programs that can help create picture boards that use universally accepted symbols to depict events and actions. Information on obtaining Boardmaker is included in the electronic resources section of this chapter.

Routines and Structure

Establishing routines and structure aids in managing and instructing students with ASD. Children with ASD often demonstrate inappropriate behavioral responses when new or incongruent information is presented in a random or haphazard manner. Routines with set beginning and end points allow for more predictability and help to reduce sensory overload. Routines are also useful in introducing new information or behaviors. By keeping some information familiar and gradually introducing new information, students can respond appropriately. Routines also help to reduce verbal directions and allow children to work independently.

The following scenario illustrates a typical routine that incorporates pictures and can be useful in physical education. Before Justin goes to physical education class, a classroom teacher gives Justin a picture of the physical education teacher and says, "Justin, it is time for PE." The picture of the physical education teacher allows Justin to understand what is going to happen next. When the class enters the gym, Justin gives the picture card to the physical education teacher. The physical education teacher then uses a communication board with pictures to relay to Justin the lesson from start to finish. For example, a picture of a child stretching could indicate the warm-up, and a picture of a child doing curl-ups could indicate the fitness portion of the lesson. Further, the specific focus could be identified, such as a picture of a soccer ball. Finally, goalposts can be used to indicate the game activity. Figure 10.2 presents a sample schedule for a physical education lesson. The components of the schedule can remain the same, but the actual activities can be manipulated to prepare the child for the daily lesson. When using words, each activity can be erased after it is completed. This way Justin understands that the activity has ended and the next activity will soon begin.

As noted previously, children with ASD have difficulty with sensory overload. When they are entering a new environment, such as a gym, the atmosphere might create extreme sensory overload (Janzen, 2003). Structure helps alleviate this stress by creating environments that are easily understood and manageable. In physical education, teachers can structure their space so that the environment is predictable. First, the teacher needs to identify for the child where activities are done (in the gym, on the field, on a mat), where things are located (balls in bin, ropes on hangers, rackets on hooks), and how to move from one place to another (rotating stations, rotating positions, moving from inside to outside). Second, the teacher needs to establish concrete boundaries. For example, if a child is to remain on one-half of the field, cones indicating the halfway point should be in place. Labels can also help organize space. For example, equipment boxes should be clearly labeled so that the child can easily retrieve and put away equipment.

At the conclusion of the lesson, the physical education teacher should have a consistent cue to transition the child back to the classroom. This could be a picture of the classroom teacher or a desk. Forewarning is another effective way to transition a child back to the classroom. For example, the teacher might say, "Justin, in three minutes PE will be over." This helps the child better understand time and prepare for the change in routine. A second warning might be given at two minutes and a third at one minute. Through proper preparation, anxiety levels are reduced because the child begins to understand that a change in the task will occur after the one-minute signal from the instructor. Again, the child must understand what will be happening next. When he arrives back in the classroom, physical education can be crossed off his daily schedule.

The implementation of routines and structure might at first seem time consuming for the teacher. However, once these systems are in place, dramatic improvements in behavior and participation usually occur, making the extra time and effort worthwhile.

Natural Environmental Cues and Task Analysis

In teaching new skills to children with ASD, instructors are urged to use natural cues within the environment and to minimize verbal cues. If the goal is for the child to kick a soccer ball into a goal, the natural cues would be a soccer ball and a goal. To achieve the desired objective, the instructor might need to break the task down into smaller steps or task analyze the skills. Task analysis is the systematic breakdown of skills into their component parts in order to enhance success. For example, when shooting a soccer ball into a goal, the following steps may be used: (1) Line the child up at the shooting line, (2) place the ball on the shooting line, and (3) prompt the child to take a shot. The skill may be further broken down by placing a poly spot in front of the child to initiate a stepping action with the opposite kicking foot and prompting the child with either a verbal cue or physical assist to use the kicking foot to make

Physical Education Schedule

Warm-up   Stretching

Fitness   Push-ups

Focus   Soccer drills

1. Dribbling

2. Passing to a partner

Game   Soccer game

Closure   Review lesson.

Shoot ball in goal.

Hold ball and listen.

FIGURE 10.2 Physical education sample pictorial schedule. The pictures allow the student to understand what is going to happen in the lesson from start to finish.

contact with the ball. The degree to which skills should be task analyzed will depend on the task and the learner.

Demonstrations also prove helpful in the acquisition of new skills. If the child performs the task correctly, continue with the lesson. For example, the teacher might teach the child how to stop a ball being passed to the shooting line. If the child is unsuccessful in shooting the ball toward the goal, the teacher could use physical assistance to help the child gain a better understanding of what the task requires, allowing the child to repeat the task until no physical assistance is needed. Once the child has performed the task correctly, the teacher would

FIGURE 10.3 Shooting a soccer ball into a goal can be broken down into steps. Here the child is taking step 3, where the assistant prompts the child to take a shot.

Photo courtesy of Cathy Houston-Wilson.

move on to the rest of the lesson. Figure 10.3 depicts a child working on soccer skills with assistance.

Correction Procedure Rule

Another effective technique in instructing children with ASD is the correction procedure rule, which is applied by taking the child back to the last component of the skill done correctly. Using batting as an example, say a child maintains a proper batting stance and properly swings the bat at the ball, but then she runs to first base with the bat; in this case, following the correction procedure rule, the instructor would ask the child to repeat the swing and then physically assist her in placing the bat on the ground before running to first. The instructor returns the child to the last correct response before the incorrect response. The following application example is another scenario in which the correction procedure rule can be used.

Parallel Talk

To promote language and skill acquisition, instructors are encouraged to embed language throughout the lesson. One way to accomplish this is using parallel talk, in which the teacher verbalizes the actions of the learner. For example, if Marci is rolling a red ball to the teacher, the teacher would say, "Marci is rolling the red ball." Parallel talk can also help children associate certain skills with their verbal meaning, such as spatial concepts (e.g., in, out, under, over) and motor skills (e.g., dribbling, shooting, striking). Another way to foster language acquisition is to create print-rich physical education environments. Pictures, posters, and action words should be displayed prominently around the gym. Labeling the action as it is being performed helps students acquire both receptive and expressive language skills.

Learning Modalities

Learning modalities, or learning styles, refer to the way in which students learn best. The three common categories of learning include auditory, motor, and visual. Auditory learners tend to learn by following commands or prompts and may be easily distracted by background noise. Children who are motor or kinesthetic learners tend to learn by doing. They are active learners and would

APPLICATION EXAMPLE

Importance of Visual Cues

Setting: Physical education field

Students: Elementary physical education class

Task: Participating in a tee-ball game

Application: Using visual cues to create a positive learning environment

Kiera is seven years old and has autism. Her physical education teacher, Mr. Greer, has been teaching her how to play tee ball. They have practiced swinging the bat at the ball (in a hand-over-hand manner), making contact with the ball, putting the bat down, and running to first base. It appeared that Kiera had the hang of the skill, so Mr. Greer allowed her to bat independently. Kiera stood in the ready position; Mr. Greer placed the ball on the tee and took a step back. Just then a gust of wind came, and the ball fell off the tee. Kiera immediately placed the bat on the ground and began running to first base even though she did not make contact with the ball. This showed that Kiera still did not understand the purpose of the game, which was to contact the ball with the bat before running.

Mr. Greer then demonstrated to Kiera what to do if the ball fell off the tee. Mr. Greer put the ball on the tee loosely so that it would fall off. When the ball fell off, he picked up the ball, replaced it on the tee, and struck it with the bat. Mr. Greer then signaled to Kiera to try. Again he placed the ball loosely on the tee and gave the bat to Kiera. The ball fell off the tee and Kiera picked up the ball and replaced it on the tee. She then struck the ball and ran to first base. This example illustrates the need for students with autism to visually see and understand a task. In no way was Kiera being uncooperative or off task. She simply did not understand the task. When she understood the task, she was able to participate in the game independently.

Photo courtesy of Cathy Houston-Wilson.

Kiera practices her swing in tee ball.

rather do than watch; they enjoy hands-on projects. Children who are visual learners tend to learn by watching and looking at pictures, and they can be easily distracted by surrounding activities and noise. Research indicates that students with ASD tend to be visual learners (Janzen, 2003), although all learning modalities should be employed from time to time. As indicated previously, the use of pictures and communication boards is by far the most effective teaching strategy used to communicate with and teach students with ASD.

Support Personnel

Teachers should take advantage of support personnel to assist them in implementing programs. Teaching assistants, teacher aides, and peer tutors are all valuable resources that can help in providing individualized instruction to students with ASD in physical education. Teachers can request support personnel through the child's IEP as a necessary component to support the learning of children with ASD.

APPLIED BEHAVIOR ANALYSIS

The following section presents behavior management techniques that can be useful when teaching children with ASD in order to reduce the occurrence of inappropriate behaviors, such as verbal outburst or self-injury, or to promote appropriate behaviors, such as on-task behavior and motor and language skill acquisition.

Positive Behavior Support

As discussed in chapter 9, it may be appropriate to conduct a functional behavioral analysis (FBA) when children are experiencing difficulties controlling their behavior. The FBA is a system of gathering information about behavior from a variety of sources. An essential component of the FBA is to note the functional cause or antecedent of the behavior. Antecedents are events that occur within the environment that yield a response or a behavior. Often a connection can be made between the antecedent and the inappropriate behavior. By understanding what triggers the behavior, a behavioral intervention plan (BIP) can be created to minimize or distinguish inappropriate behaviors. Rather than giving consequences or punishment for each infraction, the environment is manipulated to create a positive learning environment, also known as positive behavior support (PBS), to change the behavior.

Token Economy and Premack Principle

The token economy system and the Premack principle, which were described in chapter 6, are also effective behavior management strategies to use with students with ASD. A token economy is a system in which the student is rewarded with a reinforcer that can be collected and later redeemed for a desirable object or privilege. For example, if Justin enjoyed roller-skating, he would need to collect a certain number of coins or tokens in order to be permitted to skate. Similarly, the Premack principle encourages the student to participate in a less preferred activity before the preferred activity. Once again, using Justin's preferred activity of roller-skating, he would be required to participate in other physical education–related activities before he could skate. Extreme caution should be used with the Premack principle, because if it is misused, a desirable object, privilege, or preferred activity may soon become nonpreferred. If Justin is constantly forced to do things he does not enjoy in order to skate, it may quickly become a nonpreferred activity.

Finally, instructors should be aware that students with ASD may experience meltdowns. Despite best efforts, structure, and routines, there will be times when students with ASD find it difficult to participate in any activity. Allowing the child to sit it out or go to a quiet space and regain composure may be the best option. When the episode has subsided, the child would be positively reinforced and encouraged to participate in the planned activity.

INCLUSION

The techniques described in this chapter are useful in helping physical educators include children with ASD in physical education. Keeping in mind that adapted physical education is a program, not a placement, these ideas are easy to incorporate in an inclusive setting. Using resources within the IEP, physical educators can request support personnel to help provide any one-on-one teaching that might be necessary throughout the lesson. In addition, supplemental aids and equipment that might be required to more successfully include the child should be identified on the IEP. Goals and objectives developed for children with ASD should parallel the physical education curriculum. In some instances, children with high-functioning autism or Asperger syndrome might not need any form of modification or an IEP to be successfully included in the class. Determining whether to include students with ASD in regular physical education must be based on the individual needs of the learner. In some instances, inclusion is most appropriate; in others, it is not. Responding to the unique needs of the learner is the best approach.

SUMMARY

This chapter provided an overview of ASD and implications for physical education. Disorders include autism, Asperger syndrome, Rett's disorder, CDD, and PDD-NOS. Each of these conditions has been explained in detail. The cause of ASD is unknown, but research indicates that the disorders are probably attributed to a genetic or neurological link. The incidence of ASD, especially autism, has increased significantly over the last several years. Many attribute this increase to better screening and detection.

Research on the physical and motor characteristics of students with ASD varies depending on the condition. Although it appears that some children with Asperger syndrome, Rett's disorder, CDD, and PDD-NOS have physical and motor delays, the physical and motor status of children with autism is less clear. Additional research is needed in this area.

Many treatment approaches have been used to help students with ASD live more productive lives. This chapter provided a review of the following approaches: ABA, the TEACCH program, the DIR or Floortime approach and its counterpart ABLC, and social stories and comic strips. These approaches all have merit, and each has led to significant gains in participants. Using these treatment approaches, strategies for teaching and managing the behavior of students with ASD in physical education were presented. The teaching focus is on developing effective communication strategies, using the strengths of the learner (e.g., structure, routines), and maintaining a positive learning environment.

REFERENCES

American Medical Association (AMA). (2004). *Immunization safety review: Vaccines and autism.* Washington, DC: National Academies Press.

American Psychiatric Association (APA). (2000). *Diagnostic and statistical manual of mental disorders (DSM IV)* (4th ed.). Washington, DC: Author.

Bruey, C.T. (2004). *Demystifying autism spectrum disorders.* Bethesda, MD: Woodbine House.

Centers for Disease Control and Prevention (CDC). (2008). *Autism Information Center frequently asked questions: Prevalence.* Atlanta: Author.

Cohen, M.J., & Sloan, D.L. (2007). *Visual supports for people with autism.* Bethesda, MD: Woodbine House.

Courchesne, E., Carper, R., & Akshoomoff, N. (2003). Evidence of brain overgrowth in the first year of life in autism. *Journal of the American Medical Association, 290,* 337-344.

Friend, M. (2007). *Special education: Contemporary perspectives for school.* Upper Saddle River, NJ: Pearson.

Gray, C. (1994). *Comic strip conversations.* Arlington, TX: Future Horizons.

Gray, C. (2000). *The new social story book.* Arlington, TX: Future Horizons.

Greenspan, S.I. (1998). A developmental approach to problems in relating and communicating in autistic spectrum disorders and related syndromes. *SPOTLIGHT on Topics in Developmental Disabilities, 1* (4), 1-6.

Greenspan, S., & Lewis, D. (2002). *Affect-Based Language Curriculum (ABLC): An intensive program for families, therapists and teachers.* Bethesda, MD: ICDL.

Houston-Wilson, C., & Lieberman, L. (2003). Strategies for teaching students with autism in physical education. *Journal of Physical Education, Recreation and Dance, 74* (6), 40-44.

Individuals with Disabilities Education Improvement Act of 2004 (IDEA). 20 USC 1400.

Janzen, J.E. (2003). *Understanding the nature of autism: A guide to the autism spectrum disorders.* San Antonio: Therapy Skill Builders.

Levinson, L.J., & Reid, G. (1993). The effects of exercise intensity on the stereotyped behaviors of individuals with autism. *Adapted Physical Activity Quarterly, 10,* 255-268.

Lovaas, O.I. (1987). Behavioral treatment and normal educational and intellectual functioning in young autistic children. *Journal of Consulting and Clinical Psychology, 55,* 3-9.

Mesibov, G.B., Shea, V., & Schopler, E. (2005). *The TEACCH approach to autism spectrum disorders.* New York: Kluwer Academic/Plenum.

National Institute of Mental Health (NIMH). (2008a). *Autism spectrum disorders (pervasive developmental disorders).* Bethesda, MD: Author

National Institute of Mental Health (NIMH). (2008b). *What are the autism spectrum disorders?* Bethesda, MD: Author.

National Institute of Neurological Disorders and Stroke (NINDS). (2008). *Rett syndrome fact sheet.* National Institute of Health, Bethesda, MD: Author.

Ozonoff, S., Dawson, G., & McPartland, J. (2002). *A parent's guide to Asperger syndrome and high-functioning autism.* New York: Guilford Press.

Reid, G., & Collier, D. (2002). Motor behavior and the autism spectrum disorders: Introduction. *Palaestra, 18,* 20-27/44.

Reid, G., & O'Connor, J. (2003). The autism spectrum disorders: Activity selection, assessment, and program organization—part II. *Palaestra, 19,* 20-27/58.

Reid, G., O'Connor, J., & Lloyd, M. (2003). The autism spectrum disorders: Physical activity instruction—Part III. *Palaestra, 20,* 20-26/47.

Rimland, B. (1964). *Infantile autism: The syndrome and its implications for neural theory of behavior.* New York: Appleton-Century-Croft.

Sigman, M., & Capps, L. (1997). *Children with autism: A developmental perspective.* Cambridge, MA: Harvard University Press.

Sulzer-Azaroff, B., & Mayer, R. (1991). *Behavior analysis for lasting change.* Fort Worth, TX: Holt, Reinhart & Winston.

WRITTEN RESOURCES

Greenspan, S.I., & Wieder, S. (2006). *Engaging autism: Using the Floortime approach to help children relate, communicate, and think.* Cambridge, MA: Da Capo Lifelong Books.

An instructional resource for implementing the DIR or Floortime approach. Includes information on neuroscience research into the effects of the Floortime approach to teaching children with ASD. Unlike approaches that focus on changing specific behavior, Greenspan's program promotes the building blocks of healthy emotional and behavioral development.

Kluth, P. (2003). *"You're Going to Love this Kid!": Teaching students with autism in the inclusive classroom.* Baltimore: Paul H. Brookes.

A guidebook for including students with autism in both primary and secondary school classrooms. Provides first-person accounts that give readers insight into the experience of having autism. This book shows educators how to adapt their environments to support student participation in classwork, school routines, social activities, and more.

Koegel, R.L., & Koegel, L.K. (2006). *Pivotal response treatments for autism communication, social, and academic development.* Baltimore: Paul H. Brookes.

Describes pivotal response treatment, which uses natural learning opportunities to target and modify key behaviors in children with autism, leading to widespread positive effects on communication, behavior, and social skills.

Neisworth, J.T., & Wolfe, P.S. (Eds.). (2004). *The Autism Encyclopedia.* Baltimore: Paul H. Brookes.

An A-to-Z reference source on ASD and PDD. Includes more than 500 terms, alphabetically listed and clearly described, on such topics as causes, incidence and prevalence, interventions, behavior, education, and many more.

Shapiro, B.K., Pasquale J., & Accardo, P.J. (Eds.). (2008). *Autism frontiers: Clinical issues and innovations.* Baltimore: Paul H. Brookes.

Provides cutting-edge information on ASD based on applied research. Includes information on early diagnosis and intervention, language and social reciprocity, overlapping syndromes, complementary and alternative medicine, autism and epilepsy, parent advocacy, and a new screening protocol for detecting autism.

AUDIOVISUAL RESOURCES

Autism and applied behavioral analysis [VHS and DVD]. (2001). Films for the Humanities & Sciences, P.O. Box 2053, Princeton, NJ 08543.

Provides an overview of two children with autism who participate in ABA DTT. Although the degree of improvement attributable to ABA varies from child to child, the gains noted appear to be of great value to the children and their families. Running time is approximately 22 minutes.

Autism: A world apart [VHS and DVD]. (1990). Films for the Humanities & Sciences, P.O. Box 2053, Princeton, NJ 08543.

Presents the day-to-day life of three families who have a child with autism. Depicts the struggles they face and the importance of special education in helping these children and their families to live more fulfilled lives. Running time is approximately 52 minutes.

Breakthrough: How to reach students with autism [VHS and curriculum manual]. (1998). Child Development Media, Inc., 5632 Van Nuys Blvd., Ste. 286, Van Nuys, CA 91401.

Follows a preschooler in a school setting and demonstrates how the use of high expectations, physical prompting, modeling, and attending to task increases the child's educational progress. Running time is approximately 26 minutes.

The child who couldn't play [VHS and DVD]. (1996). Films for the Humanities & Sciences, P.O. Box 2053, Princeton, NJ 08543.

This is a comprehensive overview of autism. It is filmed at the Princeton Child Development Institute and depicts the Institute's highly successful scientific approach to teaching children with autism. Running time is approximately 46 minutes.

On the spectrum: Children and autism [VHS and DVD]. (2002). First Signs, Inc., P.O. Box 358, Merrimac, MA 01860.

Assists professionals in recognizing the early warning signs of ASD and understanding the impact of early intervention. The video outlines the diagnostic criteria for ASD, provides guidelines for conducting a developmental screening, and describes how to relay developmental concerns to parents. Differences in development are demonstrated through filmed examples of typical and atypical behavior in children from 4 to 36 months of age. Running time is approximately 24 minutes.

Struggling with life: Asperger's syndrome [VHS and DVD]. (1996). Films for the Humanities & Sciences, P.O. Box 2053, Princeton, NJ 08543.

Follows three children with various obsessions and explains the neurological disorder of Asperger syndrome. Includes research studies conducted at Yale University on children with Asperger syndrome. Running time is approximately 14 minutes.

ELECTRONIC RESOURCES

Autism Society: www.autism-society.org.

The Autism Society is the leading grassroots autism organization in the United States that exists to improve the lives of all affected by autism. Its goal is to increase public awareness about the day-to-day issues faced by people on the spectrum, advocate for appropriate services across the life span, and provide the latest information regarding treatment, education, research, and advocacy. The Autism Society is the leading source of trusted and reliable information about autism and was instrumental in the passage of the 2006 Combating Autism Act, the first federal autism-specific law in the United States.

Autism Speaks: www.autismspeaks.org.

Autism Speaks is dedicated to funding global biomedical research into the causes, prevention, treatments, and cure for autism; to raising public awareness about autism and its effects on individuals, families, and society; and to bringing hope to all who deal with the hardships of this disorder.

Boardmaker: www.mayer-johnson.com.

This software program enables teachers to create interactive symbol-based communication and educational materials to aid in communicating with children with ASD.

National Autism Association: www.nationalautism association.org.

The National Autism Association was created to educate and empower families affected by autism and other neurological disorders. Their mission is to educate society that autism is not a lifelong, incurable genetic disorder but one that is biomedically definable and treatable.

11

Specific Learning Disabilities

Barry W. Lavay

Calvin is 13 years old and he has been receiving special education services since first grade, when he was first diagnosed with a specific learning disability and ADHD. This year Calvin is attending seventh grade at Lexington Middle School, and the first two periods of the school day are spent working on math and reading in a special education resource room. During the remaining five periods, Calvin is included in regular education classes with his peers without disabilities, including regular physical education.

Calvin struggles with physical education class; the acoustics and the noise level make it difficult to concentrate and understand class instructions. Calvin also finds the large gym space with the different floors markings to be a distraction. Every three weeks after a sport unit is completed, Mr. Santos gives the class a 15-minute written rules tests that Calvin has difficulty reading and completing in such a short amount of time. Recently, two of the more skilled boys whose team he played on in a basketball unit began to make fun of him and taunted him with such names as "Clumsy Cal" each time he dropped the ball. When Mr. Santos comes over to help Calvin, he gets nervous and drops the ball even more. He doesn't want Mr. Santos to find out that he has a learning disability and is different from the other kids.

As the adapted physical education specialist assigned to Lexington Middle School, how can you assist Calvin and Mr. Santos? You can start by identifying each of the unique behaviors and specific challenges that Calvin faces in class. Next, provide possible teaching strategies and accommodations to assist Mr. Santos in helping Calvin have a more positive learning experience.

As you read this chapter, think about Calvin and other children with a specific learning disability, ADHD, or poor motor skills and consider the challenges each one faces. Keep in mind that not all children with a learning disability have ADHD or poor motor skills, but some do. Skill levels for children with a specific learning disability can vary along a spectrum from highly skilled, such as the star athlete, to unskilled or clumsy. No two children with a specific learning disability are alike; a wide range of characteristics exist. Children with a specific learning disability will often be included in regular physical education classes. Consider how you can use the information in this chapter to provide a more successful learning experience. Topics include definitions, causes, and incident rates of specific learning disabilities; common behavioral characteristics; general educational approaches; and recommendations for teaching physical education and sport.

WHAT IS A SPECIFIC LEARNING DISABILITY?

No other disability has been more misunderstood and caused more confusion among professionals and parents than the condition identified as learning disability. In the past, terms commonly used to identify this population have been *perceptually handicapped, brain injured, minimal brain dysfunction, dyslexia,* and *developmentally aphasic.*

In 1963, Sam Kirk of the University of Illinois, who is considered the father of the field of learning disabilities, coined the term *learning disability* in a meeting of parents and professionals in Chicago. He shared with conference attendees that he had been using the term to refer to children who had learning problems but showed no signs of mental retardation or emotional disturbance. Parents quickly adopted the term as a more appropriate label than those used at the time (Dunn & Leitschuh, 2006; Smith, 2007).

Learning Disability Defined

Professionals are unable to agree on one specific definition of learning disability (Kavale & Forness, 2000; Smith, 2007). What experts do agree on is that this group has trouble learning for a variety of reasons. Many believe that children with a learning disability have a **neurological disorder** that results in problems with storing, processing, and producing information in the central nervous system, thus causing a deficit in understanding spoken or written words.

A learning disability can manifest itself in a less-than-perfect ability to listen, think, speak, read, write, spell, do mathematical calculations, or motor plan. Other possible indications can be when people consistently have difficulty remembering newly learned information, expressing thoughts orally or in writing, understanding information presented, following directions and routines, or moving in space from one activity to the next. More specific difficulties include reversal of letters or words, difficulty with the steps necessary to complete an addition or division math problem, or trouble with spatial awareness (e.g., bumping into objects).

Since the mid-1970s, the Individuals with Disabilities Education Act (IDEA) definition has been used in public schools to determine if a child with a learning disability qualifies for special education services. Here is that definition:

> "Specific learning disability" means a disorder in one or more of the basic psychological processes involved in understanding or in using language, spoken or written, that may manifest itself in an imperfect ability to listen, think, speak, read, write, spell, or do mathematical calculations. The term includes such conditions as perceptual disabilities, brain injury, minimal brain dysfunction, dyslexia, and developmental aphasia. The term does not apply to children who have learning problems that are primarily the result of visual, hearing, or motor disabilities; of mental retardation; or of environmental, cultural, or economic disadvantage. (IDEA, 2004)

The IDEA definition of a specific learning disability has undergone little change since being introduced in 1975. The definition still includes such terms as *minimal brain dysfunction, dyslexia,* and *developmental aphasia.* Many professionals believe that this definition is difficult to operationalize or put into practice and fails to provide significant insight into the true nature of a condition (Kavale & Forness, 2000). Despite this controversy, the IDEA definition continues to be used in public schools to determine if a child qualifies for special education services.

Learning Disabilities Are Specific

The term **specific** was added to learning disabilities to underscore that these children have learning difficulties only in specific areas (e.g., reading, speaking, calculating) and that there are other areas of learning in which they are at least of average ability or even gifted in their learning. To some degree, most children have difficulty in some of these areas at one time or another. But when these behaviors occur in more than one setting, persist over an extended time, and interfere with learning, they need special attention. In addition, learning disabilities vary among children; one child may have trouble in math only whereas another child may have difficulty in both reading and writing.

Unexpected Underachievement

Experts agree that a defining feature of a learning disability is that an identified **educationally significant discrepancy** exists between measured intellectual potential and actual academic achievement. Educationally significant discrepancy in this context refers to unexpected underachievement in such academic areas as math, reading, and written language that is not attributed to other disabilities. A learning disability cannot be explained by cultural differences, lack of educational opportunities, poverty, or other such conditions. Experts believe that the problem is the result of an inability to store, process, and produce information in the central nervous system. Although the majority of students with a learning disability possess normal intelligence, their academic performance lags behind that of their peers, and they do not perform at grade level. This population has difficulty learning in traditional ways, but a learning disability affects *how* people learn, not *how well* they learn (Kavale & Forness, 2000; Smith, 2007).

The Hidden Disability

A specific learning disability is not easily recognized or accepted. It is considered a hidden disability because no easily identifiable physical signs exist. When a person is missing a limb or using a wheelchair, for instance, her disability is easily visible. However, when a person's disability involves dysfunction to the central nervous system and processing information, it is often not visible at all. Many people with a specific learning disability exhibit deficits in the perceptual–motor process, such as when taking in, storing, and retrieving information (Waugh & Sherrill, 2004). Chapter 20 includes an overview of information processing and the tactile, kinesthetic, visual, and auditory sensory systems.

Because they are often hidden, learning disabilities are frequently misunderstood; sometimes the main problem is in educating people who do not have the disability. Recognition is made even more difficult because many people with a specific learning disability spend much of their time and energy hiding their disability. They might not read in public, for example, or they might shy away from activities on the playground. Parents might be in denial about their child's disability and feel that it will go away or can be quickly fixed. The truth is that a learning disability presents lifelong challenges to children and their families. However, with modifications and the right type of intervention, many children with learning disabilities will go on to be productive members of society. For example, Ben Franklin, Woodrow Wilson, Albert Einstein, and Winston Churchill did not perform well in school and are believed to have had a learning disability involving some type of attention deficit that was later adjusted.

Learning Disabilities and Coexisting Disabilities

Learning disability does not occur as a result of other conditions, but it might coexist with other conditions, such as attention deficient/hyperactivity disorder (ADHD) and developmental coordination disorder (DCD). The prevalence of children with learning disabilities who display **comorbidity**, meaning the disability coexists with other conditions of ADHD and DCD, makes it important to discuss these two conditions in this chapter. However, children with ADHD and DCD are not recognized as a distinct disability category under IDEA, and children with these disabilities do not automatically qualify for special education services.

Children with ADHD who do qualify for services must have, as their primary disability, one of the 14 disabilities identified in IDEA. The primary disability category is usually a specific learning disability or a behavioral disability (see chapter 9). Some children with ADHD can qualify under the category of other health impairments in IDEA if it can be shown that the child's deficit results in heightened alertness to environmental stimuli that limits alertness to the educational environment and adversely effects educational performance (Smith, 2007). Although IDEA does not recognize motor disabilities alone as a diagnosis for a learning disability, most authorities believe that a higher-than-average percentage of children with learning disabilities have perceptual–motor and movement-related difficulties that require intensive intervention (Harvey & Reid, 2003; Sherrill, 2004; Waugh & Sherrill, 2004).

Because IDEA does not clearly identify and recognize ADHD and DCD as distinct conditions, programming for students with learning disabilities and the coexisting conditions of ADHD and DCD has become problematic (Beyer, 1999; Waugh & Sherrill, 2004). For example, Henderson and Henderson (2002) believe that the high degree of overlap between DCD and other childhood disorders appears to deemphasize its acceptance as a distinct syndrome. Other professionals feel it is not important what labels children wear as long as they receive services designed to meet their unique educational needs. In this chapter, the terms *specific learning disability*, *ADHD*, and *DCD* denote that the information provided applies to students with one or more of these conditions.

What Is Attention Deficit/ Hyperactivity Disorder?

ADHD is an official clinical label clearly defined and recognized by the American Psychiatric Association (APA). The diagnostic criteria to determine a person has ADHD are shown in the diagnostic criteria sidebar (APA, 2000). No single test to determine ADHD

exists, and a comprehensive battery of assessment tests administered by a qualified professional, such as a school psychologist, is necessary for diagnosis.

ADHD is divided into three subtypes: **combined type**, **predominantly inattentive type**, and **predominantly hyperactive–impulsive type** (see sidebar). The defining features of ADHD are inattention and hyperactivity–impulsivity. Based on the criteria used to diagnose this condition, ADHD is defined as a persistent pattern of inattention or hyperactivity with impulse behaviors that are more inappropriate, excessive, frequent, and severe than are observed in children of comparable development (criterion A). Six or more of these symptoms from category 1 or 2 must be excessive and present over at least six months. Some hyperactive–impulsive or inattention symptoms must be present before the age of seven; exhibited in multiple (at least two or more) settings such as the home, school, and or social settings (criterion B); and not be explained by another disorder (see sidebar). The hyperactivity must be excessive, inappropriate, and occur in various settings. Children with ADHD are easily distracted by irrelevant stimuli and frequently shift from one incomplete activity to the next. Inattention occurs in academic, occupational, or social situations and is more difficult to observe than hyperactivity (APA, 2000). Children who exhibit inattention without hyperactivity may even be hypoactive. Everyone can exhibit inattention, hyperactivity, and impulsive behaviors from time to time; however, with ADHD

Diagnostic Criteria for Attention Deficit/ Hyperactivity Disorder

A. Meets either 1 or 2:

1. Six or more of the following symptoms of inattention have persisted for at least six months to a degree that is maladaptive and inconsistent with developmental level:

INATTENTION

a. Often fails to give close attention to details or makes careless mistakes in schoolwork, work, or other activities.

b. Often has difficulty sustaining attention in tasks or play activities.

c. Often does not seem to listen when spoken to directly.

d. Often does not follow through on instructions and fails to finish school-work, chores, or duties in the workplace (not due to oppositional behavior or failure to understand instructions).

e. Often has difficulty organizing tasks and activities.

f. Often avoids, dislikes, or is reluctant to engage in tasks that require sustained mental effort (such as schoolwork or homework).

g. Often loses things necessary for tasks or activities (e.g., toys, school assignments, pencils, books, or tools).

h. Is often easily distracted by extraneous stimuli.

i. Is often forgetful in daily activities.

2. Six or more of the following symptoms of hyperactivity–impulsivity have persisted for at least six months to a degree that is maladaptive and inconsistent with developmental level:

HYPERACTIVITY

a. Often fidgets with hands or feet or squirms in seat.

b. Often leaves seat in classroom or in other situations in which remaining seated is expected.

c. Often runs about or climbs excessively in situations in which it is inappropriate (in adolescents or adults, may be limited to subjective feelings of restlessness).

d. Often has difficulty playing or engaging in leisure activities quietly.

e. Often on the go or acts as if driven by a motor.

f. Often talks excessively.

IMPULSIVITY

a. Often blurts out answers before questions have been completed.

b. Often has difficulty awaiting turn.

c. Often interrupts or intrudes on others (e.g., butts into conversations or games).

B. Some hyperactive–impulsive or inattentive symptoms that caused impairment were present before age 7.

C. Some impairment for the symptoms is present in two or more settings (e.g., at school and at home).

D. There is clear evidence of clinically significant impairment in social, academic, or occupational functioning.

E. The symptoms do not occur exclusively during the course of pervasive development disorder (PDD), schizophrenia, or other psychotic disorders and are not better accounted for by another mental disorder (e.g., mood disorder, anxiety disorder, dissociative disorder, personality disorder).

Code Based on Type

ADHD, combined type: if both criteria A1 and A2 are met for the past six months

ADHD, predominantly inattentive type: if criterion A1 is met but criterion A2 is not met for the past six months

ADHD, predominantly hyperactive–impulsive type: if criterion A2 is met but criterion A1 is not met for the past six months

Coding note: For people (especially adolescents and adults) who currently have symptoms that no longer meet full criteria, *in partial remission* should be specified.

Taken from American Psychiatric Association. (2000). *Diagnostic and statistical manual of mental disorders* (4th ed.). Washington DC: Author.

these types of behaviors are chronic and adversely affect academic, social, and life skills (Smith, 2007).

What Is Developmental Coordination Disorder?

Since 1987, DCD has been officially recognized as an independent disorder by the APA, which identifies four diagnostic criteria (APA, 2000; Henderson & Henderson, 2002):

1. Performance in daily activities must be substantially below that expected for a person's age and intelligence.

2. The motor deficiency must interfere with academic achievement or activities of daily living.

3. The motor deficiency cannot be caused by a known general medical condition, such as cerebral palsy, muscular dystrophy, or PDD. For example, children with ADHD might fall and bump into things, but this is usually a result of distractibility or impulsiveness.

4. If mental retardation is present, the motor difficulties must be in excess of those associated alone with this disability.

DCD is operationally defined as performing two standard deviations below age norms on a standardized motor test. In general, children with DCD demonstrate a marked delay in meeting motor developmental milestones, such as walking, and the child appears clumsy; exhibits poor handwriting, balance, and spatial ability; and performs behind age-level peers in sport. Children with DCD often do not exhibit the classic neurological signs of clumsiness, but they lack the motor competence required to cope with the everyday demands of living (Henderson, 1994). Approximately 50 percent of children with DCD do not grow out of their motor difficulties; thus, DCD can be a lifelong challenge (Clark et al., 2005).

Suspected Causes of Specific Learning Disability, ADHD, and DCD

A specific learning disability is complex, multidimensional, and possibly the culmination of many causes. Presently, the most common theory is that it is a neurological condition, such as a dysfunction in the central nervous system in producing, processing, or storing information. **Central nervous system dysfunction** means that brain or neurological damage is present that impedes motor or learning abilities. Teachers must recognize the uncertainty about what causes learning disabilities and not make assumptions that brain damage exists when there is no physical evidence or an actual medical diagnosis. Labeling students with such terms as *brain injured* might lead educators and parents to presume that nothing can be done to remediate the educational difficulties, and consequently student expectations might be set too low, with educational potential never met (Smith, 2007). Other possible causes of learning disabilities include brain damage from an accident; lack of oxygen before, during, or after birth; and genetics (Kavale & Forness, 2000).

As is the case with learning disabilities, the exact cause of ADHD is unclear and controversial, though experts agree it is a multidimensional disability caused primarily by an interaction of neurological, genetic, and psychosocial factors. Several studies support the theory that the condition is biological, because certain regions of the brain such as the frontal lobes and prefrontal cortex are associated with ADHD. In addition, there is a high probability that the condition can be inherited and is genetic, because it frequently runs in families (Children and Adults with Attention Deficit/Hyperactivity Disorder [CHADD], 2008). For example, if one person in a family is diagnosed with ADHD, a 25 to 35 percent probability exists that another family member also has ADHD (versus a 4-6 percent probability in the general population). Physical educators must be aware of the probable biological basis for the lack of social control that students with ADHD might exhibit and that this behavior can become more erratic in environments with decreasing amounts of social support (Harvey & Reid, 2003).

Incident Rates of Specific Learning Disability, ADHD, and DCD

Approximately 2.9 million students (5.6 percent) enrolled in public schools in the United States are identified as having a specific learning disability, which makes this group easily the largest special education category served. This category has grown considerably, from 20 percent of special education students in 1976 to over 40 percent in 2006 (U.S. Department of Education, 2007). Although criteria are based on the federal IDEA definition, interpretation of the definition and identification of students can vary slightly from state to state and district to district, with statistics of students identified as having a specific learning disability ranging from 1.7 to 5.8 percent.

The number of students categorized as having a specific learning disability is large because the definition of this disability is so exceptionally broad, and because children who are not succeeding in general education classes are often incorrectly identified as having a specific learning disability. The learning disability label has become a dumping ground for students who are unsuccessful in general education as well as students with other disabilities, such as ADHD, and it is often used to qualify children for special education placement (Smith, 2007).

A high percentage of children with learning disabilities (25-50 percent) also display ADHD (CHADD, 2008). About half of the children identified with ADHD also have ADD or conduct disorder (APA, 2000). The symptoms of this condition are more likely to occur in a group setting, such as a playground or classroom, than in an individualized setting. This fact has important implications for physical education, in which most activities occur in large-group settings.

There is a lack of agreement as to how many students have ADHD. The prevalence of ADHD in school-aged children is between 3 and 7 percent, but estimates have been reported as high as 20 percent, depending on the population sampled (APA, 2000). Within this group, 50 percent do not qualify for special education services. It has long been believed that boys with ADHD may outnumber girls as much as 9 to 1 (Smith, 2007). However, many experts believe that females with ADHD are underrecognized and that the actual number of females might be closer to the number of males. The incident rate of children aged 6 to 11 identified with DCD has been estimated to be as high as 6 percent (APA, 2000).

BEHAVIORS PRESENT UNIQUE CHALLENGES

Figure 11.1 is a flowchart that includes a general list of the possible behavioral and environmental factors that can affect children's movement, the most widely used educational approaches in schools today, and the specific physical education methods and activities that have been effective when teaching children with a learning disability, ADHD, and DCD. This chart serves as an overview and helps the reader to better understand the remainder of the information provided in this chapter.

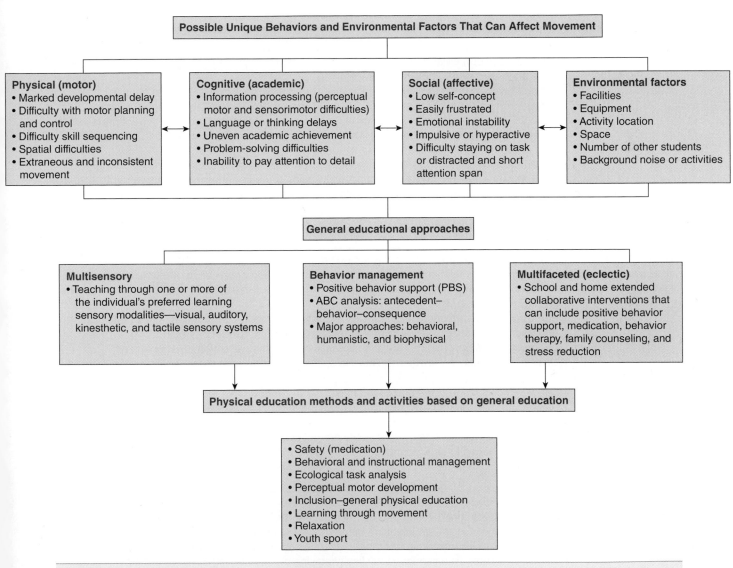

FIGURE 11.1 Unique behaviors and environmental factors that can affect movement when teaching physical education to children with a specific learning disability, ADHD, or DCD.

The movement behaviors of people with specific learning disabilities, ADHD, or DCD can vary. Some might be skilled movers and exceptional athletes, but most are at risk for developmental delays compared with peers without disabilities (Harvey & Reid, 2003). In general, this population exhibits a wide range of physical, cognitive, and social behaviors that affect the ability to move (Grosshans & Kiger, 2004; Milne, Haubenstricker, & Seefelt, 1991). Some behaviors, such as a short attention span, are not specific motor problems but can make it difficult to attend to directions, and consequently they affect movement outcomes (Horvat et al., 2002).

Table 11.1 describes unique physical, cognitive, and social behaviors that students with a specific learning disability, ADHD, or DCD may display that can affect movement. Teachers need to be aware of these behaviors because they can interfere with the ability of the student to learn. Other perceptual motor and sensory behaviors are discussed later in this chapter and more specifically in chapter 20. In order to provide students with a safe and positive experience, the physical educator must carefully consider all of the listed behaviors and their relationships when designing and teaching activities. For example, in the physical behavior section under skill sequencing, the physical educator can ask,

Table 11.1 Physical, Cognitive, and Social Behaviors That May Affect Movement for People With a Specific Learning Disability, ADHD, or DCD

Behavior	Characteristics
Physical (developmental delay)	*Marked developmental delay:* Lag behind their same-age peers in fundamental gross motor skills such as running, throwing, and catching. *Difficulty with motor planning and an inability to control movements*: Rush to complete the activity and do not perform at a pace or speed needed to successfully perform the task. *Difficulty with skill sequencing:* Unable to initiate a movement that puts the correct parts into a proper sequence, such as breaking down or analyzing the movements needed to successfully plan and perform the skill. *Extraneous movements that are not performed in a smooth and efficient manner:* Require extra movements and the use of unnecessary body parts to perform skills. Movements appear clumsy or uncoordinated and there is difficulty moving one body part independently from others. *Inconsistency in skill performance*: Skill levels vary from practice session to practice session and even within the same session. Skill retention is difficult.
Cognitive (average or above-average intellectual ability)	*Processing information:* More time is required to take in, organize, and produce instructional information. They take in too much extraneous information or stimuli at one time and have difficulty remaining focused on the specific instruction or task. Difficult to take in more than one given direction at a time. *Perceptual and sensory difficulties:* Difficulties with tactile, proprioception, kinesthetic, visual, and auditory systems; may be hyper- or hyporesponsive to sensory stimuli. *Language/thinking delays:* Delays in expressive, receptive, retention, or sequencing. *Uneven academic achievement:* There is uneven development among educational subject areas. *Difficulty completing tasks and problem solving in allotted time:* Avoid or fail to stay on tasks that require a sustained mental effort. Overall, have difficulty organizing, planning, and solving tasks. *Inability to pay attention to details:* Tasks are not completed or are finished quickly; make careless mistakes in order to move on to the next task. *Perseveration:* Inability to shift easily from one activity to the next. This is the opposite of distractibility.
Social (lack of social expectations and low self-esteem)	*Low self-concept:* Easily frustrated and have a low perceived competence level. *Impulsive:* Act before thinking and do not consider the consequences of actions. Often interrupt others. Show little inhibition before speaking or acting in front of others. *Hyperactive, easily distracted, and short attention span:* Demonstrate excess energy that is difficult to control. This can lead to difficulty staying on task, taking turns, or remaining focused.

These common behavioral characteristics can affect movement and will vary from person to person.

Adapted from Bishop & Beyer, 1995; Milne, Haubenstricker, and Seefelt, 1991; Sherrill, 2004; Waugh and Sherrill, 2004.

"Why does the student have difficulty performing this skill and what can I do to help this student? Is the student having skill-sequencing difficulty? Can I use a task-analysis teaching method and break the skill into manageable parts to help the student learn and be successful?" Many other teaching strategies to help offset these physical, cognitive, and social behaviors and environmental factors, as well as to support student learning, are presented throughout the remainder of the chapter.

GENERAL EDUCATIONAL APPROACHES

Because students with learning disabilities, ADHD, and DCD are a heterogeneous group, it follows that physical educators will be involved in various educational approaches and ways of teaching to meet these students' needs. General educational approaches used by educators in other disciplines need to be used by physical educators in order to collaborate effectively with other professionals to meet student needs. Currently, no one educational approach is universally supported; rather, several approaches have been successful with students with learning disabilities, ADHD, and DCD. The three most widely used educational approaches—multisensory, behavior management, and multifaceted—are described briefly here. For consistency and when practical, the physical educator might want to determine which approach is used in the student's classroom or home and follow that same approach in the physical education setting. More specific methods and activities for teaching physical education and sport are included toward the end of the chapter under Recommendations for Teaching Physical Education and Sport.

Multisensory Approach

A child's sensory system has a direct effect on his ability to learn. Children with learning disabilities, ADHD, or DCD can have deficits related to their sensory systems, including poor spatial orientation, difficulty with body awareness, immature body image, poor visual–motor coordination, clumsiness or awkwardness, coordination deficits, or poor balance. See table 11.1 for more possible sensory deficits under the physical and cognitive categories of the chart that may affect movement. When taking these deficits into consideration, effective instruction needs to include a multisensory teaching approach with an understanding of the

perceptual–motor development process and the sensory systems (as described in greater detail in chapter 20).

Many students with a specific learning disability, ADHD, or DCD have difficulty learning in traditional ways. To increase each student's opportunity to learn, it is important to determine the student's preferred learning style. The **multisensory approach** emphasizes teaching by combining one or more of the sensory systems in which the child learns best. The most typical sensory systems are visual, auditory, kinesthetic, and tactile and are included in the VAKT (visual, auditory, kinesthetic, tactile) multisensory teaching method (Smith, 2002). For example, the student can look at a picture or watch a demonstration of a movement (visual), listen to the teacher describe the movement (auditory), and be physically manipulated by the teacher and feel the movement (kinesthetic and tactile). In another example, a student might learn alphabet letters by looking at a printed letter (visual), hearing the sounds of the letters (auditory), moving the entire body to form the letters (kinesthetic), and feeling the shape by tracing the letters (tactile).

Behavior Management

The foundation of effective instruction is managing student behavior. **Positive behavior support (PBS)** and the blending of approaches to behavior management are used to maintain and increase appropriate behaviors and prevent or redirect inappropriate behaviors in children with learning disabilities, ADHD, or DCD (see figure 11.1 on page 221). In PBS, the teacher analyzes the behaviors of the student or class by focusing on the actions occurring before the behavior (i.e., antecedents) and the consequences occurring after the behavior. This ABC analysis (antecedents-behaviors-consequences) helps the teacher evaluate the student or class and make appropriate changes (usually to the environment) to alter the behavior.

Three major approaches to behavior management used either separately or collectively are behavioral, humanistic or psychodynamic, and biophysical (Lavay, French, & Henderson, 2006, 2007). A more detailed discussion of these three approaches and effective behavior management strategies are presented in chapter 6. Also, see Recommendations for Teaching Physical Education and Sport later in this chapter for strategies for organizing the physical education instructional setting to effectively manage behaviors of students with learning disabilities, ADHD, or DCD.

Multifaceted Approach

As stated earlier, students with specific learning disabilities, ADHD, or DCD often have difficulty learning in traditional ways, and no one method works best. Rather, an eclectic or multifaceted approach is required, one that offers a combination of program services based on what is best for each student. Taking a multifaceted, eclectic approach means that a variety of approaches are used in conjunction (Smith, 2007). Such an approach needs to be long term, consistent, and systematic. In many cases, a team approach among school personnel and other appropriate individuals (e.g., the special education classroom teacher and the child's family) works best. A multifaceted approach that develops both school and home interventions with educators and families forming a partnership can require educational (i.e., PBS), medical (i.e., medication; see sidebar), and behavioral and psychological (i.e., behavioral therapy, family counseling, relaxation techniques) interventions (National Resource Center on ADHD, 2008).

RECOMMENDATIONS FOR TEACHING PHYSICAL EDUCATION AND SPORT

For many students with a specific learning disability, ADHD, or DCD, physical education can be a series of miserable failures, such as repeatedly being the last student picked when choosing teams or dropping a fly ball in front of peers. For physical education to be a positive and successful experience, effective programming must be based on the teacher's understanding of the relationships among the many factors that can affect student learning. In the next section, recommendations and best teaching practices are provided that have proven effective in physical education and sport for students with a learning disability, ADHD, or DCD. The section includes information, methods, and activities regarding safety, medication, behavioral and instructional management, task analysis, perceptual motor development, inclusion, interdisciplinary teaching, relaxation, and youth sport (see figure 11.1 on page 221).

Safety

Always keeping student safety first and foremost in mind, physical educators must be aware of any potentially harmful activities and regularly check all facilities and equipment for potential hazards. Equipment needs to be developmentally appropriate for the student's age, body type, and skill level. Unstructured physical activity designed to blow off steam is contraindicated because it may overstimulate students, especially those with ADHD. When this occurs, the potential exists for students to get out of control and become confused and frustrated. Instead of using unstructured activities, provide students with opportunities to perform skills under control and at a slower rate, allowing time to motor plan before performing the activity. Physical educators must remember that some students may be taking medication to help manage behavior and learning (see sidebar on medication).

Physical educators need to protect students from both physical and psychological harm. Many students with a learning disability, ADHD, or DCD have low self-esteem from others making fun of them (Waugh & Sherrill, 2004), which can happen during school activities if educators are not watchful. Making fun of one another must never be tolerated, and discussions should be held in class about respecting individual differences. Instructors must design their programs to promote cooperation and positive interactions among students. When possible, a buddy or teammate may be assigned to socialize with a student with a learning disability, ADHD, or DCD. Strategies for inclusion and activities that involve cooperation are described throughout this book.

Behavioral and Instructional Management

A supportive, structured, consistent, and proactive approach to behavior management is important to student success. Organizing the environment and using instructional strategies that are supportive of students with learning disabilities, ADHD, or DCD is an effective way for the teacher to emphasize student success and provide a positive experience. Being proactive means spending time before class designing an instructional setting consisting of clear rules, consistent routines, smooth transitions with signals for changing activities, and reinforcement methods that motivate students to participate. During instruction, these methods are consistently implemented and practiced so that students clearly understand and follow class expectations. For example, during instruction, the physical educator can tell students to look, think,

Medication: What the Physical Educator Should Know

Ritalin (methylphenidate) and Dexedrine (dextroamphetamine) are two of the most common medications taken by children identified as hyperactive or who have attention difficulties. Each is a stimulant to the central nervous system that has a paradoxical effect by calming the hyperactivity, increasing the student's attention and ability to focus on learning by stimulating the parts of the brain that are not filtering out distractions (National Resource Center on ADHD, 2008). During the past 40 years, Ritalin, the medication most often prescribed by physicians, has been safely and successfully used in the treatment of millions of children with ADHD (Huber & Duhuis, 2002). Research conducted on medication and its effects on learning is well documented; however, the majority of the work has focused on the classroom and not on motor performance in physical education settings (Beyer, 1999).

Medication must never be viewed as an educational panacea or an easy fix but rather as part of the student's entire treatment package. Professionals caution against the quick prescription of any medications and believe they should only be prescribed after other interventions have been explored. Medications such as Ritalin are not to be taken by students six years and younger. These stimulant drugs are fast acting and can take effect within one to eight hours, with Ritalin taking effect within one to four hours (National Resource Center on ADHD, 2008).

Physical educators need to consider a number of factors regarding medication and students with a specific learning disability, ADHD, or DCD (Howell, Evans, & Gardiner, 1997; Lavay et al., 2006). They should identify those students who are on medication by receiving a list from the school nurse, asking the student's special education teacher, checking school files, or sending a note home to the student's parents asking them to provide general information about their child. Though physical educators will not be required to dispense medication, it is still important to be aware of medication type, dosage, schedule, and possible side effects. Poor motor performance and an elevated heart rate can be potential adverse side effects. Students on medication may exhibit drowsiness, fatigue, headaches, loss of sleep, dizziness, blurred vision, irritability, and mood swings. There is also the possibility of the rebound effect that occurs when the medication wears off, causing irritability and mood swings. Physical educators must insist on being informed of those students who are taking medication and their schedule, such as any drug holidays when the student is taken off the medication or transitional periods when the physician adjusts the dosage to determine optimal medication.

and act or focus, plan, and move. The section that follows provides behavior management strategies to promote class structure and organization. For other effective behavior management methods to increase appropriate behaviors and redirect inappropriate behaviors, see chapter 6.

Class Structure

A structured class format is recommended for students with a learning disability, ADHD, or DCD, and it is important to design clear, concise rules and routines that are posted and followed consistently during each class session. Students must know where to go when entering and exiting the gym. Starting class the same way each time allows students to feel comfortable with the program (Lavay et al., 2007). For example, class can start in the same location with an exercise warm-up and certain activities each student knows and feels comfortable with before introducing new activities. To help alleviate apprehension, the instructor should briefly explain the activities of the day.

Provide clear **transitions**, using signals for changing activities or moving from one activity area to the next. This will alert students that a change is about to occur. Consistent transitions and routines will help students stay comfortable in class and learn what is expected of them. Examples of possible transition signals include hitting a tambourine, clapping hands, tossing a scarf into the air, playing music, or counting down (e.g., "5, 4, 3, 2, 1"). After the transition signal, students freeze and listen for the next set of instructions. It might be helpful to establish an area, such as a big circle in the middle of the gym, where students know to go. Before each transition, consider giving a two-minute verbal warning. Provide a one-on-one cue or a secret signal for a student having difficulty following transitions, and signal the student a few minutes before the transition is to occur.

Class Organization

Effective class organization helps students stay active and on task, cuts down on wait time, and reduces behavior problems. Shortening lines, providing each student with a piece of equipment, and individualizing instruction can also increase skill-learning opportunities. Consider using one-on-one instruction (self-paced), partner work, small groups, and learning stations or obstacle courses.

Learning stations allow students to perform activities at their own pace and ability level and free instructors to work with students who need extra time for instruction. Remember to minimize distractions and reduce irrelevant stimuli at learning stations by using marked cones, chalking the area, or positioning folding gymnastic mats vertically (Bishop & Beyer, 1995).

Another effective strategy to minimize distractions is to position students in learning stations away from the center of the gym with their backs toward the extraneous stimuli or in a quiet area with reduced background noise. For more information, see the section on teaching stations in chapter 7 on page 132).

When teaching students with learning disabilities and ADHD, try to eliminate irrelevant stimuli that might cause distractions. Many educators are aware that it is important to improve classroom acoustics in rooms used by students with hearing difficulties but unnecessary to do so for those students with normal hearing. However, many students without hearing disabilities, including students with learning disabilities and those with auditory processing difficulties, can benefit from better acoustics (Acoustical Society of America, 2008). Poor room acoustics and increased noise levels can make it difficult to concentrate and understand instructions. When listening conditions are difficult, physical educators can use teaching prompts or cues to increase student learning.

Teaching Prompts or Cues

Some students with learning disabilities, ADHD, or DCD may have difficulty attending to the relevant aspects of the learning task. A **prompt** or a **cue** is a verbal, physical, or environmental signal to help the student remember to perform a task. The teacher can help students focus on only the most relevant teaching prompts or cues by keeping directions simple and not providing too much information. This is especially important for students with limited attention spans. During instruction, it may also be helpful to position the student directly in front of the instructor. To ensure an optimal view for the entire class, position all of the students so they are not facing the sun. The application example provides the reader with a variety of **verbal**, **physical**, and **environmental** prompting or cueing strategies for a student with a short attention span who demonstrates difficulty staying on task.

Positive Feedback

For all students, but especially students who do not effectively hear instructions or who have difficulty staying on task, it is reinforcing for the teacher to provide positive feedback. Trocki-Ables, French, and O'Connor (2001) found that boys with ADHD stayed on task and performed better when verbal praise and tokens were used to reinforce their mile-run fitness performance. **Nonverbal positive feedback** can be a high-five or thumbs-up. Verbal positive feedback should be specific and provided for student effort and staying on task. For example, say, "Nicole, that's great—you remembered to step with your opposite foot when throwing the ball!" Provide positive feedback to students who are accurate and move under control rather than those who demonstrate speed or how quickly they can complete an activity. Consider spending a shorter amount of time on an activity than you might with same-age peers. Frequently changing the activity adds variety, keeping students on task and motivated.

Ecological Task Analysis

Traditional task analysis and ecological task analysis (ETA), described in chapters 4 and 7, is a major teaching approach that is useful when teaching students with a learning disability, ADHD, and DCD. The teacher must not only consider the student's strengths and weaknesses but must also be able to carefully observe the movements (task or skill) by using **task analysis**, or breaking down

APPLICATION EXAMPLE

Prompting and Cueing Strategies

Setting: Elementary to high school physical education class

Student: Students with specific learning disabilities, ADHD, and DCD who have a short attention span

Issue: What are some possible strategies for handling this situation?

Application: Prompting and cueing strategies for getting and keeping student attention during instruction

▸ Have the student make eye contact, listen, and do not let her begin the activity until the directions are completed.

▸ Give one set of age-appropriate directions at a time, and provide time for the student to take in the information and respond to the directions. Have the student repeat the instructions before performing the task to determine if he is paying attention.

▸ Encourage verbal mediation or self-talk in which the student plans ahead and states aloud the task to be conducted; this strategy will help the student get organized.

▸ Provide verbal reference points. For example, to teach a soccer throw-in, the teacher can say, "Danielle, hold the ball with both arms above your head with your thumbs together."

▸ Determine the form of instruction or teaching cue that works best for each student, including demonstration, visual aids (such as a poly spot or footprint), hand signals (visual), verbal instruction such as specific feedback (auditory), and physical guidance (kinesthetic or tactile).

▸ Use as few prompts or cues as possible. Start by providing verbal instructions, followed by a picture, demonstration, or model, followed by physical guidance. For example, the teacher might say, "Calvin, turn your body to the side before you throw the ball." Have Calvin then try to the throw the ball. Give Calvin time to respond to the directions. If he's unsuccessful, say, "Watch me," and then demonstrate or model the throw. Again, provide time for Calvin to respond to the demonstration. If Calvin is still having difficulty, then physically assist him: "Let me help you turn your body to the side." Be careful not to overassist. Many students with learning disabilities might feel more comfortable watching peers before starting the activity.

▸ Provide visual or environmental cues such as cones, footprints, poly spots, pictures, or a sign with an arrow that marks where and when to move. This will make the directions more concrete, gain students' attention, and help students who have difficulty listening and reading directions. In the previous example of Calvin throwing the ball, footprints or a hula hoop could be placed on the floor to prompt Calvin where to step. A more complex example of cuing or prompting is stating, "Calvin, take five steps forward, turn toward the cone, and run in the direction of the arrow on the cone, and I'll throw you the Frisbee."

skills into components. When necessary, teachers should make modifications, particularly to the environment, including equipment and facilities. For example, provide enough equipment to accommodate task changes and various skill levels, such as making available several types (e.g., bats, rackets) and sizes of striking implements and speed of balls (e.g., balloons, beach balls).

Perceptual–Motor Development

As discussed earlier, people with a learning disability, ADHD, or DCD may exhibit a variety of perceptual and sensory challenges (see table 11.1 on page 222) that will affect their movement and consequently their success in physical education (Waugh & Sherrill, 2004). However, perceptual difficulties can be managed and sometimes overcome by a physical educator who teaches fun and positive movement activities that help develop the tactile, kinesthetic, visual, and auditory sensory systems. See chapter 20, Perceptual–Motor Development, for activities that contribute to development in these areas.

Inclusion in Regular Physical Education

The majority of students with a specific learning disability, ADHD, or DCD are taught in a regular physical education class with their peers without disabilities. Schools need to avoid placing a large group of students with learning disabilities, ADHD, and DCD in the same regular physical education class based on schedule convenience; instead, they should assign students across a range of classes. Further, if inclusion is to be successful, it is not an educationally sound practice to place a student with a disability into a regular physical education class setting without a plan that includes school, administrative, and teacher support (Rizzo & Lavay, 2000; Tripp, Rizzo, & Webbert, 2007).

The teacher will need to include many of the teaching practices discussed in this chapter. It is important to be patient and perhaps provide students with a learning disability, ADHD, or DCD with more time to complete certain tasks. This includes providing the student with plenty of repetition and practice. Break skills down into simple parts, progressing from one step to the next in a well-planned sequential order from simple to complex. For example, kick a stationary ball before progressing to a moving ball, or strike a ball off a tee before trying to hit a pitched ball.

Peer tutor programs are one of the most effective methods to promote inclusion. A major benefit is that the student with a learning disability, ADHD, or DCD receives increased instruction, practice, reinforcement, and feedback on a continual, individual basis from the tutor (Lieberman & Houston-Wilson, 2009). However, peer tutors must

never overassist or treat a student with a disability in any way other than as a member of the class. When possible, an effective method to use with students with a mild learning disability, ADHD, or DCD is **reciprocal peer tutoring**, in which the entire class is placed in pairs and takes turns tutoring. For example, one student tutors and provides feedback while the other performs the activity, and then the partners switch roles. Mach (2000) believes that providing students with a learning disability, ADHD, or DCD the opportunity to be a peer tutor to classmates or younger students can improve self-esteem and motivation.

Learning Through Movement

Learning through movement, or **interdisciplinary teaching**, is an educational process where two or more subject areas are integrated to promote learning in each subject area (Cone et al., 1998). Interdisciplinary teaching lends itself well to the multisensory approach because many children with learning disabilities, ADHD, or DCD are concrete learners who learn best through movement. Conceptual information that is abstract is presented in a concrete manner that actively engages student learning. Movement or motor activities taught in physical education (i.e., perceptual motor activities) can be integrated with other subject areas throughout the school curriculum. Learning through movement in education has been used successfully for over 40 years (Cratty, 1976; Humphrey, 1965).

Recently, there has been a resurgence of interdisciplinary teaching in physical education (learning through movement). Advantages of using the movement medium include the following (Cone et al., 1998; Pangrazi, 2007):

- Helps in learning abstract concepts.
- Promotes active rather than passive involvement in learning.
- Effective for students who are kinesthetic learners (see the previous section on the multisensory approach).
- Stimulates expression and communication.
- Reinforces learning in a fun and meaningful way.
- Helps promote collaboration among professionals, such as the physical educator working with the classroom teacher.

This approach must never be viewed as a substitute for a sound, well-rounded physical education curriculum, and it is certainly not a panacea to overcome all the academic difficulties of students with learning disabilities, ADHD, or DCD. Rather, it should be understood as a fun, multisensory strategy that will motivate students and enhance movement and learning.

Initially, physical educators can start simple and integrate the motor, cognitive, and affective learning domains into a lesson. For example, they might ask a young child with language delays who is striking a balloon (i.e., motor) to tell them the color of the balloon (i.e., academic). Young students with a learning disability, ADHD, or DCD can work with a peer tutor or in a small group (i.e., affective) to shape their body (i.e., motor) in various ways to form letters or words (i.e., academic) (figure 11.2).

The physical educator and classroom teacher can collaborate on a thematic approach and present such themes as the human body, animals at the zoo, transportation, holidays, seasons, the Olympics, and cultures from around the word. For example, students can move as if they were animals at the zoo or on a farm. Using transportation as a theme, the teacher can guide children to move as if they were a plane, car, boat, or train. Another approach is to link a subject area such as math to movement. For example, the teacher can ask students to take a certain number of jumps, such jumping once, twice, or three times, or students can toss beanbags onto a number grid to solve addition and subtraction problems. To supplement spelling, the teacher can have the student hop on a letter grid and spell out words.

Relaxation

Relaxation is a socially appropriate way for all students to control their emotions when they are upset and to handle stressful situations. It can be an essential teaching tool when working with students with a specific learning disability, ADHD, or DCD who may demonstrate difficulty attending to a task and moving under control. Relaxing unneeded muscle groups conserves energy; makes for smoother, more coordinated movements; and helps students solve problems and motor plan. When students lose focus, become too excited, or encounter stressful situations, the physical educator can immediately begin relaxation methods, such as having the student take a few slow, deep breaths. Ending with a relaxing cool-down or closure activity might help calm individual students or the group before heading to the next scheduled class. Surprisingly, relaxation in physical education is often overlooked as a way of helping students focus their attention.

Relaxation methods used in physical education might include progressive relaxation, yoga, tai chi, static stretching, imagery, and impulse-control games (Lavay et al., 2006). The teacher can introduce a **progressive relaxation activity**, where muscle groups are tightened for 5 to 10 seconds and then relaxed for 15 seconds. Using a calm voice in a setting that is as quiet as possible with the lights dimmed to reduce stimuli, students lie in a comfortable position and take slow, deep breaths, inhaling through the nose and exhaling through the mouth while maintaining a rhythm. Soft background music can be played to help students relax.

Physical educators should consider setting aside a few minutes of the class to teach students to move under control and apply proper force to movements. For example, impulse-control games can be introduced by instructing students to move their body parts as slowly as possible by walking on the moon, moving in a sea of gelatin, or being a slowly melting ice cream cone on a hot summer day. Many

FIGURE 11.2 Having students shape their bodies to form letters is an example of learning language through movement.

students with learning disabilities, ADHD, and DCD think in pictures (Waugh & Sherrill, 2004), and the teacher can use **visual imagery** with the student to imagine a pleasant scene, such as walking in a forest along a stream, sitting by a campfire, or watching a sunset. Edwards and Hofmeier (1991) believe it is important for the instructor to use descriptive terms when teaching relaxation. For example, a relaxed muscle is loose and soft, like a sock, and a tense muscle is hard and tight, like a stick. Instructors can develop relaxation training scripts, asking students to make their arms loose like a dog's tongue or to pretend they have a wet sponge or washcloth in their hands and squeeze all the water out as hard as possible (Ballinger & Heine, 1991).

Youth Sport

Students with a learning disability, ADHD, or DCD can enjoy the same benefits of youth sport participation as their peers without disabilities. However, difficulty with movement skills or the inability to socially interact with others often creates barriers that inhibit successful sport participation (Decker & Voege, 1992). Physical educators can help students overcome these barriers by teaching skills that are required in youth sport programs. Physical educators can also be resources for students and their parents by telling them about youth sport programs that exist in their community (Lavay & Seamark, 2001). Initially, an individual sport that a student enjoys, such as dance, karate, tennis, or swimming, might be a better choice than a team sport because the student will receive more individual attention and the complexities of working with teammates are minimized. Many individual sports can become lifelong leisure activities.

Proper coach selection is important for students with a learning disability, ADHD, or DCD. Parents can assist the coach by providing all the necessary information about their child. For example, parents can provide the coach with such information as the child's unique behaviors, strategies for overcoming these behaviors, reinforcements that motivate, and learning strategies that have worked well with the child.

SUMMARY

For many students with a specific learning disability, ADHD, or DCD, physical education might be the one area in which they can experience success during the school day because there is seldom the requirement to sit still, read, or write. When this is the case, physical educators can showcase these students' movement skills. For others with a learning disability, ADHD, or DCD whose movement performances need maturing, physical education can still be an enjoyable experience when conducted in a manner that does not dwell on the student's movement deficits. This chapter has examined the importance of being sensitive to the behaviors and unique needs of students with a learning disability, ADHD, or DCD when designing a program to promote student success.

When preparing to support and teach students with a learning disability, ADHD, or DCD, physical educators can ask the following questions: What are the student's strengths and needs or present level of performance? How does this student best learn (e.g., multisensory approach)? How can I as the teacher change the environment and the task to help this student learn (e.g., ETA)? What approaches and programs are already in place for this student at school and at home (e.g., multisensory approach, multifaceted approach)? What support systems will I need (e.g., behavior management approach, collaboration with other professionals for inclusion), and how will I work to get them? And, finally, how can I collaborate with others to ensure this student's success?

To help answer these questions, this chapter has examined the most effective educational approaches used in the schools today, including the multisensory, behavior management, and multifaceted approaches. Also included are specific recommendations and activities based on students' unique behavior needs and environmental factors for physical education and sport, including safety; behavioral and instructional management, including class structure and organization, teaching prompts or cues, and positive feedback; ETA; perceptual–motor development; inclusion in regular physical education; learning through movement; relaxation; and youth sport. Positive movement experiences can translate into a healthy lifestyle and a lifetime of quality physical activity for students with a learning disability, ADHD, or DCD.

REFERENCES

Acoustical Society of America. (2008). Classroom acoustics. Retrieved July 1, 2008, from http://asa.aip.org/classroom/booklet.html.

American Psychiatric Association (APA). (2000). *Diagnostic and statistical manual of mental disorders (DSM IV)* (4th ed.). Washington, DC: Author.

Ballinger, D.A., & Heine, P.L. (1991). Relaxation training for children—A script. *Journal of Physical Education, Recreation and Dance, 62* (2), 67-69.

Beyer, R. (1999). Motor proficiency of boys with attention deficit/hyperactivity disorder and boys with learning disabilities. *Adapted Physical Activity Quarterly, 16,* 403-414.

Bishop, P., & Beyer, R. (1995). Attention deficit/ hyperactivity disorder (ADHD): Implications for physical educators. *Palaestra, 11* (4), 39-46.

Children and Adults with Attention Deficit/Hyperactivity Disorder (CHADD). (2008). Fact sheet #1. Retrieved January 24, 2008, from www.CHADD.org.

Clark, J.E., Getchell, N., Smiley-Owen, A.L., & Whitall, J. (2005). Developmental coordination disorder: Issues, identification, and intervention. *Journal of Physical Education, Recreation and Dance, 76* (4), 49-53.

Cone, T.P, Werner, P., Cone, S.L, & Woods, A.M. (1998). *Interdisciplinary teaching through physical education.* Champaign, IL: Human Kinetics.

Cratty, B. (1976). *Active learning: Games to enhance academic abilities.* Englewood Cliffs, NJ: Prentice Hall.

Decker, J., & Voege, D. (1992). Integrating children with attention deficit disorder with hyperactivity into youth sport. *Palaestra, 8,* 16-20.

Dunn, J.M., & Leitschuh, C.L. (2006). *Special physical education: Developmental, individualized and developmental* (8th ed.). Dubuque IA: Kendall/Hunt.

Edwards, V.D., & Hofmeier, J. (1991). A stress management program for elementary and special populations children. *Journal of Physical Education, Recreation and Dance, 62* (2), 61-64.

Grosshans, J., & Kiger, M. (2004). Identifying and teaching children with learning disabilities in general physical education. *Journal of Physical Education, Recreation and Dance, 75* (6), 18-20, 58.

Harvey, W.J., & Reid, G. (2003). Attention-deficit/ hyperactivity disorder: A review of research on movement skill performance and physical fitness. *Adapted Physical Activity Quarterly, 20,* 1-25.

Henderson, S.E. (1994). Developmental coordination disorder editorial. *Adapted Physical Activity Quarterly, 11,* 111-114.

Henderson, S.E., & Henderson, L. (2002). Toward an understanding of developmental coordination disorder. *Adapted Physical Activity Quarterly, 19,* 11-31.

Horvat, M., Eichstaedt, C., Kalakian, L., & Croce, R. (2002). *Developmental/adapted physical education: Making ability count* (4th ed.). San Francisco: Benjamin Cummings.

Howell, K.W., Evans, D., & Gardiner, J. (1997). Medication in the classroom: A hard pill to swallow. *Teaching Exceptional Children, 29,* 58-61.

Huber, J., & Duhuis, P. (2002). Ritalin and ADHD—Recent developments. *Palaestra, 18* (3), 12.

Humphrey, J. (1965). *Child learning.* Dubuque, IA: Brown.

Individuals with Disabilities Education Improvement Act (IDEA). (2004). *Amendments of 2004* (PL 108-446), U.S. Department of Education.

Kavale, K.A., & Forness, S.R. (2000). What definitions of learning disability say and don't say: A critical analysis. *Journal of Learning Disabilities, 33* (3), 239-256.

Lavay, B., French, R., & Henderson, H. (2006). *Positive behavior management in physical activity settings* (2nd ed.). Champaign, IL: Human Kinetics.

Lavay, B., French, R., & Henderson, H. (2007). A practical plan for managing the behavior of students with disabilities in general physical education. *Journal of Physical Education, Recreation and Dance, 78* (2), 41-48.

Lavay, B., & Seamark, C. (2001). Everyone plays: Inclusion of special needs children into youth sport programs. *Palaestra, 14* (4), 40-43.

Lieberman, L.J., & Houston-Wilson, C. (2009). *Strategies for inclusion: A handbook for physical educators.* (2nd ed.). Champaign, IL: Human Kinetics.

Mach, M.M. (2000). Teaching and coaching students with learning disabilities and attentional deficits. *Strategies, 13* (4), 12, 29-31.

Milne, D.C., Haubenstricker, J.L., & Seefelt, V. (1991). Remedial motor education: Some practical suggestions. *Strategies, 4* (4), 15-18.

National Resource Center on ADHD. (2008). Diagnosis and treatment. Retrieved January 24, 2008, from www.help4ADHD.org/en/treatment.

Pangrazi, R.P. (2007). *Dynamic physical education for elementary school children* (15th ed.). San Francisco: Pearson Benjamin Cummings.

Rizzo, T., & Lavay, B. (2000). Inclusion: Why the confusion? *Journal of Physical Education, Recreation and Dance, 71* (4), 32-36.

Sherrill, C. (2004). *Adapted physical activity, recreation and sport: Crossdisciplinary and lifespan* (6th ed.). Boston: McGraw-Hill.

Smith, D.D. (2007). *Introduction to special education: Making a difference* (6th ed.). Boston: Pearson.

Smith, N.B. (2002). *American reading instruction* (special ed.). Newark, DE: International Reading Association.

Tripp, A., Rizzo, T.L., & Webbert, L. (2007). Inclusion in physical education: Changing the culture. *Journal of Physical Education, Recreation and Dance, 78* (2), 32-36, 48.

Trocki-Ables, P., French, R., & O'Connor, J. (2001). Use of primary and secondary reinforcers after performance of a 1-mile walk/run by boys with attention deficit/

hyperactivity disorder. *Perceptual and Motor Skills, 93,* 461-464.

U.S. Department of Education, National Center of Educational Statistics. (2007). Digest of educational statistics: Table 47 Children 3-21 years served in federally supported programs for the disabled. Retrieved June 11, 2008, from http://nces.ed.gov/programs/digest/d07/tables/dt07_047.asp?referrer=report.

Waugh L.M., & Sherrill, C. (2004). Dyslexia: Implications for physical educators and coaches. *Palaestra, 20* (3), 20-25, 47.

WRITTEN RESOURCES

Bishop, P., & Beyer, R. (1995). Attention deficit/hyperactivity disorder (ADHD): Implications for physical educators. *Palaestra, 11* (4), 39-46.

Provides a variety of useful teaching suggestions for the physical education setting.

Grosshans, J., & Kiger, M. (2004). Identifying and teaching children with learning disabilities in general physical education. *Journal of Physical Education, Recreation and Dance, 75* (6), 18-20, 58.

Includes information on the definition and causes of learning disabilities, how to recognize various types of learning disabilities, and tips for teaching this population in an inclusive physical education setting.

Harvey, W.J., & Reid, G. (2003). Attention-deficit/hyperactivity disorder: A review of research on movement skill performance and physical fitness. *Adapted Physical Activity Quarterly, 20,* 1-25.

Provides the most comprehensive review to date of research on the movement performance and physical fitness of children with ADHD.

Smith, D.D. (2007). *Introduction to special education: Making a difference* (6th ed.). Boston: Pearson.

Provides a comprehensive chapter on learning disability and another chapter on ADHD in the classroom, and includes definitions, identification types, history, incidence rates, causes and prevention, learning characteristics, and general educational interventions.

AUDIOVISUAL RESOURCES

Lavoie, R.D. *Beyond F.A.T. City: A look back, a look ahead: A conversation about special education* [DVD]. (2005). PBS Video.

This program builds on the international success of the F.A.T. City workshop and provides parents and teachers with thought-provoking discussions of how to play a more effective role in the lives of children with a learning disability. Discusses major trends, issues, and future challenges for this population. Includes a viewer guide and teacher guide with teaching tips and discussion topics. PBS offers other DVDs and videos regarding learning disabilities and other disability topics.

ELECTRONIC RESOURCES

Children with Attention Deficit Disorders (CHADD), 8181 Professional Place, Ste. 1501, Landover, MD, 20785; phone: 800-233-4050; fax: 301-306-7090; Web site: www.chadd.org.

This organization's Web site provides a series of fact sheets and information on conferences, legislation, news releases, local chapters, and research studies. In addition, go to the National Resource Center on ADHD link which is a program of CHADD at www.help4ADHD.org, a clearinghouse since 2002 for the latest science-based information about all aspects of ADHD.

Council for Learning Disabilities (CLD), 11184 Antioch Rd. Box 405, Overland Park, KS, 66210; phone: 913-491-1011; fax: 913-491-1012; Web site: www.cldinternational.org.

This is an international organization that for the past 20 years has been concerned with current issues and has promoted research for students with learning disabilities. The site offers conference information, updates on scholarly initiatives, and general information about learning disabilities, legislation, and research reports.

Division for Learning Disabilities (DLD), one of the special interest groups within the Council for Exceptional Children (CEC), 1110 N. Glebe Rd., Ste. 300, Arlington, VA 22201; phone: 866-915-5000; fax: 703-264-9494; Web site: www.cec.sped.org (CEC) and www.teachingld.org (DLD).

The CEC is the largest international professional organization dedicated to improving educational outcomes for students with exceptionalities, students with disabilities, and the gifted. The exceptionality section includes the division on learning disability, consisting of a mission statement, events calendar, resources, and publications. Also included is the DLD Web site, which offers an electronic newsletter that provides trustworthy and up-to-date professional resources and information about teaching students with learning disabilities.

Visual Impairments

Lauren J. Lieberman

Mr. Joseph has two students with visual impairments in his regular middle school physical education classes. Peter has partial vision due to **retinitis pigmentosa**. Sarah is totally blind. Both of her eyes were removed due to **retinoblastoma**, and she now wears prosthetic eyes. Throughout the year, Mr. Joseph teaches units in which Peter and Sarah can participate with minimal adaptations, and he includes the students in inclusive physical education on a flexible schedule. Mr. Joseph is beginning a basketball unit and the other physical educator is beginning a swimming unit, so Mr. Joseph gives Peter and Sarah the option of deciding which unit they each would like to participate in.

Sarah opts for swimming. She has no sight, making it difficult for her to play basketball and similar sports that depend heavily on seeing a ball. But Sarah can participate in swimming with few adaptations. Peter opts for basketball. His neighbors enjoy shooting hoops and Peter hopes to improve his game enough so he can join them.

On one particular afternoon, Peter stands ready to receive the basketball from a sighted peer but is not aggressively moving toward the ball in the scrimmage. The teacher makes the teammates pass Peter the ball twice. In each case the ball is immediately stolen. Mr. Joseph, who thought all students were involved in his physical education class, sees that Peter's actual involvement is 15 seconds of contact with the ball over a 35-minute class. Such a low level of participation goes against Mr. Joseph's philosophy of teaching.

Mr. Joseph rereads the chapter on children with visual impairments in his college text on adapted physical education, browses the Internet for additional appropriate adaptations, and makes a call to his district's adapted physical education specialist. One week later the scene in Peter's physical education class is quite different. Two-thirds of the class time is now devoted to skill practice and the final third devoted to game play. Rules have been changed. To teach passing skills and cooperation, teams are now required to pass the ball to each team member before scoring. Peter and his teammates always wear yellow jerseys to increase their visibility. There is a five-second rule when Peter has the ball—no defense for five seconds. His teammates can verbalize to indicate where they are and the other team has to remain silent until he passes the ball. On this day Peter scores two baskets for his team and passes the ball 10 times!

Just like people with sight, people with visual impairments want to be accepted and respected as individuals; their visual impairment is just one of many personal characteristics, not the defining characteristic. Educators should keep in mind this quote inspired by athlete Tim Willis: "Tim Willis lost his sight, but he never lost his vision." This means that just because a student has a vision loss does not mean she cannot participate in sports and games with her sighted peers; in fact, a vigorous physical education program is important. The challenge for physical educators, as it is for Mr. Joseph, is planning and teaching so that students with visual impairments can actively participate in physical education, recreation, and sport in school and throughout life.

However, sometimes the accommodations to minimize visual impairments are the least of the teacher's concerns. Often it is the emotional and social issues resulting from how others treat people who are blind that present the greater challenge. Further, *learned helplessness* results when family members and others are overprotective of the person with visual impairment. Well-intended acts can undermine independence and overall personal development when a child is never allowed to experience personal control. Much of this chapter seeks to provide ideas for accommodating the visual impairment and promoting **self-determination** among young people with visual impairments and blindness. So, the task for the physical educator is to make the activity adaptations as needed but also to expect students with visual impairments to do much on their own and to be active, contributing members of the class and community (Lieberman, Modell, & Jackson, 2006).

DEFINITION OF VISUAL IMPAIRMENT

What is a visual impairment? Who is blind? The educational definition from the Individuals with Disabilities Education Act (IDEA) is as follows:

> Visual impairment, including blindness, means an impairment in vision that, even when corrected, adversely affects a child's educational performance. The term includes both partial sight and blindness. (Office of Special Education and Rehabilitative Services, 2006)

These classifications of visual impairments are presented in table 12.1.

Most people with visual impairments still have some usable sight. Perhaps one in four people with visual impairments is blind. Among students with visual losses, about half became blind before or at birth.

Table 12.1 Classification of Visual Impairments

Classification	Description
Visual impairment	Umbrella term encompassing total blindness and partial sight.
Partial sight	Can read print through use of large print or magnification.
Blind	Unable to read large print even with magnification.
Legal blindness	Acuity of 20/200 or less in the better eye with best possible correction or a field of 20° or less diameter in the better eye.
Travel vision	Able to see at 5-10 ft (1.5-3 m) what the normal eye can see at 200 ft (60 m) (5/200 to 10/200). Motion perception: Able to see at 3-5 ft (1-1.5 m) what the normal eye can see at 200 ft (60 m); this ability is limited almost entirely to the perception of motion.
Light perception	Able to distinguish a strong light at a distance of 3 ft (1 m) from the eye but unable to detect a hand movement at 3 ft (1 m) from the eye (<3/200).
Total blindness	Unable to recognize a strong light shining directly into the eyes.

CAUSES OF VISION LOSS

There are multiple causes of vision loss. Though most causes are associated with aging, occasionally loss of vision occurs before or at birth (**congenital**) or in childhood or later (**adventitious**). Some causes of blindness are as follows.

Before Birth

- **Albinism:** Total or partial lack of pigment causing abnormal optic nerve development; may or may not affect skin color. People with albinism may have one or more of the following conditions: decreased visual acuity, photophobia (sensitivity to light), high refraction error (the shape of the eye does not refract light properly so the image seen is blurred), astigmatism (blurred vision), nystagmus (uncontrollable eye movements that are involuntary, rapid, and repetitive), central scotomas (a blind or partially blind area in the visual field), and strabismus (the inability of one or both eyes to look directly at an object at the same time).

- **Retinoblastoma:** A malignancy of the retina in early childhood that usually requires removal of the eye and can occur in one or both eyes.

- **Retinopathy of prematurity (ROP):** Occurs in some infants who are born prematurely, resulting in reduced acuity or total blindness. ROP occurs when abnormal blood vessels grow and spread throughout the retina, the tissue that lines the back of the eye. These abnormal blood vessels are fragile and can leak, scarring the retina and pulling it out of position. This causes a retinal detachment, the main cause of visual impairment and blindness in ROP.

After Birth or Progressive

- **Cataracts:** Opacity of the lens that restricts the passage of light, usually bilateral. Reduces acuity, resulting in blurred vision, poor color vision, photophobia, and sometimes nystagmus. Visual ability fluctuates according to light (figure 12.1*a*).

- **Cortical visual impairment (CVI):** Caused by a brain problem rather than an eye problem. Children with CVI have variable vision; visual ability can change day to day and minute to minute. One eye may perform significantly worse that the other, and depth perception can be very limited. The field of view may also be severely limited, and visual processing can take a lot of effort.

- **Glaucoma:** Causes increased pressure in the eye because of blockage in the normal flow of the aqueous humor. Visual loss may be gradual, sudden, or present at birth. People with glaucoma may also have an increased sensitivity to light and glare.

- **Macular degeneration:** Progressive degeneration of the macula. The macula governs central vision; therefore, macular degeneration affects central vision, resulting in photophobia, poor color vision, and normal peripheral vision (figure 12.1*b*).

- **Retinitis pigmentosa:** Retinitis pigmentosa is caused by a variety of inherited retinal defects, all of which affect the ability of the retina to sense light. It is a progressive disorder that causes loss of peripheral vision, night blindness, tunnel vision, decreased acuity and depth perception, spotty vision because of retinal scarring, and photophobia (figure 12.1*c*).

CHARACTERISTICS OF PEOPLE WITH VISUAL IMPAIRMENTS

There is tremendous diversity among people with visual impairments, but many share certain characteristics. The following sections discuss some of these characteristics. Remember that these are only generalities and are not true of all people with visual impairments.

Affective and Social Characteristics

Habits such as rocking, hand waving or finger flicking, and digging the fingers into the eyes are examples of repetitive movements that some people with visual loss or multiple disabilities develop. These repetitive movements are also known as **blindisms** or **self-stimulation**. There is continuous debate as to the reason for these movements. Regardless of the cause, parents and teachers can simply accept

FIGURE 12.1 Three photos of what a person with a visual impairment might see. *(a)* In cataracts, clouding of the lens causes reduced ability to see detail. *(b)* In age-related macular degeneration, central vision is impaired, making it difficult to read or do close work. *(c)* In retinitis pigmentosa, night blindness develops, and tunnel vision is another frequent result.

these movements as variations of nervous habits most people show, or they may decide that it is in the child's best interest to stop these movements in certain situations. If the movements are not affecting the child's education or others around the child, then some self-stimulating behaviors may be best overlooked (McHugh & Lieberman, 2003).

Fearfulness and dependence may characterize some people with visual losses, whether the loss is due to congenital or adventitious blindness. These characteristics may develop not as a result of the lack of vision but rather as a result of overprotection. This overprotection usually leads to reduced opportunities for students to freely explore their environments, thus creating possible delays in perceptual, motor, and cognitive development (Stuart, Lieberman, & Hand, 2006).

Socialization Opportunities

Socialization opportunities for children with visual impairments are characterized by less

extensive social networks and fewer friendships compared with sighted peers. Observations of children with visual impairments in inclusive settings have shown that children often are in the vicinity of their teacher and seldom socialize with sighted children. Children with visual impairments have described schools as unfriendly, lonely places or as places where they are teased and ignored by other children. Robinson and Lieberman (2004) found that children with visual impairments had low levels of perceived control over their ability to make and retain friendships. Children who experience movement difficulty often experience lower self-perceptions and self-worth (Shapiro et al., 2008). These poor self-perceptions are likely to lead to reduced movement confidence and often extend beyond the athletic domain, resulting in adverse psychosocial consequences.

Implications: Socialization opportunities must be nurtured and self-advocacy must be taught. For example, when a teacher has students partner up, the child with the visual impairment can have a say as to whom he wants as his partner. In addition, disability awareness must be taught so the child's classmates know what he can see and what modifications are made and why. If paraeducators or aides are used, they must be taught when to step out of the way to encourage social opportunities, because they can inhibit such opportunities if they are not aware. These types of choices must be taught and social opportunities must be created as much as possible.

Implications for Teaching Physical Education: Motor and Fitness Characteristics

The lack of sight does not directly cause any unique motor or physical characteristics. However, the reduced opportunity to move, which often accompanies blindness, may result in many distinct characteristics (Stuart et al., 2006). The following are possible motor, physical, and fitness characteristics of visual impairments and corresponding implications.

Motor delays in young children with visual impairments are often due to the following situations: reduced opportunity for rough-and-tumble play with parents, heightened protective instincts of parents and caregivers, the child's own fear of being moved suddenly, the lack of vision that motivates movement, and the lack of opportunity to observe others moving.

Implications: Students with visual losses must be provided with the opportunity and be encouraged to move in a safe environment to minimize the development of motor delays. Enthusiastically encourage and positively reinforce movements by physically demonstrating or prompting and verbally encouraging students that it is safe to move. Motor delays are not usually observed among people who are blind but who were sighted for years. Those with adventitious blindness need corrective feedback from observers as a substitute for monitoring their own movements so that skills once mastered are retained.

Postural deviations may be prevalent among people with visual impairments or blindness who hold the head in unique positions to maximize vision. Postural deviations may be more pronounced among people who have been blind since birth and have never had the opportunity to see how others sit, stand, and move. Examples include a shuffling gait, forward tilt, or rounded shoulders.

Implication: Corrective postural exercises may help improve posture and thereby reduce stress on the body. Verbal or physical prompts can remind the person to "sit up tall" and keep the "head up."

Body image and balance may also be delayed among students who are blind (Casselbrant et al., 2007). This may be due to decreased opportunities for regular physical activity through which balance and body image are refined. Also, sight enhances balance because it allows people to see a reference point for aiding stability.

Implication: Participation in activities such as dance, yoga, movement education, and any age-appropriate activity can be excellent means of developing body image and balance.

Gait difficulties may appear in people with visual impairments and many who are blind. This can be demonstrated by asking sighted students to close their eyes and walk across the room. When unaided by sight, their gait usually shows shorter strides, a pronounced shuffle, a slower pace, more time spent in the support phase, and a tendency to veer away from the stronger leg over a distance.

Implication: If gait is impeding movement and learning, physical educators can improve running gait by generating greater hip extension during the drive phase and greater hip flexion during the recovery stage of the sprint run. Using the guide-running techniques presented in this chapter can improve running gait. Running gait may also be improved by increasing the time students walk or run, which can be motivated by using talking pedometers (Lieberman et al., 2006).

Health-related fitness levels of people with visual impairments are generally below those of their sighted peers (Kozub, 2006). This may be of particular concern because Buell (1966) suggests that people with visual impairments need higher levels of physical fitness than their sighted counterparts. He notes that there are many instances in which people without sight need to spend more energy to reach the same goals as those with sight.

Implication: Health-related fitness levels of people who are blind have the potential to match those of their sighted peers. Lack of opportunity to train and difficulty arranging for sighted guides for running can be obstacles to developing fitness. It is important for physical educators to develop fitness programs for students with visual impairments and to work with families in finding fitness activities that students can pursue at home, such as rope jumping, weight training, aerobics, bicycling (single in a clear area or tandem), or walking.

In summary, the missing component in the development of functional movement and fitness abilities among students with visual impairments is the opportunity to experience physical activity, not ability. The physical educator must encourage students to feel safe and good about their movements. This can be accomplished both through instruction in physical education and through collaboration with parents, caregivers, and other influential people in the child's life. The following section offers suggestions for helping students with visual impairments enjoy physical activity.

TEACHING STUDENTS WITH VISUAL IMPAIRMENTS IN INCLUSIVE PHYSICAL EDUCATION

With the current emphasis on inclusive education, many students with disabilities are taught in regular physical education classes. Inclusion can work well if support systems are provided. When teaching students with visual impairments in physical education, keep in mind that these students can do all of the same physical activities as their sighted peers. Thoughtful modifications, such as changing the ball color to one that contrasts sharply with the background, are sometimes the only adjustments needed to enable the student with partial sight to participate fully in class. Research has shown that children with cortical visual impairments benefit from objects that have more color and are moving (Cohen-Maitre & Haerich, 2005). Other times, more extensive support is needed, such as team teaching or consultation with an adapted physical education specialist to help a student with visual impairment learn in physical education. Further, children with visual impairments can have needs in other areas or even coexisting conditions that require the reader to refer to other chapters in this book.

All too often, students with visual impairments are placed in inclusive physical education classes without the necessary support systems. This dumping under the guise of inclusion is unfair to the student, the classmates, and the teacher. A result of this dumping can be the failure of children with visual impairments to develop lifelong movement skills. They become adults who are unable to enjoy basic movement opportunities and who remain inactive over the life span. Research has shown that children with visual impairments become less active as they get older (Kozub & Oh, 2004). This pattern develops even though people with visual impairments have the capacity to enjoy a host of activities, such as bike riding, in-line skating (with a friend serving as a guide), or jogging in a safe area with a partner. Activities such as bowling, dance, horseback riding, and many other lifetime sports can be done safely and lead to social networks of friends, enabling people with visual impairments to remain within their capabilities but extend beyond their experience.

Members of the child's multidisciplinary team are keys to appropriate inclusion. Parents and other caregivers may advocate for appropriate support systems. In addition, collaboration with a resource specialist in adapted physical education, the vision teacher, an orientation and mobility specialist, and others can be major factors in successful inclusion. The child's paraeducator or teacher's aide can also be a great resource for information and a great teaching assistant in physical education if prepared correctly (McKenzie & Lewis, 2008). Needed support services should be recorded on the child's individualized education program (IEP).

The child with a visual impairment can provide input on appropriate inclusion strategies. Teachers can use the child as a source of ideas for adaptations. The student with the visual impairment and all students in the class are also excellent sources of ideas for adaptations. Teachers have had much success in developing accommodations through class efforts.

The curriculum and programming for students with visual impairments should include a mix of **open and closed sports**. Open sports have variables that change often, such as tennis, volleyball, football, soccer, and lacrosse. In other words, the game is unpredictable and the speed, angle, and direction of the ball and defenders change often and without notice. Closed sports are consistent and predictable. Examples of closed sports are archery, bowling, the shot put and discus, and bocce. Skill in and love of movement can be developed through active participation in physical education. Students with visual impairments should be introduced to all sports, games, and activities that their peers learn. Lifetime activities such as tandem biking, running, goalball, swimming, wrestling, judo, and bowling should be included as well.

The following three sections present ideas for adapting instruction for students with visual impairments based on learning about the student's abilities, fostering the student's independence, and exploring options for instructional modifications. Please refer to the Inclusion of a Student With Impaired Vision application example.

APPLICATION EXAMPLE

Inclusion of a Student With Impaired Vision

Setting: Middle school physical education class

Student: Andrea is an active sixth-grade student who enjoys biking, swimming, in-line skating, and studying judo after school and on weekends. She has retinitis pigmentosa, resulting in a progressive visual impairment. She has some residual vision and is adjusting to her current visual ability.

Issue: Andrea's IEP states that she must be fully included in her two 45-minute physical education classes each week, but her teacher believes that her blindness limits her abilities. He has her exercising on a stationary bike and walking the perimeter of the gym while her classmates are involved in physical activities and games. Andrea is becoming more and more frustrated, and this is affecting her performance in other subject areas.

Application: The following were determined as a result of a meeting with the school administrator, the teacher of the visually impaired, and the physical educator:

▶ Andrea will participate in all physical education activities with her peers.

▶ To help him adapt games, sports, and activities, the physical educator will purchase books such as *Games for People With Sensory Impairments*, *Adapted Physical Education and Sport*, and *Adapted Physical Activity, Recreation, and Sport*.

▶ The teacher will search the Internet for information and adaptations to assist him in supporting Andrea in an inclusive setting.

▶ The school will buy brightly colored balls and auditory balls, and it will set up a guide-wire system in the gym and outside on the track.

▶ The curriculum will include a variety of games and activities conducive to full participation by Andrea, such as weight training, aerobics, goalball, and cross-country skiing.

▶ Three of Andrea's friends will be trained as peer tutors to assist her in class.

▶ An additional physical education class with supplemental instruction will be offered should Andrea need more time to grasp a skill or activity.

Learning About Students' Abilities

An important step in learning about students' abilities is to determine each student's present level of performance. Generally, students with visual impairments are capable of taking the same formal assessments and attaining the same standards as students with sight. In case of mobility limitations due to blindness, teachers can modify standards for mobility test items, use assistive devices, or use sighted guides based on suggestions throughout this chapter. For example, auditory cues may be added so students know where to throw and how far to skip or run. However, caution should be used when interpreting test norms that do not include students with visual impairments or that are based on test items that have been modified. The Brockport Physical Fitness Test (BPFT) (Winnick & Short, 1999) assesses the health-related fitness of young people who are blind. Refer to chapter 5 for additional information on measurement and evaluation. The teacher may seek answers to the following five questions in addition to assessing current performance:

1. *What can the student see?* Ask the student, "What can you see?" rather than "How much can

you see?" Ask the same question of others familiar with the student's vision, including the student's previous teachers, parents, caregiver, and low-vision specialist. Read the student's educational file for further information regarding what the student can see. Use this important information when teaching.

2. *When (at what age) was the loss of vision experienced, and over what period of time did it progress? Is it still progressing?* Ask the student when the vision loss was experienced. Certain skills are acquired before the ages of 8 to 10 in sighted children, so if a student gradually lost all vision due to disease before the ages of 8 to 10, she may require less time preparing for specific activities, such as hitting a sound-emitting softball and running to a sound-emitting base, than a student who is congenitally blind and has never had the chance to see a game of baseball. A student with congenital blindness may need more detailed explanations that do not depend on analogies for which the student has no basis of understanding. For example, the teaching cue "Jump like a bunny" may not be useful to a child who does not have any visual memory of rabbits moving. The teacher may wish to teach the child how to jump like a bunny.

3. *How can the instructor maximize use of existent sight?* Learn from the students what helps them see best. For most types of visual impairments, bright lighting maximizes vision. For some conditions, such as glaucoma and albinism, however, glare is a problem. Teach these students in lighting free of glare to maximize vision. When outside, these students may need tinted glasses or hats to reduce glare.

4. *Are there any contraindicated physical activities?* To determine if there are any contraindicated (not recommended) physical activities, seek medical consultation. Note the cause of blindness. It is important to consult reference texts on the etiology of visual impairments and read about the student's specific visual impairment. There are few contraindications for people with total blindness since there is no sight to preserve. For people with partial sight, there might be activity restrictions imposed in an effort to preserve the remaining sight. Discuss the condition with the student's eye specialist to determine what, if any, restrictions are necessary, especially following recent eye surgery. For example, jarring movements that could cause further detachment are usually contraindicated with a detached retina. Contact sports, as well as diving and swimming underwater, may need to be

modified. Glaucoma occurs when the fluid within the eye is unable to drain and pressure increases within the eye, causing blindness. Inverted positions and swimming underwater are often contraindicated with glaucoma because of increased pressure in the eye.

5. *What are the student's favorite scholastic, social, and physical activities?* Students may be asked what adaptations they prefer. For example, how do they like to run? With a sighted guide? Using a guide wire? Independently on a clearly lined track? It is important to learn about the opportunities that exist for the child to participate in physical activities with family and friends as well as in the community. The opportunity to try all the options is important because students may not know their preferences until they have had repeated opportunities to try each one. These activities and adaptations can be incorporated into the child's physical education program.

6. *What instructional approach does the child prefer?* A child with limited vision will need some physical support to learn new skills. It is important to ask children if they prefer one teaching approach, such as physical guidance over tactile modeling, or perhaps they prefer not to be touched at all (O'Connell, Lieberman, & Petersen, 2006). In this case, clear explanations may work best for them.

Fostering Independence

To be independent, students must have the skills, socialization, stamina, and strength to complete everyday tasks. Through physical activity, students with visual impairments can acquire the necessary stamina, socialization, strength, and skills to be independent. Consider the following suggestions for teaching.

Have a positive attitude about all students. The teacher's attitude is the determining factor in the classroom. If the teacher is truly interested in teaching all students, including a student with a visual impairment, and if she provides accommodations and makes adaptations to meet the diverse needs of all students without a fuss, then the students in the class will pick up on this attitude and they will be more likely to also accept students with visual impairments or other differences.

Encourage participation of all students in physical activities. To encourage participation, find out how students feel about various activities. Address any fears students might express, and create a safe environment so they are willing to participate in physical activity. The following incident illustrates the importance of talking with students to understand their concerns and encouraging them to participate. A young girl who had been totally blind since birth performed well in swimming, but she seemed unable to learn to swim underwater. When asked why she had such difficulty learning to swim underwater, she replied, "No one will see me if I go underwater. That scares me." After it was explained that water is clear and can be seen through, the girl was reassured and soon learned to swim underwater.

Use parents as resources. Parents are most children's biggest advocates. Further, in some cases parents can have a negative impact on physical activity if their fears about the safety of their child influence activity levels. Based on their fears for the child who does not have use of a major sense organ, some caregivers may dwell on what the child can't do rather than on what he can do. In these cases the child will rarely have the opportunity at home to try new things, play games that sighted children play, or take risks. Physical educators can collaborate with parents about their children's capabilities by sending home assessment data, personal notes, or newsletters with descriptions of students' accomplishments, photographs of the student doing activities, and lists of the student's favorite physical activities. By learning about their children's current performance and abilities, parents may have a better understanding of their children's potential and may allow more opportunities for physical activity at home and in the community.

Challenge students with visual impairments so they can be successful. To help improve self-esteem and motivate students to continue to work on their next goals, reward and recognize their accomplishments. Using a realistic test that includes assessment of process, product, and level of independence will assist the student in observing improvement. An example of this type of assessment specifically for children with visual impairments is the Camp Abilities Activity Analysis Checklist (www.campabilities.org). Teachers work with the student to set realistic goals and recognize achievements. Bulletin boards, student newspapers, progress reports, and announcements are all ways to recognize student achievement.

Expect the student to move as independently as possible during physical education. At the beginning of the school year and then at the start of each unit, the person with a visual impairment should be oriented to playing fields, gymnasiums, locker rooms, and equipment to increase indepen-

dence and feelings of security. Landmarks that can help students orient themselves (e.g., a landmark might be the mats along the walls at either end of the gymnasium in contrast to the paneling along the sidewalls) can be identified. Students may be encouraged to walk around and touch everything as often as needed in order to create the visual map in their minds that will enable them to negotiate the area with confidence. Equipment should be kept in the same position in the gymnasium, and students should have extra time before class to orient themselves to any new configuration of equipment. In the locker room, the locker should be in an easily accessible location, and a lock that opens with a key or push-button number rather than a combination should be provided. Accessible locks can be purchased through the American Printing House for the Blind (www.aph.org). A trained peer tutor may be most helpful with mobility, skill acquisition, and feedback for children who are totally blind. Training the peer tutor is imperative to ensure safety, improved skill acquisition, and communication. In addition to the initial training, it is advantageous to meet with the student and peer tutor a few minutes before each class to introduce the student to the concepts and movements to be taught that day. The sidebar offers more suggestions of things to keep in mind when teaching students with visual impairments. These suggestions must be shared with the peer tutor.

Provide additional incentives for young children. Young children with visual impairments need additional incentives to move. Fundamental **phylogenetic skills** (those skills that humans inherently develop such as crawling, sitting, walking, and so on) are more difficult to learn due to the deprivation of the most motivating sense—sight. Parents, specialists, teachers, and therapists must work together to give the child a reason to move and develop basic motor skills such as sitting, scooting, crawling, rolling, and walking. Increasing play behaviors will provide increased opportunity for social interaction for children with visual impairments (Celeste, 2006). The following are some suggested activities to instill a yearning for movement in the young child with a visual impairment:

■ Bell Balloon Bash: The child chases a balloon with a bell in it around the room while crawling, walking, or running. Guide the child if necessary, and encourage the child to kick the balloon when possible.

■ Parachute Swing: Two people swing a parachute while the child is inside.

When Teaching Students Who Are Blind or Visually Impaired, Remember . . .

- What seem like ordinary, everyday happenings might need to be explained. Narrate during a game so students can understand what everyone is doing, or appoint a student narrator.

- Some experiences are not part of every student's direct experience. For instance, tell the child about the martial art of judo and allow the child to experience it.

- Students might need help putting parts together to form a whole concept. Allow children to feel the entire playground set, the entire gym space, and so on. Allow time for this before class if possible.

- Make a raised tactile map of the playing area that the child can feel to understand the boundaries of the game. Boundaries in soccer,

basketball, volleyball, goal ball, or the pool can be more easily understood by this technique of a small tactile map. Pipe cleaners, twine, or felt glued on cardboard or on the back of a clipboard are all that is needed. Ask the vision teacher or orientation and mobility instructor for help if necessary.

- Imitation is hard. Physically guide or tactile model students through movements rather than showing them.

- Feedback is needed because students cannot always tell how they are doing. Tell students where they threw the ball, or even better, use a beeping ball so they know where they threw the ball.

- Incline Roll: Place the child on top of a low incline and allow the child to roll or crawl to a motivating sound source at the bottom.

- Scooter Pull: The child sits on a scooter and holds one part of a hula hoop. The teacher holds the opposite part of the hula hoop and pulls the child around the gymnasium. The teacher then decreases support until the child is doing the movements herself. Children can also lie on a scooter and pull themselves up a rope that is tied to a table or wall.

- Therapy-Ball Push: In an assisted sitting position (an adult sits directly behind the child, helping to support the child's back), the child pushes a large, heavy therapy ball to a sound source or a person. This builds upper-body strength to assist in crawling and creeping.

- Rebounder Heaven: The child jumps on a rebounder (minitrampoline) while holding the wall, the teacher, or a bar for support.

- Movement Exploration: Place the child on a mat and ask the child to move forward, backward, high, low, fast, slow, and so on.

- Jump Rope Madness: Standing on a mat, allow the child to explore a variety of jump rope movements (e.g., forward, backward, fast, slow). A jump rope kit specifically for

children with visual impairments is available through the American Printing House for the Blind (www.aph.org).

No matter what activity is being taught to young children with visual impairments, it is important to offer choices. Choice making in physical activities, such as size of objects, sounds, colors, or textures, can generalize across settings, items, and individuals (Clark & McDonnell, 2008).

Exploring Options for Instructional Modification

So much of what people learn is not directly taught but learned through watching and listening to what is happening around them. **Incidental learning** occurs when information is not directly taught but rather is observed from the surroundings. When there is a visual impairment, the opportunity for incidental learning is dramatically reduced, and teachers need to directly teach much more information. Every opportunity should be used to explain what is happening around the child and why. The teacher and paraeducator must take the time to ensure the child understands the surrounding environment, such as the volleyball net and boundaries or the baseball bases and pitching mounds, as well as the concepts of the game and all relevant terminology.

Students with visual impairments learn with various levels of prompting and instructional techniques. Some students may need a physical demonstration for certain skills, yet others may learn through verbal instruction. In some cases the complexity of the activity will drive the level of instruction. This varied level of instruction is often referred to as the *system of least prompts*. The following system of least prompts provides examples specific to teaching children with visual impairments. Note that the instructor may use one or more of the following teaching strategies to help the student perform the skill. Instructors should know that physical guidance and tactile modeling have both been shown to improve self-efficacy in novel tasks for children with visual impairments (O'Connell et al., 2006).

Verbal explanations *by the instructor*

- Explain what the child is to do in simple terms.
- Use the child's preferred mode of communication.
- If the child does not understand the first time, repeat in a different way.
- If the child has any usable vision, demonstrate to increase understanding.
- Give feedback using precise, unambiguous descriptions. A statement such as "Hold the racket three to four inches above your left shoulder" provides more feedback than "Hold the racket like this." Precise language benefits all students, with or without visual impairments.
- Include students with visual impairments during spectator events by assigning a student announcer to describe the action for spectators, much as a radio announcer describes a ball game. Select an announcer with a lively sense of humor to make the event more fun for everyone.

Demonstrations *by the instructor or peer*

- Show the child the desired skill or movement.
- Demonstrate within the child's field of vision.
- Ask someone close to the student's size and ability to model.
- Use whole-part-whole teaching when possible. Demonstrate the whole skill, then the parts (based on task analysis), and then the whole task again.

Physical assistance or guidance *from the instructor or peer*

- Assist the student physically through the movement with either partial physical assistance—touching the elbow for the crawl stroke—or with total physical assistance—moving their arms through the motion of batting.
- Record which skills require physical assistance, including how much and where on the student's body the assistance was modeled. If asked for legal purposes, the teacher can explain when, where, and why he touched a student.
- Forewarn the student before giving physical assistance in order to avoid startling the student.
- Fade assistance to minimal physical prompts as soon as possible.

Tactile modeling *of the instructor or peer*

- Allow the student to feel a peer or the instructor execute a skill or movement that was previously difficult to learn using the three previous approaches.
- Tell the student where and when to feel you or a peer executing a skill.
- Document how much assistance was given, when and where the student felt you or a peer, and why (for legal purposes).
- Repeat tactile modeling as many times as necessary to ensure understanding.
- Combine tactile modeling with the other teaching methods to increase understanding.

Addition of sound devices

- For softball, use a large playground ball that is hit off a bounce, or use a beeper ball (a ball with an audible buzzer inside is available for purchase at www.aph.org). The base coach calls continuously to direct the batter to the base.
- Make playground balls audible by cutting the ball, inserting bells, and then resealing the ball with a bicycle tire patch.
- Make scoring a goal audible by tying bells onto net goals. Everyone can hear the jingling sound when a goal is scored.
- Make a basket audible by tying a can with rocks to a string and to the rim and having a peer jiggle the string to emit an audible sound.

Enhancement of visual cues

- Most people with visual impairments have some residual vision. Evaluate each activity to decide what types of visual cues are needed and how to highlight them. Color, contrast, and lighting are important. Be sure to ask students what enhances their vision. For example, a student may not be able to distinguish between a blue and a red pinny but can see a yellow pinny clearly.

- Use colored tape to increase the contrast of equipment with the background, such as high jump standards and poles or the edges of a balance beam. Use rope with tape over it to delineate the end of a balance beam or the center of a trampoline.

- Use brightly colored balls, mats, field markers, and goals that contrast with the background for most students with visual impairments. Some people with albinism and glaucoma, however, need solid-colored objects under nonglare lights.

- Make the gymnasium lighting brighter (or darker for students who have difficulty with glare or who tend to self-stimulate with the bright lights).

SPORTS FOR ATHLETES WITH VISUAL IMPAIRMENTS

There are two major organizations for athletes who have visual impairments. The goal of the United States Association of Blind Athletes (USABA) and the International Blind Sports Federation (IBSA) is to promote competitive sport opportunities for athletes with visual impairments throughout the world. These organizations also seek to change attitudes toward people with visual impairments.

United States Association of Blind Athletes (USABA)

USABA is the major sport organization in the United States for athletes 14 years of age and older who have a visual impairment. Organized in 1976, USABA provides competitive sport opportunities at the local, state, regional, national, and international levels. People with visual impairments may choose to participate in integrated sport with their sighted peers, in sport exclusively for people with visual impairments, or both. Many people with visual impairments participate in sport for the blind because of the opportunity to meet and compete with others who are also blind. Physical educators are encouraged to contact USABA (www.usaba.org) for the location of the nearest sport organization and then share this information with students who are blind. The USABA can also provide the teacher with local role models who will come and speak to the school about competing in international sports against others with visual impairments.

Although there are increased recognition and opportunities for elite athletes who are blind, there remain few programs designed to bring young people with visual impairments into sport. Physical educators can help by reviewing their physical education curriculum, noting those sports offered that are also USABA sports. While teaching those sports, physical educators are encouraged to make an extra effort to promote them among any students with visual impairments and assist students in learning how to pursue them through USABA.

USABA offers competition in nine sports:

Alpine and Nordic skiing

Athletics (track and field)

Five-a-side soccer

Goalball

Judo

Powerlifting

Swimming

Tandem cycling

Wrestling

USABA athletes who reach an elite athletic level compete in the World Blind Championships and in the Paralympics. USABA classification for competition is based on residual vision, as shown in table 12.2. Rules for each sport are modified slightly from those established by the national sport organizations. For example, track and field follows most National Collegiate Athletic Association (NCAA) rules, except guide wires are used in sprints, sighted guides may be used on distance runs, hurdles are eliminated, and jumpers who are totally blind touch the high bar and then back off and use a one- or two-step approach. The use of guides depends entirely on the athlete's visual classification and the particular event. Guides facilitate the activity by running alongside the athlete, with both runners holding on to a tether. Alternatively, stationary guides are positioned around the track

Table 12.2 USABA Classification for Sport Competition

Level	Classification
B1	No light perception in either eye up to light perception; unable to recognize the shape of a hand at any distance or in any direction.
B2	Able to recognize the shape of a hand up to visual acuity of 20/600 or a visual field of less than 5° in the best eye with the best practical eye correction.
B3	From visual acuity above 20/600 and up to visual acuity of 20/200 or a visual field of less than 20° and more than 5° in the best eye with the best practical eye correction.
B4	From visual acuity above 20/200 and up to visual acuity of 20/70 and a visual field larger than 20° in the best eye with the best practical eye correction.

to call directional signals to the runner. The following list provides descriptions of various guiding techniques for running.

- **Sighted guide:** The runner grasps the guide's elbow, shoulder, or hand depending on what is most comfortable for the runner and guide (figure 12.2a).

- **Tether:** The runner and guide grasp a tether (i.e., short string, towel, shoelace). This allows the runner full range of motion of the arms while remaining in close proximity to the sighted runner (figure 12.2b).

- **Guide wire:** The runner holds onto a guide wire and runs independently for time or distance. A guide wire is a rope or wire pulled tightly across a gymnasium or track. A rope loop, metal ring, or metal handle ensures that the runner will not receive a rope burn and allows for optimal performance. The runner holds onto the sliding device and runs independently for as long as desired. Guide wires can be set up permanently or temporarily (figure 12.2c).

- **Sound source from a distance:** The runner runs to a sound source such as a clap or a bell. This can be done as a one-time sprint or continued for a distance run.

- **Sound source:** The guide rings a bell or shakes a noisemaker for the runner to hear while running side by side. This works best in areas with limited background noise.

- **Circular running:** In a large, clear, grassy area, a 20- to 25-foot (6-8 m) rope is tied to a stake. The student takes the end of the rope, pulls it taut, and runs in circles. The circumference of the circle can be measured to determine the distance, or the athlete can run for time. A beeper or radio can be placed at the starting point to mark the number of laps completed.

- **Sighted guide's shirt:** The runner with partial vision runs behind a guide with a bright shirt. Ask the runner what color she can see best to ensure maximum vision. This must be done in areas that are not too crowded.

- **Independent running:** A runner with travel vision runs independently on a track marked with thick white lines.

- **Treadmill:** Running on a treadmill provides a controlled and safe environment. Select a treadmill with the safety feature of an emergency stop.

- **Wheelchair racing:** A person who is blind and in a wheelchair can use any of the previous adaptations as needed. Aerobic conditioning results from pushing over long distances, whether around a track, on neighborhood sidewalks, or along a paved path.

Running is fundamental to many sports and activities. It is crucial to allow the student opportunities to experience each technique and decide which technique is preferred. Students may even prefer one technique for speed and another for distance.

Talking pedometers have been successfully used to improve walking performance in children with visual impairments to the healthy fitness level of 11,000 to 13,000 steps per day recommended by the President's Challenge (2007). The three brands of talking pedometers on the market are equally valid (Beets et al., 2007). Talking pedometers can also be used in physical education classes with students with visual impairments. In addition, RT3 activity monitors are useful for measuring short-term physical activity by adolescents with visual impairments (Kozub, Oh, & Rider, 2005).

Photo courtesy of Carla Rodriguez.

Photo courtesy of Carla Rodriguez.

Photo courtesy of Carla Rodriguez.

FIGURE 12.2 Running using *(a)* a sighted guide, *(b)* a tether, and *(c)* a guide wire.

Wrestling rules are modified slightly to require that opponents maintain physical contact throughout the match. Wrestlers with visual impairments have a long history of victories and state championships against sighted opponents (Buell, 1966).

Gymnasts compete according to USA Gymnastics rules, except for the following: Vaulters who are blind may start with their hands on the horse and use a two-bounce takeoff, coaches on the balance beam may warn competitors when they near the end of the beam and no jumps are used, competitors may count their steps to the edge of the mat during the floor exercise, and music may be placed anywhere near the mat to aid directionality.

Swimming follows NCAA rules. Athletes commonly count their strokes so that they can anticipate the end of the pool. Coaches may also tap a swimmer on the shoulder, using a long pole with soft material at the end such as a tennis ball, or 4 inches (10 cm) of a pool noodle to signal the upcoming end of the pool. For the backstroke, flags are hung low over the pool to brush the swimmers' arms to signal the end of the pool. Water can be sprayed on the surface of the pool to designate the end of the lane, either for one swimmer or across the end of all lanes. When necessary, a spotter may use a kickboard to protect a swimmer's head from hitting the wall at the end of the lane.

Goalball is a sport specifically designed for athletes with visual impairments. The object of the game is to roll a ball that contains bells past the opposing team's end line (figure 12.3).

International Blind Sports Federation (IBSA)

The international counterpart of USABA is IBSA. For international competition, athletes participate in the Paralympic Games and the World Blind Championships.

Photo courtesy of Carla Rodriguez.

FIGURE 12.3 Physical educators might introduce goalball in an integrated class as a challenge to students who are sighted.

National Beep Baseball Association (NBBA)

Beep baseball, a popular modification of baseball, is governed by the National Beep Baseball Association (NBBA). Competition culminates with the NBBA World Series. Further details on beep baseball are provided in chapter 26.

SUMMARY

This chapter has focused on physical education for students with visual impairments. Whether the students are in an inclusive physical education setting or in a segregated class, it is important to know their abilities and focus on what they can do. It is up to the physical education teacher to make the modifications necessary to ensure a quality experience that will prepare the student for experiences in physical activity.

REFERENCES

Beets, M., Foley, J., Tindall, D.W., & Lieberman, L.J. (2007). Accuracy of voice-announcement pedometers for youth with visual impairment. *Adapted Physical Activity Quarterly, 24* (3), 218-227.

Buell, C.E. (1966). *Physical education for blind children.* Springfield, IL: Charles C. Thomas.

Casselbrant, M.L., Mandel, E.M., Sparto, P.J., Redfern, M.S., & Furman, J.M. (2007). Contribution of vision to balance in children four to eight years of age. *Journal of Ontology, Rhinology & Laryngology, 116* (9), 653-657.

Celeste, M. (2006). Play behaviors and social interaction of a child who is blind: In theory and practice. *Journal of Visual Impairment and Blindness, 100,* 75-90.

Clark, C., & McDonnell, A.P. (2008). Teaching choice making to children with visual impairments and multiple disabilities in preschool and kindergarten classrooms. *Journal of Visual Impairment and Blindness, 100,* 397-409.

Cohen-Maitre, S.A., & Haerich, P. (2005). Visual attention to move and children with cortical visual impairment. *Journal of Visual Impairment and Blindness, 99,* 389-402.

Kozub, F.M. (2006). Motivation and physical activity in adolescents with visual impairments? *RE:view, 37,* 149-160.

Kozub, F.M., & Oh, H. (2004). An exploratory study of physical activity levels in children and adolescents with visual impairments. *Clinical Kinesiology, 58* (3), 1-7.

Kozub, F.M., Oh, H., & Rider, R.A. (2005). RT3 accelerometer accuracy in estimating short-term physical activity in individuals with visual impairments. *Adapted Physical Activity Quarterly, 22,* 265-276.

Lieberman, L.J., Modell, S., Jackson, I. (2006). *Going PLACES: A transition guide to physical activity for youth with visual impairments.* Louisville, KY: American Printing House for the Blind.

Lieberman, L.J., Stuart, M.E., Hand, K., & Robinson, B. (2006). An investigation of the motivational effects of talking pedometers among youth with visual impairments and deaf-blindness. *Journal of Visual Impairment and Blindness, 100* (12), 726-736.

McHugh, B.E., & Lieberman, L.J. (2003). The impact of developmental factors on incidence of stereotypic rocking among children with visual impairments. *Journal of Visual Impairment and Blindness, 97* (8), 453-474.

McKenzie, A.R., & Lewis, S. (2008). The role and training of paraprofessionals who work with students who are visually impaired. *Journal of Visual Impairment & Blindness, 102,* 459-471.

O'Connell, M., Lieberman, L., & Petersen, S. (2006). The use of tactile modeling and physical guidance as instructional strategies in physical activity for children who are blind. *Journal of Visual Impairment & Blindness, 100* (8), 471-477.

Office of Special Education and Rehabilitative Services (OSE/RS), 34 CFR 300 (2006).

The President's Challenge. (2007). Washington, DC: U.S. Department of Health and Human Services.

Robinson, B., & Lieberman, L.J. (2004). Effects of visual impairment, gender, and age on self-determination. *Journal of Visual Impairment and Blindness, 98* (6), 351-366.

Shapiro, D., Moffett, A., Lieberman, L.J., & Dummer, G. (2008). Domain-specific importance ratings and global self-worth in children with visual impairments. *Journal of Visual Impairment and Blindness, 102,* 232-243.

Stuart, M.E., Lieberman, L.J., & Hand, K. (2006). Parent–child beliefs about physical activity: An examination of families of children with visual impairments. *Journal of Visual Impairment and Blindness, 100* (4), 223-234.

Winnick, J., & Short, F. (1999). *The Brockport Physical Fitness Test manual.* Champaign, IL: Human Kinetics.

WRITTEN RESOURCES

Kuusisto, S. (1998). *Planet of the blind: A memoir.* New York: Dial Press.

This acclaimed writer has been legally blind since birth. Readers gain insights into his experiences with blindness through his excellent prose.

Lieberman, L.J., Modell, S., & Jackson, I. (2006). *Going PLACES: A transition guide to physical activity for youths with visual impairments and deafblindness.* Louisville, KY: American Printing House for the Blind.

The purpose of this book is to walk adolescents through the process of choosing sports and recreational activities for their future. It also promotes advocacy and self-determination.

Mastro, J., & Hassing-Bonnette, T. (2006). Our noisy national pastime revisited. *Palaestra, 22,* 32-36.

This article is about the sport of beep baseball.

Runyan, M., & Jenkins, S. (2002). *No finish line: My life as I see it.* New York: Berkley Trade.

Marla Runyan is a world-class runner who competed in the Paralympics and the Olympics in track and field and the marathon. This is an autobiography of her life so far.

Steber, R. (2005). *No end in sight.* Prineville, OR: Two Star.

This book is about Rachael Scdoris, a young woman with a visual impairment who competed in several Iditarod races.

Weihenmayer, E. (2002). *Touch the top of the world.* New York: Penguin Group.

This book is the story of a climber named Erik Weihenmayer, who has climbed the highest peak on each continent and happens to be blind.

AUDIOVISUAL RESOURCES

Access sports model [VHS]. (1996). Western Michigan University.

This 15-minute videotape describes modifications and adaptations to boundaries, equipment, and rules to increase success in sport and physical activity for people who are visually impaired or blind.

Portraits of possibility [VHS]. (1996). Insight Media, 2162 Broadway, P.O. Box 621, New York, NY 10024-0621; fax 212-799-5309.

This 20-minute videotape explores issues raised by participation in sport for people who are blind. Training methods are included.

Teaching children with visual impairments in physical education [VHS]. (2008). www.campabilities.org.

A video that describes teaching techniques that will assist teachers in integrating children with visual impairments or deafblindness into physical education. See www.campabilities.org to download this video.

ELECTRONIC RESOURCES

American Foundation for the Blind (AFB). 11 Penn Plaza, New York, NY 10001; phone: 800-232-5463; Web site: www.afb.org.

Provides information about advocacy, resources, programs, and publications by AFB, a major organization serving people who are blind.

Camp Abilities. Lauren Lieberman, director, SUNY Brockport, Department of Physical Education, Brockport, NY 14420; phone: 585-395-5361; e-mail: llieberm@brockport.edu; Web site: www.campabilities.org.

A developmental sport camp for children who are visually impaired, blind, or deafblind.

International Blind Sport and Recreation Association (IBSA). Enrique Sanz, IBSA president, c/o Quevedo, 1-1 28014, Madrid, Spain; phone: 3491-589-45-33/34/36; fax: 3491-589-45-37; e-mail: ibsa@ibsa.es; Web site: www.ibsa.es.

The international counterpart of USABA.

National Beep Baseball Association (NBBA), 9623 Spencer Hwy., La Porte, TX 77571; phone: 713-476-1592; Web site: www.nbba.org.

Offers information about NBBA competitions and how to play beep baseball.

chapter 13

Hard of Hearing, Deaf, or Deafblind

Lauren J. Lieberman

Mrs. Goodwin was an elementary physical education teacher who loved her job. At the beginning of her fourth year, her class of second-graders included a girl named Rachel. Rachel was Deaf and used sign language to communicate. She had a full-time educational interpreter named Ms. Colgan. Mrs. Goodwin had had several students who were Deaf and knew some strategies but had to learn more. She wanted to make sure she did the right thing, so she referred to some Web sites and talked to a teacher of the Deaf. She learned about the instructional modifications she could make to ensure that Rachel accessed everything she was teaching. Mrs. Goodwin made sure she had picture descriptions and clear explanations for her fitness warm-up at all the stations. She flashed the lights on and off once to signal when she wanted the students to stop and look at her. She made sure the class was in a semicircle during instruction and used lots of demonstrations with checks for understanding along the way.

Mrs. Goodwin felt Rachel was learning everything she was teaching, yet she noticed that Rachel hung back to watch the other children before moving. Ms. Colgan and Mrs. Goodwin decided that learning a few signs in Rachel's language would solve some of these problems and also help her feel part of the class. Mrs. Goodwin knew that she needed to learn the signs not only to communicate to Rachel (expressive language) but also to understand what Rachel was communicating back to her (receptive language). To achieve this, Mrs. Goodwin took a few minutes out of each day and learned the signs for that day's lesson. When she was teaching kicking, she learned signs such as kick, hard, soft, far, short, stop, start, good job, more, and try again from Rachel and from her interpreter. Each class she learned a few signs, and she and Rachel taught the other students the signs as well. Some of the kids were starting to pick up other signs that Ms. Colgan shared with them throughout the day, and before long, Rachel could communicate with a few of her peers. Mrs. Goodwin was becoming skilled at the physical education signs, and she noticed Rachel was trying harder than ever! She was one of the most skilled students in the class, and the next time Mrs. Goodwin said "Go," Rachel was off and running at the same time as her peers.

Teaching children who are Deaf, hard of hearing, or deafblind can be difficult if the instructor does not plan appropriately and become proactive about instruction. This chapter discusses the definition of hearing loss, types of hearing loss, general characteristics of Deaf students and students who are hard of hearing, considerations for teaching, cochlear implants and physical education, inclusion strategies (including how to use interpreters), and sport opportunities for the Deaf community. Also covered is information on teaching children who are deafblind, including types of deafblindness, general characteristics of children who are deafblind, and adaptations for teaching students who are deafblind.

DEFINITIONS OF HEARING LOSS

According to the Hearing Loss Association (HLA) (2006), "Hearing loss is the number one disability in the United States. One in every 10 Americans and 3 school age children per 100 have a significant hearing loss," and "the proportion of people who are Deaf is small (less than 1%) when compared to the number of individuals who are hard of hearing." *Hard of hearing* refers to people who have difficulty understanding speech through their ears either with or without amplification. "Even though most people with hearing loss are not culturally Deaf, the majority of hearing loss services and accommodations often go to this group" (Reich, 2007b). According to the HLA (2006), the umbrella term for all people who have hearing loss is *people with hearing loss. People* is the optimum word. For example, do not say, "*The* hearing impaired, *the* deaf, or *the* hard of hearing." In general, it is important to use person-first terminology and not categorize people by their disability (Reich & Lavay, 2009, p. 10).

However, Gallaudet University (2007) suggests using the words *Deaf* and *hard of hearing* to describe all people with hearing loss. Unlike members of most populations with disabilities, most who are deaf do not want person-first terminology used to describe them; instead, they prefer to be called a *Deaf person* rather than a *person who is deaf*. The use of the uppercase D in the word *Deaf* is a succinct proclamation by the Deaf that they share more than a medical condition; they share a culture and a language—sign language. One of the reasons Deaf people do not like the term *hearing impaired* is that they think nothing is wrong with them and nothing needs to be fixed; thus, nothing is impaired.

Understanding the perspective of the Deaf culture makes effective teaching of Deaf students in physical education more likely. Awareness of this perspective might begin with the knowledge that many Deaf people do not consider themselves disabled but rather members of a cultural and linguistic minority.

Deaf refers to a severe or profound hearing loss in which hearing is insufficient for comprehension of auditory information, with or without the use of a hearing aid. The Individuals with Disabilities Education Act (IDEA) defines *deaf* as having a hearing loss so severe that the person is unable to process language through hearing, with or without the use of an amplification device. The loss must be severe enough to adversely affect the student's educational performance (IDEA, 2004).

Hard of hearing refers to a hearing loss that makes understanding speech through the ear alone difficult but not impossible. Amplification with a hearing aid or remedial help in communication skills often benefits people who are hard of hearing. IDEA defines hard of hearing as having a hearing loss that might be permanent or fluctuating and that adversely affects the student's educational achievement or performance (IDEA, 2004).

Most people with hearing losses are hard of hearing, not totally deaf. It is also important to note that two students might have the same degree of hearing loss but use their residual hearing differently because of age differences when the hearing loss occurred, the age when they received their first amplification device, or the amplification device itself. Motivation, intelligence, presence of disabilities, environmental stimulation, and response to a training program might also affect the degree to which residual hearing is used.

Degree of hearing loss and residual hearing are described in terms of decibel (dB) levels. The ability to detect sounds in the 0 to 15 dB range is considered normal for children. Ordinary conversation occurs in the 40 to 50 dB range, whereas noises in the 120 to 140 dB range are painfully loud. Degrees of hearing loss are presented in table 13.1.

Children with hearing loss use several communication modes depending on parental influence, educational background, speech therapy, and technological enhancements (such as cochlear

Table 13.1 Degrees of Hearing Loss

Hearing threshold	Degrees of hearing loss	Levels of loudness
27-40 dB	Mild	Faint or quiet speech
41-55 dB	Moderate	Normal speech
56-70 dB	Moderate-severe	Loud speech
71-90 dB	Severe	Extremely loud speech
Greater than 90 dB	Profound	Extremely loud or inaudible

implants). Deaf culture typically uses American Sign Language (ASL) only and frowns on cochlear implants and any other type of sign language. Communication ranges from the following: speaking and hearing; using Signed Exact English (SEE) with speech (also known as *total communication*); using cued speech, a combination of speaking and signs around the mouth to represent specific sounds; using pidgin sign language (PSE), a combination of SEE and ASL; and using strictly ASL. Some children use a combination of these methods depending on audience, experience, and comfort level.

TYPES AND CAUSES OF HEARING LOSS

The three major types of hearing loss are conductive, sensorineural, and mixed. With a **conductive loss**, sound is not transmitted well to the inner ear (analogous to a radio with the volume on low). There is no distortion, but words are faint. Most children with conductive loss have intelligible speech. Because a conductive loss is a mechanical problem in which nerves remain undamaged, it can often be corrected surgically or medically. Typically, hearing aids effectively increase volume. A frequently observed condition is serous otitis media, or middle ear effusion, which often is treated by placing a plastic tube through the eardrum for several months to allow fluid to drain from sound-conducting inner ear bones.

According to the American Speech-Language-Hearing Association (ASHA), a **sensorineural hearing loss** occurs when there is damage to the inner ear (cochlea) or to the nerve pathways from the inner ear (retrocochlear) to the brain. Sensorineural loss cannot be medically or surgically corrected. It is a permanent loss. Sensorineural hearing loss not only involves a reduction in sound level, or the ability to hear faint sounds, but it also affects speech understanding, or the ability to hear clearly.

In comparison to a conductive loss, sensorineural loss can be more severe and likely to be permanent. Children with a sensorineural loss (analogous to a radio that is not well tuned) often have more difficulties with speech than those with a conductive loss do. Sensorineural losses affect fidelity as well as loudness, so there is distortion of sounds. The words might be loud, but they can be distorted and garbled. Though raising one's voice or using a hearing aid might help the voice be heard, the words still might not be understood. Also, note that only 20 to 30 percent of speech is visible on the lips even by the best lip readers.

Students with a severe to profound sensorineural loss will likely use sign language, are less likely to use speech, and might have balance difficulties as a consequence of damage to the semicircular canal. A **mixed loss** is a combination of conductive and sensorineural losses.

Among Deaf students, approximately two-thirds have congenital deafness (present at birth) and one-third have acquired deafness (developed some time after birth). Medical advances have enabled more severely premature babies and children with meningitis and encephalitis to survive. These survivors might have multiple disabilities, including hearing loss. Injuries, autoimmune conditions, genetic conditions, allergies to drugs, repeated exposure to loud sounds, infections such as herpes viruses, and toxoplasmosis can all cause hearing loss, just to name a few.

CHARACTERISTICS OF STUDENTS WITH HEARING LOSS

People who are classified as hard of hearing typically can hear speech from up close but still need accommodations (see the sidebar for communication suggestions) to hear as far away as necessary in physical education conducted in outdoor playing areas or noisy gymnasiums. Their hearing losses from slight to moderate might not present major obstacles to speech. Also, most people who are postlingual profoundly Deaf or prelingual severely or profoundly Deaf might have unique characteristics caused by the need to communicate through a means other than spoken language. These characteristics are the focus of the following section.

Language and Cultural Characteristics

American Sign Language (ASL) is the preferred means of communication within the Deaf culture in the United States. This shared language is the basis of the shared identity in Deaf culture. Just like English, ASL is a language used to communicate and has its own grammar and structure to convey subtle nuances of abstractions in addition to describing concrete objects. Most hearing people see only the signs that name objects and directions (figure 13.1) and are unaware of the concepts of ASL. Currently, many prelingually Deaf children do not develop intelligible speech despite speech training and cochlear implants, especially if they do not receive implants until several years after loss is diagnosed. So, communication between hearing and Deaf people remains a major problem until more hearing people learn ASL. Courtesies to aid communication between hearing and Deaf people are presented in the sidebar.

Deaf students and students who are hard of hearing in the hearing community have fewer opportunities for *incidental learning* than hearing students do because they cannot overhear conversations. Rarely do hearing parents, teachers, and friends sign or ensure understanding when not addressing the child with hearing loss. Thus, there is little opportunity to oversee conversations, and continuity with life events is often missing. This is where the use of sign language becomes important in the socialization and language development of children with hearing loss.

Behavioral and Affective Characteristics

Sometimes students with hearing loss are regarded as slow learners or having behavior problems when their inappropriate behavior is actually a result of an undetected mild hearing loss. The incidence of perceived impulsivity seems to be greater among students with hearing loss than among hearing

When Communicating With a Deaf Person, Remember . . .

- Maintain eye contact throughout the conversation.
- Use paper and pencil to augment conversation.
- Signal that you understand only when you really do (do not pretend to understand).
- Use polite ways to gain a Deaf person's attention.
- Use instant messaging, e-mail, teletypewriter (TTY), or video relay to communicate.
- Discourage interruptions to the conversation.
- Correct a Deaf person's English only if asked.

Graybill & Cokley, 1993.

students. Perhaps this is because these students learn visually and want to look around to check their surroundings more frequently. Some behavioral problems may be a direct result of frustrations on the part of the child with hearing loss that are caused by a lack of understanding and communication.

Motor Characteristics

If the semicircular canals of the inner ear are damaged as a part of the hearing loss, as in sensorineural deafness, balance problems are likely. These balance problems—which occur as a result of vestibular damage, not deafness—can in turn cause developmental delays and motor ability delays. Research results that show poor motor performance for Deaf students as a group could reflect the poor performance of those students with vestibular damage along with the average performance of the other Deaf students. Given equal opportunity to learn movements and participate in physical activity, Deaf children should equal their same-age peers in motor skills (Lieberman, Volding, & Winnick, 2004). If these children are not afforded equal opportunity, they might lag behind in motor skills.

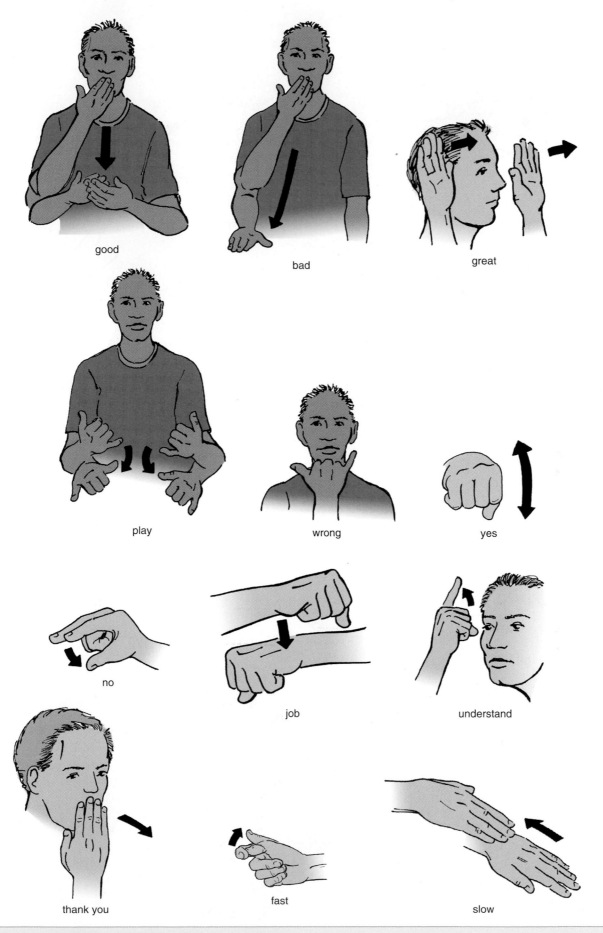

good

bad

great

play

wrong

yes

no

job

understand

thank you

fast

slow

FIGURE 13.1　Signs for physical education. (*continued*)

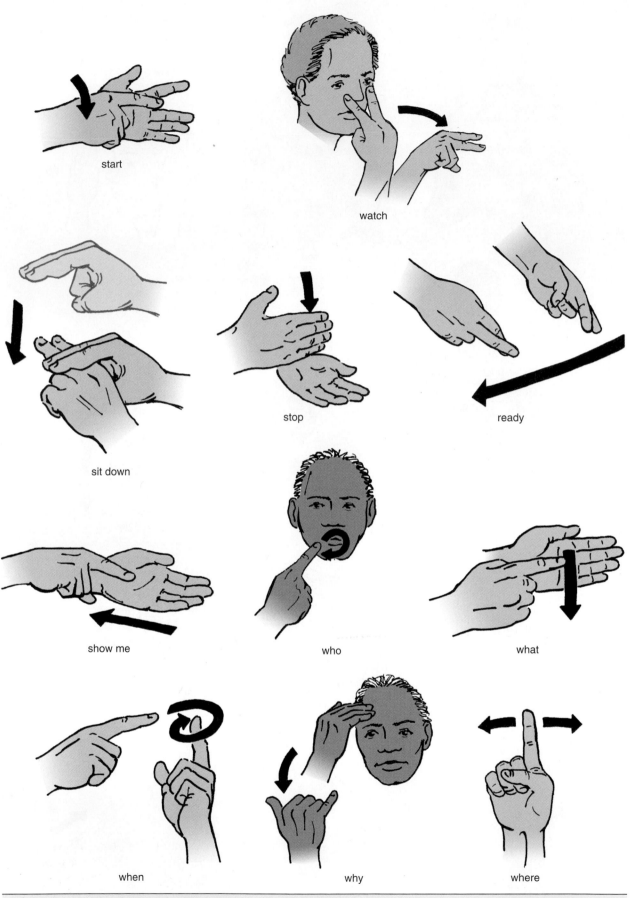

start

watch

sit down

stop

ready

show me

who

what

when

why

where

FIGURE 13.1 *(continued)*

When comparing the results of fitness testing of young people with hearing losses against standardized norms, the outcome becomes drastically different, with Deaf children showing acceptable fitness levels (Ellis, 2001; Ellis et al., 2005; Winnick & Short, 1986). The only reason some fitness scores were low was due to higher levels of body mass index (BMI) among some Deaf children (Dair, Ellis, & Lieberman, 2006). Ellis (2001) reported that because hearing loss is a sensory rather than physical disability, there is no reason for Deaf students to demonstrate lower fitness levels than their hearing peers. Thus, Ellis set out to determine what factors influenced the physical fitness of Deaf children. Both studies (Dair, et al., 2006; Ellis, 2001) found that two primary factors influenced the physical fitness of Deaf children: physical activity participation (just as with hearing children) and parental influence. It was also discovered that Deaf children with Deaf parents had greater encouragement and activity participation than Deaf children with hearing parents (Ellis, 2001; Stewart, 1991).

GENERAL CONSIDERATIONS FOR TEACHING PHYSICAL EDUCATION TO STUDENTS WITH HEARING LOSS

Although movement is an area that does not heavily depend on auditory cues, receiving feedback about movement can be problematic. Usually, visual cues can be substituted for the auditory cues that are distorted or absent. According to Graziadei (1998), teaching conceptual aspects of physical education to Deaf students in a hearing class with a teacher who is not fluent in sign language can be problematic. The concepts, meaning, and purpose of movements and skills may be hard to express to the child with limited communication. It is also important for the teacher to use plenty of demonstrations for students who are hard of hearing. It is recommended that students with hearing loss demonstrate learned skills in order to increase involvement and understanding.

Recall the scenario at the beginning of this section. Rachel had a physical education teacher and friends who had basic means of communication with her. But she still faced some complex problems. It is unlikely that subtle sport strategy and rule concepts could be completely conveyed to her. Interpreters seldom have the sport-specific

ASL vocabulary with which to explain subtle movement or sport concepts.

Deaf students who are included in regular schools often experience isolation, social deprivation, and ridicule from teachers and peers because they lack a common language with their hearing classmates (Graziadei, 1998; Nowell & Innes, 1997). If a Deaf student is placed in an inclusive classroom, a peer-tutor program should be available to alleviate these problems. Peer tutors have been shown to improve physical activity in inclusive physical education classes (Lieberman et al., 2000). As tutors learn more signs, new opportunities for appropriate socialization among peers emerge. Additional information on peer tutor programs can be found in Lieberman and Houston-Wilson (2009).

TEACHING CONSIDERATIONS FOR STUDENTS WITH COCHLEAR IMPLANTS

Cochlear implantation is a surgical procedure that implants a device into the inner ear. The implant consists of an external speech processor that communicates with the internal implant. The internal device electrically stimulates the auditory nerve and bypasses the damaged cochlea of the inner ear. The goal of the implant is to improve recognition of speech and acoustic information over the benefit of a hearing aid (see figure 13.2). "Good verbal development can result when children receive cochlear implantation early in life (Schlumberger, Narbona, & Manrique, 2004). Early cochlear implantation has also been shown to improve motor abilities (Schlumberger et al., 2004; Wright et al., 2002)" (Reich and Lavay, 2009, p. 9). Although the National Association of the Deaf (NAD) does not promote cochlear implants, they are being implanted in children with sensorineural loss more and more.

Students with cochlear implants have unique needs when it comes to physical education. The following are teaching considerations for students with cochlear implants according to Hilgenbrinck and colleagues (2004):

■ Avoid sports that might result in serious blows to the head, such as American football, hockey, lacrosse, soccer, wrestling, tumbling, and other contact sports. These activities might be modified to eliminate contact and can be enjoyed with adaptations.

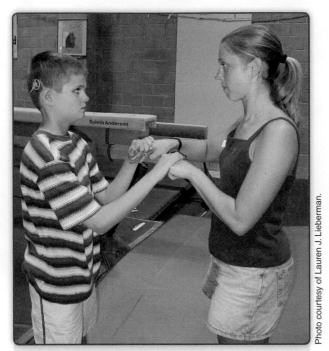

FIGURE 13.2 Tactile sign language with a student with a cochlear implant.

Photo courtesy of Lauren J. Lieberman.

■ Avoid activities that increase the risk of falls or blows to the head, such as in-line skating, skateboarding, using a scooter, and climbing walls. With proper instruction, removal of the implant device, and use of helmets, these activities might be enjoyed.

■ Use caution when participating in winter activities, such as skiing, snowboarding, sledding, and ice-skating. These situations might create uncomfortable sensations around the head and neck.

■ During water activities, remove the device parts and place them in watertight containers. This eliminates any hearing the student had with that ear, so follow the teaching techniques for Deaf students when the student does not have the device connected.

■ Excessive sweating creates moisture inside the device. This might cause motorboating (i.e., unwanted and unnecessary noise). Students should either take the device off before vigorous activity or wear a headband or hat to keep the device dry.

■ At the time of implant, each implant is calibrated by an audiologist to custom fit each recipient. This is called *mapping* the device. The interference of static electricity might demap the device, rendering it unusable. Avoidance of static electricity (balloons, rubber, dry mats, plastic slides) reduces the risk of demapping the device.

■ The implant may break, leaving the child without hearing while it is being fixed.

Several of these situations suggest taking the implant off for safety reasons. This will leave the student with no usable hearing. If the student does not sign or have an interpreter, it will be necessary to teach him signs related to the activities being taught. It is better to teach the student sign language and not self-created signs so the signs can be used in other situations.

INCLUSION STRATEGIES FOR TEACHING STUDENTS WITH HEARING LOSS

When teaching students with hearing loss, physical educators might find it helpful to learn the answers to the following questions. When seeking answers to these questions, the student should be asked, if possible. It is also important to review the student's individualized education program (IEP) and ask questions of the parents or caregivers, educational audiologist, Deaf educator, and educational interpreter (if there is one). In-service education sessions by the educational audiologist for all students with audiology needs may help answer the following questions:

■ What hearing situations are most difficult (Reich, 2007a; Reich & Lavay, 2009)?

■ What is the student's preferred mode of communication? How can the teacher maximize communication with the student?

■ Are there any contraindications or activities that should be avoided? How can these activities be modified?

■ Does the student wear hearing aids? Excessive noise and reverberation caused by substandard room acoustics interfere with speech intelligibility, especially in children with hearing aids or cochlear implants (Reich & Lavay, 2009; United States Access Board, 2007).

Most students with hearing loss have no restrictions on participation in physical education. Children with frequent ear infections might have tubes placed in their ears, so they might need to wear earplugs when swimming. Not all students with hearing loss have balance problems; however, if there are balance issues, it is necessary to work on tasks to improve balance.

Students with hearing loss might benefit from the use of an interpreter. The role of an educational interpreter is to facilitate communication between Deaf or hard-of-hearing students and others, such as teachers, service providers, and peers within the educational environment. In inclusive physical education classes, the following suggestions from Graziadei (1998) and Best, Lieberman, and Arndt (2002) improve success, communication, and socialization:

- Encourage the interpreter to stand next to the teacher.
- Give lesson plans to the interpreter days in advance so both the interpreter and student can review and understand the lesson before it begins. Include a list of any specialized vocabulary.
- Face the student (not the interpreter) when addressing the student.
- Meet with the interpreter before beginning each unit to clarify sport terminology, instructional cues, and idioms that are likely to be used.
- Teach sport-specific signs at the beginning of each new unit.
- Pair each Deaf student with a hearing peer, *not* the interpreter.
- Use the interpreter to communicate with Deaf students. Do not ask students to speak if they do not feel comfortable using their voice; allow them to use their interpreter to communicate.
- Understand that the interpreter's role does not include reprimanding a student, working with other students, or assisting with small jobs.
- The interpreter is not a teacher's assistant and should not be expected to take attendance or distribute and collect equipment.
- Include the Deaf student in information taught during teachable moments.

For students with enough residual hearing to hear background noises, Graziadei (1998) makes these suggestions:

- Minimize background noise—turn off any music (Reich & Lavay, 2009), and expect silence when others are speaking.

- Encourage the student to remove the hearing aid or adjust the volume if there is excessive unavoidable background noise.

The following are general considerations when teaching or coaching students with hearing loss in either integrated or segregated settings:

- Use visual teaching cues when instructing activities that are easily understood.
- Give students with hearing loss copies of lessons modified to their reading levels.
- Use stations with cue cards providing written explanations and illustrations.
- Use clear signals for starting and stopping activities, such as arms up, flags, lights, or signs.
- Use demonstrations liberally.
- Use a scoreboard and a visual timer if playing a game.
- Use highly recognizable and easily visible signals for communication at a distance.
- Make sure there is eye contact before passing a ball.
- When possible, stand near the student with hearing loss and tap the student on the shoulder to gain attention.
- Face the student so that lips and facial expressions are fully visible.
- Avoid chewing gum or covering the mouth; consider shaving a beard or mustache.
- Position the student directly in front of the teacher.
- When outdoors, take care that the student does not face into the sun. Ensure that the teacher is not standing directly in front of the sun or a bright light.
- When indoors, provide adequate lighting (behind the student).
- Assess the distance at which the student can hear your speech. The distance will change in different rooms and situations (Reich, 2007a; Reich & Lavay, 2009). Preference is within 6 feet (2 m) even in a quiet room.
- Check for understanding. Ask all students if they understand the activity before beginning. Help hearing students appreciate that if the students with hearing loss do not follow the rules, it might be because they do not understand them and not because they intend to cheat or seek unfair advantage.

- Promote leadership skills among students with hearing loss, such as being team captains, group leaders, and referees. Also, allowing these students to do demonstrations, set out and clean up equipment, or be squad leaders promotes leadership (Lieberman, Arndt, & Daggett, 2007).
- Ensure that any movie or instructional video is captioned (Reich & Lavay, 2009).
- Give students choices and honor them.
- Have students with hearing loss help hearing students as well as vice versa.
- Provide clear instructions so students with hearing loss do not need to wait and watch others before participating.
- Repeat questions or comments from other students or incorporate students' comments into the answer.

The following recommendations are specifically for Deaf students:

- If teaching students who sign, learn as much sign language as possible. A hearing person is encouraged to practice and learn sign language, which takes as much effort as learning any other language. With this practice, a hearing person can look forward to improved communication with Deaf people.
- Include Deaf students in information taught during teachable moments. These moments often occur in the middle of a game, when an interpreter is on the sidelines and the Deaf student is down the field. Two options for including Deaf students are to review the teachable moments at the end of the lesson with either the entire class or only the Deaf students or to gather all students along with the interpreter together on the field during a teachable moment (Graziadei, 1998).
- Dance and rhythms can be especially important for Deaf students. To help students better feel the vibrations of music, place speakers facedown on a wooden floor, turn up the bass, and dance in bare feet. Butterfield (1988) suggests adding strobe lights that flash in rhythm with the music to provide visual cues. Balloons can be used so students can feel the music through their hands by feeling the vibrations through the rubber of the balloon.
- Allow Deaf students the option of taking written tests with an interpreter to clarify and sign test questions. In this way, physical education knowledge is tested, not the Deaf students' knowledge of English, a second language (Graziadei, 1998). Refer also to the application example for an example of including a Deaf student in physical education class.
- When there is only one Deaf student in the class, teach signs to the entire class so there is clear communication no matter who is in the student's group.
- Schedule Deaf students into the same physical education class and encourage them to work together during class so they can help each other understand the lesson.
- Hold the same expectations for hearing and Deaf students regarding motor performance, fitness, and behavior. Clearly communicate these expectations in writing to Deaf students. Educators who offer excessive assistance when students are not prepared for class teach Deaf students that they can rely on others rather than accept responsibility for their own actions. It is suggested that teachers ask themselves, "Am I really helping? Is the assistance I am giving helping students to cope more effectively with the world that they will be living in after graduation? Or is it better to let them experience the real consequences of their behavior?"
- Encourage students to become involved in Deaf sport. The USA Deaf Sports Federation (USADSF) can be contacted through its Web site, www.usdeafsports.org.

Most physical fitness and motor tests can be administered to Deaf students, provided that visual cues are substituted for auditory cues. Examples of this are dropping the arm in addition to shouting "Go!" to signal the start of an event, or using strobe lights or cable lights as starting signals when doing a shuttle-run test. ASL is not semantically similar to English, so care must be taken when signing instructions. The person giving instructions should be skilled in signing and able to give signed instructions that are semantically identical to spoken instructions (Stewart, Dummer, & Haubenstricker, 1990). Deaf children whose native language is ASL perform better on motor tests when the test is administered in ASL instead of English.

The strategies described previously apply to individualized segregated and integrated settings for students with hearing loss. In addition to a quality physical education program, Deaf students need quality sport opportunities in hearing and Deaf sport.

Inclusion of a Student With Hearing Loss

Setting: Elementary school physical education class

Student: Samuel is a fourth-grader who is hard of hearing and benefits from sign language and speech. Samuel has been going to his elementary school since kindergarten and has many friends. When he was in second grade, Samuel's parents asked for an interpreter to assist him in his academic areas. Ms. Bowie has been his interpreter for two years, and Samuel likes her a lot. Unfortunately, Ms. Bowie takes her break during physical education class. The administrators made this decision because they viewed physical education as visual and felt there was no need for an interpreter. Many of Samuel's friends know some sign language and use it on the bus and in classes. They also understand his speech when they are not in a noisy environment. They only know the signs he teaches them and a few they have picked up from the interpreter in passing.

Issue: Samuel loves physical activity but is reserved in physical education because he does not always understand the directions. He always waits a minute or two at the start of each activity to be sure he knows what the activity involves before starting. Mr. Wineberg has noticed Samuel's reservations and is concerned. Samuel misses at least six minutes of activity during each class as he watches his peers participate in fear of doing the wrong thing. Mr. Wineberg does not know enough sign language to ask him what was wrong, so he asked to make an appointment with the school administrator, the Deaf education consultant, the educational audiologist, the interpreter, and Samuel and his parents.

Application: The following was determined as a result of a meeting with the school administrator, the Deaf education consultant, the educational audiologist, the interpreter, Samuel and his parents, and Mr. Wineberg:

▸ Samuel will continue to participate in physical education with his peers.

▸ The interpreter, Ms. Bowie, will take short breaks at reading time, lunch, and recess instead of during physical education.

▸ Mr. Wineberg will meet with Ms. Bowie before each unit and learn the necessary signs so he can start to communicate with Samuel himself during class. Ms. Bowie will also teach Samuel's peers the signs commonly needed for each unit so they can communicate with him during class.

▸ Mr. Wineberg and Ms. Bowie will create an appropriate list of modifications to activities, such as using start and stop signals, sitting in a semicircle instead of rows, and facing Samuel when instructing students.

▸ Mr. Wineberg will start a peer tutor program with trained peer tutors so that when Samuel is in class and he cannot see the interpreter or if he is playing a game, the peer tutor can relay important information to him using speech and signs. This will also increase his self-confidence, the number of peers he can communicate with, and his depth of conversation.

▸ An additional class with supplemental physical education instruction will be offered should Samuel need more time to grasp a skill or activity, such as dancing or in-line skating.

DEAFBLINDNESS

People who are deafblind do not have effective use of either of the distance senses (vision and hearing). Although the term *deafblind* suggests that these people can neither hear nor see, this is rarely the literal truth. Most people who are deafblind receive both visual and auditory input, but information received through these sensory channels is usually distorted. So, the term *deafblind* is often misleading—it is frequently more accurate to say that these people are both hard of hearing and partially sighted. Only in rare instances, such as with Helen Keller, is a person totally blind and profoundly deaf. Each person with the label *deafblind* has a unique history, and it is important to gather information from the team to understand what the student might be able to see and hear. See the sidebar on page 264 for considerations when teaching students with deafblindness.

Deafblindness has many causes. Understanding the cause might give an indication of the age of onset and whether remaining vision and hearing are likely. Usher syndrome is the major cause of adult-onset deafblindness in the United States, and when students have Usher syndrome, it is important to know the amount of hearing and vision they have. Usher syndrome is a congenital disability characterized by hearing loss present at birth or shortly thereafter and the progressive loss of peripheral vision. Usher syndrome type I is congenital deafness and progressive retinitis pigmentosa, whereas type II is adventitious deafness and progressive retinitis pigmentosa. Today there are three types of Usher syndrome.

The leading cause of child-onset deafblindness is CHARGE syndrome. The diagnosis of CHARGE syndrome is still clinically based on the medical features seen in the child. An evaluation for possible CHARGE syndrome should be made by a medical geneticist who is familiar with the syndrome. The clinical diagnosis is made using a combination of major and minor features. Major features are characteristics that are common in CHARGE syndrome but relatively rare in other conditions and are, for the most part, diagnosable in the newborn period. Minor features are characteristics that are also common in CHARGE but not quite as helpful in distinguishing CHARGE from other syndromes. Major features in children with CHARGE include vision problems, swallowing and nasal issues, hearing difficulties, and growth delays. CHARGE syndrome is a leading cause of deafblindness at birth. Because children with CHARGE experience so many medical complications, it is imperative that they be taught to their functional ability. As they get stronger and experience fewer visits to the hospital, the instructor can increase the length, duration, and intensity of activities offered.

Deafblindness can also be associated with meningitis, prematurity, parental use of drugs, sexually transmitted diseases (STDs), other syndromes, and unknown causes (McInnes, 1999). People who have both vision and hearing loss often have additional disabilities. These disabilities may include cerebral palsy, intellectual disability, autism, or a combination of several disabilities. No matter what disabilities are present, it is most important to focus on the student's functional ability and communication. For example, if Megan has low vision and is hard of hearing, the instructor would need to provide demonstrations at close distances with plenty of explanation, physical assistance, and feedback. For many children, this level of instruction would necessitate a one-on-one teaching situation.

Characteristics of Children With Deafblindness

Though there is often a tendency for caregivers to focus on the medical aspects of deafblindness, physical educators can help parents begin to focus on the quality of life of their child with deafblindness. Physical educators can work to introduce students who are deafblind to activities that they may come to enjoy. They can help these students experience joy in living rather than focus only on survival. Teaching students who are deafblind is a unique experience that requires hands-on work; it is a topic that is difficult to cover comprehensively in the limited time allotted in professional preparation courses. Camp Abilities, a developmental sport camp for young people with visual impairments and deafblindness, is held for one week each summer at State University of New York (SUNY) at Brockport and in other locations throughout the United States. This camp is an excellent opportunity for students to learn how to teach young people who are deafblind. For more information on Camp Abilities, see www.campabilities.org. See the resource list for more great resources for educating students who are deafblind.

A major consideration with students with deafblindness is isolation (Alsop, 2002). Some people who are deafblind move to communities where there are several others who are deafblind. Many attend camps for people who are deafblind. Physical education and sport can provide opportunities to reduce this isolation and introduce the person who is deafblind to activities such as in-line skating, swimming, biking, and gymnastics to increase socialization. Deafblindness presents limited opportunities for *incidental learning*. This means that the student needs to be specifically taught everything. It is becoming more common to use an intervenor, a person who works one on one with the student, signing exactly what is happening in the environment (Morgan, 2001). For example, the intervenor signs when a child is on the swings over there, when a certain classmate recently entered the room, or who is saying what in a discussion. The range of communication methods is similar to the range for children who only have hearing loss. The exception with a child who is deafblind is that signing may need to be done in the child's limited field of vision. This may be close up to the child's face, far away from the child, or in a limited space. If there is no vision, signing may be done tactually in the child's hand. See figure 13.2 earlier in the chapter for an example of tactile sign language.

Communication During Physical Activity

Communication during physical activity with a child who is deafblind can be difficult unless it is planned and discussed. Research by Arndt, Lieberman, and Pucci (2004) helped create steps for setting up clear, planned communication during activity. Follow these steps for communication during physical activity with children who are deafblind:

1. Allow the child to explore the equipment and environment to gain a better understanding of the activity. This may include a bicycle, canoe, volleyball court and ball, or pool. Exploration time will help the child understand the environment and equipment before beginning to learn skills or an activity. The tactile exploration needs to be accompanied by clear terminology of what is being felt. For instance, a bike would open up the concepts of wheels, chain, handlebars, seat, and frame.

2. It is important to listen to the expert, including the child, paraeducator, and intervenor or interpreter. When children have a question or concern, or if they are apprehensive about a new activity, their feelings and communication must be addressed. For example, if a child is swimming in the shallow end of the pool with a life vest and he points to the deep end, it is likely that he has experienced swimming and is skilled enough to

swim in the deep end. Ask questions and explore what the child's communication is conveying.

3. Make sure that new continuous activities are made discrete until the child feels comfortable. Continuous skills are skills such as biking, running, rock climbing, swimming, and in-line skating. They are activities that do not have a clear beginning or ending. Discrete activities include those that have a definite beginning and ending. Examples include the shot put, bowling roll, or free throw in basketball. When children who are deafblind engage in a continuous activity for the first time, it may be scary and they may not know when they can stop, when they will have a chance to communicate what they need, or when they will get feedback. Making a continuous activity discrete will allow the child to choose to continue, ask a question, or receive important feedback. For example, if a child is swimming in the deep end and she is afraid, she can swim for five strokes and then stop and get feedback, rest, or ask a question. Planning ahead of time when communication will happen will minimize fears and allow the child to get more feedback as well as increase opportunities for communication.

4. Make sure the child has the opportunity to receive and express communication with others. This will take careful planning, discussion, and often positioning before the activity, but it is vital to success. For example, if the physical education teacher plans for the child to pull himself prone on a scooter and he uses tactile signing, the teacher, intervenor (interpreter), and child will need to plan time for instruction, activity, and feedback before the child starts moving.

Adaptations for Teaching

Many students who are deafblind will need modifications to successfully participate in regular activities. The teaching tips for children with visual impairments and for Deaf children also apply for students who are deafblind. Refer to the sidebar on page 264 for additional considerations when teaching students with deafblindness. Keep in mind that a multisensory approach is preferred when teaching these students. Modifications might include changing the rules, equipment, instruction, or environment, as described in chapter 2.

Students with deafblindness uncomplicated by additional disabilities can participate in most sports at both a competitive and recreational level. Weightlifting, dance, in-line skating, swimming, skiing, bowling, hiking, goalball, track and field, cycling,

When Teaching Students With Deafblindness, Remember . . .

- Offer activities that promote movement, such as swimming, swinging, biking, walking, and climbing (Lieberman & MacVicar, 2003).
- Use multiple teaching modes, such as explanation, demonstration, tactile modeling, and physical assistance.
- Encourage choice making, such as choice of activity and equipment.
- Set up the environment to accommodate the students' strengths. For example, if the student will be batting, offer bats and balls in a variety of sizes, colors, and textures as well as several ways to deliver the ball, such as on a string, on a tee, or from a pitch. This way the student can choose the size, weight, and color of the bat and ball and the preferred trajectory of the ball.
- Be flexible, patient, and creative.
- Facilitate socialization because students who are deafblind often experience isolation and loneliness (Lieberman & MacVicar, 2003). This can be done by implementing a peer tutor program, teaching the student's mode of communication to classmates, or encouraging the student who is deafblind to become involved in after-school programs and community activities.
- Provide all incidental information.
- Link movement to language. Teach the word for each skill learned and explain the purpose of each sport and activity.
- Learn the student's form of communication, including gestures and body language.
- Help students find activities in their homes to engage in with and without siblings and peers (Lieberman & Pecorella, 2006).

and canoeing are some of the possibilities. As with students who are visually impaired, it is important to teach a combination of open and closed skills. Deafblind athletes wishing to compete might choose to compete in sports for people who are blind (e.g., via USABA) or Deaf (e.g., via USADSF).

An experience with a student named Eddie illustrates the importance of not placing ceilings on expectations for students who are deafblind. Eddie was a 15-year-old student with deafblindness who asked to learn to ride a unicycle. Using the same task analysis his physical education teacher had used to learn to ride, Eddie learned to ride the unicycle independently. Teaching students who are deafblind challenges physical educators to adapt appropriately to enable these students to learn. See a video of the process at www.youtube.com/watch?v=lLYp4b_p_wg.

SPORT OPPORTUNITIES

The greatest sport opportunities for most Deaf students usually come from after-school and community sport programs. It is important for physical educators and coaches to encourage participation with hearing peers. Another opportunity for involvement in sport for Deaf students is Deaf sport through the USADSF (www.usdeafsports.org).

David Stewart's (1991) view of segregated Deaf sport follows:

There is something about being "Deaf" that is quietly comforting to those who have this identity . . . Deaf sport can be thought of as a vehicle for understanding the dynamics of being deaf. It facilitates a social identification among Deaf people that is not easily obtained in other sociocultural contexts. . . . It relies on a Deaf perspective to define its social patterns of behaviors, and it presents an orientation to hearing loss that is distinctly different from that endorsed by hearing institutions. Essentially, Deaf sport emphasizes the honor of being Deaf, whereas society tends to focus on the adversity of hearing loss. (p. 1)

Physical educators have the important role of introducing Deaf students to both hearing and Deaf sport. For many Deaf students attending public schools, the majority of their exposure to Deaf culture is through Deaf sport. Many Deaf athletes choose to compete against other Deaf athletes under the auspices of the USADSF. The organization was established as the American Athletic Association for the Deaf (AAAD) in Ohio in 1945. People with moderate or severe hearing loss (55 dB or greater in the better ear) are eligible for USADSF competition. No hearing aids or cochlear implants are permitted during USADSF competition.

The USADSF includes the following sports for men and women:

Badminton

Baseball

Basketball

Bowling

Curling

Cycling

Golf

Hockey

Martial arts

Orienteering

Shooting

Skiing and snowboarding

Soccer

Swimming

Table tennis

Tennis

Team handball

Track and field

Triathlon volleyball

Water polo

Wrestling

The worldwide counterpart of USADSF is the Comité International des Sport des Sourds (CISS), which translates to the International Committee of Sports for the Deaf (ICSD). Currently, CISS is not a member of the International Paralympic Committee (IPC). Instead of participating in the Paralympic Games, Deaf sport holds its own summer and winter Deaflympics every four years. Winter events include Alpine and Nordic skiing, speed skating, and ice hockey.

The rules followed by the USADSF and CISS are nearly identical to those used in national and international competitions for hearing athletes.

To equalize competition, athletes are not allowed to wear hearing aids. A few changes have been made to use visual rather than auditory cues. For example, in team sports a whistle is blown and a flag is waved to stop play. Strobe lights are used at the starting blocks for swimming events. In track, lighting systems placed 50 meters in front of the starting blocks and to the side of the track are used to signal the start of a race.

Involving young people in Deaf sport is an important objective of USADSF. The Deaf Youth Sports Festival, held in Louisville, Kentucky, is designed for the participation of 6- to 18-year-old Deaf students (Paciorek & Jones, 2006). This event is particularly important in fostering pride in Deaf sport and increasing involvement among Deaf youths who will form the future of Deaf sport. Refer to the electronic resources of this chapter to learn more about student involvement in Deaf sport and to share this information with Deaf students.

The sport skills of Deaf athletes span the range found in the hearing population, from unskilled to highly skilled. Deaf athletes are capable of competing as equals with hearing athletes, and some do so with significant success. As far back as 1883, Deaf athletes were competing in professional sport in the United States. In that year, Ed Dundon became the first recorded Deaf professional baseball player and is reported to be the reason for the development of umpire hand signals. Curtis Pride is Deaf and competed in Major League Baseball, and Jeff Pollock from Salt Lake City is on the U.S. snowboarding team and won medals in the 2005 Deaflympics in that event. Deaf athletes have also excelled in sports such as swimming, wrestling, bowling, and American football. In fact, the huddle is said to have been first used by the Gallaudet University football team to prevent competing Deaf teams from eavesdropping on their plays.

SUMMARY

This chapter reviews types of deafness, characteristics, strategies for teaching, issues related to cochlear implants, deafblindness, and Deaf sport. Children with sensory impairments are born with the same potential as their hearing and sighted peers. Early intervention and exposure to a variety of sports and physical activities increases fitness and skill level and helps maintain a high quality of life. Physical educators are key in instilling confidence in movement in Deaf, hard-of-hearing, and deafblind students.

REFERENCES

Alsop, L. (2002). *Understanding deafblindness: Issues, perspectives and strategies.* North Logan, UT: Home Orientation Program Essentials.

Arndt, K.L., Lieberman, L.J. & Pucci, G. (2004). Communication during physical activity for youth who are deafblind. *Teaching Exceptional Children Plus, 1* (2), Article 1.

Best, C., Lieberman, L.J., & Arndt, K. (2002). The use of interpreters in physical education. *Journal of Physical Education, Recreation and Dance, 73* (8), 45-50.

Butterfield, S.A. (1988). Deaf children in physical education. *Palaestra, 6* (4), 28-30, 52.

Dair, J., Ellis, M.K., & Lieberman, L.J. (2006). Prevalence of overweight among deaf children. *American Annals of the Deaf, 151* (3), 318-326.

Ellis, K.M. (2001). Influences of parents and school on sports participation and fitness levels of deaf children. *Palaestra, 17* (1), 44-49.

Ellis, K., Lieberman, L.J., Fittipauldi-Wert, J., & Dummer, G. (2005). Passing rates of deaf children on health-related fitness: How do they measure up? *Palaestra, 21* (3), 36-43.

Gallaudet University. (2007). Overall style requirements for proposal and final document. Writing style. Retrieved July 31, 2007, from http://aaweb.gallaudet.edu/Documents/Academic/GSPP/Dissertation_and_Masters_Thesis_Handbook_11_2007_OVERALLSTYLE.pdf.

Graybill, P., & Cokely, D. (1993). *Introduction to the Deaf community.* Burtonsville, MD: Sign Media.

Graziadei, A. (1998). *Learning outcomes of deaf and hard of hearing students in mainstreamed physical education classes.* Unpublished doctoral dissertation, University of Maryland, College Park.

Hearing Loss Association (HLA). (2006). Advocacy. Retrieved October 8, 2006, from www.hearingloss.org/advocacy/accessibility.asp.

Hilgenbrinck, L., Pyfer, J., & Castle, N. (2004). Students with cochlear implants: Teaching considerations for physical educators. *Journal of Physical Education, Recreation and Dance, 75* (4), 28-33.

Individuals with Disabilities Education Act Amendments of 2004 (IDEA) (PL 108-446), 20 U.S.C. 1400 (2004).

Lieberman, L.J., Arndt, K.L., & Daggett, S. (2007). Promoting leadership in physical education and recreation. *Journal of Physical Education, Recreation, and Dance, 78,* 46-50.

Lieberman, L.J., Dunn, J.M., van der Mars, H., & McCubbin, J.A. (2000). Peer tutors' effects on activity levels of deaf students in inclusive elementary physical education. *Adapted Physical Activity Quarterly, 17* (1), 20-39.

Lieberman, L.J., & Houston-Wilson, C. (2009). *Strategies for inclusion: A handbook for physical educators* (2nd ed.). Champaign, IL: Human Kinetics.

Lieberman, L.J., & MacVicar, J. (2003). Play and recreation habits of youth who are deaf-blind. *Journal of Visual Impairment and Blindness, 97* (12), 755-768.

Lieberman, L.J., & Pecorella, M. (2006). Activity at home for children and youth who are deafblind. *Deaf-Blind Perspectives, 14,* 3-7.

Lieberman, L.J., Volding, L., & Winnick, J.P. (2004). A comparison of the motor development of Deaf children of Deaf parents and hearing parents. *American Annals for the Deaf,* July.

McInnes, J.M. (1999). *A guide to planning and support for individuals who are deafblind.* Toronto: University of Toronto Press.

Moores, D.F. (1996). *Educating the Deaf: Psychology, principles, and practices* (4th ed.). Boston: Houghton Mifflin.

Morgan, S. (2001). "What is my role?" A comparison of the responsibilities of interpreters, intervenors, and support service providers. *Deaf-Blind Perspectives, 9* (1), 1-3.

Nowell, R., & Innes, J. (1997). *Educating children who are deaf or hard of hearing: Inclusion.* Retrieved from ERIC database. (E557)

Paciorek, M.J., & Jones, J.A. (2006). *Disability sport and recreation resources* (4th ed.). Carmel, IN: Cooper.

Reich, L. (2007a). *Accommodating the unique needs of individuals who are specifically hard of hearing during physical education, sport, and exercise training.* Thesis project dissertation, California State University, Long Beach.

Reich, L. (2007b). Hard of hearing or deaf vs. culturally deaf person: Who receives the services? Retrieved October, 2009, from www.lorireich.com/hoh/index_files/Page633.htm.

Reich, L., & Lavay, B., (2009). Physical education and sport adaptations for students who are specifically hard of hearing. *Journal of Physical Education, Recreation, & Dance, 80* (3), 1-60.

Schlumberger, E., Narbona, J., & Manrique, M. (2004). Non-verbal development of children with deafness with and without cochlear implants. *Developmental Medicine & Child Neurology, 45,* 599-606.

Stewart, D.A. (1991). *Deaf sport: The impact of sports within the deaf community.* Washington, DC: Gallaudet University.

Stewart, D., Dummer, G., & Haubenstricker, J. (1990). Review of administration procedures used to assess the motor skills of deaf children and youth. *Adapted Physical Activity Quarterly, 7,* 231-239.

United States Access Board. (2007). Implementing classroom acoustics standards: A progress report. Retrieved July 8, 2007, from www.access-board.gov/acoustic/index.htm.

Winnick, J.P., & Short, F.X. (1986). Physical fitness of adolescents with auditory impairments. *Adapted Physical Activity Quarterly, 3,* 58-66.

Wright, M., Purcell, A., & Reed, V. (2002). Cochlear implants and infants: Expectations and outcomes. *Annals of Otology, Rhinology & Laryngology, III* (pt. 2), 131-137.

WRITTEN RESOURCES

McInnes, J.M. (1999). *A guide to planning and support for individuals who are deaf-blind.* Toronto: University of Toronto Press.

This book takes an international perspective on teaching students who are deafblind. Teaching strategies, modifications, communication techniques, and curriculum ideas are abundant in this resource.

Smith, T. (2002). *Guidelines: Practical tips for working and socializing with deafblind people.* Burtonsville, MD: Sign Media.

This resource offers a step-by-step guide to working and socializing with deafblind people.

ELECTRONIC RESOURCES

American Academy of Audiology: www.audiology.org.

The American Academy of Audiology is the world's largest professional organization of audiologists. More than 10,000 audiologists join together to provide the highest quality of hearing health care service to children and adults.

American Association of the Deaf-Blind (AADB), 814 Thayer Ave., Ste. 302, Silver Springs, MD 20910-4500; TTY: 301-588-6545; relay: 800-735-2258; fax: 301-588-8705; Web site: www.aadb.org.

The Web site of the AADB provides information about annual activities, membership, and current issues.

National Consortium on Deafblindness (NCDB): www.nationaldb.org.

The NCDB is a national technical assistance and dissemination center for young people who are deafblind. Funded by the U.S. Department of Education's Office of Special Education Programs (OSEP), the NCDB provides technical assistance, the information services and dissemination activities of the DB-LINK database, and information related to personnel training.

USA Deaf Sports Federation (USADSF): 911 Tierra Linda Dr., Frankfort, KY 40601-4633; TTY: 801-393-7916; fax: 801-393-2263; Web site: www.usdeafsports.org.

Provides information about USADSF competition, events, calendar, history of the organization, and news.

14

Cerebral Palsy, Traumatic Brain Injury, and Stroke

David L. Porretta

He was once one of the most feared defensemen in the National Hockey League. But following a near-fatal automobile accident, Vladimir Konstantinov acquired a brain injury severe enough that he might never skate independently again. Within a short time he went from a highly skilled athlete to someone who needed to relearn many motor and sport skills he had once taken for granted. No doubt, Vladimir Konstantinov may play hockey again—but it might be in a wheelchair or on an adapted sled and in a game adapted to his needs. Traumatic brain injury (TBI) and other conditions that cause damage to the brain, including cerebral palsy (CP) and stroke, are addressed in this chapter. Physical education teachers and coaches must be aware of problems associated with damage to the brain and the ways in which brain conditions can affect the learning process. With the help of adapted physical educators, allied health professionals, and physicians, people such as Konstantinov can enjoy physical education and sport in settings that are safe, enjoyable, and beneficial to health.

Although CP, stroke, and TBI have their own causes, each of these conditions results in damage to the brain. Thus, people with CP, stroke, and TBI might exhibit common motor, cognitive, and behavioral characteristics. Discussing these conditions together in this chapter highlights their commonalties. People with CP, stroke, or TBI at one time were restricted from physical activity for fear that it would aggravate their conditions. Now they are encouraged to participate in a wide range of physical activities.

CEREBRAL PALSY

Cerebral palsy (CP) refers to a group of permanent disabling symptoms resulting from damage to the motor control areas of the brain. It is a nonprogressive condition that might originate before, during, or shortly after birth, and it manifests itself in a loss or impairment of control over voluntary musculature. The term *cerebral* refers to brain and *palsy* to disordered movement or posture. Depending on the location and the amount of damage to the brain, symptoms vary widely, ranging from severe (total inability to control bodily movements) to mild (only a slight speech impairment). Damage to the brain contributes to abnormal reflex development in most people, resulting in difficulty coordinating and integrating basic movement patterns. It is rare for damage to be isolated in a small portion of the brain. For this reason, the person with CP commonly exhibits many other impairments, possibly including seizures, speech and language disorders, sensory impairments (especially those involving visual–motor control), abnormal sensation and perception, and intellectual disability. People with CP also commonly exhibit secondary medical complications, such as impaired bone growth, joint abnormalities, respiratory conditions, and accelerated cardiovascular disease.

CP can result from a myriad of prenatal, natal, or postnatal causes. Some of the more common causes are rubella, Rh incompatibility, prematurity, birth trauma, anoxia, meningitis, poisoning, brain hemorrhages or tumors, and other forms of brain injury caused by accidents or abuse. Many medical professionals now believe that CP results from causal pathways rather than any single factor. For example, a premature infant is five times more likely than a full-term baby to have CP, but prematurity is not the cause of CP; rather, it is one factor that can lead to CP.

Incidence

According to the most recent figures published by United Cerebral Palsy (2010), there are an estimated 800,000 children and adults in the United States with CP. Of this number, only about 10 percent of the cases are acquired—that is, they occur after birth during the first two years of life. Most acquired cases are a consequence of some form of head trauma. The number of new cases of children with CP has increased 25 percent over the past decade. It is estimated that about 8,000 babies and infants are diagnosed with CP each year. In addition, about 1,200 to 1,500 preschool-aged children are identified each year as having CP. Recent data from eight European countries suggest that their figures are similar to those of the United States (Johnson, 2002).

Classifications

People with CP typically exhibit a variety of observable symptoms, depending on the degree and location of brain damage. Over the years, classification schemes have evolved that categorize CP according to **topographical** (anatomical site), **neuromotor** (medical), and **functional perspectives**, of which the functional classification is the most recent.

Topographical Classification

The topographical classification is based on the body segments affected and is typically used by the medical community. Classes include the following:

- Monoplegia—any one body part involved
- Diplegia—major involvement of both lower limbs and minor involvement of both upper limbs
- Hemiplegia—involvement of one complete side of the body (arm and leg)
- Paraplegia—involvement of both lower limbs only
- Triplegia—any three limbs involved (a rare occurrence)
- Quadriplegia—total-body involvement (all four limbs, head, neck, and trunk)

Neuromotor Classification

The American Academy for Cerebral Palsy and Developmental Medicine (AACPDM) currently uses a neuromotor classification system to describe CP. This classification has undergone revisions over the years. Today, three main types are commonly described (United Cerebral Palsy, 2010). The characteristics described under each type might overlap; they are not as distinct as one might assume. The most common overlapping symptoms include spastic and athetoid movements.

Spasticity

Spasticity results from damage to motor areas of the cerebrum and is characterized by increased muscle tone (hypertonicity), primarily of the flexors and internal rotators, which might lead to permanent contractures and bone deformities. Strong, exaggerated muscle contractions are common, and in some cases muscles continue to contract repetitively. Spasticity is associated with a **hyperactive stretch reflex**. The hyperactive reflex can be elicited, for example, when muscles of the anterior forearm (flexors) are quickly stretched in order to extend the wrist. When this happens, receptors that control tone in the stretched muscles overreact, causing the stretched muscles to contract. This results in inaccurate and jerky movement, with the wrist assuming a flexed position as opposed to an extended or middle position. If muscles of the upper limb are prone to spasticity, the shoulder will be adducted, the arm will be carried toward the midline of the body, and the forearm will be flexed and pronated. The wrist will be hyperflexed, and the hand will be fisted.

Lower-limb involvement results in hip flexion, with the thigh pulling toward the midline, causing the leg to cross during ambulation. Lower-limb involvement causes flexion at the knee joint because of tight hamstring muscles. Increased tone in both the gastrocnemius and soleus muscles, along with a shortened Achilles tendon, contributes to excessive plantar flexion of the foot. A scissoring gait characterized by flexion of the hip, knee, and ankle along with rotation of the leg toward the midline is exhibited (figure 14.1). With this narrow base of support, people with a scissoring gait typically have problems with balance and locomotor activities. Because of increased muscle contraction and limited range of motion, they might have difficulty running, jumping, and throwing. Intellectual disability, seizures, and perceptual disorders are more common in spasticity than in any other type of CP.

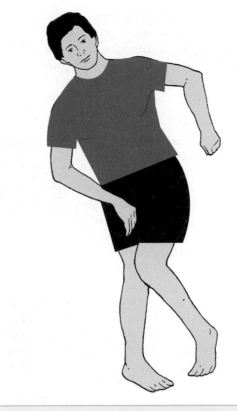

FIGURE 14.1 Person exhibiting spastic cerebral palsy.

Athetosis

Damage to the **basal ganglia** (masses of gray matter composed of neurons deep within the cerebral hemispheres of the brain) results in an overflow of motor impulses to the muscles, a condition known as *athetosis*. In some cases basal ganglia damage can be caused by blood incompatibility (Rh) problems during birth. However, most blood incompatibility problems can now be controlled. Because slow, writhing movements are uncoordinated and involuntary, athetosis is also known as *dyskinetic CP*. Muscle tone tends to fluctuate from hypertonicity to hypotonicity, and the fluctuation typically affects muscles that control the head, neck, limbs, and trunk. Severe difficulty in head control is usually exhibited, with head drawn back and positioned to one side. Facial grimacing, a protruding tongue, and trouble controlling salivation are common. The person has difficulty eating, drinking, and speaking. Because lack of head control affects visual pursuit, people with athetosis might have difficulty tracking thrown balls or responding to quick movements made by others. They will have difficulty performing movements that require accuracy, such as throwing a ball to a target or kicking a moving ball. A lordotic standing posture in which the lumbar spine assumes an abnormal anterior curve is common. In compensation, the arms and shoulders are placed in a forward position. People with athetosis typically exhibit aphasia (impairment or loss of language) and articulation difficulties.

Ataxia

Damage to the **cerebellum**, which normally regulates balance and muscle coordination, results in a condition known as *ataxia*. The cerebellum is located below and behind the cerebral cortex (figure 14.2). Muscles show abnormal degrees of hypotonicity. Ataxia is usually not diagnosed until the child attempts to walk. When trying to walk, the person is extremely unsteady because of balance difficulties and lacks the coordination necessary for proper arm and leg movement. A wide-based gait is typically exhibited. Nystagmus, a constant involuntary movement of the eyeball, is commonly observed, and people who are able to ambulate will frequently fall. People with mild forms of ataxia are often considered clumsy or awkward. They have difficulty with basic motor skills and patterns, especially locomotor activities such as running, jumping, and skipping.

Functional Classification

A **functional classification** scheme is commonly used today in the field of education. According to this classification system, people are placed into one of eight ability classes according to the severity of the disability (table 14.1). Class I denotes severe

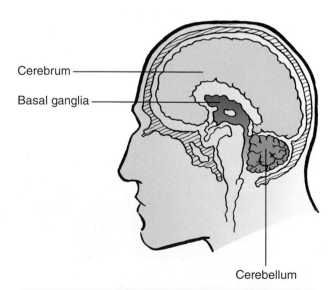

Cerebrum

Basal ganglia

Cerebellum

FIGURE 14.2 Areas of the brain involved in major neuromotor types of cerebral palsy.

impairment, whereas class VIII denotes minimal impairment. This scheme has important implications for physical education and sport because people are categorized according to ability. For example, participants in classes VII and VIII might be good candidates for inclusion in several regular physical education activities. Teachers and coaches can also use this system, as do the BlazeSports National Disability Sports Alliance (BNDSA) and the Cerebral Palsy International Sports and Recreation Association (CPISRA), to assist in equalizing competition among participants. In activities requiring competition between two people, players of the same classification can compete against each other. In team activities, players of the same class can be placed on separate teams so that each team comprises players of similar functional levels. These suggestions for equalizing competition can be followed in either inclusive or noninclusive settings.

General Educational Considerations

Because CP is not a disease, most medical professionals agree that CP is not treated but rather managed. Management is aimed at alleviating symptoms caused by damage to the brain and helping the person achieve maximum potential in growth and development. This consists of managing both motor and other associated disabilities. Managing motor dysfunction usually entails developing voluntary muscle control, emphasizing muscle relaxation, and increasing functional motor skills. In some instances, braces and orthotic devices are used to help prevent permanent contractures or to support affected muscle groups; this is especially true for people with spasticity. Surgery can be performed to lengthen contracted tendons (especially the Achilles tendon) or to reposition an unimpaired muscle to perform the movement of an impaired one. For instance, the Eggers procedure relieves flexion at the knee joint and helps to extend the hip by transferring the insertion of the hamstrings from the pelvis to the femur. In rare instances, brain surgery can be performed to alleviate extreme hypertonicity. Implantation of stem cells into selected areas of the brain is now being studied with the potential for improved brain function. Additional research advances such as new neuroimaging techniques, better understanding of the neurobiology of early central nervous system damage, and mechanisms of neural repair such as brain plasticity (recruiting other areas of the brain to perform functions that have been lost) are now being employed.

Table 14.1 Functional Classification Profiles for Cerebral Palsy Used by BNDSA and CPISRA

Class	Description	Locomotion	Object control
I	Severe spasticity or athetosis with poor functional range of motion and strength in all extremities; poor to nonexistent trunk control	Uses motorized wheelchair or assistance for mobility.	Only thumb opposition and one finger possible; can grasp only beanbag.
II	Severe to moderate spastic or athetoid quadriplegic; poor functional strength in all extremities, and poor trunk control; classified as II lower if one or both lower extremities are functional; otherwise classified as II upper	Propels wheelchair on level surfaces and slight inclines (lower class II with leg only); sometimes might be able to ambulate short distances with assistance.	Can manipulate and throw a ball (II upper).
III	Moderate quadriplegic or triplegic; severe hemiplegia; fair to normal strength in one upper extremity	Can propel wheelchair independently but might walk a short distance with assistance or assistive devices.	Normal grasp of round objects but release is slow; limited extension in follow-through with dominant arm.
IV	Moderate to severe diplegic; good functional strength and minimal control problems in upper extremities and torso	Assistive devices used for distances; wheelchair is usually used for sport.	Normal grasp is seen in all sports; normal follow-through is evident pushing a wheelchair or throwing.
V-A	Moderate to severe diplegic or hemiplegic; moderate to severe involvement in one or both legs; good functional strength; good balance when assistive devices are used	No wheelchair; might or might not use assistive devices.	Minimal control problems in upper limbs; normal opposition and grasp seen in all sports.
V-B	Moderate to severe diplegic; some moderate to minimal limitation in upper limbs particularly when throwing; good functional strength	Does not use assistive devices for track competition.	Hand function is normal; opposition and prehensive grasp and release in dominant hand in all sports.
VI	Moderate to severe quadriplegic (spastic, athetoid, or ataxic); fluctuating muscle tone producing involuntary movements in trunk and both sets of extremities; greater upper-limb involvement when spasticity or athetosis present	Ambulates without aids; function can vary; running gait can show better mechanics than when walking.	Spastic–athetoid grasp and release can be significantly affected when throwing.
VII	Moderate to minimal spastic hemiplegic; good functional ability on nonaffected side	Walks and runs without assistive devices but has marked asymmetrical action; obvious Achilles tendon shortening when standing.	Minimal control problems with grasp and release in dominant hand; minimal limitation seen in dominant throwing arm.
VIII	Minimal hemiplegic, monoplegic, diplegic, or quadriplegic; might have minimal coordination problems; good balance	Runs and jumps freely with little to no limp; gait demonstrates minimal or no asymmetry when walking or running; perhaps slight loss of coordination in one leg or minimal Achilles tendon shortening.	Minimal incoordination of hands.

Adapted, by permission, from National Disability Sports Alliance, 2008. Available: www.ndsaonline.org/class_cp.htm.

Because of central nervous system damage, many people with CP exhibit abnormal reflex development that interferes with the acquisition of voluntary movement. If abnormal reflex patterns are present, young children with CP most likely receive some type of physical therapy designed to inhibit abnormal reflex activity in addition to enhancing flexibility and body alignment. However, recent scientific data show that passive activities and manipulations during the early years might not provide as much assistance in the remediation of abnormal reflex activity as once thought. Treatment emphasis should be directed toward having people perform and refine motor tasks through active self-control. Functional motor skills such as walking, running, and throwing should be developed and attained. Damiano (2004) suggests five aims when working with people with CP: (1) reducing musculoskeletal impairments to improve function and quality of life, (2) enabling children to function optimally given their existing impairments, (3) preventing or limiting development of secondary implications, (4) altering the natural course of the disorder, and (5) promoting wellness and fitness over the life span.

Attention must also be given to the psychological and social development of people with CP. The conditions associated with CP increase the possibility of adjustment problems. Because of the negative reactions that other people might have to their disability, people with CP might not be totally accepted. As a result, guidance from psychologists or professional counselors should be sought for both parents and children when emotional conflicts arise.

The primary concern should be for the total person. From an educational perspective, a team approach in which both medical and educational personnel work together with the parents and, when appropriate, with the student is strongly recommended.

TRAUMATIC BRAIN INJURY

Traumatic brain injury (TBI) refers to an injury to the brain that might produce a diminished or altered state of consciousness and result in impairment of physical, cognitive, social, behavioral, and emotional functioning. Possible physical impairments include lack of coordination, difficulty planning and sequencing movements, muscle spasticity, headaches, speech disorders, paralysis, and seizures as well as a variety of sensory impair-

ments, including vision and hearing problems. Physical impairments often cause varying degrees of orthopedic involvement that require the use of crutches or wheelchairs. Even when people exhibit no loss of coordination, motor function deficits, or sensation, apraxia might be evident.

Cognitive impairments many times result in short- or long-term memory deficits, poor attention and concentration, altered perception, communication disorders in such skills as reading and writing, slowness in planning and sequencing, and poor judgment. Social, emotional, and behavioral impairments might include mood swings, lack of motivation, lowered self-esteem, self-centeredness, inability to self-monitor, difficulty with impulse control, perseveration, depression, sexual dysfunction, excessive laughing or crying, and difficulty relating to others. These impairments vary greatly depending on the extent and location of damage to the brain and the success of the rehabilitation process. Thus, impairments could range from mild to severe. However, with immediate and ongoing therapy these impairments sometimes decrease in severity. Because of the developmental nature of the central nervous system, children with TBI recover motor and verbal skills faster than adults. However, children's head injuries tend to be more diffuse than focal. A diffuse injury might affect the entire range of academic achievement and thus have significant educational implications for the child.

TBI is often referred to as the silent epidemic because impairments continue although no external visible signs are present on or around the face and head area. TBI can result from motor vehicle, sport and recreation accidents, child abuse, assaults and violence, and accidental falls. In addition, TBI can be caused from lack of oxygen (anoxia), cardiac arrest, or near drowning. Motor vehicle accidents, violence, and falls are the leading causes of TBI. For active-duty military personnel in war zones, blasts are the leading cause of TBI (Brain Injury Association of America, 2008). As a subgroup, children are especially at risk for brain injury. Head injuries in children and adolescents are commonly caused by the following:

- Traffic accidents (e.g., pedestrian, passenger, cyclist)
- Falls from buildings, play equipment, or trees
- Injuries from objects (e.g., golf club, ball, firearms)
- Child abuse

- Sport-related injuries (e.g., horseback riding, skateboarding, in-line skating, American football)
- Seizures and other causes of lost consciousness

With a greater number of children and adolescents participating in sport, the number of brain injuries is increasing. These injuries are common in contact sports such as football, soccer, rugby, lacrosse, and ice hockey. However, only a few first-time direct blows to the head result in severe head trauma. The majority of brain injuries in such sports result from repeated blows to the head resulting in various degrees of concussion or what some authorities term *mild traumatic brain injury* (Powell, 2004). TBIs cause more deaths than any other sport injury.

Because TBI is so common, it is now identified as a separate categorical condition in the Individuals with Disabilities Education Act (IDEA). In addition, in 2008, Congress reauthorized the Traumatic Brain Injury Act (PL 110-206), authorizing federal agencies to produce and disseminate data, conduct studies, and establish innovative programs with respect to TBI.

Incidence

TBI is the leading killer and cause of disability in children and young adults under 45 years of age in the United States. It is estimated that 5.3 million people in the United States live with functional loss resulting from brain injuries, and every year about 1.4 million people sustain a new TBI (Brain Injury Association of America, 2008). Of this number, hundreds of thousands die or sustain an injury severe enough to require hospitalization. Of those who survive, approximately 85,000 have a permanent disability. Each year about 500,000 children sustain a TBI. Males are about 1.5 times as likely as females to sustain a TBI, and the two age groups at highest risk are infants to 4-year-olds and 15- to 19-year-olds (Langlois, Rutland-Brown, & Thomas, 2006).

Classification

There are two classifications of head injury: **open head injury** and **closed head injury**. An open head injury might result from an accident, gunshot wound, or blow to the head by an object, leading to a visible injury. A closed head injury might be caused by severe shaking, anoxia, and cranial hemorrhages, among other causes. If the head injury is closed, damage to the brain is usually diffuse, but if the head injury is open (e.g., a bullet wound), damage is usually to a more limited area of the brain. In a closed head injury, the brain is shaken back and forth within the skull, bruising or tearing nerve fibers in the brain that send messages to other parts of the central nervous system and all parts of the body. TBI can range from mild to severe. Severe brain injury is characterized by a prolonged state in which the person is unconscious (comatose) and a number of functional limitations remain following rehabilitation. An injury to the brain can be considered minor when no formal rehabilitation program is prescribed and the person is sent directly home from the hospital. However, minor brain injury should never be treated as unimportant.

The Rancho Los Amigos Scale describes eight levels of cognitive functioning and is typically used in the first few weeks or months following injury. These levels consist of the following:

Level 1—No response: deep sleep or coma

Level 2—Generalized response: inconsistent and nonspecific response to stimuli

Level 3—Localized response: might follow simple commands in an inconsistent and delayed manner; vague awareness of self

Level 4—Confused or agitated response: severely decreased ability to process information; poor discrimination and attention span

Level 5—Confused and inappropriate response: consistent reaction to simple commands; highly distractible; in need of frequent redirection

Level 6—Confused and appropriate response: responses might be incorrect because of memory loss but are appropriate to the situation; retention of tasks relearned; inconsistently oriented

Level 7—automatic and appropriate: oriented and appropriate behavior but lacks insight; poor judgment and problem solving; requires minimal supervision

Level 8—purposeful and appropriate: ability to integrate recent and past events; requires no supervision once new activities are learned

This scale should not be used in the years following the injury as a gauge for improved function.

General Educational Considerations

Many people with TBI need an individualized rehabilitative program. People suffering from severe injury initially need intense rehabilitation in which therapy begins as soon as the patient is medically stable. An interdisciplinary team of medical professionals (e.g., physicians, nurses, speech and occupational therapists) provides such a therapy program, which usually lasts three to four months, depending on the injury. For people of school age, the rehabilitative program takes precedence over educational considerations. According to Wehman et al., (2001), reentry planning needs to occur immediately following hospital admission. Hospital outreach personnel (e.g., social worker) should contact appropriate school personnel. Ongoing communication should include discussing the child's status and prognosis, discussing implications for school services, accessing school records, and providing education to family, school personnel, and peers.

Following the acute rehabilitation program comes the long-term rehabilitation program, which provides a structured environment for those who make slow improvements. As long as progress is being made, school-aged students remain at this level of rehabilitation and typically receive their educational program within the rehabilitative facility.

Some people with severe injuries require extended therapy programs following long-term care. These extended, structured therapy programs might last from 6 to 12 months following injury and usually emphasize cognitive skills, speech therapy, activities of daily living, relearning of social skills, recreation therapy, and, when appropriate, prevocational and vocational training. Individualized educational programming continues in this environment. Only after patients have attained the maximum benefit of the rehabilitation programs will they reenter their local educational environment.

Educators play a key role in the rehabilitation and educational process. Ylvisaker and Feeney (1998) stress that educational reentry programs need to be flexible and creative. Because of the uniqueness of each person, no one reentry program fits every student with TBI; rather, educators should rely on basic principles to guide the implementation of their reentry programs. These principles include the following: Each student presents unique cognitive, behavioral, and psychosocial challenges; assessments need to be functional, collaborative, and contextualized; supports (e.g., teacher's aide) need to be systematically reduced when appropriate; and collaborative decision making (among educators, rehabilitation professionals, parents, student, and possibly others) should be fostered.

Educators need to work closely with the student's family to ensure the best reentry program possible. Walker (1997) recommends that when building effective parent–professional partnerships, teachers should do the following:

■ Remember that collaboration means sharing control with parents in educational planning.

■ Acknowledge the value of parents as the primary decision makers in determining quality-of-life and intervention decisions on behalf of their child.

■ Strive to establish and maintain rapport and trust in relationships with parents in order to negotiate family-centered decisions.

■ Strive for educational programs that include equal proportions of parent and professional goals.

■ Work to resolve disagreements and interpersonal tension with parents. Establishing positive relationships with parents of students with TBI is important. This can be a stressful time for parents, who up to this point in their child's education did not need to interact with special education teachers and therapists.

The development and implementation of transitional plans for high school students with TBI is of particular importance. Educators are encouraged to follow a transitional approach to functional skills. Transitional skills related to physical education include recreation and leisure activities such as bowling, cycling, or swimming, as well as accessing community recreation facilities. Regardless of the transitional outcomes agreed on, educators must plan appropriate school experiences and establish links with community and postschool (e.g., vocational or technical schools) resources. See the application example for more information.

Several instructional strategies are recommended for teachers and coaches. Top-down instruction (Driver, Harmon, & Block, 2003) emphasizing functional activities is one such strategy. First, the instructor identifies functional physical activities that the student enjoys and that can be performed within the community. The instructor then assesses the student to determine what elements of the

APPLICATION EXAMPLE

Transition

Setting: Carlos is a 14-year-old male with TBI. Before his injury, Carlos enjoyed participating in interscholastic athletics. However, he has lost many of the sport skills he learned previous to his injury. Now, Carlos uses a wheelchair.

Task: Teach functional sport, recreation, and leisure skills so that Carlos can successfully maintain a healthy, active lifestyle during his high school years and adulthood.

Application: Skills and activities once deemed important in regular secondary physical education might now need to be reevaluated relative to Carlos' functional needs. To determine the functional sport, recreation, and leisure skills and activities to be learned, the physical education teacher needs to

▶ be part of Carlos' individualized education program (IEP) team;

▶ consult with therapists and other educators;

▶ talk with Carlos' parents about their hopes and expectations for him during high school and after graduation;

▶ consult with school officials to include Carlos to the maximum extent possible should he be interested in continuing participation in interscholastic athletics;

▶ seek Carlos' input about his interests and desires in sport and leisure activities;

▶ identify, contact, and visit community resource centers (e.g., the local YMCA, recreation, and adult fitness centers) that can provide services to Carlos after graduation; and

▶ implement Carlos' physical education program in at least one site (when feasible) to aid him in the transitional process.

activity need to be learned for the student to be successful. Some additional instructional strategies include using frequent reminders regarding tasks to be completed, providing additional time for review, rewriting or reexplaining complex directions in simple steps, using cooperative learning activities so that the student is not required to complete an entire task alone, having the student use a diary or datebook to help organize information, breaking up a task into smaller and distinct sequential parts so that they can be put together meaningfully at the end, and color coding materials for each class or activity.

STROKE

Stroke, or **cerebrovascular accident** (CVA), refers to damage to brain tissue resulting from faulty blood circulation. CVA can result in serious damage to areas of the brain that control vital functions. These functions might include motor ability and control, sensation and perception, communication, emotions, and consciousness, among others. In certain cases, CVA results in death. People who survive CVA have varying degrees of disability, ranging from minimal loss of function to total dependency. Because of the nature of the cerebral arterial system, CVA commonly causes partial or total paralysis on either the left or right side of the body. This might be one limb (monoplegia) or body segment or one entire side (hemiplegia). People with right-sided hemiplegia are likely to have problems with speech and language; they tend to be slow, cautious, and disorganized when approaching new or unfamiliar problems. People with left-sided hemiplegia are likely to have difficulty with spatial–perceptual tasks (e.g., ability to judge distance, size, position, rate of movement, form, and how parts relate to the whole) and tend to overestimate their abilities. They often try to do things they cannot do and that might be unsafe. This trait has significant implications for those performing in physical education, leisure, and sport settings.

According to Ådén (2009), neonatal (birth through the first month of life) CVA is now an increasingly recognized condition. The peak age for CVA is the first year of life, in which one-third of all cases are reported. In such cases there might be no detectable neurological signs at onset. Rather, neurological signs might appear during the first year after CVA as motor skills develop, and those who survive typically have hemiparesis. Children who have had CVAs tend to exhibit significant long-term disabilities, including cognitive and sensory impairments, CP, and epilepsy.

Several factors contribute to the occurrence of CVA, including uncontrolled hypertension (high blood pressure), smoking, diabetes mellitus, diet, drug abuse (such as heroin and cocaine), obesity, and alcohol abuse, among others. Many of these risk factors can be controlled through lifestyle changes. The past few years have seen a substantial increase in the amount of knowledge regarding CVA and how it is treated, especially regarding the promotion of healthful behaviors such as performing regular physical activity. In an article summarizing 23 research studies, Lee, Folsom, and Blair (2003) found that moderate and high levels of physical activity are associated with a reduced risk of CVA. As a result of better education and treatment, more people are living who otherwise might have died because of CVA.

Depending on the location of the damage, symptoms mirror those of CP and TBI. However, people with TBI and CVA can expect varying degrees of improvement following their injury, whereas those with CP cannot. People who have had CVA might exhibit cognitive or perceptual deficits, motor deficits, seizure disorders, and communication problems, which is why a collaborative approach to CVA rehabilitation is necessary. Research indicates that children show more improvement following brain trauma (TBI and CVA) than adults do.

Incidence

CVA is a leading cause of long-term disability in the United States. About 4.7 million Americans are living with neurological impairment because of CVA. About 780,000 Americans experience CVA each year; of these, about 600,000 are first attacks and 180,000 are recurrent attacks (American Heart Association, 2008). Females generally account for about 60 percent of all CVA fatalities, and about 30 percent of all infants die after CVA. It is the third largest cause of death in the world following heart disease and cancer (Hankey, 2005). Recent statistics also indicate that more than half of all people experiencing their first CVA will survive, although only about 10 percent completely recover. Males have

a higher incidence rate than females at younger ages but not at older ages, and African Americans are more prone to CVA than Caucasians. Typically, it affects older segments of the population and is a common form of adult disability. CVA occurring in infants, children, and adolescents is relatively rare but has significant implications for educators.

Classification

Although there are many types, CVA can generally be divided into two categories: **hemorrhagic** and **ischemic**. Hemorrhage within the brain is a result of an artery that loses its elasticity and ruptures, resulting in blood flowing into and around brain tissue. This type of hemorrhage is commonly called *cerebral hemorrhage* and is the most serious form of CVA. Ischemia, on the other hand, refers to the lack of an appropriate blood supply to brain tissue and causes the majority of CVAs. The lack of blood results from a blocked artery leading to or within the brain itself. Typically, the blockage results from a progressive narrowing of the artery or from an embolism. An embolism is usually a blood clot or piece of fat deposit (plaque) that lodges in small arteries. An insufficient or absent blood supply means that oxygen, vital for brain functioning, is absent or diminished. This interruption might be permanent or for a brief time. If the attack is very brief, it is a transient ischemic attack (TIA). About 10 percent of all CVAs are preceded by a TIA, which might occur days, weeks, or months before a major CVA. This type of ischemia results in full recovery but might indicate a future attack that is more severe. Aside from a TIA, when a person experiences a hemorrhagic or ischemic CVA, brain tissue (cells) dies, which results in long-term reduced brain function or death. In addition to medications designed to dissolve clots, medical treatment includes the removal of clots by inserting a catheter into a leg artery and physically removing the clot.

General Educational Considerations

Although CVA may strike without warning, some people receive warning signs. Teachers and coaches should be aware of common warning signs, including sudden weakness or numbness of the face or an arm and leg on one side of the body, sudden dimness or loss of vision in only one eye, sudden loss of speech or trouble understanding speech, sudden severe headache with no apparent cause, and unexplained dizziness, unsteadiness, or sudden falls, especially with any of the previous symptoms. Teachers and coaches should have students with any of these symptoms seek medical attention immediately. If a student showing one or more symptoms has heart or circulatory problems or has experienced a previous CVA or brain injury, consider the situation an emergency.

Immediately following CVA, survivors will need to be placed on a planned, systematic, and individualized rehabilitation program. The intensity and duration of the rehabilitation program depends on the degree of disability. Someone who exhibits paresis (muscle weakness) or paralysis in one limb and retains normal voluntary movement for the remainder of the body will need little in the form of therapy. But someone who exhibits complete paralysis of all four limbs will need intense, long-term therapy. From an educational standpoint, students will follow a school reentry program similar to that followed by students with TBI, as described in the previous section.

PROGRAM IMPLICATIONS

All people with CP, TBI, or CVA can benefit from physical education and sport activities. The type and degree of physical disability, motor educability, interest level, and overall educational goals determine the modifications and adaptations required. Taking these factors into account, an IEP can be planned and implemented.

General Guidelines

Several guidelines apply to programs for students with CP, TBI, or CVA. The guidelines that follow pertain to safety considerations, physical fitness, motor development, psychosocial development, and implications for sport.

Safety Considerations

All programs should be conducted in a safe, secure environment in which students are free to explore the capabilities of their own bodies and to interact with surroundings that nurture their physical and motor development. Teachers and coaches should closely monitor games and activities, especially for students who are prone to seizures or who lack good judgment (e.g., those with TBI). About 60 percent of people with CP have tendencies toward seizures (Laskin, 2003). Many take anti-seizure medication, and as a result, side effects

(e.g., slowed physiologic responses to exercise, irritability, hyperactivity) might affect the person's performance in physical education and sport.

Students with severe impairments need special equipment, such as crutches, bolsters (to support the upper body while in the prone position), standing platforms (to assist them in maintaining a standing posture), orthotic devices, or seating systems to help them perform certain motor tasks (figure 14.3). Most students with mild impairments require no specialized equipment. Because many people with physical disabilities have difficulty maintaining an erect posture for extended amounts of time, some activities are best done in a prone, supine, or seated position. Students with physical limitations should be encouraged to experience as many postures as possible not only in physical education classes but also throughout the school day. This is particularly important for people in wheelchairs.

Because of abnormal muscle tone and reduced range of motion, many people with neuromotor involvement have difficulty moving voluntarily. The teacher might need to assist by getting a student into and out of activity positions, physically supporting her during activity, or helping her perform a skill or exercise. The teacher might also need to position students by applying pressure with the hands to key points of the body, such as the head, neck, spine, shoulders, elbows, hips, pelvis, knees, or ankles. An example is applying both hands symmetrically to both elbows in order to reduce flexion at the elbow joints. However, these techniques should be performed only after instruction by a therapist or physician.

The ultimate aim of handling, positioning, and lifting people with CP is to encourage them to move as independently as possible. This is accomplished by gradually reducing the amount of support to key points of the body over time. When possible, teachers should consult with therapists in an effort to coordinate these procedures, especially for students possessing severe physical disabilities. Finnie (1997) provides excellent information on appropriate ways to handle children with characteristics associated with CP. In addition, teachers should closely monitor the physical assistance that a student with a disability receives from trained peers. Peer assistance should be discouraged if it poses a safety risk.

Because the conditions described in this chapter are of medical origin, it is important that physical educators and coaches consult medical professionals when establishing programs to meet unique

FIGURE 14.3 Athletes with cerebral palsy using crutches to assist in running.

Photo courtesy of Challenge Publications, Ltd./Palaestra Magazine.

needs. This is especially important for students with TBI or those receiving physical or occupational therapy, such as students with CP and CVA.

Physical Fitness

It is generally agreed that appropriate levels of health-related physical fitness assist people with disabilities in performing activities of daily living, recreation, and leisure activities, which, in turn, promote a healthy lifestyle. Although the health-related physical fitness needs of people with CP, TBI, or CVA are similar to the needs of people without disabilities, some aspects of fitness are particularly important to them. Reduced muscular strength, flexibility, and cardiorespiratory endurance are common in people with CP, TBI, or CVA and might lead to the inability to maintain balance, independently transfer or move one's body, perform activities of daily living, or participate in functional leisure activities.

Because restricted movement is common, it is vital that strength and flexibility be developed to the maximum extent possible. If unattended, weak musculature and limited range of motion will lead to permanent joint contractures that result in significant loss of movement capability. For example, people with more severe forms of spastic CP might have significant range-of-motion and flexibility needs. People who have experienced TBI or CVA might need to develop and sustain an adequate level of

aerobic activity, especially if the trauma is recent. Whatever health-related profiles people with CP, TBI, or CVA exhibit, a personalized approach to enhancing health-related fitness is recommended.

The **Brockport Physical Fitness Test** (BPFT) (Winnick & Short, 1999a) is the most recent fitness assessment instrument used for people with CP, TBI, or CVA. This criterion-referenced test provides test items, modifications for disabilities, and criterion-referenced standards for achieving fitness. The test includes components of aerobic functioning, body composition, and musculoskeletal functioning (flexibility, muscular strength, and endurance) vital for achieving health-related physical fitness. Various test items may be selected within each of the three components, depending on the student's desired profile (e.g., target aerobic movement test, upper-arm skinfold measures for body composition, modified Apley test for flexibility, seated push-ups for muscular strength and endurance). The BPFT incorporates the eight-level functional classification system used by CPISRA and BNDSA (see table 14.1), which identifies the person's functional level. Based on the functional level, specific test items are selected. Detailed information regarding this test can be found in chapter 4.

As is true for anyone who has a low health-related fitness level, certain precautions might need to be taken as programs are established for students with CP, TBI, or CVA. It is especially important that the teacher be sensitive to the frequency, intensity, duration, and mode of exercises and activities. Fatigue might cause the person to become frustrated, which could adversely affect proper performance. The instructor should permit rest breaks and player substitutions when endurance-related activities such as soccer and basketball are offered. It might be beneficial for those with reduced fitness levels to perform exercises and activities more frequently but with less intensity and duration. Exercises and activities should be selected that the student finds enjoyable. Performing enjoyable exercises and activities increases the likelihood that health-related fitness will be maintained over a lifetime.

Motor Development

CP, TBI, and CVA restrict people from experiencing normal functional movement patterns essential to normal motor development. As a result, delays in motor control and development are common. People with CP typically exhibit motor delays because they have fewer opportunities to move, lack movement ability, or have difficulty controlling movements. People with varying degrees of TBI or CVA might have difficulty planning and performing movements because of damage to the motor control and related areas of the cerebrum. Children with CP and TBI are frequently unable to execute fundamental movements in an appropriate manner.

Physical education programs should encourage the sequential development of fundamental motor patterns and skills essential for participation in games, sports, and leisure activities. Authentic assessment, which emphasizes the evaluation of functional skills, should be used in physical education programs. When attempting to enhance motor development, the physical educator should be concerned primarily with the manner in which a movement is performed rather than with its outcome. One means of enhancing motor development is the use of ecological task analysis (ETA), where task requirements, environmental contexts, and learner constraints are taken into account when instruction takes place. The goal of every physical education program should be to encourage students to achieve maximum motor control and development related to functional activities (e.g., recreation and daily living activities). Standardized motor development tests recommended for use with younger students include the Denver Developmental Screening Test, the Milani-Comparetti Motor Development Screening Test, and the Peabody Developmental Motor Scales (PDMS-2).

Psychosocial Development

Many people with CP, TBI, or CVA lack self-confidence, have low motivational levels, and exhibit problems with body image. An appropriately designed physical education program can provide successful movement experiences that motivate students and help them gain the self-confidence they need to develop a positive self-image, which is vital for emotional well-being. A realistic body image can be developed when the physical education teacher does not expect students to perform skills and activities perfectly. It is far more important that the student perform the activity as independently as possible with a specified degree of competence. The teacher should promote the attitude that it is acceptable to fail at times when attempting activities, because failing is a natural part of the learning process. Physical activities perceived as fun rather than hard work can motivate students to perform to their maximum potential.

Implications for Sport

Physical education teachers are encouraged to integrate many of the activities described in the adapted sport section of this chapter into their programs. For example, the club throw, a BNDSA field event, can be incorporated into a physical education program as a means of developing strength and also offers an opportunity for sport competition. The club resembles a thin wooden bowling pin. The athlete grasps the thin portion of the club and throws the club in the air as far as possible. Other events such as bowling, archery, cycling, and bocce can be taught. Bowling, bocce, and cycling are excellent lifelong leisure activities. Team games and sports might include volleyball, basketball, soccer, and floor hockey.

Individual and dual activities include tennis, table tennis, riflery, archery, badminton, horseback riding, billiards, and track and field. Winter activities, including ice hockey, ice-skating, downhill and cross-country skiing, tobogganing, and sledding, are also popular in colder regions. All of these games and sports can be offered with a view toward future competition or leisure activity.

Disability-Specific Guidelines

The previous section described general program guidelines applicable to CP, TBI, and CVA. However, there are also several guidelines specific to each condition. These guidelines focus chiefly on health-related physical fitness and motor ability.

Cerebral Palsy

According to Winnick and Short (1999a), people with CP should possess the ability to sustain moderate physical activity (aerobic functioning), have body composition consistent with positive health, and musculoskeletal function (muscular strength and endurance, flexibility) so that participation in a variety of sport and leisure activities is possible. Sustaining moderate physical activity (70 percent of maximum predicted heart rate adjusted for mode of exercise) for 15 minutes represents the general aerobic standard for young people with CP (Winnick & Short, 1999a). The ability to perform this general standard has positive implications for sport and leisure activities. Minimum and preferred general standards are also presented for body composition and musculoskeletal functioning.

Inappropriate reflexive behavior in people with CP contributes to reduced aerobic activity and imbalances in muscle functioning and flexibility throughout regions of the body. Inappropriate reflexive behavior can also contribute to difficulties with motor coordination and equilibrium, which can compromise the ability to attain acceptable health-related fitness and to learn and perform certain motor skills, especially those needed to perform recreation and leisure activities. Because of either restricted or extraneous movements, a person with CP might exert more energy than a person without impairment to accomplish the same task. Even with more energy output, people with CP can exhibit a 50 percent reduction in physical work capacity when compared with peers without disabilities (Laskin, 2003). In addition, the greater energy output requires a greater degree of endurance, and therefore the duration of physical activities might need to be shortened.

When a child is receiving therapy for inappropriate reflexive behavior, it is important for the physical educator to work in conjunction with therapists to foster the suppression of certain abnormal reflexes and the facilitation of righting and equilibrium reactions. Although many physical education activities help in the development of righting and equilibrium reactions, others might elicit abnormal reflexes. Some of the more common reflexes affecting the performance of physical education and sport skills include the asymmetrical tonic neck reflex (ATNR), the symmetrical tonic neck reflex (STNR), the crossed extension reflex, and the positive supporting reflex. The ATNR can

prevent the effective use of implements such as bats, rackets, and hockey sticks. Children exhibiting the ATNR typically jump asymmetrically and may roll to one side when performing a forward roll. When present, the STNR can affect the ability to perform scooter-board activities in the prone position or other activities requiring the chin to be tucked toward the chest (e.g., looking down to control a soccer ball or catch a ground ball). Children exhibiting the STNR can have difficulty swinging on a swing. Difficulty in kicking from a standing position can be affected by the crossed extension and positive supporting reflexes.

As the student ages, inappropriate reflexes will not be inhibited even with therapy. Thus, professionals responsible for the student's physical education program must pursue attainment of functional skills, including sport skills. The attainment of functional skills such as creeping, walking, running, and throwing are important to future skill development and should be incorporated into the student's program. Asking students with CP to repetitively perform activities that elicit unwanted reflexes will not aggravate the condition of CP once children have aged beyond seven or eight years. The following sections address components of strength, flexibility, speed, motor coordination, and perceptual–motor disorders as they pertain to physical education and sport.

Strength

In addressing strength development, it is important to note that muscle-tone imbalances between flexor and extensor muscle groups are common in people with CP. For those with spastic tendencies, flexor muscles might be disproportionately stronger than extensors. Thus, strength development should focus on strengthening the extensor muscles. For example, even though a student might have increased tone of the forearm flexors, he might perform poorly on pull-ups. This being the case, one should not continue to develop the forearm flexors as opposed to the forearm extensors. The goal is to develop and maintain a balance between flexor and extensor muscles throughout the body. When muscular strength imbalances are present among regions of the body, DiRocco (1999) suggests that people with CP can use handheld weights or flexible tubing so that the appropriate resistance is applied to a particular body segment or region.

It is commonly known that strength training does not increase spasticity. However, when participating in a resistance training program, some people might temporarily exhibit increased spasticity in the involved limb or segment of the body when a contralateral nonspastic limb is involved in a resistance exercise. It is suggested that strength-building exercises be performed at a moderate speed rather than a fast speed to reduce the spasticity. Baxter and Lockette (1995) suggest that increased spasticity is a temporary phenomenon and the increased spasticity should subside soon after the session. In any case, spastic muscles should not be subjected to workloads above 60 percent of maximum (DiRocco, 1999).

People with CP can benefit from rigorous strength training programs. Isokinetic resistance exercises are particularly useful for developing strength, probably because they provide constant tension through the full range of motion and help inhibit jerky movements that are extraneous and uncontrolled. Moving limbs in diagonal patterns (e.g., moving the entire arm across the body in a diagonal plane) encourages muscle groups to work in harmony. A variety of gross motor activities such as throwing, striking, and kicking can elicit such movements.

Flexibility

Tight muscles in both the upper and lower limbs and the hip region contribute to reduced flexibility, especially for students with spastic CP. If left unattended, restricted range of motion leads to contractures and bone deformities. Thus, flexibility exercises and activities should be a regular part of physical education and sport programs. People with spastic CP benefit from a prolonged warm-up (15 to 20 minutes) of static flexibility exercises (DiRocco, 1999). The instructor might want to begin a flexibility session by helping students relax target muscle groups. This can be accomplished by teaching students relaxation techniques, which they can then perform independently. According to Surburg (1999), stretching exercises should be static rather than ballistic, and they should be done both before and after strength and endurance activities. If a student is participating in a ballistic type of activity such as a club throw, ballistic stretching can be used, but static stretching should precede it. Surburg also recommends that stretching exercises for more severely affected body parts possessing spasticity should be done on a regular basis. When flexibility exercises are done, it is recommended that fewer repetitions and longer periods of stretching be performed.

When possible, students should perform stretching exercises on their own. This type of stretching (performed with no assistance) is active range of motion. Should the teacher or coach need to assist a student with spasticity in performing flexibility exercises (active–assistive range of motion), her hand should be placed on the extensor muscle, not the flexor (spastic) muscle (Mushett, Wyeth, & Richter, 1995). For people who cannot voluntarily move their body part because of severe spasticity or limited motor control, passive range of motion (movement performed entirely by the teacher or coach without assistance from the student) can be performed under general medical supervision.

Speed

Many students with CP have difficulty with games and sport skills that include a speed component because quick movements tend to activate the stretch reflex. However, an appropriate program can permit students with CP to increase their movement speed. Speed-development activities for students with CP differ little from those for students without impairments except that such activities should be conducted more frequently for students with CP (daily activities are recommended). Students with CP should be encouraged to perform movements as quickly as possible but to do them in a controlled, accurate, and purposeful manner. Activities with a speed component include throwing and kicking for distance, running, and jumping. Initially, the student should concentrate on the pattern of the movement while gradually increasing the speed of execution. To develop arm and leg speed, the student can throw or kick a ball (or some other object) in a soft manner to a target; gradually, the throw or kick can increase in speed.

Motor Coordination

Varying degrees of incoordination (dyspraxia) are common in people with CP and contribute to delayed motor control and development. Those who are significantly uncoordinated might have problems ambulating independently or with appliances and might need to wear protective headgear. Because they frequently fall, they should be taught to fall in a protective manner. Because of abnormal movements and posture, people with CP have difficulty controlling balance and body coordination. Obstacle courses, horseback riding, bicycling and tricycling, and balance beam and stability-board activities can assist in controlling movements.

Difficulties with motor control notwithstanding, people with CP (as well as those with TBI and CVA) can learn to become more accurate in their performance. Because people with CP can have difficulty planning movements involving accuracy, they should be allowed sufficient time to plan the movement before executing it. Many times, the use of a weighted ball, bat, or other implement assists in decreasing abnormal flailing or tremor movements. Adding weight to the implement helps reduce exaggerated stretch reflexes, which in turn aids in controlling movements. People with CP possessing deficiencies in motor control resulting from athetoid, tremor, or ataxic tendencies can be expected to throw or kick for distance better and to exhibit freer running patterns than people with CP who have limited range of motion because of spastic or rigid tendencies.

Loud noises and stressful situations increase the amount of electrical stimulation from the brain to the muscles. This tends to increase abnormal and extraneous movements, which make motor activities difficult to perform. In an attempt to deal with this situation, students should be taught to concentrate on the activity they are performing. People exhibiting spastic tendencies tend to relax more when encouraged to make slow, repetitive movements that have a purpose, whereas those with athetoid tendencies perform better when encouraged to relax before moving. Highly competitive situations that promote winning at all costs might increase abnormal movements. Thus, competitive situations might need to be introduced gradually. Teaching relaxation techniques, which consciously reduce abnormal muscle tone and prepare the student for activity and competition, is beneficial. Another way to help students with CP improve general motor control and coordination is to have them construct a mental picture of the skill or activity prior to performance. This technique, called **mental imagery**, might help to integrate thoughts with actions.

In motor skill development for students with CP, the skills taught should be broken down into components and presented sequentially. This method is particularly useful for uncoordinated students seeking to learn more complex motor skills. However, because of the general lack of body coordination, activities should initially focus on simple repetitive movements rather than on complicated ones requiring many directional changes. Thus, activities that help to develop basic fundamental motor skills and patterns, such as walking, running, jumping, throwing, catching, and so forth, should be taught.

Perceptual–Motor Disorders

Perceptual–motor disorders also contribute to poor motor performance. Because of these disorders, many children with CP exhibit short attention spans and are easily distracted by objects and people in the immediate environment. Activities might need to be conducted in an environment as free from distractions as possible, especially during early skill development.

Visual–perceptual disorders are common among students with CP and can adversely affect activities and events that involve spatial relations. These might include player positioning in team sports such as soccer, remaining in lanes during track events, and determining distances between objects such as bocce balls. Students might have difficulty with accuracy and aiming tasks, such as throwing, tossing, or kicking an object to a specified target, as well as with activities involving fine motor coordination, such as rifle shooting, angling, or pocket billiards.

Traumatic Brain Injury and Stroke

Before their brain trauma, people with TBI once learned and performed physical education and sport skills in the same way as people without disabilities. Learning motor skills requires varying amounts of cognition, depending on the level of difficulty. Skills once thought to be quite simple to learn now require constant practice and planning by the person with TBI or CVA. Depending on the age at the time of trauma, some skills might have already been learned for quite some time (e.g., running, throwing, catching), whereas other skills have not yet been acquired (e.g., specific sport skills). Although some people with TBI or CVA might fully recover the motor skills lost, others with more significant and permanent injury might never regain them. For students with TBI and CVA to regain skills to their maximum potential, physical education and sport programs need to be individualized and offered regularly.

Because of the nature of the disability, students with TBI or CVA might commonly exhibit weak muscles and balance difficulties. Thus, exercises and activities are necessary to regain functional balance, walking, manipulation, and strength. Inadequate balance might hinder the performance of many physical education and sport activities. Readers interested in exercise testing and programming for people with CVA and head injury should consult the writing of Palmer-McLean and Harbst (2003). The following sections address physical fitness and motor coordination as they pertain to physical education and sport.

Physical Fitness

Acquiring and maintaining an adequate level of health-related physical fitness is important. This is especially true for people who have been severely injured through TBI and those who have been immobile for long periods of time after CVA. Their health-related fitness needs can be considered similar to those of people with CP. As such, people with CVA or TBI need to develop and sustain at least moderate levels of aerobic activity to maintain body composition consistent with good health and musculoskeletal functioning sufficient to participate in sport and leisure activities. Thus, depending on individual need, the physical education program should allow for activities to develop and maintain these health-related components. The BPFT (Winnick & Short, 1999a) highlights items and standards that can be used in the assessment of health-related fitness for people with disabilities. A personalized process might be used to design a test for students with CVA and TBI.

Many students will fatigue easily, especially as they begin their reentry into school. Thus, fitness exercises and activities should be introduced gradually, and sufficient rest should occur between activities, especially if physical education is near the end of the school day. For students who are immobilized for large amounts of time, aerobic activities should be preceded by progressive muscular strength and endurance activities.

The neurological deficits associated with head injury often affect the ability to ambulate efficiently. Thus, the person with head trauma uses a significant amount of energy that would otherwise not be used. According to Palmer-McLean and Harbst (2003), appropriately planned fitness programs can improve cardiorespiratory endurance and muscle strength, thereby allowing students to raise energy levels to perform locomotor activities (e.g., sport, leisure, activities of daily living) in a more efficient manner. Raising functional health-related fitness levels also increases the chance of living a more fulfilling and productive life.

Some students who exhibit spasticity (similar to CP) will need to focus on relaxation and flexibility exercises. Other students exhibiting partial paralysis need to maintain residual functioning through muscular strength and endurance exercises and activities. Weight training and flexibility activities will not be new to the person recovering from TBI or CVA, because physical and occupational therapy rehabilitation programs typically focus on these areas. In addition to describing a number of rehabilitation programs, Petrofsky, Petrofsky, and Bweir (2004) provide detailed information on flexibility and strength development.

Universal gym equipment is convenient and safe to use to develop strength and endurance because students need not be concerned with placing free weights on barbells and dumbbells. Except for the bench press, students can stay seated in their wheelchairs (although getting out of the wheelchair is important and should be encouraged). For people who can remove themselves from their chairs either independently or with assistance, isokinetic equipment is also beneficial. However, according to DiRocco (1999), weight machines might not be the choice of equipment for people with TBI or CVA. Muscle weakness on one side of the body might prevent the successful use of weight machines because several exercises require the use of both arms or both legs at once. This considered, free weights, which allow limbs to be exercised individually, should be made available. For students who do not have free weights available, stretch bands are an economical way to conduct resistance training.

Because people with more severe brain injury are more likely to be sedentary, aerobic activities, which develop cardiorespiratory endurance, should be performed regularly. These might take the form of low-impact aerobics for students who can ambulate or a recumbent bicycle for those with balance difficulties. Aerobic activities can be done from a sitting position for those using wheelchairs. Those who can perform activities from a standing position but who have limited endurance should have a stationary object available for rest or support as needed. Aquatic activities are especially good for developing physical fitness. People with TBI and CVA should participate in physical fitness programs that address all areas of fitness. *The Brockport Physical Fitness Training Guide* (Winnick & Short, 1999b) includes additional exercise and activity suggestions for promoting health-related fitness.

Motor Control

Depending on the location and severity of injury, people with TBI or CVA have difficulty planning, initiating, and controlling gross and fine motor movements. People with TBI typically have difficulty performing movements sequentially. This has important implications for physical education and sport activities, especially when combinations of separate skills need to be linked together in succession. Students with TBI or CVA typically need to relearn movements and movement patterns they could easily perform before the injury. To assist in this process, more complex skills should be broken down into simpler subskills, which should be practiced sequentially. Because these students typically have problems processing information, allow enough time for movements to be planned before they are executed.

As is true for people with CP, visual perception might also be affected in people with TBI or CVA. Thus, they might exhibit difficulty with activities requiring spatial relationships and those requiring object control, such as catching, kicking, and striking. Of course, activities incorporating object control need to be individualized. Adolescents with TBI or CVA should be given choices about the type of sport and leisure activities they will learn in physical education classes. This gives the adolescent a needed sense of independence and self-control and contributes to a smooth transition from school to community.

INCLUSION

Unless otherwise decided by IEP team members, students with CP, TBI, or CVA should be included in regular physical education classes. Of course, such a decision must be made on an individual basis. Generally, students with mild to moderate degrees of impairment can be safely and effectively included in regular physical education settings. Physical education teachers can use both universal design and differentiated instruction to foster inclusion in regular physical education. Universal design focuses on equipment that can be used by all students regardless of ability, and differentiated instruction uses various instructional techniques to maximize learning for all students regardless of learning style. Unless they are severely intellectually impaired, most students with CP, TBI, or CVA will understand verbal and written directions as well as rules and strategies for games and sports. In certain cases, teachers might need to structure activities to suit participants' abilities. For example, students with CP affecting the lower limbs could play goalie in soccer or floor hockey and could pitch or play first base in softball. In addition, class VIII athletes with CP have such a mild degree of impairment that they may easily compete on their interscholastic track and field team. Providing appropriate inclusive environments gives these students opportunities for enhancing social and emotional development.

ADAPTED SPORT

At almost all ages, people with CP, TBI, or CVA have the opportunity to become involved in competitive sport. They are included in BNDSA competition, as well as a select group of sports for athletes with other physical disabilities, including muscular dystrophy, multiple sclerosis, and osteogenesis imperfecta. As the national governing body, the BNDSA is responsible for the conduct and administration of approved sports in the United States. In 2008, the NDSA became a division of BlazeSports America and therefore falls within its organizational structure. Now called the BNDSA, it offers a variety of modified sporting events, such as the distance kick (see figure 14.4) and club throw. In addition to local and regional competitions, the BNDSA holds annual national championships. The BNDSA is responsible for formulating the rules, policies, and procedures for its events and is also responsible for selecting athletes to represent the United States in international competition.

The BNDSA is a member of the Committee on Sports for the Disabled (COSD) of the United States Olympic Committee (USOC) and a member of the International Sport Organization for the Disabled (ISOD). BNDSA athletes are eligible to participate in international competition governed by the ISOD as long as they meet classification standards and qualify for events. The ISOD oversees the Paralympic Games, World Championships, World Games, and World Cup. The Paralympic Games are organized every fourth year, with competition in

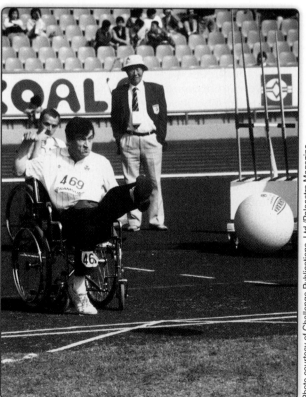

Photo courtesy of Challenge Publications, Ltd./Palaestra Magazine.

FIGURE 14.4 Athlete with cerebral palsy performing the distance kick.

multidisabled games and sports. World Championships are organized for specific sports; participants generally have single or multiple disabilities. The World Games, on the other hand, are organized for competition in one or more sports for specific disability groups (e.g., CP) or games that might deviate from existing rules. Finally, World Cup competition refers to international competition for national or club teams in team and individual sports. The international governing body for BNDSA is CPISRA.

Competition for athletes with CP, TBI, or CVA is based on the eight-level classification system described at the beginning of this chapter (see table 14.1). Athletes are placed in a specific class through two testing procedures. In the first, a functional profile is established through observa-

tion and questioning regarding the person's daily living skills. The second testing procedure involves the measurement of speed, accuracy of movement, and range of motion for upper-extremity and torso function and, for ambulant athletes, the assessment of lower-extremity function and stability. Athletes generally compete within their designated classes in a variety of events. Table 14.2 identifies events and associated classification levels.

BNDSA competition is divided into three age divisions: youth (up to 18 years of age), open (ages 19-39), and masters (over 40 years of age). The youth division is subdivided into five groups: futures (age 6 and under), division A (ages 7-9), division B (ages 10-12), division C (ages 13-15), and division D (ages 16-18). There are sports for

Table 14.2 Classes Eligible for BNDSA Events

Events	Classes
Archery	I-VIII (all classes)
Bocce (wheelchair—individual and team)	I and II only
Bowling	I-VIII (all classes)
Cross country (3,000 m)	V-VIII
Cycling • Bicycling • Tricycling	 V-VIII II, V, and VI
Equestrian	I-VIII (all classes)
Powerlifting (bench press)	I-VIII (all classes)
Slalom	I-IV
Soccer • Seven-a-side soccer • Indoor wheelchair soccer	 V-VIII I-VIII (all classes)
Swimming	I-VIII (all classes)
Shooting	II-VIII
Table tennis	III-VIII
Track • 60 m weave (wheelchair) • 100 m, 200 m, 400 m, 800 m • 1,500 m • 4 × 100 m relay, 4 × 400 m relay	 I II-VIII III-IV and VI-VIII II-VIII
Field events • Soft shot, precision throw, height toss, soft discus • Medicine ball thrust, distance kick • Club throw • Shot, discus • Javelin throw • Long jump	 I II II-VI II-VIII III-VIII VI-VIII

Adapted, by permission, from National Disability Sports Alliance, 2002, *NDSA sports rules manual*, 6th ed. (Kingston, RI: National Disability Sports Alliance), 6-13. © BlazeSports American/NDSA.

both wheelchair and ambulatory classes in all three age divisions. The futures subdivision stresses participation rather than competition. Depending on age and classification, youth athletes compete in events that are the same as those for adult athletes (e.g., ambulatory soccer, swimming). The BNDSA hosts or sanctions several regional events across the United States each year. It also hosts the annual Youth Nationals Competition, which brings together young athletes from across the United States. Each year, the BNDSA holds clinics for professionals and volunteers that focus on coaching, training, and officiating techniques. The BNDSA publishes an approved sport rules manual (BNDSA, 2002) and a separate training guide.

SUMMARY

This chapter has described the conditions of CP, TBI, and CVA as they relate to physical education and sport. In addition, physical and motor needs were described and suggestions for programs and activities were presented. Because of the medical nature of these conditions, teachers and coaches are encouraged to plan activities with the input of physicians and allied health professionals.

REFERENCES

Ådén, U. (2009). Neonatal stroke is not a harmless condition. *Stroke, 40,* 1948-1949.

American Heart Association. (2008). *Heart disease and stroke statistics.* Dallas: Author.

Baxter, K.F., & Lockette, K.F. (1995). Resistance training with stretch bands: Modifying for disability. In P.D. Miller (Ed.), *Fitness programming and physical disability* (pp. 91-100). Champaign, IL: Human Kinetics.

BlazeSports National Disability Sports Alliance (BNDSA). (2002). *Sports rules manual* (6th ed.). Newport, RI: Author.

Brain Injury Association of America. (2008). Fact sheet. Retrieved from www.biausa.org/factsheets.htm.

Damiano, D. (2004). Physiotherapy management in cerebral palsy: Moving beyond philosophies. In D. Scrutton, D. Damiano, & M. Mayston (Eds.), *Management of the motor disorders of children with cerebral palsy* (2nd ed., pp.161-169). London: MacKeith Press.

DiRocco, P.J. (1999). Muscular strength and endurance. In J.P. Winnick & F.X. Short (Eds.), *The Brockport physical fitness training guide* (pp. 39-73). Champaign, IL: Human Kinetics.

Driver, S., Harmon, M., & Block, M. (2003). Devising a safe and successful physical education program for children with a brain injury. *Journal of Physical Education, Recreation, and Dance, 74* (7), 41-48, 55.

Finnie, N.R. (1997). *Handling the young child with cerebral palsy at home* (3rd ed.). Boston: Butterworth-Heinemann.

Hankey, G. (2005). *Stroke treatment and prevention: An evidence-based approach.* Cambridge, UK: Cambridge University Press.

Johnson, A. (2002). Prevalence and characteristics of children with cerebral palsy in Europe. *Developmental Medicine and Child Neurology, 45,* 633-640.

Langlois, J., Rutland-Brown, W., & Thomas, K. (2006). Traumatic brain injury in the United States: Emergency department medical visits, hospitalizations, and deaths. Atlanta: CDC, National Center for Injury Prevention and Control.

Laskin, J. (2003). Cerebral palsy. In J.L. Durstine & G.E. Moore (Eds.), *ACSM's Exercise management for persons with chronic diseases and disabilities* (2nd ed., pp. 288-294). Champaign, IL: Human Kinetics.

Lee, C., Folsom, A., & Blair, S. (2003). Physical activity and stroke risk: A meta-analysis. *Stroke, 34,* 2475-2482.

Mushett, C.A., Wyeth, D.O., & Richter, K.J. (1995). Cerebral palsy. In B. Goldberg (Ed.), *Sports and exercise for children with chronic health conditions* (pp.123-134). Champaign, IL: Human Kinetics.

Palmer-McLean, K., & Harbst, K.B. (2003). Stroke and brain injury. In J.L. Durstine & G.E. Moore (Eds.), *ACSM's exercise management for persons with chronic diseases and disabilities* (2nd ed., pp. 238-246). Champaign, IL: Human Kinetics.

Petrofsky, J., Petrofsky, A., & Bweir, S. (2004). Stroke: Present therapy and treatment, part 2. *Palaestra, 20* (3), 35-43.

Powell, J. (2004). Diagnosis, management, and prevention. In M. Lovell, R. Echemendia, J. Barth, & M. Collins (Eds.), *Traumatic brain injury in sports: An international neuropsychological perspective* (pp. 23-34). Lisse, Netherlands: Swets & Zeitlinger.

Surburg, P.R. (1999). Flexibility/range of motion. In J.P. Winnick & F.X. Short (Eds.), *The Brockport physical fitness training guide* (pp. 75-119). Champaign, IL: Human Kinetics.

United Cerebral Palsy (2010). Cerebral palsy information. Retrieved from www.ucp.org/uploads/CP_Fact_Sheet_10Feb18.pdf.

Walker, B.R. (1997). Creating effective educational programs through parent–professional partnerships. In A. Glang, G.H. Singer, & B. Todis (Eds.), *Students with acquired brain injury: The school's response* (pp. 295-322). Baltimore: Paul Brookes.

Wehman, P., Keyser-Marcus, L., West, D., Targett, P., & Bricout, J. (2001). Applications for youth with traumatic brain injury. In P. Wehman (Ed.), *Life beyond the classroom: Transition strategies for young people with disabilities* (3rd ed., pp. 449-490). Baltimore: Paul H. Brookes.

Winnick, J.P., & Short, F.X. (1999a). *Brockport physical fitness test manual.* Champaign, IL: Human Kinetics.

Winnick, J.P., & Short, F.X. (Eds.). (1999b). *Brockport physical fitness training guide.* Champaign, IL: Human Kinetics.

Ylvisaker, M., & Feeney, T.J. (1998). School re-entry after traumatic brain injury. In M. Ylvisaker (Ed.), *Traumatic brain injury rehabilitation: Children and adolescents* (2nd ed., pp. 369-387). Boston: Butterworth-Heinemann.

WRITTEN RESOURCES

Fitness Canada. (1994). *Moving to inclusion: Cerebral palsy.* Ottawa, ON: Active Living Alliance for Canadians with a Disability.

This is one in a series of nine manuals designed to provide physical education teachers with practical ways in which to integrate students with disabilities into regular physical education classes. This manual includes programming for inclusive physical education, manipulation skills, sport skills, fitness, outdoor education, intramural and interschool programs, and professional support services. The manual can be obtained for a nominal fee by writing to Active Living Alliance for Canadians with a Disability, 720 Belfast Rd., Ste.104, Ottawa, ON, Canada, K1G O25; by phoning 800-771-0663; or by e-mailing info@ala.ca.

Martin, S. (2006). *Teaching motor skills to children with cerebral palsy and similar movement disorders: A guide for parents and professionals.* Bethesda, MD: Woodbine House.

This book is designed to help parents (as well as professionals without a movement background) teach fundamental motor skills (e.g., walking, crawling) through various exercises and activities that can be conducted in the home or other nontherapy settings. The book has a number of excellent illustrations to show how to teach the various movements.

AUDIOVISUAL RESOURCES

Aerobics for cerebral palsy [VHS]. (n.d.). Disabled Sports USA/Videotapes, 451 Hungerford Dr., Ste. 100, Rockville, MD 20850.

This video illustrates vigorous exercise for ambulatory and nonambulatory people with muscular coordination difficulties. The program features a prolonged warm-up followed by exercise using easy-to-follow upper-body movements. Low-impact, rhythmic full-body actions are demonstrated.

Physical activity [VHS]. (n.d.). American Heart Association, 7272 Greenville Ave., Dallas, TX 75231.

This video illustrates how regular physical activity can help reduce heart attack and stroke risk as well as improve overall health.

A stroke survivor's workout [VHS]. (n.d.). American Heart Association, 7272 Greenville Ave., Dallas, TX 75231.

This 28-minute video contains flexibility and strength exercises. Some exercises are done from a standing position and, if needed, using the support of a chair; other exercises are done seated in a chair or wheelchair.

ELECTRONIC RESOURCES

Brain Injury Association of America: www.biausa.org.

The Brain Injury Association of America is the national clearinghouse for information related to brain injury. The organization promotes awareness, understanding, and prevention of brain injury through education, advocacy, and research.

Amputations, Dwarfism, and Les Autres

David L. Porretta

Although **South African Natalie Du Toit** finished the 2008 Olympic swimming marathon in 16th place, she accomplished a feat no other female Olympic athlete can claim: Natalie was the first athlete with a below-the-knee amputation to compete in the Olympics since George Eyser, an American, won three gold medals in gymnastics on a wooden leg in 1904. Natalie swims without a prosthetic device. She has been a competitive swimmer from a young age, even before her amputation resulting from a motor scooter accident in 2001. Following her amputation, Natalie has continued to swim competitively. Because she can only move one leg, she has half the kicking power of her Olympic opponents, so she compensates with her left arm. Nonetheless, she finished fourth in the 10,000-meter marathon (equivalent to 6.2 mi) at the 2008 world championships to earn a spot at the Olympics. Natalie has already won five gold medals and a silver medal at the Paralympics, and she will continue to compete at that venue. But because of her hard work and dedication to swimming, Natalie will no doubt be in contention for a medal at the next Olympic Games.

eople with amputations, dwarfism, and les
autres (a French term meaning "the others")
impairments were at one time restricted
from physical activity for fear that it would aggravate their conditions. Today, they are encouraged
to participate in many physical education and sport
activities, and they are now approaching many of
the national records set by athletes without disabilities. An overview of amputations, dwarfism,
and les autres impairments within a physical education and sport context is presented in this chapter,
including specific information relating to program
and activity perspectives.

AMPUTATIONS

Amputations are the loss of an entire limb or a limb
segment. They are categorized as either acquired or
congenital. Acquired amputations can result from
diabetes, tumor, or trauma, whereas congenital
amputations result from failure of the fetus to
properly develop during the first three months of
gestation. In most cases, the cause of partial and
total congenital limb absence is unknown. Generally, there are two types of congenital deformities.
In one type, a middle segment of a limb is absent
but the proximal and distal portions are intact;
this is known as **phocomelia**. In phocomelia, the
hand or foot is attached directly to the shoulder
or hip without the remaining anatomical structures
present. The second type of deficiency is similar to
surgical amputation, in which no normal structures,
such as hands or fingers, are present below the
missing segment. In many cases, however, fingerlike buds are present; this deficiency is usually
below the elbow and is unilateral.

Incidence

It is estimated that approximately 1.7 million
people in the United States are amputees (National
Limb Loss Information Center, 2008). About 6 percent of those with missing limbs are under 18 years
of age and about 23 percent are between 18 and
44 years of age. Across all age groups, the leading
cause of limb loss is due to some form of cancer or
vascular disease. Congenital limb loss accounts for
about 60 percent of all amputations in children, and
of this percentage, upper-limb deficiencies occur
1.6 times more often than lower-limb deficiencies.

Males are more than twice as likely as females to
have a missing limb due to trauma.

Classification

Amputations can be classified according to the site
and level of limb absence or from a **functional**
point of view. Nine classes, which are now in use
by Disabled Sports USA (DS/USA) and the International Sport Organization for the Disabled (ISOD),
are identified as follows:

- Class A1—Double above the knee (AK)
- Class A2—Single AK
- Class A3—Double below the knee (BK)
- Class A4—Single BK
- Class A5—Double above the elbow (AE)
- Class A6—Single AE
- Class A7—Double below the elbow (BE)
- Class A8—Single BE
- Class A9—Combined lower- plus upper-limb
  amputations

According to this system, class A8 represents
functional ability greater than class A1. Information
on sport competition can be found in the Adapted
Sport section of this chapter.

General Educational Considerations

In nearly all cases, a **prosthetic device** is prescribed and selected for the amputee by a team
of medical specialists. The prosthetic device is
designed to compensate, as much as possible, for
the functional loss of the limb. Devices are chosen
according to the size of the person and the area
and extent of limb absence. It is important that
lower-limb prostheses are fit properly because if
they are not, amputees are at risk for secondary
conditions such as osteoarthritis, osteoporosis,
and back pain. Most authorities favor the use of
a prosthetic device as early as possible following
the loss of the limb because the device tends to
be more easily incorporated into the person's
normal body actions the earlier it is introduced.
Learning to use a device takes time and effort,
and some people with more extensive lower-limb
amputations need training with canes or crutches.

However, children with limb deficiencies tend to adapt better than adults to prostheses. Special consideration within the educational environment is needed for students with prosthetic devices. For example, classroom teachers can assist therapists in helping students acquire and maintain important fine motor skills, such as cutting, pasting, and drawing. Physical education teachers can assist therapists in helping students acquire and maintain important gross motor skills, such as catching, throwing, and handling implements such as bats and rackets.

With recent technological advances, new types of both upper- and lower-limb prosthetic devices are now commonly seen in educational and sport settings. New types of lower-limb prosthetic devices are commonly used to provide athletes with the most realistic sense of normal foot function. These devices provide an active push-off in which the device propels the body in a forward or vertical fashion. These prostheses, made of carbon fiber, contain a type of dynamic response in that they can store and release energy, simulating the function of a normal foot. They respond smoothly, gradually, and proportionally to pressure applied by the user. Amputees are fit individually with the assistance of computer-generated designs. As such, many athletes with both BK and AK amputations use these prostheses for competitive purposes in sports such as volleyball, basketball, American football, and sprint and distance running (figure 15.1). Cosmetic foot covers are also available that simulate the form and look of the natural foot. These natural-looking foot covers are shells that accommodate prostheses. Unless closely examined, they make the limb look as if nothing is missing. Of course, the use of these cosmetic devices is a personal choice.

Photos courtesy of Ossur Americas, www.ossur.com.

a

b

FIGURE 15.1 *(a)* Kelly Bruno and *(b)* Roderick Green, two elite athletes performing with state-of-the-art prosthetic devices.

People with limb deficiencies often have additional educational needs in the psychosocial domain. Many feel shame, inferiority, and anxiety when in social and educational settings—feelings that might result from stares or comments from their school-age peers. The new cosmetic covers might be of help, especially if students are self-conscious about their prosthetic devices within an educational setting. Finally, counseling by a psychologist or professional counselor might be necessary to promote healthy emotional functioning. To address the social stigma associated with limb loss in children, the Amputee Coalition of America has created a school-based curriculum titled the Limb Loss Education and Awareness Program (LLEAP). Through multisensory activities, children are taught to recognize and appreciate differences in themselves and others. The Amputee Coalition of America also publishes a magazine called *Expectations: Parenting Children and Teens with Limb Differences*. The publication is for parents and caregivers of young amputees. It addresses topics of interest to parents, including adjustment issues, prosthetics, funding, peer support, advocacy, insurance reimbursement, technology, and prevention of secondary conditions.

DWARFISM

Dwarfism is an umbrella term that describes several hundred conditions of short stature that often have associated hormonal, intrauterine, nutritional, and psychosocial problems (Adelson, 2005). The average height of an adult with dwarfism is typically 4 feet (120 cm). When compared with the general population, people with dwarfism are shorter than 98 percent of all other people. Generally, dwarfism results from either the failure of cartilage to form into bone as the person grows or from a pituitary irregularity. Aside from their short stature, people with dwarfism are no different from people without dwarfism. Most people with dwarfism prefer to be called *little people*. The largest organization devoted to people of short stature is the Little People of America (LPA). It was formed in 1957 by actor Billy Barty and now has more than 5,000 members.

Incidence

About 150,000 people in the United States possess a degree of dwarfism. More than 80 percent of people with dwarfism are born to average-sized parents with no family history of dwarfism. **Achondroplasia** is the most common type of disproportionate dwarfism. According to the LPA (2008), as many as 1 in 26,000 infants are born with achondroplasia.

Classification

Dwarfism can be classified into two categories: **proportionate** and **disproportionate**. People with proportionate dwarfism have proportionate body parts but are very short. This type of dwarfism results from a deficiency in the pituitary gland, which regulates growth. Short arms and legs with a normal torso and a large head, on the other hand, characterize disproportionate dwarfism. This type of dwarfism might be caused by a faulty gene that results in failure of the bone to fully develop. People with disproportionate dwarfism are the most prevalent, and this type of achondroplasia is most common.

Achondroplasia means the absence of normal cartilage formation and growth, and it begins in utero. This type of dwarfism can manifest itself in a waddling gait, lordosis, limited range of motion, and bowed legs. Additional anatomical features include a large head and flattened face. Many people with achondroplasia are overweight or obese. Because of the abnormal stature, additional weight is carried in the buttocks, hips, and legs. The average adult height in achondroplasia is about 4 feet (122 cm) for men and women. In more severe cases in which spinal involvement as well as additional bone deformities are present, people with achondroplasia might require ambulation devices such as crutches. Lumbrosacral spinal stenosis with compressed spinal cord or nerve roots is common. This condition is a structural abnormality of the spine in which the canal that houses the spinal cord is too small. As a result, muscle weakness, pain, and loss of sensation might occur. In severe cases, spinal surgery can alleviate the condition.

Some people with dwarfism who do not have achondroplasia might have cervical vertebrae abnormalities, similar to atlantoaxial instability in Down syndrome, which might lead to serious neck injury. As such, the Dwarf Athletic Association of America (DAAA) requires a medical screening for all nonachondroplasic athletes before participation in running, jumping (e.g., basketball), or swimming (e.g., diving start) events.

General Educational Considerations

In general, a physical education program for people with dwarfism should follow the same guidelines as a program developed for people without disabilities. On an intellectual level, students with dwarfism do not function any differently from students without dwarfism. Thus, they should be treated the same as other students with regard to cognitive ability and academic achievement. Delayed motor milestones and otitis media are common in children with achondroplasia. In addition, Adelson (2005) identifies a number of psychosocial implications for children with dwarfism, and thus students with dwarfism should have the opportunity to develop a positive self-image in a psychologically safe educational environment. Many times students with obvious physical differences and limitations are subject to ridicule. It is the responsibility of the teacher to maintain an environment that encourages positive interactions and social contact among all students.

Physical education teachers and coaches need to be aware of certain factors associated with physical education and sport activities for people with dwarfism. Because of delayed motor milestones in children with achondroplasia, elementary physical education programs should focus on the attainment of fundamental motor skills and patterns before the performance of more advanced activities. In addition, because of limited stature and disproportionate body segments, people with dwarfism might have a disadvantage in certain activities, such as track and field, tennis, baseball, softball, and basketball. From a safety perspective, because of joint defects, certain activities (e.g., gymnastics, acrobatics, contact sports) that place stress on joints should be modified.

LES AUTRES

Les autres is used in this chapter as a categorization for several disabilities. These include muscular dystrophy, juvenile rheumatoid arthritis, osteogenesis imperfecta, arthrogryposis, multiple sclerosis, Friedreich's ataxia, myasthenia gravis, and Guillain-Barré syndrome.

Muscular Dystrophy

Muscular dystrophy is a group of inherited diseases characterized by progressive, diffuse weakness of various muscle groups. Muscle cells within the belly of the muscle degenerate and are replaced by adipose and connective tissue. The dystrophy itself is not fatal, but secondary complications of muscle weakness predispose the person to respiratory disorders and heart problems. It is common for people with dystrophy in advanced stages of the disease to die from a simple respiratory infection or as a result of myocardial involvement. Disease symptoms might appear any time between birth and middle age, but most cases affect children and young people.

There are various types of muscular dystrophy, including the myotonic, facioscapulohumeral, limb-girdle, and Duchenne types. **Myotonic muscular dystrophy**, or Steinert's disease, manifests itself through muscle weakness and affects the central nervous system, heart, eyes, and endocrine glands. It is a slowly progressing disease generally occurring between the ages of 20 to 40 years. Congenital myotonic dystrophy is rare, occurring almost exclusively in infants of mothers with the adult form. With appropriate care, their condition often improves; however, delayed motor development and intellectual disabilities in late infancy and early childhood are common. **Facioscapulohumeral muscular dystrophy** initially affects muscles of the shoulders and face and, in some instances, the hip and thigh. Life expectancy is usually normal because this type of dystrophy might arrest itself at any time. In **limb-girdle muscular dystrophy**, degeneration might begin in either the shoulder or the hip girdle, with eventual involvement of both. Unlike the facioscapulohumeral type, degeneration continues at a slow rate. Facioscapulohumeral dystrophy manifests itself during adolescence or adulthood. The limb-girdle type might be exhibited at any time from late childhood on, though it usually occurs during the teenage years. Males and females are equally affected by both facioscapulohumeral and limb-girdle dystrophy.

Duchenne muscular dystrophy (DMD) is the most common and severe childhood form of the disease. It affects more boys than girls, and symptoms usually occur between ages 2 and 6. An almost identical form of DMD is called **Becker muscular dystrophy**. However, it is much less severe, and onset is typically between 2 and 16 years of age. Many times Becker muscular dystrophy is not diagnosed until an adolescent or young adult cannot fully participate in physical education or recreational activities. The Duchenne type is commonly referred to as **pseudohypertrophic muscular dystrophy**. A pseudohypertrophic appearance, especially of the calf and forearm muscles, results from an excessive accumulation of adipose and connective tissues within the interstitial spaces between degenerated muscle cells. It is yet to be determined precisely how this happens; however, the gene responsible for causing Duchenne dystrophy has been identified. Linked to this gene is a protein called *dystrophin*. This protein allows muscle cells to function properly; without it, the muscle cells eventually die. In people with Duchenne dystrophy, this protein is absent. Research has shown that dystrophin is attached to other proteins at the edge of muscle fibers and that it most likely helps anchor the fibers to connective tissue surrounding them.

DMD manifests itself in atrophy and weakness of the thigh, hip, back, shoulder girdle, and respiratory muscles. The tibialis anterior muscle of the lower leg becomes extremely weak, resulting in a drop foot, meaning the foot remains angled downward, making the person prone to falling. Steady and rapid progression of the disease usually leads to the inability to walk within 10 years after onset. The child exhibits characteristics that include

- a waddling gait,
- difficulty climbing stairs,
- a tendency to fall, and
- difficulty rising from a recumbent position.

An additional characteristic is a high level of creatine phosphokinase (CPK), a protein commonly appearing in muscle. In addition to muscle biopsy, DNA analysis, clinical examination, and electromyography, an abnormal CPK level in blood serum is an important laboratory finding in the diagnosis of DMD.

Lordosis frequently develops from weakness of the trunk musculature (figure 15.2). As the disease progresses, the child eventually needs to use orthopedic devices (e.g., leg braces, walker) in order to continue walking. However, even with these devices and continued physical therapy, the child eventually becomes confined to a wheelchair and is likely to grow obese. Contractures might form at the ankle, knee, and hip joints, and muscle atrophy is extensive. Soon after the child begins using a wheelchair, scoliosis (lateral curvature of the spine) also develops. Although weakness of the arms is present in the early stages of the disease, it does not cause real problems until the person begins using a wheelchair. At that time, progressive loss of strength in these muscles continues until it becomes impossible to lift objects or even lift the hands to the mouth. Death often results in about the third decade of life. With continued research on treatments such as dystrophy gene transfer and various medications and injections of compounds to restore the production of dystrophin in those with DMD, a cure might be forthcoming. However,

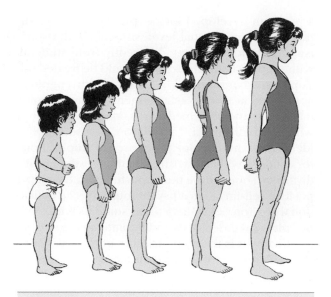

FIGURE 15.2 The developmental posture sequence of a child with DMD. Notice the increased lordosis as the child gets older.

at present no treatment exists to stop muscle atrophy; any treatment given is symptomatic. A major treatment goal is to maintain ambulation as long as possible through daily exercise and activity.

Cognitive difficulties are present in some children with DMD, but many exhibit above-average intelligence. Sometimes slowness of movement and limitations in physical abilities are misinterpreted as cognitive difficulties. Should a child have cognitive difficulties, they are stable and do not worsen as the disease progresses.

Physical education can play an important role in managing muscular dystrophy, especially when exercises and activities are performed during the initial stage of the disease. Regular muscular strength and endurance activities can have a positive effect on muscular development and can help counteract muscular atrophy. Particular attention should be given to the development of the lower leg, hip, abdomen, and thigh because muscles of these areas are used for locomotion. For people with weak respiratory muscles, especially those confined to wheelchairs, breathing exercises and activities should be given priority and performed on a daily basis in order to slow the loss of vital capacity and forced expiratory flow rate (see the application example for more information). Strength and endurance can be developed through aquatic activities that use water as resistance. Aquatic activities can keep muscles toned without putting undue stress on them. Performed regularly,

APPLICATION EXAMPLE

Breathing Activities

Setting: The parents of Janine, a child with muscular dystrophy, ask the adapted physical education teacher to suggest a couple of breathing activities that can be done at home so that she can maintain appropriate function of her respiratory muscles.

Student: Janine, an 8-year-old girl with muscular dystrophy beginning to exhibit weak respiratory muscles

Application: The adapted physical education teacher recommends that Janine perform the following two activities with a friend, sibling, or parent on a daily basis:

▶ Janine and a partner face each other about a yard (1 m) apart and try to keep a balloon in the air as long as possible by blowing it to each other without letting it touch the ground.

▶ While sitting and facing each other at opposite ends of a small table about a yard (1 m) long, Janine and her partner attempt to blow a table-tennis ball across each other's goal (end of table).

flexibility activities help to develop or maintain range of motion so that permanent joint contractures do not develop; flexibility activities that keep the child's attention might be chosen. Low-intensity aerobic activities are also helpful in managing obesity, which is common in people with muscular dystrophy. Dance movements are particularly helpful for improving flexibility and cardiorespiratory efficiency. Arm and upper-body movements for students in wheelchairs can be performed to music. Postural exercises and activities help reduce postural deviations and give the student an opportunity to perform out of the wheelchair.

Juvenile Rheumatoid Arthritis

Juvenile rheumatoid arthritis (JRA), or Still's disease, manifests itself in childhood and is one of several forms of juvenile arthritis. Whereas the American College of Rheumatology uses the term *JRA*, the European League Against Rheumatism uses the term *juvenile chronic arthritis (JCA)*. JRA is the most common type of arthritis in children and one of the more frequent chronic diseases in children today (Cassidy et al., 2005). As with adult rheumatoid arthritis, the cause of JRA is unknown. Depending on the degree of involvement, JRA affects joint movement. Joints become inflamed, resulting in reduced range of motion. In some cases, permanent joint contractures develop, and

muscle atrophy is pronounced. Some authorities suggest that inflammation of the joints results from abnormal antibodies of unknown origin that circulate in the blood and destroy the body's normal structures. The disease is not inherited, nor does it seem to be a result of climate, diet, or patterns of living.

JRA is characterized by a series of remissions and exacerbations (attacks). One cannot predict how long affected children will remain ill or how long they will be symptom free. Generally, the prognosis for JRA is encouraging—only about 15 percent of children with JRA will have moderate to severe functional disability in adulthood. The highest frequency of onset is between 1 to 3 years of age and before the age of 16. According to recent figures, about 294,000 infants, children, and teenagers possess some form of arthritis, of which JRA is the most common (Arthritis Foundation, 2008). There are three main types of JRA: polyarticular, pauciarticular, and systemic. **Polyarticular JRA** affects five or more joints, which might include hand and finger joints as well as the knees, hips, ankles, feet, neck, and jaw. It affects more girls than boys. The same joints on both sides of the body are typically affected. Malformation of the temporomandibular joint can result in slower jaw growth; other symptoms could include a low-grade fever and anemia.

Pauciarticular JRA affects four or fewer joints, which can include knees, ankles, and elbows. Children with pauciarticular JRA have the highest probability for developing uveitis (chronic eye inflammation), which is seen most frequently in girls. Pauciarticular JRA typically affects one side of the body, particularly the knee. The **systemic** type of JRA affects the entire body, including joints and internal organs. It is the least common form of JRA and affects boys and girls equally. In addition to joint inflammation, symptoms include a high spiking fever lasting for weeks or months and a body rash. In some instances, there is inflammation of the heart and lungs along with enlarged liver or spleen. In a majority of cases, the high spiking fever and inflammation of the internal organs might disappear completely; however, joint inflammation will be chronic.

At present, there is no cure for juvenile arthritis. However, research is now being conducted in the areas of genetics and immunology. Treatment for severe periods of exacerbation consists of controlling joint inflammation, which is accomplished through medicine, rest, appropriately designed exercises, and, in some cases, surgery. During acute stages, complete bed rest is strongly recommended, and excessive weight bearing by inflamed joints should be avoided. In some instances, surgery might be performed to remove damaged tissue from the joint to prevent greater deterioration to bone and cartilage. Total hip replacements are now performed in some cases with great success.

Even during acute stages of JRA, joints should be exercised through the greatest possible range of motion at least once or twice a day so that range of motion can be maintained. For people who are unable to exercise independently, teachers or therapists can provide partial or total assistance.

The physical education program should stress exercises and activities that help increase or maintain range of motion so that permanent contractures do not develop and normal bone density is maintained (e.g., swimming, bike riding). Muscular strength and endurance activities should also be offered to decrease muscle atrophy. Isometric activities, such as hooking the fingers of both hands together and trying to pull them apart or placing the palms together and pushing, may be particularly helpful to encourage the development of the hand muscles. Another hand exercise involves squeezing objects of various sizes and shapes. Hand exercises are most important in order to maintain manipulative skills. Most people with severe joint limitation or deterioration should refrain from activities that twist, jar, or place undue stress on the joints; activities such as basketball, volleyball, and tennis might need to be modified accordingly.

Osteogenesis Imperfecta

Osteogenesis imperfecta (OI), also known as *brittle bone disease*, is an inherited condition in which bones are imperfectly formed. An unknown cause produces a defect in the protein matrix of collagen fibers. The defect reduces the amount of calcium and phosphorus (bone salts), which in turn produces a weak bone structure. Bones are easily broken, and when healed, they take on a shortened, bowed appearance. According to the Osteogenesis Imperfecta Foundation (2006), up to 50,000 people in the United States might be affected with OI. The disease occurs with equal frequency among males and females as well as all racial and ethnic groups.

There are four types of OI, which vary in characteristics and severity. The mildest and most common form of OI is type I, in which the bones are easily susceptible to fractures. People with type I experience most fractures before puberty, and bone deformity is minimal or nonexistent. Collagen fibers are normal but about half the normal amount. People with type I attain normal stature, but they have a tendency toward spinal curvature and a triangular-shaped face. Abnormal joint elasticity and low muscle tone are present. In addition, people with type I exhibit a thinning sclera (white portion of the eye) that takes on a blue, purple, or gray tint. About 50 percent of people with type I OI acquire a hearing loss in early adulthood. Many people with type I do not exhibit all the characteristics described here.

The most severe and least common form of OI is type II, which results in death at or shortly after birth. In type II, the child is born with multiple severe deformities and fractures, is of small stature, and has underdeveloped lungs. In type II, collagen fibers are improperly formed.

Children with type III OI have fractures present at birth, and bone deformity is often severe. They have poor muscle development and abnormal joint elasticity. They are short of stature and exhibit a barrel-shaped chest, a triangular face, and spinal curvatures. As in type I, eye sclera is abnormal in color, and hearing loss is possible. In type III, collagen fibers are improperly formed.

Type IV is between types I and III in severity. People with type IV have easily fractured bones; most fractures occur before puberty. Children tend to be shorter than average and have moderate bone deformity, a barrel-shaped chest, a tendency for spinal curvature, and a triangular face. Similar to types II and III, people with type IV have collagen fibers that are improperly formed. As with types I and III, hearing loss is possible, but unlike types I and III, eye sclera is normal in color.

Students with severe fractures and deformities might require the use of wheelchairs. Multiple fractures over a prolonged time have resulted in limb deformities and significant lower-limb limitations. People with milder types of OI can ambulate independently, whereas those with more moderate degrees of impairment need to use canes or crutches. There is no cure for the disease. At the present time, surgery, which consists of reinforcing the bone by inserting a steel rod lengthwise through its shaft, is the most effective treatment.

Physical activities such as swimming, bowling (with the use of a ball ramp), and the use of beach balls for striking and catching are safe because they do not place undue stress on the joints or bones. Because of abnormal joint elasticity, strength-building exercises and activities, which can increase joint stability, should be encouraged. This might be accomplished in a swimming environment because water buoyancy promotes movement without risk of new fractures. Most people with the disorder should not play power volleyball, basketball, or American football unless the games are modified appropriately.

Arthrogryposis

Arthrogryposis, or multiple congenital contractures, is a nonprogressive congenital disease of unknown origin. About 500 infants in the United States are born with arthrogryposis each year. The condition affects some or all of the joints and is characterized by stiff joints (contractures) and weak muscles. Instead of normal muscle tissue surrounding the joints, fatty and connective tissue is present. The severity of the condition varies; a person might be in a wheelchair or only minimally affected. Limbs commonly exhibit deformities and can be fixed in almost any position. In addition, affected limbs are usually small in circumference, and joints appear large. Surgery, casting, and bracing are usually recommended for people with deformities. Most typically, upper-limb involvement includes turned-in shoulders, extended and straightened elbows, pronated forearms, and flexed wrists and fingers; trunk and lower-limb involvement includes flexion and outward rotation of the hip, bent or straightened knees, and feet turned in and down. People with arthrogryposis typically have partially or completed dislocated hips. Other conditions associated with arthrogryposis include congenital heart defects, respiratory problems, and facial abnormalities. People with arthrogryposis almost always possess normal intelligence and speech.

Because people with arthrogryposis have restricted range of motion, their physical education program should focus on exercises and activities that increase flexibility. In addition, they should be taught games and sports that make effective use of leisure time. In most cases, exercises and activities appropriate for students with arthritis are also acceptable for those with arthrogryposis and OI. Swimming, an excellent leisure activity, encourages the development of flexibility and strengthens weak muscles surrounding joints. Other activities, modified when needed, include cycling, miniature golf, bowling, shuffleboard, bocce, and track and field.

Multiple Sclerosis

Multiple sclerosis (MS) is one of the most common central nervous system diseases among young adults. It is estimated that MS affects 2.5 million people worldwide and 400,000 people in the United States (National Multiple Sclerosis Society, 2008). It is a slowly progressive neurological disorder that might result in total incapacitation. About two-thirds of all those afflicted with the disease experience onset between the ages of 20 and 40, and the disorder affects more women than men. The disease might manifest itself in young children or the elderly as well, but this is rare. MS is characterized by changes in the white-matter covering (myelin sheath) of nerve fibers at various locations throughout the central nervous system (brain and spinal cord). The cause of MS is unknown, but most scientists believe that the disease involves a genetic susceptibility of the brain and spinal cord nerves to lose the ability to transmit electrical signals in combination with a viral infection and an immune response. Current research studies are focusing on myelin formation and its changes, drug therapy, immunotherapy, and diagnostic tests, among others. MS is diagnosed through a variety of tests, including neurological examination, blood tests, and magnetic resonance imaging (MRI), which can show lesions in the central nervous system.

In MS, the myelin sheath (which helps transmit signals) is destroyed and replaced by scar tissue; a lesion might vary from the size of a pinpoint to about 1 or 2 centimeters in diameter. People with MS exhibit various symptoms, depending on the location of the damage. The most common symptoms are extreme fatigue, heat intolerance, hand tremors, loss of coordination, numbness, general weakness, double vision, slurred speech, staggering gait, and partial or complete paralysis. According to current estimates, about 75 percent of people with MS experience extreme fatigue. The early stage of the disease is characterized by periods of exacerbation followed by periods of remission. As scar tissue continues to replace healthy tissue, symptoms tend to continue uninterrupted.

Because most people with MS are stricken in the most productive and enjoyable years of life, many have difficulty coping emotionally with the disease. Additional stress results from the fact that there is no established treatment to cure it. The main treatment objective is to maintain the person's functional ability as long as possible. Treatment should be directed toward preventing loss of range of motion (which would result in permanent contractures) and preserving strength and endurance. Many times, the disease progresses to a point at which the person needs braces or a wheelchair. Intensive therapy or physical conditioning during acute phases of MS might cause general body fatigue. An electrical stimulation device is now available to assist those who exhibit balance and lower-body coordination loss. The lightweight device is strapped to the leg just below the knee and triggers electrical impulses to leg and foot muscles.

Recent evidence suggests that moderate physical activity, judiciously programmed on a regular basis, significantly reduces non-activity-related fatigue, which a vast majority of people with MS experience. In addition to the physiological effects, regular physical activity provides psychological benefits as well. According to the National Multiple Sclerosis Society (2008), although current fatigue medications are helpful, moderate, regular physical activity seems to be more effective. Mild forms of physical activity that emphasize strength and endurance should be performed for short amounts of time. However, the duration and intensity of the activity should be programmed according to the person's level of exercise tolerance. Activities such as bowling, miniature golf, and table tennis are acceptable if regular rest breaks are provided. Stretching exercises and activities are also recommended to maintain range of motion. Activities incorporating balance and agility components might prove to be helpful for those exhibiting a staggering gait or varying degrees of paralysis. Many of these activities can be done in water. However, because of heat intolerance by many people with MS, water temperature must remain in the 80s (27-32 degrees Celsius).

Friedreich's Ataxia

An inherited neurological disease, **Friedreich's ataxia** usually manifests itself in childhood and early adolescence (boys and girls aged 10-15 years), but it can occur as late as the age of 20. Early onset is usually associated with a more serious course of the disease. Worldwide, Friedreich's ataxia affects about 1 in every 50,000 people, making it the most common in a group of hereditary ataxias (Muscular Dystrophy Association [MDA], 2006a). The disease was first identified in the 1860s by German neurologist Nikolaus Friedreich, who described the disease as a gradual loss of motor coordination and progressive nerve degeneration. The sensory nerves of the limbs and trunk (peripheral nerves) are affected and tendon reflexes are lost; the disease might progress either slowly or rapidly. When the disease progresses quickly, many people become wheelchair users by the late teens and early 20s.

Early symptoms include poor balance and lack of limb and trunk coordination, resulting in a clumsy, awkward, wide gait almost indistinguishable from the gait of ataxic cerebral palsy (CP). This is caused by the inability of the brain to regulate the body's posture and the coordination of its muscle movements. Fine motor control of the upper limbs tends to be impaired because tremors might be present. Atrophy is common in muscles of the distal limbs. People with the disease typically exhibit slurred speech and are prone to seizures. Most develop foot deformities such as clubfoot, high arches, and hammertoes, a condition in which the toes are curled because of tight flexor tendons of the second and third toes. As the disease progresses, spinal deformities, such as kyphosis and scoliosis, are common. Most people exhibit heart problems, such as heart murmur, enlarged heart, and constriction of the aorta and pulmonary arteries, making heart failure a leading cause of death in Friedreich's ataxia. Diabetes develops in 10 to 40 percent of people with Friedreich's ataxia. Visual abnormalities include nystagmus and poor visual tracking.

There is no known cure at this time, but researchers have recently identified a defective gene (frataxin) that is responsible for energy production in the cell. Therapy consists of managing foot and spinal deformities and cardiac conditions. Medication might be prescribed to control diabetes as well as cardiac, tremor, and seizure disorders. Certain experimental drugs have shown great promise for slowing and even reversing the fundamental cardiac abnormalities of the disease.

Some common diagnostic tests include the electromyogram, which measures electrical activity of muscle cells; nerve conduction velocity, which measures how fast nerves are transmitting impulses; and electrocardiogram, which determines if heart abnormalities exist.

Physical education activities should be planned to promote muscle strength and endurance and body coordination. Activities that develop muscles of the distal limbs such as the wrist, forearm, foot, and lower leg are recommended. The development of grip strength is essential for activities requiring implements, such as rackets and bats. Students exhibiting poor balance and lack of coordination are in need of balance training and activities that encourage development of fundamental locomotor movements. For those who have difficulties with fine motor control, activities might take the form of riflery, billiards, or archery. Remedial exercises are recommended for people with foot and spinal deviations. Games, exercises, and activities should be programmed according to individual tolerance levels of people with cardiac conditions; those who are prone to seizures should be closely monitored.

Myasthenia Gravis

Myasthenia gravis (MG), which means "grave muscular weakness," is a neuromuscular disease characterized by a reduction in muscular strength ranging from minimal to severe. In Western countries, MG affects about 2 to 7 out of every 10,000 people (MDA, 2006b). The disease was first identified and named in 1890 by a German medical professor, Wilhelm Erb. Even when strength is greatly reduced, the person still has enough strength to perform activities, but often this demands maximum or near-maximum effort. MG may be easily confused with muscular dystrophy because it is a neurological disease where muscle weakness affects the back, lower extremities, and intercostal muscles. It affects more females than males. Women often develop MG in their late teens and early 20s, whereas men usually acquire it after the age of 60. Although the exact cause is unknown, nerve impulses are prevented from reaching muscle fibers because the immune system produces destructive antibodies that block the muscle receptors at the neuromuscular junctions (points at which nerve endings meet muscle cells).

One of the main symptoms is abnormal fatigue. Muscles generally appear normal except for some disuse atrophy. Weakness of the extraocular and lid muscles of the eye occurs in about half of all cases; this results in drooping of the eyelid (ptosis) and double vision (strabismus). Because facial, jaw, and tongue muscles become easily fatigued, people might have problems chewing and speaking. Weakness of the neck muscles might prevent holding the head erect. Back musculature might also be weakened, which leads to misalignment of the spinal column, which can further restrict movement. Muscle weakness makes the execution of daily activities difficult and contributes to low levels of cardiorespiratory efficiency. When properly treated, most people can remain physically active. The disease is not progressive; it might appear gradually or suddenly. It commonly goes into remission for weeks, months, or years. Thus, those who are affected live in fear of recurrent attacks. MG is commonly treated with drugs that help strengthen the neuromotor transmission or suppress the immune system. However, these drugs have serious side effects when taken over a prolonged time. Most recently, a blood-flow exchange is now being used that removes antibodies from the blood that might interfere with the transmission of nerve impulses.

Physical activities should focus on the development of physical fitness. Because people with MG fatigue easily, their activities should be programmed in a progressive manner and according to individual tolerance levels that take into account the duration, intensity, and frequency of the activity. When the respiratory muscles are weakened, breathing activities are strongly recommended. It is important to strengthen weak neck muscles, especially when the program includes such activities as heading a soccer ball or hitting a volleyball. Fitness levels can be maintained during acute stages via swimming activities. Poor body mechanics resulting from weak musculature will ultimately affect locomotor skills; thus, remedial posture exercises and activities should be offered.

Guillain-Barré Syndrome

Guillain-Barré syndrome (GBS), also known as *infectious polyneuritis*, is a neurological disorder characterized by ascending paralysis of the peripheral nerves resulting in acute and progressive paralysis. Initially, the lower extremities become easily fatigued, and numbness, tingling, and symmetrical weakness are present. Paralysis, which usually originates in the feet and lower legs, progresses to the upper leg, continues to the trunk and upper extremities, and finally affects the facial muscles. Symptoms usually peak within a few weeks.

Typically symptoms then stabilize for a number of days, weeks, or months and recovery may be as short as a few weeks or as long as a few years. About one-third of those affected will have some weakness after three years. When initially affected, people involved in locomotor activities of an endurance nature, such as distance running, typically find themselves stumbling or falling as muscles of the feet and lower legs fatigue prematurely. The condition is frequently preceded by a respiratory or gastrointestinal infection, which suggests that a viral or bacterial infection might be the cause. Some authorities believe that the syndrome is an autoimmune disease. Neurologists, immunologists, and virologists are cooperatively investigating the syndrome.

Although rare, GBS occurs worldwide, affecting both genders equally and all ages and races. The National Institute of Neurological Diseases and Strokes (2008) reports that the syndrome affects about 1 person per 100,000. It can affect both infants and the elderly but seems to cluster in childhood and middle age. About 90 percent recover either completely or with minimal paralysis, and most walk unassisted. However, about 10 percent can die as a result of pulmonary complications. Acute-stage treatment includes passive range of motion, exercise, and rest.

For people who have made a complete recovery, no restrictions in physical activities are needed. However, those who do not completely recover exhibit weakness in limb and respiratory muscles. Their activities can focus on maintaining or improving cardiorespiratory endurance and strength and endurance of unaffected muscles. When significant weakness remains in the lower extremities, activities might need to be modified accordingly.

PROGRAM IMPLICATIONS

All people with amputations, dwarfism, or les autres conditions can benefit from physical education and sport. Should modifications or adaptations be needed, the type and degree of physical involvement, motor educability, interest level, and overall educational goals will determine them. Especially for people with unique physical and motor needs, physical education instruction needs to individualized and personalized.

General Guidelines

Several guidelines can be applied to programs for people with amputations, dwarfism, and les autres conditions. The guidelines that follow pertain to safety considerations, physical fitness, motor development, and implications for sports.

Safety Considerations

The physical impairments presented in this chapter are of a medical origin, and as such, the physical education teacher or coach needs to be aware of key safety considerations. People with physical limitations should be encouraged to experience as many postures as possible so that contractures do not develop, thus leading to decubitus ulcers that might require hospitalization. This is especially true for people in wheelchairs, such as students with advanced cases of DMD. Before getting a student into or out of a wheelchair or positioning a student who has obvious physical limitations, it is important to consult the student's special education teacher and physical therapist or occupational therapist (should the student be receiving such services). Safe handling of students is of the utmost concern, especially for those who are medically fragile. For example, it is especially important to never pull, push, or twist the limbs of children with arthritis, OI, or arthrogryposis.

Students with disabilities described in this chapter might tire easily, especially when performing large-muscle activities for an extended time. Fatigue exhibited in MS and DMD, for example, might cause someone to become frustrated, which in turn adversely affects performance. The instructor should permit rest breaks and player substitutions when endurance activities such as soccer and basketball are being played. Should teachers fail to take this fatigue into account and program activities without regard to students' personal intensity and duration levels, the risk of medical problems is high, especially for students with cardiopathic conditions. For example, children with DMD typically have cardiopathic involvement as an accompanying condition to muscle degeneration.

Thus, it is important that physical educators consult medical professionals before establishing physical education and sport programs to meet unique needs. This is especially important for students currently under the care of a physician and those receiving physical or occupational therapy. Teachers also should be in direct contact with the school nurse. Typically, the school nurse understands the student's medical condition and knows whether the student is taking any prescribed medications. Usually, the nurse has direct contact with the child's parents and personal physician should medical problems arise during the school day. Athreya and Lindsley (2005) provide excellent information on special health care needs during the school day for children with rheumatic diseases, and the information has direct relevance for all children who are chronically ill. The topics include administration of medications, emergency planning and procedures, selected exercises to prevent injury, and communication with school staff.

Physical Fitness

A sufficient amount of evidence suggests that appropriate levels of health-related physical fitness contribute to the overall wellness of people with amputations, dwarfism, and les autres conditions. The Amputee Coalition of America promotes a youth fitness program called *bio-fit*. The fitness program is designed for children with amputations, as well as their parents and caregivers, in which physical activities are led by Paralympians. (To learn more about the bio-fit program, visit www.amputee-coalition.org.) Winnick and Short (1999) recommend that young people with amputations and congenital anomalies be evaluated and achieve physical fitness standards that promote functioning consistent with positive health. This level of functioning includes appropriate fitness levels to adequately perform activities of daily living, including physical education and sport activities. The Brockport Physical Fitness Test (BPFT) (Winnick & Short, 1999) provides selected test items as well as projected standards for the evaluation of aerobic functioning, body composition, and musculoskeletal functioning (flexibility, muscular strength, and endurance).

Because the conditions described in this chapter are of a medical nature, certain precautions might need to be taken as health-related fitness programs are established and implemented. It is especially important that the teacher be sensitive to the frequency, intensity, duration, and mode of exercises and activities. With low fitness levels, it is recommended that intermittent training be used, especially for students who fatigue easily. Activities performed with greater frequency and with less intensity and duration are recommended. Exercises and activities that are enjoyable will tend to be continued over time, which increases the chances of these students adopting lifelong active lifestyles.

Because restricted movement is common in people whose conditions are described in this chapter, it is important that strength and flexibility be developed to appropriate levels of physical fitness. Range of motion is basic to overall fitness. Maximizing range of motion allows the opportunity to perform physical education and sport skills as well as activities of daily living in the most efficient and effective manner possible. Weak musculature and limited range of motion, if unattended, lead to permanent joint contractures that result in significant loss of movement capability, which in turn reduces the level of health-related fitness. Surburg (1999) provides flexibility and range-of-motion guidelines and exercise and activity examples that can be applied to people with physical conditions such as amputations, MS, DMD, and JRA.

Motor Development

Many times, amputations and les autres impairments (and to a lesser extent dwarfism) prevent people from experiencing movement patterns essential to normal motor development. As a result, delays in the development of motor skills and patterns are common. Lack of ability to control movements contributes to the performance of inappropriate motor skills and patterns. Children with congenital amputations, for example, are frequently unable to execute fundamental movements in an appropriate manner. Children born with the absence of an upper limb or with multiple limb deficiencies may have motor delays due to the inability to use their arms to crawl, pull to a stand, or manipulate objects (e.g., toys, balls), whereas children born with the absence of a lower limb might be delayed in acquiring locomotor patterns such as walking and running. Muscle atrophy or weakness prevents people from developing the strength and endurance levels needed to perform fundamental movements vital to overall health.

Physical education programs should encourage the sequential development of fundamental motor patterns and skills essential for participation in games, sport, and leisure activities. When attempting to enhance motor development, physical educators should be concerned primarily with the manner in which a movement is performed rather than with its outcome. For example, they should be concerned with the mechanics of the movement within the physical limitations of the student (e.g., dwarfism). The goal of every physical education and sport program should be to encourage students to achieve maximum motor control and development within their ability levels. The motor development of young people with disabilities covered in this chapter might be assessed using standardized tests as well as less formal procedures, including ecological task analysis (ETA) and rubrics. Interested readers are encouraged to consult chapter 4 for information on assessment of motor development and skills.

Implications for Teaching Sport in Physical Education

Physical education teachers are encouraged to integrate many of the sport activities described in the Adapted Sport section of this chapter into their physical education programs. For example, sitting volleyball, a DS/USA event, can be incorporated into a physical education program as a means of developing eye–hand coordination as well as offering an opportunity for sport competition. Other events included in organized competition such as DAAA competition (e.g., bowling, archery, cycling, bocce) can be taught.

Amputations

In general, a physical education program for students with amputations can follow the same guidelines as those for students without disabilities. Aside from missing limbs, people with amputations are considered able bodied. However, the location and extent of the amputations might require modifications in some activities.

Most students with amputations typically use prosthetic devices in physical education activities. A person with unilateral lower-limb amputation usually continues to use the device for participation in American football, basketball, volleyball, and most leisure activities. As previously stated, more mechanically efficient devices are now being worn by athletes with unilateral lower-limb amputations. In some situations, a unilateral BE, AE, or shoulder amputee might consider the device a hindrance to successful performance and discard it during participation; this is common in baseball or softball. Such was the case with Jim Abbott, a former Major League Baseball pitcher who did not wear a prosthetic device for his BE congenital amputation. Of course, in some activities, such as swimming, the prosthetic device must be removed. Currently, the National Federation of High Schools (NFHS) allows participating athletes to wear prosthetic devices for interscholastic sports such as football, basketball, gymnastics, soccer, baseball, and field and ice hockey. However, a device cannot be used if it is more dangerous to other players than a corresponding human limb or if it gives the user an advantage over an opponent (NFHS, 2008).

Participation in physical education and sport requires some adaptations depending on the location and extent of the amputation and the type of activity. Table 15.1 provides some general participation guidelines for people with amputations.

Physical Fitness

Similar to people with other physical conditions, people with amputations might need to increase their levels of health-related physical fitness. The BPFT can be used to assess the health-related fitness of young people with amputations and congenital anomalies. Depending on the site of amputation, various test items might be chosen to assess aerobic functioning, body composition, and musculoskeletal functioning. For example, a person with a unilateral AK amputation would perform the Target Aerobic Movement Test (TAMT) to assess aerobic functioning. In this test, appropriate physical activities can be chosen to assess aerobic functioning. An activity would be deemed appropriate if it is of sufficient intensity to reach a minimal target heart rate and sustain that rate within a given target zone. Sustaining a level of moderate physical activity for least 15 minutes would be a minimal general standard for young people with amputations and congenital anomalies. Other BPFT items for a student with a unilateral AK amputation would be triceps and subscapular skinfold measures (body composition) and a bench press (muscular strength and endurance).

Students with bilateral BK or AK amputations often have lower levels of aerobic functioning level than upper-limb amputees because their locomotor activities might be severely restricted. For long-term aerobic training programs for students with lower-limb amputations, activities should be chosen that do not cause overuse injuries or skin breakdown (Pitetti & Pedrotty, 2003). Suggested aerobic activities include swimming, using an arm-propelled tricycle, or using arm, rowing, and cycle ergometers. To further encourage aerobic development, the physical educator could offer activities in which a wheelchair can be used, such as marathon racing or slalom events.

Muscular strength and endurance and flexibility should be developed for all parts of the body, even at the site of the amputation or anomaly. The remaining muscles surrounding the site also need to develop so that they remain in balance with the unaffected side. For a person with only a partial limb amputation, such as an ankle or wrist disarticulation, exercises and activities should be programmed to encourage the most normal possible use of the remaining limb segment. Absence of a limb can also affect balance and leverage when performing resistance activities. Some strength activities are better and more safely performed without the use of a prosthetic device. According to DiRocco (1999), if a force of resistance runs

Table 15.1 **Participation Guide for Students With Amputations in Selected Activities**

Activity	Upper extremity	Lower extremity (BK)	Lower extremity (AK)
Archery	R A	R	R
Baseball or softball	R	R	R A
Basketball	R	R	WC A
Bicycling	R	R	R
Bowling	R	R	R
Field hockey	R	I	WC A
Football	R	R	I
Golf	R A	R	R
Rifle shooting	R A	R	R
Skiing (downhill)	R	R	R A
Cross-country skiing	R	R	R A
Soccer	R	R	I
Swimming	R	R	R
Table tennis	R	R	R
Tennis	R	R	I
Track	R	R	WC A
Volleyball	R	R	WC A

Note: A = adapted; R = recommended; I = individualized; WC = wheelchair.

Adapted from Adams and McCubbin, 1991.

through the shaft of the prosthetic device, then it would be acceptable to wear it for that particular exercise. For example, it would be acceptable if a person were wearing a prosthetic device when performing the bench press, because the weight would be distributed through the shaft of the prosthesis when the person attempted to lift the weight.

Both unilateral and bilateral AK amputees have a tendency to be obese and thus should be encouraged to follow a weight-reduction diet along with a program of regular, vigorous physical activity. Short, McCubbin, and Frey (1999) describe several desirable characteristics of a weight loss physical activity program for people with disabilities. Some of these characteristics include raising daily total energy expenditure, deemphasizing activity intensity and emphasizing activity duration, exercising daily, participating with partners or small groups, and doing well-liked activities. Before a student begins a physical activity program, Lockette and Keyes (1994) recommend that amputation type, functional range of motion, strength, balance and stability, and skin integrity be assessed.

Motor Skills

Limb deficiency of the upper or lower limb can affect a person's level of motor skills. For example, acquired BE, AE, BK, or AK amputations of the dominant limb can initially result in awkward or clumsy performance of motor skills. This might be more pronounced for adolescents and adults who have already mastered motor skills with their dominant limbs (e.g., overarm throwing, kicking a ball). The absence of a limb most often affects the center of gravity, to a greater degree in lower-limb amputees than in upper-limb amputees. The result is difficulty with activities requiring balance. Developing static and dynamic balance is crucial to the performance of locomotor skills such as walking, running, or hopping as well as sitting in a wheelchair. Activities that foster the development of balance and proper body alignment should be encouraged; these might include traversing an obstacle course, performing on a minitrampoline, or walking a balance beam. Speed and agility might also be adversely affected, especially in people with lower-limb deficiencies. People with unilateral

AK and bilateral BK or AK amputations are most affected and might have difficulty in locomotor activities that require quick changes of direction, such as basketball, football, soccer, and tennis.

Although unilateral BK or BE amputees can participate effectively in physical education and competitive sport, those with bilateral upper or lower amputations will have activity restrictions. Bilateral upper-limb amputees can successfully engage in activities that involve the lower extremities to a significant degree—for example, skating, soccer, and jogging.

Unilateral AK amputees can effectively participate in activities such as swimming, water skiing, snow skiing, weightlifting, and certain field events (e.g., shot put and javelin) that do not emphasize locomotion and agility. Those with bilateral BK amputations will be more limited in activities such as track events, football, or basketball, which involve jumping, hopping, or body contact. Bilateral AK amputees are much more restricted in their activities, usually relying on a wheelchair part time and crutches at other times. Activities such as archery, badminton, and riflery, which can be performed from a sitting or prone position, are appropriate.

Dwarfism

Students with dwarfism should be encouraged to perform in regular physical education and sport activities. The development of health-related physical fitness and motor skills are important aspects of any physical education program, and students with dwarfism should have the same opportunities to develop them as other students. This is especially true because many people with achondroplasia are overweight or obese. However, certain considerations need to be addressed in programs for developing physical fitness and motor skills.

Physical Fitness

Restricted range of motion, obesity, and joint defects might predispose people to dislocations and joint trauma, and this is especially true for people with achondroplasia. Thus, maintaining flexibility, especially at the elbow joint, is important. Exercises and activities that place undue stress on weight-bearing joints should be avoided or modified to accommodate this limitation. For example, jogging can be replaced with walking or riding a bicycle, and volleyball can be performed with a lighter ball. Swimming, which promotes flexibility and cardio-respiratory endurance, is an excellent activity for

people with achondroplasia because it does not place undue stress on the joints.

Motor Skills

Because of shorter limbs, movement quality might be affected in some activities, including ball throwing and catching, striking, and locomotor skills such as running, jumping, and hopping. Implements such as golf clubs, rackets, and hockey sticks will need to be adjusted according to the size of the student. Failure to use appropriately sized implements results in inappropriate or inefficient execution of motor skills.

Les Autres

Atrophied or weak muscles (e.g., DMD), reduced range of motion (e.g., JRA), and balance and coordination problems (e.g., Friedreich's ataxia) may hinder students with les autres conditions in performing physical activities. Many of the conditions presented in this chapter are progressive (e.g., DMD, Friedreich's ataxia, MS, MG); that is, muscles become weaker regardless of the amount of exercise or activity. As a result, it is important to maintain current levels of muscular strength and endurance as long as possible. DiRocco (1999) suggests that people with progressive muscular disorders not go beyond 50 percent of their maximum resistance weight when performing muscular strength activities. According to DiRocco, the exercise intensity is too great if functional strength does not return within 12 hours of exercise; this should be monitored closely by the teacher or coach. When affected muscles are weaker than antigravity strength (e.g., DMD), added weight resistance (e.g., formal weights) is of no use in developing strength (Tarnopolsky, 2003). Rather, the goal is to maintain full range of motion against gravity. Once this is accomplished, gradual resistance exercises can be employed.

Exercises and activities that are fun increase the likelihood that students will perform them regularly. For young children, activities should be short and might include rhythmic activities, active lead-up games, and obstacle courses. For adolescents, emphasis should be placed on lifelong activities such as racket sports, skating, cycling, hiking, and swimming. Students in wheelchairs can participate in activities such as sledge hockey, rugby, seated aerobics, and wheelchair tennis.

Because limitations presented in this chapter prevent extended periods of activity, low aerobic fitness levels are common. For example, people with MS typically exhibit general body fatigue (not related to exercise), which reduces their capacity to perform physical activity over an extended length of time. This inactivity makes people with les autres conditions prone to obesity (e.g., DMD, amputations) and ultimately places them at greater risk for coronary heart disease and other associated conditions (e.g., osteoporosis). For students with moderate degrees of orthopedic impairments, low-impact aerobics, cycling, swimming, and brisk walking can achieve aerobic gains. Maintaining a satisfactory level of health-related fitness reduces the risk of associated debilitating conditions, such as osteoporosis.

Severe limitations in strength and flexibility can also hinder people with les autres conditions from acquiring the motor skills they need to become successful in sport and leisure activities. The inability to perform these skills reduces the chances of being physically active and thus places these students at greater risk of reduced health.

Whether physical activity is performed for purposes of fitness or enhanced motor skills, proper warm-up and cool-down activities that emphasize flexibility are needed. This is especially true for people with conditions that limit joint flexibility, such as JRA, OI, and other les autres conditions that might elicit spasticity. Daily range-of-motion exercises are recommended for those who have joint-limiting conditions such as JRA, arthrogryposis, and GBS. Surburg (1999) offers several excellent recommendations for the development of flexibility and range of motion for people with disabilities.

INCLUSION

As is true for other disabilities, students with amputations, dwarfism, and les autres conditions must be encouraged to participate in regular physical education classes unless the individualized education program (IEP) team decides otherwise. Most people with these conditions can be safely and effectively included in regular physical education settings. And, unless students with les autres conditions are severely physically impaired, most can also be safely and effectively included in regular physical education settings. Even students with severe physical impairments can succeed in regular physical education settings as long as appropriate activities are performed and support services (e.g., teachers' aides) are provided.

Both universal design and differentiated instruction can be used to foster inclusion in regular physical education. Universal design focuses on equipment that can be modified and used by all students regardless of ability, whereas differentiated instruction uses various instructional techniques to maximize learning for all students regardless of learning styles. In all cases, decisions about inclusion must be made on an individual basis in consultation with the student's IEP team. The impairments described in this chapter affect physical functioning, not intellectual functioning, so students will clearly understand verbal and written directions as well as rules and strategies for games and sports. In certain cases, teachers might need to structure activities to suit the participants' abilities.

Students with amputations or other lower-limb deficiencies could play goalie in soccer or floor hockey and could pitch or play first base in softball, and they could be provided the option of riding a stationary bike when students without disabilities are required to run over a long distance. Students with dwarfism can be safely and effectively included in regular physical education classes as long as the proper-sized equipment is used to accommodate short limbs, including shorter and lighter implements such as bats, rackets, and hockey sticks.

Students with reduced muscular strength and aerobic capacity (e.g., muscular dystrophy, MS, Friedreich's ataxia) can also be safely and effectively included in regular physical education classes as long as activities are modified or activity options are provided. For example, when programming activities for the development of arm and shoulder strength, students with reduced strength can perform modified push-ups (with knees touching the floor) or chin-ups with a horizontal bar (performed from a supine position on the floor) while students without disabilities perform push-ups and chin-ups in a traditional manner.

Students with joint limitations or deficiencies, such as those with JRA, arthrogryposis, and OI, can also benefit from regular physical education classes. For example, when programming activities to enhance aerobic capacity, these students can swim or participate in low-impact aerobics while students without disabilities participate in more traditional forms of rope jumping, jogging or running over distance, and bench stepping.

ADAPTED SPORT

At almost all age levels, people with amputations, dwarfism, and les autres conditions now have the opportunity to become involved in competitive sport. Organizations such as DS/USA and DAAA assist people in reaching their maximum potential in sport. DS/USA and DAAA offer a variety of sporting events that in many cases have been modified for specific disabilities. Athletes are able to participate in these events on the basis of their functional abilities. These organizations are members of the Committee on Sports for the Disabled (COSD) of the United States Olympic Committee (USOC) and members of the ISOD.

Amputations

DS/USA sponsors organized competition for athletes with amputations (as well as competition for people with birth defects, visual impairments, and neurological conditions). Founded in 1967 by Vietnam veterans with disabilities, DS/USA is the largest multisport and multidisability organization in the United States. National and international competition for athletes with amputations is based on the nine-level classification system described earlier in this chapter. People with combinations of amputations not specified in the classification system are assigned to the class closest to the actual disability. For example, a combined AK and BK amputee would be placed in class A1, whereas a combined AE and BE amputee would be in class A5. People with single-arm paralysis are tested for muscle strength of the arms and hands. The following movements are tested and scored on a scale from 0 to 5, with 5 being the greatest function:

- Shoulder flexion, extension, abduction, and adduction
- Elbow flexion and extension
- Wrist dorsal and volar flexion
- Finger flexion and extension at the metacarpophalangeal joints
- Thumb opposition and extension

Classification for participants with single-arm paralysis is limited to A6 (AE) or A8 (BE).

Amputee competition at both the national and international levels takes place in track events such as the 100-, 200-, and 400-meter dashes and 800- and 1,500-meter runs, and in field events such as the shot put, discus, javelin, long jump, and high jump. National and international competition might also be offered in basketball, volleyball, lawn bowling, pistol shooting, table tennis, cycling, archery, weightlifting, and swimming (100 m backstroke, 400 m breaststroke, 100 and 400 m freestyle,

and 4 × 50 m individual medley). Volleyball and basketball are offered in both sitting and ambulatory categories. In each sport, athletes of similar classifications compete with prostheses, except for those with double AK or combined upper and lower amputations.

In addition to national and regional competitions sponsored by DS/USA, amputees are eligible to compete in events sponsored by Wheelchair and Ambulatory Sports, USA (WASUSA), the NWBA, and the National Foundation of Wheelchair Tennis (NFWT) as long as they have an amputation of the lower extremity and require the use of a wheelchair.

Dwarfism

The DAAA was established in 1985 for the purpose of providing organized sport competition to people with dwarfism. Although independent of the LPA, the DAAA maintains ties with that organization. Sports include track (15 m, 20 m, 40 m, 60 m, and 100 m runs and 4 × 100 m relay), field (shot put, tennis and softball throw, discus, soft discus, and javelin), swimming (freestyle, backstroke, and breaststroke at 25, 50, and 100 m), basketball, bocce (individual and team), equestrian sports, soccer, volleyball, table tennis, and powerlifting. Separate competition is offered for men and women except for basketball, volleyball, and team bocce, in which both men and women play on the same team. Skiing is offered in the winter.

Athletes are classified for open division (ages 16-39) track, field, and swimming events. There are three classes for track alone, which are based on a ratio of standing height to sitting height, and three classes for field and swimming, which are based on the ratio of arm span to biacromial breadth. This system, which is now being refined, is used only for national DAAA events. For international events, the ISOD functional classification system is used.

To be eligible for competition, people with disproportionate dwarfism must be equal to or less than 5 feet (152 cm) in height, whereas people with proportionate dwarfism must be equal to or less than 4 feet, 10 inches (147 cm) in height. Athletes participate in one of five divisions (open, youth, master, wheelchair, or futures). Youth events (7-15 years) emphasize achieving one's personal best, whereas the futures division is for children younger than 7 years of age. In this division, a limited number of events are offered on a noncompetitive basis. The DAAA also offers clinics and developmental events.

Les Autres

Historically, the les autres movement was associated with CP sport. Les autres athletes performed at the National Cerebral Palsy Games in 1981 and 1983 along with CP athletes. At the National Cerebral Palsy/Les Autres Games in Michigan in 1985, they participated in their own separate competition. In 1988, the United States Les Autres Sports Association (USLASA) held a national competition in Nashville. Currently, the BlazeSports National Disability Sports Alliance (BNDSA) serves les autres athletes. These athletes compete among themselves in events such as track and field, swimming, volleyball, archery, bocce, cycling, shooting, table tennis, wheelchair team handball, and powerlifting. Currently, the classification system for les autres athletes coincides with that of the ISOD. Classes are divided into wheelchair and ambulatory sections. The number of eligible classes might vary with each event. Currently, for track and field competition, there are five wheelchair classes and five ambulatory classes, with the recent addition of three jumping classes for certain field events.

SUMMARY

This chapter has described the conditions of amputations, dwarfism, and les autres as they relate to physical education and sport. Physical and motor needs were described and program and activity suggestions presented. Recognizing the medical nature of these conditions, teachers and coaches are encouraged to plan activities in consultation with allied medical professionals and the student's personal physician.

REFERENCES

Adelson, B. (2005). *Dwarfism*. Baltimore: Johns Hopkins University Press.

Arthritis Foundation. (2008). *Juvenile arthritis fact sheet*. Atlanta: Arthritis Foundation.

Athreya, B.H., & Lindsley, C.B. (2005). A general approach to management of rheumatic diseases in children. In J.T Cassidy, R.F. Petty, R.M. Laxer, & C.B. Lindsley (Eds.), *Textbook of pediatric rheumatology* (3rd ed., pp.184-203). Philadelphia: Elsevier.

Cassidy, J.T., Petty, R.E, Laxer, R.M., & Lindsley, C.B. (Eds.). (2005). *Textbook of pediatric rheumatology* (3rd ed.). Philadelphia: Elsevier.

DiRocco, P. (1999). Muscular strength and endurance. In J.P. Winnick & F.X. Short (Eds.), *The Brockport physical fitness training guide* (pp. 39-73). Champaign, IL: Human Kinetics.

Little People of America (LPA). (2008). Frequently asked questions. Retrieved from www.lpaonline.org/mc/page.do?sitePageId=84634.

Lockette, K.F., & Keyes, A.M. (1994). *Conditioning with physical disabilities*. Champaign, IL: Human Kinetics.

Muscular Dystrophy Association (MDA). (2006a). *Facts about Friedreich's ataxia*. Tucson, AZ: Author.

Muscular Dystrophy Association (MDA). (2006b). *Facts about myasthenia gravis*. Tucson, AZ: Author.

National Federation of State High School Associations (NFHS). (2008). *Football rules book*. Indianapolis: Author.

National Institute of Neurological Diseases and Strokes. (2008). *Guillain-Barré syndrome*. Bethesda, MD: National Institutes of Health.

National Limb Loss Information Center. (2008). Fact sheet. Retrieved from www.amputee-coalition.org/fact_sheets/amp_stats_cause.html.

National Multiple Sclerosis Society. (2008). Just the facts. Retrieved from www.nationalmssociety.org/multimedia-library/brochures/index.aspx.

Osteogenesis Imperfecta Foundation. (2006). *OI: A guide for medical professionals, individuals, and families affected by OI*. Gaithersburg, MD: Author.

Pitetti, K.H., & Pedrotty, M.H. (2003). Lower-limb amputation. In J.L. Durstine & G.E. Moore (Eds.), *ACSM's exercise management for persons with chronic diseases and disabilities* (2nd ed., pp. 230-235). Champaign, IL: Human Kinetics.

Short, F.X., McCubbin, J., & Frey, G. (1999). Cardiorespiratory endurance and body composition. In J.P. Winnick & F.X. Short (Eds.), *The Brockport physical fitness training guide* (pp. 13-37). Champaign, IL: Human Kinetics.

Surburg, P. (1999). Flexibility/range of motion. In J.P. Winnick & F.X. Short (Eds.), *The Brockport physical fitness test training guide* (pp. 75-119). Champaign, IL: Human Kinetics.

Tarnopolsky, M.A. (2003). Muscular dystrophy. In J.L. Durstine & G.E. Moore (Eds.), *ACSM's exercise management for persons with chronic diseases and disabilities* (2nd ed., pp. 254-261). Champaign, IL: Human Kinetics.

Winnick, J.P., & Short, F.X. (1999). *The Brockport physical fitness test manual*. Champaign, IL: Human Kinetics.

WRITTEN RESOURCES

Arthritis Foundation. (2006). *When your student has arthritis*. Atlanta: Author.

This brochure provides an overview of arthritis for teachers. It includes a school activities checklist for students as well as information on education rights and how teachers can help. The brochure can be obtained by writing to the Arthritis Foundation, P.O. Box 932915, Atlanta, GA 31193, or by visiting their Web site at www.arthritis.org.

inMotion magazine, 900 East Hill Ave., Ste. 205, Knoxville, TN 37915; Web site: www.amputee-coalition.org.

This is a bimonthly publication of the Amputee Coalition of America for amputees, caregivers, and health care professionals.

Osteogenesis Imperfecta Foundation. (2006). *Therapeutic strategies for osteogenesis imperfecta: A guide for physical therapists and occupational therapists.* Gaithersburg, MD: Author.

This brochure provides information on the condition, safe handling procedures, adaptive equipment, specific care tasks, and more. Although written for therapists, it is highly relevant for regular physical education teachers and adapted physical education specialists.

AUDIOVISUAL RESOURCES

Aerobics for amputees. [VHS]. (n.d.). Disabled Sports USA, 451 Hungerford Dr., Ste. 100, Rockville, MD 20850.

This video depicts vigorous exercises for ambulatory people (e.g., with impaired balance or coordination) who can exercise standing up but cannot do fancy footwork that might upset balance.

Take control with exercise [DVD]. (2006). Arthritis Foundation, P.O. Box 932915, Atlanta, GA 31193.

This 60-minute fitness DVD provides a balanced exercise routine for people with arthritis. The DVD includes two optional endurance routines to create a more challenging workout and a relaxing guided imagery segment to help manage stress.

What is DS/USA? [VHS]. (n.d.). Disabled Sports USA, 451 Hungerford Dr., Ste. 100, Rockville, MD 20850.

This video features the organizational structure of DS/USA as well as competition footage and interviews of DS/USA athletes and staff.

Yoga for MS and related conditions [VHS]. (2000). National Multiple Sclerosis Society NW, Ste. 750, Washington, DC 20036.

This video is for anyone with limited mobility from conditions such as MS, mild arthritis, chronic fatigue, and chronic illness. The video describes various yoga positions along with frequency and duration. It can be obtained by the national chapter at the address listed here or by contacting your local National Multiple Sclerosis chapter.

ELECTRONIC RESOURCES

Amputee Coalition of America: www.amputee-coalition.org.

This Web site provides information and education regarding limb loss and limb differences. The organization provides publications, peer support, and various programs and events (e.g., bio-fit), with special attention to young people.

Spinal Cord Disabilities

Luke E. Kelly

Jerry and Rick are playing one-on-one basketball, and whoever reaches 15 first wins. The score is 14 all, and Jerry has the ball. Rick is on defense and knows he has to stop Jerry, or he will have to listen to him bragging the rest of the day. Rick positions himself in the center of the lane and gives Jerry an alley to his right. Rick knows Jerry has no left-hand shot and figures he can overplay his right side. Jerry starts at midcourt and drives toward Rick. Jerry makes a head fake first to the left and then to the right and then pulls up and shoots. Rick immediately yells "Travel!" as the shot swishes through the net.

"Travel? Who are you kidding?" responds Jerry. "You overcommitted and got skunked."

"Keep dreaming," says Rick. "You took four pushes on your rims without dribbling before taking that shot—that's traveling in my book."

Jerry smiles. "I didn't think you could count and play defense at the same time."

Rick takes the ball out and drives to Jerry's right. Jerry moves to block the lane. Rick does a 180 in his chair, dribbles the ball once on the floor, puts the ball on his lap, gives two quick pushes on his rims, picks up the ball, and shoots. "That's all she wrote!" he yells as the ball banks off the backboard and in.

"Nice move," says Jerry. "Another game?"

Rick and Jerry both have spinal cord injuries resulting in the loss of the use of their legs. They met at a rehabilitation center after their injuries and began playing wheelchair basketball. They now both play on the local wheelchair basketball team.

The focus of this chapter is to review the common spinal cord disabilities and their implications for physical education. After reading this chapter, teachers should be able to modify their programs or develop appropriate alternative programs to accommodate the needs of students with spinal cord disabilities. Spinal cord disabilities are conditions that result from injury to, or disease of, the vertebrae or the nerves of the spinal column. These conditions are almost always associated with some degree of paralysis caused by damage to the spinal cord. The degree of the paralysis is a function of the location of the injury on the spinal column and the number of neural fibers subsequently destroyed. Three such spinal cord disabilities are examined in this chapter: traumatic injuries to the spine resulting in tetraplegia and paraplegia, poliomyelitis, and spina bifida. This chapter also reviews several common spinal column postural deviations that can adversely affect body mechanics and predispose the spine to injury: scoliosis, kyphosis, lordosis, spondylolysis, and spondylolisthesis. Finally, this chapter covers orthotic devices commonly associated with spinal cord disabilities as well as physical education and sport implications.

CLASSIFICATIONS

The physical education teacher should be aware of the systems for categorizing spinal cord disabilities. Medical classifications are based on the segment of the spinal cord that is impaired, whereas sport organizations classify people by their abilities in order to match similarly able athletes for competition.

Medical Classifications

As illustrated in figure 16.1, spinal cord injuries are medically labeled or classified according to the segment of the spinal column (i.e., cervical, thoracic, lumbar, or sacral) and the number of the vertebra at or below which the injury occurred. For example, a person classified as a C6 complete has a fracture between the sixth and seventh cervical vertebrae that completely severs the spinal cord. The location of the injury is important because it provides insight related to the functions that might be affected. The extent of the spinal cord lesion is

ascertained through muscle, reflex, and sensation testing.

The actual effect of a spinal cord injury is best understood in terms of what muscles can still be used, how strong these muscles are, and what can functionally be done with the muscles in the context of self-help skills (eating, dressing, grooming), movement (wheelchair, ambulation, transfers, bed), vocational skills, and physical education skills.

Table 16.1 provides a summary of the major muscle groups innervated at several key locations along the spinal column, with implications for the movements, abilities, and physical education activities that might be possible with lesions at these locations. The functional abilities remaining are cumulative as one progresses down the spinal column. For example, someone with a lesion at or below T1 would have all the muscles and abilities shown at and above that level.

Sport Classifications

Sport organizations that sponsor athletic events for people with spinal cord disabilities use different classification systems to equate athletes for competition. The most widely used system is the one used by Wheelchair and Ambulatory Sports, USA (WASUSA) (2010), formerly the National Wheelchair Athletic Association (NWAA) and Wheelchair Sports, USA. This system classifies athletes by functional ability into one of several classes based on the sporting event, degree of **muscular functioning**, and actual performance during competition. Muscular functioning includes the evaluation of such actions as arm function, hand function, trunk function, trunk stability, and pelvic stability in relation to their importance in performing a given sporting event. This classification system provides an efficient way of equating competition among a diverse group of athletes with varying types of spinal cord disabilities. The functional classification system is illustrated in table 16.2. Note that although functional abilities are the key criteria in functional classification systems, there is a relation between these sport classifications and the level of spinal cord damage. The approximate spinal cord lesion level associated with the National Wheelchair Basketball Association (NWBA) and several of the functional sport classifications are shown in figure 16.2 on page 322.

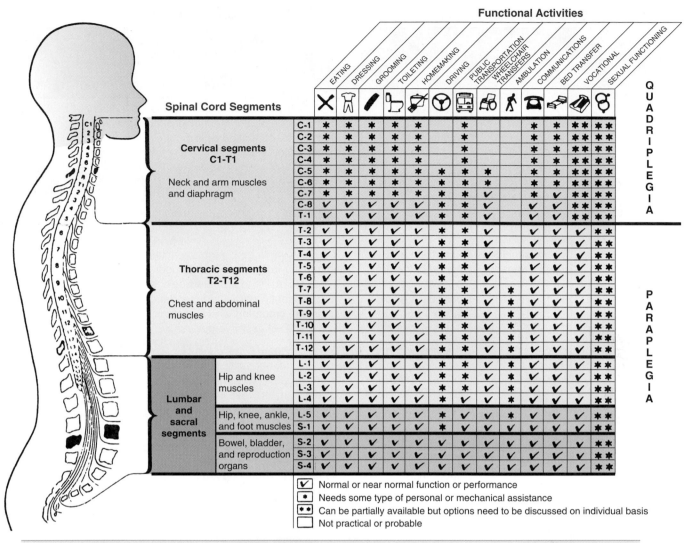

- ✔ Normal or near normal function or performance
- ∗ Needs some type of personal or mechanical assistance
- ∗∗ Can be partially available but options need to be discussed on individual basis
- ☐ Not practical or probable

FIGURE 16.1 Functional activity for spinal cord injuries.

Courtesy of Healthsouth Harmarville Rehabilitation Hospital, Pittsburgh, PA 15238.

SPINAL CORD INJURIES

Damage to the spinal cord can occur as a result of infectious diseases or a variety of genetic and environmental causes. This section describes the common causes of spinal cord disabilities and the implications for planning and delivering physical education.

Traumatic Tetraplegia and Paraplegia

Traumatic tetraplegia and paraplegia refer to spinal cord injuries that result in the loss of movement and sensation. **Tetraplegia**, or quadriplegia, is used to describe the more severe form, in which all four limbs are affected. **Paraplegia** refers to the condition in which primarily the lower limbs are affected.

The amount of paralysis or loss of sensation associated with tetraplegia and paraplegia is related to the location of the injury (how high on the spine) and the amount of neural damage (the degree of the lesion). Figure 16.1 shows a side view of the spinal column, accompanied by a description of the functional abilities associated with various levels of injury. The functional abilities indicated for each level should be viewed cautiously because the neural damage to the spinal cord at the site of the injury might be complete or partial. If the cord is severed completely, the person will have no motor control or sensation in the parts of the body innervated below that point.

Table 16.1 Potential Functional Abilities by Select Lesion Locations

Lesion locations	Key muscles innervated	Potential movements	Associated functional abilities	Sample physical education activities
C4	Neck, diaphragm	Head control, limited respiratory endurance	Can control an electronic wheelchair and other computer electronic devices that can be controlled by a mouth-operated joystick.	Riflery, bowling
C5	Partial shoulder, biceps	Abduction of the arms, flexion of the arms	Can propel a wheelchair with modified rims, can assist in transfers, can perform some functional arm movements using elbow flexion and gravity to extend the arm.	Swimming
C6	Major shoulder, wrist extensors	Abduction and flexion of the arms, wrist extension, possibly a weak grasp	Can roll over in bed; might be able to transfer from wheelchair to bed; improved ability to propel wheelchair independently; partial independence in eating, grooming, and dressing using special assistive devices.	Billiards, putting
C7	Triceps, finger extensions, finger flexions	Stabilization and extension of the arm at the elbow, improved grasp and release but still weak	Independent in wheelchair locomotion, bed, sitting up, and in many cases, transferring from bed to wheelchair; increased independence in eating, grooming, and dressing.	Archery, crossbow, table tennis
T1	All upper-extremity muscles	All upper body lacks trunk stability and respiratory endurance	Independent in wheelchair and bed transfers, eating, grooming, dressing, and toileting; can ambulate with assistance using long leg braces, pelvic band, and crutches.	Any activities from a wheelchair
T6	Upper-trunk muscles	Trunk stability, improved respiratory endurance	Can lift heavier objects because of improved stability, can independently put own braces on, can ambulate with low spinal attachment, pelvic band, long leg braces, and crutches using a swing gait but still depends on wheelchair as primary means of locomotion.	Track and field, bowling, weightlifting
T12	Abdominal muscles and thoracic back muscles	Increased trunk stability, all muscles needed for respiratory endurance	Can independently ambulate with long leg braces including stairs and curbs, uses a wheelchair only for convenience.	Competitive swimming, marathon racing
L4	Lower back, hip flexors quadriceps	Total trunk stability, ability to flex the hip and lift the leg	Can walk independently with short leg braces and bilateral canes or crutches.	Some standing activities
S1	Hamstring and peroneal muscles	Bend the knee, lift the foot up	Can walk independently without crutches, might require ankle braces or orthotic shoes.	Normal physical education

Table 16.2 Functional Classifications

Sport or class	Description
ARCHERY	
AR1	Defined as tetraplegic archers in a wheelchair. The archer with upper cervical lesions and triceps not functional against resistance (i.e., test grades 0-3) and the archer with lower cervical lesions and normal triceps power (i.e., test grades 4-5), wrist extensors, and flexors but no finger flexors or extensors of functional value (i.e., below grade 3 on the muscle test scale) might use a release, compound or recurve bow, strapping, and body support. All AR1 archers are allowed to use a compound bow, a release or finger, or any combination of these. The equipment will be standard International Archery Federation (FITA) equipment except for the addition of the release and compound bow. The sighting aids must be according to current FITA shooting rules, (A) outdoor target archery, article 504, archer's equipment, (a) (v). Archers who use mechanical release may receive assistance in putting arrow in their bows.
AR2	An open class for wheelchair archers. The archers use equipment according to FITA rules. For AR2 division, there must be no more than 15 cm slackness in the back upholstery of the wheelchair to be measured from the front of the main vertical support of the chair back. No strapping to the chair is allowed in the AR2 classification. The height of body support from the top of the chair to the armpit shall be no less than 11 cm.
AR3	A standing division for disabled archers will be permitted at some events sanctioned by Wheelchair Archery, USA.
FIELD EVENTS	
F51	Events: Club, discus *Functional level* No grip with nonthrowing arm. (Use resin or adhesive-like substance for grip.) Discus: Have little control of the discus because finger movements are absent. Throw with a flat trajectory. Club: May throw forward or backward over head. Use either thumb and index finger, index and middle finger, or middle and ring finger grip. (When throwing backward, the athlete is using strong elbow flexors.) *Neurological level* C6 *Anatomical level* Have functional elbow flexors and wrist dorsiflexors. May have elbow extensors (up to power 3) but usually not wrist palmar flexors. May have shoulder weakness. Have no sitting balance. *Old level* 1A Complete *Note:* This system applies to the spinal-injured athlete. Athletes whose disability is a result of polio or other causes may show different movement and function than described here. However, the total function of the athlete in this specific event shall be similar to that of the spinal cord injury description.
F52	Events: Shot, discus, and javelin *Functional* Have difficulty gripping with nonthrowing arm. Shot: Unable to form a fist, and therefore do not usually have finger contact with the shot at the release point. Unable to spread fingers apart. Discus: Have no functional finger flexors (i.e., unable to form a fist). Have difficulty placing fingers over the edge of the discus, but might do so with the aid of contracture or spasticity. Javelin: Usually grip the javelin between the index and middle fingers, but may use the gap between the thumb and index finger or between the middle and ring fingers. These athletes might have slight function between the digits of the hand. *Neurological level* C7

(continued)

Table 16.2 *(continued)*

Sport or class	Description
FIELD EVENTS	
F52 *(cont'd)*	*Anatomical capability* Functional elbow flexors and extensors, wrist dorsiflexors, and palmar flexors. Have good shoulder muscle function. May have some finger flexion and extension but not functional. *Old level* 1B Complete: No sitting balance. 1A Incomplete: Have ability to lift trunk off the back of a chair and to perform backward and forward movement. May also be able to rotate the trunk. *Note:* This system applies to the spinal-injured athlete. Athletes whose disability is a result of polio or other causes may show different movement and function than described here. However, the total function of the athlete in this specific event shall be similar to that of the spinal cord injury description.
F53	Events: Shot, discus, and javelin. *Functional* Have nearly normal grip with nonthrowing arm. Shot: Usually a good fist can be made. Can spread the fingers apart but not with normal power. Can grasp the shot put when throwing. Discus: Have good finger function to hold discus. May be able to import spin on the discus. Are able to spread and close the fingers, but not with normal power. Javelin: Usually grip the javelin between the thumb and index finger. Have ability to hold the javelin because of hand muscles that spread and close the fingers. *Neurological level* C8 *Anatomical capability* Have full power at elbow and wrist joints. Have full or almost full power of finger flexion and extension. Have functional but not normal intrinsic muscles of the hand (demonstrable wasting). *Old class* 1C Complete (no sitting balance) 1B Incomplete with trunk movements
F54	Events: Shot, discus, and javelin *Functional* Have no sitting balance. Usually hold onto part of the chair while throwing. Complete class 2 and upper class 3 athletes have normal upper limbs. They can hold the throwing implement normally. They have no functional trunk movements. Incomplete 1C athletes who have trunk movements with hand function like F3. *Neurological level* T1-T7 *Anatomical capability* See above Functional section for this classification. *Old class* 1C Incomplete 2 Complete Upper 3 Complete
F55	Events: Shot, discus, and javelin *Functional* Three trunk movements might be seen in this class: 1. Off the back of a chair (in an upward direction) 2. Movement in the backward and forward plane 3. Some trunk rotation These athletes have fair to good sitting balance. They cannot have functional hip flexors (i.e., ability to lift the thigh upward in the sitting position). They may have stiffness of the spine that improves balance but reduces the ability to rotate the spine.

Sport or class	Description
	FIELD EVENTS
F55 *(cont'd)*	Shot and javelin: Tend to use forward and backward movements. Discus: Predominantly use rotary movements. *Neurological level* T8-L1 *Anatomical capability* Normal upper-limb function. Have abdominal muscles and spinal extensors (upper or more commonly upper and lower). May have nonfunctional hip flexors (grade 1). Have no adductor function. *Old class* Lower 3, Upper 4 Amputee: Bilateral hip disarticulation
F56	Events: Shot, discus, and javelin *Functional* Have good balance and movements in the backward and forward plane. Have good trunk rotation. Can lift the thighs (i.e., off the chair; hip flexion). Can press the knees together (hip adduction). May have the ability to straighten the knees (knee extension). May have some ability to bend the knees (knee flexion). *Neurological level* L2-L5 *Anatomical capability* See above Functional section for this classification. *Old class* Lower 4/Upper 5 Amputee: Bilateral transfemoral amputations whose residual limb length is less than half of the distance from the olecranon process to the tip of the middle finger.
F57	Events: Shot, discus, and javelin *Functional* Have good sitting balance and movements in the backward and forward plane. Usually have good balance and movements toward one side (side-to-side movements) due to presence of one functional hip abductor, on the side that movement is toward. Usually can bend one hip backward (i.e., push the thigh into the chair). Usually can bend one ankle downward (i.e., push the foot onto the foot plate). The side that is strong is important when considering how much it will help functional performance. *Neurological level* S1-S2 *Anatomical capability* See above Functional section for this classification. *Old class* Lower 5/Class 6 Amputee: Bilateral transfemoral amputations whose residual limb length is greater than half of the distance from olecranon process to tip of middle finger. Single hip disarticulation.
F58	Events: Shot, discus, and javelin *Functional* Have normal sitting balance and trunk movements in all planes. Usually are able to stand and possibly walk with braces or by locking knees straight. Are unable to recover balance in standing position when balance is challenged and will fall when attempting throws with full effort in standing. Not more than 70 points in the lower limbs in those who choose to compete from a seated position because of poor dynamic standing balance. Amputee: Single transfemoral amputation, bilateral transtibial amputations competing in a seated position.

(continued)

Table 16.2 *(continued)*

Sport or class	Description
	TRACK
T51	*Functional* May use elbow flexors to start (back of wrist behind pushing rim). Hands stay in contact or close to the pushing rim, with the power coming from elbow flexion. The old technique is to use the palms of the hands to push down on the top of the wheel in a forward direction. *Neurological level* C6 *Anatomical capability* Have functional elbow flexors and wrist dorsiflexors. Have no functional elbow extensors or wrist T1 palmar flexors. May have shoulder weakness. *Old class* 1A Complete
T52	(Adults, Juniors, and International) *Functional* Usually uses elbow flexors to start, but might use elbow extensors. Power from pushing comes from elbow extension, wrist dorsiflexion, and upper chest muscles (Matson technique). Additional power may be gained by using the elbow flexors when the hands are in contact with the back of the wheel. The head may be forced backward (by the use of neck muscles), producing slight upper-trunk movements. *Neurological level* C7 *Anatomical capability* Have functional pectoral muscles, elbow flexors and extensors, wrist dorsiflexors, radial wrist movements, and some to all palmar flexors, and may have ulnar wrist movements. May have finger flexors or extensors. Do not have the ability to perform finger abduction and adduction (spread fingers and bring them together). *Old class* 1B Complete
T53	*Functional* Have normal or nearly normal upper-limb function. Have no active trunk movements. When pushing, the trunk is usually lying on the legs. The trunk may rise with the pushing action. Usually use a hand flick technique for power (or friction technique). May use the shoulder to steer around curves. Interrupt pushing movements to steer and have difficulty resuming the pushing position. When braking quickly, the trunk stays close to pushing position. *Note:* Scoliosis (curvature of the spine) usually interferes with abdominal and back muscle function. *Neurological level* T1-T7 *Anatomical capability* Have normal or nearly normal upper-limb function. Have no abdominal function. May have weak upper spinal extension. *Old class* Incomplete 1C 2 Upper 3

Sport or class	Description
TRACK	
T54	*Functional* Have backward movement of the trunk. Usually have rotation movements of the trunk. May use trunk movements to steer around curves. Usually do not have to interrupt pushing stroke rate around curves. When stopping quickly, the trunk moves toward an upright position. Use abdominal muscles for power, particularly when starting but also when pushing. *Neurological level* T8-S2 *Anatomical capability* Have back extension, which usually includes both upper and lower extensors. Usually have trunk rotation (i.e., abdominal muscles). *Old class* Lower 3 4-5-6
SWIMMING	
S1-S10	Freestyle, backstroke, butterfly
S1	Tetraplegia or polio comparable to a complete lesion below C5. Very severe quadriplegia with poor head and trunk control and very limited movements of all limbs for propulsion. Severe arthrogryposis affects all four limbs with severely restricted movement in the upper limbs and limited propulsion in the lower limbs.
S2	Tetraplegia or polio comparable to a complete lesion below C6. Tetraplegia comparable to a complete lesion below C7 with additional plexus paralysis or restriction in one arm. Very severe quadriplegia with very limited function in range of movements of the two upper limbs for propulsion. Severe musculoskeletal impairment with very poor shoulder function comparable to complete tetraplegia below C6.
S3	Tetraplegia or polio comparable to a complete lesion below C7. Some incomplete tetraplegics below C6 or comparable polio. Severe spastic quadriplegia with poor trunk control and asymmetrical movement of the upper limbs for propulsion. Severe quadriplegia with spasticity and athetosis involving poor head and trunk control, limited coordination for propulsion in all four limbs. Moderate quadriplegia, poor trunk control. Spasticity and athetosis or ataxia with moderate propulsion in all four limbs. Severe dysmelia in all four limbs or amputation of all four limbs with short stumps. Severe muscular atrophy of both upper and lower limbs. Arthrogryposis affecting all four limbs with moderate to fair propulsion of the lower limbs only.
S4	Tetraplegia or polio comparable to a complete lesion below C8 with good finger extension. Incomplete tetraplegia below C7 or comparable polio. Severe diplegia with involvement of the trunk and limited propulsion in shoulders and elbows. Musculoskeletal impairment comparable to complete tetraplegia below C8. Severe dysmelia of three limbs. Arthogryposis affecting all four limbs with moderate to fair propulsion from the upper limbs and possible restricted movement in the lower limbs.
S5	Complete paraplegia or polio comparable to below T1-T8. Incomplete tetraplegia below C8 with reasonable trunk function or comparable polio. Severe diplegia with fair trunk control and fair propulsion in shoulders and elbows. Severe hemiplegia. Severe to moderate athetosis or ataxia and spasticity. Musculoskeletal impairment comparable to incomplete tetraplegia below C8. Achondroplasia not more than 130 cm for women and 137 cm for men with additional handicap (what causes propulsion problems). Moderate dysmelia in three limbs. Arthrogryposis affecting all four limbs with moderate to fair propulsion in upper and lower limbs.

(continued)

Table 16.2   *(continued)*

Sport or class	Description
SWIMMING	
S6	Complete paraplegia or polio comparable to below T9-L1 with no leg function suitable for swimming. Moderate diplegia with fair trunk control and fair to good propulsion in shoulders and elbows. Moderate hemiplegia with severe restriction in the more affected upper limb. Moderate athetosis or ataxia. Above-elbow and above-knee amputation of the same side. Double above-elbow amputation. Congenital amputations of three limbs. Dysmelia with shortened arms (2/3 or normal) and above-knee amputation. Achondroplasia not more than 130 cm for women and 137 cm for men. Above-knee amputation plus severely functionally restricted shoulder or the same side.
S7	Complete paraplegia or polio comparable to below L2-L3. Moderate diplegia with minimal upper-body and trunk involvement. Moderate hemiplegia. Double below-elbow amputation. Double above-knee amputation, shorter than 1/2. Above-elbow and above-knee amputation on opposite sides. One paralyzed upper limb and severely restricted functions of the leg on the same side.
S8	Complete paraplegia or polio comparable to below L4-L5. Minimal diplegia with minimal trunk involvement. Minimal evidence of hemiplegia. Minimal spasticity in four limbs. Double above-knee amputation, stumps longer than 1/2. Double below-knee amputation, not longer than 1/3. Single above-elbow amputation or comparable functionally complete brachial plexus lesion. Double hand amputation, 1/4 or palm inclusive. Severe joint restriction in the lower limbs.
S9	Walking paraplegia with minimal involvement in limbs. Polio with one nonfunctional leg. Slight overall functional coordination problems. Single above-knee amputation. Single through-knee amputation. Double below-knee amputation, stumps longer than 1/3. Single through-elbow amputation. Single below-elbow amputation. Partial joint restriction in the lower limbs, one side more affected.
S10	Polio and cadua equina syndrome S1/2 minimal affective lower limbs. Clear evidence of slight spasticity or ataxia in the specific tests. Paresis on one leg. Severe restriction of one hip joint. Single below-knee amputation. Double foot amputation. Hand amputation with loss of 1/2 of hand.
SB1-SB10	Breaststroke
SB1	Tetraplegia or polio comparable to a complete lesion below C6. Tetraplegia comparable to a complete lesion below C7 with additional plexus paralysis or restriction in one arm. Very severe quadriplegia with limited function in range of movement of the upper limbs from propulsion. Severe quadriplegia with spasticity and athetosis involving poor head and trunk control. Limited coordination for propulsion in all four limbs. Severe musculoskeletal impairment with very poor shoulder function comparable tetraplegia below C6. Severe dysmelia in all four limbs or amputation of all four limbs with very short stumps. Severe arthrogryposis affecting all four limbs with severely restricted movement in the upper limbs.
SB2	Tetraplegia or polio comparable to a complete lesion below C7. Some incomplete tetraplegia below C6 or comparable polio. Moderate quadriplegia, poor trunk control, spasticity and athetosis or ataxia with moderate propulsion in all four limbs. Severe dysmelia of three limbs. Severe muscular atrophy of both upper and lower limbs. Musculoskeletal impairment comparable to complete tetraplegia below C7.
SB3	Tetraplegia or polio comparable to a complete lesion below C8, with good finger extension. Incomplete tetraplegia below C7 or comparable polio. Complete paraplegia or polio comparable to below T1-T5. Complete paraplegia T1-T8 with surgical rods from T4/6, which includes the lumbar spine or severe contractures in the hips that result in balance being affected. Severe diplegia with involvement of the trunk; limited propulsion in shoulders and elbows. Musculoskeletal impairment comparable to complete tetraplegia below C8. Moderate dysmelia in three limbs. Arthrogryposis affecting all four limbs with moderate to fair propulsion from the upper or lower limbs and severely restricted movement in the upper or lower limbs.

Sport or class	Description
SWIMMING	
SB4	Complete paraplegia or polio comparable to below T6-T10. Complete paraplegia T9-L1 with surgical rods from T4/6, which includes the lumbar spine or severe hip contractures that affect balance. Incomplete tetraplegia below C8 with reasonable trunk function or comparable polio. Severe diplegia with fair trunk control and fair propulsion in shoulders and elbows. Severe hemiplegia. Severe to moderate athetosis or ataxia and spasticity. Musculoskeletal impairment comparable to incomplete tetraplegia below C8. Arthrogryposis affecting all four limbs with moderate to fair propulsion in the upper and lower limbs.
SB5	Complete paraplegia or polio comparable to below T11-L1 with no leg function useful for swimming. Complete paraplegia L2-L3 with surgical rods from T4/6, which includes the lumbar spine or severe hip contractures that affect balance. Moderate diplegia with fair trunk control and fair to good propulsion in shoulders and elbows. Severe to moderate hemiplegia. Severe to moderate athetosis or ataxia. Above-elbow and above-knee amputation of the same side. Double above-knee amputation, stumps shorter than 1/2. Achondroplasia not more than 130 cm for women and 137 cm for men with additional handicap that causes propulsion problems. Above-knee amputation plus severely functionally restricted shoulder of the same side. Dysmelia with shortened arms and additional dysfunctions of legs.
SB6	Complete paraplegia or polio comparable to below L2-L3. Moderate diplegia with minimal upper-body and trunk involvement. Moderate hemiplegia. Moderate athetosis or ataxia. Double above-knee amputation, stumps longer than 1/2. Achondroplasia not more than 130 cm for women and 137 cm for men. Dysmelia with shortened arms (2/3 of normal) and above-knee amputation. One paralyzed upper limb and severely restricted function of the leg of the same side.
SB7	Complete paraplegia or polio comparable to below L4-L5. Minimal diplegia with minimal trunk involvement. Moderate hemiplegia. Minimal spasticity in four limbs. Double above-elbow amputation, Double below-knee amputation, stumps shorter than 1/2. Above-elbow amputation and above-knee amputation on opposite sides. Severe joint restrictions in the lower limbs.
SB8	Walking paraplegia with minimal involvement in lower limbs. Polio with one nonfunctional leg. Slight overall functional coordination problems. Slight evidence of hemiplegia. Double below-elbow amputation. Single through-elbow amputation. Single-above elbow amputation or comparable functionally complete brachial plexus lesion. Single below-elbow amputation, stump less than 1/4. Double below-knee amputation, stumps lower than 1/2. Single above-knee amputation. Single through-knee amputation. Single below-knee amputation, stump less than 1/4. Partial joint restriction in the lower limbs, one side more affected.
SB9	Polio minimally affected lower limb and cauda equina syndrome S1/2. Clear evidence of slight spasticity or ataxia in specific tests. Single below-knee amputation, stump longer than 1/4. Single below-elbow amputation, longer than 1/4. Foot amputation. Hand amputation, less than 1/3. Incomplete Erb's palsy or brachial plexus lesion. Perthes disease with restriction in hip mobility. Severe hip restriction combined with further dysfunctions of the leg. Ankylosis of both ankle joints combined with minimal leg weakness.

Note: WASUSA also has functional classifications for table tennis and weightlifting.

| | Old Wheelchair Sports, USA | Functional Wheelchair Sports, USA | | NWBA Basketball |
		Track	Field	
C1				
C2				
C3				
C4				
C5				
C6	IA	T51(C6)	F51(C6)	I
C7	IB	T52(C7-C8)	F52(C7)	
C8	IC		F53(C8)	
T1	II	T53(T1-T7)	F54(T1-T7)	
T2				
T3				
T4				
T5	III			
T6				
T7				II
T8		T54(T8-S2)	F55(T8-L1)	
T9				
T10	IV			
T11				
T12				
L1				
L2	V		F56(L2-L5)	III
L3				
L4				
L5				
S1			F57(S1-S2)	
S2				
S3				
S4				

FIGURE 16.2 Spinal cord levels associated with functional sport classification systems.

Reprinted, by permission, from Wheelchair and Ambulatory Sports, USA, 2010, *2010-2011 Competition rules for track and field and road racing* (St. Peters, MO: Wheelchair Sports USA).

This loss will be permanent because the spinal cord cannot regenerate itself. In many cases, however, damage to the spinal cord is only partial, resulting in retention of some sensation and motor control below the site of the injury. In a case involving partial lesion, the person might experience a gradual return of some muscle control and sensation over several months following the injury. This is a result not of regeneration of damaged nerves but rather the alleviation of pressure on nerves at the injury site caused by bruising or swelling. Although damage to the spinal cord currently results in a permanent loss of function, a wealth of research is looking for ways to reverse this process. Promising research results have been found in animals using innovative drug therapies, reactivating dormant nerve cells, and using embryonic transplant therapy. For additional information on these and other advances, consult the resources at the end of this chapter.

Incidence

The National SCI Statistical Center (2008) estimates that about 12,000 people suffer spinal cord injuries each year in the United States. Among the major causes are automobile accidents (42 percent), falls (27.1 percent), acts of violence (15.3 percent), athletic injuries (7.4 percent), and other accidents (8.1 percent). Unfortunately, a large percentage of these

First Aid for Suspected Neck Injury

The American Medical Association (2000) recommends the following procedures whenever a neck injury is suspected:

A neck injury should be suspected if a head injury has occurred. *Never* move a victim with a suspected neck injury without trained medical assistance unless the victim is in imminent danger of death (from fire, explosion, or a collapsing building, for example). WARNING: Any movement of the head (forward, backward, or side-to-side) can result in paralysis or death. (pp. 191-192)

▶ **Immediate Treatment If the Victim Must Be Moved**

Do not wait and hope someone else will know what to do in this situation. Do the following:

1. Immobilize the neck with a rolled towel or newspaper about 4 inches (10 cm) wide wrapped around the neck and tied loosely in place. (Do not allow the tie to interfere with the victim's breathing.) If the victim is being rescued from an automobile or from water, place a reasonably short, wide board behind the victim's head and back. The board should extend to the victim's buttocks. If possible, tie the board to the victim's body around the forehead and under the armpits. Move the victim very slowly and gently. Do *not* let the body bend or twist.

2. If the victim is not breathing or is having great difficulty in breathing, tilt the head slightly back to provide and maintain an open airway.

3. Restore breathing and circulation if necessary.

4. Summon paramedics or trained ambulance personnel immediately.

5. After moving the victim, place folded towels, blankets, clothing, sandbags, or other suitable objects around the head, neck, and shoulders to keep the head and neck from moving. Place bricks or stones next to the blankets for additional support.

6. Keep the victim comfortably warm.

---

injuries happen to students of high school age, with the incidence being greater among males (82 percent) than females (18 percent). When spinal cord injury is suspected, proper handling of the patient immediately after the injury can play a major role in minimizing additional damage to the spinal cord.

Treatment and Educational Considerations

The treatment of people with spinal cord injuries usually involves three phases:

1. Hospitalization
2. Rehabilitation
3. Return to the home environment

Although the three phases are presented as separate, there is considerable overlap between the treatments provided within each phase. During the **hospital phase**, the acute medical aspects of the injury are addressed, and therapy is initiated. Depending on the severity of the injury, the hospital stay can last up to several months. Many people with spinal cord injuries are then transferred from the hospital to a rehabilitation center. As indicated by its name, the **rehabilitation phase** centers on adjustment to the injury and mastery of basic living skills (e.g., toileting, dressing, transfers, and wheelchair use) with the functional abilities still available. Near the end of the rehabilitation phase, a transition is begun to move the person back into the home environment. In the case of a student, the transition involves working with parents and school personnel to make sure that they have the appropriate skills and understanding of the student's condition and needs and that they know what environmental modifications will be required to accommodate those needs.

The abilities outlined in table 16.1 are those that can potentially be achieved by people with spinal cord injuries. To achieve these abilities, people must accept their conditions, not be hindered by any secondary health problems, and be highly motivated to work in rehabilitation.

One of the major secondary problems associated with spinal cord injuries is psychological acceptance of the limitations imposed by the injury and the loss of former abilities. Counseling is usually a major component of the treatment plan during rehabilitation. The rate of adjustment and the degree to which people learn to cope with their disabilities vary tremendously.

People with spinal cord injuries are susceptible to a number of secondary health conditions. One of their most common health problems is pressure sores or **decubitus ulcers**. These are caused by the lack of innervation and reduced blood flow to the skin, and they most commonly occur at pressure points where a bony prominence is close to the skin (buttocks, pelvis, and ankles). Because of the poor blood circulation, these sores can easily become infected and are extremely slow to heal. The prevention of pressure sores involves regular inspection of the skin, the use of additional padding in troubled areas, and regular pressure releases (changes in position that alleviate the pressure). Individually designed seat cushions are used by many people to help better distribute pressure and avoid pressure sores. Keeping the skin dry is also important because the skin is more susceptible to sores when it is wet from urine or perspiration.

A problem closely related to pressure sores is bruising of the skin. Because no sensation is felt in the limbs that are not innervated, it is not uncommon for them to be bruised or irritated from hitting or rubbing against other surfaces. Injuries of this nature are common in wheelchair activities such as basketball if appropriate precautions are not taken. Because these bruises are not felt, they can go unnoticed and eventually can become infected.

A third health problem commonly encountered by people with spinal cord injuries is urinary tract infections. Urination is controlled by some form of catheterization on an established schedule. Urinary infections occur when urine is retained in the bladder and backs up into the kidneys. Urinary tract infections can be severe and usually keep the patient bedridden for a prolonged time, which is counterproductive for attitude, rehabilitation, and skill development. Bowel movements must also be carefully monitored to prevent constipation and incontinence. Bowel movements are usually controlled by a combination of diet and mild laxatives. In cases where bowel movements cannot be controlled by diet, a tube is surgically inserted into the intestine. The tube exits through a small opening in the side of the body and is connected to a bag that collects the fecal excretions.

Two other closely associated problems that frequently accompany spinal cord injuries are spasticity and contractures. **Spasticity** is an increase in muscle tone in muscles that are no longer innervated because of the injury. This increased muscle tone can nullify the use of still-innervated muscles. The term *spasm* is frequently used to describe sudden spasticity in a muscle group that can be of sufficient force to launch someone out of a wheelchair. The best treatment for spastic muscles is to stretch them regularly, particularly before and after rigorous activity. **Contractures** can frequently occur in the joints of the lower limbs if they are not regularly, passively moved through the full range of motion. A high degree of spasticity in various muscle groups can also limit the range of motion and contribute to contractures.

The last problem commonly associated with spinal cord injuries is a tendency toward obesity. The loss of function in the large-muscle groups in the lower limbs severely reduces the calorie-burning capacity of people with spinal cord injuries. Unfortunately, a corresponding loss in appetite does not also occur. Many people with spinal cord injuries tend to resume their habitual caloric intake or even increase it because of their sedentary condition. Weight and diet should be carefully monitored to prevent obesity and the secondary health hazards associated with it. Once weight is gained, it is extremely difficult to lose.

A major key to success in rehabilitation and in accepting a disability is motivation. Many people with spinal cord disabilities initially have great difficulty accepting the loss of previous abilities and, subsequently, are reluctant to work hard during the tedious and often painful therapy. Recreational and sport activities are commonly used in both counseling and therapy to provide reasons for working hard and as distractions. A physical educator should be sensitive to the motivational needs of a student returning to a program with a spinal cord disability. Although sport can be a motivator for many, it can also highlight the loss of previous skills and abilities.

The physical education teacher should anticipate needs in the areas of body image, upper-body strength, range of motion, endurance, and wheelchair tolerance. These needs, together with the student's functional abilities, should be analyzed to determine what lifetime sport skills and wheelchair sports are most viable for future participation. These activities then become the annual instructional goals for the physical education program.

Although a student with a spinal cord injury is still learning to deal with the injury, the physical educator can assist by anticipating the person's needs and planning ahead (see the student placement application example). This might involve reminding the student to perform **pressure releases** at regular intervals (lifting the weight off the seat of the chair by doing an arm press on the arm supports of the chair or just shifting the sitting position) or bringing extra towels to class to absorb extra moisture in the chair. Because spasticity and spasms are common, stretching at the beginning of class and regularly during the class is recommended. Finally, pads should be provided to prevent bruising in active wheelchair activities. As the student becomes accustomed to the condition, most of these precautions will become automatic habits. A student who has an external bag should be reminded to empty and clean it before physical education class. In contact activities, care should be taken to protect the bag from contact. For swimming, the bag should be removed and the opening in the side covered with a watertight bandage.

Poliomyelitis

Poliomyelitis, commonly called *polio*, is a form of paralysis caused by a viral infection that affects the motor cells in the spinal cord. The severity and degree of paralysis vary with each person and depend on the number and location of the motor cells affected. The paralysis might be temporary, occurring only during the acute phase of the illness (in which case the motor cells are not destroyed), or it may be permanent if the motor cells are destroyed by the virus. Bowel and bladder control, as well as sensation in the involved limbs, are not affected in this condition.

Incidence

The occurrence of polio is rare in school-age children today because of the widespread use of the Salk vaccine. The Centers for Disease Control and Prevention (CDC) (2000) has reported that no new cases of polio have been reported in the United States for the past 20 years. This is in comparison to over 20,000 reported cases in the United States

APPLICATION EXAMPLE

Student Placement

Setting: Individualized education program (IEP) committee meeting

Student: Fran is 16 years old and returning to school after suffering a complete T6 spinal cord lesion as a result of a motorcycle accident. Prior to the accident, Fran was an excellent athlete. During rehab Fran was cooperative and worked hard. She has expressed concerns about returning to school, particularly physical education class.

Issue: What is the best way to transition Fran back into physical education? What would be the most appropriate physical education placement?

Application: On the basis of the previous information and a meeting with Fran, her parents, and the rehab staff, the following is decided:

▸ Fran will receive an adapted physical education program, which will include an individually designed strength training and endurance program.

▸ The program will be initiated in a weight training unit in an integrated setting with support services as needed.

▸ Prior to inclusion in the integrated setting, the physical education staff will work with Fran on learning how to safely perform the exercises in her routine.

▸ Special arrangements will be worked out with Fran to address any concerns she has related to changing clothes for physical education.

As Fran's strength and endurance improve, she will begin to train to participate in the school's 5K race that is held each spring.

in 1952. Although new cases of polio are uncommon, many people who have previously had polio have experienced a recurrence of the symptoms of polio later in life. This reoccurrence of symptoms, referred to as *post-polio syndrome*, affects about 25 percent of former polio victims, usually 35 to 40 years after the original onset of the disease. This condition is caused by the overuse of the remaining muscle fibers over time, resulting in muscle pain, joint pain, increased fatigue, and loss of strength.

Treatment and Educational Considerations

During the acute, or active, phase of the illness, the child is confined to bed. The illness is accompanied by a high fever and pain and paralysis in the affected muscles. After the acute phase, muscle testing is conducted to determine which muscles are affected and to what degree. Rehabilitation is then begun to develop functional abilities with the muscles that remain.

Depending on the severity of the paralysis, a child might require instruction in walking with crutches or long leg braces or using a wheelchair. When the lower limbs have been severely affected, it is not uncommon for bone deformities to occur as the child develops. These deformities can involve the hips, knees, ankles, or feet and frequently require surgery to correct.

Specific activity implications are difficult to provide for people who have had polio because their range of abilities can be so great. Physical educators need to accurately evaluate the abilities and limitations imposed by the condition for each student and then make appropriate placement and instructional decisions.

Many people with only one involved limb or mild involvement of two limbs will already have learned to compensate for the condition and can participate in an integrated physical education setting. Others with more extensive or severe involvement might require a more restrictive setting for the provision of adapted physical education services. Care should be taken not to totally remove these children from inclusive physical education. Whatever the degree of involvement, these children have typical play interests and the desire to be with their classmates.

Regardless of the physical education placement, the emphasis should be on optimal development of the muscles the student does have. Priority should be given to lifetime sport skills and activities that can be carried over and pursued for recreation and fitness when the school years are past. Swimming is an excellent example of an activity that promotes lifetime fitness, provides recreation, and prepares one for other activities such as sailing and canoeing.

Spina Bifida

Spina bifida is a congenital birth defect in which the neural tube fails to close completely during the first four weeks of fetal development. Subsequently, the posterior arch of one or more vertebrae fails to develop properly, leaving an opening in the spinal column. Spina bifida can be detected prior to birth, usually during the 16th to 18th weeks, by a combination of blood tests, amniocentesis, and sonograms. There are three classifications of spina bifida, based on which structures, if any, protrude through the opening in the spine.

Myelomeningocele is the most severe and, unfortunately, the most common form of spina bifida. In this condition the covering of the spinal cord (meninges), cerebrospinal fluid, and part of the spinal cord protrude through the opening and form a visible sac on the back (see figure 16.3*a*). Some degree of neurological damage and subsequent loss of motor function are always associated with this form.

Spina bifida **meningocele** is similar to the myelomeningocele form except that only the spinal cord covering and cerebrospinal fluid protrude into the sac (see figure 16.3*b*). This form rarely has any neurological damage associated with it.

Occulta is the mildest and least common form of spina bifida. In this condition, the defect is present in the posterior arch of the vertebra, but nothing protrudes through the opening (see figure 16.3*c*). No neurological damage is associated with this type of spina bifida.

Once detected soon after birth and surgically corrected, the meningocele and occulta forms of spina bifida have no adverse ramifications. The greatest threat in these conditions is from infection prior to surgery.

Incidence

Because some degree of neurological damage is always associated with the myelomeningocele type of spina bifida, it will be the form discussed in the remainder of this section. About 10 children out of every 10,000 live births have spina bifida (Spina Bifida Association, 2008), and 80 percent of these children have the myelomeningocele form. The degree of neurological damage associated with spina bifida myelomeningocele depends on

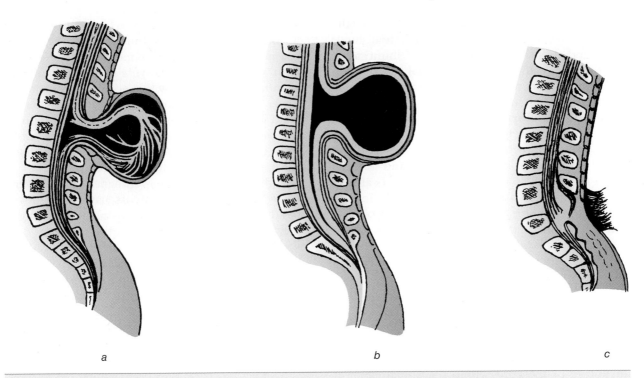

a

b

c

FIGURE 16.3 Diagram of the three types of spina bifida: *(a)* myelomeningocele, *(b)* meningocele, and *(c)* occulta.

Reprinted from *Yearbook of Physical Medicine and Rehabilitation,* G.G. Deaver, D. Buck, and J. McCarthy, Spina bifida, pg. 10, Copyright 1952, with permission from Elsevier.

the location of the deformity and the amount of damage done to the spinal cord. Fortunately, spina bifida occurs most commonly in the lumbar vertebrae, sparing motor function in the upper limbs and limiting the disability primarily to the lower limbs. Bowel and bladder control are almost always lost. The muscle functions and abilities presented in table 16.1 for spinal cord lesions in the lumbar region can also be used to ascertain what functional abilities a child with spina bifida will have.

In addition to the neurological disabilities associated with damage to the spinal cord, myelomeningocele is almost always accompanied by three other conditions: hydrocephalus, Chiari II malformation, and tethering of the spinal cord. **Hydrocephalus** is a condition in which circulation of the cerebrospinal fluid is obstructed in one of the ventricles, or cavities, of the brain. If the obstruction is not removed or circumvented, the ventricle begins to enlarge, putting pressure on the brain and enlarging the head. If not treated, this condition can lead to brain damage, intellectual disabilities, and ultimately to death. Today, hydrocephalus is suspected early in children with spina bifida and is usually treated surgically by insertion of a shunt during the first few weeks after birth (see figure 16.4, *a-c*). The shunt, a plastic tube equipped with a pressure valve, is inserted into a ventricle and drains off

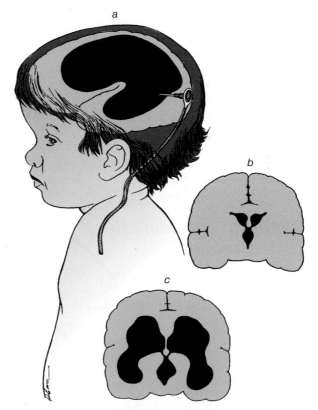

FIGURE 16.4 Shunt being used to relieve hydrocephalus: *(a)* the shunt in place, *(b)* normal ventricles, and *(c)* enlarged ventricles.

the excess cerebrospinal fluid. The fluid is usually drained into either the heart (ventriculoatrial shunt) or the abdomen (ventriculoperitoneal shunt) to be reabsorbed by the body. Additional information regarding shunts can be found in the electronic resources section at the end of the chapter.

Chiari II malformation, or Arnold-Chiari malformation (ACM), refers to a condition in which the cerebellum and lower brain stem are stretched and pulled through the base of the skull and into the top of the spinal column. This condition is always present in children with myelomeningocele. In mild cases the condition does not cause any problems and is left untreated. In more severe cases, where the functions controlled by the brain stem and cerebellum are compromised, surgery is performed to decompress the brain stem by widening the opening at the base of the skull and at the top of the spinal column.

The spinal cord should float in the spinal canal, allowing it to move up and down as the child grows. **Tethering of the spinal cord** refers to anchoring of the cord within the spinal canal at the site where the spina bifida occurred and was surgically closed. All children with myelomeningocele have tethered cords. The issue is whether the tethering results in stretching of the cord and loss of function caused by reduced circulation. Common symptoms include loss of muscular strength and tone, reductions in gait quality, and further loss of bowel and bladder functions. Tethering usually does not present problems until the adolescent growth spurt. When tethering problems are diagnosed, the problem can be treated by surgically untethering the cord. It is estimated that approximately 60 percent of all people with myelomeningocele experience tethering symptoms that could benefit from surgical treatment.

Treatment and Educational Considerations

As mentioned earlier, all forms of spina bifida are diagnosed and surgically treated soon after birth. The major treatment beyond the immediate medical procedures involves physical and occupational therapy for the child and counseling and training for the parents. The therapy has two focuses: using assistive devices to position children so that they parallel the developmental positions (e.g., sitting, crawling, standing) through which a child without disability progresses and maintaining full range of motion and stimulating circulation in the lower limbs. In conjunction with their therapy, children

with spina bifida are fitted with braces and encouraged to ambulate. Even if functional walking skills are not developed, it is important for the child with spina bifida to do weight-bearing activities to stimulate bone growth and circulation in the lower limbs. Parents are counseled to provide the child with as many normal and appropriate stimuli as possible. Many parents overprotect and confine their children with spina bifida, which results in further delays in growth and development.

Although still in the experimental stage, several innovative surgical treatments have been developed that involve surgically closing the opening in the fetus' spinal cord between the 25th and 30th weeks of the pregnancy (Bruner et al., 1999). The National Institutes of Health is currently sponsoring the Management of Myelomeningocele Study (MOMS), which is a long-term, randomized clinical trial designed to compare fetal surgery with postnatal treatment of spina bifida. Although it is still too early to evaluate the long-term impact of these new procedures, the results look promising.

There are several important similarities and differences in the treatment of spina bifida and the treatment of acute spinal cord injuries discussed earlier in this chapter. The similarities concern muscle and sensation loss and the common problems related to these deficits:

Bone deformities

Bruising

Obesity

Postural deviations

Pressure sores

Urinary tract infections

The differences are related to the onset of the conditions. Different circumstances result in different emotional and developmental ramifications.

Generally, children with spina bifida have fewer emotional problems dealing with their condition than do children with acquired spinal cord disabilities, probably because the condition has been present since birth and they have not suffered the loss of any former abilities. However, this is not to imply that they do not become frustrated when other children can perform skills and participate in activities that they cannot because of their dependence on a wheelchair or crutches.

A major ramification of the early onset of spina bifida is its effect on growth and development. The lack of innervation and subsequent use and stimulation of the affected limbs retard their physical growth. The result is a greater incidence of bone deformities and contractures in the lower limbs and a greater need for orthotics (braces) to help minimize these deformities and assist in providing functional support. A concurrent problem is related to sensory deprivation during the early years of development because of restricted mobility. This deprivation is frequently compounded by overprotective parents and medical problems that confine the child to bed for long periods of time.

Children with spina bifida are vulnerable to infections from pressure sores and bruises. Pressure sores are most common in those who are confined to wheelchairs. Bruising and skin irritation are particular concerns for children with spina bifida who use crutches and long leg braces. These children have a tendency to fall in physical activities and are susceptible to skin irritations from their braces if the braces are not properly put on each time. About 7 out of 10 children with spina bifida have also been found to have an allergic reaction to latex. Latex can be found in rubber balls and other materials used in physical education such as balloons. Physical educators must diligently check all equipment and materials used in physical education to ensure they do not contain latex.

Bowel and bladder control present significant social problems for the child with spina bifida during the early elementary school years. Bowel movements are controlled by diet and medication, which are designed to prevent constipation. Urination is commonly controlled by a regular schedule of catheterization, performed during the day with assistance by the school nurse or an aide. This dependence on others for help with personal functions and the inevitable occasional accident in class can have negative social implications for children with spina bifida and their classmates.

Finally, children with spina bifida have a tendency toward obesity. Several causes contribute to this tendency. The loss of the caloric expenditure typically made by the large-muscle groups in the lower limbs limits the number of calories that can be burned. Caloric expenditure is frequently further limited by the sedentary environment of these children and their limited mobility during the early years. Control of caloric intake is essential to avoid obesity. Unfortunately, food is frequently highly gratifying to these children and is overprovided by indulging parents and caregivers. It is a primary reinforcer that is probably desired more by this population as a result of issues described earlier, such as social isolation due to health issues, restricted mobility, and diet restrictions for bowel control. Obesity should be avoided at all costs because it further limits the children's mobility and predisposes them to other health problems.

Children with spina bifida will most likely be placed initially in some combination of adapted and regular physical education settings during the early elementary years and will be fully integrated into regular physical education settings by the end of the elementary years. It is important not to remove these children unnecessarily from inclusive physical education settings. They have the same play and social needs as the other students in their classes. On the other hand, the primary goal of physical education, to develop physical and motor skills, should not be sacrificed purely for social objectives. If the student's physical and motor needs cannot be met in an inclusive setting, the student should receive appropriate support or supplemental adapted physical education to meet these needs in a more restricted setting.

Although there has been little systematic and experimentally controlled research on the learning attributes of children with spina bifida, there is a growing body of literature that demonstrates that many children with spina bifida display a range of learning problems involving attention, memory, and organization. Although each child's needs should be assessed and individually addressed, physical educators should be aware of potential problems in these areas and how to modify their instruction accordingly to accommodate these needs.

In summary, children with spina bifida need to pursue the same physical education goals targeted for other students. As they pursue these goals, their objectives might be different. Modifications might be needed to accommodate their modes of locomotion (crutches or wheelchair) and to emphasize their upper-body development. Emphasis should be placed on physical fitness and the development of lifetime sport skills.

SPINAL COLUMN DEVIATIONS

Mild postural deviations are quite common and can often be remedied through proper instruction and practice in physical education. It is estimated that 70 percent of all children have mild postural deviations and that 5 percent have serious ones. The prevalence of serious postural deviations is much greater among students with disabilities.

Poor posture can result from any one or a combination of factors, such as ignorance, environmental conditions, genetics, physical or growth abnormalities, or psychological conditions. In many cases children are unaware that they have poor posture because they do not know what correct posture is and how their posture differs. In other cases, postural deviations can be traced to simple environmental factors, such as poorly fitting shoes. In students with disabilities, poor posture can be caused by factors affecting balance (e.g., visual impairments), neuromuscular conditions (e.g., spina bifida and cerebral palsy), or congenital defects (e.g., bone deformities and amputations). Finally, poor posture can occur as a result of attitude or self-concept. Students who have a poor body image or who lack confidence in their abilities to move tend to display defensive postures that are characterized by poor body alignment.

Physical educators should play an important role in the identification and remediation of postural deviations in all students (Horvat, Block, & Kelly, 2007). The physical educator is often the one educator in the school with the opportunity and background to identify and address postural problems. Unfortunately, postural screening and subsequent remediation are overlooked in many physical education programs. This is ironic because the development of kinesthetic awareness and proper body mechanics is fundamental to teaching physical education and is clearly within the domain of physical education as defined in the Individuals with Disabilities Education Act (IDEA).

Several excellent posture screening tests are available that can be used easily by physical educators and involve minimal preparation and equipment to administer. Two examples, included in the resources list at the end of this chapter, are the Posture Grid (Adams & McCubbin, 1991) and the New York Posture Rating Test (see figure 16.5) (New York State Education Department, 1966). Posture screening should be an annual procedure in all physical education programs. Particular attention should be paid to children with disabilities because of their generally higher incidence of postural deviation. The appropriate school personnel, such as the school nurse, and the parents or guardians of all children identified as having present and potential postural problems should be informed of and requested to pursue further evaluation of these students. The instructor can remedy most mild postural deviations within the regular physical education program by educating the children about proper body mechanics and prescribing exercises

that can be performed both in and out of class. Sample exercises are described on page 337.

Viewed from the back, the spinal column should be straight with no lateral (sideways) curves. Any lateral curvature in the back is abnormal and is referred to as **scoliosis**. Viewed from the side, the spinal column has two mild curves. The first natural curve occurs in the thoracic region, where the vertebrae are **concave** forward (curving slightly in a posterior or outward direction). An extreme curvature in this region is abnormal and is known as **kyphosis**. The second natural curve occurs in the lumbar section, where there is mild forward **convexity** (inward curvature) of the spine. An extreme curvature in this region is also abnormal and is called **lordosis**. An exaggerated lumbar curve in younger elementary children is natural but should disappear by the age of eight.

Scoliosis

Lateral deviations in the spinal column are classified according to whether the deviation is structural or nonstructural. **Structural deviations** are generally related to orthopedic impairments and are permanent or fixed changes in the alignment of the vertebrae that cannot be altered through simple physical manipulation, positioning, or exercise. **Nonstructural**, or functional, deviations are those in which the vertebrae can be realigned through positioning or removal of the primary cause—such as ignorance or muscle weaknesses—and remedied with practice and exercise.

Structural scoliosis is also frequently classified according to the cause of the condition. Although scoliosis has many possible causes, the two most common are **idiopathic** and **neuromuscular**. Idiopathic means that the cause is unknown. Neuromuscular means that the scoliosis is the result of nerve or muscle problems.

Structural idiopathic scoliosis occurs in about 2 percent of all schoolchildren. The onset of scoliosis usually occurs during the early adolescent years, when children are undergoing a rapid growth spurt. This form of scoliosis is characterized by an S-shaped curve, usually composed of a major curve and one or two minor curves. The major curve is the one causing the deformity. The minor curves, sometimes called *secondary* or *compensatory curves*, usually occur above or below the major curve and are the result of the body's attempt to adjust for the major curve. Although both genders appear to be equally affected by this condition, five times as many females have the progressive form

POSTURE RATING CHART

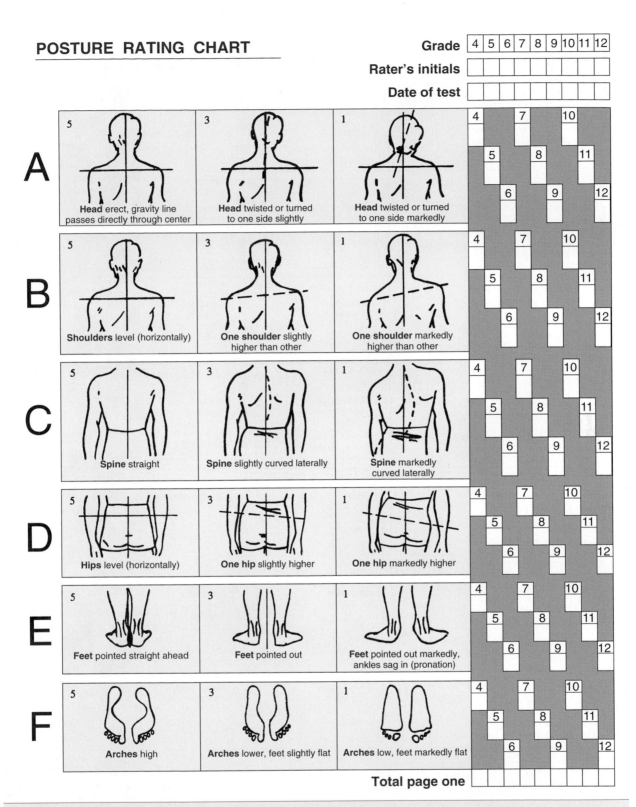

Grade | 4 | 5 | 6 | 7 | 8 | 9 | 10 | 11 | 12 |

Rater's initials

Date of test

A
- 5 — Head erect, gravity line passes directly through center
- 3 — Head twisted or turned to one side slightly
- 1 — Head twisted or turned to one side markedly

B
- 5 — Shoulders level (horizontally)
- 3 — One shoulder slightly higher than other
- 1 — One shoulder markedly higher than other

C
- 5 — Spine straight
- 3 — Spine slightly curved laterally
- 1 — Spine markedly curved laterally

D
- 5 — Hips level (horizontally)
- 3 — One hip slightly higher
- 1 — One hip markedly higher

E
- 5 — Feet pointed straight ahead
- 3 — Feet pointed out
- 1 — Feet pointed out markedly, ankles sag in (pronation)

F
- 5 — Arches high
- 3 — Arches lower, feet slightly flat
- 1 — Arches low, feet markedly flat

Total page one

FIGURE 16.5 New York State Posture Rating Chart. *(continued)*

Reprinted, by permission, from New York State Education Department, 1999, *New York State physical fitness test for boys and girls 4-12* (New York: New York State Education Department).

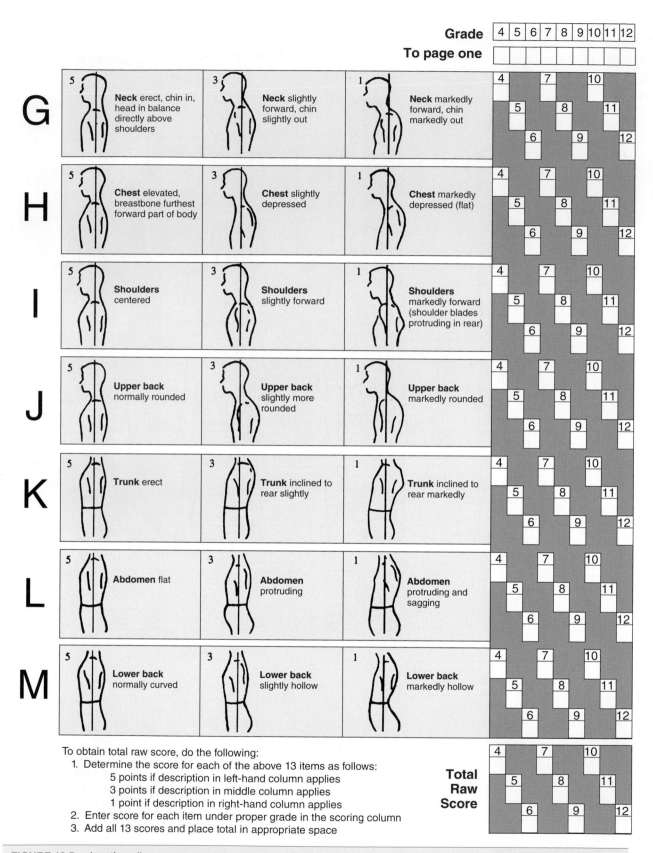

To obtain total raw score, do the following:
1. Determine the score for each of the above 13 items as follows:
   5 points if description in left-hand column applies
   3 points if description in middle column applies
   1 point if description in right-hand column applies
2. Enter score for each item under proper grade in the scoring column
3. Add all 13 scores and place total in appropriate space

FIGURE 16.5   *(continued)*

Reprinted, by permission, from New York State Education Department, 1999, *New York State physical fitness test for boys and girls 4-12* (New York: New York State Education Department).

that becomes more severe if not treated. The cause of this progressive form of scoliosis is unknown, but there is some evidence that suggests a possible genetic link in females.

A second type of structural scoliosis, more commonly found in children with severe disabilities, is caused by neuromuscular problems. This form of scoliosis is usually characterized by a *C*-shaped curve. In severe cases, this form of scoliosis can lead to balance difficulties, pressure on internal organs, and seating problems (pressure sores) for students in wheelchairs.

Nonstructural scoliosis can be the result of several causes and can be characterized by either an *S*-curve or a *C*-curve. The primary causes can be broadly classified as either skeletal or muscular. An example of scoliosis with a skeletal cause would be a curve that has resulted from one leg being shorter than the other. An example of scoliosis

with a muscular cause would be a curve that has resulted because the muscles on one side of the back have become stronger than the muscles on the other side and have pulled the spinal column out of line. Fortunately, nonstructural scoliosis can usually be treated by identification and correction of the cause—that is, inserting a lift in the child's shoe to equalize the length of the legs or strengthening and stretching the appropriate muscle groups in the back (see the application example on correcting postural deviations).

Assessment of Scoliosis

Early identification is extremely important for both structural and nonstructural scoliosis so that help can begin and the severity of the curve can be reduced. Scoliosis screening should be conducted annually for all children, particularly from the 3rd through the 10th grades, when the condition

APPLICATION EXAMPLE

Correcting Postural Deviations

Situation: During the annual posture screening of her fourth-grade students, the physical education teacher notices that one student has a mild lateral curvature to the right when viewed from behind. When the teacher asks the student to hang from a pull-up bar, the curve disappears.

Student: This 10-year-old boy is very coordinated and active in many sports. His favorite sport is baseball, and he was the star pitcher last year. The physical educator deduces that this student has a nonstructural postural deviation probably caused by his baseball pitching, which overdeveloped and tightened the back muscles on the right side.

Application: On the basis of the information presented here, the physical educator takes the following actions:

▶ Develops an exercise routine designed to stretch the muscles on the right side

of the upper back and strengthen the muscles on the left side of the upper back.

▶ Contacts the parents and informs them that their son has a mild, nonstructural postural deviation of his back. She tells them that at this time the deviation can be corrected by a routine of exercises. She asks for their assistance in encouraging their son to regularly perform the exercises and in monitoring the remediation of the deviation. She also asks them to identify a reward their son can earn for doing his exercise routine.

▶ Meets with the student and explains the problem and how it can be corrected by a regular exercise routine. The teacher demonstrates the exercises and has the student perform them a few times to ensure they are done correctly.

▶ Develops a progress chart that she and the student can use to monitor the degree of his curvature and his exercise compliance. She gives the student a copy of this chart each month to share with his parents.

is most likely to occur. If a child is suspected of having scoliosis, the parents or guardians and appropriate school personnel should be notified and further evaluation conducted. Students suspected of having scoliosis should be monitored frequently, approximately every three months, to ascertain if the condition is progressing. A scoliosis assessment, which can be performed in less than a minute, involves observing the student shirtless. The assessments should be done individually and by an assessor of the same gender as the children being assessed because children of these ages are usually self-conscious about the changes occurring in their bodies and about being seen undressed.

To perform a scoliosis assessment, check the symmetry of the child's back while the child is standing and then when the child is bent forward. First, with the child standing erect, observe from a posterior view any differences between the two sides of the back, including the following points (see figure 16.5, rows A-D, on page 331):

1. Does the spinal column appear straight or curved?

2. Are the shoulders at the same height, or does one appear higher than the other?

3. Are the hips at the same horizontal distance from the floor, or does one appear higher than the other?

4. Is the space between the arms and trunk equal on both sides of the body?

5. Do the shoulder blades protrude evenly, or does one appear to protrude more than the other?

Then ask the child to perform the Adam's position, bent forward at the waist to about 90 degrees (figure 16.6). Examine the back from both a posterior and an anterior view for any noticeable differences in symmetry, such as curvature of the spine or one side of the back being higher or lower than the other, particularly in the thoracic and lumbar regions.

Treatment of Scoliosis

The treatment of scoliosis depends on the type and degree of curvature. As mentioned earlier, nonstructural scoliosis can frequently be corrected when the cause is identified and the condition remedied through a program of specific exercises and body awareness. With structural scoliosis, the treatment varies according to the degree of curvature. Children with mild curvatures (less than 20 degrees) are usually given exercise programs

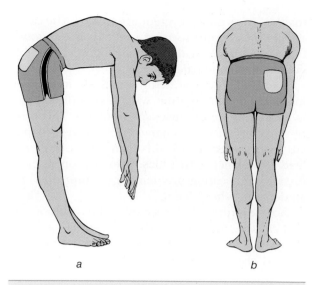

FIGURE 16.6 Adam's position showing normal spinal symmetry: *(a)* side view, *(b)* back view.

to keep the spine flexible and are monitored on a regular basis to make sure the curves are not becoming more severe.

Children with more severe curves (20-40 degrees) are usually treated with braces or orthotics, which force the spine into better alignment or prevent it from deviating further. The purpose of the bracing is not to correct the condition but to keep it from becoming worse. Historically, the Milwaukee brace has been reported as the most effective, however there have been problems with compliance in wearing the brace due to the visible cervical collar. Today, most scoliosis braces are made of molded orthoplast and are custom fitted to the individual. These braces are also known as low-profile braces, TLSO (thoracic lumber sacral orthosis) braces, or underarm braces and have been found to be effective in treating mild and moderate curves (see figure 16.7). One of the major advantages of the orthoplast braces is that they are less conspicuous and tend to be worn more consistently. These braces must be worn continuously until the child reaches skeletal maturity—in many cases, for four to five years. The brace can be removed for short periods for activities such as swimming and bathing. The treatment of scoliosis in people who are wheelchair-bound might also involve modifying the chair to improve alignment and to equalize seating pressures. For the latest information on braces used to treat scoliosis, check the electronic resources listed for this chapter.

In extremely severe cases of scoliosis, in which the curve is greater than 40 degrees or does not

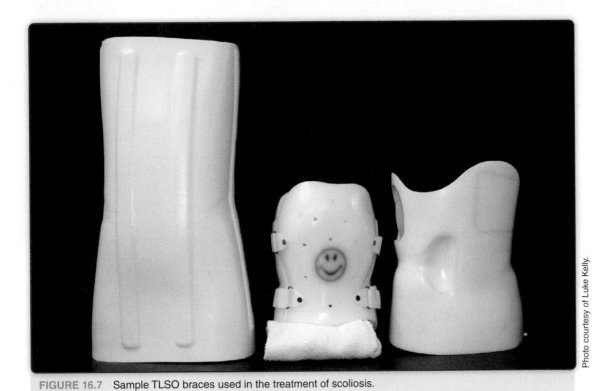

FIGURE 16.7 Sample TLSO braces used in the treatment of scoliosis.

Photo courtesy of Luke Kelly.

respond to bracing, surgery is employed. The surgical treatment usually involves fusing together the vertebrae in the affected region of the spine by means of bone grafts and the implantation of a metal rod. Following surgery, a brace is typically worn for about a year until the fusion has solidified.

Kyphosis and Lordosis

Abnormal concavity forward (backward curve) in the thoracic region (kyphosis) and abnormal convexity forward (forward curve) in the lumbar region (lordosis) are usually nonstructural and the result of poor posture (figure 16.5, rows G-M, on page 332). These deformities are routinely remedied by exercise programs designed to tighten specific muscle groups and stretch opposing muscle groups and through education designed to make students aware of their present posture, proper body mechanics, and the desired posture.

The physical educator can assess kyphosis and lordosis by observing children under the conditions described previously for scoliosis screening but from the side view. Look for exaggerated curves in the thoracic and lumbar regions of the spinal column. Kyphosis is usually characterized by a rounded appearance of the upper back. Lordosis is characterized by a hollow appearance of the back and a protruding abdomen.

Structural kyphosis, sometimes called *Scheuermann's disease* or *juvenile kyphosis*, is similar in appearance during the early stages to the nonstructural form described earlier, but it is the result of a deformity in the shape of the vertebrae in the thoracic region. Although the cause of this vertebral deformity is unknown, it can be diagnosed by X-rays. This form of kyphosis is frequently accompanied by a compensatory lordotic curve. The prevalence of this deformity is not known, but it appears to affect both genders equally during adolescence.

Early detection and treatment of structural kyphosis through bracing can result in effective remediation of the condition. The treatment typically involves wearing a brace continuously for one to two years until the vertebrae reshape themselves. A variety of braces and orthotic jackets have been developed for the treatment of this condition. The Milwaukee brace used for the treatment of scoliosis is considered one of the more effective braces for treating this form of kyphosis.

Spondylolysis and Spondylolisthesis

Spondylolysis is a congenital malformation of the neural arches of the fourth or, more commonly, fifth lumbar vertebra. People with spondylolysis might or might not experience any back pain, but they are predisposed to acquiring spondylolisthesis. Spondylolisthesis is similar to spondylolysis, except that the fifth lumbar vertebra has slid forward. The displacement occurs because of the lack of the neural arch structure and the ligaments that normally hold this area in place. Spondylolisthesis can be congenital or can occur as a result of trauma to the back. It is usually associated with severe back pain and pain in the legs.

Treatment in mild cases involves training and awareness of proper posture. Individuals with spondylolisthesis frequently have an exaggerated lordotic curve in the back. In more severe cases, surgery is performed to realign the vertebrae and fuse that section of the spine.

Medical consultation should be pursued before any students with spondylolysis or spondylolisthesis participate in physical education. Children with mild cases might be able to participate in a regular physical education program with emphasis on proper posture, additional stretching, and avoidance of activities that involve extreme stretching or trauma to the back. In more severe cases, an adapted physical education program might be required to provide more comprehensive posture training and exercises and to foster the development of physical and motor skills that will not aggravate the condition.

Working With Students With Spinal Column Deviations

As discussed earlier, physical educators can play a major role in screening for postural deviations in the spinal column. Children identified as having mild, nonstructural postural problems should receive special instruction and exercises to remediate their problems. Following are several guidelines that should be considered whenever a physical educator is designing, implementing, or monitoring an exercise program to correct postural deviations.

- Establish and follow policies and procedures for working with students suspected of having structural or serious postural deviations of the spinal column.

- In an exercise program to remediate a postural deviation, the objective is to strengthen the muscles used to pull the spinal column back into correct alignment and to stretch or lengthen the muscles that are pulling the spinal column out of alignment. The stretching program should be performed at least twice a day, and muscle-strengthening exercises should be performed at least every other day. A number of exercise and stretching routines should be developed to add variety and keep the exercise routine interesting. Setting the exercise routines to music and establishing reward systems are also recommended, especially for students who are not highly motivated to exercise.

- All exercise and activity programs should begin and end with stretching exercises, with the greatest emphasis on static stretching. Stretches should each be performed five times and held for a count of 15 seconds.

- The exercise program should be initiated with mild, low-intensity exercises that can be easily performed by the children. The intensity of the exercises should be gradually increased as the children's strength and endurance increase.

- In most cases, individual exercise programs should be initiated and taught as part of adapted physical education. After learning the exercise routine, the student can perform the routine in the regular physical education class, monitored by the regular physical education teacher. First, explain to the student the nature of the postural deviation being addressed, the reasons why good posture is desirable, and the ways in which the exercises will help. The exercises should then be taught and monitored until the child clearly understands how to perform them correctly. The importance of making the student aware of the difference between the present posture and the desired posture cannot be overemphasized. Many children with mild postural deviations are simply unaware of the problem and thus do not even try to correct their postures. Mirrors and videotapes are useful for giving students feedback on posture. When working with students with visual impairments, the teacher will need to provide specific tactile and kinesthetic feedback to teach them the feeling of the correct postures. Cratty (1971) has described a tactile posture board composed of a series of movable wooden pegs projecting through a vertical board that can be placed along a student's spine to provide tactual feedback related to both postural deviations and desired postures.

■ Children should follow their exercise programs at home on the days they do not have physical education. Some form of monitoring system, such as a log or progress chart, should be used. Periodically the children should be evaluated and given feedback and reinforcement to motivate them to continue working on their exercise programs.

■ Exercises that make the body symmetrical are recommended. The use of asymmetric exercises, especially for children being treated for scoliosis, should be used only following medical consultation.

■ When selecting exercises to remediate one curve (e.g., the major curve), take care to ensure that the exercise does not foster the development of another curve (e.g., the minor curve).

■ The exercise program should be as varied and interesting as possible to maintain the student's motivation and involvement. Alternating between routine exercises and activities such as swimming and rowing will usually result in greater compliance with the program. Motivation is an even greater concern with students with intellectual disabilities, who might not comprehend why they need to exercise or why better posture is desirable; they will require more frequent feedback and reinforcement. Showing students random digital photos is a good technique for keeping their attention on their postures and rewarding them when they are displaying the desired postures.

■ Students wearing braces such as the Milwaukee brace can exercise and participate in physical education, although activities that cause trauma to the spine (e.g., jumping and gymnastics) might be contraindicated. As a general rule, the brace will be self-limiting.

Recommended Exercises

Using the guidelines just presented and drawing on an understanding of the muscles involved in a spinal column deviation, a physical educator should be able to select appropriate exercises and activities. The following lists include sample exercises for the upper and lower back that can be used in the remediation of the three major spinal column deviations discussed in this chapter. These exercise lists provide examples and are far from complete. Several resources that provide additional exercises and more detailed descriptions of their performance are listed at the end of this chapter.

Sample Upper-Back Exercises

The following sample exercises can be used to remediate nonstructural deviations in the upper spine.

■ Symmetrical swimming strokes such as the backstroke and the breaststroke. If a pool is not available, the arm patterns of these strokes can be performed on a bench covered with a mat. Hand weights or pulley weights can be used to control the resistance.

■ Rowing using either a rowboat or a rowing machine. The rowing action can also be performed with hand weights or pulley weights.

■ Various arm and shoulder lifts from a prone position on a mat. Small hand weights can be used to increase resistance.

■ Hanging from a bar. This is a good stretching exercise.

■ Lateral (sideways) trunk bending from either a standing or a kneeling position. Forward bending should be avoided.

Sample Lower-Back Exercises

The following sample exercises can be used to remediate nonstructural deviations in the lower back.

■ Any form of correctly performed sit-ups commensurate with the student's ability. Emphasis should be placed on keeping the lower back flat and performing the sit-ups in a slow, continuous action, as opposed to performing a large number of repetitions. Raising the hips and sudden jerky movements should not be allowed.

■ Pelvic tilt. This can be done from a supine position on a mat or standing against a wall.

■ Alternating or combined knee exchanges (bringing the knee to the chest) from a supine position on a mat.

■ Doing a bicycling action with the legs from a supine position on a mat.

■ Leg lifts. Any variation of leg lifts is appropriate as long as the lower back is kept flat and pressed against the floor.

New techniques and treatments for spinal column postural deviations are constantly being developed. To find the latest information, review the electronic resources at the end of the chapter.

IMPLICATIONS FOR PHYSICAL EDUCATION

Assessment is the key to successfully addressing the physical education needs of students with spinal cord disabilities. Physical educators must work as part of a team to obtain the assessment data they need to provide appropriate instruction. By consulting with each other, the physical educator and the physical or occupational therapist can share essential information about goals and objectives for each student. The physical therapist can provide pertinent information about the muscles that are still innervated and those that have been lost, the existing muscle strength and prognosis for further development, the range of motion at the various joints, and the presence or absence of sensation in the limbs. The physical or occupational therapist can also provide useful information about adapted appliances (e.g., a device to hold a racket when a grip is not possible) as well as practical guidance on putting on and removing braces, adjusting wheelchairs, positioning and using restraints in wheelchairs, lifting and handling the student, and making transfers to and from the wheelchair.

Within the domain of physical education, the physical educator must be able to assess the physical fitness and motor skills of students with spinal cord disabilities. There is currently only one health-related, criterion-referenced physical fitness test available, the Brockport Physical Fitness Test (BPFT) (Winnick & Short, 1999a), that is designed to accommodate people with spinal cord disabilities and provides appropriate standards for the evaluation of physical fitness for this population. The BPFT recommends that people with spinal cord injuries be evaluated in the areas of aerobic functioning, body composition, and musculoskeletal function. Criterion-referenced test items are provided for each area, with modifications for levels of functioning based on the level of the spinal cord injury. For example, the following test items would be recommended for a student who is a paraplegic and uses a wheelchair: for aerobic functioning, the 15-minute target aerobic movement test; for body composition, the sum of the triceps and subscapular skinfold test; and for musculoskeletal function, the seated push-up, dominant grip strength, and modified Apley tests.

In general, students with spinal cord disabilities have placed significantly below students without disabilities at the same age level on physical fitness measures and in motor skill development. Winnick and Short (1985), for example, have reported that 52 to 72 percent of people with spinal cord disabilities in their Project UNIQUE study had skinfold measures greater than the median value for same-age subjects who were not impaired and that only about 19 percent of the girls and 36 percent of the boys with spinal cord disabilities scored above the nonimpaired median on grip strength. Winnick and Short (1984) have also reported that young people with paraplegic spinal neuromuscular conditions have generally lower fitness levels than their peers without disabilities of the same age and gender and that they do not demonstrate significant improvement with age or show significant gender differences as do their peers without disabilities. These results should not be misinterpreted to mean that people with spinal cord disabilities cannot develop better levels of physical fitness. Research has shown, on the contrary, that with proper instruction and opportunity to practice, they can make significant improvements in physical fitness. The key is appropriate instruction and practice designed to address individual needs.

Fitness programs for students with spinal cord disabilities should focus on the development of all components of physical fitness. Although flexibility in all joints should be a goal, particular emphasis should be placed on preventing or reducing contractures in joints in which muscles are no longer innervated. These situations require a regular routine of stretching that moves the joints through the full range of motion.

Strength training should focus on restoring or maximizing the strength in the unaffected muscles. Care must be taken not to create muscle imbalances by overstrengthening muscle groups when the antagonist muscles are affected. Most common progressive resistance exercises are suitable for people with spinal cord disabilities with little or no modification. Posture and correct body mechanics should be stressed during all strength training activities.

One of the most challenging fitness areas for people with spinal cord disabilities is cardiorespiratory endurance. Work in this area is frequently complicated by the loss of the large-muscle groups of the legs, which makes cardiorespiratory training more difficult. Research has shown that people with paraplegia typically have about only half the cardiac output compared with people without spinal cord injuries, and people with tetraplegia tend to have about only a third of the cardiac output of people with paraplegia (ACSM, 2003). In these cases, the principles of intensity, frequency, and duration must be applied to less traditional aerobic activities that use the smaller muscle groups of the arms and shoulders. A number of wheelchair ergometers and hand-driven bicycle ergometers have been designed specifically to address the cardiorespiratory needs of people with spinal cord disabilities. Although it is more difficult to attain the benefits of cardiorespiratory training using the smaller muscle groups of the arms and shoulders, it is not impossible. There are several highly conditioned wheelchair marathoners who clearly demonstrate that high levels of aerobic fitness can be attained.

Obesity is common in people with spinal cord disabilities, largely because the loss of the large-muscle groups of the lower limbs diminishes their capacity to burn calories. Weight control is a function of balancing caloric intake with caloric expenditure. Because caloric expenditure is often limited to a large degree by the extent of muscle damage and the subsequent activities that can be undertaken, the obvious solution is to control food intake.

When working on physical fitness with people with spinal cord injuries, safety must be a major concern. People with spinal cord injuries, particularly those with injuries above T6, are subject to a number of problems, such as hypotension, problems of thermoregulation, and limits on their maximal exercise heart rates. **Hypotension** (low blood pressure) is caused by a disruption of the sympathetic nervous system. During aerobic exercise, the body depends on the large muscles in the legs to contract and assist in pumping blood back to the heart. When the legs are not involved, blood can pool in the legs, reducing the amount of blood returned to the heart and, subsequently, the stroke volume of the heart. Some precautions that can be taken to reduce hypotension include exercising in a reclined position and including appropriate warm-ups and cool-downs as part of the workout so the body can gradually adapt to the increased workload.

Thermoregulation refers to the ability of the body to regulate its internal temperature in response to the outside temperature. The higher the injury on the spine, the greater the problems with thermal regulation. When thermal regulation is an issue, care should be taken to avoid exercising in extremely cold or hot environments. Physical educators should also keep cool compresses available to help students cool down after aerobic workouts.

People with spinal cord injuries above T6 are also subject to autonomic dysreflexia and limitations in their maximal exercise heart rates. **Autonomic dysreflexia** refers to a rapid increase in heart rate and blood pressure to dangerous levels, which can be triggered by several factors, including bowel or bladder distension, restrictive clothing, or skin irritation. In reaction to these events, a reflex is triggered to constrict blood vessels and increase blood pressure. Another set of reflexes should also be triggered that monitors and subsequently relaxes these blood vessels. Normally, these reflexes would monitor the heart rate and blood pressure and respond to these changes at the spinal cord level without conscious thought on the part of the individual. In people with T6 and higher lesions, the second set of reflexes is not triggered, possibly resulting in dangerously high blood pressure levels. Care should be taken to ensure that people empty their bowels and bladders before exercise and that their heart rates and blood pressures are monitored before and during exercise. If not monitored and treated in a timely fashion, this can be a life-threatening condition. Disruption to the integration of the parasympathetic and the sympathetic nervous systems also limits the maximum heart rate in people with injuries above T6 to approximately 120 beats per minute, which limits the aerobic training effects that can be achieved.

In recent years, several excellent resources have been published to assist physical educators in planning and implementing safe fitness programs for individuals with spinal cord injuries (ACSM, 2003; Frontera, Slovik, & Dawson, 2006; Goldberg, 1995; Lockette & Keyes, 1994; Miller, 1995; Rimmer, 1994; Winnick & Short, 1999b). The American College of Sports Medicine (ACSM) in collaboration with the National Center on Physical Activity and Disability (NCPAD) has also created a fitness certification, the Certified Inclusive Fitness Trainer, for fitness professionals who work with people with disabilities.

In addition to physical fitness and motor skills, physical educators should concentrate on posture and body mechanics. People with spinal cord disabilities frequently have poor body mechanics as a result of muscle imbalances and contractures. Exercises and activities that contribute to body awareness and alignment should thus be stressed.

In terms of sport skills, the most valuable activities are those with the greatest carryover potential for lifetime participation. The selection of activities should provide a balance between warm- and cold-weather sports as well as indoor and outdoor sports. Preference should be given to sports that promote physical fitness and for which there are organized opportunities for participation in the community. Just about any sport (e.g., softball, golf, tennis, swimming, skiing) can be adapted or modified so that people with spinal cord disabilities can participate. Figure 16.8 shows several people with disabilities playing a game of wheelchair volleyball on an indoor court.

INCLUSION

The goal of assessment is to obtain the most accurate and complete data possible so that the most appropriate placement and instruction can be provided (Kelly & Melograno, 2004). Physical educators must be willing to devote both the time and effort required to obtain this assessment data if they wish to help their students reach their maximum potential in physical education. Because of the uniqueness of each spinal cord disability, physical educators need to use their skills in task analysis to develop their own authentic assessment tools and scoring rubrics to evaluate and teach functional motor skills (Horvat et al., 2007). Working cooperatively with a team is the key to maximizing staff efficiency and the benefits for the students. Additional information on assessment and development of physical fitness and motor development is presented in other chapters in this text.

Once goals and objectives have been established for a student with a spinal cord disability, the next challenge is how to provide the instruction to achieve these goals in as inclusive a physical education setting as possible. Some physical education content, such as physical fitness, lends itself to inclusion because the content must be individualized for all of the students. Physical educators should know the principles of universal design and ensure that all the equipment is accessible and useable by all students. Because all students are at different levels of fitness in terms of their flexibility, strength, and endurance, it is common to develop individual routines based on the students' assessed needs and then to use a circuit approach to have students work on their programs. In an individualized setting like this, it is easy to accommodate the unique needs of students with spinal cord disabilities by defining fitness routines to meet their unique needs at the same stations as the other students.

Other physical education content, such as working on sport skills (e.g., the volleyball serve), can initially appear more difficult to modify because such skills are traditionally taught to the class as a whole, and then activities and games are used in which everyone is expected to perform the same skill. For example, how do you include a student with a spinal cord injury who uses a wheelchair in a volleyball game if the student cannot hit the ball hard enough to serve the ball over the net and cannot move quickly enough in the wheelchair to

FIGURE 16.8 Sports, such as volleyball, can be modified to allow for participation by people with disabilities.

© BOLD STOCK / age fotostock

defend part of the court? What are some possible modifications? The weight of the ball could be adjusted. The student could be allowed to serve closer to the net. The student could be given a smaller zone to defend on the court after the ball is served. More students could be assigned to each side to reduce the amount of space needing to be defended. Physical educators should also apply the principles of differentiated instruction and learning to ensure that students are provided multiple options for learning and demonstrating their understanding and skill.

Although the physical educator is responsible for creating an inclusive setting in which the needs of all students are addressed, it is also important that students with spinal cord disabilities be taught how to advocate for themselves. This form of self-advocacy involves students being able to analyze new games and activities and then offer suggestions on how the activities could be modified so that they can successfully participate. This is a critical skill for all students with disabilities because the physical educator will not always be there to orchestrate the modifications. A common transition step from teacher-directed accommodations to those that are student directed is to have the class help to develop modifications and accommodations. This process also sensitizes the other students to the value of making activities appropriate for all participants. The golden rules to making accommodations are that the activity must still serve its original purpose and people with disabilities must be working on the same skills or similar skills modified to meet

their unique needs. Assigning students with spinal cord impairments to roles such as scorekeeper because they are in wheelchairs is not appropriate inclusion because they are not developing the skills they need to live and maintain an active healthy lifestyle. In the long term, inclusive physical education settings are beneficial for everyone. Inclusion requires that instruction be based on assessment and be individually designed. It also requires successful participation of all students in the planned drills, games, and activities, which should result in positive learning outcomes for all students.

ORTHOTIC DEVICES

Because of the neuromuscular limitations imposed by spinal cord disabilities, many people with these disabilities use orthotics to enhance their functional abilities. **Orthotic devices** are splints and braces designed to provide support, improve positioning, correct or prevent deformities, and reduce or alleviate pain. The use of orthotic devices is not limited to people with spinal cord disabilities. For example, the Milwaukee and Charleston braces are commonly used to treat scoliosis, which can occur in any adolescent. Orthotic devices are prescribed by physicians and fitted by occupational therapists, who also instruct users in wearing and caring for the devices. Examples of the more common orthotics are shown in figure 16.9. They are used both by people who are ambulatory to provide better stability and by people in wheelchairs to prevent

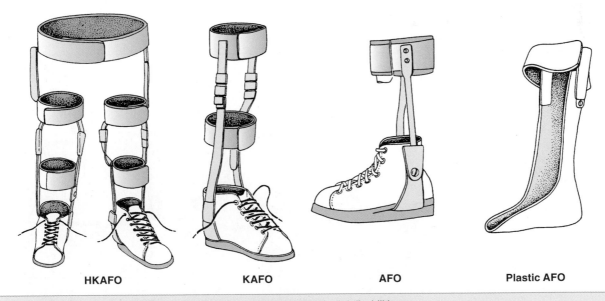

HKAFO   KAFO   AFO   Plastic AFO

FIGURE 16.9 Common orthotic devices worn by people with spinal cord disabilities.

deformities. These devices are commonly referred to by abbreviations that describe the joints they cover: AFO (ankle-foot orthotics), KAFO (knee-ankle-foot orthotics), and HKAFO (hip-knee-ankle-foot orthotics). Additional information on orthotics can be found in the electronic resources at the end of the chapter.

Many of the newer plastic orthotics can be worn inside regular shoes and under clothing. Under normal circumstances, orthotics should be worn in all physical education activities with the exception of swimming. In vigorous activities, physical educators should periodically check that the straps are secure and that no abrasion or skin irritation is occurring where the orthotics or straps contact the skin. Orthotics can also be used to improve positioning to maximize sensory input. Figure 16.10 shows a series of assistive devices often used with children with spina bifida. The purpose of these orthotics is to allow children with spina bifida to view and interact with the environment from the developmental vertical postures that they

cannot attain and maintain on their own. The last device is a parapodium, or standing table, which allows people who otherwise could not stand to attain a standing position from which they can work and view the world. The parapodium frees the individual from the burden or inability to balance and bear weight and also affords complete use of the arms and hands. The parapodium can be used effectively in physical education to teach skills such as table tennis. In recent years, several companies have devised ingenious modifications of the parapodium so that the table can be easily adjusted to many vertical and horizontal positions.

A secondary category of orthotic devices includes canes and walkers used as assistive devices for ambulation. The **Lofstrand** or **Canadian crutches** are most commonly used by people with spina bifida and spinal cord disabilities who ambulate with leg braces and crutches. Physical educators should be aware that a person using only one cane or crutch employs it on the strong side, thus immobilizing the better arm. This should

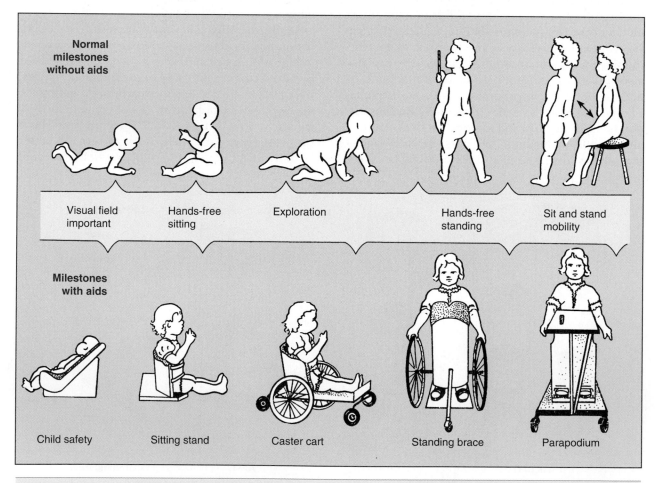

FIGURE 16.10 Orthotic devices help children with spina bifida attain normal developmental postures.

be considered, and appropriate modifications (i.e., to maintain balance) should be made for skills in which use of the better arm is desired. For additional information on canes and crutches, consult the electronic resources at the end of the chapter.

ADAPTED SPORT ACTIVITIES

Today, many organizations sponsor athletic programs and sporting events for people with spinal cord disabilities. These organizations have evolved from the need to provide athletic and recreational opportunities for people with spinal cord disabilities who want to participate in sport.

The NWAA, now known as Wheelchair and Ambulatory Sports, USA (WASUSA), was formed in 1956 and is one of the most notable organizations sponsoring athletic events for people with neuromuscular disabilities resulting from spinal cord injuries, spina bifida, or polio. WASUSA sponsors competitive events in pistol shooting, riflery, swimming, table tennis, weightlifting, archery, fencing, billiards, basketball, wheelchair slalom, and track and field. Competitors are classified into divisions by age and functional ability (table 16.2). There are two age divisions: adult, for people aged 16 and older, and junior, for young people 8 to 15 years old. As discussed earlier in this chapter, there is growing interest in replacing the system with a functional classification system (figure 16.2), which is now used for international competitions.

Disabled Sports USA (DS/USA) plays a major role in organizing and sponsoring both competitive and noncompetitive winter sport events for people with disabilities They also sponsor events in volleyball, swimming, cycling, powerlifting, and track and field. DS/USA was formally called National Handicapped Sports (until 1994) and the National Handicapped Sport and Recreation Association (until 1976). DS/USA is a leader in the development and dissemination of recreation and fitness and training materials related to sport and recreation for people with disabilities. DS/USA also serves as the official governing body for sport competitions for people with amputations.

Several special organizations sponsor athletic competitions in a specific sport. Although many of these organizations employ the WASUSA classification system, the National Wheelchair Basketball Association (NWBA) has its own system. The NWBA was formed in 1949 and sponsors competition for men, women, and youth. In the NWBA classifica-

tion system, each player is classified as I, II, or III, depending on the location of the spinal injury and the degree of motor loss. Each class has a corresponding point value of 1, 2, or 3. A team can comprise players in any combination of classes as long as the total point value for the five players does not exceed 12 and there are not more than three class III players playing together at the same time. The classifications are made according to the following criteria (NWBA, 2008):

Class I: Complete motor loss at T7 or above or comparable disability in which there is total loss of muscle function originating at or above T7.

Class II: Complete motor loss originating at T8 and descending through and including L2 in which there might be motor power of hips and thighs. Also included in this class are people with amputations with bilateral hip disarticulation.

Class III: All other physical disabilities related to lower-extremity paralysis or paresis originating at or below L3. All lower-extremity amputees are included in this class except those with bilateral hip disarticulation (see class II).

The NWBA classification system provides an excellent model for equating team sport competition in physical education classes that include integrated students with spinal cord disabilities. A similar classification system based on students' skill levels could also be designed and used in physical education classes.

Over the past decade, wheelchair sports have evolved from primarily recreational activities into highly sophisticated and competitive events. Many of the initial advances in wheelchair sports were the direct result of technical advances in wheelchair design and research related to the postural and body mechanics of wheelchair propulsion. In recent years, attention has shifted to defining and improving training and conditioning programs for wheelchair athletes (Ferrara & Davis, 1990; Gayle & Muir, 1992; Wells & Hooker, 1990).

Specialized, organized sport programs serve as an extension of the physical education curriculum. Such programs provide students with spinal cord disabilities with equal opportunities to gain the benefits and experiences all athletes derive from sport, and they are also a good source of motivation. These activities give participants an opportunity to meet and interact socially with others who have similar characteristics, interests, and needs. Finally, these sport experiences expose students with spinal cord disabilities to positive role models who demonstrate the difference between having a disability and being handicapped. To maximize the probability that students with disabilities will both attempt and succeed in sport, physical educators must ensure that the physical education curriculum provides instruction in the fundamental sport skills and the appropriate transition from skill development to skill application in actual sport situations.

SUMMARY

People with spinal cord disabilities need to pursue the same physical education goals as other students. This chapter includes the information that teachers and other professionals need to successfully meet the needs of these students. Physical educators must have a thorough understanding of the nature of the disabilities and the functional abilities that can be attained. They can then build on this knowledge base to determine the most appropriate placement and instructional programming for each student. Particular emphasis should be placed on body awareness and proper body mechanics to minimize the negative impact of spinal column deviations. In addition, special attention should be given to physical fitness. Many people with spinal cord disabilities are predisposed to obesity and have imposed constraints on how they can train because of their disability. Finally, all programs for people with spinal cord disabilities should be designed so that they leave the program with functional lifetime sport skills that can be used to maintain their health and fitness. Adapted sport, using functional ability classification systems, provides excellent opportunities for people with spinal cord disabilities to apply and practice the skills learned in physical education.

REFERENCES

Adams, R.C., & McCubbin, J.A. (1991). *Games, sports, and exercises for the physically disabled* (4th ed.). Philadelphia: Lea & Febiger.

American College of Sports Medicine (ACSM). (2003). *ACSM's exercise management of persons with chronic diseases and disabilities* (2nd ed.). Champaign, IL: Human Kinetics.

American Medical Association (AMA). (2000). *Handbook of first aid and emergency care*. New York: Random House.

Bruner, J.P., Tulipan, J., Paschall, R.L., Boehm, F.H., Walsh, W.F., Silva, S.R., Hernanz-Schulman, M., Lowe, L.H., & Reed, G.W. (1999). Fetal surgery for myelomeningocele and the incidence of shunt-dependent hydrocephalus. *Journal of the American Medical Association, 282,* 1819-1825.

Centers for Disease Control and Prevention (CDC). (2000). Polio vaccine: What you need to know. Retrieved August 14, 2008, from www.cdc.gov/vaccines.

Cratty, B.J. (1971). *Movement and spatial awareness in blind children and youth*. Springfield, IL: Charles C. Thomas.

Ferrara, M.S., & Davis, R.W. (1990). Injuries to wheelchair athletes. *Paraplegia, 28,* 335-341.

Frontera, W.R., Slovik, D.M., & Dawson, D.M. (2006). *Exercise in rehabilitation medicine* (2nd ed.). Champaign, IL: Human Kinetics.

Gayle, G.W., & Muir, J.L. (1992). Role of sportsmedicine and the spinal cord injured: A multidisciplinary relationship. *Palaestra, 8* (3), 51-56.

Goldberg, B. (Ed.). (1995). *Sports and exercise for children with chronic health conditions*. Champaign, IL: Human Kinetics.

Horvat, M., Block, M.E., & Kelly, L.E. (2007). *Developmental and adapted physical activity assessment*. Champaign, IL: Human Kinetics.

Kelly, L.E., & Melograno, V. (2004). *Developing the physical education curriculum: An achievement-based approach*. Champaign, IL: Human Kinetics.

Lockette, K., & Keyes, A.M. (1994). *Conditioning with physical disabilities*. Champaign, IL: Human Kinetics.

Miller, P.D. (Ed.). (1995). *Fitness programming and physical disability*. Champaign, IL: Human Kinetics.

National SCI Statistical Center. (2008). Spinal cord injury facts and figures at a glance 2008. Retrieved August 14, 2008, from www.spinalcord.uab.edu.

National Wheelchair Basketball Association (NWBA). (2008). *National Wheelchair Basketball Association official rules and case book 2007-2008*. Colorado Springs: Author.

New York State Education Department. (1966). *New York State physical fitness test for boys and girls grades 4-12*. Albany, NY: Author.

Rimmer, J. (1994). *Fitness and rehabilitation programs for special populations*. Madison, WI: WCB Brown & Benchmark.

Spina Bifida Association (SBA). (2008). How often does spina bifida occur? Retrieved August 14, 2008, from www.spinabifidaassociation.org.

Wells, C.L., & Hooker, S.P. (1990). The spinal injured athlete. *Adapted Physical Activity Quarterly, 7,* 265-285.

Wheelchair and Ambulatory Sports, USA (WASUSA). (2010). *2010-2011 Competition rules for track and field and road racing*. St. Peters, MO: Author.

Winnick, J.P., & Short, F.X. (1984). The physical fitness of youngsters with spinal neuromuscular conditions. *Adapted Physical Activity Quarterly, 1*, 37-51.

Winnick, J.P., & Short, F.X. (1985). *Physical fitness testing of the disabled*. Champaign, IL: Human Kinetics.

Winnick, J.P., & Short, F.X. (1999a). *The Brockport physical fitness test manual*. Champaign, IL: Human Kinetics.

Winnick, J.P., & Short, F.X. (Eds.). (1999b). *The Brockport physical fitness training guide*. Champaign, IL: Human Kinetics.

WRITTEN RESOURCES

American College of Sports Medicine (ACSM). (2003). *ACSM's exercise management of persons with chronic diseases and disabilities* (2nd ed.). Champaign, IL: Human Kinetics.

This book provides guidelines for exercise testing and programming for people with spinal cord injuries, polio, and post-polio syndrome. Excellent recommendations are provided regarding safety and precautions that should be taken to reduce risks during exercise.

New York Posture Rating Test. (1966). In *New York State physical fitness test for boys and girls grades 4-12*. Albany, NY: New York State Education Department.

This is any easy-to-use and comprehensive screening test for upper- and lower-back postural deviations.

Posture Grid. (1991). In R.C. Adams & J.A. McCubbin, *Games, sports and exercises for the physically disabled* (4th ed., pp.155-162). Philadelphia: Lea & Febiger.

This document describes how to make your own posture grid, which can then be used to evaluate postural deviations of the head, spine, legs, and feet.

AUDIOVISUAL RESOURCES

AbleData, 8630 Fenton St., Ste. 930, Silver Spring, MD 20910; phone: 800-277-0216.

AbleData provides consumer information for people with disabilities about assistive technology products and rehabilitation resources available from domestic and international sources. Among these materials are over 20 videotapes designed for ages ranging from babies to senior citizens with various physical disabilities. Two examples are the following:

Fitness for everyone, a 30-minute aerobic dance video for people with paraplegia and quadriplegia

Theracise, a video of exercises for people with upper-extremity disabilities that focuses on range of motion, strength, and function

National Center on Physical Activity and Disability (NCPAD); phone: 800-900-8086; Web site: www.ncpad.org/videos/.

The NCPAD is housed at the University of Illinois and funded by a grant from the CDC. It offers a number of videos that address the physical and recreation needs of individuals with disabilities. Two examples are the following:

Exercise program for individuals with spinal cord injuries: Paraplegia [video, Quick Series Booklet].

Exercise program for individuals with spinal cord injuries: Tetraplegia [video, Quick Series Booklet].

National Scoliosis Foundation, 5 Cabot Place, Stoughton, MA 02072; phone: 800-673-6922; e-mail: NSF@scoliosis.org.

This is an excellent source for movies on the history, nature, and treatment of scoliosis. Films range in length from 8 to 60 minutes and in cost from $5 to $50.

ELECTRONIC RESOURCES

Association for Spina Bifida and Hydrocephalus: www.asbah.org.

This site contains the latest information on the treatment of spina bifida and shunts used to treat hydrocephalus.

National Spinal Cord Injury Association: www.spinalcord.org.

This site provides extensive coverage of the current treatment and latest research developments related to spinal cord injuries.

Scoliosis Research Society: www.scoliosis.org.

This Web site provides links to educational and informational resources on the treatment of scoliosis.

chapter 17

Other Health-Impaired Conditions

Francis M. Kozub

Jesse is a six-year-old boy who has recently been diagnosed with viral-induced asthma. What this means is that when Jesse gets a cold, he is susceptible to asthma attacks. On most days this condition does not affect Jesse's ability to participate in physical education; however, during periods of illness, he must use an inhaler frequently in order to breathe normally. The medication contained in these treatments has side effects that affect motor performance and attention. Further, Jesse's teacher has expressed concern over being responsible for helping him with the inhaler if an attack occurs during physical education. What activity modifications must a physical educator consider for Jesse?

This chapter provides information to program planners about other health-impaired (OHI) conditions, including the addition of Tourette syndrome in the most recent reauthorization of the Individuals with Disabilities Education Act (IDEA) (Code of Federal Regulations, 2006).

According to the most recent regulations (Electronic Code of Federal Regulations, 2008), OHI means having limited strength, vitality, or alertness, including heightened alertness to environmental stimuli that results in limited alertness with respect to educational environment, that

(i) Is due to chronic or acute health problems such as asthma, attention deficit disorder or attention deficit hyperactivity disorder, diabetes, epilepsy, a heart condition, hemophilia, lead poisoning, leukemia, nephritis, rheumatic fever, and sickle cell anemia, and Tourette syndrome; and

(ii) Adversely affects a child's educational performance.

Recent statistics by the U.S. Department of Education indicated an incidence rate of 1 in 100 children, making OHI a disability on the rise in public schools (Data Accountability Center, 2007).

OHI is defined in school-aged children based on the impact that chronic or acute health problems have on educational programs. This chapter focuses on the majority of the conditions found in the IDEA definition, including diabetes, seizures, asthma, cancer, cardiovascular disease, anemia, AIDS, and Tourette syndrome. Further, conditions covered by OHI can require regular medications that may influence behavior and motor performance. These side effects may be negligible and require no program modification; however, it is important that physical educators and coaches consider this issue when providing physical activity programming for a child with OHI. The physical education implications and a checklist for successful inclusion of children with OHI are provided for each condition in the section on inclusion.

DIABETES MELLITUS

Diabetes mellitus is a condition affecting the body's ability to process, store, and use glucose. The incidence of type 1 and type 2 diabetes is just under 8 people per 10,000. **Type 1 diabetes** is the more serious form and affects more children than type 2. There has been substantial growth in the incidence of **type 2 diabetes** in children (CDC, 2007). Today, type 2 diabetes accounts for 45 percent of the new diabetes cases in this target age group.

The human body must maintain adequate blood glucose levels. In this process, the pancreas secretes insulin, which is needed to break down glucose and store it in the liver. Without insulin (**hyperglycemia**), glucose is not broken down into glycogen and stored in the liver, resulting in damage to other parts of the body such as the kidneys, eyes, heart, and blood vessels. Alternatively, when too much insulin is present in the bloodstream due to improper management of injections, food intake, or exercise (which can facilitate the production of insulin in people with type 1 diabetes) a serious condition known as **hypoglycemia** (i.e., low blood sugar) can result. If left untreated, hypoglycemia can result in sudden coma. See the sidebar for symptoms and treatment of hypoglycemia and hyperglycemia.

Physical Education and Students With Diabetes

Many factors such as diet, growth, stress, and insulin injection levels are not directly controllable by physical educators, and therefore cooperation by educational team members is necessary. In this team, parents are the first line of defense along with teachers and other school support staff. Without a collaborative effort, younger children in particular run the risk of repeated problems with low and high blood sugar, resulting in complications later in life. To avoid low blood sugar, regular monitoring of glucose levels is encouraged. This involves using a pinprick to draw a small sample of blood that is then placed on a strip and either compared with a chart or placed in a monitor. Both provide estimates of blood sugar that can be used to adjust food or insulin intake.

When people with diabetes are about to exercise, proper attention to food intake, insulin levels, and exercise amount is critical. Balancing these factors also requires attention to the type of physical activity anticipated. In people with diabetes, insulin and blood sugar levels vary depending on the physical activity, making it difficult sometimes to estimate nutritional needs. For example, Colberg (2000) highlights research showing that intense exercise such as lifting weights can actually cause

Symptoms and Treatment of Insulin Shock and Diabetic Coma

Insulin shock results from excessive insulin in the bloodstream (hypoglycemia). Diabetic coma results from too much glucose and not enough insulin (hyperglycemia).

Insulin Shock (Hypoglycemia)

▸ **Symptoms**

Rapidly occurring symptoms such as fast pulse, dizziness, weakness, irritability, and eventual loss of consciousness occur with insulin shock.

▸ **Treatment**

If the person is conscious, provide some fast-acting sugar, such as honey, juice, or soda (nondiet).

Diabetic Coma (Hyperglycemia)

▸ **Symptoms**

Slower-acting symptoms occur, developing more gradually than with insulin shock. They include thirst and frequent urination over a number of days coupled with nausea and other signs of distress, such as irregular breathing and abdominal pain.

▸ **Treatment**

Take the person to an emergency room immediately. This is a serious medical situation and you may not have adequate knowledge on how much or what type of insulin to inject. A person who is in a diabetic coma needs prompt medical care.

The symptoms for these diabetic conditions are similar, and it is helpful to talk with the affected person (if possible) before deciding whether or not to treat symptoms as hypoglycemia or hyperglycemia. However, insulin shock can occur quickly, and if a person loses consciousness, seek medical attention immediately.

The American Red Cross, 2008.

blood sugar to rise due to increases in counter-regulatory hormones. These and other factors, such as stress, temperature, and growth spurts, make it important to monitor blood sugar levels regularly, and children are encouraged to learn to manage their diabetes by learning to estimate energy expenditure. In physical activity settings, coordinating nutrition, the student's response to exercise, insulin, and curricular offerings is important.

An important consideration for people with diabetes is exercise intensity. As stated earlier, intense exercise has the potential to increase blood glucose without increasing insulin secretion, making it difficult to regulate glucose levels (Marliss & Vranic, 2002). This condition, known as **exercise-induced hyperglycemia**, is in contrast to **exercise-induced hypoglycemia**, where lower-intensity exercise has the potential to increase insulin sensitivity. The effect of low-intensity exercise on injected insulin creates issues such as an increased risk of hypoglycemia in both trained and untrained people. Horton (1995) has recommendations for preexercise meals and insulin injections to counter hypoglycemia and monitoring to help avoid hyperglycemia. Children

and adults with diabetes who exercise have to learn to regulate their insulin intake to account for the decrease in insulin requirements during exercise.

New methods for insulin delivery in children with type 1 and type 2 diabetes require additional attention by physical activity providers (Colberg & Walsh, 2002). The use of an **insulin pump**, connected to the abdomen with a small needle to inject insulin in the fatty tissue under the skin (American Diabetes Association, 2010), is now used by some people with diabetes. If the pump fails to deliver insulin during exercise, the onset of the life-threatening hyperglycemia is increased due to the lack of insulin and the heightened physical activity. Instructors responsible for programming in situations involving students who use insulin pumps must be aware of the importance of maintaining the pump as well as the integrity of the infusion site. Further, temperature is a concern since high or low temperatures degrade the insulin in the pump (Colberg & Walsh, 2002).

Physical educators must be aware of circulation problems in children with diabetes, especially concerns over foot health and general skin care. It is not recommended for people with diabetes to participate in physical activity while barefoot (Conti & Chaytor, 1995). Socks, water slippers, and other types of appropriate footwear are available for use during physical activity to avoid the risk of cuts, blisters, and other foot injuries.

SEIZURE DISORDERS

Seizures in children and adults are common, and many people with seizure disorders fail to take part in regular physical activity because of concerns over safety (Dubow & Kelly, 2003). Misunderstandings about seizures and potential contraindications with physical activity are important concerns for physical educators. First, the nature of seizures must be understood. Seizures result when abnormal electrical activity occurs in the brain, causing involuntary movements; varied sensations, perception, and behavior; and altered levels of consciousness. Although seizures are common, occurring in 1 out of 10 people (Colson Bloomquist, 2003), the focus of this section is **epilepsy**, where seizures occur with relative frequency. This occurs in about 1 percent of children. Uncontrolled and prolonged seizures have the potential to result in serious long-term and even fatal consequences. For this reason, proper attention to help reduce seizures as well as monitor the frequency and duration of episodes is necessary.

Types of Seizure Disorders

Types of seizure disorders depend on the system used for categorization. Common in educational settings and supported by the Epilepsy Foundation (2008) are classifications of seizures as either generalized or partial seizures. **Generalized seizures** can be **tonic-clonic (grand mal)** and result in a loss of consciousness and jerking movements, or they may produce a sudden change in muscle tone, with the child perhaps falling. Further, seizures can be categorized as partial and result from disturbance in a single portion of the brain, thus affecting one area of control or mental activity. Whether or not a person remains conscious further differentiates partial seizures as either **complex partial** or **partial**. Children are less frequently affected by partial seizures than adults. More common in children are generalized tonic-clonic seizures, or the noticeable loss of consciousness followed by thrashing movements, foaming at the mouth, and loss of bladder control. Grand mal seizures are the most common, and an important aspect to note is that an **aura** or warning precludes many seizures. Also, a trigger or common factor may stimulate the occurrence of a seizure in many people. These triggers include flashing lights, intense pain, psychological stress, and even fatigue.

Medications are a common treatment for seizures. Each person with epilepsy is different; some

First Aid for Tonic-Clonic (Grand Mal) Seizures in Physical Education

1. In many situations, children who have experienced repeated seizures have an aura or warning sign that a seizure is about to happen. In this case, help the child to the floor and be sure to cushion the head.

2. If a child wears glasses, remove them. Further, if a child has some type of mouth guard or prosthetic dental work, if possible remove it so the airway remains open. Turning the head to the side allows saliva to drain and keeps the airway open.

4. Do not attempt to restrain or put any object in a child's mouth. Also, make sure the child is safe from bumping into objects during the seizure.

5. Make sure to note the length of the seizure since a prolonged loss of consciousness or convulsive part of the seizure is a medical emergency. For seizures lasting more than a few minutes, first-time seizures, or seizures occurring in the water, the American Red Cross recommends calling emergency medical personnel.

6. If emergency medical personnel are not needed, be sure to let the child who has had a seizure rest if needed and inform the child of what happened. Be sure to discuss missed events or information with the child.

The American Red Cross, 2008.

may have a lifetime need for medication, while others may be able to discontinue use if seizure activity ceases with age. Medication and avoiding triggers that may spur an episode are common treatments. However, seizures can occur despite consistent efforts to avoid them. First aid is an important aspect of helping children to manage seizures. Basic first aid information for educators is included in the sidebar. Care must be taken to maintain the dignity of the student when urination or other embarrassing situations occur during the seizure. Having the rest of the class go to another area away from the child who is having a seizure may help maintain control so no further injury occurs and may preserve the dignity of the child.

Physical Education and Students With Seizure Disorders

Exercise is an important part of the routine necessary for children to normalize the electrical function of the brain (Colson Bloomquist, 2003). Regular exercise has a positive impact on the brain activity believed to be responsible for seizure activity (Dubow & Kelly, 2003). However, the intensity and stress-related factors of competitive sport may promote seizure activity in some students who are active and experience fatigue or hyperventilation. Athletics and other milder forms of physical activity are not triggers for seizures; however, Dubow and Kelly (2003) note that some types of seizures are prone to occur in children who are physically active during high humidity and excessive temperatures. High-risk activities such as swimming, climbing, and other activities where risk of falling is a concern require close monitoring for children with seizures. If a child's seizures are under control, the risks in most forms of physical activity are minimal (Dubow & Kelly, 2003). For specific recommendations for aquatic activities, see chapter 25.

ASTHMA

Asthma is both a common childhood condition and a life-threatening illness. It is a chronic inability to breathe accompanied by wheezing, coughing, and swelling in the bronchial tubes. Asthma is attributed to **extrinsic** allergens or **intrinsic** factors where the cause of asthma attacks is not readily apparent. Further, as is the case in seizure disorders, different people have different triggers for asthma attacks. Exercise, upper-respiratory infections, and other

factors can trigger attacks in people who otherwise experience no breathing difficulties. Asthma is on the rise worldwide, and the Centers for Disease Control and Prevention (CDC) (2009) estimates that 14 to 15 million Americans are at risk for this condition. Most notably, asthma affects 5 million children, or 8.5 percent prevalence (Moorman et al., 2007), making it one of the most common OHI childhood conditions.

Symptoms and Treatment of Asthma

Exacerbation of asthma in susceptible students is first observed in an inability to breathe or a persistent cough. Physical educators should be aware of children in their class who have a documented pattern of asthma and should have access to fast-acting inhalers. Some children do not use inhalers but might require medication administration via more involved nebulizers that require an electrical outlet and 20 minutes to administer (figure 17.1). Knowledge about each child's triggers, rate of decline, and treatment is important for helping children engage in structured physical activity. In addition to time needed for a child to return to normal breathing after the use of an inhaler, keep in mind that these medications typically have a stimulant effect, raising the heart rate, and can affect behavior.

Physical Education and Students With Asthma

Asthma as a condition affecting physical activity is most noted when exercise is the trigger. This occurs in a large percentage of people with asthma and is referred to as **exercise-induced asthma** (EIA) or **exercise-induced bronchospasm** (EIB). Whether exercise induced or activated by other triggers, asthma presents a challenge to physical activity programmers (McFadden, 1999). Young children or developmentally immature learners might lack an understanding of time and might not be able to regulate hourly dosages or even be able to remember when they last took their medicine. Further, physical educators might not always be told when inhalers were last used. For this reason, parents and educators should come up with a system of documenting and communicating when inhalers are used so that the child is not overmedicated. Some additional recommendations for dealing with children with asthma include the following:

Photo courtesy of Francis Kozub.

FIGURE 17.1 Various types of equipment such as a nebulizer are used by people with asthma to deliver short-term relief for breathing difficulties.

- Be sensitive to times when children might not be functioning at their best. Prolonged intense physical activity during asthmatic episodes is not recommended.
- Children with EIA might need to avoid physical activity in conditions such as high humidity.
- If fitness levels are low, gradual increases in exercise intensity might help the child with EIA tolerate higher levels of physical activity.
- Children with asthma are prone to having higher body mass indexes (BMIs) than children without asthma (Gannotti, Veneri, & Roberts, 2007), so attention has to be given to health-related fitness variables.

CANCER

Although often perceived as a single disease, cancer involves many conditions and symptoms that can influence short- and long-term well-being. The American Cancer Society's 2007 report on cancer statistics indicates that this condition affects about 15 children out of every 100,000 (ages 0-14); additionally, **bone tumors** affect adolescents at a higher rate than adults. Thus, it is very possible that educators in the public schools will have students who are facing this potentially disabling condition.

Physical activity will play a vital role in helping children recover and adjust to any permanent outcomes of the disease.

Cancer Types

Background information about cancer focuses on two factors: the nature of the disease and the treatment. Cancer is categorized based on the tissue affected. In cancer, cells grow at an abnormal rate and replace healthy tissue. The mechanism of cell growth and division is not clearly understood, but any body cells can be attacked. Treatment varies and may include surgery to remove the abnormal growths, radiation to destroy or reduce tumor mass, and chemotherapy, which involves drugs that retard growth in cancerous cells. Prolonged hospital stays and the side effects from chemotherapy might affect normal development in children. Children might experience pain, anemia, loss of hair, and other side effects from treatment, which might create extra program considerations in physical education.

Physical Education and Students With Cancer

All children, including those diagnosed with cancer, can develop fitness. Physical activity plays an important role in recovering from the physical effects of treatments (San Juan et al., 2007). However, caution in prescribing exercise for children with cancer is warranted based on the lack of research specific to children. A general recommendation is to provide programs that influence multiple systems in the child. Obesity and osteoporosis are major problems in long-term cancer survivors (Van der Sluis & Van den Heuvel-Eibrink; 2008; Warner, 2008). Awareness of these trends and links to inactivity is important to help children with cancer combat obesity and avoid fractures during the various phases of the disease. Specifically in relation to osteoporosis, load-bearing activities are recommended to stimulate new bone growth (Van der Sluis & Van den Heuvel-Eibrink, 2008). Finally, games and exercise help children by providing normalization effects where play and fitness activities are opportunities for interaction with peers and support emotional well-being.

CARDIOVASCULAR DISORDERS

Cardiovascular disorders include children with disease affecting the heart, veins, or lymphatic system. A child can either have a **congenital defect** or acquire the condition from some other illness. Congenital defects occur in about 40,000 newborns per year, and it is estimated that 154,000 cardiovascular procedures are performed on children aged 15 years and younger (American Heart Association, 2003). Depending on the nature of the cardiovascular disorder, some exercise prescription may or may not be warranted at the time of acute symptoms. However, in the long term, all children need physical education, and even children with serious conditions warranting heart replacement benefit from appropriate levels of exercise.

Rheumatic Heart Disease

Rheumatic heart disease is a condition resulting from a streptococcal infection that then progresses to **rheumatic fever** and eventually may result in permanent damage to the heart (in about half of all cases). More often than not, mild effects on the heart occur when a child is infected with streptococcal infections. This occurs without obvious symptoms in about 15 to 20 percent of children (Kaplan, 2004). However, in some people the cardiac problems associated with rheumatic fever are present and result in heart murmurs, cardiomegaly (enlarged heart caused by additional stress on the muscle itself), **pericarditis** (swelling around the lining of the heart), and congestive heart failure. Symptoms of rheumatic heart disease include shortness of breath, weight gain, dizziness, edema, and palpitations (Kaplan, 2004).

Treatment for infections resulting from rheumatic fever include antibiotics, which have little impact on the development of cardiac problems once rheumatic attack occurs (Kaplan, 2004). When damage to the heart valves results, treatment can include surgery to repair or replace the heart. Prevention is the best measure, and educators who find students with severe sore throats should refer them to the school nurse, given the high prevalence of streptococcal infections in school-aged children. An important concern is that rheumatic heart disease is associated with low socioeconomic status and is found in places where there is a lack of community education on symptoms of streptococcal infections (Kaplan, 2004).

Physical Education and Children With Cardiovascular Disorders

Factors that need to be considered in planning physical education experiences include the nature of the disorder and the treatment, specifically the medication being used and the accompanying side effects. Program providers should consult physicians to learn about potential interactive effects between medications and how prescribed medications affect physical activity. In general, basic weight-bearing and large-muscle movements help the recovery process for people with cardiovascular disorders.

Intensity, frequency, and duration of exercise vary depending on the physician's recommendations for the student with a cardiovascular disorder. Consultation with medical personnel should be done before programming to ensure that students with cardiovascular disorders exercise for both recovery and health-related fitness. Further, people with cardiovascular disease should never engage in vigorous or high-intensity resistance training without spending time training at more moderate levels (Williams et al., 2007). Progression of exercise intensity is checked using heart rate monitors or other objective measures. Depending on physician recommendations, it may be appropriate to have children engage in light (35-54 percent of maximal heart rate), moderate (55-69 percent of maximal heart rate), or vigorous exercise (>70 percent of maximal heart rate).

ANEMIA

Anemia has many causes, including poor diet and heredity. In anemia, there is a marked reduction in red blood cells or general change in quality of **hemoglobin**. This in turn affects the oxygen-carrying capabilities of the blood, forcing the heart to increase output to compensate for the needs of cells in the body. The most common form of anemia is iron deficiency, which can result in shortness of breath, lack of energy, dizziness, and digestive problems. Also considered as part of OHI is sickle-cell anemia, a genetic condition most frequently found in African Americans. Sickle-shaped cells resulting from defective **hemoglobin** occur in about 10 percent of African Americans carrying the abnormal gene. The symptoms most likely to affect physical activity participation include fatigue, bone and joint pain, and leg ulcers (Porth, 2005).

Physical Education and Students With Anemia

Children with anemia require close communication among educators, parents, child, and physician to address various symptoms. As Sigler and Zinkham (1995) explain, specific physical activity recommendations for people with anemia are difficult because each condition is different, and personal motivation, abilities, and levels of conditioning will affect recommendations. In general, children with all types of anemia should be encouraged to exercise and even engage in individual sport. However, caution is warranted in competitive and high-impact activities for children who lack experience and may not understand their potential physical limitations as a result of anemia (Sigler & Zinkham, 1995). This includes higher heart rates resulting from lower oxygen in the blood during aerobic exercise, joint inflammation, and heart problems associated with anemia that may go unnoticed (Barden et al., 2000; Moheeb, Wali, & El-Sayed, 2007; Single & Zinkham, 1995).

AIDS AND HIV

The CDC (2005) reports that almost 5,000 children in the 33 states that reported data were infected with human immunodeficiency virus (HIV) or diagnosed with acquired immunodeficiency syndrome (AIDS) in 2004 alone. As a result of these numbers and increased social pressure for integration, educators must be well informed and equipped to serve learners with AIDS. Most important is making educators aware that being **HIV positive** is not the same as having AIDS. Only some people who are infected with the virus (HIV positive) develop AIDS symptoms. From a disease-control standpoint, those who are HIV positive are carriers of the virus and thus able to infect others. This is perhaps the issue that most alarms communities and creates resistance to the notion that children with HIV or AIDS can integrate into schools without putting peers and teachers at risk.

Facts About HIV and AIDS

It has long been known that HIV, the virus that causes AIDS, is present in the bodily fluids of those who are infected. However, it is only through direct contact from an open wound, sexual intercourse, or shared needles that the disease spreads. Airborne exposure or general casual contact will not spread AIDS, and the CDC monitors the spread of the disease to ensure that children and adults are not put at undue risk. Although the reported number of AIDS cases has declined since 1992, it is likely that children with HIV will attend public schools. New drugs (increasing life expectancy and decreasing viral load) and a more informed public have opened the doors for children with HIV to lead normal lives.

Physical Education and Students With HIV or AIDS

Physical education modifications for children with AIDS depend on the presence of secondary opportunistic illnesses. Once acute symptoms such as open sores, cough, or diarrhea begin to show up, children might need program modifications depending on the extent of the symptoms. In general, these are conditions that might be present in any child, and notification of appropriate school personnel about medical and hygiene issues is important. Children with AIDS should be treated in a manner consistent with all students when blood, vomit, or other biohazards are present and at risk for exposing others. In general, all institutions should have a plan or universal precautions for handling biohazards, whether children with AIDS or HIV are present or not.

Knowledge about children with AIDS and exercise primarily has been generalized from adult studies. The positive effects of exercise are noted in light of many side effects of the medications used to treat the disease. Specifically, many medications are now being linked to redistribution of fat and general weight gain. From the standpoint of health-related fitness, children with AIDS or HIV can benefit both mentally and physically from exercise without further complications (Spence et al., 1990). Resistance training has also had positive effects on strength and lean body mass (Roubenoff et al., 1998). However, there is some evidence to suggest that adults with HIV or AIDS are prone to fatigue and decreased muscular performance during anaerobic activities (Scott et al., 2007). Addressing the social issues related to children who are HIV positive or have AIDS is more of a concern than physical limitations inferred from studies on adults.

TOURETTE SYNDROME

Tourette syndrome is a neurological disease that affects the ability to control movement and in some cases speaking. This condition is present in about 1 in 1,000 people in the United States (Berardelli et al., 2003). The involuntary actions and comments are called **tics** and are typically noticed during early childhood between ages 3 and 8 (Copur et al., 2007). Tics can range from mild throat clearing or eye movements to more noticeable rapid movements or sounds repeated over and over. Tourette syndrome varies over the life span, with the worst symptoms occurring during the teen years (Hendren, 2002). Medications are used in some cases that can have side effects such as increased BMI, school phobia, depression, and damage to the liver (Copur et al., 2007).

Physical Education and Students With Tourette Syndrome

There are many examples of athletes with Tourette syndrome, including baseball pitcher Jim Eisenreich and soccer goalie Tim Howard, who are able to participate at high levels. Aside from the medical side effects noted earlier and the social stigma associated with this condition, necessary physical education modifications are few. Physical educators and peers of children with Tourette syndrome should be aware that tics are involuntary, may occur in bouts, and can be absent for long periods of time (Hendren, 2002).

Tourette syndrome can exist with other conditions such as OCD, behavior problems, attention deficits, and issues with visual–motor integration (Murray, 1997). These situations can interact with physical activity programming if a child with Tourette syndrome is placed in an integrated setting where competitive and social situations are part of the curriculum. Care has to be taken to obtain specific information about each child to determine if **triggers** exist for tics. Stress and anxiety can influence the frequency of tics for some children (Hendren, 2002). For this reason, physical education in integrated settings should include information sharing for the entire class to avoid misinformation. Further, children with Tourette syndrome may benefit from programming that is low in stress. Children with Tourette syndrome need physical education and an opportunity to engage socially with peers so that physical activity skills are present later in life, when symptoms are likely to diminish or disappear altogether.

INCLUSION

Inclusion for children with OHI provides a challenge to educational teams because of the need for case-by-case modifications based on unique learner needs. Table 17.1 outlines some of the considerations related to medical conditions discussed in this chapter. This checklist is recommended when the disability warrants concern for involvement in physical activity. Physical educators are encouraged to address each of these points at a student's individualized education program (IEP) meeting to ensure that appropriate activities are selected, attention is paid to medical aspects of the disability, the child's social needs are addressed, parents understand implications for home programming, and appropriate placement occurs.

SUMMARY

OHI is a broad category including many conditions that potentially affect the educational outcomes of children with disabilities. Changes to this category include the addition of Tourette syndrome to IDEA classification in 2004, and other medical conditions may come under the heading of OHI in future reauthorizations. This chapter included information to help promote educational, healthful, and safe involvement in physical education for students with OHI conditions. What separates

Table 17.1 Inclusion Checklist for Children With Other Health Impairments

	Diabetes	Seizures	Asthma	Cancer	Cardio-vascular disorders*	Anemia	AIDS	Tourette syndrome
Exercise intensity	I	S	S	S	I	I	S	N
Social interactions	S	N	N	I	N	N	I	I
Overemphasis on illness	I	S	S	S	S	S	S	N
Regular parental support	I	S	I	I	I	I	I	S
Appropriate-ness of select curricular offerings	N	S	N	S	S	I	S	S

Note: These are general areas to focus on prior to inclusion that are not necessarily an issue for each child; it is a checklist to begin gathering information critical for the IEP process and successful integration experiences.

I—Important consideration that needs to be addressed for many children with this condition.

S—In some cases, this issue may warrant consideration for successful inclusion.

N—No more of a concern than for any other child without a disability.

OHI from other disabilities are chronic or acute medical conditions that place this category more in line with disease than disability.

REFERENCES

American Cancer Society. (2007). *Cancer statistics 2007: A presentation from the American cancer society.* Retrieved March 4, 2008, from www.cancer.org/downloads/STT/Cancer_Statistics_Combined_2007.ppt.

American Diabetes Association. (2010). Diabetes basics. Retrieved March 5, 2010, from www.diabetes.org/diabetes-basics/common-terms/common-terms-f-k.html.

American Heart Association. (2003). *Statistical fact sheet: Populations.* Retrieved March 5, 2008, from www.americanheart.org/downloadable/heart/1059110431975FS11YTH3REV7-03.pdf.

American Red Cross. (2008). *SafetNet: Staying safe at home and at work.* Washington, DC: Author.

Barden, E.M., Zemel, B.S., Kawachak, D.A., Goran, M.I., & Ohene-Fempong, K. (2000). Total and resting energy expenditure in children with sickle cell disease. *Journal of Pediatrics, 136,* 73-79.

Berardelli A., Currà A., Fabbrini G., Gilio F., & Manfredi, M. (2003). Pathophysiology of tics and Tourette syndrome. *Journal of Neurology, 250,* 781-787.

Centers for Disease Control and Prevention (CDC). (2005). *HIV/AIDS surveillance report, 2004* (Vol. 16). Retrieved September 2008 from www.cdc.gov/hiv/topics/surveillance/resources/reports/2004report/pdf/2004SurveillanceReport.pdf.

Centers for Disease Control and Prevention (CDC). (2007). Crude and age-adjusted incidence of diagnosed diabetes. Retrieved September 12, 2008, from www.cdc.gov/diabetes/statistics/incidence/fig2.htm.

Centers for Disease Control and Prevention (CDC). (2009). Asthma: Basic information. Retrieved March 5, 2010, from www.cdc.gov/asthma/faqs.htm.

Colberg, S.R. (2000). Practical management of type 1 diabetes during exercise. *Journal of Physical Education, Recreation, and Dance, 71* (2), 24-27, 35.

Colberg, S.R., & Walsh, J. (2002). Pumping insulin during exercise: What healthcare providers and diabetic patients need to know. *Physician and Sportsmedicine, 30* (4), 33-36.

Colson Bloomquist, L.E. (2003). Epilepsy. In J.L. Durstine & G.E. Moore (Eds.), *ACSM's exercise management for persons with chronic diseases and disabilities* (pp. 262-280). Champaign, IL: Human Kinetics.

Conti, S.F., & Chaytor, E.R. (1995). Foot care for active patients who have diabetes. *Physician and Sportsmedicine, 23* (6), 53-68.

Copur, M., Arpaci, B., Demir, T., & Narin, H. (2007). Clinical effectiveness of quetiapine in children and adolescents with Tourette's syndrome. *Clinical Drug Investigation, 27,* 123-130.

Data Accountability Center (DAC). (2007). Individuals with disabilities education act (IDEA) data. Retrieved February 21, 2008, from https://www.ideadata.org/index.html.

Dubow, J.S., & Kelly, J.P. (2003). Epilepsy in sports and recreation. *Sports Medicine, 33,* 499-516.

Electronic Code of Federal Regulations. (2008). GPO Access Title 34: Education, part 300—assistance to states for the education of children with disabilities. Retrieved December 30, 2008, from http://ecfr.gpoaccess.gov/cgi/t/text/text-idx?c=ecfr&sid=eaa7f55ca11b5ce22b3539d633e0fcd8&rgn=div8&view=text&node=34:2.1.1.1.1.1.36.7&idno=34.

Epilepsy Foundation. (2008). Seizure types. Retrieved September 10, 2008, from www.epilepsyfoundation.org.

Gannotti, M., Veneri, D., & Roberts, D. (2007). Weight status and physical activity in third graders with chronic health conditions. *Pediatric Physical Therapy, 19,* 301-308.

Hendren, G. (2002). Tourette syndrome: A new look at an old condition. *Journal of Rehabilitation, 68* (2), 22-26.

Horton, E.S. (1995). Diabetes mellitus. In B. Goldberg (Ed)., *Sport and exercise for children with chronic health conditions* (pp. 356-372). Champaign, IL: Human Kinetics.

Kaplan, E.L. (2004). *Rheumatic fever and rheumatic heart disease.* Geneva: World Health Organization.

Marliss, E.B., & Vranic, M. (2002). Intense exercise has unique effects on both insulin release and its roles in glucoregulation. *Diabetes, 51,* 271-283.

McFadden, E.R. (1999). *Exercise-induced asthma.* London: Informa Health Care.

Moheeb, H., Wali, Y.A., & El-Sayed, M.S. (2007). Physical fitness indices and anthropometrics profiles in schoolchildren with sickle cell trait/disease. *American Journal of Hematology, 82,* 91-97.

Moorman, J.E., Rudd, R.A., Johnson, C.A., King, M., Minor, P., Bailey, C., Scalia, M.R., & Akinbami, L.J. (2007). National surveillance for asthma: United States, 1980-2004. *Morbidity and Mortality Weekly Report, 56,* 1-14.

Murray, J.B. (1997). Psychophysiological aspects of Tourette's syndrome. *Journal of Psychology, 131,* 615-626.

Office of Special Education and Rehabilitative Services (OSE/RS), 34 CFR 300 (2006).

Porth, C.M. (2005). *Pathophysiology: Concepts of altered health states* (7th ed.). Hagerstown, MD: Lippincott Williams & Wilkins.

Roubenoff, R., McDermott, A., Wiess, L., Suri, J., Wood, M., Block, R., & Gorbach, S. (1998). Short-term progressive resistance training increases strength and lean body mass in adults infected with human immunodeficiency virus. *AIDS, 13,* 231-239.

San Juan, A.F., Fleck, S.J., Chamorro-Vina, C., Mate-Munoz, J.L., Moral, S., Garcia-Castro, J., Ramirez, M., Madero, L., & Lucia, A. (2007). Early-phase adaptations to intrahospital training in strength and functional mobility of children with Leukemia. *Journal of Strength and Conditioning Research, 21,* 173-177.

Scott, W.B., Oursler, K.K., Katzel, L.I., Ryan, A.S., & Russ, D.W. (2007). Central activation, muscle performance and physical function in men infected with human immunodeficiency virus. *Muscle & Nerve, 36,* 374-383.

Sigler, A.T., & Zinkham, W.H. (1995). Anemia. In B. Goldberg (Ed.), *Sport and exercise for children with chronic health conditions* (pp. 279-299). Champaign, IL: Human Kinetics.

Spence, D.W., Galantino, M., Mossbert, K.H., & Zimmerman, S.O. (1990). Progressive resistance exercise: Effect on muscle function and anthropometry of select AIDS population. *Archives of Physical Medicine and Rehabilitation, 71,* 644-648.

Van der Sluis, I.M., & Van den Heuvel-Eibrink, M.M. (2008). Osteoporosis in children with cancer. *Pediatric Blood Cancer, 50,* 474-478.

Warner, J.T. (2008). Body composition, exercise and energy expenditure in survivors of acute lymphoblastic leukemia. *Pediatric Blood Cancer, 50,* 456-461.

Williams, M.A., Haskell, W.L., Ades, P.A., Amsterdam, E.A., Bittner, V., Franklin, B.A., Gulanick, M., Laing, S.T., & Stewart, K.J. (2007). Resistance exercise in individuals with and without cardiovascular disease. *Circulation Journal of the American Heart Association, 116,* 572-584.

WRITTEN RESOURCES

Barfield, J.P., & Michael, T.J. (2002). Responses to physical activity among children and youths with exercise-induced asthma. *Palaestra, 18* (2), 26-32.

Misconceptions about exercise and children with EIA are discussed. Recommendations for educators are provided.

Durstine, L.J., & Moore, G.E. (2003). *ACSM's exercise management for persons with chronic diseases and disabilities* (2nd ed.). Champaign, IL: Human Kinetics.

This is an excellent source of current medical implications for children with the disabilities covered in this chapter. Specifically, it provides activity recommendations and other tables to help determine appropriate frequencies and intensities.

Verity, L.S., & Aufsesser, P.M. (1999). Type 2 diabetes and disabilities, a dangerous duo: What are the recommendations? *Palaestra, 15* (4), 43-48.

Provides basic information on type 2 diabetes and blood glucose monitoring as well as detailed information on activity recommendations based on the needs of people with type 2 diabetes.

AUDIOVISUAL RESOURCES

Cancer: A personal voyage [VHS and DVD]. (1997). Films for the Humanities & Sciences, P.O. Box 2053, Princeton, NJ 08543.

Covers issues associated with cancer from the perspective of a younger male. Mortality is discussed with relation to terminal cancer and the two-year chronicle of a person's struggle with cancer. Running time is 58 minutes.

Diagnosing and treating diabetes [VHS]. (1998). Films for the Humanities & Sciences, P.O. Box 2053, Princeton, NJ 08543.

Provides factual information about diagnosing and treating diabetes, including information about the metabolic facts related to diabetes, diet, and exercise. Running time is 22 minutes.

ELECTRONIC RESOURCES

American Cancer Society: www.cancer.org.

This site contains information on cancer that is geared to all audiences. Educators, parents, and children can access this site and gain valuable information about treatment and other medical aspects of cancer.

American Diabetes Association: www.diabetes.org.

This site provides information about symptoms preceding diabetic coma that will help educators understand the early warning signs of this medical emergency.

chapter 18

Students With Temporary Disabilities and Other Special Conditions

Christine B. Stopka

Two high school students were participating in the Special Olympics Unified Sports program. During the first half of the basketball game, the student without a disability slightly sprained her ankle. Immediate care for this injury was administered; rest, cold, compression, and elevation were immediately applied. During the second half of the game, one of the participants with an intellectual disability sustained a similar injury and the same type of care was provided. The following week both students were in their physical education classes. Although these injuries were simply mild sprains, the physical education teacher followed the appropriate protocols, which are described in this chapter, to enhance full participation and recovery.

As noted in chapter 5, students without a designated disability but with unique physical education needs should have an individualized physical education program (IPEP). For example, a middle school student who has Osgood-Schlatter disease might not be able to engage in all types of physical activities. Similarly, a person with an injured ankle might be temporarily limited in the physical education setting (figure 18.1). People with long-term disorders benefit from physical education programs modified to meet their unique needs. In addition, some of the information offered in this chapter to help students with temporary disorders may apply to students with disabilities. Also, topics discussed under the section on long-term disorders are conditions that people with disabilities commonly exhibit. Thus, the content of this chapter is applicable to both students with and without disabilities.

FIGURE 18.1 Student with a temporary limitation.

ACTIVITY INJURIES AND REHABILITATIVE EXERCISES

Students might sustain activity or sport injuries in various settings. Although some injuries might originate in a physical education class, more occur during free time or recreational pursuits.

If an injury occurs in physical education, immediate care should be provided in the **RICE** (rest, ice, compression, elevation) sequence: *Rest* should be given immediately to the injured part or joint. *Ice* or a cold application should be administered immediately and removed after 20 minutes. Cold may be reapplied in 60 to 90 minutes, depending on the extent of injury. The unavailability of commercial cold packs should not deter this critical treatment; food storage bags can be filled with ice cubes or crushed ice. An even more convenient home method is to place a bag of frozen vegetables on the injured area—frozen corn or peas conform nicely to an injured joint. *Compression* and *elevation* reduce internal bleeding and swelling. Unfortunately, these procedures are not always followed in the recreational setting, and the injury might be exacerbated. Without the ice and compression, intra-articular pressure from the swelling might stretch structures, such as ankle ligaments, just as if the joint had been twisted. Some type of immobilization or rest is needed for musculoskeletal injuries; rest promotes healing and reduces the risk of a prolonged recovery.

Unless injured students are on an athletic team, there is probably no type of rehabilitation service available to them at their school. Still, although physical educators cannot act in the capacity of athletic trainers, they might provide valuable assistance. If an injury is not being managed in an appropriate manner, the physical educator might recommend that the student see a medical professional. Many hospitals provide sports medicine services; these clinics or departments are staffed by sport physical therapists or athletic trainers.

If the injured student is progressing normally toward recovery, the physical education class might provide an opportunity for activities that ameliorate the condition. The Brockport Physical Fitness Test (BPFT) (Winnick & Short, 1999a) is health related and criterion referenced. This test may be used to assess aerobic functioning, body composition, musculoskeletal functioning, and flexibility development following recovery from activity injuries.

Ankle

Ankle sprains are a risk for anyone who engages in sport or physical activity. Jumping and other movements might cause a person to roll over on an ankle and stretch the medial or lateral side of the joint. Because of the structural configuration of the bones and ligaments of this joint, 85 percent of all ankle sprains are of the inversion type (in which the ligaments on the lateral side of the ankle are stretched).

Table 18.1 provides an exercise protocol for inversion sprains after primary care and treatment have been administered. Although eversion sprains are less frequent, they tend to be more serious and entail a longer recovery. Most of the exercises listed in table 18.1 could be used for an eversion sprain; however, the eversion exercises, being the mechanism of injury for this type of sprain, should be eliminated.

Although the primary focus of this chapter is activity and exercise, other rehabilitative measures might be used. Hydrotherapy and cryotherapy are used to treat sprained ankles; taping the ankle or wearing an ankle brace are other modes that might be used for participation in physical education class. Sports medicine practitioners differ on the value, duration, and methods of taping or strapping. If ankle taping has been prescribed by sports medicine personnel, compliance by the student should be encouraged. The physical educator, however, should not make a practice of taping ankles; it is more prudent to refer these students to a certified athletic trainer or other appropriate medical personnel.

Table 18.1   Rehabilitation Protocol for a Moderate Inversion Sprain of the Ankle

Stage	Activity	Purpose
I. Control and decrease foot swelling and pain.	A1. Flexion, extension, and spreading of toes 2. Exercises for noninvolved leg and upper extremities 3. Crutch walking with touch weight bearing	A1. Work on intrinsic muscles and certain muscles that go across the ankle. 2. Keep rest of body in good condition. 3. Involve ankle in a minimal amount of motion, but replicate a normal gait pattern as closely as possible.
II. Begin restoration of strength and movements.	B1. Ankle circumduction movements 2. Toe raises 3. Eversion exercises (isometric then isotonic) 4. Achilles tendon stretch in sitting position with toes in, out, and straight ahead 5. Shifting body weight from injured side to uninjured side	B1. Involve ankle in the four basic movements of the joint. 2. Begin to develop plantar flexors. 3. Reinforce side of ankle that has been stretched. 4. Improve dorsiflexion and slight inversion and eversion. 5. Begin to retain proprioception.
III. Restore full function to ankle.	C1. Ankle circumduction 2. Achilles tendon stretching in standing position 3. Eversion exercises 4. Plantar flexion, dorsiflexion, and inversion exercises	C1. Continue to improve range of motion. 2. Work on dorsiflexion. 3. Improve strength for protection. 4. Develop main muscle groups of ankle.
IV. Restore full function of ankle.	D1-4. As in previous stage 5. Tilt-board exercises 6. Walk–jog 7. Jog faster, stop 8. Run and sprint 9. Jog figure eights 10. Run figure eights 11. Cutting—half-speed 12. Cutting—full speed 13. Run Z-shaped patterns 14. Backward running	D1-4. As in previous stage. 5. Work on proprioception. 6. Develop function and sport-specific activities.

Knee

A variety of conditions and situations involving the knee might affect physical education performance. Table 18.2 provides basic rehabilitation programs for common knee problems. A common condition in adolescents and young adults, especially females, is patellofemoral pain syndrome (PFPS), which is usually caused by overuse accompanied by a less-than-optimal joint alignment. PFPS often includes a painful knee condition termed **chondromalacia patella**, which refers to a degeneration or softening of the posterior surface of the patella or the femoral cartilage.

Quad sets are isometric contractions of quadriceps femoris muscle groups. A six-second contraction of this muscle group constitutes a repetition. Straight-leg lifts involve having a student assume a supine position and flex one leg at the hip while keeping the knee in complete extension. Short-arc exercises are isotonic knee extensions done from 30 or 40 degrees of knee flexion to full or 0 degrees of knee extension. For chondromalacia patella, 30 to 0 degrees is appropriate, whereas for anterior cruciate ligament (ACL) problems, 90 to 45 degrees of motion is recommended. An individualized exercise program is used for each of these problems. A protocol that might be used in the latter stages of a rehabilitation program is **daily adjustable progressive resistance exercise** (DAPRE), developed by Dr. Ken Knight (Prentice & Arnheim, 2008). This strength-development program provides precise modification between sets of an exercise session and between workouts (see table 18.3).

Shoulder

The shoulder is composed of several major joints: sternoclavicular, acromioclavicular, scapulocostal, and glenohumeral. In many instances, activity-related strains or overuse syndromes involve the glenohumeral joint. Rotator cuff impingement syndrome, tendinitis, bursitis, and other glenohumeral problems might benefit from a general mobilizing and conditioning program for this joint (table 18.4). This program, however, is contraindicated

Table 18.2   Rehabilitation Exercise Programs for Common Knee Problems

Diagnosis	Rehabilitation areas to stress	Method
Chondromalacia patella, subluxating patella, s/p surgery for chronic dislocations or chronic irritative processes	Strengthen the quads, particularly VMO, without putting additional stress on patellofemoral surface. Achieve or maintain full ROM. Strengthen hamstrings, abductors, adductors, and lower-leg musculature.	Use quad sets, straight lifts, terminal extensions, lifts, short arcs with progressive resistance. (ROM and strengthening of hamstrings, abductors, and adductors can be done conventionally.)
Anterior cruciate–deficient knees, chronic or acute; s/p casting; s/p reconstruction, intra-articular or extra-articular	Achieve full ROM. Emphasis is on strengthening secondary stabilizers to the anterior cruciate.	Use active ROM exercise. Hamstring strength aims to equal quad strength of the nonaffected leg, done with programs of isometrics, isotonic with concentric and eccentric contractions, and isokinetics. Quad strength to be elevated by use of isometrics at 90°, 60°, 30°, and full extension; isotonic resistance done only in 90°-45° flexion.
Medial collateral ligament sprains, chronic or acute, s/p reconstruction; s/p immobilization	Place special emphasis on strengthening quads and adductors. Work on general ROM. Strengthen hamstrings, adductors, and lower-leg musculature.	Achieve or maintain full ROM. Use quad sets, straight leg lifts with progressive resistance in hip flexion and adduction, and isotonics and isokinetics for quads and hamstrings.

s/p = status/post (i.e., immediately following).

VMO = vastus medialis oblique muscle.

ROM = range of motion.

Table 18.3 — Daily Adjustable Progressive Resistance Exercise (DAPRE)

Set	Weight	Repetitions
1	50% of working weight	10
2	75% of working weight	6
3	100% of working weight	Maximum
4	Determined by repetitions done in third set*	Maximum number determines working weight for next session

WORKING WEIGHT ADJUSTMENTS		
Repetitions during third set*	Working weight for fourth set	
0-2	Decrease 5-10 lb (2.25-4.5 kg)	
3-4	Decrease 0-5 lb (0-2.25 kg)	
5-7	Keep the same	
8-10	Increase 2.5-5 lb (1.1-2.25 kg)	
More than 10	Increase 5-10 lb (2.25-4.5 kg)	
Repetitions during fourth set	Working weight for next session*	
0-2	Decrease 5-10 lb (2.25-4.5 kg)	
3-4	Keep the same	
5-7	Increase 2.5-7.5 lb (1.1-3.5 kg)	
8-10	Increase 5-10 lb (2.25-4.5 kg)	
More than 10	Increase 10-15 lb (4.5-6.8 kg)	

* From Knight, K. Rehabilitating chondromalacia patellae. *The Physician and Sportsmedicine,* 1, 147-148.

Table 18.4 — Shoulder Exercise Protocol for the Glenohumeral Joint

Stage	Activity	Purpose
I. During immobilization	A1. Isometric contractions of major muscle groups of shoulder 2. Isotonic wrist exercises of involved extremity 3. General conditioning exercises for the other three extremities	A1. Reduce muscle atrophy. 2. These muscles might be kept in condition without involving shoulder muscle. 3. These muscle groups should be kept in good condition.
II. Mobilization of the shoulder	B1. Moving the shoulder through abduction and external rotation 2. Codman's exercise[a] 3. Wall-climbing exercise 4. Continued conditioning of other extremities	B1. Begin to gain appropriate range of motion. 2. Begin to enhance four motions of the shoulder. 3. Help to develop abduction and external rotation. 4. Improve body fitness.
III. Development of the shoulder	C1. Isotonic exercises that involve shoulder flexion, extension, abduction, adduction, medial rotation, and lateral rotation 2. Specific exercise involvement: bench press, pullovers, push-ups, parallel bar dips 3. PNF[b] exercises, replicating arm positions without the use of sight 4. Resistance movements that replicate sport activities	C1. Develop muscles that cause specific motions. 2. Develop muscles for aggregate muscle action. 3. Improve kinesthesis. 4. Conform to the principle of specificity.

Note: Not to be used with glenohumeral dislocations.

[a] Explained in text under the heading, Selected Exercises.

[b] PNF = proprioceptive neuromuscular facilitation.

for students suffering from anterior glenohumeral dislocation. In its chronic form, this condition is sometimes called a *trick shoulder*.

Mobilization for this condition consists primarily of adduction or internal rotation exercises. During the immobilization stage, isometric exercises are the exercises of choice; following immobilization, the exercise regimen might progress from isometric exercises, such as pulling against rubber tubing, to pulley or free-weight exercises that emphasize adduction and internal rotation. Note that external rotation and abduction are movements associated with the mechanism of injury.

An important phase of many rehabilitation programs is the development of proprioception and kinesthesia. Because of this position-sense deficit, a comprehensive rehabilitation and conditioning program should include proprioceptive neuromuscular facilitation (PNF) exercises (Voss, Knott, & Iona, 1986) as well as other exercises, such as moving the arm into functional positions without the benefit of sight.

Types of Exercises

Open and closed kinetic chain exercises are lower-extremity exercises used in rehabilitation and physical fitness programs to develop strength, flexibility, and proprioception. **Open kinetic chain exercises** are non-weight-bearing exercises where the distal end (foot) is free to move; they generally involve motion in one joint. Common examples of open kinetic chain exercises include seated, or prone, knee flexion and extension.

Closed kinetic chain exercises are weight bearing, with the distal segment in contact with a supporting surface and several joints involved in the execution of movement. A half deep-knee bend would be an example of a closed kinetic chain exercise. This type of exercise is often suggested for people with certain types of knee injuries, such as ACL problems and patellofemoral problems. It has been suggested that closed kinetic chain exercises put less strain on the ligament (Fitzgerald, 1997).

A question that naturally arises is, "What is the best type of exercise?" The answer is that both open and closed kinetic chain exercises should be part of a rehabilitation and physical fitness program. If one thinks of a basic movement, such as walking, there are both open (swing phase) and closed (stance phase) components to this motor skill.

Open and closed kinetic chain exercises might apply to proprioception and kinesthesis. Closed kinetic chain exercises can be thought of as a means to promote proprioception. The tilt-board exercise described in the next section is a closed kinetic chain exercise. Exercises such as PNF might help kinesthesis, or the sense of the position of the joint in space, in addition to improving flexibility. For more information on PNF, consult *Maximize Your Stretching Potential* (Stopka, 2008) and chapter 4 of *The Brockport Physical Fitness Training Guide* (Surburg, 1999). This type of stretching can be carried out in regular physical education classes as well to stretch any muscle groups (Stopka, 2010). Most commonly, stretches include the hamstrings and gluteal muscles, calves, hip flexors and quadriceps, hip adductors, shoulders, the triceps and deltoids especially, and so on. Kinesthetic and proprioceptive defects are present not only after an injury but for students who have certain physical and learning disabilities.

Selected Exercises

This section describes selected exercises for rehabilitation programs (tables 18.1-18.4) that might be unfamiliar. Table 18.1 refers to **tilt-board** exercises. The apparatus used with this exercise, which is available commercially or could easily be constructed, is basically a circle of 3/4-inch (2 cm) plywood that is 1 foot (30 cm) in diameter (figure 18.2*a*). Attached to the center of the board is half of a pool ball or similar wooden ball. Standing with both feet on the board, the student attempts to balance on the board. This apparatus could be used to develop proprioceptive capabilities following an injury to the lower extremity. This exercise would be appropriate for balance and proprioceptive training of students with and without disabilities.

Terminal extension exercises are listed as strength exercises for quadriceps development in the exercise programs for common knee problems (table 18.2). Ideally, these exercises are done with a knee extension machine rather than a weight boot or weights wrapped around the ankle. Weights around the ankle cause a traction or pulling effect on the knee, which could stretch ligaments. Terminal extension exercises are initiated with the knee completely extended and resistance applied to the extremity (figure 18.2*b*). In subsequent exercise sessions, isotonic contractions are started with 5 degrees of extension; over several sessions, the degree of extension increases until the person can extend against resistance through 25 degrees of motion.

In table 18.4, **Codman's exercise** is listed as an exercise to mobilize the shoulder. In this exercise, the participant bends at the waist to achieve 90 degrees of trunk flexion and holds onto a chair or the end of a table. In this position, the arm of the affected side should hang in a relaxed state. The person initiates motion first in a flexion–extension direction, then adduction–abduction, and finally circumduction. All of these motions are pendular without the benefit of muscular contractions at the shoulder joint. Progressions in this exercise include wider circumduction motions and holding 2.5- and 5-pound (1.1 and 2.25 kg) weights as motions are performed (see figure 18.2c). As with the tilt board for proprioceptive development, Codman's exercise

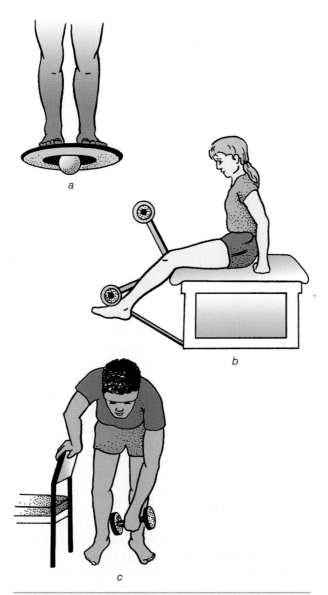

FIGURE 18.2 *(a)* Tilt-board exercise for common ankle problems, *(b)* DAPRE, and *(c)* shoulder exercise protocol for the glenohumeral joint.

may be used to promote range of motion and flexibility of students with certain types of disabilities.

SUGGESTED ADAPTED PHYSICAL ACTIVITIES FOR LONG-TERM DISORDERS

This section deals with several conditions classified as long-term disorders. The designation implies a condition or a problem that lasts longer than 30 days. This time span is a somewhat arbitrary designation because, for example, a third-degree ankle sprain might not be completely rehabilitated within 30 days. Several conditions (i.e., fractures, common knee and foot anomalies, adolescent hip diseases, weight-control problems) are the primary focus here, but the principles and procedures relevant to these conditions may also be applied to the integration of students with virtually any long-term disorders or conditions into regular physical education classes.

Fractures

Bones in the upper and lower extremities are often fractured in activity-related accidents, such as when landing on an outstretched arm. Although the focus of this chapter is activity, fractures might result from other situations, such as child abuse and pathologic bone-weakening conditions (e.g., cancer, osteopenia, osteoporosis, osteogenesis imperfecta). For physical educators, a student with a fracture presents two challenges: developing a program for a student immobilized in a cast and providing assistance after removal of the cast to integrate the student into the regular physical education program.

The first challenge must be dealt with from the perspective that three-fourths of the extremities have normal movement. A student with a broken arm has no problem with ambulation and can easily maintain a high level of cardiorespiratory fitness. Strength development of three extremities can be pursued with only minimal modification or adaptation. With a broken arm, certain lifts such as the bench press would have to be eliminated, but triceps development of the nonaffected arm could be accomplished through other exercises, such as elbow-extension exercises. Involvement of the affected arm should be predicated on recommendations from the physician and on good judgment. For example, any type of isometric exercise involving muscles immobilized in a cast should be approved by the physician. Any exercises involving joints above or below the cast area should also have physician approval; however, this does not mean that exercises are contraindicated for these joints.

Participation in physical education is based on the nature of the activities in the curricular unit. Although a track unit might mean little restriction for the student with a broken arm, a unit on gymnastic activities might require considerable restriction. For the person with a broken radius of the nondominant arm, a badminton unit will need little modification, whereas an archery unit, although less vigorous, does require use of both upper extremities. However, the student could use a crossbow for archery, which needs dexterity of one arm and could be mounted on a camera tripod. When unit activities preclude participation because of a fracture, physical fitness of the remaining three extremities might be the focus of the student's involvement in physical education.

Once the cast is removed, the curricular focus should be on integrating the student into regular class activities. Part of this integration process might be to help develop range of motion, flexibility, strength, and muscular endurance in the affected limb. This assistance might be critical for students from low socioeconomic levels who do not have the benefit of appropriate medical services. Most students can benefit from a systemic reconditioning program. Activities and exercises described in an earlier section (Activity Injuries and Rehabilitative Exercises) might be incorporated into this program. The student's total integration into the regular physical education program depends on a group of factors: the nature of the fracture, the extent of immobilization, the duration of the reconditioning period, the physician's recommendations, and the nature of activities involved in the unit.

Common Knee and Foot Conditions

A long-term condition of the knee that often presents a dilemma for the physical educator is Osgood-Schlatter condition, often known as Osgood-Schlatter disease. The condition is not actually a disease but instead involves incomplete separation of the epiphysis of the tibial tubercle from the tibia. Whether the condition is a result of singular or plural causes, it affects primarily adolescents during their most rapid growth. The treatment varies from immobilization in a cast to restriction of explosive extension movements at the knee, such as jumping and kicking (Prentice & Arnheim, 2008). Treatment depends on the severity of the condition and the philosophy of the attending physician concerning its management.

The physical educator should help the student with this condition during both its stages: the acute stage of involvement and the recovery stage. Because 60 to 75 percent of all cases are unilateral, affected students might have normal status for three-fourths of their extremities. In essence, the approach discussed in the earlier section on fractures might be applied here. The comparison is applicable not only from a programmatic standpoint but also from a causality perspective, because with Osgood-Schlatter condition there is a type of avulsion or fracture of bone from the tibial tuberosity.

Involvement of the affected knee in activity must be based on a physician's recommendation. For example, certain physicians might approve isometric contractions of the quadriceps and stretching of the hamstrings in the affected extremity. Ankle exercises might also be considered appropriate for the affected limb. When all symptoms have disappeared and the physician has approved full participation, the student should begin a general mobilizing program in physical education class. Development of strength and flexibility of the affected limb should be part of the student's physical education program. Exercises such as straight-leg raises, short-arc exercises, and wall-slide arcs are used to improve quadriceps strength. Stretching of the quadriceps and hamstrings should be part of the student's fitness program (Prentice & Arnheim, 2008). The physical educator should evaluate the student's gait pattern following the occurrence of Osgood-Schlatter condition. Consider the application example concerning weight training for a student with Osgood-Schlatter condition.

Knock-knees, or **genu valgum**, refers to a valgus alignment problem in which the tibia bow outward from the midline and the knees are too close to midline (often they are actually touching; compare figure 18.3b with the normal alignment shown in 18.3a). Genu valgum is a common postural deviation in children who are obese. Poor alignment of the knee results in a disproportionate amount of weight being borne by the medial aspect of the knee and predisposes the joint to strain and injury. Physical educators should carefully consider this point when selecting physical activity for students with this condition. Activities that increase the possibility of trauma to the knees (e.g., jumping from heights, running on hard or uneven surfaces,

APPLICATION EXAMPLE

Weight Training

Setting: Middle school physical education class

Student: A 13-year-old student with Osgood-Schlatter condition

Task: Develop a suitable strength program for a weight training unit.

Application: The physical educator might include the following modifications:

▸ Use DAPRE for all waist-up exercises and the uninvolved leg.

▸ For the leg with Osgood-Schlatter condition, work on strength exercises for the ankle and hip.

▸ Do flexion and extension range-of-motion exercises for the knee with Osgood-Schlatter condition.

---

playing games or sports in which the knees could be hit laterally) should be avoided.

Bowlegs, or **genu varum**, refers to a varus alignment in which the tibia bows inward from the midline, resulting in the ankles touching; the knees are too separated, far apart from the midline (compare figure 18.3*c* with the normal alignment shown in 18.3*a*). The bowing, usually bilateral, can occur in either the femur or the tibia but is most common in the tibia. This structural deformity is frequently accompanied by compensatory deformities in the feet. When the condition is suspected, the physical educator's major responsibility is to refer the child to a physician for possible treatment.

Although many foot deformities can be caused by skeletal and neuromuscular abnormalities, most are caused by compensatory postures required to offset other postural misalignments in the legs, hips, and spine. Physical educators should review the medical files and be aware of any students who have foot deformities. In most cases, the students will be able to participate in the regular physical education setting; however, the physical educator might need to monitor specific students to ensure they are wearing any needed braces or orthotics and that they are performing exercises as prescribed by their physicians.

Talipes deformities, which involve deformities of the foot and ankle, refer to a number of conditions, such as **talipes equinus**, a result of a plantar-flexed ankle caused by tight tendo-Achilles structures, and **talipes calcaneus**, the opposite condition, usually caused only iatrogenically (e.g., by the surgeon), a result of overzealous TAL (tendo-Achilles lengthening) surgery. Two others conditions are not uncommon: **talipes varus**, in which the foot and ankle are inverted (the toes and sole of the foot are turned inward, or supinated, so the person walks on the outside edge of the feet), and **talipes valgus**, in which the foot and ankle are everted (the toes and soles of the feet are turned outward, or pronated, so the person walks on the inside edge of the feet). Mild forms of the conditions are treated with special shoes with orthotics. More severe forms might require braces, surgery, or a combination of the two.

Pronation is a foot deformity in which the person walks on the medial (inside) edge of the feet. The condition is frequently accompanied by the toes facing laterally (outward). The use of corrective shoes (or surgery in severe cases) can help minimize the deformity and relieve any associated pain. **Pes planus**, or flatfoot, is usually a congenital condition that results in a lowered, or flattened, longitudinal arch. Pain is a common symptom, and obesity exacerbates the condition. Students might need to be referred to a physician for evaluation for surgery, orthotics, or exercises to relieve the pain and, in severe cases, correct the alignment.

Hollow foot, or **pes cavus**, the opposite of flatfoot, is characterized by an extremely high longitudinal arch that, because of a finite flexor tendon length, results in a flexion of the toes that appears clawlike—thus the nickname, clawfoot. This condition is usually congenital and associated with an extremely high arch, which reduces the ability of the foot to absorb and distribute force. Although surgery might be indicated in severe situations, the use of orthotics is often sufficient to relieve pain and prevent further deformities.

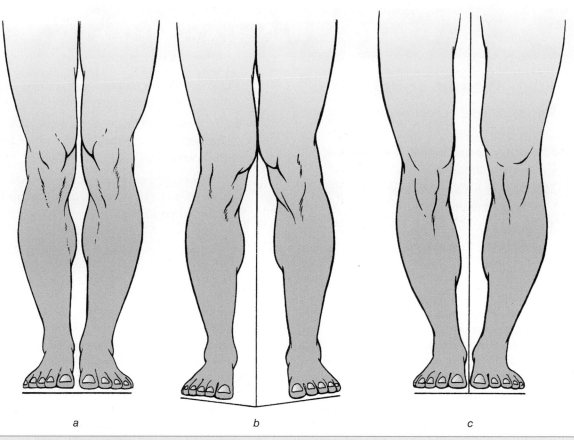

FIGURE 18.3 *(a)* Normal (in line), *(b)* knock-kneed (inward, valgus stress; thus having genu valgum), and *(c)* bowlegged (outward, varus stress; thus having genu varum) alignment of the lower extremities.

Adolescent Hip Diseases

Legg-Calvé-Perthes disease (LCPD) and **slipped capital femoral epiphysis** (SCFE) are two common hip diseases affecting children and adolescents, mostly males. LCPD, or osteochondrosis of the capital epiphysis of the femur, is characterized by the degeneration of the femoral head. It occurs in children 3 to 12 years old and runs a definitive course of pain, necrosis, and regeneration, often with some degree of residual deformity (Stopka & Todorovich, 2008). SCFE involves the subluxation, or slippage, of the head of the femur at the epiphyseal plate. It usually affects children during their periods of rapid growth, 10 to 16 years of age (Stopka & Todorovich, 2008). SCFE is similar to Osgood-Schlatter condition in that they both involve an epiphysiolysis, or a degeneration of a physis (growth plate). Rather than a degeneration of an apophysis (growth plate of a tubercle), as in Osgood-Schlatter condition, SCFE involves the degeneration of the growth plate through the entire femoral head.

In both LCPD and SCFE, early diagnosis is essential to minimize the damage. But early diagnosis can be a challenge because both conditions involve pathologies of the center of the hip bone, the femoral head, in which pain is not easily perceived; indeed, this relatively internal pain is referred to the knee region, similar to the referred pain experienced when other internal organs are damaged. Thus, in a child or adolescent complaining of nonspecific, generalized knee pain, the hip should always be evaluated (at least radiographically) to rule out LCPD or SCFE. If these conditions are left untreated until the student can no longer bear weight on the hip, the damage is so severe that, in most cases, only surgery can provide hope for a full recovery. For example, in SCFE, the hip must undergo an innominate osteotomy—that is, an actual reshaping (cutting of the hip and placement of pins for the duration of the healing).

The physical educator's job is clear: When students complain of diffuse, nonspecific knee pain for no apparent reason, refer them to medical authorities. After diagnosis, the treatment will be directed at prevention of further involvement, avoidance of weight bearing through crutches, casting or bracing, and possibly surgery. Although these directives must be observed, safe, appropriate physical education activities are essential at this time. Specifically, all activities are indicated in which the child can participate successfully and safely in the brace. Activities that aggravate the hip are contraindicated; the hip must heal by removal of pressure on the femoral head and the acetabulum. Strength, endurance, flexibility, coordination, and balance must be maintained and trained as much as possible. To improve participation, self-confidence, and overall health, acceptance of the full treatment program of bed rest, wheelchair use, or brace wearing (while providing safe, motivating activities for the student) is essential (Stopka & Todorovich, 2008).

Weight-Control Problems

Many people associate weight-control problems with the obese person going for the fourth serving at an all-you-can-eat smorgasbord. In reality, there are two types of weight-control problems, overweight and underweight, and both pose serious threats to students' health. Weight control might be the only condition a student must cope with, or it might be an accompanying condition of a disability.

Underweight

Only recently have the terms *anorexia nervosa* and *bulimia* become familiar to the general public. School staff and faculty, including physical educators, should realize that a coordinated effort among parents, students, physicians, and school personnel is needed to deal with these problems.

Anorexia nervosa is a preoccupation with being thin that is manifested in self-starvation and might be accompanied by excessive physical activity. People with anorexia have a distorted body image, and may have primary or secondary amenorrhea if they are female. There is also the female athlete triad, which consists of eating disorders, amenorrhea, and osteoporosis. Increases in stress fractures are related to the third element in this triad, osteoporosis (Murphy & Gutekunst, 1997; Rencken, Chestnut, & Drinkwater, 1996). During the early stages of anorexia, both parents and student might be unaware that the condition is developing. As it progresses, the student becomes emaciated and hungry but denies the existence of the problem. Anorexia nervosa is not to be regarded lightly, for mortality rates range from 5 to 15 percent among those who are diagnosed with it. Death is the result of circulatory collapse or cardiac arrhythmias caused by electrolyte imbalance.

Bulimia is a condition associated with anorexia nervosa; it involves obsessive eating with ritualistic purging of ingested food through means of self-induced vomiting or laxatives. This condition is not exclusive to girls but is also common in male gymnasts and wrestlers, who engage in these practices to make their weight classes (Prentice & Arnheim, 2008). These practices can lead to electrolyte imbalance, impaired liver and kidney functioning, stomach rupture, tooth decay, and esophagitis.

The goals of treatment to promote weight gain in these conditions are simple in nature but challenging in execution. Hospitalization in a medical or psychiatric unit might be needed to initiate treatment, with a brief stay of two weeks or a longer stay of several months to a year. Treatment consists of behavior modification, vitamin and mineral supplements, appropriate diet, and psychotherapy for the student and family. Low self-esteem, guilt, and anxiety are often part of the student's underlying problems.

The physical educator might be one of the first to recognize these problems. Anorexic or bulimic students are often compliant high achievers. A preoccupation with thinness, apparent weight loss, and an increasing involvement in aerobic activities might be signs that referral to an appropriate health professional is needed. Whatever the stage of the student's disorder, physical education activities must be monitored to ensure an appropriate level of exertion. A caloric deficit—more calories being used than are taken in—should not be allowed to develop through physical education activities. Fitness enhancement should be a gradual process, with strength gains achieved before cardiorespiratory endurance is attempted. Precautions or exercise contraindications for students with cardiovascular conditions, discussed in chapter 17, are applicable in this situation. Dual and individual sports, some with certain modifications, are of suitable intensity and good for promoting social interaction. A priority with students who have these eating disorders should be enhancement of self-esteem.

Overweight and Obesity

Obesity is defined as an excessively high amount of body fat or adipose tissue in relation to lean body mass (Winnick & Short, 1999a). Body-fat distribution can be estimated by skinfold measures, waist-to-hip circumference ratios, or techniques such as ultrasound, computed tomography, or magnetic resonance imaging (MRI). The body mass index (BMI) is a mathematical formula that is commonly used for determining whether someone is overweight or obese. BMI is calculated by determining body weight in kilograms and dividing the result by the square of the height in meters (i.e., weight divided by height squared). Although this method is imperfect because it lacks precision for mesomorphic (heavily muscled) and ectomorphic people (producing artificially high or low scores), it remains a popular method because of its convenience and overall validity and reliability. According to the Centers for Disease Control and Prevention (CDC) (2007), the term *overweight* is defined by having a BMI ranging from 25 to 29.9; people with a BMI of 30 or more are considered obese.

Incidence

Behind smoking, obesity is the second leading preventable cause of death in the United States. Thus, a major public health concern today is the rapidly growing numbers of overweight and obese students. Furthermore, the CDC (2007) reports that the percentage of children defined as overweight has more than doubled since the early 1970s, and there are almost three times as many overweight adolescents as there were in 1980. By 1999, an estimated 61 percent of U.S. adults were either overweight or obese (an increase of 74 percent since 1991); by 2000, nearly 40 million American adults were classified as obese; and most recently, findings indicate that "no state met the Healthy People 2010 objective of only 15% obesity; 30 states were 10 or more percentage points away" (CDC, 2007).

Demographic variables related to obesity include gender, age, and socioeconomic level. Although women, especially those of Hispanic and African American descent, have higher percentages of obesity, this epidemic is pervasive and affects all ages, ethnicities, disabilities, and gender. It is critical that teachers provide physical education experiences for overweight and obese students. When students with disabilities (who might have less mobility than others and thus are at higher risk for becoming obese) grow older, it is important that they have the desire and skills to engage in an active adult lifestyle that maintains their physical fitness and improves their overall health and well-being while combating the ravages of a sedentary lifestyle.

Causes

The causes of overweight and obesity are multifaceted. At least three factors seem to play a significant role: (1) behavior—eating too many calories teamed with not getting enough physical activity is a bad combination; (2) environment—home, work, school, and community significantly influence opportunities for an active lifestyle; and (3) genetics—heredity plays a large role in determining how susceptible people are to overweight and obesity. Genes also influence how the body burns calories for energy or stores fat. The behavioral and environmental factors are the two principal contributors to overweight problems and obesity; fortunately, they provide the greatest opportunities for prevention and treatment. In addition, emotional factors seem to play a significant role. For example, some people eat as a means of compensation or to reduce feelings of anxiety; others eat excessively when content and happy.

An increase in the number (hyperplastic obesity) or size (hypertrophic obesity) of the fat cells that make up adipose tissue may lead to obesity. There are two times in the life span when there are rapid increases in fat-cell production (hyperplasia): the third trimester of fetal development through the first year of life, and the adolescent growth spurt. Thus, the need for providing adolescents with appropriate education in nutritional choices and physical activity programs is enormous.

Characteristics and Associated Problems and Health Consequences

People who are overweight are more likely to develop health problems such as heart disease, stroke, diabetes, cancer, gallbladder disease, sleep apnea, and osteoarthritis. The more overweight the person is, the more likely it is that these health problems will occur. The CDC (2007) provides an exhaustive list of health consequences related to these health problems, which people with BMIs of 25 and above are at increased risk to experience. These unfortunately common physical ailments are numerous and severe (see sidebar). Without question, quality strategies for weight control, including excellent teaching content and methods, motivating activities, opportunities for athletic participation, and the skills to implement a safe, active way of life through adulthood and beyond, are crucial to combat the obesity epidemic (CDC, 2007).

Strategies for Controlling Weight

The physical educator is one member of a team who may help a student with a weight-control problem. Just as exercise alone cannot remediate a weight problem, the physical educator alone cannot solve this problem. A team effort is needed, with the physician overseeing medical and dietary

Health Consequences of Being Overweight or Obese

- High blood pressure and hypertension
- High bad cholesterol (LDL) and low good cholesterol (HDL) levels
- Type 2 (non-insulin-dependent) diabetes
- Insulin resistance (decreased insulin sensitivity) and glucose intolerance
- Coronary heart disease and stroke
- Atherosclerosis, peripheral vascular disease, and intermittent claudication
- Congestive heart failure
- Gallstones and gout
- Diabetic retinopathy, angiopathy, nephropathy, and neuropathy
- Osteoarthritis

- Obstructive sleep apnea and respiratory problems
- Some types of cancer (such as endometrial, breast, prostate, and colon)
- Pregnancy complications
- Poor female reproductive health (such as menstrual irregularities, infertility, and irregular ovulation)
- Bladder control problems (such as stress incontinence)
- Psychological disorders (such as depression, eating disorders, distorted body image, and low self-esteem)

matters, the parents providing appropriate diet and psychological support, and the physical educator selecting the exercises and activities best for the student who is overweight or obese.

There are three main ways to lose weight: diet, exercise, and a combination of the two. Diet alone is the most common method used by adults and is often the most abused method. The criterion frequently used to judge success with this approach is how quickly the maximum number of pounds can be lost. A crash diet may even trigger a starvation reaction, which causes the basal metabolic rate to diminish, thus triggering the body to use fewer calories throughout the day, both at rest and during physical activity. In this way, the body counteracts certain effects of the crash diet and does not lose the desired weight. A far more effective method is to use a gradual approach with a reduction of 500 calories a day, which equals 3,500 calories per week—the number of calories needed to lose a pound (.5 kg) of fat. Under the direction of a physician, an obese student may be on a diet that reduces intake by more than 500 calories per day.

Several key words may be provided to students to help with the diet phase of the weight-control program, including **pyramid**, **plastic**, **fast food**, and **drinks**. Students should be reminded that the food pyramid guidelines promote the need for daily exercise, as well as reinforce that the foods of choice are fruits, vegetables, whole grains, and low-fat dairy products. Students should be advised to avoid eating anything wrapped in plastic, such as candy and potato chips. Lunch should include fruits and vegetables and not food from fast-food restaurants. Finally, students should be cautioned about what they drink. Water should be selected over diet sodas, yet diet sodas should be chosen over sugared sodas. Necessary nutrients are plentiful in reduced-calorie fruit juices and fat-free milk.

Dietary and Physical Activity Considerations for Weight Loss

In spite of the fact that there seems to be a genetic component to some forms of obesity, in all cases, a healthy diet combined with the proper types, durations, frequencies, and intensities of physical activities can successfully improve body weight and body composition for the long term. This works because participation in physical activity affects body composition and weight favorably by facilitating fat loss while preserving or even increasing lean body mass, the rate of weight loss is positively related to the frequency and duration of the physical activity session as well as to the duration (e.g., months, years) of the physical activity program, and the rate of weight loss resulting from increased

Dietary Considerations to Promote Weight Loss

- Restrict calories to 10 calories per pound (.5 kg) of body weight (e.g., 1,600 calories per day for a 160 lb [73 kg] person).

- Reduce intake of saturated fats (daily intake should not exceed 30 percent of total calories, and saturated fats, including trans fatty acids, should not exceed 10 percent of total caloric intake).

- Increase intake of dietary fiber and complex carbohydrate (starches).

- Reduce intake of simple carbohydrate (sugars).

- Use lean meats and trim excess fat.

- Reduce or eliminate use of cooking oils and fats in the preparation of foods (e.g., substitute canola or olive oil; again, minimize saturated fat and avoid trans fat as much as possible).

- Avoid fried foods; broil or bake instead.

- Reduce sugar and fat in all recipes.

- Seek out fat-free and cholesterol-free alternatives.

- Feature fruits and vegetables at snack time.

- Avoid fast-food restaurants.

Adapted from Short, McCubbin, & Frey, 1999.

Physical Activity Guidelines for Weight Loss

- Expending at least 1,000 calories per week in physical activities is a goal for everyone.

- For children aged 10 to 17, a frequency of four to seven days a week is recommended, with a duration of 30 to 60 minutes of accumulated activity time per day. The intensity should be 55 to 75 percent of maximal heart rate (approximately 115-145 beats per minute, or 5-7 metabolic equivalent tasks [METs], at a rate of perceived exertion of 12-13).

- For students with disabilities, the frequency and total duration are similar, but each exercise bout may need to be more intermittent (with more breaks). The intensity may need to be adjusted depending upon the amount of actively engaged lean body mass (actively working muscles) and the initial fitness level.

Adapted from Short, McCubbin, & Frey, 1999.

physical activity is enhanced compared with engaging in physical activity alone or dieting alone. Thus, an effective weight-loss program must include both diet and physical activity considerations. Specific examples of diet and physical activity guidelines are presented in the sidebars.

Finally, it is important to select the appropriate type, or mode, of exercise. To accomplish this, the FITT principle (frequency, intensity, time, and type) is often employed. Activities that facilitate the acquisition of more lean body mass, such as resistance exercises, have a positive effect on the basal metabolic rate by increasing it throughout the day. This is possible because muscle mass requires more calories for maintenance than does adipose tissue.

Also of critical importance is the acquisition of cardiorespiratory endurance, which burns calories while it is being performed and for several hours after the exercise session has ceased. The types of activities selected should engage large-muscle groups and be rhythmic and continuous in nature. Such activities can include swimming, jogging, cycling, rowing, wheeling, dancing, hiking, cross-country skiing, in-line skating, and walking. Additional characteristics of a desirable weight training program for students who are overweight or obese are shown in the sidebar.

Physical Education and Students Who Are Overweight

A well-designed physical education program for students who are overweight and obese may contribute to increased caloric expenditure. There are, however, certain limitations the physical educator must deal with in developing such a program. These barriers include lack of motivation, time,

Characteristics of a Desirable Training Program for Students Who Are Overweight or Obese

- The activity should emphasize the use of large-muscle groups in low-impact, aerobic activities.
- Intensity should be deemphasized and duration should be stressed.
- The frequency of activities should be daily or nearly so, thus raising the total daily energy expenditure.
- There should be a gradual increase in frequency, time, and intensity.
- Participation time (daily duration) can be accumulated throughout the day; thus, intermittent

activities should be encouraged, especially for younger children and those beginning an exercise program, as well as participation in daily activities such as household chores.

- The activities should be well liked and pain free.
- Encouraging the participation of others such as partners, small groups, and especially family members is helpful for program maintenance, motivation, and enjoyment.

Adapted from Short, McCubbin, & Frey, 1999.

facilities, and equipment; anxiety and previous negative experiences; and poor balance, discomfort, or pain related to the weight problem.

The physical education teacher is in an excellent situation to offer appropriate activities and advice to deal with these barriers. For example, it may be helpful to provide evidence of successful weight control by assessing the percent of weight lost rather than the pounds lost. The teacher can help celebrate the progress that is being made. Time in each physical education class may be devoted to weight control. Physical education provides access to both facilities and equipment to enhance a weight-control program. An atmosphere of commitment to students' goals and positive feedback from teacher and peers can counter previous negative experiences.

Many activities are suited to students with excessive weight. The physical education teacher may work on balance and proprioception and provide activities such as water aerobics that minimize weight on joints and reduce reliance on balance skills. The physical educator should ease a student into a physical activity program and provide activities that are enjoyable. This is the best antidote for anxiety. Appropriate activities that reduce intensity, duration, and weight-bearing situations will minimize or eliminate discomfort and pain associated with exercise.

The physical education program should be developed to provide successful experiences for the student who is overweight or obese. Activities that

require lifting or excessively moving body weight will not result in positive experiences. Gymnastic activities, distance running, rope climbing, and field events such as the long jump might need extensive modification for students who are overweight or obese. Gradual enhancement of endurance capabilities should be part of the program. Fast walking, bicycle riding, and certain swimming activities might help to develop aerobic endurance. Students can wear pedometers to measure distances covered throughout the day. Awards can be given for such progress through the President's Council on Physical Fitness and Sports, individualized Physical Best programs (from AAHPERD), or the teacher's own programs.

Additionally, the reader is encouraged to consult *The Brockport Physical Fitness Training Guide* (Winnick & Short, 1999b), which provides specific details regarding assessment guidelines for weight loss and much more. Items from the BPFT (Winnick & Short, 1999a) might be used to evaluate health-related components of fitness. Preferred general standards of body fat for children and adolescents range from 7 to 25 percent for males and 13 to 32 percent for females (Meredith & Welk, 2007).

Aquatic activities are well worth the extra effort needed in making them part of a program. They are usually appropriate for nearly all special populations since the constraints of gravity are reduced to allow those with physical limitations to not only acquire aquatic skills but also experience more freedom of movement and thus an improvement in flexibility, strength, and endurance (Dunn & Leitschuh, 2006). Indeed, students with conditions causing them to be underweight, including those lagging behind in coordination and motor skills, often find the water to be a forgiving and positive learning environment. For example, learning locomotor skills in the water eliminates the fear of falling or looking uncoordinated in front of peers and is terrific for skill learning, balance, and fitness. It even invites positive social interactions (it is hard to skip or gallop in waist-deep water without laughing and just having fun).

In addition, for students who are obese, activities such as water calisthenics might reduce stress on joints such as the knees, ankles, and feet. As the students gain in fitness, they can gradually work out in shallower water, thus eventually gaining the ability to tolerate the higher gravitational stresses of the land-based environment. Also, if swimming skills are an objective, excessive buoyancy might be counterproductive, as Sherrill (2004) points out, because this force might keep parts of the body out of the water, thus impeding the execution of certain swimming strokes. So, the varying amount of buoyancy offered by the water allows it to be an individualized, effective medium for all. It can be enjoyed by people of all ages and with virtually any disability, and it may offer an extremely therapeutic and positive experience.

Activities for Achieving Cardiorespiratory Endurance and Weight Loss

It is critical that instructors planning weight-loss programs carefully consider the factors that motivate participants to engage in the activities and continue the program. Students must understand how to incorporate physical activity into their personal lifestyles (Twisk, 2001). If they are going to participate in sport or other activities, they must learn the skills to do so. For example, one cannot expect a student to participate in a lap swimming program without having learned the necessary swimming skills. Often such details are overlooked. For most children and adolescents, participation in games and sports that have a lifetime emphasis are especially desirable to make the activity both enjoyable and inviting to family and friends.

Developmentally appropriate activities are also essential. Children cannot be expected to experience success on a basketball or soccer team when they have not yet mastered their basic locomotor and manipulative skills such as running, skipping, sliding, dribbling, and kicking. Well-planned obstacle courses and climbing activities are excel-

lent for younger children for motivating enjoyment and the development of motor skills. Slightly older children might benefit significantly by participating in creative dance and music games as well as lead-up games that encourage teamwork and allow the practice of motor skills. Once these skills are learned, older children can successfully participate in team sport and sport-related conditioning and training activities, if so desired. Other types of activities that downplay team competition but encourage the learning of skills on a more individual basis are walking, hiking, swimming, jogging, running, skiing, cycling, skating, rowing, and hiking. Group activities such as aerobic dance, aqua aerobics, spinning, and similar activities encourage socialization without requiring participation with a specific team. See the sidebar for suggestions that may enhance participation in physical activities.

Many of the typical units covered in a physical education class may need considerable modification for students who are obese. A basketball or American football unit may focus on developing certain fundamental skills such as passing, catching, kicking, and shooting. Softball may include the development of fundamental skills and may involve modification of some rules, such as allowing for courtesy or pinch runners. Dual and individual sports with modifications such as boundary or rule changes (i.e., the ball may bounce twice in handball) are appropriate activities. Golf, archery, and bowling need no modification, whereas tennis and racquetball may be feasible only in doubles play.

All curricular experiences should be oriented toward helping obese and overweight students develop a positive attitude toward themselves and toward physical activity. Physical education experiences—whether doing a caloric analysis of energy expenditures, learning to drive a golf ball, or being permitted to wear sport clothing other than the typical gym uniform—should help obese and overweight students cope with their condition and should contribute directly or indirectly to solving the weight-control problem. Finally, any strategy to improve self-image will help these students deal with their situation. Likewise, any strategy that changes the other students' attitudes toward their peers with weight problems will facilitate integration of students who are overweight or obese into the social environment. In the final analysis, the focus of a physical education class must be suitable physical activity. Short, McCubbin, and Frey (1999) provide helpful physical activity guidelines for weight loss in chapter 2 of *The Brockport Physical Fitness Training Guide*.

Suggestions to Enhance and Maintain Participation in Physical Activities

- Select activities that are developmentally appropriate.
- Ensure that students have the necessary skills to participate successfully and safely.
- Select well-liked activities in pleasant surroundings.
- Emphasize that accumulated physical activity is beneficial.
- Give guidance regarding the amount of activity, intensity, and duration.
- Start easy and progress gradually; avoid doing too much, too fast, too soon.
- Teach skills for lifetime activities and those that invite the involvement of others.

- Provide individualized guidance, reinforcement, and personal attention.
- Empower participants by encouraging self-assessment and self-monitoring.
- Provide feedback regarding physiological and other skill improvements.
- Develop knowledge, understanding, and values regarding health-related fitness.
- Develop and implement award systems and other incentives for participation.

Adapted from Short, McCubbin, & Frey, 1999.

SUMMARY

This chapter has addressed conditions that both students with and without disabilities may experience. Although activity injuries and long-term disorders may be found among all students, these conditions should not preclude participation in physical education class or physical activity outside the school setting. Suggestions for appropriate physical activity and physical fitness experiences have been provided for students with activity injuries, long-term disorders, and weight-control problems.

REFERENCES

Centers for Disease Control and Prevention (CDC) & National Center for Chronic Disease Prevention and Health Promotion (NCCDPHP). (2007). Obesity in U.S. Adults, 2007, Behavioral Risk Factor Surveillance System (BRFSS). Retrieved from www.cdc.gov/Features/dsObesity/.

Dunn, J.M., & Leitschuh, C.A. (2006). *Special physical education* (8th ed.). Dubuque, IA: Kendall/Hunt.

Fitzgerald, G.K. (1997). Open versus closed kinetic chain exercise: Issues in rehabilitation after anterior cruciate ligament reconstructive surgery. *Physical Therapy*, 77, 1747-1754.

Meredith, M.D., & Welk, G. J. (2007). *Fitnessgram/Activitygram test administration manual* (4th ed.). Champaign, IL: Human Kinetics.

Murphy, S., & Gutekunst, L. (1997). *Disordered eating among athletes: The athletic trainer's role*. Champaign, IL: Human Kinetics.

Prentice, W., & Arnheim, D. (2008). *Arnheim's principles of athletic training: A competency-based approach* (13th ed.). Boston: McGraw-Hill.

Rencken, M.L., Chestnut, C.H., & Drinkwater, B.L. (1996). Bone density at multiple skeletal sites in amenorrheic athletes. *Journal of the American Medical Association, 276*, 238-240.

Sherrill, C. (2004). *Adapted physical activity, recreation, and sport: Crossdisciplinary and lifespan* (6th ed.). Boston: McGraw-Hill.

Short, F., McCubbin, J., & Frey, G. (1999). Cardiorespiratory endurance and body composition. In J. Winnick & F. Short (Eds.), *The Brockport physical fitness training guide*. Champaign, IL: Human Kinetics.

Stopka, C. (2008). *Maximize your stretching potential: Use the "ultra-stretch" for safe and effective results!* Blacksburg, VA: PE Central.

Stopka, C. (2010). Increasing student flexibility—The ultra-stretch way! *Palaestra, 24* (4), 31-35.

Stopka, C., & Todorovich, J. (2008). *Applied special physical education and exercise therapy* (5th ed.). Boston: Pearson.

Surburg, P. (1999). Flexibility/range of motion. In J. Winnick & F. Short (Eds.), *The Brockport physical fitness training guide.* Champaign, IL: Human Kinetics.

Twisk, J.W. (2001). Physical activity guidelines for children and adolescents: A critical review. *Sports Medicine, 31* (8), 617-27.

Voss, D., Knott, M., & Iona, B. (1986). *Proprioceptive neuromuscular facilitation.* Philadelphia: Harper & Row.

Winnick, J.P., & Short, F.X. (1999a). *The Brockport physical fitness test manual.* Champaign, IL: Human Kinetics.

Winnick, J., & Short, F. (1999b). (Eds.). *The Brockport physical fitness training guide.* Champaign, IL: Human Kinetics.

WRITTEN RESOURCES

Surburg, P.R., & Schroder, J.W. (1997). Proprioceptive neuromuscular facilitation techniques in sports medicine: A reassessment. *Journal of Athletic Training, 32,* 34-39.

This article explains the basis of PNF, the types of techniques, and the use of these techniques by athletic trainers. It compares the use of PNF techniques between these dates and a previous study and provides ideas regarding practical applications.

U.S. Department of Health & Human Services (USDHHS). (2008). Healthy People 2020. www.healthypeople.gov.

Office of Disease Prevention and Health Promotion dietary guidelines and other documents and publications are available from this site.

Winnick, J., & Short, F. (1999). *The Brockport physical fitness training guide.* Champaign, IL: Human Kinetics.

This training manual provides information regarding the development of health-related physical fitness of children and adolescents with disabilities. An introductory chapter on health-related physical fitness concepts is included as well as three chapters on cardiorespiratory endurance and body composition, muscular strength and endurance, and flexibility and range of motion.

ELECTRONIC RESOURCES

Centers for Disease Control and Prevention (CDC). (2007). Overweight and obesity health consequences. www.cdc.gov/nccdphp/dnpa/obesity/consequences.htm.

This Web site details the health consequences experienced by people who are overweight or obese. References include the latest National Institutes of Health (NIH) clinical guidelines for the identification, evaluation, and treatment of overweight and obesity in adults.

Centers for Disease Control and Prevention (CDC) & National Center for Chronic Disease Prevention and Health Promotion (NCCDPHP). (2007). Obesity in U.S. Adults, 2007, Behavioral Risk Factor Surveillance System (BRFSS). www.cdc.gov/Features/dsObesity/.

This Web site gives details about the 2007 BRFSS study and concludes that "no state met the Healthy People 2010 objective of only 15% obesity; 30 states were 10 or more percentage points away."

part three

Developmental Considerations

This part of the book focuses on early childhood development and services for children with disabilities at the youngest ages. Chapters 19 through 22 discuss motor development (chapter 19), perceptual–motor development (chapter 20), adapted physical education services for infants and toddlers (chapter 21), and early childhood adapted physical education (chapter 22).

The information presented in chapters 19 and 20 is intended to review and build on foundational knowledge related to motor development classes taken in a student's professional program. Chapter 21, which deals with the infant and toddler population, opens with a discussion of the physical education teacher's role in programs for infants and toddlers. Following this, topics include assessment, goals, and objectives for programs along with recommendations for interacting with infants, toddlers, and their families. Chapter 22 provides information related to program objectives, developmentally appropriate teaching approaches and activities, and assessment.

chapter 19

Motor Development

John C. Ozmun and David L. Gallahue

Do you remember when you were young, about four or five, and wanted to complete what now is a simple task, to just tie your shoelaces? Back then it was a monumental accomplishment. First, there were the fine motor requirements of the task itself (T). Second, there were the individual differences in the rate of learning among you and your preschool playmates (I). Finally, there were environmental factors, such as the fact that your mom or dad may have dressed you in shoes with Velcro fasteners and you had little need to learn how to tie laces (E). Motor development and the learning of new movement skills involve a transaction among the requirements of the specific task and a variety of personalized factors within the individual and the environment. Keep the letters *T, I, E* in mind as you read this chapter, focusing on how the task, the individual, and the environment combine to determine the sequence rate and extent of learning any movement skill.

For years the topic of motor development has been of considerable interest to physical educators in general and adapted physical educators in particular. Without knowledge of the development process, teachers can only guess at appropriate educational techniques and intervention strategies to use to maximize students' learning potential. Educators who use developmentally based instruction incorporate learning experiences geared to the needs of their students. They reject the all-too-frequent textbook ideal of all students being at the same level of development at given chronological age markers. In fact, one of the most valuable outcomes of studying human development has been less reliance on the concept of age appropriateness and more attention paid to the concept of individual appropriateness.

In a very real sense, adapted physical education is developmental education. Program content and instructional strategies are designed to meet individual developmental needs. Unfortunately, human development is frequently studied from a compartmentalized viewpoint—that is, the cognitive, affective, and motor domains are viewed as unrelated entities. Although valid perhaps from the standpoint of basic research, such a perspective is of little value when it comes to understanding the learning process and devising appropriate interventions. It is essential for teachers of students with developmental disabilities to be knowledgeable about the typical process of development so that they have a baseline for comparing the students with whom they are working. The totality and integrated nature of the student must be recognized, respected, and accommodated in the educational process.

In this chapter, the focus is on defining motor development and describing the categories of human movement. Developmental theory is briefly examined from the viewpoints of two popular theoretical frameworks: dynamic systems theory and the phases of motor development. Applications and variations as they relate to adapted physical educators and students with disabilities are discussed throughout the text.

MOTOR DEVELOPMENT DEFINED

Development is a continuous process of change over time, beginning at conception and ceasing only at death. **Motor development**, therefore, is progressive change in movement behavior throughout the life cycle. Motor development involves continuous adaptation to changes in a person's movement capabilities in a never-ending effort to achieve and maintain motor control and movement competence. Such a perspective does not view development as domain specific, nor does it view development as stagelike or age dependent. Instead, a life-span perspective suggests that *some* aspects of a person's development can be conceptualized into domains, as being stagelike and age-related, whereas others cannot. Further, the concept of achieving and maintaining competence encompasses all developmental change, both positive and negative.

Motor development can be studied as both a **process** and a **product**. As a process, it is viewed from the standpoint of underlying factors that influence motor performance and movement capabilities from infancy through old age. As a product, motor development may be studied from a descriptive or normative standpoint and is typically viewed in broad time frames, phases, and stages.

Dynamic systems theory (Kamm, Thelen, & Jensen, 1990; Thelen & Smith, 1993) is popular among developmentalists as a means of better understanding the *process* of development, whereas the **phases of motor development** (Gallahue & Ozmun, 2006) serve as a descriptive means for better understanding and conceptualizing the *product* of development. Both concepts are briefly discussed after an initial overview of the categories of human movement.

CATEGORIES OF MOVEMENT

Both the processes and products of motor development are revealed through changes in a person's movement behavior across the life span. During all developmental stages—infancy, childhood, adolescence, and adulthood—humans are involved in learning how to move with control and competence in response to the daily movement challenges they face. Educators can observe developmental differences in motor behavior by observing changes in body mechanics and motor performance. In other words, a window is provided through which the student's movement behavior can be observed.

Observable movement takes many forms and may be grouped into categories. One technique involves three categories—stability, locomotion, and manipulation—and combinations of the three (Gallahue & Donnelly, 2003; Gallahue & Ozmun, 2006). **Stability** is the most basic form of movement and is present to a greater or lesser extent in all movement. A stability movement is any movement that places a premium on gaining and maintaining equilibrium in relation to the force of gravity. Gaining control of the muscles of the head, neck, and trunk is the first stability task of the newborn. Sitting with support, sitting unaided, and pulling oneself to standing are important stability tasks for most developing infants. Standing without support, balancing momentarily on one foot, and being able to bend and stretch, twist and turn, and reach and lift are all important stability tasks of childhood through old age.

Many disabling conditions are associated with deficits in stability and can result in the delay of some of the movement tasks. Central nervous system disorders such as cerebral palsy can delay the onset of independent sitting, standing, and walking in infants. Muscular strength deficits associated with conditions such as Down syndrome can inhibit children from developing key stability skills often mastered during childhood. Because of various orthopedic conditions or sensory impairments, an older adult might lack the necessary stability to prevent falls.

The **locomotion** movement category refers to movements that involve a change in location of the body relative to a fixed point on the surface. To walk, run, jump, hop, skip, or leap is to perform a locomotor task. In this use of the term, activities such as a forward or backward roll might be considered to be both locomotive and stability movements—locomotive because the body is moving from point to point, and stability because of the premium placed on maintaining equilibrium in an unusual balancing situation.

The development of the locomotor skills used with a wheelchair might involve moving the chair forward, backward, or in a zigzag pattern. More advanced locomotor skills include moving the chair forward or backward while riding on two wheels in a wheelie position. People with lower-limb amputations might also need to modify their locomotor patterns to compensate for the use of a prosthesis.

The **manipulation** movement category refers to both gross and fine motor manipulation. The tasks of throwing, catching, kicking, and striking objects are all gross motor manipulative movements. Activities such as sewing, cutting with scissors, and typing are fine motor manipulative movements.

The development of basic manipulative movements, such as grasping and releasing a fork or raising a spoon to the mouth with control and accuracy, is of significant importance for the person who is severely disabled. A person with a spinal cord injury that is high enough on the spinal column to be classified as tetraplegia might strive for the development of these manipulative skills in an effort to decrease dependence on others. On the other hand, a person missing an upper-body limb may modify a prosthetic device to participate in sports that require the skills of throwing and catching.

Many movements involve a combination of stability, locomotive, and manipulative movements. In essence, all voluntary movements involve an element of stability. This is why stability is the most basic category of movement—and why it is absolutely essential for progressive development in the other two categories. For people with disabilities, certain strategies might be necessary to provide the requisite stability to carry out a variety of movement tasks. Using supportive devices such as balance bars, walkers, or peer assistance might be sufficient to compensate for the lack of stability and facilitate the performance of many movement skills.

MOTOR DEVELOPMENT AS A DYNAMIC SYSTEM

Theory should undergird all research and science, and the study of motor development is no exception. Motor development theory is based on the observation of people without disabilities as they acquire and refine movement skills. This information provides insight into the influence of developmental disabilities on the learning of new movement skills, thereby permitting adoption of appropriate instructional strategies.

To be of practical benefit, developmental theory must be **descriptive** and **explanatory**. It is important to know about the products of development in terms of what people are typically like during particular ages (description). It is equally important, however, to know what causes these changes (explanation). Many motor developmentalists use explanatory models in an attempt to understand more about the underlying processes that govern development. Dynamic systems theory is popular among many (Caldwell & Clark, 1990; Kamm et al., 1990; Thelen, 1989; Thelen & Smith, 1994).

The term *dynamic* conveys the concept that developmental change is **nonlinear** and **discontinuous**, rather than linear and continuous. Because development is nonlinear, it is a discontinuous process—that is, individual change over time is not necessarily smooth and hierarchical, and it does not necessarily involve moving toward ever higher levels of complexity and competence in the motor system. People are encumbered by impairments that tend to impede their motor development, especially if they have disabling conditions. For example, children with cerebral palsy are frequently delayed in learning to walk independently. When independent walking is achieved, the gait pattern will be individualized and achieved at a point in time appropriate for each child. Although development by definition is a continuous process, it is also a discontinuous process. In other words, from a dynamic perspective, development is a continuous–discontinuous process. The dynamics of change occur over time but in a highly individual manner influenced by critical factors within the system.

The term *systems* conveys the concept that the human organism is self-organizing and composed of several subsystems. A human is self-organizing in that it is natural for humans to strive for motor control and movement competence. It is the subsystems—namely, the task, the individual, and the environment—operating separately and in concert that determine the rate, sequence, and extent of development. In other words, a person's development does not follow some preprogrammed universal plan that unfolds on an inflexible schedule.

Dynamic systems theory attempts to answer the *why* questions—that is, the process questions that result in the observable product of motor development. For instance, what are those enabling factors (affordances) that allow or promote developmental change, and what are those inhibiting factors (rate limiters) that restrict or impede development? For children with cerebral palsy, rate limiters are neurological and biomechanical, whereas affordances might include assisted support, handholds, encouragement, and guided instruction.

For years, developmentalists have recognized the interactive role of two primary systems—heredity and environment—on the developmental process. Interestingly, many have now taken this view one step further in recognizing that the demands of a movement task itself actually transact with the individual (i.e., hereditary or biological factors) and the environment (i.e., experience or learning factors) in the development of

stability, locomotor, and manipulative movement abilities. Such a transactional model implies that factors within various subsystems of the task, individual, and environment not only interact with one another but also have the potential for modifying and being modified by the other as a person strives to gain motor control and movement competence. These factors serve as variables on which task analyses and ecological task analysis (ETA) of skills should be founded. The adapted physical educator should be prepared to manipulate these variables to stimulate optimal teaching and learning (figure 19.1).

Both the processes and the products of motor development should constantly remind us of the individuality of the learner. Individuals have their own timetables for the development and extent of skill acquisition. Although our biological clocks are rather specific when it comes to the **sequence** of movement skill acquisition, the **rate** and **extent** of development is individually determined and dramatically influenced by the specific performance demands of the task itself. Typical ages of development are just that—typical—and nothing more. Age periods merely represent approximate time ranges during which certain behaviors might be observed for the mythical average person. Overreliance on

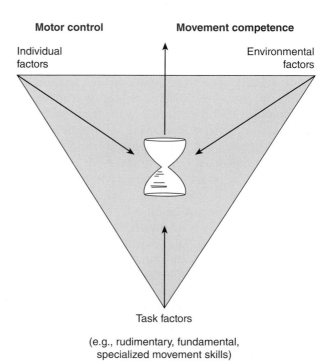

FIGURE 19.1 A transactional model of causality in motor development and movement skill acquisition.

these time periods would negate the concepts of continuity, specificity, and individuality in the developmental process, and the time periods are of little practical value when working with people with developmental disabilities.

PHASES OF MOTOR DEVELOPMENT

If movement serves as a window for viewing motor development, then one way of studying development is through examining the typical sequential progression in the acquisition of movement abilities. The phase of motor development (figure 19.2) and the developmental stages within each phase (table 19.1) serve as a useful descriptive model for this study (Gallahue & Ozmun, 2006).

Reflexive Movement Phase

The first movements noted in humans are reflexive and can be observed as early as the fourth month of fetal life. **Reflexes** are involuntary, subcortically controlled movements. Through reflex activity, the infant gains information about the

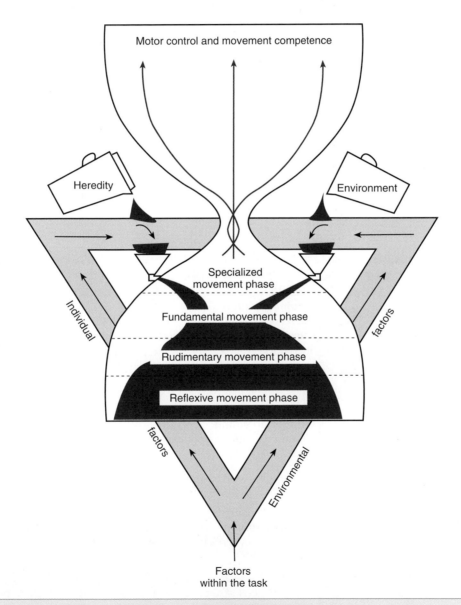

FIGURE 19.2 The hourglass: Gallahue's life-span model of motor development.

From D. Gallahue and J. Ozmun, 2006, *Understanding motor development: Infants, children, adolescents, adults,* 6th ed. (New York: McGraw-Hill Companies). Reproduced with permission of The McGraw-Hill Companies.

immediate environment. The infant's reactions to touch, light, sounds, and changes in pressure trigger involuntary movements. These movements, coupled with increasing cortical sophistication in the early months of life, play an important role in helping children learn more about their body and the outside world. Involuntary movements are typically referred to as **primitive reflexes** or **postural reflexes**.

Primitive reflexes are information-gathering, nourishment-seeking, and protective responses. Postural reflexes resemble later voluntary movements and are used to support the body against gravity or to permit movement. See tables 19.2 and 19.3 for a summary of common primitive and postural reflexes. The reflexive movement phase may be divided into the two overlapping stages of information encoding and decoding.

Table 19.1   Phases and Stages of Motor Development

Phase of motor development	Approximate periods of development	Stages of motor development
Reflexive movement phase	In utero to 4 mo 4 mo-1 yr	Information-encoding stage Information-decoding stage
Rudimentary movement phase	Birth-1 yr 1-2 yr	Reflex inhibition stage Precontrol stage
Fundamental movement phase	2-3 yr 4-5 yr 6-7 yr	Initial stage Elementary stage Mature stage
Specialized movement phase	7-10 yr 11-13 yr 14 yr+	Transition stage Application stage Lifelong utilization stage

From D. Gallahue and J. Ozmun, 2006, *Understanding motor development: Infants, children, adolescents, adults*, 6th ed. (New York: McGraw-Hill Companies). Reproduced with permission of The McGraw-Hill Companies.

Table 19.2   Sequence of Emergence of Selected Primitive Reflexes of the Newborn

Reflex	Onset	Inhibition	Stimulus	Behavior
Moro	Birth	3 mo	**Supine position** Rapid or sudden movement of infant's head caused by sudden loud noise.	Stimulation will result in extension of the infant's extremities, followed by a return to a flexed position against the body.
Tonic neck (asymmetrical)	Birth*	6 mo	**Supine position** Neck turned so head faces left or right.	Extremities on side of body facing head position extend; those on side opposite flex.
Tonic neck (symmetrical)	Birth*	6 mo	**Supported sitting** Flexion or extension of infant's neck.	Extension or flexion of neck will result in extension of arms and flexion of legs.
Grasping	Birth	4-6 mo	**Supine position** Stimulation of palm of the hand or ball of the foot.	Stimulation will result in a grasping action of the fingers or toes.
Babinski	Birth	6 mo	**Supine position** Stimulation by stroking the sole of the foot.	Stimulation will result in extension of the toes.
Sucking	Birth	3 mo	**Supine or supported sitting** Stimulus applied directly above or below the lips.	Touching area of mouth will result in a sucking action of the lips.

*Not seen in all children.

Table 19.3	Sequence of Emergence of Selected Postural Reflexes of the Newborn			
Reflex	Onset (age)	Inhibition (age)	Stimulus	Behavior
Labyrinthine righting	2 mo	12 mo	**Supported upright position** Tilting trunk forward, rearward, or to side.	Infant will attempt to keep head in an upright position by moving head in opposite direction from tilt.
Supportive reactions	4 mo (arms) 9 mo (legs)	12 mo	**Prone or upright supported** Movement of the child's extremities toward a surface.	Extension of the extremities to a position of support.
Pull-up	3 mo	4 mo	**Upright sitting supported by hands** Tilting of child from side to side and front and back.	Infant will flex arms in an attempt to maintain equilibrium.
Stepping	2 wk	5 mo	**Supported upright position** Infant is held in upright position and soles of feet are allowed to touch a surface.	Lower extremities perform definite stepping action.
Crawling	Birth	4 mo	**Prone unsupported position** Stimulus is applied to sole of one foot.	Crawling action exhibited by both the upper and lower extremities.
Swimming	Birth	5 mo	**Prone held over water** Infant is held over or in water.	Swimming movements elicited in both the upper and lower extremities.

Information-Encoding Stage

The information-encoding (gathering) stage of the reflexive movement phase is characterized by observable involuntary movement during the fetal period until about the fourth month of infancy. During this stage, lower brain centers are more highly developed than the motor cortex and are in command of fetal and neonatal movement. These brain centers are capable of causing involuntary reactions to stimuli of varying intensity and duration. During this stage, reflexes serve as the primary means through which the infant is able to gather information, seek nourishment, and seek protection through movement.

Information-Decoding Stage

The information-decoding (processing) stage begins around the fourth month of postnatal life. There is a gradual inhibition of many reflexes as higher brain centers continue to develop. Lower brain centers gradually relinquish control over skeletal movements and are replaced by voluntary movement mediated by the motor area of the cerebral cortex. The decoding stage replaces sensorimotor activity with perceptual–motor behavior—that is, the infant's development of voluntary motor control involves processing sensory stimuli with stored information, not merely reacting to stimuli.

Developmental Divergence

The evaluation of an infant's reflexes is a much-used method of screening for developmental problems. One means of diagnosing possible central nervous system disorders in the infant is through observation and reflex testing. The complete absence of a reflex is usually less significant than a reflex that remains too long. Other evidence of possible neurological problems might be found in a reflex that is too strong or too weak. In addition, a reflex that elicits a stronger response on one side of the body than on the other might indicate dysfunction of the central nervous system. An asymmetrical tonic neck reflex, for example, that shows full arm extension on one side of the body and only weak extensor tone when the other side is stimulated might provide evidence of developmental complications. The list below summarizes the reflexive behaviors that might indicate neurological dysfunction:

- Nonexistence of reflex response
- Weakness of reflex response
- Asymmetrical reflex response
- Persistence of reflex response

Examination of reflexive behaviors in the neonate serves as a primary means of diagnosing central nervous system integrity in full-term, premature, and at-risk infants. Further, such examination serves as a basis for intervention by the physical and occupational therapists and the adapted physical education specialist working with students displaying pathological reflexive behavior. One such intervention is represented by the use of a small treadmill to elicit the stepping reflex in developmentally delayed infants. Dr. Beverly Ulrich and Dr. Dale Ulrich have been able to demonstrate that when supported in an upright position with feet placed on the treadmill, an infant will begin stepping reflexively once the treadmill belt begins to move (Ulrich et al., 2008; Wu et al., 2007). The Ulrichs and their associates have demonstrated that treadmill-trained infants with Down syndrome tend to walk independently much sooner than infants with the same condition who did not train. They speculate that the treadmill training plays a role in muscular strength development as well as promoting practice of the movement pattern of walking. In addition to Down syndrome, similar investigations have been initiated with conditions such as spina bifida and cerebral palsy.

Rudimentary Movement Phase

The first forms of voluntary movement are rudimentary. **Rudimentary movements** are maturationally determined behaviors seen in the normally developing infant from birth to about age 2. Rudimentary movements are characterized by a highly predictable sequence that is resistant to change under normal conditions. The rate at which these abilities appear, however, varies from child to child and relies on biological, environmental, and task-specific factors. The rudimentary movement abilities of the infant represent the basic forms of voluntary movement required for survival. See table 19.4 for a descriptive profile of selected rudimentary stability, locomotor, and manipulative abilities.

The rudimentary movement phase can be subdivided into two stages: reflex inhibition and precontrol. These stages represent progressively higher orders of motor control and movement competence.

Reflex Inhibition Stage

The **reflex inhibition stage** of the rudimentary movement phase begins at birth. Although reflexes dominate the newborn's movement repertoire, movements are increasingly influenced by the developing cortex. Development of the cortex and the lessening of certain environmental constraints cause several reflexes to gradually disappear. Primitive and postural reflexes are replaced by voluntary movement behaviors. At the level of reflex inhibition, voluntary movement is poorly differentiated and integrated—the neuromotor apparatus of the infant is still at a rudimentary stage of development. Movements, though purposeful, appear uncontrolled and unrefined. If, for example, the infant desires to make contact with an object, there will be global activity of the entire hand, wrist, arm, shoulder, and even trunk. In other words, the process of moving the hand into contact with the object, although voluntary, lacks control.

Precontrol Stage

Around one year of age, most developing children begin to bring greater precision and control to their movements. The process of differentiating between sensory and motor systems and integrating perceptual and motor information into a more meaningful and congruent whole takes place. The rapid development of higher cognitive processes as well as motor processes makes for rapid gains in rudimentary movement abilities during this stage. Children learn to gain and maintain their equilibrium, manipulate objects, and locomote throughout their environment. The maturational process might partially explain the rapidity and extent of development of movement control during this stage, but the growth of motor proficiency is no less amazing.

Developmental Divergence

A number of disabling conditions exist that place an infant or toddler at risk for delayed development of rudimentary movements. Central nervous system disorders, orthopedic conditions, and mental disabilities can hinder motor development during

Table 19.4 Developmental Sequence of Selected Rudimentary Movement Abilities

Movement pattern	Selected abilities	Approximate age of onset
Control of head and neck	Turns to one side Turns to both sides Held with support Chin off contact surface Good prone control Good supine control	Birth 1 wk 1 mo 2 mo 3 mo 5 mo
Control of trunk	Lifts head and chest Attempts supine-to-prone position Success in supine-to-prone roll Prone-to-supine roll	2 mo 3 mo 6 mo 8 mo
Sitting	Sits with support Sits with self-support Sits alone Stands with support	3 mo 6 mo 8 mo 6 mo
Standing	Supports with handholds Pulls to supported stand Stands alone	10 mo 11 mo 12 mo
Horizontal movements	Scooting Crawling Creeping Walking on all fours	3 mo 6 mo 9 mo 11 mo
Upright gait	Walks with support Walks with handholds Walks with lead Walks alone (hands high) Walks alone (hands low)	6 mo 10 mo 11 mo 12 mo 13 mo
Reaching	Globular ineffective Definite corralling Controlled	1-3 mo 4 mo 6 mo
Grasping	Reflexive Voluntary Two-hand palmar grasp One-hand palmar grasp Pincer grasp Controlled grasping Eating without assistance	Birth 3 mo 3 mo 5 mo 9 mo 14 mo 18 mo
Releasing	Basic Controlled	12-14 mo 18 mo

From D. Gallahue and J. Ozmun, 2006, *Understanding motor development: Infants, children, adolescents, adults,* 6th ed. (New York: McGraw-Hill Companies). Reproduced with permission of The McGraw-Hill Companies.

this initial phase of voluntary movement. Sensory impairments can also represent hurdles in the developmental process. In particular, infants and toddlers with visual impairments often experience delays in motor development (Elisa et al., 2002; Prechtl et al., 2001). Intervention strategies, however, can help minimize such delays. By incorporating auditory cues where visual cues usually exist, infants with visual impairments can be stimulated to interact with their environment and smooth the progress of their motor development.

Fundamental Movement Phase

The fundamental movement abilities of early childhood are an outgrowth of the rudimentary movement phase of infancy. Fundamental movements are basic movement skills, such as walking, running, throwing, and catching, that are building blocks for more developed and refined movement skills. This phase of motor development represents a time when young children are actively involved in exploring and experimenting with the movement capabilities of their bodies. It is a time for discovering how to perform many of the basic stabilizing, locomotor, and manipulative movements, first in isolation and then in combination with one another. Children who are developing fundamental patterns of movement are learning how to respond with motor control and movement competence to a variety of stimuli. Tables 19.5, 19.6, and 19.7 present an overview of the typical developmental sequence of fundamental stability, locomotor, and manipulative movements.

Several researchers and developers of assessment instruments have attempted to subdivide fundamental movements into a series of identifiable sequential stages (Gallahue & Ozmun, 2006; Haubenstricker & Seefeldt, 1986; McClenaghan & Gallahue, 1978; Roberton & Halverson, 1984). Within this chapter, the entire fundamental movement phase will be viewed as having three separate but often overlapping stages: the initial, elementary, and mature stages.

Initial Stage

The **initial stage** of a fundamental movement phase represents the child's first goal-oriented attempts at performing a fundamental skill. Movement itself is characterized by missing or improperly sequenced parts, markedly restricted or exaggerated use of the body, and poor rhythmical flow and coordination. In other words, the spatial and temporal integration of movement is poor during this stage.

Elementary Stage

The **elementary stage** involves greater control and better rhythmic coordination of fundamental movements. The temporal and spatial elements of movement are better coordinated, but patterns of movement are still generally restricted or exaggerated. Children without delays in intellectual or physical functioning tend to advance to the elementary stage primarily through the process of maturation. Many people, adults as well as children, fail to get beyond the elementary stage in many fundamental patterns of movement.

Table 19.5 **Sequence of Emergence of Selected Fundamental Stability Abilities**

Movement pattern	Selected abilities	Approximate age range of onset
Dynamic balance Dynamic balance involves maintaining one's equilibrium as the center of gravity shifts.	Walks 1 in. (2.5 cm) straight line. Walks 1 in. (2.5 cm) circular line. Stands on low balance beam. Walks on beam 4 in. (10 cm) wide for a short distance. Walks on same beam, alternating feet. Walks on 2-3 in. (5-8 cm) beam. Performs basic forward roll. Performs mature forward roll.*	2-4 yr 3-5 yr 2-3 yr 2-4 yr 3-5 yr 2-5 yr 5-7 yr 6-7 yr
Static balance Static balance involves maintaining one's equilibrium while the center of gravity remains stationary.	Pulls to standing position. Stands without handholds. Stands alone. Balances on one foot 3-5 sec. Supports body in basic three-point inverted positions.	7-10 mo 9-11 mo 10-12 mo 3-5 yr 4-6 yr
Axial movements Axial movements are static postures that involve bending, stretching, twisting, turning, and the like.	Axial movement abilities begin to develop early in infancy and are progressively refined to a point where they are included in the emerging manipulative patterns of throwing, catching, kicking, striking, trapping, and other activities.	2 mo-6 yr

*The child has the developmental potential to be at the mature stage. Actual attainment will depend on task, individual, and environmental factors.

From D. Gallahue and J. Ozmun, 2006, *Understanding motor development: Infants, children, adolescents, adults,* 6th ed. (New York: McGraw-Hill Companies). Reproduced with permission of The McGraw-Hill Companies.

Table 19.6 **Sequence of Emergence of Selected Fundamental Manipulative Abilities**

Movement pattern	Selected abilities	Approximate age range of onset
Reach, grasp, release Reaching, grasping, and releasing involve making successful contact with an object, retaining it in one's grasp, and releasing it at will.	Shows primitive reaching behaviors. Corrals objects. Shows palmar grasp. Shows pincer grasp. Shows controlled grasp. Shows controlled releasing.	2-4 mo 2-4 mo 3-5 mo 8-10 mo 12-14 mo 14-18 mo
Throwing Throwing involves imparting force to an object in the general direction of intent.	Body faces target, feet remain stationary, ball thrown with forearm extension only. Same as before but with body rotation added. Steps forward with leg on same side as the throwing arm. Boys exhibit more mature pattern than girls. Mature throwing pattern.*	2-3 yr 3.5-5 yr 4-5 yr 5 yr+ 4-6 yr
Catching Catching involves receiving force from an object with the hands, moving from large to progressively smaller balls.	Chases ball; does not respond to aerial ball. Responds to aerial ball with delayed arm movements. Needs to be told how to position arms. Fear reaction (turns head away). Basket catch using the body. Catches using the hands only with a small ball. Mature catching pattern.*	18-24 mo 2-3 yr 2-5 yr 3-5 yr 3-5 yr 5-6 yr 6-7 yr
Kicking Kicking involves imparting force to an object with the foot.	Pushes against ball but does not actually kick it. Kicks with leg straight and little body movement (kicks *at* the ball). Flexes lower leg on backward lift. Greater backward and forward swing with definite arm opposition. Mature pattern (kicks *through* the ball).*	14-18 mo 18-36 mo 3-4 yr 4-5 yr 5-6 yr
Striking Striking involves sudden contact with objects in an overarm, sidearm, or underhand pattern.	Faces object and swings in a vertical plane. Swings in a horizontal plane and stands to the side of the object. Rotates the trunk and hips and shifts body weight forward. Mature horizontal pattern with stationary ball.	2-3 yr 4-5 yr 4-6 yr 5-7 yr

*The child has the developmental potential to be at the mature stage. Actual attainment will depend on environmental factors.

From D. Gallahue and J. Ozmun, 2006, *Understanding motor development: Infants, children, adolescents, adults,* 6th ed. (New York: McGraw-Hill Companies). Reproduced with permission of The McGraw-Hill Companies.

Mature Stage

The **mature stage** of the fundamental movement phase is characterized by mechanically efficient, coordinated, and controlled performances. The majority of available data on the acquisition of fundamental movement skills suggests that most children can and should be at the mature stage in most fundamental skills by five or six years of age. However, manipulative skills, which require tracking and intercepting moving objects (catching, striking, volleying), develop somewhat later because of the sophisticated visual–motor requirements of the tasks.

Developmental Divergence

As children advance through the preschool and elementary years, their movement requirements become increasingly complex. As they grow older, children with disabilities might experience a widening of the gap between themselves and their peers without disabilities. This disparity might be due to a child's physical limitations, limited learning capabilities, or inadequate instruction. Children with physical limitations might benefit from an instructional focus on the outcome of a task (i.e., how far, how fast, how many) rather than the mechanics of a particular skill. A child who has limited learning capabilities might

Table 19.7 Sequence of Emergence of Selected Fundamental Locomotor Abilities

Movement pattern	Selected abilities	Approximate age range of onset
Walking Walking involves placing one foot in front of the other while maintaining contact with the supporting surface.	Rudimentary upright unaided gait. Walks sideways. Walks backward. Walks up stairs with help. Walks up stairs alone—follow step. Walks down stairs alone—follow step.	9-15 mo 13-16 mo 14-17 mo 18-20 mo 20-24 mo 22-25 mo
Running Running involves a brief period of no contact with the supporting surface.	Hurried walk (maintains contact). First true run (nonsupport phase). Efficient and refined run. Speed of run increases, mature run.*	14-18 mo 2-3 yr 4-5 yr 4-6 yr
Jumping Jumping takes three forms: jumping for distance, jumping for height, and jumping from height. It involves a one- or two-foot takeoff with a landing on both feet.	Steps down from low objects. Jumps down from object with one foot lead. Jumps off floor with both feet. Jumps for distance (about 3 ft [1 m]). Jumps for height (about 1 ft [30 cm]). Mature jumping pattern.*	14-18 mo 18-24 mo 24-28 mo 4-5 yr 4-5 yr 5-6 yr
Hopping Hopping involves a one-foot takeoff with a landing on the same foot.	Hops 3 times on preferred foot. Hops 4-6 times on the same foot. Hops 8-10 times on same foot. Hops distance of 50 ft (15 m) in about 11 sec. Hops skillfully with rhythmical alteration, mature pattern.*	2-3 yr 3-4 yr 4-5 yr 4-5 yr 5-6 yr
Galloping The gallop combines a walk and a leap with the same foot leading throughout.	Basic but inefficient gallop. Gallops skillfully, mature pattern.	3-5 yr 5-6 yr
Skipping Skipping combines a step and a hop in rhythmic alteration.	One-footed skip. Skillful skipping (about 20% can do this). Skillful skipping for most.*	3-4 yr 5-6 yr 5-7 yr

*The child has the developmental potential to be at the mature stage. Actual attainment will depend on task, individual, and environmental factors.

From D. Gallahue and J. Ozmun, 2006, *Understanding motor development: Infants, children, adolescents, adults,* 6th ed. (New York: McGraw-Hill Companies). Reproduced with permission of The McGraw-Hill Companies.

possess the ability to complete a task but might not grasp the concept of a required set of movements. By breaking down a task into meaningful parts, the student might be able to experience a certain degree of success (see the application example). Inadequate instruction might require the intervention of parents or other advocates to discuss achievable strategies with school administrators.

Specialized Movement Phase

The specialized phase of motor development is an outgrowth of the fundamental movement phase.

Instead of continuing to be closely identified with learning to move for the sake of movement itself, movement now becomes a tool applied to specialized movement activities for daily living, recreation, and sport pursuits. This is a time when fundamental stability, locomotor, and manipulative skills are progressively refined, combined, and elaborated so that they can be used in increasingly demanding situations. The fundamental movements of hopping and jumping, for example, might now be applied to jumping rope, performing folk dances, and performing the triple jump (hop-step-jump) in track and field.

APPLICATION EXAMPLE

Improvement of Throwing and Catching Skills

Setting: An adapted physical education class

Students: A group of students with intellectual disabilities

Task: The adapted physical education teacher is interested in improving the students' throwing and catching skills. The objective is for them to be able to use these fundamental manipulative skills more effectively in play, game, and sport activities.

Application: Assess the students' present skill levels in overhand throwing and ball catching, and use this information when engaging students in individually appropriate skill-development activities. Use the four-step approach that follows:

▶ *Preplan* a partner throwing and catching activity to create a situation for observing the students' present levels of developmental skills (i.e., initial, elementary, mature).

▶ *Assess* each student's present skill level from a location in which unobtrusive observation is possible. While they are playing catch, do a total-body configuration analysis by watching each student's entire throwing or catching pattern. After identifying students who are at less than the mature level, do a segmental analysis by breaking their movement pattern down and observing individual body segments.

▶ *Plan and implement* a series of individually appropriate movement lessons designed to bring lagging body parts in line with more advanced ones.

▶ Take time to *evaluate students* and revise lessons. Use ongoing observation and evaluation to determine if they have made progress in throwing and catching. Make modifications in subsequent lessons as appropriate.

The onset and extent of skill development within the specialized movement phase depends on a variety of task, individual, and environmental factors. Task complexity; physical, mental, and emotional limitations; and environmental factors such as opportunity for practice, encouragement, and instruction are but a few of these factors. There are three identifiable stages within the specialized movement phase: the transitional stage, application stage, and lifelong utilization stage.

Transitional Stage

Somewhere around seven or eight years of age, children commonly enter a **transitional stage** in their movement skills. They begin to combine and apply fundamental movement skills to the performance of specialized skills in sport and recreational settings. Walking on a rope bridge, jumping rope, and playing kickball are examples of common transitional skills. These skills contain the same elements as fundamental movements, but

greater form, accuracy, and control of movement are required. The fundamental movement skills that were developed and refined for their own sake during the previous phase now begin to be applied to play, game, and daily living situations. Transitional skills are simply an application of fundamental movement patterns in somewhat more complex and specific forms.

Application Stage

From about age 10 to age 13, interesting changes take place in skill development. During the previous (transitional) stage, children's limited cognitive abilities, affective abilities, and experiences, coupled with a natural eagerness to be active, caused the normal focus (without adult interference) on movement to be broad and generalized to all activity. During the **application stage**, increased cognitive sophistication and a broadened experience base enable children to make many learning and participation decisions based on a variety of factors. Children begin to make conscious decisions for or against participation in certain activities. These decisions are based largely on their perceptions regarding the extent to which factors within the task, themselves, and the environment either enhance or inhibit chances for personal enjoyment and success.

Lifelong Utilization Stage

The **lifelong utilization stage** typically begins around age 13 and continues through adulthood. This stage represents the pinnacle of the motor development process and is characterized by the use of one's acquired movement repertoire throughout life. The interests, competencies, and choices made during the previous (application) stage are carried over to this stage, further refined, and applied to a lifetime of daily living, recreational, and sport-related activities.

Developmental Divergence

Continuing to develop motor skills through adolescence and adulthood is an extremely important endeavor for people with disabilities. The enhancement of movement skills plays a significant role in maintaining or increasing the level of independence a person with a disability possesses. Certain locomotor and manipulative skills are needed to access opportunities in the community, be they occupational or recreational. The development of movement skills also increases the options for physical activity, which in turn enhances the potential for health benefits and functional daily living, particularly in the older adult.

SUMMARY

The acquisition of motor control and movement competency is an extensive process beginning with the early reflexive movements of the newborn and continuing throughout life. The process through which a person progresses from the reflexive movement phase, through the rudimentary and fundamental movement phases, and finally to the specialized movement skill phase is influenced by factors within the task, individual, and environment.

Reflexes and rudimentary movement abilities are largely maturational. They appear and disappear in a fairly rigid sequence, deviating only in the rate of their appearance. They form an important base on which fundamental movement abilities are developed.

Fundamental movement abilities are basic movement patterns that begin developing around the same time a child is able to walk independently and lead to freely moving through the environment. These basic locomotor, manipulative, and stability abilities go through a definite, observable process from immaturity to maturity. Three stages within this phase have been identified for a number of fundamental movements: the initial, elementary, and mature stages. Attainment of the mature stage is significantly influenced by opportunities for practice, encouragement, and instruction in an environment that fosters learning. These same fundamental skills will be elaborated on and refined to form the specialized movement abilities so highly valued for recreational, competitive, and daily living tasks.

The specialized skill phase of development is an elaboration of the fundamental phase. Specialized skills are more precise than fundamental skills. They often involve a combination of fundamental movement abilities and require a greater degree of exactness in performance. Specialized skills have three related stages. From the transition stage onward, children are involved in the application of fundamental movement skills and their purposeful use in play, games, sport, and daily living tasks. If the fundamental abilities used in a particular activity are not at the mature stage, the person will have to use less mature patterns of movement.

Principles of development emerge as researchers continue to study the process of growth and motor development. These principles serve as an avenue for theory formulation. Dynamic systems theory and the phases of motor development are helpful for conceptualizing both the process and the product of motor development.

People with disabilities might experience a delay in their motor development; in some cases, development occurs that diverges somewhat from the usual course of progression. By examining the characteristics of the individual, task demands, and environmental factors, intervention strategies can be devised to increase the opportunity for successful motor performance across the life spans of all people.

REFERENCES

Caldwell, G.E., & Clark, J.E. (1990). The measurement and evaluation of skill within the dynamical systems perspective. In J.E. Clark & J.H. Humphrey (Eds.), *Advances in motor development research*. New York: AMS Press.

Elisa, F., Josee, L., Oreste, F., Claudia, A., Antonella, L., Sabrina, S., & Giovanni, L. (2002). Gross motor development and reach on sound as critical tools for the development of the blind child. *Brain & Development, 24,* 269-275.

Gallahue, D.L., & Donnelly, F.C. (2003). *Developmental physical education for all children.* Champaign, IL: Human Kinetics.

Gallahue, D.L., & Ozmun, J.C. (2006). *Understanding motor development: Infants, children, adolescents, adults.* Boston: McGraw-Hill.

Haubenstricker, J.L., & Seefeldt, V.D. (1986). Acquisition of motor skills during childhood. In V.D. Seefeldt (Ed.), *Physical activity and well-being* (pp. 42-102). Reston, VA: AAHPERD.

Kamm, K., Thelen, E., & Jensen, J.L. (1990). A dynamical systems approach to motor development. *Physical Therapy, 70,* 763-774.

McClenaghan, B.A., & Gallahue, D.L. (1978). *Fundamental movement: A developmental and remedial approach.* Philadelphia: Saunders.

Prechtl, H., Cioni, G., Einspieler, C., Bos, A., & Ferrari, F. (2001). Role of vision on early motor development: Lessons from the blind. *Developmental Medicine and Child Neurology, 43,* 198-201.

Roberton, M.A., & Halverson, L.E. (1984). *Developing children—their changing movement: A guide for teachers.* Philadelphia: Lea & Febiger.

Thelen, E. (1989). Dynamical approaches to the development of behavior. In J.A.S. Kelso, A.J. Mandell, & M.E. Schelsinger (Eds.), *Dynamic patterns in complex systems* (pp. 348-362). Singapore: World Scientific.

Thelen, E., & Smith, L.B. (Eds.). (1993). *A dynamic systems approach to development: Applications.* Cambridge, MA: MIT Press.

Thelen, E., & Smith, L.B. (1994). *A dynamic systems approach to the development of cognition and action.* Cambridge, MA: MIT Press.

Ulrich, D.A., Lloyd, M.C., Tiernan, C., Looper, J., & Angulo-Barroso, R.M. (2008). Effects of intensity of treadmill training on developmental outcomes and stepping in infants with Down syndrome. *Physical Therapy Journal, 88* (1): 114-22.

Wu, J., Looper, J., Ulrich, B.D., Ulrich, D.A., & Angulo-Barroso, R.M. (2007). Exploring effects of different treadmill interventions on walking onset and gait patterns in infants with Down syndrome. *Developmental Medicine and Child Neurology, 49,* 839-845

WRITTEN RESOURCES

Block, M.E. (2007). *A teacher's guide to including children with disabilities into general physical education* (3rd ed.). Baltimore: Paul H. Brookes.

This is a user-friendly, theoretically grounded text containing developmentally appropriate instructional strategies for teaching students with disabilities.

Gallahue, D.L., & Donnelly, F.C. (2003). *Developmental physical education for all children.* Champaign, IL: Human Kinetics.

This text contains an expanded and updated version of the fundamental movement pattern assessment instrument originally developed by McClenaghan and Gallahue in 1978. Assessment guidelines for conducting both total-body configuration and segmental analysis are provided for 23 fundamental movement skills. Corresponding videotapes, developed by Arlene Ignico, are also available.

Gallahue, D.L., & Ozmun, J.C. (2006). *Understanding motor development: Infants, children, adolescents, adults.* Boston: McGraw-Hill.

This source contains a wealth of information on 23 fundamental movement skills. Line drawings depict initial, elementary, and mature stages of each.

Ulrich, D.A. (2000). *Test of Gross Motor Development* (2nd ed.). Austin, TX: Pro-Ed.

This is a 12-item test of selected fundamental movement skills with norm-referenced and criterion-referenced interpretations.

Wessel, J.A., & Zittel, L.L. (1995). *Smart Start: A preschool movement curriculum for children of all abilities.* Austin, TX: Pro-Ed.

This source describes a comprehensive program of motor and play skills for all preschool children, including those with special developmental and learning needs.

ELECTRONIC RESOURCES

AHEMD Project, joint research project between Motor Development Laboratories of the Instituto Politécnico Viana do Castelo (Portugal) and Texas A&M University: www.ese.ipvc.pt/~dmh/AHEMD/ahemd.htm.

This project represents the development of a unique observational research instrument to assess the quality and quantity of motor development affordances in the home for children from birth to 3 years.

Center for Motor Behavior and Pediatric Disabilities, Division of Kinesiology, University of Michigan: www.kines.umich.edu/research/cmbpd/index.html.

This site describes cutting-edge research in the area of motor development with infants and children who have various disabilities.

Perceptual–Motor Development

Barry W. Lavay and Joseph P. Winnick

Margaret is a 4-year-old with total blindness who would like to move independently in her preschool gymnasium. Her teacher has encouraged her to orient herself to the different play areas according to the specific sound cues associated with each. In essence, she is encouraging Margaret to develop her auditory perceptual abilities to help compensate for her loss of sight. Do you feel that Margaret's teacher should continue to help her develop her auditory perceptual abilities? If yes, which components of auditory perception need to be developed, and what are some fun and challenging physical education activities that could help Margaret?

The ability to learn and function effectively is affected by **perceptual–motor development**, which permits an individual to receive, transmit, organize, integrate, and attach meaning to sensory information and formulate appropriate responses. These responses are important for the individual to move and to learn while moving in a variety of environments. Thus, they have a direct impact in physical education and sport.

Ordinarily, perceptual–motor development occurs without the need for formal intervention. Sometimes, however, perceptual–motor abilities need attention because they have not developed satisfactorily. For example, deficits related to perceptual–motor ability are often named as characteristics of people with learning disabilities. These deficits might include poor spatial orientation, difficulty with body awareness, immature body image, clumsiness or awkwardness, coordination deficits, and poor balance. The higher incidence of perceptual–motor deficits among people with cerebral palsy or intellectual disability is well known. Perceptual–motor experiences are particularly important in cases in which sensory systems are generally affected but residual abilities might be enhanced and in cases where perceptual–motor abilities must be developed to a greater degree to compensate for loss of sensory abilities. People with visual or auditory disabilities exemplify these situations.

In this introductory section, it is important to comment on the influences of perceptual–motor programs. In the 1960s and early 1970s, such programs were strongly advocated and supported because of the belief that they led to a significant improvement in academic and intellectual abilities; however, research conducted has not supported this notion (Gallahue & Ozmun, 2006; Kavale, & Mattison, 1983; Payne & Issacs, 2007). On the other hand, research indicates clearly that perceptual–motor abilities, as measured by various tests, may be attained through carefully sequenced programs (Cheatum & Hammond, 2000; Sherrill, 2004; Winnick, 1979). For example, it is clear that balance, a perceptual–motor ability basic to movement skill, might be enhanced through systematic training. Because perceptual–motor abilities are fundamental to many motor, academic, and daily living skills, the nurturing or remediation of these skills is vital to physical education and adapted physical education.

After reading this chapter, it should be clear that all the movement activities experienced in physical education are perceptual–motor experiences. When perceptual–motor abilities require nurturing or when they have developed inadequately, there might be a need to plan programs to enhance their attainment. This chapter is designed to serve as a resource for planning and program implementation.

OVERVIEW OF THE PERCEPTUAL– MOTOR PROCESS

To implement perceptual–motor programs effectively, it is helpful to have an understanding of how the process works. A simplified four-step schematic of perceptual–motor functioning is presented in figure 20.1.

Sensory Input

The first step in the perceptual–motor process, **sensory input**, involves receiving energy forms from the environment and from within the body itself as sensory stimuli and processing this information for integration by the central nervous system. Tactile (touch), kinesthetic (movement), vestibular (balance), visual (sight), and auditory (hearing) sensory systems gain information that is transmitted to the central nervous system through sensory (afferent) mechanisms.

Sensory Integration

The second step in the perceptual–motor process involves **sensory integration**. Present and past sensory information is integrated, compared, and stored in short- or long-term memory. An important phase occurs as the person selects and organizes an appropriate motor output based on the integration. The resultant decision becomes part of long-term memory, which is transmitted through the motor (efferent) mechanisms.

Motor–Behavioral Output and Feedback

The third major step in the perceptual–motor process is **motor–behavioral output**. Overt move-

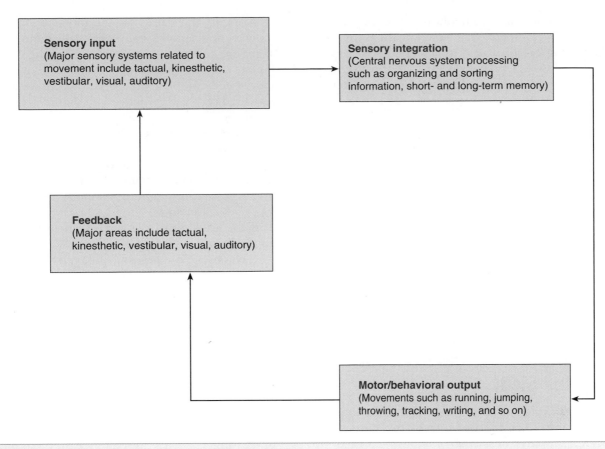

FIGURE 20.1 A simplified model of the perceptual–motor process.

ments or behaviors occur as a result of decisions from the central nervous system. This is the actual movement response, such as running, jumping, and throwing. As output occurs, information is also continually fed back as sensory input about the ongoing response by the human organism. This feedback constitutes step 4 and serves as sensory information to continue the process. Similar to sensory input, feedback in movement settings is usually kinesthetic, tactile, visual, or auditory. During **feedback**, the adequacy or nature of the movement response is evaluated or judged. If it is judged inadequate, adjustments are made; if it is successful, adjustments are not required.

Terminology of the Perceptual–Motor Process

Terms associated with the perceptual–motor process are used in many ways. The following are definitions of some terms used in this chapter.

Perception is the monitoring and interpretation of sensory information or knowledge resulting from the interaction between sensory and central nervous system processes. Perception occurs in the brain and enables an individual to derive meaning from sensory information. **Perceptual–motor development** is the process of enhancing the ability to integrate sensory stimuli arising from or relating to observable movement responses. It involves the ability to combine kinesthetic and tactual perceptions with and for the development of other perceptions, the use of movement to explore the environment and develop perceptual–motor abilities, and the ability to perceive both tactually and kinesthetically. Perception occurs as sensory information is interpreted or given meaning. Because the perceptual–motor process includes both an interpretation of and response to sensory stimulation, it requires cognitive ability. On the other hand, **sensorimotor activity** occurs at a subcortical level and does not involve meaning, interpretation, or cortical-level functioning. Sensorimotor activity is characterized by motor responses to sensory input. Sensory integration results in perception and other types of sensory data synthesis. Thus, perception is one aspect of sensory integration.

During the 1980s and continuing today, the physical education literature has developed a view on perception that has implications for perceptual–motor development. This view, known as the direct or **ecological approach** to perception, is based on the writings of J.J. Gibson (1977, 1979) and emphasizes that perception is specific to each person and that the environment is perceived directly in terms of its usefulness for the perceiver. Humans perceive the environment in terms of the actions they can exert on it—that is, the **affordances** provided by the environment. For example, children might perceive a chair predominantly in terms of their ability to crawl under it, whereas adults perceive it as an object to sit on (although they might also recognize its other possibilities). Advocates of this orientation feel that perceptual deficits might be defined in terms of inadequate perception of affordance. Thus, perception might become a prime candidate in the search for potential rate-limiters in children with movement problems (Burton, 1990; Davis & Broadhead, 2007; Davis & Burton, 1991).

Example of a Perceptual–Motor Skill

Batting a pitched softball can be used to illustrate these introductory concepts of the perceptual–motor process described in figure 20.1. As the pitched ball comes toward the plate, the batter focuses on the ball and tracks it. Information about speed, direction, spin, and other flight characteristics is picked up (stimulus reception) by the visual system (sensory input) for further processing. The information is transmitted via sensory neurons to the central nervous system, where it undergoes sensory integration. Because of the characteristics of the environment, the nature of the sensory information, and past experience, the incoming object is perceived as a softball (perception) to be hit (perceptual–motor or observable movement response). The batter's past experience will influence the ability to fixate and track the softball and process information about how to hit it. How to hit it involves comparative evaluations in which, for example, the arc of the ball is compared with that from previous instances when the act was performed (feedback).

The batter decides on the appropriate swing (decision about motor behavior) on the basis of earlier steps in the process. This decision becomes part of the long-term memory to be used for future reference. During the pitch, the brain is constantly kept informed about the position of the bat and the body (kinesthetic) and will use this information to enhance the overt behavior or movement response

of swinging the bat. Once the motor behavior or movement response has been determined, messages are sent to appropriate parts of the body to initiate the response (motor output). As the batter moves and completes the task, the information is provided on which to judge whether the response is successful or inadequate (feedback). If the pitch was missed, the batter might decide that adjustments such as moving closer to home plate or moving the hands higher on the bat handle are necessary in similar future instances; this information is stored in long-term memory and serves as a basis for learning.

If the ecological perspective on perception is applied to this example, the ball will be perceived by each observer in terms of ability to hit the ball or to hit the ball to a particular place on the field given one's body size and skill rather than in terms of ball velocity, spin, and so on. Thus, people perceive the ball in terms of their ability to hit it, and based on this perception, they decide what to do and respond accordingly (Davis & Broadhead, 2007).

Perceptual–Motor Deficit

Because figure 20.1 depicts perceptual–motor processing, it is a useful reference for breakdowns in the process, including breakdowns at the input, integration, output, and feedback sites. A breakdown at the input site might occur for a variety of reasons. For example, people with sensory impairments such as blindness or deafness might not be able to adequately take in visual or auditory information from the environment, and the result is that this information does not reach the central nervous system. Students with intellectual disabilities, learning disabilities, attention deficient/hyperactivity disorder (ADHD), or autism might not attend to, and thus might not receive, relevant information. People with neuromuscular impairments might be inhibited by the lack of appropriate kinesthetic, vestibular, or tactual information basic to quality input. For example, a young child with cerebral palsy and faulty kinesthetic perception may demonstrate difficulty with balance during playground climbing activities and be unable to keep up with peers.

Sensory integration might be affected by factors such as intellectual disability or neurological conditions that impair the functioning of the central nervous system. Also, sensory integration might be influenced by the quality of information received and the ability to process sensory input. For example, a student with a learning disability might have difficulty with motor planning needed to dribble, shoot, and pass a ball during a basketball game.

Motor output can be affected by inappropriate functioning during previous steps as well as conditions influencing movement, including transmission of information. Conditions associated with cerebral palsy, muscular dystrophy, and other neurological or orthopedic impairments are examples. Breakdowns at the feedback site can result from factors that affect earlier steps and any additional factors that bear on the ability to modify or correct behavior. The child with developmental coordination disorder (DCD), for example, might lack body awareness because of faulty kinesthetic perception, which would impair the adequacy of receiving appropriate feedback.

Related to the ecological approach, it has been suggested that perception be examined more closely when movement problems occur (Burton, 1987, 1990; Davis & Broadhead, 2007; Hutzler, 2007). Consistent with this view, it is suggested that perceptual judgments be assessed using actual performance as a criterion to determine if the motor outcomes are due to faulty perception. Golf provides a good example of this concept. In golf, the club used for a particular shot is selected on the basis of distance, height desired, and so on. If the golfer makes a shot short of the target, it is possible that this inadequate performance resulted from selecting the wrong club (faulty perception of shot requirements) rather than from poor skill. For example, the golfer might have underestimated the distance, wind resistance, and so on. Although the shortness of the shot might have been caused by other reasons, the possibility for faulty perception exists and needs to be assessed.

Many factors causing perceptual–motor deficits are associated with student disabilities seen in the school environment. Because of the influence of disabilities on perceptual–motor development, physical educators might need to develop programs to nurture development or remediate performance. The nature of an individualized program depends on the cause of the perceptual–motor breakdown, the student's perception and abilities, and the purpose of the program. In the case of a student with total blindness, for example, it might be necessary to focus on heightening auditory perceptual–motor components to improve orientation to school grounds and focus on kinesthetic perception to enhance movement in the environment. Table 20.1 presents an analysis of prominent perceptual–motor need and deficit areas as a function of specific disability.

Sensorimotor Stimulation

As stated earlier, perceptual–motor deficits might be a result of sensory input and processing problems. Physical educators who have reviewed and analyzed research and literature on the value of sensory stimulation (Cheatum & Hammond, 2000;

Table 20.1   Analysis of Prominent Perceptual–Motor Need and Deficit Areas

Disability	Prominent need and deficit areas
Visual disability (visual impairments)	Need to focus on the development of residual visual perceptual abilities and to help the child compensate for visual perceptual–motor deficits by enhancing auditory, vestibular, tactual, and kinesthetic perception. Give particular attention to **input** and **feedback** steps in the perceptual–motor process.
Auditory (Deaf and hard of hearing)	Need to focus on the development of residual hearing and vestibular abilities (if affected) and help the child compensate by enhancing development associated with sensory systems that are intact. Give particular attention to **input**, **integration**, and **feedback** steps in the perceptual–motor process.
Haptic disabilities that include vestibular, kinesthetic, and tactual perception (primarily children with orthopedic, neuromuscular, or neurological impairments)	Need to focus on the development of vestibular, kinesthetic, and tactual perception and to integrate motor experiences with visual and auditory perception. There may be a particular need to focus on **input**, **motor response**, and **feedback** steps in the perceptual–motor process.
Mental or affective disabilities (children with intellectual disabilities, emotional disturbance, and the like)	Need to focus on needs determined through assessment of perceptual–motor abilities. Involvement throughout the perceptual–motor process might exist.

Cratty 1986a, 1986b; Seaman, et al., 2007; Sherrill, 2004) believe that sensorimotor stimulation enhances development and learning. There is also agreement in the literature that acceptable levels of sensorimotor development generally occur without the need for special intervention by professionals. However, programs including sensorimotor activity are sometimes recommended for people with disabilities, especially those exhibiting severe disabilities. This stimulation is designed to overcome sensorimotor developmental delays or deficits caused by such factors as inadequate central nervous system development or functioning, diseases, disabilities, and opportunities for development. Programs designed to nurture sensory systems have been conducted by professionals, including educators as a part of early childhood or physical education, movement therapists as a part of movement education programs, and occupational therapists as a part of sensory integration programs. Goals of programs established by professionals will influence program purposes and approaches. Sensorimotor stimulation is recommended to promote adequate perceptual–motor and motor development.

Programs designed for sensorimotor nurturing emphasizing movement have several identifiable commonalties. First, they are closely associated with the major sensory modalities associated with movement (tactile, kinesthetic, vestibular, visual, and auditory). Second, they focus on subcortical activity—that is, activity not dependent on cerebral cortex and cortical tracts. A key distinction between sensorimotor activity and perceptual–motor activity is that the former is subcortical and the latter includes cognition. Third, during program implementation, there is considerable overlap in sensorimotor and perceptual–motor activities. In fact, perceptual–motor functioning depends on sensorimotor functioning because sensory information is processed, integrated, and organized in the cerebral cortex, and this activity is key to perceptual–motor functioning. For example, if a child is blindfolded and is holding a wet sponge and it feels squishy, that is sensorimotor functioning. When the child gives meaning to what is felt and says it is a wet sponge, that is perceptual–motor functioning. So perceptual–motor functioning is when meaning is given to sensorimotor information.

Factors that affect sensorimotor function include muscle and postural tone, reflexes and postural reactions, and sensory input systems (Sherrill, 2004). In this regard, this chapter is delimited to an introduction of activities associated with the

stimulation of sensory systems. The information presented in table 20.2 serves as a beginning resource for physical educators called on to provide or coordinate programs designed to nurture sensory input systems. Components and sample activities typically associated with such programs are shown in table 20.2. The components include tactile, kinesthetic, vestibular, visual, and auditory integration. Although activities are grouped with a single component, most activities involve two or more components as they are conducted. These components correspond closely to the perceptual–motor components to be discussed subsequently in the chapter.

Facilitating Development

The teacher has an important role in the nurturing or remediation of perceptual–motor abilities. The exact role and teaching styles need to vary with the characteristics of the learner. Because perceptual–motor abilities appear to develop optimally between ages 2 and 7, indirect teaching styles such as movement exploration, guided discovery, and open-ended tasks that allow more than one response are generally appropriate. As children reach ages 6 and 7, more direct teaching styles requiring a specific movement response are developmentally appropriate and thus more effective.

Burton (1987) suggested two implications for teaching that might be important for enhancing perceptual–motor development. First, he emphasized that teachers should provide **purposeful movement** because it is most motivating and encourages attention to the information in the environment. Movements are most purposeful when they are performed in natural settings as a means to an end rather than as the end itself. Key to the provision of purposeful movement is to select an activity involving an objective beyond the actual movement itself. For example, assume that the teacher wishes to improve the accuracy of kicking a playground ball. A purposeful movement would be to kick the ball into a goal in a soccer lead-up activity. This is more motivating and fun than a drill of kicking a ball for the sake of kicking a ball.

A second teaching implication is for students to become more accurately attuned to **affordances in the environment** (Burton, 1987; Davis & Broadhead, 2007). One way this is accomplished is by encouraging students to make perceptual judgments and to assess the accuracy of their judgments. Applied to a golf example, the question posed might be "Can I hit the ball to the green using

Table 20.2 **Components and Activities Associated With Sensorimotor Development**

Components	Typical activities
Tactile integration	Water, sand, mud, and clay activities; massage; stroking; partner touching activities; bare-footed activities; movement education activities; activities performed on various surfaces; handling objects of various textures such as a sponge; crawling through tunnels, rolling on a mat, or sitting on a carpet square; tactual discrimination between familiar and unfamiliar objects, including identifying objects, textures, or shapes in a bag while blindfolded
Kinesthetic integration	Naming body parts such as in Simon Says; moving body parts for purposeful movement such as bending to the right or left, up or down; active movements that develop a knowledge of body parts and their position in self and general space; the ability to move to different time, space, force, and flow of movement
Vestibular integration	Activities involving equilibrium, posture, and balance, including rocking and cradling on boards, cribs, or chairs; simple bouncing activities on spring-type or trampoline equipment; simple spinning and swinging activities using hammocks or other simple swing-type activities on a playground; sliding down an incline; therapy-ball activities; riding a scooter board; sitting and standing postures; nonlocomotor movements
Visual integration	Activities involving object manipulation, including ball handling in which speed, distance, size, color, and mass are modified; recognition and tracking of objects, including following a swinging or moving ball or beam of light; looking; sorting; fundamental visual–motor activities including eye–hand coordination, such as catching and striking, and eye–foot activities, such as kicking; finding objects
Auditory integration	Activities involving sound recognition, including finding a hidden beep ball; auditory discrimination, including differentiating between finding a loud and soft sound; sound localization, including pointing in the direction of a whistle; auditory figure–ground, including recognizing spoken words or a tambourine over music; listening and responding to auditory stimuli, including following spoken directions; making sounds and talking activities, including auditory memory

the nine iron?" In another example, the question might be "Can I pass the ball to a teammate without it being intercepted by a defensive player?" In these situations, the congruency between perception and movement is evaluated. The accuracy of one's perception of the environment or the affordances available is evaluated. The influence of perception on motor performance might be evaluated to determine if poor performance results from faulty perception.

SENSORY SYSTEMS

Many sensory systems are associated with perceptual–motor development. The remainder of this chapter discusses tactual, kinesthetic, visual, and auditory perception. Each sensory system is first described and then followed by examples of physical education and sport activities. The application example suggests perceptual–motor activity stations designed to promote the sensory systems in fun and challenging ways.

During a movement response, the sensory systems work collectively and simultaneously. For example, visual–motor coordination combines the use of the visual, kinesthetic, and tactual sensory systems. A multisensory approach that emphasizes using more than one sensory system is one of the more accepted instructional practices used to teach children with disabilities. Chapter 11, Specific Learning Disabilities, includes further discussion of the multisensory approach.

Tactile Perception

Tactile perception is the ability to interpret sensations from the layers of the skin. Tactile perception is related to external sensations and responds to touch, feel, and manipulation. Through these aspects of the tactile system, the student experiences sensations that contribute to a better understanding of the environment. For example, tactile perception enables one to distinguish wet from dry, hot from cold, soft from hard, and rough from smooth. For students with a learning disability, instruction is enhanced and made more concrete when they touch, feel, hold, and manipulate objects. The term *soft* becomes more meaningful

APPLICATION EXAMPLE

Fun Activity Stations to Promote the Sensory Systems

Setting: Ms. Sayers, the adapted physical education specialist, has designed four stations in the gymnasium for her class.

Students: A group of 12 children in the third and fourth grades with developmental and mild intellectual disabilities. She has assigned a fifth-grade peer tutor to assist at each station.

Issue: Promote the sensory systems for children in fun and challenging ways.

Application: Station 1, Spiderweb, is a web made out of yarn intertwined between two volleyball stands. To promote spatial awareness, the children move individually and then cooperate as a group holding hands through the web openings, with each child moving through the openings without touching the web (Kress & Lavay, 2006). At station 2, Walk the Pirate's Plank, the children move up, across, and down the five sets of bleachers in the gymnasium to promote functional dynamic balance. To challenge students to climb to the top, each student must touch a picture of a pirate located on the highest bleacher. Directionality is reinforced at station 3, Drive Your Car, where each child travels on a scooter board holding a small hula hoop as a steering wheel, following arrows on the gym floor and moving around large pylon cones without bumping into classmates' cars. Station 4, Surprise Bag, promotes tactual awareness; as the children sit in chairs while blindfolded, they place their hands in four bags and tell the peer tutor the contents of each bag (sand, clay, a wet sponge, and gummy worms).

and tangible when students feel something soft and distinguish it from something hard.

Some students might have a disorganized tactile system and consequently exhibit **tactile dysfunction**. A lack of tactile perception or the inability to localize touch might occur with children with learning problems related to a lack of body awareness (discussed in the proprioception section of this chapter). Other children (i.e., with serious emotional disturbance) might be **tactile defensive** and very sensitive to normal touch. For example, the feeling of clothes or a touch on the body causes a negative or painful reaction. They perceive touch as irritating and avoid contact with objects and people. They dislike tag games, tumbling, and contact sports such as football, wrestling, and soccer. Other children who have not received necessary amounts of stimulation might be tactile deprived and crave touch (Cheatum & Hammond, 2000). For example, a child with autism who is tactile underresponsive may wear a weighted vest because the vest provides some of the tactile stimulation the child craves.

Gross motor activities in physical education and sport offer many opportunities to use tactile perception. Relevant activities include those involving contact of the hands or the total body with a variety of surfaces, such as touching body parts with a wet sponge. Tactile perception combines with kinesthetic sensations as children crawl through a tunnel, walk along a balance beam, jump on a minitrampoline, climb a ladder, wrestle, or tumble. Students might walk barefoot on floors, lawns, beaches, balance beams, or mats or in swimming pools, or they might climb ropes, cargo nets, ladders, playground equipment, and a low-ropes adventure course (Kress & Lavay, 2006). Swimming activities are particularly important because of the unique sensations that water provides.

Proprioception

Proprioception consists of perceptual–motor abilities that respond to stimuli arising within the body. These include sensory stimuli arising from skin, muscles, tendons, joints, and vestibular sense receptors. Such abilities emphasize movement and are discussed within the categories of kinesthetic perception and balance.

Kinesthetic Perception

It is apparent even to the casual observer that we use information gained through auditory and visual receptors to move within and learn from the environment. Just as we know a sight or sound, we also have the ability to know a movement or body position. We can know an action before executing it, and we can feel the correctness of a movement. The awareness and memory of a planned movement and position is **kinesthetic perception** and is related to internal sensations. It develops from impulses that originate from the body's proprioceptors. Because kinesthetic perception is basic to all movement, it is associated with visual–motor and auditory–motor abilities.

Similar to all perceptions, kinesthetic perceptions depend on sensory input (including kinesthetic acuity) provided to the central nervous system. The central nervous system processes this information in accordance with the perceptual–motor process. Certain conditions might cause kinesthetic perception to be impaired. For example, in the case of a person who has had an amputation, all sensory information that normally would be processed by a particular extremity could be missing. Cerebral palsy, muscular dystrophy, and other disabilities or conditions affecting the motor system might result in a pattern of input or output different from that of a person without disabilities. A student with a learning disability and DCD might have difficulty selecting appropriate information from the many sources in the body to successfully complete a planned movement. Inadequate kinesthetic perception might manifest itself in clumsiness due to lack of opportunity for participation in movement experiences. Abilities closely associated with kinesthetic perception are body awareness, laterality, and verticality.

Body Awareness

Body awareness is an elusive term that has been used in many ways to represent different but related disciplines. Used here, **body awareness** is a comprehensive term referring to the ability to derive meaning from the body and includes body schema, body image, and body concept or knowledge.

Body schema is the most basic component and is sometimes called the *sensorimotor compo-*

nent because it depends on information supplied through activity of the body itself. It involves awareness of the body's movement capabilities and limitations, including the ability to create appropriate muscular tensions in movement activities and awareness of the position in space of the body and its parts. Body schema helps people know where the body ends and external space begins. Thus, an infant uses feedback from body action to become aware of the dimensions and limitations of the physical being and begins to establish separateness of the body from external surroundings. As body schema evolves, higher levels of motor development and control appear and follow a continuous process of change throughout life.

Body image refers to the feelings one has about one's body. Body image is affected by biological, intellectual, psychological, and social experiences. It includes the internal awareness of body parts and how they function. For example, people learn that they have two arms and two legs or two sides of the body that sometimes work in combination and other times function independently.

Body concept, or body knowledge, is the verbalized knowledge one has about one's body. It includes the intellectual operation of naming body parts and the understanding of how the body and its parts move in space. Body concept builds on body schema and body image.

The importance of movement experiences for the stimulation and nurturing of body awareness and the importance of body awareness for movement are obvious. Virtually all gross motor activities involve body awareness at some level. Movement experiences that might enhance body awareness in the developmental years include those in which parts of the body are identified, named, pointed to, and innervated (e.g., playing Simon Says). Imitation of body-part movements, balance activities, rhythmic or dance activities, scooter-board activities, mimetic activities, movement exploration, swimming games, activities conducted in front of a mirror, and stunts and tumbling are all examples of helpful movement experiences (figure 20.2). Thus, instructors who desire to enhance body awareness must provide children with many positive movement opportunities in a variety of fun, challenging, and safe settings.

Laterality and Verticality

Laterality and verticality refer to internal awareness of the body's right and left and up and down. **Laterality** is the **internal awareness** of both sides of

FIGURE 20.2 Scooter-board activities enhance body awareness during the developmental years.

the body and their relations as well as differences. With good laterality, a child can catch a ball on the right side with the right hand, the left side with the left hand, or toward the center of the body with both hands. He can also use the two limbs of the body to perform opposite tasks, such as using one hand to hold a paper and the other hand to write (Cheatum & Hammond, 2000). **Verticality** refers to an internal awareness of up and down and includes, for example, the ability to raise the body from a horizontal to upright position (Sherrill, 2004). Development of verticality is also believed to be enhanced through experimentation in upper and lower parts of the body. Laterality and verticality are very much related to body awareness. Laterality and verticality are included in many physical education activities, and nurturing these abilities enhances their successful development and performance. Examples include most balance activities such as walking up steps, locomotor activities such as jumping and leaping, and object-control activities such as moving the body up, down, and to both sides to catch a ball.

Balance

As mentioned previously, proprioception includes sensation pertaining to vestibular sense reception. The vestibular system provides information about the relation of the body to gravitational pull and thus serves as the basis for balance or equilibrium. Vestibular sense perception combines with multiple sources such as visual, auditory, kinesthetic, and tactual information to enhance the attainment of **static** (stationary) and **dynamic** (moving) forms of balance.

Balance is a key element in the performance of movement activities. Many activities might be used to nurture or remediate balance during the perceptual–motor developmental years. These include activities conducted on tilt boards, balance boards, surfaces such as stepping stones, low-ropes courses, and balance beams. Examples of everyday functional activities that require balance are stepping off a sidewalk curb to get on a bus or walking up bleachers to attend a game. Mimetic activities, stunts and tumbling, and a variety of games can also be used to develop balance.

Visual Perceptual–Motor Development

Visual perceptual–motor abilities are important in academic, physical education, and sport settings. In the academic setting, visual perceptual abilities are used in writing, drawing, reading, spelling, and arithmetic. In physical education and sport, they are important for performing such fundamental movements as running; catching, throwing, and kicking objects; playing tag; and balancing. Age-appropriate visual perceptual–motor abilities are built on visual acuity, which affects the ability to see, fixate, and track and thus is required for the input step of the perceptual–motor process. On the basis of input, people develop the components of visual perceptual–motor process associated with central nervous system processing and output. Components closely associated with this process that affects movement include visual figure–ground perception, spatial relationships, visual perceptual constancy, and visual–motor coordination.

Figure–Ground Perception

Figure–ground perception involves the ability to distinguish the main figure or target from its background and give meaning to the forms or the combination of forms or elements that constitute the figure. It requires the ability to differentiate and integrate parts of objects to form meaningful wholes and to appropriately shift attention and ignore irrelevant stimuli. Visual figure–ground perception is needed, for example, when students are asked to pick out a specific letter of the alphabet from a field of extraneous items. Students with inadequate perception might exhibit difficulties in differentiating letters, numbers, and other geometric forms; combining parts of words to form an entire word; or sorting objects. For instance, in the classroom, the child who has difficulty with figure–ground perception might place her paper closer to her face to block out background information (Cheatum & Hammond, 2000).

In physical education, figure–ground perception is required in games that depend on tracking moving objects, observing lines and boundaries, and concentrating on relevant stimuli. These include activities in which children move under, over, through, and around tires, hoops, or playground equipment as well as activities in which they follow or avoid the lines and shapes associated with obstacle courses, geometric figures, maps, mazes, hopscotch diagrams, or footprints. In sport, figure–ground perception is clearly demonstrated in baseball—a batter must distinguish a white ball from a background in attempting to hit it.

Spatial Relationships

The perception of **spatial relationships** means locating objects in space relative to oneself, or self-space (egocentric localization), and locating objects relative to one another or general space (objective localization). **Egocentric localization**, or perception of position in space, is demonstrated as students attempt to move through hoops without touching them. **Objective localization** is seen as a player attempts to complete a pass to a guarded teammate.

Spatial relationship, which affects virtually all aspects of academic learning, involves direction, distance, and depth. Position in space is basic to the solution of reversal or directional problems (such as the ability to distinguish *d*, *p*, and *q*; 36 and 63; *saw* and *was*; and *no* and *on*). Perception of spatial relationship also encompasses temporal ordering and sequencing. Students who have difficulty placing objects in order will have difficulty in various academic areas, including arithmetic sequencing problems (performing operations in correct order). In physical education, students who have difficulty with spatial relationship seem to be lost in space and may need to be oriented to their position on the court or field. Some authors have contended that spatial awareness is preceded by body awareness and that the awareness of relationships in space grows out of an awareness of relationships among the parts of one's own body.

Visual Perceptual Constancy

Perceptual constancy is the ability to recognize objects despite variations in their presentation. It entails recognizing the sameness of an object even though the object might in actuality vary in appearance, size, color, texture, brightness, shape, and so on. For example, an American football is recognized as having the same size even when seen at a distance. It has the same color in daylight as in twilight and maintains its shape even when only its tip is visible during a spiral pass. Development of perceptual constancy involves seeing, feeling, manipulating, smelling, tasting, hearing, naming, classifying, and analyzing objects. Inadequate perceptual constancy affects the recognition of letters, numbers, shapes, and other symbols in various contexts. Physical education and sport provide a unique opportunity for nurturing perceptual constancy because objects are used and manipulated in many ways and are viewed from many perspectives.

Visual–Motor Coordination

Visual–motor coordination is the ability to coordinate vision with body movements. It is the aspect of visual perceptual–motor ability that combines visual with tactual and kinesthetic perception; thus, it is not an exclusively visual ability. Although coordination of vision and movement might involve many parts of the body, eye–hand and eye–foot coordination are usually most important in physical education and sport activities. Effective eye–limb coordination is also important in such pursuits as cutting, pasting, finger painting, drawing, tracing, coloring, scribbling, using the chalkboard, and manipulating clay and toys. Eye–limb coordination is particularly important in writing. It is also necessary for such functional activities of daily living as putting on and tying shoes, putting on and buttoning clothes, eating or drinking without tipping glasses and plates, and using simple tools. In physical education, eye–limb coordination is needed for object-control skills used in games and sport, such as throwing, catching, kicking, dribbling, and striking. For example, in figure 20.3, the teacher can assist children with visual–motor challenges by using larger equipment during striking activities.

Development of Visual Perceptual–Motor Abilities

Many experiences in physical education and sport call on visual perceptual–motor abilities. Although motor activities are not generally limited to the development of one ability, some activities are especially well suited for figure–ground development. These include rolling; throwing; catching; kicking; striking; dodging; chasing a variety of objects in a variety of ways; moving under, over, through, and around tires, hoops, geometric shapes, ropes, playground equipment, and pieces of apparatuses;

following or avoiding lines associated with obstacle courses, geometric shapes, maps, mazes, hopscotch games, or grids; stepping on or avoiding footprints, stones, animals, or shapes painted on outdoor hard surfaces or floors; imitating movements as in Leap-frog, Follow the Leader, or Simon Says; and doing simple rope activities, such as moving under and over ropes and jumping rope.

Spatial relationships are involved in tumbling, swimming, rope jumping, rhythms and dance, and obstacle courses. Activities particularly useful in helping to develop spatial abilities include moving through tunnels, tires, hoops, mazes, and perception boxes. Activities in which one must locate objects in space relative to oneself (egocentric localization or self-space) or relative to one another (objective localization or general space) also promote perception of spatial relations.

Visual–motor coordination is clearly important in physical education and sport. Students exhibiting difficulty moving around other players and objects, not tracking an object, and turning their head or blinking when attempting to catch a ball are all examples of potential visual problems. Games that include throwing, catching, kicking, and striking balls and other objects are among those activities requiring such coordination. Age-appropriate games are highly recommended because they enhance the purposefulness of movement and motivate the learner.

Auditory Perceptual–Motor Development

Age-appropriate **auditory perceptual–motor abilities** are built on auditory acuity and perception. The ability to receive and transmit auditory stimuli as sensory input is the foundation of auditory figure–ground perception, auditory discrimination, sound localization, temporal auditory perception, and auditory–motor coordination.

Auditory Figure–Ground Perception

Auditory figure–ground perception is the ability to distinguish and attend to relevant auditory stimuli against a background of general auditory stimuli. It includes ignoring unimportant auditory sensations or irrelevant stimuli (such as those in a noisy gym in which several activities are conducted simultaneously) and attending to relevant stimuli, such as the teacher's directions. In situations in which irrelevant stimuli are present, people with inadequate figure–ground perception might have difficulty concentrating on the task at

Photo courtesy of David Nelson.

FIGURE 20.3 A child finds success with striking by using a large foam hockey stick to hit a large beach ball.

hand, responding to directions, and comprehending information received during the many listening activities of daily life. They might not attend to a honking horn, a shout, or a signaling whistle. Their problems in physical education and sport might be associated with transitions when beginning, changing, and ending activities are signaled through sound. Visual methods and signals to use with students with auditory difficulties to ensure smooth transitions include tossing a scarf in the air or using a hand signal. Other examples of transition signals are discussed in chapter 11 in the section on behavior management under class structure.

Auditory Discrimination

Auditory discrimination is the capacity to distinguish among frequencies, qualities, and amplitudes of sound. It involves the ability to recognize and discriminate among variations of auditory stimuli presented in a temporal series as well as auditory-perceptual constancy. The latter is the ability to recognize an auditory stimulus as the same under varying presentations. Auditory discrimination thus involves the ability to distinguish pitch, loudness, and constancy of auditory stimuli. People with inadequate auditory discrimination might exhibit problems in games, dances, and other rhythmic activities that depend on this ability. Another potential problem with auditory discrimination is the player who cannot distinguish the official's whistle from the noise of the crowd.

Sound Localization

Sound localization—the ability to determine the source or direction of sounds in the environment—is used, for example, during a basketball game to find an open player calling for the ball. Sound localization is basic to goalball, in which blindfolded players attempt to stop a ball emitting a sound. Another fun and challenging way to reinforce sound localization is to hide an object in the gym that emits a sound, such as a beep ball, and have the students find the object.

Temporal Auditory Perception

Temporal auditory perception involves the ability to recognize and discriminate among variations of auditory stimuli presented in time. It entails distinguishing rate, emphasis, tempo, and order of auditory stimuli. Students with inadequate temporal auditory perception might exhibit difficulties in rhythmic movement and dance, singing games, and other physical education activities.

Auditory–Motor Coordination

Auditory–motor coordination is the ability to coordinate auditory stimuli with body movements. This coordination is readily apparent when a student responds to a beat in music (ear–foot coordination) or to a particular cadence when football signals are called out. Auditory–motor coordination is evident as a dancer, skater, or gymnast performs a routine to musical accompaniment.

Development of Auditory Perceptual–Motor Abilities

Physical education and sport offer many opportunities to develop auditory perception. Participants might follow verbal directions or perform activities in response to music, and the activities might be suggested by the music itself. For example, children might walk, run, skip, or gallop to a musical beat; they might imitate trains, airplanes, cars, or animals as suggested by music. Dances and rhythmic activities with variations in the rate and beat are useful, as are games and activities in which movements are begun, changed, or stopped in response to various sounds. Triangles, drums, tambourines, bells, sticks, or whistles might direct children in movement or serve as play equipment. A teacher conducting such activities should minimize distracting stimuli and vary the tempo and loudness of sound. It might be necessary to speak softly at times so that students must concentrate on listening.

SUMMARY

Perceptual–motor development is the process of enhancing the ability to integrate sensory stimuli arising from or relating to observable movement experiences. It is associated with all the sensory systems. This chapter discussed sensorimotor stimulation and perceptual–motor development, focusing on how movement activities are involved in and can be used for sensorimotor stimulation and perceptual–motor development as well as how they thereby contribute to students' development and consequent movement experiences.

REFERENCES

Burton, A.W. (1987). Confronting the interaction between perception and movement in adapted physical education. *Adapted Physical Activity Quarterly, 4,* 257-267.

Burton, A.W. (1990). Assessing the perceptual–motor interaction in developmentally disabled and handicapped children. *Adapted Physical Activity Quarterly, 7,* 325-337.

Cheatum, B.A, & Hammond, A.A. (2000). *Physical activity for improving children's learning and behavior.* Champaign IL: Human Kinetics.

Cratty, B.J. (1986a). *Adapted physical education in the mainstream.* Denver: Love.

Cratty, B.J. (1986b). *Perceptual motor development in infants and children.* Englewood Cliffs, NJ: Prentice Hall.

Davis, W.E. & Broadhead, G.D. (Eds.). (2007). *Ecological task analysis and movement.* Champaign, IL: Human Kinetics.

Davis, W.E., & Burton, A.W. (1991). Ecological task analysis: Translating movement behavior theory into practice. *Adapted Physical Activity Quarterly, 8,* 154-177.

Gallahue, D.L., & Ozmun, J. C. (2006). *Understanding motor development: Infants, children, adolescents and adults* (6th ed.). Boston: McGraw-Hill.

Gibson, J.J. (1977). The theory of affordance. In R. Shaw & J. Bransford (Eds.), *Perceiving, acting, and knowing: Toward an ecological psychology.* Hillsdale, NJ: Earlbaum.

Gibson, J.J. (1979). *The ecological approach to visual perception.* Boston: Houghton Mifflin.

Hutzler, Y. (2007). A systematic ecological model for adapting physical activities: Theoretical foundations and practical examples. *Adapted Physical Activity Quarterly, 24,* 287-304.

Kavale, K.A., & Mattison, P.D. (1983). One jumped off the balance beam: A meta-analysis of perceptual motor training programs. *Journal of Learning Disabilities, 16,* 165-173.

Kress, J. & Lavay, B., (2006). Traveling on the OUTBAC: Challenging children with disabilities on a low ropes course. *PALAESTRA, 22* (2), 20-26, 43.

Payne, V.P., & Issacs, L.D. (2007). *Human motor development: A lifespan approach* (7th ed.). Boston: McGraw-Hill.

Seaman, J.A., DePauw, K.P., Morton, K.B., & Omoto, K. (2007). *Making connections: From theory to practice in adapted physical education* (2nd ed.). Scottsdale, AZ: Holcomb Hathaway.

Sherrill, C. (2004). *Adapted physical activity, recreation, and sport: Crossdisciplinary and lifespan* (6th ed.). Boston: McGraw-Hill.

Winnick, J.P. (1979). *Early movement experiences and development: Habilitation and remediation.* Philadelphia: Saunders.

WRITTEN RESOURCES

Cheatum, B.A, & Hammond, A.A. (2000). *Physical activity for improving children's learning and behavior.* Champaign IL: Human Kinetics.

Provides a comprehensive, easy-to-read approach to neurological development and the sensory systems. Part II of the text devotes a chapter to each of the sensory systems.

Cowden, J.E., & Torrey, C.C. (2007). *Motor development and movement activities for preschoolers and infants with delays: A multisensory approach for professionals and families* (2nd ed.). Springfield, IL: Clarke C. Thomas.

Emphasizes organizing and conducting movement intervention programs for infants, toddlers, and preschoolers with delays or disabilities. Provides exercises and activities for increased muscle tone and strength, decreased muscle tone and reflex integration, and sensory motor development (postural reactions and vestibular stimulation, visual–motor control, auditory discrimination, tactile stimulation, and kinesthetic and spatial awareness).

Davis, W.E., & Broadhead, G.D. (2007). (Eds.). *Ecological task analysis and movement.* Champaign, IL: Human Kinetics.

Presents the ecological task analysis (ETA) model through research and instruction by bringing together the work of over 25 contributors. The book shows instructors how to apply the ETA model to the dynamics of movement behavior by examining the interacting constraints of the performer, environment, and task in coaching, teaching, and therapy.

Huettig, C., Pyfer, J., & Auxter, D. (2005). *Gross motor activities for young children with special needs.* (10th ed.). Boston: McGraw-Hill.

A supplement handbook to the textbook, *Principles and Methods of Adapted Physical Education*, this source offers more than 200 activities and suggested songs for professionals serving young children. Activities are designed to promote central nervous system development (equilibrium, sensory stimulation and discrimination, body image, basic locomotor skills, motor planning, object-control skills, cross-lateral integration, aerobic fitness, animal actions, and cooperative play and games).

Johnson-Martin, N.M., Attermeier, S.M., & Hacker, B.J. (2004). *The Carolina curriculum for infants and toddlers with special needs* (3rd ed.). Baltimore: Paul H. Brookes.

This text includes chapters on sensorimotor development, with curriculum sequences related to visual pursuit and object permanence, auditory localization and object permanence, understanding space, and visual perception. A chapter on gross motor skills includes posture and locomotion, stair activity, jumping, and balance.

Johnson-Martin, N.M., Attermeier, S.M., & Hacker, B. (2004). *The Carolina Curriculum for preschoolers with special needs* (2nd ed.). Baltimore: Paul H. Brookes.

This source presents gross and fine motor chapters with curriculum sequences encompassing object manipulation, locomotion (walking, galloping, skipping, running, and hopping), stair activities, jumping, balancing, and ball throwing and catching.

Kranowitz, C.S. (2003). *The out-of-sync child has fun: Activities for kids with sensory integration dysfunction.* New York: Perigee.

This book features more than 100 enjoyable activities that reinforce the sensory systems for young children.

AUDIOVISUAL RESOURCES

Educational Activities, Inc., 1937 Grand Ave., Baldwin, NY 11510; phone: 800-797-3223; fax: 516-623-9282; Web site: www.edact.com.

Another excellent source for perceptual–motor development materials.

Kimbo Educational, P.O. Box 477, Long Branch, NJ 07740-0477; phone: 800-631-2187; fax: 732-870-3340; Web site: www.kimboed.com.

CDs, DVDs, and books related to sensorimotor stimulation, perceptual–motor development, and interdisciplinary teaching may be purchased from this company.

ELECTRONIC RESOURCES

Center for the Ecological Study of Perception and Action: http://ione.psy.uconn.edu/.

This site features a discussion on the ecological approach to perception and action in the tradition of the late James J. Gibson.

Kimbo Educational: www.kimboed.com.

The Kimbo Educational Web site provides educational teaching tips for teaching perceptual–motor activities.

Sportime: www.sportime.com.

Sportime has four online catalogs, each with products designed to aid professionals who implement movement programs. The Abilitations catalog and Web site link has many ideas for movement, positioning, sensorimotor, and perceptual–motor activities for people with unique needs. At the Sportime Web site, go to the Activity Guide link to preview the equipment and activity ideas, many designed to reinforce perceptual–motor activities.

chapter 21

Infants and Toddlers

Cathy Houston-Wilson

Maria, an early childhood adapted physical educator at Early Learning Center, sets up her motor room with incline mats, soft balls, scarves, and tunnels to accommodate infants and toddlers with special needs and their caregivers. She has specific objectives for each child: weight bearing for Adam, balancing and ambulating for Molly, and visual tracking for Juan. The children and their caregivers enter the motor room and immediately begin acting on the equipment that has been set out for them. Maria greets the children individually as they enter and talks with their caregivers about the progress the children are making and what objectives have been developed for the day with the equipment that has been set up. Maria and the caregivers follow the young children's lead as they begin to play with the equipment.

This chapter presents an overview of adapted physical education as it relates to infants and toddlers with unique needs. The following topics are covered: legislative mandates and implications for early intervention services; the role of teachers in early childhood adapted physical education; assessment and its role in identifying infants and toddlers with unique needs and subsequent program planning; goals and objectives of early childhood motor programs for young children with and without unique needs, in particular the need for sensory stimulation and play-based experiences; appropriate ways to interact with infants and toddlers; and the importance of families in the development of infants and toddlers.

LEGISLATION

Infants and toddlers, caregivers, and adapted physical education—do these groups belong together? The answer is yes. As a result of federal legislation, particularly PL 99-457, the Education of the Handicapped Act Amendments of 1986, now reauthorized as PL 108-446, the Individuals with Disabilities Education Improvement Act of 2004 (IDEA), infants and toddlers with developmental delays or at risk for developmental delays are to be provided with early intervention services to enhance their development and minimize the potential for delays.

According to IDEA, infants and toddlers who are eligible for early intervention are defined as children under three years of age who are experiencing developmental delays in one or more of the following **functional areas** as measured by appropriate diagnostic instruments and procedures: cognitive development, physical development, communication development, social or emotional development, and adaptive development. In addition, those who have a diagnosed physical or mental condition that has a high probability of resulting in developmental delay are eligible. Infants and toddlers with disabilities might also include, at the state's discretion, **at-risk** infants and toddlers. An at-risk infant or toddler is defined as a child under three years of age who would be at risk of experiencing a substantial developmental delay if early intervention services were not provided (IDEA, 2004).

States are given flexibility in determining actual **criteria for eligibility**; however, professional opinion can serve as a basis for eligibility. In addition to professional opinion, in New York State, for example, a child would qualify for early intervention services if any of the following conditions were met (New York State Department of Health, 2005):

- A child is experiencing a 12-month delay in one or more functional areas.
- A child is experiencing a 33 percent delay in one functional area.
- A child is experiencing a 25 percent delay in two areas.
- A child scores two standard deviations below the mean in one functional area.
- A child scores one and a half standard deviations below the mean in two or more functional areas.

Early childhood experts agree that determining eligibility for children who are so young is a complex process. A variety of methods for determining eligibility are thus recommended, including direct observation, play-based assessment, standardized tests or developmental inventories, clinical opinion, and, most important, reports by parents or caregivers. Young children do not typically respond on cue, so reports by parents or caregivers cannot be underestimated. Given the complexity of assessing such young children, authentic assessments have also begun to be used in the evaluation process. Rubrics, checklists, and rating scales can be helpful in determining if the child has reached certain milestones or desired levels of functioning. In addition, authentic assessments are helpful in maintaining data to determine progress. This form of data maintenance is known as **formative assessment**. Finally, a family may choose to be involved in what is known as a **family assessment**. With this process, family members identify their concerns, priorities, and resources in relation to maximizing the potential for their child's development and then share these wishes with the early intervention team (New York State Department of Health, 2005).

To determine if the child is experiencing a developmental delay in one or more of the functional areas listed previously, a comprehensive **multidisciplinary assessment** must be conducted on the child. Tests used to determine unique needs must be valid and administered by trained professionals from the multidisciplinary team. Members of the multidisciplinary team include parents, a service coordinator, advocates, professionals from at least two disciplines (e.g., a speech and language specialist, an occupational therapist, or a teacher of adapted physical education), and any other person with an interest in the child. The team members engage in various forms of data collection to determine the strengths and needs of the child. Once a developmental delay has been established, an **individualized family service plan** (IFSP) is developed by the team members. The IFSP is a written document that contains the following information (Office of Special Education and Rehabilitative Services, 2006):

- The child's present level of performance in the five functional areas of development
- A statement of the family's resources, priorities, and concerns relating to enhancing the development of the child
- A statement of major outcomes expected to be achieved and the criteria, procedures, and timelines used to determine the degree to which progress is being made and whether modifications or revisions are necessary
- A statement of early intervention services necessary to meet the unique needs of the child and the child's family, including transportation, frequency, intensity, and method of delivery
- A statement of the natural environments in which early intervention services shall be provided, including a justification of the extent, if any, to which the services will not be provided in a natural environment (the child's home or day care)
- The projected dates for initiation of services and the anticipated duration of the services
- The identification of the service coordinator from the profession most immediately relevant to the child's or family's needs who will be responsible for implementation of the plan and coordination with other agencies and individuals
- The steps to be taken to support the transition of the toddler with a disability to preschool or other appropriate services

TEACHERS OF EARLY CHILDHOOD ADAPTED PHYSICAL EDUCATION

Where do teachers of early childhood adapted physical education fit into this process? Infants and toddlers with developmental delays, whether they be cognitive, physical, or emotional, might also demonstrate psychomotor delays. Psychomotor delays are a major disadvantage because movement serves as an important basis from which children initially learn. For example, if children lack the ability to maintain an upright position or ambulate across a room, they are unable to interact with their environments in a meaningful way. Teachers of early childhood adapted physical education are in a unique position to develop and implement motor programs that can stimulate and enhance the movement abilities of infants and toddlers with special needs. These teachers may serve as valuable members of the multidisciplinary team by conducting motor assessments or observing motor behavior, thereby helping to select goals and objectives to enhance the child's development. They may provide direct teaching services or serve as consultants to early intervention providers and parents. As resource consultants, they can provide appropriate activities that stimulate development in areas beyond the motor domain, including cognitive, social, emotional, communication, and adaptive development.

In summary, teachers of early childhood adapted physical education conduct assessments and provide direct service or serve as consultants to caregivers of infants and toddlers with special needs. Because the ability to conduct valid assessments is essential to determining eligibility for services, the following section provides information that can help teachers of early childhood adapted physical education to accurately test and assess the motor needs of infants and toddlers with developmental delays.

ASSESSMENT

Assessment serves as the primary means of determining eligibility for and implementing early intervention services. Various assessment techniques are used to determine the status of infants and toddlers. These techniques and examples of each are described in the following sections.

Screening

Prior to a comprehensive assessment, infants and toddlers might first be screened to determine if there is a probable delay. On completion of the screening procedure, recommendations are made regarding the need for further evaluation. Screening can be either informal or formal. Informal screening includes observations, checklists, rating scales, and authentic assessments such as rubrics of developmental milestones. Formal screenings are commercially available and are often done at medical offices or at early intervention centers.

One example of a formal motor screening test is the Milani-Comparetti Motor Development Screening Test for infants and young children (Stuberg et al., 1992). The Milani-Comparetti was designed to test the development of children from approximately birth to two years of age. The majority of the test items are scored within the first 16 months of a child's life; however, the test provides the most detailed information about children between the ages of 3 and 12 months. The test assesses primitive reflexes, righting reactions, protective reactions, equilibrium reactions, postural control, and active movement. Another popular screening test is the Denver II Developmental Screening Test (Frankenburg et al., 1992). The Denver II assesses children from birth to six years of age in the areas of personal and social development, language, fine and gross motor ability, and adaptive behavior. The Denver II relies heavily on the input of caregivers and direct observation of developmental tasks to determine performance level. Teachers of early childhood adapted physical education should have a solid background in motor development so that these screening tests and subsequent assessments can be administered with relative ease.

Standardized Assessment

After initial screening, if it is determined that a child might have a delay, a more extensive formal assessment may be conducted. One way to determine the unique needs of infants and toddlers is through the use of standardized assessments. Standardized assessments are often used because they lend themselves to the determination of developmental status, are technically sound, and are relatively easy to administer. Standardized assessment instruments might be norm referenced, criterion referenced, or both. **Norm-referenced assessments** allow testers to compare the child against others of similar age and characteristics, whereas **criterion-referenced assessments** compare the child's performance against preestablished criteria. Tests that are both norm and criterion referenced help not only with identification of unique needs but also with program planning and implementation.

One example of a motor assessment instrument that is both norm and criterion referenced is the Peabody Developmental Motor Scales (PDMS-2) (Folio & Fewell, 2000). This test provides in-depth

assessment and training of gross and fine motor skills for children from birth through age 5. The test is broken down into six subtests that measure reflexes, stationary positions, locomotion, object manipulation, grasping, and visual–motor integration. The test yields fine motor and gross motor quotient scores as well as a total motor quotient score. The total motor quotient is the best estimate of the child's overall motor abilities. The PDMS-2 also provides a motor activity program with units of instruction organized developmentally by skill area to aid in the development and implementation of appropriate goals and objectives to meet the unique needs of the child.

Another example of a standardized test that is both norm and criterion referenced is the Brigance Inventory of Early Development II (IED-II) (Brigance, 2008). This test is unique in that it contains both a screening test and formal assessment. Once the child has been screened and a delay is suspected, the child is further evaluated with the formal assessment. The Brigance system provides tools for assessing children from birth to seven years. Areas assessed include motor skills, self-help skills, speech and language, general knowledge and comprehension, and early academic skills. The Brigance IED-II is one of the most widely used comprehensive assessments because it targets all areas of functional development, generating a valid picture of the child's current level of performance.

Curriculum-Based Assessment

Curriculum-based assessment has become a popular means by which to generate data relative to a child's present level of performance. It takes place in natural environments and is based on a predetermined set of curriculum objectives. The Carolina Curriculum for infants and toddlers with special needs (Johnson-Martin, Attermeier, & Hacker, 2004) and the Hawaii Early Learning Profile (HELP) Strands (Parks, 2007) are both examples of curriculum-based assessment. The Carolina Curriculum was developed for infants and toddlers from birth to 24 months, whereas the HELP Strands was developed for infants and toddlers from birth to 36 months. Both tests assess the child in five functional areas of development: cognitive skills, communication and language, social–emotional adaptation, fine motor skills, and gross motor skills. Each assessed area is embedded in a naturally occurring activity. Based on the assessment data, a profile of the child is developed. Because these assessments are linked to a curriculum, there is a smooth transition from the assessment phase to the intervention phase. Both the Carolina Curriculum and the HELP Strands provide activities to develop skills assessed.

Transdisciplinary Play-Based Assessment

Another form of assessment that is appropriate for use with infants and toddlers is transdisciplinary assessment. Transdisciplinary assessment differs from traditional forms of assessment in several ways. Traditional forms of assessment typically involve experts in various domains determining the strengths and needs of the child for a particular domain. For example, a teacher of adapted physical education might provide data related to motor abilities, and a speech and language teacher might provide information regarding communication. These experts then come together and report their findings and generate a comprehensive picture of the child's current level of performance.

Transdisciplinary assessment, or arena assessment, calls for a play facilitator to interact with children, their parents, and a peer. The interactions are based on a set of criteria observed unobtrusively in both structured and unstructured play environments by representatives from various disciplines who are knowledgeable about all areas of development. Linder (2008) is credited with the development of the Transdisciplinary Play-Based Assessment (TPBA 2). Throughout the testing, professionals observe cognitive, social–emotional, communication and language, and sensorimotor development. Based on the observations, developmental level, learning style, interaction patterns, and other relevant behaviors are analyzed and recorded onto observation sheets, which are later transferred to summary sheets during postobservation sessions (Linder, 2008).

The role of the parents in the TPBA 2 cannot be overemphasized. Parents are involved in the process from start to finish by completing a developmental checklist, directly interacting with the child during the assessment, and developing the IFSP. This form of assessment has many benefits; most notably it helps to provide an accurate picture of the child's present level of performance, because data are collected in natural environments with caregivers directly involved in the assessment process. Children are typically more at ease and

perform more as they normally would with this type of assessment. In addition, by using a play facilitator, the child is exposed to only one professional individually assessing the child rather than the traditional three to five members of an assessment team. Teachers of early childhood adapted physical education can easily serve as play facilitators, because their primary means of developing motor abilities is through the use of play.

Authentic Assessment

The final form of assessment discussed in this chapter is authentic assessment. Although the tests described previously can be useful in screening and evaluating young children and determining their eligibility for services, they have their limitations. For example, some children will not respond on cue or may act differently with strangers than they would in a typical setting. In addition, the previous assessments tend to be summative; that is, the information gained presents a picture of the child's present level of performance but does not incorporate a mechanism to monitor ongoing performance or formative data. Authentic assessment, then, can be used as a mechanism to screen and evaluate infants and toddlers and can provide both formative and summative assessment data. The term *authentic assessment* is derived from the fact that the assessment is conducted in authentic or real-life situations. The assessment is often created based on the outcome, or the overall goal to be achieved (e.g., sliding down a slide), and skills needed to be mastered in order to reach this outcome (e.g., climbing stairs).

The most common form of authentic assessment is a rubric. A rubric is a rating method that uses a fixed scale describing characteristics of each point of the scale. Rubrics often provide a detailed guideline for making scoring decisions. The specific scoring criteria are used to evaluate student performance and progress (Jackson & Larkin, 2002). Scoring is qualitative rather than quantitative. Criteria may reflect the ability of the child to always, sometimes, rarely, or never accomplish a task.

Another form of authentic assessment is the checklist. A checklist identifies a list of tasks the child should be able to accomplish and performance is measured against the list. Checklists in early childhood are related primarily to developmental tasks such as reaching certain milestones in the five areas of development.

Finally, rating scales can be used to determine the quality of performance (e.g., excellent, very good, good, fair, and poor). Rating scales can be especially helpful when assessing children who require physical assistance to perform tasks. The assessor can determine the level of assistance needed to perform a given task (e.g., total physical assistance, partial physical assistance, or independent) and use that as the basis for present level of performance. As the child is able to accomplish more tasks independently, the scale can be updated and progress can be continually monitored.

Because well-prepared teachers of adapted physical education should be able and willing to provide assessment services, they might serve as valuable members of the multidisciplinary team responsible for direct screening and assessment of motor behaviors for infants and toddlers with disabilities. In addition to the ability to provide screening and assessment data, teachers of early childhood adapted physical education can help infants and toddlers achieve their motor objectives by providing developmentally appropriate activities and environments. The next section identifies goals and objectives of early childhood motor programs for infants and toddlers.

GOALS AND OBJECTIVES OF MOTOR PROGRAMS FOR INFANTS AND TODDLERS

Infants and toddlers learn by experiencing their environments in several ways: through their senses (seeing, hearing, tasting, smelling, and kinesthetically), through reciprocal adult–child interactions, and through movement actions and reactions (Bredekamp & Copple, 1997). For example, when an infant cries, a natural reaction on the part of the parent or caregiver is to interact with the child to determine his needs. Similarly, if a child swats at a mobile (i.e., movement action), the natural reaction is for the mobile to move. These constant interactions among the child, the environment, and those within the environment serve as the basis for cognitive, affective, and psychomotor development. Since children learn by moving, creating environments that facilitate movement will aid in the total development of the child. Thus, the primary goal of motor programs for infants and toddlers is the development of motor milestones and the acquisition of motor skills.

In this text, Gallahue depicts his hourglass model of motor development (see chapter 19). Within the model, four phases of motor development are noted. The phases are reflexive movement, rudimentary movement, fundamental movement, and specialized movement. Infants and toddlers operate within the reflexive, rudimentary, and fundamental movement phases.

The reflexive movement phase is characterized by involuntary movements elicited by external stimuli. Reflexes are either primitive (used for survival or precursors to voluntary movement) or postural (the body's attempt to keep itself in an upright position). Most reflexes are inhibited or integrated between 4 months and 12 months of life (Gallahue & Ozmun, 2002). The rudimentary movement phase is the first form of voluntary movement. Rudimentary movements are purposeful, although they may not be as precise as later forms of movement. During the rudimentary phase of development, stability, locomotion, and manipulative skills begin to emerge. Stability—the ability to maintain control of the head, neck, and trunk—serves as the basis for locomotion and manipulation. The enhanced motor ability that comes with rudimentary movement, such as crawling, creeping, and walking, allows infants and toddlers to move freely within their environments, and the ability to reach, grasp, and release allows infants and toddlers to make meaningful contact with objects within the environment.

Together, these movement interactions help to shape the overall development of infants and toddlers and lead to more refined movement forms, known as *fundamental movement*. Fundamental movement includes both locomotor and object-control skills that become more fully refined over time and through a variety of experiences. Other forms of active movement, such as rhythm and dance, gymnastics, aquatics, and games, can also enhance the motor skills of children. The need for active movement cannot be overstated. The National Association for Sport and Physical Education (NASPE) (2002) developed a position statement that notes, "All children birth to age five should engage in daily physical activity that promotes health-related fitness and movement skills" (p. 2). Note that young children are not miniature adults and the methods for increasing fitness levels in adolescents and adults differ significantly from the methods used for infants and toddlers. The intent is to provide infants and toddlers with opportunities for movement to foster active lifestyles over time. The NASPE guidelines regarding active movement for infants and toddlers are presented here, along with a brief explanation of these guidelines and suggestions for implementation.

Infant Guidelines

1. Infants should interact with parents or caregivers in daily physical activities dedicated to promoting the exploration of their environment.

2. Infants should be placed in safe settings that promote physical activity and do not restrict movement for prolonged amounts of time.

3. Infants' physical activity should promote the development of movement skills. Infants need opportunities to practice their newly developed skills, such as sitting up, rolling over, and crawling, and caregivers and instructors are responsible for creating environments that are safe and encourage this practice. If an infant is kept in a playpen or infant seat for extended periods of time, delays in motor milestones will occur. Additionally, research suggests that inactivity in children leads to inactive adults (NASPE, 2002). Baby games such as peekaboo and patty-cake are ideal, as is placing children on their stomachs with objects nearby for them to reach at and interact with. This tummy time is especially important since the only safe sleeping position for infants is on the back. As a result, many babies don't get the stretching and strengthening of the back and neck muscles they need, which can lead to early motor delays (American Academy of Pediatrics, 2008). Equipment that the baby interacts with should be easy to grasp, brightly colored, and varied in texture. Blocks, stacking toys, nesting cups, squeeze toys, and baby gyms are all ideal (NASPE, 2002).

4. Infants should have an environment that meets or exceeds recommended safety standards for performing large-muscle activities. Ensuring the safety of the baby goes without saying. Infants should always be supervised and never placed on equipment or heights that are intended for older children. NASPE (2002) recommends a minimum of a 5- by 7-foot (1.5 by 2 m) rug or blanket for playing, rolling, and other large-muscle activities.

5. People responsible for the well-being of infants should be aware of the importance of physical activity and promote the child's movement skills.

6. Babies are totally dependent on their caregivers to provide opportunities for motor movement and exploration. Providing the environment, however, is not enough. Caregivers must also take an active role in interacting with child and showing interest and approval in the baby's discoveries. These adult–child interactions not only enhance motor development but also help children in their social–emotional and cognitive development.

Toddler Guidelines

1. Toddlers should accumulate at least 30 minutes daily of structured physical activity.

2. Toddlers should engage in at least 60 minutes and up to several hours of daily, unstructured physical activity and should not be sedentary for more than 60 minutes at a time except when sleeping.

3. Toddlers should develop movement skills that are building blocks for more complex movement tasks. Toddlers' newfound upright movement abilities open a new world for them. The child will seemingly move from an awkward walking gait to running in the blink of an eye. Other skills such as kicking and throwing will also emerge. Though maturation plays a part in this rapid development, environmental opportunities greatly influence these behaviors. Toddlers who are not provided with equipment or opportunities to engage in these behaviors often demonstrate motor delays (NASPE, 2002). These rudimentary manipulative movements also serve as a basis for more refined fundamental motor skills. Rhythms and musical instruments should be incorporated into the environment to stimulate movement and creative expression. In addition, toddlers may be capable of acting out stories, touching body parts, and playing chasing games. The recommended time frame stated earlier reinforces the need for the child to have both structured (motor environment with specific goals and objectives embedded in the activities) and unstructured (free time to interact within the environment) motor time. The premise is that the toddler needs ample time to move, discover, and interact in a play-based environment.

4. Toddlers should have indoor and outdoor areas that meet or exceed recommended safety standards for performing large-muscle activities. NASPE (2002) recommends that a minimum of 50 square feet (15 m^2) of accessible outdoor play space be available to toddlers. Additionally, a minimum of 5- by 7-feet (1.5 by 2 m) should be available per child for active movement. Finally, play spaces should be childproofed, accessible, and inviting.

5. People responsible for the well-being of toddlers should be aware of the importance of physical activity and promote the child's movement skills. Caregivers create the environments for increased physical activity and set appropriate boundaries based on the toddler's physical capabilities. They provide activities for imitation as well as imagination. They engage with and reassure the toddler as she gains new skills (NASPE, 2002).

Creating a movement environment in which infants and toddlers can thrive is another goal of the motor program. Environments should be child centered and stimulate the child's interests and abilities to act on the environment. Figure 21.1 is an example of a play-based motor environment for infants and toddlers.

Colorful walls and equipment are used to intrigue the child and elicit movement. Crawling and climbing areas are scaled appropriately. Open space, toys that elicit cause and effect, and toys with differing shapes, sizes, and textures should also be available. Similarly, adults who follow the child's lead playfully and delight in the child's newfound discoveries help to foster the child's confidence and overall abilities. Thus, another goal of motor programs for infants and toddlers is to create child-centered learning environments.

A final goal of motor programs for infants and toddlers is to aid in the development of independence. Though infants might not be ready to function independently of their caregivers, they should be provided opportunities to engage in isolated activities independently from time to time. Toddlers, however, will need guidance and support as they begin to release their total dependence on their parents or caregivers and learn to function more independently. This need for independence helps shape positive psychosocial behaviors later

in life. Play is crucial to the development of independence or autonomy because it allows children to function within their own boundaries, not the boundaries established by others.

As children attempt new skills, they need to feel successful so that they will continue to attempt either the same skill, leading to more refined movement, or try out new skills. **Self-initiated repetition** is one way to foster this independence (Bredekamp & Copple, 1997). Teachers of early childhood adapted physical education are responsible for developing environments that allow for ample opportunities to practice both already learned skills and new skills. For example, if a toddler finds rolling a ball stimulating, balls with various shapes and sizes should be available to the child. Since young children are egocentric, they should be provided with ample equipment so that they do not have to wait for a turn or to share. Figure 21.2 depicts a group of children who are provided with similar riding toys, allowing for maximum participation.

In summary, motor programs for typically developing infants and toddlers should provide opportunities for motor activities that allow infants and toddlers to use their newfound motor skills, such as crawling, walking, grasping, and releasing, so that they may have meaningful contacts with people and objects within their environments and remain

Photo courtesy of Cathy Houston-Wilson.

FIGURE 21.1   Example of a play-based environment at the Strong National Museum of Play, Rochester, New York.

FIGURE 21.2 Plenty of similar toys should be readily available.

active most times of the day. These combined goals realized through a series of objectives help to shape motor development as well as cognitive and social development in infants and toddlers. Additionally, motor programs should be child centered and provide opportunities for young children to gain independence in a safe and nurturing environment.

Infants and toddlers with unique needs, however, might have motor delays that inhibit their abilities to move freely and interact with their environments. Whereas the goals and objectives previously discussed are applicable to all infants and toddlers, the following section identifies unique motor needs that teachers of early childhood adapted physical education might encounter as well as strategies to promote the development of children with unique needs.

GOALS AND OBJECTIVES OF MOTOR PROGRAMS FOR INFANTS AND TODDLERS WITH UNIQUE NEEDS

Although typically developing infants and toddlers move from the stage of reflexive movement to rudimentary movement in a smooth, integrated fashion, infants and toddlers with special needs might demonstrate unique motor problems that benefit through intervention.

Cowden and Torrey (2007) identify several areas of emphasis in which motor programs for infants and toddlers with unique needs are developed. The first deals primarily with increasing muscle tone and strength. Infants and toddlers lacking in muscle tone are said to be **hypotonic**. Disabilities associated with hypotonicity include Down syndrome, muscular dystrophy, and metabolic disorders. Infants with low muscle tone often demonstrate delays in primitive reflex integration, especially with the tonic neck group of reflexes. Teachers of early childhood adapted physical education should provide physical assistance as needed to move the child through various strength-enhancing activities.

Strength-control activities should occur in four positions: prone, supine, side lying, and upright (Cowden & Torrey, 2007). In the prone position, the child is developing greater control of the head and trunk. These prerequisite skills aid in the development of locomotor movements, such as crawling and creeping. A typical prone position stimulus that elicits head control involves squeaking or rattling a favorite toy above the child's head (see figure 21.3). The child will attempt to reach for the toy and in so doing will lift his head from the floor.

Control of the trunk can be realized by encouraging and even helping the child to roll from stomach to back. Again, a favorite toy just out of reach will motivate the child to roll over. After the child has accomplished the task, it is important to allow her to interact with the toy. Once head and trunk control have been established, crawling and creeping positions should be maintained.

Activities in the supine and side-lying positions also stimulate muscle strength. However, for children with extremely high or low muscle tone, supine positions should be avoided and activities should be done in the side-lying position for greater control. A typical supine or side-lying activity involves offering the child a toy just slightly out of reach. The child will then reach for the toy (extend arms), obtain it, and bring the toy into midline (flex arms). These types of activities can be repeated in several ways using a variety of equipment to stimulate the child's interest.

Finally, activities that enhance strength can be attained in upright positions. For example, in a sitting position, children can interact with caregivers and their environments. Repeating over and over again any activity that maintains the child's interest, such as peekaboo, may stimulate a child and foster an upright position. As the child gains additional strength, standing and finally walking will be achieved.

The second area of motor emphasis for infants and toddlers with special needs is to decrease muscle tone and enhance reflex integration (Cowden & Torrey, 2007). Increased muscle tone, also known as **hypertonicity**, results from delayed reflex integration. Infants and toddlers with spastic cerebral palsy exhibit hypertonicity. The lack of reflex integration interferes with typical movement skills, thus creating substantial motor delays. Activities that involve relaxation techniques, massage, therapy exercise balls, and appropriate positioning help to minimize and alleviate hypertonicity. Figure 21.4 illustrates a young child being placed in a prone position on a therapy ball with legs slightly separated and toes pointed outward. The child is gently rocked forward and backward. This position on the therapy ball helps to normalize muscle tone by relaxing the muscles.

Stimulation and development of the sensory motor system are also areas of emphasis for infants and toddlers with unique needs. Cowden and Torrey (2007) and chapter 20 of this book identify five components of the sensory system and provide activities to enhance each. These components include vestibular integration, visual integration, auditory integration, tactile integration, and kinesthetic integration. Vestibular integration activities are needed so that children can right themselves, or

FIGURE 21.3 Eliciting head lifting with a toy fosters the infant's control of the head.

FIGURE 21.4 A child using a therapy ball to help normalize muscle tone.

maintain an upright position. Infants and toddlers who lack the ability to right themselves can easily be injured and demonstrate delayed locomotion and balance abilities. Therapy balls are useful for enhancing postural reactions. With the child lying over the ball, the ball is rolled forward so that the child extends the arms in a protective fashion. Activities that use incline mats, balance boards, and scooters are all appropriate for enhancing postural reactions because they stimulate opportunities for movement in several positions and situations.

The ability to track objects, discriminate between shapes and sizes, and distinguish objects from a background is all part of visual integration (figure 21.5). Activities that can enhance children's visual integration should be incorporated in early childhood motor programs. Simple tasks such as tracking a rolling ball, matching shapes, and walking on overlapping geometric shapes are all appropriate for enhancing visual integration.

Having children search for sounds in a room, move their bodies to the rhythm of music, and follow simple directions can enhance auditory integration. Some children might be hypersensitive to touch or lack reactions to touch. In these instances, carefully sequenced tactile integration activities can be incorporated into the program. Allowing the child to interact with a variety of textured equipment such as scooters, mats, balance boards, and ropes will help improve the child's ability to distinguish hard and soft objects. Physically stroking a child with various textures in a manner that is tolerated by the child is also helpful. Finally, kinesthetic integration can be enhanced by providing activities that allow the child to move through space, such as obstacle courses with tunnels, mats, and scooters.

The ability to manipulate objects might also be a needed area of emphasis for infants and toddlers with unique needs. The ability to reach, grasp, hold, and release is crucial for acquiring self-help skills, such as eating, and for making meaningful contacts within the environment, such as swinging on a swing.

In summary, areas of emphasis associated with infants and toddlers with unique needs might include increasing muscle tone and strength, decreasing muscle tone and enhancing reflex integration, stimulating the sensory motor system, and enhancing manipulative abilities. The following section describes developmentally appropriate interactions that parents, caregivers, and teachers of early childhood adapted physical education should embrace when implementing programs.

FIGURE 21.5 Tracking a slow-moving scarf is one way to enhance visual–motor control.

DEVELOPMENTALLY APPROPRIATE INTERACTIONS WITH INFANTS AND TODDLERS

Traditional formats for teaching physical education obviously do not apply to teaching infants and toddlers. Teachers of early childhood adapted physical education are primarily responsible for setting up an environment that is intriguing to children and their parents or caregivers. Direct teaching is not recommended with such young children; rather, indirect approaches to attain goals such as guided discovery and exploration are embedded within the learning environment. Infants and toddlers should be free to explore and engage in self-initiated repetition as much as desired. Teachers and caregivers should use indirect teaching strategies, such as following the child's lead in activities that are initiated by the child rather than the teacher or caregiver. This method is **child directed** or **child initiated**, and the adult teaches from behind, meaning the adult responds to the child's interactions. One way of teaching from behind is by describing

APPLICATION EXAMPLE

Developing an Appropriate Motor Environment

Setting: Motor room at a day care facility

Students: Toddlers with and without unique needs

Task: Setting up a developmentally appropriate motor environment that promotes the movement of the young children

Application: The environment contains the following areas:

▸ Push toys for fine motor development

▸ Stack toys for fine motor development

▸ Balls for gross motor development

▸ Tunnels for gross motor development

The teacher allows the children to interact with the environment and follows their lead as they move from one piece of equipment to another. Children with special needs might need to be brought to various areas if they are unable to ambulate independently. Choosing an area should be encouraged.

what the child is doing rather than telling the child what he should be doing (McCall & Craft, 2000). For example, if a young child is interacting with blocks, the caregiver can label the blocks by their colors or shapes with statements such as, "Shannon is stacking the red block."

Adults also play a role in providing choices for young children. They provide the environment that the child acts upon. The environment allows for guided discovery in which children explore and interact with the equipment that has been set out for them. For example, a motor room might contain push toys, stacking toys, balls, and tunnels. Any of these activities would be suitable since each has specific embedded values. Tunnels and balls allow children to enhance their gross motor abilities, whereas push toys and stacking toys enhance fine motor abilities. Activity participation will have naturally occurring consequences; that is, if a child climbs to the top of the slide, the natural consequence would be to slide down. These activities contribute to an understanding of the environment and enhance sensorimotor development. Refer to the application example, which describes a developmentally appropriate motor environment.

As noted, typically parents or caregivers will accompany the young child in the motor environment; thus, teachers of early childhood adapted physical education need to respect and embrace the role of parents and caregivers in their programming. The following section provides tips for interacting with parents or caregivers to enhance the child's development.

INTERACTING WITH FAMILIES

Teachers of early childhood adapted physical education for infants and toddlers should understand that their programs should be based on a **family-centered** philosophy and that goals and objectives are developed not in isolation of the family but rather in conjunction with them. One of the underlying assumptions of IFSP development is that infants and toddlers depend on their families for survival (McGonigel, 1991); thus, the role of families in early intervention cannot be minimized.

Bennett, Lingerfelt, and Nelson (1990) developed family-centered principles that teachers of early childhood adapted physical education may adopt for interacting with families. The first principle deals with basing intervention efforts on the needs and aspirations identified by the family. Fiorini, Stanton, and Reid (1996) identify several questions one might ask regarding motor development, such as the following: "What types of activities would you like your child to be doing now that she is not doing at the present time?" "What worries you most about your child's motor ability?" "What are you most excited about in terms of your child's motor ability?" This process enables parents to set the goals and objectives they feel are important to their child's development. The role of the early childhood adapted physical educator is to help prioritize the goals.

The second family-centered principle is based on expanding and developing the family's repertoire of skills and competencies. Teachers of early childhood adapted physical education can consult with and demonstrate appropriate motor interactions that parents or caregivers can model. As parents or caregivers engage the child in developmentally appropriate activities and see gains in motor development, confidence in their abilities to do so is strengthened.

Finally, the most important family-centered principle is communication. Teachers of early childhood adapted physical education need to maintain constant open communication with parents or caregivers. The development of the young child is based on the combined efforts of parents and supportive professionals whose major role is to guide the family in the development of their child, not to direct the development of the child. With a strong collaborative partnership, infants and toddlers with special needs and their families can benefit from early intervention services, and the child's development can be significantly enhanced.

SUMMARY

This chapter has illustrated the role of teachers of early childhood adapted physical education as it relates to infants and toddlers with unique needs. As noted, teachers of early childhood adapted physical education might be involved in early intervention services for infants and toddlers with unique needs by serving as members of the multidisciplinary team convened to determine unique needs, conduct valid assessments of motor abilities, develop appropriate motor goals and objectives for the IFSP, and implement motor programs. In some instances, teachers of early childhood adapted physical education might serve as consultants to caregivers or parents on providing appropriate motor programs.

Although all infants and toddlers can benefit from developmentally appropriate motor programs, infants and toddlers with unique needs will have specific goals and objectives embedded in their activities. Goals might include increasing muscle tone and strength, decreasing muscle tone and enhancing reflex integration, stimulating the sensory motor system, or enhancing manipulative abilities. A variety of activities were presented in this chapter to help teachers of early childhood adapted physical education realize these goals; however, the reader is encouraged to seek out the recommended resources in this chapter to further develop motor programs for infants and toddlers with unique needs.

Finally, this chapter has highlighted the importance of family in the lives of infants and toddlers. It is suggested that teachers of early childhood adapted physical education embrace three family-centered principles when working with infants and toddlers with unique needs. These family-centered principles include basing intervention efforts on the needs and aspirations identified by the family, expanding and developing the family's repertoire of skills and competencies, and maintaining open communication.

Teachers of early childhood adapted physical education are in a unique position to help minimize further delays of infants and toddlers by creating movement environments that allow children to discover, explore, and interact with their environments. These interactions enhance motor development and improve cognitive and social development.

REFERENCES

American Academy of Pediatrics. (2008). *A parents' guide to safe sleep*. Elk Grove Village, IL: Author.

Bennett, T., Lingerfelt, B.V., & Nelson, D.E. (1990). *Developing individualized family support plans: A training manual*. Cambridge, MA: Brookline Books.

Bredekamp, S., & Copple, C. (1997). *Developmentally appropriate practice in early childhood programs— Revised*. Washington, DC: National Association for the Education of Young Children.

Brigance, A. (2008). *Brigance Inventory of Early Development II (IED-II)*. Billerica, MA: Curriculum Associates.

Cowden, J.E., & Torrey, C.C. (2007). *Motor development and movement activities for preschoolers and infants with delays*. Springfield, IL: Charles C. Thomas.

Fiorini, J., Stanton, K., & Reid, G. (1996). Understanding parents and families of children with disabilities: Considerations for adapted physical activity. *Palaestra, 12* (2), 16-23.

Folio, M.R., & Fewell, R. (2000). *Peabody developmental motor scales* (2nd ed.). Austin, TX: Pro-Ed.

Frankenburg, W.K., Dodds, J., Archer, P., Bresnick, B., Maschka, P., Edelman, N., & Shapiro, H. (1992). *Denver II training manual* (2nd ed.). Denver: Denver Developmental Materials.

Gallahue, D.L., & Ozmun, J.C. (2002). *Understanding motor development: Infants, children, adolescents, adults*. Boston: McGraw-Hill.

Individuals with Disabilities Education Improvement Act of 2004 (IDEA). 20 USC 1400.

Jackson, C.W., & Larkin, M.J. (2002). Teaching students to use grading rubrics. *Teaching Exceptional Children, 35*, 40-44.

Johnson-Martin, N., Attermeier, S.M., & Hacker, B.J. (2004). *The Carolina Curriculum for infants and toddlers with special needs* (3rd ed.). Baltimore: Paul H. Brookes.

Linder, T. (2008). *Transdisciplinary play-based assessment*. Baltimore: Paul H. Brookes.

McCall, R., & Craft, D.H. (2000). *Moving with a purpose: Developing programs for preschoolers of all abilities*. Champaign, IL: Human Kinetics.

McGonigel, M.J. (1991). Philosophy and conceptual framework. In M.J. McGonigel, R.K. Kaufman, & B.H. Johnson (Eds.), *Guidelines and recommendations for the individualized family service plan*. Bethesda, MD: Association for the Care of Children's Health.

National Association for Sport and Physical Education (NASPE). (2002). *Active Start: A statement of physical activity guidelines for children birth to five years*. Reston, VA: Author.

New York State Department of Health. (2005). *Standards and procedures for evaluations, evaluation reimbursement, and eligibility requirements and determination under the early intervention program*. New York: Author.

Office of Special Education and Rehabilitative Services (OSE/RS), 34 CFR 306 (2006).

Parks, S. (Ed.). (2007). *HELP strands: Curriculum-based developmental assessment birth to three years*. Palo Alto, CA: VORT.

Stuberg, W., Dehne, P., Miedaner, J., & Romero, P. (1992). *Milani-Comparetti Motor Development Screening Test manual*. Omaha: Munroe-Meyer Institute for Genetics and Rehabilitation, University of Nebraska Medical Center.

WRITTEN RESOURCES

Bardige, B. S. (2009). *Talk to me, baby! How you can support young children's language development*. Baltimore: Paul H. Brookes.

Uses movement-based activities to stimulate language development.

Chen, D. (Ed.). (2009). *Early intervention in action*. Baltimore: Paul H. Brookes.

Uses a cross-disciplinary approach for providing early intervention services. Provides video clips of children to demonstrate key concepts.

Cowden, J.E., & Torrey, C.C. (2007). *Motor development and movement activities for preschoolers and infants with delays*. Springfield, IL: Charles C. Thomas.

Uses a pediatric adapted physical education approach to enhance motor development of young children with special needs. Provides many hands-on practical activities that can easily be implemented by practitioners.

Pretti-Frontczak, K., & Bricker, D. (2004). *An activity-based approach to early intervention* (3rd ed.). Baltimore: Paul H. Brookes.

Details how activity-based assessment can be used to link assessment, goal development, intervention, and evaluation for children from birth to age 5. Useful in developing IFSPs and individualized education programs (IEPs).

Widerstrom, A.H. (2004). *Achieving learning goals through play* (2nd ed.). Baltimore: Paul H. Brookes.

A practical guide that uses play to help young children with and without special needs learn. Provides ready-to-use strategies and plans to achieve learning goals.

AUDIOVISUAL RESOURCES

And you thought they were just playing: Transdisciplinary Play-Based Assessment [VHS]. (1995). Paul H. Brookes, P.O. Box 10624, Baltimore, MD 21285.

Demonstrates how children can be assessed while playing in natural environments. Provides detailed instructions and application of this assessment approach. Running time is approximately 65 minutes.

Infants and young children with special health needs: Motor development [VHS and DVD]. (1992). Films for the Humanities & Sciences, P.O. Box 2053, Princeton, NJ 08543.

Demonstrates proper positioning of children with hypotonia and hypertonia to increase their abilities to develop motor skills. Running time is approximately 25 minutes.

Observing Kassandra: A Transdisciplinary Play-Based Assessment of a child with severe disabilities [VHS]. (1996). Paul H. Brookes, P.O. Box 10624, Baltimore, MD 21285.

Uses the TPBA to observe a child with severe disabilities. Provides detailed instructions and application of this assessment approach. Includes an accompanying booklet. Running time is approximately 50 minutes.

ELECTRONIC RESOURCES

Council for Exceptional Children, Division of Early Childhood (DEC): www.dec-sped.org.

Provides information on laws and best practices related to early intervention programs for children with disabilities.

National Association for the Education of Young Children (NAEYC): www.naeyc.org.

This is the primary site for resources and best practices for the education of young children from birth to nine years.

Zero to Three: www.zerotothree.org.

The leading resource in the United States on the first years.

22

Early Childhood Adapted Physical Education

Lauriece L. Zittel

Mr. Sanchez and Ms. Brooks are elementary physical education specialists at North Ridge Elementary School. Both teachers have experience modifying their instruction to successfully include children with disabilities in their K-3 program. Recently, their district instituted an inclusive early childhood program for preschoolers. Young children with disabilities or developmental delays who have been identified as needing special education services are enrolled in this program. The district combined this special education program with an already existing preschool program housed in the elementary school.

The Individuals with Disabilities Education Act (IDEA) requires that all preschool-aged children with diagnosed disabilities or developmental delays receive special education programming. Additionally, those children experiencing motor delays are entitled to receive adapted physical education services at the discretion of individual states. The teachers decided that rather than just providing instruction to the children with developmental delays, they would design a preschool physical education program for all of the children in this new program. The teachers are aware that the majority of children in the preschool program have communication delays in addition to their disability diagnosis or general developmental delay. They are anxious to collaborate with the classroom teachers and speech therapist to develop a movement program that will enhance motor and communication skills. The challenge is to design a preschool program that will build a skill foundation for the children as they prepare to enter their elementary physical education program.

The early childhood physical education instructors in this vignette are not alone. It is not uncommon to find preschool classrooms for children with developmental delays in an elementary school building. Many physical educators have had experience teaching children with disabilities in kindergarten through the third grade, but teaching a preschool population might be new to them. The purpose of this chapter is to present information about accurately assessing the abilities of young children, understanding the developmental differences between preschool children and those entering elementary school, and planning for instruction and developmentally appropriate teaching practices for children aged three to nine.

IDENTIFYING YOUNG CHILDREN WITH DEVELOPMENTAL DELAYS

IDEA was passed to enhance opportunities for young children with special needs. According to the act, children aged three through nine who are experiencing developmental delays are to be provided early educational opportunities and might qualify for these services if they are

(1) . . . experiencing developmental delays, as defined by the State and as measured by appropriate diagnostic instruments and procedures, in one or more of the following areas: physical development, social or emotional development, or adaptive development; and (2) Who, by reason thereof, [need] special education and related services. (Federal Register, 2006, p. 46756)

In preschool and early childhood (ages 3-9), a noncategorical approach is used to classify students as eligible to receive special education services. This noncategorical approach allows for programming based on the functional areas of development of each child rather than disability-specific programming. Federal legislation also requires that instruction be provided to these children in the least restrictive and most natural learning environment. Thus, inclusive programs designed to accommodate children with and without unique needs should be the norm rather than the excep-

tion. Teachers of physical education are thus faced with the challenge of determining if movement delays exist and structuring movement programs to meet the needs of young children with varying levels of abilities.

Accurately assessing children's abilities will enhance the planning and implementation of early childhood adapted physical education programs. Children with diagnosed developmental delays and disabilities present individual challenges for instructors. In the next section, appropriate assessment procedures are presented to assist teachers of early childhood adapted physical education in determining the functional abilities of the young children in their classrooms. Identifying a gross motor developmental delay is essential in determining a child's eligibility to receive an individualized adapted physical education program. Planning and implementing developmentally appropriate physical education instruction for children with gross motor delays depends on the accuracy of the assessment.

ASSESSMENT OF PERFORMANCE

Making accurate decisions about children's individualized program needs requires an understanding of their current ability. Professional guidelines and federal legislation recommend that assessment information come from several measures and sources. Additionally, children at risk for developmental delay should be observed in a variety of settings. A complete picture of a young child's present level of performance (in all areas of learning) can be drawn from a group of people most familiar with the child's routines and behaviors. A multidisciplinary team should collect screening information while observing the child in structured settings as well as unstructured play environments. Members of the multidisciplinary team should include classroom teachers, adapted or regular physical educators, therapists, parents or guardians, and others who see the child on a regular basis. These team members will develop the child's individualized educational program (IEP) and participate in the IEP planning committee.

The assessment may be completed using a formal, standardized procedure or an informal, play-based procedure (Linder, 2008), the difference lying primarily in the level of intrusiveness. Before selecting an instrument to assess young children, the purpose of testing should be clear (Zittel, 1994). Will the results be used to document a developmental delay, or is information needed for planning and teaching? Norm-referenced, standardized tests are administered to determine a child's gross motor developmental level and provide comparison information of same-age children without delays. Criterion-referenced instruments typically provide more information about delays in skill areas (e.g., locomotor, object control) to assist with teaching and program planning.

Standardized Formal Testing

Standardized test instruments that are both norm and criterion referenced will assist adapted physical education specialists in making eligibility decisions and provide instructional information. Instruments that incorporate flexible testing procedures (i.e., equipment selection and testing environments) will be more sensitive to the testing characteristics of young children with disabilities and thus lead to more accurate results. Examples of standardized, norm- and criterion-referenced tools used to assess the gross motor skills of young children include the Brigance Inventory of Early Development (IED-II) (Brigance, 1991), the Peabody Developmental Motor Scales (PDMS-2) (Folio & Fewell, 2000), and the Test of Gross Motor Development (TGMD-2) (Ulrich, 2000).

Each of these assessment instruments is designed to assist early childhood physical education specialists in determining a child's gross motor developmental level as well as to provide information for instructional programming. Additionally, each of these tools will assist specialists in developing goals and objectives for the child's IEP. The testing procedures outlined for the Brigance IED-II, the PMDS-2, and the TGMD-2 provide test administrators with flexibility in the way the test environment is structured, what equipment is selected, and how instructions are provided. For example, the PDMS-2 test manual suggests that a station-testing format be used for evaluating several young children at a time, and the materials used to administer the PMDS-2 are those commonly found in preschool or primary programs and familiar to most children.

Federal guidelines encourage early childhood teachers to use data from multiple observations and measures for gathering information to make decisions about performance ability. Information collected in standardized settings should be combined with observations made in natural play environments.

Informal Testing

The authenticity of data collected in natural settings provides instructors with useful information about the child's preferences and functional abilities. The ability to write accurate instructional objectives and structure an effective teaching environment is maximized when teachers observe and record behaviors of children during typical games and activities and watch them interact with age-appropriate equipment. Criterion-referenced skill checklists are used in curriculum-based assessment and yield information about the child's abilities in the context of a predetermined set of curriculum objectives (McLean, Wolery, & Bailey, 2004). For a child who may not find success performing some objectives within the curriculum, a functional motor development assessment (FMDA) should be completed. The FMDA will provide information about what skills a child can do and how the child performs the skills.

In the area of early childhood adapted physical education, two curriculum-based tools are recommended to assist physical education teachers in securing performance assessment data. *Smart Start: A Preschool Movement Curriculum* (Wessel & Zittel, 1995) and *I CAN Primary Skills: K-3* (Wessel & Zittel, 1998) are programs that include skill checklists for teachers to use to collect information for individualized movement programs. In both programs, the authors have organized the skill checklists into a LOOP model. The Smart Start preschool checklists include **l**ocomotor (e.g., jumping, hopping), **o**rientation (e.g., body awareness, imitative expressive movements), **o**bject-control (e.g., throwing, kicking) and **p**lay skills (e.g., parachute play, tricycle riding). The I CAN K-3 skill checklists also include the fundamental skill areas (**l**ocomotor, **o**rientation, and **o**bject control), but instead of play skills, **p**ersonal–social participation (e.g., problem solving, self-control) skills are assessed. Participation checklists were added to the I CAN K-3 curriculum because of a need expressed by teachers. The LOOP organization in both of these early childhood programs allows instructors to assess children according to skill areas relevant for both the preschool and elementary years. Additionally, the model gives instructors the freedom to select skill objectives from different areas for different units of instruction. For example, a preschool adapted physical educator might choose to assess three locomotor skills (vertical jumping, hop, gallop) and two play skills (parachute play, tricycle riding) to organize one six-week unit of instruction. Similarly, an elementary adapted physical educator may select two locomotor skills and four object-control skills for a six-week unit.

The Carolina Curriculum for preschoolers (Johnson-Martin, Attermeier, & Hacker, 1990) and the Assessment, Evaluation, and Programming System (AEPS) for infants and children (Bricker, Capt, & Pretti-Frontczak, 2002) are multidomain, curriculum-based programs designed for preschool-aged children with disabilities or those who are at risk of developmental delays. The Carolina Curriculum assesses children in five learning domains and provides a curriculum sequence in each area. The gross motor domain assesses skills in locomotion, stair climbing, jumping, balance, balls, and outdoor equipment. The AEPS includes a functional skill assessment across six learning domains and a curriculum to provide programming and teaching suggestions for instructors. The gross motor domain includes two skill strands. Strand A is balance and mobility in standing and walking and focuses on stair-climbing. Strand B is play skills and includes five goals for children in these areas: Jump forward; run avoiding obstacles; bounce, catch, kick, and throw; skip; and ride and steer a two-wheel bicycle.

Teacher-made checklists and rubrics can also be useful for assessing functional motor and play skill performance. Standards of performance can be written to address the unique movement abilities of children, and progress on those standards can be used to evaluate improvement on instructional objectives. These methods give teachers the freedom to collect performance information on skills or behaviors that might not be found in published checklists. Additionally, task analyzing skills for children with ambulatory difficulties or severe disabilities will give early childhood teachers the opportunity to assess functional abilities by individualizing the critical elements in a checklist. For example, a teacher might be assessing the galloping abilities of preschool children while they pretend that yardsticks are their horses. One child in the class with cerebral palsy uses a gait trainer and, with the horse attached, is working on stepping. Another child who uses a wheelchair may feed the horses and in doing so work on upper trunk stability and overhand throwing. In this example, the teacher might use the Smart Start galloping and overhand throwing checklist for some of the children in the class and create his own stepping and upper-trunk stability checklist to evaluate the ability of the children with ambulatory difficulties.

Portfolio assessment is a means of gathering information about a child in order to monitor progress on teaching objectives or to inform teaching practice (Lynch & Struewing, 2001). In collaboration with the classroom teacher, information from the movement environment can be added to a child's portfolio, or the adapted physical educator can begin a portfolio system for a child on her own. Because the purpose of a portfolio is to enhance teaching, collaboration is recommended. Ideally, movement skills will be practiced not only in the physical education class but also at home and during movement times that the classroom teacher arranges. All who work with a child should add samples of the child's activity or practice on certain IEP objectives. Written comments from teachers, parents, or teaching assistants in addition to videotapes, photos, and drawings related to movement skills and practice are examples of items to include in a movement portfolio. At the end of each evaluation period, the adapted physical educator should organize all of the material and provide an overview and reflection about the child's year. For children who will remain in a preschool program for multiple years, the portfolio can be used to document progress and then be shared with the elementary specialists during the transition to kindergarten.

Whether gathered formally or informally, performance data should provide a direct link to designing and evaluating an individualized intervention plan. The activities a teacher uses should address each child's gross motor strengths and challenges. Teachers of early childhood adapted physical education should become familiar with curriculum designs and instructional strategies that are both age and individually appropriate.

EARLY CHILDHOOD PROGRAM STANDARDS AND LEARNING OBJECTIVES

The development of early childhood physical education programs should be aligned with best practices in early childhood education and early childhood special education. Young children experiencing delays in their motor development should receive opportunities and instruction designed to parallel what their same-age peers receive but modified to address individual challenges. Early childhood movement programs should provide children with the opportunity to explore and act on objects in their physical environment. A well-designed movement curriculum for preschool through third grade should focus on fundamental movement abilities in the preschool years and specialized movement abilities in the early elementary years.

The preschool years give instructors the opportunity to guide children through games and activities in order to build a skill foundation. This fundamental movement phase should focus on stability, locomotor, and object-control skills (see chapter 19 for a review of the fundamental movement phase). It follows, then, that the early elementary years (kindergarten-third grade) allow the teacher to integrate the knowledge and skills that children have acquired and begin to refine fundamental skills required for more advanced games and activities. The specialized movement phase will give children the opportunity to use several fundamental skills to complete a single activity that is more specialized (see chapter 19 for a review of the specialized movement phase).

The importance of seeing the connection between the fundamental movement phase and specialized movement phase in the early childhood years is critical for physical education curriculum development. As a guide, national standards for physical education (NASPE, 2004) have been written for elementary children in the United States. These six physical education standards are in place for five- to nine-year-old children and are written to reflect what children should be able to do after participation in a quality physical education program. PE Metrics (NASPE, 2008) is a valid and reliable tool developed to assess the first national physical education standard, which reads "Demonstrates competency in motor skills and movement patterns needed to perform a variety of physical activities" (NASPE, 2004, p. 11). A quality physical education program for elementary-aged children should follow national standards and build upon the fundamental movement skill programs introduced in preschool.

However, early learning standards vary state by state for preschool-aged children. To assist early childhood educators, the National Institute for Early Education Research (NIEER) has organized a standards database of what states have identified as educational priorities for children of prekindergarten age (NIEER, 2008). Using learning standards to guide programming for children with and without disabilities through the early childhood years can be beneficial in all domains of learning, including physical health and development. Early childhood physical educators should be knowledgeable about learning standards and assessing them and how they contribute to program development. Mastering fundamental movements and skills and integrating them into games and activities are processes.

Activity environments designed to provide instruction for young children with developmental delays and those with disabilities should be individualized according to assessment information. Arbitrarily selecting games and activities because they seem fun and the children appear to enjoy them is not necessarily in line with good practice. Specifically, learning environments should parallel the strengths and challenges identified during the assessment process and written in the IEP as instructional objectives. Instruction is based on a good understanding of each child's present level of performance. An activity setting should be carefully planned to build on what children already know and promote the acquisition of new skills.

Developmental theorists support instruction that encourages children to explore and manipulate their environment in order to construct meaning (Piaget, 1952; Vygotsky, 1978). Individualizing instruction for each child in the class is the challenge faced by teachers providing early childhood adapted physical education in an integrated setting. Using a differentiated instructional approach will help teachers address the diverse learning needs of several children in the same class (Sands & Barker, 2004). An understanding of the child's developmental abilities (physical, social, and cognitive) and the effect that a certain disability might have on this development must be considered.

Developmental Differences Between Preschoolers and Primary-Aged Children

The cognitive and social developmental status of a four-year-old differs from that of a six-year-old. As children develop cognitively and socially, they incorporate their movement strategies in new ways. Teachers providing adapted physical education must understand age-related developmental differences in order to construct appropriate learning environments for children who exhibit delays in one or more areas of learning.

Developmentally appropriate movement environments designed for preschool-aged children (three-five years of age) differ from those planned for kindergarten and elementary school children (six-eight years of age). A watered-down kindergarten curriculum presented to children in preschool is not appropriate. Games, activities, and equipment meaningful to a four-year-old might be of little interest to a seven-year-old and vice versa. For example, preschoolers love to experiment with speed, direction change, and space. Figure 22.1 shows a young boy making his way through a tunnel placed within a larger activity area. With a little creativity and imagination, teachers of early childhood physical education can create stimulating and motivating learning environments. A refrigerator box that has holes cut for climbing and hiding might lure a preschooler to explore and move for a long time. Preschoolers are intrigued by new spaces and the opportunity to explore these seemingly simple environments. On the other hand, a seven-year-old might find these activities simplistic and boring. She would be much more interested and challenged by moving under and through a parachute lifted by classmates. A child in first or second grade (six or seven years old) might be challenged by activities that encourage a higher level of problem solving. Children at this age have greater ability to reason and logically integrate thoughts than younger children do. For a three- or four-year-old, a parachute activity that includes anything more than moving the parachute up and down is often frightening and unpredictable.

The NAEYC (Bredekamp & Copple, 1997) provides guidelines for developmentally appropriate practice in early childhood and discusses the differences between preschool and primary-aged children in their physical, social, cognitive, and language development. Teachers providing adapted physical education should keep in mind that the cognitive and social development of young children cannot be ignored when developing goals and objectives in the psychomotor domain. The interplay between each of these functional areas of learning and an individual child's development within each area must be considered when planning movement environments and instruction.

Developmental Considerations for Young Children With Disabilities

The effect of a disability on the communication, social, cognitive, or motor development of a child must be recognized before planning instruction. Knowing how a child's disability affects motor learning and performance is essential for the development of an appropriate physical education program. Young children with orthopedic impairments, for example, might begin independently exploring their physical environments by using a walker, wheelchair, or crutches but might also

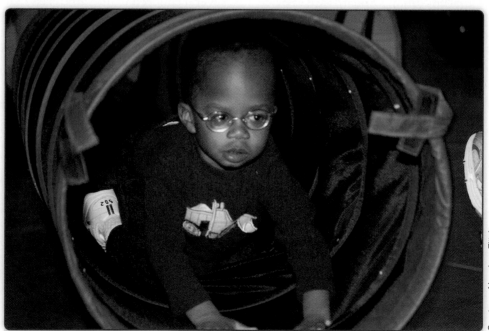

Courtesy of Lauriece Zittel.

FIGURE 22.1   A young boy makes his way through a tunnel, a familiar play space for preschoolers.

require accommodations in order to benefit from age-appropriate activities. Instructors should be aware of physical barriers that exist in the activity setting and design the environment in a way that encourages interactions with peers and equipment. Assistive devices that allow children with orthopedic impairments to initiate tasks that are both physically and intellectually challenging should be available to promote independence.

Young children with delays in social interaction, for example children with autism, require modifications in the introduction and delivery of games and activities. Small- or large-group activities might be difficult for children with autism, and practicing motor skills might need to occur in social environments that offer options for solitary and parallel play. For young children with autism, interaction with others might not be the best instructional approach or least restrictive environment for learning new skills. On the other hand, children with intellectual disabilities often benefit from an environment that is consistent, predictable, and repetitive. As shown in figure 22.2, a predictable

Photo courtesy of NIU. Photographer: Molly Coleman.

FIGURE 22.2 Consistent and predictable environments promote learning among children with disabilities.

environment with familiar equipment and routines will enhance opportunities for learning.

Physical educators need to be aware of the characteristics of young children with disabilities and plan activities and environments accordingly.

Facilitating Communication in a Movement Lesson

Interacting with others requires some level of communication. Some young children with disabilities use speech and language to communicate, whereas others who are nonverbal might use alternative methods and strategies. Although speech or language impairment is considered the most prevalent disability category among preschoolers, children with many diagnoses might have communication needs (U.S. Department of Education, 2005). The movement setting, typically a motivating setting for young children, can be an ideal environment to enhance communication skills. Collaboration with classroom teachers and speech therapists will assist the early childhood physical educator in determining what communication goals and objectives can be integrated within the physical education setting. Further, collaboration might be necessary to determine which communication strategies work best for children according to their IEP goals and objectives.

Young children with disabilities or developmental delays who are verbal might use speech and language to communicate with peers and teachers. The movement setting is a natural place to incorporate concepts such as under, over, more, through, and around. To reinforce the meaning of movement concepts and model the use of speech, a physical educator should talk with children as they participate in each movement lesson. For example, as children are pretending to be in the jungle climbing over rocks (bolsters under mats) and jumping over cutout ants and snakes (taped to the floor), a teacher might say, "I like the way everyone is jumping *over* the creatures in the jungle. Everyone find a creature and say 'over' as we jump. Ready?" Prompting children to use the words to identify the concept (e.g., over) as they practice the skill (e.g., horizontal jump) reinforces the meaning of commonly taught concepts in early childhood and encourages children to use speech. Similarly, identifying shapes, colors, or equipment can become a natural part of an early childhood movement setting.

The end of a class session or particular activity is an appropriate time to talk about what happened during that lesson. Asking children to reflect on the lesson or activity encourages them to speak, which can be a confidence booster. Talking about the snakes in the jungle or asking children to name the color of the scarf they used for a catching activity is a good strategy for prompting children to talk.

Children with speech and language delays or those who are nonverbal as a result of a particular disability or multiple disabilities might use augmentative and alternative systems to communicate (DiCarlo, Banajee, & Stricklin, 2000). Sign language and picture systems are nonverbal options used by teachers to communicate with young children. Sign language is a popular method of communicating with young children of all abilities; however, children with communication delays and those who are hard of hearing might benefit in particular. Physical educators not proficient in sign language should consult with classroom teachers, interpreters, or speech therapists to learn the signs used by young children in the classroom.

Picture systems can also be used in a movement setting to increase communication between the child and teacher. Young children with autism often have sophisticated picture systems in place to assist with identifying activities, equipment, activity directions, and transitions. Picture systems can increase the probability that children with communication delays have the opportunity to engage in movement activities to the maximum extent possible. Helping a child understand what to do and when to do it often decreases the time needed to manage unwanted behaviors. Pictures posted in the activity area or taped to pieces of equipment are a great communication strategy for all children. A sequence of pictures, or visual schedule, posted to a board or paper is a functional method for communicating an activity, skill sequence, or transition to a child who is verbal or nonverbal. Visual schedules help children to manage their environment while many times decreasing the amount of adult intervention needed. Figure 22.3 is an example of a young boy removing a picture of a completed activity from his schedule. The other pictures remaining on the schedule give him a clear indication of activities to follow. Depending upon the learning style of the child, all pictures can be on the board at the beginning of the class, or pictures can be added as the activity is presented.

Voice output devices are another method used to communicate with children who are nonverbal. A voice output system makes use of pictures and symbols along with prerecorded words and phrases (DiCarlo et al., 2000). Programming movement

Courtesy of Lauriece Zittel.

FIGURE 22.3 Visual schedules help children manage their environments.

concepts, names of equipment or activities, and general statements provides a child with functional communication during physical education. For young children using a voice output system, a movement setting might reinforce practice with a new voice output device.

Stories and songs are great methods for integrating movement and communication skills. Reading books such as *The Balancing Girl* (Rabe, 1981) after a balancing lesson or *We're Going on a Bear Hunt* (Rosen, 1989) during a lesson emphasizing concepts such as under, over, and through might prompt a dialogue. Asking children to communicate about the story as they are acting it out or to tell the story using key words related to movements they used might promote verbal and nonverbal communication. Pantomime is yet another method to integrate movement and communication (Gabbei & Clemmens, 2005). Collaboration with classroom teachers to develop a reading list or vocabulary list for use in the classroom and movement setting is a functional strategy to address communication skills during movement lessons.

PLANNING FOR INSTRUCTION

A curriculum, including assessment and instruction, should be designed according to what is known about how children learn (Bredekamp & Rosegrant, 1992). What is age appropriate must be balanced with what is individually appropriate when designing physical education instruction for young children with disabilities or developmental delays. The three Cs of curriculum design—content, construction, and contact (Wessel & Zittel, 1995, 1998)—can serve as a guide for teachers of adapted physical education working toward attaining this balance for preschool and primary-aged children.

First, the skills selected as instructional **content** must be considered. The instructional focus of a preschool physical education program might include community-based, neighborhood activities such as tricycle riding or pulling a wagon, whereas it might be appropriate to teach primary-aged children how to use a jump rope. The selection of appropriate content depends on how well the teacher has examined assessment information and understands the developmental differences between children of the same or similar chronological age.

Second, **construction** of a teaching environment must be carefully planned. How the teacher of adapted physical education constructs the physical environment and how activities are introduced will differ for preschool and primary-aged children. Given the developmental premise that a three-year-old differs from a seven-year-old, the manner in which children of different ages interact in a physical environment will vary. Physical environments should be designed to promote interactions for the purpose of skill development. The organization of the physical environment, as well as how and when activities are introduced, must be considered.

Finally, a critical consideration in planning for instruction is the thought given to strategies that maximize the **contact** a young child has with equipment and peers versus contact time with adults (teachers). Regardless of developmental level, young children must be given the opportunity to explore their physical environment in order to develop impressions about their world. Young children with disabilities or developmental delays might require additional prompting during exploration so they are not denied opportunities to interact with equipment and peers. Instructors working with young children have the primary responsibility of promoting interactions within the movement environment as an alternative to direct instruction. Table 22.1 lists strategies physical educators can use to promote effective teacher and environmental interactions.

Organization of the curriculum might vary from program to program. Teachers of early childhood adapted physical education might choose to set up an instructional unit to focus on a certain fundamental skill area at a certain time of the year or to introduce skills in a particular sequence. For example, a specialist might design a unit that targets locomotor skills at the beginning of the school year. All games and activities during that unit include the ongoing assessment and teaching of skills such as hopping, jumping, and galloping.

Table 22.1 Key Indicators in Becoming an Effective Facilitator

Teacher interaction	Effective implementation
Teacher as observer	Pursue student involvement. Collect data on the needs and interests of the children. Monitor activity environment to ensure success.
Teacher as facilitator	Allow for choice making (assist when necessary). Maximize opportunities to practice skills with child-directed repetition. Maintain physical proximity and provide support as needed. Model activity behavior, challenge present performance level, and guide or redirect to alternative activity if necessary. Encourage development of positive social skills (helping, sharing, negotiating).
Environmental interaction	**Effective implementation**
Equipment	Use familiar, meaningful objects mixed with novel, challenging objects. Arrange according to spatial and safety constraints to allow for active involvement. Provide enough material for multiple trials without waiting.
Peers	Create a motivating environment in which children can model appropriate skill performance, demonstrate alternative play activities, and encourage task persistence.

Reprinted from J.A. Wessel and L.L. Zittel, 1995, *SMART START: Preschool movement curriculum designed for children of all abilities* (Austin, TX: PRO-ED). By permission of L.L. Zittel.

Other instructors might choose to organize instructional material around themes (Clements, 1995). Often, the theme approach is used in collaboration with classroom teachers and the instructional concepts they are teaching. For example, a physical education day at the zoo or day at the circus provides children with the opportunity to practice fundamental and motor fitness skills while interacting within a familiar theme. The curricular vehicle used to organize instruction (units or themes) often depends on the instructor's style of teaching and comfort level with this age group. The number of skill objectives taught and the time needed to learn each objective depends on the severity of the child's delay. However, what should never be compromised in any early childhood program is developmentally appropriate instruction.

DEVELOPMENTALLY APPROPRIATE TEACHING APPROACHES

The following sections will deal with developmentally appropriate teaching approaches. These approaches should be used for planning and delivering adapted physical education programs for preschool and primary-aged children.

Preschool-Aged Children

Preschool classrooms typically include 12 to 18 children with one teacher and an assistant. Classrooms for young children with severe developmental delays and disabilities often have fewer children. One challenge in providing instruction for this age group is that many preschool programs have multiage classrooms, meaning that children aged three to five are taught in the same class. As stated earlier in this chapter, planning instruction requires teachers to consider early learning standards, assessment results, and the developmental status of each child in the class, regardless of chronological age or how a disability might affect development. Although ages and abilities might differ for children in the same class, the approach to intervention should remain similar for this age group.

Developmentally appropriate practice in preschool physical education emphasizes the role of the teacher as guide or facilitator. Teachers structure the environment with objectives in mind, for example throwing and kicking, and guide students toward these movement objectives. Environments are adapted to allow for several choices to meet learning objectives and for maximum active participation (Mithaug & Mithaug, 2003). This child-directed style of teaching differs from the teacher-directed style of instruction in which the instructor focuses on one task at a time and students move as a group from one activity to the next on the teacher's signal. It would be developmentally inappropriate to expect preschool children to respond to a teacher-directed format.

One example of a child-directed approach to early childhood education is activity-based intervention (ABI) (Pretti-Frontczak et al., 2003). ABI is designed to embed each child's IEP goals and objectives within activities that are naturally motivating to young children. Teachers can use strategies to design activity areas that are motivating for children and that encourage skill practice within the environment (see application example). Young children with disabilities or developmental delays benefit from structured movement environments that incorporate the following principles:

- Child-directed versus teacher-directed learning
- Opportunity for choice
- Self-initiated exploration
- Experience with novel and familiar equipment
- Exposure to peer models

The following scenario highlights how these principles of best practice can be seen within one preschool physical education setting.

Emma and her classmates are on their way to physical education class, where they will soon discover that today is an adventure with wheel toys. As they enter the activity area, they see tricycles, ride toys, wagons, and scooters scattered throughout the area. They also notice that jump ropes have been laid down to create pathways, cardboard trees have been spaced throughout the activity area, and arches held up with orange cones have been scattered around as obstacles to move under and through. As Mr. Sanchez welcomes the children into the activity environment, he announces, "Let's take a ride through the park today."

As the children scurry into the activity area to select their mode of transportation, Mr. Sanchez takes notice of Emma. He knows that Emma has autism, and from reviewing her IEP he is aware that she has a gross motor IEP objective focused on pulling an object around obstacles, a social skill objective focused on initiating social interac-

tions, and a communication objective focused on making verbal requests. He notices that Emma gets on a ride toy and begins to maneuver through the park. As Emma crosses the room, she slows down to take notice of a teddy bear sitting in a wagon. Emma knows that she has been given a ride in a wagon before and decides that she will give the teddy bear a ride.

Mr. Sanchez sees that Emma has directed her attention toward the wagon. Knowing that pulling an object is one of her objectives, he begins to interact with Emma, telling her how nice it is that she is giving the teddy bear a ride. Emma continues to pull her wagon through the pathways and around the cardboard trees. Mr. Sanchez is able to promote communication (another of Emma's IEP objectives) by suggesting that Emma ask Misha if she would like to go for ride. Once Misha is in the wagon, Mr. Sanchez suggests that Emma ask Misha where she would like to go. In this manner, Mr. Sanchez is facilitating work on Emma's IEP objective for initiating social interactions. Misha's request will encourage Emma to move through her physical environment, encountering various inanimate obstacles in the park as well as other children moving with wheel toys.

A structured movement environment should allow children to direct the process through which they manipulate the physical environment. **Child-directed learning** is *not* synonymous with free play. Teachers of preschool adapted physical education are responsible for designing environments to motivate children to initiate practice on skills outlined in their individualized plans. Interaction with equipment and practice on certain IEP objectives will be far more probable and children will persist with the task much longer if they initiate the interaction themselves. The teacher then becomes a facilitator within the movement environment. She follows the child's lead and promotes challenges based on the choices the child has made.

The intensity with which children practice a skill or explore a new task depends on how interested they are in the task itself. The fact that Emma recognized the teddy bear sitting in the wagon and related that to her previous experiences was enough to interest her in the task and encourage further exploration. Mr. Sanchez was able to accommodate the interests and abilities of all the children in his class by using multiple pieces of equipment and structuring his activity environment around one theme. The opportunity to view peer models and initiate social interactions was built into the structure of the activity. This activity design now gives Mr. Sanchez the opportunity to facilitate the children's viewing of peer models. For example, he may now prompt Erik to follow Emma while riding his tricycle.

APPLICATION EXAMPLE

Child-Directed, Teacher-Facilitated Lesson

Setting: The early childhood teacher has selected the following content objectives: body and space awareness (under, over, through) and jumping down.

Issue: What environmental construction would be appropriate to ensure child-directed learning?

Application: The goal in this setting is to minimize teacher interaction and maximize each child's interaction with peers and equipment. The learning environment should contain multiple opportunities to practice the lesson objectives. Children will choose equipment, and teachers will facilitate learning by providing verbal prompts, demonstrations, physical assistance, or redirection. The following equipment will prompt child-directed activity:

▶ Tunnels, cardboard boxes, and archways with scarves attached will prompt movement through and under.

▶ Bolsters covered with mats will prompt climbing over.

▶ Various platforms or steps with pictures of letters, numbers, smiley faces, or bugs will prompt stepping up and jumping down.

Primary-Aged Children

Primary school classes, including kindergarten through third grade, typically vary in size in accordance with school policies. One approach in primary education is to incorporate multiage class groupings. In this structure, kindergarten and first-grade students may be educated in the same classroom. Designing developmentally appropriate instruction for this age group can only follow if a good assessment of individual abilities has been completed. As children grow and mature physically, discrepancies in movement abilities among children in the same age range might become more evident. However, young children with disabilities or developmental delays between six and eight years of age will have an interest in participating in the same physical activities as their same-age, typically developing counterparts.

Planning instructional content for this age group should focus on fundamental movement skills (locomotion, object control, perceptual motor) and build on the rudimentary skills learned in preschool. For some children this means refining skills, and for others it will be a time to begin to integrate fundamental skills into organized games and activities. Integrating fitness concepts within the curriculum will also become important. Regardless of the curricular focus, it is critical that children learn to move and enjoy movement at this age in order to increase the possibility that they will continue to be physically active as they mature. Following the guidelines and grade level expectations set forth in the national standards for physical education (NASPE, 2004) will provide teachers with the content that they need to develop an age-appropriate program.

Designing instructional settings for primary-aged students of differing abilities should combine movement exploration and guided-discovery techniques with specific skill practice. With an exploration style of teaching, the teacher selects the instructional materials to be used and designates the area to be explored (Pangrazi, 2007). Rather than having the environment already set up with embedded goals and objectives, students choose a piece of equipment and figure out ways to interact with the equipment. Teachers might offer directives such as, "Get a hoop and see how many ways you can make it spin." This teaching style takes advantage of children's desire to move and explore. It emphasizes self-discovery, which is a necessary part of learning, and allows children to note variations in movement forms and equipment usage. However, when using this teaching style, the instructor should avoid praising students for their creative movements too early because this might lead to imitative or noncreative behavior (Pangrazi, 2007).

Guided discovery is used when there is a predetermined choice or result that the teacher wants students to discover (Pangrazi, 2007). With this approach to teaching, students are presented with many methods to perform a task and then are asked to choose the method that seems to be most efficient or that works best. Students with disabilities might often find that their movement choice differs from what typically developing peers choose as the appropriate movement form. This discovery reinforces the idea that just because a movement form is different does not mean it is incorrect.

Children should also have the opportunity to use fundamental skills in low-organization games. Equipment and instruction should be modified, if necessary, to accommodate the physical, sensory, behavioral, and cognitive abilities of each child in the class. The activity environment should be organized to accommodate the varying learning styles (visual, kinesthetic) of the children (Coker, 1996). General principles for the design of developmentally appropriate adapted physical education for primary students include

- using different teaching styles to individualize instruction for the variety of learning styles (visual, auditory) present in one classroom,
- providing varied equipment (e.g., different-sized rackets) to incorporate student choice,
- having rule flexibility in tasks to encourage creativity and problem solving,
- varying classroom designs (activity stations, small group, large group), and
- providing the opportunity for peer observation and interaction.

The following scenario provides an example of how the principles can be used to accommodate children in a first-grade classroom.

Louis is selected as the line leader by his classmates as they prepare to leave for physical education. Ms. Brooks greets the children outside of their classroom and walks with them to the gym. As they walk together, Ms. Brooks explains to the children that they will continue working on striking activities today. Once inside the gym, the children see a familiar sight. Ms. Brooks has set up five activity stations, each with a different task to complete. Ms. Brooks asks the children, "What type of implements do we use for striking?"

The children's responses to Ms. Brooks' question are varied. As they look around the gym, they are reminded of some answers.

"We strike with bats," says Claire.

"We can use Styrofoam rackets," yells Mia.

"I like the hockey sticks," exclaims Jose.

Ms. Brooks explains that everyone will have an opportunity to use all of the implements today as they spend time at each activity station. She informs the children that they will select an implement out of the station bin and practice at one station until they hear the sound of the drum. At that time they will put their implements back into the bin and follow the floor arrows to the next station, select their new implement, and begin the task.

Ms. Brooks has asked Louis to begin at the racket and balloon station. As Ms. Brooks designates other stations for children in the class, Louis turns to Sammy and whispers, "That's my favorite!" Ms. Brooks is familiar with Louis' IEP and has written his gross motor objectives. Striking is a focus for Louis in addition to increasing his static and dynamic balance. He will be working on both today. Louis has spina bifida and uses braces on his legs. He ambulates slowly but is proud of the fact that over the summer months before first grade began, he stopped using his walker for most activities. The activities that Louis will participate in today are functional for him. He will work on striking, just like the rest of his classmates, but this activity will also address his balance goals as he swings different implements and moves among stations.

Ms. Brooks has constructed enough activity stations to give this class of 28 children the opportunity to explore various movements with various striking implements. The equipment used to accomplish the skill objective in a few of the stations has been changed (e.g., some stations have rackets whereas others might have bats), but for the most part the students are familiar with the activity structure and have been practicing their striking for several classes now. This activity environment allows Ms. Brooks to individualize instruction, provide specific skill feedback to children, and modify equipment and tasks to accommodate the learning abilities of all the children in the class.

In Ms. Brooks' next first-grade class, she will see Micah. He has a severe mental disability, and Ms. Brooks will use a location-station approach for him. This means that she will use the same environmental structure to practice striking, but when the drum sounds Micah will remain in the same balloon-striking station, and his cross-age peer model will assist him in selecting another implement to strike

the balloon. The rest of the class will rotate stations. All of this has been planned by Ms. Brooks because she is familiar with the children she teaches and their ability levels. So, for now, she admires Louis' stability as she watches him swing the racket to hit the suspended balloon to his classmate Bryce. As Bryce tracks the balloon and gets ready to hit it back, he exclaims, "Here it comes, Louis!"

ACTIVITIES

Developmentally appropriate activities for preschool and primary-aged students are those selected, designed, sequenced, and modified to maximize learning and active participation. Fundamental motor skills and patterns form the basis for higher-level movement sequences and skills and should thus be emphasized in early childhood motor programs. Activities that promote body awareness, perceptual motor skills, communication, and academic abilities should also be incorporated into the program. Using the strategies presented in this chapter, physical educators can select games and activities to meet IEP goals and objectives that are both age and developmentally appropriate and are presented in a way that fosters child-directed interactions.

SUMMARY

The increase in early childhood motor programs has brought new challenges to physical educators. Children as young as three years old might be included in adapted physical education programs designed to meet their unique needs. Although some physical educators might have experience working with older students with developmental delays or disabilities, the opportunity to work with young children presents new and exciting challenges. This chapter has provided information to assist teachers of early childhood adapted physical education by suggesting strategies and tools necessary for the development of appropriate goals, objectives, and activities for young children with unique physical education needs. Specifically, information related to assessment, program planning, and program implementation has been highlighted. With an understanding of what constitutes developmentally appropriate intervention, teachers of adapted physical education should be able to positively influence the movement abilities of young children. Intervention that is planned and delivered in settings that challenge and reinforce motor learning in a positive manner provide young children with opportunities to experience success and enjoy movement.

REFERENCES

Bredekamp, S., & Copple, C. (1997). *Developmentally appropriate practice in early childhood programs* (revised). Washington, DC: NAEYC.

Bredekamp, S., & Rosegrant, T. (Eds.). (1992). *Reaching potentials: Appropriate curriculum and assessment for young children* (Vol. 1). Washington, DC: NAEYC.

Bricker, D., Capt, B., & Pretti-Frontczak, K. (Eds.). (2002). *AEPS test for birth to three years and three to six years.* Baltimore: Paul H. Brookes.

Brigance, A. (1991). *Brigance diagnostic inventory of early development.* Billerica, MA: Curriculum Associates.

Clements, R. (1995). *My neighborhood movement challenges.* Oxon Hill, MD: AAHPERD.

Coker, C.A. (1996). Accommodating students' learning styles in physical education. *Journal of Physical Education, Recreation and Dance, 67,* 66-68.

DiCarlo, C., Banajee, M., & Stricklin, S. (2000). Embedding augmentative communication within early childhood classrooms. *Young Exceptional Children, 3* (3), 18-26.

Federal Register. (2006, August 14). *Assistance to states for the education of children with disabilities and preschool grants for children with disabilities.* 34 CFR Parts 300-301. Vol. 71, No. 156. Washington, DC: Department of Education.

Folio, M.R., & Fewell, R. (2000). *Peabody developmental motor scales-2.* Austin, TX: Pro-Ed.

Gabbei, R., & Clemmens, H. (2005). Meaningful creative movement sequences from children's story books: Going beyond pantomime. *Journal of Physical Education, Recreation & Dance, 76,* 32-37.

Johnson-Martin, N., Attermeier, M.A., Hacker, B.J. (1990). *The Carolina Curriculum for preschoolers with special needs.* Baltimore: Paul H. Brookes.

Linder, T. (2008). *Transdisciplinary play-based assessment* (2nd ed.). Baltimore: Paul H. Brookes.

Lynch, E., & Struewing, N. (2001). Children in context: Portfolio assessment in the inclusive early childhood classroom. *Young Exceptional Children, 5* (1), 2-10.

McLean, M., Wolery, M., & Bailey, D. (2004). *Assessing infants, toddlers and preschoolers with special needs.* Upper Saddle River, NJ: Pearson, Merrill, Prentice Hall.

Mithaug, D.K., & Mithaug, D.E. (2003). Effects of teacher-directed versus student-directed instruction of self-management of young children with disabilities. *Journal of Applied Behavior Analysis, 36,* 133-136.

National Association for Sport and Physical Education (NASPE). (2004). *Moving into the future: National standards for physical education* (2nd ed.). Reston, VA: Author.

National Association for Sport and Physical Education (NASPE). (2008). *PE Metrics: Assessing the national standards, standard 1: Elementary.* Reston, VA: Author.

National Institute for Early Education Research (NIEER). (2008). State standards database. Retrieved from http://nieer.org/yearbook.

Pangrazi, R.P. (2007). *Dynamic physical education for elementary school children* (15th ed.). Needham Heights, MA: Allyn and Bacon.

Piaget, J. (1952). *The origins of intelligence in children.* New York: International Universities Press.

Pretti-Frontczak, K.L., Barr, D.M., Macy, M., & Carter, A. (2003). Research and resources related to activity-based intervention, embedded learning opportunities, and routines-based instruction: An annotated bibliography. *Topics in Early Childhood Special Education, 23.*

Rabe, B. (1981). *The balancing girl.* New York: Penguin.

Rosen, M. (1989). *We're going on a bear hunt.* New York: Simon & Schuster.

Sands, D.I., & Barker, H. B. (2004). Organized chaos: Modeling differentiated instruction for preservice teachers. *Teaching and Learning, 19,* 26-49.

Ulrich, D.A. (2000). *Test of motor development* (2nd ed.). Austin, TX: Pro-Ed.

U.S. Department of Education. (2005). *Twenty-seventh annual report to Congress on the implementation of the Individuals with Disabilities Education Act.* Retrieved from www.ed.gov.

Vygotsky, L. (1978). *Mind in society: The development of higher psychological processes.* Cambridge, MA: Harvard University Press.

Wessel, J.A., & Zittel, L.L. (1995). *Smart Start: Preschool movement curriculum designed for children of all abilities.* Austin, TX: Pro-Ed.

Wessel, J.A., & Zittel, L.L. (1998). *I CAN primary skills: K-3.* Austin, TX: Pro-Ed.

Zittel, L.L. (1994). Gross motor assessment of preschool children with special needs: Instrument selection considerations. *Adapted Physical Activity Quarterly, 11,* 245-260.

WRITTEN RESOURCES

Bricker, D., & Waddell, M. (2002). *AEPS curriculum for three to six years.* Baltimore: Paul H. Brookes.

Activities in this curriculum correspond with goals and objectives in the AEPS test.

Clements, R.L., Fiorentino, L., & Fiorentino, L. (2004). *Child's right to play: A global approach*. Westport, CT: Greenwood.

A historical look at play in early childhood is presented along with the moral and ethical dimensions of play. Types of play and how these types are beneficial for children are emphasized.

Clements, R.L. & Schneider, S.L. (2005). Excerpts from movement-based learning: Academic concepts and physical activity for ages three through eight. *Strategies, 19,* 31-32.

Practical ready-to-use activities are presented for those teaching in child care settings or school settings. Accommodations for children with disabilities are highlighted.

Cowden, J.E., & Torrey, C.C. (2007). *Motor development and movement activities for preschoolers and infants with delays: A multisensory approach for professionals and families*. Springfield, IL: Charles C. Thomas.

Principles of motor development theory are linked to practical intervention for parents, caregivers, and teachers. The impact of specific disabilities or delays is outlined.

Landy, J., & Burridge, K. (2000). *Motor skills and movement station lesson plans for young children*. West Nyack, NY: Center for Applied Research in Education.

This is a motor skills program for teachers, professionals, and parents teaching fundamental motor skills to children who have coordination difficulties.

Linder, T. (1999). *Storybook activities for young children: Read, play, and learn*. Baltimore: Paul H. Brookes.

This play-based, storybook-oriented curriculum allows teachers to incorporate skills in all domains of learning while providing a motivating experience for the young learner.

Linder, T. (2008). *Transdisciplinary play-based intervention*. Baltimore: Paul H. Brookes.

This resource offers play-based interventions for children across all domains and help to generalize skills to new situations and settings.

McCall, R., & Craft, D. (2000). *Moving with a purpose: Developing programs for preschoolers of all abilities*. Champaign, IL: Human Kinetics.

This resource provides information to teachers responsible for structuring movement programs for preschool children. Games and activities are presented. A section is also devoted to children with special needs.

National Association for Sport and Physical Education (NASPE). (2002). *Active start: A statement of guidelines for children birth to five years*. Reston, VA: Author.

This provides physical activity recommendations for children 5 to 12 years old. This is written as a guide for teachers, caregivers, and parents.

National Association for Sport and Physical Education (NASPE). (2002). *Physical activity for children: A statement of guidelines for children ages 5-12* (2nd ed.). Reston, VA: Author.

Guidelines provide information regarding the amount and type of physical activity recommended for children ages 5 to 12. Concepts regarding appropriate physical activity and models of service delivery are presented.

Winders, P. (1997). *Gross motor skills in children with Down syndrome*. Bethesda, MD: Woodbine House.

This resource addresses the physical development of children with Down syndrome and suggests guidelines for promoting gross motor development. Activities and strategies are provided.

AUDIOVISUAL RESOURCES

Pica, R., & Gardzina, R. (1990). *More music for moving and learning*. Champaign, IL: Human Kinetics.

This is a set of six audiocassettes with 62 songs that focus on typical early childhood themes, a great package for both the preschool and elementary school years.

ELECTRONIC RESOURCES

Beyond the Journal: Young Children on the Web: www.naeyc.org/yc/pastissues.

The site publishes practical papers to assist teachers.

Boardmaker: www.mayer-johnson.com.

Boardmaker is an electronic resource used to create symbol-based communication and educational materials.

National Association for the Education of Young Children: www.naeyc.org.

This Web site serves as the primary site for resources and best practices for the education of young children.

four

Activities for Individuals With Unique Needs

Part IV includes chapters on physical fitness (chapter 23); rhythmic movement and dance (chapter 24); aquatics (chapter 25); team sports (chapter 26); individual, dual, and adventure sports and activities (chapter 27); winter sports (chapter 28); and the enhancement of wheelchair sport performance (chapter 29). Although the content of each chapter is influenced by the nature of the activities discussed, there are several common threads. To the extent relevant and appropriate, the chapters identify skills, lead-up activities, modifications, and variations associated with activity areas. In many instances, these include modifications and variations used in established organized sport programs. Some chapters provide information on organized sport programs. All chapters provide information helpful for the enhancement of education in a variety of settings, including inclusive settings. The importance of the use of wheelchairs in physical education and sport is recognized by including an entire chapter (chapter 29) on ways of enhancing performance when using wheelchairs.

Although this section is last in the book, it is of great importance, because it applies much information presented earlier to the content associated with physical education and sport. It focuses on how the content of the program is adapted or modified to meet unique needs. It is this part of the book that will serve as a great resource to service providers on the job, since it provides answers on how they may modify an activity to help a specific student with unique needs to be active, be physically educated, and work toward self-actualization.

chapter 23

Health-Related Physical Fitness and Physical Activity

Francis X. Short

Mr. Barnett, a social studies teacher, and Ms. Novak, a physical education teacher, were in the teachers' lounge.

"What are you working on?" Mr. Barnett asked.

"I'm just planning some fitness activities for my third-period class."

"Isn't that the class with the students in wheelchairs? How are they doing? Are the athletes in the class treating them okay?"

"Well," said Ms. Novak with a smile, "some of my students who use wheelchairs *are* athletes, but what I do in my class is more health related than sport related."

"Health related? Is that really necessary? I mean, I haven't heard of too many junior high school students dying of heart attacks lately."

"Well, that's right, but good fitness and physical activity habits should be established early, and besides, health-related fitness, especially for kids with disabilities, is not just about reducing the risk of disease. Having good health-related fitness also means having the independence to perform important day-to-day skills, like pushing a wheelchair uphill or even getting dressed. In fact, fitness might actually be more important to students with disabilities than it is for the general student body.

"By the way," continued Ms. Novak, "your 'general student body' looks like it could stand some health-related fitness."

"Hey . . ." said Mr. Barnett while sucking in his stomach.

Physical fitness has long been viewed as an important vehicle for improving both sport performance and health. From the ancient Greeks to the modern athlete, people have used physical activity to enhance their fitness and improve their athletic prowess. The relationships among activity levels, fitness development, and improved *sport performance* are often obvious, and sometimes dramatic. The relationships among physical activity, physical fitness, and *health*, however, usually are less obvious; we cannot observe, for instance, the reduced risk of acquiring coronary heart disease, diabetes, or some forms of cancer associated with good levels of fitness. Nevertheless, many people have attempted to get into shape because of the common belief that being fit is good for you.

These relationships might accurately be expressed by the notion that increases in physical activity lead to increases in physical fitness, which in turn lead to improvements in health status. This observation, of course, is true, but it is also incomplete. It turns out, for instance, that physical activity can lead to improvements in health even without increases in physical fitness. Each of these constructs (activity, fitness, and health) can influence and be influenced by each of the others, as represented in figure 23.1. Increases in physical activity and in physical fitness can both contribute to positive health status. Increases in physical activity usually result in improved physical fitness, and improved physical fitness will likely affect the potential types (e.g., exercise, sport) and patterns (e.g., frequency, intensity, duration) of physical activity available to an individual. Finally, reductions in health status (i.e., negative health) typically reduce participation in physical activity and restrict progress in physical fitness.

The relations among physical fitness, physical activity, and health are explored further in this chapter. Particular attention is paid to how physical activity can be used to promote health-related physical fitness, but developing the skill-related components of fitness is necessary to foster certain types of physical activity (e.g., sport performance). Although some examples of modifications for students with disabilities are provided, the chapter is written primarily from a noncategorical perspective; that is, most of the information is generic and not specific to any one category of disability. Disability-specific fitness information can be found in other chapters of this book.

DEFINITIONS

Physical activity is defined as any bodily movement produced by skeletal muscle resulting in a substantial increase in resting energy expenditure. Bouchard and Shephard (1994), citing seven categories of physical activity (exercise, sport, training, play, dance, work, and domestic chores), suggested that patterns of physical activity can be described by manipulating the variables of frequency (how often), intensity (how hard), and time (how long).

Health has been defined as "a human condition with physical, social, and psychological dimensions, each characterized on a continuum with positive and negative poles. Positive health is associated with a capacity to enjoy life and to withstand challenges; it is not merely the absence of disease. Negative health is associated with morbidity and, in the extreme, with premature mortality" (Bouchard & Shephard, 1994, p. 84). Winnick and Short (1999) suggested that in broad terms, health can be categorized by physiological or functional aspects. **Physiological health** relates to the organic well-being of the person. Indices of physiological health include traits or capacities associated with well-being, absence of a disease or a condition, or low risk of developing a disease or condition. **Functional health** relates to physical capability. Indices of functional health include the ability to perform important tasks independently and the ability to independently sustain the performance of those tasks (see figure 23.1).

Caspersen, Powell, and Christenson (1985) defined **physical fitness** as a "set of attributes that people have or achieve that relates to the ability to perform physical activity" (p. 129). The components of physical fitness can be categorized into two groups: one related to health and the other to skills that are necessary for athletic ability. **Heath-related physical fitness** refers to those components of fitness that are affected by habitual physical activity and relate to health status. It is defined as a state characterized by (a) an ability to perform and sustain daily activities and (b) demonstration of traits or capacities that are associated with a low risk of premature development of diseases and conditions related to movement (modified from Pate, 1988). Most experts agree that the components of health-related fitness include aerobic functioning, body composition, muscular endurance, muscular strength, and flexibility (the latter three are sometimes referred to as *musculoskeletal functioning*). The components of **skill-related physical fitness**, or performance-related fitness, generally include agility, balance, coordination, speed, power, and reaction time.

PHYSICAL FITNESS AND HEALTH

Since the 1980s, researchers have been working to improve their understanding of the relations between physical fitness and health. It is now known, for instance, that acceptable levels of aerobic capacity are associated with a reduced risk of hypertension, coronary heart disease, obesity, diabetes, some forms of cancer, and other health problems. For these reasons, measures of aerobic capacity are thought to be linked to physiological health. A similar relation exists between body composition and physiological health. Obesity has been associated with an increased risk of diabetes, coronary heart disease, high blood pressure, arthritis, and several forms of cancer. Obesity has also been linked to higher rates of all-cause mortality and to increased risk factors for heart disease in children.

Researchers have had a more difficult time establishing relations between muscular strength and muscular endurance and physiological health, although relations between strength and low back pain and osteoporosis are suspected. Still, there is a logical relation between muscular strength and endurance and functional health. Clearly, minimal levels of muscular strength and endurance are necessary to perform many activities of daily living and to participate in leisure activities. Similarly, a logical relation exists between flexibility and functional health—that is, having sufficient range of motion in the joints to perform daily activities. There is also some evidence that hamstring flexibility is linked to low back pain in some people.

Over the years, several studies have compared the physical fitness performance of young people

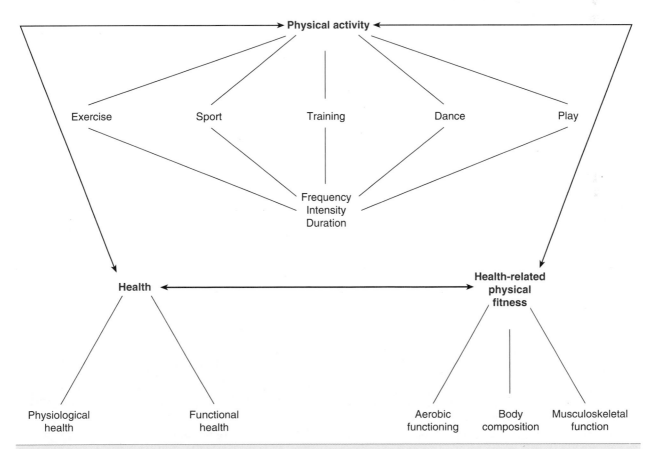

FIGURE 23.1   Relations among physical activity, health, and health-related fitness.

Reprinted, by permission, from F.X. Short, J. McCubbin, and G. Frey, 1999, Cardiorespiratory endurance and body composition. In *The Brockport physical fitness training guide*, edited by J.P. Winnick and F.X. Short (Champaign, IL: Human Kinetics), 24.

with disabilities against that of their peers without disabilities. With few exceptions, research using subjects with intellectual disabilities, cerebral palsy, spinal cord injuries, visual impairments, and developmental coordination disorder (DCD) has found that the fitness performance of young people with disabilities is below that of their peers without disabilities. To the extent that the fitness of young people with disabilities falls below acceptable levels, it is probable that they are at greater risk for the health concerns mentioned previously than are students without disabilities.

PHYSICAL ACTIVITY AND HEALTH-RELATED PHYSICAL FITNESS

People with or without disabilities generally can improve their health-related physical fitness through physical activity. For children, though, the relationship between activity and fitness is believed to be weaker than it is for adults. This is because age, maturation, coordination, and other factors can affect children's fitness more than physical activity (Pangrazi & Corbin, 2008). Still, the physical fitness of children does respond to training and adapt to physical activity (Welk & Blair, 2008), and this is true both for students with and without disabilities.

This section of the chapter focuses on improving the health-related physical fitness of students with disabilities through physical activity. The first two subsections deal with the importance of personalizing physical fitness and how physical activity can be measured and arranged into patterns to achieve fitness objectives. The third subsection addresses physical activity recommendations for promoting the components of health-related fitness, and the final subsection discusses a few general considerations for fitness development.

Personalizing Physical Fitness

When programming for students with disabilities, the physical educator must first ask, "Physical fitness for what purpose?" Objectives may vary widely from student to student. Fitness objectives for a student with a disability can be influenced by several factors, including present level of physical fitness, functional motor abilities, physical maturity,

age, nature of the disability, student interests or activity preferences, and availability of equipment and facilities. In an adapted physical education program, objectives can range from fitness for the execution of rudimentary movements (e.g., sitting, reaching, creeping) to fitness for the execution of specialized movements (e.g., sport skills, recreational activities, vocational tasks) to fitness for the pursuit of a healthier lifestyle (e.g., better daily functioning and reduced risk of acquiring diseases or conditions) (see figure 23.2).

With the help of the student as much as is appropriate, teachers should design personalized fitness programs. In personalizing physical fitness, certain elements of the fitness program are emphasized for each student. For instance, for each student the teacher might ask the following questions (with examples of possible answers for a student with lower-limb paralysis):

- What are the top-priority fitness needs for this student (including any health-related concerns), and what would be the objectives of the program (or personalized profile)? *Example: Develop upper-body fitness to promote the ability to lift and transfer the body independently and to self-propel a wheelchair.*

- Which components of health-related or skill-related physical fitness should be targeted for development given the identified needs and objectives? Which areas of the body will be trained? *Example: Focus on muscular strength and endurance for the shoulders, arms, and hands.*

- Which tests will be used to measure physical fitness for this student, and which standards will be adopted for evaluative purposes? *Example: Use test items (seated push-ups, dominant grip strength, and dominant dumbbell press) and standards provided by the Brockport Physical Fitness Test (BPFT) to assess progress. (The BPFT is a health-related, criterion-referenced test; see chapter 4 for more information.)*

Patterns of Physical Activity

Once the objectives of the personalized program have been established and baseline testing has been conducted, the teacher must arrange patterns of physical activity for the student in such a way that fitness is improved and objectives are attained. As

Photo courtesy of Amanda Tepfer.

FIGURE 23.2   Personalizing physical fitness can apply to sport skills for students with and without disabilities.

shown in figure 23.1, patterns of physical activity can be arranged by manipulating the variables of **frequency**, **intensity**, and **time** of various **types** of activity (e.g., games, sports, exercise, dance). The acronym *FITT* (frequency, intensity, time, and type) often is used to identify the variables that determine patterns of physical activity.

Monitoring appropriate levels of frequency and time is fairly straightforward. Frequency generally is expressed in the number of times a day or days in a week that activity is performed (e.g., three to five days per week; twice a day for five to seven days per week). Time is simply monitored by charting the length of the activity (e.g., 6-10 seconds, 20-40 minutes) or counting the number of repetitions of an exercise. Time of activity also can be measured by the number of steps one might take as counted by a pedometer.

Tracking intensity, however, is somewhat less objective and a bit more difficult, particularly in a field setting. Different indices of intensity are used with different components of fitness. For instance, for muscular strength and endurance, intensity could be estimated from the degree of exertion or the amount of resistance (e.g., a certain percentage of the maximum weight that can be lifted one time). In the case of flexibility, intensity could be a function of perceived discomfort or length of a stretch (e.g., touching toes rather than ankles). The intensity of activity selected to improve either aerobic functioning or body composition might be measured by heart rate, rating of perceived exertion (RPE), or estimated metabolic equivalents (METs) (see table 23.1). Heart rate monitors are becoming increasingly popular in schools and provide an easily determined, objective measure of intensity.

Table 23.1 Estimating Activity Intensity by Three Methods

Intensity	METHOD		
	% HRmax	RPE	METs
Very light	<35	<10	<2
Light	35-54	10-11	2-4
Moderate	55-69	12-13	5-7
Vigorous	70-89	14-16	8-10
Very vigorous	>90	17-19	>10
Maximal	100	20	12

Adapted from U.S. Department of Health and Human Services, 1996.

Pulse rate taken manually by either teachers or students provides an inexpensive alternative to the heart rate monitor. Maximal heart rate is usually estimated from the simple formula 220 – age (e.g., the estimated maximal heart rate for a 10-year-old is 210).

RPE provides a subjective but valid measure of intensity in which participants gauge effort by sensations such as perceived changes in heart rate, breathlessness, sweating, muscle fatigue, and lactate accumulation. Participants then translate these sensations to a numerical scale, such as the one suggested by Borg (1998) that ranges from 6 (no exertion) to 20 (maximal exertion). Borg's RPE scale has good utility for adapted physical education programs and has been used successfully in research projects employing subjects with intellectual disabilities, asthma, spinal cord injuries, and cerebral palsy.

MET values represent multiples of resting energy expenditure. For instance, when a person participates in an activity that is 4 METs, the body is using four times more oxygen than it does at rest. Estimated MET values, often published in charts in exercise physiology and fitness books, reflect the theoretical average person's energy expenditure for a particular activity (e.g., running a 10-minute mile = 10.2 METs, playing basketball = 8.3 METs). In adapted physical education, the use of METs to estimate intensity has the most relevance for students without physical disabilities (e.g., intellectual disabilities, visual impairments) and the least relevance for students who have physical disabilities (e.g., cerebral palsy, spinal cord injuries, amputations) because the theoretical average person does not have a physical disability.

Physical Activity Recommendations for Health-Related Physical Fitness

Recommendations for developing health-related fitness follow for aerobic functioning, body composition, muscular strength and endurance, and flexibility and range of motion. Adjustments to those recommendations for students with disabilities, as well as some suggested activities, are also included.

Aerobic Functioning

Aerobic functioning refers to the component of physical fitness that permits one to sustain large-muscle, dynamic, moderate- to high-intensity activity for prolonged periods of time. Aerobic functioning can be estimated by measuring aerobic capacity (an index of physiological health) or aerobic behavior (an index of functional health). **Aerobic capacity** refers to the highest rate of oxygen that can be consumed by exercising and ordinarily is the preferred measure of aerobic functioning. Field tests of aerobic capacity include a 1-mile run and the PACER (a 15 or 20 m multistage shuttle run). Estimating aerobic capacity in a field setting, however, is not always possible for students with disabilities because the estimates are based on equations developed for people without disabilities. **Aerobic behavior** provides an alternative measure of aerobic functioning and refers to the ability to sustain physical activity of a specific intensity (e.g., >70 percent of maximum heart rate [HRmax]) for a particular duration (e.g., 15 minutes). Field tests of aerobic behavior include measuring the length of time one can exercise in a target heart rate zone (e.g., the BPFT's Target Aerobic Movement Test [TAMT]). Aerobic behavior can be measured in anyone who can sufficiently elevate the heart rate through physical activity.

Frequency, intensity, and time guidelines for improving the aerobic functioning of students are summarized in table 23.2. In essence, children are encouraged to be active on all or most days of the week for at least 30 to 60 minutes each day. The intensity of activity ranges from deemphasized for younger children to moderate (and sometimes vigorous) for older children. Adolescents may reduce their frequencies and times somewhat in exchange for higher levels of intensity (moderate to vigorous). Higher levels of intensity are usually necessary to improve aerobic capacity.

Table 23.2   Guidelines for Developing Aerobic Functioning

Group	Frequency	Intensity	Time
Adolescents (ages 13-17)	3-5 days/wk	55-90% HRmax (~115-180 beats/min) 12-16 RPE 5-10 METs	20-60 min/day (accumulated, >10 min per bout)
Older children (ages 10-12)	4-7 days/wk	55-70% HRmax* (~115-145 beats/min) 12-13 RPE* 5-7 METs*	30-60+ min/day (accumulated, intermittent)
Younger children (ages 6-9)	4-7 days/wk	Deemphasized; participation encouraged	30-60+ min/day (accumulated, intermittent)
Adjustments for students with disabilities	No change unless disability can be exacerbated by regular activity	Reduced as a function of fitness level; THRZ adjusted for students using arms-only activity and for students with quadriplegia	More intermittent activity accumulated or total time reduced if necessary

* These values represent moderate physical activity; ideally, this level will be exceeded to vigorous levels at times.

Reprinted, by permission, from F.X. Short, J. McCubbin, and G. Frey, 1999, Cardiorespiratory endurance and body composition. In *The Brockport physical fitness training guide,* edited by J.P. Winnick and F.X. Short (Champaign, IL: Human Kinetics), 24.

Many students with disabilities can meet these guidelines without modification. Some adjustments, however, are appropriate in certain situations. Ordinarily, frequency will not have to be adjusted; as with students without disabilities, students with disabilities should be encouraged to participate regularly in aerobic activity. Greater periods of recovery from physical activity, however, might be necessary for students with neuromuscular diseases, arthritis, or other disabilities requiring greater rest. Similarly, students with disabilities should strive to attain the same time guidelines as their peers without disabilities. When students with disabilities cannot maintain continuous activity for the recommended length of time, the first alternative would be to accumulate more intermittent activity (i.e., shorter bouts of activity more often to achieve the recommendations) before electing to reduce the time guidelines.

Adjustments to intensity will likely be necessary when students have a history of inactivity. For these students, activity might be more appropriately conducted at lighter intensities, particularly if the frequency and time guidelines can be achieved. Intensity should be gradually increased over time. If intensity is being measured via heart rate, it will be necessary to adjust the target heart rate zone (THRZ) for students who use their arms to propel wheelchairs, for those who engage in other arms-only forms of activity, or for those with spinal cord injuries. Subtracting 10 beats per minute from

the THRZ values given in table 23.2 constitutes a reasonable adjustment in intensity for arms-only activity.

A range of activities can be used to meet the aerobic functioning guidelines in table 23.2. Teachers should select age-appropriate developmental activities for children (ages 6-12). Included in this group might be jump rope activities, relay races, obstacle courses, climbing activities (e.g., jungle gyms or monkey bars), active lead-up games, active games of low organization, and rhythmic activities, including creative dance and moving to music.

Adolescents (ages 13-18) generally are ready for more sport-related activities and should be exposed to activities that have a lifetime emphasis. Appropriate activities might include fast walking, jogging or running, swimming, skiing, racket sports, basketball, soccer, skating, cycling, rowing, hiking, parcourse (fitness trail) activities, and aerobic dance or aerobic aquatics.

Many students with disabilities can participate in most of the activities listed in the previous paragraphs, although some modifications might be necessary. As with all good teaching in physical education, teachers should start with the student and select, modify, or design appropriate activities rather than start with an activity and hope that it is somehow appropriate for the student. Students in wheelchairs or those who are blind may require alternative activities (or activity modification) to meet the aerobic functioning guidelines. Some ideas for students using wheelchairs might include slalom courses, freewheeling (i.e., jogging in a wheelchair), speed-bag work (i.e., rhythmically striking an overhead punching bag), arm ergometry, seated aerobics, and active wheelchair sports (e.g., sled hockey, basketball, track, rugby, team handball). Students with visual impairments might participate in activities such as calisthenics, rowing, stationary or tandem cycling, wrestling, judo, step aerobics, aerobic dance, swimming, or track.

Body Composition

Body composition refers to the percentage of body weight that is fat versus the percentage that is muscle, bone, connective tissue, and fluids, or it indicates the appropriateness of body weight to height. Skinfold measures can be used in field settings to estimate percent body fat, whereas body mass index (BMI), a weight-to-height ratio, is often used to assess the appropriateness of one's weight. Some schools are now using bioelectric impedance analyzers (BIAs) to determine percent body fat and BMI. BIAs measure the conductivity of a low-level electric current; a body with more fat will have greater resistance to current flow.

This section of the chapter focuses on weight-loss strategies associated with physical fitness. When people fall outside the appropriate range of body composition, most do so because they are too fat (or too heavy for their heights). However, some students might be outside the healthy range because they are too lean (or too light for their heights). Excessive leanness is also a health-related concern. When physical educators believe that a student's excessive leanness might be a result of an inadequate diet, an eating disorder, or the possible existence of a medical condition, the school's medical staff should be consulted.

Strategies for improving body composition (i.e., for weight loss) are similar to those associated with aerobic functioning. In most cases, weight-loss recommendations can be achieved by following the guidelines for improved aerobic functioning (see table 23.2); there would be little reason to ever adjust those recommendations for achieving weight loss in children. In the case of adolescents, however, there may be circumstances in which weight loss might be a more important goal than improved aerobic functioning. In such cases, the aerobic functioning guidelines could be adjusted slightly to meet weight-loss recommendations for adolescents (and adults). These weight-loss recommendations would be to participate in moderate-level activity, four to seven days per week, for 30 to 60 or more minutes per day. When compared with the aerobic functioning guidelines for adolescents, the recommendations for weight loss generally are less intense, more frequent, and for longer durations.

Another weight-loss recommendation is to attain a minimal energy expenditure of at least 1,000 kilocalories (kcals) per week. If MET estimates are available, kilocalories can be calculated from the following equation:

kcals/min = METs × 3.5 × body weight (kg) / 200.

As mentioned earlier, published MET estimates might not be particularly appropriate for students with physical disabilities. This is because of differences in mechanical efficiency that might exist between participants with disabilities and those without disabilities. Estimating kilocalorie expenditure for students with physical disabilities, however, is still possible. Assume Eddie is a 14-year-old, 150-pound (68 kg) boy with spastic paraplegia. He uses forearm crutches to walk and run. He enjoys playing floor hockey, and his dad has devised a way to attach the blade of a floor hockey stick to the end of one of his crutches so that he can play in his regular physical education class. Because there are no MET estimates for people with cerebral palsy playing floor hockey with forearm crutches and a modified stick, energy cost will have to be estimated in another way. Eddie's teacher, for instance, could determine Eddie's average heart rate during the game. (This most easily could be done with a monitor but could also be done by taking manual pulse rates periodically.) If Eddie averaged 155 beats per minute over the course of the game, he would have been working at about 75 percent of his maximal heart rate (220 − 14 = 206; 155 / 206 = 0.75). By consulting table 23.1, the teacher can see that Eddie is at the low end of vigorous activity. The low end of vigorous intensity roughly corresponds to 8 METs (the range for vigorous intensity is 8-10 METs). If 8 METs are used to estimate the energy cost of Eddie's activity, his energy expenditure in kilocalories per minute would be

kcals/min = 8 × 3.5 × 68 / 200 = 9.5.

To expend 1,000 kilocalories for the week, Eddie will need to participate in floor hockey (or some other 8-MET activity) for 105 minutes (1,000 / 9.5 = 105). If he plays twice a week, he could meet the goal of 1,000 kilocalories if he played for 53 minutes each time (105 / 2 = 52.5), or he could play three times per week for 35 minutes each time to reach 1,000 kilocalories. Activities that are less intense require greater frequencies or durations to meet the goal.

Muscular Strength and Endurance

Muscular strength is the ability of the muscles to produce a maximal level of force over a short time. Strength can be measured by using dynamometers (e.g., grip strength) or by recording the maximum amount of weight that can be lifted in a single repetition. **Muscular endurance** refers to the ability to sustain submaximal levels of force over an extended length of time. Curl-ups and flexed arm hangs are examples of field-based tests of muscular endurance. Exercise is traditionally the type of physical activity selected to improve muscular strength and muscular endurance. Recommendations generally call for an activity pattern characterized by performing 8 to 10 dynamic (i.e., isotonic or isokinetic) exercises at least twice a week with at least one day of rest between each session. It is also recommended that one set of 8 to 12 repetitions maximum be performed when strength is the primary goal and 12 to 15 repetitions maximum when endurance is being targeted. Often the intensity of the activity is viewed as a function of the amount of resistance that can be overcome within the range of maximum repetitions. The American College of Sports Medicine (ACSM) (2006) suggests that RPE also can be used to estimate the intensity of strength and endurance activities.

Exercise tends to be the preferred mode of activity for strength and endurance because muscle groups can be more easily isolated and intensity more easily monitored. For gains in strength and endurance to be made, muscles must be overloaded; that is, they must work at a greater level than normal. To achieve overload, resistance of some kind (e.g., gravity, body weight, free weights, exercise machines, elastic bands, medicine balls, weighted cuffs) is usually necessary. When resistance is used, a light load (or possibly no load at all) is recommended initially, followed by a progressive increase in resistance as exercise skill is mastered and muscles develop. The level of resistance generally should never require maximum exertion to attain a single repetition (i.e., 1-repetition max) in prepubescent children.

The exercise recommendations discussed in this section are appropriate for a wide range of people, including many students with disabilities.

Some students with disabilities might need to work at lighter intensities (lower resistance) but might still be able to meet the frequency and repetition guidelines given earlier. Others might also benefit from fewer separate exercises recommended per day (down from 8 to 10) or from a pattern that increases the frequency of exercise but reduces the intensity and time (see table 23.3). Programs for students with medical conditions should be developed with medical consultation.

Although exercise may be the preferred type of activity for enhancing strength and endurance, children will likely benefit from a wide range of developmentally appropriate activities. Activities that require children to move their own weight or the weight of an object against gravity might be most appropriate. Examples include climbing on monkey bars, jungle gyms, ropes, or cargo nets; crawling through obstacle courses; pushing a wheelchair up a ramp; propelling scooter boards with legs or arms or by pulling on a rope; and emphasizing fundamental movements that require power, such as throwing, kicking, jumping, leaping, and hopping.

Flexibility and Range of Motion

Flexibility is conceptualized as the extent of movement possible in multiple joints while performing a functional movement. The back-saver sit-and-reach test and the shoulder stretch are measures of flexibility. **Range of motion** (ROM) is defined as the extent of movement possible in a single joint. An objective measure of ROM can be obtained through goniometry; the BPFT target stretch test provides a subjective alternative (see appendix C). As with muscular strength and endurance, exercise is usually the preferred activity mode for improving flexibility and range of motion. Again, properly selected exercises can be used to isolate muscles or muscle groups, and intensity can be monitored or controlled. When exercises are used by teachers to improve flexibility and ROM, general recommendations call for performing exercise sessions at least three days per week. Each exercise should be conducted for 15 to 30 seconds and repeated three to five times per session. The intensity of a flexibility exercise is judged by a feeling of mild discomfort; that is, muscles should be stretched to a point at which a slight pulling or burning sensation is felt and then held there for 15 to 30 seconds.

Although some stretching activities are generally recommended at the start of a physical activity program for warming up, specific flexibility and ROM

Table 23.3 Guidelines for Developing Muscular Strength and Endurance

Group	Frequency	Intensity	Time and type
Adolescents (ages 13-17)	2-3 nonconsecutive days/wk	Low initial resistance, gradually increased; initial RPE 12-13, with RPE goal 15-16+	8-10 dynamic exercises; 1 set of 8-15 reps
Older children (ages 10-12)	2-3 nonconsecutive days/wk	Lower resistances with emphasis on exercise technique	8-10 dynamic exercises; 1 set of 12-15 reps
Younger children (ages 6-9)	4-7 days/wk	Intense exercise deemphasized; participation in physical activity encouraged	Dynamic exercise deemphasized; 30-60+ min/day of developmentally appropriate physical activity
Adjustments for students with disabilities	No change (unless number of exercises is decreased)	First option for adjustments: decreasing resistance	Second option: decreasing number of exercises/session (consider rotating number of exercises across greater frequencies); no change in reps

Notes: Summarized and modified from several sources, primarily DiRocco (1999) and ACSM (2006). The term *dynamic exercise* refers to isotonic or isokinetic exercises that target specific muscle groups.

training will be more successful when conducted toward the end of the activity session. Muscular and collagenous tissues are more likely to be warm toward the end of the session and more receptive to stretching (Surburg, 1999). Several stretching techniques may be used to improve flexibility and ROM, including passive stretching, active-assisted stretching, active stretching, and proprioceptive neuromuscular facilitation (PNF).

In **passive stretching**, the participant is not actively involved in the exercise. The muscle is stretched by some outside force (e.g., weight, sandbag, gravity, machine, therapist). Passive stretching is generally used in rehabilitative settings when participants are weak, when muscles are paralyzed, or when exercise protocols require sustained stretches. Nevertheless, passive stretching can be used in educational settings as well. Physical educators who wish to employ passive stretching techniques should consult qualified professionals.

Active–assisted stretching combines the efforts of the participant and a partner assistant (e.g., teacher, therapist, aide). The participant stretches the muscle as far as she can, and then the partner assists the movement through the full (or functional) ROM.

Active stretching is characterized by the participant moving the joint through its full (or functional) ROM without outside assistance. Active stretching exercises have been categorized as static (slow stretches to a point of mild discomfort held for 6-45 seconds) and ballistic (momentum exercise in which bouncing or twisting movements are used to elongate a muscle for a brief time) (Surburg, 1999). Although ballistic stretching might replicate certain sport-related movements, it generally is not recommended for improving flexibility and ROM. The preferred method is static stretching.

Proprioceptive neuromuscular facilitation (PNF) is an exercise system designed to improve strength, coordination, and kinesthesia as well as flexibility. Surburg (1999) has described five PNF techniques used specifically to increase flexibility and ROM:

- Rhythmic stabilization: The participant performs rhythmical, alternating, isometric contractions of agonists and antagonists.
- Contract–relax: A partner or teacher passively stretches the muscle to elongation, the participant contracts the muscle against resistance provided by the partner until the

body part has returned to its original resting position, and the muscle is relaxed for five seconds before the next repetition (five to six repetitions).

- Hold–relax: A partner or teacher passively stretches the muscle to elongation; the participant then performs a six-second isometric contraction in that position followed by a five-second rest.
- Hold–relax–contract: This stretch is the same as hold–relax except that following the isometric contraction of the target muscle (i.e., the muscle to be stretched), the participant contracts the opposite muscle group isotonically and without resistance.
- Contract–relax–contract: This stretch is similar to contract–relax but adds an isotonic contraction of the antagonist following the isotonic contraction of the target muscle (the agonist).

Most students with disabilities will benefit from one or more of the stretching techniques just described. The general recommendations for frequency, intensity, and time described at the beginning of this section also may be appropriate when students have unique flexibility and ROM needs, though some modification might be necessary. Although intensity (stretches to a point of mild discomfort) ordinarily would remain the same, flexibility and ROM training for students with unique needs likely should consist of greater frequency (exercise sessions conducted two to

three times daily) and duration (individual stretches lasting 10 minutes or more). For longer stretches (more than five minutes), it would be appropriate to limit the number of exercise repetitions to one (see table 23.4).

General Considerations

When developing programs of physical fitness, the physical educator should be aware of students' initial fitness levels and select activities accordingly. (See the application example.) In all cases, the procedure should be to start slowly and progress gradually. Students should be taught to warm up before a workout and cool down afterward. The physical educator should motivate students to pursue higher levels of fitness by keeping records, charting progress, and presenting awards. Selecting enjoyable activities will also help maintain interest in physical fitness; for instance, charting all students' cumulative running distances on a map for a cross country run will be more interesting and motivating than simply telling students to run three laps. The physical educator should also be a good role model for students; this includes staying fit and participating in class activities whenever appropriate. Finally, the physical educator should view physical fitness as an ongoing part of the physical education program and not just one unit of instruction. Although several units will be taught throughout the year, activities within a unit (exercises, games, and drills) should be arranged to enhance or at least maintain physical fitness.

Table 23.4 Guidelines for Developing Flexibility and Range of Motion

Group	Frequency	Intensity	Time and type
Adolescents (ages 13-17) and older children (ages 10-12)	3+ days/wk	Point of mild discomfort	3-5 reps of specific stretches; 15-30 sec for each repetition
Younger children (ages 6-9)	4-7 days/wk	Participation in general physical activity encouraged	30-60+ min/day (accumulated, intermittent)
Adjustments for students with disabilities	No change unless restrictions exist, then up to 2-3 sessions/day	No change	No change unless restrictions exist; then stretches may range from 15 sec to 10+ min (reps may be reduced for longer stretches)

Note: Summarized and modified from several sources, primarily Surburg (1999) and ACSM (2006).

APPLICATION EXAMPLE

Physical Fitness

Setting: A 15-year-old girl with a thoracic spinal cord injury is in an inclusive physical education class. One of the class goals is to improve the students' physical fitness. Present level of performance (i.e., baseline data) was established using the BPFT. Improvements in aerobic functioning and body composition (i.e., weight loss) were identified as the primary fitness objectives.

Issue: What strategies should be used to help the student achieve these goals?

Application: The teacher might recommend or pursue the following strategies:

▶ Use Activitygram (or some other self-report instrument) to monitor activity levels.

▶ Encourage the student to achieve the CDC–ACSM recommendation to engage in at least moderate-level activity—with a minimum heart rate of 103 beats per minute ($220 - 15 = 205 \times 0.55 = 112.75 - 10$ for arm activity $= 102.75$)—for at least 30 minutes per day on most, preferably all, days of the week.

▶ If the student has difficulty achieving these guidelines, reduce criteria for intensity (i.e., heart rate) but maintain frequency and duration (i.e., days and minutes).

▶ If the student is able to achieve these guidelines on a regular basis, modify the activity pattern so that some of the activity is done within a THRZ of 134 to 164 (i.e., 70-85 percent of predicted HRmax with a 10-beat adjustment for arm-only activity) for at least 20 minutes a day for three days of the week. (Such a pattern more likely will contribute to improved aerobic functioning.)

▶ Recommend enjoyable aerobic-based activities for use in and outside of class, such as wheelchair slaloms, freewheeling, speed-bag work, swimming, arm ergometry, seated aerobics and dance, scooter-board activities, and wheelchair sports.

▶ Consult with parents on the nature of the program; encourage their support at home and possibly include a dietary component with their help.

PHYSICAL ACTIVITY AND HEALTH

Although it certainly is true that physical activity can enhance physical fitness and thus positively influence one's health, the idea that regular participation in physical activity in and of itself can enhance health status regardless of fitness also is now firmly established. Regular physical activity can reduce the risk of premature mortality and the risk of acquiring coronary heart disease, hypertension, colon cancer, and diabetes mellitus; it also appears to reduce depression and anxiety, improve mood, and enhance ability to perform daily tasks (U.S. Department of Health and Human Services [USDHHS], 1996). Physical activity was one of the 10 leading health indicators in the Healthy People 2010 goals for the United States and is prominent among proposed objectives for Healthy People 2020. "The health benefits of moderate and vigorous physical activity are not limited to adults. Physical activity among children and adolescents is important because of the related health benefits (cardiorespiratory function, blood pressure control, and weight management) and because a physically active lifestyle adopted early in life may continue into adulthood" (USDHHS, 2000, pp. 22-23).

As a result of the relation between physical activity and health, the Centers for Disease Control and Prevention (CDC) and the ACSM published joint recommendations that all Americans accumulate at least 30 minutes of moderate physical activity on most, preferably all, days of the week (Pate et al., 1995). Perhaps the most significant aspect of this recommendation is the notion that moderate activity is of sufficient intensity to act as a buffer against certain diseases and conditions. In contrast, recommendations for improving physical fitness generally require more vigorous levels of intensity. Furthermore, the CDC–ACSM recommendation suggests that *any* moderate activity can enhance health status. Traditional activity recommendations for the development of physical fitness, on the other hand, have focused on specificity of training and have been dominated by one form of activity—exercise.

The Council on Physical Education for Children (COPEC) has suggested that the CDC–ACSM recommendation be modified for children. In defense of a modified recommendation, COPEC cites some significant differences when comparing children and adults, including a relatively short attention span, a tendency toward concrete rather than abstract thought, normal activity patterns that are more intermittent than continuous, a weaker relation between physical activity and physical fitness, and the possibility that participation in intense activities will be perceived as too difficult, thus leading to withdrawal from physical activity. The COPEC guidelines include the following (NASPE, 2004):

- Children should accumulate at least 60 minutes, and up to several hours, of age-appropriate physical activity on all or most days of the week. This daily accumulation should include moderate and vigorous physical activity, with the majority of the time being spent in activity that is intermittent.

- Children should participate in several bouts of physical activity lasting 15 minutes or more each day.

- Children should participate each day in a variety of age-appropriate physical activities designed to achieve optimal health, wellness, fitness, and performance benefits.

- Extended periods (two hours or more) of inactivity are discouraged for children, especially during the daytime hours.

Although there is relatively little data on the physical activity habits of people with disabilities, it is generally believed that people with disabilities are less active than those without disabilities. The USDHHS (2000), for instance, estimated that 36 percent of all adults without a disability did *not* participate in leisure-time physical activity in 1997, compared with 56 percent of adults with a disability. Inactivity among people with disabilities is thought to be due to a variety of barriers that they encounter. Scelza, Kalpakjian, Zemper, and Tate

(2005) surveyed 72 people with spinal cord injuries and reported three types of barriers to their participation in physical activity: intrapersonal or intrinsic (motivation, energy, interest), resources (expenses, transportation), and structural or architectural (accessibility of facilities, access to knowledgeable instructors). In addition, only 47 percent of those surveyed said their physician recommended they participate in an exercise program.

Though barriers may exist (including the misperception by some that physical activity is inappropriate for people with disabilities), it is important that children and adolescents with disabilities are encouraged to be physically active. Citing several sources, Crawford, Hollingsworth, Morgan, and Gray (2008) noted that participation in moderate levels of physical activity can have positive psychological and health benefits for people with disabilities. Among the psychological benefits listed were a better acceptance of disability, a more independent attitude, enhanced moods, a greater sense of life control, fewer suicidal tendencies, and greater levels of self-satisfaction, feelings of well-being, self-esteem, and perceived health. Among the health benefits listed were a decrease in the development of secondary conditions and need for medical care and an increase in functional independence, energy, and physical capacity. Further, when these authors surveyed more than 600 people with mobility impairments, they found a more positive health status and superior community participation among survey respondents who reported the highest levels of physical activity.

Rimmer (2008) has described a framework for conquering barriers and increasing physical activity among people with disabilities: RAMP, which stands for **r**estoring **a**ctivity, **m**obility, and **p**articipation. It consists of four components that build on each other and ultimately lead to a sustainable lifestyle change. The model seems appropriate for both school and community settings. The first component of the model is to provide access and includes the need for accessible transportation, buildings, equipment, and programs. If a person with a disability cannot get to, or get into, a facility; use the exercise equipment; or take part in the physical activity programming offered in the facility, little else matters. Many professionals from architects to physical educators are calling for the application of universal design principles to buildings, equipment, and even curricula. Universal design holds that we always should plan with all participants in mind rather than plan for the majority now and awkwardly modify for the rest later.

The second component of RAMP is to increase participation. Whereas access primarily is about availability, participation primarily is about usability, which may depend on the presence of adapted equipment, modified programs, and trained personnel so that people with disabilities can benefit from the facility, equipment, services, and programs to which they have access. People often require differentiated programming, and though there may be thousands of ways to differentiate, it may be helpful for teachers to think about differentiating based on content (what is being learned or practiced), process (the way it is being learned or practiced), and product (the desired and actual outcomes) and adjust accordingly (Friend, 2008). Physical educators often are in a unique position to mentor and advocate for additional activity opportunities outside of school for students with disabilities. This advocacy might take place with community recreation providers or with local pediatricians, who may not always appreciate the potential benefits of physical activity.

The third component of the model is to promote adherence, which, according to Rimmer (2008), represents a significant challenge to securing the health benefits associated with physical activity. People with and without disabilities must sustain physical activity to benefit from it. Possible strategies for increasing adherence among people with disabilities include varying the types of activities and the location of activities and developing social networks that connect people who can reinforce each other's physical activity behavior. In schools, adherence can be encouraged by tracking the physical activity of students with and without disabilities through a computer program such as Activitygram (Cooper Institute, 2007), by participating in award programs such as those sponsored by the President's Council on Physical Fitness and Sports (2007), and by selecting activities that are enjoyable to students (see figure 23.3).

At the top of RAMP is the fourth and final component, improving health and function. The goal of the sustained physical activity program is to improve quality of life and lower the risk of acquiring various health conditions.

Physical education teachers who work with students with disabilities may find that it is easier to follow either the CDC–ACSM or COPEC recommendations for physical activity than the exercise prescriptions for improving physical fitness discussed earlier in the chapter. This may be true for several reasons. First, it might be difficult or impossible to measure fitness in some students

FIGURE 23.3 Selecting activities that are fun will promote activity adherence and a healthier lifestyle.

Photo courtesy of Amanda Tepfer.

with disabilities, especially those with more severe disabilities. Second, because the CDC–ACSM and COPEC recommendations tend to be less intense, they might be more attainable by some students with disabilities. Finally, a wider range of possible activities is available to meet the CDC–ACSM or COPEC guidelines than is usually recommended for fitness development. Consequently, it is not only appropriate to pursue the CDC–ACSM or COPEC guidelines for students with disabilities, but it may be preferred over the exercise prescriptions for fitness for some students.

Nevertheless, it is the recommendation here that whenever appropriate, teachers' first priority should be to design physical activity programs for students with disabilities with the goal of improving health-related physical fitness. This recommendation is based on several reasons: (a) It is more likely that an exercise prescription approach could be supported by a typical physical education class schedule (CDC–ACSM and COPEC guidelines likely will require time outside of school to achieve); (b) exercise prescriptions will contribute to meeting the CDC–ACSM or COPEC guidelines (even if they are not the intended goal); (c) it is believed that additional physiological health benefits may be derived from vigorous, as opposed to moderate, physical activity (ACSM, 2006; USDHHS, 1996) and the exercise prescriptions tend to be more vigorous than the activity recommendations; and, most importantly, (d) improved fitness levels may be associated with additional functional health-related benefits, including those that may contribute to a student's independence. As Rimmer (2008) suggests, low physical fitness in combination with functional impairments (such as spasticity) and secondary health conditions (such as obesity) may limit physical independence and preclude participation in activities that require moderate to high levels of energy expenditure (such as community ambulation or pushing a wheelchair up a ramp).

SUMMARY

Physical fitness is critical to the person with a disability. In addition to improved performance, health, and appearance, high levels of fitness can foster independence, particularly among people with physical disabilities. The goals of a fitness program for students with unique needs depend on the type and severity of the disability and current levels of physical fitness. Increasing fitness for developing physiological or functional health and for improving skill or performance are all reasonable goals in adapted physical education. Fitness programs should be personalized to meet the goals of each student. Teachers must understand that, with few exceptions, students with disabilities will exhibit a favorable physiological response to increases in physical activity. Increased physical activity likely will result in improvements in both health status and physical fitness. In many cases, the recommendations for frequency and time of activity for improving fitness do not differ significantly from those for students without disabilities; the type and intensity, however, frequently must be modified to provide an appropriate workout. At the very least, students with and without disabilities should pursue the CDC–ACSM guidelines or the COPEC adjustments for physical activity: at least 30 minutes of moderate-intensity activity on most, preferably all, days of the week.

REFERENCES

American College of Sports Medicine (ACSM). (2006). *ACSM's guidelines for exercise testing and prescription* (7th ed.). Philadelphia: Lippincott Williams & Wilkins.

Borg, G.A. (1998). *Borg's perceived exertion to heart rate and pain scales.* Champaign, IL: Human Kinetics.

Bouchard, C., & Shephard, R.J. (1994). Physical activity, fitness, and health: The model and key concepts. In C. Bouchard, R.J. Shephard, & T. Stephens (Eds.), *Physical activity, fitness and health: International proceedings and consensus statement.* Champaign, IL: Human Kinetics.

Caspersen, C.J., Powell, K.E., & Christenson, G.M. (1985). Physical activity, exercise, and physical fitness: Definitions and distinctions for health-related research. *Public Health Reports, 100,* 126-131.

Cooper Institute. (2007). *Fitnessgram/Activitygram test administration manual.* Champaign, IL: Human Kinetics.

Crawford, A., Hollingsworth, H.H., Morgan, K., & Gray, D.B. (2008). People with mobility impairments: Physical activity and quality of participation. *Disability and Health Journal, 1,* 7-13.

DiRocco, P. (1999). Muscular strength and endurance. In J.P. Winnick & F.X. Short (Eds.), *The Brockport physical fitness training guide.* Champaign, IL: Human Kinetics.

Friend, M. (2008). *Special education: Contemporary perspectives for school professionals* (2nd ed.). Boston: Pearson.

National Association of Sport and Physical Education (NASPE). (2004). *Physical activity for children: A statement of guidelines for children ages 5-12* (2nd ed.). Reston, VA: Author.

Pangrazi, R.P. & Corbin, C.B. (2008). Factors that influence physical fitness in children and adolescents. In G.J. Welk & M.D. Meredith (Eds.), *Fitnessgram/Activitygram reference guide.* Dallas: Cooper Institute.

Pate, R.R. (1988). The evolving definitions of fitness. *Quest, 40,* 174-178.

Pate, R.R., Pratt, M., Blair, S.N., Haskell, W.L., Macera, C.A., Bouchard, C., et. al. (1995). Physical activity and public health: A recommendation from the Centers for Disease Control and Prevention and the American College of Sports Medicine. *Journal of American Medical Association, 273,* 402-407.

President's Council on Physical Fitness and Sports. (2007). *The President's challenge.* Retrieved February 11, 2008, from www.presidentschallenge.org.

Rimmer, J.H. (2008). Promoting inclusive physical activity communities for people with disabilities. *Research Digest, President's Council on Physical Fitness and Sports, 9* (2), 1-8.

Scelza, W.M., Kalpakjian, C.Z., Zemper, E.D., & Tate, D.G. (2005). Perceived barriers to exercise in people with spinal cord injury. *American Journal of Physical Medicine and Rehabilitation, 84,* 576-584.

Surburg, P. (1999). Flexibility/range of motion. In J.P. Winnick & F.X. Short (Eds.), *The Brockport Physical Fitness training guide.* Champaign, IL: Human Kinetics.

U.S. Department of Health and Human Services (USDHHS). (1996). *Physical activity and health: A report of the Surgeon General.* Atlanta: Author.

U.S. Department of Health and Human Services (USDHHS). (2000). *Healthy People 2010* (2nd ed.). Washington, DC: Government Printing Office.

Welk, G.J. & Blair, S.N. (2008). Health benefits of physical activity and fitness in children. In G.J. Welk & M.D. Meredith (Eds.), *Fitnessgram/Activitygram reference guide.* Dallas: Cooper Institute.

Winnick, J.P., & Short, F.X. (1999). *The Brockport physical fitness test manual.* Champaign, IL: Human Kinetics.

WRITTEN RESOURCES

American College of Sports Medicine (ACSM). (2003). *Exercise management for persons with chronic diseases and disabilities.* Champaign, IL: Human Kinetics.

Provides information on how to effectively manage exercise for someone with chronic disease or disability. This source includes 49 chapters categorized by disabilities, diseases, or conditions written by people with research or clinical experience in exercise programming. Prominent in the book are suggestions for exercise testing and exercise programming.

Lockette, K.F., & Keyes, A.M. (1994). *Conditioning with physical disabilities.* Champaign, IL: Human Kinetics.

This book covers general principles of physical conditioning, including strength, aerobic, and flexibility training, and applies these principles to a number of physical disabilities, including cerebral palsy, stroke, head injury, spinal cord injury, spina bifida, poliomyelitis, amputations, visual impairments, and multiple sclerosis. Separate chapters for upper-extremity, abdominal and trunk, and lower-extremity exercises are included.

Miller, P. (Ed.). (1995). *Fitness programming and physical disability.* Champaign, IL: Human Kinetics.

This excellent book provides information on principles of conditioning for the development of health-related physical fitness; guidelines for developing resistance-training programs; modifications for using stretch bands or tubing as the mode of exercise; ways of maintaining and developing flexibility; exercises for the neck, shoulder, elbow, wrist, trunk, hip, knee, and ankle; and other topics.

Murphy, N.A., Carbone, P.S., & the Council on Children with Disabilities. (2008). Promoting the participation of children with disabilities in sports, recreation, and physical activities. *Pediatrics, 121* (5), 1057-1061. (May also be available at http://aappolicy. aappublications.org.)

A clinical report by the American Academy of Pediatrics summarizing the benefits of participation and the preparticipation considerations for children with disabilities. Includes a section on advice for pediatricians. Could be helpful to physical educators who consult with physicians on appropriate activity programs for students with disabilities.

Winnick, J.P., & Short, F.X. (Eds.). (1999). *The Brockport physical fitness training guide.* Champaign, IL: Human Kinetics.

This guide is designed to be used in conjunction with the BPFT. Provides principles for fitness development in the areas of cardiorespiratory endurance, body composition, muscular strength and endurance, and flexibility and ROM. CDC–ACSM physical activity guidelines are incorporated. Focuses on young people with intellectual disabilities, visual impairments, cerebral palsy, spinal cord injury, and amputations.

AUDIOVISUAL RESOURCES

Fitness for everyone [VHS series]. (1995). Disabled Sports, USA, 451 Hungerford Dr., Ste. 100, Rockville, MD 20850.

Developed by the National Handicapped Sports and Recreation Association (NHSRA), this series includes an aerobics video for those with quadriplegia, cerebral palsy, paraplegia, and amputations; another video in the series demonstrates strength and flexibility training for people with a variety of disabilities.

ELECTRONIC RESOURCES

Fitness Challenge software. (1999). Human Kinetics, P.O. Box 5076, Champaign, IL 61825-5076.

Supports the BPFT. Prints goals, results, and fitness plans for individual students; separate reports can be generated for instructors or parents. Also includes the technical manual for the BPFT, which provides validity and reliability information for test items.

Fitnessgram/Activitygram software. (2007). Human Kinetics, P.O. Box 5076, Champaign, IL 61825-5076.

Provides a sophisticated computerized system for administering the Fitnessgram. Has both teacher and student components. The student component allows students to enter their own scores and track their progress. It also provides a system for monitoring their levels of physical activity through Activitygram, a subcomponent of the software.

National Center on Physical Activity and Disability (NCPAD): www.ncpad.org.

The mission of this information center is to promote the substantial health benefits that can be gained by people with disabilities through participation in regular physical activity.

President's Challenge: www.presidentschallenge.org.

Provides information on the four programs related to physical fitness and physical activity sponsored by the President's Council on Physical Fitness and Sports.

24

Rhythmic Movement and Dance

Boni B. Boswell

Shawn dreaded his fifth-grade creative educational dance class. His success rate in physical education was close to zero and would sink even lower in dance. Extreme muscle tightness made throwing and kicking look like slashing and punching. Playing the usual ball games using his wheelchair wasn't considered cool. Dance would be another round of trying to copy the movements of people with perfect bodies.

Shawn felt encouraged when the teacher explained that creative educational dance focused on discovering ways of moving by changing things such as speed and energy level. The class tried different ways of reaching into space at different levels and traveling at different speeds. Several classes later, Shawn's perception of both dance and his ability to dance began to change. Students were asked to travel on a straight path, stop, and slowly show strong movements that changed levels. The teacher described the movements as deliberate, tense, and forceful, calling it *pressing*. Students changed to fast, strong movements, described as punching, thrashing actions.

The teacher asked students to create a sequence that included traveling quickly, pausing, pressing, and punching. As Shawn created his sequence, he noticed that his body demonstrated these qualities easily. He felt good about sharing his sequence with the class. He felt shocked when the teacher used his movements as a model for the class. As students began creating dances based on Shawn's movements, he was beginning to think that dance was his favorite class.

What if someone told you that a joyous and meaningful part of your physical education curriculum was missing? When rhythmic activities and dance are omitted from a physical education program, this is indeed the case. Rhythmic activities and dance offer opportunities not only to improve motor skills but also to have fun and gain valuable learning experiences in problem solving and creative expression. This chapter presents a practical approach that teachers with little or no dance background can use to present rhythmic movement and dance in physical education programs for students with a wide range of ability levels.

TEACHING DANCE: WHAT IS IT?

Typically, dance in physical education includes three movement forms: rhythmic movement, creative educational dance (CED), and structured dance (e.g., folk, social). This chapter presents an overview of these forms, suggestions for ways to include students with disabilities, and sample lessons. Although in most cases these dance forms are taught separately, there are important links between them. These links include movement principles that relate to balance, transfer of weight, and alignment as well as to such movement concepts as time, space, and force. The degree of emphasis on these principles and concepts differs among movement forms, but each content can lead into the others, supporting and strengthening student development in them. Through overlapping activities from these movement forms, teachers can provide a richer base for achieving student objectives than could be achieved using one of these movement forms exclusively.

TEACHING DANCE: WHAT IS IT NOT?

It is important to note differences as well as commonalities between dance therapy and educational dance used with students with unique needs. First, the purpose of each is strikingly different. Whereas dance therapy is a psychotherapeutic use of movement focused on the emotional and physical integration of participants, educational dance

is designed to meet the educational and aesthetic needs of students with and without disabilities. Dance therapy is a treatment used primarily with clients with mental illness or emotional and behavioral problems.

Dance therapists earn a degree that qualifies them as therapists. Clearly, teachers of educational dance classes are not therapists—they are instructors—and the participants are not clients—they are students. On the other hand, anyone with or without a disability who dances can experience therapeutic effects. For example, any student who moves rhythmically can release tension, both physically and psychologically, and thus derive therapeutic benefit. Although educational dance and dance therapy have different goals, they both offer potential therapeutic effects.

SELECTION OF AGE-APPROPRIATE CONTENT

Each of these three movement forms contains age-appropriate content, but each form can be extended or simplified to accommodate a range of age and ability levels. For example, CED content is considered most applicable to kindergarten through fifth grade, but by extending CED content to focus on progressively more complex forms for creative expression, teachers can easily adapt the content for sixth- through eighth-grade students. Structured or pattern dance content might be considered most age appropriate for upper-elementary and middle school students, but many folk dances are easily modified for kindergarten students. Although some social dances, such as the salsa and tango, might be best suited for high school students, other social dances are age appropriate for middle school students. Selection of age-appropriate content is guided primarily by practical information about the developmental needs, social behaviors, and interests of students. For an overview of the general order of dance forms suggested for kindergarten through grade 12 in regard to traditional age-appropriate dance content, Kassing and Jay (2003) present the sequence shown in figure 24.1.

RHYTHMIC MOVEMENTS

"Of all the ingredients in . . . dance, rhythm is the most persuasive and most powerful element"

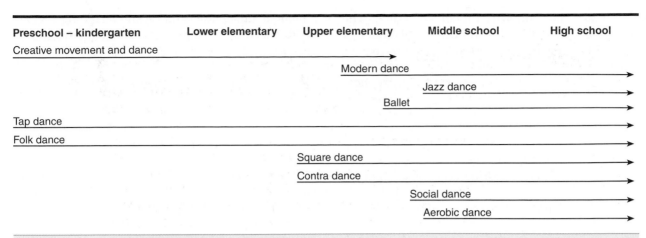

Preschool – kindergarten	Lower elementary	Upper elementary	Middle school	High school

Creative movement and dance ─────────────────────────────→

Modern dance ───────────────────────────────────────→

Jazz dance ─────────────────────────→

Ballet ─────────────────────────────→

Tap dance ───→

Folk dance ──→

Square dance ──────────────────────────→

Contra dance ──────────────────────────→

Social dance ──────────────→

Aerobic dance ─────────────→

FIGURE 24.1 Sample curriculum overview of dance for kindergarten through grade 12.

Reprinted, by permission, from G. Kassing and D. Jay, 2003, *Dance teaching methods and curriculum design* (Champaign, IL: Human Kinetics), 200.

(Humphrey, 1980, p. 104). The primary purpose of a rhythmic movement program is to provide opportunities for students to become competent in moving to rhythmic patterns. In their simplest form, rhythmic movements can be described as a balance of contracting and expanding movements that are connected and repeated, such as inhaling and exhaling. When two movements are connected and repeatedly performed, a rhythm is created. Try the following exercise. Lift and then lower one arm. Perform these two movements as if they were parts of the same movement. In other words, connect the movements. Repeat the connected movements several times without stopping. Notice the resulting rhythmic pattern? You can continue to perform rhythmic arm movements in sync with an internal rhythm, such as your breathing, or you can match the movements to an external rhythm, such as a drumbeat.

Rhythm and Movement

As an integral part of movement, rhythm can be said to characterize the quality of movement. Although all children possess a sense of rhythm, they do not all possess the same degree of rhythmic sense. For several reasons, such as lack of appropriate rhythmic experience, poor concentration, and physical differences, some children might appear to lack a sense of rhythm. When students experience difficulty in moving rhythmically, their movements often appear choppy or awkward. In truth, a sense of rhythm can be developed and refined by carefully selecting appropriate rhythmic activities that offer fun but challenging opportunities. When students develop

a refined sense of rhythm, the quality of their movements reflects this change.

Content of Rhythmic Movement Programs

The content of a rhythmic program includes four elements: pulse, tempo, accent, and patterns. The **pulse** is the underlying beat of the rhythm. It repeats continuously, with each beat taking an equal amount of time, unless the tempo of the pulse slows down or speeds up. Students need opportunities to explore internal rhythms—in other words, to explore movements at their own speed—before being challenged to demonstrate movements in sync with external beats. **Tempo** can be defined simply as the speed of the rhythm. Pulse and tempo are the simplest of the four rhythmic elements for students to master.

An **accent** is the emphasis or stress placed on certain beats. Students need opportunities to listen to a variety of rhythms for the sole purpose of identifying which beats are accented. Students should know that accents reflect the basic structure of the rhythm, and to understand the basic structure of rhythm, they should know that beats are grouped together in measures. **Measures** are composed of series of beats in twos, threes, or fours. In most popular music in the United States, the first beat in each measure is accented. As each measure or series of beats is repeated, the first beat in each measure continues to be accented, and there continues to be the same number of beats in each measure. When students are able to hear or feel the accented beats, they can count the number of beats in each measure.

In music, measures are fundamental units. The **meter** of a musical piece reflects the number of beats in each measure and what kind of note equals one beat. For example, music with a meter of 3/4 has three beats in each measure, and a quarter note receives one beat. Music with 4/4 meter has four beats in each measure, with a quarter note receiving one beat. Understanding this aspect of rhythm is especially important in structured dance because the steps in these dances (folk, social, and square dance) reflect the basic structure of the rhythmic accompaniment.

The term **rhythmic patterns** connotes variety in rhythm and presents a level of complexity not found in pulse, tempo, and accent. Simply stated, rhythmic patterns are reoccurring groups of beats or movements in which each group includes different tempos. For example, if a rhythmic pattern is composed of a group of four steady beats, a combination of two or more tempos would be included within the four beats. Translating this into movement, this four-count rhythmic pattern can include two walking steps (counts 1 and 2) and four running steps (counts 3 and 4). Locomotor patterns such as galloping, sliding, rolling, or skipping can be used in this example by replacing the walking steps (counts 1 and 2) with the new locomotor pattern followed by the four running steps (counts 3 and 4). After teacher-guided practice combining movements of different tempos to match a group of set beats, students should be encouraged to create their own rhythmic patterns using other movements. Most students need to feel a rhythmic pattern while stationary by clapping or tapping the pattern before moving through space using the pattern.

Teaching Style

Guided discovery offers a natural avenue for presentation of rhythmic activities. The teacher guides students by asking questions and presenting tasks that require students to engage in self-discovery. The rhythmic movement lesson presented in this chapter also includes opportunities for problem solving. Students are asked to solve movement problems that relate to the rhythmic material explored. Through the process of solving these problems, students generate a broad range of solutions or responses. Depending on the developmental level of the students, the solutions could range from a brief sequence of simple movements that reflect the students' breathing rhythms to a move-

ment sequence focusing on the changing accents combined with changes in direction, pathway, and levels.

Speaking Rhythmically

A significant part of presenting rhythmic activities is the skill of beginning the class in unison and in rhythm with the beat of the activity. The beginning signal given by the teacher or student leader is traditionally a verbal cue presented by speaking rhythmically—speaking loudly, clearly, and in rhythm with the beat of the activity. An example of speaking rhythmically would be counting an introductory set of eight beats and ending the set of counts with, "five, six, ready, and." Instructions given during the activity for changing the task must be announced before the change is to take place. For example, the instructor would say, "five, six, ready, change." For students with auditory difficulties, verbal cueing must be accompanied by visual cues. In these classes, simple hand responses, such as beating in time with the tempo of the activity, can be easily added.

Developmental Progression of Activities

Perhaps all teachers would agree that rhythmic activities should be presented in a developmental manner, but often teachers present rhythmic challenges that are too complex for many of their students. The following guidelines can help teachers sequence rhythmic activities for a range of developmental levels.

- Focus on internal rhythmic awareness before focusing on external rhythms.
- Provide opportunities for listening to the pulse before moving to the pulse.
- Begin with nonlocomotor movements before using locomotor movements.
- Begin with nonlocomotor movements using hand movements before using other body parts.
- Gradually increase the number of and difficulty of the concepts introduced. For example, use the concept of moving forward before incorporating other directions.
- Begin with students moving individually, then moving with partners, and then moving with a small group.

Suggestions for Students With Differences

The following suggestions apply to any students who need to increase awareness of internal rhythms and develop awareness of external rhythmic patterns. This might include not only students with severe disabilities but also students who appear to lack a sense of rhythm. As mentioned previously, lack of appropriate rhythmic experiences, poor concentration, and physical differences can hinder rhythmic ability. Initially, these students might demonstrate difficulty moving to an external rhythm. Teachers can begin working with rhythms that originate from the students themselves by encouraging students to explore nonlocomotor and locomotor movements at their own speed before introducing activities that require moving in sync with external beats.

One teaching strategy for students who need to develop initial rhythmic awareness is to match these students with peers or cross-age tutors. Matching students (with or without disabilities) with partners requires careful consideration of many variables, including level of maturity, student preferences, body weight, and level of rhythmic ability. In regard to students using wheelchairs, teachers might ask selected peers to attend an introductory class so that partners can be introduced to each other and the strengths of each student can be emphasized. Relevant information about wheelchairs and assistive devices can be highlighted. For students who remain in their wheelchairs during the rhythmic activities, peers can sit in chairs facing their partners or sit side by side. When appropriate, instruction can be presented to partners of students with severe disabilities about providing physical support, such as physically helping to guide a partner's hands through movements. To actively engage and foster responses of students with severe cognitive and physical disabilities in rhythmic movements, the following steps are suggested: (1) focus attention by securing eye contact, (2) provide opportunities for passive movements, (3) provide opportunities for mirroring movements of a partner, and (4) provide opportunities for creating original movement responses.

Clarifying the objectives for a class is a crucial step in developing a rhythmic program. These might be based on national curriculum guides, state or locally developed guidelines, or knowledge of typical development. The objectives of the Beginning Rhythmic Movement sample lesson are based on typical rhythmic development. The activities included in the lesson were adapted from a program designed for middle school students with severe differences. Even though the original discussion (Boswell & Vidret, 1993) focused on students with severe cognitive and physical disabilities, the activities lend themselves to a wide range of adaptations.

The following example of a beginning lesson was designed for students who need opportunities to move to their internal rhythms and to increase awareness of external rhythms (figure 24.2). The content of this sample lesson is primarily rhythmic movement, but it includes group activities leading to readiness in structured dances.

Sample Lesson: Beginning Rhythmic Movement

Student Objectives

1. Show awareness of internal rhythms by demonstrating movements that reflect breathing patterns.
2. Match a partner's rhythmic pattern with movements.
3. Move in sync with simple external rhythm by demonstrating tapping movements while stationary.

Warm-Up Activity: Modified Structured Dance—Seven Jumps

Instructions: The class listens to the music "Seven Jumps" for two or three minutes (perhaps while the teacher checks roll). The teacher stops the music and explains that the music alternates between the melody heard for 32 counts and a series of single, long notes of 4 to 8 counts. The teacher replays the music and provides a physical signal, such as lifting

(continued)

FIGURE 24.2 This sample lesson focuses on rhythmic movement, but it includes group activities leading to readiness in structured dances.

her arms, when the series of long notes is heard. Each time the melody stops and the long, single notes are heard, a long note is added. Thus, one long note is heard after the first melody change, then two long notes after the second melody change, proceeding in an add-on pattern until seven long notes are heard.

The following is a modification of the traditional steps of the simple folk dance, Seven Jumps. In circular formation, students travel when they hear the melody, then stop and reach in any direction, changing body parts, when they hear the long notes. Students can use any locomotor pattern that is appropriate. Stepping on the beat is not emphasized. With each long note, students reach out into space; thus, during the last section of long notes, students reach seven times in different directions.

Communicate the Goal of the Class to Students

The goal of the class is to increase awareness of rhythms, beginning with breathing. Explain that everyone has a comfortable rhythm of breathing, and the rhythm of one person's breathing might differ from that of others.

Sequence of Activities

1. Explore internal rhythm of breathing. Ask students to focus on their natural rhythm of breathing. Stress that it doesn't matter if exhalations and inhalations last two or eight counts—the point is to be aware of the rhythm. If any students need additional structure to focus on their breathing, ask them to count to five as they exhale and to five again as they inhale.

  a. Ask students to add movements that reflect the rhythm of their breathing. Describe and demonstrate. While inhaling, add lifting of both arms forward and high. While exhaling, add lowering of arms down and backward. Students match arm movements to their breathing pattern, using their own pace.

  b. Students add lateral rocking with breathing. Describe and demonstrate. Begin with palms of both hands touching the floor or a chair at the sides of the body. When inhaling, lean the trunk to one side and lift the opposite arm over the head, then reverse the movement when exhaling. Students are encouraged to move at their own pace.

  c. Students mirror a partner's rhythm. One in each pair of students is designated as the mirror and copies his partner. Facing each other, the mirror student matches his partner's breathing and movement pattern. Partners take turns mirroring each other's breathing as movements are added.

  d. Present a movement problem. Ask students to create a rhythmic sequence of four breaths with at least two different arm movements, repeated twice.

  e. After independent practice creating a sequence including various movements, partners can volunteer to perform their sequences for the class.

  f. The teacher provides feedback and encourages students to observe variations in tapping rhythms.

2. Explore tapping to a simple external rhythm.

  a. Provide an external rhythm with any instrument, such as a drum.

  b. Explain that tapping movements are short, gentle movements performed quickly. Demonstrate tapping using a variety of body parts. Students explore tapping fingers or hands on knees, shoulders, feet, or floor.

  c. Provide a steady, moderate-tempo drumbeat. Ask students to match their tapping movements to the beat.

  d. Provide a steady beat using a different instrument, such as a tambourine. Ask students to travel through space to the tambourine beat and tap in place to the drumbeat.

  e. The teacher divides the class in half. One half performs its sequence while the other half observes, and then groups switch roles.

  f. The teacher provides feedback and encourages students to observe variations in tapping rhythms.

Closure

Ask students to demonstrate the movements they liked best as they take deep breaths and review the purpose of the lesson.

FIGURE 24.2 *(continued)*

CREATIVE EDUCATIONAL DANCE

CED is a movement form that focuses on refining natural movements as students explore the elements of movement (i.e., space, time, force, and body). In this discussion, an integral part of CED is creating dances through problem solving. The simplest dance created through this process is a movement sequence that includes a clear beginning and ending as well as a middle section that demonstrates creative use of the elements of movement. As students learn and master the content, they begin to create dances that communicate ideas or themes. One of the joys of CED for students comes from giving form to their natural movements so that they can communicate ideas as they perform their dances for their peers. There are many avenues to approaching the process of creating dances. This chapter focuses on creating dances through the process of solving movement problems.

Several terms have been used to describe programs that focus on exploration of space, time, and force. Related terms include *movement education*, *creative movement*, and *creative dance*. Kassing and Jay (2003) summarize the history of these related dance forms, highlighting the influence of Margaret H'Doubler and Rudolf Laban. Although these terms might stress different aspects of exploration of the elements and different outcomes, Kassing and Jay underscore that "regardless of what titles they are given," these approaches "provide age-appropriate movement and dance experiences that support learning in other dance forms, other art forms, and in physical education" (2003, p. 215).

Teaching Style

Similar to rhythmic movement, CED lends itself to the use of guided discovery and divergent teaching styles. The teacher poses questions that encourage students to analyze and explore the body and movement concepts. For example, the teacher might ask, "Can you jump higher if you use a different body shape?" The terms *exploration* and *improvisation* are used frequently in relation to CED. The heart of each CED lesson is **exploration** of the elements of movement. In this context, exploration is defined as "a systematic investigation, examination, search for making specific discoveries and learning about something" (Smith-Autard, 2000, p. 80). The process of exploring CED content is filled with **improvisation**, which is defined as spontaneously responding to a stimuli, or "invention without preparation" (Smith-Autard, 2000, p. 80).

In CED lessons, exploration is replete with questions and **movement problems** (i.e., assignments) that require students to consider possible **spontaneous responses** and then select one of the responses to include in the dance. Specifically, in implementing exploration, teachers present questions that guide students in using **improv** as a strategy for exploring. For example, a teacher might ask his students, "What body parts can make an angular shape like the letter *S*? Now, how can you create a different angular *S* shape with a different body part? Select one of these shapes and explore making that shape at different levels." Clearly, there are many levels of improvisation. Teachers can pose highly specific questions that offer few options, or they can ask questions that are completely open ended.

Figure 24.3 presents students engaged in an improvisation activity. To begin, one student is asked to perform a nonlocomotor rhythmic movement accompanied by a sound. Dancers are asked to individually add their rhythmic movements and sounds to the rhythmic movement of the first dancer, thus creating a rhythm machine. Dancers reverse the process of adding movements so that each dancer individually breaks away from the rhythm machine, leaving the initial dancer to end the dance.

When teachers present problem-solving activities that have many possible solutions, they provide opportunities for divergent thinking. Movement problems are posed that require students to create a dance that adheres to boundaries related to aspects of space, time, and force, but there are many possible solutions. Through the process of solving movement problems, students can create a diverse collection of dances, ranging in scope from the flickering movements of a candle to the powerful movements of a hurricane.

Content

The heart of CED is exploring the elements of movement: space, time, force, and the body. Space, time, and force are concepts that allow us to analyze movement. These concepts are defined in physical education and dance texts, but terminology varies from text to text. For example, the term *force* might be replaced by other terms, such as *effort*, *energy*, or *weight*. The following brief descriptions of the elements are similar to definitions found in physical education texts, such as *Children Moving: A*

Photo courtesy of Tony Rumple, ECU News Bureau.

FIGURE 24.3 The rhythm machine performed by an inclusive dance troupe at East Carolina University, Greenville, North Carolina.

Reflective Approach to Teaching Physical Education (Graham, Holt/Hale, & Parker, 2007), and texts on creative dance, such as *First Steps in Teaching Creative Dance to Children* (Joyce, 1994).

Space is the medium in which our bodies move and create designs, and it includes terms that relate to specific areas in space. Typically, space is described as self-space or general space and includes a description of level and focus. The area closest to the body is called *self-space* or kinesphere. The area beyond the body's reach is termed *general space*. Levels in space are described as high, middle, or low. The focus of the body in space can be near or far away and can be directed to a certain level in space. Space designs related to the body include shape, size, direction, and pathway. Body shapes can be small or large. Identification of the direction of

a movement is based on where the body is facing: forward, backward, diagonally, or sideward. One of the first ways to explore direction is to ask the students to lead with various parts of their bodies. For example, leading with the back, students travel backward, and when leading with one side of the body, students travel sideways. The term *pathway* describes a different aspect of space. The pathway the body follows can be described as the floor pattern, such as straight, curved, or any combination. Thus, you can move backward (direction) while traveling on a curved pathway (floor pattern).

Force describes the energy level of movements. Other related terms include *quality* and *flow*. Force can be powerful, described as strong or weak (or light). Quality refers to how the energy moves the body, often described as swinging, smooth (sustained), sharp (sudden), or shaking. Flow describes whether the energy is bound (controlled, tensed) or free (uncontrolled, free flowing).

Time includes the terms *beat, tempo, accent,* and *pattern. Beat* refers to the underlying pulse of the rhythm. *Tempo* describes whether the beat is fast or slow. Stressed beats (or emphasized movement) are *accents. Patterns* refer to combinations of rhythms created by changing tempos, changing accent placement, or including uneven rhythms. Uneven rhythmic patterns simply include both quick and slow movements or beats, such as the rhythm of galloping (quick, quick, slow).

Suggested CED Themes

In concert with Graham, Holt/Hale, and Parker (2001), each of the elements can be considered a movement theme that serves as a basis for lesson development. A suggested progression of movement themes for planning a series of lessons is shown in table 24.1. In this progression, space and body are combined. It is suggested that teachers begin with the level A themes of body and space, progressing from left to right and incorporating movement themes from the level A themes of time and force. Teachers can build on these by adding themes from level B and then level C.

Although using various images can motivate students to explore the elements of movement, many images support stereotypic movements and actually distract students from exploring movement. Animal images, such as bunnies and dogs, are especially difficult to use because students fall into stereotypic movements and thereby miss exploration of movement.

Table 24.1 CED Progression of Movement Themes

Body and space themes	Time themes	Force themes
A. EXPLORING MOTION AND STILLNESS	**A. EXPLORING INTERNAL RHYTHMS AND EXTERNAL RHYTHMS**	**A. EXPLORING MOVEMENT QUALITIES**
• Travel short distances and stop (stillness) on cue. • Change ways of travel (galloping, jumping) and stop (stillness) on cue. • Create a traveling sequence with two points of stillness without teacher cue. • Travel, rise to high level, show stillness, and hold a high body shape. • Travel, rise to high level, sink to low level, and stop with low body shape. • Create traveling sequences with two rising and sinking movements and two points of stillness. Begin with body lifted and end holding body close to floor. • Travel using any locomotor pattern with a partner, stop, and one rises while the other sinks; reverse roles.	• Stationary—Sit and focus on internal beats (heartbeats and breathing), lifting and lowering arms in rhythm with breathing. • Tap fingers to internal rhythm on different body parts. • Draw circles with body parts to internal rhythm. • Stationery—using internal, natural rhythm, sway side to side 4-6 times, turn, then stop. Repeat using natural, internal rhythm. • Stationary—play Navajo greeting game, hands patting knees and floor with verse. • Listen to steady drumbeat and sway side to side. • Travel using internal rhythm, stopping on teacher's cue and swaying side to side in rhythm to drum. Repeat. • Create sequence—traveling to internal rhythm, stopping on teacher's cue, and tapping and swaying to external, even beatdrum.	• Stationary—explore qualities of shaking, tapping, swinging, bending, twisting, reaching. • Body isolations—use different body parts to perform qualities. • Travel, stop, and perform various qualities with teacher cues. • Create sequence of traveling and stopping (independently) and performing qualities, adding level changes.

(continued)

Table 24.1 (continued)

Body and space themes	Time themes	Force themes
B. EXPLORING SPATIAL RELATIONSHIPS	**B. EXPLORING CHANGING TEMPO**	**B. EXPLORING STRONG AND LIGHT**
• Stationary—different body parts reach toward various spatial areas: front, back, side, high, low. • Stationary—body parts perform qualities of force (shaking, swinging) in different spatial locations. • Travel through space, stopping, reaching with various body parts into spatial areas. • Create a traveling sequence including body parts reaching into spatial areas and two stationary points with body parts performing selected qualities of force; begin and end with body shape that includes reaching away from body into space. • Travel with partner in any locomotor pattern, stop, reach out into space with any body part, and repeat, replacing reaching with shaking various body parts.	• Stationary—sit and tap quickly on floor, then hands slowly clapping. • Stationary—echo teacher's clapping: four slow claps, then two quick claps; repeat. • Travel, changing from slow to fast. • Create a traveling sequence, changing tempo and adding stillness. • Select two body shapes, changing quickly from one shape to another, then slowly. Repeat several times. • Create a sequence traveling quickly and slowly, with two points of stillness in which the body pauses then quickly changes shape.	• Stationary strong movements—explore punching, pushing, stamping. • Stationary light movements—explore tapping, brush, patting, rocking. • Travel using strong then light force. • Create sequence of traveling, stopping, and using strong and light force.
C. EXPLORING BODY SHAPES	**C. EXPLORING ACCENTS AND PATTERNS**	**C. EXPLORING FLOW**
• Stationary—shake whole body and then freeze to hold shaking shape. • Stationary, whole-body control—body reaches wide and holds shape, then reaches to expand into large shapes. • Large shapes change into small shapes. • Travel with large shapes, then travel with large shapes changing into small shapes. • Isolate body parts, exploring shapes focusing on back (e.g., cat back, long back) shoulders, heads, and so on. • Balance using various body parts as base of support and holding shapes. • Create a shape dance sequence, beginning with large, whole-body shapes; isolating a body part and changing shape of that body part; adding traveling; and forming definite ending shape.	• Stationary—sit and listen to a steady 4/4 rhythm, accent on first beat of the four counts by clapping. Repeat, adding voice on accented beat. • Stationary—clap three beats, accenting first beat by clapping at high level. • Stationary—sit or stand and perform a punching movement on the accented beats of 4/4 rhythm. • Travel and accent the first beat of every four counts with voices of students counting, "One." • Play African rhythm game—students repeat a rhythm using stomp, clap, pat, and hold (rest) for a beat.	• Stationary, energy flowing: Explore swinging, free movements with individual body parts and then whole body. • Stationary, energy bound: Explore tight, frozen movements with body parts and then whole body. • Travel with free-flowing energy sequence from earlier. • Create sequence combining traveling and stationary movements using free and bound flow.

Lesson Format

CED content is organized into lessons that include objectives, a warm-up, and a closure phase. In addition, the CED lesson format includes four sequential phases that provide a framework for students to explore, create, and respond (perform). The following format can be used with a broad range of ability levels.

1. *Exploration.* This is the heart of the lesson. The teacher guides the students in exploring selected elements.

2. *The teacher presents movement problem or assignment.* Problems are based on the material covered in exploration. The problem is similar to an assignment, specifying the parameters or boundaries that students follow to create dances.

3. *Students create dances.* Individually, with a partner, or in a small group, students create dances by following the boundaries or instructions specified in the problem.

4. *Respond (perform).* Students share their dances with peers. Responses after each performance focus on how the content of the dances solved the movement problem.

The following sample CED lesson was designed for a range of ability levels and would be appropriate for most typically developing primary school students (figure 24.4). Although the content of this lesson is primarily CED, it includes valuable opportunities for rhythmic development.

Sample Lesson: CED

Student Objectives

1. Demonstrate traveling and stopping with auditory and visual cues.

2. Demonstrate stopping and showing a shape with a round back and a shape with an arched back.

3. Travel for three beats and hold on fourth beat; repeat to music.

Warm-Up Activity

Directions: Students travel through space, carefully avoiding colliding with others, as the teacher beats a drum at a moderate tempo. When the beats stop, students stop and extend any body part into space for four counts. (Another percussion instrument such as a bell or maracas can be played to provide an auditory cue for reaching into space, or the teacher can verbalize the sequence.) The teacher repeats the sequence—travel, stop, reach—several times, changing the tempo of the drumbeat. If developmentally appropriate, other nonlocomotor movements can be added, such as an elbow tapping a knee or a hand tapping the sole of a foot for four counts. Teachers can guide students to use certain body parts for tapping or twisting for four counts. By varying the tempo of the sequence (travel, stop, reach, tap, and twist), teachers can add complexity as needed. For children with hearing losses, simple visual cues can easily be added. Depending on the developmental level of the students, teachers might add several visual cues, such as a color code in which certain colors are matched with specified movements.

Communicate the Goals of the Class to Students

1. Demonstrate body control while traveling, stopping, and shaping with round and arched backs.

2. Create a dance that includes shapes with rounded and arched backs.

▸ *Exploration.* Students melt to the floor in four counts and explore shapes with rounded backs on count 5. The teacher uses age-appropriate feedback to encourage students to repeat melting and shaping with rounded backs. Elementary school students might begin exploration by focusing on the size of the shape. For example, the teacher asks the students to keep their rounded back shapes while they change the size of their shapes. As suggested in table 24.1 under the section on exploring body shapes, students' small, rounded shapes can grow into large ones while maintaining rounded backs and vice versa. The teacher can add traveling while changing the size of the shapes or ask students to travel through

(continued)

FIGURE 24.4 This lesson focuses on creative educational dance but it also include valuable opportunities for rhythmic development.

Sample Lesson: CED   *(continued)*

space and then stop on a certain cue before shaping with rounded backs. After students demonstrate traveling and shaping with rounded backs, the teacher may guide students in exploring shapes with arched backs. Slowly stretching into a shape with an arched back and then slowly curving into a rounded back provides opportunities for students to refine upper-body control while increasing awareness of their abdominal muscles. To add complexity, the teacher can ask students to explore changing level as well as shape and size: "Can you lift and expand your arched back shape to a high level and then change to a small, rounded back shape as you melt toward the floor?"

▶ *Movement problem (assignment).* The teacher creates a shape dance that includes traveling and shaping with rounded and arched backs and that begins and ends with definite shapes. Complexity is added to the problem to match the abilities of the students by including size, level, and tempo changes.

▶ *Creation of dances.* Students create dances independently (or with a partner). The teacher circulates through the class and provides feedback and encouragement. As students complete the assignment, the teacher asks them to repeat their dances and think of possible titles for their dances.

▶ *Respond (perform).* Half the students share their dances while the other half observe quietly. Then the groups switch roles so that all students perform their dances. The teacher encourages all students to watch for the rounded and arched shapes and to focus on how other students solved the movement problem.

▶ *Closure.* Students form a circle and breathe deeply as they stretch high, melt low, reach into the circle, reach out of the circle, turn, and stretch. Cue words for the sequence include *reach up*, *down*, *in*, *out*, *turn*, and *stretch*. Repeat the sequence several times and verbally review the purpose of the lesson.

FIGURE 24.4   *(continued)*

Extending the Content

When students create dances that demonstrate their understanding of the basic content (space, time, force, and the body), teachers can offer greater challenges by extending the content into exploration of the qualitative aspects of movement. In this discussion, examination of qualitative aspects of movements is limited to the introduction of the eight basic effort actions, as presented in table 24.2. The eight effort actions correspond to eight qualities of movement. They are described as basic effort actions "because they form the base from which more subtle qualities are drawn" (Preston-Dunlop, 1990, p. 60). Although performing even simple movements such as reaching for a glass of water might contain a blend of effort actions, the quality or dynamics of reaching for the glass can be described in terms of the overall use of space, time, and force. For example, the movement of reaching slowly, lightly, and directly toward the glass can be described as the effort action called *gliding*. In contrast, if the movement of reaching is performed quickly, with strong force, and directly, the movement can be described as the effort action

thrusting or *punching*. As presented in table 24.2, in addition to gliding and thrusting, the eight basic effort actions include slashing, floating, wringing, pressing, flicking, and dabbing.

Lessons devoted to exploration of the eight basic effort actions provide opportunities for students to refine their movements in terms of force, space, and time and improve their abilities to use movement in creative expression. As students master the effort actions, teachers can provide meaningful opportunities to concentrate on refining creative expression. Presenting words that clarify the moods or feelings associated with effort actions can help students understand the various expressions characterized by each effort. For example, words such as *quietness*, *balance*, and *peaceful* can be used when exploring the effort actions of floating or gliding. Using words such as *sparkling*, *sharp*, *glittering*, and *excited* with the effort actions of flicking and dabbing helps students become more aware of the connection of movement qualities and expression.

To help students understand how to work with the effort actions, teachers may use the following sequence:

Table 24.2 Eight Basic Effort Actions

Basic effort action	Space	Time	Force
Float	Indirect	Sustained	Light
Wring	Indirect	Sustained	Strong
Press	Direct	Sustained	Strong
Glide	Direct	Sustained	Light
Dab	Direct	Sudden	Light
Flick	Indirect	Sudden	Light
Slash	Indirect	Sudden	Strong
Punch	Direct	Sudden	Strong

■ Begin focusing on one aspect of the elements of movement.

■ Introduce the notion that each element ranges on a continuum in respect to the selected aspect.

■ Progress to focusing on how these elements of movement combine to create the basic effort actions.

In regard to space, a teacher might focus on the aspect of pathway, which ranges from indirect to direct.

Space: Movements ranging from indirect to direct express the continuum of space.

Indirect· · · · · · · · · ·**SPACE**· · · · · · · · · ·**Direct**

When students enter a classroom to find a seat, they might travel on a straight path directly to a seat or wander around the room before finding a seat. If the person looks straight ahead and moves through the room on a straight path with a definite idea of where to go, the spatial focus of that person is direct. If another person scans the room and wanders through space, weaving freely between seats before finally spiraling into a seat, her spatial focus is indirect. Students need to explore moving both indirectly and directly, when stationary in self-space and when traveling through general space.

Time: Movements varying from slow to sudden or abrupt express the time continuum.

Slow· · · · · · · ·**TIME**· · · · · · · · · ·**Sudden**

To simplify this discussion, time is considered only in respect to tempo. Slow movements extend into time, whereas sudden movements are performed quickly. Cows often demonstrate slow and sudden movements simultaneously. Typically, cows grazing in a green field travel slowly from one grassy spot to another. But at the same time the cows' bodies are moving slowly, their tails are moving suddenly and repeatedly to swish away flies and mosquitoes.

Force: Movements described as light and resisting gravity ranging to movements that are strong and powerful express the continuum of force.

Light· · · · · · · · ·**FORCE**· · · · · · · · · ·**Strong**

Force can be described as an amount of energy. Force relates to gravity in that it is influenced by the degree of energy needed to overcome the pull of gravity on the weight of the body or an object. For example, if you need to move a piano, you will need to use your weight (with gravity) and push with a strong force. However, if you are moving a delicate crystal vase, you need to withhold your full body weight and use light force.

So, what happens when aspects of space, time, and force of a movement are clarified? The result is that you can identify the effort action that describes the quality of that movement. Simply stated, when a movement is described in respect to time (fast or slow), space (direct or indirect), and force (light or strong), one of the basic effort actions is identified. Exploration of the effort actions builds on the basic CED content. In other words, students explore effort actions while exploring the body and aspects of the other elements, such as direction, size, level, and shape. For example, pressing (direct, slow, strong) can be explored at a low level using the whole body or at a high level using an isolated body part. Teachers can gradually increase the complexity of the movement problem from lesson to lesson, thus allowing students time to learn and master the concepts while continuing to present new and challenging content.

Exploring the eight basic effort actions in pairs of opposites is suggested for beginning students (Preston-Dunlop, 1990). Working with opposite effort actions within one lesson allows teachers to focus primarily on one effort, using the opposite one to balance the experience. For example, exploring effort actions characterized by strong force and fast tempo interspersed with light, slow actions provides opportunities to experience the contrast of the two actions and provides recovery time for the body. Using opposite effort actions, teachers would pair the effort actions as follows: wringing with dabbing, slashing with gliding, punching with floating, and pressing with flicking.

One quick and easy way to begin exploring opposite effort actions is to ask students to work with partners using a structured activity, such as Together and Apart. In this activity, partners begin several feet apart from each other, then travel together (toward each other), and then travel apart (back to their beginning point). Students focus on only one element of movement, such as time, before broadening their focus to include force and then space. For example, to explore floating and punching using Together and Apart, students can begin by focusing on the time continuum. Students travel together (toward a partner) in slow motion, pause, and then rush quickly apart. The teacher adds the concept of force to the exploration of time. In other words, students travel slowly with light or gentle force, pause, and then separate and travel apart quickly with strong force. After experiencing the contrast between slow, light movements and quick, strong movements, students add a layer related to space. Teachers guide students to explore traveling indirectly, slowly, with light force together and directly while traveling quickly and forcefully apart.

APPLICATION EXAMPLE

Exploring Opposite Pairs of Effort Actions

Setting: Using words to guide and motivate students in exploring an opposite pair of basic effort actions: floating and thrusting

Students: A middle school class, including a student with hypertonia (excessive muscle tightness) who walks with a scissors gait

Application: The physical educator presents exploration floating and thrusting by offering a variety of movement choices and using age-appropriate descriptor words.

▸ Students are asked to travel in slow motion for eight drumbeats, pause, and then with the speed of light they clap, stamp, or jump for four drumbeats. Students can use any form of traveling as long as they use slow tempo. Using a variety of travel words, such as *plodding*, *creeping*, or *lingering*, or descriptive words, such as *sleepily*, *calmly*, *serenely*, *quietly*, *gradually*, or *leisurely*, can help students move in slow motion.

▸ Students are asked to perform the stationary, quick movements with any body parts, such as a knee, elbow, wrist, or shoulder, and focus on force. The teacher might say, "As you travel, breathe deeply and move gently, drifting along, then surprise me with strong, vigorous, jolting, powerful, exploding movements with any body parts. You can clap, stamp, jump, or use any movements. Your sequence is drift, pause, explode."

▸ Words used to characterize the use of space for floating include *vaporous*, *roundabout*, *carefree*, or *meandering*. Making sure to clearly highlight the contrast of the direct use of space of thrusting actions, the teacher describes them as pointed, piercing, or jabbing movements.

When teachers provide a wide range of possible movements that can be used to explore the effort actions, students with disabilities can be included more easily. In other words, traveling can be rolling, scooting, or any form of moving through space. To bring the basic effort actions to life and give meaning to the exploration, teachers and students can match the movements to selected traveling or descriptive words. Selection of words used to motivate students to explore these effort actions is based on the developmental level and interests of the students. The application example includes potential words for exploring opposite pairs of basic effort actions and many possible movements.

CED and Students With Disabilities

All students should have opportunities to explore the interactions of space, time, and force, but how can students with severe physical disabilities participate? The following discussion introduces an approach based not on normalizing the movements of students with disabilities but on perceiving differences associated with disabilities as potential sources of artistic material. The approach requires expansion of the definition of dance to include a new aesthetic—the aesthetics of disability. Within the scope of this chapter, a detailed description of this approach is not possible; instead, a brief overview of the key components is offered.

As described by Elin and Boswell (2004), the process of re-envisioning dance begins with adopting the notion that all students bring talents to class and that sometimes these talents are disguised as limitations. In other words, whether students present postural misalignments, limited mobility, lack of range of motion, or other obvious differences, they enter class bringing strengths. In addition, what appears to be a limitation can be perceived as an asset. This process allows students to begin to see motor differences associated with disabilities as potential sources of artistic expression. Recognition of the potential value of movements previously considered unacceptable is a central theme in the process.

The concept of motif is an integral component of re-envisioning dance. A motif is a single movement, spatial design, or brief movement phrase used as the basis for creating a dance. An excellent discussion of motif and development by Blom and Chaplin (1982) clarifies motif as a device or method for building dances:

The motif is manipulated; it is performed upside down, backward, inside out. Its original sequence (order of its parts) is not sacred as in theme and variation. Fragments of the movement are used and developed separately, then put together with no specific regard for the original order. But there is a definite sense of form that comes from developing the motif. (pp. 101-102)

Re-envisioning dance involves guiding students to explore the development of motifs as they focus on the effort actions. As highlighted in the opening scenario, the movements of students with disabilities can serve as the basis of motifs. At first, these movements might appear to be unacceptable for dance, but teachers are encouraged to re-envision these movements as potential sources of artistic material. Note that as teachers increase the opportunities for students with disabilities to develop dance skills and knowledge, the options for these students to continue their studies in higher education remain limited.

STRUCTURED DANCE

Building on the knowledge and skills gained in rhythmic activities and CED, students can discover the joy of learning structured or patterned dances. Structured dances, as the name implies, have specific sequences of steps. The terms *structured, patterned*, and *recreational* can be used interchangeably and include many types of dances, such as international folk dances, American heritage dances (e.g., the Virginia reel), contemporary line dances, and social dances (e.g., swing and salsa) (Pittman, Waller, & Dark, 2009).

The degree of structure varies greatly from dance to dance, but there are important commonalities that thread through most structured or patterned dances. These commonalities include the following:

- Basic steps
- Formations
- Figures

Many folk and social dances are characterized by a basic step. These basic steps are made up of combinations of locomotor patterns and are further discussed under the content section. Structured dances also have a range of group formations, such as a circle, line, or square, as well as common figures or movement designs performed by two or more people that characterize the dance. Common dance figures in folk dances include the do-si-do for partners and turning under arches for three dancers.

Musical Accompaniments

Use of age-appropriate music is especially important in middle school and high school. Many folk and social dances can be adapted to contemporary music, which can motivate older students to participate. When high school students are motivated to participate and have opportunities to increase their skills and confidence in social dances, they can learn that dance is a lifelong physical activity that provides social as well as physical benefits throughout their lives.

Start the Music!

Learning a structured dance should be accomplished in a minimum amount of time and music should be added as quickly as possible. Dance steps can be shortened and simplified so that the class can quickly be ready to practice selected steps with music. Quickly adding music while practicing dance steps often results in a feeling of accomplishment. Variations of locomotor and nonlocomotor movements previously experienced in rhythmic activities and CED are the basic ingredients. For example, moving from exploring running with a partner to learning a structured dance that uses running as the basic step is a natural progression. Also, progression from exploring ways of traveling using a wheelchair with a partner to discovering ways of moving together to learn a structured dance is a natural transition.

Content

The basic nonlocomotor (bend, reach, twist) and locomotor (walk, run, jump, hop, leap) movement patterns are the basic materials of structured dances. Combinations of these locomotor movements produce the gallop, slide, and skip. Variations and combinations of these locomotor patterns form the traditional dance steps, such as the two-step, schottische, polka, grapevine, and waltz. Most folk and line dances consist of one or two of these basic steps performed in sequence. The sequence of steps is performed repeatedly to a simple rhythmic pattern. Many references for folk dances classify the dances according to the basic step used. One of the guidelines for selecting a structured dance for a class is to review the

basic step in light of the students' developmental level. The step should already be part of the students' movement repertoire, and it should be easily modified so that all students can participate. The movement content of the dance should match the developmental level of the students to ensure that the class can learn the dance easily and practice it quickly with a sense of enjoyment and accomplishment.

Teaching Style and Method of Presentation

One teaching style that incorporates verbal cues with each step was developed by Phyllis S. Weikart (1989, 1997). She provides an excellent description of her teaching style, Say and Do, which involves verbalizing cue words as steps are performed. As well as capitalizing on the power of verbalizing the steps as they are performed, this procedure includes a developmental analysis of the movements included in folk dances. Dances are grouped developmentally into levels of motor difficulty.

The following list presents dances grouped according to general motor complexity. Developmental considerations include the difficulty of locomotor patterns, number of weight transfers, complexity of rhythm, and directional information (knowing left and right). Other factors such as previous motor experience, cultural differences, and levels of social development must be considered when selecting dances for a particular class.

Level 1 (kindergarten-grade 2)
>   Seven Jumps
>   Apat Apat
>   Irish Stew
>   Sneaky Snake
>   La Raspa

Level 2 (grades 3-5)
>   Close Encounters
>   Alley Cat
>   Hustle
>   Popcorn
>   Cotton-Eyed Joe

Level 3 (grade 6 and up)
>   Dirlada
>   Jambo
>   Mayim Mayim

Tarantella

Korobushka

Misirlou

Polka

Many international folk dances as well as American heritage dances may be accessed on YouTube or by searching online for "ethnic dances." Teachers and students may need to watch several YouTube presentations of a specific dance to find the most appropriate version. For example, keying in "Dirlada" may provide a dozen options, of which only two may show a version that matches the steps that you have selected to teach.

In respect to teaching styles that may be most appropriate for older students, Kassing and Jay (2003) provide a description of the inclusive teaching style, which is based on allowing students to work on variations of the content. This style can include using stations that allow students to work on variations of the steps. For example, some students might be refining the grapevine step at station 1 while other students who use wheelchairs are working at station 2, traveling forward on a curved path with a partner. The teacher can present options to the entire class or to small groups of students. Teaching variations of certain steps when presenting structured dances is an essential part of including all students.

The method of presentation will vary according to the features of the dance and the needs of the students. The teaching process outlined in the following list is primarily the add-on method. As the name implies, after specific steps are learned, remaining steps are added. Depending on the complexity of the dance and the developmental level of the students, use of the part–whole–part method might be appropriate. Regardless of presentation method, students need to hear the music and have opportunities to listen to the beat at the beginning of the lesson. For students who are Deaf or hard of hearing, the instructor should use visual cues. Also, sitting close to a speaker on the floor might allow these students to feel vibrations of the music. Clapping in time to the music emphasizes the underlying beat and can help students identify accented beats.

1. Students listen and clap or tap to the music. Emphasize the tempo and meter.

2. The teacher (or student leader) provides a brief demonstration of the dance with the musical accompaniment and introduces verbal cues. Students with visual differences can be paired with a peer who verbally describes the steps as performed by the instructor.

3. Introduce the basic step. This activity can serve as a warm-up. Demonstrate the step, facing the same direction as the students, and suggest a modification if needed. In circular formation or while traveling across the room, the class performs the step to music or a drumbeat.

4. If a difficult step is included, it can be pulled out of the entire sequence and taught separately. Modifications are explored and developed to match the students' developmental level. The step is practiced with music.

5. The remaining steps are combined, and the sequence is performed to music. Teacher cues (verbal and visual) and additional demonstrations are provided as needed.

Dance and Students With Autism

Often the unique behaviors of students with autism present significant challenges to physical and dance educators. A primary concern is that the environment and the procedures have not been adequately adapted so that these students can participate successfully. One physical activity program that offers a structure in which dance can be included is the Success in Physical Activity (SPA) program. As described by Schultheis, Boswell, and Decker (2000), SPA was based on adaptations of the Treatment and Education of Autistic and related Communication-handicapped CHildren (TEACCH) recreational program (Schopler, Mesibov, & Hearsey, 1995; Zikratch, 1997).

Dance has been integrated into this program by including an assigned dance step that is clearly defined and practiced for a specific amount of time in a designated location that is defined by room dividers. This is accomplished with student schedules that are posted at the entrance of the room. TEACCH schedules present each student's assigned activities and the order in which they are to be completed during that session. Upon arrival, each student is guided to check her individualized schedule and remove the top activity card. The activity card presents a symbol (photo of dance step being performed) and is color coded to correspond to the color posted at the dance station. The student goes to the dance station, places the activity card in the designated pocket folder, and completes the dance step for the prescribed amount of time. The time duration as well as the dance step is individualized to fit the student's abilities and preferences.

These activities may be completed independently, but assistance is provided as needed. At the dance station, an assistant sets a timer indicating the amount of time allotted, guides the student to follow the visual cues (color-coded feet cutouts), and if needed, provides assistance in turning on the music. For example, if the waltz step is the appropriate dance step, the cutouts are arranged on the floor to present the foot placement. After completing the waltz step, the student returns to the schedule board, removes the next activity card, and proceeds to the next dance station, which may be twisting or a single swing step. For a more detailed description of accommodations for unique characteristics of students with autism, please review the program suggestions of Schultheis, Boswell, and Decker (2000).

Problem Solving in Structured Dance

An inclusive teaching style used in teaching structured dances can be extended to incorporate a divergent teaching style. Kassing and Jay (2003) suggest that this extension could engage students in problem solving. In other words, students can work not only on learning different levels of the same combination but also on discovering new variations of the steps. Many students with physical disabilities can engage in problem solving to create their own movements that replace or add to the traditional steps. Once students understand the sequence of steps, the figures, and how the steps reflect the phrasing of the music, the teacher can use these as parameters in the movement problem.

To incorporate problem solving in teaching structured dances, the teacher must allow changes in the original dance that might alter the essential pattern and style. The teacher must carefully consider what changes are appropriate and set acceptable boundaries for changes to the dances. Changes that distort any semblance of the original pattern and style of the dance might not be acceptable. But if altering certain steps and eliminating others allows all students to participate with enthusiasm and to develop a love for movement and dance, the result likely outweighs the loss of authentic-

ity. See the following section on modifications for more details.

Modifications for Meeting Unique Needs

Possible ways to modify dances will evolve as the teacher and students engage in problem solving. The following questions are offered to encourage teachers to be inventive in the process. It is better to change certain aspects of the dance than to exclude any students or to abandon the dance altogether.

- If the dance consists of several sections, can a section be eliminated or shortened? Dancing only two of three sections might help students remember the dance and leave the class with a feeling of accomplishment.
- If the dance includes movements that require considerable balance skills, such as hops or jumps, how can these movements be modified? What movements can be substituted for them?
- Can the tempo of the music be slowed or can the movements be performed using twice as many counts? Acquiring a music player with variable speed control allows teachers to easily adjust the tempo of the music.
- If the dance includes a difficult turn, in what other ways can the turn be performed? What other movements might be substituted?

Participation in structured dances offers lifetime health and social benefits. Moving in unison with others to music should be a fun activity that students return to with pleasure and develop as a meaningful lifetime activity. Also, learning international folk dances provides excellent opportunities for students to increase their understanding of other cultures. Introductory information such as country of origin and cultural significance of the dance can be covered quickly and reinforced through handouts.

The following sample lesson was designed for any students who have responded successfully to changing tempos while performing nonlocomotor and locomotor movements (figure 24.5). These students can dance with a partner or small group and follow simple sequences of movements performed to an external rhythm. Although the content is primarily structured dance, the lesson includes opportunities for rhythmic development.

Sample Lesson: Structured Dance

Student Objectives

1. Demonstrate the basic step, the schottische, to a steady external beat.
2. Demonstrate two of the three sections of the African Creole folk dance, Bele Kawe, with music.
3. Explore variations for the movements in the third section of Bele Kawe, the four-count turn or jump.

Warm-Up Activity: Movements to "Happiness Runs in a Circular Motion"

Instructions: Students listen to the song ("Happiness Runs in a Circular Motion") and sway side to side in rhythm to the four simple lines of verse. The teacher asks students to watch as she demonstrates a basic step, the schottische, composed of three walking steps and a hop. She repeats the schottische step several times and then asks the students to perform the step (or an appropriate variation) with her without the music. To practice with music, students divide into two or three groups to form small circles. Each circle travels forward on the circular path, in the same direction, repeating the schottische step (or an appropriate modification) to music.

Communicate Goals of the Lesson to Students

Perform two of the three sections of Bele Kawe with a small group to music. Explore variations of the step that includes a turn or jump.

Sequence of Activities

1. Listen to the music for Bele Kawe and clap or tap in sync with the beat.

2. Students learn part 1. Facing the same direction as the students, the instructor demonstrates a simple version of the step–touch. Beginning with either foot, the first step is forward and the other foot touches (no transfer of weight) close to the first; then the step–touch is repeated to the back. In circular formation, the class practices the step with the instructor and then performs the step to music.

3. Students use the same procedure for learning part 2, touch heel–step. Students touch the heel of the foot forward, then step with the same foot. They alternate feet and practice in circular formation with the teacher.

4. Students practice parts 1 and 2 to music.

5. The teacher demonstrates the three-step turn or jump and asks students to brainstorm variations for this movement. Examples of variations include performing the basic schottische step forward (four counts) and backward (four counts) or repeating the step for two sets of eight counts.

6. Students independently explore variations for the third section and select one to perform to music.

7. The students divide into groups of six to eight, share their variations, and select the best fit to the music.

Closure

The class performs the schottische step to contemporary music with a moderate or slow tempo in a circular path. The teacher slows the tempo and asks the class to use walking steps as she reviews the purpose of the lesson.

FIGURE 24.5 This lesson focuses on structured dance, but it also includes opportunities for rhythmic development.

SUMMARY

The guiding theme of this chapter is that rhythmic movement and dance are powerful content areas for developing problem solving, creative expression, and motor skills of students with and without disabilities. Rhythmic movement can be considered the beginning point for dance, a beginning that is strengthened through participation in CED and structured dance. Structured dances enable teachers to involve students quickly in physical activity and provide meaningful opportunities to learn a lifetime physical activity. Although the content of these movement forms can be taught separately, each can lead into the others, thus resulting in a more powerful medium for strengthening student development. This chapter also emphasized that the content of CED can be extended into exploration of the basic effort actions. This expansion of content provides opportunities for students to refine their ability to communicate through movement; it also provides opportunities for teachers to re-envision movements associated with disabilities as potential sources of artistic material.

REFERENCES

Blom, L.A., & Chaplin, T.L. (1982). *The intimate act of choreography*. London: Dance Books.

Boswell, B., & Vidret, M. (1993). Rhythmic movement and music for adolescents with severe and profound disabilities. *Music Therapy Perspectives, 11*, 37-41.

Elin, J., & Boswell, B. (2004). *Re-envisioning dance: Aesthetics of disability*. Dubuque, IA: Kendall Hunt.

Graham, G., Holt/Hale, S., & Parker, M. (2007). *Children moving: A reflective approach to teaching physical education* (7th ed.). New York: McGraw-Hill.

Humphrey, D. (1980). *The art of making dances*. New York: Grove Press.

Joyce, M. (1994). *First steps in teaching creative dance to children* (3rd ed.). Palo Alto, CA: Mayfield.

Kassing, G., & Jay, D.M. (2003). *Dance teaching methods and curriculum design*. Champaign, IL: Human Kinetics.

Pittman, A.M., Waller, M.S., & Dark, C.L. (2009). *Dance awhile: A handbook for folk, square, contra, and social dance*. San Francisco: Pearson Benjamin Cummings.

Preston-Dunlop, V. (1990). *Modern educational dance* (rev. ed.). Boston: Plays Inc.

Schopler, E., Mesibov, G.B., & Hearsey, K. (1995). Structured teaching in the TEACCH system. In E. Scholper & G.B. Mesibov (Eds.), *Learning and cognition in autism* (pp. 243-267). New York: Plenum Press.

Schultheis, S., Boswell B., Decker, J. (2000). Successful physical activity programming for students with autism. *Focus on Autism and Other Developmental Disabilities, 15* (3), 159-162.

Smith-Autard, J.M. (2000). *Dance composition* (4th ed.). London: Routledge.

Weikart, P.S. (1989). *Teaching movement and dance* (3rd ed.). Ypsilanti, MI: High Scope Press.

Weikart, P.S. (1997). *Teaching folk dance: Successful steps*. Ypsilanti, MI: High Scope Press.

Zikratch, H. (1997). TEACCH training and structured recreation. Presentation given at the Riverside Unified School District teacher training, Riverside, CA.

25

Aquatics

Monica Lepore

Jack is an eight-year-old boy needing full physical assistance to participate in his general physical education class. Jack's parents have asked the school district for a physical education assessment to determine if Jack is benefiting from his current support and placement. Jack's parents have noticed that he exhibits more independence when placed in a flotation device in his backyard pool than he does anywhere else. Thus, they have asked that a swimming component be part of the assessment.

During the land portion of the physical education assessment, it is evident that Jack cannot participate in physical activities without adult intervention. He is unable to consistently perform voluntary movements against gravity and cannot raise his heart rate unless physically assisted. In contrast, during the pool assessment, Jack is able to raise his heart rate by 40 beats per minute using a head–neck flotation device without teacher intervention. In addition, he continually moves his arms and legs for nine minutes without prompting. On the basis of this information, Jack's individualized education program (IEP) committee has decided that he should receive adapted aquatics instruction at the expense of the school district in addition to general physical education instruction.

I t is apparent from the preceding scenario that adapted aquatics instruction can be a needed complement to a land-based adapted physical education program. The purpose of this chapter is to identify the benefits of aquatics, illustrate the best practices in adapted aquatics, and provide information for meeting the needs of students with disabilities in aquatics programs.

BENEFITS OF ADAPTED AQUATICS

Swimming and aquatic activities for children with disabilities can foster physical fitness and motor skill development within a physical education program and during recreational pursuits. In the opening scenario, Jack's parents are within their legal rights to request swimming as part of their son's IEP because aquatics is listed as a component of physical education under the Individuals with Disabilities Education Act (IDEA). Aquatics instruction for students with disabilities is neither a luxury nor a therapeutic (related) service. **Adapted aquatics** means modifying the aquatic teaching environment, skills, facilities, equipment, and instructional strategies for people with disabilities. It can include aquatic activities of all types, including instructional and competitive swimming, small-craft boating, water aerobics, and skin diving or scuba diving (AAHPERD-AAALF, 1996).

Physical educators, school administrators, parents, related service personnel, and special education teachers must be educated about the benefits of aquatics and its role in a child's physical education. The physical and psychosocial benefits of aquatics for students with disabilities are more pronounced and significant than for students without disabilities. Because of the buoyancy afforded by water, many people whose disabilities impair mobility on land can function independently in an aquatic environment without the assistance of braces, crutches, walkers, or wheelchairs. Although adapted aquatics does not focus on therapeutic water exercise, warm water facilitates muscle relaxation, joint range of motion (ROM), and improved muscle strength and endurance (Koury, 1996). Swimming strengthens muscles that enhance the postural stability necessary for locomotor and object-control skills. Water supports the body, enabling a person to possibly walk for the first time, thus increasing strength for ambulation on land. Adapted aquatics also enhances breath control and cardiorespiratory fitness. Blowing bubbles, holding one's breath, and inhalation and exhalation during the rhythmic breathing of swimming strokes improve respiratory function and oral motor control, aiding in speech development (Martin, 1983; see figure 25.1).

Benefits are not limited to the physical realm. Water activities that are carefully planned and implemented to meet individual needs provide an environment that contributes to psychosocial and cognitive development. As a student with a physical disability learns to move through the water without assistance, self-esteem and self-awareness improve. Moreover, the freedom of movement made possible by water boosts morale and provides an incentive to maximize potential in other aspects of rehabilitation (Koury, 1996).

The motivational and therapeutic properties of water provide a stimulating learning environment. Some instructors even reinforce academic learning, successfully integrating cognitive concepts during water games and activities centered on math, spelling, reading, and other concepts. Participants might count laps, dive for submerged plastic letters, or read their workouts from a whiteboard. These types of activities also help participants improve judgment and orientation to the surrounding environment.

GENERAL TEACHING SUGGESTIONS

Each person is unique, and individualization is the key to safe, effective, and relevant programming. Thus, it should never be assumed that all characteristics associated with a disability are endemic to each person with that diagnosis. Generalizations merely present a wide scope of information that might pertain to swimmers with any particular disability. Each swimmer should be taught sufficient safety and swimming skills to become as safe and comfortable as possible during aquatic activities. Choice and presentation of skills should be tailored to meet the needs of each individual (Lepore, Gayle, & Stevens, 2007).

Before instruction begins, the teacher must gather information from written, oral, and observational sources. In addition to reading previous records and interviewing the swimmer and significant others, an aquatic assessment must be conducted to determine present level of functioning. General instructional suggestions include writing long-term goals and short-term performance objectives, task analyzing aquatic skills, determining proper lift and transfer methods, establishing communication signals, and developing holding and positioning techniques to facilitate instruction. Knowledge of typical growth and developmental patterns is helpful in understanding the difference between movements that are developmentally inappropriate and movements that have just not developed yet. For example, doing a bicycle kick is a developmentally appropriate sequence for most children who are learning to swim, but after more experience and decreased fear, this type of kick is inappropriate during freestyle movements.

Teaching basic safety skills first, such as mouth closure, rolling over from front to back, changing directions, recovering from falling into the pool, vertical recovery from front and back positions, and holding onto the pool wall, helps to alleviate fear of more difficult skills. A balanced body position in the water is an important prerequisite for skills. The instructor must experiment with horizontal and vertical rotation and appropriate placement of arms, legs, and head to teach the development of proper buoyancy, balance, and water comfort in relation to the student's unique physical characteristics. One method of teaching balance and body positions in adapted aquatics is the Halliwick method (Stanat & Lambeck, 2001).

Finally, presenting swimming cues in a concise manner and connected to something that the student already is familiar with strengthens learning. Because swimming takes place in a unique setting, swimmers with disabilities need cues that refer to situations or movements they already know or know how to do. An example is using the phrase, "Move your hands as if you are opening and closing curtains," to depict the movement of the hands while treading water or sculling.

AQUATIC ASSESSMENT

Individualized instructional planning begins with defining which skills a participant needs to learn and assessing the present level of performance in those skills. Before performing the assessment, an instructor should determine the skills to be

FIGURE 25.1 Breath-control exercises help improve oral motor control.

assessed. To help prioritize skills, questions such as these should be asked of the participant or caregiver:

- What is the participant interested in learning?
- What are important safety skills for the participant to acquire?
- Where will the participant use the skills outside of class?
- What are same-age peers performing in aquatics?
- What equipment does the family have available?
- What are the medical, therapeutic, educational, and recreational needs of the participant?

After looking at all the possible skills that are important for a participant, the instructor looks at the list to determine if there are any repeat skills. Skills common to many of the questions just listed should become the priorities to assess (and then be taught, if they are lacking). Assessment items that determine the present level of performance in these skills should be developed (Block, 2007).

Swimming instructors typically use curriculum-based or ecologically based assessment checklists or rubrics to determine the extent of a student's aquatic skills (figure 25.2). Curriculum-based assessment items include skills that the swimmer needs to function effectively within an integrated class. The American Red Cross progressive swim levels (American Red Cross, 2004), YMCA swim levels (YMCA, 1999b), and SwimAmerica programs (SwimAmerica, n.d.) are examples of curricula from which a swim instructor would draw skills for a curriculum-based assessment checklist.

An ecologically based aquatic assessment might also be considered. Ecologically based assessments include skills needed for a person's current and future environment. Aquatic skill assessments of this nature might include components of the curriculum-based assessment but also include skills not addressed in the regular curriculum, such as entering and exiting the pool area, dressing, using appropriate language in a swim group, performing stretching exercises before swimming, knowing how to swim in a lane, using a flotation device, or clearing the mouth of water. These are skills that need to be learned but would not usually appear within a regular swim curriculum because they are prerequisite skills that are typically acquired through incidental learning before formal swim

lessons commence. Ecologically based assessments are recommended to assess all areas of the aquatic experience. These assessments should be developed based on individual needs.

ADAPTING SWIMMING SKILLS

Before adapting skills to meet a student's needs, the instructor must first look at why the skill is needed and how and where the skill will be used. Some swimmers might want to pass the competencies for the American Red Cross swim levels, some might want to improve cardiorespiratory functioning, and yet others might want to enter a swim meet. These differing purposes for performing the front crawl (freestyle) might cause an instructor to take a different approach to adapting strokes and other aquatic skills. Important considerations in adapting strokes include the following:

- What are the physical constraints of the disability?
- What is the most efficient way to propel through the water, given the constraints?
- What movements will cause or diminish pain or injury?
- What adaptations can be used to make the stroke or skill as much like the nonadapted version as possible?
- What equipment is available to facilitate the skill?
- Why does the swimmer want to learn this skill (competition, relaxation)?

The instructor might need to
- adjust the swimmer's body position by adding flotation or light weights,
- change the propulsive action of the arms or legs, or
- adapt the breathing pattern.

Adjusting the swimmer's body position is typical for people who have disabilities such as cerebral palsy (CP), stroke, traumatic brain injury, spina bifida, obesity, limb loss, muscular dystrophy, post-polio syndrome, or traumatic spinal cord injury. Because of variations from the norm in regard to muscle mass and body fat in many people with physical disabilities, the center of gravity and center of buoyancy might be atypical. It is important to find an efficient body position and experiment

Aquatic Skill Evaluation Chart

Student: _____

Scoring codes:

O = cannot perform   V = needs verbal cues to perform   G = needs gesture cues to perform
I = independent   PC = needs picture cues to perform   P = needs physical cues to perform

• More than one code might describe a step (e.g., V, PC).

Target steps and skills	Date/scoring
I. Entries	
▸ Ladder entry	_____
▸ Stomach slide in	_____
▸ Jump: shallow	_____
▸ Jump: deep	_____
▸ Dive: kneel	_____
▸ Dive: compact	_____
▸ Dive: stride	_____
▸ Dive: standing	_____
II. Exits	
▸ Ladder	_____
▸ Pull-up (side of pool)	_____
III. Water orientation	
▸ Washes face	_____
▸ Puts chin in water	_____
▸ Puts mouth in water	_____
▸ Puts mouth and nose in water	_____
▸ Puts face in water	_____
▸ Puts whole body in water	_____
▸ Blows bubbles	_____
▸ Blows bubbles with face in water	_____
▸ Blows bubbles lying on front with face in water	_____
▸ Blows bubbles with full body underwater	_____
▸ Bobs 5 times in shallow water	_____
▸ Bobs 10 times in shallow water	_____
▸ Bobs 5 times in deep water	_____
▸ Bobs 10 times in deep water	_____
IV. Front propulsion	
▸ Pushes off side with face out of water	_____
▸ Pushes off side with face in water	_____

Target steps and skills	Date/scoring
▸ Pushes off side with face in water and kicks	_____
▸ Arm stroke while walking	_____
▸ Arm stroke with underwater recovery (5 ft or 1.5 m)	_____
▸ Arm stroke with underwater recovery, face in water (5 ft or 1.5 m)	_____
▸ Arm stroke with underwater recovery, face in, kicking (10 ft or 3 m)	_____
▸ Arm stroke with over-water recovery (10 ft or 3 m)	_____
▸ Arm stroke with kick (20 ft or 6 m)	_____
▸ Front crawl with rhythmic breathing to front (20 ft or 6 m)	_____
▸ Front crawl with breathing to side (20 ft or 6 m)	_____
V. Breaststroke	
▸ Push-off in streamlined position for beginning breaststroke	_____
▸ Breaststroke arms (on deck)	_____
▸ Breaststroke arms while standing in water	_____
▸ Breaststroke arms over a noodle (30 ft or 9 m)	_____
▸ Breaststroke kick correctly on deck (5 times)	_____
▸ Breaststroke kick over a noodle (30 ft or 9 m)	_____
▸ Breaststroke combined arms and kick (30 ft or 9 m)	_____
VI. Back propulsion	
▸ Back float (5 sec)	_____
▸ Back glide off wall with a noodle	_____
▸ Back glide (10 ft or 3 m)	_____

(continued)

FIGURE 25.2 This checklist helps instructors determine a student's aquatic skills.

From J. Winnick, ed. 2011, *Adapted physical education and sport, fifth edition* (Champaign, IL: Human Kinetics).

Aquatic Skill Evaluation Chart   *(continued)*

▸ Back glide with kick (20 ft or 6 m)   _____

▸ Back glide with finning
   or sculling (10 ft or 3 m)   _____

▸ Back crawl arms (on deck)   _____

▸ Back crawl arms over a noodle   _____

▸ Back crawl arms with kick
   (20 ft or 6 m)   _____

VII. Side propulsion

▸ Sidestroke glide   _____

▸ Sidestroke legs (on deck)   _____

▸ Sidestroke legs while holding
   a noodle (20 ft or 6 m)   _____

▸ Sidestroke arms (on deck)   _____

▸ Sidestroke arms with a noodle
   (20 ft or 6 m)   _____

▸ Sidestroke (30 ft 9 m)   _____

FIGURE 25.2   *(continued)*

From J. Winnick, ed. 2011, *Adapted physical education and sport, fifth edition* (Champaign, IL: Human Kinetics).

with flotation devices and weights (e.g., scuba diving and ankle weights, inflatable arm floaties, foam swim noodles, rescue tubes, life jackets, ski belts). A body position close to horizontal is the most streamlined and effective.

The swimmer's arm and leg actions might need to be adjusted as well. Typical propulsive action might not be feasible because of contractures, muscle atrophy, or missing limbs. Adaptations such as changing the ideal *S* curve of the arms in the front crawl to a modified *C* or *J* should be experimented with. Lower-body propulsive adaptations might include bending the knees more during flutter kicking, using the scissors kick while breathing in the front crawl, or using fins while doing the dolphin kick during any of the strokes.

Breathing patterns can be changed from one-side breathing to alternate-side breathing, front breathing, rolling over onto the back to breathe, or using a snorkel. Swimmers can be taught explosive breathing, breathing using the mouth only, or breathing using a closed-throat technique. Finally, nonphysical adaptations include developmentally appropriate progressions, frequent practice of skills, detailed traditional and ecological task analysis (ETA), verbal and visual cues, repeating of directions, and altered skill objectives.

ORIENTATION TO WATER

Acquisition of aquatic skills is based on the learner's readiness to receive the skill, readiness to understand the goal, opportunities to practice at a challenging but manageable level, and ability to receive feedback. Orientation to water focuses on the readiness of the learner and other psychological and physiological factors. Physiological factors are those in which anatomical and physiological variations in the body affect how and what the person learns. This includes how disability and medication affect each body system. A swimmer might not be neurologically ready to perform a skill because of brain damage, lack of central nervous system maturity, or developmental delays. When the instructor understands the effect of a disability on learning and provides developmentally appropriate skill progressions, learning increases (Langendorfer & Bruya, 1995).

Psychologically, each person is unique and learns at an individual rate, depending on several psychological factors. People with disabilities might have psychological characteristics that hinder the acquisition of aquatic skills. Certain psychological factors, such as anxiety and cognitive readiness, should be examined before developing instructional strategies.

Most anxiety during swim instruction stems from fear and discomfort and inhibits mental adjustment to the aquatic environment. Although mental adjustment takes time for new or frightened swimmers, it might be even more difficult for students with disabilities. Poor breath control as a consequence of oral muscle dysfunction, asthma, or high- or low-muscle tone limits the ability to develop breath holding and rhythmic breathing. These and other issues, such as not being able to grasp and hold the pool gutter, make it likely that some people with disabilities are at high risk of having fear and anxiety affect their openness to learning.

Factors that might cause anxiousness include fear of drowning, past frightening water experiences, submerging unexpectedly and choking on water, fear reinforced by warnings (e.g., "Don't go near that water or you'll drown"), capsizing in a boat, being knocked down by a wave, or feelings of insecurity caused by poor physical ability or unfamiliar surroundings (Lepore et al., 2007). Fear stimulates physiological responses, such as heightened muscle tone, increased involuntary muscle movements, and inability to float. In short, fear and insecurity prevent success in swimming. Helping participants get past fear and anxiety to practice aquatic skills that will make them safer in the water is an initial step in teaching swimming. When participants are free of fear, they are free to learn. The following tips, taken from the YMCA's *Parent/Child and Preschool Aquatic Program Manual* (1999a), will promote comfort and reduce fear. These suggestions can be used for participants of all ages:

- Allow reluctant participants extra time for water-acclimation activities.
- Use patience without pampering.
- Gently guide; don't force.
- Explain everything in a calm, quiet, matter-of-fact voice.
- Teach in shallow water (e.g., on pool steps, water tables, or water docks) or on a gradually sloping ramp.
- Emphasize noncompetitive activities.
- Provide a mask or goggles if water in the eyes is an issue.
- Redirect crying or anxious behaviors by using a colorful piece of equipment or discussing the swimmer's favorite food.
- Use the swimmer's name frequently; smile and praise small steps in the progression of water adjustment.
- Assess a student's readiness for swim lessons using a tool such as the Aquatic Readiness Assessment by Langendorfer and Bruya (1995). Areas to assess with this tool are water entry, breath control, buoyancy and body position, arm actions, leg actions, and combined movements.

Fear is diminished when the instructor and swimmer easily communicate. In addition to communication skills, a thorough understanding of participant positioning, guiding, and supporting is essential. Proper methods of transferring, touching, and supporting participants in the locker room, on the pool deck, and in the pool will also develop relationships based on trust. Knowing how to use the adapted equipment, wheelchairs, and flotation devices provides an atmosphere of efficiency and safety that makes everyone feel comfortable. Like-

wise, holding someone with a firm and balanced grip as close as safety and comfort allow communicates care and establishes trust and rapport (Lepore et al., 2007). In addition, an environment in which the instructor exhibits a consistent personality, provides discipline methods that are flexible but consistent, uses caring verbal assurances, and provides balanced, controlled physical handling promotes trust, security, and mental adjustment.

The instructor should use fun activities instead of drills to promote a more comfortable atmosphere. Games, music, and props help a fearful student become more ready to accept the aquatic setting. Activities such as a flower hunt with plastic flowers inserted into the gutters help acclimate the fearful student in a nonthreatening manner. Other activities include square dance and social dance; physical education games, such as cooperative musical chairs using hoops; land games; and activities such as basketball and sponge tossing to inflatable tubes. These activities build on familiar activities, and the instructor can progress from there.

FACILITY AND EQUIPMENT CONSIDERATIONS

For participants and instructors alike, facilities and equipment must be accessible and safe and lend themselves to successful, satisfying experiences. Familiarity with the Americans with Disability Act (ADA) accessibility guidelines (ATBCB, 2004), state and local health codes for aquatic facilities, and resources for equipment and supplies that promote aquatic participation (see the references and resources of this chapter) help provide quality swimming experiences.

Facilities

Facility characteristics should be discussed with the participant before the first session. This discussion should center on information about the locker room, pool deck, and pool itself. Locker rooms can cause frustration for people with disabilities. Factors such as shower handles and locker shelves too high for people with dwarfism, inadequate lighting for people with visual impairment, and combination-only lockers that impede people with arthritis do not motivate people to use a facility. Other factors inhibiting independence include benches cemented into the floor in front of lockers, shower-area ledges or lips that limit access for participants in wheelchairs, and lack of Braille signs on lockers, entrances, and exits. Since the Architectural and Transportation Barriers Compliance Board (ATBCB) published their final ruling on accessibility and recreation facilities, it is easier to know exactly what facilities meet the standards (ATBCB, 2004).

Facility design must enable participants to make transitions between the locker area, pool deck, and water. Newly designed, newly constructed, or significantly altered pools must have at least one primary means of access (lift or sloped entry) plus a secondary means of access if the pool has over 300 linear feet (91 m) of pool wall or if access is limited to one place (e.g., a lazy-river pool at a water park) (Brown, 2003). A lift (figure 25.3*a*) or sloped entry (figure 25.3*b*) is called a primary means of access; secondary means can be a lift, a sloped entry, a transfer wall (see figure 25.3*c*), a

transfer system (see figure 25.3*d*), or pool stairs that meet the ADA code (Scott, 2003). A sloped entry (wet ramp) connects the deck directly to the water through a gradual-slope entry ramp. It has handrails and a flat landing area at the bottom.

Another primary means for access could be a lift (which is generally categorized as equipment and thus is covered in the next section). Secondary access to the pool may be provided via one of the means just mentioned or by a transfer wall, a transfer system, or pool stairs (not the ladders built into the walls of the pool). A transfer wall (sometimes called a *dry ramp* because it is outside the pool on the deck) is constructed so that the deck of the pool slopes down below the pool edge so that it is flush with the wheelchair seat. This method of access is the least used because of its limitations for exiting the pool and the extensive strength and stability required to use it. Another

a

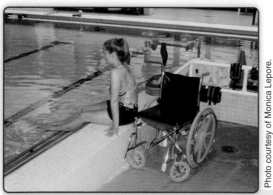

c

Photo courtesy of Monica Lepore.

b

Photo courtesy of Monica Lepore.

d

Photo courtesy of Monica Lepore.

FIGURE 25.3 *(a)* Lifts are a primary means of access according to the ADA guidelines. *(b)* Gradual-slope entry is a primary means of access. *(c)* A dry ramp provides access to a transfer ledge. *(d)* A transfer system can be a secondary means of access.

means of access is a transfer system (discussed in the equipment section). Gradually sloping steps are a helpful adaptation for many pool participants. They are either built into the pool or are portable and placed into the pool as needed. These steps must meet the ADA accessibility guidelines for depth, height, and width.

Facilities already in existence can use any or all of the access means mentioned here to make reasonable accommodations to remove existing architectural and service barriers. New guidelines will set a high standard for reasonable accommodations (ATBCB, 2004), so facility managers would be prudent to develop a long-term barrier-removal plan to bring their pool up to code.

In addition to the structure and architecture, pool temperature and chemical composition must be compatible with the groups it serves. In general, children with disabilities perform better with water temperature between 86 and 90 degrees Fahrenheit (30 and 32 degrees C); air temperature should be about 4 degrees higher. Participants should be made aware of the type of water purification used because some people have chemical sensitivity to chlorine.

Equipment

Appropriate equipment and supplies are even more important for classes serving people with disabilities than for the general population. Adapted equipment is often necessary for entry and exit, safety, maintenance of a proper body position in the water, arm and leg propulsion, fitness purposes, and motivation.

Safe entrances and exits are crucial to accessible swim instruction. In addition to the method of entry afforded by the facility design, lifts, portable ramps, stairs, and transfer systems are important items for entrance and exit when equipment is not built into the facility. Lifts often provide primary access to pools for people with severe orthopedic disabilities (figure 25.3a). A lift is a pneumatic, water-powered, mechanical, or fully automated electrical assistive device that permits a user to transfer from a wheelchair to a seat or sling and move from deck to pool using little strength. According to the newest guidelines (ATBCB, 2004), the lift must be capable of unassisted operation from both deck and water levels and should have a hard plastic seat with a backrest rather than a sling (cloth) seat. Independent usage is best facilitated when hand controls are located at the front edge of the seat, are operational with one hand, do not require tight grasping, and require 5 pounds (2.25 kg) or less of force to operate.

Portable ramps and gradual steps have been used for many years to offer access to pools when the facility design does not provide any other means of access. These items take up extra room on the deck when they are removed and do not provide the most independent access (because users need to rely on staff to place them in the water when needed). Portable equipment also breaks more frequently as a result of wear and tear from removal and storage.

For people who have good upper-body function but cannot negotiate stairs or ladders because of lower-body involvement, a transfer system often allows more independent pool access. A transfer system is a platform 19 by 24 inches (48 by 61 cm) wide and 16 to 19 inches (41-48 cm) above deck (see figure 25.3d). This platform is connected to a series of steps (14-17 in. [36-43 cm] deep by 24 in. [61 cm] wide) that participants use to gradually lower themselves into the water from the chair to the platform to each step. The process is reversed for exiting.

Another useful piece of equipment is an aquatic chair with push rims, especially if the pool has a gradually sloped ramp as its primary means of access. Aquatic facilities should provide an aquatic wheelchair that can be used on the sloped entrance because personal wheelchairs are not appropriate for submersion.

Safety equipment is mandatory to an adapted aquatics program. It includes typical rescue equipment, a floor covering to decrease slippage, closed-cell foam mats for use during seizures, and transfer mats to cover pool gutters.

Equipment used to maintain body position is the most prominent equipment typically seen in an adapted aquatics program. Support equipment useful in an adapted swim program might include personal flotation devices (PFDs), foam noodles, sectional rafts, and flotation collars. A large variety of flotation devices, including PFDs, water wings, pull buoys, dumbbell floats, and sectional rafts, give an extra hand when working with people who are dependent on others to stay above the water. Flotation devices can ensure safety (if they are Coast Guard–approved PFDs) and might also reduce or even eliminate fear. Because flotation devices help to support, stabilize, and facilitate movement, they open a new world to people with mobility impairments, allowing freedom of movement not possible on land.

Although flotation devices are useful, they might pose certain concerns. For example, they might impair independence if swimmers rely on them too long after they should have progressed to independent, unaided swimming. Also, devices typically tested on people without disabilities often fall short of their goal when used with swimmers who have atypical body postures, uneven muscle development or tone, or poor head control. Thus, if students use flotation devices for support, proper supervision must be provided, even if the PFDs are Coast Guard approved. Generally speaking, each person with a disability has unique needs and thus it is difficult to make blanket statements or recommendations regarding safety and buoyancy. It is important to know each swimmer's abilities. In addition, an assessment should be performed to determine body control and horizontal balance through experimentation (under supervision) with buoyancy and floating in various positions. Buoyancy can be used to resist or assist movement or to support the swimmer (Koury, 1996).

Propulsion equipment affords participants with a disability the ability to move in ways they might not be able to on land. Propulsion is affected by variances in streamlined position, difficulty with horizontal and lateral body positions, inadequate strength, poor ROM, atypical buoyancy, and other factors, including poor coordination and disproportionate body shape contributing to drag (Prins & Murata, 2008). The first step to efficient propulsion is to put the body in the most streamlined and balanced position possible, using other support as necessary. If the participant is still having difficulty with propulsion, try other devices such as hand paddles and fins to increase surface area for pressing against the water for propulsive efficiency. Remember that in official competition, these devices are not allowed. Those who have part or all of their arms missing might be able to use a swimming hand prosthesis or Plexiglas paddles attached to the residual limb segment. For ideas and possible uses of these devices, see Paciorek and Jones (2001) and Summerford (1993).

An increased interest in water fitness has resulted in a greater diversity of fitness supplies. Underwater treadmills, aquacycles, water workout stations, and aqua exercise steps provide cardiorespiratory conditioning, muscle toning, and strength training. Water fitness participants also use supportive and resistive equipment and supplies in the water that are handheld, pushed, or pulled, including finger and hand paddles, balance-bar floats, upright flotation vests and wraps, aqua shoes, webbed gloves, waterproof ankle and wrist weights, workout fins, buoyancy cuffs, water-ski belts, aqua collars, and water jogging belts.

Motivational equipment provides swimmers of all ages the push necessary to attempt and complete tasks that might be otherwise overwhelming or boring. The developmental levels, interests, and attention spans of participants in adapted aquatics require a unique approach to instruction and recreation. Attractive, brightly colored equipment; nontoxic, sturdy supplies; toys; flotation devices; and balls enhance instructional strategies that focus on fun. Other devices include swim belts, bubbles, and foam squares, many of which come with modules to increase or decrease flotation. Water logs (i.e., water noodles, woggles) are hefty, flexible buoyant logs that encourage water exploration and kicking in a fun way.

MEETING PARTICIPANTS' UNIQUE NEEDS

To meet the needs of a variety of people in providing safe, effective, and relevant aquatic opportunities, it is necessary to know the unique attributes of learners. However, it is important not to assume that these attributes apply to every person in an identified category. Suggestions for teaching people with intellectual disabilities, visual impairments, or deafness are quite similar to land-based teaching tips; thus, readers can generalize the information in chapters 8 through 13 to an aquatic setting.

Participants With Cerebral Palsy

People with CP exhibit a variety of skills depending on the type and severity of CP and the body parts affected. See the tips in the sidebar for teaching swimming to students with CP.

Participants With Orthopedic Disabilities

Although people with orthopedic disabilities have a range of characteristics, certain similarities can be considered within the aquatic environment. Balance, buoyancy, body position, and ROM might be affected. People with arthrogryposis, amputations, dwarfism, spina bifida, spinal cord injuries, osteogenesis imperfecta, traumatic brain injury, stroke, spinal cord injury, orthopedic disabilities, multiple sclerosis, muscular dystrophy, or myasthenia gravis might benefit from the teaching tips in the sidebar on page 492.

Suggestions for Teaching Swimming to Participants With Cerebral Palsy

- Many stroke adaptations are based on limited ROM; try having the person use an underwater versus out-of-water recovery of the arms, especially for the front crawl.

- Maintain water temperature between 86 and 90 degrees Fahrenheit (30 and 32 degrees C) and air temperature 4 degrees higher than the water temperature.

- Guard against sudden submersion of the face; people with CP often have a weak cough and cannot clear water from the throat effectively.

- Consider hand paddles for participants with wrist flexion contractures.

- Develop strokes executed in the back-lying position, eliminating the need for head control with rhythmic breathing.

- While in a prone position, have the participant wear a ski belt or rescue tube across the chest and under the armpits (with closing clip on back) to elevate the chest and face.

For people with primitive reflex retention, the following suggestions apply:

- Sudden noises, movements, or splashing may cause sudden reflex activity, possibly causing the participant to lose a safe position. Maintain a position at or near the participant's head to prevent sudden submersion.

- Consider allowing participants to wear a flotation collar to hold their heads above water.

- Neck hyperextension or turning of the head to the side may affect arm and leg control in swimmers with reflex retention. Encourage a full-body roll for breathing or the use of a snorkel.

- Avoid quick movements and sudden hands-on and hands-off movements. Slow movements and a steady touch are best with swimmers who have high muscle tone.

- Be aware of sudden spastic movements during transfers in and out of the pool. Have adequate personnel for transfers and use a mat under the transfer area.

- Encourage participants to flex their heads slightly while on their backs. When the head is in extension while lying on the back, the mouth tends to open and the arms tend to extend.

- Keep the participant stable; unstable positions in the water or a feeling of falling causes the body to stiffen, the arms and legs to involuntarily extend and flex, and the mouth to open.

- Use positions that inhibit reflexes, such as a neutral or slightly tucked chin and the head in midline of the shoulders. Hips and knees should be slightly flexed.

- Use symmetrical activities as much as possible (both sides of the body doing the same thing at the same time) such as the breaststroke, elementary backstroke, inverted breaststroke, finning, or sculling.

- Use caution with the scissors kick and the flutter kick because they promote the crossed extension reflex, causing scissoring of the legs. If scissoring occurs, place a comfortable piece of cushioning between the knees during swimming.

Participants Who Are Seizure Prone

Participants with seizure disorders need instructors who have a plan of action in case of a seizure incident. Current practice suggests that steps be taken to ensure that the person having the seizure has an open airway and is protected from physical injury caused by contact with other people or objects and water ingestion or aspiration. When in doubt, always activate the emergency medical system (EMS). This section describes how to manage a seizure effectively.

The first-aid objectives for assisting a person having a seizure in the pool are to keep the face above the water, to maintain an open airway, and

Suggestions for Teaching Swimming to Participants With Orthopedic Disabilities

- Use in-water benches or docks for people with fatigue or who have short stature and cannot stand on the bottom of the pool.

- Look for ways to streamline the body, such as changing head position or attaching flotation devices or weights to lower or raise body position. Achieve a balanced body position by experimenting within proper safety limits.

- Check skin for abrasions before and after swimming if the person has decreased sensation.

- Encourage use of aqua shoes to decrease lesions caused by transferring and scraping the feet when swimming.

- Be aware that muscle spasms and strange sensations may sometimes interrupt the aquatic session.

- Become knowledgeable about proper assistance in taking off and putting on braces and other orthotic devices.

- Alter stroke mechanics as necessary for uneven muscle strength and abnormal centers of gravity and buoyancy. Change strokes as little as possible from normal efficiency. If necessary, use smaller ROM or sculling arm movements with participants.

- If upper-body impairment causes difficulty in lifting the head to breathe, a participant should use a mask and snorkel or roll over onto the back to breathe. Initially, teach the back crawl or elementary backstroke.

- Ensure that all excretion collection bags are emptied before swimming.

- Allow the participant to wear a neoprene vest or wet suit to keep warm in cooler pools.

- Provide assistance for balance problems while on deck.

to prevent injury by providing support with a minimal amount of restraint. One position that meets these objectives is standing low in the water behind the person's head and placing the body in a supine position. Then support the person under the armpits, shoulders, and head. Provide only the support needed to keep the participant's face out of the water; unnecessary restraint might cause injury to the participant or instructor. Remove the person from the water as soon as it is safe to do so. Do not allow the person to remain in the pool if the seizure lasts for more than several minutes, if seizures continue in rapid succession, or if injury or hypothermia is imminent. The Epilepsy Foundation (2008) offers the following suggestions: If a seizure occurs in water, support the person's head and keep her face out of the water. Bring her to the shore or side of the pool and place her on her side. Check her airway. If water has been ingested or breathing is labored, get medical treatment.

Refer to the tips in the sidebar for more information about swimming safety for people who are seizure prone.

SWIMMING AS A COMPETITIVE SPORT

As with other sports, integration of athletes with disabilities into regular competition has been a goal of disability sport advocates for over a decade. In the United States, USA Swimming has done an exemplary job of advocating for vertical integration, or the inclusion of people with disabilities into regular aquatic meets and teams. USA Swimming is the national governing body for all U.S. swimming competition and has a national adapted swimming committee. The organization's Disability Swimming Committee acts as a consultant to the USA Swimming Disability Championships and advocates for swimmers with disabilities. The committee has written several resources for coaches, local swim committees, officials, meet directors, parents, and swimmers with disabilities (USA Swimming, n.d.). The *USA Swimming Rules and Regulations* manual (2008) has guidelines for officiating swimmers with a disability.

Suggestions for Teaching Swimming to People Who Are Seizure Prone

- Obtain medical clearance and a list of any contraindicated activities.
- Maintain supervision during aquatic activities.
- Factors provoking onset of seizure include playing games of holding the breath as long as possible; hyperventilation before underwater swimming; excessive drinking of pool water, which can lead to hyperhydration or hyponatremia; hyperthermia; and excessive looking into the sun.

- Discuss scuba diving with participants and their physicians before attempting deep dives.
- Be aware that some seizure medications increase photosensitivity. When outdoors, it may be important to swim in the early evening. Use sunscreen or wear a shirt over a swimsuit.
- Fill out an appropriate incident report following a seizure.

The goal of USA Swimming is for swimmers with disabilities to train with their local swim clubs and participate in swim meets combining swimmers with and without disabilities during events. In addition to integrated swim meets, the USA Swimming Disability Championships are held once a year. This multidisability swim championship is conducted for elite disabled swimmers who have met qualifying times for their events. USA Swimming rules and regulations apply during these meets; however, disability sport classifications are used so that swimmers can compete against others of similar functioning. Swimmers with disabilities often have atypical stroke mechanics or atypical power because of missing limbs, neurological issues, cognitive delays, or paralysis that do not allow them to compete equally with one another or even with swimmers who have the same disability. Swimmers are classified into categories according to their functional ability rather than merely separated by gender and swim stroke.

USA Swimming encourages the integration of swimmers with disabilities into meets by providing reasonable accommodations to barriers that might otherwise preclude their participation. According to USA Swimming (n.d.), local swim committees are encouraged to develop administrative procedures and circumstances that encourage swimmers with disabilities to participate, such as the following:

- Include a statement inviting swimmers with disabilities to provide notice of needed accommodations.
- Develop standards for seeding swimmers that do not interfere with the timeline and flow of the meet and do not place undue spotlight on the athlete with a disability. (For example, swimmers who have CP might be placed in a 100 m event but swim 50 m if their 50 m time is similar to the 100 m times of peers without disabilities.)
- Waive qualifying time standards.

Additional guidelines for officiating swimmers with disabilities meets might include some of the following accommodations from the 2008 USA Swimming rules and regulations:

- Allowing the swimmer to start in the water
- Allowing the swimmer's assistant on the deck to assist the start
- Using a visual starting system (e.g., a strobe light or hand signals) for deaf and hard-of-hearing participants
- Being lenient regarding the time it takes to get into starting positions
- Modifying starting positions on blocks, deck, or gutter (see figure 25.4)
- Using tappers for swimmers with vision impairments (assistants who hold a pole with a soft tip to tap the swimmer at turns and finishes)
- Using physical touch to signal relay swimmers when their teammates have touched the wall
- Not judging a part of the body that is absent or not used as part of a stroke technique

Although most competitive training in the United States takes place in USA Swimming clubs, the

Photo courtesy of Joe Kusumoto.

FIGURE 25.4 One reasonable accommodation in competitive swimming for athletes with disabilities might be to allow modified starting positions.

YMCA and other organizations conduct integrated club teams as well. For those who prefer training with only swimmers who have disabilities, segregated disability sport organizations such as Special Olympics (for athletes with intellectual disabilities) and the USA Deaf Sports Federation (USADSF) provide segregated competitive opportunities within disability-specific meets (although Special Olympics offers some unified swimming events that provide reverse inclusion of athletes without disabilities). Deaf or hard-of-hearing swimmers may participate in the Deaflympics through the USADSF, people with dwarfism may participate as members of the Dwarf Athletic Association of America (DAAA) in the organization's regional and national games, athletes with cognitive disabilities may swim in Special Olympics events, and swimmers who are blind or visually impaired may participate in United States Association of Blind Athletes (USABA) competitions. These competitions are limited in number and are usually far from a swimmer's home pool.

Although swimming is the primary means of aquatic competition in disability sport, competitive diving (Special Olympics) and water polo (USADSF) are other options. However, they generally need to be pursued in inclusive team settings.

OTHER AQUATIC ACTIVITIES

Activities such as water skiing, scuba diving, and boating can help increase independence and empowerment. People with disabilities of all ages enjoy water sport as much as their counterparts without disabilities. Water sport provides aquatic recreational opportunities with peers, families, and community members. With legal mandates for accessibility, more chances exist for participation in instructional, recreational, and competitive water sport. The ATBCB (2004) rulings on accessibility and recreation facilities include boat docks and fishing piers.

Water Skiing

Prerequisites to water skiing include consultation with a swimmer's physician, acquisition of basic swim skills, and knowledge of using a PFD. All skiers should practice using PFDs for support and buoyancy in a controlled environment before using them in open water. The driver of the boat, the observer, and the skier should agree beforehand on communication techniques (e.g., hand or head-movement signals) to make the activity safe for all.

To make skiing easier for the beginner and for those with disabilities, equipment modifications must be made, especially for those with lower-extremity involvement. A ski bra is one piece of equipment that keeps the skis together for those with leg weakness or paralysis. A kneeboard, ski biscuit (inflatable inner tube with a cover), or specially designed sit-ski can accommodate the skier who cannot stand up. Liquid Access is one provider dedicated to the design and manufacture of adapted equipment for water skiing in the United States (www.liquidaccess.org).

In addition, several adaptations to ski progressions might be combined with equipment modifications, as evidenced by UCanSki2, a USA Water Ski–affiliated ski club directed by Ann O'Brine Satterfield of Winter Park, Florida (www.ucanski2.com). She and her staff conduct dry-land instruction followed by the use of a boom off the side of the boat as a first step to skiing. A triple bar in back of the boat allows another progression with one instructor on either side of a student.

The Water Skiers with Disabilities Association (WSDA), an official sport division of USA Water Ski, offers an adaptive water-skiing certification program in addition to an adaptive coaches certification. This group also puts together the national championship each August and sponsors the 14-member U.S. Disabled Water Ski Team to represent the United States at the world championships. Events include slalom, audio slalom, tricks, and jumps. There are eight classification groupings for physically disabled skiers and three for skiers with visual impairments (www.usawaterski.org).

Scuba Diving

Traditionally, scuba diving was not a sport open to people with disabilities, but scuba and snorkeling have become a core part of adventure-based activities offered to people with numerous disabilities. Before beginning training, the instructor and diver need to discuss water access and entry from the poolside, beach, or boat (Petrofsky, 1995; Robinson & Fox, 1987) as well as medical issues that affect breathing, mobility, and vision. Once in the water, no architectural barriers prevent interaction with nature, and mobility is enhanced by a minimal amount of gravity. Some modifications to equipment might include pressure gauges that have Braille numbers or that emit auditory signals, divers tethered together, hand paddles or swim mitts, diving boots, low-volume masks, octopus regulators, jacket-type buoyancy compensators, flexible vented fins, Velcro on wet suits, and diver propulsion vehicles for those who cannot propel themselves (Jankowski, 1995; Paciorek & Jones, 2001).

Handicapped Scuba Association International (HSA International) has programs to train people with disabilities to scuba dive and also trains scuba instructors to meet the needs of divers with disabilities. Founded in 1981 by Jim Gatacre, HSA International uses a multilevel credential that classifies divers according to physical performance standards regardless of disability type. Level A consists of diving students who can care for themselves and others, level B includes students who need partial support and must dive with two buddies, and level C includes students who need full support (two dive buddies, one of whom who is trained in dive rescue). Another international organization is the International Association for Handicapped Divers (IAHD), founded in 1993. Based in the Netherlands, the IAHD is similar to HSA International in that it has three levels of divers and conducts instructor training programs. The IAHD publishes a newsletter for its members and conducts seminars, symposiums, and dive conventions.

Although all agree that certified divers should possess requisite knowledge and skills for a safe and successful experience, controversy surrounds the subject of medical clearance and certification. Scuba diving has been generally accepted for most people with orthopedic, vision, and auditory disabilities. However, secondary disabilities such as limited breathing capacity, osteoporosis, poor circulation, temperature-regulation disorders, psychological conditions, and medical conditions such as seizure disorders, insulin-dependent diabetes, and asthma present a real concern for physicians and dive instructors (Lin, 1987; Petrofsky, 1995). Presently, the only sound advice for the prospective diver with a disability is to consult a physician experienced in hyperbaric medicine, use caution when diving, and be conservative.

Boating

Boating activities are enjoyed by all but are especially good for people with lower-body involvement because paddling, rowing, and sailing emphasize upper-body strength. Adaptations to equipment are the primary concern, along with embarking, disembarking, seating, and balance. People with cognitive disabilities have similar needs for instructional modifications in boating as they do in swimming: Simplify, demonstrate, and repeat. People with vision impairments should have land-based training and a chance to practice their skills in shallow water or a pool. This land practice is important because it is difficult for people who need to use tactile modeling (putting hands on the person demonstrating to feel movements) to be out in a boat and unable to move around because of safety or capsizing concerns. Two-person tandem kayaks are ideal for paddlers who have visual impairments to use with a sighted partner.

Paddlers with mobility disabilities often need modifications to the access points of paddle sports. Hard-surface runways on beachfronts—including accessible routes to accessible launch ramps, slips, and boarding piers—are needed for those who use wheelchairs, crutches, or canes and those who have balance problems. When runways are not available, a beach wheelchair could be made available. Once a person with a mobility disability reaches the boat, it is recommended that a mat or cushion be placed over the gunwale, the boat steadied, and a plan of action for embarking established. Entry and exit procedures can be modified in several ways. For example, a modification might be as simple as the instructor standing or swimming in the water and stabilizing a boat or two assistants helping to lift a boater onto a transfer mat from the dock to the bottom of a boat. If the riverbed or lakebed is firm enough, it might be possible to push a water wheelchair into shallow water for water entries, with assistants, if necessary, to help lift and transfer.

Commercial equipment for seating is available, such as sling-back seats, rubber materials to prevent slipping on the seat, and materials to protect people with sensitive skin. Several models of canoes and kayaks lend themselves to various needs. Instructors should analyze the movements, stability, cognitive ability, and strength of the participant to determine what type of canoe or kayak would be best. Open-decked or sit-on-top kayaks are advisable for warm water and for people who have difficulty in transferring. These vessels are easy to enter and exit but have a high center of gravity and don't lend themselves to seating adaptations (Adaptive Adventures, n.d.). People who need adaptive seating systems or have poor balance would work best in an inflatable kayak (duckie). Sea kayaks are helpful for those who need seating systems because they have deep wells and come in many shapes.

Propulsion in paddle sports can be adapted by using mitts or tubing to secure a paddler's hands to the paddle shaft. Further equipment modifications to enhance propulsion include printing the words *right* and *left* on the opposite paddle blades on a double-blade paddle or on the inside of the boat to help a paddler with an intellectual impairment, painting the inside of the boat with nonslip paint, using suction-cup bath mats on the bottom or seats of the boat, keeping a variety of paddle lengths available, and having participants use rubber or leather-palm gloves for a better grip.

In the United States, the primary organization for paddle sports is the American Canoe Association (ACA). The ACA sponsors the Adaptive Paddling Program (APP), which promotes canoeing, kayaking, and rafting as lifetime recreational activities for people with disabilities. In addition, its mission includes full integration of paddlers with varying abilities in all aspects of paddle sports. The APP is a clearinghouse on adaptations to equipment and accessibility to instruction as well as a resource for instructors who want to include paddlers with disabilities. Adaptive paddling workshops are conducted nationally and provide already-certified paddling instructors with the information needed to integrate paddlers with disabilities into their programs (ACA, 2004). On completion of the four-day workshop, which includes classroom instruction, hands-on learning, and pool and open-water sessions, the adaptive paddling endorsement is achieved by certified paddling instructors. Because of new accessibility regulations for marinas, advancements in technology, and creative designs of adapted seating and paddles, more people with disabilities can now experience boating.

In addition to canoeing and kayaking, sailing opportunities have expanded rapidly through new programs and adapted boats for people with disabilities. Worldwide, the International Association for Disabled Sailing (IFDS) makes positive contributions to the sport and is the governing body of Paralympic sailing (IFDS, 2007). The IFDS promotes disabled sailing through the publication of worldwide events on its Web site, reports of recent events, and articles pertinent to the sport. The IFDS publishes *IFDS Bulletin*, which contains information related to current and future trends in adapted sailing, upcoming races, and race results. The organization also conducts the Disabled Sailing World Championship, which is a qualifier for Paralympic competition. There are three events in Paralympic sailing: single-person keelboat, two-person keelboat, and three-person keelboat. The IFDS was recognized in 1991 by the International Sailing Federation (ISAF) as a committee, and sailors with physical disabilities have been able to compete in Paralympic sailing since its demonstration in 1996 and full medal status in 2000.

Nationally, the United States Sailing Association (US Sailing) promotes sailing at all levels. Created in 1998, the US Disabled Sailing Team (USDST) ranks American sailors with disabilities and serves as the U.S. representative of sailing to the IFDS. For those who want to compete but are not at the elite level, the Council for Sailors with Disabilities exists within US Sailing.

Sailors with intellectual disabilities may participate in international competition through Special Olympics, which has included sailing in its world games since 1995. Special Olympics individual, team, and Unified Sports categories exist at the local, national, and international levels. Athletes are placed in divisions according to age, gender, and ability.

One of the first adapted sailing programs in the United States, the Lake Merritt Adapted Boating Program of the Office of Parks and Recreation in Oakland, California, began in 1981. Glo Webel, boating programs coordinator, pioneered the development of sailing facilities for people with disabilities. Another pioneer and innovator in sailing is

Harry Horgan, founder of Shake-A-Leg of Newport, Rhode Island. His boat design with adapted seating proved successful, and participants consider it to be the benchmark of modified sailing vessels.

People with disabilities also pursue rowing for recreation or competition. At the international level, adaptive rowing is a commission within the International Rowing Federation (FISA), an advocate for inclusion of rowers with disabilities into races such as the World Rowing Championships. The goals of the commission are to oversee all areas of international adaptive rowing, increase participation in adaptive rowing on all levels, promote and monitor trends, and provide advice on adaptive rowing. The commission has been instrumental in the development of a classification and ranking system for racing. It applied to the International Paralympic Committee (IPC) for adaptive rowing as a Paralympic sport for the first time in the 2008 Games and it was successful. At present, there are four boat classes with separate categories for men and women under the 1x class (FISA Adaptive Rowing Commission, 2010):

Class LTAMix4+: Four athletes (mixed gender) in a shell who can row using legs, trunk, and arms; one coxswain (sliding-seat boat)

Class LTAIDMix4+: Four athletes with intellectual disability (mixed gender) in a fixed-seat shell using legs, trunk, and arms with a coxswain

Class TAMix2x: Two athletes (mixed gender) in a fixed-seat shell who can use their trunk and arms to row

Class ASW1x: Single fixed-seat shell for women who can only use arms for rowing

Class ASM1x: Single fixed-seat scull for men who can only use arms for rowing

USRowing is the national governing body for rowing in the United States and is a member of FISA. Its adaptive rowing committee has been active in recruiting members for the national team since its inception in 2002. One of the most active programs is the Philadelphia Rowing Program for the Disabled, held in the prestigious boathouse-row section of the Schuylkill River.

Safety and risk management are concerns for everyone in boating, but some people with disabilities need to take extra precautions. Those who are interested can become certified as instructors through the ACA or through USRowing. Zeller (2009) suggests that safety planning of any boating class should include swim skills assessment

of participants, considerations for accessibility to the boating site, review of medical information, and considerations involved with any medical condition. In addition, it is crucial to assess what the participant can do on land and determine what medical information needs to be shared with others in the group in relation to an emergency action plan. Other safety issues include stumbling over unseen items on the boat or dock for boaters with vision impairments, failure to hear a shouted warning for Deaf boaters, bowel and bladder management issues for participants who are incontinent, change of weather conditions for those with temperature-regulation disorders, and balance problems due to rough seas or reduced ability to grip and thus hold on.

The amount of responsibility a paddler, sailor, or rower should have depends on functional ability. It is important to test the balance, stability, and buoyancy of the boat with the person in it while in shallow, calm water and to test equipment before undertaking a river or lake trip. Other elements of safety include planning for embarkation and disembarkation, instructor-to-student ratio, and—as with all water sports—an emergency action plan. To determine which boat, method, and paddle are most appropriate, consider the participant's balance, grip strength and endurance, coordination, and upper-extremity ROM. Consider, too, how much sight and hearing the person possesses, the ability to make decisions, and knowledge of cause and effect.

Water orientation should include instruction in safety, personal rescue, and proper PFD use. After the water orientation, boat orientation may begin on land, move into a pool and then calm outdoor water, and finally progress to moving and open water. Boat orientation should take into account terminology that is understandable to the participants, exploration of the boat by participants who are blind, entry and exit procedures, and propulsion and steering techniques. Participants and instructors must work together to modify equipment through trial and error based on knowledge of available commercial equipment.

INCLUSION IN AQUATIC ACTIVITIES

Including a student with a disability in an aquatic activity with peers without disabilities requires the teacher to review the results of the individual skill assessment and to look at the goals of the program, class, or activity in which the student will be placed. Even if a student is included in a regular physical education environment on land, several questions must be answered by the IEP team before the student begins an aquatics program within an inclusive setting. Typical questions might include the following: How many of the participant's targeted goals and objectives match those that are possible within the regular aquatics program? Can the participant follow rules and guidelines within the regular program so as not to compromise the safety of all? Is an age-appropriate class available? Does the placement provide an emotionally and physically safe environment? Is the ultimate goal of the placement to be able to participate in aquatic activities in an integrated setting? Does the placement meet other goals in addition to instructional goals (e.g., recreational or therapeutic goals)? Refer to the application example for a practical situation describing the inclusion of a student with disabilities.

A critical factor in the successful inclusion of students with disabilities into the regular aquatics program is the instructor. Instructors should work with swimmers and their caregivers to provide the most appropriate placement and curriculum for

teaching aquatic skills. Studies show that aquatics instructors have more positive attitudes toward including students with mild disabilities and that in order to feel more successful with all inclusion programs, aquatics instructors have expressed perceived needs in the areas of adapted aquatics training, equipment, and class management (Conatser, Block, & Lepore, 2000). Currently, there are two formal adapted aquatics training programs in the United States: the Adapted Aquatics Instructor credential from the AAHPERD-AAPAR Council for Aquatic Professionals and the YMCA Swim Lessons for Individuals with Disabilities Instructor certification.

Another critical factor for successful aquatics inclusion programs is matching the participants' prerequisite skills with the programs or classes they are put in. Participants should have a minimal level of skill competencies and possess several prerequisite skills for safe and successful experiences in an integrated class. Participant prerequisites might include such factors as social, cognitive, and aquatic readiness skills vital to inclusive group integrity and learning. Medical and health conditions are also concerns. Lepore and colleagues (2007) contend

APPLICATION EXAMPLE

Diving

Setting: A child with multiple physical disabilities has been included in the regular sixth-grade aquatics class during her physical education class. The class is learning how to dive, but the child does not have the prerequisite skills to participate.

Student: This 12-year-old girl has no cognitive disabilities but has spastic CP and uses a power wheelchair. She has head control and can close her mouth in response to splashing water. She can also hold onto the pool gutter and use her arms to do a modified elementary backstroke.

Application: The adapted aquatics instructor suggests the following modifications:

▶ An additional instructor trained in adapted aquatics should be available.

▶ While the rest of the class is practicing kneeling or standing dives, the student practices sitting on the pool edge with maximal support while wearing a life jacket. Assistants in the water and on deck help the student to fall into the pool and recover on her back.

▶ While the others are practicing diving, she can work on surface dives in the deep end with an aide to assist her in plunging under the water and then recovering onto her back.

▶ Have the student work on her IEP aquatic goals in the shallow end.

▶ Encourage the student to work on diving prerequisites, such as streamlined body position and pike or tuck position, but not the dive itself.

that some medical and health conditions, such as the following, might warrant a segregated setting, such as a hospital or therapy-oriented facility, or even a suspension of aquatic activities:

- Open sores, such as decubitus ulcers
- Uncontrolled seizures leading to emergency removal from the pool and causing clearing of the pool for each seizure incident
- Tracheotomy tubes or ventilator dependency that might require shallow water, qualified health care professionals, heavily grounded electrical cords, and calm water with no splashing
- Neuromuscular conditions that require a water temperature not available in the regular facility
- Neurological conditions that require gradual change from water to air temperature because of inadequate thermoregulation systems
- High susceptibility to infection, requiring more sterile environments
- Allergies to chlorine, requiring pools with alternative chemical, UV, or ozone disinfection
- Behavior disorders, such as uncontrolled aggression, compromising the safety of others
- Hemophilia, possibly requiring calm water, limited bumping into other participants and equipment, and modified pool temperatures because of arthritic conditions
- Detached retinas, requiring the need to avoid projectiles and any bumping of the head and face

Aquatic skill prerequisites are necessary for success in swimming classes. Regardless of whether the tasks are as simple as holding the pool gutter, closing the mouth when someone splashes, or not drinking pool water, these skills might be necessary for success and safety in the regular class. Support services are often needed to assist with skill prerequisites.

Unlike land-based physical activities, some students with disabilities cannot safely participate in aquatics with same-age peers without disabilities because of lack of ability. For example, if an entire instructional unit is taking place in a diving well and the student with a disability is overly fearful, the caregiver and the student must communicate with the instructor about what is needed, desired, and feasible.

Ways to enhance inclusion include modifications to equipment, rules, instruction, and the environ-ment. Many suggestions have been integrated into the information in this chapter. Here are other strategies to try:

- Provide an alternative swimming activity (e.g., participants can complete a cannonball jump instead of a dive).
- Use an aide to provide physical support within an inclusive aquatics class. (AAPAR Adapted Aquatics Instructors can provide training and award a credential titled Adapted Aquatics Assistant.)
- Provide a temporary segregated program in a small group or one on one when the skills in the inclusion group do not match the goals or abilities of the swimmer.
- Have the swimmer work with an adapted aquatics instructor in another area of the pool.
- Use peers trained as water safety aides or adapted aquatics teaching assistants who can provide assistance (e.g., repeating directions or providing positive reinforcement).

SUMMARY

Aquatics can be an important part of a physical education program for students with disabilities. This chapter summarized the benefits of adapted aquatics, the importance of assessment, issues related to facilities and equipment, and general teaching tips for adapted aquatics. Physical educators should be familiar with the many possibilities afforded by water and advocate for aquatic experiences within the physical education program for students with disabilities. After-school recreational and competitive opportunities also exist in other aquatic pursuits, including swim team, boating, water skiing, and scuba.

REFERENCES

Adaptive Adventures. (n.d.). Adaptive canoeing, kayaking and rafting: A level paddling field. Retrieved from www.adaptiveadventures.org.

American Alliance for Health, Physical Education, Recreation and Dance (AAHPERD), & American Association for Active Lifestyles and Fitness (AAALF). (1996). *Adapted aquatics: Position paper*. Reston, VA: Author.

American Canoe Association (ACA). (2004). The ACA and adaptive paddling. Retrieved from www.americancanoe.org.

American Red Cross. (2004). *Water safety instructor's manual*. Boston: StayWell.

Architectural and Transportation Barriers Compliance Board (ATBCB). (2004). Americans with Disabilities Act accessibility guidelines for buildings and facilities; final rule. *Federal Register*, 36 CFR Parts 1190 and 1191, July 23, 2004.

Block, M.E. (2007). *A teacher's guide to including students with disabilities in regular physical education* (3rd ed.). Baltimore: Paul H. Brookes.

Brown, A. (2003). Access points: Ground rules. *Aquatics International, 15* (2), 14-16.

Conatser, P., Block, M.E., & Lepore, M. (2000). Aquatic instructors' attitudes toward teaching students with disabilities. *Adapted Physical Activity Quarterly, 17,* 197-207.

Epilepsy Foundation of America. (2008). First aid in special circumstances. Retrieved from www. epilepsyfoundation.org/about/firstaid/seizurespecial. cfm.

FISA Adaptive Rowing Commission. (2010). FISA adaptive classifiers instruction manual. Retrieved July 9, 2010, from www.worldrowing.com/index.php?pageid=17.

International Association for Disabled Sailing (IFDS). (2007). *IFDS Bulletin, September 2007*. Retrieved from www.sailing.org/disabled.

Jankowski, L.W. (1995). *Teaching persons with disabilities scuba diving*. Montreal: Quebec Underwater Association.

Koury, J.M. (1996). *Aquatic therapy programming*. Champaign, IL: Human Kinetics.

Langendorfer, S.J., & Bruya, L. (1995). *Aquatic readiness*. Champaign, IL: Human Kinetics.

Lepore, M., Gayle, G.W., & Stevens, S.F. (2007). *Adapted aquatics programming: A professional guide* (2nd ed.). Champaign, IL: Human Kinetics.

Lin, L.Y. (1987). Scuba divers with disabilities challenge medical protocols and ethics. *Physician and Sportsmedicine, 15* (6), 224-228, 233, 235.

Martin, K. (1983). Therapeutic pool activities for young children in a community facility. *Physical and Occupational Therapy in Pediatrics, 3,* 59-74.

Paciorek, M.J., & Jones, J.A. (2001). *Disability sport and recreation resources* (3rd ed.). Traverse City, MI: Cooper.

Petrofsky, J.S. (1995). Diving with spinal cord injury: Part I. *Palaestra, 10* (4), 36-41.

Prins, J., & Murata, N. (2008). Stroke mechanics of swimmers with permanent physical disabilities. *Palaestra, 24* (1), 19-25.

Robinson, J., & Fox, A.D. (1987). *Diving with disabilities*. Champaign, IL: Human Kinetics.

Scott, J.P. (2003). Access points: The fine print. *Aquatics International, 15* (3), 16-18.

Stanat, F., & Lambeck, J. (2001). The Halliwick method. *AKWA, 15* (1), 39-41.

Summerford, C.F. (1993). Apparatus used in teaching swimming to quadriplegic amputees. *Palaestra,* Spring, 54-57.

SwimAmerica. (n.d.) Organizational documents provided by SwimAmerica. 2101 N. Andrews Ave., Ste. 107, Fort Lauderdale, FL 33311.

USA Swimming. (n.d.). *Including swimmers with a disability*. Colorado Springs: Author.

USA Swimming. (2008). *USA Swimming rules and regulations*. Colorado Springs: Author.

YMCA of the USA. (1999a). *The parent/child and preschool aquatic program manual*. Champaign, IL: Human Kinetics.

YMCA of the USA. (1999b). *The youth and adult aquatics program manual*. Champaign, IL: Human Kinetics.

Zeller, J. (2009). *Canoeing and kayaking for people with disabilities*. Champaign, IL: Human Kinetics.

WRITTEN RESOURCES

USA Swimming. (n.d.). *Including swimmers with a disability*. Colorado Springs: Author. www. usaswimming.org.

USA Swimming has published a series of five brochures, including guides for coaches, officials, swimmers and parents, meet directors, and local swimming committees. These are excellent resources that cover in-depth issues related to inclusion of swimmers with a variety of disabilities into regular swim competitions and teams.

AUDIOVISUAL RESOURCES

Courage Center. (1997). *Aquatics for children with disabilities* [VHS]. Available from Courage Center of Minnesota, Golden Valley, MN (www.couragecenter. com).

This video includes training about swimming for children with disabilities. Running time is approximately 30 minutes.

International Halliwick Therapy Network (IHTN). *The Halliwick method* [PowerPoint and videoclips]. www. halliwick.net.

This video presents critical factors to consider when working with individuals with disabilities in the water using the Halliwick method.

Introduction to adapted aquatics [DVD]. (2009). Rothhammer International.

This best practices DVD includes segments on aquatic assessment, inclusive groups, and a variety of commonly seen disabilities in children's adapted aquatics programs.

ELECTRONIC RESOURCES

Aquatic Access: www.aquatic-access.com.

This site includes information related to aquatic lifts and ADA pool access.

International Paralympic Committee (IPC): www. paralympic.org.

This organization conducts the Paralympics and creates classification procedures for athletes, including swimmers and boaters with disabilities.

National Center on Accessibility: www.ncaonline.org.

This site contains information on all types of accessible recreation, including the swimming pool access project. It also includes an extensive bibliography on accessibility and pools.

USA Swimming: www.usaswimming.org.

The national governing body of swimming in the United States has information on adapted competitive swimming and brochures (previously mentioned) included on this Web site.

USRowing Association: www.usrowing.org.

This site presents information about rowing programs, including the adaptive rowing committee.

OTHER RESOURCES

Access to Recreation. 8 Sandra Ct., Newbury Park, CA 91320; phone: 800-634-4351; Web site: www.accesstr. com.

Offers adapted products designed to put people with disabilities into recreation and physical activities, including pool lifts and ramps, bath and shower chairs, pool floats, beach access chairs, and adapted water skis.

chapter

26

Team Sports

David L. Porretta

Joe, a 15-year-old, has just moved to a new school district and is to receive regular physical education with his peers of the same chronological age. Joe is functioning academically at grade level, is socially well adjusted, and has a mobility impairment that requires him to use a wheelchair. Joe's physical education teacher, Mr. Bailey, was consulted about whether Joe could safely and effectively participate in regular physical education. Mr. Bailey believes that students with disabilities should be included with peers without disabilities whenever possible, so he agreed to the arrangement knowing that some accommodations would need to be made, especially because the curriculum has many team sport units. Although unsure about how these accommodations will be made, Mr. Bailey will do his best—he is committed to teaching *all* students.

In this chapter, variations and modifications of selected team sports are presented to promote the inclusion of students with disabilities into team sports. These variations and modifications are designed to help teachers such as Mr. Bailey provide the best possible physical education programs for students with disabilities.

GETTING INVOLVED

Team sports are a popular way for people with disabilities to become involved in physical activity. In elite or inclusive settings, people with disabilities have excelled and continue to excel in amateur as well as professional team sports, and many interscholastic and recreational sport programs encourage the integrated participation of people with disabilities.

Fully integrated sport is especially encouraged for people with auditory impairments. As early as the late 19th century, people with auditory impairments were excelling in sport with people without disabilities. For example, William Ellsworth "Dummy" Hoy played Major League Baseball from 1886 to 1902 and was the first person with profound deafness to become a superstar in the game. He is regarded as the first person to use hand signals typically used by umpires and coaches. Hoy was inducted into the Cincinnati Reds Hall of Fame in 2003. Kenny Walker (professional football) and Curtis Pride (professional baseball) are other examples of Deaf athletes who have excelled in sport. Both got signals from managers or coaches and team players while on the field. In sports that are played in a relatively small area, including floor hockey, basketball, and volleyball, few modifications might be needed. In volleyball, an official pulling the net might signal the beginning or ending of play. On the other hand, sports played outdoors on a large field might require more modification. For instance, in American football and soccer, flags and hand gestures can supplement whistles as signals. For Deaf players, a bass drum on the sideline might signal the snap of the ball instead of the quarterback's verbal cadence (National Federation of High Schools, 2008). There are teams composed entirely of Deaf players who compete against players without disabilities.

Many organizations now provide sport programs for athletes with disabilities. The USA Deaf Sports Federation (USADSF) and its international counterpart, the International Committee of Sports for the Deaf (CISS), offer competition solely for those with hearing impairments. CISS is a member of the International Olympic Committee (IOC). The USADSF and CISS are independent of both U.S. Paralympics and the International Paralympic Committee (IPC). USADSF team events include baseball, basketball, ice hockey, soccer, team handball, and volleyball, in which athletes are classified according to gender and degree of hearing loss. These sports are regularly featured at the Deaflympics and follow international sport federation rules with some minor adjustments. The Deaflympics occur every two years, alternating between the summer and winter games. Because few modifications are needed for people with hearing impairments to participate in team sport, the focus in the remainder of this chapter is people with other types of disabilities.

Other sport organizations, such as the National Beep Baseball Association (NBBA), Special Olympics, and BlazeSports National Disability Sports Alliance (BNDSA) , have been formed to meet the needs of people with disabilities for segregated sport competition. However, Special Olympics promotes team sport competition for people with intellectual disabilities in totally inclusive settings in its Unified Sports program. Beep baseball, goalball, quad rugby, and wheelchair softball are relatively new team sports designed for players with disabilities.

Only the significant modifications of each sport are presented in this chapter. A more detailed description of the rules and regulations can be obtained from each sponsoring sport organization.

BASKETBALL

Basketball is a popular activity in both physical education and sport programs. It incorporates the skills of running, jumping, shooting, passing, and dribbling. Modifying skills, rules, or equipment can allow students with disabilities to effectively participate in the game. Generally, most ambulatory people can participate in basketball with few or no modifications. However, those with severe mental disabilities or mobility problems might need greater modifications—for example, wheelchair basketball for people in wheelchairs.

Game Skills

Important basketball game skills include shooting, passing, and dribbling. Selected modifications are provided for each skill.

■ *Shooting and passing.* Bounce passing is advised for partially sighted players because the sound of the bounce lets them know from which direction the ball is coming. Bounce passing also provides more time for players with unilateral upper-limb involvement to catch the ball. One-hand shots and passes should be encouraged for players who have upper-limb impairments. Players in wheelchairs find the one-hand pass useful for long passes; when shooting at the basket, however, they often prefer the two-hand set shot (especially for longer shots) because both arms can put more force behind the ball. For people with ambulation difficulties, a net placed directly beneath the basket during shooting practice facilitates return of the ball. Players with upper-limb involvement might find it helpful to trap or cradle the ball against the upper body when trying to catch a pass.

■ *Dribbling.* For players with poor eye–hand coordination or poor vision, dribbling can be performed with a larger ball. For those with poor body coordination, it might be necessary to permit periodic bouncing when running or walking, although they can dribble the ball continually when standing still. Players in wheelchairs will need to dribble to the left or the right of the chair and carry the ball in the lap when wheeling.

Lead-Up Games and Activities

Lead-up games and activities are important prerequisites to learning the game of basketball. Selected lead-up games and activities are provided.

■ *Horse.* Two or more players might play this shooting game, competing against each other from varying distances from the goal. To begin the game, a player takes a shot from anywhere on the court. If the shot is made, the next player must duplicate the shot (e.g., type of shot, distance). Failure to make the shot earns that player the letter H. If, however, the second player makes the shot, an additional shot may be attempted from anywhere on the court for the opponent to match. Players attempt shots that they feel their opponents might have difficulty making. The first person to acquire all of the letters *H-O-R-S-E* loses.

■ *Circle shot.* This activity involves shooting a playground ball in any manner to a large basket about 45 inches (1 m) high from six spots ranging from about 2 feet (.5 m) to 5 feet (1.5 m) away from the basket. Two shots are attempted from each spot for a total of 12 shots. The player's score is the number of successful shots.

■ *Other activities.* Other basketball lead-up activities might include bouncing a beach ball over a specified distance and shooting or dropping a playground ball into a large barrel or container.

Sport Variations and Modifications

Basketball is an official sport of the Dwarf Athletic Association of America (DAAA). The only modification to the game is that players use a slightly smaller ball (the size used by women in international play) for better dribbling and shooting control.

In Special Olympics competition, the game follows rules developed by the International Basketball Federation (FIBA) for all multinational and international competition (Special Olympics, 2008a). Both full-court (5v5) and half-court basketball (3v3) are offered by Special Olympics. The only significant modifications are as follow:

■ A smaller basketball 28.5 inches (72.5 cm) in circumference and 18 to 20 ounces (510-567 g) in weight might be used for women's and junior division play.

■ A shorter basket of 8 feet (2.4 m) might be used for junior division play.

■ Players might take two steps beyond what is allowable. (However, if the player scores or escapes the defense, a violation is called.)

The National Wheelchair Basketball Association (NWBA) (2007) has also modified the game for wheelchair users. Examples of some major rule modifications include the following:

■ The wheelchair is considered part of the player.

■ Players must stay firmly seated in the chair at all times.

■ An offensive player shall not remain for four seconds in the key.

■ Dribbling consists of simultaneously wheeling the chair and dribbling the ball (a player cannot take more two consecutive pushes without bouncing the ball).

- Taking more than two consecutive pushes results in a traveling violation.
- No player of the team with a throw-in into the front court shall enter the free-throw lane until the throw-in starts.
- Personal fouls are charged to players who block, push, charge, or impede the progress with either the body or wheelchair.

Skill Event Variations and Modifications

Special Olympics offers individual skills competition in shooting, dribbling, and passing for people with lower ability levels who can't yet play the game. Scores for all three events are added to obtain a final score. The shooting competition is called *spot shot* and measures the athlete's skill in shooting a basketball. Six spots are marked on the basketball floor—three spots to the left of the basket and three spots to the right of the basket. The athlete attempts two shots from each of the six spots. The first six shots are taken from the right of the basket, and the second six shots are taken from the left of the basket. Points are awarded for every field goal made. The farther the spot is from the basket, the higher the point value. For any shot that hits the backboard or rim and does not go into the basket, one point is scored. The athlete's score is the sum of all 12 shots.

The 10-meter event requires the athlete to dribble with one hand as fast as possible for a distance of 10 meters. If control of the ball is lost, the athlete can recover the ball. If, however, the ball goes outside of the designated 1.5-meter lane, the ball may be retrieved, or a backup ball placed 5 meters outside of the lane at the start of the event might be picked up. Points are awarded depending on how long it takes to dribble the entire 10 meters. A one-second penalty is added for each illegal (e.g., two-handed) dribble. Two trials for this event are allowed. The athlete's score is the better of the two trials.

In the target pass event, the athlete must stand within a 3-meter square and pass the ball in the air to a 1-meter-square target 1 meter from the floor from a distance of 2.4 meters. Five attempts are allowed. The athlete receives 3 points for hitting the inside of the target, 2 points for hitting the lines of the target, 1 point for hitting the wall but no part of the target, and 1 point for catching the ball on the return from the wall. The final score is the sum of all five passes.

Other Variations and Modifications

Game rules might be simplified by reducing the types of fouls players are allowed to commit. A playground ball might be used, and the basket can be lowered or enlarged. The game area might be restricted to half-court for players with mobility impairments, such as those using lower-limb prostheses. Shorter play periods and frequent substitutions might be incorporated into the game for players with cardiac or asthmatic conditions. Those with insufficient arm strength can use lighter balls.

FLOOR HOCKEY

The game of floor hockey has gained popularity in physical education and sport programs across the United States. Game skills include stick handling, shooting, passing, checking, and goalkeeping. With appropriate variations and modifications, students with disabilities can play the game.

Game Skills

Important floor hockey game skills include stick handling, shooting, passing, checking, and goalkeeping. Selected modifications are provided for each skill.

- *Stick handling.* The key to successful stick handling is being able to keep the head up. Keeping the head up allows the player to attend to the field of play and opponents rather than the puck. To promote better stick handling, the stick blade can be enlarged for players with motor-control problems or visual impairments. The size and length of the stick are important factors for some players. Lighter sticks should be available for smaller players and those with muscle weaknesses, and shorter sticks should be provided for those in wheelchairs. Players with crutches might use the crutch as a stick to strike the puck, as long as sufficient balance can be maintained. Those with crutches or leg braces can hit the puck more successfully from the stationary position. Players with unilateral upper-limb deficiencies or amputations can control the stick with the nonimpaired limb because sticks are light. However, for those with poor grip or poor arm or shoulder strength, the stick can be secured to the limb with a Velcro strap. Players in wheelchairs might need to stress passing or shooting rather than dribbling past opponents.

When moving the chair, they usually place the stick in their laps.

■ *Shooting and passing.* Shooting and passing require quickness, accuracy, and the ability to shoot the puck when moving. Making a pass is a difficult skill and requires good timing and eye–hand coordination. In the initial stages of learning this skill, the player should make passes from a stationary position to a player who is also in a stationary position. More advanced stages of passing might include passing the puck from a stationary position to a moving player. When passing or shooting on goal, players with visual impairments can push the puck with the stick rather than using a backswing before striking the puck. They will find it helpful to play with a larger, brightly colored puck. It is also helpful if a coach or a sighted teammate calls to them when the puck is passed in their direction.

■ *Checking.* Checking requires the player to gain control of the opponent's puck. The player positions the stick under the opponent's stick and attempts to lift the opponent's stick away from the puck. Once the opponent's stick is raised, the puck can be controlled. Players should first practice checking slowly while in a stationary position, gradually increasing in the speed of movement. The highest level of checking is when both players are moving.

■ *Goalkeeping.* Goalies try to keep the puck from going into the goal and thus need to make quick movements. They might stop the puck in several ways, with either the stick or feet or by blocking it with the body or catching it. Once the puck is controlled, it may be put back into play by using the stick or actually throwing it into the playing area. Goalies need a larger stick and wear a face mask, pads, and gloves. Players with asthma or poor cardiorespiratory endurance can be successful at the goalie position because little running is needed.

Lead-Up Games and Activities

Lead-up games and activities are important prerequisites to learning the game of floor hockey. Selected lead-up games and activities are provided.

■ *Stop the Puck.* Three players face the net at a distance of 5 meters. One player is positioned in front of the net, and the other two players position themselves 3 meters to the left and right of the middle player. Each of the three players has two

pucks. On command, players shoot their pucks at the goal in rapid succession, attempting to score. The goalie makes as many saves as possible.

■ *Puck dribble race.* The player starts the race from behind a starting line. On command, the player dribbles the puck as quickly as possible in a forward direction for a distance of 10 meters.

■ *Other activities.* Additional activities include pushing a puck to the goal as fast as possible using a shuffleboard stick, kicking the puck with the feet as fast as possible to the goal, dribbling the puck as quickly as possible around a circle of cones, and shooting a sock stuffed in the shape of a ball (sockball) with a poly hockey stick into a large box turned on its side.

Sport Variations and Modifications

As played under Special Olympics rules (2008b), floor hockey is similar to ice hockey. The game can be played on any safe, level, properly marked surface with minimum dimensions of 12 meters by 24 meters and maximum dimensions of 15 meters by 30 meters. The backs of the goals are set 1.2 meters from the end lines to allow play behind them. Additional official floor dimensions (e.g., center circle, goal line, face-off circles) can be found in the winter sports rule book (2008b). Six players compose a team (one goalkeeper, two defenders, and three forwards). Players use wooden or fiberglass sticks that resemble broom handles, except for the goalie, who uses a regulation ice hockey stick. The goalie must wear a mask, helmet, and protective gloves; pads may be used if desired. All other players must wear helmets with protective cages and shin guards; pads, gloves, and mouth guards can also be worn. All players wear a shirt with distinctive team markings.

The puck is a circular felt disc (about 20 cm in diameter and 2.5 cm thick) with a 10-centimeter hole in the center. The end of the stick is placed in the hole to control the puck. Face-offs, offsides, and minor and major violations are part of the game. Games consist of three nine-minute periods of running time, with one minute of rest between periods. There are three line shifts per period, during which all on-ice players from one team are replaced by substitute players. For penalties, frozen-puck situations, time-outs, and line changes, the clock is stopped.

Floor hockey can also be played by people who use power wheelchairs. The playing surface is the size of a basketball court. Players use plastic hockey sticks and instead of a rubber puck, a hollow plastic ball 2 inches (5 cm) in diameter is used. The goalie uses a stick with a larger blade than other players. Nets used for goals measure approximately 6 feet (183 cm) wide by 3 feet (91 cm) high by 1.5 feet (46 cm) deep and are placed at both ends of the floor. If players are unable to hold or grip the hockey stick, they use athletic tape to secure the stick to the chair or arm. Teams are composed of five on-floor players (including a goalie).

In order to equalize competition, players are classified into one of three levels. The classification is based solely on physical strength. In general, level 1 players possess the greatest function. They have the upper-body strength to hold the stick, lift it, and hit the ball a good distance and with speed. Level 2 players range in ability to lift the stick, and they hit the ball with fair distance and speed to players who rely on the momentum of the chair to shoot and pass the ball. These players generally keep the stick on one side of the chair or hold the stick between the legs. Level 3 players tape or mount the stick to their chairs. These players rely entirely on the momentum of the chair to shoot, pass, and control the ball. Only two level 1 players can be on the floor at the same time, and at least one level 3 player must be on the floor. Although there is no official limit on the speed of the chairs, any modifications to increase the speed of the chair to be excessively faster than the other chairs is prohibited. Players are free to wear protective equipment such as helmets, knee pads, or arm pads. The game consists of three 15-minute periods. There are various major and minor penalties. For more information on the game, visit the Web site listed at the end of the chapter under the electronic resources section.

Skill Event Variations and Modifications

Special Olympics offers individual skills competition for floor hockey in shooting (two events), passing, stick handling, and defense for players with lower ability levels, not for athletes who can already play the game. A final score is determined by adding the scores of all five events.

The shooting competition has two events: shooting around the goal and shooting for accuracy. In shooting around the goal, the athlete takes one shot from five locations around the goal, with each location 6 meters from the goal. One puck

is placed at each location before the athlete starts shooting, and the athlete has a 10-second time limit to shoot all the pucks. Each puck that goes into the goal is worth 5 points. The score is the total of the five shots. In the shooting-for-accuracy event, the athlete takes five shots directly in front of the goal from a distance of 5 meters. The goal is divided into the following point sections: 5 points for a shot entering the goal in either of the upper two corners, 3 points for a shot entering the goal in either of the lower two corners, 2 points for a shot entering the goal in the upper-middle sections, 1 point for a shot entering the goal in the lower-middle section, and 0 points for a shot not entering the goal.

The passing event requires the athlete to make five passes from behind a passing line located 8 meters from two cones placed 1 meter apart. The athlete earns 5 points each time the puck passes between the two cones; 3 points are awarded whenever the puck hits a cone and also crosses the line. The total score is the sum of scores for the five passes.

In the stick-handling event, the athlete handles the puck in a figure-eight fashion past six cones 3 meters apart for a distance of 21 meters and then shoots the puck at the goal. The time elapsed from the beginning of the event to the shot on goal is subtracted from 25. One point is also subtracted for each cone missed, and 5 points are added to the score if the goal is made.

In the defensive event, the athlete gets two attempts to steal the puck from two opponents within a 12-meter-square area. The athlete gets 15 seconds for each attempt, and each steal is worth 10 points. If the puck is not stolen, the athlete might score up to 20 points for pressing opponents, stick-checking the opponent with the puck, or staying between opponents.

Other Variations and Modifications

To accommodate players with differing abilities, the game might be played on a smaller playing surface and with larger or smaller goals. To make the game less strenuous, a Wiffle ball, sockball, foam ball, or large reinforced beanbag might be used. If players have impaired mobility, increasing the number of players on each team might be helpful. Body contact can be eliminated for players with bone or soft tissue conditions, such as juvenile rheumatoid arthritis or osteogenesis imperfecta. Penalties might be imposed on players who deliberately bump into opponents in wheelchairs.

FOOTBALL

American football uses the skills of passing, catching, kicking, blocking, and tackling. Most people can participate effectively in football or some variation of it. People with mild impairments who are in good physical condition can play the regulation game of tackle football. A small number of players possessing partial sight participate on high school and collegiate teams, and people who are legally blind can be successful placekickers. However, people with total blindness are unable to play the regulation game. People with unilateral amputations either below the knee or above or below the elbow will be able to participate in regulation football as long as their prostheses do not pose a safety risk. Flag or touch football is more commonly offered in physical education and recreation programs. Most people with intellectual disabilities, except those with severe or profound impairments, can be safely integrated with other players. Players with significant physical impairments might prefer modified or less-integrated participation.

Game Skills

Important football game skills include passing, catching, and kicking. Selected modifications are provided for each skill.

■ *Passing.* Players possessing partial sight are able to pass the ball as long as distances are short and receivers wear bright-colored clothing. For players with poor grip strength or pronounced contracture of the hand or wrist or for those on crutches, a softer, smaller ball might be used to promote holding and gripping. People in wheelchairs will be able to pass the ball if they have sufficient arm and shoulder strength. Wheelchair users will find it almost impossible to perform an underhand lateral pass while facing the line of scrimmage, so this type of pass must be performed facing the receiver.

■ *Catching.* Players with partial or no available sight and those who are wheelchair users should be facing the passer when attempting to catch the ball. Instead of trying to catch with the hands, they should cradle the ball with both hands or trap the ball at the midsection. The ball should be passed from short distances without great speed; a foam ball should be used for safety purposes. Players who have unilateral arm deformities should catch the ball by stopping it with the palm of the non-impaired hand and trapping it against the body. Wheelchair users will be able to catch effectively if the ball is thrown accurately (using a chair limits catching range).

■ *Kicking.* Players with partial or no available sight might be encouraged to practice punting without shoes so they can feel the ball contacting the foot. In learning the punt, players should be instructed to point the toes (plantarflex the foot) while kicking. A player with unilateral arm amputation can punt the ball by having it rest in the palm of the nonimpaired hand. A punting play might begin with the player already holding the ball instead of with a snap from center.

Lead-Up Games and Activities

Lead-up games and activities are important prerequisites to learning the game of football. Selected lead-up games and activities are recommended here.

■ *Kickoff football.* The game is played on a playground 30 yards (27.5 m) by 60 yards (55 m) by two teams of six to eight players each. The object of the game is to return the kickoff as far as possible before being touched. The football is kicked off from the center of the field. The player with the ball returns it as far up the field as possible without being touched (two-handed) by any opponents. The team returning the ball might use a series of lateral passes to advance it; forward passes are not permitted. Play stops when the ball carrier is touched. The other team then kicks off from the middle of the field. The winner is the team advancing farthest up the field.

■ *Football-throw activity.* A player attempts to pass a football from a distance of 30 feet (9 m) through a hole of a large rubber tire suspended 4 feet (1.2 m) from the ground on a rope. Ten attempts are given, and the player's score is the number of successful passes out of 10.

■ *Other activities.* Other lead-up activities include placekicking or punting the ball for distance, centering the ball to a target for accuracy, performing relays in which players hand the ball off to each other, and guessing the number of throws or kicks it will take to cover a predetermined distance.

Sport Variations and Modifications

Wheelchair football has steadily gained in popularity since it began in 1948. Because of its growing popularity, the Universal Wheelchair Football Association (UWFA) was formed in 1997 to promote the game. Wheelchair football is played on any hard, flat surface. The boundaries for a standard basketball court work well. The degree of physical contact is determined by how hard one blocks or tackles others. Some players, through mutual consent, like to play more aggressively. Most contact occurs wheelchair to wheelchair. With few exceptions, the game is similar to touch football. Team size varies, but six per side is preferred to avoid too much on-field confusion. A standard foam football is used, and players can participate in manual chairs, motorized chairs, or scooters. Protective equipment is optional but could include a bike helmet, gloves, seatbelt, and eyewear.

Players are classified into one of three levels according to their ability to catch the ball and ability to tag (tackle) a player. For example, a level 1 player (with fully functional arms and hands) must catch and hold onto the ball, whereas a level 3 player (with minimal or no arm movement) has caught the ball when the ball hits anywhere above the waist from the front or the side of the body or in the back of the head or headrest. People without disabilities are encouraged to play the game (using wheelchairs); of course, they would be classified as level 1 players. Each team should have players of similar ability on the field at the same time. Major rule modifications are as follows:

- Throwing the ball down the field simulates a kickoff or punt.
- The game can be played with a delayed rush. However, the defense must count off three seconds before beginning the rush.
- One blitz is allowed per series of downs.
- A first down is from the foul line on the basketball court to half-court or any equivalent distance identified (a first down could be two parking spaces).
- Contact behind the opponent's rear axle is considered clipping; grabbing an opponent's chair is considered holding.
- When playing indoors, the walls behind the end zones are considered in the field of play for kickoffs and punts. Balls hitting the walls are considered in play until the player takes

possession of the ball and is tackled (or downs the ball).

Each year elite teams from around the United States compete in the Xtreme Bowl (formerly the Blister Bowl), a national tournament. The USADSF is the only multisport organization for athletes with disabilities that has flag football as an official sport.

Skill Event Variations and Modifications

Various skill events are possible. A catching event might require a player to run a specified pattern (e.g., down and out) and catch the ball. Five attempts are given, with the total number of catches constituting the player's score.

In a field-goal event, players attempt to placekick a football over a rope suspended 8 feet (2.4 m) from the ground between two poles 50 feet (15.2 m) apart. Kicks might be attempted from 5 yards (4.6 m), 10 yards (9.1 m), 15 yards (13.7 m), 20 yards (18.3 m), or 25 yards (22.9 m) from the rope. Ten kicks are given; players might kick from any or all of the five distances. Points are awarded according to the distance kicked: 1 point for a 5-yard kick, 2 points for a 10-yard kick, 3 points for a 15-yard kick, 4 points for a 20-yard kick, and 5 points for a 25-yard kick. The total number of points after 10 successful kicks is the player's score.

Other Variations and Modifications

Simplified game situations that include only the performance of specific game skills can be used. For example, only passing plays might be allowed. The field can be shortened and narrowed, and the number of players on each team can be reduced. In addition, first-down yardage can be reduced to less than 10 yards (9.1 m). Players of low skill might play the game with a kickball or volleyball. People with arm or leg deformities or visual impairments can play most line positions.

SOCCER

Soccer is included in many physical education and sport programs. Skills in soccer include running, dribbling, kicking, trapping, heading, and catching (goalie only) the ball. Because of the large playing area and continuous play, soccer requires stamina. However, the game can be varied or modified so that people with disabilities can participate in any setting. For those with minimal impairments (e.g., mild learning disability), no modifications in the game are necessary. When regular sport competition is not possible, the BNDSA and Special Olympics provide competition for players with disabilities.

Game Skills

Important soccer skills are kicking, trapping, heading, and goalkeeping. Selected modifications are provided for each skill.

■ *Kicking.* Whether for dribbling, passing, or shooting, kicking is of paramount importance in soccer. People with upper-limb amputations can learn to kick the ball effectively, but they might have difficulty with longer kicks because the arms are normally abducted and extended to maintain balance. People with unilateral lower-limb amputations might use a prosthesis for support when passing or shooting the ball. Players might be unable to kick the ball effectively with a prosthetic device and thus might wish to play in a wheelchair. Wheelchair users will be able to dribble the ball by using the footrests of the chair to contact the ball and push it forward. They are also allowed to throw the ball because they do not have use of the lower limbs.

■ *Trapping.* Most players can learn to trap the ball effectively. Foam balls are good for players who are hesitant to have the ball hit the body. Players in wheelchairs might have some difficulty trapping because the sitting position impedes the reception of the ball on the chest and abdomen. However, some players learn to trap the ball in their laps.

■ *Heading.* Most players can learn to head the ball successfully, although heading should not be encouraged for players with conditions such as brain injury or atlantoaxial instability. Players with mental or visual impairments might find using a balloon or beach ball helpful for learning to head because these balls are soft and give players time to make body adjustments before ball contact. Players with upper-limb amputations can be very effective in heading the ball. Players in wheelchairs will be able to head the ball as long as it comes directly to them. However, the distance the player can head the ball will be limited because the backrest of the chair and the sitting position limit the player's ability to exert force on the ball.

■ *Goalkeeping.* Goalkeeping requires that the goalie be able to catch (or at least trap the ball with the hands) and kick the ball. It also requires that the goalie be able to react quickly to the ball. Because playing this position requires little cardiorespiratory endurance, many players with limited endurance can successfully play goalie. Those in wheelchairs can catch effectively as long as upper-limb involvement is minimal. Most players with one arm find it difficult to catch in the goalie position. In this case, they should be encouraged to slap, trap, or strike the ball. For some players with limited mobility, reducing the size of the goal can help.

Lead-Up Games and Activities

Lead-up games and activities are important prerequisites to learning the game of soccer. Selected lead-up games and activities are provided.

■ *Line soccer.* The game might be played on a playground with two teams, preferably of 8 to 10 players each. Players on each team stand beside each other about .5 meter apart. Both teams face each other from a distance of about 8 meters. Players on each team try to kick a soccer ball below shoulder level past their opponents. After each score, players on both teams rotate one position to the right. A team scores 1 point each time the ball passes the opponents' line, and 1 point is scored against a team that uses hands to stop the ball.

■ *Accuracy kick.* This activity involves kicking a playground ball into a goal area 1.5 meters wide from a distance of 3 meters. A player is allowed three kicks from either a standing or sitting position. The player receives 3 points each time a ball is kicked into the goal, 2 points each time the ball hits a flagstick (placed at either side of the goal) but does not pass through the goal, and 1 point each time the ball is kicked in the direction of the goal but does not reach the goal. Following three kicks, players' scores are compared.

■ *Other activities.* Additional activities include heading a beach ball into a large goal area from a short distance, dribbling a soccer ball in a circle around stationary players as fast as possible, throwing a soccer ball inbounds for distance, keeping a balloon in the air by kicking it, punting a soccer ball for distance, and playing scooter soccer.

Sport Variations and Modifications

Modifications in the sport of soccer have been introduced by several sport organizations. Disabled

Sports USA (DS/USA) sponsors soccer competition for players with amputations. Players missing part or all of one leg participate on forearm crutches; the crutch is treated as an extension of the arm.

Sport modifications have also been introduced by the BNDSA, which sponsors both indoor wheelchair soccer and seven-a-side soccer. For indoor wheelchair soccer, players are assigned to one of two divisions (division A or open division). Generally, open-division players have higher skill levels than division A players. Players are assigned to one of five classes. These classes generally follow the BNDSA eight-level functional classification system presented in chapter 14; in this system, assignment to one of the higher classification levels (e.g., class VII) is a result of greater function than players assigned to one of the lower classification levels (e.g., class II). Class assignment is based on the player's ability and function related to catching, throwing, and manipulating the ball, in addition to his degree of sitting balance and wheelchair operation. Class I players have less function than class V players. For example, class I players use a motorized wheelchair because they are not able to propel a manual wheelchair, whereas class V players have near-normal function of the upper extremities and good to normal trunk control and thus use manual wheelchairs. Each team must field at least one player who uses a motorized chair and no more than two players from class V. Teams are composed of at least four but not more than six on-court players, one of whom is the goalie. The game is composed of two 25-minute halves. A 10-minute sudden death overtime is played if the score is tied after regulation play. The following are modifications to indoor wheelchair soccer:

- The game is played on a gym floor with boundaries not less than 50 feet (15.2 m) wide and 94 feet (28.6 m) long, or not more than 50 feet (15.2 m) wide and 100 feet (30.5 m) long.
- A rubber playground ball 10 inches (25.4 cm) in circumference is used.
- The goal measures 5 feet, 6 inches (1.7 m) high; 5 feet (1.5 m) wide; and 3 to 5 feet (.9-1.5 m) deep.
- Penalty boxes are located at midcourt on the opposite side of team benches.
- Penalty shots and power plays are used.
- Goalies might leave the goal area with the ball or to gain possessions of the ball.
- The ball is considered tied up when a team is unable to move the ball for two seconds.

- The wheelchair, a limb, or any part of the body can be used to move the ball.
- Dribbling the ball with one or both hands simultaneously is permitted.
- Players are not permitted to rise from the wheelchair to gain an advantage.
- A maximum of three seconds are permitted for a player to hold or maintain possession of the ball before attempting a pass, dribble, or shot.
- Unnecessary roughness, holding, hooking, or ramming into another wheelchair results in penalties.

Players who can ambulate (BNDSA classes V-VIII) are eligible to play seven-a-side soccer. Rules generally follow Fédération Internationale de Football Association (FIFA) standards (CPISRA, 2005). Along with the seven-player limit, some modifications are as follows:

- One class V or class VI player must be a member of the team, and one of these players must be on the field at all times.
- Players are not allowed to use crutches.
- No offside rule is applied.
- An underhand throw-in is permitted.
- Teams might consist of male and female players.
- The field dimensions are 82 yards (75 m) by 60 yards (55 m); standard junior-size goals are 19 feet (5.8 m) by 7 feet (2.1 m).

In Special Olympics, the sport is played as either 11-a-side or 5-a-side soccer, and FIFA rules are followed (Special Olympics, 2008a). There are no major modifications for 11-a-side soccer. However, the standard length of the game (two 45-minute periods) can be shortened to account for players' ability levels and physical condition. The following modifications, among others, are applied for 5-a-side soccer:

- The field dimensions must be a maximum of 50 meters by 35 meters and a minimum of 40 meters by 30 meters. The smaller field is recommended for lower-ability teams.
- The goal should be about 4 meters by 2 meters.
- A ball over the sideline results in a kick-in by a player from the opposing team to the player who last touched it.
- There are two 25-minute periods.

The game of soccer is also modified for players in motorized wheelchairs. Known as *power soccer*, it originated in France in the early 1970s and was introduced in the United States in the 1980s. Because many countries developed their own versions of the sport, an international meeting was held in Paris in 2005. At that meeting the Fédération Internationale de Powerchair Football Association (FIPFA) was created, and in 2006 the United States Power Soccer Association (USPSA) was formed. The USPSA promotes both national and international play and sponsors an officials training program. The organization is working toward getting power soccer recognized as a Paralympic sport. The game is played on an indoor court (regulation basketball court) with a 33-centimeter soccer ball. Teams are composed of four players each, either male or female. The strategy is similar to rugby. Bumpers on footrests (to maneuver the ball and protect the chair and player) and anti-tip bars on chairs are mandatory for safety and ball control. To score, the ball must travel through a goal at the end of the court designated by two cones 7.6 meters apart.

Both the American Youth Soccer Association (AYSO) and the United States Youth Soccer Association (USYSA) offer modified programs for young people with disabilities. AYSO sponsors a VIP (Very Important Players) program where children with physical and intellectual disabilities play a modified game. Players are matched with volunteer buddies. Teams can have as few as three players and may be composed of both boys and girls. Teams are balanced by ability levels and age when numbers allow. For more information on the VIP soccer program, visit the AYSO Web site (www.ayso.org). USYSA sponsors a similar modified program for young people with disabilities—TOPSoccer—and offers grants to communities interested in starting a TOPSoccer program. TOPSoccer players are placed on teams according to ability, not age. Each community program is unique in that it is created around the needs of its participants. For more information on TOPSoccer, visit the USYSA Web site (www.usyouthsoccer.org).

Skill Event Variations and Modifications

Special Olympics offers individual skills competition for athletes with lower ability levels. Three events consist of dribbling, shooting, and running and kicking. Athletes perform each event twice, and all scores are then added for a total score. In the dribbling event, the player dribbles the ball 15 meters down a 5-meter lane into a 5-meter finish zone marked with cones. The clock stops when both the player and the ball are stopped inside the finish zone. If players overdribble the finish zone, they must dribble the ball back into the zone to finish. If the ball runs over the sideline, the referee places another ball in the center of the lane opposite the point at which the ball went out. The elapsed time it takes to do this is converted into points. The maximum number of points that can be obtained is 60, and the minimum is 10 (less a deduction of 5 points each time the ball runs over the sideline or a player touches the ball with her hands).

In the shooting event, the player runs forward a distance of 2 meters and then kicks a stationary ball into a goal 4 meters wide by 2 meters deep from a distance of 6 meters. Once the kick is made, the player returns to the starting line. A total of five kicks are allowed, and each successful kick is worth 10 points.

In the run-and-kick event, the player stands 4 meters from four balls (one to the left, one to the right, one in front, and one in back). The player begins by running to any ball and kicking it 2 meters through a target gate that is 2 meters wide and formed by cones. Play continues until all four balls have been kicked. From when the player starts to when the last ball is kicked, total time is recorded in seconds. The time is then converted into points. The maximum number of points is 50; the minimum number is 5. In addition, a bonus of 5 points is added for each ball kicked successfully through the target.

Other Variations and Modifications

For a simplified game, fewer than 11 players can participate, and field dimensions can be reduced. For players with low stamina, a partially deflated ball (which does not travel as fast as a fully inflated ball) can be used, and frequent rest breaks, substitutions, or time-outs can be incorporated into the game. A soft foam soccer ball or a cage ball can be used. Players with upper-limb deficiencies might be allowed to kick the ball inbounds on a throw-in. Additional players might be situated along the sidelines to take throw-ins for their teams. Penalty kicks can be employed for penalties occurring outside of goal areas. To avoid mass convergence on the ball, players can be required to play in specific zone areas.

SOFTBALL

Softball uses the skills of throwing, catching, fielding, hitting, and running. With certain modifications, the game can be played in an integrated setting by most people with disabilities, although players with visual or mobility impairments might find competing in a segregated setting more appropriate. The National Wheelchair Softball Association (NWSA) sponsors competition for athletes in wheelchairs, the NBBA sponsors competition for players with blindness, Special Olympics sponsors competition for players with intellectual disabilities, and the DAAA sponsors competition for players with dwarfism. The DAAA follows Amateur Softball Association of America (ASA) rules with no modifications.

Game Skills

Game skills important to softball are throwing, catching, fielding, and batting. Selected modifications are offered for each skill.

■ *Throwing.* People with visual impairments throw with better accuracy if the person receiving the ball communicates verbally with the thrower. For players with small hands or hand deformities, the use of a smaller or foam ball is recommended. Because of control problems, people with cerebral palsy might prefer using a slightly heavier ball. People with lower-limb disabilities will be able to throw the ball quite well; however, they will have difficulty throwing for distance because body rotation might be limited. A player with one upper limb will be able to throw the ball without much difficulty.

■ *Catching and fielding.* Players with visual impairments will learn to catch more easily if a large, brightly colored ball is initially rolled or bounced. A beep baseball, described in the Sport Variations and Modifications section, will be most helpful. People using wheelchairs and those with crutches or with braces might wish to use a large glove. Players with one upper limb will be able to catch with one hand as long as eye–hand coordination is well developed. A glove is helpful to most players with one arm who have a remaining segment of the affected limb, provided they have mastered the technique of catching the ball and then freeing it from the glove for a throw. (After the catch, the player removes the glove with the ball by placing it under the armpit of the limb segment; the hand is then quickly drawn from the glove to grasp the ball for the throw). Jim Abbott, a former Major League pitcher, used this technique.

■ An oversize glove can facilitate fielding for players with poor eye–hand coordination. Fielders should face the direction from which the ball is being hit, and players with visual impairments should be encouraged to listen for a ground ball moving along the ground. Players with assistive devices or in wheelchairs can be paired with sighted players without disabilities for assistance in fielding. Although a fielder in a wheelchair should be able to intercept a ball independently, the assisting player can retrieve it from the ground after interception and hand it to the player with a disability for the throw.

■ *Batting.* Players with one upper limb will be able to bat as long as the nonimpaired limb possesses enough strength to hold and swing the bat. To promote hitting, the player might use a lighter bat, grasping it not too close to the handle. Players in wheelchairs or on crutches must rely more on arm and shoulder strength for batting because they will be unable to shift their body weight from the back leg to the front leg to provide power for the swing. Plastic bats with large barrels will be helpful for people with poor arm and grip strength or poor eye–hand coordination. In this case, a large Wiffle ball should be used.

Lead-Up Games and Activities

Lead-up games and activities are important prerequisites to learning the game of softball. Selected lead-up games and activities are provided.

■ *Home-run softball.* The game is played on a softball field with a pitcher and catcher, a batter, and one fielder. The object of the game is for the batter to hit a pitched softball into fair territory, then run to first base and return home before the fielder or pitcher can get the ball to the catcher. The batter is out when three strikes are made, a fly ball is caught, or the ball reaches the catcher before the batter returns home.

■ *Lead-up team softball.* The game is played in any open area, with six players constituting the team. Players position themselves in any manner about 3.5 meters from each other. To begin play, the first player throws the ball to the second player. Each player attempts to catch the softball and throw it (in any manner) to the next one. When the sixth player catches the ball, he attempts to throw it to a 1-meter-square target from a distance of 4 meters. Following that throw, players rotate positions until each player has had an opportunity to throw the ball to the target.

■ *Other activities.* Additional activities include throwing beanbags in an underarm manner through a hoop suspended from the floor, hitting balls for distance from a batting tee, punching a volleyball pitched underarm, keeping a balloon in the air by hitting it with a plastic stick, and batting a ball suspended from the ceiling or a tetherball pole.

Sport Variations and Modifications

Beep baseball, designed for athletes with visual impairments, is sanctioned by the NBBA. The object of the game is for the batter to hit a regulation 16-inch (40.6 cm) audio softball equipped with a special sound-emitting device and to reach base before an opposing player fields the ball. (The ball is manufactured by Qwest Communications International and distributed by the Denver Beep Ball Group in Colorado. To obtain a beep ball, visit the NBBA Web site at www.nbba.org.) The TelecomPioneers, a volunteer organization, has been largely responsible for the success of beep baseball (figure 26.1).

Teams are composed of six players. Each team might have two additional teammates on the roster; they play blindfolded only when no other player with visual impairment is available to play. All

Photo courtesy of David L. Porretta.

Photo courtesy of David L. Porretta.

FIGURE 26.1 Beep baseball competition.

players, even those with visual impairment, must wear blindfolds. In addition to the two teammates who might be on the roster, two sighted players function as the pitcher and catcher. The pitcher throws the ball (from a distance of 20 ft [6.1 m]) in an underarm motion to the batter in an attempt to give up hits. The pitcher must give two verbal cues to the batter before the pitch: "ready" and "pitch" (or "ball"). The catcher assists batters by positioning them in the batter's box, and she also retrieves pitched balls.

On defense, both sighted players (spotters) stand in the field and assist their six teammates in fielding the ball by calling out the number of the defensive player closest to the ball. The spotters cannot field balls themselves. If a hit ball presents a chance of injury to a player, the spotter might yell a warning. Also, a spotter might knock down an unusually hard-hit ball headed directly toward a player; however, a run will be awarded to the offensive team. To assist players and spotters, position markers can be spray painted on the field to identify defensive positions. A batter gets four strikes before being called out. A batter might allow one ball to go by without penalty, and any additional pitched balls that are not swung at are strikes. Bunting is not allowed. Each side has three outs per inning, and there are six innings to an official game unless more are needed to break a tie.

On hitting the ball beyond the foul line (see figure 26.2), the batter runs to one of two bases (one located down the third baseline and one located down the first baseline) that are at least 122 centimeters high. Bases are padded cylinders that contain battery-powered, remotely controlled buzzers that emit a steady buzz when activated; the umpire predetermines which buzzer is to be activated by giving a hand signal to the base operator before the ball is hit. The bases are located off the foul line to prevent a defensive player from colliding with a base runner. To score a run, the batter must touch the appropriate base before an opposing player cleanly fields the ball. However, if the opposing player fields the ball before the batter reaches base, the batter is out.

The game of softball has been modified for players in wheelchairs by the NWSA (see figure 26.3). The game is played under official rules for 16-inch (40.6 cm) slow-pitch softball as approved by the ASA with the following major modifications:

■ Manual wheelchairs with foot platforms must be used.

■ The field is a smooth, level surface of blacktop or similar material.

■ Bases are 50 feet (15.2 m) in length from each other; home plate to second base is a distance of 70 feet, 8 inches (21.5 m).

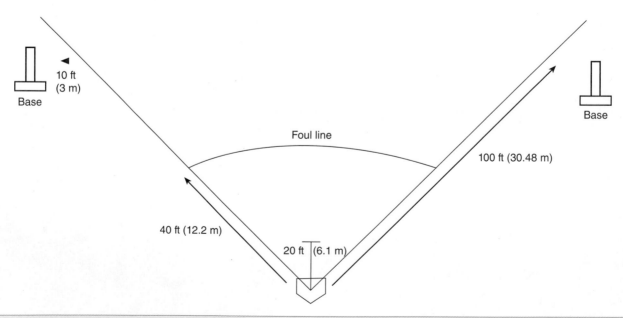

FIGURE 26.2 Beep baseball field.

- The pitching stripe is located 28 feet (8.5 m) from home plate.
- Second base is composed of a circle with a 4-foot (1.2 m) diameter; first and third bases are composed of 4-foot (1.2 m) semicircles.
- Teams are balanced by a point system.
- Neither a hitter nor a fielder (when playing the ball) can have any lower extremity in contact with the ground.
- Fielders cannot play the ball with any lower extremity in contact with the ground.
- Teams must have a player with quadriplegia on the team and in active play.
- Each team is composed of 10 players.

The game of softball is also modified for Special Olympics (2008a). Official events include slow-pitch team competition and tee-ball competition. Both events follow International Softball Federation (ISF) and national governing body rules for slow-pitch softball. The following are some modifications used for the slow-pitch game:

- The distance from home plate to the pitching rubber can be modified to a distance of 40 feet (12.2 m).
- A 12-inch (30.5 cm) restricted-flight softball must be used.
- Ten players play defense at any one time.

- An extra player may be used. If one is used, he must play the entire game. The extra player might be substituted at any time.
- If an extra player is used, all 11 players must bat, and any 10 are allowed to play defense.
- If the batter has two strikes and fouls off the third pitch, the batter is out.
- The catcher must wear a face mask and batter's helmet.

For young people with disabilities, additional modified programs are available. The Little League Challenger division offers the opportunity to participate to boys and girls with physical or intellectual disabilities who are 5 to 18 years of age or who remain in school. Players are assigned teams based on ability, not age. Little League players without disabilities who are 11 to 12 years of age serve as buddies. The Challenger division has three levels: tee ball, coach pitch, and player pitch. For additional information, visit the Little League Web site (see the electronic resources). For communities where Little League is not available, community organizers can offer a similar modified program through the Miracle League. Children and children with various physical or intellectual disabilities participate with community children who serve as buddies. What makes the Miracle League unique is that games are played on a specially designed field with a rubber surface similar to that used in

FIGURE 26.3 Players participating in a wheelchair softball game.

Photo courtesy of David L. Porretta.

wheelchair softball. For more information on the program, visit the Miracle League Web site (www.miracleleague.com).

Skill Event Variations and Modifications

Special Olympics offers individual skills competition for athletes with lower abilities (not for athletes who can already play the game) in four events: baserunning, throwing, fielding, and hitting. The scores for each event are added to obtain the athlete's final score. In the baserunning event, the player must start at home plate, run the bases (positioned 65 ft [19.8 m]) apart, and return home as fast as possible. The time in seconds needed to run the bases is subtracted from 60 to determine the point score; a 5-second penalty is given for each base missed or touched in improper order. The better of two trials is counted.

In the throwing event, the object is to throw a softball as far and as accurately as possible. Two attempts are given, and the player's score is the distance of the longest throw (measured from the restraining line to the point where the ball first touches the ground). The score reflects the throwing distance in meters minus the error distance (the number of meters the ball landed to the left or right of a perpendicular throwing line marked from the restraining line). Similar events sponsored by the BNDSA include a soft shot and a club throw for distance. BNDSA junior events also include a softball throw. Distance-throwing events such as the shot and club throws are also offered in competition sponsored by Wheelchair and Ambulatory Sports, USA (WASUSA).

The fielding event requires the player to stand between two cones 10 feet (3 m) apart and catch a total of 10 ground balls (five attempts per trial for a total of two trials) thrown by an official from 65 feet (19.8 m) away. The throw from the official must hit the ground before traveling 20 feet (6.1 m). The athlete can move aggressively to the thrown ball. Catching the ball in the glove or trapping it against the body but off the ground earns 5 points and blocking the ball scores 2 points.

The hitting event requires the player to bat for distance by hitting a softball off a batting tee. Three attempts are allowed, and the longest hit is the player's score. The distance is measured in meters from the tee to the point at which the ball first touches the ground. If the score falls between meters, the score is rounded down to the lower meter.

Other Variations and Modifications

To accommodate players' varying ability levels, the number of strikes a batter is allowed can be increased. In some cases, fewer than four bases can be used, and distances between bases can be shortened. Half-innings might end when three outs have been made, six runs have been scored, or 10 batters have come to bat. In addition, lighter-weight and large-barreled bats might be used. For players with poor eye–hand coordination, such as those with cerebral palsy or traumatic brain injury, the ball might be hit from a batting tee. A larger ball or restricted-flight softball, which travels a limited distance when hit, might be used. For players with more severe impairments, the ball might be rolled down a groove or tubelike channel when they are at bat. A walled or fenced area is recommended for players with mobility impairments so that distances can be shortened. In addition, a greater number of players on defense might be allowed, especially if players have mobility problems. The game can also be modified so that it is played in a gym with a Wiffle ball and bat.

VOLLEYBALL

Volleyball is a popular game included in most programs. Game skills include serving, passing, striking, and spiking the ball. Most people with disabilities can be integrated into the game. However, for players with severe intellectual disabilities or those with significant visual or mobility impairments, the game might require modifications.

Game Skills

Important volleyball game skills consist of serving and striking. Selected modifications are provided for each skill.

■ *Serving*. Players with disabilities can learn to serve quite effectively. It is helpful to begin with an underhand serve. The nondominant hand is beneath the ball, and the dominant hand (fisted) strikes the ball in an underhand motion. Very young players or those with insufficient arm and shoulder strength can move closer to the net. As players develop coordination, they can progress to the overhand serve. Players with one functional arm can serve overhand by tossing the ball into the air with the nonimpaired arm and then hitting it with the same arm. Wheelchair users will be able to perform both the underhand and overhand serves, though for the underhand serve, it is important to be in a chair without armrests.

■ *Striking.* Players with visual impairments can competently hit the ball with two hands if the ball is first allowed to bounce. This gives the player more time to visually track the ball. Because of limited mobility, players on crutches will need to learn to return the ball with one hand. However, players in wheelchairs can use both hands to return the ball within their immediate area. As these players become more adept in predicting the flight of the ball, they are able to make a greater percentage of returns.

Lead-Up Games and Activities

Lead-up games and activities are important prerequisites to learning the game of volleyball. Selected lead-up games and activities are provided.

■ *Keep It Up.* This game is played by teams that form circles about 15 to 20 feet (4.6-6.1 m) in diameter. Any number of teams of six to eight members each may play. To begin the game, a team member tosses the volleyball into the air within the circle. Teammates use both hands to keep hitting the ball into the air (it must not hit the ground). A player may not strike the ball twice in succession. The team that keeps the ball in the air the longest scores 1 point; the team with the most points wins the game.

■ *Serving activity.* A player hits a total of 10 volleyballs, either underhand or overhand, over a net and into the opposite court. Point values are assigned to various areas within the opposite court, with areas farther away from the net having higher values. The player's score is the point total for all 10 serves.

■ *Other activities.* Additional activities might include setting a beach ball or large balloon to oneself as many times as possible in succession, serving in the direction of a wall and catching the ball as it returns, or spiking the ball over a net about 1 foot (30 cm) higher than the player.

Sport Variations and Modifications

DS/USA, DAAA, and Special Olympics offer team sport competition in volleyball. Volleyball competi-

tion is governed internationally by the International Wheelchair and Amputee Sports Federation (IWAS) and the International Paralympic Committee (IPC). Players are classified according to functional ability, especially for DS/USA competition. For example, players with amputations are classified according to the site and degree of amputation. Two modifications of the sport under the DAAA consist of a slightly lowered net and smaller court dimensions. National competition for DAAA follows USA Volleyball rules and regulations. Finally, sitting volleyball was first introduced in the Netherlands as early as the mid 1950s (figure 26.4). In 1980, it became an official Paralympic sport. Table 26.1 illustrates the differences between sitting and standing volleyball.

Special Olympics volleyball competition is based on Fédération Internationale de Volleyball (FIVB) rules and the rules of each country's national governing board. Some modifications of the game (Special Olympics, 2008a) include the following:

■ Hitting the ball with any part of the body on or above the waist

■ Moving the serving area closer to the net but no closer than 4.5 meters

■ Using a lightweight ball no heavier than 226 grams

Skill Event Variations and Modifications

Special Olympics competition includes three skill events: overhead passing (volleying), serving, and passing (forearm). These events are designed for athletes with lower ability levels, not for those who can already play the game. Scores obtained in each event are added to obtain a final score. For the overhead passing event, the player stands 2 meters from the net and 4.5 meters from the sideline on a regulation-size court. A tosser provides the player with 10 two-handed underhand balls from the backcourt 4 meters from the baseline and 4.5 meters from the sideline in the left back position. The player sets the tossed ball to a target (a player standing 2 m from the net and 2 m from the front left sideline position). If any toss is not high enough for the player to set, it is repeated. The peak of the arc of each set should be above net height. The height of each set is measured. Participants earn 1 point for setting the ball 1 meter above the athlete's head, 3 points for setting the ball above net height, and 0 points for illegal contact (a ball that goes lower than head

FIGURE 26.4 Participation in sitting volleyball.

Photo courtesy of USA Volleyball.

height or goes over the net outside the court). The final score is the sum of all points awarded for the 10 attempts.

Serving competition requires the athlete to serve a ball into the opponent's side of the court. That court is divided into three areas of equal size, and a point value is assigned to each area. One point is awarded for a serve landing in the area of the opponent's court closest to the net, 3 points are awarded for a serve landing in the middle third area, and 5 points are awarded for a serve landing in the area closest to the opponent's end line. For serves that land on a line, the athlete receives the higher point value. The final score is the total number of points made in 10 serves.

In the forearm passing event, the athlete stands on a regulation court at the right back position 3 meters from the right sideline and 1 meter from the baseline. A tosser standing on the same side of the net in front center court 2 meters from the net makes a two-hand overhead toss. The athlete returns the toss with a forearm pass to a target (person standing on the same side of and 2 m from the net and 4 m from the side away from the tosser). Varying point values are marked on the frontcourt. This is repeated with the athlete at the left back position. To receive the maximum number of points, the peak of the arc of the pass must be at least net height. A ball landing on a line is assigned the higher point value. One point is received if the ball passes below net height. The final score is determined by adding the five attempts from both the left and right sides.

Other Variations and Modifications

Volleyball is easily modified for most players with disabilities. Most often, court dimensions are reduced, the net is lowered, and the serving line is brought closer to the net to accommodate varying abilities of players, especially for players in wheelchairs. Balls might be permitted one bounce before players attempt to return them over the net, or an unlimited number of hits by the same team might be allowed before the ball is returned. Players with arm or hand disabilities can be allowed to carry on a hit or return. To serve, players might throw the ball over the net rather than hitting it, and they might catch the ball before returning it. Players might have greater success by using a large, colored beach ball or a foam ball. Players who have mobility problems, such as those using

Table 26.1 **Basic Rule Differences Between Sitting and Standing Volleyball**

Game characteristics	Sitting	Standing
Court dimensions	32 ft, 8 in. (10 m) x 19 ft, 7 in. (6 m)	59 ft (18 m) x 29 ft, 5 in. (9 m)
Attack lines	6 ft, 5 in. (2 m) from the middle of the centerline	9 ft, 8 in. (3 m) from the middle of the centerline
Net size	21 ft, 7 in. (6.5 m) x 2 ft, 6 in. (.8 m)	31 ft, 2 in. (9.5 m) x 3 ft, 3 in. (1 m)
Net height	3 ft, 8 in. (1.15 m) (men) 3 ft, 4 in. (1.05 m) (women)	7 ft, 9 in. (2.43 m) (men) 7 ft, 3 in. (2.24 m) (women)
Equipment	Not allowed to sit on thick materials	NA
Play	Positions of players are determined by the position of their buttocks.	Positions of players are determined by the position of their feet contacting the ground.
	Players are not allowed to lift their buttocks from the court when carrying out any type of attack hit.	NA
	When serving, the server must be in the service zone and buttocks must not touch the court.	When serving, the server's feet must be in the service zone and must not touch the court.
	Only front-row players are allowed to block the opponent's service.	It is a fault to block the opponent's service.

crutches or walkers, might play the game from a seated position, or the number of players on each team might be increased.

GOALBALL

Goalball, a sport invented almost 60 years ago in Europe, was created primarily for sport and rehabilitation for World War II veterans with visual impairments. The game was first introduced to world competition at the 1976 Paralympics in Toronto. Goalball requires players to use auditory tracking, agility, coordination, and teamwork. The game is played in a silent arena in which blindfolded players attempt to score goals by rolling a ball across an opponent's goal line. Game skills are throwing, shot blocking, and ball control. Goalball follows rules established by the International Blind Sport Association (IBSA).

Males and females compete separately. To remove any advantages for players possessing partial sight, all players are blindfolded, even those who are totally blind, using blacked-out swim or ski goggles. A hard rubber ball 76 centimeters in circumference and weighing about 1.25 kilograms

is used. Each ball contains bells that allow players to track it during play. Information on purchasing goalballs can be obtained from the United States Association of Blind Athletes (USABA) by referring to the electronic resources section at the end of the chapter.

Many players wear protective padding covering the knees, elbows, and hips, similar to the padding worn in volleyball or ice hockey. Some players prefer to wear American football pants and pads or soccer goalie pads combined with other pants for protection. Coaches are not permitted to communicate with their players outside of halftime or official time-outs. Spectators must also remain silent so that players can hear the ball. However, the rules permit communication between players in the form of talking, finger snapping, or tapping on the floor.

The game consists of two 10-minute periods, and halftime lasts 3 minutes. Running time is not used; rather, the clock is stopped at various points in the game (e.g., a scored goal). Three 45-second team time-outs are allowed during regulation play. Whistles are used to communicate clock times to players. Each team is allowed a total of six players. Three players are on the court at any one time, and each team is allowed three substitutions per game.

Players must remain within their respective play zones. Boundaries are marked with any type of textured tape about 5 centimeters wide. To assist players in remaining in their zones, a heavy string covered by tape can line the boundaries (figure 26.5). Play begins with a throw by the designated team. During the game, the ball must touch the floor at least once between the two overthrow lines (neutral area). If it does not touch, the throw counts but cannot result in a score. The ball might be passed twice before each throw on goal.

All three players may play defense. Defensive players might assume a kneeling, crouching, or lying position to contact the ball, but they cannot assume a lying position on the playing surface until an opponent has thrown the ball. Defenders might move laterally within their team area. However, they cannot rush forward into the throwing area to intercept the ball except to follow a deflection. A player must throw the ball within 10 seconds after defensive control has been gained.

Should a personal or team penalty be assessed, the offending team must defend a penalty throw. In the case of a personal penalty, the player committing the penalty is the only player to defend against the penalty throw. In the case of a team penalty, the player who made the last throw before the penalty was awarded will defend the throw. If a team penalty is awarded before a throw has been taken, the player to defend the throw will be at the coach's discretion. Should the game end in a tie, two additional three-minute periods are played. The team scoring the first overtime goal is the winner.

The USABA encourages and promotes goalball development camps across the country and provides technical assistance and professional support to members who are interested in offering these camps. The camps are designed to assist new players in learning the game.

Game Skills

Important goalball skills are throwing, blocking, and ball control. Selected modifications are offered for each skill.

■ *Throwing.* Most players can easily accomplish throwing. The ball is thrown in an underhand manner so that it rolls along the ground. People with poor upper-body strength or poor motor control might need to use a lighter ball. Players with one arm can effectively throw the ball, whereas players with orthopedic impairments who use scooters might need to push the ball with both hands along the ground rather than throwing it underhand. In other cases, players on scooters can throw the ball by striking it with a sidearm motion when it is located at their side.

■ *Blocking and ball control.* Blocking and ball control are essential skills because defensive players must stop the ball from entering the goal area. Once the ball is blocked, it is brought under control with the hands so that a throw can be made. It might be helpful to have players with intellectual disabilities see the ball when learning to block so that they can more effectively coordinate body movement with the sound of the ball. Players with amputations can wear prosthetic devices to assist

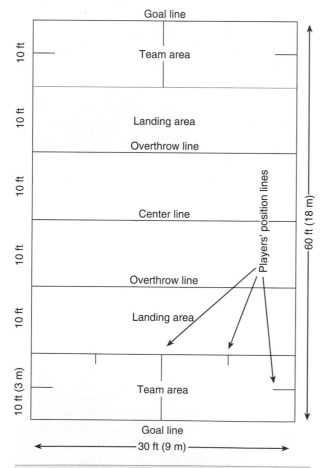

FIGURE 26.5 Goalball arena. (According to IBSA rules, all measurements are to be within a half-meter of these.)

in blocking, as long as the ball does not damage the device or vice versa.

Lead-Up Games and Activities

Lead-up games and activities are important prerequisites to learning the game of goalball. Selected lead-up games and activities are provided.

■ *Heads-Up.* This game involves one-on-one competition with players positioning themselves in their half of the arena. A player is given possession of the ball with the object of scoring a goal. The ball must be continuously rolled as the offensive player moves about; the player cannot carry the ball. The defensive player can take control of the ball from the offensive player by deflecting or trapping a shot on goal. The first player to score three goals wins the game.

■ *Speedy.* This game involves two teams of three players each who play within an enclosed area. Players on each team assume a crouching or kneeling position and form a triangle with a distance of 12 feet (3.7 m) between players. Players position themselves on small area rugs and face the middle of the triangle. On command, a designated player rolls a goalball as quickly as possible to the player on the immediate right, who controls the ball and rolls it to the next player on the right, and so on. If the player to whom it was rolled does not control the ball, that player must retrieve the ball and return to the area rug before rolling to the next player. Each time the ball returns to the player who started the game, a point is scored. The team scoring the most points in one minute wins the game. Teams compete one at a time so that players can hear the ball.

■ *Other activities.* Other activities include throwing for accuracy to the goal and passing the ball as quickly as possible between two players for a set amount of time.

Sport Variations and Modifications

Goalball has quickly gained popularity in the United States and is an official USABA competitive sport. People with other types of disabilities as well as people without disabilities can participate in the game as long as blindfolds are worn.

Other Variations and Modifications

The game might be modified by increasing or decreasing the size of the play arena and the number of players on a side. People with mobility challenges might play on scooter boards, and a lighter ball might be used for players with poor upper-arm and shoulder strength.

QUAD RUGBY

Quad rugby (internationally known as wheelchair rugby), originally called *murderball*, was developed in the late 1970s by wheelchair athletes from Manitoba, Canada. In 1981, the game was introduced in the United States and quickly gained popularity. The United States Quad Rugby Association (USQRA) was formed in 1988 to promote and regulate the game at both the national and international levels. The USQRA is the national governing body for quad rugby in WASUSA competition. To further advance the sport, the USQRA sponsors a number of instructional clinics each year around the country. Today, quad rugby is the fastest growing wheelchair sport in the world. Stoke Mandeville in England was the site of the first international competition in 1990. In 1996, the game was played at the Paralympics as an exhibition sport. The International Wheelchair Rugby Federation (IWRF) holds a world championship every four years, and in 2000 the sport attained full medal status at the Paralympics.

Quad rugby is designed for players who have quadriplegia that prevents them from participating in other sports, such as wheelchair basketball. People who exhibit upper- and lower-extremity limitations caused by spinal cord injuries, cerebral palsy, spina bifida, and les autres conditions are eligible to compete. Quad rugby is a combination of American football, ice hockey, and wheelchair basketball. Teams are composed of four on-court players. To equalize competition, players are classified according to functional ability by a point system. Players are provided a classification number from one of seven classifications ranging from .5 (most impaired) to 3.5 (least impaired). The player classified as .5 has function comparable to C5 quadriplegia, whereas a player classified as 3.5 has function comparable to C7 to C8 incomplete quadriplegia. The combined classification points cannot exceed 8 for the four on-court players.

Because of the classification process, males and females can compete on the same team. A complete copy of quad rugby rules and regulations can be obtained from the IWRF Web site (www.iwrf.com). For additional information on how to become a referee or classifier, visit the USQRA Web site (www.quadrugby.com).

Quad rugby is played on a regulation basketball court. Cones placed at the end of each line identify the goal lines at each end of the court. In front of each goal line is a key area 8 meters by 1.75 meters. The object of the game is to carry the ball (regulation volleyball) over the opponent's goal line. Players try to gain possession of the ball by forcing a bad pass or a violation. The team with the most goals at the end of the game wins. At no time can all four defensive players be in the restricted area. Full chair contact is allowed, and any form of hand protection might be used; however, whatever is used cannot be harmful to other players (e.g., hard or rough material). The game is composed of four eight-minute periods. Should the game end in a tie, three-minute overtime periods are played. The team scoring the first overtime goal is the winner.

The ball handler can make an unlimited number of pushes, but the ball must be either passed or bounced within 10 seconds or else a turnover is assessed. A player has 15 seconds to advance the ball into the opponent's half of the court. Although only three defensive players can be in the key area at any one time, all four offensive players are allowed in the key area for 10 seconds at a time. Players committing personal fouls must serve time in a penalty box, which gives the opposing team a power play.

Game Skills

Important quad rugby game skills consist of wheelchair mobility, throwing, and catching. A brief description of each skill is provided.

■ *Wheelchair mobility.* Chair mobility is essential in quad rugby. Mobility skills consist of maneuvering the chair with the ball, picking, and sprinting. To maneuver effectively, the player must place the ball securely in the lap. Maneuverability consists of being able to move forward and backward as fast as possible in addition to being able to turn the chair quickly to the left or right. Players also must be able to bounce and pass the ball while the chair is in motion. Players

set picks to gain an offensive advantage. A set pick is where an offensive player maneuvers to the side or behind a defensive player guarding an offensive teammate. This creates an offensive advantage in that the offensive player (not the one creating the pick) can move or drive around the pick. Players having the ability to quickly start from a stopped position have an advantage over other players, especially when sprinting down the court. Sprinting up and down the court places the offensive player in a better position to score and places the defensive player in an advantageous position to defend against a score.

■ *Throwing and catching.* Throwing (accuracy and distance) and catching are essential skills in the game of quad rugby. The nature of the game requires that the ball be advanced, and throwing (passing) the ball is the quickest way to do it. Depending on ability level, a one-hand or two-hand throw can be thrown. Those with more severe upper-limb impairments might need to throw two-handed. The skill of catching needs to be mastered while the chair is either moving or stationary. Of course, the ability to catch while the chair is in motion is an advantage. For players who do not have full control of the hands, catching (trapping) the ball can be done with closed fists, wrists, or forearms.

Lead-Up Games and Activities

Lead-up games and activities are important prerequisites to learning the game of quad rugby. Selected lead-up games and activities are provided.

■ *Mobility relay.* Relay teams are composed of three or more players. Three cones are placed at 4-meter intervals from a starting line. The distance from the starting line to the third cone is 12 meters. The object of the relay is to wheel forward as fast as possible in a figure-eight fashion around each of the three cones. Rounding the third cone, the player returns to the starting line by wheeling backward. The first team to successfully complete the relay wins.

■ *Accuracy passing.* A passing line is marked on a court floor 5 meters from a wheelchair situated on the court. The start line is situated 3 meters behind the passing line. The total distance between the start line and the wheelchair is 8 meters. On command, the player begins moving forward and passes the ball to the wheelchair (facing the player) before crossing the passing line. The player gets a total of five throws. The final score is the number of times the player hits the wheelchair in the air. Should the player go over the passing line before the ball is thrown, a fault is called and the pass does not count.

■ *Other activities.* A battery of quad rugby skill tests (consisting of sprinting, passing, picking, and maneuvering) has been validated (Yilla & Sherrill, 1998). Each of these skills can be used in practice for the competitive sport or can be used as lead-up activities in physical education classes.

INCLUSION

During physical education, and at times in athletics, players with disabilities can be included in regular or adapted sports of basketball, floor hockey, volleyball, football, soccer, and softball. The games of goalball and quad rugby are designed for people with specific disabilities. However, participants with disabilities as well as those without disabilities might play them. As long as certain techniques are applied, most players with disabilities can be successfully and safely integrated into the sports identified in this chapter. Many variations and modifications have already been presented. In addition, other techniques have also been successfully implemented, as shown in the following application example. One technique is to match abilities and positions; teachers and coaches should attempt to assign positions based on players' ability levels. In football, for example, players with mild intellectual disability possessing good catching skills could play end positions, whereas others with good speed could play the backfield. Players with upper-arm impairments can be the placekickers in football. In specific instances, a physical disability can be used to advantage. For example, Tom Dempsey, whose partial amputation of the kicking foot allowed for a broader surface with which to kick the ball, was a successful placekicker in the National Football League.

Teaching to players' abilities can also enhance integration. When teaching or coaching players with intellectual disabilities, emphasize concrete demonstrations over verbal instructions. Any verbal instructions should be short, simple, and direct, as when coaching first and third base in softball. In football and basketball, a few simple plays that have been overlearned can promote success, and the player holding the ball can shout or call out to help a partially sighted player with ball location.

Equipment modifications can also foster integration. For players with visual impairments, the teacher or coach can place audible goal locators in goal areas for sports such as basketball, soccer, and floor hockey. Goals can be brightly painted or covered with colored tape. For example, the crossbar

APPLICATION EXAMPLE

Transition

Setting: Interscholastic freshman football

Students: Players with mild intellectual disabilities or specific learning disabilities

Application: To accommodate the learning needs of these players, the coach could, among other strategies,

▶ require players to play only on special teams (e.g., kickoff, punt return) so that they will not need to know multiple play assignments,

▶ use task analysis for the learning of complex skills and assignments,

▶ allow players to wear a wristband to remind them of their play assignments,

▶ have teammates remind players of their play assignments in the huddle, and

▶ teach new plays and new skills at the beginning of practice and then review the new plays and new skills at the end of practice.

and goalposts in soccer could be brightly painted. In games played on an indoor court, such as floor hockey or basketball, mats might be placed along the sidelines to differentiate the playing surface from the out-of-bounds area.

Special Olympics promotes competition with players without disabilities provided the Special Olympics athletes have demonstrated the ability to participate in team sport. This ability includes not only the attainment of certain skills but also teamwork and team strategy. In addition to a comprehensive Unified Sports coaching guide (Special Olympics, 2003) covering history, partner eligibility, and program benefits, Special Olympics provides Unified Sports rules for basketball, floor hockey, soccer, softball, and volleyball (Special Olympics, 2008a, 2008b).

SUMMARY

This chapter described a number of popular team sports included in physical education and sport programs. Team sports included in competition sponsored by sport organizations such as the USADSF, DAAA, NBBA, DS/USA, NWBA, NWSA, Special Olympics, USABA, and BNDSA and international sport organizations (e.g., IBSA, IWRF, UWFA) were also discussed. Game skills and variations and modifications specific to each sport were identified. Also presented were lead-up games and activities, as well as rules and strategies, corresponding to those found in programs for players without disabilities. Finally, suggestions for integrating people with disabilities into team sports were offered in addition to the many modifications and variations presented earlier to promote inclusion.

REFERENCES

Cerebral Palsy International Sports and Recreation Association (CPISRA). (2005). *Classification and sports rules manual* (9th ed.). Bad Neuenahr-Ahrweiler, Germany: Author.

National Federation of High Schools (NFHS). (2008). *Football rules book*. Indianapolis: Author.

National Wheelchair Basketball Association (NWBA). (2007). *2007-2008 Official rules and casebook*. Colorado Springs: Author.

Special Olympics. (2003). *Unified Sports coaching guide*. Retrieved from www.specialolympics.org/coaching_guide_unifiedsports.aspx.

Special Olympics. (2008a). *Special Olympics summer sports rules*. Retrieved from www.specialolympics.org/sports.aspx.

Special Olympics. (2008b). *Official Special Olympics winter sports rules*. Retrieved from www.specialolympics.org/sports.aspx.

Yilla, A.B., & Sherrill, C. (1998). Validating the Beck battery of quad rugby skill tests. *Adapted Physical Activity Quarterly, 15*, 55-67.

WRITTEN RESOURCES

Special Olympics. (2007). *Young athletes activity guide*. Washington, DC: Author.

This guide describes a new program sponsored by Special Olympics. It is designed for children aged two to eight. The guide covers areas such as walking and running, balance and jumping, throwing and catching, striking, and kicking that lead to the development of various team sports skills.

Spirit: The magazine of Special Olympics. Special Olympics, Inc., 1325 G St. NW, Ste. 500, Washington, DC 20005.

This is a quarterly publication focusing on such topics as sports, athletes, families, volunteers, world games, celebrities, and fund-raising.

AUDIOVISUAL RESOURCES

Introduction to goalball [VHS]. (n.d.). USABA, 33 N. Institute St., Colorado Springs, CO 80903. www.usaba.org.

This video provides an overview of the sport of goalball. It can be purchased for a nominal fee by writing to USABA or by visiting www.usaba.org.

Risotto, D., & Sandy, S. (2007). *Dummy Hoy: A Deaf hero* [DVD]. Da-Cor Pictures. www.dacorpictures.com.

This documentary film is about the life of Major League Baseball player William "Dummy" Hoy. Many credit Hoy for incorporating the use of hand signals typically used by umpires, coaches, and players into the game. The film can be acquired by visiting the company's Web site.

ELECTRONIC RESOURCES

Little League Baseball Challenger division: www.littleleague.org.

This site provides information on the Challenger division designed for players with disabilities. It includes the history of the division, its grant program to foster local development, and a series of brochures detailing various aspects of the program.

United States Association of Blind Athletes (USABA): www.usaba.org.

This site provides information on membership, general information, and sport specific events such as goal ball. Information is also available on how to purchase goal balls.

U.S. Electric Wheelchair Hockey Association: www. powerhockey.com.

This site provides information on the game of floor hockey for people using power wheelchairs. Includes topics such as rules, equipment, news, and events.

World Organization Volleyball for Disabled (WOVD): www.wovd.info.

This site provides information on volleyball for people with physical disabilities. Sections such as history, constitution, competition schedules, statistics, refereeing, and rules (in English and Spanish) are included.

chapter 27

Individual, Dual, and Adventure Sports and Activities

E. Michael Loovis

Kevin approached the physical education instructor at a local college and inquired about signing up for the beginning tennis course. The instructor told Kevin he was welcome, and Kevin appeared at the first class. After the normal introductory lecture, students were paired up for some basic drills. Initially, only one student would pair up with Kevin; everyone seemed to think that he was incapable of doing well in tennis. It soon became obvious, however, that Kevin was quite capable, and other students wanted to be paired with him. Kevin picked up the forehand and backhand strokes quickly. He did have some difficulty with the serve, but even in this area he was ahead of most of the class. Kevin completed his competency testing before anyone else in the class and was patiently waiting for the class tournament to begin. When it did, Kevin quickly dispatched all his opponents! Although he needed to play while seated in a wheelchair, Kevin had clearly become the best tennis player in the class.

This chapter examines individual, dual, and adventure sports and activities in which people with unique needs can participate successfully. Participation is analyzed from two perspectives: within the context of sanctioned events sponsored by sport organizations and as part of physical education programs. In terms of organized competition, discussion is limited to the rules, procedural modifications, and adaptations that are in use and that are the only approved vehicle for participation. The remainder of the chapter is a compendium of modifications for several activities and sports, including the use of lead-up games and activities for players with disabilities.

TENNIS

Tennis can be played in one form or another by all people except those with the most severe disabilities. It can be played as a singles or doubles activity, so the skill requirements (both psychomotor and cognitive) can be modified in many ways to encourage participation. Regardless of the variations and modifications, the objective remains the same: to return the ball legally across the net and prevent the opponent from doing the same.

Sport Skills

Most people can play tennis using only the forehand and backhand strokes and the serve. For the ground strokes, good footwork or effective wheelchair mobility along with good racket preparation—moving the racket into the backswing well in advance of the ball—are fundamental to execution. Under normal circumstances, racket preparation and movement into position to return the ball are performed simultaneously.

Lead-Up Activities

Adams and McCubbin (1991) describe an elementary noncourt lead-up game, Target Tennis, that is appropriate for both students in wheelchairs and ambulatory students and that can be played indoors with limited space. Players position themselves behind the end-zone line, which is 10 feet (3 m) from a target screen. The screen has five openings, each 10 inches (25.4 cm) in diameter, which are the targets. The player tosses a tennis ball into the air and uses an overhand swing to bounce the ball midway between the end-zone line and the target so that the ball goes through one of the five openings. A bonus serve is permitted for every point scored. No points are awarded if the ball bounces twice.

Special Olympics (2008) offers four developmental events that can serve as lead-up activities: target stroke, target bounce, racket bounce, and return shot. In the target stroke, the athlete gets 10 attempts to drop-hit the ball within the boundaries of the opponent's singles court; 1 point is awarded for each successful hit. In the target bounce, the athlete bounces a tennis ball on the playing surface using one hand; the score is the highest number of consecutive bounces in two trials. In the racket bounce, the athlete bounces the ball off the racket face as many times consecutively as possible; the score is the most consecutive bounces in two trials. In the return shot, the athlete waits for the ball to bounce once and then attempts to return it over the net and into the opponent's singles court. One point is awarded for each successful hit, and the greatest number of successful consecutive attempts in two rounds is counted.

Sport Variations and Modifications

In 1980, the National Foundation of Wheelchair Tennis (NFWT) was founded to develop and sponsor competition. In 1981, the Wheelchair Tennis Players Association (WTPA) was formed under the aegis of the NFWT with the purpose of administering the rules and regulations of the sport. The United States Tennis Association (USTA) approved the formation of the Wheelchair Tennis Committee in 1996, and in 1998, it merged with the WPTA, making the USTA the governing body for wheelchair tennis.

The rules for wheelchair tennis are the same as for regular tennis except that the ball is allowed to bounce twice before being returned (International Tennis Federation [ITF], 2008). The first bounce must land in-bounds; the second bounce can land either in-bounds or out-of-bounds. Before serving, the player must be stationary and in the legal service position. The player can then take one push before striking the ball. At no time can any wheel of the player's chair exceed the baseline or cross the center mark or sideline. Players with quadriplegia who cannot serve in the conventional manner may drop the ball or have someone drop the ball for them. Once this type of serve is chosen, it must be used consistently throughout the match. Players who are unable to propel their chairs with the wheel may use one foot; however, that foot may not be in contact with the court during the forward swing of the racket, including when contact is made with the ball.

The USTA (2007) sanctions the following singles and doubles divisions: men's and women's open; men's A, B, and C; women's A, B, and E (novice); and boys' and girls' junior. There is also a senior doubles event. The quad division (open, A, and B) was established for players with limited power, mobility, and strength in at least three limbs as a result of accidents, spinal cord injuries, or other conditions. Also included in this division are players with quadriplegia with the ability to walk, players who use power wheelchairs, and players with three amputations.

Special Olympics (2008) offers the following events: singles, doubles, mixed doubles, Unified Sports doubles, Unified Sports mixed doubles, and individual skills competition. The latter consists of the forehand volley, backhand volley, forehand ground stroke, backhand ground stroke, serve into deuce court, serve into advantage (ad) court, and alternating ground strokes with movement. A player's final score is the cumulative score of all seven events.

Other Variations and Modifications

If mobility is a problem, the court size can be reduced to accommodate players with disabilities. This can be accomplished by having players without disabilities defend their entire regulation court while players with disabilities defend half of their court. It could also be accomplished by permitting players to strike the ball on the second bounce. Variations in the scoring system can promote participation. An example is scoring by counting the number of consecutive hits, which structures the game as cooperative rather than competitive. If the player with a disability has extremely limited mobility, the court could be divided into designated scoring areas, with those closest to that player receiving higher point values. Racket control might be a concern for some students because the standard tennis racket might be too heavy. There are several solutions to this problem, including shortening the grip on the racket, using a junior-

size racket, or substituting a racquetball racket. In the case of a player with an amputation, the racket can be strapped to the stump (if one remains) to allow for effective leverage and racket use.

If mobility or racket preparation is a problem, reducing the court size, at least initially, assists in learning proper racket positioning and stroking (because footwork is minimal). If players are still unsuccessful, they can be placed in the appropriate stroking position with the shoulder of the non-swinging arm perpendicular to the net. This way, they only have to move into and swing at the ball.

To serve, the player tosses the ball into the air with the hand opposite the one holding the racket. In preparation for striking the ball at the optimal height, the racket is moved in an arc from a position in front of the body down to the floor and up to a position behind the back. At this point, the racket arm is fully extended to strike the ball as it descends from the apex of the toss. For people who lack either the coordination or strength to perform the serve as described, an appropriate variation is to bring the racket straight up in front of the face to a position in which the hand holding the racket is even with the forehead or slightly higher. Although serving in this manner reduces speed and produces an arc that is considerably higher than normal, it allows players to serve who might otherwise not learn to serve correctly. To accomplish the toss, a player with a single-arm amputation might grip the ball in the racket hand by extending the thumb and first finger beyond the racket handle and hold the ball against the racket. The ball is then tossed in the air and hit in the usual way. A player with a double-arm amputation and the racket strapped to a stump uses a different approach. The ball lies on the racket strings, and, with a quick upward movement, the ball is thrust into the air and then struck either in the air or after it bounces.

TABLE TENNIS

As is true of tennis, all but the severely disabled can play table tennis or a version of it. Table tennis can be played in singles or doubles competition, and although the requisite skills are less adjustable than in tennis, the available mechanical modifications make this sport suitable for people with disabilities. Regardless of the variations and modifications, the objective of the game remains the same: to return the ball legally onto the opponent's side of the table in such a way as to prevent the opponent from making a legal return.

Sport Skills

As in tennis, the basic strokes are the forehand and backhand. Unlike tennis, the service is not a separate stroke. A serving player puts the ball in play with either a forehand or backhand stroke. The ball must strike the table on the server's side before striking the table on the receiver's side. In addition, servers must strike the ball outside the boundary at their end of the court.

Lead-Up Activities

Appropriate for use in physical education programs is surface table tennis, an adapted table tennis game created at the Kluge Children's Rehabilitation Center at the University of Virginia Hospital. Two or four people can play this game, which involves hitting a regulation table tennis ball so that it moves on the surface of the table and passes through a modified net. The net is constructed from two pieces of string strung parallel and attached a half-inch (1.25 cm) apart at the top of official standards, and two or three pieces of string strung parallel and attached three-quarters of an inch (2 cm) apart at the bottom of the standards with a 2-inch (5 cm) opening in the middle (Adams & McCubbin, 1991). At the start of play, the ball is placed on the table, and the player strikes it so that it rolls through the opening in the net into the opponent's court. Points are awarded to the player who last made a legal hit through the net. Points are lost when a player hits the ball over the net either on a bounce or in the air, when the ball fails to pass through the net, or when a player hits the ball twice in succession.

Another lead-up game, Corner Ping-Pong, was developed at the University of Connecticut (Dunn & Leitschuh, 2006). It is played in a corner in an area 6 feet (2 m) high and 6 feet wide on each side of the corner. One player stands on either side of the centerline. The server drops the ball and strokes it against the floor to the forward wall. The ball must rebound to the adjacent wall and then bounce onto the floor of the opponent's area. If the server fails to deliver a good serve, 1 point goes to the opponent. The ball may bounce only once on the floor before the opponent returns it. The ball must be hit against the forward wall within the opponent's section of the playing area so that it rebounds to the adjacent wall and onto the floor in the server's area. Failure to return the ball is 1 point for the server. Scoring is similar to that for table tennis. Each player gets five consecutive serves. A ball that is hit out-of-bounds is scored as 1 point for the other player. The winning score is 21 points, and the winner must win by 2.

Special Olympics provides three developmental events that can serve as lead-up activities: the target serve, racket bounce, and return shot (Special Olympics, 2008). In the target serve, the athlete serves five balls from the right side and five balls from the left side of the table; 1 point is awarded for each ball that lands in the correct service area. In the racket bounce, the athlete bounces the ball off the racket face as many times consecutively as possible in 30 seconds; the score is the most consecutive bounces in two trials. The return shot involves returning a tossed ball to the feeder's side of the table; 1 point is awarded if the ball is successfully returned, and 5 points are earned if the ball lands in one of the service boxes. The athlete attempts to return five balls, with a maximum of 25 points possible.

Sport Variations and Modifications

Table tennis is included in competitions offered by Wheelchair and Ambulatory Sports, USA (WASUSA); the Dwarf Athletic Association of America (DAAA); the USA Deaf Sports Federation (USADSF) through its affiliate, the U.S. Deaf Table Tennis Association; and Special Olympics. For the most part, competition is based on the rules established by the International Table Tennis Federation (ITTF) (2010) and International Paralympic Table Tennis Committee. Some modifications are permitted. For example, the DAAA permits the use of a riser or an elevated platform. In WASUSA competition (2008a), the following rules apply:

- Competitors' feet and footrests may not touch the floor.
- Service shall be called a let if the ball leaves the table by either of the receiver's sides, if on bouncing on the receiver's side the ball returns in the direction of the net, or if the ball comes to rest on the receiver's side of the playing surface.
- The playing surface shall not be used as a support with the free hand while playing the ball; a player may use the playing surface to restore balance after a shot has been played as long as the table does not move.
- Strapping is permitted only below the knee.

■ The playing area may be reduced, but it should not be less than 8 meters long and 7 meters wide.

■ There are no exceptions to the playing rules for players who stand.

Special Olympics (2008) sanctions the following events: singles, doubles, mixed doubles, wheelchair competition, individual skills competition, Unified Sports doubles, and Unified Sports mixed doubles. In wheelchair competition, players who are serving may project the ball upward in any manner; they are not required to deliver the ball from the palm of the free hand. The individual skills competition is composed of five events, including the hand toss, racket bounce, forehand volley, backhand volley, and serve. Scores from all five events are added for a final score.

Other Variations and Modifications

Several assistive devices are available for players with severe disabilities (e.g., muscular dystrophy and other disorders that weaken or affect the shoulder). A ball-bearing feeder provides assistance for shoulder and elbow motion by using gravity to gain a mechanical advantage and makes up for loss of power resulting from weakened muscles. The bihandle paddle, which consists of a single paddle with handles on each side, is designed to encourage larger range of motion for participants. Its greatest asset is increased joint movement resulting from the bilateral nature of hand and finger positioning. A strap-on paddle has been designed for players with little or no functional finger flexion or grasp. The paddle is attached to the back of the hand with Velcro straps. The major disadvantage is that it precludes use of a forehand stroking action. A table tennis cuff is useful for players with limited finger movement and grip strength. The cuff consists of a clip that attaches to a metal clamp on the paddle handle and a Velcro strap that holds the cuff securely to the hand (Adams & McCubbin, 1991).

Another device, the space ball net, can replace the paddle for players who are blind (Dunn & Leitschuh, 2006). This device consists of a lightweight metal frame that supports a nylon lattice or webbing and held in two hands. The net is large and provides an adequate rebounding surface to make participation feasible for players who are blind. Additionally, a special table has been designed for players with visual impairments or blindness. The table is all white and, when combined with a special orange ball containing metal beads, it accommodates players who have visual impairments.

ANGLING

The American Casting Association (ACA) is the governing body for tournament fly and bait casting in the United States. It sets the rules by which eligible casters can earn awards in registered tournaments. None of the sport organizations for people with disabilities sponsors competition in angling, and the activity is rarely seen in physical education programs. It is most likely used as a recreational sport.

Lead-Up Activities

Angling requires the mastery of casting and other fishing skills. In terms of lead-up activities, at least two casting games deserve mention. The game of skish involves accuracy in target casting at various distances. Each participant casts 20 times at each target, and 1 point is awarded for each direct hit (plug landing inside target or similar goal). Three targets can be used simultaneously to speed up the game, with players changing position after each has cast 20 times at a target. The player with the greatest number of hits at the end of 60 casts is the winner. The second game, speed casting, is a variation of skish. Each player casts for 5 minutes at each target, and the player with the high score at the end of 15 minutes is the winner (Adams et al., 1982).

Variations and Modifications

Major assistive devices for use in angling have become popular in recent years. For example, the Strong Arm rod holder (see figure 27.1) is a 6-ounce (170 g) sleeve into which the rod fits, enabling people with quadriplegia to cast. Other devices include the Ampo Fisher I, Van's EZ Cast, Batick Bracket, and Handi-Gear. Several lines of electronic fishing reels are also available through Access to Recreation, Inc.

ARCHERY

Shooting the longbow is usually a six-step procedure. The steps are assuming the correct stance, nocking the arrow, drawing the bowstring, aiming at the target, releasing the bowstring, and following

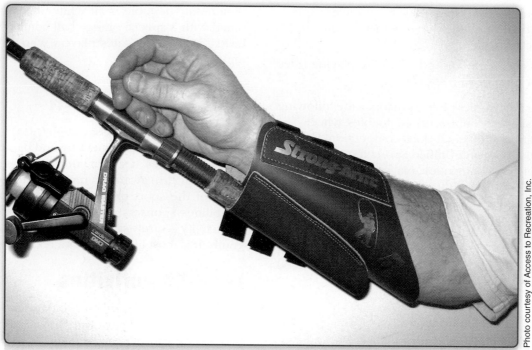

FIGURE 27.1 Strong Arm rod holder.

Photo courtesy of Access to Recreation, Inc.

through until the arrow makes contact with the target. One or more of these steps might be problematic and thus may require some modification in the archer's technique.

Sport Variations and Modifications

Target archery is an athletic event sponsored nationally by WASUSA and internationally by the International Paralympic Committee (IPC). These groups observe the rules established by the International Archery Federation (FITA), with certain modifications. The following are adjustments that might encourage participation by students in wheelchairs, including les autres athletes (IPC, 2007/2008; WASUSA, 2008b):

- An adjustable arrow rest and arrow plate and any movable pressure button or pressure point on the bow may be used, provided they are not electric or electronic and do not offer any additional aid in aiming; a draw-check indicator that is audible or visible but not electric or electronic may be used.

- Archers with quadriplegia (class AR1) may use strapping and body support.

- Only archers with bow-arm disability may have the bow bandaged or strapped into the hand. Archers with bow-arm disability may use an elbow or wrist splint; they may also have someone load their arrows into the bow for them.

- Archers with quadriplegia may use compound bows, and they may use a mechanical release aid with recurve and compound bows.

- Archers with functional use of only one side of their bodies can use a bow stand that holds the bow vertical to the target (only in junior divisions at WASUSA events).

Other Variations and Modifications

Several assistive devices are available to aid the archer who has a disability. These include the bow sling, commercially available from most sport shops, which helps stabilize the wrist and hand for bow control; the below-elbow amputee adapter device (see figure 27.2), which is held by the terminal end of the prosthesis and requires a slight rotation of the prosthesis to release the string and the arrow; the wheelchair bow stringer, which consists of an in-ground post with two appropriately spaced bolts around which the archer places the bow in order to produce enough leverage to string it independently; and the elbow brace, which is

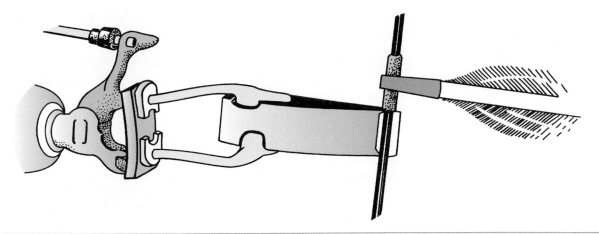

FIGURE 27.2 Amputee adapter device for archery.

used to maintain extension in the bow arm when the archer has normal strength in the shoulder but minimal strength in the arm, possibly because of contractures (Adams & McCubbin, 1991). Additionally, the vertical bow set can accommodate people with bilateral upper-extremity involvement (Wiseman, 1982).

Other program adjustments include the use of a crossbow with the aid of the tripod assistive device for bilateral upper-extremity amputees. Various telescopic sights are also commercially available for the archer with partial sight.

Although the United States Association of Blind Athletes (USABA) does not sponsor competition in archery, several modifications can promote participation by people with visual impairments (Hattenback, 1979):

- Using foot blocks to ensure proper orientation with the target
- Placing an audible goal locator behind the target to aid in directional cueing
- Using a brightly colored target for people with partial sight
- Placing balloons on the target as a means of auditory feedback

BADMINTON

Special Olympics (2008) sponsors competition in badminton, but it is classified as a recognized sport only, which means it can be included in Special Olympics training and competitive programs but probably has not generated enough interest to be included in their regular sport offerings. Badminton

was added as a new medal sport by the DAAA in 1998. The International Committee of Sports for the Deaf (CISS) sponsors competition in badminton at the Deaflympics. Currently, badminton is an inactive sport under the USADSF. Hearing aids and external cochlear implants are forbidden. Competition is based on the rules of the International Badminton Federation (IBF). The game is ideally suited for people with disabilities and is played routinely in physical education classes.

Sport Skills

Badminton can be played using only the forehand and backhand strokes and the underhand service. Beyond these strokes, development of the clear, smash, drop shot, and drive will depend on the participant's ability.

Lead-Up Activities

There are at least two lead-up games that deserve mention. Loop badminton (Dunn & Leitschuh, 2006) is played with a standard shuttlecock, table-tennis paddles, and a 24-inch (61 cm) loop placed on top of a standard 46 inches (1.2 m) in height. The object of the game is to hit the shuttlecock through the loop, which is positioned in the center of a rectangular court 10 feet (3 m) long and 5 feet (1.5 m) wide. Scoring is the same as in the standard game of badminton. Loop badminton is well adapted for people with restricted movement who wish to participate in an active game that requires extreme accuracy. A second modified game is balloon badminton (Adams & McCubbin, 1991), where a balloon is substituted for the shuttlecock and table-tennis paddles are used instead of badminton rackets. People with visual impairments can play this game if a bell is placed inside the balloon to aid in directional cueing.

The three lead-up activities Special Olympics provides for badminton are the target serve, return volley, and return serve (Special Olympics, 2008). In the target serve, the participant has 10 chances to hit the shuttlecock within the boundaries of the opponent's singles court; 1 point is awarded for each successful hit. In the return volley, the athlete has 10 chances to return the shuttlecock feed from the opponent's midcourt area to the opponent's single court; 1 point is awarded for each successful hit. The return serve involves attempting to return a serve to anywhere in the opponent's court; 1 point is awarded for each successful return up to a maximum of 10 points.

Sport Variations and Modifications

Special Olympics sanctions the following events: singles, doubles, mixed doubles, and Unified Sports doubles, and individual skills contests. The latter is unique to Special Olympics and includes six events: hand feeding, racket feeding, the ups contest, forehand stroke, backhand stroke, and serve. A final score is determined by adding the scores of all six events. In Special Olympics competition (2008), the following rules apply to wheelchair athletes:

- Athletes may serve an overhand serve from either the right or left serving areas.
- The serving area is shortened to half the distance.

The DAAA (1998) permits the following rules modifications:

- Sidearm serving is allowed.
- No overhead serves are permitted.

Other Variations and Modifications

Some standard modifications are routinely used: reducing the court size, strapping the racket to the stump of the person with a double-arm amputation, and using Velcro on the butt end of the racket and on the top edge of the cork or rubber base of the shuttlecock to aid in shuttlecock retrieval (Weber, 1991). Several assistive devices are used to promote participation in badminton. The extension-handle racket involves splicing a length of wood to the shaft of a standard badminton racket. This is helpful for a wheelchair player or a player with limited movement. Another device is the amputee serving tray. Attached to the terminal end of the prosthesis, the tray permits easier service and promotes active use of the prosthesis. See also the application example.

BOWLING

Both people who are ambulatory and people who use wheelchairs can participate in bowling with a high degree of success. Usually, the ambulatory bowler demonstrates a procedure that incorporates the following actions: approach (which may be

---

APPLICATION EXAMPLE

Individual, Dual, and Adventure Sports and Activities

Setting: Middle school physical education class

Student: A seventh-grade student with muscular dystrophy who uses a wheelchair and is able to push himself

Unit: Badminton

Task: Serving the shuttlecock

Applications: The physical educator might make reasonable accommodations in the following ways:

- ▶ Modify regular equipment to make it lighter or more manageable.
- ▶ Permit serving into a larger court area.
- ▶ Lower the net.
- ▶ Shorten the distance of the serve.

modified if lower-extremity involvement exists); delivery, including the swinging of the ball; and release. A bowler who uses a wheelchair will eliminate the approach and either perform the swing and release independently or use a piece of adapted equipment to assist this part of the procedure. Two organizations that have significantly influenced the lives of bowlers with disabilities are the American Blind Bowling Association (ABBA) and the American Wheelchair Bowling Association (AWBA).

Lead-Up Activities

Special Olympics (2008) sponsors two developmental events that qualify as lead-up activities: target bowl and frame bowl.

■ *Target bowl.* In this activity, participants roll two 2-pound (1 kg) bowling balls in the direction of two regulation bowling pins positioned on a standard bowling lane modified to equal half its normal length. Participants bowl five frames using the standard scoring systems of the United States Bowling Congress (USBC).

■ *Frame bowl.* In this activity, the bowler rolls two frames (two rolls per frame) using plastic playground balls 30 centimeters in diameter. The object is to knock down the greatest number of plastic bowling pins from a traditional 10-pin triangular formation. The lead pin is set 5 meters from a restraining line. Bowlers either sit or stand and may use either one or both hands to roll the ball; the ball must be released behind the restraining line. Pins that are knocked down are cleared between the first and second rolls, and pins are reset for each new frame. A bowler's score equals the number of pins knocked down in two frames. Five bonus points are awarded when all pins are knocked down on the first roll of a frame; 2 bonus points are awarded when all remaining pins are knocked down on the second roll of the frame.

Sport Variations and Modifications

Bowling is a sanctioned event in the Special Olympics. The USBC rules are followed. CISS and USADSF also sponsor bowling with the use of hearing aids and external cochlear implants prohibited during competition. The BlazeSports National Disability Sports Alliance (NDSA, 2001) has developed the following procedures and rules for competition:

■ There are four divisions, two chute and two nonchute.

■ Nonchute divisions include classes 3 through 8, in which bowlers do not use specialized equipment; the retractable ball handle is permitted in these divisions.

■ Chute divisions are for classes 1 through 6, in which bowlers use specialized equipment. There are two divisions: closed chute, for class 1 and 2 bowlers, who need assistance with equipment (wheelchair, chute, or ball), and open chute, for bowlers in classes 3 through 6, who do not require assistance with their equipment.

■ All bowlers must be able to bowl each ball independently within 60 seconds.

Special Olympics (2008) sponsors competition in bowling and follows the rules established by the USBC and the Women's International Bowling Congress (WIBC). It sponsors singles (ramp unassisted and ramp assisted) competitions; doubles (male, female, mixed, and Unified Sports male, female, and mixed) competitions; and team (male, female, mixed, and Unified Sports male, female, and mixed) competitions. Modified rules for use in Special Olympics are as follows:

■ Ramps and other assistive devices are permitted for singles competition only.

■ Bowlers using ramps shall compete in separate divisions. There are two classifications of ramp bowling: unassisted (where athletes aim the ramp by themselves, place the ball on the ramp, and push the ball down the ramp toward the target) and assisted (where an assistant aims the target based on verbal or visual cues from the athlete).

■ Bowlers are permitted to bowl up to three consecutive frames.

Other Variations and Modifications

Ambulatory bowlers use several types of assistive devices. The handle-grip bowling ball, which snaps back instantly on release, is ideal for bowlers with upper-extremity disabilities and for people with spastic cerebral palsy, especially those who have difficulties with digital control. The USBC has approved the handle-grip ball for competitive play. People with upper-extremity amputations who use a hook can use an attachable neoprene sleeve to hold and deliver a bowling ball. The sleeve can compress using a spring and expand for release with the identical action used to open the conventional hook. Stick bowling, which is similar to the use of a shuffleboard cue, was designed for people with upper-extremity involvement, primarily grip problems. The AWBA permits stick bowling in its national competitions, provided the bowlers apply their own power and direction to the ball.

Bowlers who are wheelchair users have several assistive devices available that facilitate participation. The recently approved chute/ramp division within AWBA permits bowlers with severe disabilities to compete at national competitions. The counterpart of stick bowling for people who use wheelchairs is the adapter-pusher device, originally designed for wheelchair bowlers lacking sufficient upper-arm strength to lift the ball. The handlebar-extension accessory, used in conjunction with the adapter-pusher device, assists ambulatory bowlers who do not have enough strength to lift the ball. Also available is the bowling ball–holder ring (third arm), a device that attaches to the wheelchair arm and holds a ball while the bowler wheels down the approach lane.

Although USABA does not sponsor competition in bowling, the International Blind Sports Federation (IBSA) sponsors 9-pin bowling (skittles) and 10-pin bowling. There are several modifications that can enhance participation in the sport for people with visual impairments. These modifications include

- use of a bowling rail for guidance, which is the standard method employed by most bowlers in the ABBA National Blind Bowling Tournament;
- use of an auditory goal locator placed above or behind the pins; and
- a scoring board system that tactually indicates the pins that remain standing after the ball is rolled.

FENCING

Sir Ludwig Guttmann introduced fencing as a competitive event for people with disabilities in 1953 as part of the Stoke Mandeville Games in Stoke Mandeville, England, and it was included in the Paralympic Games in Rome in 1960. The objective in fencing is to score by touching the opponent's target while avoiding being touched. If fencing is included in physical education, several possible variations and modifications make achievement of the primary objective feasible for people with disabilities.

Sport Variations and Modifications

Competition in fencing for people who use wheelchairs is normally conducted according to the rules of the International Wheelchair Fencing Committee (IWFC) of the International Stoke Mandeville Wheelchair Sports Federation (ISMWSF) (see figure 27.3). In competition, the following classes are recognized for all weapons: C, B, and A, which represent the old classification of 1A and 1B, class 2, and class 3 and 4, respectively. This classification system represents competitors with no sitting balance and a severely affected fencing arm all the way to competitors with good sitting balance and support legs and a functional fencing arm. When appropriate, fencers in these classes with significant loss of grip or control of the sword hand may bind the sword to the hand with a bandage or similar device (IWFC, 2008). Participants eligible to compete in wheelchair fencing include people with cerebral palsy, spinal cord injuries, amputations, and les autres. Among the modified rules to ensure equal opportunity for all participants in wheelchair fencing, the following are important:

- A fencing frame must be used; the fencer with the shortest arms determines the length of the playing area.
- Fencers cannot purposely lose their balance, leave their chairs, rise from their seats, or use their legs to score a hit or to avoid being hit. The first offense is a warning, with subsequent offenses penalized by awarding one hit for each occurrence; accidental loss of balance is not penalized.
- The legs and trunk below the waist are not valid targets for any weapon, the target area for the épée and saber is exactly the same (i.e., any part of the body above the waist), and the target area for the foil is the torso above the waist, excluding the arms and head.

Other Variations and Modifications

Fencing is ordinarily conducted on a court measuring 6 by 40 feet (1.8 by 12.2 m); however, to accommodate wheelchair participants, the dimensions of

FIGURE 27.3 In wheelchair fencing, the wheelchairs are fixed in place to the floor by metal frames to keep the chairs from tipping.

Shariff Che'Lah/fotolia.com

the standard court may be changed to 8 by 20 feet (2.5 by 6 m), or a circular court 15 to 20 feet (4.6-6 m) in diameter may be used (Adams et al., 1982). Fencers who are blind will require a smaller, narrower court, which may conceivably be equipped with a guide rail (Dunn & Leitschuh, 2006).

The only piece of adaptive equipment is the lightweight sword, which permits independent participation, especially for people with upper-extremity disabilities. In cases where no modification is necessary, the épée is recommended for ease of handling rather than the foil or saber (Orr & Sheffield, 1981).

HORSEBACK RIDING

The North American Riding for the Handicapped Association (NARHA), founded in 1969, is the primary advisory group to riders with disabilities in the United States and Canada. NARHA does not sponsor competition; however, it advises therapeu-

tic, recreational, and competitive riding programs. NARHA also certifies riding instructors, accredits therapeutic riding facilities, and provides guidelines for operating safe programs.

Sport Skills

The Cheff Therapeutic Riding Center in Augusta, Michigan, and Equest Therapeutic Horsemanship in Dallas, Texas, are two of the largest instructor training programs for therapeutic riding in the United States. Horseback riding involves, among other skills, mounting, maintaining correct positioning on the mount, and dismounting. Most therapeutic riding programs engage their students in lessons that emphasize mounting, warm-up exercises, riding instruction, games, and dismounting (NAHRA, 2008). Special consideration should be given to the selection and training of horses used for therapeutic riding programs (Spink, 1993). The horses should be small because children are less likely to be fearful of smaller animals. Smaller horses also permit helpers to be in a better position for assisting unbalanced riders; the shoulder of the helper should be level with the middle of the rider's back.

Lead-Up Activities

Several possibilities exist for using games in the context of horseback riding. The origin of some of these games is pole bending, which is common in Western riding. It is used to teach horses how to bend and riders how to compensate during the bending movement. One game that encourages stretching of the arms involves placing quoits over the poles; this activity is conducted in relay fashion, with two- or three-member teams competing. Another game consists of throwing balls into buckets placed on a wall or pole. This activity has similar benefits to quoits. The traditional game Red Light, Green Light can be played to reinforce certain maneuvers, such as halts, that are taught to riders.

Sport Variations and Modifications

Currently, Special Olympics is the only governing body that offers equestrian competition or show. The BNDSA used to sponsor equestrian competition but no longer coordinates Paralympic events in the United States. Special Olympics (2008) offers the following events: dressage; English equitation;

stock seat equitation; Western riding; working trails; gymkhana events including pole bending, barrel racing, figure-eight stake race, and team relays; drill teams of two or four; prix caprilli; showmanship at halter and bridle classes; and Unified Sports team and drill relays. There are eight divisions to which riders are assigned based on a rider profile completed by the coach prior to any competition: CS, CI, BSP, BS, BIP, BI, AP, and A. Distinctions among divisions range from division CS, which requires a leader (horse handler) and one or two sidewalkers to act as spotters (figure 27.4), to division A, in which a rider is expected to compete with no modifications to national governing body rules. Special Olympics (2008) has designated the following rules for riding:

▪ Riders who must wear other footwear as the result of a physical disability must submit a physician's statement with their entry; English tack-style riders must use Peacock safety stir-

rups, *S*-shaped stirrups, or Devonshire boots; and Western tack-style riders must use safety stirrups.

▪ All riders must wear protective helmets with full chin harness approved by the Safety Equipment Institute-American Society for Testing and Materials (SEI-ASTM) or British Horse Society (BHS).

▪ Riders may use adaptive equipment without penalty but must in no way be attached to the horse or saddle.

▪ An athlete with Down syndrome who has been determined to have atlantoaxial instability is prohibited from competing in equestrian competition.

The IPC offers competition in the following dressage tests according to the rules established by the International Para-Equestrian Committee (IPEC): dressage, including grades 1 through 3 (walk

Fieldstone Farm Therapeutic Riding Center—Chagrin Falls, Ohio.

FIGURE 27.4 Division CS of Special Olympics requires that the rider has one or two sidewalkers and a leader.

only, walk and trot, and walk, trot, and canter), and grade 4 in derby and freestyle to music and pairs competition. For further details about the individual dressage test, consult the IPEC Web site (www.ipec-athletes.de). The IPEC (2009) has the following rules:

- No equipment is permitted that would in any way affix a rider to a horse or saddle, with the exception of Velcro to keep the rider attached to the saddle and elastic rubber bands to keep feet in the stirrups.

- Readers or callers (called *commanders*) are permitted for riders with intellectual impairments, visual impairments, or head injury in all events including freestyle; commanders may use radio communication if supervised by a steward.

- For dressage tests, riders with visual impairments may either have callers or use beepers for purposes of location.

Other Variations and Modifications

Mounting is the single most important phase of a riding program for people with disabilities. Because the typical method of mounting is impossible for some people (i.e., placing the left foot in the stirrup, holding onto the cantle, and springing into the saddle), alternatives are available. Several mounting procedures are used by riders with disabilities, ranging from totally assisted mounts, either from the top of a ramp or at ground level, to normal mounting from the ground (NARHA, 2008).

Once the person is mounted, many pieces of special equipment can make riding an enjoyable and profitable learning experience. One commonly used item is an **adapted rein bar**, which permits riders with a disability in one arm to apply sufficient leverage on the reins with the unaffected arm to successfully guide the horse; use of this bar is faded as soon as the rider learns to apply pressure with the knees. Another adaptation is the **Humes rein**, consisting of large oval handholds fitted on the rein; this allows riders with involvement of the hands to direct the horse with wrist and arm movement.

Body harnesses are used extensively in programs for riders with disabilities. They consist of web belts about 4 inches (10 cm) wide with a leather handhold in the back, which a leader can hold onto to help maintain a rider's balance. Most riders who have disabilities also use the **Peacock stirrup**, which is shaped like a regular stirrup except that only one side is iron and the other side has a rubber belt attached to the top and bottom. This flexible portion of the stirrup releases quickly in case of a fall, reducing the chance of catching a foot. The **Devonshire boot** is used frequently if a rider has tight heel cords (Achilles tendons) or weak ankles. Designed much like the front portion of a boot, it prevents the foot from running through the stirrup, and consequently it promotes keeping the toes up and heels down, which can be invaluable if heel-cord stretching is desirable.

GYMNASTICS

Gymnastics has enjoyed considerable popularity because of its visibility in the Olympic Games. As a result, people with disabilities have begun to participate in gymnastics programs when opportunities are available.

Sport Skills

Beyond possessing the physical attributes necessary to participate in gymnastics (e.g., strength, agility, endurance, flexibility, coordination, and balance), participants must learn to compete either in one or more single events or in all events (the all-around). Under normal conditions, men compete in the following events: pommel horse, rings, horizontal bar, parallel bars, and floor exercise. Women compete in balance beam, uneven parallel bars, vaulting, and floor exercise. In both men's and women's competitions, participation in all events qualifies athletes for a chance to win the all-around title.

Lead-Up Activities

The closest thing to lead-up activities in gymnastics can be found in the Special Olympics sport skills program and in select developmental events offered as part of the Special Olympics Games. In its sport skills program manuals, *Artistic Gymnastics Coaching Guide* and *Rhythmic Gymnastics Coaching Guide* (Special Olympics, 2008), general conditioning exercises with emphasis on flexibility and strength are recommended. Doubles tumbling and balance stunts are also suggested. As an introductory experience, educational gymnastics, which uses a creative, problem-solving approach, can be used to teach basic movement concepts. This could eventually allow participants to compete in more advanced forms of gymnastic competition.

Sport Variations and Modifications

Gymnastics is offered in the Special Olympics Games. Events for men include vaulting, parallel bars, pommel horse, horizontal bar, rings, and floor exercise. Women's events include vaulting, uneven parallel bars, balance beam, and floor exercise. Both men and women can compete in the all-around competition. Mixed-gender events include vaulting, wide beam, floor exercise, and tumbling with an all-around competition. Only women compete in rhythmic gymnastics in the following events: rhythmic floor exercise, ribbon, ball, hoop, and all-around competition consisting of the four events. Level A, which is mixed gender, also competes in rhythmic gymnastics individual compulsory routines either sitting or standing. There are also Unified Sports events and group routines performed by groups of four to six athletes. Each individual competition (i.e., mixed gender, men's, and women's) has a Unified Sports event for each of the events that make up the specific category. No significant rule modifications are required, and each participant's performance is judged according to the rules established for that event by the International Gymnastics Federation (FIG) and the national governing body (Special Olympics, 2008).

Special Olympics (2008) rules to ensure equitable competition include the following:

■ Gymnasts with visual impairments have the option of performing the vault with no run, one step, two steps, a multiple bounce on the board (with hands starting on the horse), or a two- or three-bounce takeoff; audible cues may be used in all routines.

■ In the floor exercise, the coach may signal gymnasts with hearing impairments to begin the routine.

■ Gymnasts using canes or walkers may have a coach walk onto the floor and remove (and replace) walkers and other aids as needed without any deduction of points.

■ Gymnasts with visual impairments may use audible cues during all routines; during the floor exercise, music may be played at any close point off the mat, or the coach may carry the music source around the perimeter of the mat.

■ Gymnasts in level A perform their rhythmic gymnastics routines while seated either in a wheelchair or a sturdy chair. Gymnasts who are blind can have audible cues during competition, and Deaf athletes can have a visual cue to start with music.

Other Variations and Modifications

Few modifications are used in gymnastics competition. If gymnastics is included in physical education programs, all of the modifications observed by the sport organizations in the conduct of their competitions would be valid.

WRESTLING AND JUDO

The sports of wrestling and judo require strength, balance, flexibility, and coordination. If people with disabilities possess these characteristics and if they can combine knowledge of techniques with an ability to demonstrate them in competitive situations, then there is no reason why they cannot experience success in wrestling and judo.

Sport Skills

Wrestling consists of several techniques that are essential for success. These include takedowns, escapes and reversals, breakdowns and controls, and pin holds. When learned and performed well, these maneuvers assist in accomplishing the objective in wrestling, which is to dominate opponents by controlling them and holding both shoulders to the mat simultaneously for one second. Judo, on the other hand, consists of three primary branches: throws, groundwork (i.e., strangles, joint locks, and chokes), and striking techniques, including kicks and punches.

Lead-Up Activities

The development of lead-up activities for wrestling and judo has apparently not been an area of creative activity. If lead-up activities are desirable, then one can conceivably use certain elementary physical education self-testing activities that have some relation to wrestling. Two such activities are listed here:

- *Hand wrestling.* Standing, two people face each other and grasp right hands; each person lifts one foot off the ground. On a signal, each attempts to cause the other to touch either the free foot or hand to the ground.
- *Indian leg wrestle.* Two people lie side by side but facing in opposite directions. Hips are adjacent to the partner's waist, and inside arms are hooked. Each person raises the inside leg to a count of three; on the third count, they bend knees, hook them, and attempt to force the other person into a backward roll.

Sport Variations and Modifications

USABA used to sponsor competition in the open division. International freestyle rules as interpreted by IBSA were used. USABA is currently not offering wrestling competition due to a lack of interest; IBSA, on the other hand, has completely eliminated wrestling and now offers competition in judo exclusively.

Both Greco-Roman wrestling (which prohibits holds below the waist and use of the legs in attempting to take opponents to the mat) and freestyle wrestling are sanctioned events in competitions governed by the USADSF. These events are conducted according to the rules established by the International Federation of Associated Wrestling Styles (FILA). Hearing aids and external cochlear implants are forbidden during competition.

Competition in judo is also sanctioned by USABA. Judo is contested according to the rules of the International Judo Federation (IJF) as interpreted by IBSA. In the Paralympic Games, world championships, and regional championships, competition for all weight classifications is combined for classes B1, B2, and B3. There are individual men's and women's competitions and men's and women's team competitions. The basic sport adaptation for judo (for B1 and B2 competitors) is to have opponents start with a grip on each other's gi (the traditional judo garment).

Other Variations and Modifications

Wrestling and judo are not for everyone. For people with disabilities who want to attempt these sports, several modifications can be used. For those with lower-extremity difficulties that prevent ambulation, all maneuvers should be taught from the mat with emphasis on arm technique. Bilateral upper-extremity involvement will probably restrict participation in all but leg wrestling maneuvers. After removal of prostheses, single-arm amputees can participate with emphasis placed on leg maneuvers.

TRACK AND FIELD

Because all major sport organizations for people with disabilities offer competitive opportunities in track and field, this section will focus on rule modifications that maximize participation. For each organization, the track portion is discussed first, followed by the field events. No attempt is made to examine sport skills, variations and modifications, or lead-up activities except as related to Special Olympics.

Wheelchair and Ambulatory Sports, USA (WASUSA)

Track and field competitions are governed by the rules of The Athletic Congress (TAC). WASUSA sponsors a classed division in track and field events. Classes include T51, T52, T53, and T54 for track events and F51, F52, F53, F54, F55, F56, F57, and F58 for field events. Standing athletes compete under the F42, F43, and F44 classifications. There is also a junior division starting with a futures category for children through 6 years of age. It then has divisions A through E that include children from 7 to 21 years of age.

Classes T51 and T52 compete in 100-, 200-, 400-, 800-, 1,500-, and 5,000-meter races as well as a 4 × 100-meter circular relay. Classes T53 and T54 compete in the same races but also compete in a 10,000-meter race and a 4 × 100-meter circular relay. T51, T52, T53, and T54 athletes also contest 10-, 15-, and 20-kilometer races as well as half- and full marathons. In field events, all classes compete in the discus, shot put, and javelin, except class F51, which does not put the shot and which substitutes the club throw for the javelin event. Class F2 can choose between the club throw and javelin. Additionally, all classes compete in the pentathlon, which consists of five individual events. F51 competes in a 100-meter race, club throw, 400-meter race, discus, and 800-meter race. Classes F52 and F53 compete in the shot put, javelin, discus, and 100- and 800-meter races. Classes F54 through F58 substitute 200- and 1,500-meter distances. There is also a junior division that contests mostly similar events but also includes races at shorter distances, such as 60 meters, as well as medley relays (all male, all female, and mixed).

WASUSA (2008b) has designated the following rules:

- Wheelchairs shall have at least two large wheels and one small wheel with only one round hand rim for each large wheel, no mechanical gears or levers shall be allowed in any sanctioned WASUSA competition, and only hand-operated mechanical steering devices are permitted.

- Batons are not exchanged in relay races; the takeover shall be a touch on any part of the body of the outgoing competitor within the takeover zone.

- Athletes must ensure that no part of their lower limbs can fall to the ground or track during an event; if used, strapping must be of a nonelastic material.

- Approved hold-down devices can be used to stabilize competitors' chairs in field events. Classes F1 to F6 must have at least one part of the upper leg or buttock in contact with the cushion or seat until the implement is released; F7 and F8 competitors are permitted lifting as long as one foot is in contact with the ground inside the throwing circle.

- Competitors cannot use any device (e.g., taping two or more fingers together) to assist in making throws, and gloves are not allowed. F1 through F3 may use strapping on the nonthrowing hand to anchor it to the chair.

United States Association of Blind Athletes (USABA)

The International Association of Athletics Federations (IAAF) rules are employed in track and field competitions. Within the USABA structure, there are three visual classifications: B1, B2, and B3. The following events are provided for males and females across all three classes: 100-, 200-, 400-, 800-, 1,500-, 5,000- and 10,000-meter races. Men and women in all classes also run a marathon. There are two relays for men and women: a 4 × 100 meter and a 4 × 400 meter with combined visual classes. Both men and women in all three classes compete in long jump, high jump, triple

jump, discus, javelin, and shot put. Men in all three classes throw the hammer. There are pentathlons contested by all classes and both genders. Both men and women compete in the long jump, discus, and 100-meter events. Men throw the javelin while women put the shot. Men run a 1,500-meter event, and women run an 800-meter race. Two divisions of youth events, junior and intermediate, are also contested. IBSA (2009) has determined that the following rule modifications are necessary to provide more suitable competition for athletes with visual impairments:

- Class B1 sprinters may run the 100 meter with the help of not more than two callers, one of whom must remain behind the finish line; the second caller has no restriction on position taken but may not cross the finish line ahead of the athlete.

- Guides are allowed for B1 and B2 in the 200-meter through marathon events. When guides are used in events between 200 and 800 meters, there is an allowance of two lanes per competitor.

- Competitors may also decide what form guidance will take. They may choose an elbow lead, a tether, or running free. At no time will the guide push or pull the competitor, nor will the guide ever precede the athlete. The runner may receive verbal instructions from the guide.

- Acoustic signals (a caller) are permitted for B1 and B2 athletes in field events.

- Class B1 high jumpers may touch the bar as an orientation before jumping; B2 jumpers are permitted to place a visual aid on the bar (e.g., hanging strips of 2 in. [5 cm] black or bright orange tape from the crossbar).

- Class B1 and B2 shot-put, discus, and javelin throwers may enter the throwing circle or runway (run-up track) only with the assistance of a helper, who must leave the area before the first attempt.

USA Deaf Sports Federation (USADSF)

Competition for Deaf athletes conforms to CISS rules and regulations. Therefore, events sponsored by the USADSF parallel the 44 CISS events. Track competition for men includes races at standard distances from 100 meters through 10,000 meters. It also includes the 110- and 400-meter hurdles, 3,000-meter steeplechase, 4 × 100-meter relay, 4 × 400-meter relay, and marathon. Women's competition in track and field parallels that described for men with one exception: they compete in the 100-meter hurdle instead of 110-meter hurdle. Along with the standard field events, such as shot put, discus, javelin, high jump, long jump, and triple jump, the USADSF also provides competition in pole vaulting and the hammer throw. Additionally, there are a decathlon and a heptathlon.

Special Olympics

Special Olympics offers more track and field events than any other sport organization for people with disabilities. Included in the list of possible events that can be offered at a sanctioned competition are 100-, 200-, 400-, 800-, 1,500-, 3,000-, 5,000-, and 10,000-meter races as well as walking races of 400 and 800 meters. Women compete in 100-meter hurdles whereas men compete in 110-meter hurdles. Additionally, there are 4 × 100- and 4 × 400-meter relays; each of these events has a Unified Sports counterpart. In field competition, the following events are contested: long jump, high jump, shot put, and pentathlon. There are also track and field events for athletes in wheelchairs. Long-distance events combining racing and walking have expanded to include 1,500-, 3,000-, 5,000-, and 10,000-meter competitions. There is also a half-marathon and a full marathon. IAAF rules are employed in competitions sanctioned by Special Olympics (2008). Modifications to those rules include the following:

- In running events, a rope or sighted guide can be used to assist athletes with visual impairments; a tap start can be used only with an athlete who is deafblind.

- In walking races, athletes are not required to maintain a straight advancing leg while competing.

- In the softball throw, athletes can use any type of throw.

- In all races 400 meters and below, athletes have the option of using starting blocks.

- Athletes with Down syndrome who have recognized atlantoaxial instability may not participate in either the high jump or the pentathlon.

Special Olympics (2008) gets close to describing lead-up activities. It does this through the provision of 18 developmental events, including the 25- and 50-meter dashes or walks, 100-meter walk, 10-, 25-, and 50-meter assisted walks, softball throw, 10- and 25-meter wheelchair races, 30-meter wheelchair slalom, 4 × 25-meter wheelchair shuttle relay, 30- and 50-meter motorized wheelchair slaloms, 25-meter motorized wheelchair obstacle race, tennis ball throw for distance, and standing long jump.

BlazeSports National Disability Sports Alliance (BNDSA)

Competition sanctioned by the BNDSA is governed by rules established by TAC. Events are contested via an eight-class system and consist of races as short as 60 meters (weave) for class 1 athletes in electric wheelchairs up to 3,000 meters and cross country running for classes 5 through 8. There are 4 × 100-meter and 4 × 400-meter open relays for classes 2 through 8, including wheelchair and ambulatory events. The following events constitute the field portion: shot put, discus, javelin, club throw, and long jump. Additional events include the precision throw, soft shot, distance kick, high toss, and medicine ball thrust. There is also a pentathlon for classes 3 through 8. Modifications of rules used to ensure equitable competition include the following (NDSA, 2001):

- Class 5 athletes who use canes or crutches must use their assistive devices in a manner such that they make contact with the surface of the track a minimum of one time approximately every 10 meters.

- Athletes in wheelchair relays must make personal contact with their team member to complete a successful changeover. This contact can be on any part of the outgoing teammate; either the incoming or outgoing competitor may initiate the tag within the change zone.

The BNDSA (NDSA, 2001) incorporates the following additional modifications in its field events:

- An attendant or approved holding device may secure the chair in place; however, neither an attendant nor the apparatus may be inside the throwing area.

- The soft shot (cloth 5 in. [13 cm] in diameter weighing a maximum of 6 oz [170 g]), precision throw, high toss, and soft discus are used for class 1 only.

- The distance kick and medicine ball thrust are offered for class 2 athletes who cannot engage in routine throwing events. In the distance kick, a 13-inch (33 cm) playground ball is placed on a foul line; the competitors initiate a backswing and then kick the ball forward while remaining seated in their chairs. Distance of the kick is the criterion. In the medicine ball thrust, a 6-pound (2.7 kg) medicine ball is used. Competitors may not kick the ball; rather, the foot must remain in contact with the ball throughout the entire movement until release.

Dwarf Athletic Association of America (DAAA)

The DAAA sanctions the following track events: 20-meter run for children under 7 years of age (futures), 20-meter run for juniors aged 7 to 9 years, 40-meter run for juniors aged 7 to 9 and 10 to 12 years, and 60-meter run for juniors aged 10 to 12 and 13 to 15 years and athletes over 40 years of age (masters). There is also a 100-meter open race and a 4 × 100-meter relay. The rules of TAC and wheelchair competition are typically followed.

Field events contested in DAAA competition include the shot put, discus, and javelin in open classes and shot put and discus in masters classes. Juniors (13-15 years old) may participate in shot put and discus. Other juniors and futures events include the softball throw, flippy flyer (soft discus), and tennis ball throw (DAAA, 1998).

GOLF

Golf has been an event in the Special Olympics since 1995. It is also an activity that can be effectively included in physical education programs for students with disabilities. Professional golf achieved infamous recognition in 1998, when Casey Martin, a golfer with a chronic and debilitating circulatory disorder in his leg, sued the Professional Golfers' Association (PGA) under the provisions of the Americans with Disabilities Act (ADA) to traverse the course using a cart. He won the right to use a cart in PGA events.

Sport Skills

Golf typically requires a person to grasp the club and address the ball using an appropriate stance. Being able to swing the golf club backward and then forward through a large arc including a follow-through is also a requisite task.

Lead-Up Activities

An appropriate lead-up activity is miniature golf. This popular version of golf is quite suited to people with disabilities, and for many it might represent the extent to which the golf experience is explored. Holes should range from 8 to 14 feet (2.4-4.3 m) from tee mat to hole with a width of 3 feet (1 m), which accommodates reaching a ball lying in the center of the course from a wheelchair.

Sport Variations and Modifications

Special Olympics (2008) has created rules based on the rules of golf as written by the Royal and Ancient Golf Club of St. Andrews and the United States Golf Association (USGA). Official events include an individual skills contest (level 1), alternate-shot team play competition (level 2), Unified Sports team play (level 3), individual stroke play competition of 9 holes (level 4), and individual stroke play competition of 18 holes (level 5). Individual skills contests are designed to train athletes to compete in basic golf skills. Competition is held in short putting, long putting, and chipping, as well as the pitch shot, bunker shot, iron shot, and wood shot. The alternate-shot team play competition involves pairing one Special Olympics athlete with one golfer without disabilities who serves as a coach and mentor. The format is a 9-hole tournament played as a modified four-person scramble. Level 3 is Unified Sports team play that is designed to provide the opportunity to play in a team format with a partner without intellectual disabilities but with similar ability. Level 4 enables athletes to play in regulation 9-hole golf competition, whereas level 5 is suitable for play in 18-hole competitions.

Other Variations and Modifications

Because of limitations experienced by people with disabilities, the essential sport skills are often problematic. Dunn and Leitschuh (2006) have detailed many practical considerations necessary for successful participation by golfers with disabilities. These include using powered and adaptable carts for those who lack stamina to walk the golf course but who can physically play the game or for those who have significant mobility issues (see figure 27.5); having a player whose right arm is missing or incapacitated play left-handed or vice versa; providing a chair for players who cannot balance on one crutch or who are unable to stand (those using a chair or sitting in a wheelchair should have the chair turned so they are facing the ball) (Longo, 1989); and eliminating the preliminary movement of the club (waggle) for blind golfers because this could produce an initial malalignment of the club with the ball. Additionally, information about distance to the hole can be gained by tapping on the cup or by asking others how far they are positioned from the cup; some wheelchair players also use extra-long clubs to clear the footplates.

The Putter Finger is an assistive device that consists of a molded rubber suction cup designed to fit on the grip end of any putter. It is used to retrieve the ball from the hole (Adams & McCubbin, 1991). J.H. Huber (personal communication, January 1971) developed another adaptation that enables golfers who are blind to practice independently. Three pieces of material, all of which produce a different sound when struck, are hung 15 to 20 feet (4.6-6 m) in front of golfers as they practice indoors. Golfers are instructed about the positions of the pieces of material and the sound made by each. Because feedback about the line of flight of the ball is available, they can determine whether the ball went straight, hooked, or sliced. The golf chirper (Cowart, 1989) is used to develop independent putting skills; it serves as a cup locator and audio feedback device. Finally, an amputee golf grip developed by TRS, Inc. fits any standard prosthetic wrist. It permits full rotation during backswing, squared clubface at impact, and complete follow-through. Additionally, it has an energy storing capacity during backswing that promotes more powerful strokes.

© BOLD STOCK / age fotostock

FIGURE 27.5 Practical considerations, such as an adapted golf cart, allow for successful participation by golfers with disabilities.

POWERLIFTING

Powerlifting has developed over the years as an extremely popular sport for people with disabilities. In this chapter, powerlifting as a sport is distinguished from routine weight training.

Sport Skills

As administered by the ISMWSF, the sport includes two lifts: the bench press and the powerlifting press. In IPC competition, the sport is restricted to the bench press. Participants are classified by weight; however, braces and other devices are not counted in the total weight. WASUSA makes adjustments to recorded weight according to the site of an amputation.

Sport Variations and Modifications

WASUSA, DAAA, NDSA, and USABA offer competitive powerlifting programs. Special Olympics also offers powerlifting but only as a demonstration event. IBSA (2009) sanctions three events: the bench press, squat, and deadlift. Special Olympics (2008) offers the bench press, deadlift, and squat. It also offers two combination events: deadlift and bench press, and the deadlift and squat. WASUSA provides competition in the powerlift press and bench press. Each organization has specific rules that accommodate its athletes. Some of the more significant modifications are the following:

- A safety device engineered to protect lifters against the clasp knife reflex (exaggerated stretch reflex) is mandatory in all sanctioned events (NDSA, 2001).
- Strapping the legs to the bench is permissible either just above the knees or at the ankles as long as it is done with the strap provided by the organizing committee; for above-the-knee amputees, strapping is permitted between the hip and the remainder of the amputated limb (WASUSA, 2002).
- A lifter who has a physical disability may be strapped to the bench between the ankles and the hips with a strapping not to exceed 10 centimeters in length (Special Olympics, 2008).
- An athlete with Down syndrome with a recognized atlantoaxial instability may not compete in the squat lift (Special Olympics, 2008).

- Athletes may bench-press with legs straight or with knees bent and feet flat on the bench (DAAA, 1998).

CYCLING

Cycling, whether bicycle, tricycle, or handcycle, is a useful skill for lifelong leisure pursuit. It can also be a strenuous sport pursued for its competitiveness. To compete, participants must develop a high level of fitness and learn effective race strategy. For example, Challenge Alaska sponsors the Sadler's Alaska Challenge, which is the longest handcycle race in the world. In 2009 the race covered 267 miles (430 km) in seven days with a total of approximately 16,000 feet (4,877 m) of ascent during the race.

Sport Skills

Under most circumstances, cycling requires the ability to maintain balance on a cycle and to execute a reciprocal movement of the legs to turn the pedals. Technological advances have opened cycling to people who would never have thought previously about cycling as a leisure pursuit or as a competitive event.

Sport Variations and Modifications

The USADSF through the United States Deaf Cycling Association (USDCA) sponsors three events: the 1,000-meter sprint, a road race, and a time-trial race on the road. At the international level, CISS sponsors the following competition for men: a 1,000-meter sprint, a 29K individual time trial, a 90.4K individual road race, and a 50K points race. For women, it sponsors a 29K individual time trial and a 60.1K individual road race. The BNDSA sponsors events in four divisions, including divisions 1 and 2 for tricycles and Divisions 3 and 4 for bicycles. The tricycle events include a 3K to 10K time trial and a 10K to 40K road race for classes 2, 5, and 6. The bicycle events include a 10K to 20K time trial and a 35K to 75K road race for classes 5 to 8. Classes 5 to 8 also compete in a velodrome or cycling track event, a flying 200, a pursuit 3K and 4K, and a kilo. Hand-propelled tricycles are not permitted in BNDSA competitions (NDSA, 2001).

IBSA (2009) offers four event categories: road races, track races, individual pursuit, and sprints.

Within each category are races for men, women, and mixed tandems. Road races are 100 to 135 kilometers for men, 60 to 70 kilometers for women, and 65 to 80 kilometers for mixed teams. Track races are 1,000 meters for men and mixed teams and 500 meters for women. Individual pursuit events are 4 kilometers for men and 3 kilometers for women and mixed teams. Sprint competitions are contested over a distance of 1,000 meters for men, women, and mixed teams. With few exceptions, the rules for IBSA cycling are the same as those for the United States Cycling Federation (USCF). The primary exception is that the pilot (front rider) in tandem riding events must be sighted and have a group 1 permit; the stoker (back rider) can be from any vision class and must have a group 2 permit.

Special Olympics offers the following events: 500-meter time trial; 1K, 5K, and 10K time trials; 5K, 10K, 15K, 25K, and 40K road races; and 500-meter Unified Sports tandem time trial. All events are governed by the rules established by the Union Cycliste Internationale (UCI) (Special Olympics, 2008).

Other Variations and Modifications

Riding a bicycle can be difficult. People with impaired balance or coordination might require some adaptation. Three- and four-wheeled bicycles with or without hand cranks can facilitate cycling for people with disabilities. If riding a two-wheeled bicycle is the desirable approach, then training wheels suitable for full-size adult bikes can be constructed. Additionally, tandem cycling can be used when total control of the bicycle is beyond the ability of the person with a disability (e.g., visual impairment). Handcycling (figure 27.6) is now an IPC sport with athletes competing in three divisions with separate events for men and women. Events include road races and individual time trials.

FIGURE 27.6 Handcycling is now an International Paralympic Committee sport with athletes competing in three divisions.

Imago/Icon SMI

BOCCIA

Boccia, the Italian version of bowling, is generally played on a sand or soil alley 75 feet (23 m) long and 8 feet (2.4 m) wide. The playing area is normally enclosed at the ends and sides by boards 18 inches (46 cm) and 12 inches (30 cm) high, respectively.

Boccia made its initial appearance in the Paralympics at the 1992 Barcelona Games. Boccia is the only Paralympic sport in which men and women compete together in all events.

Sport Skills

The game requires that players roll or throw wooden balls (see figure 27.7) in the direction of a smaller wooden ball, or jack. The object is to have the ball come to rest closer to the jack than any of the opponent's balls. To do this, players try to roll balls in order to protect their own well-placed shots while knocking aside their opponent's balls.

Lead-Up Activities

The Empire State Games for the Physically Challenged pioneered Crazy Bocce, a game that consists of throwing two sets of four wooden balls alternately into rings of various sizes for specified point totals. Three smaller rings sit inside one large ring that is 13 feet (4 m) in circumference. Points are awarded only if the ball remains inside the large ring. If the ball lands inside the large ring (but not in any of the smaller rings), 1 point is awarded. If the ball lands inside the small blue or red ring, 2 points are earned. Landing inside the small yellow ring nets 3 points. The game is usually played with the large ring in a small wading pool. The large ring can also be attached to swimming pool sides using a suction-cup attachment. The game can be played in the snow, on the beach, on the lawn, and on carpet. Crazy Bocce is enjoyed by people of all ages.

Sport Variations and Modifications

Both individual and team boccia are sanctioned events in the national competition of the BNDSA, the DAAA, and Special Olympics. A minor adjustment to established rules permits the use of ramps or chutes by DAAA athletes. In the Paralympic Games, athletes eligible for individual competition are classified as BC1, BC2, BC3, and BC4 according to the Cerebral Palsy International Sports and Recreation Association (CPISRA) and the International Boccia Commission. There are also pairs events for BC3 and BC4, as well as team competition for BC1 and BC2. Special Olympics (2008) offers the following events: singles, doubles, and team competitions

FIGURE 27.7 The game of boccia requires that players roll or throw wooden balls.

Shariff Che'Lah/fotolia.com

and Unified Sports doubles and team competitions. Major modifications to the rules in either BNDSA (NDSA, 2001) or DAAA (1998) events include the following:

- The court is laid out on a tile or wood gym floor or other hard surface and measures 12.5 by 6 meters; stools, chairs, or other sitting devices are permitted in the thrower's box during matches.

- An assistant is allowed to adjust ramps or chutes and the player's chair position within the throwing box; however, all direction for adjustments must be initiated by the player. Assistive devices should not contain any mechanical device that aids in propulsion, such as a spring-loaded device.

- BC1 players who have difficulty holding or placing the balls can receive assistance from one aide; however, they must throw, kick, strike, push, or roll the ball independently. Players may use more than one assistive device during a match only after the referee has indicated it is their turn to throw.

- All balls must be thrown, rolled, pushed, struck, or kicked into the court; use of a head pointer, chin lever, or pull lever is acceptable.

Other Variations and Modifications

There are several ways to modify boccia for participation by people with disabilities. A major concern is a lack of sufficient strength to propel the ball toward the jack. In such cases, substitution of a lighter object, such as a foam ball or balloon, or reduction of the legal court size would facilitate participation. Another area of concern is upper-extremity involvement, which could prohibit rolling or throwing the ball. This concern can be overcome if the player is permitted to kick the ball into the target area or perhaps to use a bowling cue or stick.

ADVENTURE ACTIVITIES

A programming area that has gained considerable momentum over the past 25 to 30 years is the adventure curriculum. Perhaps the best-known program is Project Adventure, started by Bob Lentz in 1971. Project Adventure uses a sequence of activities that encourage the development of individual

and group trust, cooperation, confidence, courage, independence, and competence. These goals are achieved through trust activities, cooperative games, initiative problems, ropes-course elements, and high-ropes courses. Over the years it became clear that these experiences would benefit people with disabilities just as they benefit those without disabilities. In 1992, with the encouragement of Project Adventure, M.D. Havens published *Bridges to Accessibility*. The theme of this text is the provision of integrated adventure experiences that are accessible rather than adapted.

People with disabilities engage in adventure activities such as canoeing (Wachtel, 1987), whitewater rafting (Roswal & Daugherty, 1991), kayaking (Kegel & Peterson, 1989), and backpacking (Huber, 1991). Still others participate in activities considered by many to be high-risk, nontraditional experiences, at least for people with disabilities. These include rock climbing (Roos, 1991), mountain biking (see figure 27.8), mountain trekking, and mountaineering.

FIGURE 27.8 Adventure activities, such as mountain biking, provide another area of programming for people with disabilities.

THEOBALD/BSIP/age fotostock

Hal O'Leary, who is the recreation program director at the National Sports Center for the Disabled (NSCD) in Winter Park, Colorado, indicates that white-water rafting for people with disabilities is not much different than it is for people without disabilities (personal communication, October 1998). In the case of wheelchair users, the chair is placed on the floor of the raft, which is contrary to where one is normally positioned. Also, air mattresses or inflatable seats can be fitted in the boat to provide support and comfort. For people with severe disabilities, the NSCD uses beanbag chairs to position rafters to participate comfortably in the experience.

Huber (1991) reported on the successful through-hike of the Appalachian Trail by Bill Irwin. Irwin lost his sight to an eye disease at the age of 28. He made the hike from Springer Mountain, Georgia, to Mount Katahdin, Maine, in a little over eight months accompanied by only his guide dog.

Rock climbing (Roos, 1991) is becoming a favorite sport of people with disabilities. Mark Wellman was the first paraplegic to climb the sheer 3,000-foot (914 m) granite face of El Capitan in Yosemite National Park. Erik Weihenmayer was the first person with blindness to climb El Capitan; he likewise was the first to climb the 20,320-foot (6,194 m) summit of Denali in Alaska. More recently, mountaineering has become the talk of the world of sport for people with disabilities with the successful climb of Mount Everest in 1998 by Tom Whittaker, who has a below-the-knee amputation. The equally successful 1998 All Abilities Trek accompanied Whittaker's summit. A group of five people with disabilities and seven trekkers without disabilities attempted to reach the Mount Everest base camp located at 17,000 feet (5,182 m). These Kripples in the Kumboo, as they called themselves, became the first group of people with disabilities to reach base camp; it took 41 days. In 2001, Erik Weihenmayer succeeded in his quest to climb Mount Everest. He has also climbed the Seven Summits, the tallest mountain peaks on every continent. More recently, he guided a group of Tibetan teenagers who were blind to the 21,500-foot (6,553 m) base camp on the north side of Mount Everest.

Many of these adventure activities are conducted in a one-day format. Also available is the adventure or wilderness trip that might last for days or weeks. Several organizations provide separate wilderness experiences for people with disabilities, whereas others offer integrated experiences for people of all abilities. The more prominent organizations providing these experiences include the following:

SPLORE (Special Populations Learning Outdoor Recreation and Education), 880 East 3375 South, Salt Lake City, UT 84106; 801-484-4128.

C.W. HOG (Cooperative Wilderness Handicapped Outdoor Group), Idaho State University, Student Union, Box 8128, Pocatello, ID 83209; 208-282-3912.

Wilderness Inquiry II, 808 14th Avenue SE, Minneapolis, MN 55414; 612-676-9400.

BOEC (Breckenridge Outdoor Education Center), P.O. Box 697, Breckenridge, CO 80424; 970-453-6422.

Challenge Alaska, 3350 Commercial Dr., Ste. 208, Anchorage, AK 99501; 907-344-7399.

Bradford Woods, 5040 State Rd. 67 North, Martinsville, IN 46151; 765-342-2915.

INCLUSION

The variations and modifications highlighted in this chapter reflect good practice in physical education as well as in sanctioned sport programs (e.g., limiting the play areas is an adaptation technique used in several sports such as tennis, badminton, and boccia). Individual, dual, and adventure sports and activities provide a unique opportunity for inclusion of people with disabilities with their peers without disabilities. From elementary school through high school, variations and modifications can be used to alter sports in subtle ways (e.g., maintaining physical contact while wrestling). As a result of this approach, students with disabilities can participate in inclusive physical education and sport programs, and they not only derive the benefits of instruction in activities that are themselves normalizing but also receive that instruction in the least restrictive environment. Because of the reduced temporal and spatial demands of most of the individual, dual, and cooperative sports and activities, there is every reason to believe that success in activities such as those highlighted in this chapter will be readily attainable within accessible programs in inclusive settings.

As it relates to inclusion in adventure activities, the Cooperative Wilderness Handicapped Outdoor Group (C.W. HOG) at Idaho State University uses the common adventure principle. This means that all participants engage in planning, decision making, expense, and execution of the experience, regardless of their ability level.

SUMMARY

This chapter presented individual and dual sports currently available in the competitive offerings of the major sport organizations serving athletes with disabilities. In each case, the particular skills needed in the unmodified version of the game or sport were detailed. Additionally, lead-up activities were suggested in addition to variations and modifications for use in competitive sport or in physical education programs. It is worth noting that the rules governing sport for people with disabilities continue to undergo subtle modifications. National governing bodies and international federations have changed rules in ways that permit fewer and fewer modifications. Space limitations prevented discussion of other activities such as riflery and air pistol, shuffleboard, darts, wheelchair racquetball, and billiards; information on these activities can be found in Adams and McCubbin (1991). Also highlighted were accessible adventure activities, including the common adventure principle. It is likely that wilderness experiences for people with disabilities will be a burgeoning area of interest in the early decades of the 21st century.

REFERENCES

Adams, R.C., Daniel, A.N., McCubbin, J.A., & Rullman, L. (1982). *Games, sports, and exercise for the physically handicapped* (3rd ed.). Philadelphia: Lea & Febiger.

Adams, R.C., & McCubbin, J.A. (1991). *Games, sports, and exercise for the physically handicapped* (4th ed.). Philadelphia: Lea & Febiger.

Cowart, J. (1989). Golf chirper for the blind. *Palaestra, 5* (3), 34-35.

Dunn, J.M., & Leitschuh, C. (2006). *Special physical education* (8th ed.). Dubuque, IA: Kendall/Hunt.

Dwarf Athletic Association of America (DAAA). (1998). *Athletic handbook.* Lewisville, TX: Author.

Hattenback, R.T. (1979). Integrating persons with handicapping conditions in archery activities. In J.P. Winnick and J. Hurwitz (Eds.), *The preparation of regular physical educators for mainstreaming* (pp. 50-54). Brockport, NY: State University of New York, College at Brockport. Retrieved from ERIC database. (ED222028)

Havens, M.D. (1992). *Bridges to accessibility: A primer for including persons with disabilities in adventure curricula.* Hamilton, MA: Project Adventure.

Huber, J.H. (1991). An historic accomplishment: The first blind person to hike the Appalachian trail. *Palaestra, 7* (4), 18-23.

International Blind Sports Federation (IBSA). (2009). *IBSA technical rulebook.* Madrid: Author.

International Paralympic Committee (IPC). (2006). *IPC handbook.* Retrieved January 6, 2009, from www.paralympic.org.

International Paralympic Committee (IPC). (2007/2008). *IPC archery rules and regulations.* Bonn, Germany: Author.

International Para-Equestrian Committee (IPEC). (2009). *Rules for para-equestrian dressage events* (2nd ed.). Lausanne, Switzerland: Author.

International Table Tennis Federation (ITTF). (2010). *ITTF para table tennis: Rules and regulations* (8th ed.). Lausanne, Switzerland: Author.

International Tennis Federation (ITF). (2008). *Wheelchair tennis handbook 2008.* London: Author.

International Wheelchair Fencing Committee (IWFC). (2008). *Official rules for fencing.* Bucks, UK: International Stoke Mandeville Wheelchair Sports Federation.

Kegel, B., & Peterson, J. (1989). Summer splash: A water sports symposium for the physically challenged. *Palaestra, 6* (1), 17-19.

Longo, P. (1989). Chair golf. *Sports 'N Spokes, 15* (2), 35-38.

National Disability Sports Alliance (NDSA). (2001). *NDSA sports rules manual* (6th ed.). Newport, RI: Author.

North American Riding for the Handicapped Association (NARHA). (2008). *NARHA instructor training handbook.* Denver: Author.

Orr, R.E., & Sheffield, J. (1981). Adapted épéefencing. *Journal of Physical Education, Recreation and Dance, 52* (6), 42, 71.

Roos, M. (1991). Pass the adrenaline, please. *Palaestra, 8* (1), 44-46.

Roswal, G.M., & Daugherty, N. (1991). Whitewater rafting: An outdoor adventure activity for individuals with mental retardation. *Palaestra, 7* (4), 24-25.

Special Olympics. (2008). *Special Olympics summer sports rules, 2008.* Retrieved January 6, 2009, from www.specialolympics.org.

Spink, J. (1993). *Developmental riding therapy: A team approach to assessment and treatment.* Tucson, AZ: Therapy Skill Builders.

United States Tennis Association (USTA). (2007). *USTA/ITF wheelchair rules reference.* White Plains, NY: Author.

Wachtel, L.J. (1987). Thoughts on a wilderness canoe trip. *Palaestra, 3* (4), 33-40.

Weber, R.C. (1991). Using Velcro to assist badminton players who are disabled or elderly. *Palaestra, 7* (3), 10-11.

Wheelchair and Ambulatory Sports, USA (WASUSA). (2008a). *American wheelchair table tennis association.* St. Peters, MO: Author.

Wheelchair and Ambulatory Sports, USA (WASUSA). (2008b). *Competition rules for track and field and road racing.* St. Peters, MO: Author.

Wiseman, D.C. (1982). *A practical approach to adapted physical education.* Reading, MA: Addison-Wesley.

WRITTEN RESOURCES

Grosse, S. (Ed.). (1991). *Sport instruction for individuals with disabilities: The best of practical pointers.* Reston, VA: AAHPERD.

This book contains previously published pointers as well as new articles on increasing opportunities for people with disabilities to participate in instructional sport programs. Adaptations are presented for students with crutches and with unilateral and bilateral upper-arm amputations in badminton, golf, archery, bowling, tennis, and table tennis.

Ladies Professional Golf Association (LPGA). (2006). *Accessible golf: Making it a game fore all.* Champaign, IL: Human Kinetics.

This how-to manual provides all the essential tools for implementing a comprehensive golf program for individuals with disabilities, including modifications to equipment and instructional techniques.

Paciorek, M.J., & Jones, J.A. (2001). *Disability sport and recreation resources* (3rd ed.). Traverse City, MI: Cooper.

Perhaps the most comprehensive resource currently available, this manual uses a cross-categorical approach in discussing sport and recreation for people with disabilities. Information is provided on sport-governing bodies for people both with and without disabilities. An overview of each sport, along with adapted equipment suppliers and manufacturers, accompanies each description.

Special Olympics. (2008). *Special Olympics summer sports rules, 2008.* Washington, DC: Author.

This manual contains information that organizers will need to conduct equitable competitions, including how to conduct official sporting events, how to place athletes in appropriate ability groups, and how to prepare athletes for competition.

United States Tennis Association (USTA). (2006). *Manual for teaching adaptive tennis.* White Plains, NY: Author.

This manual is designed to assist those interested in teaching tennis to people with a variety of disabilities as well as those with differing abilities or circumstances.

AUDIOVISUAL RESOURCES

Beyond the barriers [VHS]. (1998). Aquarius Health Care Videos, 5 Powerhouse Ln., P.O. Box 1159, Sherborn, MA 01770.

This video features Mark Wellman, the first paraplegic to climb El Capitan in Yosemite National Park, and other people with disabilities engaging in such activities as sailing, bodyboarding, scuba diving, and hang gliding. It demonstrates the breadth of activities in which individuals with disabilities can engage and provides an inspirational message for people of all ability levels.

Farther than the eye can see [DVD]. (2006). Serac Films, 1135 Pearl St. #7, Boulder, CO 80302.

This DVD documents the historic expedition that resulted in Erik Weihenmayer becoming the first climber who is blind to ascend Mount Everest.

Making of a champion: Track and field [VHS]. (n.d.). Special Olympics, Inc., 1325 G Street, NW, Ste. 500, Washington, DC 20005.

This video can be used as a training aid for athletes. It provides instruction on various techniques used to prepare athletes for competition.

Summer sports officials/coaches training video [VHS]. (n.d). United States Association of Blind Athletes (USABA), 33 N. Institute St., Colorado Springs, CO 80903.

This video provides information about fundamentals, rules, and their modifications from companion sports for athletes without disabilities. Special equipment and adaptations are addressed. Sports include track and field, gymnastics, powerlifting, and wrestling.

ELECTRONIC RESOURCES

Access to Recreation : www.accesstr.com.

This is the online catalog of a nationally recognized equipment retailer. It services the needs of people with disabilities as it relates to adaptive equipment for fishing, hunting, swimming, cycling, bowling, and other recreational activities.

Equest Therapeutic Horsemanship: www.equest.org.

This is the home of the nationally recognized and accredited equine-assisted therapy and rehabilitation program for children and adults with mental, emotional, and learning disabilities located in Dallas, Texas.

National Sports Center for the Disabled (NSCD): www.nscd.org.

This is the home of the innovative, nonprofit organization in Winter Park, Colorado, that serves the year-round recreational needs of children and adults with disabilities.

Success Oriented Achievement Realized (SOAR): www.soarnc.org.

This is the home of SOAR, which sponsors success-oriented, high-adventure programs, such as wilderness backpacking, rock climbing, white-water rafting and canoeing, mountaineering, and wildlife studies for students with disabilities or attention deficient/hyperactivity disorder (ADHD) at six locations in North and Central America.

TRS: www.oandp.com.

TRS, Inc. designs and manufactures high performance prosthetic appliances for use in sports and recreation.

chapter 28

Winter Sport Activities

Luke E. Kelly

> **I**t's **7:00 a.m.,** going to be partly sunny, high around 15 degrees, with winds out of the west today," blares the DJ on the radio as Andrew and Emily drive into the sunrise toward the mountains.

"It's going to be a great day for skiing," Emily says.

"Yeah," Andrew agrees. "I hope they have the black diamond run open. I want to get some big air off that run of moguls near the top."

"Come on!" says Emily. "You can't get big air! The way you ski, you'll be lucky if you don't get taken out by a tree. I know—let's make a little wager on who can get down the black diamond the fastest."

Andrew grins. "Sorry, but no way—you're not getting another free lunch off me."

As they approach the lodge, Andrew says, "You want me to drop you off here, and I'll go park?"

"That would be great," says Emily. "Get my chair set up, and I'll take our skis and get in line for the lift tickets." Andrew gets Emily's wheelchair out of the trunk and sets it up. While Emily transfers from the car seat to her wheelchair, Andrew gets the skis off the roof.

"You sure you can carry your skis and mine?" asks Andrew.

"No problem," says Emily. "Just don't get lost parking the car and make me pay for the lift tickets."

The reason Andrew did not want to bet Emily on a race down the black diamond run is that she is a world-class sit-skier. Emily broke her back in a skiing accident when she was 13 and lost the use of both legs. After the injury, she took up sit-skiing because she loved to ski and wanted an activity she could do outdoors with her friends. She lives in Colorado, so skiing was the natural choice.

This chapter introduces winter activities that can be included in physical education and sport programs for people with disabilities. It is not within the scope of the chapter to cover in detail how each winter sport should be taught. Instead, general guidelines are provided along with a brief description of each activity and suggested adaptations for participants with various disabilities.

VALUE OF WINTER SPORT

A major goal of physical education for both students with and without disabilities is to provide the knowledge, skills, and experiences they need to live healthy and productive lives. At the completion of their school physical education programs, students should have the basic physical fitness and motor skills required to achieve this goal. It would be logical to assume that the emphasis on sport skills in the school curriculum would reflect the students' needs in terms of carryover value and the likelihood of continuing participation after the school years. However, one area—winter sport skills—is frequently underrepresented in the physical education and sport curriculum. This is a serious omission for all students and especially students with disabilities. In many parts of the United States, the winter season is the longest season during the school year. Winter sport activities provide opportunities for people with disabilities to

- maintain or improve physical fitness levels,
- participate in community recreation activities, and
- pursue athletic competition.

Failure to provide winter sport skills to students with disabilities limits their recreational options during the winter months. This in turn might affect their fitness and isolate them from many social activities and settings.

Given proper instruction and practice, people with disabilities can pursue and successfully participate in many winter sports, including alpine skiing (downhill), snowboarding, cross-country skiing (Nordic), ice skating, ice picking, sledding, curling, and hockey. Instructional programs for people with disabilities should be guided by equal attention to safety, motivation (fun), and skill development. Safety concerns should encompass the areas of

physical and motor readiness, appropriate clothing and equipment, and instructor qualifications (National Ski Patrol, 2008).

ALPINE SKIING

Alpine (downhill) skiing is a winter sport in which most people with disabilities can participate with little or no modification. Skiing frees many people from limitations that hinder their mobility on land and allows them to move with great agility and at great speeds (figure 28.1). For many people with physical, mental, and sensory impairments, skiing offers a unique opportunity to challenge their environment.

The key to learning to ski is controlling one's weight distribution and directing where the weight is applied on the surface (edges) of the skis. The goal of any introductory ski program is to provide students with the basic skills needed to enjoy and safely participate in the sport. The basic skills of downhill skiing can be grouped into six categories:

- Putting on and taking off equipment independently
- Using rope and chairlifts independently
- Falling and standing
- Walking (sidestepping, herringbone)
- Stopping (wedge, parallel)
- Turning (wedge, parallel)

Instruction

Ski instruction should be preceded by a conditioning program and the development of basic skills such as falling and standing. When actual ski instruction begins, the skill sequence must be matched to the needs and abilities of the learners to ensure safety and maximize enjoyment. Although independent recovery (standing back up on the skis) is a required skill for independent skiing, it might not be appropriate to concentrate on this skill during early learning. For many people with disabilities, learning to stand up on skis after falling is strenuous and often frustrating. Students who are made to master this skill first are likely not to experience much success or fun and will soon become disenchanted with the idea of skiing. Initial instruction should focus on actual skiing skills, such as a wedge stop, and the instructor should

FIGURE 28.1 A skier maneuvers down the slope using a monoski and outriggers.

AP Photo/Nathan Bilow

provide assistance to compensate for the lack of other skills, such as the ability to independently recover from falls. This form of instruction provides students with confidence and some of the thrills of moving on skis (figure 28.2). As skill and enjoyment increase, students become more motivated to work on mastering the other essential skills, such as independent recovery.

Assistive Devices

Assistive devices have been developed to offset some of the limitations imposed by disabilities and to compensate for the general low fitness and poor motor coordination common to many people with disabilities. The most commonly used device is the **ski bra**, which is mounted to the tip of the skis and serves two primary functions. First, it stabilizes the skis while allowing them to move independently. Second, it assists the skier in positioning the skis in a wedge position, which improves balance and makes for easier stopping and turning. The ski bra

can be used as a temporary learning device for any skier (e.g., those with intellectual disabilities, visual impairments) during the early stages of learning to assist with balance and control of the skis. The ski bra may also be used as a permanent assistive device for people with lower-extremity orthopedic impairments who lack sufficient strength or control of their lower limbs.

Canting wedges are another common modification used to assist skiers with disabilities. Small, thin wedges are placed between the sole of the ski boot and the ski. The wedges adjust the lateral tilt of the boot and subsequently affect the distribution of weight over the edges of the skis. Canting wedges are commonly used to assist skiers who have trouble turning to one side or the other.

Outriggers (see figure 28.3) are common assistive devices used by skiers with amputations and other orthopedic impairments who require additional support primarily in the area of balance. The outriggers are made from a Lofstrand crutch with a short ski attached to the bottom. The ski on the

FIGURE 28.2 A student learning to sit-ski while tethered to the instructor.

Carl D. Walsh / Aurora Photos

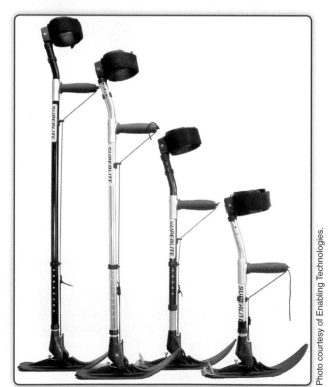

FIGURE 28.3 Outriggers come in a range of sizes. From left to right, tall, medium, monoski adult, and sit-ski adult.

Photo courtesy of Enabling Technologies.

end of the crutch can be placed in a vertical (up) position and used as a crutch or positioned in a horizontal position for use as an outrigger. *Three-track* and *four-track skiing* are common terms used to describe skiing with outriggers. Three-track skiing refers to people who use only one ski and two outriggers—for example, single-leg amputees. Four-track skiing refers to those who use two skis and two outriggers.

Sit-skiing is more similar to sledding than skiing, but it is included here because it is performed on ski slopes and is the skiing method used by skiers with paraplegia and quadriplegia. Sit-skiing involves the use of a special sled. The skier is strapped into the sled, which contains appropriate padding and support to hold the skier in an upright sitting position. The top of the sled is covered by a water-repellent nylon skirt to keep the skier dry. The bottom of the sled is smooth, with a metal runner or edge running along each side. Skiers control the sled by shifting their weight over the edge in the direction they want to go. A single kayak-type pole or two short poles can assist in balancing and controlling the sled. Special mittens are available to allow people with limited grip strength to hold onto the poles. For the protection of both the sit-skier and other skiers on the slope, the beginner sit-skier should always be tethered to an experienced ski instructor. Modified sit-skis are also available and can be used by people with paraplegia for cross-country skiing. Consult the electronic resources at the end of this chapter to find the latest advances in sit-skiing equipment.

Ski instructors use various forms of physical assistance to help skiers with disabilities. Instructors must be able to provide sufficient physical assistance during early learning to ensure safety and success. Providing physical assistance to a moving beginner requires skills that must be learned and perfected. As the skills of a skier with a disability increase, the instructor must also know how to gradually fade out the physical assistance to verbal cues and eventually to independence.

In addition to the more universal assistive devices described previously, many other devices have been created to address the needs of skiers with disabilities. Special prosthetic limbs, for example, have been developed to allow single- and double-leg amputees to ski. Many of these devices are homemade by ski instructors trying to help specific students. Watching a national ski competition for people with disabilities may provide an idea of the range of devices that can be created to assist skiers with various disabilities.

SNOWBOARDING

The latest winter sport to evolve for athletes with disabilities is **snowboarding**. Snowboarding is comparable to skateboarding on snow but using a slightly longer and wider board. The snowboarder's feet are attached perpendicular to the length of the board by bindings that require special boots (see figure 28.4). Snowboarding can be done at any facility that offers alpine skiing. The necessary snowboarding equipment costs between $250 and $600. Most beginners use slightly longer, wider, and heavier boards. The average board should be about mouth level when stood end to end and as wide as the feet (in boots) are long. Most ski resorts that offer adapted ski instruction also offer snowboard instruction for people with disabilities.

An adapted snowboard instructor should be consulted when selecting and adapting snowboard equipment. With modified equipment, most people with disabilities can learn and participate in snowboarding. The United States of America Snowboard

FIGURE 28.4 An amputee snowboards using two outriggers.

Carl D. Walsh / Aurora Photos

Association (USASA) is the governing body for snowboarding competition. The USASA has a division for adaptive snowboarders at its regional and national competitions and offers events in alpine, freestyle, and boardercross (USASA, 2007). Special Olympics initiated snowboarding as an official event in the 2001 World Winter Games in Anchorage, Alaska. Athletes compete in three divisions (novice, intermediate, and advanced) in three events: super giant slalom (super G), giant slalom, and slalom.

In 1998, the U.S. Deaf Skiers Association was renamed the U.S. Deaf Ski and Snowboard Association (USDSSA). The USDSSA offers regional competitions in snowboarding that culminate in competition at the Winter Deaflympics. The instructional recommendations provided for alpine skiing also apply to teaching snowboarding. Many of the assistive devices used in teaching downhill skiing, such as outriggers and tethers, are also used when teaching snowboarding. The Professional Ski Instructors of America (PSIA) and the American Association of Snowboard Instructors (AASI) produce three manuals that should be consulted when preparing to teach snowboarding: *Adaptive Snowsports Instruction Manual* (2003), *AASI Snowboard Manual* (1998), and *AASI Snowboard Movement Analysis Handbook* (2003).

CROSS-COUNTRY SKIING

Cross-country skiing has become a popular winter sport in recent years, partly because it is an excellent physical fitness and recreational activity. Because both the arms and the legs are used in cross-country skiing, it develops total-body fitness. Two other advantages of the sport are that it costs nothing after the initial equipment is purchased and that it can be done almost anywhere (e.g., golf courses, parks, open fields). The major disadvantage of cross-country skiing when compared with downhill skiing is that the skier must create the momentum to move. This difference precludes participation of many people with more severe orthopedic impairments who lack either the strength or the control to generate the momentum needed to cross-country ski. However, because the activity is performed on snow and does not require that the feet actually be lifted off the ground, many people with cerebral palsy who have difficulty walking (shuffle gait) can successfully cross-country ski.

A complete cross-country skiing outfit (skis, poles, gaiters, and shoes) is relatively inexpensive. For beginners, waxless (fish-scale or step-pattern)

skis are recommended over wax skis. Waxless skis require no maintenance or preparation before use, and they provide more than sufficient resistance and glide for learning and enjoying cross-country skiing.

Initial instruction should take place in a relatively flat area with prepared tracks (figure 28.5). Most beginning cross-country skiers tend to simply walk wearing their skis, using their poles for balance. This, unfortunately, is incorrect and very fatiguing. The key in learning to cross-country ski is getting the feel of pushing back on one ski while the weight is transferred to the front foot and the front ski slides forward. Instructors should focus on demonstrating this pattern and contrasting it with walking. An effective technique is to physically assist the beginning skier through this pattern so that the learner can feel what it is like (a method that works particularly well with skiers with intellectual disabilities or visual impairments). Cross-country skiers with visual impairments must be accompanied by sighted partners who usually ski parallel to them and inform them of upcoming conditions (turns, dips, changes in grades). The forward push-and-glide technique is the preferred pattern for most skiers with disabilities, as opposed to the more strenuous and skill-demanding skating technique used by world-class Nordic skiers.

COMPETITIVE SKIING FOR PEOPLE WITH DISABILITIES

Skiing for people with disabilities is sponsored by several sport associations that conduct local, state, and national skiing competitions. Three of the largest and most prominent sponsors of ski competitions are Special Olympics, which sponsors competitions for people with intellectual disabilities; Disabled Sports USA (DS/USA), which sponsors national skiing competitions for people with disabilities; and the United States Association of Blind Athletes (USABA), which sponsors an annual national competition for skiers with visual impairments.

Special Olympics sponsors local, state, and national ski competitions (Special Olympics, 2008). Competition is offered in both alpine and Nordic events. The alpine events include downhill, giant slalom, and slalom races. The Nordic events include the 500-meter, 1K, 3K, 5K, 7.5K, and 10K races as well as a $4 \times 1K$ unified relay race and a $4 \times 1K$ relay race. Athletes are classified for competition into one of three classes—novice, intermediate, or

FIGURE 28.5 Double-leg amputee cross-country skiing in a prepared track.

Boomer Jerritt/All Canada Photos/age fotostock

advanced—on the basis of preliminary time trials in each event. There are no age or gender divisions. Special Olympics also offers developmental (noncompetitive) alpine and Nordic events. The developmental alpine events include a 10-meter walk, glide event, and super glide. The Nordic developmental events include 10-, 50-, and 100-meter cross-country skiing race and glide events. Special Olympics also offers 100-meter, 200-meter, 400-meter, 800-meter, 1,600-meter, 5K, and 10K races as well as 4 × 100-meter and 4 × 400-meter relay races.

DS/USA sponsors national ski championships each year. The nationals are preceded by a series of regional meets in which athletes must qualify for the nationals. The national meets involve competition in three categories: alpine (downhill, slalom, giant slalom), Nordic (5K, 10K, 15K, 20K, 30K, biathlon, relays), and sit-skiing (as listed for alpine and Nordic). Athletes are classified according to the site and severity of their disabilities and the type of adapted equipment used in skiing (DS/USA, 2001). Skiers with orthopedic impairments are divided into 12 classes, described briefly in the next section.

Classification of Skiers With Orthopedic Disabilities

The following is a list of the DS/USA classifications for people with orthopedic disabilities (2001).

Standing Classes

Class L0—No measurable disability

Class L1—Disability of both legs above the knees; skiing with outriggers and using two skis or skiing on one ski using a prosthesis

Class L2—Disability of one leg; skiing with outriggers or poles and on one ski

Class L3/1—Disability in both legs below the knees, amputations, severe cerebral palsy, severe neurological impairments; skiing on two skis with poles; point score 36 to 60 out of 80

Class L3/2—Disability of both legs below the knees, partial paraplegia, mild cerebral palsy, or nerve disorder; skiing on two skis with poles; point score 61 to 80 out of 80

Class L4—Disability of one leg; skiing on two skis with poles

Class L5—Disability of both arms or hands; skiing on two skis with no poles

Class L6—Disability of one arm or hand; skiing on two skis with one pole

Class L9/1—Disability of a combination of arm and leg, partial quadriplegia, above-knee amputations, severe cerebral palsy, or neurological impairment; using equipment of choice

Class L9/2—Disability of a combination of arm and leg, partial quadriplegia, below-knee amputation, mild cerebral palsy, or neurological impairment; using equipment of choice

Monoski Classes

Class L10—Athletes with disabilities in the lower limbs, no functional sitting balance or significant impairment of the upper limbs (e.g., tetra, para classes 1, 2, and upper 3), standing L classes with impairment of the lower limbs together with a significant functional impairment in the upper limbs or trunk; point score 0 to 8 points

Class L11—Athletes with disabilities in the lower limbs and fair sitting balance (e.g., para classes lower 3 and 4), standing L classes with impairment of the lower limbs together with a significant functional impairment of the trunk and hips, any function in the lower limbs may not be used outside of the equipment at any time during the race; point score 9 to 15 points

Class L12/1—Athletes with disabilities in the lower limbs, paraplegia only with good sitting balance; point score 16 to 18 points

Class L12/2—Athletes with disabilities in the lower limbs, amputations, and standing L classes L1, L2, L3/1, L3/2, L4, L9/1, and L9/2 with good sitting balance; point score 16 to 18 points

Classification of Skiers With Vision Disabilities

Skiers with visual impairments are divided into three classes on the basis of visual acuity with maximum correction. These classifications are used by both USABA and DS/USA for their ski competitions. The following are the three most common classifications for people with visual disabilities:

Class B1—Totally blind; can distinguish between light and dark, but cannot discern all shapes.

Class B2—Partially sighted; best correctable vision up to 20/600 or visual field of 5 degrees.

Class B3—Partially sighted; best correctable vision from 20/600 to 20/200 or field of vision from 5 degrees to –20 degrees.

For its national ski competition, USABA offers giant slalom and downhill alpine events as well as 5K, 10K, and 25K Nordic events (USABA, 2003). Separate competitions are offered for each gender within each classification; there are no age divisions. Sighted guides are used in all events to verbally assist the skiers who are visually impaired. USABA sponsors several Nordic skiing training camps each year to promote skiing for people with visual impairments.

In addition to the DS/USA classifications just described, there are three age divisions: ages 0 through 16 (juniors), ages 17 through 39 (open division), and age 40 and over (masters division). Separate competitions are offered for each gender in each age division except when there are not enough participants of one gender to compose a heat. The same classifications apply for both alpine and cross-country skiing. The only difference between the men's and women's events is that women are limited to the 5K and 10K cross-country events.

Sit-Skiing Classifications

Sit-skiing competition is conducted only in the United States; thus, athletes competing in this category are not classified according to an international classification system. Sit-skiers are classified into one of two groups. Group 1 is composed of athletes with disabilities in the lower limbs, with injury between T5 and T10 inclusive. (Athletes with higher injuries, above T5, typically are not able to sit-ski.) Group 2 is for athletes with all other disabilities resulting from injury below T10 and conditions such as spina bifida, amputation, cerebral palsy, polio, and muscular dystrophy.

ICE SKATING

Ice skating is an inexpensive winter sport easily accessible in many regions. Most people with disabilities who can stand and walk independently can learn to ice-skate successfully. For those who cannot, a modified form of ice skating, ice picking, is available. Although skating is common in many areas on frozen lakes and ponds or water-covered tennis courts, the preferred environment for teaching ice skating is an indoor ice rink. An indoor rink offers a more moderate temperature and an ice surface free from the cracks and bumps commonly found in natural ice. Ice rinks frequently can be used by physical education programs during off times, such as daytime hours on weekdays.

Properly fitting skates are essential for learning and ultimately enjoying ice skating. Ice skates should be fitted by a professional experienced in working with and fitting people with disabilities. Either figure or hockey skates can be used. The important consideration is that the skates provide good ankle and arch support so that the skater's weight is centered over the ankles and the blades of the skates are perpendicular to the ice when the skater is standing.

As discussed earlier, instruction should be guided by safety and success. The greatest obstacle in learning to ice-skate is the fear of falling. Although falling while first learning to skate is inevitable, steps can be taken to minimize the frequency and severity of the falls and, consequently, the apprehension. At the same time, the early stages of learning must be associated with success, which gives learners confidence that they will be able to learn to skate. It is recommended that padding be used around the major joints most likely to hit the ice during a fall. Knee and elbow pads reduce the physical trauma of taking a fall and also provide psychological security that alleviates the fear of falling. When teaching people with disabilities to ice skate, elbow pads and American football pants with knee, hip, and sacral pads are beneficial during the early stages. See the application example on overcoming fear.

The locomotor skill of ice skating is similar to walking. Weight, the center of gravity, is transferred in front of the base of support and from side to side as the legs are lifted and swung forward to catch the weight. The back skate is usually rotated outward about 30 degrees to provide resistance to sliding backward as the weight transfers to the forward skate. Because success during the early lessons is essential, one-on-one instruction from an experienced instructor is highly recommended.

APPLICATION EXAMPLE

Overcoming Fear

Setting: A physical education class is starting an ice hockey skills unit. Most of the students can skate forward well and are working on increasing speed, changing direction, and skating backward.

Student: John is an 11-year-old with mild intellectual disabilities who recently moved to Michigan from Florida. He has slightly below-average coordination for his age but is generally willing to try new skills. John has recently become a big Michigan State hockey fan.

Issue: John had a negative experience with ice skating the first time he tried it and now is extremely fearful and unwilling to put skates on.

Application: Based on the information available and a meeting with John's parents, the physical educator decides on the following strategies:

▶ Meet individually with John to discuss his fears of ice skating and to explain how these fears will be addressed.

▶ Contact the local university and borrow some official Michigan State hockey pads and a helmet of appropriate size.

▶ John will start using a padded Hein-A-Ken skate aid to give him confidence. He will then transition to using a hockey stick as a balance aid.

▶ Prepare an aide to work with John during the initial lessons to ensure he is successful and to prevent any new negative experiences.

Special Olympics has excellent coaching guides available for both figure skating (2006) and speed skating (2003).

The primary aid used in teaching ice skating is physical assistance. Some people with orthopedic and neuromuscular impairments might benefit from the use of polypropylene orthoses to stabilize their ankles. Ankle–foot orthoses are custom made and can be worn inside the skates. Skating aids, such as the Skate Coach Early Skating Trainer (from Skatebuys), are devices that do not interfere with the skating action of the legs and provide the beginning skater with a stable means of support independent from the instructor. The skate aid can be used for temporary assistance during the early stages of learning for students who need a little additional support or confidence; it can also be a more permanent assistive device for skaters with more severe orthopedic impairments. It is beneficial to add some foam padding to the top support bar in the front of the skate aid to further reduce the chance of injury from falls. If skate aids are not available, chairs can be used in a similar fashion.

Ice picking is a modified form of ice skating in which the participant sits on a **sledge** (a small sled with blades on the bottom) and uses small poles (picks) to propel the sledge on the ice. Ice picking can be performed by almost anyone and is particularly appropriate for people who have only upper-limb control (e.g., people with paraplegia or spina bifida). Ice picking is an excellent activity for developing upper-body strength and endurance. All skating activities and events (speed skating and skate dancing) can be modified and performed in sledges. Because people with and without disabilities can use the equipment, ice picking offers a unique way to equalize participation and competition in integrated settings.

Special Olympics sponsors ice skating competitions in two categories: figure skating and speed skating (Special Olympics, 2003). The figure-skating events include singles, pairs, and ice dancing; the speed-skating events include the 100-, 200-, 300-, 500-, 800-, 1,000-, and 1,500-meter races and 4 × 20-lap relay; and Unified Sports 4 × 20-lap relay. For each event, athletes are divided into three classifications—novice, intermediate, and advanced—on the basis of preliminary performance and time trials. Developmental (noncompetitive) ice-skating events are also offered. These include the skills competition and the 100-meter oval, 25-meter straightaway, and 50-meter half-lap race.

SLEDDING AND TOBOGGANING

In snowy regions, sledding and tobogganing are two common recreational activities universally enjoyed by children and adults. Many people with disabilities, however, avoid these activities because they lack the simple skills and confidence needed to successfully take part in them. The needed skills and confidence can easily be addressed in a physical education program. Given proper attention to safety and clothing, almost all children with disabilities can participate in sledding and tobogganing. Sleds and toboggans can be purchased or rented at minimal cost. Straps and padding can be added to sleds and toboggans to accommodate the specific needs occasioned by people with disabilities. Even students with the most severe disabilities can experience the thrill of sledding or tobogganing when paired with an aide who can control and steer the sled.

HOCKEY

Ice hockey is a popular winter sport in the northern areas of the United States and is the national sport of Canada. The game is played by two teams who attempt to hit a puck into the opposing team's goal using their hockey sticks. Hockey is a continuous, highly active, and exciting sport. Because of these features, many modifications and adaptations have been made to accommodate players with disabilities. Some common modifications are as follows:

- Use soft plastic balls, plastic pucks, or doughnut-shaped pucks instead of the traditional ice hockey pucks.
- Use shorter and lighter sticks made of plastic, which are more durable, easier to handle, and less harmful to other players.
- Use a less slippery surface, such as a gym floor or tennis court.
- Change the size of the goals.
- Change the boundaries, number of players per team, or length of playing periods to accommodate players' abilities.

Modifications can easily be made with tape and Velcro to enable players with physical impairments to hold sticks or use sticks from wheelchairs. A wide range of abilities can be accommodated in a game if the teams are balanced and the players' abilities are matched to the various positions.

Special Olympics sponsors local, state, and national competition in floor hockey. A stick similar to a broomstick with a vinyl coating on the end is used in conjunction with a doughnut-shaped puck. The goalkeeper uses a regular hockey goalie stick. The goals are 1.8 meters wide and 1.2 meters high. The playing area is 30 meters by 15 meters, or the size of a typical basketball court. Special Olympics offers team competition, Unified Sports team competition, and a 10-meter puck dribble event.

Sledge hockey is a modified form of ice hockey played on sledges. The only difference from the regulation game of ice hockey is that sledge hockey is played from a sledge and the puck is struck with a modified stick called a *pick*. The pick is about 30 inches (76 cm) long. One end has metal points that grip the ice and allow the athlete to propel the sledge. The other end, the butt, is rubber coated. The butt end is held while the sledge is being propelled. When the athlete wants to hit the puck,

the hand slides down the shaft of the pick to cover the spiked end, and then the butt end of the pick is used to strike the puck.

Sledge hockey is an excellent recreational and fitness activity. Using sledges is also an ideal way of allowing students with and without orthopedic disabilities to participate in the same activity. The United States won the gold medal in sledge hockey in the 2002 Paralympics and the 2010 Paralympics and the bronze medal in the 2006 Paralympics. Figure 28.6 shows a picture from a sledge hockey game. For more information on sledge hockey, consult the electronic resources for this chapter.

Logical modifications should be made to the regulation game of hockey to accommodate beginners, such as reducing the playing area, increasing the number of players on each team, increasing the size of the goal, playing without goalkeepers, or changing the size or type of puck (e.g., substituting a playground ball). The goal of all modifications should be to maximize participation and success in the basic sledge and hockey skills while gradually progressing toward the regulation game.

FIGURE 28.6 In this sledge hockey game from the 2006 Paralympics, Norway makes an attempt for a goal against the U.S. goalie.

LaPresse/Zuma Press/Icon SMI

CURLING

Curling is a popular sport in Europe and Canada. The playing area is an ice court 46 yards (42 m) long and 14 feet (4.3 m) wide, with a 6-foot (1.8 m) circular target, called a *house*, marked on the ice at each end. The game is played by two teams of four players, with pieces of equipment called *stones* (a kettle-shaped weight 36 in. [1 m] in circumference and weighing about 40 lb [18 kg], with a goose-neck handle on top). A game is composed of 10 or 12 rounds called *heads*, which consist of each player delivering (sliding) two stones. Players on each team alternate delivering stones until all have been delivered. After each stone is delivered, teammates can use brooms to sweep frost and moisture from the ice in front of the coming stone to keep it straight and allow it to slide farther. At the end of a round, a team scores a point for each stone they have closer to the center of the target than the other team. The team with the most points at the end of 10 or 12 rounds is the winner. If the score is tied, an additional round is played to break the tie.

Curling can easily be modified to accommodate people with just about any disability. The distance between the houses and the weight of stones can be reduced to facilitate reaching the targets. The size of the targets can also easily be increased to maximize success. Audible goal locators can be placed on the houses to assist players with visual impairments. The sweeping component of the game might be difficult to modify to include players who are nonambulatory or have visual impairments. In these cases, mixed teams could be formed of players with various disabilities or combining players with and without disabilities so that each team has a few members who could do the sweeping. Finally, assistive devices similar to those used in bowling (ramps and guide rails) could be used to help players with more severe disabilities deliver the stones. For the latest information on curling, check the electronic resources for this chapter.

INCLUSION

Although competition is available for most winter sports, most students learn winter sports so that they can participate in them as recreational activities. As such, winter sports lend themselves to inclusion, and many modifications can be made to allow people with even the most severe disabilities to participate. The goal of all modifications should be to capitalize on the abilities of the students and maximize their participation. For winter activities such as skiing, snowboarding, cross-country skiing, ice skating, and sledding, modifications can easily be made to the equipment to increase stability and control and to the terrain to slow the activity down to ensure success and allow inclusion of all students in the same activity. In many cases the specialized equipment used by students with disabilities draws the interest and respect of students without disabilities. Seeing a student with a spinal cord injury ski down a slope on a monoski and then get on the chair lift commands the admiration of any skier who is having trouble staying up on two skis. In fact, it is not uncommon for students without disabilities to want to try skiing with a monoski.

Simple modifications can also be made to team events such as floor hockey, sledge hockey, and curling to promote inclusion. These typically involve modifying how the equipment is held to increase control, reducing the distances and boundaries to minimize the limitations imposed by reduced mobility, and defining safe areas if the students must be protected from physical contact or require a little more time to react during the game. Again, the goal should be to build on the students' strengths and maximize participation. Given the physical fitness and social benefits associated with winter activities, every effort should be made to ensure that all students with disabilities have functional competency in these activities so that they can participate in them throughout their lives.

SUMMARY

Winter sports are excellent all-around activities. They develop motor skills, strength, and physical fitness, and at the same time they provide participants with functional recreational skills they can use for the rest of their lives. For many people with disabilities, winter sports performed on snow and ice allow them to move with agility and speed not possible under their own power on land. Thus, winter sports should be an essential component in physical education and sport programs, especially for students with disabilities. For this reason, activities have been discussed in this chapter with particular focus on ways to modify them for people with unique needs.

REFERENCES

Disabled Sports USA (DS/USA). (2001). DS/USA alpine competition rules. Retrieved December 8, 2008, from www.dsusa.org/programs-winter-competition-disclassrules.html.

National Ski Patrol. (2008). Safety information. Retrieved December 4, 2008, from www.nsp.org/slopesaftey/slope_safety.aspx.

Professional Ski Instructors of America (PSIA) and American Association of Snowboard Instructors (AASI). (1998). *AASI snowboard manual*. Lakewood, CO: Author.

Professional Ski Instructors of America (PSIA) and American Association of Snowboard Instructors (AASI). (2003). *AASI snowboard movement analysis handbook*. Lakewood, CO: Author.

Professional Ski Instructors of America (PSIA) and American Association of Snowboard Instructors (AASI). (2003). *Adaptive snowsports instruction manual*. Lakewood, CO: Author.

Special Olympics. (2003). Coaching guide for speed skating. Retrieved December 4, 2008, from www.specialolympics.org/speed_skating.aspx.

Special Olympics. (2006). Coaching guide for figure skating. Retrieved December 4, 2008, from www.specialolympics.org/figure_skating.aspx.

Special Olympics. (2008). Winter sports rules. Retrieved August 19, 2008, from www.specialolympics.org/sports.aspx.

United States of America Snowboard Association (USASA). (2007). *Rulebook for USASA 2007-2008 season*. Retrieved August 19, 2008, from www.usasa.org.

United States Association of Blind Athletes (USABA). (2003). Alpine and Nordic skiing. Retrieved October 20, 2003, from www.usaba.org.

WRITTEN RESOURCES

O'Leary, H. (1994). *Bold tracks: Teaching adaptive skiing*. Boulder, CO: Johnson Books.

This book is a must for anyone who is going to be teaching skiing to people with disabilities.

Special Olympics. (2007). *The Special Olympics alpine skiing coaching guide*. Washington, DC: Special Olympics, Inc.

This manual provides a how-to approach for teaching the basic skills involved in alpine skiing, including teaching suggestions, sample drills, and activities.

Special Olympics. (2007). *The Special Olympics floor hockey coaching guide*. Washington, DC: Special Olympics, Inc.

This manual provides a how-to approach for teaching the basic skills involved in floor hockey. Teaching suggestions, sample drills, and activities are provided for each skill.

AUDIOVISUAL RESOURCES

Canadian Association for Disabled Skiing (CADS): www.disabledskiingontario.com.

This Web site contains online videos of the 2004 and 2005 CADS festivals that show a variety of individuals with disabilities skiing with assistive devices.

International Paralympic Committee (IPC) Archive Collection: www.paralympic.org/Media_Centre/Footage/index.html.

This Web site provides contact information on accessing video of past Paralympic Summer and Winter games.

National Center on Physical Activity for Disability (NCPAD). (2005). Skiing videos. Retrieved December 8, 2008, from www.ncpad.org/videos/fact_sheet.php?sheet=247&section=1602.

This site provides basic information on different forms of skiing for people with disabilities along with short video clips.

ELECTRONIC RESOURCES

AbleData Database of Assistive Technology for Winter Sports: www.abledata.com/abledata.cfm?pageid=19327&ksectionid=19327.

This Web site provides information and links to the latest assistive devices that can be used to help people with disabilities participate in a variety of sport and recreational activities, including winter sports.

International Paralympics Committee: www.paralympic.org/IPC/Reference_Documents/.

This site provides the official rules, classifications, and competitions for all paralympic sports.

Sitski.com: www.sitski.com.

This site provides information and pictures of the latest advances in sit-skiing equipment.

Skatebuys: www.skate-buys.com.

This site provides online access to all types of skates and skating accessories. It also provides information on how to buy and match skates to different ability levels.

United States of America Snowboard Association (USASA): www.usasa.org.

USASA is the national governing body for all snowboarding competition. This site contains the official rules and events as well as information on regional and national competitions.

U.S. Deaf Ski and Snowboard Association (USDSSA): www.usdssa.org.

This is the official site of the USDSSA, which governs ski and snowboard competitions for Deaf people. The site contains information on the organization and its history as well as information on upcoming events.

USA Curling: www.usacurl.org.

This site provides information on curling history, rules, and strategies.

chapter 29

Enhancing Wheelchair Sport Performance

Abu B. Yilla

So this was it: the Paralympic Games, London, 2012. It had been a long road from the small high school where Karim's adapted physical education teacher had first shown him a DVD of athletes racing in wheelchairs. Memories of the long, hard days of training in all weather were mixed with those of triumph in local, national, and international competitions. The court cases that finally resulted in him contributing points to his high school's state University Interscholastic League's championship, the competitions as part of the collegiate track team, and the battles in the world championship had finally come to this: the T54 100-meter dash final at *the* Games. And all because his high school adapted physical education teacher knew about wheelchair racing. "Racers. On your marks, set. . ." and the starting gun fired.

From Oscar Pistorius' battle to be included in the Beijing Olympics and his triple-gold-medal performance at the Paralympics to Natalie Du Toit's inclusion in the Olympics and her five-gold-medal performance at the Paralympics, the 2008 Beijing Paralympic Games were a showcase for the development of disability sport. As always, at the heart of the Games were the wheelchair events.

The Oscar-nominated documentary *Murderball* (Shapiro, 2005) showcased the ability and motivations of wheelchair rugby athletes, wheelchair racers have continued to break records, and wheelchair basketball competition has thrilled crowds. Athletes who compete in wheelchair sport combine themselves, their chairs, and their skills into performance systems to achieve levels of excellence unheard of in the days of medically driven attitudes and regulations. The combination of body and wheelchair into a performance system has opened elite disability sport to a new dimension far from that envisioned by early pioneers. There is now a functional perspective in wheelchair sport that places disability second to the demands of the specific sport. This transition has been spearheaded by the athletes themselves, and they have been instrumental in developing many of the innovations in equipment and technique.

It was once possible for athletes with disabilities to compete at a world championship level in a number of sports, but this is no longer the case. Sport for athletes with disabilities now parallels the world of athletes without disabilities, and to reach the highest levels, athletes must find the sport (and often the event or position) for which they are best suited. Suitability for specific sports is most commonly determined by the athlete's interest, disability type, body size and shape, and psychological makeup. In order to maximize wheelchair sport performance, event selection should be based on a systems approach that takes into consideration both the athlete and the wheelchair. Taking all of these changes and advances into consideration, this chapter covers the process of selecting both a sport and an appropriate chair as well as training and performance considerations.

ATHLETE AND WHEELCHAIR: A SYSTEMS APPROACH

The athlete and the wheelchair combined can be viewed as a performance system. This reflects the functional model of disability sport now prevalent in both the design of wheelchairs and the functional classification systems employed in elite disability sport competition. Much of the early research on wheelchair sport examined either the athlete or the wheelchair. Many of these studies also examined wheelchair users outside of their preferred environment—that is, their competitive wheelchair. These approaches employed instruments such as ergometers that had scientific but not ecological validity. In appreciating the functional development in wheelchair sport, it is necessary to understand the importance of a systems approach. This approach combines athlete and wheelchair into a performance system that is defined by the needs of the specific sport. This chapter examines performance enhancements for wheelchair athletes, provides a brief description of the equipment, and then examines the combination of the athlete and the wheelchair into a performance system (see figure 29.1).

Athlete

Success in wheelchair sport requires that an athlete be suited to meet the performance considerations of that sport. For example, success in basketball requires height for the forward and center positions and speed and agility in the guard positions. In general, athletes with predominantly fast-twitch muscle fibers should focus on sprint events; those with slow twitch, the endurance events. Those with the psychological profile that includes subsuming the self into a team mold should, of course, focus on team events; those with an individual orientation should focus on the appropriate individual sport. Though this approach is somewhat of a truism in sport for athletes without disabilities, in the past, wheelchair athletes have not always been able to match their personal goals to the appropriate athletic challenge. After identifying the appropriate event, the athlete needs to focus on meeting the demands of the particular sport by identifying a training regime.

Training

Wheelchair users respond to physical training in a similar manner to each other and to the nondisabled population (Shephard, 1990; Wells & Hooker, 1990). In addition to developing a foundation of health-related fitness (see chapter 23) when identifying the training requirements in a given sport, the

Joe Giddens/PA Photos

FIGURE 29.1 Basketball performance system.

athlete should develop levels of fitness associated with performance for that sport. The athlete should also consider factors such as individual orientation to specific sports and body anthropometry. Performance-related fitness includes components such as movement, coordination, agility, power, speed, and balance (Gallahue & Ozmun, 2002). These components are applicable to wheelchair performance and should be developed in a sport-specific manner. Ultimately, the trained athlete will demonstrate improved performance in the sport under examination (Curtis, 1981b).

Training regimens for athletes with disabilities parallel those for athletes without disabilities, and in many cases they appear identical. When modifications are necessary, it is usually due to the smaller active muscle mass and to the lack of alternative training modes available. For example, runners can train the legs through running, jumping, stair-climbing, cycling, or weight training. Athletes who use wheelchairs are usually limited to weight training, pushing their chairs, or arm cranking (if

they have access to this specialized equipment). This makes repetitive overuse injuries a concern, although reported injury rates for athletes with disabilities are less than those reported for athletes in American football and soccer (but more than in running basketball) (Ferrara & Peterson, 2000).

Underpinning most athletic performances is the development of a sound cardiorespiratory base. However, training the cardiorespiratory system presents unique problems to the wheelchair athlete. Cardiorespiratory endurance is produced by stressing the heart and respiratory system through the use of major muscle groups, which expend large amounts of energy over prolonged lengths of time. For athletes without disabilities, running, cycling, and swimming use the large muscles of the trunk and lower limbs and are excellent modes of exercise. The wheelchair athlete, however, is limited to using the relatively small muscles of the arms and, in some cases, the muscles of the trunk. This smaller working muscle mass places lower demands on the heart and lungs and makes cardiorespiratory training more difficult. Training rollers, arm-crank ergometers, and upper-body exercise (UBE) systems (modalities used in cardiorespiratory endurance programs of elite wheelchair athletes) can be employed.

The intensity of training can best be gauged by using rate of perceived exertion (RPE) scales (Borg, 1998), which allow the trainer to account for the uniqueness of the athlete independent of standard measures. There is some merit in using standardized exercise tests, and Van der Woude, Bouten, Veeger, and Gwinn (2002) found that elite athletes can be evaluated using standardized aerobic and anaerobic exercise tests, provided classification and current training status are taken into account.

Though a cardiorespiratory base is essential, power more directly relates to the performance demands made in the anaerobic sports exemplified on the court (e.g., tennis, basketball, quad rugby). Because of the small muscle mass involved in wheelchair propulsion and the asymmetry of the propulsion movements, systematic strength and flexibility training is critical. Stretching, both before and after exercise, may be more important for athletes with disabilities than for athletes without disabilities. Weight training will develop strength and indirectly power, and it is a major component in the training regime of the elite athlete.

The wheelchair athlete propels the wheelchair using a relatively small range of motion at the shoulder and elbow, and this action is asymmetrical in that the forces of extension (during propulsion) are far greater than the muscular forces used in recovery. This asymmetry can lead to muscle imbalance around the shoulder joint, which in turn may cause serious overuse injury and postural problems (Curtis, 1981a). An important component of the weight training program for wheelchair users should, therefore, be development of the posterior (back) muscles. A simple rule of thumb is to pair muscles in the training program (i.e., biceps and triceps) and to include free-weight exercises that require the athlete to be facedown (prone) on the work bench. The latissimus dorsi and the trapezius muscles of the back are examples of muscles that should be targeted in a weight program, if such exercises are not contraindicated. Attention to appropriate stretching practices will also improve weight training regimes (Curtis, 1981a), and where there is a strength imbalance in the muscles due to the disability, stretching can reduce problems such as contractures. The next section examines other disability-specific medical concerns.

Medical Concerns

Wheelchair athletes face several disability-specific sports medicine problems, of which the most important are those associated with thermal regulation. Damage to the spinal cord presents problems at both high and low ambient temperatures because impairment of sensory nerves means that athletes are often unable to feel heat, cold, or pain. Thus, in cold weather they receive no sensory warning that body extremities (usually the feet) are becoming frozen. Coupled with reduced blood flow to the inactive feet, frostbite becomes an ever-present danger against which the athlete must guard.

At high ambient temperatures, the problem is damage to the nerves that initiate and control sweat production. The problem is particularly severe in athletes with quadriplegia, many of whom have little or no body sweat production and thus no way of reducing their core temperature. The provision of shade, adequate drinking fluids, and wet towels for the reduction of surface temperature can help alleviate this problem.

A particularly pernicious medical problem that has surfaced in wheelchair sport is the life-threatening but deliberate precipitation of autonomic dysreflexia by athletes with quadriplegia, a process referred to as *boosting*. Autonomic dysreflexia is a medical condition characterized by hypertension, piloerection, headaches, bradycardia, and very high levels of catecholamine. Autonomic dysreflexia is unique to people with spinal cord injury above the major splanchnic outflow at the sixth thoracic

vertebrae. Athletes with quadriplegia believe that boosting increases their athletic performance, and experimental evidence (Burnham et al., 1993; Schmid et al., 2001) supports this view. National and international sport groups are aware of the use of boosting and its dangers, and the practice is banned in Paralympic competition (Schmid et al., 2001).

Wheelchair

Developments in wheelchair design that match the chair to the demands of the sport have led to multiple choices for the athlete wishing to enhance performance (LaMere & Labanowich, 1984a, 1984b, 1984c). It is no longer feasible to expect a general wheelchair to perform to the competitive demands of a sport at the elite level. Just as the athlete without a disability wears different shoes for different sports, the elite wheelchair athlete uses different wheelchairs for different sports. Nevertheless, there are some commonalties in wheelchair design that generalize across the spectrum of competitive wheelchairs.

Wheelchair Frame

The wheelchair frame performs one major function: It holds the other components—the seat, the main wheels, and front wheels—in their proper positions (see figure 29.2). Perhaps the most important design consideration in building a wheelchair frame is to make it as light and as rigid as possible. It needs to be lightweight so that the athlete has to propel as little weight as possible during performance, and it needs to be rigid so that the energy that the athlete applies to the wheelchair is used to drive the chair rather than to bend and deform the frame. Frame flexing absorbs energy directly, but because the wheel alignment of the wheelchair changes as the frame flexes, additional energy is lost when the main wheels do not point straight ahead in the direction of travel. In addition, the frame must be matched to the body size and shape of the athlete and will vary depending on the performance considerations of the sport.

Wheels

The rear wheels of racing wheelchairs are larger in diameter and narrower in cross section than those used in other sport chairs because of the differing demands of the activity. Wheels for court chairs have to be able to withstand rotational torque and in many cases contact with other wheelchairs.

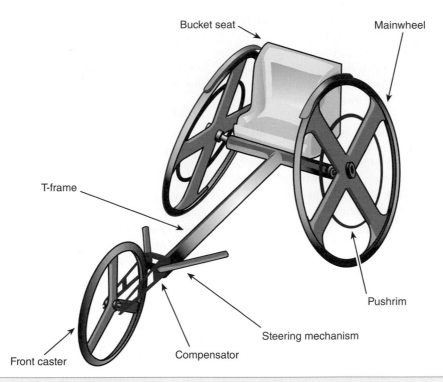

Bucket seat

Mainwheel

T-frame

Pushrim

Steering mechanism

Front caster

Compensator

FIGURE 29.2 Schematic of the racing wheelchair.

Courtesy of Per4Max Medical.

Therefore, some athletes in contact sports such as basketball and quad rugby forgo lightness for additional robustness in the main wheel and have stronger, cross-spoked wheels that can withstand these extra forces.

For racing, unless the athlete is very small, the main wheels are usually high-quality racing bicycle wheels in the European 700C or North American 27-inch size. For road racing, the narrowest possible tires (19 mm or less) are used, whereas for track racing there appears to be some benefit to using wider 23- to 28-millimeter tires. Since additional weight in the wheels of a wheelchair slows the athlete down twice as much as additional weight in the frame, racing wheels should be as light, strong, and rigid as possible. The trend for front wheels has been to use as large of a wheel as the rules allow, and front wheels with 18- and 20-inch (46 and 51 cm) diameters are common.

For court chairs such as those used in the basketball game pictured in figure 29.1, the size of main wheels ranges from 24 inches (61 cm) to the maximum permissible 26 inches (66 cm), depending on the position played (Yilla, La Bar, & Dangelmaier, 1998). The preferred front wheel now tends to be the skateboard type available at regular hobby shops.

Number of Wheels

A wheelchair remains stable as long as the center of gravity of the athlete plus the chair remains inside the wheelchair base of support. The base of support is the area of ground marked by the points at which the wheels contact the surface. In four-wheeled designs, the base of support is rectangular with the base a little narrower at the front than at the rear, whereas in three-wheeled designs, the base of support is triangular. This means that as the weight of the athlete moves forward (as she leans forward to reduce air resistance), the center of gravity gets nearer to the edge of the base of support of the three-wheeled chair and the chair becomes less stable. This lack of stability can be a problem for less experienced athletes or for some court sports, but for those who can handle them, three-wheeled chairs are faster. Three-wheel designs are faster because there is less resistance to passage over the ground for three rather than four wheels (Higgs, 1992a), and three-wheeled designs also have considerably less wind resistance than four-wheelers under most wind conditions (Higgs, 1992b).

A performance consideration in many court sports is the necessity to extend laterally forward to the right or the left, and this may require the extra stability inherent in a four-wheeled design. Caution should be exercised, therefore, in selecting a three-wheeled chair for basketball or quad rugby where stability is at a premium. For tennis and racing, elite athletes almost exclusively use a three-wheeled configuration. An additional wheel for front-to-rear stability can be attached to the back of the chair and is now popular in tennis, basketball, and rugby (see figure 29.3).

Main-Wheel Alignment

To allow the wheelchair to roll with the least resistance, it is critical that the main wheels point straight ahead. If the main wheels point slightly outward (toe out) or slightly inward (toe in), it significantly slows down the wheelchair. O'Reagan et al. (1981) showed that for some tires, toe in or toe out of as little as 3 degrees increased rolling resistance tenfold. Since the front wheels are essentially castors to allow turning, they are not subject to the same toe-in and toe-out problems as main wheels. They do, however, increase rolling resistance greatly when their bearings become worn.

Camber Angle

Sport chairs are cambered to allow for superior turning and ease of pushing. Camber is the state in which the wheels are fixed to the frame of the chair at an angle so that the top of the wheel is close to the frame and the bottom is farther away. With the wheels cambered, the hands fall naturally to the push rim. The main wheels of a racing wheelchair are cambered to allow for maximum application of force to the push rim. With court chairs, the camber significantly enhances maneuverability. The majority of athletes use camber angles between 6 and 12 degrees, with 8 to 10 degrees being most popular.

Seat Height

All other factors being equal, the most effective seat height is a function of the athlete's trunk

Photo courtesy of Per4Max Medical.

FIGURE 29.3   Tennis chair with a "fifth" wheel—although in this case it is the fourth.

and arm length and of the push-rim size that is selected. Higgs (1983) reported that at the 1980 Paralympic Games, superior performances in racing events were recorded by athletes with lower seats. Experimental work by Traut (1989) showed greater propulsion efficiency when a relatively low seat position was used. Experimental work by Meijs, Van Oers, Van der Woude, and Veeger (1989) and by Van der Woude, Veeger, and Rozendal (1990) showed a relationship between the elbow angle (when the athlete was sitting upright in a general sport wheelchair with hands placed on the top center of the push rim) and propulsion efficiency. Their results showed that efficiency was greatest when the elbow angle was 80 degrees and that the energy cost of sitting too high in the chair was greater than the penalty paid for sitting too low. However, performance considerations (height in basketball or the post position in quad rugby) offset some propulsion considerations.

Additional sport-specific considerations for wheelchairs follow. Note that there is a fundamental difference in the configuration of the racing wheelchair relative to court chairs.

Specific Considerations for Racing Wheelchairs

As can be seen in figure 29.4, the structure of the racing wheelchair has changed fundamentally since Bob Hall first pushed in the Boston Marathon.

Goosey and Campbell (1998) concluded that wheelchair design combined with disability may be more important factors in pushing efficiency than propulsion techniques. Specific considerations for racing wheelchairs involve the weight distribution of the athlete in the wheelchair, which can be modified by the anterior–posterior seat position, the size of the push rims, and the use of accessories. Detailed explanations of these considerations follow.

Anterior–Posterior Seat Position

Little is known about the optimal anterior–posterior position of the wheelchair seat, although this position affects both stability and the effectiveness of application of force to the push rim. If the athlete is too far toward the rear of the wheelchair, there is a tendency for the chair to become unstable (particularly when going uphill) and for the athlete to flip out the back. A rear seat position makes it difficult for the athlete to apply force to the front of the push rim, where the most effective application of driving force can be made. Though there is little research evidence on optimal anterior–posterior seating and positioning for elite athletes, Boninger et al. (2000) identified that adjustable axle positions greatly aid in identifying the optimal seating position for maximizing propulsion.

Push Rims

The push rims are the point at which the athlete's energy is transmitted to the wheelchair, and as such

FIGURE 29.4 Racing performance system.

dbvirago/fotolia.com

they are critical to producing optimal performance. The three most important aspects of the push rim are its diameter, its width, and the material with which it is covered.

Push-Rim Diameter

The push rim acts as the gearing for the wheelchair. If a small-diameter push rim is used, the athlete has selected a high gear that produces poor acceleration but a high top speed. Conversely, if a large-diameter push rim is used, the benefit is greater acceleration at the cost of a lower top speed. In general, stronger athletes are able to effectively push smaller-diameter push rims, and thus the optimal push-rim diameter is a function of the size of the athlete, the relative importance of acceleration and top speed in the race being run, and the strength of the athlete. Most push rims are between 14 and 16 inches (35 and 41 cm) in diameter, and athletes usually experiment to determine what works best for them. Paralympic rules require that there be only one push rim on each main wheel.

Push-Rim Width

If the push rim is made of relatively wide tubing, it is easier to grasp, which makes starts and uphill climbing easier. On the other hand, it is possible that narrower tubing would encourage higher wheeling speeds because the athlete is more likely to strike the push rim rather than hold it and push. In the absence of research studies, athletes determine their optimal push-rim width by trial and error.

Push-Rim Material

The push-rim covering is of great importance since it is this material that the hand strikes during propulsion. If it is too smooth or shiny, the hand will slip when power is applied. For this reason, a number of materials have been used for push-rim covers. Many racers also apply adhesives to increase push-rim traction. Although the frictional grip of the push rim is important, it is only half of the hand–wheelchair interface, and the hand covering used by the athlete is of equal or greater importance. Most athletes wear gloves that have been sculpted to their exact requirements by the application of hundreds of layers of adhesive tape. This glove and tape combination provides protective cushioning and high, instant grip between the hand and the push rim. Again, the athlete is encouraged to experiment with materials to find the combination that meets his needs.

Accessories

Racing wheelchair accessories are almost as numerous as the wheelchair athletes who use them, but almost all racing wheelchairs incorporate at least a steering device, a compensator, and a computer. With downhill racing speeds reaching more than 40 miles per hour (64 kph), the need for a steering mechanism to help the athlete negotiate corners is obvious, and the usual steering device is a small handle attached directly to the front wheel mounting. This lever can be moved left or right to steer the wheelchair, although steering only occurs when the lever is held in place. Once released, the front wheel returns (under spring action) to a neutral, straight-ahead position. This process is called *active steering*, since turning only occurs when steering input is applied by the racer. In addition to this active-steering mechanism, the wheelchair also incorporates a compensator.

The purpose of the compensator is to permit small, long-term adjustments to the direction in which the chair moves, and it is most important in road racing. Most road races are held on public roads that are designed with a high crown along the midline and with the road falling away for drainage toward the curb. A chair propelled along the crown would go straight, but a chair wheeled near the curb for safety would be moving forward on a sideways-sloping surface. The front of the chair would be constantly falling away from the crest of the crown, and the chair would tend to steer into the curb. A compensator applies a small offset to the front wheel to allow the chair to move straight ahead without the athlete needing to make constant, small corrective steering adjustments. The rigidity provided by a compensator system (as opposed to rotating casters) also stabilizes the wheelchair in the event of surface irregularities.

Bicycle computers are now relatively inexpensive and are almost universally found on racing wheelchairs. These computers provide essential information on distance traveled, cadence, and top and average speeds. This feedback is essential for developing and maintaining accurate training and racing logs that enhance performance.

Specific Considerations for Court Chairs

Because of similarities in configuration, it is easy to assume that a wheelchair that is appropriate for everyday use is also sufficient for sport. Although a general wheelchair may be sufficient for recreational physical activity, a first step when enhancing wheelchair sport performance is to realize the importance of sport-specific equipment. The following paragraphs contain some general guidelines that should help when selecting a wheelchair for court sports such as basketball, rugby, and tennis. Yilla (1997) has provided a more detailed explanation on selecting a wheelchair specifically for basketball, and much of this information transfers to the selection of other court chairs.

When selecting a wheelchair, athletes should seek advice from someone who has experience in court sports and understands the athlete's function level at the position played. This will help give the athlete insight into the functional demands of the sport. If it is a first court chair, it should be purchased from a reputable manufacturer.

There are now a bewildering number of options in performance wheelchairs and in their designs, many of which are experimental. It is advisable to avoid experimental designs until the athlete is comfortable with the performance demands of the sport. The athlete's first sport-specific performance chair should be adjustable both for height and for point of balance (see figure 29.8 later in the chapter) so that it can be modified. However, because of weight and performance considerations, the athlete should avoid wheelchairs that have too many adjustments. Adjustable mechanisms tend to add weight to the chair because of the need to provide a securing method that is flexible and that can be locked for rigidity. The solution is almost always heavier than the simple weld, nut, or other locking mechanism that it replaces. Performance is negatively affected because adjustment mechanisms cannot provide the same rigidity as a weld, leading to a misapplication of drive forces. Adjustments also require a level of expertise for the frame alignment to remain true.

Wheelchairs Without Wheels

Functionality is the focus of performance wheelchairs, and these chairs can diverge from the traditional concept of the wheelchair to the point that they no longer have wheels! In particular, throwing chairs for field events (figure 29.5), monoskis for snow skiing, and monoskis for water skiing (figure 29.6) are all wheelchairs without wheels.

Wheelchairs without wheels are designed to provide a rigid, stable base from which the athlete can perform optimally. Throwing chairs are firmly anchored to the ground during the throw; there is no need for wheels, and as can be seen in figure 29.5, they are no longer part of the chair design. The heavy metal frame is designed to provide stability for the athlete and to provide anchor points so that the chair can be tied down to prevent it from moving during throws. The seat is built as high above the ground as the rules allow, and since cushioning on the seat would absorb some of the power of the throw, the seat is usually hard. Sit-skis and monoskis take a similar sport-specific approach, and in meeting the functional demands of the activity, the wheels have become superfluous. Similarly, as was seen at the Winter Paralympics Games in 2010, sleds used to compete in ice hockey are an exciting addition to this category of wheelchairs.

FIGURE 29.5 A throwing chair for field events.

Imago/Icon SMI

AP Photo/The Daily Journal, James Ramsay

FIGURE 29.6 A water skier, competing in the MP-1 division for quadriplegic athletes, catches some air off the ramp during the jump portion of the U.S. National Disabled Water Ski Championships.

SYSTEMS APPROACH: COMBINING THE ATHLETE AND THE WHEELCHAIR

The process of combining the athlete and the wheelchair into a sport system will vary depending on the specific sport. However, there are some general principles that can be applied when fitting the wheelchair itself. Additionally, there are some specific performance considerations for racing wheelchairs and court chairs.

Fitting the Wheelchair to the Athlete

Proper fitting of the wheelchair to the athlete is critical for high levels of athletic performance. Most manufacturers provide retail experts who are experienced in measuring athletes for performance wheelchairs.

In fitting the frame, the two most critical dimensions are the width and the relative positions of the seat and wheels. If the frame is too narrow for the athlete, there will be insufficient clearance between the wheels and the athlete, resulting in the wheel rubbing the athlete's body. This both slows the chair and produces frictional injury to the athlete. If the frame is too wide, the push rim will be difficult to reach and even more difficult to push effectively.

The relative positioning of the seat and the main wheels is dependent on the material in the wheelchair, the sport to be played, the athlete's weight, and the athlete's fitness level. Therefore, an adjustment on the wheelchair for this relative position is essential no matter how experienced the athlete. Because manufacturers present this adjustment option in different ways, it is an important factor when selecting the chair. Refer to the application example for a list of considerations to keep in mind while helping athletes find the chair that is best for them.

System Considerations for Racing Wheelchairs

A number of system considerations apply to racing wheelchairs. The following section identifies **propulsion techniques** and how to overcome negative forces as important considerations in developing an athlete's wheelchair racing system.

Propulsion Techniques in Track and Road Racing

Coupled with the evolution of the racing wheelchair has been the development of ever more efficient propulsion techniques (Higgs, 1985). A six-phase technique (see figure 29.7) is most frequently used, although not all athletes use each phase with the same degree of effectiveness. An analysis by O'Connor, Robertson, and Cooper (1998) led the authors to conclude that there is a need for coaches to become more knowledgeable concerning appropriate wheelchair propulsion techniques.

Basic Stroke

The propulsion cycle starts with the hands drawn up as far above and behind the push rim as possible given the seating position and flexibility of the athlete. The hands are then accelerated as rapidly and forcefully as possible (acceleration phase) until they strike the push rim (see point A on figure 29.7). The moment of contact is the

APPLICATION EXAMPLE

Enhancing Wheelchair Sport Performance

Setting: A community-based junior wheelchair sport program

Student: A 16-year-old junior wheelchair basketball player needs recommendations to refine his individualized transition program to incorporate adult wheelchair sports. The player is tall, has played the center and forward positions, and wishes to purchase his own wheelchair.

Issue: What considerations should be taken into account in making recommendations to this athlete?

Application: Considerations for this athlete center on equipment, physical fitness, and individual skills.

▶ Equipment considerations

  Athlete's height

  Desire to play a certain position

  Athlete's classification level

  Adjustability for height and point of balance (being able to maximize the seat height to about 21 in. [53 cm] for the center and forward positions)

  System considerations such as strapping and mobility in the wheelchair

  Reputable manufacturer

▶ Individual physical fitness

  Strength training program that targets the upper-body muscles in paired groups (e.g., biceps and triceps)

  Cardiorespiratory conditioning program that uses an arm-crank ergometer or, preferably, a training roller

▶ Individual skills targeted

  Wheelchair mobility skills both with and without the basketball

  Shooting skills both stationary and moving

  Passing skills both stationary and moving

  Studying the sophisticated strategies involved in the adult game

---

impact energy transfer phase (point B on figure 29.7), during which the kinetic energy stored in the fast-moving hand is transferred to the slower-moving push rim. With the hand in contact with the push rim, there is a force application, or push, phase (point C on figure 29.7), and this continues until the hands reach almost to the bottom of the push rim. During the force application phase, most of the propulsion comes from the muscles acting around the elbow and shoulder.

As the hands reach the bottom of the push rim, the powerful muscles of the forearm are used to pronate the hand, which allows the thumb to be used to give a last, powerful flick to the push rim. This last flicking action is reversed by a few athletes who use supination in the rotational energy transfer phase (point D on figure 29.7) to flick the push rim with the fingers rather than the thumb,

and research indicates this type of backhand technique may be more efficient in endurance races (Chow et al., 2001).

Immediately following the rotational energy transfer, the hands leave the push rim during the castoff phase (see point E on figure 29.7). Here it is important that the hand be moving faster than the push rim as it pulls away, since a slower hand will act as a brake on the wheelchair. Often the athlete will use the pronation or supination of the rotational energy transfer phase to accelerate the hands and arms and thus allow them to be carried up and back under ballistic motion. This upward and backward motion is called the *backswing phase* (point F on figure 29.7) and is used to get the hands far enough away from the push rim to allow them to accelerate forward to strike the push rim at high speed at the start of the next stroke.

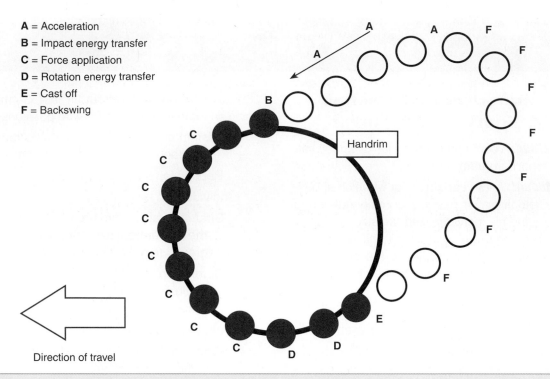

A = Acceleration
B = Impact energy transfer
C = Force application
D = Rotation energy transfer
E = Cast off
F = Backswing

Handrim

Direction of travel

FIGURE 29.7 Six-phase propulsion cycle.

Goosey, Campbell, and Fowler (2000) reported that no single identifiable stroke frequency could be recommended as best for wheelchair racing, but the athlete's own freely chosen frequency was the most economical in laboratory conditions.

This basic propulsion stroke is modified by the terrain over which the athlete is wheeling, by the tactics of the race, and by the athlete's level of disability. On uphill parts of a course, the athlete shortens the backswing and acceleration phases so as to minimize the time during which force is not applied to the push rim and during which the chair could roll backward. Tactically, the athlete is either wheeling at constant speed or is making an attack and needs to accelerate. The basic stroke described previously is used at steady speed; during bursts of acceleration, the major change in stroke takes place during the backswing. At steady speeds, the backswing is a relatively relaxed ballistic movement in which the velocity at castoff is used to raise the hand to its highest and most rearward position. This relaxed backswing is efficient and allows a brief moment of rest during each stroke. During acceleration, however, the major change in stroke dynamics is to increase the number of strokes from approximately 80 per minute to more than 120 per minute. This is achieved by a rapid reduction in the time taken for a more restricted backswing.

Race Start

The stroke is modified during the start of a race. Because the wheelchair is stationary, the hands should grip the push rim (rather than striking it), and for the first few strokes the arc of pushing will be more restricted with as rapid a recovery as possible. The key is to get three or four short, hard strokes before making the transition to a striking rather than pushing stroke.

Retarding Forces and Overcoming Them

While the athlete provides the energy to drive the wheelchair forward, the twin retarding forces of rolling resistance and aerodynamic drag act to slow it down. When propulsive forces are greater than resistance, the wheelchair accelerates, and when the retarding forces are greater, the chair is slowed. Obviously reductions in rolling resistance and aerodynamic drag translate directly into higher wheeling speeds and improved athletic performance.

Rolling Resistance

On a hard, smooth surface, the majority of the rolling resistance of the wheel occurs at the point where the tire is in contact with the ground. As the tire rotates, each part is compressed as it passes under the hub and is in contact with the road surface, and then it rebounds as it begins to rise again and contact with the surface is broken. Not all the energy used to compress the tire is recovered on the rebound, and the energy loss (called *hysteresis*) is the major determinant of rolling resistance.

Rolling resistance of racing wheelchairs is also affected by the camber angle of the main wheel. Though the evidence concerning rolling resistance and camber angle is complex, findings with regard to longitudinal wheel alignment could not be clearer: Wheels that are not parallel and pointing straight ahead dramatically increase the rolling resistance of a wheelchair. Athletes should do everything in their power to check and adjust alignment before every important race.

Aerodynamic Drag

The problem of aerodynamic drag of racing wheelchairs and athletes is unique in sport because of the relatively low speeds at which events take place. Coutts and Schutz (1988) calculated that races on the track take place at average speeds between 3 and 7 meters per second. Although the race times of wheelchairs have dramatically improved since 1988, wheelchair times are still considerably slower than the speeds found in cycling. This creates special low-speed aerodynamic conditions.

Aerodynamic drag is caused by two separate but interrelated forces called **surface drag** and **form drag**. Surface drag is caused by the adhesion of air molecules to the surface of an object passing through it, and it is very powerful at low speeds. Form drag, on the other hand, is caused by the difference in air pressure between the front and the back of an object, which in turn is created by the swirls and eddy currents formed as the wheelchair and athlete pass through the air.

For wheelchair racers, the problem is that smooth surfaces increase surface drag while decreasing form drag, and at the speeds at which wheelchair track events take place, there is uncertainty as to which type of surface gives the best overall result. Some aspects of aerodynamic drag reduction are beyond doubt, and those are the importance of reducing both surface and form drag by minimizing the drag-producing areas of the wheelchair and the athlete's clothing.

Drafting

Because aerodynamic drag represents approximately 40 percent of the force acting to slow down a wheelchair racer, methods of cheating the wind pay considerable dividends. The single most effective way in which drag can be reduced is the process of drafting. Drafting occurs when one wheelchair follows closely behind another wheelchair that acts as a wind deflector. At the end of long races, the energy saved by drafting can be a critical determinant of race outcome. Frequently teams work together, taking turns at both leading and drafting so that their overall performance will be increased.

System Considerations for Court Wheelchairs

This section does not include information on propulsion in court sports. There is less research in propulsion techniques for court sports, presumably because of the wide variability in the propulsion techniques as compared to racing; however, Vanlandewijck, Theisen, and Daly (2001) conducted a review of propulsion biomechanics that included not only wheelchair racing but also basketball and rugby. For those interested in increasing wheelchair sport performance, it is recommended reading.

Two fundamental properties affect the system considerations for court wheelchairs (Yilla et al., 1998): the horizontal (anterior–posterior) positioning and vertical positioning of the chair (see figure 29.8). Appropriate adjustments of these will facilitate development of the balance (vertical adjustment) and agility (horizontal adjustment) components of performance-related fitness.

Horizontal Positioning

Horizontal positioning of the main wheels affects the mobility of the chair. The farther forward the main wheel from a hypothesized neutral position (see figure 29.8*a*, position A), the more maneuverable the chair (see figure 29.8*a*, position B). A backward tilt to the seat rail can also be incorporated; this shifts the center of gravity of the system to the rear and further promotes mobility. Unfortunately, the farther forward the main wheel relative to the center of gravity, the more likely it is that the chair will tilt up. Therefore, the forward placement of the main wheel is restricted by the athlete's ability to force the front end of the chair down. This ability is a function of abdominal and lower-body strength and therefore is a function of the athlete's disability level. Thus, disability level has been a limiting factor in how far forward the main wheels can be placed, with more restricted athletes positioning their chairs in the more stable position, C, in figure 29.8*a*.

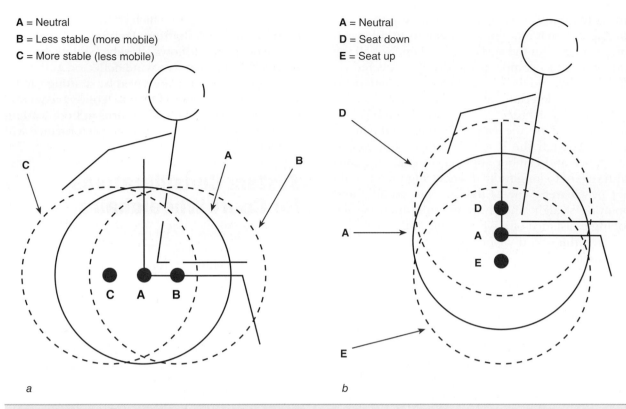

A = Neutral
B = Less stable (more mobile)
C = More stable (less mobile)

A = Neutral
D = Seat down
E = Seat up

a   *b*

FIGURE 29.8 *(a)* Horizontal and *(b)* vertical main-wheel adjustments.

This limiting factor has been somewhat mitigated by changes in the rules of basketball, quad rugby, and tennis that allow for a "fifth" wheel (see figure 29.3 on page 576). This fifth wheel can be placed on the rear of the chair, provided it stays within the area contained by the main wheel. It offsets the tendency of the chair to tilt up if the main wheel is set forward of the neutral position (position B, figure 29.8*a*), thus affording more restricted athletes the capacity to move their rear wheels forward and thereby improve their mobility. In basketball, less restricted athletes are now using the fifth wheel to aid in the tilting of the chair to gain more height, particularly when rebounding or shooting in the restricted zone.

Vertical Positioning

Vertical positioning of the main wheel affects the height at which the athlete sits and the center of gravity of the system. This fundamentally affects the handling properties of the chair. Again, using a hypothetical neutral position (figure 29.8*b*, position A), the lower the athlete sits relative to this neutral position (figure 29.8*b*, position D), the more maneuverable the wheelchair. Therefore, all other things being equal, the wheelchair athlete should

sit as low as possible. However, performance considerations place a premium on height for certain positions, such as center in basketball and the post position in quad rugby. When playing these positions, it is advantageous to position the main wheel to maximize sitting height (figure 29.8*b*, position E); however, because the center of gravity is higher, this will make the chair less maneuverable. This effect can be offset somewhat by using larger main wheels, but this will reduce the start speeds that are vital for court sports.

Therefore, when enhancing wheelchair sport performance on the court, athletes should identify the functional aspects of the game and their roles or positions. This will depend in part on the disability level of the athlete. After identifying these roles, athletes should select the wheelchair setup that will improve functionality within the roles. It is stressed that the positioning of the main wheel will fundamentally affect the performance characteristics of the chair. After the athlete has identified the appropriate wheelchair setup, consideration needs to be given to combining the athlete and the wheelchair into a performance system. This is accomplished with strapping, and where applicable, the use of orthotic and prosthetic devices.

Strapping

The relaxation of regulations that used to prohibit or limit the securing of the athlete to the wheelchair has radically altered the performances seen in basketball, rugby, and tennis. The use of strapping helps an athlete establish a base from which to perform, and it results in greater volumes of action by allowing more leaning and stretching than could occur without being secured to the wheelchair. A striking representation of this is the practice of tilting or standing the chair now common in basketball. In basketball, the player has to remain firmly seated to the chair or else a technical foul is assessed. With the advent of strapping, innovative players found a means to lean or stand the chair on one side without the buttocks leaving the seat (Vernon et al. 2003), considerably raising the height of the chair on the side that is elevated. Initially controversial, it is now accepted practice and is seen as a means of making the game more dynamic.

Level of loss of function can be used as a general indicator of the point at which the athlete should strap to the wheelchair. A National Wheelchair Basketball Association (NWBA [USA]) class III athlete (International Wheelchair Basketball Federation [IWBF], 4.5-3.5) who has good leg function may simply use a strap across the thighs. An NWBA class II athlete (IWBF, 3.0-2.0) may choose to strap at the waist and other points of the lower body. An NWBA class I athlete (IWBF, 1.5 and 1.0) may also use straps across the abdomen that are secured to the back of the chair to compensate for the lack of stomach function. These are general guidelines; the choice of strapping is ultimately based on personal preference. Similarly, the use of orthotics and prosthetics will depend on what the athlete has identified as needed to achieve maximum performance. Novice participants are encouraged to experiment with a variety of strategies to identify their best performance system. Finally combined with the wheelchair in a performance system, the athlete should next address the skill development essential for success in the specific sport.

Skill Development

Sport-specific skills are critical to the elite athlete's program. Common to skills in court sports are speed (which depends on power, which depends on strength) and maneuverability with the target object, whether it be a basketball, volleyball (as used in quad rugby), or tennis racket. Other sport-specific skills can be obtained from the research literature. Skills tests have been developed for wheelchair basketball, quad rugby, and tennis (Brasile, 1986; Brasile & Hedrick, 1996; Moore & Snow, 1994; Yilla & Sherrill, 1998).

Instructional materials that focus on the skills and strategies involved in many wheelchair sports are also available (Hedrick, Byrnes, & Shaver, 1989; Moore & Snow, 1994). Again, the systems approach should be incorporated, with athletes practicing their skills in their competitive system that includes sport-specific wheelchair, strapping, bracing, and applicable prosthesis.

As pioneer Sir Ludwig Guttmann stated, "It is no exaggeration to say that the paraplegic and his chair have become one, in the same way as a first-class horseman and his mount" (Weisman & Godfrey, 1976, p. 53). This is the essence of the systems approach to enhancing wheelchair sport performance.

INTRODUCING JUNIORS TO WHEELCHAIR SPORT

Due to the relatively lower visibility of disability sport, it is essential for adapted physical activity professionals to be aware of the opportunities that are available to juniors and to inform prospective participants of these opportunities. The Internet has become a useful tool for the acquisition of this information, and the reader is encouraged to visit the Wheelchair and Ambulatory Sports, USA (WASUSA) Web site (www.wsusa.org) and the International Paralympic Committee (IPC) Web site (www.paralympic.org) for more information. The specific court sports of basketball, rugby, and tennis also each have Web sites. Because competition equipment, especially wheelchairs, can be expensive, athletes should identify local wheelchair sport clubs because they can assist, at least in part, in the provision of this equipment. The Web sites just identified are a rich source of information in this regard.

Introducing Juniors to Track and Road Racing

Track and road racing within the United States is governed by WASUSA. Specific competition details, including eligibility information, are available within the *2010-2011 Competition Rules for Track and Field and Road Racing* (WASUSA, 2010) available for download from the WASUSA Web site.

Each IPC-affiliated country also has similar rules established for national competition.

In deciding whether wheelchair racing is a viable activity, the athlete should first address the issue of minimal disability. For the purposes of competition within the United States, WASUSA states in its manual that athletes "must have a medically diagnosed disease or impairment that causes a permanent mobility related disability. This disability must result in a substantial, or total, loss of function in one or more lower extremities" (WASUSA, 2010, p. 12). After eligibility is established, the athlete's classification should be identified. Classification is a means for athletes with disabilities to compete with each other on an equitable basis, regardless of disability. This is achieved in racing by the identification of four functional divisions, T51 through T54, within a more complex structure that covers all Paralympic sports. The four classes are outlined in table 29.1 and are composed of two quadriplegic classes (some loss of arm as well as leg function) and two paraplegic classes (no loss of arm function). In addition, junior competition is further divided by age with the categories identified in table 29.2. Consequently, qualification standards for national competition are established for both class and age. Examples of U.S. national qualification standards are presented in table 29.3. These standards can be useful both in the evaluation of

training programs and also as measurable objectives within the student's individualized education plan (IEP) where applicable.

In addition to the general training considerations identified in the first section of this chapter, race training should be tailored by some principles of progression for teaching wheelchair racing.

Introducing Juniors to Court Sports

The basic approach to getting juniors involved in court sports is outlined in the application example. In basketball and rugby, sport-specific functional classification is an important aspect of the athletes' training because classification influences the performance and function of the athlete on the court and thus should influence training strategies. The role of athletes in basketball was examined by Vanlandewijck and colleagues (2003), who found that more dynamic responsibilities such as rebounding were performed more by higher-functioning players. Similar findings were identified in rugby by Molik and colleagues (2008). There is no classification system in wheelchair tennis. Wheelchair tennis players are eligible to compete with and against non-wheelchair-using players in United States Tennis Association (USTA) competitions.

Table 29.1 Functional Classification for Wheelchair Track Racing

Class	Spinal cord injury (old)	Functionality
T51	Quadriplegic: C6 (1A)	May use elbow flexors to start (back of wrist behind push rim). Hands stay in contact or close to the push rim, with the power coming from elbow flexion.
T52	Quadriplegic: C7/C8 (1B)	Usually use elbow flexors to start, but may use elbow extensors. Power from pushing comes from elbow extension, wrist dorsiflexion, and upper chest muscles. Additional power may be gained by using the elbow flexors when the hands are in contact with the back of the wheel. The head may be forced backward, producing slight upper-trunk movements.
T53	Paraplegic: T1-T7 (1C, 2, upper 3)	Athletes have normal or nearly normal upper-limb function. Have no active trunk movements. When pushing, the trunk is usually lying on the legs. The trunk may rise with the pushing action.
T54	Paraplegic: T8-S2 (Lower 3, 4, 5, and 6)	Athletes have backward movement of the trunk. Usually have rotation movements of the trunk. Use abdominal muscles for power, particularly when starting but also when pushing.

Reprinted, by permission, from Wheelchair and Ambulatory Sports, USA, 2010, *2010-2011 Competition rules for track and field and road racing* (St. Peters, MO: Wheelchair Sports USA).

Table 29.2 WASUSA Age Divisions

Division	Age (yr)
Futures	Under 6
Division A	Under 11
Division B	Under 14
Division C	Under 17
Division D	Under 20
Division E	Under 23

Reprinted, by permission, from Wheelchair and Ambulatory Sports, USA, 2010, *2010-2011 Competition rules for track and field and road racing* (St. Peters, MO: Wheelchair Sports USA).

This makes tennis a useful inclusionary tool, and though a sport-specific chair is necessary for elite competition, beginning players can start in their everyday chair.

Students contemplating participation in enhanced-performance wheelchair sport should consider beginning their involvement by developing, assessing, and enhancing their wheelchair mobility skills and skills in various activities and sports. Davis (2011) has developed a useful guide for teaching and enhancing the involvement of young people in wheelchair sport.

Table 29.3 WASUSA National Junior Competition Qualifying Standards

CLASS/AGE	100 m M	100 m F	200 m M	200 m F	400 m M	400 m F	1,500 m M	1,500 m F
T51A/U11	1:40	2:00	2:40	3:00				
T51B/U14	1:20	1:40	2:15	2:50	4:00	4:40		
T51C/U17	1:10	1:30	2:00	2:40	3:50	5:00		
T51D/U20	1:00	1:20	1:50	2:30	3:40	4:45	11:00	13:30
T51E/U23	1:00	1:20	1:50	2:30	3:40	4:45	11:00	13:30
T52A/U11	1:20	1:24	2:00	2:15	3:30	4:00		
T52B/U14	:55	1:10	1:40	2:20	3:00	3:50	11:00	13:00
T52C/U17	:50	1:05	1:20	2:00	2:40	3:40	9:00	12:00
T52D/U20	:40	1:00	1:10	1:50	2:30	3:30	8:00	10:00
T52E/U23	:40	1:00	1:10	1:50	2:30	3:30	8:00	10:00
T53A/U11	:52	:54	1:35	1:38	3:00	3:10		
T53B/U14	:30	:40	:50	1:10	2:00	2:30	7:00	8:00
T53C/U17	:27	:33	:45	1:00	1:40	2:00	6:00	7:00
T53D/U20	:24	:30	:42	:55	1:30	1:55	5:45	6:30
T53E/U23	:24	:30	:42	:55	1:30	1:55	5:45	6:30
T54A/U11	:50	:52	1:30	1:34	2:45	2:50		
T54B/U14	:27	:32	:50	1:00	1:40	2:10	6:00	7:00
T54C/U17	:23	:28	:45	:55	1:30	1:50	5:30	6:00
T54D/U20	:21	:25	:40	:50	1:20	1:40	5:10	5:45
T54E/U23	:21	:25	:40	:50	1:20	1:40	5:10	5:45

Reprinted, by permission, from Wheelchair and Ambulatory Sports, USA, 2010, *2010-2011 Competition rules for track and field and road racing* (St. Peters, MO: Wheelchair Sports USA).

FUTURE DIRECTIONS

Technological advances and improved training techniques have changed the look of wheelchair sport dramatically. The opportunities are now seemingly endless. Professionalism is now part of many wheelchair sports, including racing, tennis, and even basketball. Elite athletes now travel around the world plying their trade, and there is reason to believe this trend will become even more prevalent.

New sports are constantly being adapted to meet the needs of people with disabilities, and with each new sport comes the need for specialized equipment designed to meet its unique demands. The popularity of quad rugby and wheelchair basketball at the 2008 Summer Paralympic Games in Beijing and sledge hockey at the 2010 Winter Paralympic Games in Vancouver were both indicators that wheelchair sport is a dynamic, evolving means of physical activity for people with mobility disabilities.

The demands of each sport and the needs of athletes involved in the sport must be systematically assessed, and suitable equipment must then be designed and built. The combining of the athlete and the wheelchair into a sport-specific, functional performance system is the trend in elite wheelchair athletics, with even greater equipment and technique specialization anticipated as the wave of the future.

SUMMARY

This chapter has dealt with information for enhancing performance in wheelchair sport. It discussed the appropriate selection of a sport by the athlete, the athlete's individual training regime, and sports medicine issues faced by athletes with disabilities. Basic types of sport wheelchairs were identified (racing and court), as were specific performance considerations that influence selection of the appropriate chair. The chapter also examined the combination of the athlete and the chair to create a performance system. Racing performance considerations (stroke analysis, starting techniques, overcoming rolling resistance, and drafting) were separated from court performance considerations (adjusting the chair and individual skill development). Finally, the chapter provided information on initiating wheelchair sport activities for prospective junior competitors.

REFERENCES

Boninger, M.L., Baldwin, M., Cooper, R.A., Koontz, A., & Chan, L. (2000). Manual wheelchair pushrim biomechanics and axle position. *Archives of Physical Medicine and Rehabilitation, 81* (5), 608-613.

Borg, G. (1998). *Borg's perceived exertion and pain scales.* Champaign, IL: Human Kinetics.

Brasile, F. (1986). Do you measure up? *Sports 'N Spokes, 12* (4), 42-47.

Brasile, F., & Hedrick, B.N. (1996). The relationship of skills of elite wheelchair basketball competitors to the International Functional Classification System. *Therapeutic Recreation Journal, 30* (2), 114-127.

Burnham, R., Wheeler, G., Bhambhani, Y., Cumming, D., Maclean, I., Sloley, B.D., Belanger, M., Eriksson, P., & Steadward, R. (1993). Performance enhancement in elite quadriplegic wheelchair racers through self-induced autonomic dysreflexia. Vista '93 Conference, May 14-20, Jasper, AB.

Chow, J.W., Millikan, T.A., Carlton, L.G., Morse, M.I., & Chae, W.S. (2001). Biomechanical comparison of two racing wheelchair propulsion techniques. *Medicine and Science in Sports and Exercise, 33* (3), 476-484.

Coutts, K.D., & Schutz, R.W. (1988). Analysis of wheelchair track performance. *Medicine and Science in Sport and Exercise, 20,* 188-194.

Curtis, K.A. (1981a). Wheelchair sportsmedicine, part 2—Training. *Sports 'N Spokes, 7* (2), 16-19.

Curtis, K.A. (1981b). Wheelchair sportsmedicine, part 3—Stretching routines. *Sports 'N Spokes, 7* (3), 16-18.

Davis, R.W. (2011). *Teaching disability sport: A guide for physical educators* (2nd ed.). Champaign, IL: Human Kinetics.

Ferrara, M.S., & Peterson, C.L. (2000). Injuries to athletes with disabilities: Identifying injury patterns. *Sports Medicine, 30* (2), 137-143.

Gallahue, D.L., & Ozmun, J.C. (2002). *Understanding motor development* (5th ed.). Dubuque, IA: McGraw/Hill.

Goosey, V.L., & Campbell, I.G. (1998). Pushing economy and propulsion techniques of wheelchair racers at three speeds. *Adapted Physical Activity Quarterly, 15* (1), 36-50.

Goosey, V.L., Campbell, I.G., & Fowler, N.E. (2000). Effect of push frequency on the economy of wheelchair racers. *Medicine and Science in Sports and Exercise, 32* (1), 174-181.

Hedrick, B., Byrnes, D., & Shaver, L. (1989). *Wheelchair basketball* [text and VHS]. Washington, DC: Paralyzed Veterans of America.

Higgs, C. (1983). An analysis of racing wheelchairs used at the 1980 Olympic Games for the Disabled. *Research Quarterly for Exercise and Sport, 54* (3), 229-233.

Higgs, C. (1985). Propulsion of racing wheelchairs. In M. Ellis & D. Tripps (Eds.), *Proceedings of the 1984 Olympic Scientific Congress, Eugene, Oregon*. Champaign, IL: Human Kinetics.

Higgs, C. (1992a). Racing wheelchairs: A comparison of three- and four-wheeled designs. *Palaestra, 80,* 28-36.

Higgs, C. (1992b). Wheeling the wind: The effect of wind velocity and direction on the aerodynamic drag of wheelchairs. *Adapted Physical Activity Quarterly, 9* (l), 74-87.

LaMere, T.J., & Labanowich, S. (1984a). The history of sport wheelchairs, part I: The development of the basketball wheelchair. *Sports 'N Spokes, 9* (6), 6-8, 10-11.

LaMere, T.J., & Labanowich, S. (1984b). The history of sport wheelchairs, part II: The racing wheelchair 1956-1975. *Sports 'N Spokes, 10* (1), 12-15.

LaMere, T.J., & Labanowich, S. (1984c). The history of sport wheelchairs, part III: The racing wheelchair 1976-1983. *Sports 'N Spokes, 10* (2), 12-16.

Meijs, P.J.M., Van Oers, C.A.J.M., Van der Woude, L.H.V., & Veeger, H.E.J. (1989). The effect of seat height on the physiological response and propulsion technique in wheelchair ambulation. *Journal of Rehabilitation Science, 2,* 104-107.

Molik, B., Lubelska, E., Kosmol, A., Bogdan, M., Yilla, A.B., & Hyla, E. (2008). An examination of the International Wheelchair Rugby Federation classification system utilizing parameters of offensive game efficiency. *Adapted Physical Activity Quarterly, 25* (4), 335-351.

Moore, B., & Snow, R. (1994). *Wheelchair tennis: Myth to reality*. Dubuque, IA: Kendall Hunt.

O'Connor, T.J., Robertson, R.N., & Cooper, R.A. (1998). Three-dimensional kinematic analysis and physiological assessment of racing wheelchair propulsion. *Adapted Physical Activity Quarterly, 15* (1), 1-14.

O'Reagan, J.R., Thacker, J.G., KauzIarich, J.J., Mochel, E., Carmine, D., & Bryant, M. (1981). Wheelchair dynamics. In *Wheelchair Mobility 1976-1981* (pp. 33-41). Charlottesville, VA: Rehabilitation Engineering Center, University of Virginia.

Schmid, A., Schmidt-Trucksaess, A., Huonker, M., Koenig., D., Eisenbarth, I., Sauerwein, H., et al. (2001). Catecholamines response of high performance wheelchair athletes at rest and during exercise with autonomic dysreflexia. *International Journal of Sports Medicine, 22,* 2-7.

Shapiro, D.A. (2005). *Murderball* [VHS and DVD]. Los Angeles, CA: Thinkfilm.

Shephard, R.J. (1990). *Fitness in special populations*. Champaign, IL: Human Kinetics.

Traut, L. (1989). Gestaltung ergonoisch relevanter Konstruktionsparameter am Antriebssystem des Greifreifenrollstuhls-Teil 1. *Orthopedaedie Technik, 7,* 394-398.

Van der Woude, L.H.V., Bouten, C., Veeger, H.E.J., & Gwinn, T. (2002). Aerobic work capacity in elite wheelchair athletes: A cross-sectional analysis. *American Journal of Physical Medicine and Rehabilitation, 81* (4), 261-271.

Van der Woude, L.H.V., Veeger, H.E.J., & Rozendal, R.H. (1990). Seat height in hand rim wheelchair propulsion: A follow up study. *Journal of Rehabilitation Science, 3,* 79-83.

Vanlandewijck, Y.C., Evaggelinou, C., Daly, D.D., Van Houtte, S., Verellen, J., Aspeslagh, V., et al. (2003). Proportionality in wheelchair basketball classification. *Adapted Physical Activity Quarterly, 20,* 369-380.

Vanlandewijck, Y., Theisen, D., & Daly, D. (2001). Wheelchair propulsion biomechanics: Implications for wheelchair sports. *Sports Medicine, 31* (5), 339-367.

Vernon, T., Tunstall, H., Mullineaux, D.R., Bishop, D.C., Horton, J., & Brooksbank, S.L. (2003). A biomechanical analysis of the tilt technique in wheelchair basketball (Abstract). *Journal of Sports Sciences, 21* (4), 253.

Weisman, M., & Godfrey, J. (1976). *So get on with it: A celebration of wheelchair sports*. Toronto: Doubleday.

Wells, C.L., & Hooker, S.P. (1990). The spinal injured athlete. *Adapted Physical Activity Quarterly, 7,* 265-285.

Wheelchair and Ambulatory Sports, USA (WASUSA). (2010). *2010-2011 Competition rules for track and field and road racing*. Retrieved July 15, 2010, from www.wsusa.org.

Yilla, A.B. (1997). Express yourself. *Sports 'N Spokes, 23,* 59-63.

Yilla, A.B., La Bar, R.H., & Dangelmaier, B.S. (1998). Setting up a wheelchair for basketball. *Sports 'N Spokes, 24* (2), 63-65.

Yilla, A.B., & Sherrill, C. (1998). Validating the Beck Battery of quad rugby skill tests. *Adapted Physical Activity Quarterly, 15* (2), 155-167.

WRITTEN RESOURCES

Davis, R.W. (2011). *Teaching disability sport: A guide for physical educators* (2nd ed.). Champaign, IL: Human Kinetics.

This book identifies methodologies for integrating a variety of disability sports, including wheelchair basketball and tennis, into the physical education curriculum. It includes descriptions of the skills to be taught and modification strategies.

TRAINING RESOURCES

Marty Morse is an expert trainer who has been associated with the notable University of Illinois at Champaign-Urbana Wheelchair Sports program. Morse has many publications and is considered a leader in the field of training elite wheelchair athletes. He publishes regularly in both *Sports 'N Spokes* and scientific journals. His work should be accessed for the most recent trends in enhancing wheelchair sport performance.

Cooper, R.A. (1998). *Wheelchair selection and configuration*. New York: Demos.

This book provides an in-depth, though somewhat technical, insight into all aspects of wheelchair design. Though it is brief in the area of sport-specific wheelchair design, it belongs on the shelf of any professional with an interest in physical activity for wheelchair users.

LaMere, T.J., & Labanowich, S. (1984a). The history of sport wheelchairs, part I: The development of the basketball wheelchair. *Sports 'N Spokes*, 9 (6), 6-8, 10-11.

LaMere, T.J., & Labanowich, S. (1984b). The history of sport wheelchairs, part II: The racing wheelchair 1956-1975. *Sports 'N Spokes*, 10 (1), 12-15.

LaMere, T.J., & Labanowich, S. (1984c). The history of sport wheelchairs, part III: The racing wheelchair 1976-1983. *Sports 'N Spokes*, 10 (2), 12-16.

These articles contain a brief history of the development of wheelchairs until 1984. Most of the landmark developments are covered, and the reader is left with a vivid impression of the relentless drive of the athletes to improve their equipment.

AUDIOVISUAL RESOURCES

Hedrick, B., Byrnes, D., & Shaver, L. (1989). *Wheelchair basketball* [text and VHS]. Washington, DC: Paralyzed Veterans of America.

The authors have all achieved considerable success as coaches in international wheelchair basketball competition. Their level of expertise is reflected in this comprehensive instructional text on wheelchair basketball and the accompanying series of videotapes.

Shapiro, D.A. (2005). *Murderball* [VHS and DVD]. Los Angeles, CA: Thinkfilm.

This Oscar-nominated documentary provides a powerful insight into the lives of wheelchair rugby players and the competitive environment that drives them.

You feel the need for speed [VHS]. (1992). K.C. Racing, 291 Comfort Dr., Henderson, NV 89014.

This instructional video, available in both North American and European VHS formats, covers all the basics of wheelchair racing. Adjustment and operation of a new chair, propulsion techniques, maintenance, and many tricks of the trade are covered. The narrator and producer of the video is Kenny Carnes, one of the top racers in the United States.

ELECTRONIC RESOURCES

Basketball

Canadian Wheelchair Basketball Association (CWBA): www.wheelchairbasketball.ca.

CommunityZero: www.communityzero.com/iwbfamzone.

This is the site of the international, North American wheelchair basketball community. At time of press, subscription is free and there is a wealth of information, including links to other sites. Subscription includes receiving an electronic newsletter that provides information on wheelchair basketball from around the world.

National Wheelchair Basketball Association (NWBA): www.nwba.org.

Quad Rugby

United States Quad Rugby Association (USQRA): www.quadrugby.com.

This is the home of the USQRA. The site includes the rules of rugby and updates on recent tournaments.

Racing

International Paralympic Committee (IPC): www.paralympic.org.

This is the home of the official governing body of the Paralympic Games. This site includes extensive resources regarding rules, eligibility, and classification for international competition.

Wheelchair and Ambulatory Sports, USA (WASUSA): www.wasusa.org.

This is the home of the official governing body for wheelchair sport in general, and racing in particular, in the United States. The site includes extensive resources regarding rules, eligibility, and classification for competition in the United States.

Tennis

International Tennis Federation (ITF): www.itfwheelchairtennis.com.

This is the wheelchair tennis site of the ITF. It provides information, including schedules and results, from the world of wheelchair tennis. There are a number of positive images of well-known tennis celebrities interacting with wheelchair tennis athletes and beginners.

Definitions Associated With the Individuals With Disabilities Education Act (IDEA)

Several definitions are associated with infants, toddlers, and children with disabilities. To a great extent, the definitions used in this book are based on those from IDEA. Those definitions are summarized here.

INFANT OR TODDLER WITH A DISABILITY

The term "infant or toddler with a disability" means an individual under 3 years of age who needs early intervention services because the individual

- is experiencing developmental delays, as measured by appropriate diagnostic instruments and procedures in one or more of the areas of cognitive development, physical development, communication development, social or emotional development, and adaptive development; or

- has a diagnosed physical or mental condition that has a high probability of resulting in developmental delay; and

- may also include, at a State's discretion, at-risk infants and toddlers. (Office of Special Education and Rehabilitative Services [OSE/RS] 34 CFR 303.16 [2006])

The term "at-risk infant or toddler" means an individual under two years of age who would be at risk of experiencing a substantial developmental delay if early intervention services were not provided to the individual.

CHILDREN WITH DISABILITIES

The term "children with disabilities" means those children having mental retardation; a hearing impairment including deafness, speech, or language impairment; visual impairments including blindness; serious emotional disturbance; orthopedic impairments; autism; traumatic brain injury; another health impairment; a specific learning disability; deaf-blindness; or multiple disabilities—and who, because of these disabilities and differences, need special education and related services. The term "children with disabilities," for children aged three through nine, may, at a State's discretion, include children

1. who are experiencing developmental delays, as defined by the state and as measured by appropriate diagnostic instruments and procedures, in one or more of the following areas: physical development, cognitive development, communication development, social or emotional development, or adaptive development; and

2. who, for that reason, need special education and related services. (Office of Special Education and Rehabilitative Services [OSE/RS] 34 CFR 300 [2006])

The terms used in this definition are defined as follows:

1. "Autism" means a developmental disability significantly affecting verbal and nonverbal communication and social interaction, generally evident before age three, that adversely affects a child's educational performance. Other characteristics often associated with autism are engagement in repetitive activities and stereotyped movements, resistance to environmental change or change in daily routines, and unusual responses to sensory experiences. The term does not apply if a child's educational performance is adversely affected primarily because the child has a serious emotional disturbance.

2. "Deaf-blindness" means concomitant hearing and visual impairments, the combination of which causes such severe communication and other developmental and educational needs that they cannot be accommodated in special education programs solely for children with deafness or children with blindness.

3. "Deafness" means a hearing impairment that is so severe that the child is impaired in processing linguistic information through hearing, with or without amplification, that adversely affects his or her educational performance.

4. "Hearing impairment" means an impairment in hearing, whether permanent or fluctuating, that adversely affects a child's educational performance but that is not included under the definition of deafness.

5. "Mental retardation" means significantly subaverage general intellectual functioning existing concurrently with deficits in adaptive behavior and manifested during the developmental period that adversely affects a child's educational performance.

6. "Multiple disabilities" means concomitant impairments (such as mental retardation and blindness, or mental retardation and orthopedic impairment), the combination of which causes such severe educational problems that they cannot be accommodated in special education programs solely for one of the impairments. The term does not include deaf-blindness.

7. "Orthopedic impairment" means a severe orthopedic impairment that adversely affects a child's educational performance. The term includes impairments caused by congenital anomaly (e.g., clubfoot or absence of some member), impairments caused by disease (e.g., poliomyelitis or bone tuberculosis), and impairments from other causes (e.g., cerebral palsy, amputations, or fractures or burns that cause contractures).

8. "Other health impairment" means having limited strength, vitality, or alertness as a result of chronic or acute health problems, such as a heart condition, attention deficit disorder, attention deficit hyperactivity disorder, rheumatic fever, nephritis, asthma, sickle cell anemia, hemophilia, epilepsy, lead poisoning, leukemia, or diabetes that adversely affects a child's educational performance.

9. "Serious emotional disturbance" is defined as follows:

   a. a condition exhibiting one or more of the following characteristics over a long period of time and to a marked degree that adversely affects a child's educational performance.

      1. An inability to learn that cannot be explained by intellectual, sensory, or health factors.

      2. An inability to build or maintain satisfactory interpersonal relationships with peers and teachers.

      3. Inappropriate types of behavior or feelings under normal circumstances.

      4. A general pervasive mood of unhappiness or depression.

      5. A tendency to develop physical symptoms or fears associated with personal or school problems.

   b. The term includes schizophrenia. The term does not necessarily apply to children who are socially maladjusted, unless it is determined that they have a serious emotional disturbance.

10. "Specific learning disability" means a disorder in one or more of the basic psychological processes involved in understanding or in using

language, spoken or written, that may manifest itself in an imperfect ability to listen, think, speak, read, write, spell, or to do mathematical calculations. The term includes such conditions as perceptual disabilities, brain injury, minimal brain dysfunction, dyslexia, and developmental aphasia. The term does not apply to children who have learning problems that are primarily the result of visual, hearing, or motor disabilities, intellectual disability, emotional disturbance, or environmental, cultural, or economic disadvantage.

11. "Speech or language impairment" means a communication disorder such as stuttering, impaired articulation, or a voice impairment that adversely affects a child's educational performance.

12. "Traumatic brain injury" means an acquired injury to the brain caused by an external physical force, resulting in total or partial functional disability or psychosocial impairment (or both) that adversely affects a child's educational performance. The term applies to open or closed head injuries resulting in impairments in one or more areas, including cognition; language; memory; attention; reasoning; abstract thinking; judgment; problem solving; sensory, perceptual, and motor abilities; psychosocial behavior; physical functions; information processing; and speech. The term does not apply to brain injuries that are congenital or degenerative or to brain injuries induced by birth trauma.

13. "Visual impairment including blindness" means an impairment in vision that, even with correction, adversely affects a child's educational performance. The term includes both partial sight and blindness.

appendix B

Adapted Physical Education and Sport Contact Information

MULTISPORT ORGANIZATIONS

American Association of Adapted Sports Programs (AAASP)

Project ASPIRE
P.O. Box 451047
Atlanta, GA 31145
404-294-0070 (phone)
404-294-5758 (fax)
E-mail: sports@adaptedsport.edu
Web site: www.aaasp.org

BlazeSports National Disability Sports Alliance (BNDSA)

BNDSA
25 West Independence Way
Kingston, RI 02881
401-792-7130 (phone)
401-792-7132 (fax)
E-mail: info@blazesports.org
Web site: www.blazesports.org

Canadian Blind Sports Association (CBSA)

7 Mill St., Lower Level
Almonte, ON K0A 1A0
Canada

613-748-5609 (phone)
613-256-8759 (fax)
E-mail: cbsa@istar.ca
Web site: www.canadianblindsports.ca

Canadian Cerebral Palsy Sports Association (CCPSA)

305-1376 Bank St.
Ottawa, ON K1H 7Y3
Canada
613-748-1430 (phone)
613-748-1355 (fax)
E-mail: ccpsa@cyberus.ca
Web site: www.ccpsa.ca

Canadian Deaf Sports Association (CDSA)

10217 Boul. Pie IX, Ste. 202
P.O. Box 202A
Montreal-Nord, QC
Canada, H1H 3Z5
514-321-4520 (phone)
514-321-8349 (fax)
E-mail: office@assc-cdsa.com
Web site: www.assc-cdsa.com

Canadian Wheelchair Sports Association (CWSA)

2255 St. Laurent Blvd., Ste. 108
Ottawa, ON K1G 4K3

Canada
613-523-0004 (phone)
613-523-0149 (fax)
E-mail: info@cwsa.ca
Web site: www.cwsa.ca

Disabled Sports USA (DS/USA)

451 Hungerford Dr., Ste. 100
Rockville, MD 20805
301-217-0960 (phone)
301-217-0968 (fax)
E-mail: information@dsusa.org
Web site: www.dsusa.org

Dwarf Athletic Association of America (DAAA)

418 Willow Way
Lewisville, TX 75067
972-317-8630 (phone)
972-966-0184 (fax)
E-mail: daaa@flash.net
Web site: www.daaa.org

National Sports Center for the Disabled (NSCD)

P.O. Box 1290
Winter Park, CO 80482
970-726-1540 (phone)
970-726-4112 (fax)
E-mail: info@nscd.org
Web site: www.nscd.org

Special Olympics

1133 19th St., NW
Washington, DC 20036
202-628-3630 (phone)
202-824-0200 (fax)
E-mail: info@specialolympics.org
Web site: www.specialolympics.org

United States Association for Blind Athletes (USABA)

33 North Institute St.
Colorado Springs, CO 80903
719-630-0422 (phone)
719-630-0616 (fax)
E-mail: mlucas@usaba.org
Web site: www.usaba.org

United States Olympic Committee (USOC)

Disabled Sports Services Dept.
1 Olympic Plaza
Colorado Springs, CO 80909-5760
719-632-5551 (phone)
Web site: www.usoc.org

USA Deaf Sports Federation (USADSF)

102 North Krohn Pl.
Sioux Falls, SD 57103-1800
605-367-5761 (TTY)
866-273-3323 (toll-free TTY)
605-367-5760 (phone)
800-642-6410 (toll-free phone)
605-367-5958 (fax)
E-mail: homeoffice@usadsf.org
Web site: www.usdeafsports.org

U.S. Paralympics

1 Olympic Plaza
Colorado Springs, CO 80909
719-866-2030 (phone)
719-866-2029 (fax)
E-mail: paralympicinfo@usoc.org
Web site: www.usparalympics.org

Wheelchair and Ambulatory Sports, USA (WASUSA)

1236 Jungermann Rd., Ste. A
St. Peters, MO 63376
636-614-6784 (phone)
636-329-1090 (fax)
E-mail: wsusa@aol.com
Web site: www.wsusa.org

Wheelchair Basketball Canada

2211 Riverside Dr., Ste. B2
Ottawa, ON K1H 7X5
Canada
613-260-1296 (phone)
613-260-1456 (fax)
E-mail: info@wheelchairbasketball.ca
Web site: www.wheelchairbasketball.ca

UNISPORT ORGANIZATIONS

Aquatics

American Canoe Association (ACA)

7432 Alban Station Blvd., Ste. B-232
Springfield, VA 22150
703-451-0141 (phone)
703-451-2245 (fax)
E-mail: aca@americancanoe.org
Web site: www.acanet.org

Aqua Sports Association for the Physically Challenged

9052-A Birch St.
Spring Valley, CA 91977

619-589-0537 (phone)
619-589-7013 (fax)

USA Swimming Adapted Swimming

1 Olympic Plaza
Colorado Springs, CO 80909
719-866-4578 (phone)
719-866-4669 (fax)
Web site: www.usa-swimming.org

USRowing

201 S. Capitol Ave., Ste. 400
Indianapolis, IN 46225
317-237-5656 (phone)
317-237-5646 (fax)
Web site: http://usrowing.org

U.S. Wheelchair Swimming, Inc.

c/o WASUSA
1236 Jungermann Rd., Ste. A
St. Peters, MO 63376
636-614-6784 (phone)
636-329-1090 (fax)

Archery

Wheelchair Archery, USA

c/o WASUSA
1236 Jungermann Rd., Ste. A
St. Peters, MO 63376
636-614-6784 (phone)
636-329-1090 (fax)

Athletics

Wheelchair Athletics of the USA

2351 Parkwood Rd.
Snellville, GA 30278
770-972-0763 (phone)
770-985-4885 (fax)

Baseball

International Baseball and Softball, Little League Challenger Division

Little League Headquarters
539 US Route 15 Hwy.
P.O. Box 3485
Williamsport, PA 17701-0485
Web site: www.littleleague.org/learn/about/divisions/challenger.htm

National Beep Baseball Association (NBBA)

5568 Boulder Crest St.
Columbus, OH 43235
614-442-1444 (phone)
E-mail: info@nbba.org
Web site: www.nbba.org

Basketball

National Wheelchair Basketball Association (NWBA)

Charlotte Institute of Rehabilitation
c/o Adaptive Sports/Adventures
1100 Blythe Blvd.
Charlotte, NC 28203
704-355-1064 (phone)
704-466-4999 (fax)
E-mail: nwba@carolinas.com
Web site: www.nwba.org

Bowling

American Blind Bowling Association (ABBA)

411 Sheriff St.
Mercer, PA 16137
412-662-5748 (phone)

American Wheelchair Bowling Association (AWBA)

P.O. Box 69
Clover, VA 24534-0069
434-454-2269 (phone)
434-454-6276 (fax)
E-mail: bowlawba@aol.com
Web site: www.awba.org

Cycling

North American Riding for the Handicapped Association (NARHA)

P.O. Box 33150
Denver, CO 80233
303-452-1212 (phone)
800-369-RIDE (toll-free)
303-252-4610 (fax)
E-mail: narha@narha.org
Web site: www.narha.org

United States Handcycling Federation (USHF)

P.O. Box 3538
Evergreen, CO 80437
303-459-4159 (phone)
E-mail: info@ushf.org
Web site: www.ushf.org

Flying

Freedom's Wings

P.O. Box 7076
East Brunswick, NJ 08816
800-382-1197 (phone)
E-mail: president@freedomswings.org
Web site: www.freedomswings.org

International Wheelchair Aviators

P.O. Box 4140
Big Bear Lake, CA 92315
951-529-2641 (phone)
E-mail: IWAviators@aol.com
Web site: www.wheelchairaviators.org

Football (American)

Universal Wheelchair Football Association (UWFA)

UC Raymond Walters College
Disability Services Office
9555 Plainfield Rd.
Cincinnati, OH 45236-1096
513-792-8625 (phone)
513-745-8300 (TTY)
513-792-8624 (fax)
E-mail: john.kraimer@uc.edu
Web site: www.rwc.uc.edu//kraimer/PAGE1.htm

Golf

Association of Disabled American Golfers (ADAG)

P.O. Box 280649
Lakewood, CO 80228-0649
303-922-5228 (phone)
303-969-0447 (fax)
E-mail: adag@usga.org

National Amputee Golf Association (NAGA)

11 Walnut Hill Rd.
Amherst, NH 03031-1713

800-633-6242 (toll free)
E-mail: info@nagagolf.org
Web site: www.nagagolf.org

U.S. Golf Association

Resource Center for Individuals with Disabilities
P.O. Box 708
Far Hills, NJ 07931
908-234-2300 (phone)
908-234-9687 (fax)
E-mail: aphipps@usgafoundation.org
Web site: www.usga.org

Hockey

U.S. Electric Wheelchair Hockey Association

U.S.EWHA Powerhockey
7216 39th Ave. N.
Minneapolis, MN 55427
763-535-4736 (phone)
E-mail: info@powerhockey.com
Web site: www.powerhockey.com

Quad Rugby

United States Quad Rugby Association (USQRA)

5593 Cedar Oak Blvd.
Sarasota, FL 34233
941-924-1804 (phone)
E-mail: edandcindy67@verizon.net
Web site: www.quadrugby.com

Racquetball

USA Racquetball

1685 West Uintah
Colorado Springs, CO 80904
719-635-5396 (phone)
719-635-0685 (fax)
E-mail: usragen@webaccess.net
Web site: www.usra.org

Road Racing

Achilles International

42 West 38th St., Ste. 400
New York, NY 10018
212-354-0300 (phone)
212-354-3978 (fax)

E-mail: achillesTC@aol.com
Web site: www.achillestrackclub.org

Sailing

Access to Sailing

Shoreline Village Dr., Ste. 423
Long Beach, CA 90802
562-501-9999 (phone)
E-mail: info@accesstosailing.org
Web site: www.accesstosailing.org

Scuba Diving

Handicapped Scuba Association International (HSA International)

1104 El Prado
San Clemente, CA 92672-4637
949-498-4540 (phone)
949-498-6128 (fax)
E-mail: hsa@hsascuba.com
Web site: www.hsascuba.com

Shooting

National Rifle Association Disabled Services

11250 Waples Mill Rd.
Fairfax, VA 22030
703-267-1450 (phone)
703-267-3941 (fax)
E-mail: competitions@nrahq.org
Web site: www.nrahq.org/compete/disabled.asp

National Wheelchair Shooting Federation (NWSF)

102 Park Ave.
Rockledge, PA 19111
215-379-2359 (phone)
215-663-9662 (fax)

Skating

Skating Association for the Blind and Handicapped (SABAH)

2607 Niagara St.
Buffalo, NY 14207
716-362-9600 (phone)
716-362-9601 (fax)
E-mail: sabah@aabahinc.org
Web site: www.sabahinc.org

Skiing

Adaptive Sports Center

P.O. Box 1639
Crested Butte, CO 81224
866-349-2296 (toll free)
970-349-2296 (phone)
Web site: www.adaptivesports.org

Ski for Light, Inc.

1455 West Lake St.
Minneapolis, MN 55408
612-827-3232 (phone)
E-mail: info@sfl.org
Web site: www.sfl.org

Soccer

American Amputee Soccer Association (AASA)

E-mail: rgh@ampsoccer.org
Web site: www.ampsoccer.org

International Paralympic Committee (IPC)

IPC Headquarters
Adenauerallee 212-214
53113 Bonn
Germany
+49 (228) 2097-200 (phone)
+49 (228) 2097-209 (fax)
E-mail: info@paralympic.org
Web site: www.paralympic.org

Softball

National Wheelchair Softball Association (NWSA)

13414 Paul St.
Omaha, NE 68154
402-305-5020 (phone)
Web site: www.wheelchairsoftball.org

Tennis

International Tennis Federation (ITF) Wheelchair Tennis

Bank Lane, Roehampton
London, SW15 5XZ
United Kingdom
011-44-208-878-6464 (phone)
011-44-208-392-4744 (fax)

E-mail: wheelchairtennis@itftennis.com
Web site: www.itfwheelchairtennis.com

National Foundation of Wheelchair Tennis (NFWT)

940 Calle Amanecer, Ste. B
San Clemente, CA 92673
714-361-3663 (phone)
714-361-6603 (fax)
E-mail: NFWT@aol.com

United States Tennis Association (USTA)

70 W. Red Oak Ln.
White Plains, NY 10604
914-696-7000 (phone)
914-696-7029 (fax)
Web site: www.usta.com
(Click on *wheelchair* for wheelchair tennis under leagues and tournaments.)

Water Skiing

USA Water Ski

c/o Water Skiers with Disabilities Association (WSDA)
1251 Holy Cow Rd.
Polk City, FL 33868
863-324-4341 (phone)
863-325-8259 (fax)
E-mail: usawaterski@usawaterski.org
Web site: www.usawaterski.org/pages/divisions/WSDA/main.htm

Weightlifting

NDSA Powerlifting

25 W. Independence Way
Kingston, RI 02881
401-792-7130 (phone)
Web site: http://disabledpowerlifting.org

United States Wheelchair Weightlifting Federation

39 Michael Pl.
Levittown, PA 19057
215-945-1964 (phone)
215-946-2574 (fax)
Web site: www.wasusa.org

INTERNATIONAL ORGANIZATIONS

Cerebral Palsy International Sports and Recreation Association (CPISRA)

P.O. Box 16
6666 ZG Heteren
The Netherlands
E-mail: cpisra_nl@hotmail.com
Web site: www.cpisra.org

International Blind Sport Association (IBSA)

Jose Ortega y Gasset, 18
Madrid, Spain 28006
34-1-589-4537 (phone)
E-mail: ibasecretary@Fibertal.com.ar
Web site: www.ibsa.es

International Committee of Sports for the Deaf (CISS)

528 Trail Ave.
Frederick, Maryland 21701
E-mail: info@ciss.org
Web site: www.ciss.org

International Paralympic Committee (IPC) Sledge Hockey

Adenaverallee 212-214
53113 Bonn
Germany
+49-228-2097-200 (phone)
+49-228-2097-209 (fax)
Web site: www.paralympic.org

International Sports Federation for Persons with Intellectual Disability (INAS-FID)

c/o Mencap
4 Swan Courtyard
Birmingham, B26 1BU
England
E-mail: info@paralympic.org

International Tennis Federation (ITF)

Wheelchair Tennis Department
Bank Lane
Roehampton
London SW15 5XZ
United Kingdom
+44 208 878 6464 (phone)
+44 208 392 4714 (fax)
E-mail: wheelchairtennis@itftennis.com

International Wheelchair and Amputee Sports Federation

Head Office
Olympic Village, Guttmann Rd.
Aylesbury, Bucks HP21 9PP
United Kingdom
E-mail: infor@iwasf.com
Web site: www.iwasf.com

International Wheelchair Basketball Federation (IWBF)

189 Watson St. #109
Winnipeg, Manitoba, R2P 2E1
Canada
204-632-6475 (phone)
Email: morchard@mts.net
Web site: www.iwbf.org

GENERAL AND OTHER ONLINE RESOURCES

National Center on Physical Activity and Disability (NCPAD)

NCPAD provides information and resources to enable people with disabilities to become as physically active as possible.
Web site: www.ncpad.org

PE Central

This site provides up-to-date information on developmentally appropriate programs for school-aged children. PE Central offers resources and lesson ideas for regular and adapted physical education classes.
Web site: www.pecentral.org

PE Links 4 U

Provides seven sections related to physical education that offer links, resources, and suggestions for programs.
Web site: www.pelinks4u.org

Project Inspire

Provides disability fact sheets for several disability types along with teaching suggestions for each. Also offers ideas for games and activities for classes.
Web site: www.twu.edu/inspire

appendix C

Brockport Physical Fitness Test

This appendix contains a brief description of the test items included in the Brockport Physical Fitness Test. Readers are reminded that a video describing the test can be found on the DVD provided in the back of the book. Although all 27 test items are presented here, a test battery for a particular individual generally includes 4 to 6 items. Test-selection guidelines are included in the test manual. For a full description of the test, please see Winnick and Short, *The Brockport Physical Fitness Test,* Human Kinetics, 1999.

AEROBIC FUNCTIONING

■ **PACER Test (20 meters and modified 16 meters):** At the sound of a tape-recorded beep, youngsters run from one line to another, either 20 meters or 16 meters away. They must arrive at the second line prior to the next beep (initially a nine-second interval). The time between beeps gradually decreases over the length of the test, so students find it increasingly difficult to keep up with the pace the longer the test goes on. The test score is the number of laps completed on pace (scoring stops when two consecutive beeps are missed; one trial is given).

■ **Target Aerobic Movement Test:** Youngsters engage in any type of activity to elevate their heart rates into a target heart rate zone (70 to 85 percent of predicted maximum heart rate). They then attempt to maintain their elevated heart rates for 15 continuous minutes (one trial).

■ **One-Mile Run–Walk:** Youngsters have one trial to complete a one-mile distance as quickly as they can.

BODY COMPOSITION

■ **Skinfold Measures:** Skinfold calipers are used to determine the youngster's skinfold thickness to estimate body fat percentage. Measures are taken at one of the following site options: triceps (only), triceps plus calf, or triceps plus subscapular. Three measures are taken at each site, and the middle score serves as the criterion.

■ **Body Mass Index:** Height and weight measures are used in a ratio to determine if individuals are overweight or underweight for their height.

MUSCULOSKELETAL FUNCTIONING

Muscular Strength and Endurance

■ **Trunk Lift:** From a prone position with hands under thighs, participants attempt to lift their chins up to 12 inches from the mat by arching the back. Allow two trials and count the better score.

■ **Dominant Grip Strength:** Youngsters squeeze a grip dynamometer as hard as possible with their preferred hand. Three trials are given; the middle score is the criterion.

■ **Bench Press:** From a supine position on a bench, youngsters are given one attempt to repeatedly lift a 35-pound barbell from the chest to a straight-arm position above the chest. Boys are limited to 50 repetitions and girls to 30 repetitions.

■ **Push-Up:** Initially, participants lie prone on a mat with hands placed under the shoulders (palms flat on the mat), elbows at 90 degrees, legs straight, and toes tucked. The participant then pushes up so that the arms (and back) are straight and the body weight is supported completely by the hands and toes. Youngsters attempt to complete as many push-ups as possible in one trial by performing one push-up every three seconds.

■ **Isometric Push-Up:** Participants are given one trial to hold the up position for the push-up for up to 40 seconds.

■ **Seated Push-Up:** Participants who are wheelchair users (paraplegic) attempt to lift their buttocks and posterior thighs off the seats of their wheelchairs by pushing up from the armrests or tires of the chairs with their hands and arms. An alternative is to lift the buttocks off a mat using seated push-up blocks. One trial is provided; the push-up is held up to 20 seconds.

■ **Dumbbell Press:** From a seated position, youngsters are given one attempt to repeatedly lift a 15-pound dumbbell from shoulder height to a straight-arm position directly above the shoulder. Boys and girls are limited to 50 repetitions.

■ **Reverse Curl:** Participants (with a spinal cord injury and quadriplegia) are given one attempt to lift a one-pound weight one time from lap level to shoulder level with a tenodesis grasp and elbow flexion.

■ **40-Meter Push–Walk:** Youngsters with certain mobility problems are given one attempt to cover at least 40 meters in 60 seconds while maintaining a low heart rate (i.e., 10-second heart rate is generally below 19 beats).

■ **Wheelchair Ramp Test:** Youngsters in wheelchairs are given one try to negotiate a standard ANSI ramp (12 inches of run for every inch of rise) up to a maximum of 30 feet.

■ **Curl-Up:** Youngsters lie in a supine position with knees bent and feet flat on the mat; arms are straight at the side with palms down and fingers at the edge of a 4.5-inch-wide cardboard strip. Youngsters lift their upper backs off the mat until the fingers slide to the far edge of the strip and then return to the starting position. Youngsters perform as many curl-ups as possible (up to 75) by doing one curl-up every three seconds (1 trial).

■ **Curl-Up (modified):** Identical to the curl-up except there is no cardboard strip. Instead, youngsters place their hands on the top of their thighs and slide them to the kneecaps during the curl-up.

■ **Flexed Arm Hang:** Participants grasp (palms forward) an overhead bar (feet off the floor) with elbows bent and chin above the bar and attempt to hold that position for as long as possible (one trial).

■ **Extended Arm Hang:** Participants grasp (palms forward) an overhead bar (feet off the floor) with elbows straight and attempt to hold that position for up to 40 seconds (one trial).

■ **Pull-Up:** Participants grasp (palms forward) an overhead bar (feet off the floor) with elbows straight. They then get one attempt to repeatedly lift the body with the arms until the chin is above the bar.

■ **Pull-Up (modified):** Using a special apparatus, students lie in a supine position and grasp a bar an arm's length above their chests. Keeping heels on the ground and their backs straight, participants pull their bodies toward the bar until the chin passes an elastic band placed seven to eight inches below the bar. Participants attempt to perform as many modified pull-ups as they can in one trial.

Flexibility

■ **Back-Saver Sit-and-Reach:** The youngster places one foot against a sit-and-reach box with a straight leg while the other leg is bent at the knee with the foot flat on the floor. With one hand placed on top of the other, the youngster attempts to reach as far across the top of the box as possible while maintaining the straight leg. One trial is given for each leg.

■ **Shoulder Stretch:** Participants attempt to touch the fingertips of their two hands behind their backs. The right hand reaches over the right shoulder between the scapulae while the left hand is brought up the back from the waist by bending the elbow. The test is repeated with the opposite arms; do one trial each.

■ **Apley Test (modified):** Youngsters attempt to touch with one hand one of three landmarks given here in descending order of difficulty: superior angle of the opposite scapula, top of the head, and the mouth. The test is repeated with the opposite hand; do one trial each.

■ **Thomas Test (modified):** Youngsters lie supine on a table and pull one knee to their chests while the tester evaluates the length of the opposite hip flexors by observing the extent of "lift" present in the opposite leg. The test is repeated with the other leg; do one trial each.

■ **Target Stretch Test:** Participants demonstrate in one attempt their maximum movement extent for a variety of single-joint actions (e.g., wrist extension, shoulder abduction, elbow extension, forearm supination), and testers estimate the extent of movement from pictorial criteria.

THE BROCKPORT PHYSICAL FITNESS TEST KIT

The *Brockport Physical Fitness Test Kit* provides a complete package for fitness testing for youths with physical and mental disabilities. The kit includes the following:

■ A comprehensive test manual that explains development of the test and testing procedures

■ A training guide to assist you in improving your students' fitness

■ *Fitness Challenge,* the companion software that makes test use much easier

■ A video that clearly demonstrates how to use the test with this population (DVD included at the back of the book)

■ Curl-up strips

■ Skin caliper

■ PACER audio CD or cassette

All materials are available from Human Kinetics Publishers at www.HumanKinetics.com.

Rating Scale for Adapted Physical Education

Name of school: _____

Address: _____

Level: _____ Number of pupils enrolled in adapted P.E.: _____

Principal: _____

Director of physical education: _____

Reviewed by: _____ Date: _____

INTRODUCTION

The purpose of the rating scale is to assist school personnel to evaluate and improve adapted physical education services.

When properly guided and developed, physical education becomes a purposeful and vital part of a student's school education. It aids in the realization of those objectives concerned with the development of favorable self-image, creative expression, motor skills, physical fitness, knowledge, and understanding of human movement. To promote self-actualization individuals need many opportunities to participate in well-conceived, well-taught learning experiences in physical education. To have the best program in place, the essentials of a quality program of physical education need to be identified.

This rating scale is designed to help schools evaluate their program as related to adapted physical education.

USE AND INTERPRETATION OF THE SCORES

The rating scale is comprised of a series of ratings on the major areas that should concern school personnel relative to adapted physical education. There are six sections to the rating scale: curriculum, required instruction, attendance, personnel, facilities, and administrative procedures.

The person(s) making the assessment should consider the criteria statement in terms of the degree of achievement that exists for the program. The rating score is on a scale form 0 to 4; 0 meaning inadequate achievement and 4 meaning fully achieved with excellent results. Each section can be rated by the total section score or a program overall rating can be obtained by totaling all sections of the rating scale.

A careful analysis should be made of each statement, section and overall rating to determine the areas in need of improvement. The interpretation of the score for each statement is:

From J. Winnick, ed. 2011, *Adapted physical education and sport, fifth edition* (Champaign, IL: Human Kinetics).

0 **Inadequate:** extremely limited

1 **Poor:** exists but needs a great deal of improvement

2 **Fair:** adequate but needs some improvement

3 **Good:** well done and only needs periodic review

4 **Excellent:** has achieved outstanding results.

Rating Scale for Adapted Physical Education

	Inadequate (0)	Poor (1)	Fair (2)	Good (3)	Excellent (4)
SECTION I: CURRICULUM					
1. The goals and objectives of the school district plan for physical education encompasses adapted physical education.					
2. Provision is explicitly made for adapted physical education in the school district physical education plan.					
3. There exists a definition of adapted physical education, which is in accord with state, federal and professional laws, regulations, or practices.					
4. Adapted physical education designed to meet unique needs may include pupils with disabilities as well as pupils without disabilities.					
5. There exists a variety of activities to meet unique pupil needs.					
6. Instruction in adapted physical education is based upon a curriculum guide which encompasses adapted physical education content.					
7. Instruction for all pupils is distributed among the following areas in accord with students' needs and abilities.					
a. Basic movement experiences					
b. Adventure and risk challenge activities					
c. Rhythms and dance					
d. Games and sports					
e. Gymnastics					
f. Outdoor education					
g. Motor movement skills					
h. Physical fitness					
i. Aquatics					
8. Appropriate literature and other resource materials regarding adapted physical education are made available to professional staff.					
9. Pupils with disabilities are provided equivalent opportunities in intramural, extramural, or extra-class activities.					

From J. Winnick, ed. 2011, *Adapted physical education and sport, fifth edition* (Champaign, IL: Human Kinetics).

	Inadequate (0)	Poor (1)	Fair (2)	Good (3)	Excellent (4)
SECTION I: CURRICULUM					
10. Guidelines pertaining to adapted physical education are evaluated at least every five years.					
11. There is a procedure for reporting pupil status and progress.					
12. The progress of pupils is continuously measured.					
13. Cumulative records pertaining to the physical education of each pupil are maintained.					
14. Indicators of performance related to program standards may be modified for individuals with unique needs.					
15. Transition programs are considered in determining the curricular thrust for individuals with disabilities.					
16. Accommodations are provided, as appropriate, to enhance participation in physical education.					
17. Activities within the curriculum may be adapted to enhance participation and success.					
18. The individual education program of a child with a disability may consider both the strengths and weaknesses of the individual.					
19. The school district plan includes criteria for eligibility for adapted physical education.					
SECTION II: REQUIRED INSTRUCTION					
1. All pupils not receiving regular physical education have an adapted physical education program.					
2. No pupil is excused from physical activity or excused from adapted physical education because of participation in extra-class programs unless by the school's committee on adapted physical education or similar committee or unless approved in a pupil's individualized education program (pupil with a disability).					
3. Instruction in adapted physical education is conducted with a time allotment, which is in accord with state regulations and in a frequency and duration which is comparable to chronological-aged peers in the school district.					
4. Class periods are scheduled in time lengths that are appropriate to pupil needs and achievement of instructional objectives.					
5. Physical education instruction is made available to every pupil with a disability.					

(continued)

From J. Winnick, ed. 2011, *Adapted physical education and sport, fifth edition* (Champaign, IL: Human Kinetics).

Rating Scale for Adapted Physical Edcuation *(continued)*

	Inadequate (0)	Poor (1)	Fair (2)	Good (3)	Excellent (4)
SECTION III: ATTENDANCE					
1. Physical education is required of all pupils, ages 3-21, and adapted physical education is provided for pupils who exhibit unique physical education needs.					
2. All pupils with disabilities ages 0-2, and/or ages 3-5 will be provided physical education consistent with physical education offerings in the general program for pupils in their age groups.					
3. Pupils with disabilities, ages 0-2 and/or ages 3-5 may be provided physical education if they exhibit unique physical education needs.					
4. Credit is provided for adapted physical education in accord with regular physical education credit.					
SECTION IV: PERSONNEL					
1. Instruction in adapted physical education for pupils ages 3-21 is provided by a certified physical education teacher.					
2. Adapted physical education for infants and toddlers is provided by an adapted physical educator.					
3. Physical educators teaching adapted physical education who have not completed at least 12 semester hours of formal higher education in adapted physical education have access to appropriate resource personnel.					
4. Extra-class activities are provided under the supervision of personnel meeting state requirements and approved by the board of education.					
5. Physical educators teaching adapted physical education for more than 50% of their teaching load have completed at least 12 semester hours of formal study in adapted physical education, have a concentration in adapted physical education from an accredited college or university, or have a state credential or endorsement in adapted physical education.					
6. Supervision and coordination of all phases of adapted physical education (instruction, intramurals, extra-class programs, interscholastic athletics) is provided by a director certified in physical education and administrative and supervisory services.					
7. Paraeducators are provided for instructional classes in physical education.					
8. The qualifications of paraeducators are in accord with appropriate state and/or local regulations.					

From J. Winnick, ed. 2011, *Adapted physical education and sport, fifth edition* (Champaign, IL: Human Kinetics).

	Inadequate (0)	Poor (1)	Fair (2)	Good (3)	Excellent (4)
SECTION IV: PERSONNEL					
9. A physician delegated by a district submits to appropriate committees/personnel medical limitations and areas of the program in which a pupil may participate when medical reasons are given to limit participation.					
10. Teachers of adapted physical education are involved in individualized education programming and placement decisions.					
11. Teachers of pupils requiring adapted physical education are involved in assessment, setting objectives and goals, and determining unique needs of pupils receiving adapted physical education.					
SECTION V: FACILITIES					
1. Pupils receiving adapted physical education have equal access to facilities required to provide equal opportunity for programmatic benefits.					
2. Indoor facilities for adapted physical education:					
a. Have adequate clear activity space					
b. Provide a safe environment for activity					
c. Have appropriate flooring and satisfactory finish					
d. Have adequate lighting					
e. Have adequate acoustical treatment					
f. Have protective padding on walls					
g. Have sufficient ceiling clearance					
h. Have adequate ventilation					
3. Equipment and supplies required for reasonable accommodations are provided.					
4. For pupils receiving adapted physical education, the dressing, showering, and drying areas include:					
a. Adequate space for peak load periods					
b. Floors constructed to facilitate ambulation and maintenance of safe and clean conditions					
c. Lockers of proper type and sufficient quantity					
d. Sufficient number of showerheads					
e. Adequate ventilation					
f. Adequate lighting					
g. Adequate heating					
h. Adequate benches, mirrors, and toilets					
i. Facilities that are clean, sanitary, and in operable condition					

From J. Winnick, ed. 2011, *Adapted physical education and sport, fifth edition* (Champaign, IL: Human Kinetics).

(continued)

Rating Scale for Adapted Physical Edcuation *(continued)*

	Inadequate (0)	Poor (1)	Fair (2)	Good (3)	Excellent (4)
SECTION V: FACILITIES					
5. The outdoor adapted physical education facilities are designed for effective instruction and safety. They are:					
a. Readily accessible					
b. Free from safety hazards (glass, holes, stones)					
c. Properly fenced or enclosed for safety and efficient usage					
d. Properly surfaced, graded, and drained					
e. Laid out and marked for a variety of activities					
f. Properly equipped (playground structures, backstops, physical fitness equipment, etc.)					
6. Qualified supervision of areas and facilities is provided during use.					
SECTION VI: ADMINISTRATIVE PROCEDURES					
1. Class sizes for adapted physical education are equitable to those specified for special education classroom teaching.					
2. Teacher load for teachers teaching adapted physical education is equitable to that of special education teachers.					
3. Teachers of adapted physical education receive support staff on the same student-teacher ratio as special education teachers.					
4. Appropriate committees use certified physical educators to assess physical education status for IEP development when unique physical education needs are suspected.					
5. Pupils with disabilities are integrated into regular physical education classes to the maximum extent appropriate.					
6. Pupils with disabilities are provided reasonable accommodations in physical education classes.					
7. Provisions are made for physical educators to refer to appropriate committees and all pupils with disabilities suspected of having unique needs in physical education.					
8. The physical education teacher is involved with individualized program development of all pupils who participate in physical education outside of regular or integrated classes.					
9. Physical education is included in the IEP of every pupil with a disability.					

From J. Winnick, ed. 2011, *Adapted physical education and sport, fifth edition* (Champaign, IL: Human Kinetics).

	Inadequate (0)	Poor (1)	Fair (2)	Good (3)	Excellent (4)
SECTION VI: ADMINISTRATIVE PROCEDURES					
10. Pupils are referred to appropriate planning committees and receive adapted physical education on the basis of objective criteria.					
11. The physical education abilities of all pupils not participating in regular physical education are assessed by a physical educator.					
12. Staff implementing adapted physical education are provided in-service education on at least an annual basis.					
13. School districts provide placement settings, which permit personalized attention in the most appropriate environment.					
14. The annual budget request for adapted physical education is prepared on the basis of an inventory of needs of the program including needs specified in individualized education programs.					
15. The adapted physical education budget includes state and federal monies earmarked for instruction and extra-curricular activity of pupils with disabilities if such pupils are receiving an adapted physical education program.					
16. A variety of up-to-date reference materials are provided for teachers providing adapted physical education.					
17. The school library contains materials on adapted physical education, which are sufficient and appropriate.					
18. Budgets for instructional, intramural, extramural, and athletic programs for pupils with disabilities are equitable to those for pupils without disabilities.					
19. The school district plan includes provisions for regular extra-class programs for qualified pupils with disabilities.					
20. Physical educators are encouraged and permitted to make referrals following accepted school district procedures for individualized education programs to appropriate committees in the school district.					

From J. Winnick, ed. 2011, *Adapted physical education and sport, fifth edition* (Champaign, IL: Human Kinetics).

Author Index

Note: The italicized *f* and *t* following page numbers refer to figures and tables, respectively.

Subject Index

Note: The italicized *f* and *t* following page numbers refer to figures and tables, respectively.

About the Editor

Joseph P. Winnick, EdD, is a distinguished service professor of kinesiology, sport studies, and physical education at The College at Brockport, State University of New York, where he has taught adapted physical education for over 40 years after teaching adapted physical education in Baltimore County, Maryland. Renowned for his research in adapted physical education, he is the coauthor of the *Brockport Physical Fitness Test Manual* and related resources, which present the best health-related physical fitness test available for young people with disabilities.

Dr. Winnick developed and implemented America's first master's degree professional preparation program in adapted physical education at SUNY Brockport in 1968. Since that time he has secured funds from the U.S. Department of Education to support the program. He has received the Professional Recognition Award and Julian U. Stein Lifetime Achievement Award from the Adapted Physical Activity Council of AAHPERD and the G. Lawrence Rarick Research Award and the Hollis Fait Scholarly Contribution Award from the National Consortium on Physical Education and Recreation for individuals with disabilities. Dr. Winnick earned his bachelor's degree from Ithaca College and his master's and doctoral degrees from Temple University.

About the Authors

Boni B. Boswell received a doctorate in kinesiology at Texas Woman's University. She is an associate professor at East Carolina University (ECU) where she teaches adapted physical education and dance in the department of exercise and sport science. Boswell also currently serves as director of the ECU DanceAbility Center. She is coauthor of *Re-envisioning Dance* as well as author of numerous articles concerning dance and inclusive settings.

Douglas H. Collier received his bachelor's and master's degrees along with a diploma in special education from McGill University and his doctorate from Indiana University. He is an associate professor in the department of kinesiology, sport studies, and physical education at the College at Brockport, State University of New York, where he teaches undergraduate courses in the teacher preparation program with an emphasis on elementary and early childhood education and graduate courses in adapted physical education. His research and writing focus on instructional strategies effective for learners with severe disabilities, the autism spectrum disorder, and positive, proactive approaches to behavior management.

Patricia L. Fegan is the president and CEO of Special Olympics Maryland, Inc. (SOMD), which serves more than 10,000 athletes. Prior to this appointment, she served as director of education for Special Olympics, Inc. She earned her doctorate from the University of Maryland in 1979 and previously directed the undergraduate and graduate adapted physical education preparation programs at Adelphi University. In 1997, she was named one of Maryland's Top 100 Women, and in 1999 she led SOMD to receive the Maryland Association of Nonprofit Organizations Standards for Excellence Award, one of only 50 nonprofits out of 16,000 statewide to achieve and maintain this standing.

Manny Felix, originally from Turlock, California, is the coordinator for undergraduate adapted physical education in the department of exercise and sport science at the University of Wisconsin at La Crosse. He received his bachelor's degree in physical education from the University of California at Davis, master's degree in adapted physical education from Northern Illinois University, and PhD in movement studies in disability from Oregon State University. Dr. Felix teaches undergraduate and graduate courses in adapted physical education and also serves as the director of the UW-La Crosse Center on Disability Health and Adapted Physical Activity.

David L. Gallahue is dean emeritus of the school of HPER at Indiana University at Bloomington. He holds degrees from Indiana University (BS), Purdue University (MS), and Temple University (EdD). He is author of several textbooks, journal articles, and edited book chapters. Dr. Gallahue is a past president of the National Association for Sport and Physical Education (NASPE) and former chair of the Motor Development Academy and the Council on Physical Education for Children (COPEC). He is a recognized leader in children's motor development and developmental physical activity.

Cathy Houston-Wilson received her doctoral degree from Oregon State University in movement studies in disability. She is a professor at The College at Brockport, State University of New York in the department of kinesiology, sport studies, and physical education, where she serves as associate chair and coordinator of student teaching. She teaches classes in adapted physical education and early childhood physical education. Her research and writing focus on inclusion, autism spectrum disorders, early childhood physical education, and fitness education for people with disabilities.

Luke E. Kelly is a professor of kinesiology at the University of Virginia, where he directs the master's and doctoral programs in adapted physical education. He received his doctorate from Texas Woman's University and his bachelor and master's degrees from SUNY Brockport. Dr. Kelly works extensively with public schools on developing functional physical education curricula based on the Achievement-Based Curriculum (ABC) model so that they accommodate the needs of all students. Dr. Kelly is a fellow in the American Academy of Kinesiology and Physical Education, a past president of the National Consortium for Physical Education and Recreation

...bilities (NCPERID), and the ... Adapted Physical Education ... Project.

...ozub is an associate professor in the ...t of kinesiology, sport studies, and physi-...cation at The College at Brockport, State ...ersity of New York. Dr. Kozub received his PhD ...t Ohio State University in 1997. Both master's and bachelor's degrees were earned at SUNY Brockport in 1996 and 1995, respectively. Dr. Kozub taught and coached in the public schools of New York as a general and adapted physical educator from 1986 until 1994.

Barry W. Lavay is a professor in the kinesiology department (KIN) at California State University at Long Beach (CSULB), where he coordinates the state adapted physical education teaching specialist credential program and directs the after-school and summer physical activity programs for children with disabilities. He is the 2001 CSULB Outstanding Professor Award recipient. He obtained his PhD in special physical education from the University of New Mexico in 1984. His scholarly activity is in the area of behavior management, and he has authored or coauthored several textbook chapters, manuals, and juried articles. He is the coauthor of *Positive Behavior Management in Physical Activity Settings, Second Edition* (2006). Dr. Lavay has been an active member with the American Alliance of Health, Physical Education, Recreation and Dance (AAHPERD) and he received the 2001 AAHPERD Adapted Physical Activity Council Professional Recognition Award.

Monica Lepore is a professor at West Chester University, where she is the coordinator of the adapted physical education programs. Her specialty is in the area of adapted aquatics, and she is the lead author of a text titled *Adapted Aquatics Programming* and a DVD, *Introduction to Adapted Aquatics*, for aquatic instructors to learn how to teach adapted swimming and water safety skills. She has received the National AAPAR and also the Pennsylvania State Adapted Physical Activity Professional of the Year awards, the International Swimming Hall of Fame Adapted Aquatics Award, and a Pennsylvania House of Representatives and Senate Citation for her advocacy for people with disabilities. She is a certified adapted physical educator, an AAPAR master teacher of adapted aquatics, a lifeguard, and a water safety instructor.

Lauren J. Lieberman is a professor of adapted physical education at The College at Brockport, State University of New York. She currently teaches undergraduate and graduate classes in adapted physical education. She has taught physical education and aquatics at the Perkins School for the Blind in Watertown, Massachusetts, in the deafblind program. She received her PhD from Oregon State University in the movement studies in disabilities program. In addition to teaching, she runs Camp Abilities, a developmental sport camp for children with visual impairments and deafblindness in various places around the United States. She also conducts research and consults in the area of people with visual impairments, deafness, and deafblindness and physical activity.

E. Michael Loovis received his PhD from Ohio State University in 1975. He is currently a professor at Cleveland State University, where he teaches adapted physical education and related courses at both the graduate and undergraduate levels. He is a fellow of the Research Consortium of AAHPERD and also the North American Society of Health, Physical Education, Recreation, Sport, and Dance Professionals. He is a recent recipient of the Fulbright Scholar Award. On an interdisciplinary basis, he teaches courses in child development and organization behavior and change in the college of education master's and doctoral programs, respectively. His research interests include the development of fundamental motor skills and patterns in typically developing children using hierarchical linear modeling.

John C. Ozmun is a professor of physical education in the College of Arts and Sciences at Indiana Wesleyan University. He holds degrees from Taylor University (BS) and Indiana University (MS, PED). He is the coauthor with David L. Gallahue of *Understanding Motor Development: Infants, Children, Adolescents, Adults*, one of the most widely used motor development textbooks nationally and internationally. His research focus is muscular strength characteristics of young children with and without disabilities.

Michael J. Paciorek received his PhD from Peabody College of Vanderbilt University. He is a professor at Eastern Michigan University, where he teaches classes in adapted physical education and sport and motor development. Dr. Paciorek is the coauthor of the popular text, *Disability Sport and Recreation Resources*. He has served on the board of directors for Special Olympics Michigan for 12 years and was co-coordinator of disabled athlete participation at the United States Olympic Festival. Additionally, he was a member of the United States

Disabled Sports Team that competed at the 1992 Paralympic Games in Barcelona.

David L. Porretta, PhD, is a professor of physical education at Ohio State University and is responsible for graduate study in adapted physical education. He earned his doctoral degree from Temple University, Philadelphia. Dr. Porretta is a fellow in the American Academy of Kinesiology and Physical Education (AAKPE) and a past president of NCPERID. He is the recipient of G. Lawrence Rarick Research Award, the Hollis Fait Scholarly Contribution Award from NCPERID, and the Professional Recognition Award from the Adapted Physical Activity Council of AAHPERD. Dr. Porretta is a former editor of the Adapted Physical Activity Quarterly (APAQ), the official scholarly journal of the International Federation of Adapted Physical Activity (IFAPA).

Francis X. Short is the dean of the School of Health and Human Performance and is a professor in the department of kinesiology, sport studies, and physical education at The College at Brockport, State University of New York. He has typically taught courses in adapted physical education and motor development. He has authored and coauthored a number of publications related to the physical fitness of people with disabilities, including the Brockport Physical Fitness Test (BPFT). In 2000 he received the Professional Recognition Award from the Adapted Physical Activity Council of AAHPERD and the G. Lawrence Rarick Research Award from NCPERID. Dr. Short holds degrees from Springfield College and Indiana University.

Christine B. Stopka earned her PhD from the University of Virginia. She is a professor of exercise therapy, adapted physical activity, and medical terminology at the University of Florida. There she established undergraduate and graduate specializations in athletic training and special physical education, the student injury care center, the exercise therapy lab, the adapted aquatics program, and community-based programs in athletic training and adapted physical activity. Her writings and research include the study of exercise therapy programs and sports medicine considerations for people with disabilities, including those with intellectual disabilities and peripheral arterial disease, as well as adapted equipment ideas to facilitate inclusive teaching. In 2007, she received the William A. Hillman Distinguished Service Award from NCPERID and the Athletic Training Service Award from the National Athletic Trainers' Association. In 2008, she received the Charles S. Williams Distinguished Service Award from the College of Health and Human Performance, the John K. Williams Adapted Aquatics Award from the International Swimming Hall of Fame, and the University of Florida Teacher of the Year Award.

Garth Tymeson, originally from Troy, New York, is a professor in the department of exercise and sport science at the University of Wisconsin at La Crosse. He received his bachelor's degree from SUNY Cortland, master's degree from SUNY Brockport, and PhD from Texas Woman's University. Dr. Tymeson teaches undergraduate and graduate courses in adapted physical education and has directed and codirected adapted physical education personnel development programs funded by the U.S. Department of Education, Office of Special Education and Rehabilitative Services. He has served as president of NCPERID and is involved with numerous programs in the UW-La Crosse Center on Disability Health and Adapted Physical Activity.

Abu B. Yilla received his master's and doctoral degrees from Texas Woman's University and two bachelor's degrees, one from the University of Nottingham, England, and one from the University of Texas at Arlington. He is a clinical assistant professor at the University of Texas at Arlington. His research focus is the explication of elite disability sport, in particular wheelchair basketball. He is a Paralympic medalist and has won 12 national championships in wheelchair basketball (8 in Great Britain and 4 in the United States). Dr Yilla is also president of the Dallas Wheelchair Mavericks, who are nine-time USA National Wheelchair Basketball Association champions, and was founding president of the United States Quad Rugby Association.

Lauriece L. Zittel earned her doctorate at Oregon State University. Currently she is an associate professor at Northern Illinois University, where she teaches graduate coursework in adapted physical activity. She is the coauthor of *Smart Start: A Preschool Movement Curriculum; I CAN K-3, Second Edition; and Principles and Methods of Adapted Physical Education and Recreation, Eleventh Edition.* She has received the Mabel Lee Award (AAHPERD), the Hollis Fait Scholarly Contribution Award (NCPERID), and the Crystal Apple Award (Michigan State University). Her research focuses on the environmental variables influencing the motor development of young children with developmental delays, particularly children exposed to severe poverty and violence.

You'll find other outstanding
physical education resources at
www.HumanKinetics.com

In the U.S. call 1.800.747.4457
Australia 08 8372 0999
Canada. 1.800.465.7301
Europe . . . . .+44 (0) 113 255 5665
New Zealand 0800 222 062

HUMAN KINETICS
The Information Leader in Physical Activity & Health
P.O. Box 5076 • Champaign, IL 61825-5076